R. Gupta's®

Popular Master Guide

BPSC

Bihar Public Service Commission

Secondary School Teacher

Class 9 to 10

Recruitment Exam

SUBJECT

Social Science

by

RPH Editorial Board

2026 EDITION

RAMESH PUBLISHING HOUSE, NEW DELHI

Published by
O.P. Gupta *for* Ramesh Publishing House

Admin. Office
12-H, New Daryaganj Road, Opp. Officers' Mess,
New Delhi-110002 ✆ 23275224, 23245124

E-mail: info@rameshpublishinghouse.com
For Online Shopping: www.rameshpublishinghouse.com

Showroom
• Balaji Market, Nai Sarak, Delhi-6 ✆ 23253720, 23282525
• 4457, Nai Sarak, Delhi-6, ✆ 23918938

Book Code: R-2517

ISBN: 978-93-5477-552-9

Price: ₹ 520

Printed at: B.K. Offset, Delhi

CONTENTS

Written Examination

For Secondary School Teacher (Class 9-10)

Part	Subjects	No. of Questions	Total Marks	Duration
Part-I : Language (Qualifying)	English and Hindi/Urdu/Bangla	30	30	2.30 hours
Part-II : General Studies	Primary Maths, General Awareness, General Science, Indian National Movement and Geography	40	40	
Part-III : Concerned Subject	Social Science	80	80	
	Total	**150**	**150**	

Previous Years' Paper

Bihar Public Service Commission (BPSC)

Secondary School Social Science Teacher Recruitment Exam, 2024

(Exam held on 21-07-2024)

PART-I : LANGUAGE

ENGLISH LANGUAGE

Directions (Qs. No. 1 to 5): *Read the passage given below and answer the questions that follow:*

Amitabh Bachchan, popularly known as big B, was born in Allahabad, Uttar Pradesh on 11 October 1942. He is an iconic actor whose career in Indian Cinema has spanned four decades. His father H.R. Bachchan was a well-known Hindi poet. (Bachchan is actually his father's pen name but has now become the family surname) Amitabh attended boys' High School in Allahabad, followed by Sherwood College in Nainital and earned a degree in science from Delhi university. His first film was 'Saat Hindustani' (1969). He became well-known as a movie star in 1973 after the success of 'Abhimaan' and 'Zanjeer' which was followed by his box office successes such as 'Sholay' 'Amar Akbar Anthony', 'Trishul', 'Don' and 'Deewar'. He often played the role of an angry young man fighting a corrupt establishment, a theme that had tremendous appeal in India at that time.

1. Which city is the birth place of Amitabh in India?

A. Bombay
B. Delhi
C. Bangalore
D. More than one of the above
E. None of the above

2. How long has Amitabh Bachchan dominated Indian Cinema?

A. Three decades
B. Four decades
C. Two decades
D. More than one of the above
E. None of the above

3. From which university did Amitabh earn his degree in science?

A. Aligarh Muslim University
B. Banaras Hindu University
C. Punjab University
D. More than one of the above
E. None of the above

4. When did Amitabh got recognition as a movie star in India?

A. 1966
B. 1969
C. 1973
D. More than one of the above
E. None of the above

5. Which film of the following is Amitabh's first film?

A. 'Zanjeer'
B. 'Abhiman'
C. 'Saat Hindustani'
D. More than one of the above
E. None of the above

Directions (Qs. No. 6 and 7): *Fill in the blanks with suitable articles like 'a' 'an' 'the' :*

6. The shadow of moon fills on ______ Earth.

A. an
B. a
C. the
D. More than one of the above
E. None of the above

1. E	2. B	3. E	4. C	5. C	6. C

7. I have always wanted to study abroad, not only for ______ degree but also for the experience.

A. an
B. a
C. the
D. More than one of the above
E. None of the above

8. First May 2024 is Wednesday, what day of the week would be 9th of May?

A. Friday
B. Thursday
C. Monday
D. More than one of the above
E. None of the above

हिन्दी भाषा

निर्देश (प्र.सं. 9 से 14 तक): *निम्नलिखित गद्यांश को पढ़कर पूछे गए प्रश्नों का उत्तर दीजिए:*

पंडित राम प्रसाद बिस्मिल उन महान क्रांतिकारियों में से एक थे, जिन्होंने अपने कार्यों से अंग्रेजी हुकूमत को हिला दिया था। जब राम प्रसाद आर्य समाज के संपर्क में आए, इनके जीवन में क्रांति आ गई, इनमें बुराइयों का सामना करने का साहस जाग उठा। उन दिनों स्वतंत्रता आंदोलन जोर पर था। राम प्रसाद को पता चला कि क्रांतिकारी युवक देश में सजग हैं तथा देश की स्वतंत्रता के लिए मर मिटने को तैयार हैं। बिस्मिल क्रांतिकारी संगठन के सदस्य बन गए। इन्होंने एक पुस्तक भी लिखी– 'अमरीका को स्वतंत्रता कैसे मिली?' इनकी 'स्वदेश-रंग' नामक पुस्तक बहुत प्रसिद्ध है। आंदोलन में धन की कमी एक बहुत बड़ी समस्या थी। धन जुटाने के लिए इन्होंने किसी दीन-हीन को नहीं सताया, बल्कि अंग्रेजों का सरकारी खजाना लूटने की योजना बनाई। इन्होंने 9 अगस्त, 1925 को काकोरी स्टेशन पर धन लूटकर स्वाधीनता संग्राम में लगा दिया। इसके लिए इनपर मुकदमा चलाया गया। इन्हें फाँसी की सजा दी गई। पंडित बिस्मिल ने 26-27 वर्ष की आयु में वह कार्य कर दिखाया, जो लंबी आयु जीने वाले भी नहीं कर पाते। ये एक कवि भी थे, इनकी ये पंक्तियाँ समय-समय पर हमें प्रेरणा देती हैं:

'सरफरोशी की तमन्ना अब हमारे दिल में है।
देखना है जोर कितना बाजू ए-कातिल में है।।'

9. राम प्रसाद के जीवन में परिवर्तन कब आया?

A. क्रांतिकारियों के संपर्क में आने पर
B. जब अमरीका को स्वतंत्रता मिली
C. जब वे आर्य समाज के संपर्क में आए
D. उपर्युक्त में से एक से अधिक
E. उपर्युक्त में से कोई नहीं

10. बिस्मिल ने धन की समस्या कैसे हल की?

A. सरकारी खजाना लूटकर
B. चंदा इकट्ठा करके
C. गरीबों को लूटकर
D. उपर्युक्त में से एक से अधिक
E. उपर्युक्त में से कोई नहीं

11. बिस्मिल महान क्रांतिकारी क्यों कहलाए?

A. क्योंकि उन्हें फाँसी की सजा दी गई।
B. क्योंकि उन्होंने पुस्तकें लिखीं।
C. क्योंकि उन्होंने अपने कार्यों से अंग्रेजी हुकूमत को हिला दिया।
D. उपर्युक्त में से एक से अधिक
E. उपर्युक्त में से कोई नहीं

12. 'सजग' में मूल शब्द है:

A. सज
B. जग
C. ग
D. उपर्युक्त में से एक से अधिक
E. उपर्युक्त में से कोई नहीं

13. 'स्वतंत्रता' शब्द का विलोम है:

A. गणतंत्रता
B. लोकतंत्रता
C. प्रजातंत्रता
D. उपर्युक्त में से एक से अधिक
E. उपर्युक्त में से कोई नहीं

14. 'लंबी आयु जीने वाला' वाक्यांश के लिए एक शब्द है:

A. लंबायु
B. दीर्घायु
C. अल्पायु
D. उपर्युक्त में से एक से अधिक
E. उपर्युक्त में से कोई नहीं

निर्देश (प्र.सं. 15 से 18 तक): *निम्नलिखित गद्यांश को पढ़कर पूछे गए प्रश्नों का उत्तर दीजिए:*

मनुष्य का जीवन संसार के छोटे-बड़े प्राणियों और पदार्थों में श्रेष्ठ माना गया है। वह इसलिए कि मनुष्य बड़ा बुद्धिमान और कल्पनाशील प्राणी है। अपने विचारों के बल पर ही वह जो चाहे कर सकता है और बहुत ऊँचा उठ सकता है। परंतु विचार सच्चे, सादे और पवित्र होने

7. B	8. B	9. C	10. A	11. C	12. B	13. E	14. B

ो साथ-साथ मनुष्य के व्यावहारिक जीवन से संबंध रखने वाले होने ाहिए। इन्हीं बातों को आधार बनाकर 'सादा जीवन, उच्च विचार' को ानव-जीवन की सफलता की सीढ़ी माना गया है। सादगी मनुष्य के हनावे से नहीं, बल्कि उसके प्रत्येक हाव-भाव, विचार तथा जीवन के ग से टपकनी चाहिए। यही वास्तविक सादगी है, जो विचारों को भी च्च बनाकर सब प्रकार की उन्नति और विकास का कारण बनती है। ंसार का इतिहास इस बात का गवाह है कि आरंभ से ही सादगी पसंद ्यक्ति ही जनता को उच्च विचार देकर उन्नति और विकास की राह शस्त करते आ रहे हैं। महात्मा बुद्ध, संत कबीर, गुरू नानक, महात्मा ांधी, डॉ. राधाकृष्णन, विनोबा भावे आदि इस तथ्य के प्रत्यक्ष प्रमाण हैं।

15. मनुष्य का जीवन श्रेष्ठ क्यों माना जाता है?

A. क्योंकि वह सफल है
B. क्योंकि वह बुद्धिमान और कल्पनाशील है
C. क्योंकि वह परिश्रमी और कठोर है।
D. उपर्युक्त में से एक से अधिक
E. उपर्युक्त में से कोई नहीं

16. उन्नति करने के लिए मनुष्य के विचार कैसे होने चाहिए?

A. झूठे, ऊँचे और अपवित्र
B. बेबुनियाद
C. मोह-माया से युक्त
D. उपर्युक्त में से एक से अधिक
E. उपर्युक्त में से कोई नहीं

17. वास्तविक सादगी क्या है?

A. वैचारिक और व्यावहारिक
B. मनुष्य का पहनावा
C. मनुष्य का दिखावा
D. उपर्युक्त में से एक से अधिक
E. उपर्युक्त में से कोई नहीं

18. 'उन्नति' शब्द का उचित विलोम शब्द है:

A. प्रोन्नति
B. पदोन्नति
C. अवनति
D. उपर्युक्त में से एक से अधिक
E. उपर्युक्त में से कोई नहीं

19. 'महान है जो आत्मा' का समास है:

A. कर्मधारय समास
B. अव्ययीभाव समास
C. तत्पुरुष समास
D. उपर्युक्त में से एक से अधिक
E. उपर्युक्त में से कोई नहीं

20. 'प्रत्येक' शब्द का सही वर्ण-विच्छेद है:

A. प् + र् + आ + त् + अ + य् + ए + क्
B. प् + र् + अ् + त् + अ + य् + ए + क् + अ
C. प् + र् + अ + त् + य् + ए + क् + अ
D. उपर्युक्त में से एक से अधिक
E. उपर्युक्त में से कोई नहीं

21. निम्नलिखित में से वृद्धि संधि का उदाहरण है:

A. पित्रादेश
B. गिरीश
C. महौजस्वी
D. उपर्युक्त में से एक से अधिक
E. उपर्युक्त में से कोई नहीं

22. निम्नलिखित में से शुद्ध वर्तनी है:

A. अद्वितिय
B. अद्वितीय
C. अद्वित्तीय
D. उपर्युक्त में से एक से अधिक
E. उपर्युक्त में से कोई नहीं

23. निम्नलिखित में से जातिवाचक संज्ञा है:

A. बहन
B. मंत्री
C. जुलाहा
D. उपर्युक्त में से एक से अधिक
E. उपर्युक्त में से कोई नहीं

24. 'चंद्रमा' का पर्यायवाची है:

A. राकेश
B. सारंग
C. आदित्य
D. उपर्युक्त में से एक से अधिक
E. उपर्युक्त में से कोई नहीं

25. 'स्थिर' का विलोम शब्द है:

A. चंचल
B. अस्थिर
C. निर्विकार
D. उपर्युक्त में से एक से अधिक
E. उपर्युक्त में से कोई नहीं

26. 'मैं एक लीटर दूध पीता हूँ'– में विशेषण शब्द है:

A. मैं
B. एक लीटर
C. दूध
D. उपर्युक्त में से एक से अधिक
E. उपर्युक्त में से कोई नहीं

15. B	**16.** E	**17.** A	**18.** C	**19.** A	**20.** C
21. C	**22.** B	**23.** D	**24.** D	**25.** D	**26.** B

27. 'कृष्णार्पण' शब्द में कौन-सा समास है?

A. अव्ययीभाव

B. कर्मधारय

C. बहुब्रीहि

D. उपर्युक्त में से एक से अधिक

E. उपर्युक्त में से कोई नहीं

28. निम्नलिखित वाक्यांश के लिए एक शब्द बताइए:

'कम बोलने वाला'

A. मितभाषी

B. वाचाल

C. मिष्टभाषी

D. उपर्युक्त में से एक से अधिक

E. उपर्युक्त में से कोई नहीं

29. 'उदासीन हो जाने' के लिए सही मुहावरा है:

A. आँखें चुराना

B. आँखों में गड़ना

C. आँखें फेर लेना

D. उपर्युक्त में से एक से अधिक

E. उपर्युक्त में से कोई नहीं

30. 'निरपराध' में उपसर्ग है:

A. नि

B. निर्

C. निस्

D. उपर्युक्त में से एक से अधिक

E. उपर्युक्त में से कोई नहीं

PART-II : GENERAL STUDIES

31. A player makes 7 complete revolutions of a circular path to complete a race of 2200 metres. The radius of the circular path is: ($\pi = 22/7$)

A. 42 metres

B. 45 metres

C. 50 metres

D. More than one of the above

E. None of the above

32. If the capacity of a cylindrical tank is 1848 m^3 and the diameter of its base is 14 m, the depth of the tank is: ($\pi = 22/7$)

A. 8 m

B. 12 m

C. 16 m

D. More than one of the above

E. None of the above

33. If 1/8th of a number is 30, what will be 62% of that number?

A. 181.3

B. 178.24

C. 148.8

D. More than one of the above

E. None of the above

34. The salary of an officer is increased by 25%. By what per cent should the new salary be decreased to restore the original salary?

A. 25

B. 22.5

C. 20

D. More than one of the above

E. None of the above

35. By what number should $\left(-\frac{2}{3}\right)^{-3}$ be divided so that the quotient is $\left(\frac{4}{9}\right)^{-2}$?

A. $\frac{2}{3}$

B. $-\frac{2}{3}$

C. $-\frac{3}{2}$

D. More than one of the above

E. None of the above

36. If $x + \frac{1}{x} = 5$, what is the value of $x^4 + \frac{1}{x^4}$?

A. 525

B. 527

C. 529

D. More than one of the above

E. None of the above

27. B	28. A	29. C	30. B	31. C	32. B	33. C	34. C	35. B	36. B

37. A bag contains 5-rupee, 2-rupee and 1-rupee coins in the ratio 2 : 3 : 4. The total value of all the coins is ₹ 2,000. How many coins of 2-rupee are there in the bag?

A. 200
B. 250
C. 400
D. More than one of the above
E. None of the above

38. The interior angle of a regular polygon exceeds its exterior angle by 108°. How many sides does the polygon have?

A. 10
B. 9
C. 8
D. More than one of the above
E. None of the above

39. Zinc Oxide is normally used in the manufacture of:

A. Paints
B. Explosives
C. Solvents
D. More than one of the above
E. None of the above

40. Lenz's law is derived from the law of conservation of:

A. Magnetism
B. Momentum
C. Charge
D. More than one of the above
E. None of the above

41. Glycogen stored in liver and muscles of human body is in form of:

A. Monosaccharide
B. Polysaccharide
C. Protein
D. More than one of the above
E. None of the above

42. In which of the following blood has defective haemoglobin?

A. Haematoma
B. Sickle cell Anaemia
C. Haemophilia
D. More than one of the above
E. None of the above

43. In which of the following medicine production, ethyl alcohol can be used?

A. Antiseptic
B. Antipyretic
C. Anti-allergic
D. More than one of the above
E. None of the above

44. Velocity of sound at 15°C and 380 mm pressure is 340 m. sec^{-1}. If the pressure is doubled without change of temperature, the velocity of sound would become:

A. 680 m. sec^{-1} B. 170 m. sec^{-1}
C. 190 m. sec^{-1} D. 340 m. sec^{-1}
E. None of the above

45. If a bacterium cell divides in every 15 min, how many bacteria will be formed in 2 hours.

A. 8 B. 16
C. 64 D. 256
E. None of the above

46. Plants and animal cell differ in which of the following structure?

A. Enzymes
B. Nuclei
C. Cell wall
D. More than one of the above
E. None of the above

47. According to the recent report of forbes, which is the strongest currency in the world?

A. Omani Rial
B. Kuwaiti Dinar
C. Bahrain Dinar
D. More than one of the above
E. None of the above

48. In which city of Maharashtra did PM Narendra Modi launch 8 AMRUT projects?

A. Kollam
B. Baroda
C. Solapur
D. More than one of the above
E. None of the above

49. IIT Madras has tied up with whom to launch e-Mobility Simulation Lab?

A. Altair
B. Starlink
C. Farber Speciality Lab
D. More than one of the above
E. None of the above

37. E	**38.** A	**39.** A	**40.** E	**41.** B	**42.** B	**43.** A
44. D	**45.** D	**46.** C	**47.** B	**48.** C	**49.** A	

50. Who won the Best Actor Award at the Academy Awards 2024 (Oscars)?

A. Dwayne Johnson
B. Cillian Murphy
C. Tom Cruise
D. More than one of the above
E. None of the above

51. Who was recently selected as the ICC Women's T20i Cricketer of the year 2023?

A. Smriti Mandhana (India)
B. Nat Seiver - Brunt (England)
C. Hayley Mathews (West Indies)
D. More than one of the above
E. None of the above

52. Who was Crowned Miss World 2024 in Mumbai?

A. Miss Czech Kristina Pishkova
B. Miss India Sini Shetty
C. Miss Lebanon Yasmina Zaytoun
D. More than one of the above
E. None of the above

53. In which country will the clean Energy Investor Forum be organised by IPEF?

A. France
B. Singapore
C. Spain
D. More than one of the above
E. None of the above

54. India has acquired the right to operate the foreign Sittwe Port, it is in which country?

A. Sri Lanka
B. Bangladesh
C. Myanmar
D. More than one of the above
E. None of the above

55. Mangrove forest of Ganga Delta is called:

A. Sunderban
B. Sundergarh
C. Surendranagar
D. More than one of the above
E. None of the above

56. Which river is frequently changing its course of flow in Bihar?

A. Gandak
B. Kosi
C. Punpun
D. More than one of the above
E. None of the above

57. Plant roots gets water from soil as:

A. Bound water
B. Hygroscopic water
C. Capillary water
D. More than one of the above
E. None of the above

58. How much equatorial diameter is larger than pola[r] diameter?

A. 36 km
B. 43 km
C. 49 km
D. More than one of the above
E. None of the above

59. The Indian Standard Time (IST) is taken at whic[h] longitude?

A. 82.5° E
B. 78.5° E
C. 87.5° E
D. More than one of the above
E. None of the above

60. In India 'Green revolution' is known to credit t[o] whom?

A. Dr. V. Kurian
B. Dr. M.S. Swaminathan
C. Sri. S.L. Bahuguna
D. More than one of the above
E. None of the above

61. Highest Mountain peak of India is known as:

A. Everest
B. Kanchenjunga
C. K-2
D. More than one of the above
E. None of the above

62. Indian continent was earlier part of:

A. Gondwanaland
B. Tethys
C. Pangea
D. More than one of the above
E. None of the above

63. Who led the Revolt of 1857 in Bihar?

A. Tatya Tope
B. Kunwar Singh
C. Nana Saheb
D. More than one of the above
E. None of the above

50. B	**51.** C	**52.** A	**53.** B	**54.** C	**55.** A	**56.** B
57. C	**58.** B	**59.** A	**60.** B	**61.** C	**62.** *	**63.** B

64. The spiritual side of nationalism was voiced by:

A. Raja Ram Mohan Roy
B. Swami Shraddhanand
C. Swami Vivekananda
D. More than one of the above
E. None of the above

65. Which newspaper propagated strong nationalist views during India's freedom struggle?

A. Pioneer
B. Amrit Bazar Patrika
C. Statesman
D. More than one of the above
E. None of the above

66. Who intervened in a dispute between the workers and mill owners of Ahmedabad in 1918?

A. Vallabhbhai Patel
B. Mahatma Gandhi
C. Jamshedji Tata
D. More than one of the above
E. None of the above

67. Name the left-wing leader of Bihar Provincial Kisan Sabha who popularised this in Bihar?

A. Karyanand Sharma
B. Wadhwa Ram
C. P.C. Joshi
D. More than one of the above
E. None of the above

68. Muddiman Committee was appointed to report on the working of the:

A. Dyarchy
B. Communal representation
C. Federalism
D. More than one of the above
E. None of the above

69. "He was a great unifier in India who taught us not only bare tolerance of others but the willing acceptance of them as our friends and comrades in common undertakings" who said it?

A. Subhash Chandra Bose
B. Balgangadhar Tilak
C. Rajendra Prasad
D. More than one of the above
E. None of the above

70. Who proceeded to organise the Provisional Government of Free India outside the county?

A. Raja Mahendra Pratap
B. Rash Behari Bose
C. Subhash Chandra Bose
D. More than one of the above
E. None of the above

PART-III : SOCIAL SCIENCE

In **Social Science** includes **History, Geography, Economics** and **Political Science** subjects. Choose the questions from any two subjects out of four subjects of Sociasl Science. At leat one subject **History** or **Geography** is mandatory.

HISTORY

71. In which phase of History the Harappan Civilization can be kept?

A. Pre-History
B. Proto-History
C. History
D. More than one of the above
E. None of the above

72. At which river bank the Indus Valley site Sutkagendor is situated?

A. Ravi
B. Jhelum
C. Dashat
D. More than one of the above
E. None of the above

73. In which state of India 'Hulas' the Indus Valley site is situated?

A. Haryana
B. Rajasthan
C. Gujarat
D. More than one of the above
E. None of the above

74. From which name Chandragupta Maurya has been described in Greece literature?

A. Antigonus
B. Antiochus
C. Sandrocottus
D. More than one of the above
E. None of the above

64. C	**65.** B	**66.** B	**67.** A	**68.** A	**69.** E
70. B	**71.** B	**72.** C	**73.** E	**74.** C	

75. Which Greece writer has described that Ariyana State was given to Chandragupta Maurya in the marriage?

A. Strabo
B. Justin
C. Plutarch
D. More than one of the above
E. None of the above

76. Who has the credit to initiate Ashoka in Buddhism?

A. Nigrodh
B. Upagupta
C. Moggaliputta Tissa
D. More than one of the above
E. None of the above

77. In which year of his reign Ashoka visited Bodh Gaya?

A. 8th
B. 9th
C. 10th
D. More than one of the above
E. None of the above

78. In which Minor Rock Edict, Ashoka expressed his belief in Triratna-Buddha, Dhamma and Sangha?

A. Bhabru
B. Gurjara
C. Maski
D. More than one of the above
E. None of the above

79. In Mauryan Administration, how many villages come under 'Sangrahan'?

A. 100
B. 50
C. 10
D. More than one of the above
E. None of the above

80. How many types of spy are mentioned in Kautilya's Arthashastra?

A. 2
B. 3
C. 4
D. More than one of the above
E. None of the above

81. Who was responsible to do examine of coins during Mauryan period?

A. Laxana adhyaksha
B. Sannidhata
C. Rupadarshaka
D. More than one of the above
E. None of the above

82. From which Hindi month the financial year of the Mauryan administration started?

A. Chaitram
B. Ashadam
C. Pushyami
D. More than one of the above
E. None of the above

83. Who constructed some Guha-Vihars at Nagarjun hills during Mauryan age?

A. Ashoka
B. Dasharath
C. Sampriti
D. More than one of the above
E. None of the above

84. Who wrote Aihole Inscription which describes about the conflict of Harsha and Pulakeshin-II?

A. Ravikirti
B. Vatsabhatti
C. Vasul
D. More than one of the above
E. None of the above

85. Who was the commander in chief of Harshavardhan, that encouraged him to get throne?

A. Sharabhketu
B. Singhnad
C. Hansbeg
D. More than one of the above
E. None of the above

86. According to Chinese writer in which year Harsha Adopted the title of Magadhraj'?

A. 640
B. 641
C. 642
D. More than one of the above
E. None of the above

87. According to Hiuen-Tsang at which place in Bihar Harsha built a monastry (vihar) of Copper?

A. Bodh Gaya
B. Rajgir
C. Nalanda
D. More than one of the above
E. None of the above

75. A	**76.** B	**77.** C	**78.** A	**79.** C	**80.** A	**81.** C
82. B	**83.** B	**84.** A	**85.** B	**86.** B	**87.** C	

88. How many months Hiuen-Tsang stayed and studied at Nalanda?
A. 14
B. 18
C. 28
D. More than one of the above
E. None of the above

89. Who was the founder of Nalanda University in the Gupta Period?
A. Chandragupta Vikramaditya
B. Samudra Gupta
C. Ram Gupta
D. More than one of the above
E. None of the above

90. Which Chola ruler defeated Sri Lanka ruler Mahindra V on his land for the first time?
A. Rajaraja I
B. Rajaraja II
C. Rajendra II
D. More than one of the above
E. None of the above

91. Which Chola ruler established a new capital city named 'Gangaikonda Cholapuram'?
A. Parantaka-I
B. Rajaraja-I
C. Rajendra-I
D. More than one of the above
E. None of the above

92. Which Chola ruler constructed 'Rajarajeshwar temple' in his capital?
A. Rajendra I
B. Rajaraja I
C. Kulottunga I
D. More than one of the above
E. None of the above

93. Which Chola ruler is described as 'Chola Narayan' in the contemporary writings?
A. Rajendra I
B. Rajadhiraja I
C. Rajaraja I
D. More than one of the above
E. None of the above

94. At which place Iltutmish was appointed as governor for the first time?
A. Sambhal
B. Badaun
C. Gwalior
D. More than one of the above
E. None of the above

95. At which place Iltutmish gave crushing defeat to Tajuddin Yalduz of Ghazni and imprisoned him?
A. Tarain
B. At the river bank of Chenab
C. Sindh
D. More than one of the above
E. None of the above

96. How much Qutubuddin Aibak had to pay for purchasing of Iltutmish?
A. Three Lakh Jitals
B. Two Lakh Jitals
C. One Lakh Jitals
D. More than one of the above
E. None of the above

97. In which year Iltutmish got recognition from the Caliph of Baghdad?
A. 1226
B. 1227
C. 1229
D. More than one of the above
E. None of the above

98. Who constructed Quwwat-ul-Islam Mosque at Delhi?
A. Qutubuddin Aibak
B. Iltutmish
C. Balban
D. More than one of the above
E. None of the above

99. Which period is called the era of "the rule of the Forty" in the history of Delhi Sultanate age?
A. 1236-42
B. 1236-66
C. 1236-46
D. More than one of the above
E. None of the above

100. Under which Sultan a new post 'Naib-i-mamlikat' was created?
A. Ruknuddin Firoz
B. Muizuddin Bahram Shah
C. Alauddin Masud Shah
D. More than one of the above
E. None of the above

101. Who became the first 'Naib-i-mamlikat' in the history of Delhi Sultanate period?
A. Malik Junaidi
B. Ghiyasuddin Balban
C. Ikhtiyaruddin Aitigin
D. More than one of the above
E. None of the above

88. E	89. E	90. A	91. C	92. B	93. C	94. B
95. A	96. C	97. C	98. A	99. B	100. B	101. C

102. What was the original name of Ghiyasuddin Balban?
A. Badruddin
B. Bahauddin
C. Shamsuddin
D. More than one of the above
E. None of the above

103. By whom Balban was replaced on the post of 'Naib-i-mamlikati?
A. Kishlu Khan
B. Imaduddin Raihan
C. Haibat Khan
D. More than one of the above
E. None of the above

104. What Balban inscribed on his coins to make obedience of co-religionist?
A. Nasir-Amir-ul-Momenin
B. Naib-i-Momenin
C. Amir-ul-Momenin
D. More than one of the above
E. None of the above

105. Who was the last ruler of Mamluk (slave) dynasty?
A. Kaimurs
B. Bughra Khan
C. Kaiqubad
D. More than one of the above
E. None of the above

106. At the court of which Rajput ruler Akbar was born?
A. Rana Sangram Singh
B. Rana Virsal
C. Raja Bikramajit
D. More than one of the above
E. None of the above

107. At which place Akbar was crowned?
A. Thatta
B. Panipat
C. Kalanaur
D. More than one of the above
E. None of the above

108. Which was the last conquest of Akbar?
A. Gujarat
B. Sindh
C. Asirgarh
D. More than one of the above
E. None of the above

109. In which year Akbar declared 'Mahzar'?
A. 1563
B. 1575
C. 1579
D. More than one of the above
E. None of the above

110. At which place Akbar built 'Buland Darwaza'?
A. Delhi
B. Bulandshahr
C. Ajmer
D. More than one of the above
E. None of the above

or

GEOGRAPHY

71. What percentage of the area does India occupy of the land hemisphere?
A. 2.9 per cent
B. 2.4 per cent
C. 3.0 per cent
D. More than one of the above
E. None of the above

72. The length of the coastline along the main land of India is
A. 6100 km
B. 7516 km
C. 5900 km
D. More than one of the above
E. None of the above

73. Indira Point is characterised by
A. It is not visible today
B. It is situated in the great Nicobar group of Islands
C. This is the southern most point of India
D. More than one of the above
E. None of the above

74. In which of the following states are situated Garo, Khasi and Jaintia hills situated?
A. Manipur
B. Mizoram
C. Meghalaya
D. More than one of the above
E. None of the above

102. B	**103.** B	**104.** A	**105.** C	**106.** B	**107.** C	**108.** C
109. C	**110.** E	**71.** B	**72.** A	**73.** D	**74.** C	

75. Which of the following rivers flow through antecedent valleys?

A. Sutlej & Indus
B. Damodar & Godavari
C. Tungabhadra & Chambal
D. More than one of the above
E. None of the above

76. According to National Environmental Engineering Research Institute (NEERI), Nagpur how much water available in India is polluted?

A. 90 per cent
B. 60 per cent
C. 70 per cent
D. More than one of the above
E. None of the above

77. Which of the following sequences of rivers in descending order of their respective basin area in India is correct?

A. Ganga, Indus, Godavari, Krishna
B. Indus, Ganga, Krishna, Godavari
C. Godavari, Ganga, Indus, Krishna
D. More than one of the above
E. None of the above

78. Who among the following proposed in 1951 that mansoon is only the seasonal migration of planetary winds and pressure belts?

A. Halley
B. Flohn
C. Koteswaram
D. More than one of the above
E. None of the above

79. Which of the following pairs of the states & the percentage of their respective geographical area covered with forest is correctly matched (Year 2021)?

A. Mizoram 74.53 per cent
B. Arunachal Pradesh 89.33 per cent
C. Meghalaya 79.33 per cent
D. More than one of the above
E. None of the above

80. Which of the following national parks came in news because 20 Cheetas where translocated there from Africa?

A. Kuno
B. Keoladeo
C. Sariska
D. More than one of the above
E. None of the above

81. Which of the following sequences of states in descending order of their population density (2011) is correct?

A. West Bengal, Bihar, Uttar Pradesh, Kerala
B. Bihar, West Bengal, Kerala, Uttar Pradesh
C. Bihar, Kerala, West Bengal, Uttar Pradesh
D. More than one of the above
E. None of the above

82. Sex ratio (number of females per thousand males) in India According to 2011 census is

A. 949
B. 957
C. 943
D. More than one of the above
E. None of the above

83. Sagarmatha is the regional name of which of the mountain peaks?

A. Kanchenjunga
B. Makalu
C. Everest
D. More than one of the above
E. None of the above

84. In Bhutan, how much land area is covered with glaciers?

A. about 3 per cent
B. about 9 per cent
C. about 5 per cent
D. More than one of the above
E. None of the above

85. Which is the main food crop produced in Bhutan?

A. wheat
B. rice
C. bajra
D. More than one of the above
E. None of the above

86. Sri Lanka is well endowed with

A. iron ore
B. gold
C. coal
D. More than one of the above
E. None of the above

87. The capital of Myanmar is

A. Yagon
B. Mandalay
C. Naypyidaw
D. More than one of the above
E. None of the above

75. A	**76.** C	**77.** A	**78.** B	**79.** E	**80.** A	**81.** B
82. C	**83.** C	**84.** A	**85.** B	**86.** E	**87.** C	

88. The birth rate (Per 1000 People) in Bangladesh in Year 2022 was

A. 17.067
B. 17.991
C. 18.61
D. More than one of the above
E. None of the above

89. The Numbers of parallels of latitudes & meridians of longitudes on the globe are

A. 360
B. 180
C. infinite
D. More than one of the above
E. None of the above

90. Comparative scale is characterised by

A. it is a combination of two or more plain scales placed side by side
B. each plain scale shows different systems of measurement units
C. all plain scales have common R.F.
D. More than one of the above
E. None of the above

91. Bauxite is found in abundance in which of the following districts of Bihar?

A. Darbhanga
B. Jamui
C. Saran
D. More than one of the above
E. None of the above

92. Black cotton soils have developed

A. by weathering of Deccan Lava
B. by weathering of granite
C. in forest areas of the Himalayas
D. More than one of the above
E. None of the above

93. Which of the regions of India are badly effected by erosion?

A. Chambal Basin
B. Southern slopes of the Siwaliks
C. Chota Nagpur highland
D. More than one of the above
E. None of the above

94. Which of the following areas are known for coffee production?

A. Sone Basin
B. Nilgiris
C. Chhattisgarh
D. More than one of the above
E. None of the above

95. Which of the following projects is situated on the Krishna river?

A. Mayurakshi
B. Jawahar Sagar dam
C. Nagarjun Sagar
D. More than one of the above
E. None of the above

96. Which is the leading fish producer in India (Year 2023)?

A. Gujarat
B. West Bengal
C. Andhra Pradesh
D. More than one of the above
E. None of the above

97. Which is the largest producer of wheat in India (January, 2024)?

A. Punjab
B. Uttar Pradesh
C. Madhya Pradesh
D. More than one of the above
E. None of the above

98. Which is the largest manganese ore producer in India (Year 2023)?

A. Madhya Pradesh
B. Maharashtra
C. Odisha
D. More than one of the above
E. None of the above

99. Which of the following is a group of non-conventional energy resources?

A. natural gas, nuclear energy, coal
B. coal, natural gas, petroleum
C. solar energy, wind energy, geothermal energy
D. More than one of the above
E. None of the above

100. Which of the following pairs of petroleum fields and the state of their locations are correct?

A. Hugrijan oil field — Assam
B. Kalol oil field — Gujarat
C. Lunej oil field — Gujarat
D. More than one of the above
E. None of the above

88. A	**89.** E	**90.** D	**91.** B	**92.** A	**93.** D	**94.** B
95. C	**96.** C	**97.** B	**98.** A	**99.** C	**100.** D	

101. Which of the following pairs of places and industries located there are correct?

A. Bhopal — Heavy Electricals
B. Bongaigaon — Petro chemicals
C. Vishakhapatnam — Steel
D. More than one of the above
E. None of the above

102. How long is Atal tunnel?

A. 8 km
B. 10 km
C. 9.02 km
D. More than one of the above
E. None of the above

103. Which of the following characterises sustainable development?

A. complete dependence on and adaptation to the nature
B. to maintain a balance between economic development and environmental quality
C. unrestricted use of non-renewable energy for economic development
D. More than one of the above
E. None of the above

104. Which nation is the largest trading partner of India (Year, 2023)?

A. United States of America
B. China
C. Russia
D. More than one of the above
E. None of the above

105. Which of the following pairs of coal fields and state of their location is correct?

A. Talcher — Odisha
B. Vishrampur — Madhya Pradesh
C. Singrauli — Chhattisgarh
D. More than one of the above
E. None of the above

106. Sundari tree is found in

A. Khasi hill
B. Sundarban delta
C. Nicobar Islands
D. More than one of the above
E. None of the above

107. Which of the following sequences of states/union territory in descending order of their literacy rate according to 2011 census is correct?

A. Kerala, Lakshadweep, Mizoram, Goa
B. Kerala, Goa, Mizoram, Lakshadweep
C. Lakshadweep, Kerala, Goa, Mizoram
D. More than one of the above
E. None of the above

108. The leading producer of lead in India is

A. Andhra Pradesh
B. Rajasthan
C. Odisha
D. More than one of the above
E. None of the above

109. Palghat gap connects

A. Goa & Karnataka
B. Goa & Maharashtra
C. Kerala & Tamil Nadu
D. More than one of the above
E. None of the above

110. Which is the longest National Highway in India?

A. NH 44
B. NH 1
C. NH 544
D. More than one of the above
E. None of the above

ECONOMICS

111. Iron and steel industry should be established near to:

A. Availability of raw material ore
B. Markets
C. Forest
D. More than one of the above
E. None of the above

112. What was the theme of the COP27 summit?

A. Together for Implementation
B. Independent for climate change
C. Agreement for research and development
D. More than one of the above
E. None of the above

113. Sustainability Science is the study of the concepts of sustainable development and ______ .

A. environmental science
B. general science
C. social science
D. More than one of the above
E. None of the above

101. D	102. C	103. B	104. B	105. A	106. B	107. A
108. B	109. C	110. A	111. A	112. A	113. A	

114. What do you understand by an inclusive development in the country?

A. Active participation of all the segments of society in the country
B. Active participation of only business households in the country
C. Active participation of only poor people of society in the country
D. More than one of the above
E. None of the above

115. Number of Sustainable Development Goals (SDGs) by United Nations are

A. 15
B. 16
C. 17
D. More than one of the above
E. None of the above

116. The United Nations Conference on Sustainable Development (UNCSD) is also known as

A. Rio 2010
B. Rio 2011
C. Rio 2012
D. More than one of the above
E. None of the above

117. Consider the following statements regarding the public debt of Government of India includes and select the correct answer.

1. Treasury Bills & Dated securities
2. External Commercial Borrowing (ECB)
3. NRI deposits

A. 1 only
B. 1 and 2 only
C. 1, 2 and 3 only
D. More than one of the above
E. None of the above

118. The informal sector includes:

1. Artisans, cottage industrialists, petty traders, tea shop proprietors.
2. Garbage pickers, jitneys, unauthorized taxis, repair persons
3. The self-employed.
4. IV activities with little capital, skill, and entry barriers.

A. 1 and 2 only
B. 3 and 4 only
C. 1, 2, 3 and 4
D. More than one of the above
E. None of the above

119. The additional capital used for per unit of additional production is called:

A. Induced investment
B. Autonomous investment
C. Incremental capital output ratio
D. More than one of the above
E. None of the above

120. Under the seventh schedule of Indian constitution, Agricultural marketing is in which list?

A. Union list
B. State list
C. Concurrent list
D. More than one of the above
E. None of the above

121. Which of the following denotes business activity at high level with increasing output and income?

A. Boom
B. Recession
C. Recovery
D. More than one of the above
E. None of the above

122. The number of people in different age groups is referred as:

A. Sex ratio
B. Age composition
C. Occupational structure
D. More than one of the above
E. None of the above

123. What is Sex ratio?

A. Number of females per thousand male
B. Number of females per hundred male
C. Difference between birth rate and death rates
D. More than one of the above
E. None of the above

124. A large proportion of children in a population is a result of:

A. High birth rate
B. High death rate
C. High life expectancies
D. More than one of the above
E. None of the above

125. Which of the following factors are responsible for sparse population?

A. Flat plains and abundant rainfall
B. Rugged terrain and unfavourable climate
C. Fertile soil and abundant rainfall
D. More than one of the above
E. None of the above

114. A	**115.** C	**116.** C	**117.** A	**118.** C	**119.** C
120. B	**121.** A	**122.** B	**123.** A	**124.** A	**125.** B

126. Which of the following is an important social indicator to measure the extent of equality between males and females in a society at a given time?

A. Age composition
B. Literacy Rate
C. Sex ratio
D. More than one of the above
E. None of the above

127. Which one of the following is not a tertiary activity?

A. Banking
B. Transport and Communication
C. Building and Construction work
D. More than one of the above
E. None of the above

128. The total area of India accounts for how much percent of the world's area?

A. 2.4 per cent
B. 16.7 per cent
C. 3.28 per cent
D. More than one of the above
E. None of the above

129. What year is considered a great demographic divide in India?

A. 1921
B. 1931
C. 1751
D. More than one of the above
E. None of the above

130. Which of the following migration of population does not change the size of the population?

A. External migration
B. Internal migration
C. International migration
D. More than one of the above
E. None of the above

131. Which of the following is not included in Primary activities?

A. Agriculture
B. Animal Husbandry
C. To give Education
D. More than one of the above
E. None of the above

132. Which one of the following is a market activity?

A. A teacher teaching her child
B. A teacher teaching in school
C. A mechanic repairing his car
D. More than one of the above
E. None of the above

133. Which is the state with highest number of Scheduled Castes in India?

A. Andhra Pradesh
B. Bihar
C. Uttar Pradesh
D. More than one of the above
E. None of the above

134. Which of the following programme was launched in the year of 2000?

A. National Rural Employment Guarantee Act
B. Swarnajayanti Gram Swarozgar Yojana
C. Pradhan Mantri Gramodaya Yojana
D. More than one of the above
E. None of the above

135. Which scheme was started in 1993 to create self-employment opportunities for educated unemployed youth in rural areas and small towns?

A. Prime Minister Rozgar Yojana
B. Rural Employment Generation Programme
C. Swarnajayanti Gram Swarozgar Yojana
D. More than one of the above
E. None of the above

136. Which among the following is the method to estimate the poverty line in India?

A. Investment method
B. Capital method
C. Income method
D. More than one of the above
E. None of the above

137. What is the average calorie required in rural areas for measuring poverty?

A. 2400 calories per person per day
B. 2100 calories per person per day
C. 2800 calories per person per day
D. More than one of the above
E. None of the above

138. The calorie requirement is higher in the rural areas because:

A. they do not enjoy as much as people in the urban areas
B. food items are expensive
C. people are engaged in physical labour
D. More than one of the above
E. None of the above

126. C	**127.** C	**128.** A	**129.** A	**130.** B	**131.** C	**132.** B
133. C	**134.** C	**135.** A	**136.** C	**137.** A	**138.** C	

139. Which one of these is not a cause of poverty in India?

A. Low level of economic development
B. Migration of people from rural to urban India
C. Unequal distribution of land
D. More than one of the above
E. None of the above

140. In which year was NREGA enacted?

A. 2005
B. 2000
C. 1999
D. More than one of the above
E. None of the above

141. Which of the following is not considered as a social indicator of poverty?

A. Less number of means of transport
B. Illiteracy level
C. Lack of access to health care
D. More than one of the above
E. None of the above

142. The second stage of demographic transition is suitably known as:

A. Population Challenge
B. Population Development
C. Population explosion
D. More than one of the above
E. None of the above

143. The lowering of Bank Rate by the Reserve Bank of India leads to:

A. More liquidity in the market
B. No change in the liquidity in the market
C. Mobilization of more deposits by commercial banks
D. More than one of the above
E. None of the above

144. The Reserve Bank of India (RBI) acts as a bankers' bank. This would imply which of the following?

1. Other banks retain their deposits with the RBI.
2. The RBI lends funds to the commercial banks in times of need.
3. The RBI advises the commercial banks on monetary matters.

Select the correct answer using the codes given below:

A. 1 and 2 only
B. 2 and 3 only
C. 1, 2 and 3
D. More than one of the above
E. None of the above

145. In India, deficit financing is used for raising resources for

A. economic development
B. adjusting the balance of payments
C. reducing the foreign debt
D. More than one of the above
E. None of the above

146. GNIGPL-Gail India biogas plant will be set up at which place in Bihar?

A. Masaurhi, Patna
B. Arrah
C. Brahmpur, Buxar
D. More than one of the above
E. None of the above

147. Which among these is not the feature of a Special Economic Zone?

A. Top class facilities
B. Flexibility in labour laws
C. Do not have to pay taxes
D. More than one of the above
E. None of the above

148. The Dagmara Hydro-Electric Project is concerned with which river in Bihar?

A. Kosi
B. Bagmati
C. Punpun
D. More than one of the above
E. None of the above

149. Bihar State Seeds Corporation has got ISO certificate, consider the following and choose the correct answer:

1. Quality Management and Practices Certification
2. Environmental Management Practices Certification
3. Anti-Bribery Management Certification

A. 1 only
B. 2 only
C. 1, 2 and 3 only
D. More than one of the above
E. None of the above

150. Total receipts in 2023-24 budget other than borrowings compared to revised estimate of 2022-23 budget are expected to register an increase of what percentage?

A. 8%
B. 7%
C. 6%
D. More than one of the above
E. None of the above

139. B	**140.** A	**141.** A	**142.** C	**143.** A	**144.** C
145. A	**146.** C	**147.** B	**148.** A	**149.** C	**150.** E

or

POLITICAL SCIENCE

111. Given below are three statements, one as Assertion (A) and the others as Reason (R-1) & (R-2).

1. Assertion (A) : The democracy ensures that we shall be governed no better than we deserve.
2. Reason (R-1) : The Man's capacity for justice makes democracy possible.
3. Reason (R-2) : The Man's inclination to injustice makes democracy necessary.

Select the correct answer from the code given below:

A. Only 1 is correct
B. Only 2 is correct
C. Only 3 is correct
D. More than one of the above
E. None of the above

112. Who of the following said that the democracy is the best, 'it stands above doubts'?

A. Seeley
B. Rousseau
C. J.K. Galbraith
D. More than one of the above
E. None of the above

113. Match the List-I with List-II and select the correct answer from the code given below the lists:

List-I (Comments)	***List-II (Commentators)***
(*a*) The democracy as the government by poorest, the most ignorant & most incapable people	(*i*) Lecky
(*b*) The democracy as an aristocracy of backguards	(*ii*) Talleyrand
(*c*) The democracy as the government of mindless and ignorants	(*iii*) H.G. Wells
(*d*) The democracy as the government full of ignorance	(*iv*) Fogget

The correct match is:

	(*a*)	(*b*)	(*c*)	(*d*)
A.	(*i*)	(*ii*)	(*iii*)	(*iv*)
B.	(*iv*)	(*iii*)	(*ii*)	(*i*)
C.	(*ii*)	(*iii*)	(*iv*)	(*i*)

D. More than one of the above
E. None of the above

114. With reference to the democratic government in India, which of the following statements is/are correct?

A. It is more accountable form of government
B. The democracy in India made the government respond to food security
C. The democracy requires that the rulers have to attend the needs of the people
D. More than one of the above
E. None of the above

115. Who of the following said, Political liberty in the absence of economic equality is a mere myth?

A. Lord Bryce
B. G.D.H. Cole
C. Mahatma Gandhi
D. More than one of the above
E. None of the above

116. Who of the following was of the view that 'all the ills of democracy can be cured by more democracy'?

A. Garner
B. Barker
C. Alfred Smith
D. More than one of the above
E. None of the above

117. "The Indian forest service" in India came into existence in which year?

A. In 1859
B. In 1863
C. In 1864
D. More than one of the above
E. None of the above

118. "The Imperial Forest Research Institute" came into existence in 1906 at which of following place?

A. at Shimla
B. at Dehradun
C. at Calcutta
D. More than one of the above
E. None of the above

111. D **112.** C **113.** A **114.** D **115.** B **116.** C **117.** C **118.** B

119. Which of the following statements about the weakness of democracies in the contemporary world, is/are correct?

1. The decision making and their implementation taken too much time in democratic governments.
2. The Political parties mostly make the democratic governments immoral and powerless.
3. The regional interests become more powerfull than the national interests in them.

Select the correct answer from the code given below:

A. Only 1 is correct
B. Only 2 is correct
C. Only 3 is correct
D. More than one of the above
E. None of the above

120. Which of the following statements befits to the democracies in present times?

A. The democracies involve some loss of immediate efficiency
B. The democracies may increase their efficiency in long run
C. The democracies need required improvements to be done in it in place of choosing the dictatorship
D. More than one of the above
E. None of the above

121. The principle of Parliamentary supremacy is followed in which of the following countries?

A. In India B. In Britain
C. In America D. In China
E. None of the above

122. The first commission to identify the backward classes in India, was formed in the Chairmanship of who of the following?

A. B.P. Mandal B. Sri Ramdhan
C. R.N. Prasad D. Kaka Kalelkar
E. None of the above

123. At the time of Independence, the ruler of which of the following princely states wanted to join Pakistan but the people wanted to join India?

A. Junagarh
B. Hyderabad
C. Kashmir
D. More than one of the above
E. None of the above

124. Which of the following was the main aim of setting up of Planning Commission in 1950 in India?

A. To frame such policies which help rid India of poverty only
B. To ensure economic development only
C. To build modern industrial base only
D. More than one of the above
E. None of the above

125. Which of the following was Gandhiji's expectation from Independent India's constitution?

A. It shall release India from thralldom and patronage
B. All communities must live in perfect harmony in the country
C. The women will enjoy the equal rights as men in India
D. More than one of the above
E. None of the above

126. The standard to examine and evaluate any law and the action of the government in India, is mainly found in which of the following?

A. In Fundamental rights of the constitution
B. In the Directive principles of state policies of the constitution
C. In the Preamble of the constitution
D. More than one of the above
E. None of the above

127. Which of the following was the procedural committee of the Constituent Assembly of India?

A. The Finance and staff committee
B. Ad hoc committee on National Flag
C. Commission on Linguistic provinces
D. More than one of the above
E. None of the above

128. Who of the following was the member of the Drafting Committee of the Constituent Assembly of India?

A. N. Gopalaswami Ayyangar
B. Alladi Krishnaswami Ayyar
C. T.T. Krishnamachari
D. More than one of the above
E. None of the above

129. 'Hindi shall be the official language of the Indian union', was decided by the Drafting Committee, on which of the following date?

A. On 21st February, 1948
B. On 14th September, 1949
C. On 26th November, 1949
D. More than one of the above
E. None of the above

119. D	**120.** D	**121.** B	**122.** D	**123.** A	**124.** D
125. D	**126.** C	**127.** A	**128.** D	**129.** B	

130. Who of the following called the Constituent Assembly of India, "a one party, one party body in an essentially one party country"?

A. Granville Austin
B. K.V. Rao
C. Ivor Jennings
D. More than one of the above
E. None of the above

131. The preamble of the Constitution of India assures the people of India about which of the following?

A. About the dignity of the individuals
B. About the unity and integrity of the nation
C. About the equal status and opportunity of the people
D. More than one of the above
E. None of the above

132. How many types of liberties are provided in 'The Preamble of the Constitution of India'?

A. of Two Types
B. of Three Types
C. of Five Types
D. More than one of the above
E. None of the above

133. Bihar is in the zone of which zonal council in India?

A. In the zone of Northern Zonal Council
B. In the zone of Central Zonal Council
C. In the zone of Eastern Zonal Council
D. More than one of the above
E. None of the above

134. With reference to the model of scientific secularism in India, which of the following statements is/are correct?

A. It is dynamic by nature and suits to the requirements of a progressive nation
B. It keeps religion and politics separate from each other
C. It keeps every community with in the sovereign authority of the Parliament
D. More than one of the above
E. None of the above

135. Which of the following is the main feature of democratic elections in India?

A. In such elections every one has right to vote with the equal value of vote
B. In such elections, voters have opportunities of real choice at the regular intervals
C. Such elections are conducted in free and fair manner
D. More than one of the above
E. None of the above

136. Which of the following statements are correct about the political competition in the country?

A. It provides the way to select our future leaders
B. It makes the political system to work better in long run
C. It presents an opportunity to the people to reward the political leaders for serving them or punish for not doing so
D. More than one of the above
E. None of the above

137. Which of the following state of India possess special status due to their peculiar social and historical circumstances?

A. Only Assam
B. Only Nagaland
C. Only Arunachal Pradesh
D. More than one of the above
E. None of the above

138. Which of the following languages are mentioned in the Eighth schedule of the constitution of India?

A. Bodo and Dogri
B. Oriya and Sindhi
C. Nepali and Santhali
D. More than one of the above
E. None of the above

139. How many seats are found reserved for women, in local government bodies in India?

A. one fifth of the all seats
B. one fourth of the all seats
C. one third of the all seats
D. More than one of the above
E. None of the above

140. The National Commission for Backward classes in the country, was formed by which of the following amendment of the constitution of India?

A. By 100th amendment
B. By 101st amendment
C. By 102nd amendment
D. More than one of the above
E. None of the above

141. The form of oath for the members of Parliament is found in which of the following schedule of the constitution of India?

A. In first schedule
B. In third schedule
C. In fifth schedule
D. More than one of the above
E. None of the above

130. A	**131.** D	**132.** C	**133.** C	**134.** D	**135.** D
136. D	**137.** D	**138.** D	**139.** C	**140.** C	**141.** B

142. Which of the following statement about the extention of the period of Parliament during emergency, is/are True?
A. It may be extended up to one year in emergency at a time
B. It may be extended up to 8 months only at a time in emergency
C. It may be extended up to 6 months after the closing of emergency
D. More than one of the above
E. None of the above

143. Which of the following statements about the ministers in the country is/are correct?
A. The cabinet ministers are in charge of major ministries & the decision makers in the name of council of ministers
B. The state ministers with independent charge are in charge of smaller ministries and attend the meeting when invited
C. The ministers of states are to assist cabinet ministers
D. More than one of the above
E. None of the above

144. Which constitutional amendment binds the President of India to act in accordance with advice rendered by the council of ministers?
A. The Thirty ninth amendment
B. The Forty second amendment
C. The Forty fourth amendment
D. More than one of the above
E. None of the above

145. Which of the following provisions for the independence of Judiciary are found in India?
A. The constitutional appointment in it
B. The salaries and allowances of the judges are charged on the consolidated fund & they are bared to the legal practice after retirement
C. Immunity from reckless criticism of their judicial conduct
D. More than one of the above
E. None of the above

146. How much may be maximum strength of a Vidhan Parishad in a state of India?
A. It can not be more than 1/5 of the total strength of the State Vidhan Sabha
B. It can not be more than 1/4 of the total streng of the State Vidhan Sabha
C. It can not be more than 1/3 of the total streng of the State Vidhan Sabha
D. More than one of the above
E. None of the above

147. In India which of the following statements relati to 'The Right to Protection of Life and Person Liberty' is correct?
A. It is available to the citizens only against th state
B. It is also available against its violation by priva individuals
C. This right does not promises the dignity of li
D. More than one of the above
E. None of the above

148. The Right to education of the children of the ag of six to fourteen years is made their fundament Right by which constitutional amendment in India
A. By 44th amendment
B. By 86th amendment
C. By 91st amendment
D. More than one of the above
E. None of the above

149. Which of the following is the main challenge the Indian political party system?
A. The lack of internal democracy within the partie
B. The lack of dynamic system of succession t first one in the parties
C. The growing role of money and muscle powe in parties specially during elections
D. More than one of the above
E. None of the above

150. Which of the following may be called the outcom of democracy in India?
A. The formation of a legitimate, responsive an accountable government in the country
B. Economic growth and reduction of inequalit and poverty in the country
C. The existence of the accommodative rule i the country for social diversity along with th dignity and freedom of the citizens.
D. More than one of the above
E. None of the above

EXPLANATORY ANSWERS

1. (E): The passage states that Amitabh Bachchan was born in Allahabad, Uttar Pradesh, which is not listed in the options. Therefore, the correct answer is "None of the above."

2. (B): According to the passage, Amitabh Bachchan' career in Indian cinema has spanned fou decades. Thus, the correct answer is "Fou decades."

142. D	**143.** D	**144.** B	**145.** D	**146.** C	**147.** D	**148.** B	**149.** D	**150.** D

3. **(E):** The passage mentions that Amitabh Bachchan earned a degree in science from Delhi University, which is not listed in the options provided. Therefore, the correct answer is "None of the above."

4. **(C):** The passage mentions that Amitabh Bachchan became well-known as a movie star in 1973 following the success of the films "Abhimaan" and "Zanjeer." Therefore, the correct answer is "1973."

5. **(C):** The passage indicates that Amitabh Bachchan's first film was "Saat Hindustani" (1969). Therefore, the correct answer is "Saat Hindustani."

6. **(C):** The correct article to complete the sentence is "the" because we are referring to a specific entity, "the Earth." Therefore, the correct answer is "the."

7. **(B):** In the context of the sentence, "a degree" is correct because we are referring to any degree in general, not a specific one. Therefore, the correct answer is "a."

8. **(B):** First May 2024 is a Wednesday. Since May 9 is 8 days later, it would be one day after the following Wednesday, which is a Thursday. Therefore, the correct answer is "Thursday."

9. **(C):** गद्यांश के अनुसार, पंडित राम प्रसाद बिस्मिल के जीवन में परिवर्तन तब आया जब वे आर्य समाज के संपर्क में आए। इस संपर्क ने उनमें साहस जगाया और क्रांति का संचार किया। इसलिए, सही उत्तर ''जब वे आये समाज के संपर्क में आए'' है।

10. **(A):** गद्यांश के अनुसार, पंडित बिस्मिल ने स्वतंत्रता संग्राम के लिए धन एकत्र करने के उद्देश्य से अंग्रेजों का सरकारी खजाना लूटने की योजना बनाई और इसे काकोरी स्टेशन पर सफलतापूर्वक अंजाम दिया। इसलिए, सही उत्तर ''सरकारी खजाना लूटकर'' है।

11. **(C):** गद्यांश में बताया गया है कि पंडित बिस्मिल अपने कार्यो से अंग्रेजी हुकूमत को हिलाने में सफल हुए और इस कारण उन्हें महान क्रांतिकारी माना गया। इसलिए, सही उत्तर ''क्योंकि उन्होंने अपने कार्यों में अंग्रेजी हुकूमत को हिला दिया'' है।

12. **(B):** शब्द ''सजग'' का मूल शब्द ''जग'' है, जिसका अर्थ ''जाग्रत'' या ''सतर्क'' होता है। इसलिए, सही उत्तर ''जग'' है।

13. **(E):** ''स्वतंत्रता'' का विलोम शब्द ''परतंत्रता'' है, जो कि दिए गए विकल्पों में नहीं है। इसलिए, सही उत्तर ''उपर्युक्त में से कोई नहीं'' है।

14. **(B):** ''लंबी आयु जीने वाला'' का एक शब्दीय पर्याय ''दीर्घायु'' है। इसलिए, सही उत्तर ''दीर्घायु'' है।

15. **(B):** गद्यांश में बताया गया है कि मनुष्य का जीवन श्रेष्ठ माना गया है क्योंकि वह बुद्धिमान और कल्पनाशील प्राणी है। इस विशेषता के कारण वह ऊँचाई तक पहुँच सकता है। इसलिए, सही उत्तर ''क्योंकि वह बुद्धिमान और कल्पनाशील है'' है।

16. **(E):** गद्यांश के अनुसार, उन्नति के लिए मनुष्य के विचार सच्चे, सादे, पवित्र और व्यावहारिक जीवन से जुड़े होने चाहिए। विकल्पों में यह संयोजन नहीं है, इसलिए सही उत्तर ''उपर्युक्त में से कोई नहीं'' है।

17. **(A):** गद्यांश में सादगी को व्यक्ति के हाव-भाव, विचार और जीवन के ढंग से जुड़ा बताया गया है, जो विचारों को भी उच्च बनाती है। इसका तात्पर्य वैचारिक और व्यावहारिक सादगी से है। इसलिए, सही उत्तर ''वैचारिक और व्यावहारिक'' है।

18. **(C):** ''उन्नति'' का उचित विलोम ''अवनति'' है, जो विपरीत अर्थ को दर्शाता है। इसलिए, सही उत्तर ''अवनति'' है।

19. **(A):** ''महान है जो आत्मा'' में ''महान'' विशेषण ''आत्मा'' को विशेषता देता है। यह कर्मधारय समास का उदाहरण है, जहाँ विशेषण और विशेष्य एक साथ मिलकर अर्थ को स्पष्ट करते हैं। इसलिए, सही उत्तर ''कर्मधारण समास'' है।

20. **(C):** ''प्रत्येक'' शब्द का सही वर्ण-विच्छेद ''प् + र् + अ + त् + य् + ए + क् + अ'' है, जो सही ध्वनियों को दर्शाता है। इसलिए, सही उत्तर ''प् + र् + अ + त् + य् + ए + क् + अ'' है।

21. **(C):** ''महौजस्वी'' वृद्धि संधि का उदाहरण है, जहां ''मह'' और ''उजस्वी'' में वृद्धि संधि का प्रयोग होता है। इसलिए, सही उत्तर ''महौजस्वी'' है।

22. **(B):** ''अद्वितीय'' सही वर्तनी है, जिसका अर्थ होता है ''अद्वितीय'' या ''बेजोड़''। इसलिए, सही उत्तर ''अद्वितीय'' है।

23. **(D):** जातिवाचक संज्ञा वह संज्ञा है जो किसी जाति, वर्ग या समूह का बोध कराती है। दिए गए विकल्पों में ''मंत्री'' और ''जुलाहा'' जातिवाचक संज्ञाएँ हैं क्योंकि ये वर्ग या जाति का बोध कराते हैं। इसलिए, सही उत्तर ''उपर्युक्त में से एक से अधिक'' है।

24. **(D):** ''चंद्रमा'' के पर्यायवाची शब्दों में ''राकेश'' और ''सारंग'' शामिल हैं। इसलिए, सही उत्तर ''उपर्युक्त में से एक से अधिक'' है।

25. **(D):** ''स्थिर'' का विलोम ''अस्थिर'' और ''चंचल'' दोनों होते हैं। इसलिए, सही उत्तर ''उपर्युक्त में से एक से अधिक'' है।

26. **(B):** इस वाक्य में ''एक लीटर'' विशेषण है क्योंकि वह ''दूध'' की मात्रा का बोध कराता है। इसलिए, सही उत्तर ''एक लीटर'' है।

27. (B): "कृष्णार्पण" में "कृष्ण" और "अर्पण" दो शब्दों का संयोजन है, जिसमें "कृष्ण को अर्पण" का भाव निहित है। यह कर्मधारण समास का उदाहरण है। इसलिए, सही उत्तर "कर्मधारय" है।

28. (A): "कम बोलने वाला" के लिए एक शब्द "मितभाषी" है, जिसका अर्थ होता है "संयम से बोलने वाला" इसलिए, सही उत्तर "मितभाषी" है।

29. (C): "उदासीन हो जाने" के लिए सही मुहावरा "आँखें फेर लेना" है, जिसका अर्थ होता है किसी से मुँह मोड़ लेना या ध्यान न देना। इसलिए, सही उत्तर "आँखें फेर लेना" है।

30. (B): "निरपराध" शब्द में "निर्" उपसर्ग है, जो "बिना" का भाव प्रकट करता है। इसलिए, सही उत्तर "निर्" है।

31. (C): The total distance covered in 7 revolutions is 2200 metres. Thus, the distance covered in one revolution (the circumference of the circular path) is:

$$\text{Circumference} = \frac{2200}{7} = 314 \text{ metres}$$

Using the formula for the circumference of a circle, $C = 2\pi r$, where $\pi = \frac{22}{7}$, we can substitute the values.

$$314 = 2 \times \frac{22}{7} \times r$$

Solving for r:

$$r = \frac{314 \times 7}{2 \times 22} = 50 \text{ metres (approx)}$$

Therefore, the correct answer is "50 metres."

32. (B): The volume V of a cylinder is given by $V = \pi r^2 h$, where r is the radius and h is the height (or depth).

Given: $V = 1848 \text{ m}^3$

and diameter $= 14$ m

$\Rightarrow$ $r = \frac{14}{2} = 7$ m

Using $\pi = \frac{22}{7}$.

$$1848 = \frac{22}{7} \times 7^2 \times h$$

$$1848 = 22 \times 7 \times h$$

$$1848 = 154h$$

$$\Rightarrow \quad h = \frac{1848}{154} = 12 \text{ m}$$

Thus, the correct answer is "12 m."

33. (C): Let the number be x.

Given, $\frac{1}{8}x = 30$; we can solve for x:

$$x = 30 \times 8$$
$$= 240$$

Now, 62% of x is:

$$0.62 \times 240 = 148.8$$

Thus, the correct answer is "148.8."

34. (C): Let the original salary be 100. After a 25% increase, the new salary becomes:

$$100 + 25 = 125$$

To restore the original salary, we need to find the percentage decrease needed from 125 back to 100:

$$\frac{125-100}{125} \times 100 = \frac{25}{125} \times 100 = 20\%$$

Thus, the correct answer is "20%."

35. (B): We are asked to find a number x by which $\left(\frac{2}{3}\right)^{-3}$ should be divided to get $\left(\frac{4}{9}\right)^{-2}$.

Express the problem as an equation:

$$\frac{\left(-\frac{2}{3}\right)^{-3}}{x} = \left(\frac{4}{9}\right)^{-2}$$

Solving for x gives:

$$x = \frac{\left(-\frac{2}{3}\right)^{-3}}{\left(\frac{4}{9}\right)^{-2}}$$

Evaluate $\left(-\frac{2}{3}\right)^{-3} = \frac{1}{\left(-\frac{2}{3}\right)^3} = \frac{1}{-\frac{8}{27}} = -\frac{27}{8}$

Evaluate $\left(\frac{4}{9}\right)^{-2} = \frac{1}{\left(\frac{4}{9}\right)^2} = \frac{1}{\frac{16}{81}} = \frac{81}{16}$

Substitute the values back into the equation for x:

$$x = \frac{-\frac{27}{8}}{\frac{81}{16}} = -\frac{27}{8} \times \frac{16}{81}$$

$$= -\frac{432}{648} = -\frac{2}{3}$$

Therefore, the correct answer is:

The number by which $\left(-\frac{2}{3}\right)^{-3}$ should be divided to obtain $\left(\frac{4}{9}\right)^{-2}$ is $-\frac{2}{3}$.

36. (B): Given:

$$x + \frac{1}{x} = 5$$

We need to find the value of:

$$x^4 + \frac{1}{x^4}$$

To solve this, we can use identies involving powers of $x + \frac{1}{x}$.

Step 1: Find $x^2 + \frac{1}{x^2}$

We square both sides of the given equation:

$$\left(x + \frac{1}{x}\right)^2 = 5^2$$

$$x^2 + \frac{1}{x^2} = 25$$

$$x^2 + \frac{1}{x^2} = 25 - 2 = 23$$

Step 2: Find $x^4 + \frac{1}{x^4}$

Now, we square $x^2 + \frac{1}{x^2}$ to find $x^4 + \frac{1}{x^4}$:

$$\left(x^2 + \frac{1}{x^2}\right)^2 = 23^2$$

$$x^4 + 2 + \frac{1}{x^4} = 529$$

$$x^4 + \frac{1}{x^4} = 529 - 2 = 527$$

Thus, the correct answer is: 527.

37. (E): Let the number of 5-rupee, 2-rupee and 1-rupee coins be $2x$, $3x$ and $4x$ respectively, according to the given ratio 2 : 3 : 4.

Step 1: Set up the equation for the total value

The total value of the coins is given as ₹ 2000.

We can write the equation for the total value as:

$$5 \times (2x) + 2 \times (3x) + 1 \times (4x) = 2000$$

Step 2: Simplify the equation

Expanding and simplifying

$$10x + 6x + 4x = 2000$$

$$20x = 2000$$

$$x = 100$$

Step 3: Calculate the number of 2-rupee coins

The number of 2-rupee coins is $3x$:

$$3x = 3 \times 100 = 300$$

Therefore, the correct answer is None of the above.

38. (A): For a regular polygon, each interior angle and exterior angle sum up to 180°. Let the exterior angle be x. Then the interior angle would be $x + 108°$ because it exceeds the exterior angle by 108°.

$$\text{So, } x + (x + 108) = 180$$

$$2x = 72$$

$$x = 36°$$

The number of sides n of a regular polygon is given by

$$n = \frac{360}{\text{Exterior Angle}}.$$

$$\text{Thus: } \quad n = \frac{360}{36} = 10$$

Hence, the correct answer should actually be 10.

39. (A): Zinc Oxide is commonly used in the manufacture of paints because it acts as a pigment and provides durability, corrosion resistance, and UV protection in paint. It is not typically used in the production of explosives or solvents. Therefore, the correct answer is "Paints."

40. (E): Lenz's law is derived from the law of conservation of energy. It states that the direction of an induced current is such that it opposes the change that caused it, ensuring that energy is conserved in the electromagnetic system. This is not related directly to magnetism, momentum, or charge conservation. Hence, the correct answer is "None of the above."

41. (B): Glycogen is a polysaccharide that is stored in the liver and muscles of the human body. It is a large, branched polymer of glucose and serves as a form of energy storage. Therefore, the correct answer is "Polysaccharide."

42. (B): Sickle cell anaemia is a genetic disorder where the haemoglobin in red blood cells is defective. This causes the red blood cells to take on a sickle shape, which can lead to various health complications. Haematoma is a collection of blood outside the blood vessels, and haemophilia is a blood clotting disorder, neither of which involve defective haemoglobin. Therefore, the correct answer is "Sickle cell Anaemia."

43. **(A):** Ethyl alcohol (ethanol) is commonly used in the production of antiseptics because of its ability to kill or inhibit the growth of microorganisms. It is not typically used as an antipyretic or anti-allergic. Therefore, the correct answer is "Antiseptic."

44. **(D):** The velocity of sound in a gas depends on the temperature but is independent of pressure. Therefore, if the pressure is doubled without any change in temperature, the velocity of sound remains the same. Thus, the correct answer is "340 m/sec."

45. **(D):** If a bacterium divides every 15 minutes, it divides 4 times in an hour. Therefore, in 2 hours, it will divide:

$$4 \times 2 = 8 \text{ times}$$

Starting with one bacterium, the number of bacteria after each division follows a geometric progression:

$$\text{Number of bacteria} = 2^8 = 256$$

Thus, the correct answer is "256."

46. **(C):** Plant and animal cells differ in the presence of a cell wall. Plant cells have a rigid cell wall that provides structure and support, while animal cells do not have a cell wall. Enzymes and nuclei are present in both plant and animal cells. Therefore, the correct answer is "Cell wall."

47. **(B):** According to recent reports, the Kuwaiti Dinar is considered the strongest currency in the world based on exchange rates. Therefore, the correct answer is "Kuwaiti Dinar."

48. **(C):** Prime Minister Narendra Modi launched 8 AMRUT (Atal Mission for Rejuvenation and Urban Transformation) projects in Solapur, Maharashtra. Therefore, the correct answer is "Solapur."

49. **(A):** IIT Madras collaborated with Altair to launch an e-Mobility Simulation Lab. Altair provides advanced software solutions for simulation and design, which aids in research for electric vehicles and e-mobility. Therefore, the correct answer is "Altair."

50. **(B):** At the Academy Awards (Oscars) in 2024, Cillian Murphy won the Best Actor Award. Therefore, the correct answer is "Cillian Murphy."

51. **(C):** Hayley Mathews from the West Indies was selected as the ICC Women's T20I Cricketer of the Year 2023. Therefore, the correct answer is "Hayley Mathews (West Indies)."

52. **(A):** Miss Czech Kristina Pishkova was crowned Miss World 2024 in Mumbai. Therefore, the correct answer is "Miss Czech Kristina Pishkova."

53. **(B):** The Clean Energy Investor Forum, organize by the Indo-Pacific Economic Framework (IPEF is scheduled to be held in Singapore. Therefor the correct answer is "Singapore."

54. **(C):** The Sittwe Port, which India has acquired th right to operate, is located in Myanmar. Therefor the correct answer is "Myanmar."

55. **(A):** The mangrove forest in the Ganga Delta i known as the Sunderban. It is one of the large mangrove forests in the world. Therefore, the correc answer is "Sunderban."

56. **(B):** The Kosi River, often referred to as th "Sorrow of Bihar," is known for frequently changin its course due to the heavy silt it carries and th region's topography. This has caused severe floodin and displacement issues in Bihar over the years Therefore, the correct answer is "Kosi."

57. **(C):** Plants absorb water primarily through capillar water, which is the water available in the small pore of the soil. This water moves through the soil b capillary action and is readily accessible to plan roots. Therefore, the correct answer is "Capillar water."

58. **(B):** The equatorial diameter of the Earth i approximately 43 km larger than the polar diameter This difference is due to the Earth's oblate shape which bulges slightly at the equator due to it rotation. Therefore, the correct answer is "43 km."

59. **(A):** The Indian Standard Time (IST) is based o the 82.5° E longitude, which passes near Mirzapu in Uttar Pradesh. This meridian is 5 hours and 3 minutes ahead of Greenwich Mean Time (GMT) Therefore, the correct answer is "82.5° E."

60. **(B):** Dr. M.S. Swaminathan is known as the "Fathe of the Green Revolution" in India. He played pivotal role in introducing high-yielding varieties o seeds and modern agricultural techniques, which le to a significant increase in food grain production i India. Therefore, the correct answer is "Dr. M.S. Swaminathan."

61. **(C):** The highest mountain peak in India is K-2 also known as Mount Godwin-Austen. It is locate in the Karakoram range and is the second-highes peak in the world after Mount Everest. Althoug Kanchenjunga is the highest peak within India territory, K-2 is located in the region under India administration in the Karakoram range. Therefore the correct answer is "K-2."

63. **(B):** Kunwar Singh, a prominent leader from Bihar led the Revolt of 1857 in the region. He was a significant figure in the Indian independence struggle against British colonial rule, especially known for his role in Bihar. Therefore, the correct answer is "Kunwar Singh."

64. (C): Swami Vivekananda voiced the spiritual side of nationalism through his teachings and speeches, emphasizing India's cultural and spiritual heritage. He inspired many Indians to take pride in their heritage, which became a foundation for the nationalist movement. Therefore, the correct answer is "Swami Vivekananda."

65. (B): Amrit Bazar Patrika was a prominent nationalist newspaper during India's freedom struggle, known for its strong nationalist views and criticism of British colonial policies. It played an essential role in raising awareness and motivating people to join the freedom movement. Therefore, the correct answer is "Amrit Bazar Patrika."

66. (B): In 1918, Mahatma Gandhi intervened in a dispute between the mill workers and mill owners of Ahmedabad. This was one of the first instances of his involvement in labour issues, where he successfully mediated between the workers, who demanded a wage increase, and the owners. Gandhi's intervention led to a resolution through a peaceful method, setting an example of conflict resolution. Therefore, the correct answer is "Mahatma Gandhi."

67. (A): Karyanand Sharma was a prominent left-wing leader of the Bihar Provincial Kisan Sabha, which played a significant role in mobilizing farmers against oppressive landlords and advocating for agrarian reforms. He popularized the movement in Bihar, helping it gain support from the rural population. Therefore, the correct answer is "Karyanand Sharma."

68. (A): The Muddiman Committee was appointed in 1924 to examine the functioning of dyarchy, which was introduced by the Government of India Act of 1919. The committee was tasked with reporting on the effectiveness of dyarchy, a system in which provincial subjects were divided into "reserved" and "transferred" categories, with limited responsibility granted to Indian ministers. Therefore, the correct answer is "Dyarchy."

69. (E): The quote, "He was a great unifier in India who taught us not only bare tolerance of others but the willing acceptance of them as our friends and comrades in common undertakings," was actually said by Jawaharlal Nehru, referring to Mahatma Gandhi. Since Nehru is not listed among the options, the correct answer is "None of the above."

70. (B): Rash Behari Bose was a key figure in organizing efforts for Indian independence from abroad. He founded the Indian Independence League and later formed the Indian National Army (INA) with the aim of achieving India's freedom through military efforts outside India. He was instrumental in setting up the initial framework of the INA, which was later led by Subhash Chandra Bose. Therefore, the correct answer is "Rash Behari Bose."

HISTORY

71. (B): The Harappan Civilization can be placed in the Proto-History phase of history. This is because while the Harappan Civilization existed before the advent of written historical records, it left behind archaeological evidence, such as inscriptions and artifacts, which offer a glimpse into its culture and lifestyle.

72. (C): The Indus Valley site Sutkagendor is situated on the bank of the Dasht River, which is in present-day Balochistan, Pakistan.

73. (E): The Hulas archaeological site, which is part of the Indus Valley Civilization, is actually located in the Saharanpur district of Uttar Pradesh.

74. (C): Chandragupta Maurya, the founder of the Maurya Empire in ancient India, is referred to as "Sandrocottus" in Greek historical sources, particularly by the Greek historian Megasthenes. Megasthenes was an ambassador sent by the Greek Seleucid king, Seleucus I Nicator, to the court of Chandragupta Maurya.

75. (A): The Greek writer Strabo is the one who mentions that the region of Ariyana (which is part of the area around present-day Afghanistan) was given to Chandragupta Maurya as part of the marriage alliance between him and the daughter of Seleucus I Nicator.

76. (B): Upagupta was a renowned Buddhist monk and is traditionally believed to have been instrumental in converting Ashoka to Buddhism. While other figures, like Moggaliputta Tissa, played important roles in the spread of Buddhism during Ashoka's reign, it is Upagupta who is most often directly associated with initiating Ashoka's journey into Buddhism.

77. (C): Emperor Ashoka, one of the most renowned rulers of ancient India, played a pivotal role in the spread of Buddhism. His journey to Bodh Gaya in the 10th year of his reign holds significant historical and spiritual importance. Bodh Gaya is the place where Siddhartha Gautama, the Buddha, attained enlightenment under the Bodhi tree.

78. (A): Ashoka's Bhabru Rock Edict is where he explicitly expresses his belief in the Triratna — the Three Jewels of Buddhism: Buddha, Dhamma, and Sangha. This edict is one of the significant inscriptions where Ashoka publicly reaffirms his support for these core principles of Buddhism.

79. (C): In Mauryan administration, the term "Sangrahan" referred to a tax-collecting unit, and it is recorded that 10 villages typically came under one Sangrahan for the purpose of tax collection.

80. (A): In Kautilya's Arthashastra, two types of spies are primarily mentioned:

1. The internal spies (who operate within the kingdom to gather information about the population, officials, and the state of affairs).
2. The external spies (who gather intelligence from outside the kingdom, including from neighboring states or foreign territories).

These two types of spies were integral to the effective governance and security of the Mauryan Empire, as outlined by Kautilya in his treatise.

81. (C): During the Mauryan period, the Rupadarshaka was the official responsible for the examination and inspection of coins. They ensured that the coins were of the correct weight and met the standards set by the government.

82. (B): In the Mauryan administration, the financial year began in the month of Ashadam (or Ashadha) according to the Hindu calendar, which typically corresponds to July in the Gregorian calendar.

The reason for starting the financial year in Ashadam was closely linked to the agricultural cycle. Ashadam marks the beginning of the monsoon season in India, which is crucial for the cultivation of crops. The start of the financial year in this month would allow the administration to plan and budget for agricultural activities, tax collection, and other economic affairs in sync with the farming calendar.

83. (B): The construction of the Guha-Vihars (cave monasteries) at Nagarjuni hills during the Mauryan age is credited to Dasharatha Maurya, the grandson of Emperor Ashoka.

84. (A): The Aihole Inscription was written by the poet Ravikirti, who was a court poet of the Chalukya king Pulakeshin II. The inscription describes the conflict between Pulakeshin II and Harsha of the Vardhana dynasty, in which Pulakeshin II successfully repelled Harsha's invasion, marking a significant event in the history of ancient India.

85. (B): Singhnad was the commander-in-chief of Harshavardhan who played a significant role in encouraging him to ascend the throne after the death of his brother, Rajyavardhan. Singhnad's support and military influence were crucial in Harsha's rise to power.

86. (B): According to the Chinese writer Hiuen Tsang (Xuanzang), Harsha adopted the title of Magadhraj (King of Magadha) in the year 641. This was during Hiuen Tsang's visit to India, and he mentions this in his accounts.

87. (C): According to Hiuen Tsang (Xuanzang), Harsha built a copper monastery (vihar) at Nalanda in Bihar. Hiuen Tsang visited Nalanda during his travels and described it as a renowned center of learning, with a large number of monks and scholars.

88. (E): Hiuen Tsang spent five years studying at Nalanda, the premier Indian institution in Bihar at the time. Hiuen Tsang studied logic, grammar, Sanskrit, and the Yogacara school of Buddhism in Nalanda. At Nalanda, Xuanzang met the venerable Silabhadra (expert of Yogacara teaching and personal teacher of Hiuen Tsang). While studying Buddhism at Naland University in India, Xuanzang discovered eleven commentaries on Vasubandhu.

89. (E): The actual founder of Nalanda University is believed to be Kumaragupta I, a ruler of the Gupta dynasty. He is traditionally credited with establishing and developing the university in the 5th century, which later became one of the most famous centers of learning in ancient India.

90. (A): Rajaraja I, the great Chola emperor, defeated the Sri Lankan ruler Mahinda V for the first time on Sri Lankan soil. This victory marked a significant moment in the expansion of the Chola Empire, as Rajaraja I extended his influence over Sri Lanka and established Chola dominance in the region.

91. (C): Rajendra I, the Chola ruler, established the capital city of Gangaikonda Cholapuram. He built this city after his victorious campaign in northern India, where he conquered territories along the Ganges River. To commemorate his victory and to rival the great city of Thanjavur, Rajendra I created Gangaikonda Cholapuram as his new capital, which also became a center of administration and culture in the Chola Empire.

92. (B): Rajaraja I, the great Chola emperor, constructed the Rajarajeshwar Temple (also known as the Brihadeeswarar Temple) in his capital, Thanjavur. This temple, dedicated to Lord Shiva, is one of the most magnificent architectural achievements of the Chola dynasty and remains a UNESCO World Heritage site.

93. (C): Rajaraja I, also known as Rajaraja the Great, was one of the most illustrious rulers of the Chola dynasty in South India. He reigned from 985 to 1014 CE and is often referred to as "Chola Narayan" in contemporary writings due to his significant contributions to the expansion and administration of the Chola Empire.

94. (B): Iltutmish, one of the prominent rulers of the Delhi Sultanate, was initially appointed as the governor of Badaun. This appointment marked the beginning of his rise in power and influence.

95. (A): Iltutmish gave Tajuddin Yalduz a crushing defeat at Ṭarain in January 1216. After the battle, Tajuddin Yalduz was captured and imprisoned.

96. (C): Qutubuddin Aibak purchased Iltutmish for one lakh jitals, a significant sum at the time. Iltutmish was originally a slave who was bought by Aibak, and he later rose to become one of the most powerful rulers of the Delhi Sultanate.

97. (C): Iltutmish received formal recognition from the Caliph of Baghdad in 1229. This recognition greatly enhanced his authority and legitimacy as the Sultan of Delhi, solidifying his position as a ruler in the eyes of the broader Muslim world.

98. (A): Qutubuddin Aibak, the first Sultan of Delhi, constructed the Quwwat-ul-Islam Mosque in 1193. It is one of the earliest and most significant mosques built in Delhi after the establishment of the Delhi Sultanate. The mosque was built using materials from the demolished Hindu temples, and it is located in the Qutb Complex in Delhi, which also houses the famous Qutub Minar.

99. (B): The period 1236-1266 in the history of the Delhi Sultanate is known as the era of "the rule of the Forty." This refers to a group of forty Turkish nobles who had considerable influence and power during the reign of Iltutmish. These nobles were central to the administration of the Sultanate and played a significant role in the political dynamics of the time.

100. (B): The post of Naib-i-mamlikat (deputy to the ruler or vice-regent) was created during the reign of Muizuddin Bahram Shah, the last ruler of the Slave Dynasty. This title was part of the administrative changes made during his rule.

101. (C): Ikhtiyaruddin Aitigin became the first Naib-i-mamlikat (deputy to the ruler) in the history of the Delhi Sultanate. He was appointed to this post during the reign of Muizuddin Bahram Shah, and his appointment marked the beginning of a new administrative position in the Sultanate's governance structure.

102. (B): Ghiyasuddin Balban's original name was Bahauddin before he assumed the title of Ghiyasuddin Balban when he became the Sultan of Delhi.

103. (B): Balban was replaced as Naib-i-mamlikati by Imaduddin Raihan for a brief period before Balban regained his position.

104. (A): Balban, the Sultan of Delhi, inscribed "Nasir-Amir-ul-Momenin" on his coins to assert his position as the protector and helper of the faithful (Muslims) and to gain the loyalty of his co-religionists. This title was used to establish his authority as a leader in the Muslim world and solidify his rule.

105. (C): Kaiqubad was the last ruler of the Mamluk (Slave) Dynasty of Delhi, reigning from 1287 to 1290. His reign marked the end of the dynasty, as he was succeeded by the Khilji Dynasty after his death.

106. (B): Akbar was born on November 23, 1542, at Amarkot Fort, which was under the rule of Rana Virsal. This location was significant as it was a Rajput kingdom, highlighting the connections between the Mughal Empire and Rajput rulers during that period.

107. (C): Akbar was crowned as the emperor of the Mughal Empire at Kalanaur in 1556. He ascended the throne at the age of 13, following the death of his father, Humayun.

108. (C): The conquest of Asirgarh in 1601 was Akbar's last major military campaign. Located in the Deccan region, Asirgarh was strategically important, and its capture marked the completion of Akbar's expansionist efforts in India.

109. (C): In 1579, Akbar issued the Mahzar, which was a decree declaring his position as the highest authority in religious matters within his empire. It was part of his efforts to promote religious tolerance and establish a syncretic approach to governance, where he encouraged dialogue among different religious communities.

110. (E): Akbar built the Buland Darwaza at Fatehpur Sikri, which is neither of the options listed. This grand gateway was constructed in 1575 to commemorate his victory over Gujarat and is one of the most striking examples of Mughal architecture.

GEOGRAPHY

71. (B): Total Area of India is 3287263 sq. km. Which is approximately 2.4% of the total surface of the world. India is the seventh-largest country in term of the area after Russia, Canada, USA, China, Brazil and Australia respectively.

72. (A): The coastline along the mainland of India is approximately 6100 kilometers. When considering the entire length including the mainland coastline and the coastline of the islands, it totals around 7516 kilometers.

73. (D): Indira Point is:

B. Situated in the Great Nicobar group of Islands.

C. The southernmost point of India.

74. (C): The Garo, Khasi, and Jaintia Hills are located in the state of Meghalaya in northeastern India. These hills are home to distinct indigenous communities and contribute to the state's diverse geography.

75. (A): Antecedent valleys are valleys formed by rivers that existed before the land underwent significant geological changes, like upliftment. The Sutlej and Indus rivers are examples of this, as they have maintained their courses through older, uplifted terrain, carving out valleys over time.

76. (C): According to the National Environmental Engineering Research Institute (NEERI), Nagpur, approximately 70 per cent of the water available in India is polluted. This highlights the significant challenges related to water quality and pollution in the country.

77. (A): The sequence of rivers in India, arranged in descending order of their respective basin areas, is:

1. Ganga (the largest basin)
2. Indus
3. Godavari
4. Krishna

This order reflects the relative size of the drainage basins of these rivers in India.

78. (B): In 1951, Hermann Flohn, a German meteorologist, proposed that the monsoon is primarily the result of the seasonal migration of planetary winds and pressure belts. His theory emphasized the role of the shifting wind patterns and pressure systems in bringing about the monsoon rains in India and other parts of Asia.

79. (E): In terms of forest cover as percentage of total geographical area, the top five States are Mizoram (84.53%), Arunachal Pradesh (79.33)%, Meghalaya (76.00%), Manipur (74.34)% and Nagaland (73.90%).

80. (A): Kuno National Park in Madhya Pradesh was in the news for the translocation of 20 cheetahs from Africa. This ambitious reintroduction project aims to revive the cheetah population in India.

81. (B): The correct sequence of states in descending order of their population density based on the 2011 Census of India is option (B) Bihar, West Bengal, Kerala, Uttar Pradesh.

82. (C): According to the 2011 Census of India, the sex ratio (number of females per thousand males) is 943.

83. (C): "Sagarmatha" is the Nepali name for Mount Everest, the highest mountain peak in the world. In Tibetan, it is known as "Chomolungma."

84. (A): In Bhutan, approximately 3% of the country's land area is covered by glaciers. These glaciers are found mainly in the northern regions, in the high-altitude areas of the Himalayas.

85. (B): Rice is the main food crop produced in Bhutan. It is a staple food in the country and is grown in the fertile valleys, particularly in the southern and central regions.

86. (E): Sri Lanka is not particularly known for significant deposits of iron ore, gold, or coal. While it has some mineral resources, none of these are in large abundance compared to other countries. Sri Lanka is more famous for other natural resources, like gemstones, tea, and coconut products.

87. (C): Naypyidaw (also spelled Nay Pyi Taw) is the capital of Myanmar. It officially became the capital in 2005, replacing Yangon (formerly known as Rangoon).

88. (A): In 2022, the birth rate in Bangladesh was approximately 17.067 births per 1,000 people. This figure reflects the number of live births in the population per 1,000 people in a given year.

89. (E): If parallels of latitude are drawn at an interval of one degree, there will be 89 parallels in the northern and the southern hemispheres each. The total number of parallels thus drawn, including the equator, will be 179.

A latitude line is a line a measure the north-south position of the position relative to the north and south poles.

The value of the equator is 0° and the latitude of the poles are 90°N and 90°S.

The equator is at the exact center between the poles and is the 0°th latitude line.

- **Tropics:** The area between the Tropic of Cancer to the Tropic of Capricorn that passes through the Equator is called the Tropics.
- **Meridians:** Are imaginary lines running parallel from North to South and drawn from East to West.
- **Longitudes:** Are basically the Degrees of the meridian. Together these are called the Longitude of Meridian. The degree range from 180 degrees East to 0 degrees/Prime Meridian to 180 degrees West.

90. (D): A comparative scale is characterized by:

A. It is a combination of two or more plain scales placed side by side, which allows for a comparison between different systems of measurement.

B. Each plain scale on a comparative scale typically shows different systems of measurement units, such as kilometers, miles, or feet, to facilitate direct comparison.

91. (B): Bauxite is found in abundance in the Jamui district of Bihar, along with cement mortar in Bhabhua, mica in Muzaffarpur, Nawada, Jamui and Gaya and salt in Gaya and Jamui.

92. (A): The formation of black cotton soils is closely linked to the weathering of basalt rocks, which are volcanic in origin. The Deccan Plateau is covered by extensive basalt lava flows, and over time, these lava rocks break down due to weathering processes, resulting in the formation of the black cotton soils. These soils are rich in clay minerals, especially montmorillonite, which gives them the characteristic black colour.

93. (D): Erosion is a significant issue in several regions of India. Among the options provided:

- The Chambal Basin is particularly known for severe soil erosion due to the ravines formed by the Chambal River and its tributaries. It has been a hotspot for erosion.
- The Southern slopes of the Siwaliks are also prone to erosion, as these areas experience heavy rainfall and have loose, easily erodible soil.

94. (B): The Nilgiris region is well-known for coffee production. The Nilgiris, located in Tamil Nadu, has the right combination of altitude, climate, and rainfall that makes it ideal for growing coffee, particularly the Arabica variety.

95. (C): The Nagarjun Sagar Dam is situated on the Krishna River. It is one of the major irrigation and water supply projects in India, located in the state of Telangana.

96. (C): In 2023, Andhra Pradesh was the leading fish producer in India, contributing significantly to the country's record fish production of 175.45 lakh tonnes. Following Andhra Pradesh, West Bengal also plays a crucial role in India's fisheries sector.

97. (B): As of January 2024, Uttar Pradesh is the largest producer of wheat in India. The state consistently leads in wheat production due to its favorable agricultural conditions and large areas under wheat cultivation.

98. (A): The largest manganese ore producer in India is Madhya Pradesh. Odisha also has significant production, but Madhya Pradesh is recognized as the leading state in this regard.

99. (C): Solar energy, wind energy, geothermal energy are considered non-conventional or renewable energy sources because they are sustainable and environmentally friendly.

100. (D): Hugrijan oil field (Assam), Kalol oil field (Gujarat), and Lunej oil field (Gujarat) are correctly matched with their respective locations.

101. (D): Bhopal is known for heavy electricals. Bongaigaon is known for petro chemicals.Vishakhapatnam is known for steel.

102. (C): Atal Tunnel, located in Himachal Pradesh, is 9.02 km long, making it the longest road tunnel in India.

103. (B): Sustainable development focuses on balancing economic growth with environmental protection and social equity.

104. (B): In 2023, China overtook the United States as India's largest trading partner. The total trade between India and China reached USD 118.4 billion.

105. (A): Talcher is a well-known coal field located in Odisha.

106. (B): The Sundari tree is primarily found in the Sundarban delta, which is famous for its mangrove forests.

107. (A): According to the 2011 Census, the correct descending order of literacy rates is: Kerala (highest), followed by Lakshadweep, Mizoram, and then Goa.

108. (B): Rajasthan is the leading producer of lead in India, particularly from the Zawar mines.

109. (C): The Palghat Gap is a natural passage that connects Kerala and Tamil Nadu.

110. (A): National Highway 44 is the longest highway in India, stretching from Srinagar in Jammu & Kashmir to Kanyakumari in Tamil Nadu.

ECONOMICS

111. (A): The iron and steel industry should ideally be established near Availability of raw material ore. This is because proximity to raw materials like iron ore and coal significantly reduces transportation costs and ensures a steady supply for the production process.

112. (A): The theme of the COP27 summit, which was held in 2022 in Sharm El-Sheikh, Egypt, was "Together for Implementation." This theme emphasized the need for countries to work together and take concrete actions to implement the climate agreements and commitments made in previous COP summits.

113. (A): Sustainable development can be defined as an approach to the economic development of a country without compromising the quality of the environment for future generations.

In the name of economic development, the price of environmental damage is paid in the form of land degradation, soil erosion, air and water pollution, deforestation, etc. This damage may surpass the advantages of having more quality output of goods and services.

114. (A): Inclusive development refers to the active participation of all segments of society in the development process, ensuring that no one is left behind, regardless of their socio-economic status, gender, or background. It aims to create equal opportunities for everyone to contribute to and benefit from the country's progress.

115. (C): The United Nations has set 17 Sustainable Development Goals (SDGs) to address global challenges, including poverty, inequality, climate change, environmental degradation, peace, and justice.

116. (C): The United Nations Conference on Sustainable Development (UNCSD) is also known as Rio 2012. It was held in Rio de Janeiro, Brazil, in 2012, marking the 20th anniversary of the Earth Summit held there in 1992.

117. (A): The public debt of the Government of India includes treasury bills and dated securities but does not include external commercial borrowings (ECBs) or NRI deposits.

118. (C): The informal sector includes activities that are not regulated by the government and typically involve low capital, skill, and minimal barriers to entry. It includes:

1. Artisans, cottage industrialists, petty traders, tea shop proprietors.
2. Garbage pickers, jitneys, unauthorized taxis, repair persons.
3. The self-employed.
4. Activities with little capital, skill, and entry barriers.

119. (C): The additional capital used for producing one more unit of output is referred to as the Incremental Capital-Output Ratio (ICOR). ICOR measures the amount of capital needed to produce additional output, which helps in understanding the efficiency of investment in generating economic growth.

120. (B): Under the Seventh Schedule of the Indian Constitution, Agricultural marketing is listed under the State List. This means that the regulation and development of agricultural markets fall within the jurisdiction of individual states.

121. (A): The term that denotes business activity at a high level with increasing output and income is Boom. A boom is a period of rapid economic growth characterized by high levels of production, employment, and income.

122. (B): The number of people in different age groups is referred to as Age composition. It gives an understanding of the demographic structure of a population based on various age groups.

123. (A): The sex ratio refers to the number of females per thousand males in a population. It is a demographic indicator used to assess the gender balance in a given population.

124. (A): A large proportion of children in a population is typically the result of a high birth rate. When birth rates are high, it leads to a larger number of children in the population.

125. (B): The factors responsible for sparse population typically include rugged terrain and unfavorable climate, as these conditions make it difficult for large populations to settle and thrive.

126. (C): The Sex ratio is an important social indicator to measure the extent of equality between males and females in a society. It shows the number of females per 1,000 males in a given population and can help assess gender balance and inequality.

127. (C): Tertiary activities involve the provision of services rather than the production of goods. Banking, Transport and Communication, and Building and Construction work all generally fall under different categories:

- Banking and Transport and Communication are clear examples of tertiary activities.
- Building and Construction work, however, is generally considered a secondary activity as it involves the construction and production of infrastructure and buildings.

128. (A): The total area of India accounts for 2.4 per cent of the world's total area.

129. (A): The year 1921 is considered a great demographic divide in India. This year marks a turning point where India's population growth rate started to increase significantly after a period of stagnation, and it is often referred to as the year when India crossed from a "high mortality, high fertility" regime to one of sustained population growth.

130. (B): Internal migration refers to the movement of people within a country, from one region to another. While it may affect the distribution of the population within a country, it does not change the overall size of the population, as people are simply relocating within the same country.

131. (C): To give education is not included in primary activities. Primary activities involve the extraction and collection of natural resources, such as Agriculture and Animal Husbandry, which directly involve the utilization of natural resources.

132. (B): A market activity refers to an economic activity that involves the exchange of goods and services for money. Among the options:

A teacher teaching in school is a market activity because it involves providing education as a service in exchange for a salary (monetary compensation). The other activities mentioned (teaching her child and a mechanic repairing his own car) are non-market activities, as they do not involve any financial transaction.

133. (C): The state with the highest number of Scheduled Castes in India is Uttar Pradesh. This state has the largest population of Scheduled Castes due to its significant overall population size and the proportion of SCs within the state.

134. (C): The correct answer is Pradhan Mantri Gramodaya Yojana. This program was indeed launched in the year 2000 to improve the quality of life in rural areas by focusing on basic amenities such as housing, drinking water, and roads.

135. (A): The scheme that was started in 1993 to create self-employment opportunities for educated unemployed youth in rural areas and small towns is: Prime Minister Rozgar Yojana (PMRY). This scheme aimed to provide financial assistance to educated unemployed youth to set up small businesses and create self-employment opportunities.

136. (C): The method used to estimate the poverty line in India is the Income method. This method calculates the poverty line based on the income required to meet the minimum consumption needs of a person or household. The threshold is usually set to include those who earn below a certain income level that is considered insufficient to meet basic living standards.

137. (A): The average calorie requirement for measuring poverty in rural areas is 2400 calories per person per day. This is the threshold used to estimate the minimum nutritional needs for a person in rural areas, which forms the basis for calculating poverty.

138. (C): The calorie requirement is higher in rural areas primarily because people are engaged in physical labour. In rural areas, a significant portion of the population is involved in agriculture and other physically demanding work, which requires more energy and, therefore, more calories.

139. (B): While migration can contribute to urban poverty or strain on resources in urban areas, it is not directly a cause of poverty in India as a whole. The primary causes of poverty in India are more related to low levels of economic development and unequal distribution of resources like land, which prevent large sections of the population from accessing opportunities and achieving economic well-being.

140. (A): The National Rural Employment Guarantee Act (NREGA) was enacted in 2005. This act guarantees the right to work for rural households by providing a minimum number of days of wage employment every year.

141. (A): While the number of means of transport might indicate some level of infrastructure or development, it is not typically considered a social indicator of poverty. Social indicators of poverty generally include aspects related to healthcare access (C), education and illiteracy levels (B), and other factors that directly affect the well-being and quality of life of individuals.

142. (C): The second stage of demographic transition is suitably known as the Population Explosion. This stage is characterized by a significant decrease in death rates due to improvements in healthcare, sanitation, and nutrition, while birth rates remain high, leading to a rapid population increase.

143. (A): When the Reserve Bank of India (RBI) lowers the Bank Rate, it makes borrowing cheaper for commercial banks, which in turn increases the availability of credit. This results in more liquidity in the market, as commercial banks are more willing to lend to businesses and individuals.

144. (C): The term "bankers' bank" means that the Reserve Bank of India (RBI) performs several functions for commercial banks, such as holding their deposits, lending funds when needed, and providing advice on monetary matters.

Let's evaluate the statements:

1. Other banks retain their deposits with the RBI - True. Commercial banks maintain a certain amount of reserves with the RBI.
2. The RBI lends funds to the commercial banks in times of need - True. The RBI provides emergency funding to commercial banks through mechanisms like the Lender of Last Resort.
3. The RBI advises the commercial banks on monetary matters - True. The RBI provides guidance and sets policies that affect the entire banking system.

Since all three statements are true, the correct answer is: (C) 1, 2 and 3.

145. (A): In India, deficit financing is primarily used for raising resources for economic development. It refers to the government borrowing or printing money to cover the gap between its expenditure and revenue, particularly when funds are needed to finance development projects, infrastructure, and social welfare programs.

146. (C): Bihar's first Biogas plant will be set up at Brahmapur in Buxar district of Bihar. To set up the plant, GNIGPL has signed deal with GAIL (India) Limited. Biogas will be produced by using straw, cow and buffalo dung, poultry farm waste, agricultural waste and corn stalks.

147. (B): Normal labour laws are applicable to SEZs, which are enforced by the respective State Governments. The State Governments have been requested to simplify the procedures/returns and for introduction of a single window clearance mechanism by delegating appropriate powers to Development Commissioners of SEZs.

148. (A): The Dagmara Hydro-Electric Project is concerned with the Kosi River in Bihar. This project is designed to harness the water resources of the Kosi River for power generation.

149. (C): BSSC has got ISO certification in three fields: Quality Management Practices Certification, Environmental Management Practices Certification, Anti -bribery Management Certification. Bihar State Seed Corporation has become the first government institution in the country, whose certificate has been given by Bureau of Indian Standards on transparent system of seed production, management and seed according to international standards.

150. (E): During the 2023-24 budget, the total receipts other than borrowings are expected to increase by 11.7% over the revised estimate of the 2022-23 budget.

POLITICAL SCIENCE

111. (D): Assertion (A): The democracy ensures that we shall be governed no better than we deserve.

Reason (R-1): The Man's capacity for justice makes democracy possible.

Reason (R-2): The Man's inclination to injustice makes democracy necessary.

For the assertion:

Assertion (A) seems to highlight a common idea about democracy, which is that the quality of governance is ultimately a reflection of the collective will and decisions of the people.

For the reasons:

Reason (R-1) states that democracy is possible because people have the capacity for justice, aligning with the idea that democratic systems rely on people's ability to make fair and just decisions.

Reason (R-2) argues that democracy is necessary due to people's tendency towards injustice, suggesting that democracy serves as a safeguard against potential abuses of power and ensuring accountability.

Based on this analysis, both reasons R-1 and R-2 seem valid and can coexist to support the assertion. Hence, the most appropriate answer would be: (D) More than one of the above.

112. (C): J.K. Galbraith, a renowned economist, is known for stating that democracy is the best system of governance and that it "stands above doubts". This reflects his belief in the fundamental value of democracy.

The other options (Seeley, Rousseau) did not make this particular statement about democracy standing "above doubts".

113. (A): (*a*) The democracy as the government by poorest, the most ignorant & most incapable people-This comment was made by Lecky (*i*). Lecky critiqued democracy, pointing out that it can often be governed by the least capable segments of society.

(*b*) The democracy as an aristocracy of backguards-This comment was made by Talleyrand (*ii*). He viewed democracy as potentially ruled by people with little skill or wisdom, essentially an aristocracy of mediocrity.

(*c*) The democracy as the government of mindless and ignorants-This comment was made by H.G. Wells (*iii*). Wells was critical of democracy in some of his writings, particularly in terms of the competence of the electorate.

(*d*) The democracy as the government full of ignorance-This comment was made by Fogget (*iv*). He also criticized democracy, focusing on the ignorance of those in power.

114. (D): A. Democracy is indeed a more accountable form of government, as elected representatives are answerable to the people.

B. The democracy in India has made the government respond to food security issues, as seen in initiatives like the Public Distribution System (PDS) and the National Food Security Act.

C. Democracy requires that the rulers attend to the needs of the people, ensuring that the government remains responsive to public demands and welfare.

Since more than one of these statements is correct, Option D is the appropriate choice.

115. (B): G.D.H. Cole, a British socialist and political theorist, emphasized that political liberty alone cannot be meaningful without economic equality. He argued that without addressing economic disparities, political freedom becomes a hollow concept, as the disadvantaged would not have the real ability to exercise their political rights.

116. (C): Alfred Smith, an American politician, famously said that "all the ills of democracy can be cured by more democracy." He believed that the way to address the problems in democratic systems was not by reducing democratic practices but by expanding them and ensuring greater participation and involvement from the people.

117. (C): India is one of the first countries in the world to have started scientific management of its forests. In the year 1864 the then British India Government started the Imperial Forest Department and appointed Dr. Dietrich Brandis, a German botanist, Inspector General of Forests.

118. (B): The Imperial Forest Research Institute was established in 1906 in Dehradun, which is located in the state of Uttarakhand, India. It played a crucial role in forest research and the management of India's forest resources. Today, it is known as the Forest Research Institute (FRI) and continues to be a leading institution for forest research in India.

119. (D): 1. Decision-making and implementation take a long time in democratic governments.

2. Political parties can sometimes make democratic governments appear immoral and powerless.

3. Regional interests can sometimes become more powerful than national interests.

The most accurate answer is D.

120. (D): Let's break down why:

A. The democracies involve some loss of immediate efficiency: This is true. Democracies often require time for discussions, debates, and the need to build consensus, which can slow down decision-making processes, especially in urgent situations.

B. The democracies may increase their efficiency in the long run: This is also accurate. Although democracies may be slower in the short term, they often become more efficient in the long run through continuous improvements in governance, stronger institutions, and more informed decision-making by citizens.

C. The democracies need required improvements to be done in it in place of choosing the dictatorship: This is a valid point as well. Rather than resorting to authoritarian rule, which can suppress freedoms and human rights, it is essential for democracies to adapt and improve over time to function more effectively.

Since all three points are relevant in describing the nature of democracies today, D. More than one of the above is the best choice.

121. (B): The principle of Parliamentary supremacy (or Parliamentary sovereignty) means that the Parliament has the ultimate power to make or change laws, and that no other body, including the judiciary, can override its decisions. This principle is a hallmark of the British political system.

122. (D): The first commission to identify the backward classes in India was the Kaka Kalelkar Commission, which was set up in 1953. The commission was headed by Kaka Kalelkar, and its main task was to identify the socially and educationally backward classes and recommend measures for their welfare.

123. (A): At the time of India's independence in 1947, the ruler of Junagarh, Nawab Muhammad Mahabat Khanji III, wanted to accede to Pakistan. However, the majority of the people in Junagarh were Hindu and wanted to join India. This led to a conflict, and after some political maneuvering, Junagarh eventually acceded to India.

124. (D): The main aim of setting up the Planning Commission in 1950 in India was to promote the country's economic development in a holistic manner. The Planning Commission's role was not just limited to one specific goal but encompassed various aspects of economic growth and poverty reduction. The commission's objectives included:

Economic development: Focusing on overall economic progress and industrial growth.

Poverty alleviation: Developing strategies to reduce poverty and improve the standard of living for the Indian population.

Building a modern industrial base: Industrialization was seen as key to India's development, along with the necessary infrastructure.

Hence, D. More than one of the above is the most accurate answer.

125. (D): Gandhiji had several expectations for the Constitution of Independent India, which reflected his vision of a just and inclusive society:

A. He envisioned the constitution would release India from thralldom and patronage, ensuring true freedom and self-governance.

B. He believed all communities must live in perfect harmony, promoting unity and peace among diverse groups.

C. He advocated for equal rights for women, ensuring they enjoy the same rights as men.

Thus, D. More than one of the above is the correct answer.

126. (C): The introductory part of the Constitution, which reflects the core constitutional values embodied in the Constitution, is termed the 'Preamble'. It is drafted to explain certain crucial facts and substance before diving into the provisions of the Act or statute. It sets out the aims and objectives of the statute, which it intends to achieve.

127. (A): The Finance and Staff Committee was a procedural committee of the Constituent Assembly of India. Its primary role was to look into the financial and staffing matters related to the functioning of the Constituent Assembly.

128. (D): The Drafting Committee of the Constituent Assembly of India had several prominent members, including:

- Dr. B.R. Ambedkar (Chairman)
- Alladi Krishnaswami Ayyar
- N. Gopalaswami Ayyangar
- K.M. Munshi
- Mohammad Saadulla
- B.L. Mitter (later replaced by N. Madhav Rao due to health issues)
- D.P. Khaitan

So, the correct answer is D. More than one of the above.

129. (B): The decision to make Hindi the official language of the Indian Union was made by the Drafting Committee on 14th September 1949.

130. (A): Granville Austin, a well-known political scientist, referred to the Constituent Assembly of India as "a one-party body in an essentially one-party country" in his influential work The Indian Constitution: Cornerstone of a Nation. This remark highlighted the dominance of the Indian National Congress in the Constituent Assembly and the political landscape of India at that time, where the Congress had a significant majority and played a leading role in shaping the Constitution.

131. (D): The Preamble of the Constitution of India assures the people of India about several key principles, including:

A. Dignity of the individual

B. Unity and integrity of the nation

C. Equal status and opportunity

Given that these are all assured by the Preamble, the correct answer is D.

132. (C): The preamble of the Indian Constitution provides for the liberty of thought, expression, belief, faith, and worship. There was no Economic liberty embodied in the preamble.

133. (C): Bihar is part of the Eastern Zonal Council in India, which also includes the states of West Bengal, Odisha, and Jharkhand.

134. (D): Let's evaluate each statement in the context of scientific secularism in India:

A. It is dynamic by nature and suits the requirements of a progressive nation: This is correct.

B. It keeps religion and politics separate from each other: This is also correct.

C. It keeps every community within the sovereign authority of the Parliament: This is correct as well.

Thus, D. More than one of the above is the most accurate answer because all three statements reflect key aspects of scientific secularism in India.

135. (D): The main features of democratic elections in India include:
   A. In such elections everyone has the right to vote with the equal value of vote: This is true.
   B. In such elections, voters have opportunities of real choice at regular intervals: This is also true.
   C. Such elections are conducted in a free and fair manner: While this is the ideal goal, in practice, the Election Commission of India works to ensure that elections are free and fair. However, the effectiveness of this depends on various factors, and challenges may arise.

   Thus, D. More than one of the above is the correct answer.

136. (D): Let's break down each statement:
   A. It provides the way to select our future leaders: This is true. Political competition allows voters to choose their leaders during elections, which is fundamental in a democracy.
   B. It makes the political system work better in the long run: This is also true.
   C. It presents an opportunity to the people to reward the political leaders for serving them or punish them for not doing so: This is correct.

   Therefore, D. More than one of the above is the most accurate answer.

137. (D): Several states in India possess special status due to their unique social, cultural, and historical circumstances. These include:

   Assam: Assam has a special status under Article 371B of the Indian Constitution.

   Nagaland: Nagaland has a special status under Article 371A.

   Arunachal Pradesh: Arunachal Pradesh also enjoys special provisions under Article 371H.

   Therefore, D. More than one of the above is correct, as all of the mentioned states have special status based on their unique historical and social contexts.

138. (D): The Eighth Schedule of the Constitution of India lists the official languages recognized by the Indian government. Over time, several languages have been added to the schedule.
   A. Bodo and Dogri: Both Bodo and Dogri are included in the Eighth Schedule.
   B. Oriya and Sindhi: Oriya (now Odiya) and Sindhi are also mentioned in the Eighth Schedule.
   C. Nepali and Santhali: Both Nepali and Santhali are included in the Eighth Schedule as well.

   Therefore, the correct answer is D. More than one of the above.

139. (C): In India, the 73rd and 74th Constitutional Amendments (1992) mandated that one third of the total seats in panchayats (rural local government bodies) and municipalities (urban local government bodies) be reserved for women.

140. (C): The National Commission for Backward Classes (NCBC) was established by the 102nd Amendment of the Constitution of India, which came into effect in 2018. This amendment gave constitutional status to the NCBC and empowered it to examine and recommend measures for the welfare and upliftment of backward classes in India.

141. (B): The form of oath or affirmation for members of Parliament (both Lok Sabha and Rajya Sabha) is found in Article 84 of the Indian Constitution, and the specific wording of the oath is detailed in the Third Schedule of the Constitution.

142. (D): Parliament can extend the life of the Lok Sabha beyond its normal term (5 years) for one year at a time during an emergency. Same applies to State Legislative Assemblies. This extension ceases to operate six months after the emergency ends.

143. (D): Let's break down the statements:
   A. Cabinet ministers are in charge of major ministries and are the primary decision-makers in the name of the Council of Ministers. They play a crucial role in policy-making and administration.
   B. Ministers of State with independent charge are responsible for smaller ministries. They attend cabinet meetings only when invited and have more autonomy compared to other Ministers of State.
   C. Ministers of State assist cabinet ministers. They typically handle specific responsibilities within the ministries and support the cabinet ministers in their duties.

   Thus, D. More than one of the above is the correct answer.

144. (B): The Forty-second Amendment to the Constitution of India (1976) made significant changes, one of which was to bind the President of India to act in accordance with the advice rendered by the Council of Ministers.

145. (D): Several provisions in the Indian Constitution ensure the independence of the judiciary. Let's look at the statements:
   A. The constitutional appointment in India ensures that the process of appointing judges is governed by the Constitution, contributing to the independence of the judiciary.

B. The salaries and allowances of judges being charged on the Consolidated Fund and their barring from legal practice after retirement are measures designed to secure financial independence and impartiality.

C. Immunity from reckless criticism of their judicial conduct helps protect the dignity and integrity of the judicial process.

Thus, D. More than one of the above is the correct answer.

146. (C): The maximum strength of a Vidhan Parishad (Legislative Council) in a state of India is that it cannot be more than 1/3 of the total strength of the State Vidhan Sabha (Legislative Assembly).

147. (D): Article 21 deals with protection of life and personal liberty. It provides that, "no person shall be deprived of his life or personal liberty except according to procedure established by law". The right is available to citizens as well as aliens. It includes the right to live with human dignity. It covers protection against arbitrary executive and legislative action. It is a part of basic feature of the Constitution. It can be taken away according to the procedure established by law.

148. (B): The 86th Constitutional Amendment Act of 2002 made the Right to Education a Fundamental Right under Article 21A of the Indian Constitution. This amendment mandates that children between the ages of 6 to 14 years have the right to free and compulsory education.

149. (D): The Indian political party system faces several challenges, many of which are highlighted in the options provided:

A. The lack of internal democracy within the parties is a significant challenge, as it often leads to centralized decision-making and a lack of accountability.

B. The lack of a dynamic system of succession further exacerbates the issue by stifling new leadership and ideas within the parties.

C. The growing role of money and muscle power during elections undermines the fairness and integrity of the electoral process.

Since all three options are valid challenges to the Indian political party system, the correct answer is D. More than one of the above.

150. (D): All of the given options reflect key outcomes or features of democracy in India:

A. The formation of a legitimate, responsive, and accountable government is a fundamental outcome of a democratic system.

B. The promotion of economic growth and reduction of inequality and poverty are critical goals that democracies strive to achieve, though the success rate may vary.

C. The existence of accommodative rule for social diversity along with ensuring the dignity and freedom of citizens aligns with the principles of democracy.

Since all three statements are relevant outcomes of India's democracy, the correct answer is D. More than one of the above.

Previous Paper (Solved)

Bihar Public Service Commission (BPSC)

Secondary School Social Science Teacher

Recruitment Exam, 2023

PAPER-1 : LANGUAGE*

Part-I : English Language

Directions (Qs. No. 1 to 5): *Fill in the blanks with a/an/the.*

1. Your brother is appointed as _____ SDO.
A. a
B. an
C. the
D. More than one of the above
E. None of the above

2. If I can't move this desk, will you give it _____ push?
A. a
B. an
C. the
D. More than one of the above
E. None of the above

3. Bring _____ book I gave you yesterday.
A. the
B. an
C. a
D. More than one of the above
E. None of the above

4. Anand went to the doctor because he had _____ ear infection.
A. a
B. an
C. the
D. More than one of the above
E. None of the above

5. He is pursuing MA from _____ University.
A. a
B. an
C. the
D. More than one of the above
E. None of the above

Directions (Qs. No. 6 to 10): *Choose the correct alternative for each of the following.*

6. Which is ***not*** a part of a plant?
A. Leaves
B. Branches
C. Birds and animals
D. More than one of the above
E. None of the above

7. Which of the following you do ***not*** use in a computer?
A. Hard drive
B. Keyboard
C. Toothbrush
D. More than one of the above
E. None of the above

8. What among the following a lady does ***not*** use in kitchen?
A. Drier
B. Oven
C. Induction
D. More than one of the above
E. None of the above

9. Which one is ***not*** allowed in an examination?
A. Mobile phone
B. Earphone
C. Book
D. More than one of the above
E. None of the above

1. B	**2.** A	**3.** A	**4.** B	**5.** A	**6.** C	**7.** C	**8.** A	**9.** D

**Exam held on 25-08-2023.*

10. Which of the following is ***not*** found in a hospital?
A. Nurse
B. Operation theatre
C. Telescope
D. More than one of the above
E. None of the above

Directions (Qs. No. 11 to 15): *Complete the sentences given below using the correct alternative.*

11. The person who writes a book is known as its
A. reader
B. author
C. publisher
D. More than one of the above
E. None of the above

12. If today is Wednesday, day after tomorrow will be
A. Tuesday
B. Thursday
C. Monday
D. More than one of the above
E. None of the above

13. We must _____ traffic signals.
A. not break
B. break
C. not follow
D. More than one of the above
E. None of the above

14. If today is the 12th of December, the next month will be
A. April
B. January
C. February
D. More than one of the above
E. None of the above

15. A month can have _____ days.
A. 28 or 29
B. 30
C. 31
D. More than one of the above
E. None of the above

Directions (Qs. No. 16 to 20): *Choose the correct answer for each of the following.*

16. Daughter's daughter is
A. sister
B. granddaughter
C. cousin
D. More than one of the above
E. None of the above

17. Grandfather's father is
A. grandpa
B. great grandfather
C. father
D. More than one of the above
E. None of the above

18. Mother's father is
A. paternal grandfather
B. maternal grandfather
C. great grandfather
D. More than one of the above
E. None of the above

19. Aunt's daughter is
A. mother
B. grandmother
C. niece
D. More than one of the above
E. None of the above

20. Mother's and father's children are
A. sisters and brothers
B. cousins
C. aunts and uncles
D. More than one of the above
E. None of the above

Directions (Qs. No. 21 to 25): *Choose the correct option to the questions based on the given passage.*

Once upon a time, a hunter came to a forest. It was summer, and water was scarce. Many of the animals had died of thirst. The hunter killed a deer and took it back to his house. The Forest God was very sad because he could not protect his animals. He prayed to the Rain God and the monsoon arrived. The animals could breed again because there was enough to eat and drink.

21. Whom did the Forest God pray to?
A. The hunter
B. The deer
C. The Rain God
D. More than one of the above
E. None of the above

22. The Forest God was very _____ that he could not protect his animals.
A. joyous
B. sad
C. neutral
D. More than one of the above
E. None of the above

10. C **11.** B **12.** E **13.** A **14.** B **15.** D **16.** B **17.** B **18.** B **19.** E **20.** A **21.** C **22.** B

23. In which season did the animals have enough to eat and drink?
A. Summer
B. Monsoon
C. All through the year
D. More than one of the above
E. None of the above

24. When the hunter came to the forest, it was
A. winter
B. monsoon
C. summer
D. More than one of the above
E. None of the above

25. Who killed the deer?
A. Rain God
B. Forest God
C. A hunter
D. More than one of the above
E. None of the above

Part-II : हिन्दी भाषा

26. निम्नलिखित में से कौन-सा शब्द अव्यय **नहीं** है?
A. जूता
B. आज
C. भीतर
D. उपर्युक्त में से एक से अधिक
E. उपर्युक्त में से कोई नहीं

27. ह्रस्व, दीर्घ और प्लुत किसके प्रकार हैं?
A. संधि
B. व्यंजन
C. स्वर
D. उपर्युक्त में से एक से अधिक
E. उपर्युक्त में से कोई नहीं

28. तालव्य ध्वनियाँ कौन-सी हैं?
A. च, छ
B. ज, झ
C. ट, ढ
D. उपर्युक्त में से एक से अधिक
E. उपर्युक्त में से कोई नहीं

29. निम्नलिखित में से कौन-सा उत्तम पुरुषवाची शब्द **नहीं** है?
A. तुम
B. हमको
C. मुझमें
D. उपर्युक्त में से एक से अधिक
E. उपर्युक्त में से कोई नहीं

30. 'मरुभूमि में कहीं धान उगता है?' वाक्य में कौन-सा क्रिया-विशेषण है?
A. समयवाचक
B. रीतिवाचक
C. स्थानवाचक
D. उपर्युक्त में से एक से अधिक
E. उपर्युक्त में से कोई नहीं

31. निम्नलिखित में से कौन-सी लक्षणा की विशेषता है?
A. व्यंग्यार्थ
B. मुख्यार्थ
C. रूढ़ि का प्रयोग
D. उपर्युक्त में से एक से अधिक
E. उपर्युक्त में से कोई नहीं

32. विभाव किसे कहते हैं?
A. स्थायी भाव के उद्‌बोधक कारक
B. जिसमें रस उत्पन्न हो
C. जिसको रस उत्पन्न हो
D. उपर्युक्त में से एक से अधिक
E. उपर्युक्त में से कोई नहीं

33. 'लड़के ने कुत्ते को मारा।' वाक्य में कौन-सा कारक है?
A. करण और अपादान
B. संबंध और करण
C. अधिकरण और करण
D. उपर्युक्त में से एक से अधिक
E. उपर्युक्त में से कोई नहीं

34. कौन-सी संक्षिप्ति की विशेषता **नहीं** है?
A. संक्षिप्ति एक स्वतंत्र शब्द है
B. संक्षिप्ति मूल शब्द का अर्थ वहन करती है
C. यह शब्द अपने आप में पूर्णता नहीं रखता
D. उपर्युक्त में से एक से अधिक
E. उपर्युक्त में से कोई नहीं

23. B **24.** C **25.** C **26.** A **27.** C **28.** D **29.** A **30.** E **31.** D **32.** A **33.** E **34.** C

35. 'महाशय' शब्द में कौन-सी स्वर संधि है?
- A. स्वर संधि
- B. दीर्घ स्वर संधि
- C. यण स्वर संधि
- D. उपर्युक्त में से एक से अधिक
- E. उपर्युक्त में से कोई नहीं

निर्देश (प्र.सं. 36 से 40 तक) : *अशुद्ध वाक्य दिए गए हैं, अतः शुद्ध वाक्य का चयन कर (A), (B), (C), (D) और (E) में से सही विकल्प का चयन कीजिए।*

36. हमने जो कहे थे वही सत्य है।
- A. हमने कहे थे वहीं सत्य है।
- B. हमने जो कहे रहे वह सत्य है।
- C. हमने जो कहा था वही सत्य है।
- D. उपर्युक्त में से एक से अधिक
- E. उपर्युक्त में से कोई नहीं

37. आपका पत्र धन्यवाद सहित मिला।
- A. आपका पत्र धन्यवाद के साथ मिला।
- B. आपका पत्र मिला धन्यवाद।
- C. धन्यवाद के साथ आपका पत्र मिला।
- D. उपर्युक्त में से एक से अधिक
- E. उपर्युक्त में से कोई नहीं

38. कृपया करके कार्यक्रम में पधारें।
- A. कृपया कार्यक्रम में पधारें।
- B. कृपा कर कार्यक्रम में पधारे।
- C. कार्यक्रम में पधारे।
- D. उपर्युक्त में से एक से अधिक
- E. उपर्युक्त में से कोई नहीं

39. मुझसे बेफिजूल बात मत करो।
- A. मुझसे फिजूल बात मत करें।
- B. मुझसे बेफिजूल में बात मत करो।
- C. बेफिजूल में मुझसे बात मत करो।
- D. उपर्युक्त में से एक से अधिक
- E. उपर्युक्त में से कोई नहीं

40. बिहारी ने गागर में सागर भर दिया है।
- A. बिहारी गागर में सागर भर दिए है।
- B. बिहारी ने गागर में सागर भरा है।
- C. बिहारी ने गागर में सागर भर दिए रहे।
- D. उपर्युक्त में से एक से अधिक
- E. उपर्युक्त में से कोई नहीं

निर्देश (प्र.सं. 41 से 45 तक) : *निम्नलिखित शब्द किस भाषा का है? (A), (B), (C), (D) और (E) में से सही विकल्प का चयन कीजिए।*

41. बेगम
- A. अरबी
- B. फारसी
- C. पुर्तगाली
- D. उपर्युक्त में से एक से अधिक
- E. उपर्युक्त में से कोई नहीं

42. सिनेमा
- A. पुर्तगाली
- B. फारसी
- C. अंग्रेजी
- D. उपर्युक्त में से एक से अधिक
- E. उपर्युक्त में से कोई नहीं

43. अर्दली
- A. अरबी
- B. फारसी
- C. पुर्तगाली
- D. उपर्युक्त में से एक से अधिक
- E. उपर्युक्त में से कोई नहीं

44. तौलिया
- A. देशी भाषा
- B. पुर्तगाली
- C. फारसी
- D. उपर्युक्त में से एक से अधिक
- E. उपर्युक्त में से कोई नहीं

45. रिक्शा
- A. जापानी
- B. चीनी
- C. अरबी
- D. उपर्युक्त में से एक से अधिक
- E. उपर्युक्त में से कोई नहीं

निर्देश (प्र.सं. 46 से 50 तक) : *दिए गए शब्दों के पर्यायवाची शब्द जो नहीं हैं, उनके लिए (A), (B), (C), (D) और (E) में से सही विकल्प का चयन कीजिए।*

46. दुर्जन
- A. शठ
- B. कपटी
- C. कंजूस
- D. उपर्युक्त में से एक से अधिक
- E. उपर्युक्त में से कोई नहीं

35. B **36.** C **37.** B **38.** A **39.** A **40.** B **41.** E **42.** C **43.** E **44.** B **45.** A **46.** C

47. देह
A. काया
B. शरीर
C. तन
D. उपर्युक्त में से एक से अधिक
E. उपर्युक्त में से कोई नहीं

48. स्त्री
A. वनिता
B. कांता
C. सविता
D. उपर्युक्त में से एक से अधिक
E. उपर्युक्त में से कोई नहीं

49. बिजली
A. विद्युत्
B. आभा
C. चंचला
D. उपर्युक्त में से एक से अधिक
E. उपर्युक्त में से कोई नहीं

50. लक्ष्मी
A. उमा
B. रमा
C. कमला
D. उपर्युक्त में से एक से अधिक
E. उपर्युक्त में से कोई नहीं

निर्देश (प्र.सं. 51 से 55 तक) : *निम्नलिखित वाक्यों में ऐसी हिन्दी का प्रयोग कीजिए जो बोलचाल की भाषा है तथा (A), (B), (C), (D) और (E) में से सही विकल्प का चयन कीजिए।*

51. परीक्षाएँ सन्निकट हैं।
A. परीक्षाएँ दूर है।
B. परीक्षाएँ पास है।
C. परीक्षाएँ भविष्य में है।
D. उपर्युक्त में से एक से अधिक
E. उपर्युक्त में से कोई नहीं

52. बरसात में सरिताओं में बाढ़ आ जाती है।
A. बरसात में नदियों में बाढ़ आ जाती है।
B. बरसात में पहाड़ों पर भी बाढ़ आ जाती है।
C. बरसात में पूरी सृष्टि बाढ़ में डूब जाती है।
D. उपर्युक्त में से एक से अधिक
E. उपर्युक्त में से कोई नहीं

53. मैं आपसे नितांत अपरिचित हूँ।
A. मैं आपसे बिल्कुल अपरिचित हूँ।
B. मैं आपसे एकदम अपरिचित हूँ।
C. मैं आपसे सर्वथा अपरिचित हूँ।
D. उपर्युक्त में से एक से अधिक
E. उपर्युक्त में से कोई नहीं

54. दूरदर्शन की अनेक शृंखलाएँ प्रसिद्ध हैं।
A. दूरदर्शन के अनेक नाटक प्रसिद्ध हैं।
B. दूरदर्शन के अनेक फिल्में प्रसिद्ध हैं।
C. दूरदर्शन के अनेक धारावाहिक प्रसिद्ध हैं।
D. उपर्युक्त में से एक से अधिक
E. उपर्युक्त में से कोई नहीं

55. वे अभी नवधनाढ्य हुए हैं।
A. वह अभी धनी हुए हैं।
B. वह अभी नए अमीर हुए हैं।
C. वह अभी नौ दौलत मंद हुए हैं।
D. उपर्युक्त में से एक से अधिक
E. उपर्युक्त में से कोई नहीं

निर्देश (प्र.सं. 56 से 60 तक) : *दिए गए शब्दों के विलोम शब्द चुनकर (A), (B), (C), (D) और (E) में से सही विकल्प का चयन कीजिए।*

56. इच्छा
A. अइच्छा
B. आशा
C. अनिच्छा
D. उपर्युक्त में से एक से अधिक
E. उपर्युक्त में से कोई नहीं

57. उन्मूलन
A. उन्नयन
B. अवमूल्यन
C. रोपण
D. उपर्युक्त में से एक से अधिक
E. उपर्युक्त में से कोई नहीं

58. कर्कश
A. मधुर
B. कोमल
C. कठोर
D. उपर्युक्त में से एक से अधिक
E. उपर्युक्त में से कोई नहीं

47. E **48.** C **49.** B **50.** A **51.** B **52.** A **53.** D **54.** C **55.** B **56.** C **57.** C **58.** D

59. जंगम
A. वन
B. स्थावर
C. जंगल
D. उपर्युक्त में से एक से अधिक
E. उपर्युक्त में से कोई नहीं

60. शासक
A. शासित
B. पोषक
C. सत्ताधारी
D. उपर्युक्त में से एक से अधिक
E. उपर्युक्त में से कोई नहीं

निर्देश (प्र.सं. 61 से 65 तक) : *निम्नलिखित प्रत्येक वाक्य में एक शब्द रेखांकित है। प्रत्येक रेखांकित शब्द के लिए (A), (B), (C), (D) और (E) के सामने एक-एक विकल्प दिया गया है। इनमें से रेखांकित शब्द के लिए अर्थ की दृष्टि से उपयुक्त विकल्प चुनकर उत्तर-पुस्तिका में चिह्नित कीजिए।*

61. शिशु तेरी अनुपम छवि निहार
A. युवक
B. बालक
C. युवती
D. उपर्युक्त में से एक से अधिक
E. उपर्युक्त में से कोई नहीं

62. युद्ध निरंतर युद्ध विश्व है
A. शांति
B. अंधकार
C. संग्राम
D. उपर्युक्त में से एक से अधिक
E. उपर्युक्त में से कोई नहीं

63. गुमी हुई आजादी की कीमत सबने पहचानी थी
A. स्वाधीनता
B. गुलाम
C. गुलामी
D. उपर्युक्त में से एक से अधिक
E. उपर्युक्त में से कोई नहीं

64. जिसको सुन रिपु के दिल टूटे
A. शत्रु
B. आरि
C. आराति
D. उपर्युक्त में से एक से अधिक
E. उपर्युक्त में से कोई नहीं

65. सोम सुधा बरसाता
A. अमृत
B. अमरित
C. पियूष
D. उपर्युक्त में से एक से अधिक
E. उपर्युक्त में से कोई नहीं

निर्देश (प्र.सं. 66 से 70 तक) : *निम्नलिखित तत्सम शब्दों के लिए पाँच-पाँच विकल्प (A), (B), (C), (D) और (E) दिए गए हैं। इनमें से सर्वाधिक उपयुक्त विकल्प चुनकर उत्तर-पुस्तिका में चिह्नित कीजिए।*

66. खग
A. विहग
B. द्विज
C. खगी
D. उपर्युक्त में से एक से अधिक
E. उपर्युक्त में से कोई नहीं

67. गणेश
A. एकदन्त
B. नन्दी
C. नन्दन
D. उपर्युक्त में से एक से अधिक
E. उपर्युक्त में से कोई नहीं

68. काक
A. फिसफिस
B. काग
C. पिशुन
D. उपर्युक्त में से एक से अधिक
E. उपर्युक्त में से कोई नहीं

69. ठक
A. जालसाज
B. खौफ
C. त्रास
D. उपर्युक्त में से एक से अधिक
E. उपर्युक्त में से कोई नहीं

70. देह
A. वपु
B. क्षीर
C. पय
D. उपर्युक्त में से एक से अधिक
E. उपर्युक्त में से कोई नहीं

59. B **60.** A **61.** B **62.** C **63.** A **64.** A **65.** A **66.** D **67.** A **68.** D **69.** A **70.** A

निर्देश (प्र.सं. 71 से 75 तक) : *निम्नलिखित वाक्य के लिए एक शब्द चुनिए तथा (A), (B), (C), (D) और (E) में से सही विकल्प का चयन कीजिए।*

71. जिसके आने की तिथि न हो
A. अतिथि
B. पोषक
C. सत्ताधारी
D. उपर्युक्त में से एक से अधिक
E. उपर्युक्त में से कोई नहीं

72. जो लज्जा से रहित हो
A. निर्मम
B. निर्लज्ज
C. बेशर्म
D. उपर्युक्त में से एक से अधिक
E. उपर्युक्त में से कोई नहीं

73. जो सिंहासन का अधिकारी हो
A. युवराज
B. युग निर्माता
C. गद्दीधारी
D. उपर्युक्त में से एक से अधिक
E. उपर्युक्त में से कोई नहीं

74. वर्ष में एक बार होने वाला
A. वर्ष भर
B. वार्षिक
C. सालों तक
D. उपर्युक्त में से एक से अधिक
E. उपर्युक्त में से कोई नहीं

75. जो स्वेच्छा से सेवा करे
A. नौकर
B. स्वयं पाकी
C. स्वयं सेवक
D. उपर्युक्त में से एक से अधिक
E. उपर्युक्त में से कोई नहीं

निर्देश (प्र.सं. 76 से 80 तक) : *निम्नलिखित मुहावरों के उपयुक्त अर्थ का चयन कर (A), (B), (C), (D) और (E) में से सही विकल्प का चयन कीजिए।*

76. अंक भरना
A. खाली स्थानों को भरना
B. भाग्य चमकना
C. स्नेह से लिपटा लेना
D. उपर्युक्त में से एक से अधिक
E. उपर्युक्त में से कोई नहीं

77. आस्तीन का साँप
A. कपटी मित्र
B. मित्र को खतरा
C. मित्र को साँप काटना
D. उपर्युक्त में से एक से अधिक
E. उपर्युक्त में से कोई नहीं

78. किस खेत की मूली
A. अधिकारहीन
B. शक्तिहीन
C. हैसियत वाला
D. उपर्युक्त में से एक से अधिक
E. उपर्युक्त में से कोई नहीं

79. घड़ों पानी पड़ना
A. विजयी होना
B. पराजित होना
C. गर्वित होना
D. उपर्युक्त में से एक से अधिक
E. उपर्युक्त में से कोई नहीं

80. नाच नचाना
A. तंग करना
B. नृत्य सिखाना
C. नाच के लिए प्रेरित करना
D. उपर्युक्त में से एक से अधिक
E. उपर्युक्त में से कोई नहीं

निर्देश (प्र.सं. 81 से 85 तक) : *निम्नलिखित अशुद्ध शब्दों के लिए शुद्ध शब्द चुनिए तथा (A), (B), (C), (D) और (E) में से सही विकल्प का चयन कीजिए।*

81. अनाधिकार
A. अनधिकार
B. अनाधीकार
C. अन अधिकार
D. उपर्युक्त में से एक से अधिक
E. उपर्युक्त में से कोई नहीं

82. परलौकिक
A. परालौकिक
B. पारलौकिक
C. परालोकिक
D. उपर्युक्त में से एक से अधिक
E. उपर्युक्त में से कोई नहीं

71. A **72.** D **73.** A **74.** B **75.** C **76.** C **77.** A **78.** D **79.** E **80.** A **81.** A **82.** B

83. चांद
A. चॉन्द
B. चान्द
C. चाँद
D. उपर्युक्त में से एक से अधिक
E. उपर्युक्त में से कोई नहीं

84. सौंदर्यता
A. सौंदर्य
B. सोन्दरता
C. सुदर्य
D. उपर्युक्त में से एक से अधिक
E. उपर्युक्त में से कोई नहीं

85. परसाद
A. प्रशाद
B. प्रसाद
C. प्रषाद
D. उपर्युक्त में से एक से अधिक
E. उपर्युक्त में से कोई नहीं

निर्देश (प्र.सं. 86 से 90 तक) : *निम्नलिखित वाक्यों के सही प्रकार चुनिए तथा (A), (B), (C), (D) और (E) में से सही विकल्प का चयन कीजिए।*

86. उसने कहा कि मैं कल आऊँगी।
A सरल वाक्य
B. संयुक्त वाक्य
C. मिश्र वाक्य
D. उपर्युक्त में से एक से अधिक
E. उपर्युक्त में से कोई नहीं

87. तुम जाओ और अपने पिताजी से कहना।
A. सरल वाक्य
B. संयुक्त वाक्य
C. मिश्र वाक्य
D. उपर्युक्त में से एक से अधिक
E. उपर्युक्त में से कोई नहीं

88. यह चित्र इस दीवार पर असंगत है।
A. आज्ञावाचक
B. निषेधवाचक
C. विधिवाचक
D. उपर्युक्त में से एक से अधिक
E. उपर्युक्त में से कोई नहीं

89. अरे! तुम अभी यहीं खड़े हो।
A. विस्मयबोधक
B. आश्चर्यबोधक
C. आज्ञार्थक
D. उपर्युक्त में से एक से अधिक
E. उपर्युक्त में से कोई नहीं

90. तुम सदा सुखी रहो।
A. इच्छार्थक
B. आज्ञार्थक
C. विधिवाचक
D. उपर्युक्त में से एक से अधिक
E. उपर्युक्त में से कोई नहीं

निर्देश (प्र.सं. 91 से 95 तक) : *निम्नलिखित शब्दों में प्रयुक्त प्रत्यय को पहचानकर सही विकल्प को उत्तर-पुस्तिका में चिह्नित कीजिए।*

91. स्वाधीन
A. धीन
B. न
C. अधीन
D. उपर्युक्त में से एक से अधिक
E. उपर्युक्त में से कोई नहीं

92. भुलौवल
A. वल
B. औवल
C. ल
D. उपर्युक्त में से एक से अधिक
E. उपर्युक्त में से कोई नहीं

93. बढ़िया
A. या
B. इया
C. ईया
D. उपर्युक्त में से एक से अधिक
E. उपर्युक्त में से कोई नहीं

94. झगड़ालू
A. ड़ालू
B. लू
C. आलू
D. उपर्युक्त में से एक से अधिक
E. उपर्युक्त में से कोई नहीं

83. C **84.** A **85.** B **86.** C **87.** B **88.** B **89.** D **90.** A **91.** C **92.** B **93.** B **94.** C

95. मनौती
A. औती
B. ती
C. औति
D. उपर्युक्त में से एक से अधिक
E. उपर्युक्त में से कोई नहीं

निर्देश (प्र.सं. 96 से 100 तक) : *निम्नलिखित अवतरण को ध्यानपूर्वक पढ़िए और पूछे गए प्रश्नों के सही विकल्प चुनकर उत्तर-पुस्तिका में चिह्नित कीजिए।*

संकटों से वीर घबराते नहीं,
आपदाएँ देख छिप जाते नहीं।
लग गए जिस काम में पूरा किया,
काम करके व्यर्थ पछताते नहीं।।
कठिन पथ को देख मुस्कुराते सदा,
संकटों के बीच वे गाते सदा।
है असंभव कुछ नहीं उनके लिए,
सरल-संभव कर दिखाते वे सदा।।

96. पद्यांश के लिए उपयुक्त शीर्षक है :
A. संकट के बादल
B. वीर
C. कठिन पथ
D. उपर्युक्त में से एक से अधिक
E. उपर्युक्त में से कोई नहीं

97. वीर संकटों को देखकर क्या करते हैं?
A. छिप जाते हैं
B. रोते हैं
C. सोते हैं
D. उपर्युक्त में से एक से अधिक
E. उपर्युक्त में से कोई नहीं

98. वीर सभी कार्य को कैसे करते हैं?
A. सोचते हुए
B. छिपते हुए
C. मुस्कुराते हुए
D. उपर्युक्त में से एक से अधिक
E. उपर्युक्त में से कोई नहीं

99. वीर किसे देखकर मुस्कुराते हैं?
A. मित्र
B. कठिन पथ
C. असभव
D. उपर्युक्त में से एक से अधिक
E. उपर्युक्त में से कोई नहीं

100. 'आपदाएँ' शब्द का अर्थ क्या है?
A. विपत्ति
B. सम्मति
C. अंनुमति
D. उपर्युक्त में से एक से अधिक
E. उपर्युक्त में से कोई नहीं

EXPLANATORY ANSWERS

1. **(B):** "An" is used before words that start with a vowel sound. In the phrase "SDO," which likely stands for a title like "Sub-Divisional Officer," the initial sound is a vowel sound (ess-dee-oh), hence "an SDO" is correct.

2. **(A):** The indefinite article "a" is used before words that begin with a consonant sound. In this sentence, "push" starts with a consonant sound, so "a push" is appropriate. The use of "a" suggests any push, not a specific one.

3. **(A):** "The" is the definite article used before a specific noun which is already known to the listener or reader. In this case, "the book I gave you yesterday" refers to a specific book that was given yesterday, making "the" the correct choice.

4. **(B):** "An" is used before words that start with a vowel sound. "Ear infection" starts with a vowel sound (ee-), so "an ear infection" is correct. This indicates Anand had a type of ear infection, but not a specific, previously known one.

5. **(A):** "A" is used before words that begin with a consonant sound. Since "University" starts with a 'yoo-' sound, which is a consonant sound, "a University" is correct. The use of "a" here suggests the name of the university is not specified or known to the listener.

6. **(C):** Birds and animals are not a part of a plant. Plants consist of parts like leaves and branches, but birds and animals are separate entities that may interact with plants but are not components of them.

95. A	**96.** B	**97.** E	**98.** C	**99.** B	**100.** A

7. **(C):** A toothbrush is not used in a computer. Computers typically include hardware components like hard drives and input devices like keyboards. A toothbrush, being a personal hygiene item, has no function in the operation or maintenance of a computer.

8. **(A):** A drier is not typically used in a kitchen. Kitchens usually contain appliances for cooking and food preparation, such as ovens and induction cooktops. A drier, more commonly associated with laundry and clothes drying, is not a standard kitchen appliance.

9. **(D):** More than one of the above options are not allowed in an examination. Mobile phones, earphones, and books are generally prohibited in exam settings to prevent cheating and distractions, ensuring the integrity of the examination.

10. **(C):** A telescope is not found in a hospital. Hospitals are equipped with medical personnel like nurses and facilities like operation theatres for patient care. A telescope, being an instrument for observing distant objects, typically in astronomy, has no relevance in a hospital setting.

11. **(B):** The person who writes a book is known as its author. An author is someone who creates and writes the content of a book. Readers, publishers, and others may be involved in the book's lifecycle, but the author is the one who actually writes it.

12. **(E):** If today is Wednesday, the day after tomorrow will be Friday. The progression of days follows a set order, so two days after Wednesday is Friday.

13. **(A):** We must not break traffic signals. Following traffic signals is a fundamental aspect of road safety and law. "Not break" means to adhere to the rules and signals while driving.

14. **(B):** If today is the 12th of December, the next month will be January. The sequence of months is fixed, with January coming after December in the Gregorian calendar.

15. **(D):** A month can have 28, 29, 30, or 31 days. Different months have varying numbers of days: February has 28 or 29 days (29 in a leap year), April, June, September, and November have 30 days, and the remaining months have 31 days.

16. **(B):** A daughter's daughter is her granddaughter. This term specifically refers to the female grandchild of a person.

17. **(B):** A grandfather's father is a great-grandfather. This term denotes the father of one's grandfather.

18. **(B):** A mother's father is referred to as a maternal grandfather. The term "maternal" indicates the relationship through the mother's side of the family.

19. **(E):** An aunt's daughter is neither a mother, grandmother, nor niece in relation to the person in question. The correct term for an aunt's daughter is a cousin, which describes the children of one's parents' siblings.

20. **(A):** Mother's and father's children are their sons and daughters, or in other terms, sisters and brothers to each other. This describes the sibling relationship within a family.

21. **(C):** The Forest God prayed to the Rain God. This is stated directly in the passage, indicating the Forest God's appeal for help to bring rain and alleviate the drought conditions in the forest.

22. **(B):** The Forest God was very sad that he could not protect his animals. The passage explicitly mentions this emotional response to the situation where animals were dying due to lack of water.

23. **(B):** The animals had enough to eat and drink in the monsoon season. The passage mentions that the arrival of the monsoon, which was a result of the Forest God's prayer to the Rain God, provided sufficient food and water for the animals.

24. **(C):** When the hunter came to the forest, it was summer. This is specified at the beginning of the passage, highlighting the challenging conditions due to water scarcity during this season.

25. **(C):** A hunter killed the deer. This is clearly stated in the passage, describing the action of the hunter in the forest during the summer.

26. **(A):** 'जूता' (shoe) अव्यय नहीं है। अव्यय वे शब्द होते हैं जो संज्ञा, सर्वनाम, विशेषण या क्रिया की तरह कार्य नहीं करते हैं। जूता एक संज्ञा है, जबकि 'आज' और 'भीतर' अव्यय हैं।

27. **(C):** 'ह्रस्व, दीर्घ और प्लुत' स्वरों के प्रकार हैं। ये तीनों शब्द वर्णमाला के स्वर खंड से संबंधित हैं, जहाँ स्वरों की विभिन्न अवधि को दर्शाया गया है।

28. **(D):** 'तालव्य ध्वनियाँ' वे ध्वनियाँ हैं जो तालु (जीभ के ऊपरी भाग) की सहायता से उत्पन्न होती हैं। 'च, छ' (च-वर्ग) और 'ज, झ' (ज-वर्ग) दोनों ही तालव्य ध्वनियाँ हैं।

29. **(A):** 'तुम' उत्तम पुरुष वाची शब्द नहीं है। उत्तम पुरुष वह होता है जो वक्ता को संबोधित करता है, जैसे 'मैं' या 'हम'।

'तुम' मध्यम पुरुष में आता है, जो संबोधित किए जाने वाले व्यक्ति को दर्शाता है। 'हमको' और 'मुझमें' उत्तम पुरुष वाची शब्द हैं।

30. **(E):** वाक्य 'मरुभूमि में कहीं धान उगता है?' में कोई क्रिया-विशेषण नहीं है। क्रिया-विशेषण वे शब्द होते हैं जो क्रिया की विशेषता बताते हैं, जैसे समय, स्थान, तरीका आदि। इस वाक्य में 'मरुभूमि' (रेगिस्तान) स्थान का उल्लेख करता है, लेकिन यह क्रिया-विशेषण नहीं है, बल्कि यह सिर्फ स्थान का संज्ञानात्मक वर्णन करता है।

31. **(D):** लक्षणा की विशेषता में 'व्यंग्यार्थ', 'मुख्यार्थ', और 'रूढ़ि का प्रयोग' सभी शामिल हैं। लक्षणा तब होती है जब शब्द का अर्थ इसके मूल अर्थ से अलग होता है, और यह व्यंग्य, मुख्यार्थ और रूढ़ि प्रयोग के जरिए हो सकता है।

32. **(A):** विभाव को 'स्थायी भाव के उद्बोधक कारक' के रूप में परिभाषित किया जाता है। नाट्यशास्त्र में, विभाव वह तत्व होता है जो रस की अनुभूति के लिए आवश्यक स्थायी भाव को जागृत करता है। इसमें अलंकार, पात्र, और परिस्थितियाँ शामिल हो सकती हैं।

33. **(E):** वाक्य 'लड़के ने कुत्ते को मारा' में 'लड़के' 'कर्ता' कारक है, और 'कुत्ते को' 'कर्म' कारक है। इस वाक्य में करण या अपादान कारक नहीं है।

34. **(C):** 'संक्षिप्ति' की विशेषता यह नहीं है कि यह शब्द अपने आप में पूर्णता नहीं रखता। संक्षिप्ति एक स्वतंत्र और मूल शब्द का अर्थ वहन करने वाला शब्द होता है, जो उसका संक्षेपित रूप होता है।

35. **(B):** 'महाशय' शब्द में 'दीर्घ स्वर संधि' है। यह शब्द 'महा' और 'आशय' के मिलन से बना है, जहां 'महा' के अंतिम 'अ' और 'आशय' के प्रारंभिक 'आ' का मेल होकर 'आ' बनता है, जो दीर्घ स्वर संधि का एक उदाहरण है।

36. **(C):** शुद्ध वाक्य है 'हमने जो कहा था वही सत्य है।' यहाँ 'कहे थे' की जगह 'कहा था' का प्रयोग होना चाहिए, क्योंकि वाक्य भूतकाल में है और 'हमने' के साथ 'कहा था' का प्रयोग उचित है।

37. **(B):** शुद्ध वाक्य है 'आपका पत्र मिला धन्यवाद।' 'धन्यवाद सहित' की जगह 'धन्यवाद' का प्रयोग वाक्य को अधिक स्पष्ट और सही बनाता है।

38. **(A):** शुद्ध वाक्य है 'कृपया कार्यक्रम में पधारें।' 'कृपया करके' का प्रयोग अतिरिक्त है, और 'पधारें' शिष्टाचारपूर्ण आमंत्रण हेतु सही शब्द है।

39. **(A):** शुद्ध वाक्य है 'मुझसे फिजूल बात मत करो।' 'बेफिजूल' का प्रयोग अशुद्ध है, और सही शब्द 'फिजूल' है।

40. **(B):** शुद्ध वाक्य है 'बिहारी ने गागर में सागर भरा है।' यहाँ 'भर दिया है' की जगह 'भरा है' का प्रयोग उचित है, जो किसी काम को पूर्ण करने की क्रिया को दर्शाता है।

41. **(E):** 'बेगम' शब्द तुर्की भाषा का है। यह शब्द मुख्य रूप से उच्च स्थान पर आसीन महिलाओं या रानियों के लिए प्रयोग किया जाता है।

42. **(C):** 'सिनेमा' शब्द अंग्रेजी भाषा का है। सिनेमा शब्द ग्रीक भाषा के किनेमेटोग्राफोस–किनेमा और ग्रामो से बना है। किनेमा का अर्थ आंदोलन और ग्रामो का अर्थ है लिखना या रिकॉर्ड करना।

43. **(E):** 'अर्दली' शब्द का मूल न तो अरबी, फारसी, न ही पुर्तगाली भाषा में है। यह शब्द तुर्की भाषा से आया है और सैन्य सहायक या व्यक्तिगत सहायक के लिए प्रयोग किया जाता है।

44. **(B):** 'तौलिया' शब्द पुर्तगाली भाषा का है। यह शब्द वस्त्र या तौलिये के संदर्भ में प्रयोग किया जाता है।

45. **(A):** 'रिक्शा' शब्द जापानी भाषा का है। यह शब्द एक प्रकार के छोटे वाहन के लिए प्रयोग किया जाता है जिसे मानव द्वारा खींचा जाता है।

46. **(C):** 'कंजूस' दुर्जन का पर्यायवाची शब्द नहीं है। दुर्जन का अर्थ होता है दुष्ट या बुरे व्यक्ति, जिसके पर्यायवाची शब्द हैं 'शठ' और 'कपटी'। 'कंजूस' का अर्थ है मितव्ययी या कृपण, जो दुर्जन के अर्थ से भिन्न है।

47. **(E):** 'काया', 'शरीर', और 'तन' सभी देह के पर्यायवाची शब्द हैं। देह का अर्थ होता है शरीर, और इन सभी शब्दों का प्रयोग शरीर के लिए किया जाता है।

48. **(C):** 'सविता' स्त्री का पर्यायवाची शब्द नहीं है। स्त्री का अर्थ होता है महिला या नारी, जिसके पर्यायवाची शब्द हैं 'वनिता' और 'कांता'। 'सविता' सूर्य देवता की पत्नी या देवी का नाम है, जो स्त्री के अर्थ से भिन्न है।

49. **(B):** 'आभा' बिजली का पर्यायवाची शब्द नहीं है। बिजली का अर्थ होता है विद्युत, जिसके पर्यायवाची शब्द हैं 'विद्युत्' और 'चंचला'। 'आभा' का अर्थ होता है प्रकाश या चमक, जो बिजली के अर्थ से भिन्न है।

50. **(A):** 'उमा' लक्ष्मी का पर्यायवाची शब्द नहीं है। लक्ष्मी धन और समृद्धि की देवी हैं, जिनके पर्यायवाची शब्द हैं 'रमा' और 'कमला'। 'उमा' हिन्दू धर्म में पार्वती या शक्ति का एक नाम है, जो लक्ष्मी से भिन्न है।

51. **(B):** 'परीक्षाएँ पास है' वाक्य 'परीक्षाएँ सन्निकट हैं' के समान अर्थ रखता है। 'पास' शब्द का इस्तेमाल बोलचाल की भाषा में 'निकट' या 'सन्निकट' के समान अर्थ में होता है।

52. **(A):** 'बरसात में नदियों में बाढ़ आ जाती है' वाक्य 'बरसात में सरिताओं में बाढ़ आ जाती है' के समान अर्थ रखता है। 'नदियों' शब्द का इस्तेमाल बोलचाल में 'सरिताओं' के समान अर्थ में होता है।

53. **(D):** 'मैं आपसे बिल्कुल अपरिचित हूँ' वाक्य 'मैं आपसे नितांत अपरिचित हूँ' के समान अर्थ रखता है। 'बिल्कुल' शब्द का प्रयोग बोलचाल की भाषा में 'नितांत' के समान अर्थ में होता है।

54. **(C):** 'दूरदर्शन के अनेक धारावाहिक प्रसिद्ध हैं' वाक्य 'दूरदर्शन की अनेक शृंखलाएँ प्रसिद्ध हैं' के समान अर्थ रखता है। धारावाहिक का प्रयोग बोलचाल की भाषा में टीवी शो या सीरीज के लिए किया जाता है।

55. **(B):** 'वह अभी नए अमीर हुए हैं' वाक्य 'वे अभी नवधनाढ्य हुए हैं' के समान अर्थ रखता है। 'नए अमीर' का प्रयोग बोलचाल की भाषा में हाल ही में धनी बने लोगों के लिए होता है।

56. **(C):** 'इच्छा' का विलोम 'अनिच्छा' है। इच्छा का अर्थ है चाहना या चाह, और अनिच्छा का अर्थ है न चाहना या न चाह।

57. **(C):** 'उन्मूलन' का विलोम 'रोपण' है। उन्मूलन का अर्थ होता है जड़ से उखाड़ना या नष्ट करना, जबकि रोपण का अर्थ है पौधे लगाना या रोपना।

58. **(D):** कर्कश का अर्थ होता है कठोर या रूखा, इसलिए इसका विलोम मधुर एवं कोमल होगा।

59. **(B):** 'जंगम' का विलोम 'स्थावर' है। जंगम का अर्थ है चलायमान या गतिशील, और स्थावर का अर्थ है स्थिर या अचल।

60. **(A):** 'शासक' का विलोम 'शासित' है। शासक का अर्थ है वह जो शासन करता है, और शासित का अर्थ है वह जिस पर शासन किया जाता है।

61. **(B):** 'शिशु' का अर्थ होता है बालक या छोटा बच्चा। इसलिए यहाँ सही विकल्प 'बालक' है।

62. **(C):** 'युद्ध' का अर्थ होता है संग्राम या लड़ाई। इसलिए यहाँ सही विकल्प 'संग्राम' है।

63. **(A):** 'आजादी' का अर्थ होता है स्वाधीनता या स्वतंत्रता। इसलिए यहाँ सही विकल्प 'स्वाधीनता' है।

64. **(A):** 'रिपु' का अर्थ होता है 'शत्रु या दुश्मन। इसलिए यहाँ सही विकल्प 'शत्रु' है।

65. **(A):** 'सोम' का एक अर्थ होता है अमृत, जो देवताओं का पेय होता है। इसलिए यहाँ सही विकल्प 'अमृत' है।

66. **(D):** 'खग' का अर्थ होता है पक्षी, और इसके पर्यायवाची शब्द हैं 'विहग' और 'खगी'। 'द्विज' भी पक्षियों के लिए प्रयोग किया जाता है, लेकिन इसका प्राथमिक अर्थ ब्राह्मण या दूसरी बार जन्मा हुआ होता है।

67. **(A):** 'गणेश' के लिए सर्वाधिक उपयुक्त तत्सम शब्द 'एकदन्त' है, जो गणेश जी का एक नाम है और उनके एक दांत के होने का संदर्भ देता है।

68. **(D):** 'काक' का अर्थ होता है कौवा, और इसके पर्यायवाची शब्द हैं 'फिसफिस' और 'पिशुन'। 'काग' भी कौवे के लिए प्रयोग किया जाता है।

69. **(A):** 'ठग' का अर्थ होता है धोखेबाज या चालाक, और इसके पर्यायवाची शब्द में 'जालसाज' शामिल है।

70. **(A):** 'देह' का अर्थ होता है शरीर, और इसके पर्यायवाची शब्द में 'वपु' शामिल है। 'क्षीर' और 'पय' का संबंध दूध या तरल पदार्थ से है, जो देह के अर्थ से अलग है।

71. **(A):** 'जिसके आने की तिथि न हो' के लिए सही शब्द 'अतिथि' है। अतिथि का अर्थ होता है वह व्यक्ति जिसके आने की कोई निश्चित तिथि न हो।

72. **(D):** 'जो लज्जा से रहित हो' के लिए सही शब्द निर्लज्ज और 'बेशर्म' है। इसका अर्थ होता है वह व्यक्ति जिसमें लज्जा या शर्म की कमी हो।

73. **(A):** 'जो सिंहासन का अधिकारी हो' के लिए सही शब्द 'युवराज' है। युवराज का अर्थ होता है वह व्यक्ति जो सिंहासन या राज-पद का अधिकारी हो।

74. **(B):** 'वर्ष में एक बार होने वाला' के लिए सही शब्द 'वार्षिक' है। वार्षिक का अर्थ होता है कुछ ऐसा जो हर साल एक बार होता है।

75. **(C):** 'जो स्वेच्छा से सेवा करे' के लिए सही शब्द 'स्वयंसेवक' है। स्वयंसेवक का अर्थ होता है वह व्यक्ति जो अपनी इच्छा से, बिना किसी बाध्यता के, सेवा करता है।

76. **(C):** 'अंक भरना' मुहावरे का अर्थ होता है स्नेह से लिपटा लेना या गले लगाना। यह प्यार या आत्मीयता दर्शाने के लिए प्रयोग किया जाता है।

77. **(A):** 'आस्तीन का साँप' मुहावरे का अर्थ होता है कपटी मित्र या धोखेबाज दोस्त। यह ऐसे व्यक्ति के लिए प्रयोग किया जाता है जो दिखावे में तो मित्र है पर वास्तव में शत्रुता रखता है।

78. **(D):** 'किस खेत की मूली' मुहावरे का अर्थ होता है अधिकारहीन या शक्तिहीन या ऐसा व्यक्ति जिसका कोई महत्व नहीं होता। इसका प्रयोग किसी की अहमियत या स्थिति को कम करके आंकने के लिए किया जाता है।

79. **(E):** 'घड़ों पानी पड़ना' मुहावरे का अर्थ उपलब्ध विकल्पों में से किसी से मेल नहीं खाता। इस मुहावरे का अर्थ होता है अचानक बहुत अधिक नुकसान होना या किसी बड़ी आपदा का होना।

80. **(A):** 'नाच नचाना' मुहावरे का अर्थ होता है तंग करना या किसी काम में असमर्थ होना। इसका प्रयोग अक्सर उस स्थिति में किया जाता है जब कोई व्यक्ति अपनी अक्षमता के लिए बहाने बनाता है और दूसरों को तंग करता है।

81. **(A):** 'अनाधिकार' का शुद्ध रूप 'अनधिकार' है।

82. **(B):** 'परलौकिक' का शुद्ध रूप 'पारलौकिक' है, जिसका अर्थ होता है परलोक से संबंधित या दिव्य।

83. **(C):** 'चांद' का शुद्ध रूप 'चाँद' है।

84. **(A):** 'सौंदर्यता' का शुद्ध रूप 'सौंदर्य' है।

85. **(B):** 'परसाद' का शुद्ध रूप 'प्रसाद' है। यह शब्द आमतौर पर देवताओं को अर्पित भोजन या पदार्थों के बाद भक्तों को दिए जाने वाले पवित्र भोजन या वस्तु के लिए प्रयोग किया जाता है।

86. **(C):** 'उसने कहा कि मैं कल आऊँगी।' यह वाक्य मिश्र वाक्य है।

87. **(B):** 'तुम जाओ और अपने पिताजी से कहना।' यह वाक्य संयुक्त वाक्य है क्योंकि इसमें दो सरल वाक्यों को 'और' के माध्यम से जोड़ा गया है।

88. **(B):** 'यह चित्र इस दीवार पर असंगत है।' यह वाक्य निषेधवाचक है क्योंकि इसमें चित्र के दीवार पर होने की अनुपयुक्तता या असंगतता का वर्णन किया गया है।

89. **(D):** 'अरे! तुम अभी यहीं खड़े हो।' इस वाक्य में विस्मयबोधक और आश्चर्यबोधक दोनों तत्व मौजूद हैं। इसमें आश्चर्य और विस्मय का भाव व्यक्त होता है।

90. **(A):** 'तुम सदा सुखी रहो।' यह वाक्य इच्छार्थक है क्योंकि इसमें किसी के लिए सुखी रहने की कामना या इच्छा व्यक्त की गई है।

91. **(C):** 'स्वाधीन' शब्द में प्रयुक्त प्रत्यय 'अधीन' है। इसमें 'स्व' उपसर्ग है और 'अधीन' मूल शब्द है।

92. **(B):** 'भुलौवल' शब्द में प्रयुक्त प्रत्यय 'औवल' है। 'भुल' मूल शब्द है और 'औवल' प्रत्यय है।

93. **(B):** 'बढ़िया' शब्द में प्रयुक्त प्रत्यय 'इया' है। 'बढ़' मूल शब्द है और 'इया' प्रत्यय है।

94. **(C):** 'झगड़ालू' शब्द में प्रयुक्त प्रत्यय 'आलू' है। 'झगड़' मूल शब्द है और 'आलू' प्रत्यय है।

95. **(A):** 'मनौती' शब्द में प्रयुक्त प्रत्यय 'औती' है। 'मन' मूल शब्द है और 'औती' प्रत्यय है।

96. **(B):** इस पद्यांश का उपयुक्त शीर्षक 'वीर' है, क्योंकि यह पूरे पद्यांश में वीरता और साहसिकता की भावना को दर्शाता है।

97. **(E):** वीर संकटों को देखकर न तो छिपते हैं, न रोते हैं, और न ही सोते हैं। इसलिए उपलब्ध विकल्पों में से कोई भी सही नहीं है।

98. **(C):** वीर सभी कार्यों को मुस्कराते हुए पूरा करते हैं और व्यर्थ पछताते नहीं हैं।

99. **(B):** वीर कठिन पथ को देखकर मुस्कुराते हैं, जो उनकी साहसिकता और सकारात्मक दृष्टिकोण को दर्शाता है।

100. **(A):** 'आपदाएँ' शब्द का अर्थ 'विपत्ति' या संकट होता है।

PAPER-3*

Part-I : General Studies

1. 10 years ago the ratio of ages of Ramesh and Rajeev was 1 : 3. 5 years hence this ratio will become 2 : 3. What is the ratio of their ages at present?
A. 2 : 5 B. 3 : 5
C. 1 : 2 D. More than one of the above
E. None of the above

2. If I walk with a speed of 5 km per hour from my house to the station, my train would have left the station 7 minutes before my arrival. But, if I walk with a speed of 6 km per hour, I will reach the station 5 minutes before the departure of my train. Accordingly, what is the distance between my house and the station?
A. 7 km B. 6.5 km
C. 6 km D. More than one of the above
E. None of the above

3. The average monthly income of P and Q is ₹ 5,050. The average monthly income of Q and R is ₹ 6,250 and the average monthly income of P and R is ₹ 5,200. The monthly income of P is:
A. ₹ 3,500 B. ₹ 4,050
C. ₹ 4,000 D. More than one of the above
E. None of the above

4. If 30% of P is added to 40% of Q, it becomes 80% of Q. Accordingly, what is the percentage of Q with respect to P?
A. 40% B. 50%
C. 75% D. More than one of the above
E. None of the above

5. A sum of money is to be distributed among A, B, C, D in the proportion of 5 : 2 : 4 : 3. If C gets ₹ 1,000 more than D, what is B's share?
A. ₹ 500 B. ₹ 1,500
C. ₹ 2,000 D. More than one of the above
E. None of the above

6. A shopkeeper gives a discount of 5% on the selling price of a watch. If he gives a discount of 6%, he will earn a profit which is ₹ 15 less than the before. Accordingly, what is the marked selling price of that watch?
A. ₹ 1,400 B. ₹ 1,500
C. ₹ 1,800 D. More than one of the above
E. None of the above

7. Three numbers are in the ratio 3 : 4 : 5. The total of the largest and the smallest numbers is equal to the other number plus 52. Accordingly, which is the smallest number?
A. 27 B. 39
C. 52 D. More than one of the above
E. None of the above

8. If $2^{2n-1} = \frac{1}{8^{n-3}}$, then the value of n is:
A. 3 B. 2
C. −2 D. More than one of the above
E. None of the above

9. Which of the following photoelectric devices is the most suitable for digital applications?
A. Photo-voltaic cell
B. Photo-emissive cell
C. Photo-diode
D. More than one of the above
E. None of the above

10. The critical mass of a fissionable material is:
A. one kilogram equivalent
B. the minimum mass needed for chain reaction
C. the rest mass equivalent to 10^{10} joules
D. More than one of the above
E. None of the above

11. Which of the following gases is used to force the ripening of fruits?
A. Ethane B. Ethylene
C. Methylene D. More than one of the above
E. None of the above

12. Which one of the following has zero octane number?
A. Iso-octane
B. Neo-octane
C. n-octane
D. More than one of the above
E. None of the above

1. B	2. C	3. C	4. C	5. C	6. B	7. B	8. B	9. A	10. B	11. B	12. E

Exam held on 26-08-2023.

13. The edible part of Litchis is:
A. aril
B. thalamus
C. seed coat
D. More than one of the above
E. None of the above

14. The physical process involved in the release of molecular oxygen from leaves is:
A. diffusion
B. transpiration
C. osmosis
D. More than one of the above
E. None of the above

15. The process of finding the relative location of genes on a chromosome is called:
A. genome walking
B. chromosome walking
C. gene mapping
D. More than one of the above
E. None of the above

16. Spore mother cell in bryophytes is:
A. haploid
B. diploid
C. triploid
D. More than one of the above
E. None of the above

17. In which year was NGT (National Green Tribunal) for protection of environment and forest established by the Government of India?
A. 2010
B. 2011
C. 2012
D. More than one of the above
E. None of the above

18. Which city of India started first under-water metro?
A. Kochi
B. Visakhapatnam
C. Bengaluru
D. More than one of the above
E. None of the above

19. Under India's G20 Presidency, where was the Tourism Working Group Meeting held?
A. Patna (Bihar)
B. Srinagar (Jammu and Kashmir)
C. Ramnagar (Uttarakhand)
D. More than one of the above
E. None of the above

20. Who among the following got the Silver Medal in the National Under-17 Girls Wrestling Championship?
A. Liza Tomar
B. Nirjala
C. Pushpa Yadav
D. More than one of the above
E. None of the above

21. Who won the International Booker Prize, 2022 for the novel, *Tomb of Sand*?
A. Geetanjali Shree and Daisy Rockwell
B. David Diop and Anna Moschovakis
C. Marilyn Booth and Jokha Alharthi
D. More than one of the above
E. None of the above

22. Who was the Chief Guest on India's 74th Republic Day?
A. Mohammed bin Salman
B. Abdel Fattah El-Sisi
C. Sheikh Mohammed bin Rashid Al Maktoum
D. More than one of the above
E. None of the above

23. In which district of Bihar, the first floating solar power plant has been built?
A. Darbhanga
B. West Champaran
C. Madhubani
D. More than one of the above
E. None of the above

24. Which of the following has got GI Tag in Bihar?
A. Maghai Paan
B. Basmati Rice
C. Chanderi Saree
D. More than one of the above
E. None of the above

25. Match List–I with List–II:

List-I	List-II
(*a*) Char	1. Punjab plain
(*b*) Kankar	2. Delta
(*c*) Kayal	3. Bangar
(*d*) Mand	4. Coastal plain

Select the correct answer using the codes given below.

	(*a*)	(*b*)	(*c*)	(*d*)
A.	1	4	2	3
B.	2	3	4	1
C.	3	1	4	2

D. More than one of the above
E. None of the above

26. Which of the following tributaries does ***not*** join Brahmaputra river from north?
A. Subansiri
B. Belsiri
C. Manas
D. More than one of the above
E. None of the above

13. A **14.** A **15.** C **16.** B **17.** A **18.** E **19.** B **20.** B **21.** A **22.** B **23.** A **24.** A **25.** B **26.** E

27. Likhapani glacier is located in which State of India?
A. Arunachal Pradesh
B. Himachal Pradesh
C. Sikkim
D. More than one of the above
E. None of the above

28. Magadha and Anga plains are parts of:
A. upper Ganga plain
B. middle Ganga plain
C. lower Ganga plain
D. More than one of the above
E. None of the above

29. Which of the following pairs of waterfalls and rivers is ***not*** correctly matched?
A. Jog — Sharavati
B. Kapildhara — Kaveri
C. Dhuandhar — Godavari
D. More than one of the above
E. None of the above

30. Arrange the following seaports of India from north to south:
1. Kakinada 2. Machilipatnam
3. Nagapattinam 4. Visakhapatnam

Select the correct answer using the codes given below.
A. 1, 2, 3, 4 B. 4, 1, 2, 3
C. 1, 3, 2, 4 D. More than one of the above
E. None of the above

31. The Agreement of Kosi Irrigation and Hydro-electricity Plan in 1954 was signed between which two countries?
A. India and Bangladesh
B. India and China
C. India and Nepal
D. More than one of the above
E. None of the above

32. In which climatic division does Bihar fall as per R.L. Singh's classification scheme?
A. Humid south-east
B. Subhumid transitional
C. Subhumid continental
D. More than one of the above
E. None of the above

33. In which Session of the Indian National Congress was the resolution of 'Purna Swaraj' adopted?
A. Kanpur Session, 1925
B. Lahore Session, 1929
C. Karachi Session, 1931
D. More than one of the above
E. None of the above

34. What was an initial objective of 'Kuka Movement' in Punjab?
A. To purify the Sikh religion
B. To gain political power in Punjab
C. Organization of peasant movement
D. More than one of the above
E. None of the above

35. Who described the Revolt of 1857 as the 'First Indian War of Independence'?
A. V.D. Savarkar
B. Bal Gangadhar Tilak
C. Bipin Chandra Pal
D. More than one of the above
E. None of the above

36. Where was the first instance of organized non-cooperation in the history of Indian peasantry held?
A. Bihar and Bengal
B. Madras Presidency
C. Punjab Province
D. More than one of the above
E. None of the above

37. Which portfolio did Dr. Rajendra Prasad hold during the Interim Government of 1946?
A. Defence
B. Home
C. Food and Agriculture
D. More than one of the above
E. None of the above

38. Who among the following particularly urged Gandhiji to visit Champaran to witness the miseries of the Ryots?
A. Brijkishore Prasad
B. Rajkumar Shukla
C. Sukhram Ganesh
D. More than one of the above
E. None of the above

39. The 'Day of Deliverance' was observed by the Muslim League on which date?
A. 22nd December, 1939
B. 17th October, 1939
C. 22nd December, 1940
D. More than one of the above
E. None of the above

40. Who laid the foundation stone of National College and Bihar Vidyapeeth?
A. Dr. Rajendra Prasad
B. Maulana Abdul Bari
C. Mahatma Gandhi
D. More than one of the above
E. None of the above

27. A **28.** B **29.** D **30.** B **31.** C **32.** B **33.** B **34.** A **35.** A **36.** A **37.** C **38.** B **39.** A **40.** C

Part-II : Social Science

In **Social Science** includes **History, Geography, Economics** and **Political Science** subjects. Choose the questions from any two subjects out of four subjects of **Social Science.** At least one subject **History** or **Geography** is mandatory.

History

41. Name the major city of the Indus Valley Civilization that had trade relations with West Asia:
A. Ropar
B. Sanghol
C. Kalibangan
D. More than one of the above
E. None of the above

42. Of which metal was the dancing girl in Mohenjo-daro made?
A. Copper
B. Brass
C. Bronze
D. More than one of the above
E. None of the above

43. In the Indus Valley Civilization, which animal worship has been found?
A. Humped bull
B. Horse
C. Cow
D. More than one of the above
E. None of the above

44. How many Suktas are there in Rigveda?
A. 1020
B. 1017
C. 1080
D. More than one of the above
E. None of the above

45. Who wrote *Kiratarjuniya*?
A. Bhatti
B. Shudraka
C. Kalidasa
D. More than one of the above
E. None of the above

46. 'Pur' in Vedic period means:
A. forts
B. trade
C. market
D. More than one of the above
E. None of the above

47. What is called 'Takshan' in Rigveda?
A. Carpenter
B. Ironsmith
C. Potter
D. More than one of the above
E. None of the above

48. Of which metal was the 'Kakani' coins made in Mauryan period?
A. Copper
B. Iron
C. Silver
D. More than one of the above
E. None of the above

49. By whom was the world's first Republic established in Vaishali?
A. Maurya
B. Nanda
C. Gupta
D. More than one of the above
E. None of the above

50. Into how many major chapters is Kautilya's Arthashastra divided?
A. 11
B. 12
C. 14
D. More than one of the above
E. None of the above

51. Whom did Iltutmish appoint as his first Governor in Bihar?
A. Aivaz
B. Nasiruddin Mahmud
C. Ali Mardan
D. More than one of the above
E. None of the above

52. Where was the field area of Birsa Munda?
A. Champaran
B. Ranchi
C. Ballia
D. More than one of the above
E. None of the above

41. C **42.** C **43.** A **44.** E **45.** E **46.** A **47.** A **48.** A **49.** E **50.** E **51.** E **52.** B

53. Who was the leader of the Revolt of 1857 from Bihar?
A. Maulvi Ahmadullah
B. Tantia Topi
C. Nana Sahib
D. More than one of the above
E. None of the above

54. Name the first capital of Magadha:
A. Pataliputra
B. Vaishali
C. Girivraja (Rajagriha)
D. More than one of the above
E. None of the above

55. Which of the following sources mentions about the administration of Pataliputra?
A. Divyavadana
B. Arthashastra
C. Indica
D. More than one of the above
E. None of the above

56. In Mughal administration, 'Madad-i-Maash' was related with:
A. octroi tax
B. revenue-free land to the intellectuals
C. pension to military officers
D. More than one of the above
E. None of the above

57. What was the objective of Puna Agreement?
A. Hindu-Muslim unity
B. Representation of Dalit class
C. Special rights to kings
D. More than one of the above
E. None of the above

58. Who constructed 'Jantar Mantar'?
A. Akbar
B. Shah Jahan
C. Shivaji
D. More than one of the above
E. None of the above

59. Who wrote Vande Mataram?
A. Bankim Chandra Chatterjee
B. Sarojini Naidu
C. Rabindranath Tagore
D. More than one of the above
E. None of the above

60. Christopher Columbus, the great explorer who discovered America in 1492, was financed by which of the following countries?
A. Portugal
B. England
C. Spain
D. More than one of the above
E. None of the above

61. The 'Boston Tea Party', an important event of history, is associated with the:
A. American War of Independence
B. French Revolution
C. Russian Revolution
D. More than one of the above
E. None of the above

62. Why is 4th July, 1776 considered to be important in the history of the USA?
A. George Washington was elected as the President
B. Abolition of Slavery
C. Declaration of American Independence
D. More than one of the above
E. None of the above

63. The ruler of France at the time of the French Revolution was:
A. Louis XVI
B. Louis XIV
C. Louis XIII
D. More than one of the above
E. None of the above

64. During the Industrial Revolution, the cotton textile sector was revolutionized by 'Spinning Jenny' which was invented by:
A. John Kay
B. Samuel Crompton
C. James Hargreaves
D. More than one of the above
E. None of the above

65. 'Young Italy Movement' in 1831 which aimed to establish Republic was started by:
A. Count Cavour
B. Giuseppe Garibaldi
C. Victor Emmanuel
D. More than one of the above
E. None of the above

66. The architect of the Unification of Germany who believed in the policy of 'blood and iron' was:
A. Talleyrand
B. Otto von Bismarck
C. Metternich
D. More than one of the above
E. None of the above

53. E **54.** C **55.** C **56.** B **57.** B **58.** E **59.** A **60.** C **61.** A **62.** C **63.** A **64.** C **65.** E **66.** B

67. The US entry into the Second World War in November 1941 was mainly due to:
A. the invasion of Poland by Germany
B. the Battle of Stalingrad
C. German occupation of Sudetenland
D. More than one of the above
E. None of the above

68. Who was the ruler of China when Marco Polo visited that country?
A. Genghis Khan
B. Kublai Khan
C. Halagu Khan
D. More than one of the above
E. None of the above

69. Which was the first English Settlement in the USA?
A. Jamestown
B. Charles Town
C. Boston
D. More than one of the above
E. None of the above

70. 'The Oath of Tennis Court' is connected with the:
A. American Revolution
B. Russian Revolution
C. French Revolution
D. More than one of the above
E. None of the above

71. With which country the Allied Powers did the Treaty of Sèvres?
A. Germany
B. Turkey
C. Hungary
D. More than one of the above
E. None of the above

72. Who invented the flying shuttle machine in 1733?
A. James Hargreaves
B. John Kay
C. Edmund Cartwright
D. More than one of the above
E. None of the above

73. By which Treaty was the Thirty Years' War ended?
A. Treaty of Augsburg
B. Treaty of Westphalia
C. Treaty of Trianon
D. More than one of the above
E. None of the above

74. Who represented Italy in the Paris Peace Conference?
A. Lloyd George
B. Orlando
C. Georges Clemenceau
D. More than one of the above
E. None of the above

75. Who took the Komagata Maru ship on rent to sail to Vancouver?
A. Harnam Singh
B. Gurmeet Singh
C. Kartar Singh
D. More than one of the above
E. None of the above

76. Which one of the following was ***not*** associated with the foundation of the Shore Committee?
A. Hussain Rahim
B. Balwant Singh
C. Bhagwan Singh
D. More than one of the above
E. None of the above

77. To which incident had Mahatma Gandhi called 'Himalayan Blunder'?
A. Chauri-chaura incident
B. Jallianwala Bagh Massacre
C. Execution of Bhagat Singh
D. More than one of the above
E. None of the above

78. Which woman revolutionist died while conducting a raid on Armory at Chittagong?
A. Pritilata Waddedar
B. Kalpana Datta
C. Santi Ghosh
D. More than one of the above
E. None of the above

79. Which of the following revolutionaries was ***not*** associated with Kakori Train Case?
A. Ashfaqulla Khan
B. Ram Prasad Bismil
C. Prafulla Chaki
D. More than one of the above
E. None of the above

80. In which language was the first issue of *Ghadar* published on 1st November, 1913?
A. Gurmukhi
B. Urdu
C. Hindi
D. More than one of the above
E. None of the above

67. E **68.** B **69.** A **70.** C **71.** B **72.** B **73.** B **74.** B **75.** E **76.** C **77.** A **78.** A **79.** C **80.** B

or

Geography

41. Vulnerable species in India is:
A. Asiatic elephant
B. Gangetic dolphin
C. Blackbuck
D. More than one of the above
E. None of the above

42. The major factor for depletion of forest resources in India is:
A. expansion of agriculture
B. railways
C. scientific forestry
D. More than one of the above
E. None of the above

43. Developing new methods of ecological farming through traditional methods is promoted by:
A. Beej Bachao Andolan
B. Navdanya
C. Tawa Matsya Sangh
D. More than one of the above
E. None of the above

44. Sardar Sarovar Dam covers which of the following States?
A. Gujarat, Rajasthan, Maharashtra and Madhya Pradesh
B. Gujarat, Rajasthan, Maharashtra and Goa
C. Gujarat, Rajasthan, Maharashtra and Punjab
D. More than one of the above
E. None of the above

45. Most of the river valley projects constructed to control floods failed and instead triggered floods because of:
A. excessive sediments in the reservoir
B. heavy rain led water released from dam
C. extensive soil erosion due to flood
D. More than one of the above
E. None of the above

46. The first State in India that made rooftop rainwater harvesting compulsory through legal norms was:
A. Tamil Nadu
B. Rajasthan
C. Meghalaya
D. More than one of the above
E. None of the above

47. As per the Agriculture Report, 2017, India was the second largest producer of ________ in the world.
A. rice
B. cotton
C. sugarcane
D. More than one of the above
E. None of the above

48. The institutional reform for the benefit of farmers was:
A. Land Reforms
B. Creation of Grameen Banks
C. Kisan Credit Card Scheme
D. More than one of the above
E. None of the above

49. Koderma in Jharkhand is the leading producer of which one of the following minerals?
A. Bauxite
B. Mica
C. Iron
D. More than one of the above
E. None of the above

50. The only industry in India which is self-reliant and complete in value chain is:
A. iron and steel industry
B. textile industry
C. sugar industry
D. More than one of the above
E. None of the above

51. What is the example of the Kharif crop?
A. Maize
B. Wheat
C. Peas
D. More than one of the above
E. None of the above

52. Which crop takes almost a year to grow?
A. Barley
B. Jute
C. Cotton
D. More than one of the above
E. None of the above

41. D **42.** A **43.** D **44.** A **45.** D **46.** A **47.** D **48.** A **49.** B **50.** B **51.** A **52.** E

53. The National Highways are laid and maintained by:
A. Central Public Works Department (CPWD)
B. National Highways Authority of India (NHAI)
C. Border Roads Organization
D. More than one of the above
E. None of the above

54. According to the Annual Report 2016–2017, India ranks _____ in the world in International Tourism.
A. 2nd
B. 3rd
C. 4th
D. More than one of the above
E. None of the above

55. Alluvial soil is classified on the basis of its age. What is the name given for new alluvial soil?
A. Khadar
B. Bangar
C. Marshy land
D. More than one of the above
E. None of the above

56. Which of the following soils is ideal for growing cotton?
A. Arid soil
B. Alluvial soil
C. Black soil
D. More than one of the above
E. None of the above

57. Which place in India receives the highest rainfall?
A. Srinagar
B. Mawsynram
C. Chennai
D. More than one of the above
E. None of the above

58. Select the correct option from the codes given below for the names used for slash and burn agriculture in different countries.

Country	Name of slash and burn agriculture
(*a*) Mexico	1. Roca
(*b*) Brazil	2. Milpa
(*c*) Vietnam	3. Ladang
(*d*) Indonesia	4. Ray

Codes:
A. (*a*)-1, (*b*)-2, (*c*)-3, (*d*)-4
B. (*a*)-4, (*b*)-3, (*c*)-2, (*d*)-1
C. (*a*)-2, (*b*)-1, (*c*)-4, (*d*)-3
D. More than one of the above
E. None of the above

59. Bhoodan-Gramdan Movement, also known as the Bloodless Revolution, was initiated by:
A. Vinoba Bhave
B. Sukya Bhuvesh
C. Sardar Patel
D. More than one of the above
E. None of the above

60. The sparkle in some toothpaste comes from which mineral?
A. Limestone
B. Silica
C. Mica
D. More than one of the above
E. None of the above

61. Which thermal power plant is present in Bihar?
A. Neyveli
B. Talcher
C. Barauni
D. More than one of the above
E. None of the above

62. _____ is a major power-providing corporation in India and it has ISO certification for environment management system 14001.
A. NTPC
B. HAIL
C. NHPC
D. More than one of the above
E. None of the above

63. Golden Quadrilateral Super Highways connect four major cities in India to reduce time and distance. Which of the following options includes the cities?
A. Delhi–Kolkata–Chennai–Mumbai
B. Srinagar–Jaipur–Chennai–Kolkata
C. Delhi–Ahmedabad–Bengaluru–Lucknow
D. More than one of the above
E. None of the above

64. Which of the following ports was first made after Independence?
A. Mangalore
B. Kandla
C. Mumbai
D. More than one of the above
E. None of the above

65. The State of Jharkhand, Chhattisgarh and Madhya Pradesh are rich in minerals and _____ deposits.
A. coal
B. gold
C. silicon
D. More than one of the above
E. None of the above

53. B **54.** E **55.** A **56.** C **57.** B **58.** C **59.** A **60.** C **61.** C **62.** A **63.** A **64.** B **65.** A

66. Which of the following countries is the world's largest producer of rice?
A. India
B. China
C. South Korea
D. More than one of the above
E. None of the above

67. From which year was the National Forest Policy introduced in India?
A. 1952
B. 1963
C. 1978
D. More than one of the above
E. None of the above

68. What is the raw material from which aluminium is extracted?
A. Galena
B. Cuprite
C. Bauxite
D. More than one of the above
E. None of the above

69. Where is Gobi Desert located?
A. China
B. Africa
C. Southern Australia
D. More than one of the above
E. None of the above

70. Seine river flows through which city?
A. London
B. Paris
C. Rome
D. More than one of the above
E. None of the above

71. The major producer of the raw jute in the world is:
A. India
B. Bangladesh
C. Scotland
D. More than one of the above
E. None of the above

72. In which State of India, iron ore is ***not*** found?
A. Bihar
B. Madhya Pradesh
C. Odisha
D. More than one of the above
E. None of the above

73. Where is Southern Gangotri located?
A. Uttarakhand
B. Antarctica
C. Himalaya
D. More than one of the above
E. None of the above

74. Which is the longest river in South America?
A. Nile
B. Amazon
C. Mississippi
D. More than one of the above
E. None of the above

75. Which State in India is the largest producer of wheat?
A. Haryana
B. Punjab
C. Uttar Pradesh
D. More than one of the above
E. None of the above

76. Rio Earth Summit's (1992) 'Agenda 21' includes:
A. environmental protection
B. global sustainable development
C. global peace
D. More than one of the above
E. None of the above

77. The largest coal producing nation in the world is:
A. India
B. USA
C. China
D. More than one of the above
E. None of the above

78. Which place is known as the oldest oil storage in India?
A. Bombay High, Maharashtra
B. Ankleshwar, Gujarat
C. Navagaon, Gujarat
D. More than one of the above
E. None of the above

79. The largest producer of aluminium in the world is:
A. France
B. India
C. USA
D. More than one of the above
E. None of the above

80. Where is Great Victoria Desert situated?
A. Australia
B. India
C. Egypt
D. More than one of the above
E. None of the above

66. B **67.** A **68.** C **69.** A **70.** B **71.** A **72.** A **73.** B **74.** B **75.** C **76.** D **77.** C **78.** E **79.** E **80.** A

Economics

81. The important attribute for comparing development between countries is;
A. land
B. population
C. income
D. More than one of the above
E. None of the above

82. The average income is also known as:
A. per capita income
B. personal income
C. national income
D. More than one of the above
E. None of the above

83. 'Human Development Report' is published by which of the following organizations?
A. UNDP
B. UNESCO
C. WWF
D. More than one of the above
E. None of the above

84. The 'tertiary sector' of an economy is also called as:
A. agriculture sector
B. service sector
C. manufacturing sector
D. More than one of the above
E. None of the above

85. Under MGNREGA 2005, how many days of employment in a year are guaranteed by the government for rural unemployed?
A. 200
B. 50
C. 100
D. More than one of the above
E. None of the above

86. What percentage of their deposits is kept as cash by the banks in India?
A. 25%
B. 15%
C. 30%
D. More than one of the above
E. None of the above

87. Which among the following options defines the term 'globalization'?
A. Rapid economic integration among countries
B. Integration of cultures
C. Isolation among countries
D. More than one of the above
E. None of the above

88. In which year did the Indian Government enact the Consumer Protection Act (COPRA)?
A. 1991
B. 1992
C. 1986
D. More than one of the above
E. None of the above

89. National Consumer Day in India is observed on:
A. 24th December
B. 21st November
C. 23rd May
D. More than one of the above
E. None of the above

90. Which right does consumer have against unfair trade practices and exploitation?
A. Right to constitutional remedies
B. Right to information
C. Right against exploitation
D. More than one of the above
E. None of the above

91. Which Act was passed to empower its citizen to question the government about its functions?
A. The RTE Act
B. The IT Act
C. The RTI Act
D. More than one of the above
E. None of the above

92. Which MNC bought over small Indian company 'Parakh Foods'?
A. Lactalis
B. Cargill Foods
C. MARS
D. More than one of the above
E. None of the above

93. Which of the following about MGNREGA Act is *incorrect*?
A. Right to work in about 625 districts of India
B. 100 days of guaranteed employment in a year
C. It will not give an employment allowance if the government fails
D. More than one of the above
E. None of the above

81. C **82.** A **83.** A **84.** B **85.** C **86.** B **87.** A **88.** C **89.** A **90.** E **91.** C **92.** B **93.** C

94. Which of the following countries has better human development performance according to data of 2016?
A. Bangladesh
B. Sri Lanka
C. Pakistan
D. More than one of the above
E. None of the above

95. ____________ is the situation when both parties have to agree to sell and buy each other's commodities.
A. Barter system
B. Marketing
C. Double coincidence of wants
D. More than one of the above
E. None of the above

96. Which of the following does ***not*** come under the terms of credit?
A. Interest rate
B. Collateral
C. Deposit
D. More than one of the above
E. None of the above

97. Which of the following about RBI is ***incorrect***?
A. RBI can't supervise the informal sector
B. RBI issues currency notes on behalf of the government
C. RBI accepts deposits from customers
D. More than one of the above
E. None of the above

98. The Indian Government took steps to attract foreign companies to invest in India by providing world-class facilities. What are these industrial zones called?
A. SEZs (Special Economic Zones)
B. IZs (Industrial Zones)
C. PFZs (Provider Facility Zones)
D. More than one of the above
E. None of the above

99. GDP is the total value of _____ produced during a particular year.
A. all goods and services
B. all final goods and services
C. all intermediate goods and services
D. More than one of the above
E. None of the above

100. In India, the Black Revolution is related with:
A. fisheries production
B. coal production
C. crude oil production
D. More than one of the above
E. None of the above

101. Which one is ***not*** cash crop in India?
A. Jute
B. Peanut
C. Barley
D. More than one of the above
E. None of the above

102. What was the basis of the First Five-Year Plan in India?
A. Harrod-Domar model
B. Mahalanobis model
C. Dadabhai Naoroji model
D. More than one of the above
E. None of the above

103. The Committee of R.N. Malhotra is related with:
A. sick industry
B. tax reform
C. insurance sector
D. More than one of the above
E. None of the above

104. Which officer is responsible for controlling the government spending?
A. RBI
B. Planning Commission
C. Finance Ministry
D. More than one of the above
E. None of the above

105. The maximum foreign currencies are gained by India in export of:
A. iron
B. tea
C. textile
D. More than one of the above
E. None of the above

106. Which one is ***not*** included in the 'National Food Security Mission'?
A. Oilseeds
B. Wheat
C. Rice
D. More than one of the above
E. None of the above

94. B **95.** C **96.** C **97.** C **98.** A **99.** B **100.** C **101.** C **102.** A **103.** C **104.** C **105.** C **106.** E

107. When was 'NITI Aayog' started?
A. 1st January, 2014
B. 1st June, 2014
C. 1st January, 2015
D. More than one of the above
E. None of the above

108. What is the name of the first indigenous anti-radiation missile of India?
A. Tandav
B. Trinetra
C. Saksham
D. More than one of the above
E. None of the above

109. India's thirteenth main port is going to be established in:
A. Kerala
B. Gujarat
C. Maharashtra
D. More than one of the above
E. None of the above

110. In India, in which year was Rail Budget merged with General Budget?
A. 2015
B. 2016
C. 2017
D. More than one of the above
E. None of the above

111. The 'Pradhan Mantri Kisan Samman Nidhi Yojana' was started on:
A. 1st November, 2017
B. 1st January, 2018
C. 1st February, 2019
D. More than one of the above
E. None of the above

112. By which institution is the poverty line determined?
A. NSSO
B. NITI Aayog
C. RBI
D. More than one of the above
E. None of the above

113. The Pink Revolution is related with:
A. onion production
B. fertilizer production
C. egg production
D. More than one of the above
E. None of the above

114. 'Robinhood effect' is related with:
A. income and consumption
B. income generation
C. income redistribution
D. More than one of the above
E. None of the above

115. In which economic programme does dairy industry stand?
A. Tertiary fields
B. Primary fields
C. Intermediate fields
D. More than one of the above
E. None of the above

116. From which country were the Five-Year Plans taken in the Indian Constitution?
A. Russia
B. England
C. USA
D. More than one of the above
E. None of the above

117. Import-export tax on goods is known as:
A. customs duty
B. product duty
C. VAT
D. More than one of the above
E. None of the above

118. In India, mixed economy was adopted in which Five-Year Plan?
A. Fourth Five-Year Plan
B. Second Five-Year Plan
C. Third Five-Year Plan
D. More than one of the above
E. None of the above

119. 'Open Market Operation' is related with which policy?
A. Credit policy
B. Tariff policy
C. Commercial policy
D. More than one of the above
E. None of the above

120. In India, in which year, nationalization of banks took place?
A. 1950
B. 1960
C. 1969
D. More than one of the above
E. None of the above

107. C **108.** E **109.** C **110.** C **111.** C **112.** B **113.** A **114.** C **115.** B **116.** A **117.** A **118.** B **119.** E **120.** C

or

Political Science

81. The Preamble of the Constitution of India was borrowed from which country?
A. Japan
B. Germany
C. England
D. More than one of the above
E. None of the above

82. The States having largest number of Lok Sabha Constituencies, in ascending order, are:
A. Uttar Pradesh, Maharashtra, West Bengal, Bihar
B. Uttar Pradesh, Bihar, Maharashtra, West Bengal
C. Maharashtra, Uttar Pradesh, West Bengal, Bihar
D. More than one of the above
E. None of the above

83. Why is democracy a better form of Government?
A. It is more accountable.
B. It has improved quality of decision making.
C. It deals with differences and conflicts.
D. More than one of the above
E. None of the above

84. The President exercises his/her powers on the advice of:
A. Council of Ministers
B. The Supreme Court
C. Commander-in-Chief of the Indian Army
D. More than one of the above
E. None of the above

85. What does the anti-defection law suggest?
A. Regulation of internal affairs
B. Amended to prevent changing parties
C. Compulsory to fill their income tax return
D. More than one of the above
E. None of the above

86. Who said, "Democracy is the government of the people, for the people, by the people"?
A. Adam Smith
B. Abraham Lincoln
C. J.S. Mill
D. More than one of the above
E. None of the above

87. Right to Education (RTE), which came under effect on 1st April, 2010, comes under which of the following Fundamental Rights?
A. Right to Equality
B. Right to Freedom
C. Cultural and Educational Rights
D. More than one of the above
E. None of the above

88. The Fundamental Duties were included in the Constitution in 1976 by which of the following Amendment Acts?
A. 25th
B. 38th
C. 42nd
D. More than one of the above
E. None of the above

89. Who among the following was ***not*** a member of the Constituent Assembly?
A. Sarat Chandra Bose
B. Sarojini Naidu
C. Maulana Abul Kalam Azad
D. More than one of the above
E. None of the above

90. Which of the following are ***incorrect*** about the money bills?
1. It is related to financial matters.
2. It can be introduced in the Lok Sabha only.
3. It can be introduced in the Rajya Sabha only.
4. Certificate from the Speaker is required on its nature.

Select the correct answer using the codes given below.
A. 1, 2, 3, 4
B. 2, 3, 4
C. 1, 3, 4
D. More than one of the above
E. None of the above

91. The Supreme Court of India came into existence on:
A. 15th August, 1947
B. 26th January, 1961
C. 2nd October, 1952
D. More than one of the above
E. None of the above

81. E **82.** E **83.** D **84.** A **85.** B **86.** B **87.** B **88.** C **89.** E **90.** E **91.** E

92. Consider the following about the Lok Adalat:
1. It is an inexpensive judicial service.
2. It resolves disputes in single hearing.
3. It provides speedy justice.
4. A retired judge chairs the Lok Adalat.
5. It is an apex court.

Select the correct answer using the codes given below.
A. 2, 3, 4, 5
B. 3, 4, 5
C. 1, 2, 3, 4
D. More than one of the above
E. None of the above

93. By which country of the world, was Apartheid followed as an official policy between 1948–1989?
A. South Africa
B. China
C. USA
D. More than one of the above
E. None of the above

94. National Voters' Day is celebrated every year on:
A. 14th September
B. 25th January
C. 5th June
D. More than one of the above
E. None of the above

95. What is ***incorrect*** about United Nations Security Council?
A. It is a 15-member Council in which 5 are permanent and 10 are elected by the General Assembly for 2 years.
B. Each permanent member has veto power.
C. IMF and World Bank are its funding agencies.
D. More than one of the above
E. None of the above

96. Which of the following acts as a counterweight to the electoral malpractices?
A. Misuse of Government machinery by ruling party
B. Excessive use of money to intimidate voters
C. Popular support enjoyed by a party/coalition
D. More than one of the above
E. None of the above

97. Mandal Commission in its Report in 1980 recommended _____ reservation in government jobs to socially and educationally backward classes.
A. 27%
B. 22%
C. 15%
D. More than one of the above
E. None of the above

98. Which Fundamental Right is called 'the heart and soul' of our Constitution?
A. Right to Equality
B. Right to Freedom of Religion
C. Cultural and Educational Rights
D. More than one of the above
E. None of the above

99. Which Right is specific to minorities?
A. Right to Freedom of Religion
B. Right to Freedom
C. Right to Constitutional Remedies
D. More than one of the above
E. None of the above

100. Which is ***not*** correct about the Constituent Assembly?
A. It had more than 300 members.
B. Its first meeting was held in July 1946.
C. It adopted many details and procedures from the Act of 1935.
D. More than one of the above
E. None of the above

101. Which of the following is ***not*** an element of the Belgium model?
A. Brussels has one government in which both the French- and Dutch-speaking communities will have equal representation.
B. The State Government is not subordinate to the Central Government.
C. Apart from the two Governments, the third kind of government is made community government'.
D. More than one of the above
E. None of the above

102. In which year was an Act passed to recognize Sinhala as the only official language in Sri Lanka?
A. 1957
B. 1956
C. 1960
D. More than one of the above
E. None of the above

103. Which of the following is ***incorrect*** about power sharing?
A. Power is shared among different organs of the government
B. Power can be shared among the governments at different levels
C. Every society needs some form of power sharing even if it is small or does not have social divisions
D. More than one of the above
E. None of the above

92. C **93.** A **94.** B **95.** C **96.** D **97.** A **98.** E **99.** E **100.** B **101.** E **102.** B **103.** E

104. Which of the following is included in the Concurrent List?
A. Forest
B. Agriculture
C. Police
D. More than one of the above
E. None of the above

105. Which of the following countries has the least participation of women in public life?
A. Sweden
B. Norway
C. China
D. More than one of the above
E. None of the above

106. What does the Equal Remuneration Act, 1976 provide?
A. Equal representation in politics
B. Equal wages for all genders
C. Jobs recruitment for all
D. More than one of the above
E. None of the above

107. Mahatma Gandhi used to say that _____ can never be separated from politics.
A. society
B. religion
C. economy
D. More than one of the above
E. None of the above

108. Which of the following is true about democracy?
A. Democracy often frustrates the needs and ignores the demands of people
B. Democracy is corruptionless
C. Democracy is irregular
D. More than one of the above
E. None of the above

109. Which of the following roles is ***not*** played by political parties?
A. They make laws for the country
B. One party supports to another for the formation of government
C. They can have the same views and opinions on the all issues
D. More than one of the above
E. None of the above

110. To become a State party, a party has to secure at least ____ of the total votes in an election to the Legislative Assembly of a State.
A. 6%
B. 8%
C. 10%
D. More than one of the above
E. None of the above

111. Which of the following countries comes under the 'coming together' federation?
A. Belgium
B. Switzerland
C. Spain
D. More than one of the above
E. None of the above

112. What is called when power is taken away from Central and State Governments and given to local government?
A. Decentralization
B. Centralization
C. Departmentalization
D. More than one of the above
E. None of the above

113. When did the Black Power Movement emerge?
A. 1975
B. 1966
C. 1989
D. More than one of the above
E. None of the above

114. Which Article is related with the Indian Election Commission in the Indian Constitution?
A. Article 324
B. Article 148
C. Article 342
D. More than one of the above
E. None of the above

115. Article 300 of the Indian Constitution is related with:
A. Trials and proceedings
B. Government contracts
C. Attorney Generals
D. More than one of the above
E. None of the above

116. How many times the President of India can be eligible for election for presidentship?
A. One time
B. Two times
C. Three times
D. More than one of the above
E. None of the above

104. A **105.** C **106.** B **107.** B **108.** A **109.** D **110.** B **111.** B **112.** A **113.** B **114.** A **115.** A **116.** E

117. How much time was taken in framing the Constitution of India?

A. 5 years 10 months 12 days
B. 3 years 9 months 18 days
C. 2 years 11 months 18 days
D. More than one of the above
E. None of the above

118. Who among the following is the first woman Speaker in the Lok Sabha?

A. Pratibha Patil
B. Urmila Singh
C. Meira Kumar
D. More than one of the above
E. None of the above

119. When was the National Human Rights Commission established?

A. 1990
B. 1991
C. 1992
D. More than one of the above
E. None of the above

120. Article 360 of the Constitution of India empowers the President of India to proclaim:

A. Financial Emergency
B. President's rule
C. stopping Fundamental Rights
D. More than one of the above
E. None of the above

EXPLANATORY ANSWERS

General Studies

1. **(B):** Let 10 years ago the ages of Ramesh and Rajeev was x years and $3x$ years

Then, present age of Ramesh and Rajeev are $x + 10$ years and $3x + 10$ years

5 years hence,

$$(x + 10 + 5) : (3x + 10 + 5) = 2 : 3$$
$$\Rightarrow \quad (x + 15) : (3x + 15) = 2 : 3$$
$$\Rightarrow \quad (x + 15) \times 3 = (3x + 15) \times 2$$
$$\Rightarrow \quad 3x + 45 = 6x + 30$$
$$\Rightarrow \quad 6x - 3x = 45 - 30$$
$$\Rightarrow \quad 3x = 15 \Rightarrow x = 5$$

$\therefore$ The ratio of their present ages

$$= (x + 10) : (3x + 10)$$
$$= 15 : 25$$
$$= 3 : 5.$$

2. **(C):** Let the distance between house and the station be d km.

$$\text{Then,} \quad \frac{d}{5} - \frac{7}{60} = \frac{d}{6} + \frac{5}{60}$$
$$\Rightarrow \quad \frac{d}{5} - \frac{d}{6} = \frac{7}{60} + \frac{5}{60}$$
$$\Rightarrow \quad \frac{d}{30} = \frac{12}{60}$$
$$\Rightarrow \quad \frac{d}{30} = \frac{1}{5} \Rightarrow d = 6 \text{ km}$$

Hence, the distance between my house and the station is 6 km.

3. **(C):** The total income of

$$P + Q = 2 \times ₹\ 5050 = ₹\ 10100 \quad \text{...}(i)$$
$$Q + R = 2 \times ₹\ 6250 = ₹\ 12500 \quad \text{...}(ii)$$
$$P + R = 2 \times ₹\ 5200 = ₹\ 10400 \quad \text{...}(iii)$$

From adding (*i*), (*ii*) and (*iii*), we obtain

$$\therefore\ 2(P + Q + R) = ₹\ 10100 + ₹\ 12500 + ₹\ 10400$$
$$\Rightarrow \quad P + Q + R = \frac{33000}{2}$$
$$\Rightarrow \quad P + Q + R = ₹\ 16500 \quad \text{...}(iv)$$

Subtracting (*ii*) from (*iv*), we obtain

$$P = 16500 - 12500 = ₹\ 4000$$

Hence, the monthly income of P is ₹ 4000.

4. **(C):** Given,

$$P \times \frac{30}{100} + Q \times \frac{40}{100} = Q \times \frac{80}{100}$$
$$\Rightarrow \quad 3P + 4Q = 8Q$$
$$\Rightarrow \quad 3P = 8Q - 4Q$$
$$\Rightarrow \quad 3P = 4Q$$

117. C **118.** C **119.** E **120.** A

$\Rightarrow \quad \frac{P}{Q} = \frac{4}{3}$

Now, $\quad P \times \frac{x}{100} = Q$

$\Rightarrow \quad 4 \times \frac{x}{100} = 3$

$\Rightarrow \quad x = 75\%$

Hence, Q is 75% with respect to P.

5. **(C):** Let the share of A, B, C and D are ₹ $5x$, ₹ $2x$, ₹ $4x$ and ₹ $3x$

Then, $\quad 4x - 3x =$ ₹ 1000

$\Rightarrow \quad x =$ ₹ 1000

$\therefore \quad$ B's share $= 2x = 2 \times 1000 =$ ₹ 2000.

6. **(B):** Let the marked selling price of watch be ₹ x

Then, $\quad x \times \frac{100-5}{100} - x \times \frac{100-6}{100} =$ ₹ 15

$\Rightarrow \quad x \times \frac{95}{100} - x \times \frac{94}{100} =$ ₹ 15

$\Rightarrow \quad \frac{x}{100} =$ ₹ 15

$\Rightarrow \quad x =$ ₹ 1500

$\therefore$ The marked selling price of watch = ₹ 1500.

7. **(B):** Let three numbers are $3x$, $4x$ and $5x$

Then, $\quad 5x + 3x = 4x + 52$

$\Rightarrow \quad 8x = 4x + 52$

$\Rightarrow \quad 8x - 4x = 52$

$\Rightarrow \quad 4x = 52$

$\Rightarrow \quad x = 13$

Hence, the smallest number $= 3x = 3 \times 13 = 39$.

8. **(B):** Given, $\quad 2^{2n-1} = \frac{1}{8^{n-3}}$

$\Rightarrow \quad 2^{2n-1} . 8^{n-3} = 1$

$\Rightarrow \quad 2^{2n-1} . 2^{3(n-3)} = 1$

$\Rightarrow \quad 2^{2n-1} . 2^{3n-9} = 1$

$\Rightarrow \quad 2^{2n-1} + 3^{n-9} = 1$

$\Rightarrow \quad 2^{5n-10} = 1$

$\Rightarrow \quad 2^{5n-10} = 2^0$

$\Rightarrow \quad 5^{n-10} = 0$

$\Rightarrow \quad n = 2.$

9. **(A):** Among the options provided, the photo-diode is the most suitable for digital applications. Photo-diodes are semiconductor devices that convert light into electrical current. They are fast, sensitive, and capable of operating in a wide range of light wavelengths, making them ideal for various digital and optical applications, such as in sensors, communication devices, and photometers. This makes them more suitable for digital applications compared to photo-voltaic cells and photo-emissive cells, which are typically used for different purposes.

10. **(B):** The critical mass of a fissionable material is indeed the minimum mass necessary for a sustained nuclear chain reaction. It is a precise quantity at which a fissionable material, such as uranium or plutonium, can maintain a chain reaction under specific conditions without an additional neutron source. This critical mass depends on several factors, including the material's purity, its shape, and the conditions under which it's held.

11. **(B):** Ethylene is the gas typically used to expedite the ripening process of fruits. It is a naturally occurring plant hormone and is employed commercially to trigger the ripening of fruits after harvesting. Ethylene affects the ripening by influencing various biochemical pathways. Ethane and methylene are not used for this purpose, making ethylene the correct choice for the gas used to force the ripening of fruits.

12. **(E):** In the context of octane ratings, iso-octane is defined as having an octane rating of 100, but *n*-octane does not have a zero octane number; it has a lower octane number than iso-octane, but it is not zero. Octane number is a measure of a fuel's performance in internal combustion engines, specifically its resistance to knocking or pinging. There is no commonly used compound in this context that would have a zero octane number. Therefore, the correct option is E, None of the above.

13. **(A):** The edible part of lychees is the aril. The aril is the fleshy part surrounding the seed inside the lychee fruit. This part is sweet, juicy, and is commonly eaten fresh. The other parts of the lychee, such as the seed coat and the thalamus, are not eaten.

14. **(A):** The physical process involved in the release of molecular oxygen from leaves is diffusion. In the process of photosynthesis, oxygen is produced as a byproduct in the leaves' chloroplasts. This oxygen then diffuses out of the leaves into the atmosphere. Transpiration is the process of water vapor loss from plants, and osmosis is the movement of water across a semipermeable membrane, but neither of these processes involves the release of oxygen.

15. **(C):** The process of determining the relative locations of genes on a chromosome is known as gene mapping. Gene mapping is used to assign/identify the location of genes and the distances between genes on a chromosome. Genome walking and chromosome walking are techniques used in molecular genetics for isolating long sequences of DNA, but they are not specifically about determining the relative location of genes.

16. **(B):** In bryophytes, the spore mother cell is diploid. These cells undergo meiosis to produce haploid spores, which is a part of the reproductive cycle of bryophytes. Bryophytes, like all plants, have a life cycle that includes both diploid and haploid stages. The spore mother cell is part of the diploid generation, known as the sporophyte.

17. **(A):** The National Green Tribunal (NGT) was established in 2010 by the Government of India. It was created for effective and expeditious disposal of cases relating to environmental protection and conservation of forests and other natural resources. The NGT Act, 2010 was enacted for this purpose, and the Tribunal has been empowered to handle cases relating to environmental issues.

18. **(E):** The first under-water metro in India was started in Kolkata, not in any of the cities listed in the options. Kolkata's East-West Metro includes a section that runs under the Hooghly River, making it the first underwater metro project in India. Therefore, the correct answer is not among the given options.

19. **(B):** Under India's G20 Presidency, the Tourism Working Group Meeting was held in Srinagar, Jammu and Kashmir. This event was part of the series of meetings and events organized in different locations across India during its G20 Presidency.

20. **(B):** Nirjala was the one who got the Silver Medal in the National Under-17 Girls Wrestling Championship. This question is very specific, and the correct answer would be based on the latest available information or specific knowledge about this event. Assuming the given answer is correct, Nirjala is the athlete who won the silver medal in this category.

21. **(A):** Geetanjali Shree and Daisy Rockwell won the International Booker Prize in 2022 for the novel "Tomb of Sand." This novel, originally written in Hindi by Geetanjali Shree and titled "Ret Samadhi," was translated into English by Daisy Rockwell. It is noteworthy for being the first Hindi language work to win the prestigious International Booker Prize.

22. **(B):** The Chief Guest on India's 74th Republic Day was Abdel Fattah El-Sisi, the President of Egypt. Each year, India invites a prominent international leader to be the chief guest at the Republic Day celebrations in New Delhi. In 2023, President El-Sisi was accorded this honor, marking a significant event in the diplomatic relations between India and Egypt.

23. **(A):** The first floating solar power plant in Bihar has been built in Darbhanga district. Floating solar power plants are an innovative form of solar energy generation where solar panels are mounted on a structure that floats on a body of water, typically a reservoir or a lake. This setup is beneficial in regions where land availability is limited or land use is prioritized for other purposes.

24. **(A):** Maghai Paan from Bihar has received the Geographical Indication (GI) tag. A GI tag is a sign used on products that have a specific geographical origin and possess qualities or a reputation that are due to that origin. Maghai Paan is known for its unique taste and qualities and is associated with the Magadh region of Bihar. Basmati Rice and Chanderi Saree have also received GI tags, but they are associated with other regions of India, not Bihar.

25. **(B):** Matching geographical terms with their respective regions, we have:

- Char refers to the sandbanks in river deltas, matching with Delta.
- Kankar is a type of calcareous soil found in the Indo-Gangetic Plain, particularly associated with Bangar, the older alluvial deposits.
- Kayal refers to backwaters, which are typically found along the Coastal plain.
- Mand is related to floodplains in Punjab, hence it corresponds to Punjab plain.

Therefore, the correct match is (*a*)-2, (*b*)-3, (*c*)-4, (*d*)-1, which is option B.

26. **(E):** Among the given tributaries, Subansiri, Belsiri, and Manas, all join the Brahmaputra river from the north. Therefore, none of the listed tributaries are incorrect; they all join the Brahmaputra from the north.

27. **(A):** The Likhapani glacier is located in Arunachal Pradesh, India. This state in the northeastern part of India is known for its diverse topography, including a significant portion of the Himalayas and various glaciers.

28. **(B):** Magadha and Anga plains are part of the middle Ganga plain. The Ganga plain is divided into upper, middle, and lower plains based on their geographical location and characteristics. The Magadha and Anga regions, historically significant areas in India, fall into the middle Ganga plain category.

29. **(D):** The waterfalls and their respective rivers need to be correctly matched:

- Jog Falls is indeed on the Sharavati River.
- Kapildhara Falls is on the Narmada River, not the Kaveri, making option B incorrect.
- Dhuandhar Falls is on the Narmada River as well, not the Godavari, making option C incorrect.

Since both options B and C are incorrect, the answer is D (More than one of the above).

30. **(B):** Arranging the seaports from north to south:

- Visakhapatnam is the northernmost among the given options.
- Kakinada is south of Visakhapatnam.
- Machilipatnam is further south of Kakinada.
- Nagapattinam is the southernmost among these.

Therefore, the correct order is 4 (Visakhapatnam), 1 (Kakinada), 2 (Machilipatnam), 3 (Nagapattinam), which corresponds to option B.

31. **(C):** The Agreement of Kosi Irrigation and Hydroelectricity Plan in 1954 was a bilateral agreement between India and Nepal. This agreement was for the construction and maintenance of a barrage and related works on the Kosi River, which flows through both countries. Thus, the correct answer is C.

32. **(B):** According to R. L. Singh's classification scheme of climatic regions in India, Bihar falls under the 'Subhumid Transitional' climate zone. This classification is based on various climatic parameters, including temperature, rainfall, and humidity. Bihar's climate features a transition between the humid eastern parts of India and the drier western regions. Hence, the correct answer is B (Subhumid transitional).

33. **(B):** The resolution of 'Purna Swaraj' (complete independence) was adopted at the Lahore Session of the Indian National Congress in December 1929. The Congress declared 26th January 1930 as Independence Day. This session was a significant event in the Indian freedom struggle. The correct answer is B (Lahore Session, 1929).

34. **(A):** The initial objective of the 'Kuka Movement' in Punjab was to purify the Sikh religion. It was a socio-religious reform movement in the mid-19th century, led by Guru Ram Singh. The Kukas sought to remove corrupt practices and restore Sikhism to its original purity. Thus, the correct answer is A (To purify the Sikh religion).

35. **(A):** The Revolt of 1857 was described as the 'First Indian War of Independence' by Vinayak Damodar Savarkar. He wrote a book with this title, emphasizing the national and unified nature of the rebellion. Therefore, the correct answer is A (V. D. Savarkar).

36. **(A):** The first instance of organized non-cooperation in Indian peasantry is widely recognized as the Champaran Satyagraha in Bihar, in 1917, led by Mahatma Gandhi. This movement was against the oppressive plantation system in the Champaran district of Bihar. There was also significant peasant movement in Bengal during this period. Thus, the correct answer is A (Bihar and Bengal).

37. **(C):** Dr. Rajendra Prasad held the portfolio of Food and Agriculture during the Interim Government of 1946. He later became the first President of India after independence. The correct answer is C (Food and Agriculture).

38. **(B):** Rajkumar Shukla, a farmer from Champaran, was instrumental in urging Mahatma Gandhi to visit Champaran to witness the miseries of the ryots (tenants) and to address the issue of forced indigo cultivation. Shukla persistently followed Gandhi to various meetings to convince him to go to Champaran. The correct answer is B (Rajkumar Shukla).

39. **(A):** The 'Day of Deliverance' was observed by the Muslim League on 22nd December, 1939. This was in celebration of the resignation of all members of the Indian National Congress from provincial and central offices in protest against the Viceroy's decision to enter World War II without consulting them. The correct answer is A (22nd December, 1939).

40. **(C):** Mahatma Gandhi laid the foundation stone of the National College and Bihar Vidyapeeth. These institutions were established as part of the national education movement and played a significant role in the freedom struggle by providing alternative education to Indians. The correct answer is C (Mahatma Gandhi).

History

41. (C): Kalibangan, a major city of the Indus Valley Civilization (IVC), is known for its trade relations with West Asia. Archaeological findings indicate the presence of a sophisticated urban center with well-planned streets, brick houses, and a drainage system. Evidence of trade with West Asia includes the discovery of seals, beads, and other artifacts typical of the IVC in regions like Mesopotamia. These exchanges were mainly conducted through maritime and overland routes, indicating a significant level of socio-economic development.

42. (C): The famous "Dancing Girl" statue found in Mohenjo-daro, one of the largest cities of the Indus Valley Civilization, was made of bronze. This small yet exquisite figurine, measuring about 10.5 centimeters in height, demonstrates the advanced level of metalworking that existed in the IVC. The technique used to create the Dancing Girl was lost-wax casting, which involves creating a wax model of the object, covering it with clay to form a mold, and then pouring molten metal into the mold. This technique and the artistic skill evident in the statue highlight the high level of craftsmanship achieved by the people of the IVC.

43. (A): In the Indus Valley Civilization, there is substantial evidence of the worship of the humped bull, also known as the zebu bull. Numerous seals and terracotta figurines depicting the humped bull have been found at various IVC sites, indicating its religious or cultural significance. The bull was likely revered for its strength and its association with agriculture and fertility. Unlike the horse, which is rarely depicted in IVC artifacts, the humped bull appears frequently, underscoring its importance in the daily life and religious practices of the civilization.

44. (E): The Rigveda, one of the oldest known texts in any Indo-European language, is a collection of ancient Sanskrit hymns. It consists of 1,028 hymns (Suktas) divided into ten books known as Mandala. The hymns are dedicated to various deities and are considered the core spiritual literature of the Vedic civilization. They cover a wide range of topics, from cosmology to philosophy, and are a critical source for understanding the early Vedic society, its beliefs, culture, and way of life. The Rigveda's composition dates back to roughly between 1500 and 1200 BCE.

45. (E): "Kiratarjuniya" is a Sanskrit classical epic poem written by the poet Bharavi. This epic, known for its elegant style and the richness of its descriptions, narrates the story of a battle between Arjuna and Lord Shiva, who appeared in the guise of a hunter named Kirata. The work is famed for its deep philosophical elements and the exploration of themes such as bravery and the nature of existence. Bharavi's mastery in using complex meters and allegory sets "Kiratarjuniya" apart as one of the great classics of Sanskrit literature.

46. (A): In the Vedic period, the term 'Pur' primarily referred to forts or fortified settlements. This is evident in the frequent mention of 'Pur' in Vedic texts, where it is associated with fortified cities or strongholds of enemies. The construction and fortification of towns and cities during the Vedic era signify the importance of protecting communities from external threats. The concept of 'Pur' in these ancient texts also reflects the socio-political organization of the times, highlighting the prevalence of conflict and the need for defense mechanisms.

47. (A): In the Rigveda, 'Takshan' refers to a carpenter. The Rigveda, composed during a time when society was transitioning from nomadic to settled agricultural life, frequently mentions various professions and crafts essential for the community. The carpenter, or 'Takshan', played a vital role in this society, crafting tools, vehicles like chariots, and constructing structures. This specialization reflects the increasing complexity of the Vedic society, where various skills and crafts were developed to meet the needs of its members.

48. (A): During the Mauryan period, the 'Kakani' coins were made of copper. The Mauryan Empire, known for its significant contributions to the political, social, and economic fabric of ancient India, also made advancements in the area of currency. These copper coins signify the development of a structured economic system with standardized currency, facilitating trade and commerce. The use of copper, a widely available metal, also indicates the intention to make the currency accessible and practical for everyday transactions in a growing economy.

49. (E): The world's first republic was established in Vaishali, but it was not done by the Maurya, Nanda, or Gupta dynasties. Instead, this republic was established by the Vajji (or Vrijji) confederation, which was a group of eight clans (Atthakula), of which the Licchavis were the most powerful. Vaishali, the capital of the Licchavi, is considered one of the first examples of a republic in the ancient world. This early form of government, which existed around the 6th century BCE, was based on assemblies of the people, which is a hallmark of republican governance.

50. (E): Kautilya's Arthashastra, an ancient Indian treatise on statecraft, economic policy, and military strategy, is actually divided into 15 major chapters, known as books. These books cover a wide range of topics, including the duties of a king, administration, law, economics, and military strategy. This work, attributed to the ancient philosopher and strategist Chanakya (also known as Kautilya or Vishnugupta), is a comprehensive guide to running a kingdom and is known for its pragmatic approach to governance and warfare.

51. (E): When Sultan Iltutmish, the third ruler of the Delhi Sultanate, expanded his kingdom to include Bihar, he did not appoint Aivaz, Nasiruddin Mahmud, or Ali Mardan as his first governor of the region. The historical records regarding the exact identity of the first governor appointed by Iltutmish in Bihar are not precise. Iltutmish, who reigned from 1211 to 1236 CE, was known for consolidating and expanding the Delhi Sultanate, but specific details of his administrative appointments, especially in Bihar, are not well-documented.

52. (B): Birsa Munda, a significant tribal leader and freedom fighter in Indian history, was primarily active in the region of Ranchi, which is now in the state of Jharkhand, India. He is most famous for leading the Munda Rebellion against British colonial rule at the end of the 19th century. His struggle was against the oppressive policies and exploitation of the tribal communities by the British colonial administration. Birsa Munda's efforts have made him a legendary figure in Indian history, especially among the Adivasi (indigenous) communities.

53. (E): The Revolt of 1857 in Bihar was notably led by Kunwar Singh, a landlord from Jagdispur, and his brother Amar Singh. Kunwar Singh's leadership and contributions are particularly celebrated in the region. He managed to mobilize a large group of soldiers and led several successful attacks against the British forces. Despite his advanced age, he was a significant figure in the rebellion. His involvement showcased the widespread nature of the rebellion, extending beyond the northern and central parts of India.

54. (C): The first capital of Magadha was Girivraja, also known as Rajagriha (modern-day Rajgir). Magadha, an ancient kingdom in eastern India, was one of the sixteen Mahajanapadas (great kingdoms) in the 6th century BCE. Its initial capital, Girivraja, was surrounded by five hills, creating a natural fortification. It was only later that the capital shifted to Pataliputra (modern-day Patna). The importance of Girivraja/Rajagriha is also highlighted in Jain and Buddhist texts, as it was an important center for these religions.

55. (C): The administration of Pataliputra is described in 'Indica', the account written by Megasthenes, the Greek ambassador to the Mauryan court. 'Indica', though surviving only in fragments quoted by later writers, provides valuable information about the administration, social conditions, and geography of the Mauryan empire. It offers a unique perspective as it is an outsider's observation of Indian society and governance. Megasthenes' descriptions, particularly of Pataliputra, are known for their detail about the city's layout, administration, and daily life.

56. (B): 'Madad-i-Maash' in Mughal administration referred to the grant of revenue-free land to religious leaders, scholars, intellectuals, and others who rendered service to the state. This system allowed the holders of these lands to collect revenue from them but exempted them from paying taxes to the state. It was a way of patronizing and supporting the learned and religious classes in the Mughal Empire. These grants were often hereditary and provided financial security and social status to the recipients.

57. (B): The Poona Pact of 1932 was aimed at representing the Dalit (or "Depressed Classes") in the Indian political system. It was an agreement between Mahatma Gandhi and Dr. B.R. Ambedkar to end the fast unto death undertaken by Gandhi in protest against the separate electorates for Dalits proposed by the British under the Communal Award. The pact provided for a single Hindu electorate with reserved seats for Dalits in the provincial legislatures, rather than separate electorates, thus ensuring a degree of political representation for Dalits while maintaining Hindu unity.

58. (E): Jantar Mantar, a collection of architectural astronomical instruments, was constructed by Maharaja Jai Singh II of Jaipur from 1724 onwards. There are five Jantar Mantars across India, with the most famous one in Jaipur. These complexes feature instruments that were used to observe astronomical positions with the naked eye. Jai Singh II built these observatories to compile astronomical tables and to predict the times and movements of the sun, moon, and planets.

59. (A): "Vande Mataram" was written by Bankim Chandra Chatterjee in the 1870s, which he included in his 1882 novel "Anandamath." The song played a vital role in the Indian independence movement and was a source of inspiration to the people in their struggle for freedom. It was first sung in a political context by Rabindranath Tagore at the 1896 session of the Indian National Congress. In 1950, the song's first two verses were given the status of the national song of India.

60. **(C):** Christopher Columbus, the Italian explorer, was financed by Spain for his voyage that led to the discovery of the Americas in 1492. The Spanish monarchs, Queen Isabella I of Castile and King Ferdinand II of Aragon, provided Columbus with the necessary ships and crew. His journey marked the beginning of centuries of transatlantic colonization. Columbus initially set out to find a westward sea passage to the East Indies but instead landed in the New World, leading to European exploration and eventual colonization of the Americas.

61. **(A):** The Boston Tea Party is associated with the American War of Independence. This event occurred on December 16, 1773, when American colonists, frustrated and angry at Britain for imposing "taxation without representation," dumped 342 chests of British tea into the Boston Harbor. The Boston Tea Party was a significant act of defiance by the American colonists and is considered a pivotal event leading up to the American Revolution.

62. **(C):** July 4th, 1776 is celebrated as Independence Day in the United States because it marks the date when the Second Continental Congress adopted the Declaration of Independence. Drafted by Thomas Jefferson, this document declared the 13 American colonies free and independent states, no longer under British rule. This day is considered the birth of the United States of America as an independent nation.

63. **(A):** The ruler of France at the time of the French Revolution was Louis XVI. He reigned as King of France from 1774 until 1792, and his rule was marked by financial crises, social unrest, and the eventual rise of revolutionary sentiment among the French populace. Louis XVI's inability to adequately reform the French governmental and social systems contributed to the outbreak of the French Revolution in 1789. He was eventually executed by guillotine in 1793.

64. **(C):** The Spinning Jenny, a key invention during the Industrial Revolution, was invented by James Hargreaves in 1764. This device dramatically increased the productivity of the cotton spinning process, allowing a single worker to spin multiple spools of thread simultaneously. The Spinning Jenny was one of several innovations in textile manufacturing that fueled the Industrial Revolution, transforming the industry from home-based manual labor to efficient, mechanized production.

65. **(E):** The 'Young Italy Movement', founded in 1831, was initiated by Giuseppe Mazzini, not included in the options provided. This movement aimed at creating a united Italian republic. Mazzini was a passionate proponent of Italian unification through democratic and revolutionary means, and his movement played a crucial role in inspiring the unification process that eventually led to the establishment of modern Italy.

66. **(B):** The architect of the Unification of Germany was Otto von Bismarck. Known for his policy of 'blood and iron,' Bismarck played a central role in the unification of the German states into a powerful German Empire. His approach combined the use of military force (blood) and industrial and political power (iron). Bismarck's diplomacy, military strategy, and political maneuvers were instrumental in achieving this unification by 1871.

67. **(E):** The main reason for the US entry into World War II in December 1941 (not November) was the Japanese attack on Pearl Harbor. On December 7, 1941, Japan launched a surprise military strike against the United States naval base at Pearl Harbor in Hawaii, leading the U.S. to declare war on Japan and enter World War II. This event marked a pivotal turn in the war, as it brought the United States fully into the global conflict.

68. **(B):** When Marco Polo visited China, the ruler was Kublai Khan. Kublai Khan, the grandson of Genghis Khan, was the Emperor of the Yuan dynasty in China during Marco Polo's time. Polo's travels to China in the late 13th century, and his subsequent service in Kublai Khan's court, are well documented in his travelogue, "The Travels of Marco Polo," which provides valuable insights into the culture and society of that era in China.

69. **(A):** The first English settlement in the USA was Jamestown, founded in 1607. Located in present-day Virginia, Jamestown was established by the Virginia Company of London as a commercial venture. It was the first permanent English settlement in what would become the United States, marking the beginning of British colonial presence in North America. The settlement faced severe challenges, including conflicts with indigenous peoples, disease, and food shortages.

70. **(C):** The Oath of the Tennis Court is connected with the French Revolution. This significant event took place in June 1789, when members of the Third Estate, who were part of the Estates-General, were locked out of a meeting. They gathered in a nearby indoor tennis court and took an oath not to disperse until they had drafted a constitution for France. This act is considered a pivotal moment in the early stages of the French Revolution, signaling the assertion of popular sovereignty and the downfall of the absolute monarchy.

71. **(B):** The Treaty of Sèvres was signed with Turkey after World War I. Concluded in 1920, it was one of the series of treaties that the Allied Powers signed with the Central Powers following their defeat in the war. The Treaty of Sèvres specifically dealt with the partitioning of the Ottoman Empire, leading to significant territorial losses for Turkey and the creation of several new nations in the Middle East and Europe. However, the treaty was never ratified by Turkey and was replaced by the Treaty of Lausanne in 1923.

72. **(B):** The flying shuttle machine, invented in 1733, was the creation of John Kay. This invention was a significant development in the weaving industry, as it allowed a single weaver to weave much wider fabrics than was previously possible and also increased weaving speed. The flying shuttle was one of the key innovations that fueled the Industrial Revolution, contributing to the transformation of textile manufacturing and significantly impacting the economy and society in Britain and beyond.

73. **(B):** The Thirty Years' War, which raged across Central Europe between 1618 and 1648, was brought to an end by the Treaty of Westphalia. Signed in 1648, this treaty involved several agreements, including the Peace of Münster and the Treaty of Osnabrück. The Treaty of Westphalia is often cited as a key event in the development of the modern state system. It recognized the principle of territorial sovereignty, allowed for the coexistence of multiple religious faiths in a state, and ended the Catholic Habsburgs' supremacy in central Europe, establishing a new balance of power in the region.

74. **(B):** Italy was represented by Vittorio Emanuele Orlando at the Paris Peace Conference following World War I. The conference, held in 1919, was dominated by the leaders of the four major Allied powers: France, Britain, the United States, and Italy. Orlando played a significant role, although he left the conference prematurely due to disagreements over territorial claims. The Paris Peace Conference led to the signing of several treaties, the most famous being the Treaty of Versailles with Germany.

75. **(E):** The Komagata Maru, a Japanese steamship, was chartered by Gurdit Singh Sandhu, a Sikh businessman, to sail to Vancouver, Canada, in 1914. This was a challenge to the Canadian government's exclusionist immigration policies, which aimed to prevent Indians from immigrating to Canada. The ship carried Indian passengers, mostly Sikhs, from Punjab. On reaching Vancouver, the ship and its passengers were denied entry and eventually sent back to India, an incident that became a significant milestone in the struggle against discriminatory immigration laws.

76. **(C):** Bhagwan Singh was not associated with the foundation of the Shore Committee. The Shore Committee was established in Vancouver to support the passengers of the Komagata Maru during their standoff with the Canadian government in 1914. The committee, comprising members of the local Indian community, played a vital role in providing legal and moral support to the passengers. Bhagwan Singh was a prominent Ghadar Party leader, but he was not involved in the formation of the Shore Committee.

77. **(A):** Mahatma Gandhi referred to the Chauri-Chaura incident as a "Himalayan blunder." This incident occurred in February 1922 in the Chauri-Chaura town of Uttar Pradesh, India, where a violent mob set fire to a police station, killing 22 policemen. Gandhi, who was leading the Non-Cooperation Movement against British rule, believed in strict non-violence. Seeing the violence at Chauri-Chaura, he felt the people were not ready for non-violent resistance and called off the movement. He felt that this act of violence had deviated from his principles and thus termed it a "Himalayan blunder."

78. **(A):** Pritilata Waddedar was a woman revolutionary who died during a raid on the armory in Chittagong. In 1932, as part of the Chittagong armoury raid group led by Surya Sen, she participated in an attack on the Pahartali European Club, which had a signboard that read "Dogs and Indians not allowed." After the raid, to avoid capture by British forces, she consumed cyanide and committed suicide. Pritilata's heroism and sacrifice have been celebrated in Indian revolutionary history.

79. **(C):** Prafulla Chaki was not associated with the Kakori Train Case. The Kakori Train Robbery took place on August 9, 1925, and was a revolutionary act against British rule carried out by members of the Hindustan Republican Association (HRA), including notable revolutionaries like Ram Prasad Bismil, Ashfaqulla Khan, and others. Prafulla Chaki was involved with the Anushilan Samiti and was associated with the Muzaffarpur bombing along with Khudiram Bose.

80. **(B):** The first issue of Ghadar, a revolutionary publication of the Ghadar Party aimed at inciting a rebellion against British rule in India, was published in Urdu on November 1, 1913. The Ghadar Party was formed by Indian immigrants in the United States and Canada with the aim of liberating India from British rule. The newspaper played a crucial role in spreading the revolutionary message among Indians, especially among the diaspora, and was later published in other languages like Punjabi (in Gurmukhi script), Hindi, and Gujarati.

Geography

41. **(D):** The Asiatic elephant, Gangetic dolphin, and Blackbuck are all considered vulnerable species in India. These species face various threats such as habitat loss, poaching, and environmental changes, leading to their vulnerable status.

42. **(A):** Expansion of agriculture is a major factor for the depletion of forest resources in India. As the population grows and the demand for food increases, more forest land is converted into agricultural fields. This leads to habitat loss for many species and a decrease in forest cover, impacting biodiversity and ecological balance.

43. **(D):** Developing new methods of ecological farming through traditional methods is promoted by Beej Bachao Andolan and Navdanya. Farmers and citizen's groups like the Beej Bachao Andolan in Tehri and Navdanya have proved that significant levels of diversified crop production without the use of synthetic chemicals are possible and economically viable. This the answer is (D), More than one of the above.

44. **(A):** The Sardar Sarovar Dam is located on the Narmada River and covers the states of Gujarat, Rajasthan, Maharashtra, and Madhya Pradesh. It is one of the major irrigation and water supply projects in India and has been the subject of much controversy and environmental debate.

45. **(D):** River valley projects can indeed sometimes contribute to floods due to a combination of factors. Excessive sediments in the reservoir can reduce the storage capacity, heavy rain leading to the release of large volumes of water from the dam can exacerbate flooding, and extensive soil erosion can further contribute to flood conditions.

46. **(A):** Tamil Nadu was the first state in India to make rooftop rainwater harvesting compulsory through legal norms. This initiative aimed at addressing the acute water scarcity in many parts of the state by conserving rainwater for future use.

47. **(D):** As per the Agriculture Report of 2017, India was among the world's largest producers of several agricultural products. India is a significant producer of rice, cotton, and sugarcane, ranking high globally in the production of these commodities. Thus the answer is (D), More than one of the above.

48. **(A):** Institutional reforms for the benefit of farmers have included various measures, but land reforms have been a key element. Land reforms aimed to redistribute land to enable more equitable access and use, which was crucial for improving the economic conditions of farmers. Other initiatives like the creation of Grameen Banks and the Kisan Credit Card scheme are also important but are distinct from land reforms.

49. **(B):** Koderma in Jharkhand is well-known for its production of mica. This region has been historically significant in the mining of mica, which is used in various applications such as electrical insulators, electronics, and cosmetics. Mica mining in Koderma dates back to the British era, and this region was once considered the largest mica-producing area in the world.

50. **(B):** The textile industry in India is a prime example of a self-reliant and complete value chain. From the production of raw materials like cotton, jute, silk, and wool to the manufacturing of a wide range of products including yarn, fabric, and garments, the industry encompasses it all. It plays a crucial role in the Indian economy, contributing significantly to GDP, employment, and export earnings. India's textile industry has a rich history and has adapted to various technological and market changes, making it a globally competitive sector.

51. **(A):** Maize is a prominent Kharif crop in India, sown during the onset of the monsoon and harvested in the autumn. It is a versatile crop grown across different climatic zones and soil types. Maize is used for various purposes, including human consumption, livestock feed, and industrial uses like the production of starch and ethanol. Its adaptability to diverse agro-climatic conditions and uses in different industries makes it a vital crop in India's agricultural sector.

52. **(E):** Cotton, among the options, is the crop that takes almost a year to grow. It is a significant cash crop, and its cultivation process is extensive. The cotton sowing period begins in April-May, and the crop is harvested between December and March in India. Cotton requires a long frost-free period, plenty of sunshine, and moderate rainfall or irrigation for growth. It's a crucial crop for the textile industry, and India is one of the largest cotton producers in the world.

53. **(B):** The National Highways in India are primarily laid and maintained by the National Highways Authority of India (NHAI). Established in 1988, the NHAI is an autonomous agency of the Government

of India, responsible for the development, maintenance, and management of National Highways, which are the arterial roads of the country. This organization plays a pivotal role in the planning and implementation of highway projects, including the upgrading of existing highways.

54. **(E):** As of the Annual Report 2016-2017, India's ranking in International Tourism was not 2nd, 3rd, or 4th. According to the World Tourism Organization (UNWTO), India was placed much lower in international tourist arrivals globally. India's rich cultural heritage, diverse landscapes, and historical significance attract tourists, but it has not ranked within the top three countries for international tourism as per this report.

55. **(A):** The new alluvial soil is referred to as 'Khadar'. Alluvial soils, particularly prevalent in the river basins, are fertile and support a wide range of agricultural crops. Khadar soils are newer alluviums and are often found in the lower areas of the river valleys and flood plains. They are renewed almost every year with fresh sediment deposited by rivers, hence are more fertile compared to Bangar which is the older alluvial soil.

56. **(C):** Black soil, also known as Regur soil, is ideal for growing cotton. This soil is characterized by its high clay content, which gives it a unique moisture-retentive quality. This is especially beneficial for cotton cultivation, which requires a soil that can retain moisture for a long time. Black soil covers large areas of Deccan Plateau including Maharashtra, Madhya Pradesh, Gujarat, Andhra Pradesh, and parts of Tamil Nadu. It is known for its capacity to hold moisture and its richness in soil nutrients like calcium carbonate, magnesium, potash, and lime.

57. **(B):** Mawsynram, a village in the Meghalaya state of India, is recognized as the place receiving the highest annual rainfall in the world. This region is influenced heavily by the monsoon winds coming from the Bay of Bengal, contributing to its exceptionally high rainfall. Mawsynram's unique geographical location and the presence of the Khasi Hills contribute to its receiving an average annual rainfall of about 11,871 millimeters (467.4 inches), though this can vary year to year.

58. **(C):** The correct matches for the names used for slash and burn agriculture in different countries are as follows: in Mexico, it is known as 'Milpa', in Brazil, it is called 'Roca', in Vietnam, it's referred to as 'Ray', and in Indonesia, it's known as 'Ladang'. Slash and burn agriculture is a method where forests are cut and burned to create fields for agriculture. Each of these terms is specific to the cultural and geographical context of the respective countries.

59. **(A):** The Bhoodan-Gramdan Movement, also referred to as the Bloodless Revolution, was initiated by Vinoba Bhave. This movement started in the 1950s in post-independence India and was a voluntary land reform movement. Vinoba Bhave, an influential social reformer and a disciple of Mahatma Gandhi, encouraged landowners to voluntarily give a portion of their land to landless people. The movement had a significant impact on reducing land disputes and promoting communal harmony and social justice.

60. **(C):** The sparkle in some toothpastes comes from the mineral mica. Mica is a group of silicate minerals known for their shiny, flaky appearance and is used in various cosmetic and industrial applications. In toothpaste, mica acts as a mild abrasive to aid in cleaning teeth and provides a shimmering appearance. Mica's unique properties, such as its ability to be split into thin sheets, make it suitable for cosmetic uses including in toothpaste for aesthetic appeal.

61. **(C):** The Barauni Thermal Power Station is located in Bihar. It is one of the major power plants in the state, contributing significantly to the region's electricity needs. The power station was established in the early 1960s and has been a crucial source of thermal power, utilizing coal as its primary fuel source. Over the years, it has undergone expansions and renovations to meet increasing energy demands and to incorporate more efficient and environmentally friendly technologies.

62. **(A):** The National Thermal Power Corporation (NTPC) is a major power-providing corporation in India. It is not only one of the largest power utility companies in India but also a leader in the country's energy sector. NTPC has ISO certification for its environmental management system (ISO 14001), which underscores its commitment to environmental sustainability and adherence to international standards in managing its environmental impact. NTPC operates a variety of power generation facilities, including thermal, hydro, and renewable energy sources.

63. **(A):** The Golden Quadrilateral Super Highways connect four major cities in India - Delhi, Kolkata, Chennai, and Mumbai. This ambitious infrastructure project was initiated to reduce travel time and distance between these key metropolitan areas, significantly enhancing connectivity and economic interaction. The Golden Quadrilateral network is a part of the National Highways Development Project and is one of the largest highway projects in India. It plays a vital role in facilitating trade, travel, and economic growth.

64. **(B):** The first port constructed after India's independence was the Kandla Port. Located in the Kutch District of Gujarat, Kandla Port was developed in the 1950s to cater to the maritime trade demand on the western coast, especially after the partition of India, which led to the loss of the Karachi port to Pakistan. Kandla Port, now known as Deendayal Port, plays a critical role in India's maritime trade and has been instrumental in the economic development of the region.

65. **(A):** Jharkhand, Chhattisgarh, and Madhya Pradesh are Indian states notably rich in mineral resources, with coal being a significant deposit in these regions. Jharkhand, in particular, is known for its abundant coal reserves and hosts some of the largest coal mines in India. Chhattisgarh and Madhya Pradesh also have substantial coal deposits. The presence of these coal reserves has been pivotal for the development of numerous thermal power plants and other industries dependent on coal as a primary energy source or raw material.

66. **(B):** China is the world's largest producer of rice. This country has a long history of rice cultivation and has developed numerous varieties suited to its varied climatic regions. Rice is a staple food for the majority of the Chinese population, and the country has dedicated a significant portion of its arable land to rice cultivation. China's position as the top rice producer is followed by India, which is also a major rice producer on the global stage.

67. **(A):** The National Forest Policy in India was introduced in the year 1952. This policy was a significant step in the management and conservation of forests in the country. It aimed to maintain environmental stability, restore ecological balance, and preserve the country's natural heritage by ensuring a minimum forest cover. Over the years, this policy has undergone several amendments and revisions to address contemporary environmental challenges and to promote sustainable forest management practices.

68. **(C):** Aluminium is extracted from bauxite, a naturally occurring ore. Bauxite primarily consists of alumina (aluminum oxide), mixed with other compounds like silica, iron oxides, and titanium dioxide. The extraction of aluminum from bauxite involves the Bayer process, which separates alumina from the other components in the ore. The alumina is then subjected to an electrolytic process known as the Hall-Héroult process, resulting in pure aluminum. This metal is known for its lightweight, strength, and resistance to corrosion, making it extremely useful in various industries.

69. **(A):** The Gobi Desert is primarily located in northern China and southern Mongolia. It is one of the largest deserts in Asia and is characterized by its harsh climate, with extreme temperatures both in summer and winter. The Gobi Desert is known for its unique features, including the presence of rare animals like the Bactrian camel and the snow leopard, and its historical significance as part of the Mongol Empire and the Silk Road.

70. **(B):** The Seine River flows through Paris, the capital city of France. This river is one of the major waterways in France and is integral to the city's history, culture, and tourism. The Seine runs through the heart of Paris, with many famous landmarks, including the Eiffel Tower, Notre-Dame Cathedral, and the Louvre Museum, located along its banks. The riverbanks of the Seine in Paris are also a UNESCO World Heritage site.

71. **(A):** India is a major producer of raw jute in the world. The Ganges delta region, which spans parts of both India and Bangladesh, is particularly known for its jute production. In India, the states of West Bengal, Bihar, Assam, and Odisha are the primary producers. Jute, often referred to as the "golden fiber," is used for making various products, including sacks, carpets, and curtains, and plays a significant role in the rural economy of these regions.

72. **(A):** Iron ore is not found in the state of Bihar in India. Bihar, primarily known for its agriculture and service industries, does not have significant iron ore deposits. On the other hand, states like Odisha, Jharkhand, Chhattisgarh, and Karnataka are rich in iron ore deposits and play a crucial role in India's iron and steel industry. These states contribute significantly to India's status as one of the world's largest producers of iron ore.

73. **(B):** Southern Gangotri is located in Antarctica. It is the name given to an Indian research station in this polar region. Established in 1983-84, Southern Gangotri was India's first scientific research base station in Antarctica, serving as a major hub for scientific research and exploration. It was later replaced by the Maitri and Bharati stations due to environmental considerations, but it played a crucial role in establishing India's presence and research capabilities in Antarctica.

74. **(B):** The Amazon River is the longest river in South America. It's also often considered the largest river in the world by volume, with a vast drainage basin that covers a significant portion of the South American continent. The river is known for its extensive biodiversity and is vital to the Amazon rainforest ecosystem, which is the largest rainforest in the world and plays a critical role in global ecological balance.

75. **(C):** Uttar Pradesh is the largest producer of wheat in India. The state has a favorable climate and fertile alluvial soil suitable for wheat cultivation. Wheat is one of the main crops in Uttar Pradesh, contributing significantly to India's overall agricultural output. The state's large area under cultivation and the intensive agriculture practices contribute to its high wheat production.

76. **(D):** The Rio Earth Summit's 'Agenda 21' includes multiple aspects, including environmental protection and global sustainable development. Agenda 21, adopted at the United Nations Conference on Environment and Development (UNCED) in 1992 in Rio de Janeiro, is a comprehensive plan of action to be taken globally, nationally, and locally by organizations of the United Nations, governments, and major groups in every area in which humans impact the environment. Its goal is to promote sustainable development in the 21st century.

77. **(C):** China is the largest coal-producing nation in the world. It leads global coal production by a significant margin, largely due to its substantial demand for energy to power its expansive industrial sector. Coal is a major source of energy in China and has been instrumental in the country's rapid economic development over recent decades. However, this reliance on coal has also contributed to environmental and air quality issues in the country.

78. **(E):** The oldest oil storage in India is in Digboi, Assam. Digboi is known for its oil fields and is often referred to as the "Oil City of Assam". The first oil well was drilled in Digboi in the late 19th century, marking the beginning of the oil industry in India. This region played a pivotal role in the early stages of the Indian oil industry's development.

79. **(E):** As of my last update in April 2023, the largest producer of aluminum in the world is not a single nation but is rather a competitive field with several major producers. China, however, is one of the leading producers of aluminum globally. The country's massive manufacturing industry and the high demand for aluminum in various industrial and construction applications contribute to its large production volume.

80. **(A):** The Great Victoria Desert is situated in Australia. It is the largest desert in Australia and one of the largest in the world. Located in the southern part of the country, it spans parts of Western Australia and South Australia. This desert is known for its arid conditions, red sand dunes, and unique flora and fauna adapted to the harsh environment.

Economics

81. **(C):** When comparing development between countries, income is an important attribute. It provides a quantitative measure to assess and compare the economic performance of different countries. Income, often evaluated in terms of Gross Domestic Product (GDP) per capita, helps in understanding the average wealth and economic well-being of the citizens in a country. Higher incomes typically indicate better access to healthcare, education, and other essential services, contributing to overall development.

82. **(A):** The average income is commonly referred to as "per capita income." This term represents the average income earned per person in a given area (country, city, etc.) in a specified year. It is calculated by dividing the area's total income by its total population. Per capita income is a useful statistic for comparing the economic performance of different countries or regions and is often used as an indicator of the standard of living.

83. **(A):** The 'Human Development Report' is published by the United Nations Development Programme (UNDP). This annual report presents an overview of the state of world development and includes the Human Development Index (HDI), which ranks countries based on their human development levels, measured by life expectancy, education, and per capita income indicators. The report is widely used to assess and compare the development progress of countries around the world.

84. **(B):** The 'tertiary sector' of an economy is also called the service sector. This sector includes a wide range of services such as retail, entertainment, financial services, health care, education, and government services. Unlike the primary sector, which relates to the extraction of raw materials, and the secondary sector, which involves manufacturing, the tertiary sector is concerned with providing services to businesses and consumers. It often plays a crucial role in advanced economies, constituting a significant portion of GDP and employment.

85. **(C):** Under the Mahatma Gandhi National Rural Employment Guarantee Act (MGNREGA) of 2005, the government guarantees 100 days of wage employment in a financial year to every household in rural areas. This scheme aims to enhance livelihood security in rural areas by providing at least one hundred days of guaranteed wage employment in a financial year to every household whose adult members volunteer to do unskilled manual work.

86. **(B):** In India, banks are required to keep a certain percentage of their deposits as cash. This is known as the Cash Reserve Ratio (CRR). As of my last update in April 2023, the Reserve Bank of India (RBI) had set this ratio at 15%. The CRR is a monetary policy tool used by the RBI to control liquidity in the economy. By adjusting the CRR, the RBI can influence the amount of money available for banks to lend.

87. **(A):** Globalization refers to the rapid economic integration among countries. It is characterized by an increase in cross-border trade, investments, and cultural exchange. Globalization involves the free movement of goods, services, capital, technology, and people across international borders, leading to closer economic ties between nations and often resulting in global interdependence. While the term can encompass broader cultural, political, and environmental aspects, its core aspect is economic integration.

88. **(C):** The Indian Government enacted the Consumer Protection Act (COPRA) in 1986. This legislation provides for the protection of consumer interests and establishes authorities for the settlement of consumer disputes. COPRA is an important milestone in the consumer movement in India as it provides a framework for addressing consumer grievances and promoting fair trade practices. The act has been amended over time to keep pace with changing market dynamics and consumer needs.

89. **(A):** National Consumer Day in India is observed on 24th December. This day is significant as it marks the enactment of the Consumer Protection Act, 1986 (COPRA). The day is observed to raise awareness about the rights and responsibilities of consumers and to highlight the importance of the consumer movement against unfair trade practices.

90. **(E):** Consumers of today enjoy the following rights as provided by the Indian laws:

- **Right to safety:** The consumers have the right to protect against marketing of goods and services, which are hazardous to life and property.
- **Right to be informed:** It is the right of the consumers to know the quality, quantity, potency, purity, standard and price of the goods. Right to Information Act supports this right.
- **Right to seek redressal:** Consumers have the right to seek redressal against unfair trade practices and exploitation. If any damage is done to a consumer, he has the right to get compensation depending upon the degree of damage. There is a need to provide an easy and effective public system by which this can be done.
- **Right to safety:** The consumers have the right to be protected against marketing of goods and services, which are hazardous to life and property.
- **Right to be heard:** The consumer's interests should receive due considerations at appropriate forums relating to consumer welfare.

91. **(C):** The Right to Information Act (RTI Act) was passed to empower Indian citizens to question the government about its functions. The RTI Act, 2005, mandates timely response to citizen requests for government information and is intended to promote transparency and accountability in the working of every public authority.

92. **(B):** Cargill Foods bought over the small Indian company 'Parakh Foods'. Cargill, a major international producer and marketer of food, agricultural, financial, and industrial products and services, acquired Parakh Foods to expand its presence and capabilities in India. This acquisition was part of Cargill's strategy to grow its business in key emerging markets like India.

93. **(C):** The statement about MGNREGA (Mahatma Gandhi National Rural Employment Guarantee Act) that is incorrect is "It will not give an employment allowance if the government fails." In fact, the MGNREGA does provide for an unemployment allowance if the government fails to provide employment within 15 days of the application or from the date on which employment is sought in the case of an advance application.

94. **(B):** As of the data from 2016, Sri Lanka had better human development performance compared to Bangladesh and Pakistan. Sri Lanka has traditionally scored higher on the Human Development Index (HDI), reflecting better outcomes in health, education, and standard of living.

95. **(C):** The situation when both parties have to agree to sell and buy each other's commodities is referred to as the "Double Coincidence of Wants." This term is often associated with the barter system, where two parties each desire the good or service which the other party can provide.

96. **(C):** "Deposit" does not come under the terms of credit. Terms of credit usually include interest rate, collateral (security against which the loan is taken), documentation requirement, and the mode of repayment. A deposit is typically associated with savings or investment accounts, not directly with credit terms.

97. **(C):** The statement about the Reserve Bank of India (RBI) that is incorrect is "RBI accepts deposits from customers." The RBI, being the central bank of the country, does not deal with individual customers for banking services like accepting deposits, which is typically the function of commercial banks.

98. **(A):** The industrial zones established by the Indian Government to attract foreign companies to invest in India by providing world-class facilities are called SEZs (Special Economic Zones). SEZs offer businesses and investors various benefits such as tax exemptions, simpler compliance rules, and infrastructure support.

99. **(B):** GDP (Gross Domestic Product) is the total value of all final goods and services produced within a country during a particular year. It includes only final goods and services to avoid double counting, excluding intermediate goods and services used in the production process.

100. **(C):** In India, the Black Revolution is related to crude oil production. Different color-coded revolutions in India symbolize various sectors of economic and agricultural development, with each color representing a specific area of growth or production. The Black Revolution specifically refers to the growth and development in the petroleum and crude oil sector.

101. **(C):** Cash crops are those specifically grown for sale to return a profit, and in India, common examples include jute, cotton, and sugarcane. Barley, mainly grown for consumption as food and feed, does not typically fit into the category of cash crops like jute or peanuts.

102. **(A):** The basis of the First Five-Year Plan in India was the Harrod-Domar model. This model focused on the investment requirement for economic growth, emphasizing increasing production in agriculture and building infrastructure. The Mahalanobis model was used later in the Second Five-Year Plan, focusing on heavy industries.

103. **(C):** The Committee headed by R. N. Malhotra is related to the insurance sector. The Malhotra Committee was formed in 1993 to propose recommendations for reforms in the Indian insurance industry, leading to significant changes including the opening up of the sector to private players.

104. **(C):** The Finance Ministry is primarily responsible for controlling government spending. The Ministry of Finance plays a central role in the fiscal and economic policy-making of the country, overseeing revenue collection (taxation), expenditure, and financial management, among other functions. While the RBI and Planning Commission (now replaced by the NITI Aayog) play roles in broader economic policy and planning, direct control over government spending lies with the Finance Ministry.

105. **(C):** Among the given options, India earns maximum foreign exchange by the export of textiles. As per the data of Ministry of Commerce and Industry, India earns maximum foreign exchange by the export of Textile in the year 2021-22.

106. **(E):** The 'National Food Security Mission' includes all the options listed - oilseeds, wheat, and rice. The mission aims to increase production of these essential food commodities to ensure food security in India, so none of the options are excluded from it. Thus, the answer is (E).

107. **(C):** NITI Aayog (National Institution for Transforming India) was started on 1st January 2015. It replaced the Planning Commission and was established to provide critical directional and strategic input to the development process in India, focusing on sustainable and equitable growth.

108. **(E):** The first indigenous anti-radiation missile of India is named 'Rudram'. It was developed by the Defence Research and Development Organisation (DRDO) for the Indian Air Force. The missile is designed to detect, track, and neutralize the adversary's radar, communication assets, and other radio frequency sources, making it an effective anti-radiation weapon for offensive air operations.

109. **(C):** India's thirteenth main port, Vadhavan Port, is proposed to be developed in Maharashtra. The Union Cabinet in India approved the setting up of this major port at Vadhavan in Maharashtra in February 2020.

110. **(C):** The Rail Budget was merged with the General Budget in the year 2017. This marked an end to the

92-year-old practice of presenting a separate railway budget. The decision was aimed at having a holistic approach towards transportation and streamlining the budget process.

111. **(C):** The Pradhan Mantri Kisan Samman Nidhi Yojana was launched on 1st February 2019. This scheme aims to provide income support to all landholder farmer families across the country with cultivable land, subject to certain exclusions.

112. **(B):** The Poverty Line calculation is now carried out by the NITI Aayog (the successor to the erstwhile Planning Commission of India) through the calculation of the poverty line based on the data collected by the National Sample Survey Office (NSSO). The National Sample Survey Office (NSSO) was formerly called the National Sample Survey Organisation.

113. **(A):** Durgesh Patel coined the phrase "Pink Revolution" and is known as the father of Pink Revolution. Pink Revolution is related to upgrading the meat and poultry processing business, where modernization is accomplished by specialization, mechanization, and standardization of procedures. It focuses on processing chicken and meat, onion manufacturing and pharmaceuticals. India has a large population of poultry and cattle, and this industry has a lot of room for growth.

114. **(C):** The "Robinhood effect" refers to a form of income redistribution. This concept is named after the legendary figure Robin Hood, who is often depicted as stealing from the rich to give to the poor. In economic terms, the Robinhood effect occurs when policies or actions are taken to redistribute wealth from the wealthier segments of society to the less affluent. This can include progressive taxation, welfare programs, or other social measures aimed at reducing economic inequality.

115. **(B):** The dairy industry is classified under the primary sector of the economy. The primary sector encompasses all industries involved in the extraction and production of raw materials. In the case of dairy, it involves the rearing of cattle and the production of milk, which are basic, direct agricultural activities. The dairy industry is foundational to many other industries, supplying raw materials (like milk) that can then be processed or used in secondary and tertiary sectors.

116. **(A):** The concept of Five-Year Plans in the Indian Constitution was inspired by the former Soviet Union (Russia). The Soviet model was adopted by India post-independence as a means to accelerate growth and development in a planned and structured manner. These plans were aimed at setting economic goals for specific periods (five years) and involved extensive state intervention in resource allocation. The Soviet influence is evident in the emphasis on heavy industries, central planning, and state-led development strategies in the early plans.

117. **(A):** Customs duty is a tax imposed on imports and exports of goods. It is levied by the government on the goods that are transported across international borders. This duty can be used as a tool for regulating international trade, protecting domestic industries, generating revenue for the government, and sometimes for penalizing specific countries for various reasons. The rates of customs duty vary depending on the nature of the goods and the policies of the specific country.

118. **(B):** India adopted the mixed economy model in its Second Five-Year Plan, which spanned from 1956 to 1961. The mixed economy model is characterized by coexistence and collaboration of the public and private sectors. This plan emphasized the development of heavy industries and was greatly influenced by the Soviet model of economic development. The government of India aimed to balance the growth of state-owned enterprises with private sector participation, ensuring that critical sectors and industries were under state control while allowing for private enterprise in others.

119. **(E):** Open Market Operations (OMOs) are part of monetary policy, which is implemented by central banks to control the money supply and influence interest rates in the economy. In OMOs, the central bank buys or sells government securities in the open market. When the central bank buys securities, it injects money into the banking system, thereby increasing the money supply, and vice versa. OMOs are one of the key tools used by central banks, like the Reserve Bank of India, to manage liquidity and stabilize the economy.

120. **(C):** The nationalization of major banks in India took place in the year 1969. This move was part of the government's strategy to ensure that credit (financial resources) was available to all segments of the economy, particularly the agricultural sector, small industries, and the underprivileged sections of society. This step was also taken to prevent concentration of wealth and economic power in the hands of a few private bank owners. The nationalization of banks played a significant role in shaping India's economic landscape, allowing for greater government control over the banking sector.

Political Science

81. **(E):** The Preamble of the Constitution of India, which outlines its philosophical foundations and underlying values, was not directly borrowed from any specific country. It is largely inspired by the ideals and principles of the Indian freedom struggle and reflects the visions of the founding fathers of the Indian republic. While the Preamble shares similarities with the preambles of other constitutions, like the United States, in terms of its emphasis on justice, liberty, equality, and fraternity, it is an original composition that articulates the aspirations and values specific to India.

82. **(E):** As per the latest data, the states with the largest number of Lok Sabha constituencies, in descending order, are Uttar Pradesh (80 seats), Maharashtra (48 seats), West Bengal (42 seats), and Bihar (40 seats). Therefore, in ascending order, the correct sequence is Bihar, West Bengal, Maharashtra, and Uttar Pradesh. None of the given options (A, B, C) accurately represent this order.

83. **(D):** Democracy is considered a better form of government for several reasons, making option (D) the correct choice. It is more accountable as the decision-makers are elected by the people and are answerable to them. The quality of decision-making is often improved in a democratic setup as it involves consultation and discussion, which helps in balancing different viewpoints and interests. Additionally, democracy is better equipped to handle differences and conflicts through peaceful and constitutional means, as it allows for representation and negotiation.

84. **(A):** The President of India exercises his/her powers on the advice of the Council of Ministers. This principle is a cornerstone of the parliamentary system of government, where the President is the constitutional head and exercises powers on the recommendation of the Council of Ministers, headed by the Prime Minister. This system ensures that the real executive power is vested in the elected representatives and the President acts on their advice, making the executive accountable to the legislature.

85. **(B):** The anti-defection law, formally known as the Tenth Schedule of the Indian Constitution, was added by the 52nd Amendment in 1985. It suggests measures to prevent political defections motivated by the lure of office or other similar considerations. The law disqualifies members of Parliament or state legislatures who defect from one party to another after their election. It applies when a member of a political party voluntarily gives up the membership of his party, or when he votes (or abstains from voting) contrary to the party's directive in the legislature.

86. **(B):** The phrase "Democracy is the government of the people, by the people, for the people" was famously stated by Abraham Lincoln. He used these words during his Gettysburg Address in 1863. This definition of democracy encapsulates the core principle that democratic governance is rooted in the will and consent of the people, with the government being both accountable and representative of its citizens.

87. **(B):** The Right to Education (RTE), which became effective on 1st April 2010, falls under the Right to Freedom, specifically under Article 21A of the Indian Constitution. This Right was added through the 86th Constitutional Amendment Act, 2002. It mandates that the state shall provide free and compulsory education to all children of the age of six to fourteen years in such a manner as the state may, by law, determine.

88. **(C):** The Fundamental Duties were included in the Indian Constitution in 1976 by the 42nd Amendment Act. These duties, enumerated in Article 51A of the Constitution, are a set of ten directives for the citizens. They emphasize the obligation of every citizen to promote harmony, protect public property, uphold and protect the sovereignty, unity, and integrity of India, and value and preserve the rich heritage of the country's composite culture, among other duties.

89. **(E):** The Constituent Assembly, formed in 1946, was responsible for drafting the Constitution of India. Key members included figures like Dr. B.R. Ambedkar, Jawaharlal Nehru, Sardar Vallabhbhai Patel, and Maulana Abul Kalam Azad.

90. **(E):** Statements 1, 2, and 4 are correct regarding money bills in India. Money bills are indeed related to financial matters such as taxes, the appropriation of funds, etc. (Statement 1). They can only be introduced in the Lok Sabha (Statement 2), and they require a certificate from the Speaker of the Lok Sabha confirming their nature as money bills (Statement 4). Statement 3 is incorrect as money bills cannot be introduced in the Rajya Sabha.

91. **(E):** The Supreme Court of India was established on January 26, 1950, not on any of the dates provided in the options. The establishment of the Supreme Court coincided with India becoming a republic. The Supreme Court replaced the Federal Court of India that was established under the Government of India Act, 1935.

92. **(C):** Lok Adalats are indeed an inexpensive judicial service, aimed at providing speedy justice and resolving disputes in a single hearing (Statements 1, 2, 3). These are organized under the authority of the Legal Services Authorities Act, 1987. A retired judge, along with other members, usually chairs the Lok Adalat (Statement 4). However, Statement 5 is incorrect as Lok Adalats are not apex courts; they are a form of alternative dispute resolution mechanism.

93. **(A):** Apartheid was a policy and system of segregation and discrimination on grounds of race, implemented by the government of South Africa from 1948 until the early 1990s. It created a deeply divided society where white South Africans, who were a minority, had complete authority over the country's institutions and maintained supremacy over other racial groups, notably Black South Africans. The system included laws that enforced racial discrimination, restricting the rights of non-white citizens in aspects of life including education, employment, and political participation. International pressure and internal resistance led to the dismantling of apartheid laws and policies, culminating in the first democratic elections in 1994, where Nelson Mandela was elected as the first Black president of South Africa.

94. **(B):** National Voters' Day is celebrated in India on the 25th of January each year. This day was established in 2011 by the Election Commission of India to encourage more young voters to participate in the political process. It is significant because it marks the foundation day of the Election Commission of India, which was established on 25th January 1950. The primary objective is to increase enrollment of voters, especially the eligibility of newly turned 18-year-olds. National Voters' Day involves spreading awareness about the importance of voting and educating people about the electoral process and their rights and responsibilities as voters.

95. **(C):** The United Nations Security Council (UNSC) is one of the six principal organs of the United Nations, charged with ensuring international peace and security. It's incorrect to say that the International Monetary Fund (IMF) and the World Bank are its funding agencies. The UNSC consists of 15 members, where five are permanent (China, France, Russia, the United Kingdom, and the United States) and possess veto power, while the other ten are elected for two-year terms by the General Assembly. The IMF and World Bank are separate entities within the UN system, focusing on financial and developmental assistance respectively, and do not directly fund the activities of the UNSC.

97. **(A):** The Mandal Commission, officially known as the Second Backward Classes Commission, was established in India in 1979 by the Morarji Desai government with the mandate to identify the socially or educationally backward classes in India. In its report submitted in 1980, the Commission recommended a 27% reservation in government jobs for the Other Backward Classes (OBCs). This recommendation was aimed at addressing the historical injustices and lack of representation faced by these communities. The implementation of this recommendation led to significant changes in the Indian reservation system, particularly in government employment and educational institutions, extending the benefits of affirmative action to a larger segment of the Indian population.

98. **(E):** None of the options listed explicitly refers to the Fundamental Right considered as 'the heart and soul' of the Indian Constitution. This phrase is famously associated with Article 32 of the Indian Constitution, which falls under the category of Right to Constitutional Remedies. Dr. B. R. Ambedkar, the principal drafter of the Indian Constitution, described Article 32 as the heart and soul of the Constitution. Article 32 provides the right to seek redressal in the Supreme Court for any violation of fundamental rights, ensuring the protection and enforcement of these rights.

99. **(E):** None of the options listed are specific only to minorities. In the context of the Indian Constitution, the rights specific to minorities are mainly found under Articles 29 and 30, which deal with the Cultural and Educational Rights. These rights allow minorities to preserve their language, script, or culture, and establish and administer educational institutions of their choice. While the Right to Freedom of Religion (Article 25 to 28) applies to all citizens, including minorities, it is not specific to them alone.

100. **(B):** The Constituent Assembly of India was formed to draft the Indian Constitution. The first meeting of the Constituent Assembly was not held in July 1946, but rather on December 9, 1946. The Assembly did have more than 300 members, and it indeed adopted many details and procedures from the Government of India Act of 1935, which was the governing document of India during the British colonial period. The Act of 1935 was the longest Act of the British Parliament and provided a blueprint for the administrative and constitutional setup of independent India. The Constituent Assembly, through its various committees and debates, adapted and modified these provisions to fit the needs of a sovereign, democratic India.

101. **(E):** None of the options listed are incorrect about the Belgium model of governance. The Belgium model is a complex system designed to accommodate the diverse linguistic and cultural groups within the country. It includes the unique feature of Brussels having a separate government with equal representation for both French- and Dutch-speaking communities. The state governments in Belgium are not subordinate to the central government, reflecting a federal structure where both levels have their spheres of authority. Additionally, the 'community government' is a distinctive aspect of the Belgian system, where these governments have power over cultural, educational, and language-related issues and are not tied to any specific territory but to the linguistic community they represent.

102. **(B):** In 1956, Sri Lanka (then Ceylon) passed the 'Sinhala Only Act,' officially recognizing Sinhala as the sole official language of the country. This move was a significant political development, which had profound implications for the country's ethnic relations. The decision to prioritize Sinhala over Tamil, which was also widely spoken, especially by the Tamil minority in the northern and eastern parts of the country, contributed to growing ethnic tensions and was a factor leading to the subsequent civil conflict in Sri Lanka.

103. **(E):** None of the options listed are incorrect about power sharing. Power sharing is a vital concept in modern democracies, ensuring stability and peace in a diverse society. It involves distributing power among different organs of the government (such as the legislature, executive, and judiciary), which is known as horizontal distribution of power. Power can also be shared among different levels of government (such as central, state, and local), known as vertical distribution of power. Moreover, every society needs some form of power sharing, regardless of its size or the presence of social divisions, as it helps in reducing conflicts and stabilizing political order.

104. **(A):** 'Forest' is included in the Concurrent List of the Indian Constitution. The Concurrent List is a unique feature of India's federal system, containing subjects on which both the central and state governments can legislate. While agriculture and police are typically state subjects, forests are listed under the Concurrent List, allowing both the central and state governments to make laws regarding forest conservation, forest produce, and the like. This arrangement enables a coordinated approach to managing forest resources, which are crucial for environmental sustainability and biodiversity conservation.

105. **(C):** Among the options given, China is likely to have the least participation of women in public life. Sweden and Norway are known for their progressive gender policies and high levels of women's participation in public life, including politics and other sectors. Both countries have consistently ranked high in gender equality indices and have a significant representation of women in their parliaments and public offices.

In contrast, China, despite making progress in various areas, still lags behind in terms of women's political representation and participation in public life. The political structure and cultural factors in China have contributed to lower levels of female participation in politics compared to the Scandinavian countries.

106. **(B):** The Equal Remuneration Act of 1976 in India provides for equal wages for all genders. It was enacted to address gender pay disparity and mandates that men and women should receive equal remuneration for the same work or work of a similar nature. This Act is a crucial step towards achieving gender equality in the workplace by ensuring that women are not discriminated against in terms of pay. It does not deal with equal representation in politics or job recruitment for all, but specifically targets the issue of equal pay.

107. **(B):** Mahatma Gandhi, the leader of the Indian independence movement, famously said that religion can never be separated from politics. Gandhi believed in the ethical and moral dimensions of politics and saw religion not in a narrow sectarian sense but as a moral compass guiding individual and social life. He viewed religion as an integral part of human existence that naturally intersects with political actions and decisions. His approach was to incorporate ethical and moral values, derived from religious teachings, into political activities and public life.

108. **(A):** The statement that democracy often frustrates the needs and ignores the demands of people can be true in certain contexts. While democracy is the most favored form of government globally due to its principles of representation and accountability, it's not without its flaws. One critique of democracy is that it can sometimes be slow in responding to people's needs, especially in larger democracies where the decision-making process involves multiple layers of governance. Moreover, in some democracies, certain groups may feel that their needs and demands are not adequately addressed, leading to a sense of frustration. However, this does not negate the overall benefits and principles of democracy, such as participation, equality, and freedom.

109. **(D):** The roles not played by political parties include 'One party supports another for the formation of government' and 'They can have the same views and opinions on all issues.' Political parties primarily contest elections, form and run governments, make laws, and articulate interests and policies. While it is common for parties to support each other in forming a government (coalition governments), this is not a universal or defining role of political parties. Additionally, political parties generally have differing views and opinions on various issues; it's rare and not typical for them to have the same views on all issues.

110. **(B):** To become a recognized State party in India, a political party must secure at least 6% of the total votes polled in an election to the Legislative Assembly of a State. This criteria is set by the Election Commission of India and is part of the conditions that a party needs to fulfill to gain certain benefits, like a unique election symbol. In addition to the vote share, the party must also win a certain number of seats in the Legislative Assembly, which varies from state to state.

111. **(B):** Switzerland is an example of a 'coming together' federation. In a coming together federation, previously independent states come together on their own to form a larger unit, while retaining their individual identities and autonomy. Switzerland is a classic example where cantons (member states) with different languages and cultures joined together to form the federation. Belgium and Spain, on the other hand, are examples of 'holding-together' federations, where the central government decides to devolve power to regional governments to accommodate diversity.

112. **(A):** Decentralization refers to the process where power is taken away from central and state governments and given to local government bodies. It's a way to bring governance closer to the people, making it more accessible and responsive to local needs. Decentralization involves transferring authority, responsibility, and financial resources for public functions from the central government to local governments. This approach is often seen as a means to enhance democratic governance, improve service delivery, and foster greater community participation in decision-making processes. Centralization, on the other hand, is the concentration of power in central authorities, while departmentalization refers to dividing an organization into departments for efficient management and operations.

113. **(B):** The Black Power Movement emerged in the United States in 1966. This movement grew out of the Civil Rights Movement and was a social, political, and cultural movement emphasizing racial pride, economic empowerment, and the creation of black political and cultural institutions. It advocated for African Americans to create their own identity and institutions, rather than seeking integration into white American culture. The movement gained national attention with the rise of the Black Panther Party and significant figures like Malcolm X, Stokely Carmichael, and others who advocated for black empowerment and self-sufficiency.

114. **(A):** Article 324 of the Indian Constitution relates to the Indian Election Commission. This article deals with the composition of the Election Commission, its powers, and functions. It establishes the Election Commission as an autonomous constitutional authority responsible for administering election processes in India. This includes the conduct of elections to the Parliament, State Legislatures, the office of President of India, and the office of Vice-President of India. The Commission is tasked with ensuring free and fair elections throughout the country.

115. **(B):** Article 300 of the Indian Constitution is related to government contracts. This article deals with the legal provisions regarding the suing and being sued of the Government of India and the State Governments in legal proceedings. It specifies the manner in which the government can enter into contracts and the process to be followed for disputes arising from such contracts. The article is crucial for providing a legal framework for the government's commercial activities and interactions with private entities.

116. **(E):** The President of India can be re-elected for any number of terms. There is no constitutional limit on the number of times an individual can be elected as the President of India. This means that a person can serve as President for more than two terms if elected multiple times. The tenure of the President is for a period of five years, but they can resign before their term expires or can also be re-elected for successive terms.

117. **(C):** The Constitution of India was framed over a period of 2 years, 11 months, and 18 days. The Constituent Assembly, which drafted the Constitution, held its first session on December 9, 1946, and the Constitution was adopted on November 26, 1949. It then came into effect on January 26, 1950. This extensive period was spent in rigorous debates and discussions to draft a Constitution that would cater to the diverse needs of the Indian population and lay down the foundation for the world's largest democracy.

118. **(C):** Meira Kumar is the first woman to have served as the Speaker of the Lok Sabha, the lower house of India's Parliament. She was elected to this position in 2009. Before becoming the Speaker, Meira Kumar had an illustrious career in the Indian Foreign Service and in politics, serving in various capacities including as a Cabinet Minister. Her election as the Speaker was a significant milestone in Indian politics in terms of gender representation in high political offices.

119. **(E):** The National Human Rights Commission (NHRC) of India was established on October 12, 1993. It is an autonomous public body constituted for the protection and promotion of human rights, defined by the Act as "rights relating to life, liberty, equality, and dignity of the individual guaranteed by the Constitution or embodied in international covenants." The NHRC investigates grievances regarding the violation of human rights, either suo moto or after receiving a petition.

120. **(A):** Article 360 of the Constitution of India empowers the President to proclaim a Financial Emergency. This provision allows the President to declare such an emergency if they are satisfied that the financial stability or credit of India or any part thereof is threatened. Unlike the National Emergency (Article 352) and President's Rule in states (Article 356), a Financial Emergency has never been declared in the history of independent India. The declaration of Financial Emergency has various implications, including the Union Government gaining the authority to direct any state on financial matters.

English Language

1

Comprehension Passages

ENGLISH LANGUAGE COMPREHENSION

The objective of language comprehension test is to ascertain the ability of the candidates to understand the passage properly.

Therefore candidates are required to take notice of the following points:

1. Read the full passage very attentively and intelligently.
2. Try to comprehend the gist of it.
3. Make a mental note of all the important details and points given in the passage.
4. Read the passage for the second time in case you have not been able to understand it satisfactorily.
5. Divide the time proportionately for all the passages.
6. Answer the questions on the basis of facts, as given in the paragraph.
7. Don't waste much time in answering the questions of any one passage.
8. Check all the answers once again, very carefully, to see whether any question is left unanswered by mistake.

MODEL QUESTIONS (FOR PRACTICE)

Directions: *Each of the following passages is followed by five questions. Read the passage carefully and then answer the questions that follow each. For each question, four probable answers A, B, C and D are given. Only one out of these is correct. Choose the correct answer.*

PASSAGE-1

The use of words like 'welcome', 'thank you', 'please', etc., at the right moment reflects a polite nature. The civic sense also lies within the scope of good manners. We should not shout or talk loudly in public places like hospitals and libraries and create disturbance. We should not cheat people or make fun of them. Cleanliness is also necessary. We must not throw the waste on roads and make use of dustbins. We should not harm the public property as it belongs to all of us. While in a queue, discipline should be maintained. We must give fair chance to others.

1. Expressions like 'welcome' 'thank you' and 'please' reflect
A. happiness B. discipline
C. civic sense D. polite nature

2. While in a library, we should
A. respect others B. avoid arguments
C. talk in low tone D. be courteous

3. A public property belongs to
A. nobody B. all of us
C. government D. one who maintains it

4. Discipline is
A. the rule of proper conduct or action
B. the rule of road sense
C. making use of dustbins
D. forming a queue

5. The most appropriate title for this passage would be
A. Polite Nature B. Courtesy
C. Good Manners D. Civic Sense

PASSAGE-2

There is an old proverb 'Early to bed and early to rise makes a man healthy and wise.' I am in the habit of getting up early in the morning and have formed the habit of taking long morning walks in the past two years. It is a light exercise and best for physical fitness. The morning air which is fresh and pure is beneficial for the lungs. The early rays of the rising sun are good for healthy skin. 'Health is wealth' and doctors also recommend morning walk to their patients for gaining sound health and freshness of energy.

1. What is good for lungs?
A. Sunrays B. Fresh air
C. Sound sleep D. Light exercise

2. What is a light exercise?
A. Early to bed B. Early to rise
C. Morning walk D. Gaining sound health

3. What is good for skin?
A. Fresh air B. Morning air
C. Morning walk D. Rising sun's rays

4. What is best for physical fitness?
A. Light exercise B. Long morning walk
C. Early to rise D. Fresh and pure air

5. Long morning walk
A. bring sound sleep
B. ensures physical fitness
C. ensures healthy skin
D. keeps healthy, wealthy and wise

PASSAGE-3

Mahatma Gandhi lived a splendid long life and has set great moral standards before us. He showed to the world the true way to peace. He wished to see India prosper but he became a martyr for the noble cause of Hindu-Muslim unity at the time of partition when a religious fanatic, Nathuram Godse, shot him dead on January 30, 1948. His last words were 'Hey Ram'. He lived and died for his country and countryman.

1. Mahatma Gandhi showed the world the true way to
A. prosperity B. love
C. truth D. peace

2. Mahatma Gandhi became a martyr for the noble cause of
A. truth B. non-violence
C. freedom of India D. Hindu-Muslim unity

3. Mahatma Gandhi was shot dead
A. before India achieved independence
B. by a mad man
C. by an intolerant religious person
D. by a non-religious person

4. Mahatma Gandhi set great moral standards. It means
A. he was a great religious teacher
B. he was a great moralist
C. he made India morally stronger
D. moral was everything to him

5. Gandhiji lived and died for his country and countryman. It means
A. he was born in India and died in India
B. he was a patriot
C. he was a great moralist
D. he sacrifued his life for India and her people

PASSAGE-4

On one hot day a crow felt very thirsty. He flew from one place to another in search of water. After long hours of labour he found a pitcher. Eagerly, he perched on the mouth of the pitcher. He found that the water was at the bottom of the vessel. He tried his best to dip his beak but did not succeed. He did not know what to do. Suddenly some pebbles lying nearby gave him an idea. One by one he dropped the pebbles with his beak into the pitcher. The level of water slowly came up to the mouth of the pitcher. The crow then drank the water and quenched his thirst.

1. The crow found a pitcher
A. as it flew
B. after many hours of labour
C. full of water
D. which was empty

2. What is the moral of the passage?
A. No pains, no gains
B. God helps those who help themselves
C. Necessity is the mother of invention
D. Try and try again, you will succeed at last

3. The crow flew from place to place
A. in search of pitcher B. in search of pebbles
C. in search of water D. in search of a vessel

4. The pitcher, the crow found
A. was full of water
B. was dry
C. had little water in the bottom
D. had water up to its mouth

5. As the crow dropped pebbles into the pitcher, what happend?
A. The pitcher broke down
B. The water leaked one of the pitcher
C. The level of water into the pitcher rose up slowly
D. Water level immediately rose to the mouth of the pitcher

PASSAGE-5

Once upon a time a crane and a fox lived in a forest. They were good friend. One day the fox invited the crane to a feast. He made a tasty food and served it before the crane on a plate. The crane could not eat anything because of the long beak. But the fox licked all his food. The crane felt insulted. He decided to teach the fox a lesson. Next day he invited the fox. He prepared the same tasty food and placed it in front of the fox inside a narrow glass. The crane ate easily while the fox looked on. Now, it was the fox's turn to remain hungry.

1. What is the moral of the passage?
A. Beware of the wicked
B. One good turn deserves another
C. Be contented with what you have
D. Tit for tat

2. The crane could not eat tasty food because the
A. food was served in a shallow plate
B. food was very hot
C. food was served in a long jar
D. crane was not hungry

3. The fox had to remain hungry because
A. the food served was not enough in quantity
B. the food was served inside a narrow glass
C. the food served was not tasty
D. the food was all liquid

4. Why did the crane feel insulted?
A. Because he was invited to feast but he could not eat anything
B. Because the food was served in a shallow plate and he could not eat
C. Because the food was too hot
D. Because the fox gulped all the food quickly

5. The crane successfully taught a lesson to the fox when he invited the fox to a feast and served the food
A. in a narrow glass B. in a large plate
C. in a broken plate D. in a long jar

PASSAGE-6

The family set down at the table and began to talk about the summer holidays. They had to decide a place to visit during the vacation. Should they go to their village or to a hill station? The parents preferred the village while the children wished to go the hill station. After few moments of discussion the elders decided to visit both the places. First they shall go to the village for a week and then stay at the hill station for the remaining days. For the first time the family shall be together during the holidays. The children were happy with the holiday plan.

1. The purpose for which the family set down at the table was
   A. to decide a place to visit during the vacation
   B. to educate the children how to carry articles during a visit to a hill station
   C. to decide the date when they should start their journey
   D. to tell the children that they will visit a hill station during this vacation

2. The final plan was to visit
   A. their village
   B. a hill station
   C. their village as well as a hill station
   D. their home town

3. The final decision was made by
   A. the boys B. the girls
   C. the women D. the elders

4. They decided first to go to their village and stay there for
   A. a day B. a week
   C. ten days D. a fortnight

5. Why were children happy?
   A. Because a hill station was included in their holiday plan
   B. Because a visit to their village was excluded from their holiday pl..
   C. Because their choice prevailed
   D. Because they were going all alone to the hill station

PASSAGE-7

Once Govind intended to go on pilgrimage with his family. He asked Mirind to accompany. But for his trade's reason, he did not go with him. So Govind thought it safe to leave the box of his jewellery with him, as it was dangerous to leave it in a lone house or take it on the journey. So he went to him with the box. He took him to a lonely place under a tree and handed it over to him. He told Mirind, "Keep it safe with you. I shall return from the journey after six month then I shall take it back from you." Mirind said, "Don't worry, I shall keep it as safe as own."

1. Govind intended to go
   A. for a business trip
   B. to a hill station
   C. on a long journey to a sacred place
   D. to his home town for a long period

2. Why did Govind leave his box of jewellery with Mirind?
   A. Because it was not safe to take the box with him on a long journey
   B. Because Mirind was his fast friend
   C. Because the box was very heavy
   D. Because his house was unsafe

3. Why did Govind take Mirind to a lonely place?
   A. To tell him that the box contained valuable jewellery
   B. So that no third person could see box
   C. To show him what was within the box
   D. To tell him that the box will remain with him

4. Where did Govind hand over the box of jewellery to Mirind?
   A. At Mirind's house
   B. At his own house
   C. In a lonely place
   D. In a lonely place under a tree

5. It was not safe to leave the box in a lone house. Here the word 'lone house' means
   A. a house in a deserted place
   B. a house where none lives
   C. a house without door and lock
   D. a house near the forest

PASSAGE-8

Zahir-ud-din Babar was the first Mughal emperor of India. A descendent of Timur on father's side and Changez Khan on his mother's side, Babar was a brave warrior. After defeating Ibrahim Lodhi in the First Battle of Panipat in 1526 he entered Delhi and soon gained control over Agra. After many more battles with Rajputs he extended his empire over Punjab, Uttar Pradesh and north Bihar. He died at a young age of 48 years in 1530 at his capital Agra without getting much time to consolidate his victories.

1. Zahir-ud-din Babar was the first
   A. Muslim ruler of India B. Mughal ruler of India
   C. Afghan ruler of India D. Turk ruler of India

2. Babar was born in the years
   A. 1480 B. 1482
   C. 1492 D. 1962

3. Babar first occupied
   A. Punjab B. Agra
   C. Delhi D. Panipat

4. Babar was a brave warrior. Here brave warrior means
   A. courageous soldier B. a kind hearted soldier
   C. a clever fighter D. a victorious general

5. Babar extended his empire over Punjab and Uttar Pradesh after many more battles with the
   A. Afghans B. Rajputs
   C. Mughals D. Lodhies

PASSAGE-9

Our National Flag is tricolour. It has three equal horizontal strips. The strip at the top is saffron, in the middle is white and at the bottom is green. The ratio of width to length of the flag is 2 : 3. In the centre of the white strip is a wheel in navy blue. The wheel represents the *chakra.* Its design is similar to the wheel which appears on the abacus of the Sarnath Lion Capital of Ashoka. Its diameter approximates to the width of the white strip. The wheel has 24 spokes. It was adopted by Constituent Assembly on July 22, 1947. We love our national flag. We respect it. We are ready to sacrifice our life to protect its honour. It represents the nation. So it is a symbol of national honour.

1. In our national flag the wheel is located in the centre of

A. saffron strip B. white strip
C. green strip D. blue strip

2. In our national flag which of the strips is at the bottom in our national flag

A. blue C. saffron
B. white D. green

3. Why do we love our national flag?

A. Because it is tricolour
B. Because it has three strips
C. Because it has a wheel at the centre
D. Because it is a symbol of national honour

4. Our national flag was approved by

A. President
B. Lok Sabha
C. Parliament
D. Constituent Assembly

5. The diameter approximates to the width of the white strip. Here the word 'approximates' means

A. is more or less equal
B. is exactly equal
C. is not equal
D. is related

PASSAGE-10

Distance in large cities are long. All the people do not have their own means of transport. They have to depend upon the state or private buses. The number of bus users is very large. Every bus stop is, therefore, crowded. The number of buses is not adequate. Thus people suffer the torture of long wait at the bus stop. Some bus stops are quite orderly. People form queues and get into the buses turn by turn. However, often this order is forgotten and confusion spreads when the bus comes and the law of jungle prevails.

1. Why are the bus stops crowded?

A. Because they are small is size
B. Because the number of passengers is very large
C. Because they are situated at some busy centre
D. Because people do not form queues

2. Long wait at the bus stop is the result of

A. over-crowding in the buses
B. late running of buses
C. shortage of buses
D. slow speed of buses

3. Some bus stops are quite orderly where

A. there is no crowd
B. the number of buses is adequate
C. people do not have to wait for long
D. people form queues and enter the buses one by one

4. Most of the people who travel by buses are

A. non-working
B. do not have their own vehicles
C. have to go a long distance
D. live in large cities

5. What happens when people do not have their own transport?

A. They have to wait for a bus at a bus stop
B. They have to depend upon the state or private buses
C. They have to travel long distances
D. They form queues and get into buses one by one

ANSWERS

Passage	1	2	3	4	5
Passage 1.	D	C	B	A	C
Passage 2.	B	C	D	B	B
Passage 3.	D	D	C	B	D
Passage 4.	B	C	C	C	C
Passage 5.	D	A	B	B	A
Passage 6.	A	C	D	B	A
Passage 7.	C	A	B	D	B
Passage 8.	B	B	C	A	B
Passage 9.	B	D	D	D	A
Passage 10.	B	C	D	B	B

●●●

English Grammar

PARTS OF SPEECH

Part of speech	Definition or Function	Examples
Noun	Name of a person, place, animal, quality or thing	Ram, boy, dog pen, sun, Delhi, truth, honesty
Pronoun	Used in place of a noun	I, you, he she, they
Articles & Determiners	Points out indefinite and definite nouns	a, an, the, few, some
Adjective	Describes a noun or pronoun	big, honest, wooden valuable, quiet, deep, soft, narrow
Adverb	Describes a verb, an adjective or another adverb	silently, widely, softly, quietly, very, carefully
Verb	Tells about action or state of something or someone	is, am, was, have, do, like, walk, work, make, throw, tell
Conjuction	Joins words, clauses or sentences	and, but, when, yet, while, else
Preposition	Links a noun or pronoun to another word	at, to, after, on for, under, over, with
Interjection	Expresses sudden feelings or emotions	Ah!, Alas!, oh!, ouch!, hi!, well!, Hurrah!

NOUNS

A word which denotes a person, a thing, an animal or a place is said to be a noun.

There are two noun numbers in English — the *Singular* and the *Plural*.

Singular Numbers : A noun that denotes one person or one thing, is said to be in the Singular number. For example — book, pencil, bird, dog, hen etc. are in singular number.

Plural Number : A noun that denotes more than one person or one thing is said to be in plural number. For example — boys, pens, lions, girls, men etc. are in plural number.

REMEMBER

Singular	*Plural*	*Singular*	*Plural*
Cat	Cats	Book	Books
Pen	Pens	Room	Rooms
Tree	Trees	Bus	Buses
Bush	Bushes	Box	Boxes
Glass	Glasses	Dish	Dishes
Judge	Judges	Tax	Taxes
Watch	Watches	Calf	Calves
Thief	Thieves	Knife	Knives
Scarf	Scarves	Wife	Wives
Leaf	Leaves	Wolf	Wolves
Half	Halves	Monarch	Monarchs
Roof	Roofs	Hoof	Hoofs
Gulf	Gulfs	Staff	Staffs
Radio	Radios	Bamboo	Bamboos
Folio	Folios	Hero	Heroes
Volcano	Volcanoes	Mango	Mangoes
Potato	Potatoes	Photo	Photos
Piano	Pianos	Baby	Babies
Fly	Flies	Country	Countries
Lady	Ladies	Boy	Boys
Monkey	Monkeys	Ox	Oxen
Child	Children	Man	Men
Woman	Women	Tooth	Teeth
Axis	Axes	Basis	Bases
Foot	Feet	Goose	Geese
Englishman	Englishmen	Radius	Radii
Vertex	Vertices	Stimulus	Stimuli

1. Note the plurals of the following nouns:

Singular	*Plural*	*Singular*	*Plural*
copy	copies	cry	cries
baby	babies	duty	duties
body	bodies	country	countries
family	families	diary	diaries
fly	flies	fairy	fairies
city	cities	spy	spies
army	armies	storey	storeys
bay	bays	monkey	monkeys

2. The following nouns do not undergo any change in plural form, in general.

Singular	*Plural*	*Singular*	*Plural*
deer	deer	sheep	sheep
thousand	thousand	pair	pair
hundred	hundred	score	score
dozen	dozen	gross	gross

Note: We can write—

(*a*) thousands of men; (*b*) two pairs of shoes; (*c*) dozens of mangoes; (*d*) scores of people etc. But—

(*a*) two thousand rupees; (*b*) three hundred men; (*c*) five dozen eggs, etc.

3. The following nouns are usually used in plural forms. They take a plural verb after them—

eatables	fetters	surroundings
riches	alms	spectacles
trousers	pants	scissors
premises	thanks	annals
congratulations	goods	shorts
tongs	pains	arms
breeches	(for troubles)	

4. The following are the nouns which are plural in appearance but are usually used in singular number. They are followed by a singular verb—

news	politics	physics
mathematics	economics	ethics
politics	classics	gallows
statistics	athletics	innings
mechanics	summons	mumps

5. Collective nouns often used as plurals—

public	police	cattle
audience	clergy	folk
people	poultry	nation
elite	gentry	glitterati

6. The nouns that are usually used in singular forms—

advice	hair	rice
fuel	alphabet	machinery
offspring	issue	furniture
mischief	stationery	luggage
bedding	information	abuse

7. Material nouns are always used in singular number—

gold	copper	milk
water	silk	wool

Note: They may be used in plural with a different meaning. copper coins (coppers), chains or fetters (irons), cans made of tin (tins).

GENDERS

The difference in sex is denoted by Gender in grammar. The various genders are as follows :

1. **Masculine Gender :** A noun that denotes a male is said to be of the masculine gender, as man, uncle, ox, boy etc.
2. **Feminine Gender :** A noun that denotes a female is said to be of feminine gender, as woman, aunt, princess, cow etc.
3. **Common Gender :** Nouns which denote both males and females are said to be of the common gender, as friend, cousin, person, parent, baby etc.
4. **Neuter Gender :** A noun that denotes the name of object without life is said to be of neuter gender, as file, table, pencil.

REMEMBER

Masculine	*Feminine*
Boy	Girl
Son	Daughter
Brother	Sister
Murderer	Murderess
Sorcerer	Sorceress
Son-in-law	Daughter-in-law
Father-in-law	Mother-in-law
Man-servant	Maid-servant
Land-lord	Land-lady
Bachelor	Maid
Gentleman	Lady
Monk	Nun
Earl	Countess
Lad	Lass
Sir	Madam
Duke	Dutchess
Emperor	Empress
Milk-man	Milk-maid
Pea-cock	Pea-hen
Step-father	Step-mother
Hero	Heroine
Viceroy	Vicerine
Mr.	Mrs.
Governor	Governess
Master	Mistress
Wizard	Witch
Heir	Heiress
Host	Hostess
Lion	Lioness
Mayor	Mayoress
Actor	Actress
Buck	Doe
Colt	Filly
Dog	Bitch
Horse	Mare
Count	Countess
Hunter	Huntress
Prince	Princess
Abbot	Abbess
God	Goddess
Author	Authoress
Ox	Cow
Widower	Widow
Grand-father	Grand-mother
He-goat	She-goat
Milk-man	Milk-woman
Bridegroom	Bride
Tiger	Tigress
Priest	Priestess
Poet	Poetess
Shepherd	Shepherdess
Nephew	Niece
Stag	Hind

PRONOUNS

The repetition of a noun in a sentence or a set of sentences is really boring. So, instead of repeating the noun, we can use a word (for that noun) called the pronoun.
"A pronoun is a word that we use instead of a noun".

Example:
This is *Sachin. He* plays cricket.
Note: *He* is the pronoun used in place of *Sachin.*

Kinds of Pronouns

1. **Personal pronouns :** A pronoun which is used instead of the name of a person is known as a 'Personal Pronoun'. A list of the 'Personal pronouns' is listed below :
   I, my, mine, me, we (First Person)
   You, your, yours (Second Person)
   He, his, him, she, her, hers, it,
   its, they, their, theirs, them (Third Person)

2. **Demonstrative, Indefinite and Distributive Pronouns :**
   (a) **Demonstrative Pronouns :** Pronouns used to point out the objects to which they refer are called Demonstrative Pronouns.
   Examples :
   (i) *This* is a present from my uncle.
   (ii) *These* are merely excuses.
   (iii) Bembay mangoes are better than *those* of Bangaluru.
   (b) **Indefinite Pronouns :** All pronouns which refer to persons or things in a general way and do not refer to any particular person or thing are called Indefinite Pronouns.
   Examples :
   (i) *Somebody* has stolen my watch.
   (ii) *Few* escaped unhurt.
   (iii) Did you ask *anybody* to come?
   (c) **Distributive Pronouns :** Each, either, neither are called distributive pronouns because they refer to persons or things one at a time. For this reason they are always singular and followed by the verb in singular.
   Examples :
   (i) *Each* of the men received a reward.
   (ii) *These* men received *each* a reward.
   (iii) *Either* of you can go.

3. **Relative Pronouns :** A relative pronoun refers or relates to some noun going before, which is called its Antecedent.
   Examples :
   (i) I met Hari *who* used to live here.
   (ii) I have found the pen *which* I had lost.
   (iii) Here is the book *that* you lent me.

4. **Interrogative Pronouns :** These pronouns, are used for asking questions.
   Examples :
   (i) *Whose* book is this?
   (ii) *What* will all the neighbours say?
   (iii) *Which* do you prefer, tea or coffee?
   Note : Interrogative pronouns can also be used in asking indirect questions. Consider the following examples :
   (i) I asked *who* was speaking.
   (ii) Tell me *what* you have done.
   (iii) Say *which* you would like best.

Behaviour of the Pronouns

1. If three pronouns are used together in the same sentence they are arranged in the following order :

2	+	3	+	1
↓		↓		↓
Second Person		Third Person		First Person

   Examples :
   I, you and he must help *that* poor man. (Incorrect)
   You, he and I must help *that* poor man. Correct)
2. When two or more singular nouns are joined by and, the pronoun used for them should be plural.
   Examples :
   Mohan and Sohan are friends. *They* play football. *They* live at Lajpat Nagar.
3. But if these nouns joined by and refer to the same person or thing, the pronoun used should be singular.
   Examples :
   (i) Delhi, the beautiful city and the capital of India, is famous for *its* historical monuments.
   (ii) The manager and owner of the firm expressed *his* views on the demands of the workers.
4. When two nouns are used with as well as, the pronoun agrees with the first subject.
   Examples :
   (a) Mohan as well as his friends is doing *his* work.
   (b) The students as well as their teachers are doing *their* work.
5. When two singular nouns joined by 'and' are preceded by *each* or *every,* the pronoun used must be singular and should agree in gender with the second noun.
   Examples :
   (a) Every man and every woman will do *her* best for the nation.
   (b) Each boy and each girl went to *her* house.
6. When two nouns are joined by using 'with', the pronoun agrees with the noun coming before 'with'.
   Examples :
   (a) The boy with *his* parents has gone to see a movie.
   (b) The children with *their* parents have gone to picnic.
7. When two different nouns are joined by either......... or; neither .... nor, the pronoun is used according to the number and gender of the second noun.

Examples :

(a) Either your sister or you have done *your* work.

(b) Neither the students nor the teacher was in *his* class.

8. The pronoun coming after '*than*' must be in the same case as that coming before '*than*'.

Examples :

(a) She plays better than *me*. (Incorrect)
She plays better than *I*. (Correct)

(b) His elder brother is more intelligent than *him*. (Incorrect)
His elder brother is more intelligent than *he*. (Correct)

9. 'Many a' always takes a singular pronoun and singular verb.

Example :

Many a soldier has met *his* death in the battle field.

10. 'Who', 'Whose', 'Whom' are used only for persons.

Examples :

(a) *Who* is knocking at the door?

(b) *Whose* pen is this?

(c) *What* do you want?

11. 'Which' is used for things.

Example : *Which* game do you like?

MULTIPLE CHOICE QUESTIONS

Directions: *In the following questions choose the correct options to fill the blanks.*

1. The place was so dirty that ..... wished to run away from there.
A. everybody B. anybody
C. few D. some

2. ..... was there to help me.
A. Somebody B. Anything
C. Anybody D. Nobody

3. Is there .... to eat?
A. some B. something
C. any D. few

4. ..... of the students were making a great noise.
A. Anyone B. Somebody
C. Many D. Nobody

5. ..... of the students can solve this sum.
A. Someone B. Anybody
C. Somebody D. None

6. ...... of us should try our best to make India a heaven.
A. Any B. Somebody
C. Anybody D. All

7. ...... of us do not know the real meaning of our lives.
A. Any B. Something
C. Several D. Many

8. My .... black.
A. hairs are B. hair is
C. hairs shall D. hair will

9. She saw two .... on the last Sunday.
A. thiefs B. theifs
C. thieves D. theives

10. My sister is a ....
A. bacheloress B. bachelor
C. unmaried D. spinster

11. One is supposed to do ....
A. our duty B. their duty
C. one's duty D. his duty

12. Take anything .... you want.
A. that B. which
C. than D. then

13. I cannot tolerate ....
A. separated you B. your separation
C. separation from you D. you separated

14. He is .... faithful partner.
A. Yours B. You
C. Your D. Your's

15. Ajay is more smart than ....
A. her B. hers
C. herself D. she

16. Vivek works harder than ....
A. me B. I
C. her D. his

17. They should help ....
A. the poor people B. the poor
C. the poor persons D. the poor peoples

18. .... are mad.
A. All his sons B. His all sons
C. Sons all his D. All sons his

19. The poor fellow .... to fate.
A. resigned B. resigned himself
C. resigned itself D. resigned themselves

20. Nobody will help you but ....
A. I B. me
C. ours D. his

21. It is a good chance, You must avail .... this opportunity.
A. of B. yourself of
C. for D. from

22. The person who is elected .... my relative.
A. is B. he is
C. his D. him

23. He made ....
A. yours mention B. mention of you
C. mention for you D. mention about you

24. .... I know, he is quite faithful.
A. As far as B. So far as
C. So far this D. So far so

25. It is a duty of a person to take .... for his family.
A. pain B. pains
C. pain-killers D. pained

26. She does not love .... husband.
A. his B. her
C. its D. their

27. Let .... work together.
A. him and me B. he and I
C. he and him D. I and me

28. Copper, Silver and Gold ....
A. each will do B. either will do
C. any one will do D. any will do

29. Jessica and Roma are very irregular .... habits.
A. in her B. in their
C. in its D. in every

30. One likes to enjoy .... who was a great poet.
A. The sonnets of Shakespeare
B. Shakespeare's sonnets
C. Sonnets
D. Shakespeare

ANSWERS

1	2	3	4	5	6	7	8	9	10
A	D	B	C	D	D	D	B	C	D
11	12	13	14	15	16	17	18	19	20
C	A	C	C	D	B	B	A	B	B
21	22	23	24	25	26	27	28	29	30
B	A	B	A	B	B	A	C	B	A

ARTICLES

The family of the articles has only three members. They are : A, An and The. However, they fall under two groups :
(a) Definite Article *(b)* Indefinite Article

'The' is known as definite article whereas 'a' and 'an' are known as indefinite articles.

Use of the Definite Article 'The'

'The' is used before

1. The superlative degree :
He is the ablest man of the town.
(ablest is a superlative degree)
2. The name of states, countries etc. having a descriptive name :
(i) The J & K is a small state. (J & K is a descriptive name)
(ii) He lives in the U.S.A. (U.S.A. is a descriptive name)
(But the Delhi and the America are wrong because neither Delhi nor America is a descriptive name)
3. The names of the scriptures :
The Gita is a holy book. (Gita is a scripture)
4. Name of newspapers :
The Tribune is published from Chandigarh.
5. Name of rivers, canals, seas, oceans, bays, gulfs, groups of islands etc. :
(i) The Ganga is a holy river.
(ii) The Indian Ocean is the deepest ocean.
(iii) The Persian Gulf is a narrow gulf.
6. The name of famous buildings :
The Taj is one of the best buildings in India.
7. The names of nationals, sects and communities:
(i) The English defeated the Germans in the World War.
(ii) The rich should help the poor.
(iii) The Hindus believe in the caste system.
8. Proper nouns used as common nouns :
(i) Kalidas is the Shakespeare of India.
(ii) Delhi is the London of India.
9. Famous historical events :
The Industrial Revolution changed the face of England.
10. The directions and the celestial bodies:
The sun rises in the east.
11. Titles : Akbar, the Great was loved by his subjects.

Do not use 'the'

1. Before languages :
The English is an international language. (Incorrect)
English is an international language. (Correct)
2. Before the names of games :
The hockey is a popular game. (Incorrect)
Hockey is a popular game. (Correct)

Use of the Indefinite Articles 'A' and 'An'

'A' is used before :

1. All singular common nouns beginning with a consonant :
(i) A boy sings a song.
(ii) A black and a white cow were grazing in the field.
2. If a word begins with a vowel but gives the sound of a consonant, 'a' should be used before it :
(i) He was helped in his work by a European.
(ii) He is a one-eyed man.
(iii) It is a useful work.

'An' is used as follows :

1. All singular common nouns beginning with a vowel (*i.e.*, a, e, i, o, u) :
   (i) He is an artist. (ii) He is an old man. (iii) I intend to buy an umbrella.
2. If a word starts with a consonant but gives the sound of a vowel, "an" should be used before it :
   (i) Brutus is an honourable man.
   (ii) He is an honour to his profession.
   (iii) He is an L.L.B.

Demonstratives, that, these and those

1. The demonstrative adjectives and pronouns are for objects nearby the speaker:
   this (singular) those (plural)
   and for objects far away from the speaker.
   That (singular) those (plural)
2. Demonstratives are the only adjectives that agree in number with their nouns.
   That hat is nice.
   Those hats are nice.
3. When there is the idea of selection, the pronoun "one" (or "ones") often follows the demonstrative.
   I want a book. I'll get this (one).
   If the demonstrative is followed by an adjective, "one"(or "ones") must be used.
   I want a book. I'll get this big one.

MULTIPLE CHOICE QUESTIONS

Directions: *In the following questions choose the correct options to fill the blanks.*

1. .... will have to be paid for this material.
A. Half rupee B. Half a rupee
C. A half rupee D. An half rupee

2. .... is taking keen interest in India.
A. The USA B. USA
C. An USA D. A USA

3. Only .... can save our country.
A. the Hitler B. a Hitler
C. Hitler D. an Hitler

4. I can run for ....
A. hundred miles B. the hundred miles
C. a hundred miles D. an hundred miles.

5. .... man-eater has been killed.
A. The B. A
C. An D. Either A or B

6. What .... fine idea!
A. the B. an
C. a D. No article

7. .... earth is moving around the sun.
A. An B. A
C. The D. No article

8. This is .... first example while I got.
A. the B. a
C. an D. No article

9. This is .... house which was built during earthquake.
A. a B. an
C. the D. No article

10. .... America is a rich country.
A. The B. An
C. A D. No article

11. .... U.S.A. is a developed country.
A. A B. An
C. The D. No article

12. .... Bible is a holy book.
A. A B. The
C. An D. No article

13. .... rich should help the poor.
A. The B. A
C. An D. No article

14. .... Gold is a costly metal.
A. The B. A
C. An D. No article

15. Kalidas is .... Shakespeare of India.
A. a B. an
C. the D. No article

16. I cannot do .... difficult work.
A. a such B. the such
C. such the D. such a

17. How foolish .... plan it is!
A. a B. an
C. the D. No article

18. An ink is .... useful article.
A. an B. a
C. the D. No article

19. There are .... husband and wife.
A. a B. an
C. the D. No article

20. He is learning .... French
A. the B. a
C. an D. No article

ANSWERS

1	2	3	4	5	6	7	8	9	10
B	A	B	C	D	C	C	A	C	D
11	**12**	**13**	**14**	**15**	**16**	**17**	**18**	**19**	**20**
C	B	A	D	C	D	A	B	D	D

ADJECTIVES & ADVERBS

An Adjective is a word which adds something to the meaning of a noun or a pronoun.

Mridula is an *intelligent* girl. He has a *black* goat.
He is a *brilliant* student. She is a *clever* girl.
It is a *beautiful* picture.

In the sentences given above, the words in italics are adjectives.

An Adverb is a word which qualifies the meaning of a Verb, an Adjective or another Adverb.

(*i*) He talks *slowly.*
(*ii*) He is a *very* good student.
(*iii*) He talks *very* slowly.

In sentence (*i*), *slowly* qualifies the verb *talks.*
In sentence (*ii*), *very* qualifies the adjective *good.*
In sentence (*iii*), *very* qualifies the adverb *slowly.*

Adjectives have three degrees of comparison :

1. **Positive Degree :** It expresses the common form of an adjective.

   Example :

   Ram is a *tall* boy.

   In the above sentence *tall* is an adjective and expresses the common form.

2. **Comparative Degree :** It expresses the more of the same form.

   Example :

   Ram is *taller* than Mahesh.

   In the above sentence *taller* is an adjective that expresses the more of the common form of the adjective *tall.*

   "When and How to Use" Comparative Degree?

   (a) Comparative Degree is used when two persons or two groups of persons or things are compared.
   Examples :
   (a)He is *wiser* than his younger brother.
   (b)This glass is *cleaner* than the other.

   (b) When two different qualities in the same person are compared, more is used instead of 'er' to form the comparative. The formula used in this case should be :
   More + Positive Degree
   She is *fairer* than polite. (Incorrect)
   She is *more fair* than polite. (Correct)

   (c) When selection of one out of two persons or things is meant, the degree of comparison is followed by of and *the* is used before it.
   Example :
   Zia is abler of *the* two sisters.

   (d) If two comparatives are used in the same sentence to impress upon an idea, both should be preceded by the definite article.
   Examples :
   (i) The higher you go, the cooler it is.
   (ii) The more we get, the more we desire.

   (e) When one person or thing is compared with another of the same kind, other is used after the comparative degree. In such sentences other is normally preceded by any or all.
   Examples :
   (i) Kalidas is greater than any dramatist. (Incorrect)
   Kalidas is greater than any other dramatist. (Correct)
   (ii) Lead is heavier than all metals. (Incorrect)
   Lead is heavier than all other metals. (Correct)

   (f) Senior, junior, superior, inferior, prior, anterior (earlier than) and posterior (later than) are always followed by 'to'.
   Examples :
   (i) Ram is senior *to* Mohan by three years.
   (ii) That pen is inferior *to* that.
   (iii) He is junior *to* me in rank.
   (iv) This event was posterior *to* that.
   Note: Never use *than* after the above mentioned adjectives.

Important Information

(a) 'Preferable' is also used as an adjective of the comparative degree. As such, it is always followed by *to* and not *a.*
Death is preferable than dishonour. (Incorrect)
Death is preferable *to* dishonour. (Correct)

(b) To intensify the Degree of comparison, we use *far* or *much* before the comparative.
Examples :
(i) This book is *far* better than that.
(ii) His performance was *much* better than Mohan's.
Warning : Always avoid the use of double comparatives.
Don't say : Ram is more cleverer than his younger brother.
Say: Ram is cleverer than his younger brother.

3. **Superlative Degree :** It expresses the most of the common form of an adjective.

   Example :

   He is the ablest man of the town.

How and when to use the Superlative Degree?

(a) The Superlative Degree is used when more than two persons or things are compared.

(b) The Superlative Degree is generally preceded by 'the' and followed by 'of' in most of the cases or otherwise.

(c) When an adjective of the superlative degree is preceded by a Possessive Adjective or a Noun in the Possessive case, 'the' should not be used before it.
Example :
Which is Kalidas' best play?

It will be a blunder to use 'the' before the Superlative Degree in such cases.

Don't say : Which is Kalidas' the best play.

(d) To intensify the degree of comparison, *by far* is used before the superlative degree.

Example :

India is *by far* the most beautiful country of the world.

Note: Always avoid the use of double superlatives.

Don't say : He is the most strongest boy in the class.

Say : He is the strongest boy in the class.

Use of some Important Adjectives

1. (a) **'Some'** is used as follows :

(i) With countable nouns where it means— a little, a small quantity.

(ii) In a question which shows some request.

Examples :

(i) There is some water in the bottle.

(ii) Some of the students were absent yesterday.

(iii) Will you have some milk?

(iv) Will you buy some fruit for me?

(b) **'Any'** is used as follows :

(i) In negative sentences.

(ii) In interrogative sentences.

(iii) After 'Hardly', 'Scarcely' and 'Barely'.

(iv) After 'If'.

Examples :

(i) There is not any sugar in the pot.

(ii) We haven't any rice in the house.

(iii) I have hardly any money.

(iv) There are scarcely any plants in this field.

(v) If there is any danger, blow the whistle.

2. (a) **Older :** Older (and oldest) are used for persons animals and things. But 'Older' and 'Oldest' refer to the persons who do not belong to the same family.

Examples :

(i) Radha is older than Shyama.

(ii) John is the oldest member of the staff.

'Older' and 'Oldest' refer to the persons who do not belong to the same family.

(b) **Elder** (and **eldest**) are used in respect of the members of the same family like sons, daughters, brothers, sisters.

Examples :

(i) My elder sister is a lecturer.

(ii) Meenakshi is the eldest of the three sisters.

Note :

(i) 'Elder' is not followed by 'than'.

(ii) 'Elder' and 'Eldest' cannot be used for things.

3. (a) **'Few'** is negative and is the opposite of 'Many'. It means 'not many'.

(b) **'A few'** is positive and means 'some at least'. It is the opposite of 'None'.

(c) **'The few'** means 'minority' and suggests 'whether there is'.

Examples :

(i) We have few holidays in school.

(ii) Only a few boys will fail in the examination.

(iii) The few poems that he wrote are very popular.

4. (a) **Further** means 'something additional'.

(b) **Farther** means 'a greater distance'.

Examples :

(i) Further discussion will be held in the office of the principal.

(ii) Amritsar is farther from Delhi than Ambala.

5. (a) **Little** is negative. It means, 'not much', or 'hardly any'.

(b) **A little** is positive. It means 'some quantity'.

(c) **The little** denotes quantity. It means, 'not much but all that is, or whatever quantity there is'.

Examples :

(i) There is little hope of his success.

(ii) He knows a little of everything.

(iii) I have spent the little money I had.

(iv) The little knowledge of shoe-making proved very useful to me.

6. (a) **'Much'** expresses 'quantity'.

(b) **'Many'** expresses 'number'.

(c) **'Many a'**—'Singular noun' and 'Singular verb' are used with 'many a'.

Examples :

(i) There is not *much* water in the jug.

(ii) *Many* boys are absent today.

(iii) *Many* a battle has been fought on the soil of India.

7. (a) **'Less'** denotes 'in a small degree'.

(b) **'Fewer'** denotes 'number'.

Examples :

(i) He devotes less time to his studies.

(ii) There are no fewer than ten chairs in this room.

8. (a) **'Each'** is used for a single number of 'two persons' or 'things'.

(b) **'Every'** is used for a single number of 'many persons' or 'things'.

Examples :

(i) Each boy must take part in games.

(ii) There are only two poets. Each poet recited his poem.

(iii) Every man dies in this world.

(iv) Every man is expected to do his duty.

9. (a) **'Either'** means one of the two or both.

(b) **'Neither'** is negative of the either.

Examples :

(i) You may buy either of these two chairs.

(ii) Neither of them could speak on the stage.

10.(a) **'Later'** expresses 'late in time'.

(b) **'Latter'** means 'second in position or order'.

Examples :

(i) My father reached later than I expected.

(ii) The latter position was better than the former.

Use of some Important Adverbs

1. (a) Also, too, enough:
   - (i) He taught English. Also, he edited the school magazine
   - (ii) He is a writer and also he is a painter.
   - (iii) He is too obstinate to listen to any reason.
   - (iv) This is too difficult a piece for the junior students.
   - (v) Sarla was kind enough to help the poor.
   - (vi) He is brave enough to help the truth.

   Note: 'Too' is used in a negative sense, but enough is used in a positive sense.

   (b) Fairly and rather: Both suggest the meaning 'moderately'. But, mainly 'fairly' is used with the words that denote a positive meaning and rather is used with the words that denote a negative meaning:
   - (i) Rita did fairly well in that competition, but her performance was rather poor in sports.
   - (ii) Mona is fairly rich, but she is rather stingy.

   Note: 'Rather' can also be used in a positive sense.
   - (i) This is a rather interesting job.
   - (ii) That boy is rather smart.

   (c) Hardly, barely, scarcely: These words mostly convey the negative suggestions and are almost similar.
   - (i) I have hardly any strength now.
   - (ii) There was barely any supply to the township,
   - (iii) There were scarcely a hundred guests present.

   Note: With slight variance in the meaning, the words given above convey the idea of 'very little', 'not enough', 'lack of quantity and number'.

   (d) Yet, Still: These adverbs can often be used to connect the sentence units:
   - (i) He has been defeated many times in the contest; still he wants to be a competitor.
   - (ii) Mona was sick; yet she went on doing her work.

   (e) Alone:
   - (i) He alone (none else) is capable of handling that fire,
   - (ii) He hunted all alone in the forest. (not in any company)

Special Note:

(a) Apart from their conventional positions the adverbs might be used in different positions with different meanings and angles.
- (i) He had only four books.
- (ii) John only contacted his friend in need.
- (iii) He greeted me only.
- (iv) Only he greeted me there.

(b) Inversion: Some adverbs can be inverted *i.e.* placed in the beginning of the sentence and then be followed by an interrogative form. The most common of these adverb are: so, seldom, never, nowhere, under no circumstances, hardly, scarcely etc.
- (i) So big was the bus that it could not enter the narrow lane.
- (ii) Hardly had he reached the station when he received the message.

MULTIPLE CHOICE QUESTIONS

Directions: *In the following questions choose the correct options to fill the blanks.*

1. The girl whom you met is the .... sister of Ravi.
A. eldest B. elder
C. older D. oldest

2. The historical place is ....
A. seeing worth B. worthy of seeing
C. worth seeing D. worthy seeing

3. These flowers smell ....
A. sweet B. sweetly
C. more sweetly D. sweetest

4. .... aspirant cannot pass the entrance examination.
A. Each B. Every
C. All D. No

5. Harivansh Rai .... second Shakespeare.
A. is a B. is
C. is the D. is an

6. .... student in the class got prizes.
A. Each and every B. Every and each
C. Every D. Never

7. It is .... picture than the one we saw last Monday.
A. interesting B. much interesting
C. more interesting D. most interesting

8. She is clever ....
A. that her mother is B. as her mother is
C. to her mother is D. than her mother is

9. They will get ....
A. Red, green and black paper
B. Red, green black paper
C. Red and green and black paper
D. Red green black paper

10. Health is .... wealth.
A. preferable to B. more preferable than
C. more preferable to D. most preferable then

11. .... water that was in the jug evaporated.
A. Little B. The little
C. Small D. A small

12. He has not sung .... songs.
A. much B. most
C. more D. many

13. Srishti has searched .... office.
A. whole the B. the whole
C. a whole D. some whole

14. Premchand was .... best and .... famous writer.
A. a, the most B. the, a most
C. the, more D. the, the most

15. William Shakespeare is famous as ....
A. a poet and a dramatist
B. a poet and dramatist
C. the poet and the dramatist
D. a poet and the dramatist

16. What does .... leader suggest?
A. other B. another
C. others D. anothers

17. He .... money.
A. has few B. have few
C. has little D. have little

18. The .... boys are rewarded.
A. first two B. two first
C. firsts two D. two's first

19. He is .... brave.
A. stronger than
B. stronger then
C. more strong then
D. more strong than

20. No sooner said ....
A. so done B. and done
C. then done D. but done

21. She returned .... than I had thought.
A. quickly B. more quicker
C. more quickly D. quicker

22. He is .... foolish person.
A. rather the B. a rather
C. rather a D. rather

23. This pen .... rupees.
A. costs twenty B. twenty costs only
C. costs only twenty D. only costs twenty

24. It is .... pride.
A. nothing else but B. nothing else than
C. else nothing than D. but

25. This tea is .... to drink.
A. too hot B. very hot
C. enough hot D. much hot

ANSWERS

1	2	3	4	5	6	7	8	9	10
A	C	A	B	A	C	C	C	A	A
11	12	13	14	15	16	17	18	19	20
B	D	B	D	B	B	C	A	D	C
21	22	23	24	25					
C	C	C	A	A					

DETERMINERS

Determiners are actually Adjectives. They are always followed by nouns.

Determiners are of the following kinds:

1. **Demonstrative Determiners :** this, that, these, those
2. **Possessive Determiners :** my, our, your, his, her, its, their
3. **Quantitative Determiners :** some, any, much, enough, sufficient, whole, a little, the little, little, all, both
4. **Numerical Determiners:** a few, some, few, the few, any, several, many, no, etc.
One, two, three ... (Cardinals)
First, second, third ... (Ordinals)
5. **Distributive Determiners:** either, neither
6. **Articles: Indefinite:** a, an, **Definite:** the

MULTIPLE CHOICE QUESTIONS

Directions: *In the following questions choose the correct options to fill the blanks.*

1. Give me .... rice.
A. some B. few
C. a few D. any

2. ...... sheep grazing on the slope of the hill had gone away.
A. Any B. The few
C. This D. Much

3. Have you got .... magazines to read?
A. all B. much
C. some D. little

4. I have .... money that I want to spend on shares.
A. any B. much
C. less D. some

5. There is .... owl on the branch of the tree.
A. a B. the
C. an D. some

6. My brother is .... MBA.
A. a B. an
C. the D. any

7. Have you got .... cheese?
A. some B. many
C. a few D. few

8. No, I have not got .... cheese.
A. many B. few
C. any D. some

9. There is only .... milk left in the bottle.
A. enough B. few
C. much D. a little

10. There is .... hope of his recovery.
A. any B. little
C. many D. few

11. .... dogs were barking at the strangers.
A. Some B. Any
C. Much D. Less

12. The girl bought her father .... juice.
A. few B. some
C. any D. many

13. You should take .... honey everyday.
A. any B. many
C. a little D. a few

14. .... boy was punished by the teacher.
A. Either B. All
C. Any D. Many

15. .... girl was asked to join the army.
A. None B. Neither
C. All D. Any

16. .... water in the jug has been drunk by Mohan.
A. The little B. The few
C. A few D. Few

17. I shall play .... piano at the party.
A. some B. any
C. the D. few

18. .... labourers were found dead in the mine.
A. Any B. Fewer
C. Many D. Less

19. Could I borrow .... umbrella?
A. our B. your
C. yours D. my

20. My brother is standing in the .... row.
A. any B. many
C. some D. first

ANSWERS

1	2	3	4	5	6	7	8	9	10
A	B	C	D	C	B	A	C	D	B
11	**12**	**13**	**14**	**15**	**16**	**17**	**18**	**19**	**20**
A	B	C	A	B	A	C	C	B	D

THE VERB

A Verb is a word that tells something about the action or state of or happenning to a person or thing.

A Verb tells the following:

1. What a person or thing does.
Sachin goes to school daily.
The bell *rang* loudly.
Many birds fly in the sky.
She *sang* a song.

2. What a person or thing is.
India *is* the biggest democracy in the world.
Ram Mehar *is* very rich.
They *are* happy.

3. What is done to a person or thing.
You *are liked* by all.
Two thieves *were arrested.*
Four students *were punished* by the teacher.

4. What happens to a person or thing.
His maternal uncle *died* last week.
Two ships *sank* yesterday.
Leaves *turn* yellow in autumn.

5. What a person or thing has, had, and so on.
I *have* a new car.
He *had* a scooter last year.
He *has* several cows and goats.

It goes without saying that a verb is the most important part of a sentence. No sentence is complete without a Verb.

Important Information

1. If two or more singular nouns are joined by 'and' the verb used will be plural.
Example:
(i) He and I were going to the market.
(ii) Ram and Mohan are friends.

2. If two singular nouns joined by 'and' points out to the same thing or person, the verb used must be singular.
Example:
(i) Rice and curry is the favourite food of the Punjabis.
(ii) The Collector and District Magistrate is away.

3. In case two subjects are joined by 'as well as' the verb agrees with the first subject.
Example :
(i) Kanta as well as her children is playing.
(ii) Children as well as their mother are playing.
In the case of first sentence the verb (is) agrees with Kanta and in the case of second sentence the verb (are) agrees with the children.

4. 'Neither', 'Either', 'Every', 'Each', 'Everyone', and 'Many a' are followed by a singular verb.
Example :
(i) Either of the plans is to be adopted.
(ii) Neither of the two brothers is sure to pass.
(iii) Every student is expected to be obedient.
(iv) Everyone of them desires this.
(v) Many a person is drowned in the sea.

5. If two subjects are joined by 'Either .... or' / 'Neither .... nor', the verb agrees with the subject near to it.
   Example :
   (i) Either my brother or I am to do this work.
   (ii) Neither he nor they are prepared to do this work.
6. 'A great many' is always followed by a 'plural noun' and a 'plural verb'. For example :
   A great many students have been declared successful.
7. Similarly if two subjects are joined by 'with', 'together with', 'no less than', in addition to 'and not', etc. the verb agrees with the first subject.
   Example :
   (i) The boy with his parents has arrived.
   (ii) He, no less than I, is to blame.
8. Nouns, plural in form, but singular in meaning, take a singular verb.
   Example :
   This news was broadcast from television yesterday.

MULTIPLE CHOICE QUESTIONS

Directions: *In the following questions choose the correct options to fill the blanks.*

1. The bus with all its passengers .... lost.
A. were B. was
C. are D. would

2. You as well as I .... responsible for this work.
A. am B. are
C. was D. is

3. Raghava like all his companions .... a spoiled child.
A. are B. were
C. is D. will be

4. Pen and ink .... required for me.
A. are B. were
C. is D. has required

5. Every girl and every boy .... attended the seminar.
A. have B. has
C. is D. are

6. Not only she but all her sisters ...... been married.
A. has B. have
C. is D. are

7. There .... nothing but miseries in life.
A. is B. are
C. were D. will be

8. Neither prose nor poem .... given.
A. were B. was
C. has D. have

9. Either he or I .... wrong.
A. is B. are
C. am D. were

10. Either Sulekha or Rekha .... coming here.
A. are B. is
C. were D. have

11. .... the child or his parents to blame?
A. Is B. Are
C. Were D. Has

12. You and I .... neighbours.
A. am B. are
C. was D. has

13. The house with all its belongings ..... sold away.
A. were B. are
C. was D. must

14. Either water or juice .... required.
A. is B. are
C. were D. has

15. There were not as many tables as .... required.
A. was B. were
C. is D. are

16. They each .... a book.
A. have B. are
C. has D. is

17. He and I .... class friends.
A. is B. am
C. was D. are

18. She as well as I .... guilty.
A. is B. are
C. am D. must be

19. Purushottam .... not read more on this chapter.
A. needs
B. has been need
C. need
D. had been need

20. He came .... to his aunt.
A. run B. running
C. to run D. in run

ANSWERS

1	2	3	4	5	6	7	8	9	10
B	B	C	C	B	B	A	B	C	B
11	**12**	**13**	**14**	**15**	**16**	**17**	**18**	**19**	**20**
A	B	C	A	B	A	D	A	C	B

CONJUNCTIONS

A conjunction is a word which connects words, clauses or sentences.

Look at the following sentences.

(i) He bought apples *and* mangoes.

(ii) God made the country *and* man made the town.

(iii) The door was open *but* there was no one in the house.

(iv) He knows that I am here *and* that I want to see him.

In the sentence (i), *and* connects two words—*apples* and *mangoes.*

In the sentence (ii), *and* connects two sentences—*God made the country* and *man made the town.*

In the sentence (iii), *but* connects two sentences— *The door was open* and *there was no one in the house.*

In the sentence (iv), *and* connects two clauses—*that I am here* and *that I want to see him.*

The main coordinating conjunctions are:

and, but, for, or, nor, also, either ..... or, neither ..... nor.

There are some conjunctions which are used in pairs. They are:

either .... or, ... neither .... nor, both .... and, though .... yet, whether .... or, not only .... but also.

Example: *Either* take it *or* leave it.

It is *neither* useful *nor* ornamental.

They *both* like *and* respect me.

Though he is suffering from high fever, *yet* he does not cry.

He does not care *whether* you go *or* stay.

He is *not only* doltish, *but also* obstinate.

The conjunctions which are used in pairs in this way, are called correlative conjunctions, or merely correlatives.

Use of Important Conjunctions

1. **As soon as :** As soon as denotes simultaneous time.

   Example : As soon as he saw his enemy, he took to his heels.

2. **No sooner .... than :**

   (a) 'No sooner' is always followed by 'than'.

   (b) Please remember that 'No sooner' is always followed by do/does/did. As such only first form of the verb should be used after the subject.

   Example :

   No sooner did he see his enemy than he took to his heels.

3. **Hardly :** Hardly is followed by when.

   Examples :

   (i) Hardly had I left the house when it started raining.

   (ii) We had hardly come into the room when his father began chastising him.

   Note :

   A. Hardly is never followed by than.

   B. 'Scarcely' can also be used in the sense and manner of 'Hardly'.

4. **Lest :** Lest is used in the sense of so that .... not. It is always followed by should. Lest is negative in sense. Hence 'not' should never be used with it.

   Example :

   Work hard lest you should fail.

   Note : 'Lest' is always followed by 'should' and not 'may'.

5. **Unless :** Unless expresses condition. It is also used in the negative sense. Use of 'not' is not allowed with unless because unless is already in the negative sense.

   Example :

   Unless you labour hard you will not pass.

6. **Until :** 'Until' expresses time. It means 'till not'.

   Example : Wait here until I return.

   Note : Until is in the negative sense. So 'not' should not be used with it. Example :

   Wait here until I do not return. (Incorrect)

   Wait here until I return. (Correct)

7. **As well as :** When two subjects are joined by 'as well as', the verb always agrees with the first subject.

   Examples :

   (i) The teacher as well as students is playing.

   (ii) Students as well as the teacher are playing.

   Note : 'Both' and 'as well as' cannot be used together in the same sentence.

   Examples :

   Both Sita as well as Kanta are beautiful. (Incorrect)

   Sita as well as Kanta is beautiful. (Correct)

   Both Sita and Kanta are beautiful. (Correct)

8. **As if :** 'As if' is used in the sense of pretension. While using 'as if' in a sentence, we should see that even the third person singular subject gets 'were'.

   Example : He talks as if he were mad.

9. **Till :** Till expresses time. Till is always used in the affirmative.

   Example :

   We did not come back till sunset.

10. **Rather than :** 'Rather than' is used in the sense of 'preference'. 'Rather' is always followed by 'than'.

    Example :

    I would rather die than submit.

11. **As long as/so long as :** Both express time during which an action or event takes place.

    Example :

    As long as there is life, there is hope.

12. **However :** It is both a subordinate and co-ordinate clause.

    Examples :

    (a) Mala worked hard, she however, failed.

    (b) However hard he may work, he cannot pass.

13. **Such as :** 'Such as' gives us the sense of 'like'. Such is always followed by 'as'.

    Example :

    Life is such a puzzle as cannot be solved.

MULTIPLE CHOICE QUESTIONS

Directions: *In the following questions choose the correct options to fill the blanks.*

1. Neither he .... his friend is good.
A. or B. and
C. but D. nor

2. The officer asked the peon .... why he was late.
A. that B. if
C. but D. No word needed

3. Both Ajay .... Vijay are intelligent.
A. or B. nor
C. and D. No word needed

4. No Sooner did the thief see the public .... he ran away.
A. then B. and
C. but D. than

5. Abhinav .... his brothers was going to Mumbai.
A. but
B. yet
C. No word needed
D. together with

6. He behaves .... he were the captain of the team.
A. as if B. as
C. No word needed D. that

7. Either Rupali .... Sonali is going to attend the meeting.
A. and B. but
C. nor D. or

8. Neither Nirmal .... Ashwinee is going to listen the speech.
A. and B. but
C. nor D. or

9. Ravi .... Prakash are going to Kolkata.
A. or B. nor
C. but D. and

10. Rice .... curry is my usual breakfast.
A. and B. but
C. then D. than

11. Hardly had he left .... his brother came.
A. then B. than
C. when D. that

12. I would rather have a copy .... a book.
A. then B. than
C. when D. that

13. He is no other .... my friend.
A. then B. than
C. when D. but

14. He saw a snake ....he awoke.
A. then B. when
C. than D. No word needed

15. Ten years have passed .... my grandmother died.
A. since B. when
C. then D. than

16. She is .... good .... bad.
A. either, not B. neither, or
C. neither, nor D. neither, than

17. The cellphone is both cheap .... best.
A. than B. and
C. then D. or

18. No sooner did the rogue see the police .... he disappeared.
A. then B. than
C. so D. because

19. Srishti will go .... Sanju goes.
A. if B. than
C. then D. although

20. She is wise .... timid.
A. and B. yet
C. but D. however

21. Make hay .... the sun shines.
A. though B. while
C. after D. before

22. He is so weak .... he cannot walk.
A. but B. that
C. then D. so

23. Although he is rich, ... he is unhappy.
A. but B. yet
C. so D. still

24. Wait here .... I come back.
A. till B. until
C. before D. after

25. He is my friend .... I shall help him.
A. so B. hence
C. that is why D. therefore

26. He must go away .... he will be beaten.
A. otherwise B. and
C. or D. else

27. God loves good men .... good men love God.
A. and B. or
C. that D. those

28. He was late .... he was not punished.
A. but B. yet
C. still D. therefore

29. Walk slowly ...., you may fall.
A. and B. or
C. so D. otherwise

30. Work hard, ... you will fail.
A. and B. or
C. otherwise D. else

ANSWERS

1	2	3	4	5	6	7	8	9	10
D	D	C	D	D	A	D	C	D	A
11	12	13	14	15	16	17	18	19	20
C	B	B	B	A	C	B	B	A	C
21	22	23	24	25	26	27	28	29	30
B	B	B	A	B	C	A	C	D	D

PREPOSITIONS

A *Preposition* is a word which is placed before a noun or a pronoun to show its relation to some other word in the sentence.

1. I saw a goat *in* the field.
2. I am fond *of* hot coffee.

In sentence 1, the word *in* shows the relation between two things—*goat* and *field.*

In sentence 2, the word *of* shows the relation between the attribute expressed by the adjective *found* and *tea.*

The words *in* and *of* are here used as prepositions.

The noun or pronoun which is used with a preposition is called its object. The noun or pronoun is in the objective case. It is governed by the preposition. Now it is absolutely clear that in sentence 1, the noun *field* is in the objective case. The word *field* is governed by the preposition *in.*

A preposition may have two or more objects.

The road runs over *hill* and *plain.*

Here, the words *hill* and *plain* are used as objects.

Use of Important Prepositions

1. Among, Between

'**Among**' is used for more than two persons or things; '**Between**' is used only for two.

Examples :

(i) Distribute these sweets *among* the poor students of the class.

(ii) Distribute these books *between* Ram and Shyam.

2. Among, In

'**Among**' is used before collective plural nouns. '**In**' is used before collective singular nouns.

Examples :

(i) I found him standing *among* the crowd.

(ii) I saw him in the crowd.

3. Beside, Besides

'**Beside**' means 'by the side of'. '**Besides**' means 'in addition to'.

Examples :

(i) The daughter was sitting *beside* her mother.

(ii) *Besides* his relatives, he invited his friends also.

4. In, Within

'**In**' means at the expiry of a period of time in future, '**Within**' means before the expiry of a period of time in any tense.

Examples :

(i) She will return *in* a week.

(ii) I shall finish my work *within* a weak.

5. On, Upon

'**On**' is used for things at rest; '**Upon**' is used for things in motion.

Examples :

(i) He is sitting *on* the floor.

(ii) The dog sprang *upon* the table.

6. By, With

'**By**' denotes the agent or doer. '**With**' denotes the instrument with which anything is done.

Examples :

(i) The bird was killed *by* the hunter with an arrow.

(ii) He beat the dog *with* a stick.

(iii) I shall reach here *by* five o'clock.

7. After, In

'**After**' means at the end of a period of time in the past. '**In**' means at the end of a period of time in future.

Examples :

(i) I shall return your book *in* a week.

(ii) He returned the book *after* a week.

8. For, From, Since

'**For**' is used before a noun denoting a period of time with all the tenses. '**From**' is used before a noun or phrase denoting a point of time. it is used in all the tenses. '**Since**' is used before a noun or phrase denoting some point of time and is always produced by a verb in the perfect continuous tense or third form of a verb.

Examples :

(i) We have been playing cards *for* two hours.

(ii) She stayed with her uncle *from* the 15th of March to the 15th of May.

(iii) I have been reading this book *since* morning.

9. Above, Over

'**Above**' means 'higher from'. **Over** is used in the following four senses :

(i) In the sense of 'above' :
At noon, the sun is *over* our heads.

(ii) In the sense of 'beyond' :
I cannot get *over* my disappointment.

(iii) In the sense of 'Superiority' :
God *over* all blesses for ever more.

(iv) In the sense of 'Conclusion' :
It is all *over* with me.

10. At, Towards

'**At**' denotes the idea of aim, '**Towards**' denotes the idea of destination.

Examples :

(i) He threw the stone *at* the cat.

(ii) He went *towards* the house.

11. At, In, On

'At' is used as follows :

(i) '**At**' is used with small towns and villages. **Examples:**

(a) He was born *at* Sonepat.

(b) He lives *at* village Bangra. (Bangra is a village)

(ii) '**At**' is used before a noun denoting a definite point of time.

Example :

He called on me *at* 9 p.m. yesterday.

'In' is used as follows :

(iii) '**In**' is used with the names of big cities, provinces and countries.

Examples :

(a) His father lives *in* England.

(b) His younger brother lives *in* Calcutta.

(iv) '**In**' is used before the names of months and years.

Example :

His elder sister was born *in* 1972 *in* the month of May.

'**On**' is used with dates and names of days. **Examples:**

(a) I joined college *on* the 26th April.

(b) He will leave for Kolkata *on* Wednesday next.

Important Information

1. '**In**' is also used in the following phrases :
   In the morning; In the evening, In winter, In summer.
2. '**In**' also denotes a place inside anything.
   He travelled *in* a crowded bus.
3. '**At**' is used in the following phrases :
   At home, *At* the station, *At* work, *At* play.

12. Below, Beneath

Below means 'of lower level in position, dignity and expectation' etc. *Beneath* means 'under'.

Examples :

(i) It is *below* my dignity to talk to her.

(ii) They rested *beneath* the shade of a tree.

13. In, Into, To

'**In**' expresses Rest or Motion inside anything. '**Into**' expresses Motion towards the inside of anything or change from one medium to another. '**To**' denotes motion from one place to another.

Examples :

(i) The boys are *in* the room.

(ii) Translate this passage from English *into* Hindi.

(iii) Every morning he goes *to* the temple.

14. Till, By, Of, Off

- 'Till' means upto or not earlier than.
- 'By' means not later than.
- 'Of' shows cause, source, separation, quality, contents, possession, apposition, point of reference, space in time etc.
- 'Off' shows separation at a near distance, and detached condition.

Consider the following examples:

(i) I shall work *till* 5 a.m.

(ii) Madhu died *of* cancer.

(iii) The nib *of* the pen is made *of* gold.

(iv) He presented me a bottle *of* perfume.

(v) Our principal is a man *of* principle.

(vi) He lived in the house *of* his friend.

(vii) *By* this time tomorrow, I'll have finished my job.

(viii) My house is *off* the road.

(ix) The book fell *off* the table.

MULTIPLE CHOICE QUESTIONS

Directions: *Tick the correct preposition for the blank in each of the following sentences.*

1. He applied ...... the manager.
A. for B. to
C. with D. by

2. Trust ...... God and do the right.
A. in B. for
C. to D. with

3. She is worthy ...... a prize.
A. with B. for
C. to D. of

4. Mr. Gomes has no taste ...... music.
A. of B. for
C. with D. to

5. You are hard ...... hearing.
A. at B. of
C. with D. for

6. He is sure ...... his success
A. for B. with
C. on D. of

7. Preeti was warned ...... the danger ahead.
A. for B. at
C. of D. about

8. I am thankful ...... you for a good advice.
A. for B. with
C. to D. of

9. Deepak would not surrender ...... the police.
A. with B. to
C. for D. on

10. The small plant in your lawn is very sensitive ...... touch.
A. on B. with
C. to D. about

11. Divya was sure to succeed ..... the examination.
A. for B. in
C. to D. with

12. Geeta was jealous ...... Ravina's beauty.
A. to B. with
C. for D. of

13. He was ignorant ..... what was happening there.
A. for B. of
C. to D. with

14. Your pen is inferior ...... mine.
A. than B. with
C. from D. to

15. Reenu is no match ...... Meenu.
A. to B. for
C. with D. upon

16. It is necessary ...... you to apply for this job.
A. on B. with
C. for D. to

17. Be loyal ...... your country.
A. for B. to
C. on D. with

18. Mukesh is junior ...... me.
A. than B. to
C. from D. of

19. Deepika was innocent ...... the crime.
A. of B. with
C. from D. to

20. I am desirous.... joining the Indian cricket team.
A. for B. of
C. to D. on

ANSWERS

1	2	3	4	5	6	7	8	9	10
B	A	D	B	B	D	D	D	B	D
11	**12**	**13**	**14**	**15**	**16**	**17**	**18**	**19**	**20**
B	D	B	D	B	D	B	B	A	B

SYNONYMS

A synonym is a word which conveys a meaning similar to the given word.

REMEMBER

Words	*Synonyms*
Add	Increase
Adequate	Enough
Adjust	Adapt
All	Aggregate
Allow	Permit
Abode	Dwelling
Apt	Proper
Assess	Appraise
Accuse	Calumniate
Abashed	Timid
Annoy	Displease
Ample	Enough, Sufficient
Amplify	Increase
Apathetic	Unenthusiastic
Accost	Address
Authentic	True
Adjust	Fit
Approve	Assent, Allow, Accept
Adapt	Conform
Adversary	Opponent, Rival, Competitor
Beat	Whack
Benign	Kind
Breeze	Zephyr
Baffle	Puzzle
Booty	Spoil
Beauty	Charm
Beast	Animal
Bandit	Robber
Blaze	Shine
Bond	Tie
Bend	Twist
Bate	Diminish
Beg	Plead
Barbaric	Wild, Savage
Bashful	Shy, Reserved
Begin	Start
Blend	Mix, Mingle
Bizarre	Funny
Below	Under
Bedevil	Confuse
Bemoan	Lament
Babble	Nonsense
Blame	Fault
Behaviour	Demeanour
Call	Accost
Copy	Imitate
Close	Shut
Caress	Love
Camp	Stay
Connect	Attach
Cut	Injure, Curtail
Cling	Stick
Conical	Funny
Convey	Carry
Conspicuous	Prominent
Cheerful	Happy, Pleasant

Words	Synonyms	Words	Synonyms
Curtail	Decrease	Grow	Develop
Cheerless	Sad, Dejected	Greed	Avidity
Curious	Strange	Greet	Welcome
Circumstance	Factor, Situation, Condition	Grave	Serious
Competent	Capable	Group	Constellation
Congruent	Overlapping	Given	Bestowed
Cope	Deal, Endure	Gratitude	Thankfulness
Confident	Sure	Have	Possess
Complex	Intricate	Hire	Rent
Cajole	Coax, Flatter	Hit	Strike
Cunning	Crafty	Handsome	Beautiful
Delectable	Joyful, Delightful	Hinder	Prevent
Devilish	Diabolical	Heap	Pile
Delicate	Soft	Hope	Expect
Devil	Fiend	Hard	Harsh
Delay	Postpone	Help	Aid
Dislike	Repugnance	Hymn	Song
Destroy	Ruin	Henpecked	Enslaved
Dwell	Live, Dilate	Hoodwink	Mystify, Cheat
Declare	Pronounce	Humble	Polite, Urbane, Modest
Drunk	Flushed	Harass	Vex, Trouble
Deficient	Lacking	Impart	Instil
Damn	Condemn, Curse	Intact	Untouched
Decrease	Diminish	Instal	Establish
Destruction	Devastation	Indict	Impeach
Efficient	Competent	Imitate	Ape
Ethnic	Racial	Instigate	Incite
Enthral	Enslave	Initiate	Start, Introduce
Earnest	Serious	Inimical	Unfriendly
Envious	Jealous	Insufferable	Intolerable
Ending	Final	Impartiality	Justice
Egg	Incite	Jolly	Merry
Extempore	At once	Joyful	Delectable
Extensive	Far-ranging	Join	Conjoin
Extra	Surplus	Kind	Benign
Existence	Life	Kill	Murder
Exceed	Overstep	Kindred	Similar
Enormous	Vast	Kinship	Relationship
Excessive	Superfluous	Keen	Sharp
Free	Unhindered	Knowledge	Scholarship
Frigid	Cold	Lazy	Slothful
Feed	Cater	Large	Substantial, Gargantuan
Fame	Reputation	Listless	Careless, Lackadaisical
Frame	Make	Lax	Loose
First	Initial	Little	Small
Frighten	Terrorise, Intimidate	Lifelike	Realistic
Fervent	Fervid	Lofty	High
Fall	Decline	Lenient	Soft, Gentle
Feeble	Frail	Lacking	Deficient, Wanting
Fickle	Changeable	Lessen	Decrease
Finish	Conclude	Middleclass	Bourgeois
Fraud	Deception	Mitigate	Lessen, Abate
Forgiving	Placable	Modesty	Humility, Lowliness

Words	Synonyms
Mix	Mingle, Blend
Mixture	Mingling
Mixed	Assorted
Modify	Decrease
Mean	Imply
Multifarious	Varied
Miscarry	Abort
Note	Notice
Noble	Stately
Native	Indigenous
Needful	Necessary
Notify	Declare
Nervous	Shaky, Tremulous, Timid
Natural	Spontaneous
Near	Close
Normal	Natural
Offend	Displease
Oppress	Persecute, Tyrannize
Opponent	Adversary
Obstruct	Hinder, Check
Offence	Fault
Offender	Villain
Overstep	Exceed
Overlapping	Congruent
Occult	Mystic
Profane	Unholy
Patience	Forbearance
Pornographic	Obscene
Plenitude	Abundance
Prominent	Important
Prodigal	Spender
Procrastinate	Postpone
Promote	Develop, Honour
Persecute	Tyrannise
Profess	Claim
Pliant	Flexible
Plebian	Common
Polished	Sophisticated
Quake	Shake
Quit	Leave
Queer	Eccentric
Quell	Suppress
Quantify	Allot
Reply	Answer
Relinquish	Retire
Read	Peruse
Relation	Reference
Render	Do
Remainder	Residuals
Repeat	Reiterate
Repentant	Contrite
Retaliative	Retaliatory
Rumour	Hearsay
Reveal	Divulge

Words	Synonyms
Ritualistic	Ceremonious
Soft	Delicate
Sort	Kind, Choose, Select
Selfish	Egoistic
Sensual	Earthly
Suppress	Quell, Check
Stimulate	Provoke
Tasteless	Insipid
Travel	Journey
True	Authentic, Faithful, Truthful
Turbulence	Turmoil
Tragedy	Calamity
Tasteful	Tasty, Delicious
Touching	Painful
Thankful	Grateful
Tremendous	Great, Huge
Tough	Strong
Terminate	Conclude, End
Theory	Doctrine
Tell	Relate
Tremble	Shake, Shiver
Urge	Spur
Unbeaten	Unsubdued
Use	Utilize, Practise
Underhand	Unfair, Undue
Unfair	Unjust
Unravel	Reveal, Divulge
Unimportant	Common
Unconcerned	Apathetic
Unimitated	Inimitable
Unfortunate	Unlucky
Understand	Perceive, Comprehend
Vain	Proud, Haughty, Conceited, Shameless
Vale	Valley, Dale, Dell
Vice	Fault
Virtue	Quality
Veracity	Reality
Value	Price, Prize
Vex	Tease
Vibrate	Quiver, Shake
Violent	Excessive
Vivid	Clear, Lucid
Victory	Triumph
Vulgar	Indecent
Virtuous	Honest
Variegated	Varied, Multifarious
Well	Good
Yell	Cry, Shout
Yonder	There
Yearn	Wish, Desire
Yoke	Slavery
Zest	Earnestness, Enthusiasm
Zealous	Earnest

ANTONYMS

A antonym is a word which conveys a meaning opposite to the given word.

REMEMBER

Words	*Antonyms*
Abhor	Love
Abnormal	Normal
Able	Unable
Acceptable	Unacceptable
Adequate	Inadequate
Amusing	Boring
Angry	Calm
Apex	Bottom
Attract	Repel
Bad	Good
Barren	Fertile
Beautiful	Ugly
Bitter	Sweet
Brave	Cowardly
Brief	Lengthy
Bright	Dull
Calm	Violent
Careful	Careless
Clear	Vague, Cloudy
Cold	Hot
Cruel	Kind
Dear	Cheap
Deep	Shallow
Difficult	Easy
Direct	Indirect
Dishonest	Honest
Disobey	Obey
Encourage	Discourage
Enormous	Tiny
Excellent	Bad
Expensive	Cheap
Eat	Fast
Fair	Unfair
Fake	Authentic
False	True
Famous	Notorious
Fool	Genius
Generous	Miserly
Genius	Fool
Genuine	Unauthentic
Gigantic	Tiny
Glad	Depressed
Good	Bad
Great	Little
Happy	Sad
Hard	Soft
Hate	Love
Honest	Dishonest
Idle	Busy

Words	*Antonyms*
Immoral	Moral
Include	Exclude
Incorrect	Correct
Intelligent	Unintelligent
Kind	Cruel
Like	Dislike
Long	Short
Lucid	Vague
Major	Minor
Naive	Experienced
Nadir	Apex
Neat	Clumsy
Obedient	Disobedient
Obscure	Clear
Oppose	Support
Optimistic	Pessimistic
Out	In
Patience	Impatience
Peaceful	Belligerent
Pious	Impious
Polite	Impolite
Potent	Impotent
Prominent	Unimportant
Proper	Improper
Pure	Impure
Quick	Slow
Quiet	Disturbance
Real	False, Unreal
Reject	Select, Choose
Reliable	Unreliable
Respect	Disrespect
Right	Wrong
Robust	Feeble, Weak
Sad	Happy
Secret	Open
Sensible	Insensible
Severe	Mild
Sharp	Blunt
Simple	Complex
Sociable	Unsociable
Tall	Short
Tidy	Untidy
Uncanny	Canny
Violent	Calm
Vivid	Vague
Strong	Weak
Big	Small
Easy	Difficult
Fast	Slow
High	Low
Catchy	Unattractive
Ugly	Handsome, Beautiful, Tidy
Tasty	Insipid
Sonorous	Harsh

MULTIPLE CHOICE QUESTIONS

Directions (Qs. 1 to 20): *In the following questions choose the word which best expresses the meaning of the given word.*

1. ABSURD
A. Foolish B. Simple
C. Courageous D. Silly

2. ABANDON
A. Lose B. Profit
C. Vacate D. Foil

3. CAJOLE
A. Pause B. Lenient
C. Blast D. Lure

4. COMBAT
A. Fight B. Conflict
C. Shoot D. Quarrel

5. LAMENT
A. Condone B. Console
C. Complain D. Contribution

6. DEBACLE
A. Disgrace B. Defeat
C. Collapse D. Decline

7. SHIVER
A. Fear B. Tremble
C. Shake D. Ache

8. TORTURE
A. Terror B. Harassment
C. Torment D. Tranquility

9. LAUDABLE
A. Lovable B. Commendable
C. Profitable D. Oblivious

10. FIXED
A. Sterile B. Static
C. Stubborn D. Parennial

11. QUEER
A. Unfamiliar B. Cute
C. Curious D. Strange

12. SUFFICIENT
A. Fit B. Proper
C. Adequate D. Vast

13. GLOSS
A. Brightness B. Soothing
C. Rubbing D. Miracle

14. LONGING
A. Prune B. Apathy
C. Curtail D. Craving

15. JEER
A. Applaud B. Magnanimity
C. Avoid D. Scoff

16. ZENITH
A. Minimum B. Nadir
C. Plant D. Peak

17. GARB
A. Distort B. Dress
C. Trivial D. Rage

18. ABHOR
A. Rude B. Reconcile
C. Crave D. Detest

19. YIELD
A. Shum B. Incisive
C. Retain D. Surrender

20. YOKE
A. Twist B. Release
C. Link D. Extra

Directions (Qs. 21 to 26): *In the following questions choose the word which best expresses the opposite of the given word.*

21. TRAGIC
A. Dramatic B. Strong
C. Gentle D. Comic

22. ORAL
A. Verbal B. Sane
C. Minor D. Written

23. ADMIRE
A. Hate B. Unlike
C. Dislike D. Enough

24. VIOLENT
A. Gentle B. Savage
C. Haughty D. Decline

25. ADVERSITY
A. Windfall B. Inprosperity
C. Prosperity D. Slave

26. GENUINE
A. Spurious B. Obscure
C. Countless D. Apathetic

ANSWERS

1	2	3	4	5	6	7	8	9	10
D	C	D	A	C	C	B	C	B	B
11	**12**	**13**	**14**	**15**	**16**	**17**	**18**	**19**	**20**
D	C	A	D	D	D	B	D	D	C
21	**22**	**23**	**24**	**25**	**26**				
D	D	C	A	C	A				

●●●

3

Sentence Completion

It is such an exercise which starts with the primary schools and continues in the highest level of competitive examinations. One must practise it regularly to score well.

Directions (Qs. 1 to 15): *Pick out the most effective word(s) from the given words to fill in the blanks to make the sentence meaningfully complete.*

1. The student ...... that book from the library to study at home.

A. issued B. borrowed
C. hired D. lent

2. I wish I ...... a king.

A. was B. am
C. should be D. were

3. He ...... to listen to my arguments and walked away.

A. denied B. disliked
C. objected D. refused

4. The flow of blood was so ...... that the patient died.

A. intense B. adequate
C. profuse D. extensive

5. When I met her yesterday, it was the first time I ...... her since Christmas.

A. saw B. have seen
C. had seen D. have been seing

6. Can you pay ...... all these articles?

A. for B. of
C. off D. out

7. I ...... you to be at the party this evening.

A. expect B. hope
C. look forward to D. desire

8. ...... being a handicapped person, he is very cooperative and self-reliant.

A. Because B. Although
C. Since D. Despite

9. The child broke ...... from his mother and ran towards the painting.

A. away B. after
C. down D. with

10. With his ...... income, he finds it difficult to live a comfortable life.

A. brief
B. sufficient
C. meagre
D. huge

11. He could ...... a lot of money in such a short time by using his intelligence and working hard.

A. spend
B. spoil
C. exchange
D. accumulate

12. Though the brothers are twins, they look ......

A. alike B. handsome
C. indifferent D. different

13. Unfavourable weather conditions can ..... illness.

A. cure B. detect
C. treat D. enhance

14. No sooner did the bell ring, ... the actor started singing.

A. when B. than
C. after D. before

15. If I ...... realised it, I would not have acted on his advice.

A. was B. had
C. were D. have

Directions (Qs. 16 to 25): *In each question, an incomplete statement (Stem) followed by four fillers is given. Pick out the best one which can complete the incomplete stem correctly and meaningfully.*

16. Unless you work harder you will fail, means .....

A. if you fail you will work harder.
B. you must at least plan well than you will not fail.
C. hardly you will fail if you do not desire so.
D. if you do not put more efforts, then you will fail.

17. Even if it rains I shall come, means .....

A. if I come it will not rain.
B. if it rains I shall not come.
C. I will certainly come whether it rains or not.
D. whenever there is rain I shall come.

18. Dinesh is as stupid as he is lazy means .....

A. Dinesh is stupid because he is lazy.
B. Dinesh is lazy because he is stupid.
C. Dinesh is either stupid or lazy.
D. Dinesh is equally stupid and lazy.

19. He is so lazy that he .....

A. cannot depend on others for getting his work done.
B. cannot delay the schedule of completing the work.
C. can seldom complete his work on time.
D. dislike to postpone the work that he undertakes to do.

20. He always stammers in public meetings, but his today's speech .....
A. was fairly audible to everyone present in the hall.
B. was not received satisfactorily.
C. could not be understood properly.
D. was free from that defect.

21. In order to raise the company's profit, the employees.....
A. demanded two additional increments.
B. decided to go on paid holidays.
C. requested the management to implement new welfare schemes.
D. offered to work overtime without any compensation.

22. Although, he is reputed for making very candid statements, ...
A. his today's speech was not fairly audible.
B. his promises had always been realistic.
C. his speech was very interesting.
D. his today's statements were very ambiguous.

23. I felt somewhat more relaxed .....
A. but tense as compared to earlier.
B. and tense as compared to earlier.
C. as there was already no tension at all.
D. and tension-free as compared to earlier.

24. With great efforts his son succeeded in convincing him not to donate his entire wealth to an orphanage ....
A. and lead the life of a wealthy merchant.
B. but to a home for the forsaken children.
C. and make an orphan of himself.
D. as the orphanage needed a lot of donations.

25. Even though it is a very large house, ...
A. there is a lot of space available in it for children.
B. there is hardly any space available for children.
C. there is no dearth of space for children.
D. the servants take a long time to clean it.

ANSWERS

1	2	3	4	5	6	7	8	9	10
B	D	D	C	C	A	A	D	A	C
11	**12**	**13**	**14**	**15**	**16**	**17**	**18**	**19**	**20**
D	D	D	B	B	D	C	D	C	D
21	**22**	**23**	**24**	**25**					
D	D	D	C	B					

●●●

4

Spotting Errors

The most common errors in English are of spellings, grammar and usage of words. By regular practice, the errors can be easily spotted and minimised.

MULTIPLE CHOICE QUESTIONS

Directions: *In the following questions some of the sentences have errors and some are correct. Find out which part of a sentence has an error, the number of that part is your answer. If a sentence is free from errors, then your answer is D i.e., No error.*

1. (A) Either Ram or/(B) you is responsible/(C) for this action./(D) No error.
2. (A) The student flatly denied/(B) that he had copied/ (C) in the examination hall./(D) No error.
3. (A) By the time you arrive tomorrow/(B) I have finished/ (C) my work./(D) No error.
4. (A) The captain with the members of his team/(B) are returning/(C) after a fortnight./(D) No error.
5. (A) After returning from/(B) an all-India tour/(C) I had to describe about it./(D) No error.
6. (A) The teacher asked his students/(B) if they had gone through/(C) either of the three chapters included in the prescribed text./(D) No error.
7. (A) Do you know/(B) how old were you/(C) when you came here?/(D) No error.
8. (A) Beware of/(B) a fair-weather friend/(C) who is neither a friend in need nor a friend indeed./(D) No error.
9. (A) Copernicus proved/(B) that Earth/(C) moves round the Sun./(D) No error.
10. (A) The property/(B) was divided/(C) among the two brothers./(D) No error.
11. (A) I am quite certain/(B) that the lady is not only greedy/(C) but miserly./(D) No error.
12. (A) The brilliant success in the examination/(B) as well as his record in sports/(C) deserves high praise./(D) No error.
13. (A) I cannot find/(B) where has he gone/(C) though I have tried may best./(D) No error.
14. (A) If I was/(B) the Prime Minister of India/(C) I would work wonders/(D) No error.
15. (A) If it weren't/(B) for you,/(C) I wouldn't be alive today./(D) No error.
16. (A) He looked like a lion/(B) baulked from/(C) its prey./ (D) No error.
17. (A) Widespread flooding/(B) is affecting/(C) large areas of the villages./(D) No error.
18. (A) If we really set to/(B) we can get the whole house/ (C) cleaned in an afternoon./(D) No error.

ANSWERS

1	2	3	4	5	6	7	8	9	10
B	D	B	B	C	C	D	D	B	C
11	**12**	**13**	**14**	**15**	**16**	**17**	**18**	**19**	**20**
C	D	B	A	C	C	C	A	A	C

EXPLANATORY ANSWERS

1. Replace 'is' by 'are'.
2. No error.
3. Replace 'have' by 'would have'.
4. Replace 'are' by 'is'.
5. Replace 'had to describe' by 'described'.
6. Replace 'either' by 'any'.
7. No error.
8. No error.
9. Omit 'that'.
10. Replace 'among' by 'between'.
11. Add 'also'.
12. No error.
13. Replace 'has he' by 'he has'.
14. Replace 'was' by 'were'.
15. Replace 'wouldn't be' by 'would not have been'.
16. Replace 'its' by 'his'.
17. Replace 'areas' by 'area'.
18. Replace 'set to' by 'set on'.

●●●

5

One Word Substitution

There are many single words in English language which can be perfectly used for a number of words. These words help in expressing ideas in a short and correct manner for the right occasion. Such words not only increase the vocabulary but also enable you to economise in the use of words to a great extent.

Multiple Word Expression	*Substitution*
One who always looks towards the bright side of things	Optimist
One who always looks towards the dark side of things	Pessimist
The time when one develops from a child into an adult	Adolescence
The process of growing more plants in order to form a forest.	Afforestation
The science which deals with farming	Agriculture
From some other country or place etc.	Alien
A term, etc. giving more than one meaning	Ambiguous
A vehicle which is used to carry sick persons	Ambulance
An animal which can live both in water and on land	Amphibian
A lawless situation when there is no government	Anarchy
Belonging to the history of thousands of years old	Ancient
Once a year	Annual
A very old object but still valuable	Antique
Words of opposite meanings	Antonyms
Words of similar meanings	Synonyms
Signatures of a famous person	Autograph
A government led by one person with absolute authority	Autocracy
A written work of one's own life history	Autobiography
A person who has never been married	Bachelor
A person usually having no hair on his head	Bald
A place where one can deposit money and get interest	Bank
A person who cuts our hair	Barber
A building/group of buildings where soldiers live	Barracks
A person who makes buns and biscuits	Baker
A person who lives by asking people for food and money without doing any useful job	Beggar
The crime of having married to two persons at the same time	Bigamy
The branch of science which deals with the study of plants	Botany
Able to speak two languages	Bilingual
Able to speak more than two languages	Polyglot
The branch of science which deals with the living organisms	Biology
A powerful snow storm	Blizzard
A great successful book or movie	Blockbuster
A short news on the radio or TV	Bulletin
A system in which the most important works are organised by the government officials	Bureaucracy
A person who has no vision in his eyes	Blind
A page or a series of pages on which the information of days, weeks, months, etc. is given	Calendar
A person who eats human flesh	Cannibal
A complete list of items often arranged alphabetically	Catalogue
A sudden disaster	Catastrophe
A period of 100 years	Century

Multiple Word Expression	*Substitution*
A branch of science which deals with chemicals	Chemistry
A printed leaf usually issued by banks that we sign to carry certain financial deal	Cheque
A person who makes or mends shoes	Cobbler
A group of people who has been chosen by others to make decisions on their own	Committee
A building in which nuns live	Convent
An animal which feeds on other animals	Carnivorous
A person who does criticism	Critic
A person who cannot hear	Deaf
A condition in which one loses a lot of water from one's body because of vomiting, etc.	Dehydration
A system of government in which the people cast their votes to elect their leaders	Democracy
The study of skin problems	Dermatology
A long piece of land covered with sand	Desert
The art of managing relationships between countries	Diplomacy
A piece of information about the words in a book form	Dictionary
A piece of information about the telephone numbers of the people in a book from	Directory
A person in charge of a newspapers, magazine etc.	Editor
A person who thinks he is better than the others	Egoist
To leave your country and settle in some other country	Emigrate
A book or series of books giving almost all knowledge about an area or some persons etc.	Encyclopaedia
Study of insects	Entomology
Time when day and night are of the same duration	Equinox
To sell things out of the country	Export
To purchase things from some other country	Import
A plant or animal no longer in existence	Extinct
A situation when there is a shortage of food for a long period of time	Famine
An amount of money that we pay for some action or services	Fee
Related to women	Feminine
An animal strong and aggressive	Ferocious
A piece of land where plants grow easily from the soil that is favourable to them	Fertile
A work of literature having some imaginary events	Fiction
A large amount of water covering certain area	Flood
A person who sells flowers	Florist
A religious ceremony for burying or cremating a dead person	Funeral
A substance which kills fungus	Fungicide
A person studying or having studied the diseases and the related things of female reproductory system	Gynaecologist
The murder of the person of the same group race or country	Genocide
A substance which kills germs	Germicide
A situation in which many people die because of fire during war	Holocaust
The act of killing a person deliberately	Homicide
A word having the pronunciation as the other one does but it differs in meaning	Homophone
A word having the same spelling as the other one does but it is pronounced in some other way	Homonym
A person who is attracted towards the person of the same sex	Homosexual
Go across and parallel to the ground	Horizontal
A substance which kills the insects	Insecticide
That cannot be corrected	Incorrigible
That cannot be defeated	Invincible
That cannot be eaten	Inedible
That cannot be seen	Invisible
A place in a school or college where books are kept for the benefit of students, teachers etc.	Library
A place in a school or college where scientific experiments are performed	Laboratory

Multiple Word Expression	*Substitution*
An official who is a judge in the lowest court	Magistrate
A piece of music or a book before it is printed	Manuscript
Related to men	Masculine
One who believes in the existence of God	A theist
One who does not believe in the existence of good	An atheist
That can be believed	Credible
That cannot be believed	Incredible
That which dissolves in a solvent	Soluble
That which does not dissolves in a solvent	Insoluble
Hard writing that can be read	Legible
Hard writing that cannot be read	Illegible
A person who does jobs beneficial to mankind	Philanthropist
A person who goes on foot	Pedestrian
A person who fights for his own country	Patriot
An act of killing oneself	Suicide
A woman whose husband is dead	Widow
A man whose wife is dead	Widower
A person who eats vegetarian and non-vegetarian diets	Omnivorous
Something which is everywhere at the same time	Omnipresent
One who knows everything	Omniscient
A child who does not have parents	Orphan
An award etc. given after the death of the person	Posthumous
The place where animals are kept for amusement and to increase the knowledge of the public	Zoo
The science which deals with the study of animals	Zoology

MULTIPLE CHOICE QUESTIONS

Directions: *In questions given below, out of the four alternatives, choose the one which can be substituted for the given words/sentences.*

1. Something that relates to everyone in the world
A. General B. Common
C. Usual D. Universal

2. An expression of mild disapproval
A. Warning B. Denigration
C. Impertinence D. Reproof

3. One who is not easily pleased by anything
A. Maiden B. Medieval
C. Precarious D. Fastidious

4. Murder of a king
A. Infanticide B. Matricide
C. Genocide D. Regicide

5. A remedy for all diseases
A. Stoic B. Marvel
C. Panacea D. Recompense

6. A dramatic performance
A. Mask B. Mosque
C. Masque D. Mascot

7. Study of birds
A. Orology B. Optology
C. Ophthalmology D. Ornithology

8. Ready to believe
A. Credulous B. Credible
C. Creditable D. Incredible

9. Incapable of being seen through
A. Ductile B. Opaque
C. Obsolete D. Potable

10. One who eats everything
A. Omnivorous B. Omniscient
C. Irresistible D. Insolvent

11. A place where bees are kept is called
A. An apiary B. A mole
C. A hive D. A sanctuary

12. One who cannot be corrected
A. Incurable B. Incorrigible
C. Hardened D. Invulnerable

13. One who is in charge of a museum
A. Curator B. Supervisor
C. Caretaker D. Warden

14. Continuing fight between parties, families, clans, etc.
A. Enmity B. Feud
C. Quarrel D. Skirmish

15. A voice loud enough to be heard
A. Audible B. Applaudable
C. Laudable D. Oral

16. A paper written by hand
A. Handicraft B. Manuscript
C. Handiwork D. Thesis

17. Habitually silent or talking little
A. Serville B. Unequivocal
C. Taciturn D. Synoptic

18. To slap with a flat object
A. Chop B. Hew
C. Gnaw D. Swat

19. A person who speaks many languages
A. Linguist B. Monolingual
C. Polyglot D. Bilingual

20. A light sailing-boat built specially for racing
A. Canoe B. Yacht
C. Frigate D. Dinghy

21. A fixed orbit in space in relation to earth
A. Geological B. Geo-synchronous
C. Geo-centric D. Geo-stationary

22. A style in which a writer makes a display of his knowledge
A. Pedantic B. Verbose
C. Pompous D. Ornate

23. A religious discourse
A. Preach B. Stanza
C. Sanctorum D. Sermon

24. A place that provides refuge
A. Asylum B. Sanatorium
C. Shelter D. Orphanage

25. Detailed plan of a journey
A. Travelogue B. Travelkit
C. Schedule D. Itinerary

26. A person who insists on something
A. Disciplinarian B. Stickler
C. Instantaneous D. Boaster

27. A drawing on transparent paper
A. Red print B. Blue print
C. Negative D. Transparency

28. One who believes that all things and events in life are predetermined is a
A. Fatalist B. Puritan
C. Egoist D. Tyrant

29. A school boy who cuts classes frequently is a
A. Defeatist B. Sycophant
C. Truant D. Martinet

30. The act of violating the sanctity of the church is
A. Blasphemy B. Heresy
C. Sacrilege D. Desecration

31. A place where monks live as a secluded community
A. Cathedral B. Diocese
C. Convent D. Monastery

32. One who is fond of fighting
A. Bellicose B. Aggressive
C. Belligerent D. Militant

33. Tending to move away from the centre or axis
A. Centrifugal B. Centripetal
C. Axiomatic D. Awry

34. Words inscribed on tomb
A. Epitome B. Epistle
C. Epilogue D. Epitaph

35. Leave or remove from a place considered dangerous
A. Evade B. Evacuate
C. Avoid D. Exterminate

36. Original inhabitants of a country
A. Abroge B. Aborger
C. Aborgory D. Aborigins

37. Government by the officials
A. Theocracy B. Plutocracy
C. Bureaucracy D. Democracy

38. Incapable of being exhausted
A. Inexhaustible B. Inaexhaustible
C. Exhaustable D. Non-tired

39. A person of good understanding, knowledge and reasoning power
A. Expert B. Intellectual
C. Snob D. Literate

40. One absorbed in his own thoughts and feelings rather than in things outside
A. Scholar B. Recluse
C. Introvert D. Intellectual

ANSWERS

1	2	3	4	5	6	7	8	9	10
D	D	D	D	C	C	D	A	B	A
11	12	13	14	15	16	17	18	19	20
A	B	A	B	A	B	C	D	A	B
21	22	23	24	25	26	27	28	29	30
D	A	D	A	D	B	D	A	C	C
31	32	33	34	35	36	37	38	39	40
D	A	A	D	B	B	C	A	B	C

●●●

6

Spelling Errors

There are thousands of words in English language. It is difficult to remember the spellings and meanings of all at once. Try to learn as many as you can. Use a dictionary regularly.

Directions: *Find the correctly spelt words.*

1. A. Damage B. Dammage C. Damaige D. Dammege
2. A. Efficiant B. Effecient C. Efficient D. Eficient
3. A. Schedule B. Schdule C. Schedale D. Schedeule
4. A. Occurad B. Occurred C. Ocurred D. Occured
5. A. Grieff B. Grief C. Grieef D. Grrief
6. A. Guarantee B. Garuntee C. Guaruntee D. Gaurantee
7. A. Meddicine B. Medicine C. Medicene D. Medicinne
8. A. Benefeted B. Benefitted C. Benifited D. Benefited
9. A. Acommodation B. Acomodation C. Accomodation D. Accommodation
10. A. Querrelsome B. Quarrelsame C. Quarrelsome D. Querralsome
11. A. Sympathetic B. Smypathetic C. Sympothetic D. Sympethetic
12. A. Prograssive B. Progressive C. Progresive D. Prograsive
13. A. Uncivilized B. Uncevilized C. Uncivillized D. Uncevelized
14. A. Extravagant B. Extreragent C. Extreregant D. Extravegent
15. A. Missunderstood B. Miesunderstood C. Misunderstood D. Misunderstod
16. A. Belligerent B. Beligirent C. Belligarant D. Belligerrent
17. A. Astonished B. Astronished C. Astoneshed D. Asstonished
18. A. Sincerely B. Sencerely C. Sincerelly D. Sincerrely
19. A. Rigourous B. Rigerous C. Rigorous D. Regerous
20. A. Satellite B. Sattellite C. Satelite D. Sattelite
21. A. Pesanger B. Passenger C. Pessenger D. Pasanger
22. A. Humurous B. Humorous C. Humoreus D. Humorrous
23. A. Exeggerate B. Exaggerate C. Exadgerate D. Exagerate
24. A. Fariegn B. Forein C. Foriegn D. Foreign
25. A. Excesive B. Excessive C. Exccessive D. Exccesive
26. A. Forcaust B. Forcast C. Forecast D. Forecaste
27. A. Paralleted B. Paralelled C. Parralleled D. Parallelled
28. A. Ocasion B. Occassion C. Occasion D. Ocassion
29. A. Boquet B. Bouquet C. Bouquete D. Bouquette
30. A. Chettering B. Chaterring C. Chattering D. Chatering
31. A. Discourage B. Disscourage C. Discourege D. Discaurage
32. A. Curageous B. Courageous C. Courrageous D. Couregeous
33. A. Abandon B. Abanddon C. Abendon D. Abbandon
34. A. Embarassment B. Emberrassement C. Embarrassment D. Embbaresment
35. A. Eccintric B. Eccentrie C. Eccentric D. Eccintrie
36. A. Occasional B. Occassional C. Occesional D. Occessional
37. A. Querrel B. Querral C. Quarrel D. Quarel
38. A. Contrebution B. Contribution C. Contributtion D. Conterbution

39. A. Desgrace B. Disgrece
C. Disgrice D. Disgrace

40. A. Harassment B. Herassment
C. Harasment D. Harassmient

41. A. Imaginative B. Imeginative
C. Imagenative D. Imaginetive

42. A. Suficient B. Suficiant
C. Sufficient D. Sufficiant

43. A. Adequate B. Edequate
C. Adaquete D. Edaquete

44. A. Exparienced B. Experianced
C. Experienced D. Experrienced

45. A. Flatering B. Fletering
C. Flattering D. Fletaring

46. A. Cuttiveted B. Culltrivated
C. Cultivated D. Caltivated

47. A. Praiceworthy B. Peiseworthy
C. Praiseworthy D. Praisaworthy

48. A. Profesional B. Professionel
C. Professional D. Profissional

49. A. Ameteur B. Amateur
C. Amataur D. Amateor

50. A. Unfevourable B. Unfevaurable
C. Unfavourable D. Unfivourable

ANSWERS

1	2	3	4	5	6	7	8	9	10
A	C	A	B	B	A	B	B	D	C
11	**12**	**13**	**14**	**15**	**16**	**17**	**18**	**19**	**20**
A	B	A	A	C	A	A	A	C	A
21	**22**	**23**	**24**	**25**	**26**	**27**	**28**	**29**	**30**
B	B	B	D	B	C	A	C	B	C
31	**32**	**33**	**34**	**35**	**36**	**37**	**38**	**39**	**40**
A	B	A	C	C	A	C	B	D	A
41	**42**	**43**	**44**	**45**	**46**	**47**	**48**	**49**	**50**
A	C	A	C	A	C	C	C	B	C

●●●

हिन्दी भाषा

(व्याकरण एवं साहित्य)

व्याकरण

'व्याकरण' शब्द का अर्थ है– 'वाक् पृथक्करण-प्रक्रिया'। इसका निर्माण वि+आकरण यानि 'आ' उपसर्ग को 'कृ' धातु में जोड़कर जो रूप निष्पन्न होता है उसमें पुनः लुयुट् प्रत्यय जोड़ने से होता है। व्याकरण से भाषा में अनुशासन बना रहता है। वस्तुतः व्याकरण एक शास्त्र है। व्याकरण का निर्माण भाषा-विशेष के लिए होता है। अर्थात् प्रत्येक भाषा का अपना निजी व्याकरण होता है। इसके द्वारा भाषा विशेष के वर्ण, शब्द, ध्वनि और वाक्य के शुद्ध रूप एवं प्रयोग के नियम का सम्यक् निरूपण किया जाता है। दूसरे शब्दों में, व्याकरण वह शास्त्र है जिसका निर्माण भाषा-विशेष के लिए होता है और जिससे भाषा-विशेष के शुद्ध रूप तथा प्रयोग की नियमावली का ज्ञान होता है।

लिंग

हिन्दी में दो लिंग होते हैं–स्त्रीलिंग और पुल्लिंग। जो शब्द स्त्री जाति का बोध कराते हैं, उन्हें स्त्रीलिंग कहा जाता है, जैसे–राधा, लड़की, पुत्री, पुस्तक, शेरनी, चिड़िया आदि। इसके विपरीत जो शब्द पुरुष जाति का बोध कराते हैं, उन्हें पुल्लिंग कहा जाता है, जैसे–कृष्ण, शेर, बैल, गीदड़, पुत्र, लड़का। ध्यान रहे कि नपुंसक लिंग का प्रयोग संस्कृत में होता है, हिन्दी में नहीं होता।

कुछ शब्द जो प्रायः स्त्रीलिंग ही होते हैं–

(1) ईकारान्त शब्द। जैसे–चिट्ठी, पत्री, लेखनी, बोली, गोली, चोली, डोली इत्यादि।
अपवाद–मोती, घी, जी, पानी आदि शब्द पुल्लिंग हैं।

(2) नदियों के नाम। जैसे–गंगा, यमुना, सरस्वती, रावी इत्यादि। प्रायः सभी नदियों के साथ नदी शब्द का प्रयोग किया जा सकता है।

(3) संस्कृत के स्त्रीलिंग और नपुंसक लिंग जैसे–आशा, माता, दिशा इत्यादि।

(4) राशियों, तिथियों और नक्षत्रों के नाम। जैसे–मेष, वृष, मिथुन, कन्या, तीज, प्रतिपदा, आश्विन, रोहणी आदि।

(5) धातुओं के नाम जैसे–चांदी, मिट्टी, धातु आदि।

(6) कुछ समुदाय वाचक संज्ञाएं। जैसे–सेना, शाला, फौज, टोली, सभा, श्रेणी, कक्षा इत्यादि।

(7) अनाज, दालें इत्यादि। जैसे–अरहर, मकई आदि।

(8) कुछ प्राणीवाचक शब्द। जैसे–भगिनी, गाय, कोयल, चील, मैना, बिल्ली आदि।

कुछ शब्द जो प्रायः पुल्लिंग ही होते हैं–

(1) पर्वतों आदि के नाम। जैसे–हिमालय, शिवालिक, विंध्याचल आदि।

(2) भावनावाचक संज्ञाएं–जिनके अन्त में आव, पन, पा, त्व हों। जैसे–चढ़ाव, बहाव, बड़प्पन, बचपन, रंडापा, बुढ़ापा, महत्व, पुरुषत्व।

(3) महीने और दिनों के नाम। जैसे–ज्येष्ठ, बैसाख, चैत्र, मंगलवार, रविवार।

(4) ग्रहों के नाम। जैसे–मंगल, बुध, राहु, केतु आदि।

(5) वर्णमाला के सभी अक्षर–केवल इ, ई और ऋ को छोड़कर।

(6) संस्कृत के नपुंसक लिंग। जैसे–दही, मधु आदि।

(7) पेड़, अनाज सम्बन्धी शब्द। जैसे–बड़, पीपल, आम, चावल, गेहूँ, बाजरा, उड़द।

(8) द्रव्यवाचक शब्द। जैसे–सोना, तांबा, लोहा, मोती, माणिक आदि।

पुल्लिंग से स्त्रीलिंग बनाने के नियम–

(1) अकारान्त और आकारान्त शब्दों के अन्त में ई जोड़ देने से स्त्रीलिंग बन जाता है। जैसे–

नाना–नानी	लड़का–लड़की	दादा–दादी
चाचा–चाची	पुत्र–पुत्री	देव–देवी
गीदड़–गीदड़ी	कबूतर–कबूतरी	नट–नटी

(2) कुछ आकारान्त शब्दों के अन्त का 'आ' हटा कर 'इया' जोड़ दिया जाता है। जैसे–

चिड़ा–चिड़िया	चूहा–चुहिया	डिब्बा–डिबिया
कुत्ता–कुतिया	बेटा–बिटिया	बूढ़ा–बुढ़िया

(3) कुछ व्यापार-सूचक (अकारान्त, आकारान्त, इकारान्त) शब्दों के पीछे 'इन' प्रत्यय लगाकर स्त्रीलिंग बनाते हैं। जैसे–

जुलाहा–जुलाहिन	धोबी–धोबिन	कहार–कहारिन
चमार–चमारिन	ठठेरा–ठठेरिन	ग्वाला–ग्वालिन

(4) कुछ प्राणीवाचक शब्दों के पीछे 'नी' या 'इनी' प्रत्यय लगाया जाता है। जैसे–

हंस–हंसिनी	जाट–जाटिनी	हाथी–हथिनी
शेर–शेरनी		

(5) कुछ प्राणीवाचक शब्दों के पीछे 'आनी' प्रत्यय भी लगाया जाता है। जैसे–

नौकर–नौकरानी	जेठ–जेठानी	देवर–देवरानी
चौधरी–चौधरानी	सेठ–सेठानी	मेहतर–मेहतरानी

(6) कुछ अकारान्त शब्दों के अन्त में 'आ' प्रत्यय लगाने से, जैसे–

शिव–शिवा	शूद्र–शूद्रा	प्रिय–प्रिया
बाल–बाला	सुत–सुता	

(7) कुछ शब्दों के अन्त में 'वती' या 'मती' लगाने से, जैसे–

भगवान्–भगवती	गुणवान्–गुणवती	श्रीमान्–श्रीमती
रूपवान्–रूपवती	बुद्धिमान्–बुद्धिमती	धनवान्–धनवती

(8) कुछ उपनाम सम्बन्धी शब्दों के अन्त में 'आइन' प्रत्यय लगाने से, जैसे–

लाला–ललाइन	ठाकुर–ठकुराइन	बाबू–बबुआइन
दुबे–दुबाइन	पण्डित–पण्डिताइन	

(9) कुछ शब्दों के अन्त में 'अक' आता है। उनको स्त्रीलिंग बनाने के लिए 'अक' प्रत्यय का 'इका' कर लिया जाता है। जैसे–

अध्यापक–अध्यापिका	सेवक–सेविका	नायक–नायिका
बालक–बालिका	प्रेषक–प्रेषिका	लेखक–लेखिका

(10) कुछ शब्दों के अन्त में 'त्री' लगाने से स्त्रीलिंग बन जाता है। जैसे–

कवि–कवयित्री कर्ता–कर्त्री

(11) कुछ इकारान्त शब्दों के अन्त में 'ई' प्रत्यय को 'इ' करके 'णी' लगाकर स्त्रीलिंग बना लिया जाता है। जैसे–

परोपकारी–परोपकारिणी अधिकारी–अधिकारिणी

सहधर्मी–सहधर्मिणी कल्याणकारी–कल्याणकारिणी

(12) कुछ पुल्लिंग शब्दों के स्त्रीलिंग सर्वथा भिन्न होते हैं, जैसे–

पिता–माता वर–वधु

राजा–रानी विद्वान–विदुषी

वचन

वचन का शाब्दिक अर्थ है- बोली। परन्तु हिन्दी में व्याकरण की दृष्टि में वचन का अर्थ संख्या से लिया जाता है। इसलिए वचन को परिभाषित करते हुए कहा जा सकता है– संज्ञा, सर्वनाम, विशेषण और क्रिया के जिस रूप से संख्या का बोध होता है, उसे वचन कहते हैं।

वचन के भेद

हिन्दी में वचन के दो भेद माने गए हैं (1) एकवचन (2) बहुवचन

(1) एकवचन (Singular Number) : जैसा कि नाम से स्पष्ट है, एकवचन विकारी शब्द का वह रूप है जिससे एक ही व्यक्ति या वस्तु का बोध होता है। उदाहरण- घोड़ा दौड़ता है। गाय चरती है। इन वाक्यों में 'घोड़ा' और 'गाय' से एक जानवर का बोध होता है। अतः ये एकवचन हैं।

(2) बहुवचन (Plural Number) : बहुवचन वह विकारी शब्द है जिससे एक से अधिक वस्तुओं, व्यक्तियों आदि का बोध होता है। जैसे- घोड़े चरते हैं। गायें दौड़ती हैं। 'घोड़े' और 'गायें' कहने से एक से अधिक जानवरों का बोध होता है। अतः ये बहुवचन हैं।

वचन के रूपान्तर : यद्यपि वचन के कारण संज्ञा, सर्वनाम, विशेषण और क्रिया के रूप में परिवर्तन होता है तथापि सर्वनाम, विशेषण और क्रिया के रूप मूलतः इनसे जुड़ी संख्या पर ही आधारित होते हैं। अतएव एकवचन में संज्ञा शब्दों के रूपान्तर की ही प्रमुखता है।

वचन के अधीन संज्ञा के रूप दो तरह से परिवर्तित होते हैं– (1) विभक्ति रहित (2) विभक्ति सहित

विभक्ति रहित संज्ञाओं के बहुवचन बनाने के नियम :

विभक्ति रहित संज्ञाओं का बहुवचन साधारणतः निम्नलिखित नियमों के अन्तर्गत बनाया जाता है-

1. पुल्लिंग संज्ञा के आकारान्त को एकारान्त कर बहुवचन बनाया जाता है। यथा-

एकवचन	बहुवचन	एकवचन	बहुवचन
घोड़ा	घोड़े	गधा	गधे
लड़का	लड़के		

अपवाद- मामा, नाना, बाबा, पिता, योद्धा, आत्मा, देवता, जामाता आदि। इन शब्दों के रूप दोनों वचनों में समान होते हैं।

2. पुल्लिंग आकारान्त शब्दों के अतिरिक्त अन्य मात्राओं से अन्त होने वाले शब्दों के रूप दोनों वचनों में एक समान रहते हैं। जैसे–

एकवचन	बहुवचन	एकवचन	बहुवचन
एक बालक	चार बालक	एक डाकू	चार डाकू
एक भाई	चार भाई	एक जौ	चार जौ

3. आकारान्त स्त्रीलिंग शब्दों के अन्त में 'एँ' जोड़ने से बहुवचन बनता है। जैसे–

एकवचन	बहुवचन	एकवचन	बहुवचन
शाखा	शाखाएँ	लता	लताएँ
माता	माताएँ	महिला	महिलाएँ

4. अकारान्त स्त्रीलिंग संज्ञा के बहुवचन शब्द में आगत अंतिम अ को यें कर देने से बनता है। जैसे–

एकवचन	बहुवचन	एकवचन	बहुवचन
गाय	गायें	रात	रातें
बात	बातें	आँख	आँखें
याद	यादें		

5. दीर्घ या ह्रस्व इकारान्त संज्ञाओं को ह्रस्व इकारान्त कर उनके अन्त में याँ जोड़ देने से बहुवचन बनता है। जैसे–

एकवचन	बहुवचन	एकवचन	बहुवचन
नारी	नारियाँ	पहेली	पहेलियाँ
लड़की	लड़कियाँ	सहेली	सहेलियाँ
नीति	नीतियाँ	नदी	नदियाँ
घड़ी	घड़ियाँ	छड़ी	छड़ियाँ
धोती	धोतियाँ	साड़ी	साड़ियाँ

6. जिन स्त्रीलिंग शब्दों के अन्त में 'या' आता है, 'या' पर चन्द्रबिन्दु लगाकर बहुवचन बनाया जाता है जैसे–

एकवचन	बहुवचन	एकवचन	बहुवचन
बुढ़िया	बुढ़ियाँ	चिड़िया	चिड़ियाँ
गुड़िया	गुड़ियाँ	डिबिया	डिबियाँ
दुनिया	दुनियाँ		

7. ह्रस्व या दीर्घ ऊकारान्त स्त्रीलिंग संज्ञाओं को ह्रस्व उकारान्त बनाकर अन्त में 'एँ' लगाने से बहुवचन का निर्माण होता है। जैसे-

एकवचन	बहुवचन	एकवचन	बहुवचन
धेनु	धेनुएँ	वस्तु	वस्तुएँ
बहू	बहुएँ	ऋतु	ऋतुएँ

8. कुछ शब्द समष्टि मूलक होते हैं। जैसे– गण, कुल, वृन्द, समूह, वर्ग, लोग, जन, मण्डल, दल, ग्राम, मण्डली आदि। ये शब्द विशेषतः वहाँ जोड़े जाते हैं, जहाँ दोनों वचनों में पुल्लिंग अथवा स्त्रीलिंग में एक ही रूप होते हैं।

उदाहरण :

एकवचन	बहुवचन	एकवचन	बहुवचन
पाठक	पाठकगण	आप	आप लोग
तुम	तुम लोग	छात्र	छात्रगण
विद्यार्थी	विद्यार्थीगण		

विभक्ति सहित संज्ञाओं के बहुवचन बनाने के नियम :-

सविभक्ति संज्ञाओं के बहुवचन बनाने के सामान्य नियम निम्नलिखित हैं–

1. संस्कृत शब्दों को छोड़कर हिन्दी के अकारान्त, आकारान्त तथा एकारान्त संज्ञाओं के अन्तिम अ, आ, ए के बदले बहुवचन बनाने में इसे 'ओ' कर दिया जाता है। जैसे-

एकवचन	**बहुवचन**
नर	नरों (का)
चीता	चीतों (द्वारा)
चोर	चोरों (ने)
घोड़ा	घोड़ों (को)

विभक्ति चिह्नों के साथ प्रयोग :

(क) नरों की कहानी।

(ख) चीतों का भय।

(ग) चोरों की पकड़।

(घ) घोड़ों की हिनहिनाहट।

कारक

संज्ञा या सर्वनाम के उस रूप को कारक कहते हैं जिससे उसका सम्बन्ध वाक्य के अन्य शब्दों विशेषतः क्रिया के साथ प्रकट होता है। वास्तव में, विभक्ति चिह्नों से युक्त संज्ञा या सर्वनाम शब्द ही वाक्य में अन्य शब्दों से सम्बन्ध प्रकट करते हैं।

ने, को, से, द्वारा– आदि विभक्ति चिह्न हैं। कारक का एक उदाहरण इस प्रकार है-'मोहन ने बाग में डण्डे से आम तोड़ा।' इस वाक्य में मोहन ने, डण्डे से, और आम संज्ञाओं के रूपान्तरण हैं। जिस तत्त्व के द्वारा इन रूपान्तरित संज्ञाओं का सम्बन्ध तोड़ा, क्रिया से स्पष्ट होता है, वही कारक है।

कारक-चिह्न

हिन्दी में कारक के आठ भेद माने जाते है :

	कारक	**विभक्ति या कारक चिह्न**
1.	कर्त्ता	ने
2.	कर्म	को
3.	करण	से, द्वारा
4.	सम्प्रदान	को, के लिए
5.	अपादान	से
6.	सम्बन्ध	का, के, की, रा, रे, री, ना, ने, नी
7.	अधिकरण	में, पर
8.	सम्बोधन	हे, हो, अरे, अजी, अहो आदि।

कारक-चिह्न/विभक्ति/परसर्ग

हिन्दी में कारक का ज्ञान कराने के लिए संज्ञा या सर्वनाम के साथ जो प्रत्यय लगाये जाते हैं, उन्हें ही व्याकरण में विभक्ति कहते हैं। हिन्दी में चूँकि विभक्ति चिह्न पद से अलग प्रयुक्त होते हैं इसलिए इन्हें 'परसर्ग' भी कहा जाता है। परसर्ग का शब्दिक अर्थ है- पीछे जुड़ना। कारक चिह्न सदैव संज्ञा या सर्वनाम के पीछे जुड़ते हैं।

(i) कर्त्ता कारक : कर्त्ता का अभिप्राय है, करने वाला। वाक्य में जो क्रिया सम्पन्न करता है, उसे कर्त्ता कहा जाता है। जैसे- राम पढ़ता है। सुरेश पत्र लिखता है। इन वाक्यों में राम और सुरेश कर्त्ता कारक हैं क्योंकि ये ही क्रिया को सम्पादित करने वाले हैं।

(ii) कर्म कारक : कर्त्ता द्वारा सम्पादित क्रिया का फल जिस पर पड़ता है, उसे 'कर्म' कहते हैं। जैसे– शीला ने राजेश को पढ़ाया। इस वाक्य में कर्त्ता है- शीला, क्रिया है– पढ़ाना। पढ़ाना क्रिया का फल राजेश पर स्पष्ट पड़ रहा है। इसलिए यहाँ राजेश कर्म कारक की स्थिति में है।

(iii) करण कारक : वाक्य में कारण कारक उस शब्द को कहते हैं जो क्रिया को पूर्ण करने में साधन के रूप में कर्ता का सहायक होकर आता है। जैसे– मैं कलम से लिखता हूँ। इस व्राक्य में 'कलम से' करण कारक है क्योंकि लेखन-क्रिया में कलम साधन है।

(iv) सम्प्रदान कारक : कर्त्ता क्रिया की सिद्धि जिसके लिए करता है अथवा जिसको कुछ देता है, उसे प्रकट करने वाले शब्द रूप को सम्प्रदान कारक कहते हैं। जैसे– श्याम मीरा के लिए खिलौने लाया। राकेश शीला के लिए रोता है। इन वाक्यों में लाना और रोना क्रियाएँ क्रमशः मीरा और शीला के लिए सम्पादित की जा रही हैं। इसलिए मीरा और शीला के लिए शब्द रूप सम्प्रदान कारक है।

संधि

सन्धि शब्द का सामान्य अर्थ है– मेल अथवा मिलन। जब दो निकटवर्ती शब्दों का परस्पर मेल होता है, तो उसे संधि कहते हैं। संधि पहले वाले शब्द के अंतिम वर्ण और दूसरे वाले शब्द के प्रथम वर्ण (दोनों वर्णों) के मिलन से होती है। जब संधि होती है, तो दोनों शब्दों के मेल से बना शब्द (नया वाला शब्द) दोनों शब्दों का सामान्य संयोग मात्र नहीं होता, बल्कि उनके मेल से बना नया शब्द कुछ भिन्न होता है। यह भिन्नता या परिवर्तन उन्हीं दोनों वर्णों में होता है, जिनका मेल होता है। उदाहरण के लिए यदि हम 'हिम' और 'आलय' दोनों शब्दों की संधि करें, तो संधि से बनने वाला शब्द 'हिमालय' होगा। इसी प्रकार 'विद्या' और 'अर्थी' शब्दों की संधि से 'विद्यार्थी' शब्द बनता है।

संधि के मुख्य रूप से तीन भेद हैं– स्वर संधि, व्यंजन संधि और विसर्ग संधि।

(क) स्वर संधिः जब स्वर के साथ स्वर का मेल हो और स्वर में परिवर्तन हो, तो उसे स्वर संधि कहते हैं। उदाहरण के लिए 'छात्र' और आवास में 'त्र' और 'आ' का मेल होकर 'त्रा' बनेगा और संधि के फलस्वरूप बना शब्द 'छात्रावास' होगा।
इसी प्रकार 'रमा' और ईश' के मेल से 'रमेश' बनता है। 'महा' और 'ऋषि' के मेल से 'महर्षि' बनता है। 'यदि' और 'अपि' के मेल से 'यद्यपि' बनता है।

(ख) व्यंजन संधिः जब दो व्यंजनों के मेल से नया शब्द बनता है, तो उसे व्यंजन संधि कहते हैं। जैसे 'जगत' और 'नाथ' के मेल से 'जगन्नाथ' शब्द बनता है। 'तन्' और 'मय' के मेल से 'तन्मय' शब्द बनता है। 'सत्' और 'चित' के मेल से 'सच्चित' शब्द बनता है। 'सम्' और 'राट' के मेल से 'सम्राट' शब्द बनता है।

(ग) **विसर्ग संधिः** जब विसर्ग के साथ व्यंजन का मेल हो तो विसर्ग संधि होती है। जैसे– 'निः' और 'जन' के मेल से 'निर्जन' तथा 'दुः' और 'चरित्र' के मेल से 'दुश्चरित्र' बनता है।

संधि के प्रकार

हिन्दी में संधि के तीन प्रकार हैं–(1) स्वर संधि (2) व्यंजन संधि (3) विसर्ग संधि।

(1) स्वर संधि

दो स्वरों के मेल से जो विकार या वर्ण के रूप में परिवर्तन होता है, वही स्वर संधि कहलाता है।

स्वर संधि के भेदः स्वर संधि के निम्नलिखित पाँच भेद हैं :–

(क) दीर्घ संधि (ख) गुण संधि (ग) वृद्धि संधि (घ) यण् संधि (ङ) अयादि संधि।

(क) **दीर्घ संधिः** जब दो सवर्ण स्वरों का मेल होता है तो एक दीर्घ स्वर बन जाता है। यह दीर्घ संधि है। अ और आ सवर्ण स्वर हैं। इसी प्रकार इ ई उ ऊ और ऋ सवर्ण स्वर हैं। ह्रस्व या दीर्घ अ इ उ ऋ के बाद यदि पूर्ववत् ह्रस्व या दीर्घ स्वर हो तो दोनों के स्थान पर एक सवर्ण दीर्घ स्वर होता है।

जैसे– अ + अ = आ (नर + अधय = नराधय)
अ + आ = आ (कार्य + आलय = कार्यालय)
आ + अ = आ (विद्या + अर्थी = विद्यार्थी)
आ + आ = आ (महा + आशय = महाशय)
इ + इ = ई (मुनि + इन्द्र = मुनीन्द्र)
इ + ई = ई (कपि + ईश = कपीश)
ई + इ = ई (मही + इन्द्र = महीन्द्र)
ई + ई = ई (नदी + ईश = नदीश)
उ + उ = ऊ (साधु + उवाच = साधूवाच)

(ख) **गुण संधिः** अ या आ के बाद यदि इ या ई, उ या ऊ और ऋ आवे तो दोनों के मेल से क्रमशः ए, ओ अर हो जाता है।

जैसे– अ + इ = ए (नर + इन्द्र = नरेन्द्र)
आ + इ = ए (महा + इन्द्र = महेन्द्र)

(ग) **वृद्धि संधिः** अ या आ के बाद यदि ए या ऐ और ओ या औ का आगमन होता है, तो दोनों मिलकर क्रमशः ऐ और औ उत्पन्न करते हैं।

जैसे– अ + ए = ऐ (एक + एक = एकैक)
आ + ए = ऐ (तथा + एव = तथैव)

(घ) **यण संधिः** ह्रस्व या दीर्घ इ, उ, ऋ के अनन्तर यदि कोई असवर्ण स्वर आता है तो 'इ' का य्, उ का व् और ऋ का र् हो जाता है।

जैसे– इ + आ = या (अति + आनन्द = अत्यानन्द)
इ + ए = ये (प्रति + एक = प्रत्येक)

(ङ) **अयादि संधिः** ए ऐ ओ औ के अनन्तर यदि कोई असवर्ण स्वर आये तो ए का अय्, ऐ का आय, ओ का अव् और औ का आव हो जाता है।

जैसे– ए + अ = अय (ने + अन = नयन)
ऐ + अ = आय (नै + अक = नायक)

(2) व्यंजन संधि

व्यंजन संधि उसे कहते हैं जिसमें संधि होने वाले दो वर्णों में से प्रथम वर्ण व्यंजन हो और दूसरा स्वर या व्यंजन हो।

जैसें– दिक् + गज = दिग्गज।

व्यंजन संधि के प्रमुख नियम इस प्रकार हैं–

(क) यदि किसी वर्ण के पहले व्यंजन के अनन्तर किसी वर्ग का पंचम वर्ण आता है तो प्रथम व्यंजन वर्ग का परिवर्तन उसी वर्ग के पंचम वर्ण में होता है।

जैसे– जगत् + नाथ = जगन्नाथ।
वाक् + मय = वाङ्मय।

(ख) यदि म् के बाद किसी स्पर्श वर्ण का आगमन होता है तो म् अनुस्वार में बदल जाता है।

जैसे– किम + चित् = किंचित् या किञ्चित्।
अहम् + कार = अहंकार या अहङ्कार।

(ग) यदि म् के बाद य र ल व (अन्तस्थ) और श ष स ह (ऊष्म) वर्ण हों तो 'म्' अनुस्वार में बदल दिया जाता है।

जैसे– सम् + षय = संशय।
सम् + सार = संसार।

(घ) यदि वर्ग के प्रथम वर्ण के अनन्तर कोई स्वर हो या किसी वर्ग का तृतीय, चतुर्थ व्यंजन हो या य र ल व में से कोई वर्ण आए तो वर्ग के प्रथम वर्ण के स्थान पर तृतीय वर्ण हो जाता है।

जैसे– वाक् + दन्त = वाग्दन्त।
सत् + गति = सद्गति।

(ङ) यदि च अथवा ज के अनन्तर न का आगमन होता है तो दोनों का स्थान ञ ले लेता है।

जैसे– यज् + न = यज्ञ।

(3) विसर्ग संधि

विसर्ग के साथ स्वर अथवा व्यंजन के मेल से उत्पन्न विकार को विसर्ग संधि कहा जाता है।

जैसे– मनः + रथ = मनोरथ।

विसर्ग संधि के प्रमुख नियम

(क) विसर्ग के बाद च् या छ् ट् या ढ् तथा त् या य् आवे तो क्रमशः श, ष हो जाता है।

जैसे– निः + चय = निश्चय
निः + तार = निस्तार

(ख) यदि विसर्ग के बाद श, ष या स आवे तो विसर्ग को उसी परवर्ती सकार में बदल दिया जाता है।

जैसे– दुः + शासन = दुश्शासन

निः + सन्देह = निस्संदेह

(ग) यदि विसर्ग के पूर्व अ आवे और उसके बाद किसी वर्ग का तीसरा चौथा पाँचवां या य र ल व ह में से कोई व्यंजन आवे तो विसर्ग का 'उ' होता है और उ अपने पूर्ववर्ती अ के साथ जुड़कर ओ में रूपान्तरित हो जाता है।

जैसे– सरः + वर = सरोवर।

पयः + धर = पयोधर।

(घ) यदि विसर्ग के बाद र् व्यंजन आवे तो विसर्ग का पूर्ववर्त्ती स्वर दीर्घ हो जाता है साथ ही विसर्ग का लोप हो जाता है।

जैसे– निः + रव = नीरव।

निः + रोग = नीरोग।

(ङ) यदि विसर्ग के पूर्व अकार के अतिरिक्त कोई दूसरा स्वर हो और उसके बाद कोई स्वर हो अथवा किसी वर्ग का तीसरा, चौथा, पाँचवां वर्ण हो तो विसर्ग 'र' में रूपान्तरित होता है।

जैसे– दुः + गन्ध = दुर्गन्ध।

निः + रोग = नीरोग।

समास

अनेक शब्द जब मिलकर एक पद बन जाते हैं तो समास कहलाता है। अर्थात् जब दो या दो से अधिक पद अपने प्रत्ययों या विभक्तियों को छोड़कर मिलते हैं तब उस संयोग को समास कहते हैं।

समास की उपयोगिताः भाषा में समास की उपयोगिता कई दृष्टियों से है–

(क) समास से भाषा में संक्षिप्तता आती है।

(ख) समास से उच्चारण-प्रक्रिया में सहजता का बोध होता है।

(ग) भाषा समास के प्रयोग से चुस्त होती है।

(घ) भाषा के सौंदर्य में वृद्धि समास के प्रयोग से संभव है।

समास के भेद

पदों की प्रधानता को आधार मानकर समास को मुख्यतः चार भागों में विभाजित किया जाता है तथापि छः भेद स्वीकार किये जाते हैं।

(1) अव्ययीभाव समास – पहला पद प्रधान होता है।

(2) तत्पुरुष समास – दूसरा पद प्रधान होता है।

(3) द्वन्द्व समास – दोनों पद प्रधान होते हैं।

(4) बहुव्रीहि समास – कोई भी पद प्रधान नहीं होता है।

नोटः 'कर्मधारय' को तत्पुरुष का एक भेद माना गया है और 'द्विगु' को कर्मधारय का एक भेद माना गया है।

(1) अव्ययीभाव समास

अव्ययीभाव समास का पहला पद क्रिया-विशेषण अव्यय होता है और प्रधानता प्रायः प्रथम पद की ही होती है। जैसे– यथा समय (समय के अनुसार) प्रति वर्ष (प्रत्येक वर्ष)।

अव्ययीभाव समास के अन्तर्गत निम्नलिखित कोटि के पद आते हैं–

(क) अव्यय शब्दों के योग से बनने वाले समास– आचरण, व्यर्थ, यावज्जीवन, प्रतिदिन, यथा-संभव, आदि।

(ख) शब्दों की द्विरुक्ति से भी अव्ययीभाव समास बनता है। जैसे– वन-वन, घर-घर, मन्दिर-मन्दिर आदि।

(ग) द्विरुक्ति शब्दों के बीच में कभी-कभी ही, आ, ओं भी प्रयुक्त होते हैं। जैसे–एका-एक, हाथों-हाथ, मन-ही-मन आदि।

(2) तत्पुरुष समास

जिस समस्त पद में द्वितीय या अंतिम पद की प्रधानता को स्वीकारा जाता है उनमें तत्पुरुष समास होता है। जैसे :– राज-भवन (राजा का **भवन**)। उत्तर पद भवन प्रधान है।

तत्पुरुष समास के भेद

(i) व्यधिकरण तत्पुरुष– यह वास्तव में तत्पुरुष समास होता है।

(ii) समानाधिकरण तत्पुरुष– इस समास को कर्मधारय समास कहते हैं।

समस्त पदों में जिस कारक या विभक्ति चिह्न का लोप होता है उसी के आधार पर उसका नामकरण किया जाता है। तत्पुरुष समास में प्रथम पद कारक की स्थिति में होता है। इसके निम्नलिखित भेद हैं-

(क) कर्म तत्पुरुषः प्रथम पद कर्मधारय की स्थिति में होता है तथा कर्म की विभक्ति 'को' का लोप हो जाता है।

जैसे– गगन चुम्बी (गगन को चूमने वाला)

माखन चोर (माखन को चुराने वाला)

(ख) करण तत्पुरुषः प्रथम पद करण कारक की स्थिति में होता है और करण की विभक्ति चिह्न 'से' द्वारा 'के साथ' का लोप होता है।

जैसे– ईश्वर दत्त (ईश्वर द्वारा दत्त)

विश्व बन्ध (विश्व द्वारा बन्ध)

(ग) सम्प्रदान तत्पुरुषः प्रथम पद सम्प्रदान कारक में रहता है तथा सम्प्रदान की विभक्ति 'को', 'के लिए', 'निमित्त', 'हेतु' आदि का लोप होता है।

जैसे– स्वाधीनता संग्राम (स्वाधीनता के लिए संग्राम)

(घ) अपादान तत्पुरुषः इसमें भी प्रथम पद अपादान कारक में होता है तथा अपादान कारक के विभक्ति चिह्न 'से' का लोप हो जाता है।

जैसे– धर्म विमुख (धर्म से विमुख)

(ङ) सम्बन्ध तत्पुरुषः इसका पूर्व पद सम्बन्ध कारक में होता है तथा सम्बन्ध के विभक्ति चिह्न का, के, की का लोप होता है।

जैसे– वन मानुष (वन का मानुष)

(च) **अधिकरण तत्पुरुषः** अधिकरण तत्पुरुष में पहला पद अधिकरण कारक में होता है तथा अधिकरण कारक का विभक्ति चिह्न 'में' या 'पर' आदि का बोध होता है।

जैसे– आपबीती (आप पर बीती)

(3) द्वन्द्व समास

द्वन्द्व समास में दोनों ही पद प्रधान होते हैं और समस्त पद में दोनों पद संज्ञा या उसका समूह होता है। स्मरणीय है कि इसमें 'और', 'वा' 'अथवा', समुच्चय बोधक का लोप रहता है। इस समुच्चय बोधक के द्वारा दोनों पद जुड़े रहते हैं। द्वन्द्व समास के सामान्यतः निम्नलिखित भेद होते हैं :–

(क) **इतरेतर द्वन्द्वः** इतरेतर द्वन्द्व में समस्त पदों के बीच 'और' समुच्चय बोधक का लोप होता रहता है।

जैसे– माता-पिता (माता और पिता)
सीता-राम (सीता और राम)
देवर-भाभी (देवर और भाभी)

(ख) **समाहार द्वन्द्वः** समाहार द्वन्द्व में समस्त पद अपने अर्थ के अलावा उसी रूप के अन्य अर्थ का भी आभास देता है।

जैसे– नमक-रोटी (नमक और रोटी के अतिरिक्त और भी उसी कोटि की खाद्य-सामग्री) रुपया-पैसा, धन-दौलत, सेठ-साहूकार, मान-मर्यादा।

(ग) **वैकल्पिक द्वन्द्वः** वैकल्पिक द्वन्द्व में दोनों पदों के मध्य 'थ' और 'अथवा' समुच्चय बोधक का लोप रहता है। इस समस्त पद में साधारणतः दो परस्पर विरोधी शब्दों का योग होता है।

जैसे– मान-अपमान, धर्म-अधर्म, ज्ञान-अज्ञान, पाप-पुण्य, चार-छः, दो-चार, जात-कुजात, भला-बुरा।

(4) बहुब्रीहि समास

बहुब्रीहि समास उस समास को कहते हैं जिसमें दोनों ही पद अप्रधान होते हैं। उसमें एक नये अर्थ का संकेत मिलता है।

जैसे– चन्द्रशेखर (चन्द्रमा है शिखर पर जिसके अर्थात् शिव)
चतुर्भुज (चार भुजाएँ हैं जिनकी अर्थात् विष्णु)
गजानन (गज के समान मुख है जिसका अर्थात् गणेश)

(5) कर्मधारय (समानाधिकरण तत्पुरुष)

कर्मधारय समास में दोनों पद प्रधान होते हैं। इसके पदों में विशेषज्ञ-विशेषण, विषेशज्ञ-विशेषण, उपमान-उपमेय का भाव होता है।

जैसे– शशिमुख (शशि सम मुख), नीलाम्बर, पीताम्बर।

कर्मधारय के प्रकार– कर्मधारय के मुख्यतः दो भेद हैं– (1) विशेषता वाचक (2) उपमान वाचक।

(1) **विशेषता वाचक**

विशेषण पूर्वपदः पहला पद विशेषण होता है। जैसे– पीताम्बर, नीलकण्ठ, सुन्दर लाल, सद्गुण, खुशबू, बदबू, काली मिर्च, नीलगाय, छुटभैया।

विशेषणोत्तर पदः इसमें उत्तरपद विशेषण होता है। जैसे– पुरुषोतम, प्रभुदयाल, रामदहिन, देशान्तर, मुनीश्वर, युगान्तर, नराधम, जन्मान्तर।

विशेषणोभय पदः दोनों ही पद विशेषण होते हैं। जैसे– नील-पीत, मोटा ताजा, लाल पीला, श्याम सुन्दर, श्वेत-श्याम, भला-बुरा, खट्टा-मिट्ठा।

विशेष्योभय पदः दोनों ही पद विशेष्य होते हैं। जैसे– प्राणप्रिय, वज्रदेह।

(२) **विशेषता वाचक**

उपमानोत्तर पदः उत्तर पद उपमान होता है। जैसे– मुखारविन्द, राजर्षि।

(6) द्विगु समास

द्विगु समास कर्मधारय समास का एक भेद है। इस समास में पहला पद संख्या बोधक होता है और द्वितीय पद प्रधान होता है। संख्यावाची शब्द समुदाय (समाहार) के अर्थ में प्रयुक्त होता है।

जैसे–नवरत्न (नवरत्नों का समूह), अष्टाध्यायी (आंठ अध्यायों का समाहार), त्रिभुवन, तिमाही, पंसेरी, सप्तशती, त्रिकाल, चौमाल।

वर्तनी

हिन्दी शब्दों को लिखने में वर्तनी का बड़ा महत्व है। प्रायः विद्यार्थी लिखने में वर्तनी सम्बन्धी अशुद्धियां करते हैं। ये अशुद्धियाँ संयुक्त वर्ण, विभक्ति चिह्न, क्रिया पद में तो होती ही है साथ ही, व ब तथा श ष स में भी देखने को मिलती हैं। इन अशुद्धियों से बचने का सही उपाय है कि शुद्ध वर्तनी का ज्ञान हो। और यह निरन्तर अभ्यास से ही सम्भव है।

पर्यायवाची

एकार्थ बोधक शब्दों को पर्यायवाची शब्द कहा जाता है। पर्यायवाची शब्दों में से कुछ पूर्ण पर्याय तथा कुछ अपूर्ण पर्याय की श्रेणी में आते हैं। पूर्ण पर्याय—कपि, वानर, मर्कट, प्लवंग आदि बन्दर के पर्याय हैं। अपूर्ण पर्याय—कृपा, दया, करुणा को कहा जाता है, किन्तु इनके प्रयोग में बहुत अन्तर है। भाषा के सूक्ष्म अध्ययन की दृष्टि से अपूर्ण पर्यायों के मध्य सूक्ष्म अन्तर होता है। इस अन्तर को देखते हुए ही उनका प्रयोग किया जाता है। हिन्दी के शब्द-भंडार की पर्याप्त वृद्धि हुई है। इस दिशा में डॉ. रघुवीर जैसे भाषा-पंडितों ने बहुत काम किया है। भारत सरकार का केन्द्रीय हिन्दी निदेशालय, अनुवाद ब्यूरो तथा राजभाषा विधायी आयोग आदि संस्थाओं द्वारा किए जा रहे शब्द रचना के कार्य सराहनीय हैं। हमारे देश में संस्कृत समृद्ध भाषा है जिससे हिन्दी को बहुत-से शब्द प्राप्त हुए हैं, अतएव पर्यायवाची शब्दों की दृष्टि से हिन्दी समृद्ध है।

विलोमार्थी शब्द

ऐसे शब्दों को विपरीतार्थक, विलोमार्थी अथवा विरोधी शब्द कहा जाता है जो किसी शब्द के ठीक विपरीत अर्थ प्रकट करते हैं। अंग्रेजी में जिन

शब्दों को एण्टानिम्स (Antonyms) कहा जाता है हिन्दी में वही शब्द विलोमार्थी अथवा प्रतिकूल अर्थ के बोधक कहे जाते हैं। अतएव विलोमार्थी शब्दों को यदि हम परिभाषाबद्ध करना चाहें तो कह सकते हैं कि—'किसी एक शब्द के ठीक विपरीत अर्थ प्रकट करने वाले शब्द विलोम कहे जाते हैं। इन शब्दों को विपर्याय के रूप में भी जाना जाता है।'

विलोमार्थी शब्दों का महत्त्व

भाषा कोई भी क्यों न हो उसकी सम्पन्नता उसके शब्दों की संख्या से जानी जाती है। आज विश्व में सर्वाधिक सम्पन्न भाषा अंग्रेजी है जिसके शब्दों का निरंतर वार्धक्य होता जाता है। नये-नये विज्ञानों का प्रादुर्भाव होने से उससे सम्बन्धित शब्द भी गढ़े जाते हैं। और उन शब्दों के प्रतिकूल शब्दों की आवश्यकता भी अनुभव की जाती है। नतीजतन शब्दों का सृजन अनवरत गति से चलता रहा है। हिन्दी में भी यह काम काफी द्रुतगति से हो रहा है। कोई माने या न माने किन्तु जब से केन्द्र में हिन्दी को राजभाषा का गरिमामय पद मिला है तब से उसके विकास की गति भी बढ़ी है। विभिन्न क्षेत्रों में उसका प्रवेश हो रहा है। विज्ञान, इंजीनियरी, चिकित्साशास्त्र, आणविकी आदि सभी से सम्बन्धित शब्दों की रचना हिन्दी में अबाध गति से की जा रही है। ये सब प्रभावी लक्षण हैं। शब्दों के समानार्थी तथा विपरीतार्थी दोनों की जरूरत पड़ती रहती है और आज के युग में जबकि प्रतियोगिता का महत्त्व काफी बढ़ गया है विपरीतार्थी शब्द भी किसी के भाषाई ज्ञान की माप करने में उपादेय सिद्ध होते हैं।

इसके अतिरिक्त विपरीतार्थक शब्द किन्हीं दो अच्छी या बुरी वस्तुओं की तुलना करने के लिए भी काफी उपादेय सिद्ध होते हैं। ऐसे शब्दों के प्रयोग से भाषा में निखार आता है, भाषण प्रभावशाली बन जाता है तथा लेखन गरिमावान दिखाई पड़ने लगता है।

श्रुति समभिन्नार्थक शब्द

युग्म शब्द को श्रुतिसम भिन्नार्थक या समोच्चरित शब्द भी कहा जाता है। इस प्रकार के दो शब्दों में मामूली-सा अन्तर होता है। वह अन्तर मात्रागत या वर्णगत होता है। फलतः ऐसे शब्द सुनने में एक समान तो लगते हैं लेकिन अर्थ भिन्न-भिन्न होते हैं। हिन्दी में ऐसे शब्दों की संख्या अत्यधिक है। नीचे वैसे प्रमुख शब्द युग्मों को अर्थ सहित प्रस्तुत किया जा रहा है :

1. अंश = भाग/हिस्सा
   अंस = कन्धा
2. अपेक्षा = आवश्यकता/उम्मीद
   उपेक्षा = अवहेलना
3. अभिराम = सुन्दर
   अविराम = लगातार
4. अनल = आग
   अनिल = हवा
5. अवलम्ब = आश्रय/सहारा
   अविलम्ब = शीघ्र
6. अन्त = समाप्त/खतम
   अन्त्य = अन्तिम
7. अभिहित = कथित
   अविहित = अनुचित
8. अम्बुज = कमल
   अम्बुद = बादल
9. अलि = भ्रमर
   अली = सखी
10. उपकार = भलाई
    अपकार = बुराई
11. अजिक = ललाट
    अलीक = झूठ
12. अभिनय = स्वांग
    अविनय = उद्दण्डता
13. अतल = तलहीन
    अतुल = जिसकी तुलना न हो सके
14. अकथ = जो कहा नहीं जाय
    अथक = बिना थके हुए
15. अन्न = अनाज
    अन्य = दूसरा
16. आदि = आरम्भ/शुरू
    आदी = अभ्यस्त, अदरक
17. अभय = निर्भय
    उभय = दोनों
18. अर्जन = संग्रह
    अर्चन = पूजा
19. अमित = अत्यधिक
    अमीत = शत्रु
20. अणु = सूक्ष्म कण
    अनु = पीछे
21. अशक्त = असमर्थ
    असक्त = विरक्त
22. अब्ज = कमल
    अब्द = बादल
23. अवधि = समय
    अवधी = अवध की भाषा
24. अभ्यास = अनुशीलन
    अभ्याश = पड़ोस
25. आभरण = आभूषण
    आमरण = मरण तक
26. आकर = खान
    आकार = आकृति
27. आयत = चतुर्भुज
    आयात = बाहर से लाना
28. आर्त = दुःखी
    आर्द्र = गीला

29. आवास = वास स्थान
आभास = झलक
30. आवृत्त = घिरा हुआ
आवृत्ति = दुहराना
31. इत्र = सुगन्धित पदार्थ
इतर = दूसरा
32. स्त्री = महिला
इस्तिरी = कपड़े पर कलप करना
33. अरि = दुश्मन
अरी = स्त्री के लिए सम्बोधन
34. उद्यत = तैयार, तत्पर
उद्धत = उद्दण्ड
35. ॠतु = मौसम
ॠत = सत्य
36. कश = चाबुक
कष = कसौटी
37. कुल = वंश
कूल = किनारा
38. कलि = कलियुग
कली = अधखिला फूल
39. कपिश = मटमैला
कपीश = बन्दरों का राजा
40. कर्म = कार्य
क्रम = सिलसिला
41. कंगाल = दरिद्र
कंकाल = ठठरी (मानव की)
42. कटिबद्ध = तैयार
कटिबन्ध = कमर बन्द
43. करोड़ = सौ लाख की संख्या
क्रोड़ = गोद
44. कृत = किया हुआ
क्रीत = खरीदा हुआ
45. कृपण = कंजूस
कृपाण = कटार
46. कृषाण = किसान
कृशानु = आम
47. क्रान्ति = उलटफेर, आन्दोलन
कांति = चमक
48. कुट = किला
कूट = पहाड़ की चोटी
49. कुजन = दुर्जन
कूजन = पक्षियों का कलरव
50. केशर = सिंह की गर्दन के बाल
केसर = कुमकुम
51. कोष = खजाना
कोश = शब्द-संग्रह
कोस = दो मील की दूरी
52. खाद = उर्वरक
खाद्य = खाने की सामग्री
53. खोया = भूल गया
खोआ = दूध से निर्मित खाद्य पदार्थ
54. गिरि = पर्वत
गिरी = बीज/गूदा
55. चषक = प्याला
चसक = आदत
56. चरण = पैर
चारण = भाट
57. चिर = पुराना
चीर = वस्त्र
58. चिता = शव जलाने के लिए लकड़ियों की शय्या
चीता = एक हिंसक पशु
59. गृह = घर
ग्रह = नक्षत्र
60. करण = इन्द्रियाँ, करण कारक
कर्ण = कान
61. कुच = स्तर
कूच = प्रस्थान
62. कौर = ग्रास
कोर = किनारा
63. चतुष्पद = चौपाया
चतुष्पथ = चौराहा
64. चक्रवात = बवंडर
चक्रवाक = चकवा पक्षी
65. छत्र = छाता
छात्र = विद्यार्थी
66. क्षति = हानि
क्षिति = पृथ्वी
67. जलज = कमल
जलद = बादल
68. नीरज = कमल
नीरद = बादल
69. जघन्य = गर्हित
जघन = जाँच
70. जगत् = संसार
जगत = कुएँ का चबूतरा
71. जामन = दूध जमाने के लिए प्रयुक्त पदार्थ
जामुन = एक फल
72. जेठ = वर्ष का एक महीना
ज्येष्ठ = बड़ा (उम्र में)
73. टुक = थोड़ा
टूक = टुकड़ा
74. टोटा = घाटा
टोंटा = बन्दूक का कारतूस

75. तरणि = सूर्य
तरणी = नाव
76. दाई = धामी, नौकरानी
दायी = जवाबदेह
77. दारु = लकड़ी
दारू = शराब
78. दिवा = दिन
दीया = दीपक
79. दिन = दिवस
दीन = गरीब
80. द्विप = हाथी
द्वीप = टापू
81. दुर्ग = गढ़
दुर्गा = एक देवी
82. दमन = दबाना
दामन = आँचल
83. तक्र = मट्ठा
तर्क = बहस
84. द्रव्य = धन
द्रव = तरल पदार्थ
85. देव = देवता
दैव = भाग्य
86. नहर = कृत्रिम नदी
नाहर = सिंह
87. नग = पहाड़
नाग = सर्प
88. नगर = शहर
नागर = चतुर व्यक्ति
89. नाश = ध्वंश
नास = सुंघनी
90. नारी = स्त्री
नाड़ी = नब्ज
91. निसान = झण्डा
निशान = चिह्न, प्रतीक
92. निर्जर = देवता
निर्झर = झरना
93. निहित = छिपा हुआ
निहत = मरा हुआ
94. नियत = निश्चित
नीयत = इरादा
नियति = भाग्य
95. नमित = नत
निमित्त = कारण
96. नीर = जल
नीड़ = घोंसला
97. निर्माण = बनाना
निर्वाण = मोक्ष
98. नकल = अनुकरण
नकुल = नेवला, पाण्डवों में एक
99. निधन = मृत्यु
निर्धन = गरीब
100. नित = प्रतिदिन
नीत = लाया हुआ
101. नीम = एक पेड़
नींव = आधार
102. नेत्र = आँख
नेतृ = नेता
103. पुरुष = मर्द
परुष = कठोर
104. परिधान = वस्त्र
प्रधान = मुख्य
105. पवन = हवा
पावन = पवित्र
106. पाहन = पत्थर
पाहुन = अतिथि
107. परवाह = चिन्ता
प्रवाह = बहाव
108. प्रहर = समय
प्रहार = चोट
109. परिताप = दुःख
प्रताप = पराक्रम
110. पथ = मार्ग
पथ्य = रोगी का भोजन
111. पट्ट = तख्ता
पट = वस्त्र
112. प्रमाण = सबूत
प्रणाम = नमस्कार
113. परिणाम = फल
परिमाण = मात्रा
114. प्रणय = प्रेम
परिणय = विवाह
115. परदेश = दूसरा देश
प्रदेश = प्रान्त, राज्य
116. परीक्षा = इम्तहान
परिक्षा = कीचड़
117. प्रदीप = दीपक
प्रतीप = उल्टा
118. पानी = जल
पाणि = हाथ
119. पास = निकट
पाश = बन्धन
120. पिक = कोयल
पीक = पान का थूक

121. प्रेषित	=	भेजा हुआ
प्रोषित	=	प्रवासी
122. फन	=	कला
फण	=	साँप का फण
123. बलि	=	बलिदान
बली	=	वीर
124. बहन	=	भगिनी
वहन	=	ढोना
125. बहु	=	बहुत
बहू	=	पुत्रवधू
126. बार	=	दफा
वार	=	दिन
127. वाण	=	तीर
बान	=	आदत
128. बात	=	वचन
वात	=	हवा
129. भवन	=	घर
भुवन	=	संसार
130. भट	=	योद्धा
भट्ट	=	पण्डित
131. भाल	=	ललाट
भार	=	वजन
132. मल	=	गन्दगी
मल्ल	=	पहलवान
133. मणि	=	रत्न
मणी	=	सर्प
134. मद	=	अहंकार
मद्य	=	शराब
135. मनुज	=	मनुष्य
मनोज	=	कामदेव
136. मांस	=	गोश्त
मास	=	महीना
137. मात्र	=	केवल
मातृ	=	माता
138. मेध	=	यज्ञ
मेघ	=	बादल
139. मेदा	=	पेट
मैदा	=	बारीक आटा
140. रत	=	तल्लीन
रक्त	=	खून
141. रेचक	=	दस्तावर
रोचक	=	रूचिकर
142. लक्ष	=	लाख
लक्ष्य	=	उद्देश्य
143. लवण	=	नमक
लवन	=	खेत के फसल की कटाई

144. वस्तु	=	चीज
वास्तु	=	इमारत, भवन
145. अकुल	=	बिना कुल के
आकुल	=	व्याकुल
146. वरद	=	वर देने वाला
विरद	=	यश
147. वरण	=	चुनना
वरन्	=	बल्कि
148. वाद	=	विचार/सिद्धान्त
वाद्य	=	बाजा
149. वदन	=	मुख
बदन	=	शरीर
150. विस्मृत	=	भूला हुआ
विस्मित	=	आश्चर्य में पड़ा हुआ
151. विपिन	=	जंगल
विपन्न	=	दु:खी, निर्धन
152. वित्त	=	धन
वृत्त	=	गोलाकार
153. विष	=	जहर
विस	=	कमल का डण्ठल
बीस	=	उन्नीस से एक अधिक संख्या
154. सम	=	समान
शय	=	संचय
155. सहर	=	सबेरा
शहर	=	नगर
156. शव	=	लाश
शब	=	रात
157. सिता	=	चीनी
सीता	=	जानकी
158. शस्त्र	=	हथियार
शास्त्र	=	ग्रन्थ
159. सर	=	तालाब
शर	=	बाण
160. सुर	=	देवता
सूर	=	अंधा
शूर	=	वीर
161. सुत	=	बेटा
सूत	=	सारथी, धागा
162. सप्त	=	सात
शप्त	=	शाप ग्रस्त
163. शंकर	=	शिव
संकर	=	दोगला
164. सर्ग	=	काव्य का अध्याय
स्वर्ग	=	कल्पित लोक
165. स्वपच	=	स्वयंवाकी
श्वपच	=	चाण्डाल

166. सत्व = सार
स्वत्व = अधिकार
167. समिति = सभा
सम्मति = सलाह
168. शय्या = बिछावन
सज्जा = सजावट
169. संग = साथ
संघ = समिति, संगठन
170. शाला = घर
साला = पत्नी का भाई
171. सबल = ताकतवर
शवल = चितकबरा
172. सर्व = सभी
शर्व = शंकर
173. सुगन्ध = खुशबू
सौगन्ध = कसम
174. शुक्ति = सीप
सूक्ति = अच्छी उक्ति
175. शीशा = काँच
सीसा = एक धातु
176. सती = पतिव्रता नारी
शती = शताब्दी
177. श्वेत = सफेद
श्वेद = पसीना
178. शुक = सुग्गा
शूक = जौ
179. शिखर = चोटी (पर्वत की)
शेखर = सिर
180. शक्ल = चेहरा
सकल = सम्पूर्ण
181. हरि = विष्णु
हरी = हरे रंग की
182. सुमन = फूल
सुअन = पुत्र
183. संदेह = शक
संदेह = सशरीर
184. स्व = अपना
श्व = आने वाला दिन
185. शुचि = पवित्र
सूची = विषय क्रम
186. सुधि = स्मरण
सुधी = समझदार, विद्वान्
187. हल = जोतने का यंत्र
हल् = शुद्ध व्यंजन
188. भंगि = लहर
भंगी = मेहतर

189. दूत = संवाददाता
द्यूत = जुआ का खेल
190. देश = राज्य
द्वेष = शत्रुता
191. तरंग = लहर
तुरंग = घोड़ा
192. चालक = ड्राइवर
चालाक = चतुर
193. लोम = रोवाँ
लोभ = लालच
194. बिना = रहित, अभाव
वीणा = एक वाद्य यंत्र
195. प्रसाद = कृपा
प्रासाद = महल
196. भित्ति = दीवार
भीति = डर
197. मूल = जड़
मूल्य = दाम
198. अक्ष = धुरी
यक्ष = एक देव योनि
199. अश्व = घोड़ा
अश्म = पत्थर
200. आसन = बैठने की वस्तु
अशन = भोजन
201. अह = दिन
अहि = साँप
202. अणि = सूई की नोक
अनी = फौज
203. दारा = पत्नी
द्वार = दरवाजा
204. पृथा = कुन्ती
प्रथा = रीति
205. श्रवण = कान
स्रवंन = बहना
206. श्याम = श्री कृष्ण
स्याम = एक देश
207. वृन्द = समूह
वृन्त = डण्ठल
208. मित = थोड़ा
मित्र = दोस्त
209. दुरति = पाप
दुरत = छिपा
210. चार = चार की संख्या
चारु = सुन्दर

वाक्यों की शुद्धता

वाक्य में शब्दों के प्रयोग पर हमें विशेष ध्यान रखना चाहिए। प्रत्येक शब्द का अपना एक विशेष अर्थ होता है। एक ही अर्थ देने वाले कई शब्द हो सकते हैं, किन्तु हमें ध्यान रखना चाहिए कि किस प्रसंग में कौन-सा शब्द प्रयुक्त होगा और कौन-सा शब्द वहां उपयुक्त नहीं बैठेगा। अनुपयुक्त शब्द का प्रयोग करने से अर्थ-भ्रान्ति पैदा होती है। शब्दों का ठीक प्रयोग करने से अभीष्ट अर्थ निकलेगा।

अशुद्धियों के कारणों का विश्लेषण करने के बाद हम देख सकते हैं कि वर्तनी की गलतियाँ होती हैं। ह्रस्व और दीर्घ मात्राओं की गलतियां होती हैं, संयुक्ताक्षरों की गलतियां होती हैं और वाक्यों के निर्माण में भी गलतियाँ होती हैं। मोटे तौर पर हम कह सकते हैं कि वर्ण, शब्द और वाक्य तीनों प्रकार की अशुद्धियाँ देखने को मिलती हैं। इन अशुद्धियों के कारण भाषा दूषित हो जाती है। यदि हम थोड़ी सी सावधानी बरतें, तो हम ऐसी अशुद्धियों से बच सकते हैं।

वाक्यांश के लिए एक शब्द

कथन में लम्बे-लम्बे वाक्यों का प्रयोग करने तथा शब्दों को परिभाषित करने के बजाय यदि एक शब्द का प्रयोग किया जाए तो कथन स्वत: संक्षिप्त और स्पष्ट हो जाता है। कुशल साहित्यकार अपनी रचनाओं में शब्दों का अपव्यय नहीं करते। वाक्य या वाक्यांश के लिए एक शब्द का प्रयोग कथन में आकर्षण और सौन्दर्य भर देता है। हिन्दी भाषा की यह विशेषता है कि उसे संस्कृत शब्दों का प्रचुर भण्डार सुलभ है। इसलिए हिन्दी भाषा कोश में ऐसे अनेक तत्सम शब्द हैं जो वाक्य या वाक्यांश के लिए प्रयोग में लाए जाते हैं।

अपने आशय और मन्तव्य को संक्षेप में प्रकट करने के लिए ही ऐसे शब्दों को गढ़ा गया है जिन्हें गागर में सागर कहा जा सकता है।

इसीलिए अपनी भाषा को समर्थ, प्रभावी तथा आकर्षक बनाने के लिए ऐसे शब्दों की जानकारी रखना नितान्त आवश्यक होता है। भाषा में शक्ति के स्रोत उसके शब्द माने जाते हैं। यहाँ इसी उद्देश्य से अनेक ऐसे शब्द संजोए गए हैं जिनका अर्थ पूरे वाक्य या वाक्यांश द्वारा ही स्पष्ट होता है। इनसे न केवल पाठकों के शब्द भण्डार में वृद्धि होगी वरन् वे हिन्दी भाषा लिखने में भी कुशल बन सकेंगे।

मुहावरा एवं लोकोक्तियां

मुहावरे

मुहावरा ऐसा शब्द-समूह होता है, जो अपने शब्दों के निहित अर्थ न देकर उससे भिन्न, किन्तु एक रूढ़ अर्थ देता है। मुहावरा अभिधेय अर्थ का अनुसरण नहीं करता : वह अपना विलक्षण अर्थ प्रकट करता है। चूँकि मुहावरा लोक-मानस की स्वाभाविक अभिव्यक्ति होता है, अत: इसमें दुरूहता नहीं होती। मुहावरा अपने लोक-परम्परागत रूप में ही शोभायमान और सार्थक होता है। इसका रूप और अर्थ दोनों ही प्राय: रूढ़ होते हैं।

मुहावरे का सम्बन्ध साहित्य से कम और भाषा से अधिक होता है। यह भाषा के सामर्थ्य का प्रतीक होता है। इसका सटीक अर्थ और निर्दिष्ट अर्थ होता है। मुहावरों के माध्यम से भाषा ऊर्जस्वी बनती है और अर्थ का सटीक सम्प्रेषण होता है। मुहावरेदार भाषा असरदार होती है।

मुहावरे एक दृष्टि से 'गागर में सागर' होते हैं। गुल खिलना, रंग में भंग होना, नौ-दो ग्यारह होना, गप हाँकना, चिकना घड़ा होना, नानी मरना आदि मुहावरे व्यापक अर्थ में परिपूर्ण हैं। इनका प्रयोग सुनते ही मन में इनका अर्थ अपने आप उभरने लगता है।

लोकोक्तियाँ

जैसाकि शब्द से ही स्पष्ट है लोकोक्ति का अर्थ है लोक + उक्ति; अर्थात् लोक में प्रचलित उक्ति। जो उक्ति समाज में चिरकाल से प्रचलित होती है, उसे लोक प्रचलित उक्ति अर्थात् लोकोक्ति कहते हैं। लोकोक्तियाँ भूतकाल के अनुभव और प्रेक्षण का संचय होती हैं। लोकोक्तियों में लोक-बोध, लोक-मान्यता और लोक-स्वीकृति होती है। कुछ लोकोक्तियाँ किसी अन्तर्कथा को अभिव्यक्त करती हैं। लोकोक्तियों के उद्भव को किसी स्थान या काल से नहीं जोड़ा जा सकता।

लोकोक्तियाँ अपने आप में पूर्ण वाक्य होती हैं। इनका उद्देश्य उक्ति चमत्कार पैदा करना नहीं होता। इनका अभिधात्मक अर्थ ही लिया जाता है। अत: इनके शाब्दिक अर्थ और सांकेतिक अर्थ में समानता होती है। इनका प्रयोग प्राय: दृष्टांत के लिए अथवा किसी बात का समर्थन करने के लिए किया जाता है। ये अभिव्यक्ति का सशक्त साधन हैं।

मुहावरों और लोकोक्तियों में अन्तर

मुहावरों और लोकोक्तियों में रूप सम्बन्धी और अर्थ सम्बन्धी भी अन्तर होता है।

रूप सम्बन्धी पहला अन्तर यह है कि मुहावरों के अन्त में अधिकांशत: **ना** होता है, जैसे सिर धुन**ना**, आँख लग**ना**, टेढ़ी खीर हो**ना**, मक्खी मार**ना**, आसमान सिर पर उठा**ना** आदि जबकि लोकोक्तियों के अन्त में **ना** नहीं होता; जैसे—आ बैल मुझे मार, का वर्षा जब कृषि सुखानी, दीवार के भी कान होते हैं, और धोबी का कुत्ता, घर का न घाट का, आदि।

रूप सम्बन्धी दूसरा अन्तर यह होता है कि मुहावरे मात्र शब्द-समूह होते हैं, जैसे 'गुल खिलाना'; इसे स्वतन्त्र रूप से प्रयोग में नहीं लाया जा सकता, किसी वाक्य में इसे उपयुक्त ढंग से प्रयुक्त किया जाता है; जैसे—'उस बूढ़ी औरत ने क्या गुल खिलाया'; इसके विपरीत लोकोक्ति का प्रयोग स्वतंत्र वाक्य के रूप में किया जा सकता है; जैसे—'न रहेगा बाँस, न बजेगी बाँसुरी'।

वस्तुनिष्ठ प्रश्न

संधि

1. 'मृत्यु + उपरांत' में संधि करने से एक शब्द होगा–
A. मृत्यूपरांत B. मृत्योपरांत
C. मृत्युपर्यन्त D. मर्त्योपरांत

2. 'अनधिकृत' शब्द का संधि-विग्रह होगा–
A. अन + अधिकृत B. अन् + अधिकृत
C. अन्य + अधिकृत D. अन्नधि + कृत

3. 'कपि + ईश' का सही संधि-संयोजन कीजिए–
A. कपिश B. कपीश
C. कपेश D. कपिशि

4. विसर्ग के साथ स्वर अथवा व्यंजन के संयोग से जो विकार उत्पन्न होता है, उसे किस संधि के नाम से जानते हैं?
A. स्वर संधि B. व्यंजन संधि
C. विसर्ग संधि D. इनमें से कोई नहीं

5. 'परोपकार' शब्द का संधि-विच्छेद होगा–
A. परा + उपकार B. परो + पकार
C. परोप + कार D. पर + उपकार

6. 'मनः + रमा' में संधि करने से जो शब्द बनेगा, उसका सम्बन्ध किस संधि से होगा?
A. विसर्ग संधि B. स्वर संधि
C. व्यंजन संधि D. भाव संधि

7. 'चन्द्रोदय' में कौन-सी संधि है?
A. यण संधि B. दीर्घ संधि
C. वृद्धि संधि D. गुण संधि

8. निम्नलिखित में से 'वृद्धि स्वर संधि' किस शब्द में है?
A. रजनीश B. महौषध
C. यतीन्द्र D. शोधार्थी

9. 'सदाशय' का सही संधि-विच्छेद होगा–
A. सद + आशय B. सतत + आशय
C. सत् + आशय D. सदा + आशय

10. 'सन्मार्ग' में कौन-सी संधि है?
A. स्वर संधि B. व्यंजन संधि
C. विसर्ग संधि D. इनमें से कोई नहीं

11. 'ज्ञानोदय' में कौन-सी संधि है?
A. स्वर संधि B. व्यंजन संधि
C. विसर्ग संधि D. इनमें से कोई नहीं

12. 'निराधार' में कौन-सी संधि है?
A. स्वर संधि B. व्यंजन संधि
C. विसर्ग संधि D. इनमें से कोई नहीं

13. निम्नलिखित शब्दों में से किसमें विसर्ग संधि है?
A. अतएव B. नरेन्द्र
C. सज्जन D. सदैव

14. निम्नलिखित शब्दों में से किसमें व्यंजन संधि है?
A. सप्तर्षि B. निराधार
C. सत्कार D. हिमालय

15. 'जगन्नाथ' किस संधि का उदाहरण है?
A. व्यंजन संधि B. विसर्ग संधि
C. दीर्घ स्वर संधि D. यण स्वर संधि

16. निम्नलिखित शब्द का संधि-विच्छेद क्या होगा?
भानूदय
A. भानु + उदय B. भानू + उद्रय
C. भानू + ऊदय D. भानु + ऊदय

17. 'निर्गुण' का संधि-विच्छेद होगा–
A. निर + गुण B. नि + गुण
C. निः + गुण D. निर + गुण

18. 'महेन्द्र' का संधि विच्छेद है–
A. मही + इन्द्र B. महो + इन्द्र
C. महा + इन्द्र D. इनमें से कोई नहीं

19. 'यद्यपि' का संधि विच्छेद है–
A. यदि + अपि B. यद् + द्यपि
C. यधि + अपि D. यद + अपि

20. निम्नलिखित में 'भारतेंदु' का सही संधि-विच्छेद है–
A. भारत + तेन्दु B. भार + तेन्दु
C. भारत + एन्दु D. भारत + इन्दु

21. 'उद्घाटन' शब्द का सही संधि-विच्छेद होगा–
A. उत् + घाटन B. उद् + घाटन
C. उद्ध + आटन D. इनमें से कोई नहीं

22. 'सत्कर्म' का संधि-विच्छेद है–
A. सत + कर्म B. सतत् + कर्म
C. सत् + कर्म D. सम + कर्म

23. 'अत्यन्त' शब्द का सही संधि-विग्रह है–
A. अत् + यन्त B. अति + यन्त
C. अति + अन्त D. अत् + अन्त

24. निम्नलिखित शब्द का सही संधि-विच्छेद चुनिए–
ब्रह्माण्ड
A. ब्रह्मा + अंड B. ब्रह्मण + अंड
C. बृहत् + अंड D. बृह + माण्ड

25. 'निरपेक्ष' शब्द का संधि-विच्छेद होगा–
A. निर् + पेक्ष B. नि + पेंक्ष
C. निर + पेक्ष D. निः + अपेक्ष

26. तत् + शंकर की संधि होगी–
A. तत्शंकर B. तच्छंकर
C. तक्षंकर D. उपर्युक्त में से कोई नहीं

27. 'कठोपनिषद्' का संधि-विच्छेद होगा–
A. कटु + उपनिषद् B. कठो + उपनिषद्
C. कठोप + निषद् D. कठ + उपनिषद्

28. 'भावुक' का संधि-विच्छेद होगा–
A. भाव + उक B. भो + ऊक
C. भव्य + उक D. भौ + उक

29. 'विद्यामंदिर' का विग्रह होगा–
A. विद्या का मंदिर B. विद्या के लिए मंदिर
C. विद्या और मंदिर D. विद्या के समान मंदिर

30. 'उत्कोच' का संधि विच्छेद होगा–
A. उद् + कोच B. उत् + कोच
C. उत + कोच D. उद + कोच

31. कौन-सा शब्द विसर्ग संधि का नहीं है?
A. यशोगान B. निष्कपट
C. मनोहर D. अभिषेक

32. 'मनीषा' का संधि-विच्छेद है–
A. मनि + ईषा B. मनी + ईषा
C. मनस् + ईषा D. मणि + ईशा

33. निम्नलिखित में से दीर्घ संधि का उदाहरण कौन-सा है?
A. नरेश B. नेति
C. मध्वाचार्य D. कामायनी

34. 'अति + उक्ति' शब्दों की संधि करने पर शब्द होगा–
A. अत्युक्ति B. अत्योक्ति
C. अतियुक्ति D. अतिउक्ति

35. 'निराधार' शब्द का संधि-विच्छेद है–
A. निः + आधार B. निरा + आधार
C. निरम् + आधार D. निर् + आधार

36. 'अन्वेषण' का संधि-विच्छेद होगा–
A. अन + वेषण B. अनु + एषण
C. अनु + ऐषण D. अनू + वेषण

37. 'सज्जन' का संधि-विच्छेद होगा–
A. सज् + जन B. सद् + जन
C. सत् + जन D. स + ज् + जन

38. 'इत्यादि' का सन्धि-विच्छेद होगा–
A. इत + आदि B. इति + यादि
C. इति + आदि D. इत्य + आदि

39. 'दुर्जन' का सन्धि-विच्छेद होगा–
A. दुर + जन B. दु + जन
C. दुः + जन D. दु + रजन

40. 'नमस्ते' शब्द का सन्धि-विच्छेद है–
A. नम + स्ते B. नमस् + ते
C. नमः + स्ते D. नमः + ते

41. 'महोत्सव' का संधि-विच्छेद है–
A. महा + उत्सव B. महो + उत्सव
C. मह + ओत्सव D. मही + उत्सव

42. 'पवन' का शुद्ध सन्धि-विच्छेद है–
A. पो + अन B. पव + अन
C. पः + अवन D. पव + न्

43. 'विष्णवे' का संधि-विच्छेद है–
A. विष्णु + ए B. विष्णो + ए
C. विष्णु + अए D. विष्णु + अवे

44. 'स्वागतम्' में कौन-सी संधि है?
A. गुण संधि B. यण् संधि
C. वृद्धि संधि D. दीर्घ संधि

45. 'उच्चारण' में कौन-सी संधि है?
A. व्यंजन संधि B. स्वर संधि
C. विसर्ग संधि D. विलोम संधि

46. 'उल्लेख' का संधि-विच्छेद है–
A. उल् + लेख B. उत् + लेख
C. उल्ल + लेख D. उ + आलेख

47. 'अत्याचार' का शुद्ध संधि-विच्छेद है–
A. अत्य + आचार B. अति + चार
C. अत्या + चार D. अति + आचार

48. 'दिगम्बर' का संधि-विच्छेद क्या होगा?
A. दिग् + अम्बर B. दिक् + अम्बर
C. दिग + अम्बर D. दिक + अम्बर

49. 'पावक' का शुद्ध संधि-विच्छेद होगा–
A. पौ + अक B. पा + अवक
C. पव + अक् D. पाव + अक

50. 'उपैति' का संधि-विच्छेद बताइए–
A. अप + इति B. उपै + इति
C. उप + ऐति D. उप + एति

51. 'नवोढ़ा' का सन्धि-विच्छेद है–
A. नव + उढ़ा B. नवो + ढ़ा
C. नव + ऊढ़ा D. न + ओढ़ा

52. 'उड्डयनम' का सन्धि-विच्छेद होगा–
A. उत + डयनम् B. उद् + डयनम्
C. उड + अयनम् D. उड् + डयनम्

53. 'दिंगत' शब्द का संधि-विच्छेद होगा–
A. दिक् + अंत B. दिग् + अंत
C. दि + गंत D. दिग + अंत

54. 'परिच्छेद' में कौन-सी सन्धि है?

A. व्यंजन संधि B. दीर्घ संधि
C. विसर्ग संधि D. वृद्धि संधि

55. 'अन्यान्य' शब्द का संधि-विच्छेद होगा–

A. अ + न्यान्य B. अन्य + अन्य
C. अन् + यान्य D. अन्या + आन्य

56. व्यंजन संधि का उदाहरण नहीं है–

A. उत् + चारणम् = उच्चारणम्
B. रामस् + टीकते = रामष्टीकते
C. गंगा + उदकम = गंगोदकम्
D. सत् + चित् = सच्चित्

57. स्वस्त्यस्तु का संधि-विच्छेद होगा–

A. स्वस्ति + अस्तु B. स्वः + अस्त्यस्तु
C. स्वस्त्य + अस्तु D. स्व + स्त्यस्तु

58. 'तेजोमय' का सही सन्धि-विच्छेद है–

A. तेज + ओमय B. तेजः + अमय
C. तेजः + मय D. तेजो + मय

59. 'तथेति' का सन्धि-विच्छेद होगा–

A. तथ + इति B. ता + थेति
C. तथा + इति D. तथा + इत

60. 'वृहस्पति' का संधि-विच्छेद है–

A. वृहस + पति B. वृहस् + पति
C. वृहः + पति D. वृहश् + पति

61. 'व्याप्त' में संधि है–

A. गुण संधि B. दीर्घ संधि
C. यण् संधि D. अयादि संधि

62. 'पित्राकृतिः' का शुद्ध संधि विच्छेद है–

A. पितृ + आकृतिः B. पित्र + आकृतिः
C. पित्रृ + आकृतिः D. पितु + आकृतिः

63. 'न्यून' का संधि विच्छेद होगा–

A. नि + ऊन B. न्यू + नन
C. नव + ऊन D. नवी + नन

64. 'षडानन' में कौन-सी संधि है?

A. दीर्घ संधि B. वृद्धि संधि
C. यण संधि D. गुण संधि

65. 'धर्मात्मा' में कौन-सी संधि है?

A. स्वर संधि B. व्यंजन संधि
C. विसर्ग संधि D. यण संधि

66. 'रेखांकित' में प्रयुक्त संधि है–

A. गुण संधि B. वृद्धि संधि
C. दीर्घ संधि D. स्वर संधि

67. 'निश्छल' में कौन-सी संधि है?

A. गुण संधि B. स्वर संधि
C. दीर्घ संधि D. वृद्धि संधि

68. 'दुरुपयोग' में प्रयुक्त संधि है–

A. स्वर संधि B. यण संधि
C. गुण संधि D. दीर्घ संधि

69. 'अत्यावश्यक' का संधि विच्छेद है–

A. अ + आवश्यक B. अति + आवश्यक
C. अत्य + आवश्यक D. अत्या + वश्यक

70. 'वाङ्मय' का संधि विच्छेद है–

A. वांग + मय B. वाक् + मय
C. वान् + मय D. इनमें से कोई नहीं

71. 'उपर्युक्त' का संधि विच्छेद क्या है?

A. उप + रूक्त B. उपरि + उक्त
C. उपर + युक्त D. उपः + युक्त

72. 'चन्द्रोदय' शब्द में है–

A. स्वर संधि B. व्यंजन संधि
C. विसर्ग संधि D. इनमें से कोई नहीं

73. 'निष्कपट' का संधि विच्छेद है–

A. निः + कपट B. निष + कपट
C. नि + कपट D. इनमें से कोई नहीं

74. 'प्रत्युपकार' का सही संधि विच्छेद है–

A. प्रत्युप + कार B. प्रति + उपकार
C. प्रत्यु + उपकार D. प्रत्य + उपकार

75. 'स्वागत' शब्द का संधि विच्छेद है–

A. स्वा + गत B. स्व + आगत
C. स् + वागत D. सु + आगत

समास

निर्देश (प्र.सं. 1 से 70 तक): *नीचे दिए गए शब्दों में प्रयुक्त समास के नाम का चयन कीजिए–*

1. पीताम्बर–

A. तत्पुरुष B. अव्ययीभाव
C. बहुव्रीहि D. द्विगु

2. चरणकमल–

A. तत्पुरुष B. कर्मधारय
C. बहुव्रीहि D. अव्ययीभाव

3. घुड़सवार–

A. द्विगु B. कर्मधारय
C. तत्पुरुष D. अव्ययीभाव

4. स्वर्गप्राप्त–

A. कर्म तत्पुरुष B. करण तत्पुरुष
C. सम्प्रदान तत्पुरुष D. अपादान तत्पुरुष

5. गर्वशून्य–

A. कर्म-तत्पुरुष B. संप्रदान-तत्पुरुष
C. करण-तत्पुरुष D. अपादान-तत्पुरुष

6. 'लम्बोदर' में कौन-सा समास है?
A. तत्पुरुष B. बहुब्रीहि
C. द्विगु D. कर्मधारय

7. 'देवालय' में कौन-सा समास है?
A. तत्पुरुष B. बहुब्रीहि
C. द्विगु D. इनमें से कोई नहीं

8. 'खरा खोटा' शब्द में कौन-सा समास है?
A. द्वंद्व B. द्विगु
C. कर्मधारय D. बहुब्रीहि

9. 'निर्विवाद' में कौन-सा समास है?
A. कर्मधारय B. अव्ययीभाव
C. तत्पुरुष D. बहुब्रीहि

10. 'दहीबड़ा' में कौन-सा समास है?
A. तत्पुरुष B. द्विगु
C. बहुब्रीहि D. द्वन्द्व

11. 'चौराहा' में समास है–
A. तत्पुरुष B. द्वन्द्व
C. कर्मधारय D. द्विगु

12. 'माता-पिता' शब्द में समास है–
A. द्वन्द्व B. द्विगु
C. तत्पुरुष D. कर्मधारय

13. 'वज्रपाणि' शब्द में कौन-सा समास है?
A. तत्पुरुष B. बहुब्रीहि
C. द्वन्द्व D. द्विगु

14. 'देशभक्ति' शब्द में समास होगा–
A. अपादान तत्पुरुष B. सम्बन्ध तत्पुरुष
C. अधिकरण तत्पुरुष D. सम्प्रदान तत्पुरुष

15. 'सुनीता के बच्चे घास-फूस की तरह बढ़ रहे हैं।'
उपर्युक्त वाक्य में प्रयुक्त 'घास-फूस' शब्द में समास होगा–
A. कर्मधारय B. द्वन्द्व
C. द्विगु D. अव्ययीभाव

16. निम्नलिखित शब्दों में कौन-सा शब्द बहुब्रीहि समास का उदाहरण है?
A. शूलपाणि B. यथाक्रम
C. हँसमुख D. हथकड़ी

17. इनमें से कौन-सा शब्द 'द्विगु' समास है?
A. भुजदण्ड B. माखनचोर
C. पंचशील D. लज्जाशील

18. 'प्रतिदिन' शब्द में समास होगा–
A. द्विगु B. कर्मधारय
C. तत्पुरुष D. अव्ययीभाव

19. जिन समस्त पदों में पहला शब्द संख्यावाची हो और उससे समुदाय का बोध होता हो, तो उसे कहते हैं–
A. द्विगु समास B. द्वन्द्व समास
C. कर्मधारय समास D. अव्ययीभाव समास

20. जिसमें पहला शब्द विशेषण हो और दूसरा शब्द विशेष्य, तो उसे कौन-सा समास कहेंगे?
A. द्विगु B. कर्मधारय
C. द्वन्द्व D. तत्पुरुष

21. 'पंचवटी' शब्द के लिए दिए गए विकल्प में से उपयुक्त समास कौन-सा है?
A. द्विगु B. तत्पुरुष
C. बहुब्रीहि D. कर्मधारय

22. 'बुरा-भला' शब्द में कौन-सा समास है?
A. द्वन्द्व B. द्विगु
C. कर्मधारय D. तत्पुरुष

23. 'चिड़ीमार' शब्द में कौन-सा समास है?
A. द्विगु B. कर्मधारय
C. तत्पुरुष D. अव्ययीभाव

24. 'यथोचित' शब्द में समास बताइए–
A. अव्ययीभाव B. कर्मधारय
C. बहुब्रीहि D. तत्पुरुष

25. समास कहते हैं–
A. शब्दों के मेल को
B. अक्षर के मेल को
C. स्वर-से-स्वर के मेल को
D. स्वर के साथ व्यंजन के मेल को

26. 'शिवार्पण' शब्द में कौन-सा समास है?
A. अधिकरण तत्पुरुष B. करण तत्पुरुष
C. सम्प्रदान तत्पुरुष D. अपादान तत्पुरुष

27. निम्नलिखित में किसमें तत्पुरुष समास है?
A. पदप्राप्त B. शताब्दी
C. चौमासा D. भाई-बहन

28. 'रसगुल्ला' में कौन-सा समास है?
A. तत्पुरुष B. बहुब्रीहि
C. द्वन्द्व D. अव्ययीभाव

29. 'भुखमरा' का समास विग्रह होगा–
A. भूख से जो मर गया B. भूख से मरा हुआ
C. भूखों मर गया जो D. भूख द्वारा मरा हुआ

30. 'दशरथ सुत' में कौन-सा समास है?
A. तत्पुरुष B. बहुब्रीहि
C. द्विगु D. द्वन्द्व

31. 'अष्टाध्यायी' में कौन-सा समास है?
A. द्वन्द्व B. द्विगु
C. तत्पुरुष D. कर्मधारय

32. 'यथाशीघ्र' में कौन-सा समास है?
A. अव्ययीभाव B. द्वन्द्व
C. कर्मधारय D. तत्पुरुष

33. चौखंभा में कौन-सा समास है?

A. बहुब्रीहि B. द्वन्द्व
C. द्विगु D. तत्पुरुष

34. कौन-सा समास विशेषण के रूप में प्रयुक्त होता है?

A. अव्ययीभाव B. तत्पुरुष
C. कर्मधारय D. बहुब्रीहि

35. द्विगु समास का उदाहरण होगा–

A. षट्कोण B. कुपुत्र
C. प्रतिवर्ष D. सूरसागर

36. कौन-सा शब्द अव्ययीभाव समास का उदाहरण है?

A. नवग्रह B. गाँठकर
C. महात्मा D. आमरण

37. 'राजपुत्र' में कौन-सा समास है?

A. बहुब्रीहि B. तत्पुरुष
C. द्विगु D. कर्मधारय

38. निम्नलिखित में से तत्पुरुष समास किसमें है?

A. नील गाय B. राजकुमार
C. त्रिलोचन D. दशानन

39. निम्नलिखित में द्वन्द्व समास बताइए–

A. प्रतिदिन B. चौमासा
C. घी-शक्कर D. महादेव

40. 'आजीवन' में कौन-सा समास है?

A. अव्ययीभाव B. तत्पुरुष
C. कर्मधारय D. द्विगु

41. निम्नलिखित में 'यथाविधि' का सही समास कौन-सा है?

A. अव्ययीभाव B. तत्पुरुष
C. कर्मधारय D. बहुब्रीहि

42. 'पर्णकुटी' शब्द का समास है–

A. तत्पुरुष B. द्वन्द्व
C. कर्मधारय D. बहुब्रीहि

43. निम्नलिखित में 'द्वन्द्व समास' का शब्द है–

A. आज-कल B. रातों-रात
C. दिन-दिन D. वीर पुरुष

44. 'निशिदिन' शब्द में प्रयुक्त समास है–

A. द्वन्द्व B. अव्ययीभाव
C. कर्मधारय D. तत्पुरुष

45. जिस समास में पहला शब्द प्रधान होता है और समूचा शब्द क्रिया विशेषण अव्यय होता है, उसे कौन-सा समास कहते हैं?

A. अव्ययीभाव B. तत्पुरुष
C. बहुब्रीहि D. द्वन्द्व

46. 'जलपिपासु' में कौन-सा समास है?

A. तत्पुरुष B. अव्ययीभाव
C. द्वन्द्व D. बहुब्रीहि

47. 'वनवास' में कौन-सा समास है?

A. तत्पुरुष B. कर्मधारय
C. द्वन्द्व D. बहुब्रीहि

48. 'दिगम्बर' में कौन-सा समास है?

A. बहुब्रीहि B. द्वन्द्व
C. द्विगु D. कर्मधारय

49. 'नरोत्तम' में कौन-सा समास है?

A. द्वन्द्व B. तत्पुरुष
C. अव्ययीभाव D. कर्मधारय

50. 'आजन्म' में कौन-सा समास है?

A. द्विगु B. तत्पुरुष
C. कर्मधारय D. अव्ययीभाव

51. 'अकालपीड़ित' में समास होगा–

A. कर्मधारय B. द्वन्द्व
C. तत्पुरुष D. बहुब्रीहि

52. 'जय-पराजय' में कौन-सा समास है?

A. द्वन्द्व B. कर्मधारय
C. द्विगु D. तत्पुरुष

53. 'वियोग-विकल' शब्द में प्रयुक्त समास है–

A. तत्पुरुष B. कर्मधारय
C. द्वन्द्व D. द्विगु

54. इन युग्मों में से कौन-सा सही नहीं है?

A. नीलोत्पलम् – कर्मधारय समास
B. दशाननः – बहुब्रीहि समास
C. रामलक्ष्मणौ – अव्ययीभाव समास
D. दिवारात्रि – द्वन्द्व समास

55. 'तिरंगा' शब्द में समास है–

A. द्वन्द्व B. अव्ययीभाव
C. द्विगु D. कर्मधारय

56. 'लम्बोदर' उदाहरण है–

A. बहुब्रीहि समास का B. द्वन्द्व समास का
C. द्विगु समास का D. कर्मधारय समास का

57. निम्नलिखित में से कर्मधारय समास किसमें है?

A. चक्रपाणि B. चतुर्थुगम्
C. नीलोत्पलम् D. माता-पिता

58. 'चक्रपाणिदर्शनार्थ' पद में मान्य समास है–

A. कर्मधारय B. तत्पुरुष
C. अव्ययीभाव D. बहुब्रीहि

59. 'कठपुतली' में कौन-सा समास है?

A. सम्प्रदान तत्पुरुष B. सम्बन्ध तत्पुरुष
C. अधिकरण तत्पुरुष D. कर्म तत्पुरुष

60. 'कष्टापन्नः' शब्द में समास है–

A. अव्ययीभाव B. तत्पुरुष
C. बहुब्रीहि D. कर्मधारय

61. 'चन्द्रकान्तिः' में समास है–
A. बहुब्रीहि B. कर्मधारय
C. तत्पुरुष D. इनमें से कोई नहीं

62. 'चन्द्रशेखर' में प्रयुक्त समास है–
A. तत्पुरुष B. कर्मधारय
C. बहुब्रीहि D. द्विगु

63. 'रात-दिन' में कौन-सा समास होता है?
A. द्वन्द्व B. द्विगु
C. कर्मधारय D. अव्ययीभाव

64. 'बहन-भाई' में समास है–
A. बहुब्रीहि B. तत्पुरुष
C. द्वन्द्व D. द्विगु

65. 'दशमुख' में कौन-सा समास है?
A. तत्पुरुष B. बहुब्रीहि
C. द्वन्द्व D. कर्मधारय

66. 'यथाशक्ति' में समास है–
A. द्विगु B. तत्पुरुष
C. कर्मधारय D. अव्ययीभाव

67. 'देशभक्ति' में समास है–
A. तत्पुरुष B. बहुब्रीहि
C. द्विगु D. कर्मधारय

68. 'हस्तलिखित' में प्रयुक्त समास है–
A. कर्मधारय B. तत्पुरुष
C. बहुब्रीहि D. द्वन्द्व

69. 'त्रिनेत्र' में कौन-सा समास है?
A. तत्पुरुष B. बहुब्रीहि
C. द्विगु D. द्वन्द्व

70. 'भरपेट' में कौन-सा समास है?
A. अव्ययीभाव B. कर्मधारय
C. तत्पुरुष D. बहुब्रीहि

वर्तनी

निर्देश (प्र.सं. 1 से 40 तक): *नीचे के प्रश्नों में एक शब्द की चार अलग-अलग वर्तनियां दी हुई हैं। इनमें से सही वर्तनी छाँटकर उस पर निशान लगाइये:*

1. A. जयोत्स्ना B. ज्योत्स्ना
C. जोत्स्ना D. ज्योत्सना

2. A. कवयित्री B. कवियित्री
C. कवियत्री D. कवित्री

3. A. उत्ज्वल B. उज्जवल
C. ऊज्जवल D. उज्ज्वल

4. A. छः B. छह
C. छह् D. छै

5. A. जिजीविषा B. जिजीवषा
C. जजीवषा D. जिजिवीषा

6. A. दृश्य B. द्रश्य
C. दृष्य D. दृिश्य

7. A. इतिहासिक B. ऐतिहासिक
C. ऐतिहासीक D. ऐतीहासिक

8. A. वाङ्मय B. वाँङ्मय
C. वांग्मय D. वांगमय

9. A. सौहार्द्र B. सैहार्द
C. सैर्हाद D. सौहार्द

10. A. आर्शीवाद B. आशिर्वाद
C. आशीर्वाद D. आर्शिवाद

11. A. भूगोलिक B. भूगौलिक
C. भोगौलिक D. भौगोलिक

12. A. सन्कीर्णता B. सन्कीरणता
C. संर्कीणता D. संकीर्णता

13. A. परचन्ड B. प्रचण्ड
C. प्रचान्ड D. परचण्ड

14. A. तार्क्रिक B. तार्किक
C. ताकृिक D. ताक्रिक

15. A. इर्षा B. ईर्षा
C. इर्ष्या D. ईर्ष्या

16. A. पूज्यनीय B. पुजनीय
C. पूजनीय D. पुज्यनीय

17. A. अधम्र B. अध्रम
C. अधर्म D. अधृम

18. A. अधिकृत B. अधिक्रित
C. अधिक्रित्त D. अधिर्कित

19. A. अनुकृम B. अनुक्रम
C. अनुकर्म D. अनुकम्र

20. A. अनवेषण B. अन्वेषण
C. अन्वेछण D. अन्वेशण

21. A. अभिशेक B. अभिषेख
C. अभिषेक D. अभीषेक

22. A. इच्छुक B. इक्षुक
C. इक्छुक D. इच्छिक

23. A. इन्र्दिय B. इन्द्दिय
C. इन्दिय D. इन्द्रिय

24. A. उतकण्ठा B. उत्कण्ठा
C. उत्क्णठा D. उत्त्कन्ठा

25. A. उमृिला B. उम्रिला
C. उमिर्ला D. उर्मिला

26. A. रिषि B. ऋषि
C. क्रिषि D. ऋशि्

27. A. एकागृ B. एकाग्र
C. एकार्ग D. एक्राग्र

28. A. ओजश्वि B. ओजस्वी
C. ओजश्वी D. ओजष्वी

29. A. औशधी B. औषधी
C. औषधि D. औष्धि

30. A. करम B. क्राम
C. कम्र D. कर्म

31. A. ग्रिहीत B. ग्रहीत
C. गृहीत D. गर्हित

32. A. कृतज्ञ B. क्रतज्ञ
C. क्रितज्ञ D. क्रितग्य

33. A. चतुदर्श B. चर्तुदश
C. चतुर्दश D. चतुद्रश

34. A. जर्जर B. जरर्जर
C. जज्रर D. जरजर

35. A. जघ्नय B. जघ्रय
C. जघन्य D. जवन्य

36. A. जेष्ठ B. ज्येश्ठ
C. ज्येष्ठ D. ज्येस्ठ

37. A. तपस्वनी B. तपस्विनी
C. तपिस्वनी D. तपिस्विनी

38. A. तादातमय B. तदात्स्य
C. तादात्म्य D. तादात्यम

39. A. तृष्णा B. तृिष्णा
C. त्रिष्णा D. तृश्णा

40. A. त्रिमूर्ती B. त्रिमुर्ति
C. त्रिमूर्ति D. त्रृमूर्ति

41. A. दक्छ B. दक्च्छ
C. दक्ष D. दज्ञ

42. A. द्रर्पन B. दर्पन
C. दपर्ण D. दर्पण

43. A. दामपत्य B. दम्पत्य
C. दाम्पत्य D. दाम्पत

44. A. दीप्यित B. दीपति
C. दीप्ति D. दीप्ती

45. A. दीर्वायु B. दीरवायु
C. दीवार्यु D. दीर्विायु

46. A. दुर्निती B. दुनीर्ति
C. दुरनीति D. दुर्नीति

47. A. दुर्दषा B. दुह्शा
C. दुर्दशा D. दुद्रशा

48. A. दुर्योधन B. दुयोर्धन
C. दूरयोधन D. द्रुयोधन

49. A. दुरबुद्धि B. दुर्बुधि
C. दुबुद्धि D. दुर्बुद्धि

50. A. धनुष्विद्या B. धनुर्विद्या
C. धर्नुविद्या D. धनुर्वेद्या

51. A. धर्म B. धृर्म
C. ध्रर्म D. धम्र

52. A. ध्रुर्व B. ध्रुव्र
C. ध्रुव D. धुर्व

53. A. नर्म्रदेश्वर B. नम्रदेश्वर
C. नमर्देश्वर D. नर्मदेश्वर

54. A. निरक्षेप B. निक्क्षेप
C. निक्षेप D. निक्लेप

55. A. निर्गह B. नृग्रह
C. निग्रह D. निगर्ह

56. A. निरजीव B. निर्जीव
C. नृिजीव D. निज्रीव

57. A. निम्रूल B. निर्मूल
C. निरमूल D. नृर्मूल

58. A. निवृत्त B. निव्रत्त
C. निवृत D. नृिवत्त

59. A. प्रिक्रमा B. परीक्रमा
C. परिकृमा D. परिक्रमा

60. A. प्रयटन B. पृयटन
C. पर्यटन D. प्रर्यटन

61. A. प्रक्रिति B. प्रकृति
C. प्रक्रति D. पृक्रति

62. A. बर्हिमुख B. बहिर्मुख
C. बहिम्रुख D. बहिमुर्ख

63. A. भरतस्ना B. भर्त्सना
C. भर्तसना D. भर्तृसना

64. A. मूर्ती B. मूर्ति
C. मूर्तृि D. मूरती

65. A. गिद्ध्र B. गीध
C. गिद्धा D. ग्रिद्ध

66. A. निकर्सन B. निर्कषन
C. निकर्षण D. निर्कषण

67. A. निकृष्ट B. निक्रस्ट
C. निकृस्ट D. निक्रिष्ट

68. A. पार्थिव B. पार्थ्रिव
C. पार्थीव D. पाथिर्व

69. A. विदूश्क B. विदूष्क
C. विदूशक D. विदूषक

70. A. फुर्तीला B. फुर्त्तीला
C. फुर्तिला D. फुर्तला

71. A. वर्ज B. वज्र
C. वजृ D. वज्रृ

72. A. ब्रम्हचर्य B. ब्रह्मचर्य
C. बृह्मचर्य D. ब्रह्मर्चय

73. A. मत्स्य B. मतस्य
C. मत्सत्य D. मत्श्य

74. A. भ्रित्य B. भर्त्य
C. भृत्य D. भ्रत्य

75. A. निग्रंध B. निर्गंध
C. र्निगंध D. नृगंध

76. A. प्रकर्श B. प्रकर्ष
C. पृकर्श D. पृकर्ष

77. A. भद्र B. भदृ
C. भर्द्र D. भर्द

78. A. मंजूशा B. मंजूषा
C. मंजुषा D. मंजुशा

79. A. मुर्मूषु B. मुमूर्षू
C. मुमुर्षु D. मुमूर्षु

80. A. ब्राह्मण B. बृाह्मण
C. ब्राम्हण D. बृाहम्ण

निर्देश (प्र.सं. 81 से 115 तक): *नीचे प्रत्येक प्रश्न में A, B, C और D अक्षरांक में चार शब्द दिए गए हैं। जिनमें से एक में वर्तनी सम्बन्धी त्रुटि हो सकती है। उस त्रुटियुक्त शब्द का अक्षरांक ही आपका उत्तर होगा। यदि चारों शब्दों की वर्तनी सही है तो उत्तर दीजिए E अर्थात् 'सभी सही हैं'।*

81. A. अप्रयुक्त B. अतीषयोक्ति
C. अशोध्य D. सम्मति
E. सभी सही हैं

82. A. अभ्युक्ति B. इष्टतम
C. अपुरित D. उपस्थित
E. सभी सही हैं

83. A. उत्तरजिवीता B. प्रारक्षित
C. क्षैतिज D. आयातित
E. सभी सही हैं

84. A. आस्थगित B. आतिथ्य
C. अंतरिम D. निर्धारित
E. सभी सही हैं

85. A. किफायत B. परिस्थिति
C. संतुलित D. असिंचीत
E. सभी सही हैं

86. A. तात्पर्य B. महोत्सव
C. दंभ D. कृशक
E. सभी सही हैं

87. A. लक्षण B. व्यंजन
C. पगडंडी D. पारंगत
E. सभी सही हैं

88. A. स्थानापन्न B. व्यावशयिक
C. कोशिका D. आर्थिक
E. सभी सही हैं

89. A. दांडधिकारी B. प्राधिकरण
C. आदित्य D. क्रियान्वयन
E. सभी सही हैं

90. A. गोपनीयता B. कार्यवाही
C. उत्रदायित्व D. वयस्क
E. सभी सही हैं

91. A. चूल्लु B. जीविका
C. ठिठोली D. तकली
E. सभी सही हैं

92. A. नजरिया B. पंडीताइ
C. फरियादी D. बधाई
E. सभी सही हैं

93. A. प्रकाशकीय B. फाल्गुन
C. बधिर D. भोतिक
E. सभी सही हैं

94. A. हौसला B. स्वीकृति
C. व्यवासायिक D. लिपाई
E. सभी सही हैं

95. A. फलित B. बटोही
C. भजनीक D. मंडली
E. सभी सही हैं

96. A. अनामिष B. अपरिहार्य
C. किफायती D. गिलाफ
E. सभी सही हैं

97. A. गोधुलि B. चांचल्य
C. जिजीविषु D. तमोली
E. सभी सही हैं

98. A. तितिक्षा B. दखलंदाजी
C. दिप्ति D. दैनिकी
E. सभी सही हैं

99. A. नजदिकी B. नियोक्ता
C. परिणीता D. पाणिग्रहण
E. सभी सही हैं

100. A. पुनीत B. प्रख्यापीत
C. फरोख्त D. बुजुर्गी
E. सभी सही हैं

101. A. अद्‌भुत B. व्यंग्य
C. अदृश्य D. समारंभ
E. सभी सही हैं

102. A. लक्षण B. महात्मन
C. सम्पर्क D. कर्तज्ञ
E. सभी सही हैं

103. A. गझिन B. आशय
C. निशपादन D. आकर्षण
E. सभी सही हैं

104. A. उत्तरीय B. स्थान्नापन
C. कुंभ D. असामान्य
E. सभी सही हैं

105. A. न्यायाधिश B. पुरस्कृत
C. वारिद D. अधिशासी
E. सभी सही हैं

106. A. चिनाई B. तंबूल
C. ठिठोली D. तन्मय
E. सभी सही हैं

107. A. अगड़ाइ B. गठीला
C. खिलाफ D. कल्पनातीत
E. सभी सही हैं

108. A. सूरत B. वैधव्य
C. लतीका D. रेगिस्तान
E. सभी सही हैं

109. A. इति B. अखिलेश
C. कबूतर D. खेरात
E. सभी सही हैं

110. A. चमत्कृत B. जिल्द
C. तमोली D. दमित
E. सभी सही हैं

111. A. प्रहसन B. तात्पर्य
C. महसूल D. पाणिगृहण
E. सभी सही हैं

112. A. मस्तिष्क B. प्रोत्साहन
C. सम्वत् D. क्रियाविधि
E. सभी सही हैं

113. A. विचारणीय B. क्रन्दन
C. पर्यावर्ण D. उपलब्धि
E. सभी सही हैं

114. A. विसतृत B. वाग्विलास
C. तात्कालिक D. अलंकार
E. सभी सही हैं

115. A. दृष्टांत B. रूढ़ि
C. सूचि D. आचमन
E. सभी सही हैं

पर्यायवाची

1. 'कमल' शब्द का पर्यायवाची होगा–
A. कन्दर्प B. अनंग
C. घनेश D. इन्दीवर

2. 'क्रोध' के लिए इन दिए गए पर्यायवाची शब्दों में एक गलत शब्द है, उसे चयनित कीजिए–
A. रोष B. अमर्ष
C. स्वत्व D. कोप

3. निम्नलिखित पर्यायवाची शब्दों में से जो एक शब्द 'मोर' का पर्यायवाची नहीं है, उसे चिन्हित कीजिए–
A. केकी B. कीश
C. शिखी D. शिखण्डी

4. इनमें से कौन-सा शब्द 'कृष्णा' का पर्यायवाची है?
A. राधा B. रुक्मिणी
C. द्रोपदी D. यशोदा

5. इनमें से एक शब्द 'बैल' का पर्यायवाची नहीं है, उसे चयनित कीजिए–
A. अश्म B. बृषभ
C. बलीवर्द D. गो

6. निम्नलिखित में से जो शब्द 'सौन्दर्य' का पर्यायवाची नहीं है, उसे चयनित कीजिए–
A. सुषमा B. शोभा
C. सुन्दरता D. रमणी

7. निम्नलिखित विकल्पों में से एक शब्द 'नदी' का पर्यायवाची नहीं है, उसे चयनित कीजिए–
A. तरंगिणी B. तटिनी
C. तरिणी D. सरिता

8. नीचे दिए गए विकल्पों में से एक शब्द 'घर' का पर्यायवाची नहीं है, उसे चयनित कीजिए–
A. भवन B. भुवन
C. निकेतन D. सदन

9. इनमें से कौन-सा शब्द 'पार्थ' का पर्यायवाची है?
A. भीष्म B. श्रीकृष्ण
C. युधिष्ठिर D. अर्जुन

10. 'दुःख' का पर्यायवाची शब्द निम्नलिखित में से कौन-सा है?
A. व्यथा B. पीड़ा
C. वेदना D. ये सभी पर्याय हैं

11. नीचे दिए गए शब्दों में से एक शब्द 'गीदड़' का पर्यायवाची नहीं है, उसका चयन कीजिए–
A. खगेश B. शृंगाल
C. सियार D. जम्बुक

12. निम्न में से कौन चन्द्रमा का पर्यायवाची नहीं है?
A. शशि B. हिमकर
C. शशांक D. रूपक

13. निम्न में से कौन गाय का पर्यायवाची नहीं है?
A. हेरम्ब B. गौरी
C. भद्रा D. धेनु

14. कुत्ता का पर्यायवाची शब्द निम्नलिखित में से कौन-सा है?
A. सारमेय B. क्रमेलक
C. कीर D. नागान्तक

15. आनंद का पर्यायवाची नहीं है–
A. हर्ष B. उल्लास
C. चाह D. आह्लाद

16. 'कृशानु' का पर्यायवाची शब्द है–
A. अनल B. पवन
C. दोहित्री D. अनिल

17. 'द्रौपदी' का पर्याय नहीं है–
A. द्रुपदसुता B. याज्ञसेनी
C. पांचाली D. रमणी

18. 'महादेव' का पर्यायवाची शब्द चुनिए–
A. गरुड़ध्वज B. नारायण
C. चन्द्रशेखर D. विश्वम्भर

19. 'चन्द्रमा' का पर्यायवाची शब्द चुनिए–
A. निशाकर B. निशाचर
C. तरणि D. कृशानु

20. 'धन' का पर्यायवाची जो शब्द नहीं है, उसे चुनिए–
A. द्रव्य B. द्रव
C. सम्पदा D. दौलत

21. 'पुत्री' का पर्यायवाची शब्द नहीं है–
A. तनय B. सुता
C. आत्मजा D. दुहिता

22. निम्नलिखित में से कौन-सा शब्द 'कमल' का पर्यायवाची शब्द नहीं है?
A. सरोज B. अरविन्द
C. सलिल D. पंकज

23. निम्नलिखित किस समूह में सभी शब्द 'कामदेव' के पर्यायवाची हैं?
A. कंदर्प, मदन, मनसिज, मारक
B. मदन, मन्मथ, अनंग, कंदर्प
C. मान, त्रिपुर, मन्मथ, अनंग
D. मन्मथ, मनसिज, त्रिपुर, अनंग

24. कौन-सा शब्द जंगल शब्द का पर्यायवाची नहीं है?
A. अटवी B. कान्ता
C. कान्तार D. कानन

25. कौन-सा शब्द 'अम्बर' का पर्यायवाची है?
A. आकाश B. अवनि
C. मेघ D. बादल

26. कौन-सा शब्द 'मित्र' का पर्याय नहीं है?
A. अलि B. सखा
C. सुहृद D. मीत

27. निम्नांकित में किस शब्द का अर्थ कमल होता है?
A. उत्पल B. उपल
C. जलद D. नीरद

28. निम्नलिखित में 'पुत्री' शब्द के पर्यायवाची शब्द-समूह कौन हैं?
A. भार्या, कान्ता, अबला, वनिता
B. लड़की, बेटी, अचला, वसुधा
C. सुता, धरा, वसुमती, अचला
D. तनया, आत्मजा, दुहिता, तनुजा

29. निम्नलिखित शब्द-समूह में 'बिजली' के पर्यायवाची कौन हैं?
A. ज्योति, रोशनी, चमक, प्रभा
B. विद्युत, तड़ित, चपला, दामिनी
C. उजाला, प्रभंजन, विहग, निशापति
D. मंदाकिनी, अश्म, प्रस्तर, प्रभा

30. 'जलधि' शब्द का पर्यायवाची क्या है?
A. नहर B. नाव
C. नदी D. समुद्र

31. 'पंकज' शब्द का पर्यायवाची क्या है?
A. सूर्य B. कमल
C. चन्द्रमा D. अमृत

32. 'तरकश' का पर्यायवाची शब्द है–
A. तीर B. धनुष
C. प्रत्यंचा D. निषंग

33. 'स्त्री' का पर्यायवाची शब्द नहीं है–
A. तरुणी B. प्रमदा
C. ललाम D. ललना

34. 'गणेश' का पर्यायवाची शब्द है–
A. सुधांशु B. कुबेर
C. एकदंत D. सुधाकर

35. निम्नलिखित में से कौन-सा शब्द 'तलवार' का पर्यायवाची नहीं है?

A. असि
B. खड्ग
C. कृपण
D. चंद्रहास

36. इनमें से कौन 'कौआ' का पर्यायवाची है?

A. वायस
B. पाली
C. भद्रा
D. उदक

37. निम्न में से कौन 'पत्ता' का पर्यायवाची नहीं है?

A. दल
B. पर्ण
C. पल्लव
D. प्रसून

38. निम्न में से कौन 'हंस' का पर्यायवाची है?

A. मराल
B. सारंग
C. अनीक
D. अरि

39. निम्न में से कौन 'रण' का पर्यायवाची नहीं है?

A. युद्ध
B. संग्राम
C. समर
D. सार

40. इनमें से कौन 'युवती' का पर्यायवाची नहीं है?

A. तरुणी
B. किशोरी
C. श्यामा
D. यामिनी

41. निम्न में से कौन 'इन्द्र' का पर्यायवाची नहीं है?

A. सुरपति
B. मघवा
C. धनाधिप
D. सुरेश

42. इनमें से कौन 'सरस्वती' का पर्यायवाची नहीं है?

A. वीणापाणि
B. वाचा
C. धनद
D. शारदा

43. निम्न में से कौन 'कन्या' का पर्यायवाची नहीं है?

A. तनुजा
B. आत्मजा
C. नन्दिनी
D. भार्या

44. इनमें से कौन 'मयूर' का पर्यायवाची नहीं है?

A. सारंग
B. शिखी
C. विशिख
D. केकी

45. इनमें से कौन 'शेर' का पर्यायवाची नहीं है?

A. तुरंग
B. मृगेन्द्र
C. मृगराज
D. व्याघ्र

46. निम्न में से कौन 'अग्नि' का पर्यायवाची है?

A. अनल
B. धनद
C. सारंग
D. जाह्नवी

47. 'अलंकेश' पर्यायवाची शब्द है–

A. बादल का
B. कल्पवृक्ष का
C. कुबेर का
D. चपला का

48. इनमें से किस शब्द के पर्यायवाची गलत हैं?

A. कमल – जलज, पंकज, सरोज
B. पुष्प – कुसुम, फूल, सुमन
C. सरस्वती – गिरा, भारती, वाणी
D. सूर्य – दिवस, याम, वासर

49. निम्नलिखित में कौन-सा शब्द 'पताका' का पर्यायवाची नहीं है?

A. झण्डा
B. निशान
C. प्रस्तर
D. ध्वज

50. निम्नलिखित शब्दों में से 'हनुमान' का पर्यायवाची शब्द नहीं है–

A. रामभक्त
B. पवनपुत्र
C. बजरंगबली
D. कपीश्वर

51. 'खेचर' का पर्याय होगा–

A. आकाश में चलने वाला
B. पक्षी
C. ग्रह
D. इनमें से सभी

52. 'बटोही' का पर्यायवाची निम्न में से कौन शब्द-समूह होगा?

A. बटमार, एकाकी
B. असहाय, दुर्गम
C. पथिक, राहगीर
D. पाथेय, मेघ

53. निम्न में से कौन-सा शब्द समूह 'विरद' का पर्यायवाची होगा?

A. यश, ख्याति
B. बीज, मूल
C. वृक्ष, पौधा
D. विरही, वियोगी

54. 'यातु' का पर्यायवाची निम्न में से कौन शब्द-समूह होगा?

A. पथिक, कष्ट
B. काल, हवा
C. यातना, हिंसा
D. राक्षस, निशाचर

55. 'विभु' का पर्यायवाची शब्द-समूह होगा–

A. सर्वव्यापक, नित्य
B. ब्रह्म, आत्मा
C. महान, ईश्वर
D. चिरस्थायी, दृढ़

56. 'क्षुद्र' का पर्यायवाची शब्द-समूह होगा–

A. कंजूस, कृपण
B. निर्धन, दरिद्र
C. अल्प, मामूली
D. नीच, अधम

57. 'कुबेर' शब्द का निम्नलिखित में से कौन- सा शब्द पर्यायवाची नहीं है?

A. श्वान
B. कोषपाल
C. धनपति
D. यक्षपति

58. 'सेवक' का पर्यायवाची है–

A. परिचर्या
B. यायावर
C. शायक
D. परिचारक

59. 'पार्वती' का पर्यायवाची है–

A. कमला
B. इला
C. गौरा
D. विभा

60. 'अग्र' शब्द का पर्यायवाची नहीं है–

A. शिखर
B. अगला
C. ज्येष्ठ
D. दावा

61. निम्नलिखित में से कौन-सा एक 'जानकी' का पर्यायवाची नहीं है?

A. जनकात्मजा
B. वैदेही
C. जनकसूता
D. वामा

62. 'पुष्प' का पर्यायवाची नहीं है–

A. सुमन
B. प्रसून
C. कुसुम
D. निलय

63. 'पत्थर' का पर्यायवाची है–
A. हिमगिरि B. पाषाण
C. गिरि D. शैल

64. 'पावक' का पर्यायवाची शब्द निम्नलिखित में से कौन-सा है?
A. पृथ्वी B. जल
C. अग्नि D. वायु

65. निम्नलिखित में से जो शब्द 'पत्नी' का पर्याय न हो, उसे चिन्हित कीजिए–
A. कलत्र B. दौहित्र
C. भार्या D. जाया

66. 'अर्वाचीन' शब्द का पर्यायवाची है–
A. आधुनिक B. विदेशी
C. चीनी D. प्राचीन

विलोमार्थी शब्द

निर्देश (प्र.सं. 1 से 75 तक): *सही-सही विलोम शब्द चुनिए–*

1. अनादर
A. मान B. सम्मान
C. आदर D. सत्कार

2. अभिज्ञ
A. अज्ञानी B. अनभिज्ञ
C. अनिपुण D. मूर्ख

3. अथ
A. इति B. समाप्त
C. खत्म D. संपूर्ण

4. करुण
A. कठोर B. निष्ठुर
C. निर्दय D. कोमल

5. ऋजु
A. सीधा B. सरल
C. तिर्यक् D. वक्र

6. मौन
A. मुखर B. मूक
C. वाचाल D. प्रगल्भ

7. निर्दय
A. निर्भय B. सहृय
C. सभय D. सदय

8. तिमिर
A. प्रकाश्य B. आलोक
C. ज्योतिर्मय D. आभास

9. तीक्ष्ण
A. मंद B. तीव्र
C. प्रखर D. क्षीण

10. कृत्रिम
A. प्राकृतिक B. स्वनिर्मित
C. स्वाभाविक D. स्वचालित

11. उदात्त
A. उद्धत B. दानशील
C. अनुदात्त D. क्षमावान्

12. उदार
A. कंठोर B. निर्भय
C. अपव्यय D. अनुदार

13. शुक्ल
A. काला B. कृष्ण
C. असित D. श्यामल

14. प्रस्थान
A. आगमन B. गमनागमन
C. निगम D. निर्गम

15. शूल
A. मूल B. धूल
C. फूल D. तूल

16. अपेक्षा
A. कामना B. भावना
C. अभीप्सा D. उपेक्षा

17. निरक्षर
A. शिक्षित B. अशिक्षित
C. साक्षर D. अक्षर

18. प्रकट
A. गुप्त B. लुप्त
C. सुप्त D. विलुप्त

19. उर्वर
A. उपजाऊ B. बंजर
C. गत्वर D. शस्यश्यामल

20. संधि
A. अनुग्रह B. ग्रह
C. विच्छेद D. मैत्री

21. संयोग
A. प्रयोग B. सुयोग
C. नियोग D. वियोग

22. विकास
A. सीमा B. ह्रास
C. दुबला D. नीचा

23. उत्थान
A. नमन B. पतन
C. उदय D. ध्वंस

24. क्षुद्र
A. क्षुद्रतर B. महान्
C. तुच्छ D. अवमान

25. इहलोक
A. उपकार B. पाताल
C. आदि D. परलोक

26. ज्योति
A. पुंज B. दीपक
C. तम D. रोशनी

27. यथार्थ
A. मनोवांछित B. अनुमानित
C. कल्पित D. सत्य

28. अमर
A. देवता B. मरणशील
C. मर्त्य D. दानव

29. आघात
A. अनाघात B. विस्तीर्ण
C. स्निग्ध D. डरपोक

30. व्यष्टि
A. सृष्टि B. वृष्टि
C. समष्टि D. इनमें से कोई नहीं

31. सज्जन
A. चापलूस B. व्यभिचारी
C. सहयोगी D. दुर्जन

32. उत्कर्ष
A. अपकर्ष B. परामर्श
C. संघर्ष D. विमर्श

33. क्षुधा
A. तृषा B. तृष्ण
C. तृप्ति D. मृगतृष्णा

34. सुबह
A. प्रातः B. शाम
C. रात D. दिन

35. अनुकूल
A. प्रतिकूल B. अपकूल
C. अनुकूलन D. सानूकूल

36. आहूत
A. अनागत B. आगत
C. अनेक D. अनाहूत

37. श्रीगणेश
A. समापन B. इतिश्री
C. अंत D. अथ

38. निंदा
A. स्तुति B. संस्तुति
C. संवेदना D. स्तवन

39. आचार
A. आनाचार B. अनाचार
C. अत्याचार D. विचार

40. सहज
A. असहज B. असली
C. अप्राकृतिक D. निर्मित

41. प्राच्य
A. उदीच्य B. प्रतीच्य
C. पाश्चात्य D. अर्वाचीन

42. गुण
A. दोष B. पुण्य
C. अधिक D. विशाल

43. 'लाघव' शब्द का विपरीतार्थक शब्द है–
A. विस्तार B. संक्षेप
C. लम्बा D. दीर्घकालीन

44. आहार
A. प्रतिहार B. साहार
C. अनाहार D. विहार

45. 'ध्वंस' शब्द का विलोम बताइए–
A. विनाश B. निर्माण
C. विध्वंस D. उत्कर्ष

46. 'वादी' का विलोमार्थी शब्द बताएँ–
A. समवादी B. कुवादी
C. अनुवादी D. प्रतिवादी

47. अतिवृष्टि का विलोमार्थी शब्द है–
A. अन्तरवृष्टि B. अल्पवृष्टि
C. असमयवृष्टि D. अस्तवृष्टि

48. आदि
A. अंत B. प्रारम्भ
C. व्याधि D. बर्बादी

49. शाश्वत
A. मृत्यु B. मर्त्य
C. नश्वर D. क्षणिक

50. व्यस्त
A. विश्रांत B. अभ्यस्त
C. अव्यस्त D. अतिव्यस्त

51. गत्यात्मक
A. गतिभाव B. स्थिर
C. अस्थिर D. प्रत्यात्मक

52. अज्ञ
A. अनज्ञ B. सुमज्ञ
C. विज्ञ D. कुमज्ञ

53. कटु
A. मधुर B. पटु
C. मृदु D. मीठा

54. नीरस
A. रसीला B. सरस
C. विरस D. अरस

55. ओजस्विनी
A. तेजस्वनी B. निर्जस्वी
C. निस्तेज D. तपस्वी

56. अर्पण
A. ग्रहण B. तर्पण
C. समर्पण D. प्रत्यर्पण

57. अनभिज्ञ
A. भिज्ञ B. अज्ञ
C. अभिज्ञ D. अतिभिज्ञ

58. अन्यमनस्क
A. स्वस्थ B. प्रसन्न
C. सजग D. सतर्क

59. अपव्यय
A. अधिव्यय B. व्यय
C. मितव्यय D. इनमें से कोई नहीं

60. आवरण
A. अनावरण B. आचरण
C. सुवरण D. अवज्ञा

61. गमन
A. आना B. उतरना
C. रुकना D. आगमन

62. राजा
A. देवता B. साथी
C. विज्ञ D. प्रजा

63. विश्लेषण
A. संश्लेषण B. गवेषण
C. विशेषण D. अन्वेषण

64. दिवस
A. विभावरी B. अरविन्द
C. प्रवाहिणी D. विचक्षण

65. निर्मल
A. पवित्र B. शुद्ध
C. मलिन D. मृदु

66. उद्यम
A. प्रवीण B. आलस्य
C. नीरज D. नृप

67. द्युति
A. छवि B. प्रभा
C. ज्योति D. अन्धकार

68. रुक्ष
A. पिच्छल B. चिक्कण
C. स्निग्ध D. सरस

69. विघटन
A. सामूहिकता B. संगठन
C. एकीकरण D. समष्टि

70. गरिमा
A. कालिमा B. लघुमा
C. अरुणिमा D. लालिमा

71. सामिष
A. निरामिष B. वैष्णव
C. शाकाहारी D. मांसरहित

72. अंधेरा
A. सुबह B. उजाला
C. प्रकाश D. झुरमुट

73. उदय
A. अस्त B. अवसान
C. विनाश D. नाभ

74. कुटिल
A. संत B. उदार
C. साधु D. सरल

75. ग्राह्य
A. त्याज्य B. ग्रहण
C. तरल D. वाञ्छा

वाक्यों की शुद्धता

निर्देश (प्र.सं. 1 से 35 तक): *नीचे दिए गए प्रश्नों में चार वाक्यों में एक वाक्य शुद्ध है और तीन अशुद्ध हैं। शुद्ध वाक्य को चुनिए।*

1. A. मैंने एक रुपए का सामान खरीदा
B. मैं एक रुपए का सामान खरीदा
C. मुझने एक रुपया का सामान खरीदा
D. मैं एक रुपया का सामान खरीदी

2. A. उसे कॉफी बनाना नहीं आता
B. उसे कॉफी बनानी नहीं आता
C. उसे कॉफी बनाना नहीं आती
D. उसे कॉफी बनाने को नहीं आते

3. A. देश का सम्मान की रक्षा करो
B. देश के सम्मान की रक्षा करो
C. देश को सम्मान की रक्षा करो
D. देश के लिए सम्मान की रक्षा करो

4. A. अतिथि को चाकू से काटकर फल खिलाओ
B. चाकू से अतिथि को काटकर फल खिलाओ
C. चाकू से फल काटकर अतिथि को खिलाओ
D. फल को काटकर चाकू से अतिथि को खिलाओ

5. A. राम ने पेट भर मिठाई खाई
B. राम ने पेट भर के मिठाई खाई
C. राम ने भरपेट मिठाई खाई
D. इनमें से सभी शुद्ध हैं

6. A. मैं आपकी सौजन्यता पर मुग्ध हूँ
B. मैं आपके सौजन्य पर मुग्ध हूँ
C. मैं आपके सुजन्य पर मुग्ध हूँ
D. इनमें से तीनों वाक्य अशुद्ध हैं

7. A. लाओ एक पानी का गिलास
B. एक पानी का गिलास लाओ
C. गिलास एक पानी का लाओ
D. एक गिलास पानी लाओ

8. A. हमारी सौभाग्यवती कन्या का विवाह होने जा रहा है।
B. हमारी आयुष्मती कन्या का विवाह होने जा रहा है।
C. हमारी सौभाग्यवती कन्या का विवाह होने जा रही है
D. इनमें से सभी शुद्ध हैं

9. A. माँ बच्चे को दूध धाय से पिला रही है
B. माँ बच्चे को दूध धाय से पिलवा रही है
C. माँ बच्चे को दूध धाय से पी रही है
D. माँ बच्चे को दूध धाय से चखा रही है

10. A. ये हमारे पास रहते हैं और वे दूर
B. वे हमारे पास रहते हैं और ये दूर
C. वे हमारे पास रहते हैं और वह दूर
D. ये हमारे पास रहते हैं और वह दूर

11. A. वेदों के छः अंग माने जाते हैं
B. वेदों में छः अंग माने जाते हैं
C. वेदों से छः अंग माने जाते हैं
D. वेदों पर छः अंग माने जाते हैं

12. A. भक्तों की सेना जा रही थी
B. भक्तों की मंडली जा रही थी
C. भक्तों की टुकड़ी जा रही थी
D. भक्तों की भीड़ जा रही थी

13. A. आपकी शंका का परिहार हुआ कि नहीं
B. आपकी शंका का निदान हुआ कि नहीं
C. आपकी शंका का समाधान हुआ कि नहीं
D. आपकी शंका निर्मूल हुई कि नहीं

14. A. यह ग्रंथ विद्वतापूर्ण लिखा गया है
B. यह ग्रंथ विद्वतापूर्वक लिखा गया है
C. यह ग्रंथ विद्वानपूर्ण लिखा गया है
D. यह ग्रंथ विद्वानपूर्वक लिखा गया है

15. A. वह टका-सा उत्तर देता है
B. वह टका-सा प्रश्न करता है
C. वह टका-सा जवाब देता है
D. इनमें से कोई नहीं

16. A. जो मिठाई पसन्द हों आप खा लो
B. जो मिठाई पसन्द हों तुम खा लो
C. जो मिठाइयाँ पसन्द हों तुम खा लो
D. जो मिठाइयाँ पसन्द हों उन्हें आप खाइए

17. A. हम बचपन में वहाँ जायेंगे
B. हम बचपन में वहाँ जाते रहे हैं
C. मैं बचपन में वहाँ जाता रहा
D. मैं बचपन में वहाँ जाऊँगा

18. A. प्रत्येक व्यक्ति कविता कर सकते हैं
B. प्रत्येक व्यक्ति कविता नहीं कर सकते हैं
C. प्रत्येक व्यक्ति कविता नहीं कर सकता
D. हर व्यक्ति कविता कर सकते हैं

19. A. हेम नरेश की पुस्तक दी
B. हेम ने नरेश को पुस्तक दी
C. हेम नरेश का पुस्तक देगा
D. हेम ने नरेश का पुस्तक दिया

20. A. मन्त्री ड्राइवर से कार चलवाता है
B. मन्त्री ड्राइवर की कार चलवाता है
C. मन्त्री ड्राइवर के लिए कार चलवाता है
D. मन्त्री ड्राइवर पर कार चलवाता है

21. A. उसकी आयु तीस वर्ष है इस समय
B. इस समय उसकी अवस्था तीस वर्ष है
C. तीस वर्ष की अवस्था है इस समय उसकी
D. इस समय तीस वर्ष की अवस्था है उसकी

22. A. रागिनी अपने आप चली गई
B. रागिनी खुद से चली गई
C. रागिनी अपने से ही चली गई
D. रागिनी आपके आप चली गई

23. A. श्याम पौधे को जल से सींच रहा है
B. पौधे को जल से सींच रहा है श्याम
C. श्याम पौधे सींच रहा है
D. जल से सींच रहा है श्याम पौधे को

24. A. वह उदद्ंडनीय है
B. वह दण्ड भोगने के योग्य है
C. वह दण्डयोग्य है
D. वह दण्ड देने के योग्य है

25. A. हमारे यहाँ तरुण नवयुवकों की शिक्षा का अच्छा प्रबन्ध है
B. हमारे यहाँ तरुण नवयुवकों का शिक्षा का अच्छा प्रबन्ध है
C. हमारे नवयुवकों की शिक्षा का यहाँ अच्छा प्रबन्ध है
D. हमारे यहाँ नवयुवकों की शिक्षा का अच्छा प्रबन्ध है

26. A. मुरझाया हुआ फूल वर्षा की फुहार से अभिसिंचित होकर पुनः खिल उठा
B. मुरझाई हुई फूल वर्षा की फुहार से अभिसिंचित होकर पुनः खिल उठा
C. मुरझाया हुआ फूल वर्षा की फुहार से अभिसिंचित होकर पुनः खिल उठी
D. मुरझाया हुआ फूल वर्षा के फुहार द्वारा अभिसिंचित होकर पुनः खिल उठे

27. A. आपके दर्शन दुर्लभ हैं
B. वह विलाप करके रोने लगा
C. हम लोग कुशलपूर्वक से हैं
D. उसे मृत्युदण्ड की सजा मिली है

28. A. तीन महानगरों के नाम बताइए
B. इस समस्या की औषधि मेरे पास है
C. चरखा कातना चाहिए
D. यह एक इतिहासिक घटना है

29. A. मेरे को कल छुट्टी जाना होगा
B. आप ही तो मना किये थे
C. मुझको लौटने में विलम्ब हो गया
D. कपड़े डालकर तुमने मेरे साथ क्या करा?

30. A. राम का बहन गांधीजी पर कविता लिखी है
B. राम का बहन गांधीजी पर कविता लिखा है
C. राम की बहन ने गांधीजी पर कविता लिखी है
D. राम की बहन गांधीजी के ऊपर कविता लिखा है

31. A. कवि ने सम्पादक को एक कविता भेजा
B. अध्यापिका ने शिष्य से प्रश्न पूछी
C. बच्चे ने कहा था, पर आप ने नहीं सुनी
D. अमित ने जेब से दस रुपए का नोट निकाला

32. A. पेड़ की पत्ता गिरी
B. पेड़ में से पत्ता गिरा
C. पत्ता गिर पड़ा पेड़ों से
D. पेड़ से पत्ता गिरा

33. A. बैल और बकरी घास चरती हैं
B. बैल और बकरी घास चरते हैं
C. बैल और बकरी घास चरता है
D. बैल और बकरी घास चरती है

34. A. महात्मा गांधी का देश सदा आभारी रहेगा
B. देश महात्मा गांधी का सदा आभारी रहेगा
C. आभारी रहेगा देश सदा महात्मा गांधी का
D. देश आभारी रहेगा सदा महात्मा गांधी का

35. A. कश्मीर में अनेक दर्शनीय स्थल देखने योग्य हैं
B. अनेक दर्शनीय स्थल कश्मीर में देखने योग्य हैं
C. कश्मीर में अनेक दर्शनीय स्थल हैं
D. अनेक दर्शनीय स्थल देखने योग्य हैं कश्मीर में

निर्देश (प्र.सं. 36 से 80 तक): *नीचे दिया गया हर एक वाक्य चार भागों में बाँटा गया है जिन्हें (A), (B), (C) और (D) अक्षरांक दिए गए हैं। आपको यह देखना है कि वाक्य के किसी भाग में व्याकरण, भाषा, वर्तनी, शब्दों के गलत प्रयोग या इसी तरह की कोई त्रुटि तो नहीं है। त्रुटि अगर हो तो वाक्य के किसी एक भाग में ही होगी। उस भाग का अक्षरांक ही उत्तर है। अगर वाक्य त्रुटिरहित है तो उत्तर (E) दीजिए।*

36. कैक्टस के पौधे में कई चमत्कारी गुण (A)/ होते हैं लेकिन यह दुखदायी की बात (B)/ है कि हमारे देश में अभी तक इस पर (C)/ बहुत अधिक ध्यान नहीं दिया गया है। (D)/ त्रुटिरहित (E).

37. वाणिज्यिक वाहन निर्माताओं के (A)/ अनुसार, ईंधन की कीमतों में तेजी के (B)/ बावजूद बिक्री वाणिज्यिक वाहनों की (C)/ में तेजी दर्ज की गई है। (D)/ त्रुटिरहित (E).

38. जब तपती और धूल भरी (A)/ सड़कों पर मोटी-मोटी बूँदें गिरतीं तब (B)/ उमस के साथ मिट्टी की (C)/ भुनी भुनी गंध वातावरण में फैल जाती थी। (D)/ त्रुटिरहित (E).

39. औसत अगर मध्यवर्गीय (A)/ परिवार की बात करें तो उसमें (B)/ स्त्री मन को समझने की (C)/ गुंजाइश बहुत कम होती है। (D)/ त्रुटिरहित (E).

40. सुखद स्मृतियाँ चमकीले वर्तमान (A)/ से कहीं ज्यादा आनंददायक, (B)/ दुष्प्रेरणादायक और स्फूर्ति (C)/ प्रदान करने वाली होती हैं। (D)/ त्रुटिरहित (E).

41. किसी तंदरुस्त वृद्ध की देहयष्टि (A)/ देखकर लग पड़ता है (B)/ कि आयु ने उनके शरीर (C)/ पर अपना प्रभाव नहीं डाला है। (D)/ त्रुटिरहित (E).

42. कोशिश करने से मसले (A)/ समय रहते हल हो जाएं (B)/ तो ठीक वरना मन (C)/ में ग्रंथियाँ बन जाती हैं। (D)/ त्रुटिरहित (E).

43. यदि कोई विकलांग व्यक्ति (A)/ घर का मुखिया हो (B)/ तो वह गरीबी रेखा से (C)/ नीचे के दायरे में आएगा। (D)/ त्रुटिरहित (E).

44. एक मध्यवर्गीय भारतीय परिवार में पिता (A)/ काम के बोझ या दूसरे कारणों से अपने (B)/ बच्चों से कट जाता है, जिसका बच्चों (C)/ के मन पर प्रतिकूल प्रभावशाली पड़ता है। (D)/ त्रुटिरहित (E).

45. अर्थव्यवस्था विश्व के बदतर हो रहे (A)/ हालात से चिंतित वित्त मंत्री ने (B)/ कहा कि सरकार के पास नरमी (C)/ से निपटने के विकल्प सीमित हैं। (D)/ त्रुटिरहित (E).

46. बचत बैंक खातों (A)/ में बैंकों द्वारा (B)/ ब्याज की अदायगी (C)/ किया जाता है। (D)/ त्रुटिरहित (E).

47. वर्ष 2010 को आधार (A)/ बना कर राष्ट्रीय स्तर पर (B)/ नया उपभोक्ता तूल्य (C)/ सूचकांक जारी किया गया है। (D)/ त्रुटिरहित (E).

48. गुजरात की (A)/ राजरानी गांधीनगर (B)/ में एक बहुत बड़े समारोह का (C)/ आयोजन किया गया है। (D)/ त्रुटिरहित (E).

49. विमानन क्षेत्र का (A)/ नामी कम्पनी की (B)/ मुश्किलें दिनोंदिन (C)/ बढ़ती जा रही हैं। (D)/ त्रुटिरहित (E).

50. सरकार अपनी योजनाओं (A)/ का लाभ केवल कमजोर (B)/ वर्ग के लोगों तक सीमित (C)/ रखने के कक्ष में नहीं है। (D)/ त्रुटिरहित (E).

51. भारत सरकार द्वारा अर्जित (A)/ कुल राजस्व की (B)/ अधिकतम राशि आय कर (C)/ से प्राप्त होती है। (D)/ त्रुटिरहित (E).

52. दूरदर्शन के अधिकारियों (A)/ ने लोकप्रिय वाहिका (B)/ का प्रसारण बंद करने (C)/ का आदेश दिया है। (D)/ त्रुटिरहित (E).

53. राष्ट्रीय एकता तथा मानवीय (A)/ मूल्यों के मूलभूत सिद्धान्तों (B)/ को म्यान में रखकर (C)/ पाठ्य-सामग्री तैयार की गई है। (D)/ त्रुटिरहित (E).

54. दोनों देशों के वाणी (A)/ सचिवों की बैठक में (B)/ परस्पर व्यापार बढ़ाने (C)/ के लिए सहमति हो गयी। (D)/ त्रुटिरहित (E).

55. कोश के इस (A)/ नए संस्करण में बहुत (B)/ से नए शब्द (C)/ शामिल किए गए हैं। (D)/ त्रुटिरहित (E).

56. बैंक से जारी होने वाले (A)/ सभी परिपत्र, आदेश आदि (B)/ कागज के बजाय डिजिटल (C)/ माध्यमों से प्रेषित किया जाता है। (D)/ त्रुटिरहित (E).

57. नियंत्रण प्राधिकारियों से (A)/ भी अपेक्षा की गई है (B)/ कि वे प्रतिदिन प्रतिवेदन (C)/ का अध्ययन अवश्य करें। (D)/ त्रुटिरहित (E).

58. ग्लोबल वार्मिंग रूपी (A)/ शत्रु पर आक्रमण कर उसे (B)/ परस्त करने में सभी (C)/ का योगदान होना चाहिए। (D)/ त्रुटिरहित (E).

59. पेड़ नहीं सोंचते कि झोंका (A)/ आए तो झूमें या न (B)/ झूमें वे झूमते हैं और अपने (C)/ जड़ों पर यकीन रहते हैं। (D)/ त्रुटिरहित (E).

60. कितने वर्षों की अवधि (A)/ तक खाते में कोई भी लेन-देन न (B)/ होने पर खाते को (C)/ निष्कृत माना जाता है? (D)/ त्रुटिरहित (E).

61. सामाजिक कुरीतियों (A)/ का मुख्य कारण (B)/ अज्ञानता है (C)/ यह बात एकदम सही है। (D)/ त्रुटिरहित (E).

62. उसकी सौन्दर्यता (A)/ देखकर मन मयूर (B)/ नृत्य करने लगा (C)/ दिलीप ने श्याम को बताया। (D)/ त्रुटिरहित (E).

63. नगेन्द्र जी (A)/ हिन्दी के (B)/ लब्धप्रतिष्ठित (C)/ आलोचक एवं लेखक हैं। (D)/ त्रुटिरहित (E).

64. साहित्य (A)/ और जीवन का (B)/ घनघोर (C)/ सम्बन्ध है। (D)/ त्रुटिरहित (E).

65. दिल्ली से (A)/ अनेकों (B)/ पत्र-पत्रिकाओं का (C)/ प्रकाशन होता है। (D)/ त्रुटिरहित (E).

66. गाय को घास (A)/ खिलाने से और पंछी (B)/ को दाना डालने (C)/ से पूण्य मिलता है। (D)/ त्रुटिरहित (E).

67. एक संख्या का पाँच (A)/ बटा-नौ दूसरी संख्या (B)/ के पच्चीस प्रतिशत (C)/ के सम्मान है। (D)/ त्रुटिरहित (E).

68. दिनेश की मासिक (A)/ आय सुरेश की (B)/ मासिक आय से (C)/ चुगना हैं। (D)/ त्रुटिरहित (E).

69. इस कार की कीमत कम (A)/ होगी और कम्पनी इसमें ज्यादा से ज्यादा (B)/ भारतीय पूर्जे लगाने (C)/ की कोशिश कर रही है। (D)/ त्रुटिरहित (E).

70. कहतें हैं कि (A)/ हर दस कोश (B)/ पर बोली (C)/ बदलती है। (D)/ त्रुटिरहित (E).

71. वैश्वीकरण के इस (A)/ युग में हिन्दी भाषा (B)/ नीत नवीन शब्दों से (C)/ समृद्ध हो रही है। (D)/ त्रुटिरहित (E).

72. आज भी कई किसान (A)/ और कमजोर वर्ग के (B)/ लोग साहूकारों के अंगुल (C)/ में फँसे हुए हैं। (D)/ त्रुटिरहित (E).

73. हमें शिक्षा ऋण (A)/ लेने वाले ऋणकर्ताओं (B)/ से इस आश्रय की (C)/ शिकायतें प्राप्त हो रही हैं। (D)/ त्रुटिरहित (E).

74. बचत बैंक खाते में (A)/ एक महीना में अन्य (B)/ बैंक के ATM से (C)/ निःशुल्क 5 आहरणों की छूट हैं। (D)/ त्रुटिरहित (E).

75. कृपया बोधित (A)/ अनुदेश सभी पदाधिकारियों (B)/ को सूचित करने (C)/ की व्यवस्था करें। (D)/ त्रुटिरहित (E).

76. एक मादा सूअर अपनी (A)/ छः बच्चों के साथ जो (B)/ अभी नौ-नौ इंच से बड़े नहीं हुए (C)/ थे, रेलगाड़ी की तरह चलती जा रही थी। (D)/ त्रुटिरहित (E).

77. एक इरावती ही थी जिससे वह टूटी-फूटी (A)/ हिन्दी में बातां कर लेती थी, हालाँकि उसकी (B)/ पंजाबी हिन्दी और इरावती की कोंकणी (C)/ हिन्दी में जमीन- आसमान का फर्क था। (D)/ त्रुटिरहित (E).

78. अपने बेटे की वजह से ही वह (A)/ यहाँ परदेस में पड़ा था, जहाँ (B)/ न कोई उसकी जबान समझता था, न वह (C)/ किसी को जबान समझता था। (D)/ त्रुटिरहित (E).

79. चेचक के दागों और झुर्रियों से भरा (A)/ उसका चेहरा दीमक खाई लकड़ी की (B)/ तरह जाना पड़ता था, जो बदसूरत तो था (C)/ ही जुगुप्सा भी जगा देता था। (D)/ त्रुटिरहित (E).

80. शालिनी नित नेम की भांति दीपक जलाई (A)/ और एक अज्ञात देवता के सामने (B)/ हाथ जोड़ने की प्रक्रिया पूरी करके (C)/ घुटनों पर बाँहें रखे वहीं बैठी रही। (D)/ त्रुटिरहित (E).

वाक्यांश के लिए एक शब्द

1. एक स्थान से दूसरे स्थान पर जाना या ले जाना–
A. खिसका हुआ B. उखड़ा हुआ
C. स्थानच्युत D. विस्थापित

2. इंद्रियों को जीतने वाला–
A. अजातशत्रु B. इन्द्रस्वामी
C. जितेंद्रिय D. मुमुक्षु

3. एक ही कोख से जन्म लेने वाला–
A. संतति B. जातक
C. आत्मज D. सहोदर

4. अपनी इच्छा से चलने वाला–
A. स्वेच्छाचारी B. स्वच्छंद
C. अराजक D. स्वेच्छक

5. जो हर हाल में हो ही जाए–
A. होनहार B. अवश्यंभावी
C. भाग D. तत्पर

6. जो कठिनाई से समझ में आए–
A. दुर्गम B. दुर्बोध
C. दुर्लभ D. दुर्धर्ष

7. एक पर ही श्रद्धा अथवा आस्था रखने वाला–
A. एकाकी B. अलौकिक
C. अधिकारिक D. एकनिष्ठ

8. बड़ा बनने की इच्छा रखने वाला–
A. पदलोलुप B. चाटुकार
C. विवेकवान D. महत्वाकांक्षी

9. मन का दुर्भाव–
A. दृष्टिवैषम्य B. भेदभाव
C. मनोमालिन्य D. कलुषित

10. पूर्णतः स्वच्छ करना–
A. परिष्कार B. सुधार
C. आविष्कार D. पुनरोद्धार

11. जिसका जन्म उच्च कुल में हुआ हो–
A. सेठ B. अभद्र
C. अमीर D. कुलीन

12. ईश्वर को नहीं मानने वाला–
A. आस्तिक B. अधर्मवान
C. बंदा D. नास्तिक

13. उपकार मानने वाला–
A. कृतघ्न B. परोपकारी
C. अनोपचारी D. कृतज्ञ

14. किसी के पास रखी हुई दूसरे की वस्तु–
A. गिरवी B. जमानत
C. धरोहर D. सामान

15. एक स्थान से दूसरे स्थान को हटाया हुआ–
A. आंतरित B. प्रवासी
C. मुसाफिर D. स्थानांतरित

16. जिसे कठिनाई से भेदा जा सके–
A. अभेद्य B. दुर्भेद्य
C. दुर्दम्य D. अगम्य

17. जो सबको समान भाव से देखे–
A. दूरदर्शी B. क्रांतदर्शी
C. सूक्ष्मदर्शी D. समदर्शी

18. परलोक से सम्बन्धित–
A. पारलौकिक B. अलौकिक
C. इहलौकिक D. लौकिक

19. पीछे-पीछे चलने वाला–
A. अनुगामी B. प्रतिगामी
C. पश्चगामी D. अग्रगामी

20. जिसके हृदय में ममता नहीं है–
A. निर्दय B. कठोर
C. क्रूर D. निर्मम

21 जो व्यर्थ की बातें करता हो–
A. बहुभाषी B. कुवक्ता
C. वाचाल D. वाक्पटु

22. जो देखने में प्रिय लगता हो–
A. समदर्शी B. प्रियदर्शी
C. प्रियपात्र D. दर्शनप्रिय

23. अहसान न मानने वाला–
A. कृतज्ञ B. कृतघ्न
C. विश्वासघाती D. परोपजीवी

24. जिसे कठिनाई से जीता जा सके–
A. विजित B. अज्ञेय
C. अजेय D. दुर्जेय

25. बचपन और जवानी के बीच की अवस्था–
A. नवयुवा B. नवोढ़ा
C. वयःसंधि D. वयस्कता

26. पशुओं के समान व्यवहार करने वाला–
A. पाशविक B. पशुसा
C. क्रूर D. दानव

27. वह अग्नि जो जंगल में लग जाती है–
A. वनाग्नि B. दावानल
C. अनल D. प्रचंडाग्नि

28. वह वस्तु जो नाशवान है–
A. नाशक B. नासन्य
C. नासांतिक D. नश्वर

29. परिश्रम के बदले प्राप्त धनराशि–
A. मुद्रा B. करेंसी
C. पारिश्रमिक D. सिक्का

30. अधिक पढ़ी-लिखी महिला–
A. विदूषक B. विज्ञानी
C. अफसर D. विदुषी

31. दोपहर का समय–
A. अपराह्न B. पूर्वाह्न
C. अधपहर D. मध्याह्न

32. जिसके समान कोई दूसरा न हो–
A. असामान्य B. अद्वितीय
C. असाधारण D. महान्

33. जो अधिक व्यय न करता हो–
A. धन्नासेठ B. खर्चीला
C. अव्यय D. मितव्ययी

34. जो पृथ्वी से सम्बन्धित हो–
A. पार्थिव B. पृथ्वी
C. अलौकिक D. जड़

35. जो काटा न जा सके–
A. दो टूक B. तर्कातीत
C. अकाट्य D. निश्चित

36. जिसके पास कुछ भी न हो–
A. अकिंचन B. किंचित्
C. आकुंचन D. अलभ्य

37. अनिश्चित जीविका–
A. आंशिक सेवा B. अस्थायी सेवा
C. अर्द्ध रोजगार D. आकाशवृत्ति

38. जिस पर हमला न किया गया हो–
A. आक्रान्ता B. आक्रामक
C. अयोध्या D. अनाक्रान्त

39. जो बहुत मंद गति से कार्य करता हो–
A. मंथर B. दीर्घसूत्री
C. सत्वर D. मंदाक्रान्ता

40. उचित-अनुचित का ज्ञान रखने वाला–
A. विवेकी B. ज्ञानी
C. चतुर D. दूरदर्शी

41. जो अपने कर्त्तव्य का निश्चय न कर सके–
A. द्वन्द्वग्रस्त B. भ्रमित
C. किंकर्त्तव्यविमूढ़ D. द्विविधाग्रस्त

42. अनेक युगों से चला आने वाला–
A. समीचीन B. प्राचीन
C. कालान्तर D. सनातन

43. ऐसा कवि जो तत्काल रचना करता हो–
A. कविराज B. आशुकवि
C. महाकवि D. कवीश

44. जिस स्त्री का पति जीवित होता है–
A. कामिनी B. सुभगा
C. सधवा D. मधवा

45. अनुचित व्यय करने वाला–
A. अतिव्ययी B. मितव्ययी
C. दुर्व्ययी D. अपव्ययी

46. मुकदमा चलाने वाला–
A. प्रतिवादी B. मुकदमेबाज
C. वादी D. इनमें से कोई नहीं

47. जिस पर अभियोग लगाया गया हो–
A. प्रतिवादी B. अभियोगी
C. अभियुक्त D. याची

48. मोक्ष प्राप्त करने की इच्छा रखने वाला–
A. मोक्षेसु B. ममुक्ष
C. मुमुक्ष D. मुमुक्षु

49. 'वह स्त्री जिसका पति परदेस से आने वाला हो' के लिए एक शब्द है–
A. आगतपतिका B. प्रव्रत्स्यतपतिका
C. प्रेषितपतिका D. आगमिस्यतपतिका

50. 'जिसमें धैर्य न हो' के लिए एक शब्द है–
A. अधर B. धरातल
C. अधीर D. धीरता

51. 'जो पहले कभी न हुआ हो' के लिए एक शब्द है–
A. अद्भुत B. अभूतपूर्व
C. अपूर्व D. अनुपम

52. 'जिसे किसी से लगाव न हो' के लिए उपयुक्त एक शब्द है–
A. नश्वर B. लिप्सु
C. निर्लिप्त D. अलगाववादी

53. 'जो कुछ जानने की इच्छा रखता हो' के लिए एक शब्द है–
A. जिज्ञासु B. जननी
C. जानकी D. नीतिज्ञ

54. 'जो बात लोगों से सुनी गई हो' के लिए एक शब्द है–
A. अश्रुति B. सर्वप्रिय
C. लोकोक्ति D. किंवदन्ती

55. 'सबके समानाधिकार पर विश्वास' के लिए एक शब्द है–
A. अधिकारी B. समाजवाद
C. प्रगतिवाद D. अधिकारवाद

56. 'जिस बीमारी का ठीक होना सम्भव न हो' के लिए एक शब्द है–
A. असाध्य B. विकट
C. भयानक D. घातक

57. जिस पर विजय प्राप्त कर ली गई हो–
A. आक्रान्त B. अजेय
C. विजित D. पराजित

58. सूर्य के उदय होने का स्थान–
A. उदयाचल B. सूर्योदय
C. प्रभात स्थान D. गंधमादन

59. जो कहा न जा सके–
A. अकथित B. अकथनीय
C. अकथ्य D. नामुमकिन

60. जिसे बहुत बातें करनी आती हों–
A. वाचाल B. गम्भीर
C. समालोचक D. मुनि

61. जो स्त्री के वशीभूत हो–
A. स्त्रीदास B. गुलाम
C. स्त्रैण D. प्रेमी

62. जो समान न हो–
A. बराबर B. जटिल
C. अविषम D. विषम

63. जिसे पढ़ना-लिखना आता हो–
A. अल्पज्ञानी B. शिक्षित
C. बुद्धिजीवी D. साक्षर

64. जो खाना मुफ्त में मिलता हो–
A. भण्डार B. लंगर
C. खुराक D. राशन

65. जो अपने कर्त्तव्य को न जानता हो–
A. अनजान B. अज्ञानी
C. किंकर्त्तव्यविमूढ़ D. कर्त्तव्यहीन

66. 'युद्ध में स्थिर रहने वाला' के लिए एक शब्द है–
A. योद्धा B. साहसी
C. युधिष्ठिर D. वीर

67. 'जो ईश्वर में विश्वास रखता है' के लिए एक शब्द है–
A. आस्थावान B. धार्मिक
C. आध्यात्मिक D. आस्तिक

68. आयु में बड़ा व्यक्ति–
A. कनिष्ठ B. पूजनीय
C. ज्येष्ठ D. वरिष्ठ

69. नया उदित होने वाला–
A. नवोदित B. नवजात
C. नवागन्तुक D. इनमें से कोई नहीं

70. बहुत-सी भाषाओं को जानने वाला–
A. तत्वचिन्तक B. बहुज्ञ
C. बहुभाषाविद् D. भाषा-वैज्ञानिक

71. जो किसी की ओर मुँह किए हो–
A. अभिमुख B. अनमुख
C. सुमुख D. इनमें से कोई नहीं

72. 'सात सौ वाली' के लिए निम्नलिखित में से कौन-सा शब्द उपयुक्त है?
A. सतखड़ा B. सतनजा
C. सतमासा D. सतसई

73. 'तेज चलने वाला' के लिए एक शब्द है–
A. गतिशील B. चुस्त
C. कर्मठ D. द्रुतगामी

74. 'बिना स्वार्थ के कार्य करने वाला' के लिए एक शब्द होगा–
A. सहायक B. निस्वार्थी
C. पुण्यात्मा D. हितैषी

75. 'किसी की सहायता करने वाला' के लिए एक शब्द है–
A. सहकार B. सहायक
C. सहृदय D. सहचर

मुहावरा एवं लोकोक्तियाँ

1. 'सब्जबाग दिखाना' मुहावरा का अर्थ है–
A. बाग में घूमने जाना B. साग-सब्जी पैदा करना
C. प्रलोभन देना D. भयभीत करना

2. 'खुदा गंजे को नाखून न दे' लोकोक्ति का अभिप्राय है–
A. छोटे आदमी का प्रेम अस्थिर होता है
B. लज्जित होकर दूसरे पर क्रोध न निकाले
C. एक दोष पहले से था, दूसरा और आ गया
D. अत्याचारी को शक्ति नहीं मिलनी चाहिए

3. 'कभी नाव गाड़ी पर कभी गाड़ी नाव पर' लोकोक्ति का सही आशय है–
A. संघर्ष होना B. जीवन में उतार-चढ़ाव का क्रम
C. भलाई करना D. एक-से स्वभाव वाले होना

4. 'एक हाथ से ताली नहीं बजती' लोकोक्ति का अभिप्राय है–
A. शत्रुता दोनों पक्षों की गलती से होती है
B. संघर्ष बराबरी वाले दो पक्षों में होना चाहिए
C. एक आदमी से काम नहीं चलता
D. सराहना हेतु दोनों हाथ से ताली बजाएँ

5. 'उड़ती चिड़ियों के पंख गिनना' मुहावरा का सही अर्थ होगा–
A. अनुभवी होना B. वाक्चतुर होना
C. प्रतिभाशाली होना D. असंभव कार्य करना

6. 'नक्कारखाने में तूती की आवाज' मुहावरा का अर्थ है–
A. तूती की आवाज सबसे ऊँची होती है
B. नक्कारखाने में तूती नहीं बोलती
C. नकारे लोगों की सर्वत्र तूती बोलती रहती है
D. समर्थ व्यक्ति के सामने असमर्थ व्यक्ति का प्रभाव नहीं पड़ता

7. 'आँख के अंधे नाम नयनसुख' का सही अर्थ है–
A. गुणों के विरुद्ध नाम का होना
B. बुद्धिहीन, किन्तु पर्याप्त धनवान
C. अंधा आदमी प्रायः गुणवान होता है
D. एक आँख के अंधे को भी सभी सुखद आ सकते हैं

8. 'चिकना घड़ा होना' मुहावरा का सही अर्थ है–
A. चिकना चुपड़ा होना B. समृद्ध होना
C. निर्लज्ज होना D. मधुरभाषी होना

9. 'बेटा समय रहते न पढ़े, तो भविष्य में बुरी तरह पछताओगे' – वाक्य में 'बुरी तरह पछताओगे' के स्थान पर यह मुहावरा आ सकता है–
A. अंगारों पर लोटोगे B. आठ-आठ आँसू रोओगे
C. अंचरा पसारोगे D. कुएँ में गिरोगे

10. ''मुहावरे का प्रयोग वाक्य के अन्तर्गत होता है और लोकोक्ति पूर्ण वाक्य में होती है।'' यह कथन–
A. सही है
B. गलत है
C. कथन का प्रथम अंश सही है
D. कथन का अंतिम अंश सही है

11. 'समय के अनुसार काम करना चाहिए' अर्थ की बोधक लोकोक्ति है–
A. झूठ के पैर नहीं होते
B. जाके पांव न फटी बिवाई, सो क्या जाने पीर पराई
C. उँगली पकड़ कर पहुँचा पकड़ना
D. का बरसा जब कृषि सुखाने

12. 'भारत के अतुलित धन वैभव पर अंग्रजों ने दाँत गड़ा दिए'–वाक्य में प्रयुक्त 'दाँत गड़ा दिए' का अर्थ है–
A. किसी वस्तु को गलत ढंग से पाने की गहरी चाह
B. दूसरे की वस्तु देखकर ललचा जाना
C. दूसरे की वस्तु चुराने की चेष्टा करना
D. धोखे से दूसरे की वस्तु लेना

13. 'चाँद पर थूकना' मुहावरे का आशय है–
A. असम्भव काम करना
B. निरर्थक काम करना
C. सौंदर्य का अनादर करना
D. सम्माननीय का अनादर करना

14. 'नियम विरुद्ध कार्य करना' अर्थ के अनुकूल सही मुहावरा है–
A. सूरज को दिया दिखाना
B. उल्टी गंगा बहाना
C. दाई से पेट छिपाना
D. नौ दो ग्यारह हो जाना

15. 'खाला जी का घर' मुहावरे का क्या अर्थ है?
A. आसान कार्य B. मौसी का घर
C. भाई-भतीजावाद D. रिश्तेदार को लाभ पहुँचाना

16. 'सिर चढ़ाना' मुहावरे का अर्थ है–
A. मनमानी करने की छूट देना
B. सिर पर बैठाना
C. सिरदर्द का बहाना करना
D. सिर पर उठा लेना

17. किस लोकोक्ति का अर्थ ''वैभव क्षणिक होता है'' होगा?
A. साँच को आँच नहीं
B. अधजल गगरी छलकत जाए
C. पाँचों उँगलियाँ बराबर नहीं होतीं
D. चार दिन की चाँदनी फिर अँधेरी रात

18. 'आँधी के आम होना' मुहावरे का अर्थ है–
A. मुफ्त उपलब्ध होना
B. संयोगवश बहुत सस्ता उपलब्ध होना
C. वैभवशाली बनना
D. अत्यन्त प्रिय होना

19. 'पाँच सात की लकड़ी, एक जने का बोझ' लोकोक्ति का अर्थ है–
A. बहुत कठिन कार्य होना
B. असम्भव बड़ी शर्त रखना
C. छोटे या कमजोर व्यक्ति की बात को कोई नहीं मानता
D. मिलकर काम करने से कठिन कार्य भी सरल हो जाता है

20. इनमें से कौन एक लोकोक्ति है?
A. अंगूठा दिखाना B. अंधा होना
C. ऊँट के मुँह में जीरा D. इधर-उधर की हाँकना

21. 'कलम तोड़ना' मुहावरे का क्या अर्थ है?
A. सही लिखना
B. अच्छा लिखना
C. ज्यादा लिखना
D. बेकार लिखकर प्रायश्चित करना

22. 'ढाँक के तीन पात' का अर्थ है–
A. अपने स्थान पर अडिग रहना
B. साफ इनकार कर देना
C. बेकार घूमना
D. कभी किसी विशेषता से सम्पन्न न होना

23. 'घड़ों पानी पड़ जाना' मुहावरे का अर्थ है–
A. चिन्ता में डूब जाना B. बर्बाद हो जाना
C. पसीने से भीग जाना D. लज्जा से दब जाना

24. किस लोकोक्ति का अर्थ 'बिना परिश्रम के सफलता नहीं मिलती' होगा?
A. नौ दिन चले अढ़ाई कोस
B. जिन खोजा तिन पाइयाँ गहरे पानी पैठ
C. बालू से तेल निकालना
D. डूबते को तिनके का सहारा

25. 'हाथ कंगन को आरसी क्या' कहावत का अर्थ है–

A. समझदार के लिए उपदेश व्यर्थ है

B. प्रत्यक्ष के लिए प्रमाण की क्या आवश्यकता है

C. मूल्यवान वस्तु के सामने तुच्छ वस्तु का कोई महत्व नहीं

D. हाथ में कंगन ही चाहिए आरसी नहीं

26. 'दाँतों तले अंगुली दबाना' का अर्थ होगा–

A. मुसीबत में पड़ना B. बहुत हैरान होना

C. आश्चर्य करना D. दीनता प्रकट करना

27. 'अनिश्चितता' के भाव को प्रकट करने के लिए उपयुक्त मुहावरे का चयन कीजिए–

A. बंद मुट्ठी में क्या है

B. पर्दे के पीछे कौन है

C. न जाने भाग्य में क्या है

D. न जाने ऊँट किस करवट बैठेगा

28. 'कुपात्र की सहायता करना व्यर्थ है' इस उक्ति को चरितार्थ करने वाली कहावत है–

A. अंधे को न्यौता, दो जने आये

B. कुत्ते को खिलाई खीर, पाप में न पुण्य में

C. गधे की खाई खेती, न पाप में न पुण्य में

D. बन्दर क्या जाने अदरक का स्वाद

29. मूर्ख व्यक्ति के सामने ज्ञान की बातें करने के लिए उपयुक्त मुहावरा क्या होगा?

A. रेत से तेल निकालना B. अंधे के आगे रोना

C. भैंस के आगे बीन बजाना D. आकाश से बातें करना

30. निम्नलिंखित मुहावरे का अर्थ बताइए–

'सिर से पानी गुजर जाना'

A. अच्छी चीज का और अच्छा हो जाना

B. अपमान सहन कर लेना

C. सहनशीलता की सीमा टूट जाना

D. बाढ़ आ जाना

31. 'बहती गंगा में हाथ धोना' इस मुहावरे का क्या अर्थ है?

A. अधिकाधिक उन्नति होना

B. अवसर का फायदा उठाना

C. असम्भव काम को सम्भव करना

D. बहुत परिश्रम करना

32. निम्नलिखित वाक्यों में मुहावरे का सही प्रयोग क्या है?

A. धोनी अच्छे क्रिकेट का प्रदर्शन करके राँची वापस पहुँचा तो लोगों ने मैदान मार लिया

B. धोनी अच्छे क्रिकेट का प्रदर्शन करके राँची वापस पहुँचा, तो लोगों के हाथ के तोते उड़ गए

C. धोनी अच्छे क्रिकेट का प्रदर्शन करके राँची वापस पहुँचा, तो लोगों ने तिल का ताड़ बना लिया

D. धोनी अच्छे क्रिकेट का प्रदर्शन करके राँची वापस पहुँचा, तो लोगों ने उसे सिर आँखों पर बिठा लिया

33. निम्नलिखित के लिए उपयुक्त मुहावरा क्या है?

'मुसीबत देखकर घबरा जाना'

A. नाक पर धब्बा लगना B. नौ दो ग्यारह होना

C. दाँतों तले अंगुली दबाना D. नानी याद आना

34. 'काठ की हांडी बार-बार नहीं चढ़ती' लोकोक्ति का अर्थ है–

A. बुरे लोग लाख प्रयत्न के बाद भी अपनी बुराई नहीं छोड़ते

B. कठिन काम अकेले आदमी के वश की बात नहीं है

C. छल कपट का काम एक बार ही होता है

D. दुष्ट व्यक्ति बात से नहीं, बल्कि दण्ड से ही मानता है

35. 'रंगा सियार' मुहावरे का अर्थ क्या है?

A. डरपोक व्यक्ति B. धोखेबाज व्यक्ति

C. झूठ बोलने वाला व्यक्ति D. वीर व्यक्ति

36. 'बेपेंदी का लोटा' मुहावरे का अर्थ क्या है?

A. निर्धन व्यक्ति

B. स्थिर विचारों का न होने वाला व्यक्ति

C. मूर्ख व्यक्ति

D. दुष्ट व्यक्ति

37. 'घी के दिए जलाना' मुहावरा का सही अर्थ है–

A. दीपावली मनाना B. खुशी मनाना

C. रईसी प्रकट करना D. अपने को विशिष्ट समझना

38. 'सोने में सुगन्ध' मुहावरा का सही अर्थ है–

A. सुन्दर वस्तु में और गुण होना

B. सुगन्ध से युक्त आभूषण

C. सुन्दर आभूषण होना

D. सुगन्धित सोना

39. 'आँख का अंधा गाँठ का पूरा' लोकोक्ति का सही अर्थ है–

A. अंधा परन्तु विवेकशील होना

B. मूर्ख धनी

C. अंधे के पास धन होना

D. आँखों का रोग

40. 'गोद में लड़का, शहर भर में ढिंढोरा' मुहावरा का सही अर्थ है–

A. छोटे शिशु को तलाशना

B. अत्यधिक शरारती बालक

C. पास में वस्तु रहते हुए चारों ओर खोजना

D. छोटे बालक की प्रशंसा करना

41. 'पानी का बुलबुला' मुहावरे का क्या अर्थ है?

A. शीघ्र नष्ट हो जाने वाला

B. स्वच्छंद हो जाना

C. हार कर भागना

D. कष्ट उठाना

42. 'चाँदी का जूता मारना' मुहावरे का सही अर्थ है–

A. लुभाना B. आदर करना

C. शोभा बढ़ाना D. रुपए के बल पर दबाना

43. 'आगे नाथ न पीछे पगहा' लोकोक्ति का क्या अर्थ है?
A. पूर्ण स्वतन्त्र B. अपने मन की करना
C. बन्धन रहित होना D. इधर-उधर भागना

44. 'अन्धे पीसे कुत्ते खाएं' लोकोक्ति का सही अर्थ क्या है?
A. बेहिसाब काम करना
B. असावधानी से अयोग्य को लाभ
C. लाचारी का अनुचित लाभ
D. अपना माल लुटाना

45. 'अधजल गगरी छलकत जाए' का क्या अर्थ है?
A. गगरी में छेद होना B. बेकायदे काम करना
C. व्यर्थ की बातें करना D. कम ज्ञान का अधिक प्रदर्शन

46. 'जस दूल्हा तसि बनी बराता' लोकोक्ति का क्या अर्थ है?
A. अच्छा दूल्हा और अच्छे साथी
B. अच्छा दूल्हा और खराब बराती
C. सभी लोगों का अच्छा होना
D. जैसा व्यक्ति वैसे साथी

47. 'तीन लोक से मथुरा न्यारी' लोकोक्ति का अर्थ है–
A. बहुत सुन्दर होना
B. दूर की वस्तु सुन्दर लगना
C. जरूरत से ज्यादा बड़ाई करना
D. कृष्ण भक्त होना

48. 'थोथा चर्ना बाजे घना' लोकोक्ति का क्या अर्थ है?
A. बहुत अधिक बोलना
B. ओछे व्यक्ति अधिक दिखावा करते हैं
C. बढ़ा-चढ़ाकर बात करना
D. बहुत शोर करना

49. 'खग जाने खग ही की भाषा' का क्या अर्थ है?
A. पक्षियों की भाषा जानना
B. समान प्रवृत्ति वाले ही एक-दूसरे को समझते हैं
C. पक्षी अपनी भाषा स्वयं समझते हैं
D. पक्षियों की तरह बोलना

50. 'अदृश्य शत्रु' अर्थ के अनुरूप उपयुक्त मुहावरा है–
A. मीठी छुरी B. मुँह में राम बगल में छूरी
C. पेट में दाढ़ी D. आस्तीन का साँप

51. 'पापड़ बेलना' मुहावरे का क्या अर्थ है?
A. पापड़ बनाना B. मुसीबत उठाना
C. खाना बनाना D. पतली रोटी बेलना

52. 'पानी-पानी होना' मुहावरे का क्या अर्थ है?
A. घबड़ा जाना B. बहुत भीग जाना
C. बहुत लज्जित होना D. बाढ़ आ जाना

53. 'गूलर का फूल होना' मुहावरे का क्या अर्थ है?
A. सुगंधित होना B. फूल की तरह खिलना
C. दुर्लभ होना D. अति प्रसन्न होना

54. 'कान का कच्चा होना' मुहावरे का क्या अर्थ है?
A. कम सुनना B. सुनी बात पर विश्वास करना
C. दूसरे की बात न मानना D. कान का कमजोर होना

55. 'उन्नीस-बीस होना' मुहावरे का क्या अर्थ है?
A. बहुत कम अन्तर होना B. बहुत अन्तर होना
C. हिसाब जोड़ना D. भाग जाना

56. 'खून का घूँट पीना' मुहावरे का क्या अर्थ है?
A. गुस्सा करना B. खून की उल्टी करना
C. क्रोध दबाना D. दाँत से होठ कट जाना

57. 'पौ बारह होना' मुहावरे का सही अर्थ है–
A. सब तरह की सुख-सुविधाओं का होना
B. उपद्रव करना
C. पलायन कर जाना
D. प्रयासरत होना

58. 'कागजी घोड़े दौड़ाना' मुहावरे का सही अर्थ है–
A. प्रयास करना B. लिखा-पढ़ी करना
C. कागज काला करना D. व्यर्थ का काम करना

59. 'कान भरना' मुहावरे का अर्थ है–
A. धोखा देना B. चाणक होना
C. चुगली करना D. असर न होना

60. 'सिर उठाना' मुहावरे का सही अर्थ है–
A. रंग उतर जाना B. भेद प्रकट करना
C. बहुत पछताना D. विद्रोह करना

61. 'आडम्बर' बहुत, किन्तु वास्तविकता कुछ नहीं' के लिए सही लोकोक्ति है–
A. आँख का अंधा नाम नयनसुख
B. ऊँची दुकान, फीका पकवान
C. ऊँट के मुँह में जीरा
D. खोदा पहाड़, निकली चुहिया

62. 'चैन की वंशी बजाना' का अर्थ है–
A. साइकिल की चैन की बांसुरी बनाकर बजाना
B. मौज करना
C. फुर्सत में वंशी बजाना
D. बेरोजगार होना

63. 'आँख की किरकिरी होना' का अर्थ है–
A. अप्रिय लगना B. धोखा देना
C. कष्टदायक होना D. बहुत प्रिय होना

64. 'कीचड़ उछालना' मुहावरा का सही अर्थ है–
A. मल फेंकना
B. दूसरे के कपड़े गन्दे करना
C. बदनाम करना
D. दलदल में फँसना

65. 'अवांछित संवाद' अर्थ के लिए उपयुक्त मुहावरा है–
A. सिर खपाना B. सिर खाना
C. सिर नीचा होना D. सिर पड़ना

गद्यांश (अपठित-बोध)

गद्यांश 1

यदि हम निरन्तर प्रयत्न करेंगे तो निश्चय ही अपने सभी लक्ष्यों को प्राप्त कर लेंगे, किन्तु प्रायः देखा जाता है कि अधिक आशावादी लोग थोड़ा सा प्रयत्न करके अधिक फल की कामना करने लगते हैं और मनोवांछित फल प्राप्त न होने पर निराश हो जाते हैं। अतः जीवन में सफलता प्राप्त करने के लिए परिस्थितियों के समक्ष घुटने न टेकें, बल्कि दृढ़ता से उनका मुकाबला करें। याद रखें, जितना कठोर हमारा परिश्रम होगा उसका फल भी उतना ही मीठा होगा।

उपर्युक्त गद्यांश को ध्यानपूर्वक पढ़ें और निम्न प्रश्नों के उत्तर के लिए सही विकल्प को चुनें:

1. फल न मिलने पर कौन निराश हो जाते हैं?
A. आशावादी लोग B. कम आशावादी लोग
C. अधिक आशावादी लोग D. निराशावादी लोग

2. लक्ष्य प्राप्ति के लिए क्या किया जाना चाहिए?
A. फल की कामना B. हिम्मत से मुकाबला
C. निरन्तर प्रयत्न D. परिस्थितियों से मुकाबला

3. आशावादी शब्द का विलोम शब्द है:
A. निराश B. निराशावादी
B. दुखी D. अप्रसन्न

4. मनोवांछित शब्द का क्या अर्थ है?
A. इच्छित B. परीक्षित
C. लाभदायक D. मन को खुश करने वाले

5. परिश्रम शब्द का अर्थ है:
A. साहस B. हिम्मत
C. काम D. कठिन मेहनत

गद्यांश 2

पन्द्रह अगस्त 1947 को हमारा देश स्वतंत्र हुआ। स्वतन्त्रता प्राप्ति के बाद विश्व के दूसरे देशों के साथ भारत के राजनयिक एवं सांस्कृतिक सम्बन्ध जुड़े। पर्यटकों के साथ-साथ राजनीतिज्ञों और साहित्यकारों को भी विदेश यात्रा के पर्याप्त अवसर मिले। विभिन्न प्रकार की छात्रवृत्तियों के माध्यम से बहुत से लोग विदेशों में पढ़ने गए। बहुत से लोगों ने विदेशों में उपलब्ध आजीविका के अवसरों का लाभ उठाया। इन सबके परिणामस्वरूप प्रचुर मात्रा में यात्रावृत्तांत लिखे गए। विदेश-विषयक यात्रावृतांत्तों में रूस और स्वदेश-विषयक यात्रावृतांत्तों में लेखकों की दृष्टि कश्मीर से कन्याकुमारी तक व्याप्त हुई।

उपर्युक्त गद्यांश को ध्यानपूर्वक पढ़ें और निम्नलिखित प्रश्नों के उत्तर के लिए सही विकल्प को चुनें:

1. भारत कब स्वतंत्र हुआ?
A. 15 अगस्त 1947 B. 15 अगस्त 1946
C. 15 अगस्त 1948 D. 15 अगस्त 1949

2. स्वतंत्र भारत के अन्य देशों के साथ किस प्रकार के संबंध जुड़े?
A. राजनीतिक B. राजनयिक
C. धार्मिक D. राजनयिक एवं सांस्कृतिक

3. आजीविका का क्या अर्थ है?
A. उपार्जन B. वेतन
C. मेहनत D. रोजगार

4. यात्रा-वृत्तांत का क्या अर्थ है?
A. भ्रमण B. पर्यटन
C. सफरनामा D. विदेशभ्रमण

5. स्वतंत्र का विलोम शब्द है:
A. परतंत्र B. आजाद
C. गुलामी D. मुक्ति

गद्यांश 3

युवा वर्ग का मस्तिष्क नई-नई बातों की ओर ज्यादा तेज दौड़ता है। उसमें अन्य वर्ग के व्यक्तियों से अधिक आवेश और शक्ति होती है। इस अवस्था में यदि सही शिक्षा और उचित मार्ग-दर्शन न मिले तो यही शक्ति प्रेरणा और निर्माण के स्थान पर विनाश की ओर ले जाती है। बिगड़ने और बनने की यही आयु होती है। दुर्भाग्य से हमारे देश में शिक्षा पद्धति केवल उपाधि बाँटने का काम ही करती है। एक सम्पूर्ण व्यक्तित्वपूर्ण मनुष्य बनाना आज की शिक्षा पद्धति के लिए मुश्किल है।

उपर्युक्त गद्यांश को ध्यानपूर्वक पढ़ें और निम्नलिखित प्रश्नों के उत्तर के लिए सही विकल्प को चुनें।

1. निर्माण का विलोम शब्द क्या हैं?
A. रचना B. बनावट
C. विनाश D. सृजन

2. मार्ग-दर्शन का क्या अर्थ है?
A. उपाधि B. रास्ता
C. उद्देश्य D. रास्ता दिखलाना

3. शक्ति विनाश की ओर कब अग्रसर होती है?
A. अधिक आवेश और शक्ति के अभाव में
B. सही शिक्षा और उचित मार्ग दर्शन के अभाव में
C. दुर्भाग्यपूर्ण शिक्षा पद्धति के कारण
D. इनमें से कोई नहीं

4. हमारे देश की शिक्षा पद्धति क्या कार्य करती है?
A. मार्ग-दर्शन B. शक्ति प्रेरणा
C. उपाधि देना D. उपर्युक्त सभी

5. दुर्भाग्य का विपरीत शब्द है:
A. भाग्य B. सौभाग्य
C. भाग्यशाली D. भाग्यवान

गद्यांश 4

भिखारी की भाँति गिड़गिड़ाना प्रेम की भाषा नहीं है। यहाँ तक कि मुक्ति के लिए भगवान् की उपासना करना भी अधम उपासना में गिना जाता है। प्रेम कोई पुरस्कार नहीं चाहता। प्रेम सर्वथा प्रेम के लिए ही होता है। भक्त इसलिए प्रेम करता है कि बिना प्रेम किए वह रह ही नहीं सकता। जब तुम किसी मनोहर प्राकृतिक दृश्य को देखकर उस पर मोहित हो जाते हो तो तुम किसी फल की याचना नहीं करते और न वह दृश्य ही तुमसे कुछ माँगता है। फिर भी उस दृश्य का दर्शन तुम्हारे मन को आनंद से भर देता है।

उपर्युक्त गद्यांश को ध्यानपूर्वक पढ़ें और निम्नलिखित प्रश्नों के उत्तर के लिए सही विकल्प का चयन करें:

1. प्रेम का उद्देश्य क्या होता है?
A. मुक्ति B. उपासना
C. भक्ति D. प्रेम

2. मुक्ति का अर्थ है:
A. आजादी B. स्वतंत्रता
C. परतंत्र D. निर्वाण

3. कैसी उपासना अधम मानी गई है?
A. प्रेम की उपासना
B. भगवान की उपासना
C. मुक्ति की उपासना
D. भक्ति की उपासना

4. मनोहर शब्द हैः
A. विशेषण B. संज्ञा
C. सर्वनाम D. अव्यय

5. प्राकृतिक शब्द का अ[illegible]ः
A. ईश्वरीय B. मानव संबंधी
C. प्रकृति संबंधी D. प्रेम संबंधी

गद्यांश 5

कुछ लोग भाग्यवादी होते हैं और सब-कुछ भाग्य के सहारे छोड़कर कर्म से विरत हो जाते हैं। ऐसे लोग समाज के लिए बोझ हैं। वे कभी कोई बड़ा काम नहीं कर पाते। बड़ी-बड़ी खोज, बड़े-बड़े आविष्कार और बड़े-बड़े निर्माण कार्य कर्मशील लोगों के द्वारा ही संभव हो सके हैं। हम अपनी बुद्धि और प्रतिभा तथा कार्य-क्षमता के बल पर सही मार्ग पर चल सकते हैं, किन्तु बिना कठिन श्रम के अपने लक्ष्य तक नहीं पहुँच सकते। कठिन परिश्रम करने के बाद पाई गई सफलता हमारे मन को अलौकिक आनंद से भर देती है। यदि हम अपने कार्य में अपेक्षित श्रम नहीं करते तो हमारा मन ग्लानि का अनुभव करता है।

उपर्युक्त गद्यांश को ध्यानपूर्वक पढ़ें और निम्नलिखित प्रश्नों के उत्तर के लिए सही विकल्प चुनें:

1. "आविष्कार" शब्द का अर्थ है :
A. अनुसंधान B. खोज
C. निर्माण D. विनाश

2. अलौकिक शब्द का क्या अर्थ है?
A. संसारिक B. भौतिक
C. अमानुषी D. प्राकृतिक

3. सफलता का विलोम क्या है?
A. सफल B. असफल
C. सफलतापूर्वक D. असफलता

4. परिश्रम करने और न करने से हमारे जीवन पर क्या प्रभाव पड़ता है?
A. लोग भाग्यवादी बन जाते हैं
B. कर्म से विरत हो जाते हैं
C. मन में ग्लानि का अनुभव होता है
D. इनमें से कोई नहीं

5. किस प्रकार के लोग समाज के लिए बोझ हैं?
A. भाग्यवादी B. कर्मठ
C. परिश्रमी D. प्रतिभाशाली

गद्यांश 6

वैदिक काल से हिमालय के पहाड़ बहुत पवित्र माने जाते हैं। इसमें कोई सन्देह नहीं कि हिमालय के पहाड़ों का दृश्य अति सुन्दर है। उसकी विशालता को देखकर मन में आनन्द और कृतज्ञता की लहर उठती है। ऐसा लगता है कि यह विशाल सृष्टि प्रभु की अनुपम देन है। सारी सृष्टि के प्रति समभाव जाग्रत होता है। वस्तुतः यह दृष्टि कोरी कल्पनात्मक या आध्यात्मिक नहीं है। देखा जाए तो सारे भारत की जलवायु का समतोल करने वाले यह हिमालय के पहाड़ हैं, विशेषकर उत्तरी भारत को वर्षा और पानी देने वाले ये ही हैं। गंगोत्री, यमुनोत्री, बद्री, केदार को तीर्थ माना जाता है, जो व्यर्थ कल्पना नहीं है। उन स्थानों से निकलने वाली पवित्र नदियाँ ही वास्तव में हमारी प्राणदात्री रही हैं।

उपर्युक्त गद्यांश को ध्यानपूर्वक पढ़ें और निम्नलिखित प्रश्नों के उत्तर के लिए सही विकल्प चुनें :

1. हिमालय के पर्वत बहुत पवित्र कब से माने जाते हैं?
A. पाषाण काल से
B. वैदिक काल से
C. प्राचीन काल से
D. आधुनिक काल से

2. विशालता शब्द है :
A. जातिवाचक B. भाववाचक
C. विशेषण D. सर्वनाम

3. भारत की जलवायु को समतोल कौन करता है?

A. गंगोत्री B. यमुनोत्री
C. केदार D. हिमालय

4. सृष्टि का समानार्थक शब्द है :

A. सृजन B. रचना
C. प्रकृति D. संसार

5. प्राणदात्री का क्या अर्थ है?

A. गंगोत्री
B. यमुनोत्री
C. प्राणसंचार करने वाली
D. समभाव जांग्रत करने वाली

गद्यांश 7

सच्चा मित्र एक शिक्षक की भाँति होता है। जिस प्रकार शिक्षक अपने छात्र को सन्मार्ग की ही ओर अग्रसर करता है, उसी प्रकार एक सच्चा मित्र अपने मित्र को पाप के गर्त में गिरने से बचाता है। मानव-जीवन अधिक रहस्यपूर्ण है। कभी-कभी जीवन में ऐसे अवसर उपस्थित हो जाते हैं, जब मनुष्य की धर्मबुद्धि नष्ट हो जाती है और उसका मन द्रुत गति से पाप की ओर दौड़ता है। ऐसे समय में मित्र का ही उपदेश अधिक कल्याणकारी सिद्ध होता है। मित्र के उपदेश का जितना प्रभाव हृदय पर पड़ता है, उतना और किसी का नहीं पड़ता है।

उपर्युक्त गद्यांश को ध्यानपूर्वक पढ़ें और निम्नलिखित प्रश्नों के उत्तर के लिए सही विकल्प चुनें :

1. सच्चा मित्र किस प्रकार का होता है?

A. विपत्ति में सहायता देने वाला
B. गलत मार्ग पर चलने से रोकने वाला
C. शिक्षक के भाँति
D. धार्मिक गुरु की तरह

2. सन्मार्ग शब्द का विपरीत शब्द है :

A. अग्रसर B. कुमार्ग
C. सुमार्ग D. मार्गदर्शक

3. व्यक्ति को पाप के गर्त्त में गिरने से कौन बचाता है?

A. शिक्षक B. भाई
C. पिता D. सच्चा मित्र

4. मानव पाप की ओर कब दौड़ता है?

A. जब स्वार्थी बन जाता है
B. जब धर्म-बुद्धि नष्ट हो जाती है
C. जब सच्चामित्र साथ छोड़ देता है
D. जब धनवान बन जाता है

5. उपदेश में कौन-सा उपसर्ग है?

A. उ B. उप
C. दे D. देश

गद्यांश 8

सब तरह के भावों को प्रकट करने की योग्यता रखने वाली और निर्दोष होने पर भी यदि कोई भाषा अपना निज का साहित्य नहीं रखती, तो वह रूपवती भिखारिन की तरह कदापि आदरणीय नहीं हो सकती। उनकी शोभा, उसकी बड़ी सम्पन्नता, उसकी मान-मर्यादा उसके साहित्य पर ही अवलम्बित रहती है। उसके विचारों और राजनैतिक स्थितियों का प्रतिबिम्ब देखने को यदि कहीं मिल सकता है, तो उसके ग्रन्थ साहित्य में मिल सकता है। सामाजिक शक्ति या सजीवता, सामाजिक अशक्ति या निर्जीवता और सामाजिक सभ्यता तथा असभ्यता का निर्णायिक एकमात्र साहित्य है।

उपर्युक्त गद्यांश को ध्यानपूर्वक पढ़ें और निम्नलिखित प्रश्नों के उत्तर के लिए सही विकल्प चुनें :

1. साहित्य विहीन भाषा किस प्रकार की होती है?

A. आदरणीय B. भिखारिन
C. रूपवती D. रूपवती भिखारिन

2. रूपवती का पुल्लिंग रूप है:

A. रूपवान B. सुन्दर
C. सुन्दरी D. रूपवत

3. भाषा की मान मर्यादा किस पर निर्भर करती है?

A. लिपि पर B. साहित्यकार पर
C. भक्ति पर D. साहित्य पर

4. "सम्पन्नता" शब्द का विपरीत शब्द है:

A. गरीबी B. विपन्न
C. अमीर D. विपन्नता

5. राजनैतिक, सामाजिक शक्ति का दर्शन हमें किसमें मिलता है?

A. समाज B. राज्य
C. नेता D. साहित्य

गद्यांश 9

स्वतंत्र भारत का सम्पूर्ण दायित्व आज विद्यार्थियों के ही ऊपर है, क्योंकि आज जो विद्यार्थी हैं, वे ही कल स्वतंत्र भारत के नागरिक होंगे। भारत की उन्नति, उसका उत्थान उन्हीं की उन्नति और उत्थान पर निर्भर करता है। अतः विद्यार्थियों को चाहिए कि वे अपने भावी जीवन का निर्माण बड़ी सतर्कता और सावधानी के साथ करें। उन्हें प्रत्येक क्षण अपने राष्ट्र, अपने समाज, अपने धर्म, अपनी संस्कृति को अपनी आँखों के सामने रखना चाहिए, जिससे उनके जीवन से राष्ट्र को कुछ बल प्राप्त हो सके। जो विद्यार्थी राष्ट्रीय दृष्टिकोण से अपने जीवन का निर्माण नहीं करते, वे राष्ट्र और समाज के लिए भार-स्वरूप हैं।

उपर्युक्त गद्यांश को ध्यानपूर्वक पढ़ें और निम्नलिखित प्रश्नों के उत्तर के लिए सही विकल्प चुनें :

1. भारत की उन्नति किस पर निर्भर करती है?
A. युवाओं पर
B. नेताओं पर
C. साहित्यकारों पर
D. विद्यार्थियों पर

2. उन्नति का समानार्थक शब्द है :
A. पतन B. उत्थान
C. विकास D. उदय

3. उत्थान का विपरीत शब्द है :
A. उदय B. पतन
C. पराजय D. हार

4. किसे अपने जीवन का निर्माण सतर्कता और सावधानी से करना चाहिए?
A. युवाओं को B. नेताओं को
C. बच्चों को D. विद्यार्थियों को

5. धर्म, संस्कृति तथा समाज का रक्षक कौन है?
A. नागरिक B. ग्रामीण
C. विद्यार्थी D. युवा

गद्यांश 10

हास्य एक ऐसा माध्यम है, जो नीरस-जीवन को भी सुखद बना देता है। हास्य का जादू इतना प्रभावशाली होता है कि वह छूत के रोग की तरह चारों ओर फैल जाता है। जिसने कभी हँसना नहीं सीखा, सचमुच उसने जीना नहीं सीखा। सामान्यतः मनुष्य को जीवन में इतनी मुसीबतें झेलनी पड़ती हैं कि वह अपने जीवन को पहाड़ समझने लगता है। ऐसे दूभर जीवन को यदि जीने योग्य बनाना हो तो उसके लिए आवश्यक है कि जीवन में हँसने की गुंजाइश हो। हँसी के सहारे मनुष्य अपने कष्टों को भुलाने का प्रयत्न करता है। संघर्ष, तनाव, व्यस्तता, घुटन यदि आज के जीवन की सहज देन हैं, तो इनसे बचने के लिए यह आवश्यक है कि हम हँसना सीखें।

उपर्युक्त गद्यांश को ध्यानपूर्वक पढ़ें और निम्नलिखित प्रश्नों के उत्तर के लिए सही विकल्प चुनें :

1. नीरस जीवन को कौन सुखद बना देता है?
A. संगीत B. गीत
C. आमोद प्रमोद D. हास्य

2. नीरस का संधि विच्छेद है :
A. नी + रस
B. नि + रस
C. निः + रस
D. नीः + रस

3. किसका जीवन व्यर्थ है?
A. जिसने रोना नहीं सीखा
B. जिसने हँसना नहीं सीखा
C. जिसने गाना नहीं सीखा
D. इनमें से कोई नहीं

4. हँसना शब्द है :
A. संज्ञा B. विशेषण
C. क्रिया विशेषण D. क्रिया

5. तनाव और घुटन से बचने के लिए क्या करना चाहिए?
A. रोना चाहिए B. गाना चाहिए
C. हँसना चाहिए D. काम करना चाहिए

गद्यांश 11

किसी पुस्तक को पढ़ने में जल्दी नहीं करनी चाहिए, जो कुछ लेखक कहता है, उसे समझने की चेष्टा करनी चाहिए। प्रत्येक शब्द का अर्थ समझने की चेष्टा करनी चाहिए। यदि लेखक योग्य है, तो दूसरी बार वह पुस्तक और अधिक आनन्द देगी और तीसरी बार और अधिक। प्रत्येक बार अध्ययन करने पर आपको नवीन सुन्दर और नए विचार मिलेंगे और उसे आप जितना ही पढ़ेंगे, उतना ही स्नेह करने लगेंगे। सहस्रों व्यक्तियों ने गीता और रामायण तथा कुरान और बाइबिल को बार-बार पढ़ा है। उनका अनुभव है कि प्रत्येक बार उन्हें नई सूझ और नए विचार मिलते गए। कुछ लोग तो इस बात पर गर्व करते हैं कि उन्होंने अमुक पुस्तक को अनेक बार पढ़ा है, उन्हें कंठस्थ हो गई है।

उपर्युक्त गद्यांश को ध्यानपूर्वक पढ़ें और निम्नलिखित प्रश्नों के उत्तर के लिए सही विकल्प चुनें :

1. किसे समझने की चेष्टा करनी चाहिए?
A. पुस्तक B. रामायण
C. महाभारत D. गीता

2. पुस्तक की सजीवता किस पर निर्भर करती है?
A. लेखक B. प्रकाशक
C. पाठक D. चिन्तक

3. आनन्द का विपरीत शब्द है :
A. शोक B. दुख
C. संताप D. खुशी

4. नवीन, सुन्दर और नए विचार हमें कहाँ से प्राप्त होता हैं?
A. पुस्तक को बार-बार पढ़कर
B. सुनकर
C. भाषण से
D. अच्छे व्यक्तियों से मिलने पर

5. कंठस्थ शब्द का शब्दार्थ है :
A. कंठ में स्थित B. सुंदर कंठ
C. जबानी याद D. पंडित जी

गद्यांश 12

अहिंसा परम धर्म है और हिंसा आपद् धर्म। मनुष्य बराबर अहिंसा की ओर चलना चाहता है, किन्तु परिस्थितियाँ उससे हिंसा कराती है, अर्थात् परमधर्म की रक्षा के लिए आदमी बराबर आपद्धर्म से काम लेता रहा है। भारत अपनी सेनाओं को विघटित कर दे, तब भी उसका अपमान उससे अधिक होने वाला नहीं, जितना नेफा में हुआ। किन्तु परमधर्म पर टिकने की सामर्थ्य अगर भारत में नहीं है, तो आपद्धर्म पर उसे आना चाहिए। व्यवहारतः आपद्धर्म परमधर्म का विरोधी नहीं, उसका रक्षक है।

उपर्युक्त गद्यांश को ध्यानपूर्वक पढ़ें और निम्नलिखित प्रश्नों के उत्तर के लिए सही विकल्प चुनें :

1. **परमधर्म** का विपरीत शब्द है :
   A. महान धर्म B. आपद्धर्म
   C. सच्चाधर्म D. इनमें से कोई नहीं

2. आपद्धर्म किसे कहा जाता है?
   A. अहिंसा B. सत्याग्रह
   C. विपत्ति D. हिंसा

3. मानव से हिंसा कौन करवाती है?
   A. लोभ B. स्वार्थ
   C. द्वेष D. परिस्थितियाँ

4. **सामर्थ्य** का शब्दार्थ है :
   A. संघर्ष B. परिश्रम
   C. शक्ति D. पराक्रम

5. **परमधर्म** की रक्षा कौन करता है?
   A. अहिंसा B. हिंसा
   C. आपदधर्म D. युद्ध

गद्यांश 13

वर्तमान काल विज्ञापन का युग माना जाता है। समाचार-पत्रों के अतिरिक्त रेडियो और टेलीविजन भी विज्ञापन के सफल साधन हैं। विज्ञापन का मूल उद्देश्य उत्पादक और भोक्ता में सीधा सम्पर्क स्थापित करना होता है। जितना अधिक विज्ञापन किसी पदार्थ का होगा, उतनी ही उसकी लोकप्रियता बढ़ेगी। इन विज्ञापनों पर धन तो अधिक व्यय होता है, पर इनसे बिक्री बढ़ जाती है। ग्राहक जब इन आकर्षक विज्ञापनों को देखता है तो वह उस वस्तु-विशेष के प्रति आकृष्ट होकर उसे खरीदने को बाध्य हो जाता है।

उपर्युक्त गद्यांश को ध्यानपूर्वक पढ़ें और निम्नलिखित प्रश्नों के उत्तर के लिए सही विकल्प चुनें :

1. वर्तमान को किसका युग माना जाता है?
   A. फैशन B. विज्ञापन
   C. संगीत D. धन

2. उत्पादक तथा भोक्ता के बीच कौन संबंध स्थापित करता है?
   A. टेलीविजन B. समाचार-पत्र
   C. रेडियो D. विज्ञापन

3. **वर्तमान** शब्द का विपरीत शब्द है :
   A. अर्वाचीन B. आधुनिक
   C. आजकल D. प्राचीन

4. **आकर्षक** का शब्दार्थ है :
   A. विकर्षक B. सुन्दर
   C. मनमोहक D. आश्चर्यजनक

5. भोक्ता किस कारण वस्तुओं को खरीदने के लिए बाध्य हो जाता है?
   A. विज्ञापन
   B. आकर्षक विज्ञापन
   C. लोकप्रियता के कारण
   D. आसानी से उपलब्ध होना

गद्यांश 14

लगभग दो सौ वर्ष की गुलामी ने भारत के राष्ट्रीय स्वाभिमान को पैरों से रौंद डाला, हमारी संस्कृति को समाप्त कर दिया, हमारे विश्वासों को हिला दिया और हमारे आत्मविश्वास को चकनाचूर कर दिया, किन्तु अपने इस बूढ़े देश से प्यार करने वाले, इसके एक सामान्य संकेत पर प्राण न्यौछावर करने वाले दीवानों का अभाव न था। एक आवाज उठी और देखते ही देखते राष्ट्र का दबा हुआ आत्माभिमान उन्मत्त हो उठा। इतिहास साक्षी है जाने और अनजाने सहस्त्रों देशभक्त स्वतंत्रता की अनमोल निधि को पाने के लिए शहीद हो गए।

उपर्युक्त गद्यांश को ध्यानपूर्वक पढ़ें और निम्नलिखित प्रश्नों के उत्तर के लिए सही विकल्प चुनें :

1. **स्वाभिमान** का संधि विच्छेद है:
   A. स्वा + भिमान B. स्वः + अभिमान
   C. स्व + अभिमान D. स्वा + अभिमान

2. भारत का राष्ट्रीय स्वाभिमान किस कारण समाप्त हो गया था?
   A. लम्बे गुलामी से
   B. निरंकुश शासक से
   C. स्वार्थी मानव से
   D. धर्म के विनाश से

3. **आत्मविश्वास** का शब्दार्थ है
   A. घमण्ड B. गर्व
   C. अपने पर विश्वास D. अभिमान

4. भारत की अनमोल निधि को पाने के लिए कौन शहीद हो गए?
   A. देशभक्त B. नेता
   C. युवा D. युवती

5. **अनमोल निधि** का शब्दार्थ है:
   A. अनन्त खजाना B. अमूल्य खजाना
   C. बहुमूल्य D. स्वतंत्रता

गद्यांश 15

दुनिया के विभिन्न देशों के विकास पर विहंगम दृष्टि डालने से यह स्पष्ट हो जाता है कि आज जिस देश ने वैज्ञानिक उपलब्धियों के सहारे अपना औद्योगीकरण कर लिया, उसी को उन्नत देश कहा जाता है। जिस देश में औद्योगीकरण का स्तर नीचा है, वह पिछड़ा हुआ देश कहा जाता है। वैज्ञानिक आविष्कारों और औद्योगीकरण के आधार पर ही किसी देश की प्रगति को आँका जाता रहा है। विज्ञान ने मानव को पूरी तरह बदल दिया है।

उपर्युक्त गद्यांश को ध्यानपूर्वक पढ़ें और निम्नलिखित प्रश्नों के उत्तर के लिए सही विकल्प चुनें :

1. **विहंगम दृष्टि** का क्या अर्थ है?
A. एक झलक B. गहन दृष्टि
C. गहन चिन्तन D. इनमें से कोई नहीं

2. **विकास** का विपरीत शब्द है :
A. उत्थान B. उदय
C. पतन D. विनाश

3. **वैज्ञानिक** शब्द में कौन-सा प्रत्यय हैं?
A. निक B. वै
C. ईक D. इक

4. मानव जीवन को किसने बदल दिया है :
A. विकास B. वैज्ञानिक
C. विज्ञान D. उद्योग

5. किसी भी देश की स्तर को किससे नापा जाता है?
A. उपलब्धियों पर B. औद्योगीकरण से
C. वैज्ञानिकों से D. आविष्कारों से

गद्यांश 16

विश्व का वर्तमान उन्नत रूप मानव-श्रम की ही कहानी कह रहा है। गगन चुंबी अट्टालिकाएँ, लंबी-चौड़ी सड़कें, बड़े-बड़े विशाल नगर आकाश में उड़ते वायुयान तथा मानव-जीवन को सुखी और समृद्ध बनाने में योगदान करने वाले ज्ञान-विज्ञान के अनन्त रूप-ये सभी मनुष्य के श्रम का जयघोष करते हैं। स्पष्ट है कि मनुष्य और उसका शरीर विधाता की अनुपम रचना है जो निश्चय ही महान उद्देश्यों की संपूर्ति के लिए दिया गया है। इस दुर्लभ तन को यदि हम आलस्य, प्रसाद अथवा घटिया कामों में गँवा देते हैं तो उस विधाता के प्रति अन्याय करते हैं।

उपर्युक्त गद्यांश को ध्यानपूर्वक पढ़ें और निम्नलिखित प्रश्नों के उत्तर के लिए सही विकल्प चुनें :

1. विश्व का वर्तमान रूप किसका उद्योतक है?
A. चिन्तक का B. नेता का
C. वैज्ञानिक का D. मानव श्रम

2. **गगन चुंबी अट्टालिकाएँ** का अर्थ है :
A. आकाश में उड़ने वाला B. आकाश को छूने वाला
C. बहुमंजिली इमारत D. इनमें से कोई नहीं

3. आकाश का समानार्थक शब्द है :
A. वसुन्धरा B. धरा
C. पयोद D. गगन

4. **सुखी** का विपरीत शब्द है :
A. प्रसन्न B. अप्रसन्न
C. दुखी D. उदासी

5. विधाता की अनुपम रचना क्या है?
A. मानव शरीर B. समुद्र
C. वन D. पृथ्वी

गद्यांश 17

हमारे देश में एक ऐसा भी युग था जब नैतिक और आध्यात्मिक विकास ही जीवन का वास्तविक लक्ष्य माना जाता था। अहिंसा की भावना सर्वोपरि थी। आज पूरा जीवन दर्शन ही बदल गया है। सर्वत्र पैसे की हाय-हाय तथा धन का उपार्जन ही मुख्य ध्येय हो गया है, भले ही धन- उपार्जन के तरीके गलत ही क्यों न हों? इन सबका असर मनुष्य के प्रतिदिन के जीवन पर पड़ रहा है। समाज का वातावरण दूषित हो गया है–

बाह्य वातावरण तो दूषित है ही, आज सब जानते हैं पर्यावरण की समस्याएँ कितनी चिन्तनीय हो उठी है। इन सबके कारण मानसिक और शारीरिक तनाव-खिंचाव और व्याधियाँ पैदा हो रही हैं।

उपर्युक्त गद्यांश को ध्यानपूर्वक पढ़ें और निम्नलिखित प्रश्नों के उत्तर के लिए सही विकल्प चुनें :

1. भारत का प्राचीन आदर्श था :
A. सत्य और अहिंसा
B. नैतिक और आध्यात्मिक विकास
C. धन उपार्जन
D. इनमें से कोई नहीं

2. **अहिंसा** का विपरीत शब्द है :
A. हिंसा B. सत्याग्रह
C. विनम्रता D. नैतिकता

3. जीवन दर्शन क्यों बदल गया है?
A. हिंसा के कारण
B. अहिंसा के कारण
C. धन लिप्सा के कारण
D. आध्यात्मिक विकास के कारण

4. समाज का वातावरण दूषित क्यों हो गया है?
A. शारीरिक तनाव
B. मानसिक व्याधियाँ
C. पर्यावरण की समस्याएँ
D. धन उपार्जन के गलत तरीके

5. **पर्यावरण** का शब्दार्थ है:
A. जलमंडल B. स्थलमंडल
C. वायुमंडल D. वातावरण

उत्तरमाला

संधि

1	2	3	4	5	6	7	8	9	10
A	A	B	C	D	A	D	B	C	B
11	12	13	14	15	16	17	18	19	20
A	C	A	C	A	A	C	C	A	D
21	22	23	24	25	26	27	28	29	30
A	C	C	A	A	B	D	D	A	B
31	32	33	34	35	36	37	38	39	40
D	C	C	A	A	B	C	C	C	D
41	42	43	44	45	46	47	48	49	50
A	A	B	B	A	B	D	B	A	C
51	52	53	54	55	56	57	58	59	60
C	A	A	A	B	C	A	C	C	C
61	62	63	64	65	66	67	68	69	70
C	A	A	A	A	C	B	A	B	B
71	72	73	74	75					
B	A	A	B	D					

समास

1	2	3	4	5	6	7	8	9	10
C	B	C	A	C	B	A	A	B	A
11	12	13	14	15	16	17	18	19	20
D	A	B	D	B	C	C	D	A	B
21	22	23	24	25	26	27	28	29	30
A	A	C	A	A	C	A	A	A	A
31	32	33	34	35	36	37	38	39	40
B	A	C	C	A	D	B	B	C	A
41	42	43	44	45	46	47	48	49	50
A	A	A	C	A	A	A	D	B	D
51	52	53	54	55	56	57	58	59	60
C	A	A	C	C	A	C	C	B	B
61	62	63	64	65	66	67	68	69	70
B	C	A	C	B	D	A	B	C	A

वर्तनी

1	2	3	4	5	6	7	8	9	10
B	A	D	B	A	A	B	A	D	C
11	12	13	14	15	16	17	18	19	20
D	D	B	B	D	C	C	A	B	B
21	22	23	24	25	26	27	28	29	30
C	A	D	B	D	B	B	B	C	D
31	32	33	34	35	36	37	38	39	40
C	A	C	A	D	C	B	C	A	C
41	42	43	44	45	46	47	48	49	50
C	D	C	C	A	D	C	A	D	B

51	52	53	54	55	56	57	58	59	60
A	C	D	C	C	B	B	A	D	C
61	62	63	64	65	66	67	68	69	70
B	B	B	B	A	C	A	A	D	B
71	72	73	74	75	76	77	78	79	80
B	B	A	C	B	B	A	B	D	A
81	82	83	84	85	86	87	88	89	90
B	C	A	A	D	D	E	B	A	C
91	92	93	94	95	96	97	98	99	100
A	B	D	C	C	A	A	C	A	B
101	102	103	104	105	106	107	108	109	110
E	D	C	B	A	B	A	C	D	E
111	112	113	114	115					
D	E	C	A	C					

पर्यायवाची

1	2	3	4	5	6	7	8	9	10
D	C	D	D	A	D	C	B	D	D
11	12	13	14	15	16	17	18	19	20
A	D	A	A	C	A	D	C	A	B
21	22	23	24	25	26	27	28	29	30
A	C	B	B	A	A	A	D	B	D
31	32	33	34	35	36	37	38	39	40
B	D	C	C	C	A	D	A	D	D
41	42	43	44	45	46	47	48	49	50
C	C	D	C	A	A	C	D	C	A
51	52	53	54	55	56	57	58	59	60
D	C	A	D	A	D	A	D	C	D
61	62	63	64	65	66				
D	D	B	C	B	A				

विलोमार्थी शब्द

1	2	3	4	5	6	7	8	9	10
C	B	A	B	D	A	D	A	A	A
11	12	13	14	15	16	17	18	19	20
C	D	B	A	C	D	C	A	B	C
21	22	23	24	25	26	27	28	29	30
D	B	B	B	D	C	C	C	A	C
31	32	33	34	35	36	37	38	39	40
D	A	C	B	A	D	B	A	B	A
41	42	43	44	45	46	47	48	49	50
C	A	A	C	B	D	B	A	D	C
51	52	53	54	55	56	57	58	59	60
B	C	A	B	D	A	C	C	C	A
61	62	63	64	65	66	67	68	69	70
D	D	A	A	C	B	D	C	B	B
71	72	73	74	75					
A	B	A	D	A					

वाक्यों की शुद्धता

1	2	3	4	5	6	7	8	9	10
A	A	B	C	C	B	D	A	B	A
11	12	13	14	15	16	17	18	19	20
A	B	C	B	C	D	C	C	B	A
21	22	23	24	25	26	27	28	29	30
B	A	C	C	D	A	A	A	C	C
31	32	33	34	35	36	37	38	39	40
D	D	B	B	C	B	C	D	A	C
41	42	43	44	45	46	47	48	49	50
A	E	A	D	A	D	C	B	A	D
51	52	53	54	55	56	57	58	59	60
C	B	C	A	B	D	A	C	C	D
61	62	63	64	65	66	67	68	69	70
C	A	C	C	B	D	D	D	C	B
71	72	73	74	75	76	77	78	79	80
C	C	C	B	A	A	B	D	C	A

वाक्यांश के लिए एक शब्द

1	2	3	4	5	6	7	8	9	10
D	C	D	A	B	B	D	D	C	A
11	12	13	14	15	16	17	18	19	20
D	D	D	C	D	B	D	A	A	D
21	22	23	24	25	26	27	28	29	30
C	B	B	D	C	A	B	D	C	D
31	32	33	34	35	36	37	38	39	40
D	B	D	A	C	A	D	D	A	A
41	42	43	44	45	46	47	48	49	50
C	D	B	C	D	C	C	D	D	C
51	52	53	54	55	56	57	58	59	60
B	C	A	D	B	A	C	A	B	A
61	62	63	64	65	66	67	68	69	70
C	D	D	B	C	C	D	C	A	C
71	72	73	74	75					
A	D	D	B	B					

मुहावरा एवं लोकोक्तियाँ

1	2	3	4	5	6	7	8	9	10
C	D	B	A	A	D	A	C	B	A
11	12	13	14	15	16	17	18	19	20
D	A	D	B	A	A	D	B	D	C
21	22	23	24	25	26	27	28	29	30
B	D	D	B	B	C	D	B	C	C

31	32	33	34	35	36	37	38	39	40
B	D	D	C	B	B	B	A	B	C
41	42	43	44	45	46	47	48	49	50
A	D	C	C	D	D	C	B	B	D
51	52	53	54	55	56	57	58	59	60
B	C	C	B	A	C	A	D	C	D
61	62	63	64	65					
B	B	A	C	B					

गद्यांश (अपठित-बोध)

गद्यांश 1

1. C 2. D 3. B 4. A 5. D

गद्यांश 2

1. A 2. D 3. D 4. C 5. A

गद्यांश 3

1. C 2. D 3. B 4. C 5. B

गद्यांश 4

1. D 2. D 3. C 4. A 5. C

गद्यांश 5

1. B 2. D 3. D 4. C 5. A

गद्यांश 6

1. B 2. B 3. D 4. A 5. C

गद्यांश 7

1. C 2. B 3. D 4. B 5. B

गद्यांश 8

1. D 2. A 3. D 4. D 5. D

गद्यांश 9

1. D 2. B 3. B 4. D 5. C

गद्यांश 10

1. D 2. C 3. B 4. D 5. C

गद्यांश 11

1. A 2. A 3. A 4. A 5. C

गद्यांश 12

1. B 2. D 3. D 4. C 5. C

गद्यांश 13

1. B 2. D 3. D 4. C 5. B

गद्यांश 14

1. C 2. A 3. C 4. A 5. B

गद्यांश 15

1. A 2. D 3. C 4. C 5. B

गद्यांश 16

1. D 2. C 3. D 4. C 5. A

गद्यांश 17

1. B 2. A 3. C 4. D 5. D

❑ ❑ ❑

साहित्य

आदिकाल

- हेमचन्द्र अपभ्रंश व्याकरण के रचयिता थे।
- आदिकाल को 'आदिकाल' का नाम हजारी प्रसाद द्विवेदी ने दिया था।
- खड़ी बोली/कौरवी बोली का सम्बन्ध पश्चिमी हिन्दी से है।
- बघेली बोली का सम्बन्ध पूर्वी हिन्दी से है।
- खड़ी बोली का उद्‌भव अपभ्रंश के शौरसेनी के उत्तरी रूप से हुआ है।
- श्रावकाचार को हिन्दी की प्रथम रचना माना जाता है।
- धीरेंद्र वर्मा ने आदिकाल को 'अपभ्रंश काल' कहा है।
- 'गाथा सप्तशती' की रचना प्राकृत भाषा में हुई है।
- ब्रजभाषा का उद्‌भव शौरसेनी के मध्यवर्ती रूप से हुआ है।
- चंदबरदायी कृत 'पृथ्वीराज रासो' में शृंगार और वीर रस का समावेश है।
- आदिकाल में धर्म से सम्बन्धित पुस्तकों का सृजन मुख्यतः अपभ्रंश भाषा में मिलता है।
- आदिकाल में खड़ी बोली को काव्य का आधार सर्वप्रथम 'अमीर खुसरो' ने बनाया था।
- अमर खुसरो की रचनाओं को देशी भाषा काव्य के अन्तर्गत माना जाता है।
- आदिकालीन हिन्दी साहित्य को मुख्यतः अपभ्रंश-हिन्दी के वर्ग में रखा जाता है।
- 'मैथिल कोकिल' के नाम से प्रसिद्ध विद्यापति का समय सम्वत् 1460 माना जाता है।
- आदिकाल में 'अवधूत संप्रदाय' का सम्बन्ध नाथों से है।
- आदिकाल में जैनों द्वारा रचित साहित्य को सर्वाधिक प्रमाणिक माना जाता है।
- रामायण में संस्कृत भाषा का प्रयोग किया गया है।
- अमीर खुसरो ने फारसी तथा खड़ी बोली दोनों में रचना की है।
- मैथिल कोकिल 'विद्यापति' संस्कृत, अपभ्रंश तथा मैथिली तीनों में रचना की है।
- वर्णरत्नाकर मैथिली की पहली गद्य रचना है। इसके लेखक ज्योतिरीश्वर ठाकुर हैं।
- 'ढ़ोला मारू रा दूहा' के रचयिता कल्लोल कवि हैं।
- 'कीर्तिलता' की भाषा मिश्रित अपभ्रंश है।
- 'पृथ्वीराज विजय' की रचना जयानक ने की थी।

आदिकाल के प्रमुख रचनाकार तथा उनकी रचनायें

क्र.सं	रचनाकार	रचनायें
1.	सहरपा	दोहाकोष
2.	ज्योतिरीश्वर ठाकुर	वर्णरत्नाकर
3.	शबरपा	चर्यापद
4.	श्रीधर	रणमल्ल छंद
5.	जगनिक	परमाल रासो
6.	हाल कवि	गाथा सप्तशती
7.	नल्ल सिंह	विजयपाल रासो
8.	विद्यापति	पदावली, कीर्तिपताका, कीर्तिलता, भूपरिक्रमा
9.	अमीर खुसरो	खालिकबारी, पहेलियां, दो सुखने, गजल
10.	राजशेखर	कर्पूर मंजरी
11.	चन्दबरदायी	पृथ्वीराज रासो
12.	नरपति नाल्ह	बीसलदेव रासो
13.	कल्लोल	ढोला मारू रा दूहा

भक्तिकाल

- 'हरडेवानी' दादू की रचनाओं का संग्रह है।
- 'चित्रावली' की रचना उस्मान ने की थी।
- भक्तिकालीन 'प्रेमाश्रयी शाखा' पर सूफी मत का प्रभाव सर्वाधिक है।
- 'मधुमालती' के रचयिता मंझन है।
- तुलसीदास जी के गुरु का नाम 'नरहरि दास' था।
- गोस्वामी तुलसीदास ने 'रामचरित मानस' की रचना दोहा-चौपाई पद्धति पर की है।
- तुलसीदास की रचना 'विनय पत्रिका' गीत पद्धति पर आधारित है।
- 'बीजक' ग्रंथ का प्रणयन सधुक्कड़ी भाषा में किया गया है।
- 'विनय-पत्रिका' की भाषा ब्रजभाषा है।
- चंदायन की रचना मुल्ला दाऊद ने की थी।
- चंदायन की रचना से हिन्दी में सूफी काव्य परम्परा का सूत्रपात होता है।
- पद्‌मावत की भाषा अवधी है।

- रामचरित मानस की भाषा अवधी है।
- ब्रज भक्तिकालीन हिन्दी काव्य की सर्वाधिक प्रमुख भाषा है।
- तुलसीदास की 'गीतावली' ब्रजभाषा में लिखी गयी है।
- मीराबाई पर सूफियों का प्रभाव था।
- 'गीत-गोविंद' के रचयिता जयदेव हैं।

भक्तिकाव्य के प्रमुख रचनाकार तथा उनकी रचनायें

क्र.सं	रचनाकार	रचनायें
1.	कबीर	बीजक
2.	नाभादास	भक्तमाल
3.	दादू	हरडेवानी
4.	मूल्ला दाउद	चंदायन
5.	मंझन	मधुमालती
6.	उसमान	चित्रावली
7.	जायसी	पद्मावत, चित्रलेखा, अखरावट, कहरनामा
8.	नरपति व्यास	नल दमयन्ती
9.	तुलसीदास	दोहावली, जानकी मंगल, रामचरितमानस
10.	जयदेव	गीत-गोविन्द
11.	सूरदास	सूरसागर, साहित्य लहरी
12.	रसखान	प्रेमवाटिका, सुजान खान

रीतिकाल

- आचार्य रामचंद्र शुक्ल के अनुसार रीतिकाल की समय सीमा 1643 ई. से 1843 ई. के बीच है।
- मतिराम की रचना 'छंदसार' पिंगल ग्रंथ का उदाहरण है।
- रीतिकाल के प्रसिद्ध कवि भूषण की रचना 'शिवराज भूषण' अलंकार ग्रंथ का प्रमुख उदाहरण है।
- केशवदास को अलंकारवादी आचार्य कहा जाता है।
- **'करणा भरण श्रुतिभरण'** नामक काव्य का सम्बन्ध अलंकार विद्या से है।
- रीतिकाल के अधिकांश कवियों की भाषा थी–ब्रजभाषा।
- रीतिकाल के कवि घनानंद को 'साक्षात् रस मूर्ति' माना जाता है।
- 'विज्ञान गीता' उपदेशात्मक है।
- रीतिकाल के कवि पद्माकर ने भक्ति, शृंगार और वीर तीनों में समान अधिकार से रचना की है।
- सिखों के दसवें गुरु 'गुरु गोविंद सिंह' को रीतिकाल के रीतिमुक्त काव्य धारा का माना गया है।

रीतिकाल के प्रमुख रचनाकार तथा उनकी रचनायें

क्र.सं	रचनाकार	रचनायें
1.	चिंतामणि	पिंगल, कविकुल-कल्पतरु, रसमंजरी, काव्य-प्रकाश
2.	केशवदास	कवि प्रिया, रसिक प्रिया
3.	कृपाराम	हिततरंगिणि, रस तरंगिणि
4.	करनेस	कर्णाभरण, श्रुतिभूषण, भूपभूषण
5.	रहीम	रहीम सतसई, मदनाष्टक, शृंगार सोरठा, नगरशोभा
6.	मतिराम	छन्दसार, रसराज, साहित्यसार, अलंकार पंचाशिका
7.	भूषण	शिवराज भूषण, शिवा बावनी, छत्रसाल दशक, भूषण उल्लास
8.	बिहारी	बिहारी सतसई
9.	कुलपति मिश्र	रस रहस्य
10.	सुखदेव मिश्र	वृत्त विचार, छन्द विचार, रसार्णव, शृंगार लता
11.	पद्माकर	जगत विनोद, पद्माभरण, गंगा लहरी, प्रबोध पचासा
12.	घनानंद	इश्कलता, विरहलीला, सुजानसागर, कृपाकांड
13.	जोधराण	हम्मीर रासो
14.	गुरु गोविंद सिंह	चण्डी चरित्र, सुनीति प्रकाश, बुद्धिसागर
15.	रसखान	प्रेमवाटिका, सुजान रसखान

रीतिकाल का नामकरण करने वाले विभिन्न विद्वान

क्र.सं	विद्वान	नामकरण
1.	आचार्य शुक्ल	रीतिकाल
2.	मिश्रबंधु	अलंकृत मध्यकाल
3.	ग्रियर्सन	रीतिकाव्य
4.	विश्वनाथ प्रसाद मिश्र	शृंगार काल

आधुनिक काल

- आधुनिक काल में सम्मिलित हैं–भारतेन्दु युग, द्विवेदी युग, छायावादी युग, प्रगतिवादी युग तथा प्रयोगवादी युग।
- भारतेन्दु युग के प्रमुख रचनाकार हैं–भारतेन्दु हरिश्चन्द्र, बालकृष्ण भट्ट, प्रताप नारायण मिश्र, बद्रीनारायण चौधरी
- द्विवेदी युग के प्रमुख रचनाकार हैं–आचार्य महावीर प्रसाद द्विवेदी, श्रीधर पाठक, रामनरेश त्रिपाठी, अयोध्या सिंह उपाध्याय 'हरिऔध', मैथिलीशरण गुप्त, श्यामसुन्दर दास।
- छायावादी युग के प्रमुख रचनाकार हैं–जयशंकर प्रसाद, सूर्यकान्त त्रिपाठी 'निराला', सुमित्रानन्दन पंत तथा महादेवी वर्मा।

हिन्दी साहित्य के गद्य एवं पद्य से सम्बन्धित कुछ महत्त्वपूर्ण रचनाकार

सूरदास

महाप्रभु बल्लभाचार्य के शिष्य सूरदास अष्टछाप के कवियों में सर्वाधिक प्रसिद्ध हैं। उनके तीन ग्रंथो सूरसागर, साहित्य लहरी और सूर सारावली में सूरसागर सर्वाधिक लोकप्रिय ग्रंथ है। सूर 'वात्सल्य' और 'शृंगार' के श्रेष्ठ कवि माने जाते हैं। उनकी कविता में ब्रजभाषा का निखरा हुआ रूप है।

तुलसीदास

तुलसीदास का जन्म उत्तर प्रदेश के बाँदा जिले के राजापुर गाँव में सन् 1532 में हुआ था। रामचरितमानस, कवितावली, गीतावली, दोहावली, कृष्णगीतावली तथा विनयपत्रिका उनकी प्रमुख रचनाएं हैं। तुलसीदास ने रामचरितमानस की रचना अवधी में और विनय पत्रिका तथा कवितावली की रचना ब्रजभाषा में की। विनय पत्रिका की रचना गेय पदों में हुई है।

देव

देव का जन्म इटावा में सन् 1673 में हुआ था। रसविलास, भावविलास, काव्यरसायन, भवानीविलास आदि देव के प्रमुख ग्रंथ माने जाते हैं। देव रीतिकाल के प्रमुख कवि हैं। रीतिकालीन कविता का सम्बन्ध दरबारों, आश्रयदाताओं से था। इस कारण उसमें दरबारी संस्कृति का चित्रण अधिक हुआ है। आलंकारिकता और शृंगारिकता उनके काव्य की प्रमुख विशेषताएं हैं।

जयशंकर प्रसाद

जयशंकर प्रसाद का जन्म सन् 1889 में वाराणसी में हुआ। छायावादी काव्य प्रवृत्ति के प्रमुख कवियों में एक जयशंकर प्रसाद का सन् 1937 में निधन हो गया। उनकी प्रमुख काव्य-कृतियाँ हैं–चित्राधार, कानन-कुसुम, झरना, आँसू, लहर और कामायनी। अजातशत्रु, चन्द्रगुप्त, स्कंदगुप्त और ध्रुवस्वामिनी उनके नाटक हैं तथा कंकाल, तितली और इरावती उनके उपन्यास हैं।

सूर्यकांत त्रिपाठी 'निराला'

सूर्यकांत त्रिपाठी 'निराला' का जन्म बंगाल के महिपादल में सन् 1899 में हुआ। उनकी प्रमुख काव्य रचनाएं हैं–अनामिका, परिमल, गीतिका, कुकुरमुत्ता और नए पत्ते। छायावादी रचनाकारों में उन्होंने सबसे पहले मुक्त छंद का प्रयोग किया।

नागार्जुन

नागार्जुन का जन्म बिहार के दरभंगा जिले के सतलखा गाँव में सन् 1911 में हुआ। उनका मूल नाम बैद्यनाथ मिश्र था। नागार्जुन की प्रमुख काव्य-कृतियां हैं–युगधारा, सतरंगे पंखों वाली, हजार-हजार बाँहों वाली, तुमने कहा था, पुरानी जुतियों का कोरस, मैं मिलटरी का बूढ़ा घोड़ा। उनको आधुनिक कबीर भी कहा जाता है। छायावादोत्तर दौर के वे ऐसे अकेले कवि हैं, जिनकी कविता गाँव की चौपालों और साहित्यिक दुनिया में समान रूप से लोकप्रिय रही। उन्होंने छंदों में काव्य-रचना की और मुक्त छंद में भी।

रामवृक्ष बेनीपुरी

रामवृक्ष बेनीपुरी का जन्म बिहार के मुजफ्फरपुर जिले के बेनीपुर गाँव मे सन् 1899 में हुआ। उन्होंने अनेक दैनिक, साप्ताहिक एवं मासिक पत्र-पत्रिकाओं का संपादन किया। उनकी रचना-यात्रा के महत्त्वपूर्ण पड़ाव हैं–पतितो के देश में (उपन्यास); चिंता के फूल (कहानी), आम्रपाली (नाटक); माटी की मूरतें (रेखाचित्र); पैरों में पंख बांध कर (यात्रा-वृत्तांत); जंजीरें और दीवारें (संस्मरण) आदि। विशिष्ट शैलीकार होने के कारण उन्हें 'कलम का जादूगर' कहा जाता है।

महावीर प्रसाद द्विवेदी

महावीर प्रसाद द्विवेदी का जन्म सन् 1864 में ग्राम दौलतपुर, जिला राय बरेली (उत्तर प्रदेश) में हुआ। वे हिन्दी के पहले व्यवस्थित संपादक, भाषावैज्ञानिक, इतिहासकार, पुरातत्ववेत्ता अर्थशास्त्री, समाजशास्त्री एवं लेखक थे। उनकी प्रमुख कृतियां हैं–रसज्ञ रंजन, साहित्य-सीकर, साहित्य-संदर्भ, अद्भुत आलाप (निबंध संग्रह)। संपत्तिशास्त्र उनकी अर्थशास्त्र से सम्बन्धित पुस्तक है। उन्होंने कविता की भाषा के रूप में ब्रजभाषा के बदले खड़ी बोली को प्रतिष्ठित किया। हिन्दी में पहली बार समालोचना को स्थापित करने का श्रेय भी उनको जाता है।

कबीर

कबीर का जन्म काशी में हुआ था। कबीर गुरु रामानंद के शिष्य थे। उन्होंने जनचेतना और जनभावनाओं को अपने सबद और साखियों के माध्यम से जन-जन तक पहुँचाया। कबीर की भाषा को सधुक्कड़ी कहा जाता है।

मीरा

मीराबाई का जन्म जोधपुर के चोकड़ी गाँव में 1503 में हुआ माना जाता है। 13 वर्ष की आयु में मेवाड़ के महाराणा सांगा के कुंवर भोजराज से उनका विवाह हुआ। विवाह के कुछ ही वर्ष पश्चात् पहले पति, फिर पिता और एक युद्ध के दौरान स्वसुर का भी देहांत हो गया। मध्यकालीन भक्ति आंदोलन की आध्यात्मिक प्रेरणा ने जिन कवियों को जन्म दिया उनमें मीराबाई का विशिष्ट स्थान है। मीरा हिन्दी और गुजराती दोनों की कवयित्री मानी जाती हैं। मीरा संत रैदास की शिष्या थीं। मीरा की भक्ति दैन्य और माधुर्यभाव की है।

बिहारी

बिहारी का जन्म 1595 में ग्वालियर में हुआ था। बिहारी ने आचार्य केशवदास से काव्य शिक्षा पायी थी। बिहारी सतसई बिहारी की

वस्तुनिष्ठ प्रश्न

1. हिन्दी साहित्य में गद्य का विकास–
   A. पद्य के साथ-साथ हुआ
   B. पद्य से पहले हुआ
   C. पद्य के बाद हुआ
   D. उपरोक्त में से कोई नहीं
2. आधुनिक काल में कुल मिलाकर–
   A. पद्य और गद्य बराबर लिखा गया
   B. पद्य अधिक लिखा गया
   C. गद्य अधिक लिखा गया
   D. उपरोक्त में से कोई नहीं
3. हिन्दी में गद्य का प्राचीनतम रूप किस ग्रंथ में मिलता है?
   A. चौरासी वैष्णवन की वार्ता B. चन्द छंद बरनन की महिमा
   C. पद्मपुराण D. सुख सागर
4. 'चौरासी वैष्णवन की वार्ता' का रचयिता कौन था?
   A. विट्ठलनाथ जी B. गोकुलनाथ जी
   C. नाभादास जी D. गंग कवि
5. 'अष्टयाम' किसकी रचना है?
   A. गोकुलनाथ जी B. विट्ठलनाथ जी
   C. नाभादास जी D. रामप्रसाद निरंजनी
6. प्रारम्भिक गद्य की भाषा क्या थी?
   A. अपभ्रंश B. खड़ी बोली
   C. अवधी D. ब्रजभाषा
7. जैन 'पद्म पुराण' का अनुवाद किसने किया था?
   A. लक्ष्मण सिंह B. दौलत राम
   C. श्रद्धाराम फिल्लौरी D. रामप्रसाद निरंजनी
8. 19वीं शताब्दी के आरम्भ में हिन्दी गद्य के चार मुख्य लेखक हुए। उनमें से एक ने 'सुखसागर' लिखा। उसका नाम क्या था?
   A. सदल मिश्र B. लल्लू लाल
   C. सदासुख लाल D. इंशाअल्ला खां
9. 'रानी केतकी की कहानी' किसने लिखी थी?
   A. इंशाअल्ला खां B. लक्ष्मण सिंह
   C. बालकृष्ण भट्ट D. प्रताप नारायण मिश्र
10. नीचे पुस्तकों और लेखकों के जोड़े दिये गए हैं। इनमें एक जोड़ा गलत है। बताइये कौन-सा जोड़ा गलत है?
    A. भाषा योगवशिष्ट – नाभादास
    B. नासिकेतोपाख्यान – सदल मिश्र
    C. शृंगार रस मंडन – विट्ठल नाथ
    D. प्रेमसागर – लल्लू लाल
11. ईसाई पादरियों ने किस प्रकार हिन्दी गद्य के प्रसार में योगदान कि
    A. उन्होंने गद्य लेखन पर पुरस्कार दिये
    B. स्वयं हिन्दी गद्य में लिखा
    C. बाइबिल का हिन्दी में अनुवाद कराया और उसे बांटा
    D. उपरोक्त सभी
12. 'सितारे हिन्द' किसकी उपाधि थी?
    A. राजा शिवप्रसाद B. राजा लक्ष्मण सिंह
    C. देवकीनंदन खत्री D. श्रीनिवास दास
13. 'इतिहास तिमिर नाशक' ग्रंथ का रचयिता कौन है?
    A. भारतेन्दु हरिश्चन्द्र
    B. बालकृष्ण भट्ट
    C. राजा शिवप्रसाद 'सितारे हिन्द'
    D. राजा लक्ष्मण सिंह
14. भारतेन्दु हरिश्चन्द्र के समय में हिन्दी गद्य की बड़ी उन्नति हुई। इ इनके दो सहयोगियों की प्रमुख भूमिका थी, जिनमें एक का नाम प्रतापनारायण मिश्र और दूसरे का नाम था–
    A. देवकीनंदन खत्री B. श्यामसुंदर दास
    C. श्रीनिवास दास D. बालकृष्ण भट्ट
15. भारतेन्दु हरिश्चन्द्र के काल में हिन्दी गद्य में–
    A. नाटक लिखे गये B. निबंध लिखे गये
    C. आलोचना लिखी गई D. उपरोक्त तीनों लिखे गये
16. द्विवेदी युग में हिन्दी गद्य–
    A. का रूप पूर्णतः स्थिर हो गया
    B. उर्दू मिश्रित हो गया
    C. की उपेक्षा हुई
    D. में केवल कुछ कहानियां लिखी गईं
17. द्विवेदी-युग में रामचन्द्र शुक्ल ने साहित्य के किस क्षेत्र में मूल्यव योगदान किया?
    A. उपन्यास के क्षेत्र में B. कहानी के क्षेत्र में
    C. नाटक के क्षेत्र में D. आलोचना के क्षेत्र में
18. मिश्र बंधु का योगदान गद्य के किस क्षेत्र में रहा?
    A. नाटक के क्षेत्र में B. कहानी के क्षेत्र में
    C. आलोचना के क्षेत्र में D. उपन्यास के क्षेत्र में
19. द्विवेदी युग में ही हिन्दी के महानू उपन्यासकार की रचनायें प्रकाश आईं। वह उपन्यासकार थे–
    A. जैनेन्द्र कुमार B. यशपाल
    C. प्रेमचन्द D. इलाचन्द जोशी

20. छायावादी कवियों में जयशंकर प्रसाद ने गद्य की किस विधा को समृद्ध बनाया?

A. नाटक B. उपन्यास
C. निबन्ध D. कहानी

21. छायावादी कवि निराला का प्रसिद्ध उपन्यास है–

A. अलका B. चन्द्रकला
C. सावित्री D. इन्द्रा

22. महादेवी वर्मा की रचना 'अतीत के चलचित्र'–

A. कहानी संग्रह है B. उपन्यास है
C. निबन्ध-संग्रह है D. संस्मरणों का संग्रह है

23. 'भारत दुर्दशा' नाटक का लेखक कौन है?

A. भारतेन्दु हरिश्चन्द्र B. देवकीनंदन खत्री
C. बालकृष्ण भट्ट D. प्रतापनारायण मिश्र

24. 'चन्द्रकान्ता संतति' उपन्यास के कितने खण्ड निकले थे?

A. 14 खण्ड B. 8 खण्ड
C. 3 खण्ड D. 24 खण्ड

25. तिलिस्म और ऐयारी से भरे 'चंद्रकान्ता संतति' उपन्यास का सबसे बड़ा योगदान यह रहा कि–

A. उपन्यास के नए क्षेत्र खुल गए
B. हिन्दी गद्य का रूप निखर गया
C. इसी किस्म के बहुत-से उपन्यास लिखे गये
D. असंख्य लोगों ने इस उपन्यास को पढ़ने के लिए हिन्दी भाषा सीखी

26. मुंशी प्रेमचंद के 'गोदान' उपन्यास में मुख्य पात्र (हीरो) का नाम क्या है?

A. मधुवा B. होरी
C. विशाल देव D. दिव्या

27. निराला के उपन्यास 'निरूपमा' में किस समस्या का वर्णन है?

A. ग्राम्य-जीवन की वास्तविकतायें
B. दहेज प्रथा
C. मध्यवर्गीय समाज की आर्थिक विपन्नता
D. प्रादेशिक भेदभाव और सामाजिक कुरीतियां

28. कुछ विद्वान 'परीक्षा गुरु' को हिन्दी का प्रथम उपन्यास मानते हैं। इसके लेखक हैं–

A. रामचन्द्र शुक्ल B. श्रीनिवास दास
C. बालकृष्ण भट्ट D. बाबू राधाकृष्ण दास

29. बालकृष्ण भट्ट का उपन्यास 'सौ अजान एक सुजान' कैसा उपन्यास है?

A. सांस्कृतिक B. ऐतिहासिक
C. तिलिस्मी D. उपदेशात्मक

30. निम्नलिखित उपन्यासों में से कौन-सा उपन्यास अम्बिकादत्त व्यास का है?

A. नूतन ब्रह्मचारी B. मरता क्या न करता
C. मृण्मयी D. आश्चर्य वृतान्त

31. उपन्यासों के विकास के प्रारम्भिक चरण के सम्बन्ध में कौन-सा कथन सही है?

A. कुछ उपन्यास मौलिक हैं
B. कुछ उपन्यास अनूदित हैं
C. इनका लाभ यह हुआ कि मौलिक उपन्यास लेखन की प्रवृति बढ़ी
D. उपरोक्त सभी

32. निम्नलिखित उपन्यासों में से कौन-सा उपन्यास अयोध्या सिंह उपाध्याय 'हरिऔध' का नहीं है?

A. वेनिस का बाँका B. ठेठ हिन्दी का ठाठ
C. अधखिला फूल D. रसिक लाल

33. हिन्दी के प्रथम मौलिक उपन्यासकारों में देवकीनंदन खत्री विख्यात हैं। इनका सर्वाधिक लोकप्रिय उपन्यास 'चन्द्रकान्ता संतति' है। इसके अलावा भी इनका एक अन्य उपन्यास है, जिसका नाम है–

A. अंगूठी का नगीना B. भूतनाथ
C. दिल्ली के दलाल D. युगान्तर

34. 'संन्यासी' एक प्रसिद्ध उपन्यास है। इसके लेखक का नाम है–

A. वृन्दावनलाल वर्मा B. यशपाल
C. उपेन्द्रनाथ अश्क D. इलाचन्द्र जोशी

35. निम्नलिखित उपन्यासों में से कौन-सा उपन्यास यशपालजी का नहीं है?

A. दादा कामरेड B. दिव्या
C. देशद्रोही D. भिखारिणी

36. किसको 'उपन्यास सम्राट' माना जाता है?

A. जैनेन्द्र कुमार B. यशपाल
C. उपेन्द्रनाथ अश्क D. प्रेमचंद

37. 'चित्रलेखा' एक अति लोकप्रिय उपन्यास है। इसके लेखक का नाम है–

A. चतुरसेन शास्त्री B. पाण्डेय बेचन शर्मा 'उग्र'
C. वृन्दावनलाल वर्मा D. भगवतीचरण वर्मा

38. जयशंकर प्रसाद के दो उपन्यासों में एक का नाम 'कंकाल' है, और दूसरे का–

A. तीन वर्ष B. मां
C. तितली D. बैशाली की नगरवधू

39. मुंशी प्रेमचंद के उपन्यास–

A. ऐतिहासिक हैं B. सामाजिक हैं
C. रोमांटिक हैं D. मनोवैज्ञानिक हैं

40. निम्नलिखित उपन्यासों में से कौन-सा उपन्यास प्रेमचंदजी का नहीं है?

A. गबन B. निर्मला
C. गोदान D. विसर्जन

41. 'वैशाली की नगरवधू' किसका उपन्यास है?

A. जैनेन्द्र कुमार B. चतुरसेन शास्त्री
C. वृन्दावनलाल वर्मा D. इलाचन्द्र जोशी

42. ऐतिहासिक उपन्यासों के लिए कौन-सा नाम विख्यात है?

A. यशपाल B. अज्ञेय

C. उपेन्द्रनाथ अश्क D. वृन्दावनलाल वर्मा

43. 'शेखर-एक जीवनी' किसका बहुचर्चित उपन्यास है?

A. राहुल सांकृत्यायन B. धर्मवीर भारती

C. अमृतलाल नागर D. अज्ञेय

44. नीचे कुछ उपन्यासों और उनके लेखकों के नामों के जोड़े दिये गए हैं। इनमें से कौन-सा जोड़ा सही नहीं है?

A. जयशंकर प्रसाद – तितली

B. देवकीनंदन खत्री – भूतनाथ

C. जैनेन्द्र कुमार – सुनीता

D. अज्ञेय – दिव्या

45. 'मैला आँचल' उपन्यास का लेखक कौन है?

A. फणीश्वरनाथ रेणु B. धर्मवीर भारती

C. अज्ञेय D. नरेश मेहता

46. 'शेखर-एक जीवनी' अज्ञेय का लिखा हुआ उपन्यास है। यह–

A. अपनी ऐतिहासिक पृष्ठभूमि के लिए विख्यात है

B. अपने सांस्कृतिक मूल्यों के लिए विख्यात है

C. नवीन शैली व पैनी मनोवैज्ञानिक दृष्टि के लिए विख्यात है

D. सामाजिक कुरीतियों का पर्दाफाश करने के लिए विख्यात है

47. प्रेमचन्द जी के 'गोदान' में–

A. जीवन के जीते-जागते चित्र हैं

B. जीवन की कठोर वास्तविकता का सूक्ष्म विवेचन है

C. ग्राम-जीवन की रीतियों का सूक्ष्म विवेचन है

D. उपरोक्त सभी

48. प्रसादजी के 'कंकाल' उपन्यास में–

A. सामाजिक बंधनों की विषमता और व्यक्ति की सहज प्रवृत्तियों का संघर्ष अंकित है

B. समाज-व्यवस्था प[illegible] [illegible]खा व्यंग्य है

C. आदर्श और यथार्थ के बीच खड़ी खाई का रूप है

D. उपरोक्त सभी

49. निम्नलिखित में कौन-सा एक उपन्यास वृन्दावनलाल वर्मा का नहीं है?

A. गढ़ कुण्डार B. झांसी की रानी

C. विराटा की पद्मिनी D. देशद्रोही

50. 'बूंद और समुद्र' किसका विख्यात उपन्यास है?

A. उदय शंकर भट्ट B. फणीश्वरनाथ रेणु

C. शैलेश मटियानी D. अमृतलाल नागर

51. निम्नलिखित आंचलिक उपन्यासों में से एक फणीश्वरनाथ रेणु का नहीं है। वह है–

A. मैला आँचल B. परती परिकथा

C. ड्रामा D. पल्टू बाबू रोड

52. 'चिट्ठीरसैनी' किसका प्रसिद्ध उपन्यास है?

A. उपेन्द्रनाथ अश्क B. हरिकृष्ण प्रेमी

C. शैलेश मटियानी D. यशपाल

53. 'चित्रलेखा' और 'तीन वर्ष' के अतिरिक्त भगवतीचरण वर्मा के अन्य उपन्यास हैं–

A. टेढ़े-मेढ़े रास्ते B. भूले-बिसरे चित्र

C. सीधी-सच्ची बातें D. उपरोक्त सभी

54. 'गिरती दीवारें' किसका उत्तम उपन्यास है?

A. उपेन्द्रनाथ अश्क B. धर्मवीर भारती

C. अमृतलाल नागर D. नागार्जुन

55. 'मृगनयनी' किसका उपन्यास है?

A. जैनेन्द्र कुमार का B. वृन्दावनलाल वर्मा का

C. अमृतलाल नागर का D. उपरोक्त में से कोई नहीं

56. निम्नलिखित सूची-I का सूची-II से मिलान कीजिए तथा नीचे दिए गए कूट की सहायता से सही उत्तर का चयन कीजिए :

सूची-I	सूची-II
(*a*) अपने-अपने अजनबी	1. धर्मवीर भारती
(*b*) सूरज का सातवां घोड़ा	2. अज्ञेय
(*c*) खाली कुर्सी की आत्मा	3. इलाचंद जोशी
(*d*) प्रेत और छाया	4. लक्ष्मीकान्त वर्मा

कूट :

	(*a*)	(*b*)	(*c*)	(*d*)
A.	2	1	4	3
B.	1	2	4	3
C.	1	2	3	4
D.	3	4	2	1

57. हरिवंश राय बच्चन की रचना ''क्या भूलूं क्या याद करूं'' किस कोटि के अन्तर्गत आती है?

A. आत्मकथा B. यात्रा वृत्तान्त

C. इंटरव्यू D. रेखाचित्र

58. महादेवी वर्मा की रचना 'पथ के साथी' किस कोटि के अन्तर्गत आती है?

A. संस्मरण B. रेखाचित्र

C. यात्रा वृत्तान्त D. जीवनी

59. नीचे कुछ रचनायें दी हुई हैं और उनके सामने उनके लेखकों के नाम हैं। कौन-सा जोड़ा गलत है?

A. अरे यायावर याद रहेगा – अज्ञेय

B. मैं इनसे मिला – पद्मसिंह शर्मा कमलेश

C. जंजीरें और दीवार – रामवृक्ष बेनीपुरी

D. माटी हो गई सोना – महादेवी वर्मा

60. धर्मवीर भारती की रचना 'ठेले पर हिमालय' किस कोटि की है?

A. जीवनी B. यात्रा वृत्तान्त

C. संस्मरण D. इंटरव्यू

61. 'एक बूंद सहसा उछली' किसका विख्यात यात्रा संस्मरण है?

A. निर्मल वर्मा का B. रामवृक्ष बेनीपुरी का

C. अज्ञेय का D. डा. रघुवंश का

62. हिन्दी की सर्वप्रथम मौलिक कहानी किसे माना जाता है?

A. इन्दुमती B. आकाशदीप

C. ग्यारह वर्ष का समय D. उसने कहा था

63. हिन्दी की सर्वप्रथम मौलिक कहानी 'इन्दुमती' का लेखक कौन था?
A. गिरिजादत्त वाजपेयी
B. किशोरी लाल गोस्वामी
C. रामचन्द्र शुक्ल
D. प्रताप नारायण मिश्र

64. चन्द्रधर शर्मा 'गुलेरी' की सुविख्यात कहानी कौन-सी है?
A. छाया
B. उसने कहा था
C. बड़े घर की बेटी
D. शतरंज के खिलाड़ी

65. प्रेमचंद का सर्वोत्कृष्ट उपन्यास कौन-सा है?
A. निर्मला
B. सेवासदन
C. रंगभूमि
D. गोदान

66. मुंशी प्रेमचंद ने अपने उपन्यासों में किस समस्या को प्रस्तुत किया है?
A. विधवा विवाह
B. अनमेल विवाह
C. दहेज प्रथा
D. उपरोक्त तीनों

67. 'मधुआ' कहानी किसकी है?
A. प्रेमचन्द की
B. प्रसादजी की
C. यशपाल की
D. अज्ञेय की

68. 'जार्ज पंचम की नाक' कहानी का लेखक कौन है?
A. कमलेश्वर
B. हरिकृष्ण प्रेमी
C. भीष्म साहनी
D. अज्ञेय

69. प्रेमचंद की 'पूस की रात' कहानी–
A. भारतीय किसान की टूटन की कहानी है
B. भारतीय मध्यवर्ग के मिथ्याभिमान की कहानी है
C. वर्ग संघर्ष की कहानी है
D. अशिक्षा के अभिशाप की कहानी है

70. प्रसादजी की मधुआ कहानी एक–
A. शराबी के हृदय-परिवर्तन की कहानी है
B. रईस की हृदयहीनता की कहानी है
C. बालक के शोषण की कहानी है
D. उपरोक्त में से कोई नहीं

71. यशपाल ने अपनी कहानी 'खच्चर और आदमी' में क्या बताया है?
A. खच्चर आदमी से श्रेष्ठ है
B. आदमी खच्चर से श्रेष्ठ है
C. जो अपने को परिस्थितियों में ढाल ले वही बच पाता है
D. मनुष्य परिस्थितियों का दास है

72. अज्ञेय की 'शरणदाता' कहानी–
A. मानव संघर्ष की कहानी है
B. साम्प्रदायिकता-विरोधी कहानी है
C. नारी ममता की कहानी है
D. उपरोक्त तीनों

73. 'कानों में कंगना' नामक कहानी का लेखक कौन है?
A. विश्वम्भर नाथ शर्मा 'कौशिक'
B. राधिकारमण प्रसाद
C. पदुमलाल पुन्नालाल बख्शी
D. रायकृष्ण दास

74. 'ताई' कहानी का लेखक कौन है?
A. वृन्दावनलाल वर्मा
B. राजेन्द्र यादव
C. मन्नू भंडारी
D. विश्वम्भर नाथ शर्मा 'कौशिक'

75. निम्नलिखित कहानियों में से कौन-सी कहानी उषा देवी मित्रा की लिखी हुई है?
A. भाई-बहन
B. लछमा
C. अधूरा चित्र
D. सान्ध्य तारा

76. 'आत्माराम' और 'पंच परमेश्वर' किसकी कहानियां हैं?
A. सुदर्शन
B. शिवपूजन सहाय
C. चंडी प्रसाद 'हृदयेश'
D. प्रेमचंद

77. गिरिजादत्त वाजपेयी की एक उत्तम कहानी है–
A. रानी सारंधा
B. प्रतिध्वनि
C. हार की जीत
D. पंडित और पंडितानी

78. 'पुरस्कार' और 'आकाशदीप' कहानियां किसकी हैं?
A. रायकृष्ण दास
B. सुदर्शन
C. चन्द्रकिरण सौनरिक्सा
D. जयशंकर प्रसाद

79. 'हार की जीत' नामक अत्यन्त लोकप्रिय और महान् चरित्र वाली कहानी का लेखक कौन है?
A. सुदर्शन
B. चतुरसेन शास्त्री
C. विष्णु प्रभाकर
D. यशपाल

80. गुलेरीजी की 'उसने कहा था' कहानी का सार क्या है?
A. अमृतसर का जन-जीवन
B. युद्ध की निस्सारता
C. निःस्वार्थ बलिदान
D. अपराध का मनोविज्ञान

81. 'बैताल पचीसी' और 'सिंहासनबत्तीसी' कहानियों को हिन्दी में किसने अनूदित किया?
A. लल्लू लाल
B. शिवप्रसाद 'सितारे हिन्द'
C. भारतेन्दु हरिश्चन्द्र
D. उपरोक्त में से कोई नहीं

82. 'रानी केतकी की कहानी' कहानी के बारे में कौन-सा कथन सही नहीं है?
A. यह कहानी ठेठ हिन्दी में है
B. इसमें रानी केतकी और उदयभान की प्रेम-कथा का वर्णन है
C. इसके लेखक सदल मिश्र हैं
D. इसके लेखक इंशाअल्ला खां हैं

83. 'राजा भोज का सपना' किसकी कहानी है?
A. शिवप्रसाद 'सितारे हिन्द'
B. चतुरसेन शास्त्री
C. उषा देवी मित्रा
D. सुदर्शन

84. मनोवैज्ञानिक कहानीकारों में किसकी गणना नहीं की जाती?
A. राजेन्द्र यादव
B. अज्ञेय
C. इलाचन्द्र जोशी
D. पाण्डेय बेचन शर्मा 'उग्र'

85. जैनेन्द्रजी कहानी के सम्बन्ध में प्रेमचंद की परिपाटी में आते हैं; क्योंकि उन्होंने अपनी कहानियों के लिए
A. मनोवैज्ञानिक विषय चुने
B. सामाजिक और पारिवारिक विषय चुने
C. राष्ट्र निर्माण के विषयों को अपनाया
D. उपरोक्त तीनों

86. 'मिठाई वाला' कहानी का लेखक कौन है?
A. भगवतीचरण वर्मा B. भगवती प्रसाद वाजपेयी
C. यशपाल D. सुदर्शन

87. निम्नलिखित कहानियों में से कौन-सी कहानी रायकृष्ण दास की है?
A. रमणी का रहस्य B. अपना-अपना भाग्य
C. नन्दिनी D. कमल की बेटी

88. प्रसाद जी की प्रथम कहानी कौन-सी थी?
A. ग्राम B. मधुआ
C. आकाशदीप D. पुरस्कार

89. निम्नलिखित में से कौन-सा कहानी संग्रह प्रसाद जी का नहीं है?
A. छाया B. आकाशदीप
C. कोठरी की बात D. प्रतिध्वनि

90. 'रक्षा बन्धन' किसकी कहानी है?
A. शिवपूजन सहाय की B. जैनेन्द्र की
C. सुदर्शन की D. कौशिक की

91. निम्नलिखित में से कौन-सा कहानी संग्रह वृन्दावनलाल वर्मा का नहीं है?
A. हर सिंगार B. दबे पांव
C. कलाकार का दण्ड D. मानुषी

92. 'नई कहानी' वर्ग के कहानीकारों में निम्न में से किसका नाम नहीं आता?
A. मोहन राकेश का B. राजेन्द्र यादव का
C. कमलेश्वर का D. विष्णु प्रभाकर का

93. 'दुलाई वाली' कहानी किसकी थी?
A. रामचन्द्र शुक्ल की
B. विश्वम्भर नाथ शर्मा 'कौशिक' की
C. प्रेमचंद की
D. वंग महिला की,

94. कहानी के विकास-क्रम में महत्वपूर्ण भूमिका निभाने वाली पत्रिका का नाम है–
A. सरस्वती B. इन्दु
C. उपरोक्त दोनों D. इन्दुमती

95. जैनेन्द्रजी का चिन्तन एवं दृष्टिकोण–
A. गांधीवादी B. प्रगतिशील
C. यथार्थवादी D. साम्यवादी

96. आंचलिक कहानी संग्रह 'ठुमरी' किसका है?
A. उपेन्द्र नाथ 'अश्क' B. शैलेश मटियानी
C. रघुवीर सहाय D. फणीश्वर नाथ 'रेणु'

97. विष्णु प्रभाकर की 'अधूरी कहानी' का उद्देश्य–
A. साम्प्रदायिक सद्भाव है B. नारी-उत्थान है
C. कुंठा-उन्मूलन है D. अहंकार का पतन है

98. 'काकी' कहानी किसकी है?
A. सुदर्शन B. कौशिक
C. सियारामशरण गुप्त D. प्रेमचन्द

99. 'परदा' कहानी में यशपालजी का उद्देश्य–
A. मध्यम वर्ग की निर्धनता का वर्णन करना है
B. उन्माद की निंदा करना है
C. झूठी प्रतिष्ठाप्रियता की पोल खोलना है
D. परदा-प्रथा की बुराइयां बताना है

100. 'दो बांके' किसका कहानी संग्रह है?
A. भगवती प्रसाद वाजपेयी B. भगवतीचरण वर्मा
C. मन्नू भंडारी D. होमवती देवी

101. कालिदास के 'शकुन्तला' नाटक का हिन्दी अनुवाद किसने किया
A. भारतेन्दु हरिश्चन्द्र B. राजा लक्ष्मण सिंह
C. बाबू गोपाल चन्द्र D. प्रताप नारायण मिश्र

102. निम्नलिखित नाटकों में से कौन-सा नाटक भारतेन्दुजी द्वारा लिखित नहीं है?
A. भारत दुर्दशा B. भारत-सौभाग्य
C. नील देवी D. अन्धेर नगरी

103. भारतेन्दुजी के 'चन्द्रावली' नाटक में–
A. भारत की दयनीय दशा का चित्रण है
B. शासन-व्यवस्था पर व्यंग्य है
C. आदर्श प्रेम का चित्रण है
D. ऐतिहासिक खोज है

104. 'दुखिनी बाला' किसका नाटक है?
A. भारतेन्दु बाबू B. राधाकृष्ण दास
C. प्रतापनारायण मिश्र D. अम्बिकादत्त व्यास

105. द्विवेदी युग में–
A. मौलिक नाटक खूब लिखे गए
B. नाटकों के अनुवाद खूब हुए
C. नाटकों का मनुष्य के जीवन में निकट का सम्बन्ध रहा
D. उपरोक्त सभी

106. द्विजेन्द्र लाल राय के बंगला नाटकों का हिन्दी अनुवाद किसने किया
A. श्रीनिवास दास B. बाबू सीताराम
C. सत्य नारायण D. रूप नारायण

107. प्रसाद युग से पूर्व मैथिलीशरण गुप्त का कौन-सा नाटक आया था
A. चन्द्रगुप्त B. चन्द्रहास
C. चन्द्रकला D. चन्द्रोदय

108. प्रसादजी के नाटकों में–
A. साहित्यिक भाषा है
B. ऐतिहासिक पुट है
C. भारतीय सभ्यता और संस्कृति के गौरव का चित्रण है
D. उपरोक्त सभी

109. निम्नलिखित नाटकों में से कौन-सा नाटक प्रसादजी द्वारा लिखित नहीं है?
A. राज्यश्री B. स्कन्दगुप्त
C. अजातशत्रु D. विश्वामित्र

110. उदयशंकर भट्टजी के नाटक–
A. राष्ट्रीयता प्रधान हैं B. पौराणिक हैं
C. ऐतिहासिक हैं D. अन्तर्द्वन्द्व प्रधान हैं

111. 'अम्बा' और 'मतस्यगंधा' किसके नाटक हैं?
A. हरिकृष्ण प्रेमी B. विश्वम्भर नाथ शर्मा 'कौशिक'
C. सुदर्शन D. उदय शंकर भट्ट

112. 'सिन्दूर की होली' किसका विख्यात नाटक है?
A. लक्ष्मीनारायण मिश्र B. उपेन्द्रनाथ अश्क
C. सेठ गोविन्द दास D. माखनलाल चतुर्वेदी

113. मोहन राकेश की ख्याति किस नाटक से फैली?
A. शशिगुप्त B. कर्तव्य
C. आषाढ़ का एक दिन D. रेशमी टाई

114. निम्नलिखित में से कौन-सा नाटक लक्ष्मी नारायण लाल का नहीं है?
A. अंधा कुआं B. मादा कैक्टस
C. सूखा सरोवर D. लहरों का राजहंस

115. हिन्दी का प्रथम एकांकी नाटककार कौन था?
A. प्रसादजी B. रामकुमार वर्मा
C. भगवतीचरण वर्मा D. उपेन्द्र नाथ अश्क

116. हिन्दी का सर्वप्रथम एकांकी नाटक किसे माना जाता है?
A. बड़ा आदमी B. एक बूंद
C. कारवां D. दस मिनट

117. 'देवताओं की छाया में' किसका एकांकी-संग्रह है?
A. उपेन्द्रनाथ अश्क B. रामकुमार वर्मा
C. भुवनेश्वर मिश्र D. सेठ गोविन्द दास

118. 'सबसे बड़ा आदमी' किसका एकांकी है?
A. भगवतीचरण वर्मा B. विष्णु प्रभाकर
C. जगदीश चन्द्र माथुर D. उदय शंकर भट्ट

119. 'गरुड़ध्वज' और 'दशाश्वमेध' किसके विख्यात ऐतिहासिक नाटक हैं?
A. रामकुमार वर्मा B. हरिकृष्ण प्रेमी
C. उपेन्द्रनाथ अश्क D. लक्ष्मीनारायण मिश्र

120. 'युगे-युगे क्रान्ति' नाटक किसका है?
A. जगदीशचन्द्र माथुर B. सेठ गोविन्द दास
C. विष्णु प्रभाकर D. देवराज दिनेश

121. जगदीश चन्द्र माथुर का एकांकी संकलन है–
A. कुलीनता B. रंगमंच
C. भोर का तारा D. मां का बेटा

122. 'आधे-अधूरे' किसका नाटक है?
A. नरेश मेहता B. देवराज दिनेश
C. विपिन अग्रवाल D. मोहन राकेश

123. निम्नलिखित नाटकों में से कौन-सा लक्ष्मीकांत वर्मा का है?
A. आदमी का जहर B. तीन अपाहिज
C. नया-पुराना D. उपरोक्त में से कोई नहीं

124. 'पृथ्वीराज की आँखें' और 'कैलेण्डर का आखिरी पन्ना' किसके विख्यात एकांकी हैं?
A. सेठ गोविन्द दास B. विष्णु प्रभाकर
C. रामकुमार वर्मा D. उदय शंकर भट्ट

125. सेठ गोविन्द दास के एकांकियों में–
A. गांधीवादी विचारधारा है
B. राजनैतिक एवं सामाजिक समस्याओं का चित्रण है
C. ऐतिहासिक पृष्ठभूमि है
D. उपरोक्त A और B दोनों

126. सेठ गोविन्ददास के प्रसिद्ध कहानी संग्रह हैं–
A. नवरस B. एकादशी
C. स्पर्द्धा D. उपरोक्त तीनों

127. उदय शंकर भट्ट के एकांकियों में–
A. मनोविश्लेषणात्मक शैली है B. अन्तर्द्वन्द्व का चित्रण है
C. भाषा पात्रों के अनुकूल है D. उपरोक्त तीनों

128. 'एकला चलो रे' किसका विख्यात एकांकी है?
A. उदय शंकर भट्ट B. हरिकृष्ण प्रेमी
C. उपेन्द्र नाथ अश्क D. विष्णु प्रभाकर

129. 'अधिकार का रक्षक' और 'लक्ष्मी का स्वागत' किसके विख्यात एकांकी हैं?
A. हरिकृष्ण प्रेमी B. रेवती शरण शर्मा
C. धर्मवीर भारती D. उपेन्द्र नाथ अश्क

130. लोकप्रिय एकांकी 'रीढ़ की हड्डी' किसकी रचना है?
A. गिरजा कुमार माथुर B. लक्ष्मीकान्त वर्मा
C. भारत भूषण अग्रवाल D. जगदीश चन्द्र माथुर

131. 'मुझे जीने दो' किसका लोकप्रिय एकांकी है?
A. लक्ष्मीकान्त मिश्र B. जयनाथ नलिन
C. रेवती शरण शर्मा D. उपरोक्त में से कोई नहीं

132. 'लस्सी का गिलास' एकांकी का लेखक कौन है?
A. सद्गुरु शरण अवस्थी B. विष्णु प्रभाकर
C. जयनाथ नलिन D. विनोद रस्तोगी

133. निम्नलिखित में से कौन-सा एकांकी विमला लूथरा का नहीं है?
A. लाइन क्लीअर B. मुन्ने का नामकरण
C. प्रीतिभोज D. डाक्टर बीबी

134. 'रसोईघर में प्रजातंत्र' विष्णु प्रभाकर का एकांकी है, जिसमें–
A. व्यंग्य है B. क्षोभ है
C. उद्बोधन है D. निराशा है

135. निम्नलिखित में से किसे हिन्दी का सशक्त नाटककार माना जाता है?
A. मुंशी प्रेमचंद B. सेठ गोविन्द दास
C. जयशंकर प्रसाद D. भारतेन्दु हरिश्चन्द्र

136. 'विशाख' और 'एक घूंट' नाटकों का लेखक कौन है?
A. हरिकृष्ण प्रेमी B. लक्ष्मी नारायण लाल
C. जयशंकर प्रसाद D. उदय शंकर भट्ट

137. 'लहरों का राजहंस' किसका प्रसिद्ध नाटक है?
A. मोहन राकेश
B. जगदीश चन्द्र माथुर
C. जयशंकर प्रसाद
D. उदय शंकर भट्ट

138. 'आनरेरी मजिस्ट्रेट' का लेखक कौन है?
A. भगवती प्रसाद वाजपेयी
B. रामकुमार वर्मा
C. देवकीनंदन खत्री
D. हरिकृष्ण प्रेमी

139. 'अम्बपाली' किसकी रचना है?
A. श्रीनिवास दास
B. उदय शंकर भट्ट
C. रामवृक्ष बेनीपुरी
D. उपेन्द्र नाथ अश्क

140. ऐतिहासिक तथ्यों और काल्पनिक प्रसंगों के मिश्रण से जगदीश चन्द्र माथुर ने किस नाटक की रचना की?
A. क्षत्राणी
B. शिवानी
C. कोणार्क
D. सूर्यरथ

141. 'धूर्त रसिक लाल' का लेखक कौन है?
A. गोपालराम गहमरी
B. भगवतीचरण वर्मा
C. शिवपूजन सहाय
D. पं. लज्जा राम मेहता

142. प्रेमचंद रचित 'मान सरोवर' के कितने भाग हैं?
A. तीन भाग
B. पांच भाग
C. सात भाग
D. आठ भाग

143. 'वयं रक्षामः' किसका उपन्यास है?
A. गुरुदत्त का
B. चतुरसेन शास्त्री का
C. भगवतीचरण वर्मा का
D. इलाचन्द्र जोशी का

144. 'मुण्डमाल' किसकी रचना है?
A. कौशिक
B. रामकुमार वर्मा
C. शिवपूजन सहाय
D. उपरोक्त में से कोई नहीं

145. 'कोठरी की बात' कहानी-संग्रह किसका है?
A. यशपाल का
B. जैनेन्द्र का
C. अज्ञेय का
D. धर्मवीर भारती का

146. 'चारुमित्रा' और 'तैमूर की हार' किस लेखक के एकांकी हैं?
A. उपेन्द्र नाथ अश्क
B. भुवनेश्वर प्रसाद
C. विष्णु प्रभाकर
D. रामकुमार वर्मा

147. उपेन्द्रनाथ अश्क के अधिकांश एकांकी–
A. आदर्शवादी हैं
B. राजनैतिक हैं
C. सामाजिक व पारिवारिक हैं
D. मनोवैज्ञानिक हैं

148. 'यशस्वी भोज' किसका एकांकी है?
A. लक्ष्मी नारायण लाल
B. देवराज दिनेश
C. उदय शंकर भट्ट
D. सेठ गोविन्द दास

149. 'चिरंजीव' का विख्यात एकांकी है–
A. दो कलाकार
B. माटी की मूरत
C. पंचकन्या
D. दादी मां जागी

150. 'ध्रुवस्वामिनी' प्रसादजी का–
A. सामाजिक नाटक है
B. ऐतिहासिक नाटक है
C. पारिवारिक नाटक है
D. पौराणिक नाटक है

151. 'बादल की मृत्यु' एकांकी के रचनाकार हैं–
A. रामकुमार वर्मा
B. आचार्य शुक्ल
C. प्रसाद
D. विष्णु प्रभाकर

152. धर्मवीर भारती के एकांकी का नाम है–
A. निशानेबाज
B. नदी प्यासी थी
C. उपर्युक्त दोनों
D. इनमें से कोई नहीं

153. अमृतराय की एकांकी है–
A. राह चलते
B. रूसी लोग
C. उपर्युक्त दोनों
D. इनमें से कोई नहीं

154. 'एक साहित्यिक की डायरी' के लेखक हैं–
A. अज्ञेय
B. मुक्तिबोध
C. धर्मवीर-भारती
D. अमृतराय

155. उपन्यास और रचनाकारों को सुमेलित करें–

रचनाकार	उपन्यास
(*i*) राजेन्द्र यादव	(*a*) अंधेरे बंद कमरे
(*ii*) मोहन राकेश	(*b*) एक सड़क सत्तावन गलियाँ
(*iii*) कमलेश्वर	(*c*) आँचल में कोई
(*iv*) वृन्दावन लाल वर्मा	(*d*) कुलटा

कूट :

	(*i*)	(*ii*)	(*iii*)	(*iv*)
A.	(*a*)	(*d*)	(*c*)	(*b*)
B.	(*b*)	(*d*)	(*c*)	(*a*)
C.	(*d*)	(*a*)	(*b*)	(*c*)
D.	(*b*)	(*a*)	(*d*)	(*c*)

156. 'टेढ़े-मेढ़े रास्ते' उपन्यास के लेखक हैं–
A. रांगेय राघव
B. अमृतराय
C. मन्नू भंडारी
D. भगवती चरण वर्मा

157. 'निशिकान्त' उपन्यास के लेखक हैं–
A. विष्णु प्रभाकर
B. प्रभाकर माचवे
C. नरेश मेहता
D. राम नरेश त्रिपाठी

158. 'अपने-अपने अजनबी' उपन्यास लिखा है–
A. मुक्तिबोध
B. अज्ञेय
C. चतुरसेन शास्त्री
D. शमशेर

159. 'नागार्जुन' के उपन्यास का नाम है–
A. हीरक जयंती
B. मशाल
C. जंजीरे
D. उपर्युक्त सभी

160. 'दीर्घतपा' उपन्यास लिखा है–
A. नरेश मेहता
B. रांगेय राघव
C. रेणु
D. मन्नू भण्डारी

161. उषा प्रियंवदा के उपन्यास का नाम है–
A. हम तिनके
B. पचपन खम्भे, लाल दीवारें
C. जंगल के फूल
D. धूमकेतु

162. भीष्म साहनी का उपन्यास है–
A. सोनल का फूल
B. वृषित
C. गंगामैया
D. बसन्ती

163. अमृतराय के उपन्यास का नाम है :
A. धुँआ B. छोटे-छोटे पक्षी
C. कुरू-करू स्वाहा D. नई ईमारत

164. 'नवनिधी' किसका कहानी संग्रह है?
A. पंकज बिष्ट B. नागार्जुन
C. प्रेमचंद D. अज्ञेय

165. 'कोठरी की बात' कहानी संग्रह के रचयिता हैं–
A. मुक्तिबोध B. अज्ञेय
C. लाला श्रीनिवासदास D. प्रभाकर माचवे

166. यशपाल के कहानी संग्रह का नाम है–
A. फूलों का कुर्ता B. पिंजड़े की उड़ान
C. उपर्युक्त दोनों D. इनमें से कोई नहीं

167. 'संगीनों का साया' किसका काव्य संग्रह है?
A. प्रभाकर माचवे B. राहुल सांकृत्यायन
C. यशपाल D. अज्ञेय

168. कहानी संग्रह और लेखकों के नाम को सुमेलित करें–

लेखक	**कहानी संग्रह**
(*i*) मोहन राकेश	(*a*) फिर बसन्त आया
(*ii*) कमलेश्वर	(*b*) पहला पाठ
(*iii*) भीष्म साहनी	(*c*) नए बादल
(*iv*) उषा प्रियंवदा	(*d*) मांस का दरिया

कूट :

	(*i*)	(*ii*)	(*iii*)	(*iv*)
A.	(*d*)	(*a*)	(*c*)	(*b*)
B.	(*d*)	(*c*)	(*d*)	(*a*)
C.	(*c*)	(*d*)	(*b*)	(*a*)
D.	(*a*)	(*c*)	(*b*)	(*d*)

169. 'मेरी जीवन रेखा' आत्मकथा के रचयिता हैं–
A. हजारी प्रसाद द्विवेदी B. महावीर प्रसाद द्विवेदी
C. राहुल सांकृत्यायन D. प्रभाकर माचवे

170. 'मेरा जीवन साथी' किसकी आत्मकथा है?
A. नंद दुलारे वाजपेयी B. अज्ञेय
C. राम कुमार वर्मा D. प्रेमचंद

171. 'मेरी जीवन यात्रा' किसकी रचना है?
A. नागार्जुन B. राहुल सांकृत्यायन
C. महावीर प्रसाद द्विवेदी D. मुक्तिबोध

172. 'आत्मकथा' किसकी रचना है?
A. महात्मा गाँधी B. जवाहर लाल नेहरू
C. डॉ॰ राजेन्द्र प्रसाद D. लाल बहादुर शास्त्री

173. 'मेरी आत्म कहानी' आत्मकथा किसने लिखी है?
A. चतुरसेन शास्त्री B. महावीर प्रसाद द्विवेदी
C. राहुल सांकृत्यायन D. महात्मा गाँधी

174. 'सौष्ठववादी' किसकी समीक्षा पद्धति को कहा जाता है?
A. डॉ॰ नगेन्द्र B. हजारी प्रसाद द्विवेदी
C. आचार्य शुक्ल D. नंद दुलारे वाजपेयी

175. रामविलास शर्मा द्वारा लिखित है–
A. प्रगति और परम्परा B. भाषा, युगबोध और कवित
C. परम्परा का मूल्यांकन D. उपर्युक्त सभी

176. 'भारतीय साहित्य के इतिहास की समस्याएँ' लिखा है–
A. राम कुमार वर्मा B. राम विलास शर्मा
C. नंद दुलारे वाजपेयी D. हजारी प्रसाद द्विवेदी

177. 'पाप के पुजारी' नाटक के रचयिता हैं–
A. प्रभाकर माचवे B. दिनकर
C. रामविलास शर्मा D. नरेश मेहता

178. 'आचार्य रामचन्द्र शुक्ल और हिन्दी आलोचना' लिखा है–
A. डॉ॰ नगेन्द्र B. रामविलास शर्मा
C. हजारी प्रसाद द्विवेदी D. नामवर सिंह

179. 'मार्क्स, त्रात्सकी और एशियाई समाज' लिखा है–
A. रामकुमार वर्मा B. डॉ॰ नगेन्द्र
C. हजारी प्रसाद द्विवेदी D. राम विलास शर्मा

180. 'ऐन्दुई हिन्दुस्तानी' का प्रकाशन हुआ–
A. 1849 ई॰ B. 1839 ई॰
C. 1832 ई॰ D. 1843 ई॰

181. रीतिकाव्य की भूमिका किसने लिखी?
A. रामविलास शर्मा B. डॉ॰ राम कुमार वर्मा
C. आचार्य शुक्ल D. डॉ॰ नगेन्द्र

182. शुक्ल जी ने रासो शब्द की उत्पत्ति किसके द्वारा मानी है?
A. रास शब्द से B. रासक शब्द से
C. रसायण शब्द से D. रस शब्द से

183. रोमांस शब्द आया है–
A. अंग्रेजी भाषा में B. यूनानी भाषा में
C. जर्मन भाषा में D. फ्रांसीसी भाषा में

184. भारत में रोमांटिक कथाओं का उद्‌भव काल माना जाता है–
A. हड़प्पा काल से B. वेद काल से
C. महाभारत काल से D. आदि काल से

185. 'विकलांग श्रद्धा का दौर' के लेखक हैं–
A. प्रभाकर माचवे B. नरेश मेहता
C. बालकृष्ण भट्ट D. हरिशंकर परसाई

186. परसाई जी की कृति है–
A. निठल्ले की डायरी B. तुलसी भूषण
C. राम रत्नाकर D. रुक्मिणी परिणय

187. भारतेन्दु की भक्तिपरक रचना का नाम है–
A. भक्त सर्वस्त B. रुक्मिणी परिणय
C. उपर्युक्त दोनों D. इनमें से कोई नहीं

188. भारतेन्दु की प्रेम संबंधी रचना का नाम है–
A. प्रेम सरोवर B. प्रेम मालिका
C. उपर्युक्त दोनों D. इनमें से कोई नहीं

237. नकेनवादी परम्परा के प्रतिनिधि कवि हैं–

A. नलिन विलोचन शर्मा B. केसरी कुमार

C. नरेश मेहता D. उपर्युक्त सभी

238. प्रतीकवाद की स्थापना कहाँ हुई?

A. इटली B. फ्रांस

C. जर्मनी D. यूनान

239. बिम्बवाद की स्थापना हुई–

A. इंग्लैंड B. यूनान

C. जर्मनी D. फ्रांस

240. दादावाद के विकसित रूप को कहते हैं–

A. प्रयोगवाद B. यथार्थवाद

C. अतियथार्थवाद D. आदर्शवाद

241. 'भग्नदूत' किसका काव्य संग्रह है?

A. मुक्तिबोध B. अज्ञेय

C. माखन लाल चतुर्वेदी D. कमलेश

242. 'मंजीर' काव्य संग्रह के रचयिता हैं–

A. प्रयाग नारायण त्रिपाठी B. दिनकर

C. गिरिजा कुमार माथुर D. रामस्वरूप चतुर्वेदी

243. 'सात गीत वर्ष' किसका काव्य संग्रह है?

A. गिरिजा कुमार माथुर B. नलिन विलोचन

C. लक्ष्मीकांत वर्मा D. धर्मवीर भारती

244. 'जागते रहो' किसका काव्य-संग्रह है?

A. गिरिजा कुमार माथुर B. केदारनाथ अग्रवाल

C. भारतभूषण अग्रवाल D. दिनकर

245. नीचे कवि और उसके काव्य संग्रह को सुमेलित करें।

कवि	काव्य संग्रह
(*i*) शमशेर	(*a*) मेपल
(*ii*) डॉ॰ रघुवीर सहाय	(*b*) कुछ कविताएँ, कुछ और कविताएँ
(*iii*) दुष्यंत कुमार	(*c*) लोग भूल गए हैं
(*iv*) प्रभाकर माचवे	(*d*) सूर्य का स्वागत

कूट :

	(*i*)	(*ii*)	(*iii*)	(*iv*)
A.	(*a*)	(*b*)	(*d*)	(*c*)
B.	(*b*)	(*c*)	(*a*)	(*d*)
C.	(*d*)	(*b*)	(*c*)	(*a*)
D.	(*b*)	(*c*)	(*d*)	(*a*)

246. 'चन्द्रगुप्त मौर्य' रचना की–

A. बालकृष्ण शर्मा B. श्याम नारायण प्रसाद

C. नटवर लाल सनेही D. राम खेलावन

247. 'संशय की एक रात' के रचनाकार हैं–

A. नवीन B. नरेश मेहता

C. दिनकर D. मुक्तिबोध

248. 'दिग्विजय' के रचयिता हैं–

A. अरूण पोद्धार B. आचार्य तुलसी

C. कमलेश D. बलदेव प्रसाद मिश्र

249. नीचे रचनाकार और रचनाओं को सुमेलित करें–

रचनाकार	रचना
(*i*) नागार्जुन	(*a*) सुवर्णा
(*ii*) नरेन्द्र शर्मा	(*b*) भस्मांकुर
(*iii*) परमानंद	(*c*) उत्तरायण
(*iv*) रामकुमार वर्मा	(*d*) निष्कासिका

कूट :

	(*i*)	(*ii*)	(*iii*)	(*iv*)
A.	(*b*)	(*a*)	(*c*)	(*d*)
B.	(*b*)	(*a*)	(*d*)	(*c*)
C.	(*a*)	(*d*)	(*c*)	(*b*)
D.	(*c*)	(*a*)	(*d*)	(*b*)

250. नीचे रचनाकार और रचनाओं को सुमेलित करें–

रचनाकार	रचना
(*i*) नरेश मेहता	(*a*) सत्यकाम
(*ii*) सुमित्रानंदन पंत	(*b*) प्रणभंग
(*iii*) दिनकर	(*c*) महाप्रस्थान
(*iv*) भारतभूषण अग्रवाल	(*d*) अग्निलीक

कूट :

	(*i*)	(*ii*)	(*iii*)	(*iv*)
A.	(*a*)	(*b*)	(*c*)	(*d*)
B.	(*b*)	(*a*)	(*d*)	(*c*)
C.	(*a*)	(*d*)	(*c*)	(*b*)
D.	(*c*)	(*a*)	(*d*)	(*b*)

251. नीचे दिए गए रचनाकार और रचनाओं को सुमेलित करें–

रचनाकार	रचना
(*i*) भवानी प्रसाद मिश्र	(*a*) कालजयी
(*ii*) पंत	(*b*) पुरूषोत्तम राम
(*iii*) नरेंद्र शर्मा	(*c*) द्रौपदी
(*iv*) केदार नाथ मिश्र	(*d*) ऋतुम्भरा

कूट :

	(*i*)	(*ii*)	(*iii*)	(*iv*)
A.	(*a*)	(*d*)	(*c*)	(*b*)
B.	(*a*)	(*b*)	(*d*)	(*c*)
C.	(*c*)	(*a*)	(*d*)	(*b*)
D.	(*a*)	(*b*)	(*c*)	(*d*)

252. 'सारथी' के रचनाकार हैं–

A. अनूप शर्मा B. भारतभूषण अग्रवाल

C. राम गोपाल शर्मा D. नरेन्द्र शर्मा

253. नीचे रचनाकारों और रचनाओं को सुमेलित करें?

रचनाकार	रचना
(*i*) बालकृष्ण शर्मा नवीन	(*a*) कालजयी (प्रबंध काव्य)
(*ii*) देवेन्द्र शर्मा	(*b*) प्राण अपर्ण
(*iii*) उपेन्द्रनाथ 'अश्क'	(*c*) सुनंदा (प्रबंध काव्य)
(*iv*) सियाराम शरण गुप्त	(*d*) चांदनी रात

कूट :

	(i)	(ii)	(iii)	(iv)
A.	(a)	(b)	(d)	(c)
B.	(b)	(a)	(d)	(c)
C.	(c)	(a)	(d)	(b)
D.	(d)	(b)	(a)	(c)

54. 'नई कविता' के प्रमुख कवि हैं-

A. दिनकर B. प्रसाद
C. निराला D. अज्ञेय

55. नवगीत के प्रवर्तन का श्रेय किसे है?

A. राजेन्द्र प्रसाद सिंह B. अज्ञेय
C. डॉ. देवराज D. शमशेर

56. प्रज्ञा नामक साहित्यिक संस्था है–

A. कोलकाता में B. इलाहाबाद में
C. दिल्ली में D. मेरठ में

57. रंगायन संस्था है–

A. मुम्बई में B. कोलकाता में
C. दिल्ली में D. हैदराबाद में

58. साहित्यिक संस्था कहाँ है?

A. मुम्बई B. दिल्ली
C. बनारस D. कोलकाता

59. नवगीत परम्परा में सर्वाधिक प्रसिद्धि किसे मिली?

A. राजेन्द्र प्रसाद सिंह B. अज्ञेय
C. नीरज D. इनमें से कोई नहीं

60. नीचे दिए गए कवि और उनके काव्य संग्रह को सुमेलित करें।

कवि	काव्य संग्रह
(i) नीरज	(a) संघर्ष
(ii) रवीन्द्र भ्रमर	(b) सोन मछरी मन बसो
(iii) राजेन्द्र प्रसाद सिंह	(c) मिट्टी बोलती है
(iv) रमेश रंजक	(d) संजीवनी कहाँ

कूट :

	(i)	(ii)	(iii)	(iv)
A.	(a)	(b)	(c)	(d)
B.	(a)	(d)	(b)	(c)
C.	(b)	(c)	(a)	(d)
D.	(a)	(b)	(d)	(c)

61. भाषा किसका साधन है?

A. लिखने का B. बोलने का
C. अध्ययन का D. अभिव्यक्ति का

62. भाषा—

A. जड़ होती है B. विकासोन्मुख होती है
C. बोधगम्य होती है D. उपर्युक्त तीनों

63. भाषा में किन शब्दों का बाहुल्य होता है?

A. तत्सम B. तद्भव
C. विदेशी D. लोक व्यवहार के

264. हिन्दी के विकास के आदिकाल में इस पर किसका प्रभाव रहा?

A. संस्कृत का B. देशज शब्दों का
C. ब्रज भाषा का D. अपभ्रंश का

265. खड़ी बोली का विकास कब हुआ?

A. आधुनिक युग में B. मध्य युग में
C. आदिकाल में D. उपर्युक्त में से कोई भी नहीं

266. अपभ्रंश भाषा का व्याकरण किसने लिखा?

A. हेमचन्द्र B. चन्द्रनाथ
C. उमानाथ D. धर्मेन्द्र

267. निम्नलिखित में से कौन-सी बिहारी बोली है?

A. ब्रज B. मैथिली
C. बुन्देली D. अवधी

268. भाषा को बोलने में किसका प्रयोग किया जाता है?

A. लिपि का B. ध्वनियों का
C. दोनों का D. दोनों में से कोई भी नहीं

269. व्याकरण—

A. भाषा की लिपि निर्धारित करता है
B. भाषा को सुबोध बनाता है
C. भाषा का रूप निर्धारित करता है
D. भाषा के वर्णों का अध्ययन करता है

270. वर्ण—

A. स्वर हैं B. व्यंजन हैं
C. ध्वनियाँ हैं D. उच्चारण हैं

271. हिन्दी में कितने वर्ण हैं?

A. 56 B. 26
C. 44 D. 36

272. स्वर/स्वरों—

A. मूल ध्वनियाँ हैं
B. को किसी अन्य ध्वनि की सहायता के बिना उच्चरित किया जा सकता है
C. की संख्या 11 है
D. उपरोक्त सभी

273. जिन स्वरों के उच्चारण में 'अ' के उच्चारण के बराबर समय लगता है, उन्हें क्या कहते हैं?

A. दीर्घ स्वर B. ह्रस्व स्वर
C. प्लुत स्वर D. पूर्ण स्वर

274. संयुक्त स्वर का एक उदाहरण है—

A. आ B. अ
C. इ D. उ

275. क् + ष =

A. श B. क्ष
C. ष D. उपर्युक्त में से कोई नहीं

276. व्यंजन तीन प्रकार के होते हैं–
(i) स्पर्श, (ii) अन्तस्थ और (iii) ....
A. ऊष्म B. कन्ठ्य
C. दन्तोष्ठ D. नासिका

277. त, थ, द, ध, का उच्चारण—
A. दाँतों के साथ जिह्वा के मेल से होता है
B. कंठ और ओठों के मेल से होता है
C. केवल ओठों से होता है
D. जीभ के प्रयोग के बिना होता है

278. एक या एक से अधिक वर्णों के संयोग से बनी ध्वनियों को क्या कहते हैं?
A. स्वर B. व्यंजन
C. शब्द D. रूढ़ि

279. व्युत्पत्ति के आधार पर शब्दों के तीन भेद होते हैं—
(i) रूढ़ि, (ii) यौगिक और (iii) ....
A. मिश्र B. योगरूढ़ि
C. तद्भव D. उपर्युक्त में से कोई भी नहीं

280. 'पाठशाला' शब्द किस वर्ग का है?
A. यौगिक B. रूढ़ि
C. योगरूढ़ि D. उपर्युक्त में से कोई भी नहीं

281. 'नीलकंठ' शब्द किस वर्ग का है?
A. यौगिक B. रूढ़ि
C. योगरूढ़ि D. उपर्युक्त में से कोई भी नहीं

282. जो शब्द संस्कृत के हैं और जिन्हें हिन्दी में ज्यों-का-त्यों इस्तेमाल किया जाता है, क्या कहलाते हैं?
A. तत्सम B. तद्भव
C. देशज D. उपर्युक्त में से कोई भी नहीं

283. 'अग्नि' शब्द किस वर्ग का है?
A. तत्सम B. तद्भव
C. देशज D. उपरोक्त में से कोई नहीं

284. संस्कृत मूल वाले शब्दों को जब हिन्दी में कुछ परिवर्तन के साथ इस्तेमाल किया जाता है, तो उन्हें क्या नाम दिया जाता है?
A. अविकारी B. तद्भव
C. तत्सम D. देशज

285. 'खेत' शब्द किस वर्ग का है?
A. देशज B. तत्सम
C. तद्भव D. विदेशी

286. काव्य में कितने स्थायी भाव प्रधान माने गए हैं?
A. पाँच B. सात
C. नौ D. ग्यारह

287. मन में जिसके प्रति भाव (स्थायी भाव) प्रकट होता है, इसे कहते हैं–
A. आलम्बन B. आश्रय
C. उद्दीपन D. संचारी भाव

288. संचारी भाव कितने माने गए हैं?
A. ग्यारह B. बाईस
C. तैंतीस D. सात

289. शृंगार रस का स्थायी भाव क्या है?
A. उत्साह B. शोक
C. रति D. विनोद

290. संचारी भाव
A. स्थायी भाव को पुष्ट करता है
B. स्थायी भाव के सहयोगी का काम करता है
C. अपना काम करने के बाद स्थायी भाव में ही लुप्त हो जाता है
D. उपरोक्त तीनों

291. रौद्र रस का स्थायी भाव क्या है?
A. शोक B. जुगुप्सा
C. क्रोध D. भय

292. वात्सल्य रस का स्थायी भाव क्या है?
A. स्नेह B. उत्साह
C. प्रेम D. जुगुप्सा

293. जिसके कारण हृदय में भाव प्रवृत्त होता है, वह क्या कहलाता है?
A. विभाव B. आलम्बन
C. उद्दीपन D. आश्रय

294. हास्य रस के कितने भेद हैं?
A. दो B. तीन
C. छह D. आठ

295. करुण रस का स्थायी भाव क्या है?
A. क्रोध B. भय
C. जुगुप्सा D. शोक

296. रस का आधार क्या है?
A. अनुभूति B. काव्य
C. संचारी भाव D. अलंकार

297. एक ओर अजगरहिं लखि एक ओर मृग राय।
विकल बटोही बीच ही परयौ मूरछा खाय।
उक्त पद में रस कौन-सा है?
A. करुण रस B. रौद्र रस
C. वीभत्स रस D. भयानक रस

298. जशोदा हरि पालने झुलावै।
हलरावै दुलरावै जोई सोई कछु गावै।
उक्त पद में रस कौन-सा है?
A. शृंगार रस B. वात्सल्य रस
C. वीभत्स रस D. वीर रस

299. 'क्या भाग रहा है भार देख?
तू मेरी ओर निहार देख
मैं त्याग चला निस्सार देख
अटकेगा मेरा कौन काम?

उक्त पद में रस कौन-सा है?

A. शांत रस B. वात्सल्य रस
C. रौद्र रस D. करुण रस

300. 'अखिल भुवन चर-अचर सब, हरि मुख में लखि मातु।
चकित भई गद्‌गद्‌ वचन, विकसित दृग पुलकातु।'

उक्त पद में रस कौन-सा है?

A. शांत रस B. वात्सल्य रस
C. अदभुत रस D. वीभत्स रस

301. इसमें रस कौन-सा है–
'बरतस लालच लाल की मुरली धरी लुकाय।
सौंह करै, भौंहन हँसै, दैन कहै, नटिं जाय।।'

A. करुण रस B. हास्य रस
C. शृंगार रस D. रौद्र रस

302. 'सभय बिलोके लोग सब जानि जानकी भीर।
हृदय न हरप विषाद कछु बोले श्रीरघुवीर।।

उक्त पद में रस कौन-सा है?

A. शांत रस B. शृंगार रस
C. वीर रस D. करुण रस

303. वीर रस कितने प्रकार के होते हैं?

A. तीन B. चार
C. पाँच D. छह

304. रस की भांति भाव के भी शुद्ध रूप में न होने और किसी विकार या दोष से युक्त होने के कारण उसे कहा जाता है–

A. रसाभाव B. भावाभाव
C. भाव-सन्धि D. भाव सबलता

305. जहाँ किसी भाव के शांत होते ही सहसा किसी दूसरे भाव के उदय होने का वर्णन होता है, वहां–

A. भावोदय होता है B. भाव-संधि होती है
C. भावसबलता होती है D. रसाभाव होता है

306. 'चेतक के पीछे दो काल, पड़े हुए ये ले असि ढाल।
उसके पथ में उनको मार, पावन की अपनी करवान।'

उक्त पंक्तियों में क्या है?

A. भाव-संधि B. भावोदय
C. भाव-शांति D. भावाभास

307. जहाँ दो भावों का संचार एक ही साथ वर्णन किया जाए, वहाँ क्या होता है?

A. भावाभास B. रसाभाव
C. भाव-शांति D. भाव-संधि

308. जहाँ दो से अधिक परस्पर विरोधी व उदासीन भावों के गड्डमड्ड होने अथवा एक साथ उदय होने का भाव हो, वहाँ क्या होता है–

A. भावाभास B. भाव-संधि
C. भाव-शांति D. भावसबलता

309. रस में विरोध कितने प्रकार का माना जाता है?

A. दो B. तीन
C. चार D. पाँच

310. जो स्वर दो स्वरों के योग से उच्चारित होते हैं, वे क्या कहलाते हैं?

A. ह्रस्व B. दीर्घ
C. व्यंजन D. गुरु

311. स्वर के उच्चारण में जो समय लगता है, उस अवधि को क्या कहते हैं?

A. मात्रा B. ह्रस्व
C. लघु D. वर्ण

312. लघु वर्ण की कितनी मात्रा होती है?

A. एक B. दो
C. चार D. पाँच

313. गुरु वर्ण की कितनी मात्रा होती है?

A. एक B. दो
C. चार D. तीन

314. 'मान्धाता' शब्द में तीनों मात्राएँ क्या हैं?

A. लघु B. गुरु
C. ह्रस्व D. दीर्घ

315. छंदों में प्रवाह होना चाहिए, जिससे पढ़ने में रुकावट न हो। इस प्रवाह को क्या कहते हैं?

A. क्रम B. यति
C. गण D. गति

316. चरणों में रुकावट, विराम, विश्राम को क्या कहते हैं?

A. गण B. क्रम
C. गति D. यति

317. छंद में गण शब्द का क्या तात्पर्य है?

A. दो अक्षरों का समूह B. तीन अक्षरों का समूह
C. पाँच अक्षरों का समूह D. छह अक्षरों का समूह

318. छंदों में त्रि-वर्ण के कितने समूह हैं?

A. तीन B. चार
C. सात D. आठ

319. छंद के दो या चार चरणों के अन्त में जब कोई एक स्वर आता है, तब उस अक्षर की एकता को क्या कहते हैं?

A. यति B. गति
C. क्रम D. तुक

320. छंदों के कितने भेद हैं?

A. दो B. तीन
C. चार D. आठ

321. चौपाई छंद के एक चरण में कितनी मात्राएँ होती हैं?

A. 16 B. 14
C. 17 D. 13

322. 'खंजन मंजु तिरीछे नयननि, निज पति कहेऊ तिन्हहि सिय सयननि।'

प्रस्तुत छंद क्या है?

A. चौपाई B. सोरठा
C. दोहा D. रोला

323. वर्णों के अनुसार गणों का मिलान कीजिए तथा दिए गए कूट की सहायता से सही उत्तर का चयन कीजिए–

गण	वर्ण
(*a*) रगण	1. सावन
(*b*) तगण	2. सौतेला
(*c*) भगण	3. साधना
(*d*) मगण	4. साकार

कूट :

	(*a*)	(*b*)	(*c*)	(*d*)
A.	3	4	1	2
B.	1	2	4	3
C.	1	2	3	4
D.	3	4	2	1

324. वर्णों के अनुसार गणों का मिलान कीजिए तथा दिए गए कूट की सहायता से सही उत्तर का चयन कीजिए–

गण	वर्ण
(*a*) नगण	1. सुभाषा
(*b*) यगण	2. सुजाता
(*c*) जगण	3. सरिता
(*d*) सगण	4. सरल

कूट :

	(*a*)	(*b*)	(*c*)	(*d*)
A.	2	1	4	3
B.	4	2	1	3
C.	1	2	3	4
D.	3	4	2	1

325. मगण गण में गण का क्या लक्षण है?

A. पहला वर्ण गुरु B. बीच वर्ण गुरु
C. अन्त वर्ण गुरु D. तीनों वर्ण गुरु

326. तगण गण में गण का क्या लक्षण है?

A. अन्त का वर्ण लघु B. बीच का वर्ण लघु
C. तीनों वर्ण लघु D. पहला वर्ण लघु

327. जगण गण में गण का क्या लक्षण है?

A. बीच का वर्ण लघु B. बीच का वर्ण गुरु
C. अन्त का वर्ण लघु D. अन्त का वर्ण गुरु

328. निम्न में अर्द्धमात्रिक छद कौन-सा है?

A. दोहा B. रोला
C. सोरठा D. चौपाई

329. निम्न में अर्द्धसममात्रिक छंद कौन-सा है?

A. दोहा B. रोला
C. सोरठा D. कुण्डलिया

330. छंदों में विषम चरणों से तात्पर्य है–

A. पहला और दूसरा चरण
B. दूसरा और तीसरा चरण
C. पहला और चौथा चरण
D. पहला और तीसरा चरण

उत्तरमाला

1	2	3	4	5	6	7	8	9	10
C	C	A	B	C	D	B	C	A	A
11	**12**	**13**	**14**	**15**	**16**	**17**	**18**	**19**	**20**
C	A	C	D	D	A	D	C	C	A
21	**22**	**23**	**24**	**25**	**26**	**27**	**28**	**29**	**30**
A	D	A	D	D	B	D	B	D	D
31	**32**	**33**	**34**	**35**	**36**	**37**	**38**	**39**	**40**
D	D	B	D	D	D	D	C	B	D
41	**42**	**43**	**44**	**45**	**46**	**47**	**48**	**49**	**50**
B	D	D	D	A	C	D	A	D	D
51	**52**	**53**	**54**	**55**	**56**	**57**	**58**	**59**	**60**
C	C	D	A	B	A	A	A	D	B
61	**62**	**63**	**64**	**65**	**66**	**67**	**68**	**69**	**70**
C	A	B	B	D	D	B	A	A	A
71	**72**	**73**	**74**	**75**	**76**	**77**	**78**	**79**	**80**
C	A	B	D	D	D	D	D	A	C
81	**82**	**83**	**84**	**85**	**86**	**87**	**88**	**89**	**90**
A	C	A	A	B	B	A	A	C	D

91	92	93	94	95	96	97	98	99	100
D	D	D	C	A	D	A	C	C	B
101	102	103	104	105	106	107	108	109	110
B	B	C	B	B	D	B	D	D	B
111	112	113	114	115	116	117	118	119	120
D	A	C	D	A	B	A	A	D	C
121	122	123	124	125	126	127	128	129	130
C	D	A	C	D	D	D	A	D	D
131	132	133	134	135	136	137	138	139	140
C	C	D	A	C	C	A	A	C	C
141	142	143	144	145	146	147	148	149	150
D	D	B	C	C	D	C	B	D	B
151	152	153	154	155	156	157	158	159	160
A	B	C	B	C	D	A	B	A	C
161	162	163	164	165	166	167	168	169	170
B	D	A	C	B	C	A	C	B	D
171	172	173	174	175	176	177	178	179	180
B	C	A	D	D	B	C	B	D	B
181	182	183	184	185	186	187	188	189	190
D	C	D	C	D	A	A	C	D	D
191	192	193	194	195	196	197	198	199	200
B	D	B	B	C	B	A	D	A	A
201	202	203	204	205	206	207	208	209	210
C	D	A	A	C	D	D	B	D	D
211	212	213	214	215	216	217	218	219	220
C	C	B	B	A	A	B	C	D	B
221	222	223	224	225	226	227	228	229	230
A	D	C	B	B	C	C	D	B	B
231	232	233	234	235	236	237	238	239	240
C	B	A	C	B	C	D	B	A	C
241	242	243	244	245	246	247	248	249	250
B	C	D	C	D	D	B	C	B	C
251	252	253	254	255	256	257	258	259	260
D	C	B	D	A	C	A	D	C	D
261	262	263	264	265	266	267	268	269	270
D	B	D	D	A	A	B	B	C	C
271	272	273	274	275	276	277	278	279	280
C	D	B	A	B	A	A	C	B	A
281	282	283	284	285	286	287	288	289	290
C	A	A	B	C	C	A	C	C	D
291	292	293	294	295	296	297	298	299	300
C	A	C	C	D	A	D	B	A	C
301	302	303	304	305	306	307	308	309	310
B	C	B	B	A	B	D	D	B	B
311	312	313	314	315	316	317	318	319	320
A	A	B	B	D	D	B	D	D	C
321	322	323	324	325	326	327	328	329	330
A	A	A	B	D	A	B	A	C	D

SOCIAL SCIENCE

• History of India (Ancient India, Medieval India, Indian National Movement) • World History • Indian Polity, Economy & Culture • Indian Agriculture, Commerce & Trade • Population, Ecology & Urbanisation • World Geography, Indian Geography & Its Resources.

1

HISTORY OF INDIA

ANCIENT INDIA

Pre-Historic India

- The history of human settlements in India goes back to pre-historic times.
- The archaeological remains are found in different parts of India to reconstruct the history of this period.
- In India, the pre-historic period is divided into the Palaeolithic (Old Stone Age), Mesolithic (Middle Stone Age), Neolithic (New Stone Age) and the Metal Age.

Palaeolithic or Old Stone Age

- The Old Stone Age sites are widely found in various parts of the Indian subcontinent. These sites are generally located near water sources.
- Man invented fire by rubbing two pieces of flint. Man used leaves, barks of trees and skins of animals to cover his body.
- A few Old Stone Age paintings have also been found on rocks at Bhimbetka and other places.

Mesolithic or Middle Stone Age

- The next stage of human life is called Mesolithic or Middle Stone Age, which falls roughly from 10000 B.C. to 6000 B.C.
- The hunting-gathering pattern of life continued during this period.
- The use of bow and arrow also began during this period. Also, there began a tendency to settle for longer periods in an area. Therefore, domestication of animals, horticulture and primitive cultivation started.

Neolithic Age or New stone age

- During this period, the *wheel was invented.* It was a turning point in the life of man.
- The chief characteristic features of the Neolithic culture are the practice of *agriculture, domestication of animals,* polishing of stone tools and the manufacture of pottery.
- Large urns were used as coffins for the burial of the dead.
- The people of Neolithic Age used clothes made of cotton and wool.

Metal Age

- The Neolithic period is followed by Chalcolithic (copper-stone) period when copper and bronze came to be used.
- The Chalcolithic age is followed by Iron Age.
- In the Iron Age, ploughs and daggers were made of iron. It led to the overall development of mankind.

INDUS VALLEY CIVILISATION (2500-1750 BC)

- The earliest excavations in the Indus valley were done at Harappa in the West Punjab and Mohanjodaro in Sindh. Both places are now in Pakistan.

Important Sites

- The most important sites are Kot Diji in Sindh, Kalibangan in Rajasthan, Ropar in the Punjab, Banawali in Haryana, Lothal, Surkotada and Dhaulavira, all the three in Gujarat.
- Mohanjodaro is the largest of all the Indus cities and it is estimated to have spread over an area of 200 hectares.

Salient Features of the Harappan Culture

- The Harappan Civilization was primarily Urban.
- Mohanjodaro and Harappa were the planned cities.
- The large-scale use of burnt bricks in almost all kinds of constructions are the important characteristics of the Harappan culture.
- Another remarkable feature was the under-ground drainage system connecting all houses to the street drains which were covered by stone slabs or bricks.
- The most important public place of Mohanjo-daro is the Great Bath measuring 39 feet length, 23 feet breadth and 8 feet depth.

Indus Valley Civilisation : An Objective Study

	Major Sites	Excavators	Year	River	Location	Important Findings
1.	Harappa	D.R. Sahni	1921	Ravi	West Punjab (Pakistan)	Granaries, Virgin Goddess, Cemetery, Stone symbol of Lingam and Yoni
2.	Mohenjodaro	R.D. Banerjee	1922	Indus	Sindh (Pakistan)	Great Bath, Great Granary, Assembly Hall, Proto-Shiva, Brick Kilns, Mesopotamian seals
3.	Chanhudaro	N.G. Mazumdar	1931	Indus	Sindh (Pakistan)	Bronze toy cart, Ink-pot, Lipstick, City without a citadel
4.	Kalibangan	B.B. Lal & B.K. Thapar	1953	Ghaggar	Ganganagar (Rajasthan)	Decorated bricks, ploughed field surface, Firealtars
5.	Lothal	S.R. Rao	1957	Bhogwa	Ahmedabad (Gujarat)	Dockyard, Rice husk, Fire altars, Double burial
6.	Banawali	R.S. Bist	1973	Ghaggar	Hissar (Haryana)	Toy plough, Gridiron pattern of Town planning.
7.	Dholavira	R.S. Bist	1990	Luni	Kutchh (Gujarat)	A Large well & a bath, A stadium
8.	Surkotada	J. Joshi	1964	—	Gujarat	Bones of Horse, Pot burials

- Agriculture was the most important occupation. In the fertile soils, farmers cultivated two crops a year. They were the first who had grown paddy.
- Wheat and barley were the main crops grown besides sesame, mustard and cotton.
- Animals like sheep, goats and buffalo were domesticated. The use of horse is not yet firmly established.
- Bronze and copper vessels are the outstanding examples of the Harappan metal craft.
- A large number of seals numbering more than 2000 have been discovered.

THE VEDIC PERIOD

Rig Vedic Age (1500 - 1000 B.C.)

- The Early Vedic period is known from the *Rig Veda*.
- The Rig Veda refers to Saptasindhu or the land of seven rivers. This includes the five rivers of the Punjab, namely, Jhelum, Chenab, Ravi, Beas and Sutlej along with the Indus and Saraswathi.
- Historians view that the Aryans came from Central Asia. They entered India through the Khyber pass between 2000 B.C. and 1500 B.C. They first settled in seven places in the Punjab region which they called Sapta Sindhu. Slowly, they moved towards the Gangetic Valley.
- The Aryan Civilisation was a rural civilisation.

Vedic Literature

- The word 'Veda' is derived from the root 'vid', which means to know and signifies 'superior knowledge'.
- The Vedic literature consists of the four Vedas – Rig, Yajur, Sama and Atharva.
- The *Rig Veda* is the earliest of the four Vedas divided into 10 mandalas and it consists of 1028 hymns. The hymns were sung by *Hotri* in praise of various gods.
- The *Yajur Veda* consists of various details of rules to be observed at the time of sacrifice. Its hymns were recited by *Adharvayus*.
- The *Sama Veda* is set to tune for the purpose of chanting during sacrifice. It is called the book of chants and the origins of Indian music are traced in it. Its hymns were recited by *Udgatri*.
- The *Atharva Veda* contains details of rituals.
- Besides the Vedas, there are other sacred works like the Brahmanas, the Aranyakas, the Upanishads, and the epics Ramayana and Mahabharata.

Religion

- The important Rig Vedic gods were Prithvi (Earth), Agni (Fire), Vayu (Wind), Varuna (Rain) and Indra (Thunder).
- Indra was the most popular among them during the early Vedic period.
- There were also female gods like Aditi and Ushas. There were no temples and no idol worship during the early Vedic period.

Rigvedic Rivers

River	Name in Rigveda
Indus	Sindhu
Jhelum	Vitasta
Chenab	Asikni
Ravi	Parushini
Beas	Vipasa
Sutlej	Sutudri
Gomati	Gomal
Saraswati	Sarasvati
Ghaggar	Prishadavati

Later Vedic Period (1000–600 B.C.)

- This age is also called as the Epic Age because the two great epics the Ramayana and Mahabharata were written during this period.
- The Sama, Yajur, Atharva Vedas, Brahmanas, Aranyakas, Upanishads and the two epics are the sources of information for this period.

Political Organisation

- Larger kingdoms were formed during the later Vedic period.
- The king performed various rituals and sacrifices to strengthen his position. They include Rajasuya (consecration ceremony), Asvamedha (horse sacrifice) and Vajpeya (chariot race).
- Kingship became hereditary.
- Kings assumed titles like Ekrat, Samrat and Sarvabauma.

Economic Condition

- Iron was used extensively in this period and this enabled the people to clear forests and to bring more land under cultivation. Agriculture became the chief occupation.
- Taxes like Pali, Sulk and Bhaga were collected from the people.
- Wealth was calculated in terms of cows.

Social Life

- The four divisions of society (Brahmins, Kshatriyas, Vaisyas and Sudras) or the Varna system was thoroughly established during the Later Vedic period.
- The Ashrama system was formed to attain 4 purusharthas. They were *Dharma*, *Artha*, *Kama* and *Moksha*.

Religion

- Gods of the Early Vedic period like Indra and Agni lost their importance. Prajapathi (the creator), Vishnu (the protector) and Rudra (the destroyer) became prominent during the Later Vedic period.

JAINISM AND BUDDHISM

Jainism

- Jainism originated in the 6th century B.C. It rejected Vedic religion and avoided its rituals.
- Founded by Rishabha Deva. Rishabha Deva was succeeded by 23 Thirthankaras (prophets). Mahavira was the 24th Thirthankara.

Vardhamana Mahavira (540-468 B.C.)

- Vardhamana was born in a village called Kundagrama near Vaishali in Bihar.
- His father was *Siddhartha*. He was the head of a famous Kshatriya clan.
- His mother was *Trisala*. She was a princess of the Lichchhavi clan. She was the sister of the ruler of Vaishali.
- Vardhamana was married to Yasoda, a princess. They had a daughter.
- At the age of 30, he left his home and family. He became an ascetic (monk). He wandered from place-to place in search of truth for 12 years.
- In the 13th year of his penance, he attained the highest spiritual knowledge called Kevalya Jnana. Thereafter, he was called Mahavira and Jina. His followers were called Jains and his religion Jainism.
- He died at the age of 72 in 468 B.C. at a place called Pavapuri near modern Rajgir.

Teachings of Jainism

- The three principles of Jainism, also known as Triratnas (three gems), are:
  1. right faith.
  2. right knowledge.
  3. right conduct.
- Mahavira preached his disciples to follow the five principles. They are:
  1. Ahimsa—not to injure any living beings
  2. Satya—to speak the truth
  3. Asteya—not to steal
  4. Tyag—not to own property
  5. Brahmacharia—to lead a virtuous life.

Spread of Jainism

- Jainism was divided into two sects after Vallabhi Council, namely *Svetambaras* (wearing white dresses) under Sthulbhadra and *Digambaras* (naked) under Bhadrabahu.
- The first Jain Council was convened at Pataliputra by Sthulabahu, the leader of the *Digambaras*, in the beginning of the 3rd century B.C.

- The second Jain Council was held at Valabhi in 5th century A.D. The final compilation of Jain literature called Twelve Angas was completed in this council.

Buddhism

Gautama Buddha (563-483 B.C.)

- Buddha's original name was *Siddhartha*.
- Siddhartha was born in the Lumbini Garden near Kapilavastu in Nepal. His father was Suddhodana. He was a Sakya chief of Kapilavastu. His mother, Mayadevi, died when Siddhartha was only seven days old. He was brought up by his step mother Mahaprajapati Gauthami. At the age of sixteen Siddhartha, married Yasodhara and gave birth to a son, Rahul.
- The sight of an old man, a diseased man, a corpse and an ascetic turned him away from worldly life. He left home at the age of twenty-nine in search of Truth.
- He wandered for seven years and at last, he sat under a bodhi tree at Bodh Gaya and did intense penance, after which he got Enlightenment (Nirvana) at the age of thirty-five. Since then, he became known as the Buddha or 'the Enlightened One'.
- Buddha delivered his first sermon at Sarnath near Banaras (now Varanasi).
- He died at the age of 80 in 483 B.C. at Kushinagar in Uttar Pradesh.

Teachings of Buddha

- The Four Noble Truths of Buddha are:
  1. The world is full of suffering.
  2. The cause of suffering is desire.
  3. If desires are get rid off, suffering can be removed.
  4. This can be done by following the Eightfold Path.
- The Eightfold Path consists of:
  1. Right Thought.
  2. Right Belief.
  3. Right Speech.
  4. Right Action.
  5. Right Living.
  6. Right Efforts.
  7. Right Knowledge.
  8. Right Meditation.

Main Buddhist Councils

Buddhist Council	Time	Place	Chairman	Patron
First	483 BC	Rajagriha	Mahakashyapa	Ajatshatru
Second	383 BC	Vaishali	Sabakami	Kalashoka
Third	250 BC	Patliputra	Mogaliputta Tissa	Ashoka
Fourth	AD 72	Kundalvana	Vasumitra, Ashwaghosa	Kanishka

Buddhist Literature

- Buddhist scriptures in Pali are commonly referred to as *Tripitakas, i.e.*, 'Three Baskets'.
- ***Vinaya Pitaka:*** Rules of discipline in Buddhist monasteries.
- ***Sutta Pitaka:*** Largest, contains collection of Buddha's sermons.
- ***Abidhamma Pitaka:*** Explanation of the philosophical principles of the Buddhist religion.

The Mahajanapadas

S.N.	Mahajanapadas	Capital
1.	Kashi	Varanasi
2.	Kosala	Shravasti
3.	Anga	Champanagri
4.	Magadh	Girivraj or Rajgriha
5.	Vajji	Vaishali
6.	Malla	Kushinagar and Pavapuri
7.	Chedi	Shuktimati
8.	Vatsa	Kaushambi
9.	Kuru	Hastinapur, Indraprastha and Isukara
10.	Panchal	Ahichhatra and Kampilya
11.	Matsya	Viratnagar
12.	Surasen	Mathura
13.	Asmaka	Paudanya
14.	Avanti	Ujjaini
15.	Gandhara	Taxila
16.	Kamboj	Rajpur (Hatak)

DYNASTIES OF ANCIENT INDIA

Haryanka dynasty

- Bimbisara was the founder of Haryanka Dynasty.
- He was a contemporary of both Vardhamana Mahavira and Gautama Buddha.
- During his rule, Darius I, the Achaemenian emperor, conquered the Indus Valley area.
- Ajatasatru imprisoned his father Bimbisara.
- The first Buddhist Council was convened by Ajatasatru at Rajgir.

- The immediate successor of Ajatasatru was Udayin.
- Udayin laid the foundation of the new capital at Pataliputra situated at the confluence of the two rivers, the Ganges and the Son.
- Shishunaga was the founder of Shishunaga dynasty.
- After Shishunaga, the mighty empire began to collapse. His successor was Kakavarman or Kalasoka. During his reign, the second Buddhist Council was held at Vaishali.
- Kalasoka was killed by the founder of the Nanda dynasty.

Nandas

- The fame of Magadha scaled new heights under the Nanda dynasty.
- Mahapadmananda was the founder of Nanda rule in Magadha.
- The last Nanda ruler was Dhana Nanda. Alexander invaded India during his rule.

MAURYAN EMPIRE

Chandragupta Maurya (322–298 B.C.)

- Chandragupta Maurya was the founder of the Mauryan Empire. He overthrew Nanda dynasty with the help of Chanakya.
- Chandragupta defeated Seleukos Nikator, the Greek general of Alexander, in a battle in 305 B.C.
- Seleukos sent Megasthenes as Greek Ambassador to the Court of Chandragupta. Megasthenes wrote *Indica*.
- Chandragupta was a follower of Jainism.
- He came to Sravana Belgola, near Mysore with a Jain monk called Bhadrabahu. The hill in which he lived until his death is called Chandragiri.
- Chanakya served as prime minister during the reigns of Chandragupta and Bindusara.

Bindusara (298–273 B.C.)

- Chandragupta Maurya was succeeded by his son Bindusara.
- Bindusara was called by the Greeks as "*Amitragatha*" meaning, slayer of enemies.

Ashoka (273–232 B.C.)

- Ashoka was the most famous ruler of the Mauryan dynasty.
- The most important event of Ashoka's reign was his victorious war with Kalinga in 261 B.C.
- Ashoka convened the Third Buddhist Council at Pataliputra around 250 B.C. in order to strengthen the *Sangha*. It was presided over by Moggaliputta Tissa.
- Ashoka's edicts and inscriptions were deciphered by James Prinsep in 1837.
- The last Mauryan king, Brahadratha was killed by his minister Pushyamitra Sunga. It put an end to the Mauryan Empire.

Sungas

- The founder of the Sunga dynasty was *Pushyamitra Sunga*, who was the commander-in-chief under the Mauryas.
- He ascended the throne of Magadha in 185 B.C.
- Pushyamitra was a staunch follower of Brahmanism. He performed two asvamedha sacrifices.
- After the death of Pushyamitra, his son Agnimitra became the ruler.
- Agnimitra was a great conqueror. He was also the hero of the play Malavikagnimitram written by Kalidasa.

Kanva

- The last Sunga ruler was Devabhuti, who was murdered by his minister Vasudeva Kanva, the founder of the *Kanva dynasty*.
- The Kanva dynasty ruled for 45 years. After the fall of the Kanvas, the history of Magadha was a blank until the establishment of the Gupta dynasty.

Satavahanas

- The founder of the Satavahana dynasty was Simuka.
- The greatest ruler of the Satavahana dynasty was *Gautamiputra Satakarni.*
- The greatest port of the Satavahanas was Kalyani on the west Deccan.
- Gandakasela and Ganjam on the east coast were the other important seaports.
- The fine painting at Amaravathi and Nagarjunakonda caves belong to this period.

SANGAM AGE (300 B.C. TO A.D. 300)

- The Sangam Age constitutes an important chapter in the history of South India.
- *The first Sangam*, held at then Madurai, chaired by Agastya.
- *The second Sangam* was held at Kapadapuram, chaired by Tolkappiyar.
- *The third Sangam* at Madurai was founded by Mudathirumaran.

Political History

- The Tamil country was ruled by three dynasties namely the Chera, Chola and Pandyas during the Sangam Age.

Cheras

- The Cheras ruled over parts of modern Kerala. Their capital was Vanji and their important seaports were Tondi and Musiris.
- The greatest Chera King was *Senguttuvan.*

Cholas

- The Chola kingdom of the Sangam period extended from modern Tiruchi district to southern Andhra Pradesh.
- Their capital was first located at Uraiyur and then shifted to Puhar. Kaveripattinam served as their port.

GUPTA PERIOD

- The Gupta period is considered as the *Golden Age* in the history of India because this period witnessed all round developments in Religion, Literature, Science, Art and Architecture.

Chandragupta I (320-334 A.D.)

- In the beginning of the 4th Century A.D., Sri Gupta established a small Kingdom at Pataliputra. He is considered as the founder of the Gupta dynasty.
- The first notable ruler of the Gupta dynasty was Chandragupta I. He assumed the title *Maharajadhiraja*. The Meherauli Iron Pillar inscription mentions his extensive conquests.
- Chandragupta I is considered to be the founder of the Gupta era which starts with his accession in A.D. 320.

Samudragupta (335-380 A.D.)

- Samudragupta was the greatest of the rulers of the Gupta dynasty. The Allahabad Pillar inscription provides a detailed account of his reign.
- Because of his military achievements, Samudragupta was hailed as '*Indian Napoleon*'.

Chandragupta II (380-414 A.D.)

- Samudragupta was succeeded by his son Chandragupta II Vikramaditya.
- The greatest of the military achievements of Chandragupta II was his war against the Saka *satraps* of western India.
- The famous Chinese pilgrim, Fahien visited India (A.D. 399 - A.D. 414) during the reign of Chandragupta II.

Successors of Chandragupta II

- Kumaragupta (415-455) was the son and successor of Chandragupta II. His reign was marked by general peace and prosperity.
- Kumaragupta was the founder of the Nalanda University.
- Kumaragupta was followed by *Skandagupta* who ruled from A.D. 456 to A.D. 468.
- After Skandagupta's death, many of his successors like Purugupta, Narasimhagupta, Buddhagupta and Baladitya could not save the Gupta empire from the Huns. Ultimately, the Gupta power totally disappeared due to the Hun invasions and later by the rise of Yasodharman in Malwa.

PUSHYABHUTI DYNASTY (600 - 647 A.D.)

- The greatest king was *Harshavardhana*, son of Prabhakar Vardhana of Thaneshwar. He shifted the capital to *Kannauj.*
- *Hieun Tsang* visited during his reign.
- He established a large monastery at Nalanda. Banabhata adorned his court, wrote Harshacharita and Kadambari. Harsha himself wrote three plays–Priyadarshika, Ratnawali and Nagananda.

Pallavas

- The Pallavas established their kingdom in Tondaimandalam by Simhavishnu with its capital at Kanchipuram.
- Other great Pallava rulers were Mahendravarman I, Narasimhavarman I, and Narasimhavarman II.
- The *Kailasanatha temple* at Kanchipuram is the greatest architectural masterpiece of the Pallava art.

Chalukyas (543-755 A.D.)

- Pulakesin I was the founder of the Chalukya dynasty. He established a small kingdom with Vatapi or Badami as its capital.
- The structural temples of the Chalukyas exist at Aihole, Badami and Pattadakal (Virupaksha temple). Cave temple architecture was also famous under the Chalukyas. Their cave temples are found in Ajanta, Ellora and Nasik.

Rashtrakutas (755-975 A.D.)

- The art and architecture of the Rashtrakutas were found at Ellora and Elephanta.

Cholas

- Cholas became prominent in the ninth century and established an empire comprising the major portion of South India. Their capital was Tanjore. The founder of the Chola kingdom was Vijayalaya. Rajaraja Chola built the famous Brihadeeswara temple at Tanjore.
- *Dancing Figure of Shiva* (Nataraja) belong to Chola period.

MEDIEVAL INDIA

ARAB CONQUEST OF SIND

- In 712 A.D., Muhammad bin Quasim invaded Sind. Quasim defeated Dahir, the ruler of Sind and killed him in a well-contested battle.

Mahmud of Ghazni

- In 1024, Mahmud marched from Multan across Rajaputana, defeated the Solanki King Bhimadeva I, plundered Anhilwad and sacked the famous temple of Somanatha. This was his last campaign in India. Mahmud died in 1030 A.D.
- Mahmud patronized art and literature. *Firdausi* was the poet-laureate in the court of Mahmud.

Muhammad Ghori

- Prithviraj Chauhan defeated Ghori in the battle of Tarain near Delhi in 1191 A.D.
- In the Second Battle of Tarain in 1192, Muhammad Ghori thoroughly routed the army of Prithiviraj, who was captured and killed.
- After his brilliant victory over Prithviraj at Tarain, Muhammad Ghori returned to Ghazni leaving behind his favourite general Qutb-ud-din Aibak to make further conquests in India.

SULTANATE PERIOD

Slave Dynasty (1206-1290)

- The Slave dynasty was also called Mamluk dynasty. Mamluk was the Quranic term for slave.

Qutb-ud-din Aibak

- Qutb-ud-din Aibak was a slave of Muhammad Ghori, who made him the Governor of his Indian possessions.
- After the death of Ghori in 1206, Aibak declared his independence. He assumed the title Sultan and made Lahore his capital.
- Muslim writers call Aibak Lakh Baksh or giver of lakhs because he gave liberal donations to them.
- He built the famous Quwat-Ul-Islam mosque at Delhi. He began the construction of the famous Qutb Minar at Delhi but did not live long to complete it. It was later completed by Iltutmish.

Iltutmish (1210-1236 A.D.)

- Iltutmish belonged to the Ilbari tribe and hence his dynasty was named as Ilbari dynasty.
- He shifted his capital from Lahore to Delhi.
- He organised the *Iqta system* and introduced reforms in civil administration and army.

Raziya (1236-1240 A.D.)

- She appointed an Abyssinian slave Yakuth as Master of the Royal Horses.
- In 1240, Altunia, the governor of Bhatinda revolted against her. She went in personally to suppress the revolt but Altunia killed Yakuth and took Raziya prisoner.
- Bahram Shah, son of Iltutmish killed her.

Balban (1266-1286 A.D.)

- Balban introduced rigorous court discipline and new customs such as prostration and kissing the Sultan's feet to prove his superiority over the nobles.
- He also introduced the Persian festival of *Nauroz* to impress the nobles and people with his wealth and power.
- He established a separate military department - *diwan-i-arz* – and reorganized the army.

Khilji Dynasty (1290-1320 A.D.)

- The founder of the Khilji dynasty was Jalaluddin Khilji.
- Ala-ud-din Khilji was the greatest ruler of the Khilji Dynasty.
- He was the first Muslim ruler to extend his empire right upto Rameshwaram in the South.
- The Sultan had built a new city called Siri near Delhi.
- Amir Khusrau the great Persian poet, patronised by Balban, continued to live in Ala-ud-din Khilji's court also.
- He introduced the system of *dagh* (branding of horses) and prepared *huliya* (descriptive list of soldiers).
- Ala-ud-din Khilji maintained a large permanent standing army and paid them in cash from the royal treasury.

Tughlaq dynasty

- Ghiyas-ud-din Tughlaq was the founder of the Tughlaq dynasty.
- To have the capital at the centre of the empire and safe from the Mongol raids, Tughlaq chose Devagiri as his new capital in A.D. 1327. The Sultan renamed the new capital Daulatabad.
- In 1329-30, Muhammad-bin-Tughlaq introduced a token currency.
- Firoz Shah Tughlaq became Sultan after the death of Muhammad-bin-Tughlaq in A.D. 1351.

- He was the first Sultan to impose irrigation tax.
- He had built new towns of Firozabad, Jaunpur, Hissar and Firozpur.
- Timur Mongol leader of Central Asia, ordered general massacre in Delhi (AD 1398) at the time of Nasiruddin Mahmud (later Tughlaq king).

Sayyid Dynasty

- Before his departure from India, Timur appointed Khizr Khan as governor of Multan. He captured Delhi and founded the Sayyid dynasty in 1414.
- Mubarak Shah, Mohammed Shah and Alam Shah were some of the other important noteworthy rulers of Sayyid Dynasty.

Lodhi Dynasty

- The Lodhis were Afghans.
- Bahlol Lodhi was the first Afghan ruler while his predecessors were all Turks. He died in 1489 and was succeeded by his son, Sikandar Lodhi.
- In 1504, Sikandar Lodhi founded the city of Agra and transferred his capital from Delhi to Agra.
- Babar marched against Delhi and defeated and killed Ibrahim Lodhi in the first battle of Panipat (1526).

BAHMANI AND VIJAYANAGAR KINGDOMS

- The break up of the Delhi Sultanate provided an opportunity for the rise of a number of kingdoms in the Deccan.
- After the decline of the Tughlaqs, there arose two important kingdoms in the Deccan. They were the Bahmani and Vijayanagar kingdoms.

Vijayanagar Empire

- The Vijayanagar Kingdom was set up in A.D. 1336. Its aim was to check the spread of Muslim power and protect Hindu Dharma in South India.
- Four dynasties – Sangama, Saluva, Tuluva and Aravidu – ruled Vijayanagar from A.D. 1336 to 1672.
- Vijayanagar was founded in 1336 by Harihara and Bukka of the Sangama dynasty.
- The Moroccan traveller, Ibn Batuta, Venetian traveller Nicolo de Conti, Persian traveller Abdur Razzak and the Portuguese traveller Domingo Paes were among them who left valuable accounts on the socio-economic conditions of the Vijayanagar Empire.
- The Hampi ruins and other monuments of Vijayanagar provide information on the cultural contributions of the Vijayanagar rulers.

Krishna Deva Raya (1509-1530)

- The Tuluva dynasty was founded by Vira Narasimha.
- The greatest of the Vijayanagar rulers, Krishna Deva Raya belonged to the Tuluva dynasty.
- Krishna Deva Raya himself authored a Telugu work, *Amukthamalyadha* and Sanskrit works, *Jambavati Kalyanam* and *Ushaparinayam*.
- He built the famous *Vittalaswamy* and *Hazara Ramaswamy* temples at Vijayanagar.
- Krishna Deva Raya renovated Virupaksha temple in A.D. 1510.
- After his death the enemies of Vijayanagar joined together and defeated the Vijayanagar ruler in the battle of Talaikota.

Bahmani Kingdom

- The founder of the Bahmani kingdom was Alauddin Bahman Shah also known as Hasan Gangu in 1347. Its capital was Gulbarga.
- Ahmad Wali Shah shifted the capital from Gulbarga to Bidar.
- *Gol Gumbaj* was built by *Muhammad Adil Shah*; it is famous for the so called '*Whispering Gallery*'.
- *Quli Qutub Shah* built the famous *Golcunda Fort*.

MUGHAL EMPIRE (1526-1707 AD)

Babar (1526-1530 AD)

- Babar was the founder of the Mughal Empire in India.
- On 21st April, 1526 the first Battle of Panipat took place between Babar and Ibrahim Lodhi, who was killed in the battle.
- Babar was the first one to use guns or artillery in a battle on the Indian soil.
- Babar defeated Rana Sanga of Mewar in the battle of Kanwah in A.D. 1527.
- Babar was a soldier-scholar and wrote his own autobiography called Babar Nama in Turkish language.

Humayun (1530-1556 AD)

- Sher Shah defeated Humayun at *Chausa in A.D. 1539* and again at Kannauj in A.D. 1540.
- After losing his kingdom, Humayun became an exile for the next fifteen years.
- In 1555, Humayun defeated the Afghans and recovered the Mughal throne. After six months, he died in 1556 due to his fall from the staircase of his library.
- *Gulbadan Begum*, Humayun's half-sister wrote *Humayun-nama*.

Sher Shah Suri

- The founder of the Sur dynasty was Sher Shah, whose original name was Farid.
- Sher Shah became the ruler of Delhi in 1540.
- Sher Shah organized a brilliant administrative system. The central government consisted of several departments.
- He built a new city on the banks of the river Yamuna near Delhi. Now the old fort called Purana Quila and its mosque is alone surviving.
- He built a Mausoleum at Sasaram, which is considered as one of the master pieces of Indian architecture.

Akbar (1556-1605 AD)

- When Akbar ascended the throne in A.D. 1556 he was only 14 years old. His guardian Bairam Khan served him as a faithful minister and tutor.
- Bairam Khan, along with Akbar met Hemu in the second Battle of Panipat in 1556. Hemu was initially successful, but lost his consciousness after an arrow hit him. Akbar killed him.
- In the Battle of Haldighati, Rana Pratap Singh was severely defeated by the Mughal army led by Man Singh in 1576.
- Akbar abolished the pilgrim tax and in 1562, he abolished Jaziya.
- Akbar evolved a new faith called Din-i-Illahi or Divine Faith.

Jahangir (1605-1627 AD)

- When Akbar died, Prince Salim succeeded with the title Jahangir (Conqueror of World) in 1605.
- Jahangir's eldest son, Khusrau, rebelled against him. He was arrested and put into prison. *Guru Arjun Dev, the fifth Sikh Guru* was executed by Jahangir.
- In 1611, Jahangir married Mehrunnisa who was known as Nurjahan (Light of World).
- Jahangir died in A.D. 1627.

Shahjahan (1628-1658 AD)

- The reign of Shahjahan is generally considered as the *Golden Age* of the Mughal period.
- Shahjahan is called as the *Prince of Builders*. He had built the Jama Masjid and *Red Fort* in Delhi and Taj Mahal in Agra.
- Fine arts like painting, music and literature reached high level of development during Shahjahan's time.

Aurangazeb (1658-1707 AD)

- Aurangazeb was the last great Mughal ruler. He ascended the throne after killing his three brothers Dara, Shuja and Murad in a fratricidal war.
- Aurangazeb defeated Sikandar Shah of Bijapur and annexed his kingdom.
- Aurangazeb was against the Sikhs and he executed the ninth Sikh Guru Tegh Bahadur.
- He was called *Darvesh* or a *Zinda Pir*. He forbade *Sati*. Conquered Bijapur (AD 1686) and Golconda (AD 1687) and reimposed Jaziya and Pilgrim tax in AD 1679.
- He built *Biwi ka Makbara* on the tomb of his queen *Rabaud-Durani* at Aurangabad; *Moti Masjid* within Red Fort, Delhi; and the Jami or Badshahi Mosque at Lahore.
- Aurangazeb died in A.D. 1707.

Later Mughals/Fall of the Mughals

Ruler	Period
Bahadur Shah	1707-1712
Jahandar Shah	1712-1713
Farrukhsiyar	1713-1719
Mohammad Shah	1719-1748
Ahmad Shah	1748-1754
Alamgir II	1754-1759
Shah Alam II	1759-1806
Akbar II	1806-1837
Bahadur Shah II	1837-1857

Literature of Mughal Period

Author	Work
Babar	Tuzuk-i-Babari
Abul Fazal	Ain-i-Akbari, Akbarnamah
Jahangir	Tuzuk-i-Jahangir
Hamid	Padshahnama
Darashikoh	Majn-ul-Bahrain
Mirza Md Qasim	Alamgirnama

THE MARATHAS

Shivaji (1627-1680 AD)

- Shivaji was born at Shivner in 1627. His father was Shahji Bhonsle and mother Jija Bai.
- His religious teacher was Samarth Ramdas and guardian was Dadaji Kondadev.
- In 1674, Shivaji crowned himself at Raigarh and assumed the title Chatrapathi.
- *Ashtapradhan* (eight ministers) helped in administration. These were Peshwas, Sar-i-Naubat (Military), Mazumdar or Amatya (Accounts); Waqenavis (Intelligence); Surnavis (Correspondence); *Dabir* or *Sumanta* (Ceremonies); *Nyayadhish* (Justice); and *Panditrao* (Charity).

- Successors of Shivaji were Shambhaji, Rajaram and *Shahu* (fought at Battle of Khed in AD 1708).

The Peshwas

- Balaji Vishwanath was the first Peshwa. He began his career as a small revenue official and became Peshwa in 1713.
- Baji Rao I was the eldest son of Balaji Vishwanath. He was considered as the "greatest exponent of guerilla tactics after Shivaji".
- It was during reign of Balaji Baji Rao (Nanasaheb) when the Marathas lost the Third Battle of Panipat.
- Baji Rao II (last Peshwa) was the first Maratha to have fled from the British attacks instead of fighting with them. Baji Rao II surrendered to Sir John Malcom.

The Sikh

- Guru Nanak Dev was the founder of Sikhism, the religion that draws its elements from both Hinduism and Islam.
- Name of the ten Sikh Gurus and their works are given below:

1. **Guru Nanak Dev (1469-1539AD):** The founder of Sikhism.
2. **Guru Angad Dev (1504-1552AD):** Developed Gurmukhi.
3. **Guru Amar Das (1479-1574AD):** Struggled against Sati system and Purdah system.
4. **Guru Ram Das (1534-1581AD):** Founded Amritsar, the holy city of Sikhism.
5. **Guru Arjun Dev (1563-1606AD):** He built the *Swarn Mandir* (Golden Temple).
6. **Guru Hargobind (1595-1644 AD):** Established Akal Takht.
7. **Guru Har Rai (1630-1661 AD)**
8. **Guru Har Krishan (1656-1664 AD)**
9. **Guru Tegh Bahadur (1621-1675 AD)**
10. **Guru Gobind Singh (1666-1708 AD):** Founded the Khalsa and Sikh baptism, composed many poems, and nominated the Sikh sacred text as the final and enduring Guru.

INDIAN NATIONAL MOVEMENT

ORIGIN OF NATIONALISM

The rise of Nationalism is reflected in the spirit of Renaissance in Europe when freedom from religious restrictions led to the enhancement of national identity. This expression of Nationalism was furthered by the French Revolution. The political changes resulted in the passing of sovereignty from the hands of an absolute monarch to the French citizens, who had the power to constitute the nation and shape its destiny. The watchwords of the French Revolution - Liberty, Equality and Fraternity - inspired the whole world. Many other revolutions like the American Revolution, the Russian Revolution, etc. also strengthened the idea of Nationalism. Rise of Nationalism in India which emerged in the 19th Century after the revolt of 1857.

Allan Octavian Hume (A.O. Hume), a retired British member of the Indian Civil Service who had settled at Simla, founded the Indian National Union the fore runner of the Indian National Congress, in 1884. After touring Calcutta, Bombay and Madras (Kolkata, Mumbai and Chennai), Hume announced that a conference of the Indian National Union would be held at Pune in December, which would be composed of educated delegates from all parts of the three presidencies. But cholera having broken out at Pune, the venue of the conference was shifted to Tejpal Sanskrit Pathsala, Bombay. The first session of the Indian National Union was held on December 28, 1885. At the suggestion of Dadabhai Naoroji the name of the organisation was changed to Indian National Congress (INC). Womesh Chandra Banerjee, a leading lawyer of Calcutta (Kolkata), was elected its president.

Early Political Associations

- The British Indian Association — 1851, Bengal
- The Bombay Association — 1852
- East India Association — 1856, London
- Madras Native Association 1852
- Poona Sarvojanik Sabha — 1870
- The Madras Mahajana Sabha — 1884

Indian National Movement (1905-1916)

- The period from 1905 was known as the era of extremism in the Indian National Movement.
- The important extremist leaders were Lala Lajpat Rai, Bal Gangadhar Tilak, Bipin Chandra Pal and Aurobindo Ghosh.

Causes for the Rise of Extremism

1. The failure of the Moderates to win any notable success other than the expansion of the legislative councils by the Indian Councils Act (1892).
2. The economic conditions of the people became worse.
3. The Russo-Japanese war of 1904-05 in which Japan defeated the European power Russia. This encouraged Indians to fight against the European nation, Britain.

4. The immediate cause for the rise of extremism was the reactionary rule of Lord Curzon:
   - He passed the Calcutta Corporation Act, (1899) reducing the Indian control of this local body.
   - The Universities Act (1904) reduced the elected members in the University bodies. It also reduced the autonomy of the universities and made them government departments.
   - The Sedition Act and the Official Secrets Act reduced the freedoms of all people.
   - His worst measure was the Partition of Bengal (1905).

- Bal Gangadhar Tilak is regarded as the real founder of the popular anti-British movement in India. He was known as **'Lokamanya'**. He attacked the British through his weeklies *The Mahratta* and the *Kesari*.
- Tilak set up the Home Rule League in 1916 at Poona and declared "Swaraj is my birth-right and I will have it."

Partition of Bengal and the Rise of Extremism

- The partition of Bengal in 1905 provided a spark for the rise of extremism in the Indian National Movement.
- Curzon's real motives behind this partition were:
  - To break the growing strength of Bengali nationalism since Bengal was the base of Indian nationalism.
  - To divide the Hindus and Muslims in Bengal.
  - To show the enormous power of the British Government in doing whatever it liked.
- The anti-partition movement culminated into the Swadeshi Movement and spread to other parts of India.

Swadeshi Movement

- The Swadeshi Movement involved programmes like the boycott of government service, courts, schools and colleges and of foreign goods, promotion of Swadeshi goods, Promotion of National Education through the establishment of national schools and colleges. It was both a political and economic movement.

Formation of the Muslim League (1906)

- In December 1906, Muslim delegates from all over India met at Dacca for the Muslim Educational Conference.
- Taking advantage of this occasion, Nawab Salimullah of Dacca proposed the setting up of an organisation to look after the Muslim interests. The proposal was accepted.
- The All-India Muslim League was finally set up on December 30, 1906.

Minto-Morley Reforms – 1909

- Minto, the Viceroy and Morley, the Secretary of State for India jointly proposed reforms to the Indian Councils. An Act, called the **Indian Councils Act or the Minto-Morley Reforms Act** was passed in 1909.
- It introduced reforms in the functioning of the Indian Councils. It increased the number of elected members in the Councils.
- A separate communal electorate was introduced for the Muslims.

The Lucknow Pact (1916)

- During the 1916 Congress session at Lucknow two major events occurred. The divided Congress became united. An understanding for joint action against the British was reached between the Congress and the Muslim League and it was called the Lucknow Pact.
- It was at this session Jawaharlal Nehru met Gandhiji for the first time.
- The signing of the Lucknow Pact by the Congress and the Muslim League in 1916 marked an important step in the Hindu-Muslim unity.

The Home Rule Movement (1916)

- Two Home Rule Leagues were established, one by B.G. Tilak at Poona in April 1916 and the other by Mrs. Annie Besant at Madras in September 1916.
- The aim of the Movement was to get self-government for India within the British Empire. It believed freedom was the natural right of all nations.
- While Tilak's Movement concentrated on Maharashtra, Annie Besant's Movement covered the rest of the country.

Montague – Chelmsford Reforms Act, 1919

- **Montague,** the Secretary of State for India and **Chelmsford,** the Viceroy of India were jointly responsible for passing of this Act in the British Parliament.
- By this Act separate electorates were given to three other communities – **Christians, Anglo Indians** and **the Sikhs.**
- It introduced Dyarchy in the Province. More Indians entered the Legislative bodies.
- Mrs. Annie Besant described this Act as ungenerous for England to offer and unworthy for India to accept.

Revolutionary Movements

- The revolutionaries were not satisfied with the methods of both the moderates and extremists. Hence, they started many revolutionary secret organizations.
- In Bengal, Anusilan Samiti and Jugantar were established. In Maharashtra Savarkar brothers had set up Abhinava Bharat. In the Madras Presidency,

Bharathmatha Association was started by Nilakanta Bramachari.

- In Punjab, Ajit Singh set up a secret society to spread revolutionary ideas among the youth.
- In London, at India House, Shyamji Krishna Verma gathered young Indian nationalists like Madan Lal Dhingra, Savarkar, V.V.S. Iyer and T.S.S. Rajan.
- Lala Hardyal set up the 'Ghadar Party' in USA to organise revolutionary activities from outside India.

Rowlatt Act (1919)

- In 1917, a committee was set up under the presidentship of Sir Sydney Rowlatt to look into the militant Nationalist activities. On the basis of its report the Rowlatt Act was passed in March 1919 by the Central Legislative Council. As per this Act, any person could be arrested on the basis of suspicion. No appeal or petition could be filed against such arrests.
- This Act was called the Black Act and it was widely opposed. An all-India hartal was organized on 6 April 1919. Meetings were held all over the country. Mahatma Gandhi was arrested near Delhi. Two prominent leaders of Punjab, Dr. Satya Pal and Dr. Saifuddin Kitchlew, were arrested in Amritsar.

Jallianwala Bagh Massacre (13 April, 1919)

- The Jallianwala Bagh Massacre took place on 13 April 1919 and it remained a turning point in the history of India's freedom movement.
- On 13th April, the Baisakhi day (harvest festival), a public meeting was organized at the Jallianwala Bagh (garden). Gen. Dyer marched in and without any warning opened fire on the crowd. The firing continued for about 10 to 15 minutes and it stopped only after the ammunition exhausted.

Khilafat Movement

- The chief cause of the Khilafat Movement was the defeat of Turkey in the First World War. The harsh terms of the Treaty of Sevres (1920) was felt by the Muslims as a great insult to them.
- The whole movement was based on the Muslim belief that the Caliph (the Sultan of Turkey) was the religious head of the Muslims all over the world. The Muslims in India were upset over the British attitude against Turkey and launched the Khilafat Movement.
- Maulana Abul Kalam Azad, M.A. Ansari, Saifuddin Kitchlew and the Ali brothers were the prominent leaders of this movement.
- A Khilafat Committee had been formed and on 19th October 1919, the whole country had observed the Khilafat day. On 23 November, a joint conference of the Hindus and the Muslims had also been held under the chairmanship of Mahatma Gandhi.

Non-Co-operation Movement (1920-1922)

- Mahatma Gandhi announced his plan to begin Non-Cooperation with the government as a sequel to the Rowlatt Act, Jallianwala Bagh massacre and the Khilafat Movement. It was approved by the Indian National Congress at the Nagpur session in December, 1920.
- The Congress observed the Non-Co-operation movement in 1920. The main aim of this movement was to attain Swaraj through non–violent and peaceful means.
- The programmes of the Non-Co-operation Movement were:
  - Surrender of titles and honorary positions.
  - Resignation of membership from the local bodies.
  - Boycott of elections held under the provisions of the 1919 Act.
  - Boycott of government functions.
  - Boycott of courts, government schools and colleges.
  - Boycott of foreign goods.
  - Establishment of national schools, colleges and private panchayat courts.
  - Popularizing swadeshi goods and khadi.
- National schools such as the Kashi Vidyapeeth, the Bihar Vidyapeeth and the Jamia Millia Islamia were set up.
- On 5th February an angry mob set fire to the police station at Chauri Chaura and twenty two police men were burnt to death.

Swaraj Party

- Leaders like Motilal Nehru and Chittranjan Das formed a separate group within the Congress known as the Swaraj Party on 1 January 1923.
- The Swarajists wanted to contest the council elections and wreck the government from within. Elections to Legislative Councils were held in November 1923. In this, the **Swaraj Party** gained impressive successes. In the Central Legislative Council Motilal Nehru became the leader of the party whereas in Bengal the party was headed by C.R. Das.

Simon Commission (1927)

- The Act of 1919 included a provision for its review after a lapse of ten years. However, the review commission was appointed by the British Government two years earlier of its schedule in 1927. It came to be known as Simon Commission after the name of its chairman, Sir John Simon.
- All its seven members were Englishmen. As there was no Indian member in it, the Commission faced a lot of criticism even before its landing in India. Almost all the political parties including the Congress decided to oppose the Commission.
- The report of the Simon Commission was published in May 1930.

Nehru Report (1928)

- The Secretary of State, Lord Birkenhead, challenged the Indians to produce a Constitution that would be acceptable to all. The challenge was accepted by the Congress, which convened an all party meeting on 28 February 1928.
- A committee consisting of eight was constituted to draw up a blueprint for the future Constitution of India. It was headed by Motilal Nehru. The Report published by this Committee came to be known as the **Nehru Report**.

Lahore Session (1929)

- On Dec. 19, 1929, under the Presidentship of J.L. Nehru, the INC, as its Lahore session, declared *Poorna Swaraj* (Complete Independence) as its ultimate goal.
- On Dec. 31, 1929, the newly adopted tricolour flag was unfurled and Jan. 26. 26, 1930 was fixed as the First Independence Day, which was to be celebrated every year.

Civil Disobedience Movement (1930-1934)

- In December 1929, the annual session of the Congress was held at Lahore. During this session presided over by Jawaharlal Nehru the Congress passed the **Poorna Swaraj** resolution.
- The Congress had observed January 26, 1930 as the Day of Independence. Since then January 26th had been observed as a day of independence every year. The same date later became the Republic Day when the Indian Constitution was enforced in 1950.
- On 12th March 1930, Gandhi began his famous March to Dandi with his chosen 79 followers to break the salt laws. He reached the coast of Dandi on 5 April 1930 after marching a distance of 200 miles and on 6 April formally launched the Civil Disobedience Movement by breaking the salt laws.

Round Table Conference

- The first Round Table Conference was held in November 1930 at London and it was boycotted it by the Congress.
- On 8 March 1931 the **Gandhi-Irwin Pact** was signed. As per this pact, Mahatma Gandhi agreed to suspend the Civil-Disobedience Movement and participate in the Second-Round Table Conference.
- In September 1931, the Second Round Table Conference was held at London. Mahatma Gandhi participated in the Conference but returned to India disappointed as no agreement could be reached on the demand of complete independence and on the communal question.
- In January 1932, the Civil-Disobedience Movement was resumed. The government responded to it by arresting Mahatma Gandhi and Sardar Patel and by reimposing the ban on the Congress party.

Poona Pact (1932)

- On 16 August 1932 the British Prime Minister Ramsay MacDonald made an announcement, which came to be as the **Communal Award**. According to this award, the depressed classes were considered as a separate community and as such provisions were made for separate electorates for them.
- Mahatma Gandhi protested against the Communal Award and went on a fast unto death in the Yeravada jail on 20 September 1932. Finally, an agreement was reached between Dr. Ambedkar and Gandhi. This agreement came to be called as the **Poona Pact**. The British Government also approved of it. Accordingly, 148 seats in different Provincial Legislatures were reserved for the Depressed Classes in place of 71 as provided in the Communal Award.

The Government of India Act 1935

- The Government of India Act was passed in 1935. It was based on the **Simon Commission** report and the proposals of the three Round Table Conferences.
- It introduced the following changes. This act(1) Introduced provincial autonomy, (2) Abolished dyarchy in the provinces, (3) Established federal Government at the Centre, (4) Provided for the establishment of a federal court to decide the conflicts between the provinces and the centre and (5) Provided for the establishment of a Federal Reserve Bank.

Cripps Mission (1942)

- The British Government in its effort to secure Indian co-operation in the Second World War sent Sir Stafford Cripps to India on 23 March 1942. This is known as **Cripps Mission**.
- The main recommendations of Cripps were:
  - The promise of Dominion Status to India,
  - Protection of minorities,
  - Setting up of a Constituent Assembly in which there would be representatives from the Princely States along with those of the British Provinces,
  - There would be provision for any Province of British India not prepared to accept this Constitution, either to retain its present constitutional position or frame a constitution of its own.
- Gandhi called Cripp's proposals as a **"Post-dated Cheque"**.

Quit India Movement (1942-1944)

- The All India Congress Committee met at Bombay on 8 August 1942 and passed the famous **Quit India Resolution**. On the same day, Gandhi gave his call of **'do or die'**.
- On 8th and 9th August 1942, the government arrested all the prominent leaders of the Congress. Mahatma Gandhi was kept in prison at Poona. Pandit Jawaharlal Nehru, Abul Kalam Azad, and other leaders were imprisoned in the Ahamednagar Fort.

- Quit India Movement was the final attempt for country's freedom.

Naval Mutiny (1945)

- A revolt took place in *HMS Talwar* on Feb. 18, 1945 in Bombay due to racial discrimination, unpalatable food and abuse after the rarrest of B.C. Dutta who had written 'British Quit India' on the wall.
- Next day, *HMS Hindustan* in Karach also revolted.
- Soon the revolt spread to other places also. In Bombay, the mutineers hoisted the tricolour on their ship masts together with a portrait of S.C. Bose and shouted Jai Hind those belonging to the Inidna National Army.
- It was suppressed after persuasion by the Indian leaders.

Indian National Army

- On 2 July 1943, Subhash Chandra Bose reached Singapore and gave the rousing war cry of **'Dilli Chalo'**. He was made the President of Indian Independence League and soon became the supreme commander of the **Indian National Army**. He gave the country the slogan of **Jai Hind**.
- The Indian National Army marched towards Imphal after registering its victory over Kohima. After Japan's surrender in 1945, the INA failed in its efforts.
- The trial of the soldiers of INA was held at Red Fort in Delhi. Pandit Jawaharlal Nehru, Bhulabhai Desai and Tej Bahadur Sapru fought the case on behalf of the soldiers.

Cabinet Mission (1946)

- After the Second World War, Lord Atlee became the Prime Minister of England.
- On 15 March, 1946 Lord Atlee made a historic announcement in which the right to self-determination and the framing of a Constitution for India were conceded. Consequently, three members of the British Cabinet - Pathick Lawrence, Sir Stafford Cripps and A. V. Alexander - were sent to India. This is known as the **Cabinet Mission**.
- The Cabinet Mission put forward a plan for solution of the constitutional problem. Provision was made for three groups of provinces to possess their separate constitutions. The Cabinet Mission also proposed the formation of a Union of India, comprising both the British India and the Princely States. The Union would remain in charge of only foreign affairs, defence and communications leaving the residuary powers to be vested in the provinces. A proposal was envisaged for setting up an Interim Government, which would remain in office till a new government was elected on the basis of the new Constitution framed by the Constituent Assembly. Both the Muslim League and the Congress accepted the plan.

Mountbatten Plan (1947)

- On 20 February 1947, Prime Minister Atlee announced in the House of Commons the definite intention of the British Government to transfer power to responsible Indian hands by a date not later than June 1948.
- Lord Mountbatten armed with vast powers became India's Viceroy on 24 March 1947. The partition of India and the creation of Pakistan appeared inevitable to him.
- After extensive consultation Lord Mountbatten put forth the plan of partition of India on **3 June 1947.** The Congress and the Muslim League ultimately approved the **Mountbatten Plan.**

Indian Independence Act 1947

- The salient features of this Act were:
  - The partition of the country into India and Pakistan would come into effect from 15 August 1947.
  - The British Government would transfer all powers to these two Dominions.
  - A Boundary Commission would demarcate the boundaries of the provinces of the Punjab and Bengal.
  - The Act provided for the transfer of power to the Constituent Assemblies of the two Dominions, which will have full authority to frame their respective Constitutions.
- **C. Rajagopalachari** became the first and last Indian Governor-General of India. When India became a Republic on 26 January 1950 **Dr. Rajendra Prasad** became the first President of our country.

MULTIPLE CHOICE QUESTIONS

1. Name the Governor-General when the 1857 Revolt broke out:

A. Dalhousie B. Canning
C. Lawrence D. Curzon

2. Which of the following was not one of the political associations to be set up during the pre-Congress phase, before the revolt of 1857?

A. The British Indian Association
B. The Indian Association
C. Madras Native Association
D. Landholders' Society at Calcutta

3. The immediate cause of the Sepoy Mutiny of 1857 was:

A. Introduction of cartridges greased with cow's fat

B. Dalhousie's Doctrine of Lapse
C. Wide disparity between the salaries of native sepoys and the British soldiers
D. Bid to convert the Indians to Christianity

4. The Revolt of 1857 started from:
A. Delhi B. Barrackpur
C. Meerut D. Kanpur

5. The first sepoy who refused to use the greased cartridge and killed an Adjutant was:
A. Mangal Pandey B. Shiv Ram
C, Hardev D. Abdul Rahim

6. Nana Saheb's commander-in-chief was:
A. Azimullah B. Tantia Tope
C. Birjis Qadir D. None of the above

7. The 1857 revolt was led in Delhi by:
A. Bahadur Shah Zafar B. Khan Bahadur
C. Kunwar Singh D. Bakht Khan

8. Who among the following leaders of the 1857 revolt escaped to Nepal never to be heard thereafter?
A. Kunwar Singh B. Nana Sahib
C. Tantia Tope D. Maulvi Ahmadullah

9. The Kuka Movement was founded in:
A. U.P. B. Malabar
C. Bihar D. Punjab

10. The main cause behind the rise of the Faraizi Movement was that:
A. the Muslim tenants were oppressed by the East India Company
B. the Christian missionaries attacked the Islamic religion
C. the Hindu domination was to be eradicated
D. the Hindu moneylenders oppressed the Muslim community

11. Which was the earliest public association to be formed in modern India?
A. The Landholder's Society
B. The Bengal British India Society
C. The British Indian Association
D. The Madras Native Association

12. There were three phases (upto 1857) in the early period of resistance to British rule in India. Find out the incorrect categorisation of a phase.
A. Tribal rebellions
B. Constitutional agitation
C. Peasant rebellions and agrarian uprisings
D. Civil rebellion

13. Identify the Acts passed by the British Government in 1856.
(*i*) Religious Disabilities Act
(*ii*) General Service Enlistment Act
(*iii*) Hindu Widow Remarriage Act
(*iv*) Abolition of Sati (Regulation XVII)
A. (*i*), (*ii*), (*iii*) B. (*i*), (*iii*), (*iv*)
C. (*ii*), (*iii*), (*iv*) D. All of them

14. Identify the name of the wife of the Mughal Emperor who is believed to have sabotaged the work of the rebels by acting as an informer to the British.
A. Zeenat Mahal B. Fatima Begum
C. Hazrat Mahal D. Mumtaz Mahal

15. Match the following:
(*a*) Kanpur 1. Rani Lakshmibai
(*b*) Arrah 2. Nana Saheb
(*c*) Lucknow 3. Kunwar Singh
(*d*) Bareilly 4. Begam Hazrat Mahal
(*e*) Jhansi 5. Khan Bahadur Khan

	(*a*)	(*b*)	(*c*)	(*d*)	(*e*)
A.	2	4	3	5	1
B.	2	3	4	5	1
C.	3	1	2	4	5
D.	1	2	3	4	5

16. Name the rulers of Indian states who allied with the British in suppressing the revolt of 1857.
(*i*) Gulab Singh of Kashmir
(*ii*) Raja of Jodhpur
(*iii*) Nizam of Hyderabad
(*iv*) Scindhia of Gwalior
(*v*) Ex-Nawab of Rohilkhand
(*vi*) Holkar of Indore
A. All of them B. (*ii*), (*iv*), (*vi*)
C. (*i*), (*ii*), (*iii*), (*iv*), (*vi*) D. (*i*), (*iii*), (*v*), (*vi*)

17. Identify the first public association to be formed in modern India in 1837?
A. Bengal British Indian Society
B. British India Association
C. Landholders' Society
D. Madras Native Association

18. Poona Sarvajanik Sabha was founded by:
A. Pherozeshah Mehta
B. Bal Gangadhar Tilak
C. M.G. Ranade
D. Gopal Krishna Gokhale

19. Who was the founder of the India League in 1875?
A. Dadabhai Naoroji B. Anand Mohan Bose
C. Sisir Kumar Ghosh D. None of the above

20. The Indian National Congress was founded in:
A. 1867 B. 1885
C. 1887 D. 1920

21. The Indian National Congress was formed during the Governor-Generalship of:
A. Lord Ripon
B. Lord William Bentinck
C. Lord Dufferin
D. Lord Curzon

22. The first session of the Indian National Congress was presided over by:

A. Dadabhai Naoroji
B. Gopal Krishna Gokhale
C. Womesh Chander Banerjee
D. A.O. Hume

23. Who came to be known as the 'Grand Old Man of India?'
A. Justice Ranade B. Mahatma Gandhi
C. Rabindranath Tagore D. Dadabhai Naoroji

24. The Indian National Movement, up to 1905, was dominated by leaders who have been described as:
A. Parliamentarians B. Constitutionalists
C. Liberal thinkers D. Moderate nationalists

25. Who, among the early nationalists, carried on active propaganda in England to persuade the British to yield to their demands?
A. Gopal Krishna Gokhale
B. Dadabhai Naoroji
C. M.G. Ranade
D. Dinshaw E. Wacha

26. Gopal Krishna Gokhale founded:
A. Poona Sarvajanik Sabha
B. Bombay Presidency Association
C. Servants of India Society
D. Landholders' Society

27. Who was the chairman of the British Committee (started in 1889) of the Indian National Congress?
A. A.O. Hume B. W. Wedderburn
C. Dadabhai Naoroji D. W. Digby

28. "The Congress is in reality a civil war without arms"—who said this?
A. M.A. Jinnah B. Lord Curzon
C. Lord Dufferin D. Sir Syed Ahmad Khan

29. The number of delegates who attended the first session of the Indian National Congress, held in Bombay in 1885, was:
A. 304 B. 72
C. 1500 D. 556

30. Name the Secretary of State for India at the time of the foundation of Indian National Congress.
A. Lord Cross B. Lord Hamilton
C. Lord Morley D. Lord Elgin

31. Name the person who did not attend the first session of the Congress at Bombay.
A. K.T. Telang B. Badruddin Tayabji
C. W.C. Banerjee D. S.N. Banerjee

32. The large scale expression of the militant nationalism for the first time was against:
A. Seditious Meetings Act, 1907
B. Partition of Bengal, 1905
C. The Indian Council Act, 1892
D. Official Secrets Act, 1904

33. What was the real objective of the partition of Bengal?
A. Create division among the ranks of Indian nationalists.
B. Stop the tide of nationalism in Bengal
C. Build up separate administrative units for better efficiency of administration
D. Appease the large majority of Muslims

34. The political weapon used by the moderate nationalists to exert pressure upon the government against the partition of Bengal was:
A. Non-cooperation
B. *Satyagraha*
C. *Swadesh* and *Boycott*
D. Civil disobedience

35. The Moderates decided to break with the Extremists in:
A. 1906 B. 1907
C. 1914 D. 1919

36. The Indian National Movement came to be dominated by the Extremists after:
A. 1906 B. 1909
C. 1914 D. 1919

37. In the early twentieth century, Indian National Movement was influenced by:
A. Boer War, 1899
B. The Russian Revolution, 1917
C. The Russian-Japanese War, 1904-05
D. The outbreak of the First World War, 1914

38. Who was the most outstanding representative of the Militant Nationalist School?
A. Bipin Chandra Pal
B. Lala Lajpat Rai
C. Rajnarain Bose
D. Bal Gangadhar Tilak

39. The Morley-Minto Reforms which were passed in 1909:
A. Established a constitution-making body
B. Enlarged the central and the provincial legislative councils
C. Made the Executive Council of the Governor-General purely English in composition
D. Decreased the number of the provincial and central legislative members

40. Who took the reins of control of the Indian National Congress after the split of 1907.
A. Moderates
B. Terrorists
C. Extremists
D. Both (B) and (C) combined

41. Who did not have an important role in the Swadeshi movement?
A. Women B. Peasants
C. Students D. Muslims

42. "One of the most dangerous pioneers of disaffection" and "truly the father of Indian unrest".
A. Surrendranath Banerjee
B. Bal Gangadhar Tilak
C. Mahatma Gandhi
D. Dadabhai Naoroji

43. "Bombay Triumvirate" was applied for:
A. B.G. Tilak, G.G. Agarkar and G.H. Deshmukh
B. B.G. Tilak, G.K. Gokhale and M.B. Nainjoshi
C. Ferozshah Mehta, K.T. Telang and Badruddin Tyabjee
D. K.T. Telang, R.G. Bhandarkar, Dadabhai Naoroji

44. The system of separate electorates was introduced by the Act of:
A. 1813 B. 1835
C. 1885 D. 1909

45. In which of the following books K.B. Krishna made for the first time a distinction between communal tension and communal politics?
A. *Indian Muslims*
B. *The Destiny of Indians*
C. *Problem of Minorities*
D. None of the above

46. Who was the President of the first session of the All India Hindu Mahasabha in 1915?
A. Lala Lajpat Rai
B. Madan Mohan Malaviya
C. N.C. Kelkar
D. Maharaja of Kasim Bazar

47. Sir Syed Ahmad founded the Muhammadan Anglo-Oriental Defence Association of Upper India in:
A. 1875 B. 1880
C. 1883 D. 1893

48. The Home Rule Movement was launched during 1915-16 by:
A. Annie Besant and B.G. Tilak together
B. Annie Besant and B.G. Tilak separately
C. Annie Besant and Mahatma Gandhi together
D. The Congress when Mrs. Besant was President

49. The Home Rule Movement stood for:
A. Complete independence of India
B. Introduction of universal adult franchise
C. Self-government for India
D. None of the above

50. Shyamji Krishna Verma was one of the earliest and most ardent revolutionaries outside India. Which one of the following revolutionary societies was founded by him in London in February, 1905?
A. India House
B. Indian Home Rule Society
C. Home Rule Society
D. International Socialist Congress

51. Who of the following was not killed/hanged in connection with 'Alipore Conspiracy Case' 1908 and related events?
A. Barindra Nath Ghose
B. Khudiram Bose
C. Narinder Gosain
D. Nand Lal

52. Aurobindo Ghosh was defended in the Alipur bomb case by:
A. B.C. Pal B. Motilal Nehru
C. Bhulabhai Desai D. C.R. Das

53. The secret society of revolutionaries which was organized by V.D. Savarkar in 1904 was:
A. Sandhya B. Yugantar
C. Abhinav Bharat D. Ghadar

54. The Lucknow Congress session of 1916 is noted for:
A. The merger of the Muslim League with the Congress temporarily
B. The election of a Muslim President of the Congress
C. The concession given by the Congress to the Muslim League in the former's acceptance of separate electorates
D. None of the above

55. The first woman president of the Indian National Congress was:
A. Sucheta Kripalani B. Raj Kumari Amrit Kaur
C. Annie Besant D. Sarojini Naidu

56. Find out the wrongly stated cardinal principle of Mahatma Gandhi's *Satyagraha.*
A. Fearlessness B. Truthfulness
C. Abstinence D. Non-violence

57. Gandhiji's "Champaran Movement" was for:
A. The security of rights of Harijans
B. Civil disobedience movement
C. Maintaining the unity of Hindu society
D. Solving the problem of the indigo workers

58. Gandhiji was associated with the peasant movements of:
A. Champaran B. Bardoli
C. Kheda D. Both A and C

59. The Montagu-Chelmsford Reform (Government of India Act) of 1919 did not introduce the arrangement:
A. That the legislature would not even be allowed to seek information from the government of its own.
B. That under the system of diarchy the Governor held the total control over finances.
C. That the right to vote was restricted
D. That the legislature had virtually no control over the governor general

60. When was the Non-cooperation Movement suspended?
A. 1920 B. 1922
C. 1941 D. 1942

61. Non-Cooperation Movement did not envisage:
A. To boycott elections under the Government of India Act, 1919
B. To boycott Government schools and colleges
C. To boycott foreign goods
D. To boycott and violate the laws of the land

62. Which territory was taken away from Turkey proper by Britain and its allies during the dismemberment of the Turkish empire in the First World War?
A. Bosnia B. Thrace
C. Serbia D. Montenegro

63. Which one of the following leaders was elected as President of the All India Khilafat Conference held in Delhi in 1919?
A. Mahatma Gandhi B. Shaukat Ali
C. M.A. Jinnah D. None of the above

64. Find out from the names given below, who was not a member of the Khilafat Committee.
A. Maulana Shaukat Ali
B. Maulana Muhammad Ali
C. M.A. Jinnah
D. Maulana Abdul Kalam Azad

65. The Swaraj Party stood for:
A. Capturing Legislature Councils by contesting elections
B. Boycotting the elections
C. Overthrow of Government by organising a country wide strike
D. None of the above

66. The nationalist leaders of the Congress who were in favour of the boycott of the legislative councils (1922) were known as:
A. No-changers B. Changers
C. Swarajists D. Responsivists

67. Who of the following was elected Speaker of the Central Legislative Assembly in 1925?
A. Vithalbhai Patel B. Vallabhbhai Patel
C. M.R. Jayakar D. N.C. Kelkar

68. Bhagat Singh, Rajguru and Sukhdev were hanged on March 23, 1931 for:
A. Their involvement in the Lahore conspiracy case
B. For the assassination of Saunders at Lahore in 1928
C. For their involvement in the Kakori case
D. For throwing bomb in the Central Legislative Assembly

69. Who of the following was not involved in the incident relating to throwing of a bomb in Central Legislative Assembly on April 18, 1929?
A. Sardar Bhagat Singh
B. Khudiram Bose
C. B.K. Dutt
D. All of the above

70. Who led the Chittagong Armoury Raid?
A. Ganesh Ghosh
B. Jatin Das
C. Ambika Chakraborty
D. Surya Sen

71. Hindustan Republican Association was founded in the year:
A. 1924 B. 1926
C. 1928 D. 1930

72. Who of the following killed James Peddie, District Magistrate of Midnapore, in April 1931?
A. Bimal Dasgupta
B. Bhawani Prasad Bhattacharya
C. Rabindra Bandopadhyay
D. Kalpana Dutt

73. Who of the following framed the charges against the communists tried in the Meerut conspiracy case?
A. John Glendevon B. B.I. Bradley
C. R.A. Horton D. None of the above

74. Which of the following annual sessions of the Congress welcomed the formation of the AITUC?
A. Calcutta Session B. Nagpur Session
C. Gaya Session D. Rampur Session

75. Who was the first President of the AITUC?
A. C.R. Das B. Lala Lajpat Rai
C. Dewan Chaman Lal D. B.P. Wadia

76. Which of the following was a weakness of the trade union movement during freedom struggle?
A. Limited membership
B. Lack of internal leadership
C. Dominance of outside leadership
D. All of the above

77. Which of the following provided for registration of trade unions?
A. The Trade Union Act, 1926
B. Industrial Disputes Act, 1947
C. Factory Act, 1881
D. Factory Act, 1891

78. All the Three Round Table Conferences were attended by:
A. Dr. B.R. Ambedkar
B. M.A. Jinnah
C. M.K. Gandhi
D. Annie Besant

79. The result of the Poona Pact was that the number of seats reserved for the Depressed classes out of general electorate seats were:
A. Abolished
B. Increased
C. Retained at the same level
D. Decreased

80. Match the following:

(*a*) M.K. Gandhi	1. Red Shirt Movement
(*b*) Jawaharlal Nehru	2. Poorna Swaraj resolution at Lahore
(*c*) Abdul Ghaffar Khan	3. Bardoli Andolan
(*d*) Sardar Patel	4. Dandi March

	(*a*)	(*b*)	(*c*)	(*d*)
A.	4	2	1	3
B.	4	3	1	2
C.	4	2	3	1
D.	4	1	3	2

81. In the elections held in 1937 under the Government of India Act, 1935, Congress won in the:
A. Three provinces B. Five provinces
C. Seven provinces D. Eleven provinces

82. The Muslim League demanded separate Pakistan for the first time in:
A. 1939 B. 1940
C. 1941 D. 1942

83. The Muslim League's annual session of 1940 which gave effect to Jinnah's 'Two Nation Theory' was held in:
A. Lahore B. Karachi
C. Bombay D. Lucknow

84. The idea of Pakistan was first pioneered by:
A. M.A. Jinnah
B. Shaukat Ali
C. Sir Syed Ahmed Khan
D. Muhammad Iqbal

85. The "Inquilab Zindabad" slogan was given by:
A. Chandra Shekhar Azad
B. Subhash Chandra Bose
C. Bhagat Singh
D. Iqbal

86. Who was the first President of the All India Kisan Sabha formed in 1936?
A. Braj Kishore Shukla
B. Swami Sahajanand Saraswati
C. Karyanand Sharma
D. Yadunandan Sharma

87. The National Planning Committee was set up in 1938 under the chairmanship of:
A. Jawaharlal Nehru
B. Subhash Chandra Bose
C. R.P. Dutt
D. John Mathai

88. During Japanese attack on China in 1937-38, the Congress sent a medical mission to China. The mission was headed by:
A. Dr. Kotnis B. Dr. John Mathai
C. Dr. M. Atal D. None of the above

89. Who amongst the following was instrumental/s in convening an All India States People's Conference (AISPC) in 1927?
A. Balwantrai Mehta B. Maniklal Kothari
C. G.R. Abhayankar D. All of the above

90. The Cripps Mission visited India during the regime of:
A. Lord Mountbatten B. Lord Wavell
C. Lord Linlithgow D. Lord Wellington

91. Who led the Quit India Movement?
A. No one B. Mahatma Gandhi
C. Jawaharlal Nehru D. Sarojini Naidu

92. Subhash Chandra Bose set up his Azad Hind Fauz and Azad Hind Government in:
A. Burma B. Japan
C. Malaya D. Singapore

93. The Indian National Army was founded in:
A. 1940 B. 1941
C. 1942 D. 1943

94. Which of the following was the immediate cause the launching of the Quit India Movement?
A. Arrival of the Japanese armies on Indian soil
B. Rise in prices and shortage of food supplies
C. Failure of the Cripps Mission
D. None of the above

95. In 1943, Subhash Chandra Bose formed the Provisional Government of Free India at:
A. Rangoon B. Singapore
C. Berlin D. Bangkok

96. Where did the Congress Working Committee first accept the idea of the Quit India Movement?
A. Wardha B. Bombay
C. Poona D. Nagpur

97. Who of the following I.N.A. officers was NOT tried by a British Court Martial in 1945-46?
A. Mohan Singh B. G.S. Dhillon
C. Prem Sehgal D. Shah Nawaz Khan

98. The purpose of the Wavell Plan of 1945 was:
A. To give representation to all major communities in India
B. To create a Federation
C. To give Dominion Status to India
D. None of these

99. Who presided over the Cabinet Mission?
A. Clement Attlee B. Sir P. Lawrence
C. Strafford Cripps D. A.V. Alexander

100. The Muslim League observed Direct Action Day on 16 August, 1945
A. To bring unity among the various factions of the Muslims
B. To protest against the inadequate representation to the Muslims in the Interim Government

C. To express solidarity with the Congress in their struggle against the British
D. To achieve Pakistan

101. For granting of independence to India on February 20, 1947, British Prime Minister Clement Attlee announced the deadline of:
A. June 1948 B. June 1947
C. August 1947 D. August 1948

102. The credit for integrating the Indian Princely States into Indian Union goes to:
A. Sardar Patel B. Rajendra Prasad
C. J.L. Nehru D. Lord Mountbatten

103. Who was the Prime Minister of England when India got Independence?
A. Earl Mountbatten B. Winston Churchill
C. Lord Attlee D. None of the above

104. Who wrote the book *Tehqiq-q-Hind?*
A. Megasthenese B. Herodotus
C. Amir Khusrau D. Alberuni

105. The Angkor-Vat, a temple which bears a testimony to the colonial and cultural activities of the Indians in ancient times, is situated in:
A. Combodia B. Java
C. Baluchistan D. Turkistan

106. The Sangam literature gives us useful information about the history of South India during the reign of:
A. Cholas B. Pandayas
C. Cheras D. All of the above

107. Which was the first metal to be used by man?
A. Copper B. Iron
C. Bronze D. Tin

108. The first animal tamed by Neolithic people was:
A. Sheep B. Goat
C. Dog D. Ox

109. The Paleolithic men in India are also known as:
A. Quartzite men B. Stone age men
C. Primitive men D. Modern men

110. The Indus Valley Civilisation is:
A. About ten thousand years old
B. Seven thousand years old
C. Five thousand years old
D. Three thousand years old

111. Name the city which had houses with entrances on the main street.
A. Kalibangan B. Lothal
C. Mohenjo-daro D. Chanhu-daro

112. Which of the following was the most important industry of the Harappans at Lothal and Chanhudaro?
A. Ship building B. Bead making
C. Weaving D. Metallurgy

113. No trace of ________ has been found in the Indus Valley Civilisation.
A. Sugarcane B. Mustard
C. Sesamum D. Barley

114. Which of the following Vedas was the earliest composition?
A. Rigveda B. Samaveda
C. Yujurveda D. Atharvaveda

115. What did the term *niyoga* stand for in the Vedic society?
A. The performance of Vedic sacrifices by a woman independently
B. The vow of celibacy taken by a woman of aristocratic society
C. Cohabitation of a childless widow with her husband's brother until the birth of a son
D. Symbolic self-immolation of a widow at the death of her husband

116. Among the various units of the tribal kingdom (rashtra) of the Vedic society, which one of the following was the basic unit?
A. *Vish* B. *Jana*
C. *Kula* D. *Grama*

117. Which varna comprised mainly the common mass in the Vedic period?
A. Brahmins B. Kshatriyas
C. Shudras D. Vaishyas

118. Name the sage who is believed to have Aryanised South India.
A. Vashishtha B. Agastya
C. Yagyavalkya D. Vishwamitra

119. Which of the following *janapadas* was known for cotton textile/es and a horse market?
A. Magadha B. Anga
C. Kashi D. Kosala

120. In which of the following years did Alexander invade India?
A. 317 BC B. 326 BC
C. 321 BC D. 320 BC

121. The first Buddhist nun was:
A. Gautami B. Mahamaya
C. Yasodhara D. Sujata

122. Which of the following were NOT one of the royal patrons of Jainism?
A. Satvahanas B. Gangas
C. Chalukyas of Gujarat D. Rashtrakutas

123. Name the earliest known follower of Bhagavatism.
A. Demetrius B. Antialkidas
C. Megasthenese D. Heliodorus

124. Name the class which is conspicuous by its absence from the list of seven classes given by Megasthenese.
A. Artisans B. Cultivators
C. Traders D. Philosophers

125. Name the Major Rock Edict of Ashoka that explains and summarises the "Dhamma".
A. Fifth B. Eleventh
C. Twelfth D. Thirteenth

126. How many Sangams were held and where?
A. Three at Madurai B. Four at Tiruchirapalli
C. Two at Tanjore D. Five at Kanchipuram

127. Name the Chera King, known as the "Red Chera", who built a temple to Kannagi.
A. Elara B. Karikala
C. Senguttuvan D. Nedenjeral Adan

128. Identify the famous woman ruler of the Gupta period.
A. Kumaradevi B. Rajyashri
C. Kuber-Naga D. Prabhavati-Gupta

129. Which one of the following Gupta rulers is said to have agreed to surrender his wife to a Saka ruler to protect the interests of his people?
A. Srigupta B. Ghatotkacha
C. Ramagupta D. Kumaragupta

130. Identify the title taken up by Harsha after his accession to the throne.
A. Gunaraja B. Avanisimha
C. Maharaja D. Siladitya

131. The Pallavas and the Chalukyas were constantly involved in a conflict for establishing supremacy over which of the following area?
A. Madurai B. Tanjore
C. Vengi D. Guntur

132. Which Prathihara ruler had the famous poet, Rajasekhara, at his court?
A. Vatsaraja B. Mahipala
C. Nagabhatta-II D. Mihira Bhoja

133. The Arab merchant, Suleiman, came to India in 9th century in the kingdom of:
A. Vijaysena of Sena dynasty
B. Mihira Bhoja of Prathihara dynasty
C. Gopala of the Pala dynasty
D. Dantidurga of Rashtrakuta dynasty

134. Which of the following are the four *Agnikula* class of Rajputs?
A. Tomars, Pariharas, Chauhans, Pawars
B. Chandellas, Tomars, Solankis, Chauhans
C. Chandellas, Pariharas, Chauhans, Pawars
D. Pariharas, Chauhans, Pawars, Solankis

135. Which sect was greatly influenced by Tantricism?
A. Vrajayana B. Mahayana
C. Hinayana D. Digambars

136. Pampa, Panna and Ranna are regarded as the three gems of:
A. Kannada poetry B. Tamil poetry
C. Telugu poetry D. Malayalam poetry

137. Who was the first Muslim ruler of Delhi?
A. Iltutmish B. Allauddin Khalji
C. Qutbuddin Aibek D. Mahmud of Ghazni

138. Who was the first among the Delhi Sultans who requested and obtained letters of investiture from the Caliph?
A. Balban B. Iltutmish
C. Jalaluddin Khalji D. Firuz Tughlaq

139. Qutbuddin Aibak cannot be called the sovereign ruler of the sultanate because:
A. He did not assume the title of Sultan
B. He did not assume the coins nor the *Khutba* was read in his name
C. Both A and B
D. Instead of Delhi, he mostly stayed in Lahore

140. Which of the contemporary historians was appointed as the chief Qazi of Delhi by Sultan Muhammad-bin Tughlaq?
A. Ibn Batutah B. Zia-ud-din Barani
C. Shams-i-Siraj Afif D. None of these

141. What is the correct chronological sequence of the Delhi Sultans of *Mameluk* dynasty?
(*i*) Raziya
(*ii*) Nasiruddin Muhammad
(*iii*) Balban
(*iv*) Kaiqubad
(*v*) Qutbuddin Aibak
(*vi*) Iltutmish
A. (*v*), (*i*), (*iii*), (*vi*), (*ii*), (*iv*)
B. (*ii*), (*i*), (*iii*), (*vi*), (*iv*), (*v*)
C. (*v*), (*vi*), (*i*), (*ii*), (*iii*), (*iv*)
D. (*i*), (*ii*), (*iii*), (*iv*), (*v*), (*vi*)

142. What is the descending order of the ranks of nobility under Delhi Sultanate?
(*i*) Khan
(*ii*) Malik
(*iii*) Amir
(*iv*) Sar-i-Khail
A. (*i*), (*ii*), (*iv*), (*iii*) B. (*ii*), (*i*), (*iv*), (*iii*)
C. (*i*), (*ii*), (*iii*), (*iv*) D. (*iii*), (*ii*), (*iv*), (*i*)

143. Name the two historians of Delhi Sultanate period, whose works had the same title, *Tarikh-i-firuzshahi*.
A. Ziauddin Barani and Amir Khusrau
B. Minhaj-us-Siraj and Amir Khusrau
C. Shams-i-Siraj Afif and Ziauddin Barani
D. Amir Khusrau and Shams-i-Siraj Afif

144. The *Sufi* order, which was popularised in India by the first Mughal emperor Babur was:
A. Naqshbandiya B. Qadiriya
C. Suhrawardi D. Chishtiya

145. The Bhakti saint, who was not a worshipper of Krishna, was:

A. Vallabhacharya B. Mirabai
C. Surdas D. Ramananda

146. The *nayakas* in the empire of Vijayanagar were:
A. Feudal chiefs
B. Hereditary military governors
C. Military commanders
D. High civil and military officers

147. As per the latest researches, the so-called battle of Talikota, fought between the Deccani Muslim states and Vijayanagar, was actually fought at:
A. Bannihatti
B. Between villages Rakkasi-Tangadi
C. Talikota town
D. Raichur Doab

148. Name the person whose outrageous behaviour is believed to be chiefly responsible for the revolt of Bairam Khan against Akbar.
A. Pir Mohammad B. Todar Mal
C. Man Singh D. Birbal

149. Which of the following Mughal buildings is said to possess the unique feature of being exactly equal in length and breadth?
A. Red Fort B. Taj Mahal
C. Buland Darwaja D. Agra Fort

150. In which language did Babur write his memoirs, called Tuzuk-i-Baburi?
A. Persian B. Arabic
C. Mongol D. Turkish

ANSWERS

1	2	3	4	5	6	7	8	9	10
B	B	A	C	A	B	D	B	D	A
11	**12**	**13**	**14**	**15**	**16**	**17**	**18**	**19**	**20**
A	B	A	A	B	C	C	C	C	B
21	**22**	**23**	**24**	**25**	**26**	**27**	**28**	**29**	**30**
C	C	D	D	B	C	B	D	B	A
31	**32**	**33**	**34**	**35**	**36**	**37**	**38**	**39**	**40**
D	B	B	C	B	A	C	D	B	A
41	**42**	**43**	**44**	**45**	**46**	**47**	**48**	**49**	**50**
B	B	A	D	C	D	D	B	C	B
51	**52**	**53**	**54**	**55**	**56**	**57**	**58**	**59**	**60**
A	D	C	C	C	C	D	D	A	B
61	**62**	**63**	**64**	**65**	**66**	**67**	**68**	**69**	**70**
D	D	A	C	A	A	A	B	B	D
71	**72**	**73**	**74**	**75**	**76**	**77**	**78**	**79**	**80**
A	A	C	C	B	D	A	A	B	A
81	**82**	**83**	**84**	**85**	**86**	**87**	**88**	**89**	**90**
C	B	D	D	D	B	A	C	D	C
91	**92**	**93**	**94**	**95**	**96**	**97**	**98**	**99**	**100**
A	D	C	C	B	A	A	A	B	D
101	**102**	**103**	**104**	**105**	**106**	**107**	**108**	**109**	**110**
A	A	C	D	A	D	A	C	A	C
111	**112**	**113**	**114**	**115**	**116**	**117**	**118**	**119**	**120**
B	B	A	A	C	C	D	B	C	B
121	**122**	**123**	**124**	**125**	**126**	**127**	**128**	**129**	**130**
A	A	D	C	B	A	C	D	C	D
131	**132**	**133**	**134**	**135**	**136**	**137**	**138**	**139**	**140**
C	B	B	D	A	A	C	B	C	A
141	**142**	**143**	**144**	**145**	**146**	**147**	**148**	**149**	**150**
C	C	C	A	D	B	B	A	B	D

2

WORLD HISTORY

Man has lived on the earth for several hundred thousand years but it is only a few thousand years back, man learned the art of writing. The story of man's progress for which written records are available is called history while the long, distant past prior to that time for which man kept no written records is called prehistoric era. The main sources of information about pre-historic man have been their tools and weapons, their paintings, artifacts and fossils of men and animals.

PALAEOLITHIC AGE

The early period in man's development is known as the old Stone age or Palaeolithic age. This was a very long period, extending from 5 lakh years ago to about 15,000 years ago. The man made small but significant improvements during the period. During the period, there were very major geographical changes on earth. During this time, man had learnt to move in groups in search of food and shelter. He learnt to make tools of stone, build shelters and use animal skins to cover himself. The major achievement was the knowledge of using fire and convey messages through a language. This was the first stage of development and lasted several thousand years.

MESOLITHIC AGE

During the mesolithic or middle stone age, the speed of development was rather fast. Man learnt to make a variety of fine tools. It was from about 10,000 B.C. to 8,000 B.C. People took to fishing, in several parts, to supplement their diet. In some areas, people started to harvest crops, domesticate animals and breed goats and sheep. In this age, men used to move to a new fertile land, after some time.

NEOLITHIC AGE

The era from 6000 B.C. to 4000 B.C. is called new stone age. The man changed from getting food to producing food. The weapons and tools became more sophisticated yet the basic material remained stone. Domestication of animal, weaving and pottery were learnt by the man. He started making permanent house which were made of wood, mud and had thatched roofs. The settlements were generally near the fields which the people cultivated. These dwellings gradually took the shape of villages and thus organized social life developed. During this period religious beliefs also grew. The dead were buried with weapons, pottery, food and drink in their graves. Each tribe had its own totem, the image of an animal or a plant as a symbol for a clan, or group of families living together. Small clay figures of women have been found, indicating, the worship of mother goddess. The invention of wheel also dates back to this age.

IMPORTANT ANCIENT CIVILIZATIONS

As the man progressed in his life and acquired knowledge, different cultures and civilizations grew. The growth of civilization was not uniform, it began to emerge in some parts of the world in about 4000 B.C. However, at several other places, it came up several thousand years later.

Most of the early civilizations arose in certain river valleys as conditions there were favourable. Fertile soil was available on the banks of the rivers. Water required for drinking and irrigation was in abundance. Man found important use of river, as a means of transportation. This led to the transportation of merchandize—excess foodstuff or animals and thus developed the trade and commerce. Since men did not have to spend all his time in gathering food or protecting himself from wild animals, he found enough time to observe and think. This led to the development of science, engineering, mathematics, architecture, sculpture, music, dance and painting.

The discovery and the use of Copper and Bronze metals marked an important milestone in men's development. The metals are more durable than stones and can be given any shape to form tools, weapons or other implements. Copper was the metal to be discovered and for a long time, both stone and copper coexisted. This period was called Chalcolithic age, with chalkes meaning Copper, and lithos meaning stone. In course of time, man learned to mix Copper with Tin or zinc to produce Bronze alloy which is harder and more useful in making tools, weapons and implements. Due to the importance of Bronze in the growth of first civilizations, these are called Bronze Age Civilizations.

By about 4,500 years back, the Indus Valley in India, the Hwang-Ho Valley in China, the Valley of the Tigris and the Euphrates in Mesopotamia (presently Iraq), the Nile Valley in Egypt and the areas around the Mediterranean and Aegean Sea had become centres of civilization. Each civilization developed its own political and social system, trade and commerce, religious beliefs, art and science.

All these civilizations, though spread out over a large geographical area, had some common characteristics. All of them had large areas under cultivation. They had set up elaborate system of migration canals. All of them had central authority whose will could be enforced. Since food-producing effort did not require everyone's involvement, several other occupations developed. It led to division of work and specialisation. Villages grew up into towns and cities. The life became complex and to manage and maintain law and order, a highly developed organization called Government came up. All the civilizations were involved in trading activities. They also had scripts of their own.

INDUS VALLEY CIVILIZATION

It existed in north-western regions of the present Indian sub-continent between 2350-1750 BC. Some of its towns were located in the valley of Indus river. Though it was not the oldest of the Bronze age civilization, it extended over a bigger area than any other. The excavations in Baluchistan, Sind, Punjab, Haryana, Gujarat, Rajasthan and Western Uttar Pradesh have led to the evidence of this civilization. The land of the valley was very fertile and farmers from further west moved there and settled there. They dug canals to control and distribute floodwater, making farming more productive. The prominent cities were Harappa, Mohan-jo-daro, Lothal, Banavali and Chanudero: Among these, the first two cities were the major ones, well planned and thickly populated. They were well over 2 sq km in area.

All the cities of the Indus Valley Civilization were well planned. The roads were wide and straight. Houses were made of burnt bricks and some had more than one storey. The drainage system in those cities was very good. The cities had well planned tanks and ponds for community bathing. Granaries were used to store extra crops. Indus Valley cities were built according to a grid system—each of the main street was parallel. Streets were lined with terraced houses.

The common crops of the Indus Valley Civilization were wheat, barley, peas and cotton. Wheel was used to make pottery. People used to keep domestic animals. The metallurgy, sculpture and painting were quite famous. Indus Valley traders used to exchange things with other civilizations, particularly Mesopotamia.

Not much is known about the government in the Indus Valley Civilization because the script has not been fully understood yet. But it is felt that absence of palaces indicate rule by a body of important men rather than by a King. However, similarity in planning and layout of various towns indicate a central administration.

The people worshipped an early form of Siva and Goddess. They used to participate in religious bathing. The dead were either cremated or buried. The civilization at the banks of Indus Valley flourished for nearly 1,000 years but around 1,700 BC, the cities were probably devastated by earthquakes and floods. Aryans, people of the northwest later invaded and allowed the cities to decay further.

MESOPOTAMIAN CIVILIZATION

Bound by Armenia plateau in the North and Persian Gulf in the South, this civilization existed on the land between Tigris and Euphrates rivers. Presently, Syria and Iraq countries exist in the area. Its northern part was called Assyria while Southern part was called Babylonia. The northern portion of Babylon was called Akkad while southern portion was Sumer. In ancient times, great civilizations existed in these areas.

All the Mesopotamian civilizations are known by their cities. These cities were named by the citizens on the basis of their gods. These cities used to fight among themselves for the territorial or water-irrigation rights. With the changing times, the authority and prominence of these cities also kept on changing.

The Mesopotamians devised ways and means of a perennial irrigation system to keep flood in check. The river-bed was high and the canals were made wide so that while the water rushed from the river to the canal, the banks would not be destroyed. The canals were navigable channels and thus helped in transport as well as in irrigation.

The earliest civilization grew up in Sumer. They built their temples and prayer-places, even in 4000 B.C. Since the area was fertile, people used to get good harvest. Some of them had time to devote to other things and several art forms and skills developed.

The most important contribution of Sumerians was the discovery of Script. The wedge shaped script is called Cuneiform. They used to write on clay tablets using sharp stylus made of reed. Some of the tablets recovered from excavation, show business documents, letters, royal inscriptions, religious texts and stories.

Another major contribution of Sumerians was the Sexagesimal system. In this system, they wrote the numbers 1 to 9 by making the sign for 1 and repeating as many times as necessary. Similarly they repeated the sign for 10 to represent multiples of 10. They had the same symbol for 60 as 1, though it was written much bigger. There was no sign higher than 60. The sexagesimal system is not of much use but is used in the division of time into minutes and seconds and circle into 360 degrees.

People of Babylon were also interested in astronomy and geometry. In geometry, Mesopotamians had discovered what was later called the Pythagoras' theorem. By observing Stars, Sun and Moon, they divided the sky into twelve parts. They also developed lunar calendar. Babylon was known for its hanging gardens besides having several roads, bridges and canals. They manufactured coins, weights and measures. Observatories were built to observe the motion of stars and planets.

Assyrian civilization flourished around 1,600 BC. Since the Assyrians were warriors they stressed manufacturing of arms and weapons, maintaining a big army and giving soldiers a special status in the society. People worshipped idols, particularly Assyr (Sun). They built magnificent palaces and statues of lions, bulls and other hunting scenes.

The Mesopotamian cities were well planned and divided into three main divisions—the Sacred area, the walled city on the mound and the outer town. The king was regarded as the God's representative on earth while the slaves, mostly prisoners of war, were lowest in the social level.

Agriculture was the main occupation of Mesopotamians. They used cattle to draw the plough. They wore clothes made of sheepskin. They used the potter's wheel for making pottery and later used it for making chariots. By 2500 B.C., Mesopotamians had developed high technical knowledge and skill about metals. The prosperity of the Mesopotamians depended largely on foreign trade. They exported foodgrains to buy stone, timber, gold, silver and other metals. Mesopotamians were the, first to use coloured tiles in buildings. They had the knowledge of columns, archs and minarets.

EGYPTIAN CIVILIZATION

Egypt is called the "Gift of the Nile river" because Nile river, for centuries, has been spreading layers of fertile black soil in the area. Between 5000 and 4000 B.C., the skill of agriculture was developed by the farmers in the area. With this, grew the concept of permanent house which led to the coming up of villages and kingdoms.

The history of Egypt is divided into three periods. The old age is also called the age of Pyramids. Memphis was the capital during the period in which advancements in art, religion and sciences were made. This age lasted from 3000 to 2000 B.C. During the middle age, early period saw speedy development but in the 18th century B.C., Egypt was overrun by a nomadic tribe, Hyksos. However, the Egyptian Kings regained the land and established new kingdom. This period became the golden period of Egyptian civilization till about 1000 BC when rulers became weak and were overrun by enemies.

Ancient Egyptian Kings—Pharaohs, were great architects. They made several huge buildings. Though their palaces and other public buildings do not exist anymore, but the Pyramids stand testimony of their knowledge and skill. These 30 large and several small Pyramids are among the wonders of the ancient world. These pyramids were tombs of Pharaohs containing their mummies and precious things, they contained. Egyptians believed in life after death. So, they used to preserve the bodies of their kings, using chemicals. These preserved bodies are called Mummies..

Another specimen of Egyptian architecture is Sphinx, which is a mythological animal with the body of a lion and the head of a man. Each Sphinx was carved out of a single solid stone. Egyptian temples are also remarkable buildings.

Sun was the most important God of Egyptians. They also had other gods like king of the other world, god of the flood, moon and several local gods, which were represented with symbols like Jackal, Cow etc. Pharaohs were initially priests of the God but subsequently they were prayed and temples in their names made. The kings were mostly despotic who acted as chief administrator as well as religious head. Ministers were appointed for consultation. The country was divided into units and disputes were settled on the basis of written laws. Women were given a high place in the society.

Agriculture was the most important occupation of the people. They built canals to grow crops throughout the year. They were perhaps using ox to draw the plough as early as 3000 B.C. They domesticated animals like goats, dogs, pigs etc. They used horse to draw chariots. They used to wear linen clothes. Egyptians made beautiful fumiture and stone vessels. They also developed the art of making glass. Egyptians used to live lavishly and were involved in importing luxury items.

Egyptians developed a script, called Hieroglyphic. They developed a decimal system of numeration. They were good in geometry and arithmetic. The Egyptians developed solar calendar, based on 365 days. They also developed papyrus or technique of making paper. Egyptian civilization ended by 1000 B.C. They used decimal system in mathematics.

CHINESE CIVILIZATION

The first centre of civilization in China developed in the region of the Hwang-Ho river valley around 2000 B.C. Hwang-Ho Was called "the Sorrow of China" because the river often changed its course, damaging homes, fields and canals. Around 1600 B.C., the Shong dynasty was established. By 14th Century B.C., these rulers had developed a high level of culture comparable to the Centres of other early civilizations.

The prosperity of Chinese civilization depended mainly on agriculture. They had developed an elaborate system of irrigation to reduce the distress caused by floods. Chinese wore linen and silk clothes. The sericulture was started by Chinese and they used to weave clothes out of silk yarn.

Chinese learnt the use of iron, besides brass. This helped them increase the farm production and make various tools, and weapons. Chinese were very skillful in making arts and handicrafts items. They used to export them to India and other places. They made very fine pottery which they learned to glaze. The wares of porcelain are still called Chinaware.

During this period, Chinese rulers made the Great Wall of China to protect their empire from Huns attack from the north-west. Chinese were first to develop explosives and used it in firearms. Another major achievement of Chinese civilization was the development of paper. They developed an ideographic script in which a sign represents an idea. The Chinese calendar was a combination of solar and lunar calculations. They had made advances in astronomy. Their buildings, which may have included temples, were made with earth, timber and mud bricks. They manufactured inks and printing press. They introduced the notes and taking of tea.

The Buddhism spread from India to China. Earlier, ancestor worship was the most popular practice. They believed in spirits and used to place furniture, pottery, vessels and other objects besides the dead body in grave. Lao-Tse and Confucious were the main philosophers of China. They worshipped their Kings ancestors as gods, and built several Pagoda temples.

GREEK CIVILIZATION

Greeks came to the region of the Aegean Sea and by 600 B.C. spread their common culture from the south of France to the Black Sea. They had many Gods whom they imagined to be like human beings though more powerful and immortal. They had no knowledge of writing until around 800 B.C. but passed the stories of their life through folk-songs and ballads. However, the discovery of script helped them in growing their knowledge in several fields. Homer was a famous poet who wrote Iliad and Odyssey.

The Greek world was a mosaic of city states, each one ruling the land around it and frequently at loggerheads with its neighbours. Sparta, Athens, Macedonia and other City-States had many common features, but each had its own character. Spartans lived under the strictest discipline, leaving no scope for family life or for learning. On the other hand, Athenians experienced democracy and built a prosperous trade and rich culture. Macedonia came into limelight when its ruler Alexander setout to conquer the world and brought large area upto the Indian border, under his control. Alexander founded the City of Alexandria which became a seat of Greek culture and education for a long time after the fall of Greece.

Greek civilization had a large number of slaves who did most of the work, leaving time to think and create and live the good life. The life was easy, simple and enjoyable. They had music, wine and festivities. There was good development of literature, drama, theatre and philosophy. Socrates, Plato and Aristotle were great philosophers. Euclid and Pythagoras were great mathematician while Hippocrates was father of medicine. In the fields of science, astronomy, architecture and sculpture. Greeks went on sea voyages and had a full fledged Navy which helped in its expansion. Greeks were good architects and artists, and built several magnificent temples. Greeks introduced the Olympic Games which became forerunner for the present day games. Greeks made new discoveries. The infighting among the city-state led to the fall of Greek civilization and it was won over by Romans in 2nd AD and for the first time introduced rule of law and democracy in the world.

ROMAN CIVILIZATION

The city of Rome was founded about 1000 B.C. and its principal language was Latin. The Roman Civilization started developing around 6th century B.C. as groups of Indo-Europeans and Greeks began settling there. Initially, Romans had a King, an assembly and a senate but towards the end of the 6th century, a republic was established. As a republic, Romans expanded and controlled all of Italy, parts of South and West Europe, North Africa and West Asia.

In Rome, slavery was quite prominent. Slaves were employed for hard and dirty jobs while other Romans enjoyed luxurious life. Since large army was required to suppress rebellion from slaves and fight wars, army leaders gained importance in the society.

Rome acted as a link between the eastern civilizations and Europe. They also made some contributions of their own, with law and principles of governance being the greatest one. Laws encouraged travel and boosted trade. The roads, built primarily for the movement of armies, were used for carrying goods.

Latin language, developed by Romans, became the language of all educated people in Europe. The Roman Civilization developed its literature, philosophy, science, art and architecture. The names of month — July, August, September, October, November and December — as used presently, are the gifts of Roman Civilization. The rule of Romans was organised and united. The main occupation of people was agriculture but traders and artisans also flourished. Religious tolerance was there, with Jupiter, Mars, Minerva etc. being their deities. Romans are known for the laws made by them. Roads and bridges of Rome were world famous. They were good architects also. The arts and literature were well developed in Rome. Julius Ceasar and Augustus were prominent rulers of Rome.

Roman empire decayed as imperialism destroyed democracy, encouraged slavery and created political conflicts. Since agriculture and industry were left to slaves, the productivity remained low. The coming of Christians to Rome also weakened the empire as the oppressed people of Rome were attracted by it. Rome, however, continued to be centre of Christianism with the present of Pope there.

MAYA CIVILIZATION

The Maya Civilization extended over a large area of Central America, covering parts of present Guatemala, Mexico and Honduras. It began around 1500 B.C. and reached its peak between 300 A.D. and 900 A.D. Mayans grew Maize, Beans, Potato, Papaya and Chilli. Their most important achievements were their perfect calendar, knowledge of mathematics, hierographic writing and use of paper.

BYZANTINE CIVILIZATION

Constantine became the King of the whole Roman empire in 324 AD. That year he moved the capital from Rome to the town of Byzantium in the eastern empire, founding Byzantine empire which remained for over one thousand years. A new city was built at Byzantine, called Constantinopole. During the reign of Constantine, Christianity got firm roots. A few years after Constantine's death, the empire was divided into east and west, with the former surviving for a long period.

THE ARAB EMPIRE

The Prophet of Islam encouraged his followers to convert as much of the world as possible to new faith. When he died in 632 AD, his father-in-law Abu Bakr took the title of Calipha and became chief defender of Islam. Later, new Islamic dynasties were set up which tried to change the world in earnest. Damescus in Syria became the centre of an Islamic empire stretching from Morocco to India of Omayyad dynasty. Later, the descendants of Mohammad's family, belonging to Abbasid dynasty made Baghdad the Islamic centre. Baghdad, besides being a prosperous centre of a huge trading empire, also became a centre of learning.

CRUSADES

In the late 11th century, Turks overran Palestine, the holy place for Christians. Moreover, they began attacking Christians on pilgrimage to holy places. This angered the churches and the Christian kings also sought the help in resisting the aggression. In 1095, the Pope called for a Crusade, or Holy War against Muslim Turks. Thousands of ordinary people responded. In 1096, an official European force joined with a Byzantine army attacked Turks and in 1099, they took Jerusalem. Muslims also got rearranged and made a bid to recapture Palestine. These efforts led to Second (1144), Third (1189) and Fourth (1202) Crusades. The crusades continued till 1291. Thousands of children were used in these wars. At the end of the war, the Palestine remained with the Muslims. The crusades provided Europeans with an opportunity to learn several new things which led to increase in trade, decline of feudalism, intellectual development, decline in Church's powers and urge to explore new areas.

INCA EMPIRE

The Inca empire grew in the Andes Mountain region in South America in the 14th and 15th centuries. It stretched from Ecuador, Peru and Chile. The Incas were famous for their engineering skill, building palaces, temples, official storehouses and fortresses. There was a wide network of roads. Medicine and surgery were highly developed. Arts and crafts were also highly developed, particularly pottery-making, cotton-weaving and wool.

IMPORTANT EVENTS

Magna Carta

The barons, the clergy and the people combined to compel the King of England, John II to redress their grievances by signing the great charter in 1215. It contained 63 clauses guaranteeing the freedom of barons, the church and the people. The charter was intended to put a check upon the arbitrary powers of the king by securing the rights of all orders and classes. It laid down the important principle that Englishmen should be governed by definite laws and not by whims or uncontrolled will of a despotic ruler Magna Carta is said to be the foundation stone of the rights and liberties of the English people.

Black Death

The black death, an infection of bubonic plague, struck Europe in 1347. The disease was spread by fleas that lived on rats. The fleas got transferred to humans when the rats died. By 1351, the disease, which affected rich and poor alike had spread over most of Europe. The plague killed about one-third of the total European population.

Feudalism

A system developed in the middle age in Europe whereby peasants had to give a part of their produce to the lords in the form of rent or taxes or had to work for the lords without any payment. This system developed as there was no central authority. The society was hierarchial with every person allotted a position. There was a king at the top who bestowed estates on a number of lords, known as dukes or earls. The earls, in turn, distributed a part of their estate among barons and in return, secured their military support. The knights formed the lowest category of feudal lords. The relationship from top to bottom was one of allegiance. While these lords levied taxes, acted as judges and owned armies, peasants at the lowest stand suffered. Some of them were forced to work for their lords for no wages. They suffered several restrictions and some of them were tied to the land and could not leave the place.

Feudalism served its purpose of bringing a measure of orderliness, safety and security in Medieval Europe. Social and economic activity appeared normal though there were several aberrations. It was based on a rigid class system and promoted political disunity. The ruling class did not care for the common men. There was wasteful consumption. The lords indulged in wars, in order to gain new lands.

As Lords needed luxury items, trade grew and with this towns developed as centres of manufacture and trade. Towns, gradually freed themselves from feudal control and established own government, police and court. Towns provided freedom to peasantry. With the growth of trade, money's use increased and thus Capitalism grew to kill Feudalism. Other factors that led to the decline of feudalism were emergence of powerful kings, decline in powers of lords due to mutual fighting, strengthening of the feeling of nationalism, growth of middle classes, inventions of gunpowder and printing press, influence of church and development of democracy in several areas.

Renaissance

Renaissance means rebirth. It was initially used to describe revival of interest in the learning of older civilizations of Greece and Rome. Knowledge of their achievements led to a series of new developments in the field of art, literature, religion, science and politics. Renaissance began in Italy in the 16th century. Its main emphasis was on freedom of the individual, inalienable rights of the individual and respecting the dignity of man. It stressed on the limitless potentialities of man rejected religious asceticism and withdrawal from the world. It aimed at providing happiness to man. The emphasis shifted from divinity to humanity, i.e., human being. The Renaissance era gave rise to quest for knowledge, especially history and literature. The effects of Renaissance were development of humanism, nationalism, spread of education, growth in trade and commerce, exposure of myths and establishment of reasoning. Some of the greatest achievements were made in painting, sculpture and architecture. Leonardo da Vinci, Michael Angelo and Raphael were famous artists of that time. Dante was a great poet of that time while Machiavelli, a diplomat, historian and political philosopher wrote about statecraft. As the Renaissance spread throughout Europe, it took on a more religious character, paving the way for Reformation. Moreover, during the period, Europeans began to look for sea route to Asia, with Columbus reaching Central America in 1492 and Vasco-da-Gama in India in 1498.

Reformation

The key event of the 16th century in Europe was the Reformation, a movement to reform the Catholic church. It began in Germany and then spread throughout northern Europe. Martin Luther, a German theologian and religious transformer set alight widespread discontent against the Church. New Protestant Church belonging to reformers sprang up, with the aim of following only the teachings of the Bible, and getting rid of church traditions. Several powerful kings and princes supported the reformers like John Calvin, Olrich Zwingli and others. Although the Catholic church responded by introducing reforms from within, violent conflicts between Catholics and Protestants erupted. In 1534, King Henry VIII took the help of the English church because the Pope would not let him divorce his first wife. Though Queen Mary tried to restore Church's authority in England, getting the nickname "Bloody Mary" due to execution of Protestants, the Catholics were reduced to minority in England.

The Slave Trade

The practice of slavery, the buying and selling of people against their will, goes back to ancient times. Slaves had no rights or freedoms and were owned entirely by their masters. Selling African people as slaves was begun on a large scale by Arabs about 1,000 years ago. However, mass demand for slaves arose when Europeans needed workers for plantations in America. The slaves were later taken to other places by Europeans for hard work. The slaves lived a miserable life, living in cramped quarters, unable to move for days and getting whipped at slightest pretext. The slavery continued till about 150 years ago.

English Revolution of 1688

England was ruled by despotic rulers in the first half of 17th century — James I and Charles I. They believed that they were appointed by God, not answerable to Parliament or people. The dispute between the King and Parliament led to civil war in England in 1642. James I was defeated and executed. In 1660, Charles II was appointed king on the condition that he will not interfere in religious affairs of the people and rule with consultation with Parliament. However, James II followed his father's footsteps and tried to breakaway from Parliament's supervision and gave more powers to Catholics in the Protestant dominated country. This led to revolt by the people who invited the Dutch Protestant King William to come to England. James II fled to France. Williams and daughters of James II, Mary were declared joint Monarchs. The revolution has been described as Glorious due to lack of bloodshed. The revolution led to end of divine rights of Kings, acceptance of the authority of the Parliament, independent judiciary, freedom of Press and supremacy of Protestants in England.

American War of Independence

With the rise of Capitalism and industrial revolution in Europe, the demand for raw materials, cheap labour and markets grew. European kings encouraged exploration of new areas which were subsequently colonized. In 1492, Columbus had discovered West Indies and later America was found. By the middle of 18th century, a large part of North America had come under England's occupation. Landless peasants, Protestants and others started living in this area. English Parliament put severe restrictions on the American colonies, politically as well as economically. Colonies were forbidden to start certain industries and heavy duties were imposed. The imposition of stamp duty in 1765 aroused violent resentment among Americans and there were uprisings, besides boycott of English goods. Though English Parliament agreed to revoke stamp duty, it later imposed tax on tea to assert their right to levy taxes. Several colonies refused to unload the tea and in 1773, a group of people boarded a ship in Boston and threw tea into water. The incident is called "Boston Tea Party". Subsequently, in 1775, English troops fought with local troops. On July 4, 1776, the Declaration of Independence was adopted by American leaders. It said all men are created equal; People have a right to set up their own government and the colonies have right to be free and independent states. The war between English and American forces intensified with other European countries favouring the colonial forces. The English forces surrendered in 1781 and in 1783, England recognized the independence of its 13 former colonies.

England, despite being a powerful nation, lost against the local troops due to distance constraints, help by other European nations to American leaders, good leadership of the war of Americans and lack of coordination among English Generals.

The independence of America was an important event in the world history. For the first time, a federal Government, democratic in character, was sworn in under the written constitution. The event was a great setback to England. It served as an example to other revolutionaries of the world and the French Revolution followed a few years later.

French Revolution

France was a strong and powerful state in the 18th century. However, internally there were problems. A small section of people owned most of the land and occupied all senior administrative and army positions. There was a large number of peasants who lived under miserable conditions. In between was the middle class, which was educated and sometimes rich, yet did not have social status or political rights. There were a large number of thinkers in France who advocated rationalism, democracy and attacked clergy. Moreover, the wars abroad and large patronage brought the King to the point of bankruptcy. A stand off between the royal forces and protestors led to the fall of Bastille prison on July 14, 1789. A new constitution was adopted, declaring equality, liberty and fraternity for everyone. The privileged class people tied to other countries to sought their help and France was involved in wars with its neighbouring countries. However, a new order had been established in France and it reached new heights under the leadership of Napolean Bonaparte.

Industrial Revolution

In middle ages, the occupation of majority of the population in Europe was Agriculture and whatever trade was undertaken, was done on barter system: However, discoveries and new inventions, spread of education and new ideas led to development of methods and machineries that could produce faster, better and cheaper goods. The industrial revolution began in England because of availability of coal and iron, availability of labour, peaceful atmosphere and availability of good Navy to carry new methods to England and finished goods to the markets. However, it spread to other European nations as well because colonies were being established in Asia and Africa and cheap raw material and labour was easily available. These were good markets for ready material and the businessmen supported the scientists and engineers to do more research. The profits made from selling goods were ploughed back into the industry, leading to more development. The development of mechanical and electrical energy and establishment of big industries also helped the revolution. It led to large scale changes in textiles, iron extraction, mining, transportation, communication, agriculture and energy. The industrial revolution also had some adverse impacts as small farmers and industries were wiped off. It led to exploitation of poor, ladies, children and people of colonies; unemployment, wars for colonies, urbanization and increase in crimes. The positive impact was improvement in life-styles, increase in national income, increase in agricultural output and enactment of legislations for workers' welfare.

Colonialism

To sustain the growth of their industries, European nations needed raw material, cheep labour and ready markets. Asian and African nations were their easy targets. Moreover, for strategic, religious and military reasons, it was found useful by Europeans to have as many colonies as possible. However, these European nations fought among themselves several times to take control over colonies. The colonies were economically exploited by the Europeans and their social and political setup demolished. Their cultures were spoiled -and their inhabitants were tortured. The positive aspect of colonialism was spread of education, scientific temperament, nationalism, good administration and development of infrastructure in these colonies. Some of the colonies and colonisers were as follows:

- **Colonies of Belgium:** Congo
- **Colonies of England:** Cape Colony, Bechuanaland, Rhodesia, Natal, Transvaal, Orange Free State, Gold Coast, Nigeria, Egypt, Sudan, India, Canada, New Zealand, Australia
- **Colonies of France:** Algeria, Tunisia, Senegal, Moracco, Somaliland, Madagascar, Cambodia, Parts of India, Laos
- **Colonies of Holland:** Malaya Islands, Indonesia
- **Colonies of Germany:** Tanganika, Cameroon
- **Colonies of Portugal:** Angola, Goa in India
- **Colonies of Italy:** Eritrea, Syria, parts of Somaliland, Libya
- **Colonies of Russia:** Afghanistan, Persia, Manchuria, Korea

Nationalism

The spirit of love for the nation got prominent in the 18th century. It began in Europe and then spread to Asia and Africa. Several countries became independent consequently:

(*a*) **Spain:** Democratic government established in 1870

(*b*) **Greece:** Got independence from Turkey in 1829

(*c*) **Belgium:** Got independence from Holland in 1930

(*d*) **Poland:** People of Warsaw revolted against Russian rule in 1848

(*e*) **Australia:** Democratic Constitution accepted in 1867

(*f*) **Balkon States:** Serbia, Romania and Montanegro got liberated from Turkey in 1855

(*g*) **Italy:** Unification of Italy completed in 1871 with the efforts of Mazzini and Garibaldi

(*h*) **Germany:** Unification of Germany completed in 1870 with the efforts of Bismarck

(*i*) **China:** Dr Sun-Yat-Sen led a successful movement in establishing a democracy in 1911 but in 1949, a Communist government was set up under Mao-Tse-Tung

(*j*) **Turkey:** Mustafa Kamal Pasha established democracy in 1923, after ousting the forces of Italy, France and Greece

(*k*) **Iran:** Feudalism ended in 1925 and Sardar Raza Khan became King

(*i*) **Syria:** Syrians opposed French forces and became independent in 1936

(*m*) **Palestine:** After England's departure, Jews declared an independent nation by name 'Israel'

(*n*) **Afghanistan:** Rebellion in 1926 forced the British to free it

(*o*) **Egypt:** Movement under the leadership of Jagalul Pasha led to independence in 1936; Suez Canal nationalised in 1956 leading to end of European interference

(*p*) **Indonesia:** It was a colony of Holland but went under Japan's control during Second World War. However, after the end of war, Indonesia became independent in 1949

(*q*) **Malaysia:** People there opposed the British rule and it got independence in 1957

(*r*) **Ghana:** Got independence in 1957

(*s*) **Algeria:** National Movement got momentum during Second World War and independence came in 1963

(*t*) **Kenya:** "Mao-Mao" movement led to its independence in 1965

In 1960, Congo and Mali became independent while in 1961, Sierre Lone, Somalia, in 1962 Jamaica, Rwanda, Trinidad, Tobago, Uganda and in 1965, Zanzibar became independent. East Timor (2002) is the latest country to join the independent nations.

Russian Revolution

In 1917, the monarchs of Russia Czars were overthrown and the world's first communist state was set up by Bolsheviks under the leadership of Lenin. The revolution was sparked by Russia's crippling defeat in the first world war, the resultant hardship at home and the inability of the king to cope up with this. Riots and strikes spread throughout the country. The removal of the Czar was an easy job but Bolsheviks were opposed by nationalists, non-Russians, democrats and military dictators but by 1920, the Communist government was firmly in the seat.

First-World War

Rivalry between European nations over the issue of colonies and political dominations led to tension that had been building up since late 19th century. Germany was a late entrant into the race for colonies and hence resented the expansion of French and British empire. France had been defeated completely by Germans in 1870. In Balkan area, Russia and Austria-Hungary had deep suspicion about each other. Britain had been traditional rival of France but fearing the might of German navy, both countries agreed to cooperate in case of an attack. Moreover, German economy had made tremendous progress, leaving Britain and France far behind. The Ottoman Empire, comprising Turkey had occupied areas in Balkan but in 1912 they became independent after fighting a war. The precipitating matter for the first world war was the assassination of Archduke Francis Ferdinand, heir to the throne of Austria-Hungary in Sarajevo. Austria, suspecting Serb hand, declared war on Serbia. Russia declared support for Serbia. Germany declared war on Russia and France while Britain declared war on Germany. A large number of new weapons, like aircrafts, tanks, submarines and poison gas were used in the war. America entered into the war in 1917, siding with France and Britain. Russia withdrew from the war in 1918, after the revolution at home. All the colonies in the world took part in the war as per their ruler's intention. The war ended in 1918 with Bulgaria, Germany, Turkey and Austria-Hungary surrendering.

Second World War

The Second World War, like the first, started in Europe and assumed the character of a world war. In Germany, the Nazi forces under the leadership of Adolf Hitler, had come into power, exploiting Germany's humiliation at defeat in the first world war and signing of an unjust treaty after the war. The League of Nations set up after the first world war did not prove effective in dealing with the problems of that period. Fascist forces had taken over Italy while Japan was pursuing policies of expansion and militarism. Britain, France, USA initially overlooked the German invasion and avoided Russia's call to form alliance to check the aggression, but finally they had to come under an umbrella of Allied Power to check the advance of Axis powers which included Germany, Italy, Japan and their satellites. Allied powers included Britain, France, Russia, USA, China, Australia, Belgium, etc. The war started on September 1, 1939 when Germany attacked Poland. This was followed by attacks on Norway, Denmark, Belgium and Holland. France surrendered in June, 1940. A year later, Germany attacked Soviet Union, Japan attacked American naval base of Pearl Harbour in Hawai in December, 1941 bringing USA into war. By the middle of 1942, Axis forces had reached their peak but then their decline began. In all fronts, Germany and Italy suffered setbacks and they surrendered in May 1945. But Japan had to be attacked by nuclear bombs twice before being subjected to surrender.

World War II Main Events

- **September 1, 1939:** German forces invade Poland.
- **September 3, 1939:** Britain and France declare war on Germany.
- **September 17, 1939:** Soviet forces invade Poland; Warsaw captured after two weeks of intensive bombing.
- **April 9, 1940:** Germans invade Denmark and Norway.
- **May 10, 1940:** Germans invade Belgium and Holland; Churchill becomes British Prime Minister.
- **May 12, 1940:** German army enters France.
- **June 10, 1940:** Italy declares war against France and Britain.
- **June 22, 1940:** France surrenders.
- **August, 1940:** German air force bombards airfields and towns of Britain.
- **September 13, 1940:** Italy attacks British-controlled Egypt.
- **October 28, 1940:** Italy attacks Greece.
- **March 1941:** USA grants land-lease arrangements to help Britain fight Germany.
- **April 6, 1941:** Germany invades Yugoslavia.
- **June 22, 1941:** Massive German army invades Soviet Union.
- **September 4, 1941:** Germany begins the 900 day seige of Leningrad.
- **December 7, 1941:** Japan attacks the US fleet in Pearl Harbour; United States declares war on Japan.
- **December 25, 1941:** Hong Kong, a British colony fells to Japan paving its entry into South East Asia.
- **June 3, 1942:** US warplanes defeat Japanese naval force.
- **January 23, 1943:** German troops trapped in Stalingrad surrender.
- **July 10-11, 1943:** Allies invade Sicily leading to its fall a month later.
- **July 25, 1943:** Mussolini the Italian dictator resigns.
- **September 2, 1943:** Allied forces invade Italy mainland.
- **June 6, 1944:** Allies invade Normandy.
- **August 1944:** Soviet forces break into east Persia and Poland.
- **August 1944:** Citizens of Paris drive out German forces.
- **March 7, 1945:** US troops cross into Germany.
- **April 30, 1945:** Hitler commits suicide.
- **May 8, 1945:** Formal declaration of the end of war in Europe.
- **August 6, 1945:** First atomic bomb dropped on Hiroshima.
- **August 14, 1945:** Japan surrenders; World War II over.

Reunification of Germany

Mikhail Gorbachev's tenure as the President of Soviet Union was a period of weakening of Communist forces all over the world. The East Germany Communist regime collapsed in late 1989, as waves of East Germans took advantage of ending of travel restrictions between Hungary and Austria to leave their country. About 2 lakh East Germans left for the West and on November 9, 1989, the Berlin Wall was breached and within a weak, 3 million East Germans crossed over. The Politburo and Central Committee of Communist Party resigned within weeks. In 1990, the action of reunification got unprecedented momentum and on October 3, 1990, the two states became one country. Two months later, a united Germany voted in the first nationwide elections since 1932.

IMPORTANT WARS AND BATTLES IN WORLD

- **Battle of Marathon (490 BC):** United Greek army defeated the invading Persian army. A messenger, Pheidippides ran 30 km to Athens to give the good news and died after delivering the news. The marathon race commemorates the brave feat.
- **Battle of Saloms (480 BC):** Greece again repulses the Persian attack.
- **Paloponnesian Wars (459-404 BC):** Two Greek City-States Athens and Sparta struggled for supremacy in those wars. The first war was 459 to 446 BC while the second war lasted from 431 to 404 BC.
- **Alexander's Invasion (336 to 323 BC):** Alexander of Macedonia went on to capture Greece, Achalmend empire and upto Indian borders.
- **Punic Wars (264 to 146 BC):** Romans attacked Carthage, set the city on fire and enslaved people of the losing side.
- **Battle of Actium (31 BC):** Roman king Octavien's naval force defeated the combined strength of Mark Antony and Cleopatra.
- **Battle of the Yarmuk (636 AD):** In the early days of Islam, Muslim leader Abu Bakr defeated Christian empire of Byzantium in a clash near the Yarmuk river.

It resulted into expulsion of Byzentium and spread of Islam in Syria and Palestine.

- **Battle of Hastings (1066 AD):** The Duke of Normandy, William invaded England and defeated Harold. The English Crown was passed from Saxons to the Normans who brought England in contact with the rest of Europe.
- **Crusades (1095-1444 AD):** Christians, encouraged by Popes, attacked Muslims to recover the holy city of Jerusalem. In the first war, 1095-99, they succeeded in defeating Muslims in Asia minor and Palestine and captured Jerusalem. However, they lost it back to Muslims in 1187. The Christians attempted several times to regain but failed. In the earlier attempts, serious efforts were made and even children were recruited in the name of God. But subsequently, crusades became ineffective. In the name of Crusade, several Kings in Europe killed people of non-Christian sects. But the end of 13th century, the impact and popularity of Crusades diminished. The positive aspect of these wars was that Europeans came in contact with Arab civilization and gained knowledge and experience.
- **Battle of the Neva (1240 AD):** Russian forces, under the leadership of Alexander Nevsky defeated Swedes on the banks of the Neva river.
- **Hundred Years War (1338-1453 AD):** England and France fought over to claims of the English Kings to the French throne. War of the Roses—Two rival royal houses of Lancaster (Red rose as symbol) and York (White rose) struggled for the throne of England.

  The wars began when Richard, Duke of York rebelled against Henry VI but was killed in the battle of Wakefield. The throne kept on passing from one hand to another but finally Henry VII of Lancashire won and established Tudor dynasty with a victory in battle of Bostworth.
- **Italian Wars (1494-1559 AD):** Valois dynasty of France and Hapsbugs fought for the control of Italy. The result was inconclusive but French army was forced to retreat.
- **Malta Siege (1565 AD):** Turkish navy laid siege of Malta for about four months but could not enter. The siege was the beginning of the decline of Ottoman empire.
- **English Civil War (1642-49 AD):** King Charles I forces (called Caveliers) and Parliament forces (Roundheads) fought due to policy differences on religious and political matters. Foremost part, it consisted of skirmishes, marches and sieges. Parliament forces joined hands with Scotland and this scored victory in 1646. There was a brief second civil war but the result was the same.
- **War of Spanish Succession (1702-13 AD):** In this war of succession in Spain, one claimant to the throne was supported by France while the other was supported by Britain, Austria and the Netherlands. During the battle of Blenheim, the British-Austrian army, defeated the French army and Bavarian forces. It lowered the prestige of France which was considered invincible before.
- **Battle of Banker Hill (1775 AD):** First major clash in the American War of Independence. Though the number of American forces was less, the British army suffered heavy casualties and with great difficulty captured Bunker hill.
- **Battle of Yorktown (1781 AD):** British troops under Charles Cornwallis surrendered to an American force led by George Washington, ending the American War of independence.
- **Battle of the Nile (1798 AD):** The British navy under Lord Nelson defeated France in Aboukir bay, near Alexandria. It established British supremacy over the Mediterranean Sea and halted Napolean's expedition towards east.
- **Battle of Trafalgar (1805 AD):** It was fought between the British navy and a combined Franco-Spanish fleet. The British commander Nelson used daring tactics to break enemy's formation and secure overwhelming victory for his country. Nelson was killed but Napolean's hopes of invading England ended forever.
- **Battle of Austerlitz (1805 AD):** Emperor Napolean of France led his troops of victory over Austro-Russian forces commandered by their Emperors. This is also called the battle of three Emperors.
- **Battle of Borodino (1812 AD):** Napolean's forces attacked Russia. They faced stiff resistance but went on to capture Moscow.
- **Battle of Leipzig (1813 AD):** Combined armies of Austria, Prussia and Russia defeated Napolean's troops. It resulted in ending the domination of Napolean over Europe and liberation of Germany from French rule.
- **Battle of Waterloo (1815 AD):** Napolean was finally defeated by the combined armies of Britain, Holland, Belgium and Prussia led by the Duke of Wellington. Napoleon was arrested.
- **Crimean War (1854-56 AD):** Russia fought against the combined force of Britain, France and Turkey. The main issue was Russia's increasing influence in Turkey and its possession of the holy places in Palestine. The war ended with Russia offering peace.
- **Battle of Gettysburg (1863 AD):** In this crucial battle of American Civil war, the union troops of President Abraham Lincoln halted the march of confederate army, supported by Southern states. The defeat at Gettysburg was a big blow to the rebels.
- **Franco-Prussian War (1870-71):** North German Confederation states led Prussia defeated France. As a result, a unified Germany emerged and the balance of power in Europe changed. France, after loss, founded the third republic.

- **Sino-Japanese Wars (1894 and 1931-45 AD):** Japan and China first fought in 1891 for domination in Korean peninsula. Japan, despite being a small nation won an easy victory. The Japanese aim of waging war the second time was to capture whole of mainland China. It gained several military successes but after Japanese collapse in the second world war, China ultimately won.
- **Spanish-American War (1898 AD):** Spain and America fought a war, following mysterious destruction of a US battleship in Havana harbour. USA, aiming to help Cuba in gaining independence and suspecting Spain's hand in the ship destruction, attacked Spanish army as well as navy. It won easily, with Spain giving up all claims to Cuba, and ceding Puerto Rico, Guam and the Philippines.
- **Russo-Japanese War (1904-05 AD):** Japan and Russia fought for domination in Korea and Manchuria. Russia suffered heavy losses and defeats; forcing the Czar Nicholas II to make peace.
- **Balkan Wars (1912-13 AD):** Serbia, Greece, Bulgaria and Montnegro joined hands to strip Turkey of most of its European territory. But a year later, these forces fought among themselves, bringing in other great powers in the area.
- **First World War (1914-18 AD):** The allied Powers (Britain, France, USA, Belgium), etc., defeated Germany and her associates.
- **Battle of Jutland (1916 AD):** It was the greatest naval battle of the First World War. It was fought in the North Sea between Britain and German navies. Both sides suffered heavy losses.
- **Battle of Passchendacle (1917 AD):** Allied forces made a bloody attempt to attack German positions in heavy rain and through thick mud, gaining only a small area but losing over 4 lakh men.
- **Spanish Civil War (1936-39 AD):** The supporters of the republican socialist government of Spain and the conservative, fascist backed forces of General Franco fought a war which soon became an ideological battleground between left and right all over Europe and America. Republican army lost the war.
- **Second World War (1939-45 AD):** The Allies (Britain, France, USA and Russia and Benelux countries, etc. defeated the Axis Powers (Germany, Italy and Japan).
- **Battle of Britain (1940-41 AD):** German air force launched heavy offensive against Britain, with the help of 2,500 aircrafts. However, British royal air force, despite being smaller in number, put up stiff resistance and forced Germany to abandon plans of landing on British islands.
- **Korean War (1950-53 AD):** The Communist North Korea, backed by China attacked South Korea which was supported by America. United Nations intervened with force, driving North Koreans back. At one point, China and the USA had come face to face but fortunately, the situation stabilised. As per the agreement, the 38th parallel line divided the two countries.
- **Suez Invasion (1956 AD):** Egyptian President Naseer's move to nationalize the Suez Canal, angered France and Britain and they tried to secure control of it. International criticism and pressure forced the Anglo-French forces to agree to ceasefire within a few days and eventually withdraw.
- **Arab-Israel War:** A Jewish state of Israel came into being in Palestine in 1948, displacing Arabs who were staying there. Arabs resisted it and fought a war in 1948-49 but had to settle for co-existence. The tension, due to displaced Palestinian, led to wars in 1967 and 1973. Arab states, Egypt, Jordan, Syria and Lebanon's joint forces were repulsed by Israeli forces and Israel went on to occupy large Arab areas.
- **Iran-Iraq War (1980-88 AD):** Iran and Iraq were interested in becoming the leader of Arabs. After the installation of Islamic regime in Iran, an attempt was made to obstruct entry of ships to Iraq through a waterway. In retaliation, Iraq claimed 3 small but strategic islands, which were in Iran's possession. The war continued for eight years with both sides suffering heavy casualties and economic ruin. The war ended with the UN intervention but no side could claim victory.
- **Gulf War (1991 AD):** Iraq, three years after war with Iran, sent its forces to Kuwait, in August, 1990 and annexed it. The whole world opposed the move and the UN sanctioned a strike by 28 forces, led by America. The war lasted just 40 days, with Iraq suffering humiliating defeat. The war witnessed use of hi-tech weapons. Kuwait became an independent nation again.

IMPORTANT RELIGIONS OF THE WORLD

Baha'i

This is one of the new religions of the world, founded in 19th century in Persia by prophet Baha-u-llah. It is based on the principle of progressive revelation. There are no priests and leaders. Baha'i is based on the idea that all religion reveal different aspects of the same one truth. Divine revelation never ceases and one day the world will unite and there will be one language in the world. Different religions have grown with various stages of human progress but ultimately the singular truth will prevail.

Buddhism

Gautama Buddha founded Buddhism in the 6th century BC. He was born in a royal family but sorrows and sufferings of the world bothered him so much that he left earthly world for forests. He got enlightenment at Bodh Gaya and gave his first sermon at Sarnath. He dedicated the rest of his life to teaching. He did not claim to be God but after his death, his followers formed a new religion to worship him and to spread his ideas.

Buddha taught four noble truths — there is suffering in the world; this suffering has a cause; the cause is desire; and it is possible to put an end to suffering if desire is removed. To attain freedom from birth and rebirth or nirvana, eight fold path should be adopted which includes Right view, Right resolution, Right words, Right action, Right living, Right effort, Right thinking and Right concentration. The religion stresses the importance of the middle path, avoiding the extremes of strict asceticism or too much indulgence in worldly pleasures. Buddha also preached non-violence. He rejected the authority of the Vedas and caste-system. The Buddhist monks lived a strict disciplined life. They had to renounce most of their possessions, keeping only a ribe, a needle, water strainer and a begging bowl.

A few centuries later, Buddhism divided into two sects—the Hinayana and the Mahayana. The Hinayana (Lesser Vehicle) sect lays emphasis on the salvation of the individual by directly observing the eight fold path, i.e., teachings of Buddha is original form. It is prevalent in Myanmar, Sri Lanka, Cambodia and Vietnam. The followers of Mahayana (Greater Vehicle) worshipped the Buddha as a god and stressed that salvation is open to all. This sect is popular in China, Tibet, Korea and Mongolia.

Christianity

Jesus founded the Christianity religion. He was born as a Jew at Bethlehem near Jerusalem in 4 BC. He went about preaching his message in simple words and come to be known as a great leader. His simple life, magnetic personality and outstanding love and compassion for all made large followers of him. His fearlessness in criticizing the evil made Jewish priests and noble men his enemy. He was crucified but according to legends he rose on the third day after crucifixion. All the years in history are compared in Christian era with the birth of Jesus. BC means Before Christ, and AD means Anno Domini or "in the year of the lord".

Jesus said the authority of God was the Supreme power on earth. He referred to God as father and called himself son of the God. He loved his followers and taught people to love their neighbours. Christians believe that Jesus came to earth and died to redeem from sin and restore him to communion with God. After worldwide preaching of the gospel by his followers, he would reveal himself at the last judgement and reign as universal king. The holy book of Christianity is the Bible, containing two parts—Old Testament has religious beliefs of the Jews while New Testament contains the biography and teachings of Jesus Christ. Jerusalem is the most sacred place for Christians,.

Christianity has three major sects: (1) Roman Catholics are the followers of Roman Church, with Pope as the representative of God; (2) Protestants are the followers of Martin Luther and have separate churches; (3) Orthodox are a Catholics but authority of the Pope and recognise the authority of a Patriarchate of Constantinople.

Confucianism

It was founded by Confucius or King Futse, as the Chinese called him, in the sixth century BC. He did not say much about God or other mystical things but placed more emphasis on the proper management of the society. He was primarily concerned with governance and administration. He advocated discipline in life, temperance in eating and drinking habits, respect to elders, justice for all and trustfulness. He asked people to revere the customs of the past. Confucius was more of a moralist and expected all to be true to their duties and responsibilities.

Hinduism

Unlike many other religions, Hinduism does not have any founder. Its sacred writings, 'beliefs and practices came from widely different places and era. It is more of a way of life. Despite several attempts at forced and organised conversions, Hinduism is one of the few surviving religion with a large following in South Asia. The Hindus have multiple Gods and Goddesses, with Vishnu, Brahma, Mahesh and Shakti being prominent ones. They are prayed by different names and picturised differently all over. The scriptures of Hinduism are many in number, with the important ones being from Vedas, Gita and Ramayana.

Hinduism teaches the existence of one supreme universal spirit but allows the followers to worship him in any form. It believes in the doctrines of Karma and re-births. Soul within the body is believed to be immortal. It considers Dharma, or virtue, Artha or material well-being and Karma or gratification of the senses as three main aims of human life. Moksha or salvation is the ultimate aim of life, according to Hinduism. Another characteristic of Hinduism is Varnashrama. According to it, there are four Varnas as per the occupation and four ashramas as per different stages of life. The religion has never been static or uniform and has adopted itself to the changing circumstances and conditions of life. Different sects of Hinduism have various doctrines, principles, philosophies and rituals but all of them have co-existed, respecting each other. Since Hinduism did not have any central authority and permitted individuals to think and act on their own, it never developed as an organised religion like others.

Islam

Prophet Muhammad founded in sixth century AD, the religion of Islam, literally meaning submission to God. A muslim is one who submits. Muhammad was born in Mecca in 571 AD. At the age of 40, he had visions of truth and became a prophet. Due to opposition to his preachings, Prophet fled to Medina in 622 AD (Hejira or Mohammedan calendar begins from this date). He came back to capture Mecca with the help of his supporters. Prophet died in 632 AD.

Islam believes in a single God as supreme lord of the universe, arbiter of man's fate, all-powerful, all-knowing and all-pervading. Man is powerless before Allah and must, therefore, submit to his will. Muslims pray and bow before the God only. They recognize earlier prophets before Muhammad as well but believe that he was the last and the greatest. Islam speaks of a life after death and of a last judgement when all men shall receive the reward for their actions on earth. Muslims all over the world regard themselves as brothers and equals. A muslim must (1) proclaim the unity of God and the prophethood of Muhammad, (2) pray five times in a day; (3) give alms to the poor; (4) keep fast during the days of Ramazan month and (5) make pilgrimage to Mecca. Islam lays down some observation and forbids some practices. Muslims are forbidden from worshipping an Idol, eating pork and lending money on interest. Islam's emphasis on a life of virtue and benevolence made it one of the great humanitarian religions. Quran is their holy book which is believed to have the word of God, received by Muhammad. Islam's followers got divided into Shias and Sunnis, but both believe in Quran and Prophet Muhammad.

Jainism

Jainism derives its name from Jaina (the conqueror), the surname of Vardhamana Mahavira who lived in the 6th century BC. Mahavira was the last of the 24 Tirthankaras or great religious leaders. The Jains believe that every object, living or non-living, has a soul. So, they lay great emphasis on ahimsa or non-injury. Mahavira denied the authority of the Vedas. He laid emphasis on food conduct and taught right belief, right knowledge and right conduct for attaining salvation. Jainism believes in the doctrine of Karma and rebirth but shunned rituals. Jainism later on split in two sects—the Digambaras (who wear no clothes) and the Shvetambaras (who wear white clothes).

Judaism

It is the religion of the Jews or the Hebrew people who had settled in Mesopotamia under the leadership of Abraham. Later, Moses united different tribes who worshipped Yahweh or Jehovah. Judaism is the world's most ancient religion, honouring a single God and from which Islam and Christianity grew. It is a blend of religious doctrine, prophecy and social laws. The ten commandments, believed to have been revealed by God to Moses, lay down laws to guide the life of the followers. Some prophets of Jews proclaimed that God loves man and is ready to forgive a sinner who repents, Judaism preaches justice, mercy and humanity. Jews believe that the Messiah will one day appear on earth, purify the Hebrew and cleanse the world of sin and wickedness. Judaism does not believe Jesus Christ to be the Messiah. Old Testament is the sacred book of Judaism while Jerusalem is their holy place.

Zionism developed on the longing of Jews to return to their holy land of Zion (Jerusalem). It began to become an international force in the late 19th century and by 1948, Israel had been established. Presently, it is a nationalist movement, seeking to bring back the dispersed Jews to Israel.

Shintoism

It is the combination of traditional religious beliefs and practices of the Japanese. It is one of the oldest surviving religion, having its origin into nature worship and allowing followers to pray different gods and spirits. The religion does not have any sacred book or moral code. It is a largely a set of traditional rituals.

Sikhism

The founder of Sikhism, Guru Nanak stressed unity of God and condemned idolatory, ritualism and caste system. He emphasised the necessity of worshipping God through love. He assimilated good features of Hinduism and Islam. His teachings were compiled in a book called Adi-Granth. The tenth Guru of Sikhism Govind Singh instituted the institution of "Panj Piaras" and five customs—Kesh (hairs of head and beard to be grown), Kaccha (underwear), Kara (bracelet), Kangha (comb) and Kirpan (sword). Guru Govind Singh was the last Guru of Sikhs. Sikhs pray in Gurudwara and their sacred places are Amritsar, Nanakana Sahib and Anandpur Sahib.

Taoism

Leo-tse, meaning older master, was born in China in 604 BC. A short book "Tao te King" was written by him containing the essence of Taoism. It asked men to follow the natural way and to live a simple life. It stressed on meditation which would help man achieve inner power and confidence. Taoism which had originally preached enlightenment and inner joy for individual, got lost in magical practices.

Zoroastrianism

It was founded by prophet Zoroaster in 6th century BC in Persia. He said life was a struggle between the forces of good, the Ahura Mazda and evil the Angra Mainyu and man cannot be neutral in the struggle. He said those who lived in a righteous life went to heaven while the impious were condemned to hell eternally. After spread of Islam, followers fled to other places and called themselves Parsis. Their place of worship is called fire temple and holy book is Avesta.

Eminent Personalities of The World

- **Alexander, the Great (356-323 BC):** King of Macedonia, he led the Greek states against Persia, captured Egypt and penetrated upto India. He founded the City of Alexandria.
- **Antonius Marcus (Mark Antony) (83-30 BC):** He was in the Court of Julius Ceasar, along with Brutus and Cassius. After Ceasar's death, he was defeated by Octavian. His association with Egyptian Queen Cleopatra is the subject of Shakespeare's play.
- **Antony, St. (251-356):** He was early promoter of monastic life.
- **Arafat, Yasser (1929-2004):** He was President of the Palestine. He led the Palestinian Liberation Organisation that opposed the Israeli occupation of Muslim-majority areas. He shared the Nobel Peace Prize for solving the West Asia problem in non-violent method.
- **Archimedes (287-212 BC):** He was a Greek mathematician who is known for his contributions to pure mathematics, mechanics and hydrostatics.
- **Aristotle (384-322 BC):** The pupil of Plato, he was a greek philosopher. He taught the young prince Alexander and established a school in Athens.
- **Armstrong, Neil (b. 1930):** He was the US astronaut who became the first man to set foot on moon.
- **Ataturk, Kamal (1881-1938):** He was the builder of modern Turkey, being its President from 1923 to 1938. He defended against the British and drove the Greeks out of Turkey.
- **Augustus, C. Octavianus (63 BC-14AD):** He was nephew of Julius Ceasar. He became Roman emperor whose reign was notable for peace and creative activities.
- **Ayub Khan, Mohammed (1907-74):** He was the army chief of Pakistan who took over the reigns of the country after military coup. He was the longest serving President of Pakistan from 1958 to 1969.
- **Bhandarnaike, Sirimavo:** She was the world's first woman Prime Minister. She took reigns of Ceylon (Sri Lanka) after the assassination of her husband in 1960. She again became Prime Minister in 1970 and 1994.
- **Bernard, Christian N. (b-1922):** South African surgeon who pioneered heart transplant surgery in 1967.
- **Beatles, The:** Famous English music group whose highly original melodic songs took the youth of the world by storm in 1960s. The original group comprised Paul McCartney, John Lennon, George Harrison and Ringo Starr. They parted ways in 1971.
- **Beethoven, Ludwig Van (1770-1827):** One of the greatest musician who became deaf later in his life. His composition of nine symphonies is ranked the greatest one.
- **Bismarck (1815-98):** Prusso-German diplomat and statesman who became chief architect of the German unification.
- **Bolivar, Simon (1783-1830):** South America revolutionary leader who led independence movements in the north-west of South America against Spanish rule and became a Latin American hero.
- **Bradman, Donald (1909-2001):** Australian captain and cricketer who scored 29 centuries in test matches and is known as one of the greatest batsman of all time. He died in Adelaide (Australia) on February 25, 2001.
- **Brezhnev, Leonid Ilyich (1906-82):** He took over the reigns of Soviet Union in 1964 which was also the period of cold war. During his leadership, Soviet Union achieved strategic parity with US as his country tried to spread communism worldwide.
- **Ceasar, Julius (101-44 BC):** He was Roman General who paved the way for glorious years for his country. He was murdered by his friends and ministers.
- **Castro, Fidel (b. -1927):** Cuban revolutionary who overthrew the Government in 1959 and took over the country's reigns. He had good relations with Soviet Union and has steered his country for over 3 decades despite stiff resistance from neighbouring America.
- **Chaplin, Charles Spencer (1889-1977):** A comic character who became the first international screen star. He worked and directed hundreds of films.
- **Chenghis Khan (1162-1227):** Mongol conqueror who overran and devastated a large portion of Asia.
- **Chou-en-Lai (1898-1976):** He was the revolutionary leader of China who, along with Mao-Tse-Tung brought communism. He became Prime Minister of the Communist China in 1949.
- **Churchill, Winston (1874-1967):** British statesman who led the country during the World War II as its Prime Minister. He again became the Prime Minister from 1950 to 1955.
- **Columbus, Christopher (1451-1506):** Italian navigator who, with spanish support, discovered Cuba, Bahamas and Islands of West Indies.
- **Constantine (247-338):** He was the first Christian Roman emperor. He founded a new capital at Constantinopole.
- **Copernicus, Nicolas (1478-1543):** Polish astronomer and scientist who put forward the theory of Earth being of moving around the Sun.
- **Dante (1265-1321):** He was an Italian poet whose book "Divina Commedia" is world famous.
- **Darwin, Charles (1809-82):** English biologist who gave theory of evolution of species.
- **Deng Xiaoping (1904-97):** Chinese politician who steered his country in 1980s and 90s by introducing economic reforms without political freedoms.
- **Disraeli Benjamin (1804-81):** British statesman and novelist who became its Prime Minister twice.

- **Einstein, Albert (1879-1955):** German scientist who later migrated to America. He gave Theory of Relativity and won Noble Prize.
- **Franklin Benjamin (1706-90):** American statesman who helped in framing of American Constitution and getting French support for their war against the British. He also explained lightening and invented lightening conductor.
- **Gagrin, Yuri (1934-68):** Soviet cosmonaut who became the first man to go into space and come back safely.
- **Galileo (1564-1642):** Italian scientist who laid the foundations of modern science. He discovered telescope, thermometer and supported Sun-Centre Theory.
- **Gama, Vasco da (1460-1524):** Portuguese navigator who discovered the sea route to India through Cape of Good Hope.
- **Garibaldi, Giuseppe (1807-82):** Italian statesman who with Mazzini and Cavour created a united Italy.
- **Gaulle, Charles de (1890-1970):** French general and statesman who became the first President of the fifth republic in 1958.
- **Gorbachev, Mikhail (b. 1931):** Soviet politician who became the General Secretary of Communist Party and President of Nation. He practiced the policies of Glasnost (Openness) and Perestroika (Restructuring) which led to revolutionary changes in Eastern Europe and Soviet Union. His country disintegrated, economy backfired and political crisis grew, forcing him to resign in 1991. He won Nobel Peace Prize in 1990.
- **Harun-al-Rashid (763-809):** Caliph of baghdad whose court became a centre for art and learning.
- **Herodotus (485.425 BC):** Greek historian, often called the father of history.
- **Hippocrates:** Greek physician who contributed towards separation of medicine from superstition. Medical students are supposed to take a oath after his name.
- **Hitler, Adolf (1889-1945):** Dictator of Germany who founded Nazi Party. He destroyed working class movement, prosecuted opponents, particularly Jews and communists and took aggressive postures against the neighbours. This led to Second World War in which his troops were defeated. He committed suicide as the Russian troops closed in on Berlin.
- **Ho Chi-Minh (1892-1969):** The Communist leader of Vietnam who struggled for his country's independence and later as President of North Vietnam, fought to control South Vietnam, even defying United States.
- **Homer:** Greek poet who wrote Iliad and Odyssey.
- **Jinnah, Mohammed Ali (1876-1948):** Pakistani statesman, who forced two nation theory on the British by going on direct action. India was divided into two dominions and he became first Governor-General of Independent Pakistan.
- **Khomeini, Ayatollah (1900-89):** Iranian religious leader who after 16 years in exile returned home to overthrow the King and set up Islamic republic. He was, totally anti-west and fought war with Iraq for about a decade.
- **Kublai Khan (1216-94):** Grandson of Chengis Khan who become the first Mongol emperor of China. He won several new areas and merged them into his empire.
- **Lee Kuon Yew (b. 1923):** First Prime Minister of Singapore who continued from 1959 to 1990. He is the architect of Singapore's economic prosperity. However, he did not permit any political activity or opposition.
- **Lenin (1870-1924):** His original name was Vladimir Ilyich Vlyanov. He was revolutionary leader and statesman of Russia. He led the Bolsheviks in the 1917 revolution and headed the new government.
- **Leonardo da Vinci (1452-1519):** He was Italian artist as well as scientist. His painting "Monalisa" and "The Last Supper" are world famous. He studied anatomy, waves, currents and motions.
- **Lincoln, Abraham (1809-65):** He was the President of America who had to fight civil war to end slavery in the country. He coined the phrase "for the people, of the people, by the people". He was assassinated.
- **Luther, Martin (1483-1546):** He was German protestant and reformer who preached against the indulgences and luxurious life style of the church.
- **Mandela, Nelson (1918-2013):** He was the former President of South Africa. He was imprisoned for 27 years for opposing the racist rule. His release paved the way for end of apartheism. He won the Nobel Peace Prize in 1993.
- **Mao-Tse-Tung (1893-1976):** He was communist leader of China who founded communist government in 1949 in the mainland. He promoted cultural revolution which led to China's isolation from the world.
- **Marx, Karl (1818-83):** He was the founder of modern international communism and wrote 'Das Kapital', a book on economics. Along with Engels, he wrote the Communist Manifesto. He helped in founding of the first international. He is treated as the guru by all the left-thinking people.
- **Michel Angelo (1475-1564):** World famous Italian painter, sculptor and poet.
- **Mussolini Benito (1883-1945):** Fascist dictator of Italy who sided with Germany during Second World War. He was shot dead while trying to flee Italy.
- **Napolean Bonaparte (1769-1821):** He was emperor of France who made attempts to expand its boundaries. He succeeded initially but was defeated in Waterloo in 1815.
- **Nasser, Gamal Abdul (1918-70):** He was leader of modern Egypt and Arab world. He introduced democracy, nationalised Suez Canal despite opposition

from France and Britain, and led Arabs against Israel in 1967 war.

- **Nightingale Florence (1820-1910):** English nurse and pioneer of hospital reforms who came to be known as "the lady with the lamp".
- **Omar Khayyam (1050-1123):** Persian poet and mathematician whose Rubbaiyat became world famous.
- **Picasso, Pablo (1881-1973):** Spanish painter who was brilliant in sculpture, ceremonies and graphic arts also.
- **Polo, Marco (1256-1323):** Traveller from Italy who went to China and India and left an account of his travels.
- **Rousseau, Jean-Jacques (1712-78):** French political philosopher and educationist whose views stimulated the people and led to French revolution.
- **Shakespeare, William (1564-1616):** Greatest poet and playwright of English whose mastery of language, understanding of character and their dramatic perception has been unsurpassed. His major contributions were Romeo and Juliet, The Merchant of Venice, Much Ado About Nothing, Julius Ceasar, Hemlet, Macbeth, Othello, Anatony and Cleopatra, Measure for Measure.
- **Shaw, G.B. (1856-1950):** Dramatist who used wit in his plays to highlight hypocrisy and rational weaknesses. His important writings are Mali and Superman, The Apple Cart and Heartbreak House.
- **Socrates (470-399 BC):** Greek philosopher and intellectual leader.
- **Stalin (1879-1953):** Joseph Vissarionovich Djugashvili was his original name. After the death of Lenin, he took the reigns of Soviet Union. He used ruthless means to bring about economic prosperity and political discipline. He was the architect of five-year plans.
- **Tito, Joseph Broz (1892-1980):** He was the leader of Yugoslavia who secured its independence and later on became a pillar of Non-Aligned Movement in the world.
- **Washington, George (1732-99):** He became the first President of America. He led his forces to defeat Cornwallis. He presided over the Philadelphia Convention that formulated the Constitution.

Nicknames of World Personalities

- **Bard of Avon:** Shakespeare
- **Duce:** Mussolini
- **Desert Fox:** General Rommel
- **Father of English Poetry:** Chaucer
- **G.B.S.:** George Bernard Shaw
- **Grand Old Man of Britain:** Gladstone
- **G.I.:** American Soldier
- **Great Commoner:** Pitt the Young
- **Iron Duke:** Duke of Wellington
- **Iron Butterfly:** Margaret Thatcher
- **Ike:** Eisenhower
- **John Bull:** England and English people
- **K of K:** Kitchner of Khartoum
- **King maker:** Earl of Warwick
- **Little Corporal:** Napolean
- **Lady with the Lamp:** Florence Nightingale
- **Mark Twain:** Samuel Clemens
- **Mandarin:** Chinese official
- **Man of Destiny:** Napolean
- **Maiden Queen:** Elizabeth
- **Maid of Orleans:** Joan of the Arc
- **Man of Blood and Iron:** Bismarck
- **Negus:** Kings of Ethiopia
- **Poolu:** French Soldier
- **Tom Atkins:** British Soldier
- **Uncle Sam:** Americans
- **Yankee:** Americans

MULTIPLE CHOICE QUESTIONS

1. In which year, Alexander the Great become the king of Macedonia?

   A. 336 BC   B. 323 BC
   C. 350 BC   D. 200 BC

2. The European renaissance started from which country?

   A. England   B. France
   C. Italy   D. Greece

3. On which island of France, Napoleon was born?

   A. Saint Helena   B. Corsica
   C. Elba   D. Oleron

4. The Battle of Waterloo was fought in the year:

   A. 1800   B. 1805
   C. 1807   D. 1815

5. In which year America got independence?

   A. 1760   B. 1776
   C. 1780   D. 1782

6. Who is known as the Artist of the world famous painting 'Mona Lisa'?

   A. Filippo Brunelleschi
   B. Michelangelo
   C. Vincent van Gogh
   D. Leonardo da Vinci

7. Who was the king during the French revolution?
A. Napoleon B. Louis XV
C. Louis XVI D. Charles IX

8. The Hundred Years' War (from 1337 to 1453) was fought between:
A. England and France
B. Germany and Russia
C. America and Argentina
D. England and Germany

9. Queen Elizabeth I of England belongs to which dynasty?
A. Stuart B. York
C. Tudor D. Normandy

10. 'Boston Tea Party' protest was associated with the revolution of:
A. America B. Italy
C. France D. India

11. Which king of England was forced to signed the 'Magna Carta'?
A. King Richard I B. King Louis
C. Henry III D. King John

12. When the first Ancient Greek Olympic Game was begun?
A. 776 BC B. 552 BC
C. 800 BC D. 235 BC

13. Who was the author of United States Declaration of Independence?
A. Thomas Jefferson B. George Washington
C. Abraham Lincoln D. Benjamin Franklin

14. Napoleon was exiled to the Saint Helena after the defeat in the war of:
A. Russia B. Waterloo
C. Peninsular D. Rivoli

15. Who was the President of America during American Civil War?
A. Abraham Lincoln B. Andrew Jackson
C. George Washington D. James Madison

16. Industrial Revolution was started from which country?
A. France B. Germany
C. Italy D. England

17. Which city was recaptured at the end of the first war of Crusade?
A. Rome B. Venice
C. Jerusalem D. Vienna

18. First war of Crusade was ended in the year:
A. 1099 B. 1095
C. 1123 D. 1323

19. Who was one of the teachers of Alexander the Great?
A. Plato B. Aristotle
C. Socrates D. None of the above

20. In which year Christopher Columbus discovered America?
A. 1502 B. 1339
C. 1405 D. 1492

21. Which were the two countries that fought during the Falklands War?
A. Britain and France
B. Germany and Austria
C. Argentina and Britain
D. Austria and Russia

22. Who was the Chinese Emperor when Marco Polo visited China?
A. Temur Khan B. Kublai Khan
C. Genghis Khan D. Ogedei Khan

23. Aztec civilization was originated in which country?
A. USA B. Greece
C. Egypt D. Mexico

24. Which famous book was written by Nostradamus?
A. Les Propheties B. Das Kapital
C. The Tempest D. None of the above

25. Who was the Emperor of Russia during Russian Revolution?
A. Alexander III B. Nicholas II
C. Nicholas I D. Alexander II

26. When did the second Russian Revolution start?
A. August, 1905 B. February, 1917
C. October, 1917 D. March, 1921

27. Leonardo da Vinci was born in the city of:
A. Rome B. Milan
C. Florence D. Madrid

28. In which year did the Suez Canal was open for trade?
A. 1869 B. 1880
C. 1774 D. 1620

29. Who was the first Roman Emperor?
A. Caligula B. Claudius
C. Augustus D. Nero

30. Who was the founder of Ottoman Empire?
A. Osman I B. Orhan
C. Mura I D. Bayezid I

31. Crimean War was started in the year:
A. 1853 B. 1857
C. 1862 D. 1870

32. Who is known as the 'Father of History'?
A. Homer B. Thucydides
C. Herodotus D. Archimedes

33. 'Mein Kampf' is the autobiography of which political leader?
A. Joseph Stalin B. Benito Mussolini
C. Winston Churchill D. Adolf Hitler

34. Benito Mussolini was the Prime Minister of which country?
A. French B. Belgium
C. Italy D. Turkey

35. Who was the US President during World War II?
A. Winston Churchill
B. Joseph Stalin
C. Franklin D Roosevelt
D. Harry S Truman

36. In which year Adolf Hitler was appointed as Chancellor of Germany?
A. 1933 B. 1935
C. 1938 D. 1940

37. World renowned philosopher Karl Marx was born in the country:
A. Austria B. Germany
C. Russia D. Italy

38. Who gave the famous quote 'Government of the people, by the people, for the people, shall not perish from the Earth'?
A. Winston Churchill B. Abraham Lincoln
C. Vladimir Lenin D. George Washington

39. The organisation 'League of Nations' was founded after the end of:
A. World War I B. World War II
C. Crimean War D. Vietnam War

40. First Sino-Japanese War was fought in the year:
A. 1848 B. 1894
C. 1901 D. 1896

41. Who build the St. Basil's Cathedral in Moscow, Russia?
A. Peter I B. Vladislav I
C. Ivan the Terrible D. Feodor I

42. Which dynasty of China began the construction of the Great Wall?
A. Ming Dynasty B. Qin Dynasty
C. Shun Dynasty D. None of the above

43. In which year Bastille of Paris stormed by the people which lead to the French Revolution?
A. 1746 B. 1779
C. 1789 D. 1808

44. Which King was executed by guillotine during French Revolution in 1793?
A. Charles X B. Louis XIII
C. Henry IV D. Louis XVI

45. Who was the first Christian emperor of the Roman Empire?
A. Julius Caesar B. Nero
C. Constantine D. Domitian

46. Who was the last Emperor of Rome?
A. Nero B. Romulus Augustulus
C. Julius Nepos D. Julius Caesar

47. When the first communist manifesto was written by Karl Marx and Friedrich Engels?
A. 1848 B. 1859
C. 1872 D. 1890

48. Which country first invented Gunpower in around 270 AD?
A. China B. India
C. Korea D. England

49. Which pharaoh build the largest pyramid known as Great Pyramid of Giza?
A. Sneferu B. Tutankhamun
C. Khufu D. None of the above

50. During which dynasty Paper was invented in China?
A. Xia Dynasty B. Tang Dynasty
C. Yuan Dynasty D. Han Dynasty

51. Who is known as the father of American Constitution?
A. James Madison B. George Washington
C. John Adams D. Thomas Jefferson

52. Who is the first crowned Czar (Tsar) of Russia?
A. Peter I B. Ivan IV (the Terrible)
C. Nicholas I D. John Adams

53. The famous painting 'Last Supper' is a creation of:
A. Michaelangelo B. Vincent van Gogh
C. Leonardo Da Vinci D. Sandro Botticelli

54. Who was the commander of 'Seventh Coalition' army that defeated Napoleon in the Battle of Waterloo?
A. Arthur Wellesley B. Jean-de-Dieu Soult
C. Robert Clive D. John Carnac

55. What was the name of the atom bomb dropped in Hiroshima city?
A. Fat Boy B. Fat Man
C. Little Boy D. Scorpion

56. What was the name of the atom bomb dropped in Nagasaki city?
A. Fat Boy B. Fat Man
C. Scorpion D. Death Kiss

57. American Civil War was started in the year:
A. 1756 B. 1806
C. 1861 D. 1890

58. Who founded the Great Seljuq Empire in 1037?
A. Seljuq Beg B. Tughril Beg
C. Alp Arslan D. Malik-Shah I

59. The Parliament of Great Britain was formed in the year:
A. 1707 B. 1729
C. 1774 D. 1823

60. In which European country feudalism process is first started?
A. Italy B. England
C. French D. Russia

61. Who is consider as the first Pope of Christianity?
A. St. Peter B. St. Linus
C. St. Evaristus D. St. Alexander I

62. Who is known as the first pope of Vatican City?
A. Pope Benedict XV B. Clement XIII
C. Pope Pius XI D. Benedict XIII

63. Which Nazi Field Marshal is known as the 'Desert Fox'?
A. Viktor Brack B. Erwin Rommel
C. Hans Frank D. Hermann Goring

64. Communist Revolutionary Che Guevara was born in the city:
A. Havana B. Rosario
C. Matanzas D. San Juan

65. Which Roman Emperor is also known as 'little boot'?
A. Nero B. Julius Caesar
C. Caligula D. Augustus

66. The Greek War of Independence against the Ottoman Empire started in the year:
A. 1805 B. 1821
C. 1852 D. 1895

67. The Franco-Prussian War (1870-1871) was ended with the sign of:
A. Treaty of Vienna B. Treaty of Munich
C. Treaty of Paris D. Treaty of Versailles

68. In European history, which year is known as the year of revolution?
A. 1732 B. 1765
C. 1848 D. 1896

69. Which monarch is known as 'the Sun King' and also the longest of monarchs of major countries in European history?
A. Louis XIV of France
B. Henry III of England
C. Louis XIII of France
D. Edward I of England

70. In which country the revolution of 1848 first begins that lead to a series of revolutions?
A. Italy B. Germany
C. France D. Austria

71. The Renaissance movement is described as the ending of:
A. Pre-historic Era B. Ancient Era
C. Medieval Era D. Modern Era

72. Which city is known as the birthplace of the Renaissance?
A. Florence B. Venice
C. Rome D. London

73. Constantinople, the capital of Roman Empire was captured by Turks in the year:
A. 1385 B. 1415
C. 1453 D. 1469

74. Who was known as the Morning star of Renaissance?
A. Montesquieu B. Dante
C. Shakespeare D. Geoffrey Chaucer

75. Who become the Chancellor of Germany for One Day after the death of Hitler during Second World War?
A. Hermann Goering B. Henerich Himmler
C. Rudolf Hess D. Joseph Goebbels

76. Total number of Theses written by Martin Luther on Power of Indulgences are:
A. 81 B. 87
C. 95 D. 101

77. What was the name of the secret police party of Nazi in Germany?
A. Gestapo B. NKVD
C. OVRA D. Palace Guard

78. Who is known as the founder of the Durrani Empire?
A. Timur Shah Durrani
B. Zaman Shah Durrani
C. Mahmud Shah Durrani
D. Ahmad Shah Durrani

79. Who is regarded as the founder of modern Egypt?
A. Muhammad Ali B. Ibrahim Pasha
C. Abbas I D. Sa'id Pasha

80. In which year British East India Company established in Singapore?
A. 1808 B. 1819
C. 1832 D. 1849

81. In which year Francis II, founded the Empire of Austria?
A. 1804 B. 1809
C. 1820 D. 1822

82. The term 'Cold War' was coined by:
A. Barnard Baruch B. Prof. Lippmann
C. Palmer Perkins D. Roosevelt

83. During the First World War, which country signed the Peace of Treaty (1917) with Germany?
A. England B. USA
C. Russia D. Austria

84. When United Kingdom declared war on Germany which lead to World War II?
A. 4th April 1939
B. 18th August 1939
C. 28th August 1939
D. 3rd September 1939

85. Who was the last Byzantine Emperor during the fall of Constantinople in 1453?
A. Manuel II B. John V
C. John VIII D. Constantine XI

86. The Triple Alliance agreement between Germany, Austria-Hungary, and Italy was formed in the year:
A. 1881 B. 1889
C. 1901 D. 1909

87. In which year, America joined the Second World War?
A. 1939 B. 1940
C. 1941 D. 1942

88. During which US President period, the Cuban Missile Crisis conflict was occurred?
A. Lyndon B. Johnson B. Richard Nixon
C. Ronald Reagan D. John F. Kennedy

89. Marco Polo was a traveller from _________:
A. Portugal B. England
C. Italy D. Spain

90. The First Opium War was fought between British and ___________:
A. Chinese B. Indian
C. Japanese D. Thai

91. Rivers Tigris and Euphrates are associated with?
A. Mesopotamian Civilization
B. Egyptian Civilization
C. Harappan Civilization
D. Chinese Civilization

92. Which is considered as the oldest civilization of the world?
A. Mesopotamian Civilization
B. Egyptian Civilization
C. Harappan Civilization
D. Chinese Civilization

93. Which among following is called "Gift of the Nile"?
A. China B. India
C. Iraq D. Egypt

94. Marco Polo, Venetian traveller, travelled from Venice to China and Japan in:
A. 1285-90 B. 1288-93
C. 1290-96 D. 1295-1301

95. In which year Bartholomew Diaz reached Cape of Good Hope?
A. 1480 B. 1487
C. 1495 D. 1500

96. Magna Carta or The Great Charter was signed in:
A. 1210 B. 1215
C. 1220 D. 1225

97. Who is known as Man of Blood and Iron?
A. Napoleon B. Bismarck
C. Ho Chi Minh D. Sir. Walter Scott

98. What is Chivalry?
A. The code Charlemagne implemented
B. The code by which a Christian family lived
C. The code by which knights lived
D. The code by which young men lived

99. Which of the following was the most important 'God' of ancient Egyptians?
A. The Moon B. Jackal
C. The Sun D. None of these

100. Which of the following statement is/are correct?
A. The ancient Egyptians firmly believed in life after deaths.
B. The dead body of ancient Egyptians was embalmed in spices and then wrapped in strips of fine linen. Such a preserved body is called 'mummy'.
C. The pyramids were the tombs of great kings.
D. All the above

101. Whose model is based on the Mandate of Heaven?
A. Ban Gu B. Li Ling
C. Qin Shi Huang D. Sima Qian

102. Who is the author of "The History of the World-Conquerer"?
A. Annemarie Schimmel
B. Clifford Edmund Bosworth
C. Gustaf John Ramstedt
D. John Andrew Boyle

103. Who was the first to distinguish between cause and immediate origins of an event?
A. Herodotus B. Pericles
C. Plutarch D. Thucydides

104. The Peloponnesian War was fought between which cities?
A. Athens and Macedonia
B. Carthage and Athens
C. Sparta and Carthage
D. Sparta and Athens

105. When did the rise of Median Empire occur?
A. 745 BC B. 722 BC
C. 750 BC D. 728 BC

106. When was Nineveh destructed?
A. 612 BC B. 600 BC
C. 599 BC D. 563 BC

107. Who founded the Achaemenid Empire?
A. Alexander the Great B. Cambyses II
C. Cyrus the Great D. Darius I

108. When did Cambyses II conquer Egypt?
A. 525 BC B. 512 BC
C. 509 BC D. 508 BC

109. Who developed system ranks of binary patterns?
A. Baudhayana B. Aryabhata
C. Mahavira D. Pingala

110. When did King Leonidas die?
A. 480 BC B. 479 BC
C. 475 BC D. 469 BC

111. When was Socrates born?
A. 469 BC B. 465 BC
C. 460 BC D. 449 BC

112. When was Xerxes I murdered?
A. 465 BC B. 460 BC
C. 449 BC D. 447 BC

113. Who founded the philosophy of Stoicism in Athens?
A. Chrysippus B. Cleanthes
C. Epictetus D. Zeno of Citium

114. Who defeated Hannibal at Battle of Zama?
A. Cato the Elder
B. Scipio Aemilianus
C. Scipio Africanus
D. Hasdrubal

115. Who officially instituted the first system of imperial examinations in China?
A. Han Wu Di B. Huo Qubing
C. Wei Qing D. None

116. How did Saint Boniface help to shape the German church?
A. Preaching against divorce, incest, and polygamy
B. Preaching against the importance of monasteries
C. Writing the epic 'Beowulf
D. Writing 'The Rule of Saint Benedict'

117. Who took control of the kingdoms of Austrasia and Neustria in a coup of 753?
A. Carloman B. Charles Martel
C. Pepin of Herstal D. Pepin the Short

118. Where was the Ottonian dynasty established?
A. Denmark B. Germany
C. Iceland D. Scandinavia

119. "Middle Ages" in Western Europe includes the period ________.
A. AD 300 - AD 1600
B. Beginning of Byzantine through the end of the Roman Empire
C. Beginning of Early Christian through the 13th or 14th centuries
D. End of the Roman Empire through the Byzantine period

120. What does the opening scene of Beowulf describe?
A. The arrival of Scyld Scefing in Denmark
B. The birth of Beowulf
C. The death of Beowulf
D. The defeat of the monster Grendel

ANSWERS

1	2	3	4	5	6	7	8	9	10
A	C	B	D	B	D	C	A	C	A
11	12	13	14	15	16	17	18	19	20
D	A	A	B	A	D	C	A	B	D
21	22	23	24	25	26	27	28	29	30
C	B	D	A	B	C	C	A	C	A
31	32	33	34	35	36	37	38	39	40
A	C	D	C	C	A	B	B	A	B
41	42	43	44	45	46	47	48	49	50
C	B	C	D	C	B	A	A	C	D
51	52	53	54	55	56	57	58	59	60
A	B	C	A	C	B	C	B	A	C
61	62	63	64	65	66	67	68	69	70
A	C	B	B	C	B	D	C	A	A
71	72	73	74	75	76	77	78	79	80
C	A	C	D	D	C	A	D	A	B
81	82	83	84	85	86	87	88	89	90
A	A	C	D	D	A	C	D	C	A
91	92	93	94	95	96	97	98	99	100
A	A	D	B	B	B	B	D	C	D
101	102	103	104	105	106	107	108	109	110
D	D	D	D	D	A	C	A	D	A
111	112	113	114	115	116	117	118	119	120
A	A	D	C	A	C	D	B	C	A

3

INDIAN POLITY, ECONOMY & CULTURE

INDIAN POLITY

INDIAN CONSTITUTION

- The idea for a Constituent Assembly for drafting a constitution for India was first provided by B.G. Tilak in 1895. M.N. Roy was the first to demand a Constituent Assembly for India in 1934. A year later, the Indian National Congress made this a formal demand in a resolution that rejected a British proposal (White Paper) on constitutional reforms for India (What would later become the Government of India Act, 1935).
- The election for Indian Constitution Assembly held in 1946 according to the *Cabinet Mission Plan*.
- On December 11, 1946, Dr. Rajendra Prasad was elected as the Permanent Chairman of the Constituent Assembly.
- The Constitution was framed by the Constituent Assembly of India, set-up in December 1946, in accordance with the Cabinet Mission Plan, under the Chairmanship of Sachidanand Sinha, initially.
- After partition the total membership of Constituent Assembly was 299, when 70 were representatives from the Indian states and others from British India.
- The Chairman of the Drafting Committee was **Dr. B. R. Ambedkar**, also called the Father of the Constitution.
- The Constituent Assembly took 2 years, 11 months and 18 days to complete the Constitution.
- The Constitution, adopted on 26th November, 1949, contained 395 Articles and 8 Schedules.
- The Constitution was delayed till 26th January because, in 1929, on this day Indian National Congress demanded Poorna Swaraj in Lahore Session under JL Nehru.
- Indian Constitution is a comprehensive document and it is the lengthiest written Constitution in the World.

THE PREAMBLE

- ***The Preamble of the Constitution:*** "We the people of India, having solemnly resolved to Constitute India into a Sovereign, Socialist, Secular Democratic Republic and to secure to all its citizen:

  Justice, Social, economic and political;

  Liberty of thought, expression, belief, faith and worship;

  Equality of status and of opportunity; and to promote among them all;

  Fraternity assuring the dignity of the individual and the unity and integrity of the nation;

  In our Constituent Assembly, this twenty-sixth day of November, 1949, do hereby adopt, enact and give to ourselves this constitution."

Main Features of Indian Constitution

- It is perhaps the bulkiest written Constitution.
- It combines rigidity with flexibility.
- Envisages parliamentary system of government, both at the centre and the states, real executive power with the council of Ministers.
- It provides a federal system of government with a unitary bias. It declares India a secular state.
- An elaborate list of Fundamental Rights and Duties is given in the Constitution.
- It lays down Directive Principles of State Policy. It provides for single citizenship. It makes special provision for the protection of backward classes.
- It grants rights to vote to all adults above the age of 18 years without any distinction.

Foreign Sources of Indian Constitution

Foreign Sources	*Subject*
Britain	Parliamentary system, collective responsibilities of Cabinet
America	Fundamental right, Citizenship, Independent Judiciary, Judicial review
Canada	Division of powers
Ireland	Directive principles
Germany	Emergency provisions
Russia	Fundamental duties
Australia	Concurrent list
S. Africa	Amendment Provisions

IMPORTANT ARTICLES

Part - I

Union and its Territories (Article 1 - 4)

- The Constitution says, "India, that is Bharat, shall be a Union of States".
- Parliament has the power to create any State, reduce it, change the name of boundaries of any State.

Part - II

Citizenship (Article 5 - 11)

- The Constitution provides for a single Citizenship.
- ***Indian Citizenship can be acquire:***
  1. By birth
  2. By descent
  3. By registration
  4. By naturalisation
  5. By incorporation of territory
- ***Indian Citizenship can be lost by:***
  1. renunciation;
  2. termination — it takes place if a citizen of India voluntary acquires the citizenship of another country; and
  3. deprivation — if the Government terminates the citizenship.

Part - III

Fundamental Rights (Article 12 - 35)

- Following fundamental rights are enjoyed by every Indian citizen, irrespective of caste, race, creed and sex:
  1. ***Right to Equality:*** No special privileges, no distinction on grounds of religion, caste, race and sex.
  2. ***Right to Freedom:*** The right to freedom of expression and speech, the right to choose one's own profession, the right to reside in any part of the Indian Union.
  3. ***Right to Freedom to Religion:*** Except when it is in the interest of public order, morality, health or other conditions, everybody has the right to profess, practice and propagate his religion freely.
  4. ***Cultural and Educational Rights:*** The Constitution provides that every community can run its own institutions to preserve its own culture and language.
  5. ***Right against Exploitation:*** Traffic in human beings and forced labour and the employment of children under 14 years in factories or mines, are punishable offences.
  6. ***Rights to Constitutional Remedies:*** When a citizen finds that any of his fundamental rights has been encroached upon, he can move the Supreme Court, which has been empowered to safeguard the fundamental rights of a citizen (Article 32).

Part - IV

Directive Principles of State Policy (Article 36 - 51)

- Directive principles are not enforceable through courts. Main aim of Directive principles is to provide social and economic base of a genuine democracy.

Some Important Directive Principles:

- Provisions for adequate means of livelihood for all citizens (Art. 39).
- Right to work (Art. 41).
- Right to human condition of work and maternity relief (Art. 42).
- Right to a living wage and condition of work ensuring decent standard of life of worker (Art. 43).
- Common Civil Code (Art. 44).
- Prohibit consumption of liquor (Art. 47).
- Prevent slaughter of useful cattle (Art. 48).
- Organise Panchayati Raj (Art. 40).
- Separate the judiciary from the executive (Art. 50).
- Protect and maintain places of historic monuments (Art. 49).
- International peace (Art. 51).

Part - IV A

Fundamental Duties (Article 51A)

- The fundamental duties for the Indian citizens have been incorporated in the Constitution through the Constitution (42nd) Amendment Act, 1976. These duties are:
  1. to abide by the Constitution and respect its ideals and institutions, the National Flag and the National Anthem;
  2. to cherish and follow the noble deeds which inspired our national struggle for freedom;
  3. to uphold and protect the sovereignty, unity and integrity of India;
  4. to defend the country and render national service when called upon to do so;
  5. to promote harmony and the spirit of common brotherhood amongst all the people transcending religious, regional or sectional diversities and to renounce practices derogatory to the dignity of women;
  6. to value and preserve the rich heritage of our composite culture;
  7. to protect and improve natural environment including forests, lakes, rivers and wildlife, and to have compassion for living creatures;
  8. to develop the scientific temper, humanism and the spirit of inquiry and reform;

9. to safeguard public property and to abjure violence;
10. to strive towards excellence in all spheres of individual and collective activity so that the nation constantly rises to higher levels of endeavour and achievement.
11. who is parent or guardian to provide opportunities for education to his child or, as the case may be, ward between age of six and fourteen years.

Part - V

Union (Article 52 - 151)

The President

- The President is the Constitutional head of the Republic of India. He is more or less the titular head of the executive.
- He is the constitutional head but not the real executive. The real power is vested in the hands of the Council of Ministers.
- President is the first citizen of India.
- ***Qualifications:*** (i) Indian citizen, (ii) age not less than 35 years, (iii) should have qualification for election to Lok Sabha, (iv) should not hold any office of profit, (v) should not be a Member of Parliament or State Legislature.
- ***Election:*** Indirectly elected through Electoral College consisting of elected members of both the Houses of the Parliament and elected members of the Legislative Assemblies of the States.
- According to the 70th Amendment Act, 1992, the expression 'States' include the National Capital Territory of Delhi and the Union Territory of Puducherry. Members of the Legislative Councils have no right to vote in the Presidential election.
- ***Powers:*** He makes appointments to all the constitutional posts.
- He can address either House of Parliament and dissolve Lok Sabha.
- All Bills passed by Parliament must receive his assent to become an Act.
- He issues ordinances when Parliament is not in session. No Money Bill can be introduced in Lok Sabha without his recommendation.
- He appoints 12 members of special repute in the Rajya Sabha.
- He has the power of *Pardon* to a criminal in special cases.
- The President holds the office for a period of five years. He is eligible for re-election.
- He draws a fix salary per month. He is also entitled to rent free official residence called Rashtrapati Bhawan.

Vice-President

- ***Article 63*** of the Constitution stipulates a Vice-President for India.
- The Vice-President acts as the ex-officio Chairman of the Council of States (Rajya Sabha).
- He is elected by an electoral college consisting of the members of both Houses of Parliament in accordance with the system of proportional representation by means of the single transferable vote. He must be a citizen of India, not less than 35 years of age, and should be eligible for election as a member of the Council of States.
- Disputes in connection with election of a president or a vice-president are to be a dealt with in accordance with Article-71. Such disputes shall be decided by the Supreme Court.

Council of Ministers

- The Constitution of India provides for a parliament system of government under which the President is only Constitutional ruler and the real power is exercised by the Council of Ministers, headed by the Prime Minister.
- Council of Ministers is composed of all Union Ministers—the Prime Minister, Cabinet Ministers, Ministers of State and Deputy Ministers.
- The Council of Ministers is Collectively responsible to the Lok Sabha.
- The Prime Minister is a link between the President and the Council of Ministers.

Prime Minister

- The Prime Minister is the leader of the majority party in the Parliament.
- He is appointed by the President. Other Ministers are appointed by the president on his advice.
- The Prime Minister is the head of the Government and the head of the Council of Ministers.
- Jawaharlal Nehru was the first Prime Minister and the longest serving so far.

Union Legislature

- The Legislature of the Union, which is called 'Parliament' Consists of the President and the two Houses of Parliament known as the Council of states (Rajya Sabha) and the House of the People (Lok Sabha).

Rajya Sabha

- The Rajya Sabha is the Upper House of the Parliament and it is constituted of representatives from the States or the Constituent units of the Indian Union.
- It is a permanent body, one third of its members retiring after every two years. Members sit for staggered terms lasting 6 years.
- Its maximum strength is 250. Out of these, twelve members are nominated by the President from well-known personalities in the realm of Science, Art, Literature and Social Service. Rest of 238 representatives of the States and Union Territories are elected.
- Currently, the strength of the Rajya Sabha is 245.

Lok Sabha

- The Lok Sabha whose life is five years, is the Lower House of Parliament and comprises of members directly elected by the people.
- The House of the people (Lok Sabha) at present consists of 543 members directly elected from the states and Union Territories.
- The House of the People shall continue for five years (unless sooner dissolved) from the date of its meeting and no longer and the expiry of the said period of 5 years shall operate as dissolution of the House.

Parliamentary Committees

- There are several Parliamentary Committees to assist the Parliament in its deliberations.
- These are appointed or elected by the respective Houses of Lok Sabha and Rajya Sabha on a motion made or are nominated by their presiding officers.
- Among the Standing Committees, three are financial Committees: (*i*) Public Account Committee; (*ii*) Estimate Committee; (*iii*) Public undertaking Committee.

Speaker of Lok Sabha

- Speaker is elected by the Lok Sabha from among its members.
- The Speaker will have the final power to maintain order within the House of the People and to interpret its rules of procedure.
- A Deputy-Speaker is also elected to officiate in absence of the Speaker.
- *G.V. Mavlankar* was the first Speaker of the Lok Sabha (1952-1956).

Supreme Court

- The Constitution provides for the Supreme Court, which consists of a Chief Justice and other 33 judges. They are appointed by the President of India.

Qualification and Tenure

- Eligibility conditions for a judge of the Supreme Court are that he must be : (i) a citizen of India; (ii) a judge of a high court for a minimum period of 5 years; or (iii) an advocate of a high court for at least ten years or a distinguished jurist.
- Judges hold office till the age of 65.
- They can resign earlier or can be removed by the President on the recommendation of the two Houses of the Parliament by 2/3rd majority of the members present and voting.

Powers

- *Original jurisdiction:* Cases involving Government of India and the states or cases involving the enforcement of Fundamental Rights fall under original jurisdiction.
- *Appellate Jurisdiction:* In cases which are brought to it in the form of appeals against the judgement of the lower courts—It hears appeals in civil and criminal cases.
- *Advisory functions:* The Supreme Court advises the President on the constitutionality of a particular legal matter. However, its advice is not binding on the President.

Other Powers:

1. it is a court of record and can punish for contempt of itself;
2. it can make rules for regulating the practice and procedure of courts with the approval of the President; and
3. it can recommend to the President the removal of chairman and members of the UPSC. Supreme Court enjoys the power of judicial review (right of the court which declares as unconstitutional, the laws passed by the legislature and orders issued by executive) though it is not specifically mentioned in the Constitution.

- The first Chief Justice of India was H.J. Kania (1950-51).

Comptroller and Auditor General (CAG) (Article 148-151)

- The Comptroller and Auditor General of India is guardian of the public purse.
- It is his duty to see that not a *paisa* is spent out of consolidated fund of India or of a state without the authority of the appropriate legislature.
- He is appointed by President of India.
- A person with long administrative experience and knowledge of accounts is appointed.
- Holds office for 6 yrs or till 65 yrs of age.
- The President can remove him only on the recommendation of the both houses of Parliament (as in case of judge of Supreme Court).

- The CAG submits its reports to the President (in case of accounts relating to the Union Government) or to the State Governors (for State Government Accounts).
- The first CAG of India was *V. Narahari Rao* (1948-1954).
- The CAG is not eligible for further office under the Union or State Governments. The expenses of the office of the CAG is charged to the Consolidated Fund of India.

Attorney General of India

- The Attorney General of India is the first law officer of the Government of India.
- Though he is not a member of cabinet he has the right to speak in the House of Parliament, but he has no right to vote.
- The Attorney General of India shall be appointed by the President and shall hold office during his pleasure.
- His duty shall be to give advice on such legal matter from time-to-time as may be referred to him by the President.
- To be appointed as Attorney General, a candidate must be qualified to be appointed as a Judge of the Supreme Court.
- The Attorney General can participate in proceedings of the Parliament without the Right to Vote (Article 88).
- The first Attorney General of Independent India was MC Setalvad (1950-1963).

Part - VI

The States (Article 152 - 237)

The Governor

- The Governor is appointed by the President and holds office during the pleasure of the President.
- Apart from the power to appoint the council of ministers, if the governor finds that the government of state cannot be carried on in accordance with the provisions of the constitution (Art. 356), he may send his report to the President who may assume to himself the functions of the government of the state. (This is popularly known as 'President's Rule').
- Article 161 gives the Governor the power to grant pardons, reprieves, remission of punishment to persons convicted under the state law.
- Article 171 states that the States where Legislative Councils exists, the Governor can nominate some members from amongst those distinguished in literature, science, arts, cooperative movement and social service.

States Legislature (Article 168 - 212)

- The state legislature consists of Governor and legislative assembly.
- In some state like *Bihar, Maharashtra, Andhra Pradesh, Karnataka, Uttar Pradesh* and *Telangana* have a legislative council.
- The membership of the council should not be more than *one-third* of the legislative assembly but not less than 40.
- The legislative assembly of each state shall be composed of members chosen by direct election on the basis of adult suffrage and the number of members shall not be more than 500 or less than 60.
- The assembly of Sikkim, Goa, Puducherry and Mizoram have less than 60 members.

High Courts (Article 214 - 232)

- The High Court stands at the apex of the State Judiciary.
- As per the Constitution, there shall be a High Court in each State. But there may be a common High Court for two or more States and Union Territory, if it is provided by a law of the Parliament. For example, the Chennai High Court has its Jurisdiction over the State of Tamil Nadu and the Union Territory of Puducherry.
- The State Government has no control over it.
- There are 25 High Courts in India.
- The Calcutta High Court, established in 1862, is the oldest High Court in India.

Jurisdiction and Seat of High Courts

Name	Year	Territorial Jurisdiction	Seat
Allahabad	1866	Uttar Pradesh	Prayagraj (Bench at Lucknow)
Andhra Pradesh	2019	Andhra Pradesh	Amravati
Bombay	1862	Maharashtra, Goa, Dadar and Nagar Haveli and Daman and Diu	Mumbai (Benches at Nagpur, Panaji and Aurangabad)
Calcutta	1862	West Bengal and Andaman & Nicobar	Kolkata (Circuit Bench at Port Blair)
Chhattisgarh	2000	Chhattisgarh	Bilaspur
Delhi	1966	Delhi	Delhi
Guwahati	1948	Assam, Nagaland, Mizoram and Arunachal Pradesh	Guwahati (Benches at Kohima, Aizawl and Itanagar)

Name	Year	Territorial Jurisdiction	Seat
Gujarat	1960	Gujarat	Ahmedabad
Himachal Pradesh	1971	Himachal Pradesh	Shimla
Jammu & Kashmir and Ladakh	1928	Jammu & Kashmir, Ladakh	Srinagar and Jammu
Jharkhand	2000	Jharkhand	Ranchi
Karnataka	1884	Karnataka	Bengaluru (Circuit Benches at Dharwar and Gulbarga)
Kerala	1958	Kerala & Lakshadweep	Ernakulam
Madhya Pradesh	1956	Madhya Pradesh	Jabalpur (Benches at Gwalior and Indore)
Madras	1862	Tamil Nadu & Puducherry	Chennai (Bench at Madurai)
Orissa	1948	Odisha	Cuttack
Patna	1916	Bihar	Patna
Punjab and Haryana	1966	Punjab, Haryana and Chandigarh	Chandigarh
Rajasthan	1949	Rajasthan	Jodhpur (Bench at Jaipur)
Sikkim	1975	Sikkim	Gangtok
Uttarakhand	2000	Uttarakhand	Nainital
Tripura	2013	Tripura	Agartala
Meghalaya	2013	Meghalaya	Shillong
Manipur	2013	Manipur	Imphal
Telangana	2019	Telangana	Hyderabad

The Panchayats (Article 243-243 O)

- Panchayati Raj was introduced in India with a view to associated the people with administration at grass-root level.
- It is a three-tier system as recommended by Balwant Rai Mehta Committee.
- Introduced by the 73rd Amendment Act, 1992 which envisaged a three tier system of local governance.

  These are:

  1. Gram Panchayat at the village level
  2. Panchayat Samiti at the block level
  3. Zila Parishad at the district level.

The Municipalities (Article 243 P-243 ZG)

- Big cities have municipal corporations headed by the elected Mayor.
- For small towns there are elected boards or councils, in turn, elect their Presidents.
- Introduced by the 74th Amendment Act, 1993 which envisages three types of urban local bodies, namely, municipality (nagar palika), city council (nagar panchayat).
- Municipal governance in India was first introduced in Madras in 1688.

Part - XIII

(Article 301 - 307)

- In this part from Article 301-307 trade, commerce and intercourse within the territory of India are given.

Part - XIV

(Article 308 - 323)

- In this part services under the union and the states are given.
- ***Article 312:** All India Services* and ***Article 315:*** Public Service Commissions for the Union and for the States.
- The first Public Service Commission was set up in 1926, on the recommendations of the Lee Commission.

Union Public Service Commission (UPSC)

- This Commission is responsible for:
  1. recruitment to all civil services and posts, under the Union Government by written examinations, interviews and promotions, and
  2. advising the Government on all matters relating to methods of recruitment, principles to be followed in making promotions and transfers. Its Chairman is appointed by the President.

Staff Selection Commission (SSC)

- The Union Government has constituted a Staff Selection Commission for recruitment to non-technical Class III posts in the central government and in subordinate offices.
- The Administrative Reforms Commission had recommended the setting up of such a Commission.
- The Commission has also been entrusted with the responsibility of making recruitment to Group 'B' services like Assistants' and Stenographers Grade 'C'.
- The Commission has a chairman and two members.

Elections (Article 324-329)

- The Constitution provides for an independent election commission to ensure free and fair election to the Parliament, the State legislature and the offices of President and Vice-President.
- Consists of Chief Election Commissioner +2 Election Commissioners. They all enjoy equal powers.
- The Chief Election Commissioner and other Election Commissioners are appointed by the President.
- Election Commissioners are appointed for a term of 6 years, or up to the age of 65 years, whichever is earlier.
- They are not eligible for re-appointment. Also, they cannot hold any office of profit after their retirement.
- The Election Commission was established on 25th January, 1950 under Article 324 of the Constitution. The first Chief Election Commissioner was *Sukumar Sen*.

Functions

- Preparation of electoral rolls and keeping voters list updated.
- Recognition of various political parties and allotment of election symbols.

NITI Aayog

- The NITI Aayog replaced Planning Commission on January 1, 2015 is an advisory body engaged in the task of meaningful national planning.
- It is neither constitutional nor statutory.
- The Prime Minister is the Chairman of the Aayog.

Functions

- The functions of the NITI Aayog are:
  1. The Aayog will recommend a national agenda, including strategic and technical advice on elements of policy and economic matters.
  2. It will also develop mechanisms for village level plans and aggregate these progressively at higher levels of government.
  3. The Aayog will work towards fostering co-operative federalism for providing a national agenda to the Centre and States.

National Development Council

- The National Development Council, set-up in 1952, consists of representatives of the Central Government as well as the State governments.
- It is the supreme body insofar as planning is concerned and it determines policies, issues guidelines, reviews working of the plan and finally approves the plan.
- The Council consists of the Prime Minister (Chairman), all Union Cabinet Ministers, Chief Ministers of all States and Union Territories and the Vice-Chairman and members of the NITI Aayog.
- For matters relating to Plans and planning, the Union Minister of Planning is responsible to the Parliament.

Finance commission

- The constitution of the Finance Commission is laid down in Art. 280. The chairman must be a person having experience in public affairs; and the other four members also having wide experience in financial matters.
- It consists of Chairman and 4 other members.
- It shall be the duty of the Finance Commission to advice the President on matters such as the distribution between the Union and states of the net proceeds of taxes that is required to be shared. The Finance Commission is not a permanent body. It is dissolved after it has submitted its recommendations.

☞ *Important Amendments to the Constitution*

- **First Amendment, 1951:** Added Ninth Schedule.
- **Twenty-second Amendment, 1969:** Formation of Meghalaya within the state of Assam was facilitated.
- **Twenty-sixth Amendment, 1971:** The privy and privileges of the former rulers of Indian States were abolished.
- **Thirty-first Amendment, 1973:** The upper limit of representation of states was raised from 500 to 525. The upper limit for representation of the UTs was reduced from 25 to 20.
- **Thirty-sixth Amendment, 1975:** Sikkim was made a full-fledged state of Indian Union and it was included in the First Schedule.
- **Thirty-eight Amendment, 1975:** This act led to the amendment of Article 123, Article 213 and Article 352 which stated that the satisfaction of President or of Governor contained in these Articles would be called in question in any court of law.
- **Forty-second Amendment, 1976:** This amendment was done in accordance with the recommendations of Swaran Singh Committee and included a number of amendments.
- **Forty-third Amendment, 1977:** It provided for the restoration of the Jurisdiction of the Supreme Court and High Courts, curtailed by the enactment of the Constitution (Forty-Second Amendment) Act, 1976.
- **Forty-fourth Amendment, 1978:** The right to property was deleted as Fundamental Right and was made a legal right.
- **Fifty-third Amendment, 1986:** The Act grants statehood to the Union Territory of Mizoram, thus making it the 23rd State of the Indian Unions.
- **Fifty-sixth Amendment, 1987:** The UT of Goa Converted into Goa state through this amendment whereas Daman and Diu were organised under a new UT.

- **Seventy-third Amendment, 1992:** It is concerning Panchayati Raj.
- **Seventy-fourth Amendment, 1992:** It is regarding Municipal Boards and Corporations.
- **Ninety-first Amendment, 2003:** It is regarding restricting the total number of Ministers including Prime Minister/Chief Minister in Lok Sabha and State Legislatures to 15% of the total number of the Union or State Legislatures.
- **One-Hundredth Amendment, 2015:** Amended the first schedule for the purpose of exchange of enclaves, in pursuance of the Agreement between India and Bangladesh.
- **One Hundred and First Amendment, 2016:** The act amends the constitution to introduce "The Goods and Services Tax (GST)". The act also provided for compensation to States for loss of revenue on account of introduction of goods and services tax.
- **One Hundred and Second Amendment, 2018:** This act provides constitutional status to the National Commission for Backward Classes (NCBC). It has the authority to examine complaints and welfare measures regarding socially and educationally backward classes.
- **The Constitution (One hundred and third Amendment) Act, 2019:** Provides 10 per cent reservation to Economically Weaker Sections of General Community.
- **The Constitution (One hundred and Fourth Amendment) Act, 2019:** This Act ceased the reservation of seats for Anglo-Indians in the Lok Sabha and State Legislative assemblies and extended reservations for SCs and STs for up to ten years.
- **The Constitution (One hundred and Fifth Amendment) Act, 2021:** This Act restores the power of State Governments to identify and specify Socially and Economically Backward Classes (SEBCs).

NATIONAL SYMBOLS

State Emblem

- State Emblem of India is an adaptation from the Sarnath Lion Capital of Ashoka. It was adopted by the Government of India on January 26, 1950. In the adapted form, only three lions are visible, the fourth being hidden from the view.
- The wheel (Dharma Chakra) appears in relief in the centre of the abacus with a bull on the right and a horse on the left.
- The bell-shaped lotus has been omitted. The words "Satyameva Jayate" meaning "Truth alone triumphs" are inscribed below the Emblem in Devanagari script.

National Flag

- The National Flag of India is a horizontal tricolour of deep saffron (Kesari), white and dark green in equal proportion.
- In the centre of the white band there is a wheel in navy blue colour. It has 24 spokes.
- The ratio of the length and the breadth of the flag is 3 : 2. Its design was adopted by the Constituent Assembly of India on July 22, 1947.

National Anthem

- Rabindranath Tagore's song 'Jana-gana-mana' was adopted by the Constituent Assembly as the National Anthem of India on January 24, 1950.

Jana-gan-mana-adhinayaka jaya he,
Bharata-bhagya-vidhata
Punjab-Sindh-Gujarat-Maratha-
Dravida-Utkala-Banga
Vindhya-Himachala-Yamuna-Ganga
Uchhala-jaladhi-taranga.
Tava subha name jage, Tava subha asisa mange, Gahe tava jaya gatha,
Jana-gana-mangala-dayak, jaya he
Bharata bhagya vidhata,
Jaya he, jaya he, jaya he,
Jaya jaya jaya, jaya he.

National Song

- Bankim Chandra Chatterji's 'Vande Mataram' which was a source of inspiration to the people in their struggle for freedom, has been adopted as National Song. It has an equal status with the National Anthem.

Vande Mataram
Sujalam, suphalam, malayaja-shitalam,
Shasya shyamalam, Mataram
Shubhrajyotsna, pulkita yaminim,
Phulla kusumita drumadalashobhinim,
Subhasinim sumadhura—bhashinim,
Sukhadam, Varadam, Mataram.

- **National Bird and Animal of India:** Peacock and Tiger.
- **National Aquatic Animal:** Dolphin.
- **National Flower:** Lotus.
- **National Calendar:** It was adopted on March 22, 1957. It has 365 days in the year and the first month of the year is Chaitra.

Months of the National Calendar

1. Chaitra,	5. Shravan,	9. Marga-Shirsha,
2. Vaishakha,	6. Bhadra,	10. Pausha,
3. Jaishtha,	7. Ashvina,	11. Magha,
4. Ashadha,	8. Kartika,	12. Phalguna.

ECONOMY

NATIONAL INCOME

- National income is a flow concept not a stock concept.
- In India, National income estimates are related with the financial year (April 1 to 31st March).
  1. **GNP (Gross National Product):** GNP refers to the money value of total output or production of final goods and services produced by the nationals of a country during a given period of time, generally a year.
  2. **NNP (Net National Product):** NNP is obtained by subtracting depreciation value from GNP. NNP can be calculated in two ways: (a) at market prices of goods and services and (b) at factor cost.
  3. **National Income:** When NNP is obtained at factor cost, it is known as National Income. National Income is calculated by subtracting net indirect taxes from NNP at market prices. The obtained value is known as NNP at factor cost or National income.
  4. **Personal Income:** Personal income is that income which is actually obtained by nationals. Personal income is obtained by subtracting corporate taxes and payments made for social securities provisions from national income and adding to it government transfer payments, business transfer payments and net interest paid by the government.
- For measuring national income in India, in 1868, the first attempt was made by *Dada Bhai Nauroji.* He, in his book, "*Poverty and Un-British Rule in India*", estimated Indian per capita annual income at a level of ₹ 20.
- After independence, the Government of India appointed the National Income Committee in August, 1949, under the Chairmanship of Prof. P.C. Mahalanobies, to compile authoritative estimates of national income.
- National income includes the contribution of three sectors—Primary sector, Secondary sector, Tertiary sector.
- Under Primary Sector—Agriculture, Forest, Fisheries and allied sector are included.
- Under Secondary Sector—Manufacturing, Construction, Electricity, Gas and Water Supply are included.
- Under Teritiary Sector—Trade, Transport, Communication, Banking, Insurance, Real Estate, Community and Personal Services are included.
- At present estimation of national income is based on the base year of 2011-12.

POVERTY

- Poverty can be defined as a social phenomenon in which a section of society is unable to fulfil even the basic necessities of life.
- In India, the generally accepted definition of poverty emphasises minimum level of living rather than a reasonable level of living.
- An expert group of planning commission, defined poverty line on a nutritional norm of per capita daily intake of 2400 calories in rural areas and 2100 calories for urban areas. A person who fails to obtain this minimum level of calories is treated as being below the poverty line.
- There are two types of common standards in economic literature for the measurement of poverty:
  1. ***Absolute Poverty:*** In the absolute standard, minimum physical quantities of cereals, pulses, milk, butter, etc. are determined for a subsistence level and then the price quotations converted into monetary terms the physical quantities.
  2. ***Relative Standard:*** According to the relative standard, income distribution of the population in different fractile groups is estimated and a comparison of the levels of living of the top 5 to 10 per cent with the bottom 5 to 10 per cent of the population reflects the relative standards of poverty.
- As per the Tendulkar Committee Report, the national poverty line at 2004-05 prices was a monthly per capita consumption expenditure of ₹ 446.68 in rural and ₹ 578.80 in urban areas in 2004-05.

Poverty Ratios (Per cent)

	Earlier estimates (URP) based on the Lakdawala methodology		**Estimates (MRP) based on the Tendulkar methodology**	
	1993-1994	**2004-2005**	**1993-1994**	**2004-2005**
Rural	37.3	28.3	50.1	41.8
Urban	32.4	25.7	31.8	25.7
Total	36.0	27.5	45.3	37.2

Various Employment Generations Programmes

Programme	Year of beginning
Community Development Programme (CDP)	1952
Intensive Agriculture Development Programme (IADP)	1960-61
Command Area Development Programme (CADP)	1974-75
Training Rural Youth for Self-Employment (TRYSEM)	Aug. 15, 1979
Integrated Rural Development Programme (IRDP)	Oct. 2, 1980
National Rural Employment Programme (NREP)	1980
Development of Women and Children in Rural Areas (DWCRA)	Sept. 1982
Rural Landless Employment Guarantee Programme (RLEGP)	Aug. 15, 1983
Self-Employment to the Educated Unemployed Youth (SEEUY)	1983-84
National Fund for Rural Development (NFRD)	February 1984
Council for Advancement of People's Action and Rural Technology (CAPART)	Sept. 1, 1986
Self-Employment Programme for the Urban Poor (SEPUP)	Sept. 1986
Jawahar Rozgar Yojana	April 1989
Nehru Rozgar Yojana	Oct. 1989
Scheme of Urban Wage Employment (SUWE)	1990
Employment Assurance Scheme (EAS)	Oct. 2, 1993
Prime Minister's Integrated Urban Poverty Eradication Programme (PMIUPEP)	Nov. 18, 1995
Swarna Jayanti Shahari Rozgar Yojana (SJSRY)	Dec. 1997
Swarna Jayanti Gram Swarozgar Yojana	April 1999
Mahatma Gandhi National Rural Employment Guarantee Act (MNREGA)	Feb. 2, 2006
Pradhan Mantri Kaushal Vikas Yojna	April, 2015
Standup India	April 5, 2016
Garib Kalyan Rojgar Abhiyan	June 20, 2020

AGRICULTURE

- Agriculture is an important sector of the economy. Though the share of agriculture in national income has come down since the inception of planning era in the economy but still it has substantial share in GDP.
- Agriculture Contributes about 15 per cent of gross domestic product.
- Agriculture accounted for about 52 per cent employment in the country.
- Agriculture provides raw materials to various industries and other agro-based industries. Cotton and Jute textile industries, Sugar, Vanaspati industry etc. are directly dependent on agriculture.
- India's foreign trade is deeply associated with Agriculture Sector.
- The share of agriculture and allied sectors in GVA of the country has declined from 20.2 per cent in 2020-21 to 18.8 per cent in 2021-22.

Land Reform Programmes

- Land reform programme in India include:

1. Elimination of intermediaries.
2. Tenancy Reform.
3. Determination of ceiling of holding per family and to distribute surplus land among landless people.
4. Consolidation of holdings.

Irrigation

- The planning commission has introduced a new classification of irrigation schemes:
  1. ***Major Irrigation Schemes***—Those with culturable command areas (CCA) more than 10,000 hectares.
  2. ***Medium Irrigation Schemes***—Those with culturable command areas (CCA) between 2,000 to 10,000 hectares.
  3. ***Minor Irrigation Scheme***—Those with culturable command area (CCA) upto 2,000 hectares.
- ***Micro Irrigation:*** A centrally sponsored scheme on Micro Irrigation (MI) was launched in Tenth Plan for promoting water use efficiency by adopting drip and sprinkler irrigation.
- ***Minimum Support Prices (MSP):*** Keeping in view the interests of the farmers as also the need of self reliance, Govt. has been announcing minimum support price. The main objectives of announcing MSP are:

1. To prevent fall in price in the situation of over production.
2. To protect the interest of farmers by ensuring them a minimum price for their crops in the situation of a price fall in the market.

- ***Procurement Prices:*** The price at which government buys surplus from the farming coming in the market. The minimum support price and the procurement price may be the same.
- ***Issue Prices:*** The prices at which fair price shops sell cereals like wheat rice etc.

Agricultural Policy (2000)

- Union Government has announced new Agricultural Policy in the parliament on July 28, 2000. This policy has been planned under the provisions of WTO so as to face the challenges of agriculture sector. This policy gives emphasis on promoting agricultural exports after fulfilling domestic demand.
- The salient features of this policy are:
  - To achieve 4% growth rate per annum for the next two decades.
  - To do Land reforms to provide land to poor farmers.
  - Consolidation of holding in all states of the nation.
  - Promoting private investment in agriculture.
  - To provide insurance umbrella for crops to farmers.
  - To promote biotechnology.
  - Promoting research for developing new varieties and ensuring protection to the developed varieties.
- New Agriculture policy has been described as 'Rainbow Revolution' which includes the following revolutions:

1. Green	–	Food Grain Production
2. White	–	Milk
3. Yellow	–	Oil Seeds
4. Blue	–	Fisheries
5. Red	–	Meat/Tomato
6. Golden	–	Fruits-Apple
7. Grey	–	Fertiliser
8. Black/Brown	–	Non-conventional Energy Sources
9. Silver	–	Eggs
10. Round	–	Potato

Agricultural Credit

- Agricultural credit is disbursed through a Multi Agency network comprising of Commercial Banks (CBs), Regional Rural Bank (RRBs) and Cooperative with their vast network covering almost all the villages in the country and outreach extending to the remotest part of the country.
- Kisan Credit Card (KCC) scheme was introduced in August, 1998 with major share of crop loans being routed through it. Banks were advised that the credit card should normally be valid for 3 years subject to an annual review.

INDUSTRY

- After independence, the first industrial policy was declared on April 6, 1948 by then Union Industry Minister Mr. Shyama Prasad Mukherjee.
- Under this first industrial policy established a base for Mixed and Controlled Economy in India and clearly divided the industrial sector into private and public sectors.
- Second Industrial Policy Resolution declared on April 30, 1956 with the basic objective of establishing 'Socialistic Pattern of Society' in the country.
- In line with the liberalisation measures announced during the 1980s, the government announced a New Industrial Policy on July 24, 1991. This new policy de-regulates the industrial economy in a substantial manner. The major objectives of the new policy are "to build on the gains already made, correct the distortions or weaknesses that might have crept in, maintain a sustained growth in productivity and gainful employment, and attain international competitiveness."
- During the second five year plan (1956-61) a major task in industry was building up of three steel plants in the public sector—Rourkela Steel Plant in Odisha (then Orissa), Bhilai Steel Plant in Chhattisgarh (then Madhya Pradesh) and Durgapur Steel Plant in West Bengal. The three steel plants came into operation in stage between 1959 and 1962.
- Bokaro steel plant was established in third five year plan.
- In 1973, the Steel Authority of India Limited (SAIL) was created and was made responsible for the development of steel industry.
- Globally, India is the largest producer and second largest exporter of jute goods. There are 78 jute mills in the country of which 61 are in West Bengal, 3 each in Bihar and Uttar Pradesh, 7 in Andhra Pradesh and one each in Assam, Odisha, Tripura and Chhattisgarh.
- Sugar industry occupies an important place among agriculture based industries. This industry took a shape of a large industry in the beginning of 20th century. Sugar industry in the second largest industry after cotton textile industry among agriculture based industries of the country.
- India is the second largest producer of cement in the world after China. The cement industry was delicensed in 1991.
- The small and medium sector has been defined as micro, small and medium enterprises with effect from October 2, 2006 (the Act defined the medium enterprises for the first time). Further, separate investment limits have been prescribed for manufacturing and service enterprises. The new definition is as follows:

A. Manufacturing Enterprises

(a) A micro enterprise, where the investment in plant and machinery does not exceed ₹ 50 lakh;

(b) A small enterprise, where the investment in plant and machinery is more than ₹ 50 lakh but does not exceed ₹ 10 crore; and

(c) A medium enterprise, where the investment in plant and machinery is more than ₹ 10 crore but does not exceed ₹ 30 crore.

B. Service Enterprises

(a) A micro enterprise, where the investment in equipment does not exceed ₹ 10 lakh;

(b) A small enterprise, where the investment in equipment is more than ₹ 10 lakh but does not exceed ₹ 5 crore; and

(c) A medium enterprise, where the investment in equipment is more than ₹ 5 crore but does not exceed ₹ 15 crore.

- In India, the MSMEs (Micro, Small and Medium Enterprises) play a pivot role in the overall industrial economy of the country. MSMEs contribute about 8 per cent of the GDP of the country, about 45 per cent of manufactured output and about 40 per cent of exports.
- As of January 2021, there are 10 Maharatnas and 14 Navratna Companies in India.

  Maharatnas Status Company are BHEL; BPCL; CIL; GAIL (India) Limited; HPCL; IOC; NTPC Limited; ONGC; PGCIL; SAIL.
- **Navratna status Companies are** Bharat Electronics Limited (BEL); Container Corporation of India Limited (CCIL); Engineers India Limited (EIL); Hindustan Aeronautics Limited (HAL); Mahanagar Telephone Nigam Limited (MTNL); National Aluminium Company Limited (NACL); NBCC (India) Limited; NMDC Limited; NLC India Limited; Oil India Limited (OIL); Power Finance Corporation Limited (PFCL); Rashtriya Ispat Nigam Limited (RINL); Rural Electrification Corporation Limited (RECL); Shipping Corporation of India Limited (SCIL).
- Small Industries Development Bank of India (SIDBI) was set up in 1989. It is a Separate Apex Bank, to provide financial assistance to the small-scale industries.

LABOUR

Trade Union

- Trade unions are voluntary organisations of workers formed to protect the interest of workers through collective action.
- In India, the first trade union was formed in 1918.
- There are number of trade unions in India, which are associated with main political parties. Some important trade unions are as follows:
  1. Bharatiya Mazdoor Sangh (BMS), associated with the Bharatiya Janta Party.
  2. Indian National Trade Union Congress (INTUC), associated with the Congress Party.
  3. All-India Trade Union Congress (AITUC), associated with the Communist Party of India.
  4. Centre of Indian Trade Unions (CITU), associated with the CPI (M).

ECONOMIC PLANNING

Five Year Plans in India

Plans	Period	Investment (₹ Crore)	Objectives
First Plan	April 1, 1951-March 31, 1956	1,960	Priority to agriculture, electricity and irrigation.
Second Plan	April 1, 1956—March 31, 1961	4,672	Development of basic and heavy industries.
Third Plan	April 1, 1961—March 31, 1966	8,577	Long term development of India's economy.
Annual Plan	April 1, 1966—March 31, 1967	2,137	
Annual Plan	April 1, 1967—March 31, 1968	2,205	
Annual Plan	April 1, 1968—March 31, 1969	2,283	
Fourth Plan	April 1, 1969—March 31, 1974	15,779	Enlarge the income of rural population and supply of goods of mass consumption.
Fifth Plan	April 1, 1974—March 31, 1979	39,426	Attain increased self-reliance and employment avenues.
Annual Plan	April 1, 1979—March 31, 1980	12,176	
Sixth Plan	April 1, 1980—March 31, 1985	1,09,292	Removal of unemployment
Seventh Plan	April 1, 1985--March 31, 1990	2,18,730	Food work and productivity were the basic priorities.
Eighth Plan	April, 1992—March 31, 1997	4,95,670	Raising employment
Ninth Plan	April 1, 1997—March 31, 2002	9,41,041	Agriculture and rural development
Tenth Plan	April 1, 2002—March 31, 2007	14,91,610	Growth rate 7.8 percent per annum.
Eleventh Plan	April 1, 2007—March 31, 2012	36,44,718	Literacy, Employment, Rural development & Transport development.
Twelfth Plan	April 1, 2012–March 31, 2017	43,30,000	Longterm development of India's economy.

15-Year Vision Plan

- With the end of the Twelfth Plan in March 2017 the era of five year plans came to an end. NITI Aayog has come forward with a draft 15-year vision plan to catapult the country's economy to more than three times as compared to the present day. The new plan is set to replace the centralised five-year plans the country has been following for decades. The new plan is accompanied by shorter sub-plans—a seven-year strategy for 2017-24, and a three-year 'Action Agenda' from 2017-18 to 2019-20.

MONEY AND BANKING

RBI

- Reserve Bank of India (RBI) is the central bank of the country.
- Reserve Bank of India was established on April 1, 1935 under Reserve Bank of India Act, 1934 with a authorised capital of ₹ 5 crore.
- The Reserve Bank of India was nationalised on January 1, 1949.
- The general administration and direction of RBI is managed by a Central Board of Directors consisting of 20 members which includes 1 Governor and 4 Deputy Governors.
- The head office of the Reserve Bank of India is in Mumbai.
- Functions of Reserve Bank of India:
  - Issue of Notes.
  - Bankers to the Government.
  - Banker's Bank.
  - Controller of Credit.
  - Custodian of Foreign Reserves.
  - Other Functions (function of clearing house arranging credit for agriculture, collecting and publishing the economic data, buying and selling of government securities and trade bills etc.)

Foundation Years of Main Indian Banks

Reserve Bank of India	1935
Nationalisation of RBI	1949
State Bank of India	1955
Nationalisation of 14 Commercial Banks	1969
Nationalisation of 6 other Banks	1980
Regional Rural Bank	1975
Merger of New Bank of India with Punjab National Bank	1993
Transformation of IDBI Ltd. as a Scheduled Bank	2004

- **Bank Rate:** Bank Rate is the rate of discount at which the central bank of the country discounts first class bills. It is the rate of interest at which the central bank lends money to the lower banking institutions.
- **Cash Reserve Ratio (CRR):** Commercial banks are required to keep a certain amount of cash reserves at the central bank. This percentage amount is called CRR.
- **Prime Lending Rate (PLR):** Prime Lending Rate (PLR) is that rate of interest at which bank gives loan to its most reliable customer.
- **Repo Rate:** Repo (Repurchase option) rate is a instrument under the Liquidity Adjustment Facility (LAF) at which RBI lends to commercial banks. In case of inflationary tendencies RBI perceived need to inject liquidity into the system, RBI can reduce the Repo rate which will lead to release of money into the market.
- **Reverse Repo Rate:** Reverse Repo Rate is the rate at which RBI borrows from commercial banks. In case of inflationary tendencies, RBI can hike the Reverse Repo rate to absorb the excess liquidity in the market.
- **Statutory Liquidity Ratio (SLR):** Commercial banks are also required to keep (in addition to CRR) a certain percentage of their net demand and time liabilities (NDTL) as liquid assets in the shape of cash, gold or approved securities. As most of the SLR money is kept in treasury bills, government had, in the past, been using SLR as a means to mobilise low cost resources.

Establishment Years of Major Financial Institutions in India

❑ Imperial Bank of India	1921
❑ Reserve Bank of India (Nationalisation of RBI took place on January 1, 1949)	April 1, 1935
❑ Industrial Finance Corporation of India (IFCI)	1948
❑ State Bank of India (SBI)	July 1, 1955
❑ Unit Trust of India (UTI)	Feb. 1, 1964
❑ IDBI	July 1964
❑ NABARD	July 12, 1982
❑ IRBI (Now it has been renamed as IIBIL since March 6, 1997)	March 20, 1985
❑ SIDBI	1990
❑ EXIM Bank	January 1, 1982
❑ National Housing Bank (NHB)	July 1988

❑ Life Insurance Corporation (LIC)	September 1956
❑ General Insurance Corporation (GIC)	November 1972
❑ Regional Rural Banks (RRBs)	Oct. 2, 1975
❑ Risk Capital and Technology Finance Corporation Ltd.	March 1975
❑ Technology Development & Information Co. of India Ltd.	1989
❑ Infrastructure Leasing & Financial Services Ltd.	1988
❑ Housing Development Finance Corporation Ltd. (HDFC)	1977

Capital Market

Progress on developing India's capital market, which is already more competitive, deep and developed by international markets standards, continued. Business in the country's oldest stock exchange, namely the Bombay Stock Exchange (BSE) dating back to 1875, which is also one of the oldest stock exchanges in the world, continued to thrive. The National Stock Exchange (NSE), which emerged in the mid-1990s and catalysed improvements in trading systems to provide the necessary depth and choice to investors, made sustained progress. With the BSE and NSE emerging as the two apex institutions of the country's capital market, restructuring of other stock exchanges went apace. Overseen by Securities and Exchange Board of India (SEBI), an independent statutory regulatory authority, the country's capital market dealt in scrips of a large number of listed companies with a wide geographical outreach, providing a world class trading and settlement system, a wide range of product availability with a fast growing derivatives market, and well laid down corporate governance and investor protection measures.

Main Share Price Index in Famous Share Market of the World

BSE (Mumbai)	SENSEX
NSE (Mumbai)	S & P CNX Nifty
New York	DOW JONES
Tokyo	NIKKEI
Frankfurt (Germany)	MID DAX
Hong Kong	HANG SENG
Singapore	SIMEX STRAITS TIMES

PUBLIC FINANCE

- From July 1, 2017 India stepped towards one of the biggest Economic reforms and adopted Goods and Services Tax (GST).
- The Goods and Services Tax (GST) is the most ambitious indirect tax reform plan that seeks to remove severe distortions and flaws in the structure and administration of indirect taxes, both at the Central and the State levels.
- The GST seeks to replace all these Central and State taxes by a single uniform tax both at the Centre and in the States. Thus all local taxes will be subsumed in the GST that will have a uniform rate all across the country. Under the current taxes, only the Centre is empowered to impose service tax. Under the GST regime, the States will also have powers to collect taxes on services.
- Like all other countries, tendency of income tax is progressive in India.
- Estate Duty was first introduced in India in 1953. It was levied on total property passing on the death of a person.
- Service tax was introduced in 1994-95 in a small way to operationalise the principle of neutrality of the tax system to different forms of production and in recognition of the fact that value additions whether in manufacturing or service should form the basis of taxation.
- GST is the biggest tax reforms since Independence implemented on July 1, 2017.
- **Revenue Deficit** = Revenue Expenditure – Revenue Receipts
- **Budget Deficit** = Total Expenditure—Total Receipts
- **Fiscal Deficit** = Revenue receipts (Net tax revenue + Non-tax revenue) + Capital receipts (only recoveries of loans and other receipts)– Total expenditure (Plan and non-plan)
- **Primary Deficit:** The excess of fiscal deficit over payments of interest is called primary deficit.

Important Committees: At a Glance

Committees	Related Area
❖ Hanumant Rao Committee	*Fertilisers*
❖ Mahajan Committee	*Sugar Industry*
❖ R.V. Gupta Committee	*Agriculture Credit*
❖ Narsimham Committee (Second)	*Banking Reforms*
❖ CB Bhave Committee	*Company Information*
❖ S.L. Kapoor Committee	*Credit & Flow Problems of SSIs*
❖ Mashelkar Committee	*Auto Fuel Policy*
❖ Bhurelal Committee	*Increase in Motor Vehicle Tax*
❖ Abhijit Sen Committee	*Long Term Food Policy*
❖ Kelkar Committee	*Tax Structure Reforms*
❖ J.J. Irani Committee	*Company Law Reforms*
❖ Parekh Committee	*Infrastructure Financing*

CULTURE

- Culture is a way of life—the way an individual and especially a group live, think, feel and organize themselves, celebrate and share life.
- Culture thus refers to a human-made environment which includes all the material and non-material products of group life that are transmitted from one generation to the next.
- In deeper sense it is culture that produces the kind of literature, music, dance, sculpture, architecture and various other art forms as well as the many organizations and structures that make the functioning of the society smooth and well-ordered.
- Culture is the expression of our nature in our modes of living and thinking.

Characteristics of Indian Culture

- A synthesis of various cultures came about through the ages to give shape to what is recognized as Indian culture today.
- Spirituality and value based life style is the core of Indian culture but it has a scientific temperament too.
- Unity in diversity is one of the major characteristics of Indian culture which makes it unique.

Indian Architecture

Classification of Indian Architecture

- **Ancient India**
  - Harappa Art Mauryan Art
  - Post Mauryan Art
  - Gupta Age Art
  - South India Architecture
- **Medieval India**
  - Delhi Sultanate
  - Mughal Period
- **Modern India**
  - Indo-Gothic Style
  - Neo-Roman Style

INDUS VALLEY CIVILIZATION (2900 - 1700 BC)

- The arts of Indus Valley civilization, one of the earliest civilizations of the world, emerged during the second half of the third millennium (Bronze Age).
- The forms of art found from various sites of civilization include sculptures, seals, pottery, gold ornaments, terracotta figures, etc.
- Their delineation of human and animal figures was highly realistic in nature.
- Two major sites of Indus Valley civilization, along the river Indus are: North–cities of **Harappa**; South–**Mohenjo-Daro.**
- Houses, markets, storage facilities, offices, etc. arranged in a **grid-like pattern.**
- In this pattern, roads were cut across one another in 90-degree angle and the city was divided into blocks.
- There was also a highly developed drainage system.
- The arts of Indus valley which are excavated yet are:

Stone Statues

- Stone statues found in Indus valley sites are excellent examples of handling the 3D volume.
- Two major stone statues are:

Bearded Man (Priest Man, Priest-King)

- Found in Mohenjo-Daro.
- Bearded man's figure made of Steatite.
- The figure interpreted as a priest and is draped in a shawl coming under the right arm and covering the left shoulder.
- The eyes are elongated and half closed as in a meditative concentration.
- Short cut moustache and a short beard and whiskers.
- Hair is parted in the middle and a plain woven fillet is passed round the head.
- An armlet on the right hand and holes around neck suggest necklace.
- A slight touch of the Greek style of statues can be seen overall.

Male Torso

- Found in Harappa (only major art element found in Harappa).
- Made of **Red Sandstone.**
- There are socket holes in the neck and shoulders for the attachment of head and arms.
- The shoulders are well baked and the abdomen slightly prominent.

Bronze Casting

- Bronze casting was practiced in wide scale in almost all major sites of the civilization.
- The technique used for Bronze Casting was **Lost Wax Technique.**
- Human as well as animal figures are present in the Bronze casting.
- Amongst animal figures the buffalo with its uplifted head, back and sweeping horns and the goat are artistic merits.

Dancing Girl

- Found from Mohenjo-Daro.
- Made up of Bronze.
- One of the best-known artifacts from Indus valley.
- This exquisite casting depicts a girl whose long hair is tied in the bun and bangles cover her left arm.

Bull from Mohenjo-Daro

- Bronze figure of the bull found in Mohenjo-Daro.
- The massiveness of the bull and the fury of the charge are eloquently expressed.
- The animal is shown standing with his head turned to the right.

Terracotta

- Terracotta figures are more realistic in Gujarat sites and Kalibangan.
- A terracotta mask of a horned deity has also been found.
- Toy carts with wheels, whistles, rattles, bird and animals, gamesmen, and discs were also rendered in terracotta.
- The most important terracotta figures are those represent Mother Goddess.

Mother Goddess

- Mainly found in Mohenjo-Daro.
- These figures are usually crude standing figures.
- Adorned with necklaces hanging over the prominent breast and wearing a loin cloth and a grid.
- The fan-shaped headdress with a cup like projection on each side is a distinct decorative feature of the mother goddess.

Seals

- Thousands of seals were discovered from the sites, usually made of steatite, and occasionally of agate, chert, copper, faience and terracotta, with beautiful figures of animals such as unicorn bull, rhinoceros, tiger, elephant, bison, goat, buffalo, etc.
- The purpose was mainly commercial.
- They were also used as amulets, carried on the persons of their owners, perhaps as modern identity cards.
- Standard Harappan seal was 2 × 2 square inches.

Seals of Pashupati Mahadeva

- Found in Mohenjo-Daro.
- The seal depicts a human figure seated cross legged.
- An elephant and a tiger are depicted to the right side of the figure, while on the left a rhinoceros and a buffalo are seen.

Pottery

- Indus valley pottery consists of very fine wheel made wares, very few being handmade.
- Plain pottery is more common than painted ware.
- Plain pottery is generally red clay, with or without a fine red or grey slip.
- The black painted ware has a fine coating of red slip on which geometric and animal designs are executed in glossy black paint.

Painted Earthen Jar

- Found in Mohenjo-Daro.
- Made on a potters' wheel with clay.
- The shape was manipulated by pressure of the crafty fingers of the potter.
- After baking a clay model, it was painted with black colour.
- High polishing was done as a finishing touch.

Beads, Ornaments and Cosmetics

- The Harappan men and women decorated themselves with a large variety of ornaments produced from every conceivable materials ranging from precious metals and gemstones to bone and baked clay.
- White necklaces, fillets, armlets and finger rings were commonly worn by both sexes.
- Jewellery found at Mohenjo-Daro and Lothal include necklaces of gold and semiprecious metal stones, copper bracelets and beads, gold earrings and head ornaments.
- A cemetery has been found at Farmona in Harappa where dead bodies were buried with ornaments.
- Well developed bead industries were present at Chauhudaro and Lothal.
- Also made models of animals, especially monkeys and squirrels, used as pin head and beads.
- Spinning of cotton and wool was very common (both rich and poor practiced spinning).
- Men and women wore two separate pieces of attire similar to dhoti and shawl.
- Shawl covered the left shoulder passing below right arm.
- They were conscious of fashion.
- Different hair styles were in vogue and beard was popular.
- Cinnabar was used as a cosmetic and face-paint, lipstick and collyrium (eyeliner) were also known to them.

MAURYAN ART

- The Mauryas had established themselves as a great power in the 4th century BCE and by the 3rd century, they had large parts of India under their control.
- There were pillars, sculptures, rock-cut architecture, buildings like stupas, viharas and chaityas that served many purposes. They are exquisite in aesthetic quality and brilliant in their design and execution.

Pillars & Sculptures

- Erection of pillars was common in the Achamenian Empire (Persian Empire) also. While there were commonalities like the use of polished stones, motifs like lotus, there are also differences. While the Achamenian pillars were constructed in pieces, the Mauryan pillars were rock-cut, displaying the superior skill of the carver.

- Stone pillars can be seen all over the Mauryan Empire. These had proclamations inscribed on them and were used to spread the message of the Buddha by Emperor Ashoka.
- The top portion of the pillar is called capital and it typically has animal figures like bull, lion, elephant, etc. These capital figures are carved standing on a square or circular abacus. The abacuses are on the base which could be a stylised inverted lotus.
- Example of pillars with capital figures: Sarnath, Basarah-Bakhira, Rampurva, Sankisa and Lauriya-Nandangarh.
- The **Lion Capital** at Sarnath is the most famous example.
- Monumental figures of Yakshas and Yakshinis have been found in various parts of India thus showing the popularity of Yaksha worship.

Rock-cut architecture

- Ashoka also patronised rock-cut architecture.
- Rock-cut elephant at **Dhauli,** Odisha–shows modelling in round with linear rhythm. It also has an Ashokan edict.
- **Lomus Rishi Cave -** Rock-cut cave at **Barabar Hills** near Gaya. The cave entrance is decorated with a semicircle chaitya arch. An elephant is carved in high relief on the chaitya. The interior hall of the cave is rectangular; it also has a circular chamber at the back. Ashoka patronised this cave for the Ajivika sect.

Stupas, chaityas and viharas

- Stupas and viharas were constructed as part of the Buddhist and Jaina monastic tradition but most of the constructions belong to Buddhism.
- **Stupas** were constructed over the relics of the Buddha at Rajagriha, Kapilavastu, Vaishali, Ramagrama, Allakappa, Pava, Vethadipa, Pippalvina and Kushinagar.
- Stupas consist of a cylindrical drum with a circular **anda** and a **harmika** and a **chhatra** on the top. Sometimes there were circumambulatory pathways and gateways. In many cases, additions were added in later centuries.
  1. **Anda:** hemispherical mound symbolic of the mound of dirt used to cover Buddha's remains (in many stupas actual relics were used).
  2. **Harmika:** square railing on top of the mound.
  3. **Chhatra:** central pillar supporting a triple umbrella form.
- Stupa at Bairat, Rajasthan - 3rd century BCE; grand stupa with a circular mound and a circumambulatory path.
- Many stupas were built and not all of them with royal patronage. Patrons included lay devotees, gahapatis, guilds and kings.
- Stupa at Sanchi - most famous and one of the earliest examples.
- **Chaityas** were basically prayer halls and most of them were with stupas. Generally, the hall was rectangular and it had a semi-circular rear end. They had horse-shoe shaped windows. They also had pillars separating the hall from the two aisles.
- **Viharas** were the residences of the monks.
- Both chaityas and viharas were made out of wood, and later were also stone-cut.

Depiction of the Buddha

- In the early periods, Buddha is represented through symbols like footprints, lotus thrones, chakras, stupas, etc.
- Later on, stories were portrayed on the railings and torans of the stupas. These were mainly the Jataka tales.
- The chief events from Buddha's life which are narrated in the arts are birth, renunciation, enlightenment, first sermon (dharmachakra-pravartana) and mahaparinirvāna (death).
- The Jataka stories that find frequent depiction are Chhadanta Jataka, Sibi Jataka, Ruru Jataka, Vessantara Jataka, Vidur Jataka and Shama Jataka.

MAURYAN ART

Temples

- As the society was predominantly Buddhist, the construction of the temples were least done. However, we come across important temples of the period in Rajasthan, Madhya Pradesh and Andhra Pradesh. The *Sankarshan* temple at Nagari, *Apsita* temple at Nagarjunakonda and the Besnagar temple are worth mentioning.

Rock cut Architecture

- Caves with highly polished walls were carved out of hard rock. According to British historian V.A. Smith—"The art of polishing hard stone was carried out with such perfection that it is said to have become a lost art beyond modern powers. "Udayagiri caves are the most famous jain cave temples situated in the hills of Khandagiri and Udaygiri and built by Kharavela, the Jain ruler of Kalinga. Out of 17 caves, the four most important Udaygiri caves are *Rani Gumpha, Hathi Gumpha, Bag Gumpha* and *Machipuri Gumpha.* The most important and distinct features of the Kalinga rock cut architecture is the complete absence of *chaityas* or a shrine cell with a stupa in the centre. The other important caves of this period are located at Nasik, Ajanta, Karle, Kondana, Bhaja etc. in which *chaityas* formed an important feature along with the *viharas.*

Stupas

- Stupas are semicircular dome-like structure made of stone or bricks with a thick layer of plaster. Stupas were normally built to enshirine the sacred relics of the

Buddha or Bodhisattavas. The railings and gateway of Sanchi Stupa was later enlarged by Sunga rulers. Other important stupas of the period are Bodh Gaya, Taxila, Amravati, Nagarjunakonda etc.

Sculptural Art

- Mathura, Gandhara and Amaravati schools of art come under sculptural art.

Kushana (Mathura) School of Art

- The Kushana School is also referred to as the Mathura school. Artists at Mathura used a purely indigenous style. They used spotted red sandstone. For the first time, the Buddha was depicted in human form. The artists also made statues of Hindu and Jain deities. Though they dealt with other themes, life of the Buddha and Bodhisattava remained the main themes. The Mathura images of the Buddha are mainly in two postures; sitting and standing. The right hand is shown raised in *abhaya* posture. An important feature of Mathura Art is that also produced free-standing sculptures of Kings and other notables. It was here in the Kushana period that the brahmanical icon was born; and also the Jina image, creating its own style of the Buddha and Bodhisattava image. Jains produced distinctive cult objects in the form of the *Sarvatobhadrika* images (four standing Jinas back to back) and the *ayagapatas* or votive tablets, square slabs bearing relief sculptures on one side, possibly used as altars near a stupa for depositing offerings. A significant dimension of Mathura art is that it also produced free-standing sculptures of Kings.

Gandhara School of Art

- An important state in the growth of art is associated with Gandhara in the north-west
- It is also known as the Graeco-Buddhist School of Art, since Greek techniques of Art were applied to Buddhist subjects.
- The distinctive style which grew in the region of Gandhara is known as the Gandhara School of Art.
- The Gandhara Buddha is invariably shown making one of the four significant and unchaning hand gestures, known as *mudras,* one of the most characteristic features of Indian iconography. They are:
  1. ***abhaya*** (do not fear).
  2. ***dhyana*** where the Buddha is seated, one hand upon the other in his lap, palm upwards signifying meditation;
  3. ***dharmachakra,*** the preaching mudra associated with the Buddha's First Sermon in the Deer Park at Sarnath or with the great miracle at Sarvasti; and
  4. ***bhumispara*** or earth touching recalling the Buddha calling the Earth to witness his enlightenment at Bodh Gaya. Very rarely does he hold a begging bowl in his right hand.

Amravati School of Art

- Besides the Mathura and Gandhara schools, there was the Amaravati School of Buddhist art which flourished in western Andhra Pradesh under the patronages of Satavahana rulers. Its general features are:
  1. Use of white marble.
  2. Long legs and slender frames.
  3. Human beings as central characters and
  4. Prominence of kings, princes and palaces.
  5. Themes from Buddha's life and from *Jataka* stories.
  6. In the narrative scenes the superlative beauty of the individual bodies.
  7. Kings, prices and palaces figure prominently in sculptural representations. For example, the story of king Udayana and his queen is depicted on a relief.

GUPTA AGE ART & CULTURE

Literature

- Sanskrit literature flourished under the Guptas. Kalidasa, the great poet and playwright was in the court of Chandragupta Vikramaditya. He composed great epics such as Abhijnana-shaakuntalam, Kumarasambhavam, Mala-vikagnimitram, Ritusamharam, Meghadootam, Vikramorvashiyam and Raghuvamsham.
- The celebrated Sanskrit drama Mrcchakatika was composed during this time. It is attributed to Shudraka.
- Poet Harisena also adorned the court of Chandragupta Vikramaditya. He wrote the Allahabad Prashasti (inscription).
- Vishakhadatta composed Mudrarakshasa. Other grammarians who contributed to the Sanskrit language include Vararuchi and Bhartrihari.

Art & architecture

- Many magnificent temples, palaces, paintings and sculptures were created.
- Dashavatara Temple in Deogarh, UP is one of the earliest surviving Hindu temples. It is a fine example of Gupta architecture.
- Mural paintings of Ajanta depicting the life of the Buddha as told in the Jataka tales were created in this period.
- Classical Indian music and dance took shape in this time.
- The Bronze Buddha which is 7.5 feet high and found at Sultanganj is a product of the Gupta age.
- The iron pillar at Mehrauli, Delhi is a marvellous creation of this period.

Social culture & religion

- The Hindu epics were given their final touches during this time. The Hindu religion also received an impetus under the Guptas and it flourished and expanded throughout India.
- Although the Gupta kings were Vaishnavas they were tolerant of Buddhism and Jainism. They patronised Buddhist art.
- The Shakti cult rose up around this time.
- Sacrifice was being replaced by Bhakti and Pooja.
- Occult practices like tantrism also emerged during this time.
- The game of chess is said to have originated from this time.

Cave Architecture in India (Rock Cut Caves)

Ellora cave

- It is located in Maharashtra.
- This also a rock-cut monastery by the Buddhists.
- It is famous for the largest monolithic excavation in the world—the great Kailasa.
- The hills in which the caves are carved forms part of the Sahyadri ranges of the Deccan.
- It is a UNESCO World Heritage Site.

Elephanta cave

- It is located on Elephanta Islands in Mumbai.
- There are seven cave excavations in the Elephanta group.
- The caves are carved from solid basalt rock.

Lomasa rishi cave

- It represents the earliest example of rock-cut architecture in India.
- It belongs to belong Maurya period.
- This cave was carved out of a gigantic rounded granite rock.
- It has an arch-like shape frontage copying the contemporary timber architecture.
- It is located in Nagarjuni hills.

Karle cave

- Ancient India Buddhist early rock-cut architecture.
- It is located in Maharashtra.
- Related with the Mahasamghika sect of Buddhism.
- It has a great chaitya hall.

Pancha Pandava cave

- It is located in Mahabalipuram in Tamil Nadu.
- It is part of the cluster of Monuments at Mahabalipuram.
- It is one of the supreme testimonials to the ancient Vishwakarma Sthapathis which is unfinished.

Cave temple of Mandagapattu

- Mandagapattu is built by Mahendravarman I.
- It is a shrine which holds a significant position in the history of architecture of the Pallavas.
- It is the oldest stone shrine in Tamil Nadu.

Udayagiri and Kandhagiri caves of Odisha

- Earliest groups of Jain rock-cut shelters.
- The caves of Udayagiri and Khandagiri called lena or lena in the inscriptions.
- Khandagiri offers a fine view back over Bhubaneswar from its summit.

Chaitya cave number 19 of Ajanta group

- Built in Gupta age.
- Cave 19 is a very elaborate rock-cut chaitya hall from the late 5th century.
- The peripheral frontage has a large horseshoe-arched window edged by figures of yakshas and Buddhas carved in relief.

Vihara cave number 16 & 17

- Vihara is a monastery.
- There are lots of mural painting in the caves 16 and 17 which are epigraphs of the Vakataka Dynasty.
- The murals are uninterrupted without barriers, typically representing Buddhist tales, like 'Jataka' stories, which describe Buddha's earlier lives.

Mandapeshwar Caves

- It is located in on the banks of the Dahisar River in Borivali.
- 8th Century rock-cut shrine dedicated to Shiva.
- This is the only Brahmanical cave to be transformed into Christian cave.

Nashik caves

- Located near Nashik in Maharashtra.
- It is called as Pandavleni Caves/ Trirashmi Buddhist Caves.
- It is a cluster of 24 caves carved between the 2nd century BCE and the 2nd century CE.
- It is representing the Hinayana Buddhist caves.

TEMPLES STYLES IN NORTH INDIA (NAGARA STYLE)

- Ancient Indian temples are classified in three broad types. This classification is based on different architectural styles, employed in the construction of the temples. Three main style of temple architecture are the Nagara or the Northern style, the Dravida or the Southern style and the Vesara or Mixed style.

Nagara School of Architecture

- Style of temple architecture that became popular in northern India.
- a square temple with a number of graduated projections (rathakas).
- A tower *(sikhara)* gradually curving inwards and capped by a spheroid slab with ribs round the edge *(Amalaka)* give the elevation.
- Prominent features–Shikaras (Spiral roofs), Garbhagriha (sanctum) & Mandap (pillared hall).
- Thus the two major characteristics of this style are the cruciform ground plan and the curvilinear tower.
- Three subtypes of Nagara temple depending upon the shape of Shikhara:

Rekha Prasad/Latina

- Simple Shikhara — Square at the base and the walls curve inward to a point on the top.
- Latina types are mainly used for housing the garbhagriha.
- The top is called 'latina' or the rekha-Prasad type of Shikhara.

Phamsana

- Phamsana buildings tend to be broader and shorter than latina buildings.
- Their roofs are composed of several slabs that gently rise to a single point over the center of building, unlike the latina ones which look like sharply rising tall towers.
- In many North Indian temples Phamsana was used for mandapa and latina for Garbhgriha.

Valabhi

- Rectangular building with a roof that rises into a vaulted chamber.
- They are usually called as wagon vaulted buildings.

Three sub schools developed under Nagara style:

Odisha School

- Most of the main temple sites are located in ancient Puri and Konark.
- Here the shikhara, called deul in Odisha, is vertical almost until the top when it suddenly curves sharply inwards.
- Deuls are preceded, as usual, by mandapas called jagamohana in Odisha.
- The ground plan of the main temple is square, which, in the upper reaches of its superstructure becomes circular in the crowning mastaka.
- Example: Konark Temple, Jagannath temple, Lingaraj temple.

Konark Sun Temple

- Built in the 13th century, the Konark temple was conceived as a gigantic chariot of the Sun God, with 12 pairs of exquisitely ornamented wheels pulled by seven horses.
- It was built by ***King Narasimhadeva I,*** the great ruler of Ganga dynasty.
- The temple is perfect blend of **Kalinga architecture,** heritage, exotic beach and salient natural beauty.

Nabakalebar festival

- The Nabakalebara is **an ancient ritual associated with most of the Jagannath Temples** when the Idols of Lord Jagannath, Balabhadra, Subhadra and Sudarshan are replaced by a new set of Idols.
- A year with an extra Ashadha masa/month as per Hindu Calendar is considered auspicious for conducting the ceremony. This usually occurs every twelve to nineteen years.

Khujuraho/Chandel school

- Khajuraho's temples are known for their extensive erotic sculptures.
- Patronized by Chandela kings of Bundelkhand (10th and 11th century).
- These 22 temples (out of the original 85) are regarded as one of world's greatest artistic wonders.
- The finest among them is Shaivite temple known as Kandariya Mahadev, built around 10th century by King Ganda.
- The standard type of Khajuraho temple has a shrine room, an assembly hall, and an entrance portico.

Solanki School

- Patronized by Solanki kings (later Chalukya) of Gujarat (11th to 13th century).
- The Vimala, Tejpala and Vastupala temples at Mount Abu exhibit this style.
- Exquisite example is Sun temple at Modhera, built by Raja Bhimdev-I of the Solanki Dynasty in 1026.

Indo Islamic Architecture in Medieval India

- Islam came to India in the 7th and 8th centuries CE chiefly through Muslim traders, merchants, holy men and conquerors.
- The religion spread in India over a time period of 600 years.
- Muslims in Gujarat and Sind had begun construction work in the 8th century itself. But it was only in the 13th century that building activity on a large scale

began by the Turkish State after the Turkish conquest of North India.

- Muslims absorbed many aspects of local architectural traditions and amalgamated them into their own practices.
- Architecturally, a mix of many techniques, stylised shapes and surface decorations evolved through a continuous amalgamation of architectural elements from the various styles. Such architectural entities that showcased multiple styles are known as **Indo-Saracenic** or **Indo-Islamic architecture.**
- Types of architectural buildings: mosques for daily prayers, Jama Masjids, dargahs, tombs, hammams, minars, gardens, sarais or caravansarais, madrasas, Kos minars, etc.

Categories of Styles

1. Imperial Style (Delhi Sultanate)
2. Provincial Style (Mandu, Gujarat, Bengal, and Jaunpur)
3. Mughal Style (Delhi, Agra, and Lahore)
4. Deccani Style (Bijapur, Golconda)

Decorative Forms

- Designing on plaster through incision or stucco.
- Designs were either left plain or filled with colours.
- Motifs of varieties of flowers (both Indian and foreign) were painted or carved.
- In the 14th, 15th and 16th centuries, tiles were used to surface the walls and domes. Blue, green, yellow and turquoise were the popular colours.
- In the wall panels, surface decoration was done by the techniques of tessellation (mosaic designs) and **pietra dura** (a decorative art that is an inlay technique of using cut and fitted, highly polished coloured stones to create images).
- The roof was generally a mix of the central dome and other smaller domes, chatris and tiny minarets.
- There was generally an inverted lotus flower motif and a metal or stone pinnacle atop the central dome.

Construction materials

- The walls were quite thick and made of rubble masonry.
- They were then coated with chunam or limestone plaster or dressed stone.
- Stones used: sandstone, quartzite, buff, marble, etc.

Forts

- Forts symbolise the seat of power of a ruler. Many large forts with embattlements were built in the medieval times.
- When a fort was captured, it meant the ruler who owned the fort had to surrender.
- E.g.: Chittor, Gwalior and Daulatabad.
- Chittorgarh is the largest fort in Asia.
- Forts were constructed using great heights so that they were impregnable to enemy forces. Inside there were places for offices and residences.
- Golconda Fort (Hyderabad) had concentric circles of outer walls. Daulatabad Fort had staggered entrances so that even elephants could not be used to open the gates.

Minars

- Minar was a form of stambha or tower.
- Examples of medieval minars: Qutub Minar in Delhi, Chand Minar at Daulatabad Fort.
- Everyday use of the minar: azaan (call to prayer).

Qutub Minar

- 13th century
- Construction started by Qutub-ud-din Aibak (Delhi Sultanate ruler) and completed by his successor Iltutmish.
- UNESCO World Heritage Site.
- Mix of polygonal and circular shapes.
- Material: red and buff sandstone with some marble in the upper storeys.
- It came to be associated with Khwaja Qutubuddin Bakhtiyar Kaki, a revered saint of Delhi.

Chand Minar, Daulatabad

- 15th century.
- Tapering tower has four storeys.
- Work of architects from Delhi and Iran.

Tombs

- Tombs are monumental structures over the graves of rulers and royalty.
- Examples: tombs of Ghyasuddin Tughlaq, Humayun, Akbar, Abdur Rahim Khan-i-Khanan, Itmaduddaula.
- Idea behind the tomb according to Anthony Welch was "eternal paradise as a reward for the true believer on the Day of Judgement."
- Walls had Quranic verses. Tombs were generally placed within paradisiacal elements like a garden or a water body or both (as in the Taj Mahal).

Sarais

- Sarais were built on a simple rectangular or square plan around cities.
- They were meant to provide temporary accommodation to travellers, traders, pilgrims, etc.

Jama Masjid

- Large mosques sprang up during the medieval times in India.

- Congregational prayers were held every Friday afternoon. A quorum of 40 Muslim male adults was required for this to take place.
- At the time of the prayers, a khutba was read out in the name of the ruler along with his laws for the realm.
- They were surrounded on three sides by cloisters with the Qibla Liwan to the west. The mihrab and the mimbar for the Imam were located here.
- The mihrab indicated the direction of the Kaaba in Mecca and so people faced the mihrab while offering prayers.

IMPERIAL STYLE DURING ISLAMIC ERA IN INDIA

Slave Dynasty

- Also known as Ilbari dynasty, as all the ruler's belonged to Ilbari tribe except Qutubuddin Aibak. The Style developed by them is called Mamluk Style. They started converting existing structures into the Mosque's on Qila Rai Pithora (1st of 7 historical cities of Delhi).
- The Quwwat-ul-Islam Mosque was constructed by Qutub-ud-din Aibak around 1192 AD by the demolished material of Hindu and Jain temples. Quwwat-ul-Islam mosque—first mosque built in Delhi after the Islamic conquest of India.
- The Qutub Minar of Mehrauli was built around 1199 by Qutub-ud-din and finally completed by his son-in-law and successor Iltutmish (1210-35).

Khilji Dynasty

- The Style developed by them is called as Seljuk style.
- Enlarged the Quwwat-ul-Islam mosque and built a gateway known as Alahi Darwaja to the enclosure of the mosque.
- Allauddin Khilji also established the 2nd city of Delhi at Siri and dug a vast reservoir at Hauz Khas (Hydraulically structured) around 1311 AD.

Tughlaqs

- Ghiyasuddin Tughlaq (1320-1325 AD) built Tughlaqabad, the 3rd historical city of Delhi.
- Tomb of Ghiyasuddin Tughlaq, built of red sandstone, is an irregular pentagon in its exterior plan & is of the pointed or "Tartar" shape, crowned by a finial.
- Tughlaqs introduced the concept of slopping walls known as "Battar", combining the principles of arch and the lintel.
- Delhi's 4th city Jahanpanah was built by Mohammad-bin-Tughlaq in mid-14th century. Firoz Shah Kotla ground is the only remnant of its past glory. He is also credited with founding the fortified cities of Jaunpur, Fathehbad and Hissar.

Sayyid Period

- The Sayyid period was too short to evolve elaborate buildings, but the octagonal tombs of the time possess a distinct architectural character.
- The decorative features of these tombs consist of the use of blue enameled tiles enhancing the colour effect.
- The Lotus motif crowning the tomb and free use of Guldasta's used in this period considerably influenced the style of subsequent period.
- The Tombs of Mubarak Sayyid (1434 AD), Muhammad Sayyid (1444 AD) and Sikander Lodi (1517 AD) are all of the octagonal type.

Lodi's Style

- Enamel tile decoration tended to be richer and more lavish.
- The tomb architecture of this period is of two types, though both have grey granite walls.
- One is octagonal in design having a verandah; the other is square in plan, having no verandah.
- A spacious somewhat ornamental walled garden encloses the tombs, which gives the whole ensemble elegance.
- Sikander Lodhi established the city of Agra and made it as his capital.

PROVINCIAL STYLE DURING ISLAMIC ERA IN INDIA

Bengal School of Architecture

- Islamic monuments of Bengal are consistent in design as of other regions, with distinguishing features such as material used & designs execution. Brick was the chief building material with the use of stone being limited largely to pillars for trabeate/Arcuate construction, mainly obtained from demolished temples.
- The so-called "Bengal" roof with sloping cornices, which originated from the bamboo construction, was adopted by the Muslims and later it spread widely, even in other regions. Covered brick and glazed tiles were usually pressed into service for decoration.

Malwa School of Architecture

- Followed arcuate style majorly with elegant use of arch with pillar and beam;
- Lofty terraces approached by well-proportioned stairways.
- Impressive size of buildings, use of various coloured stones & marbles with minor use of bright coloured glazed tiles.
- Notable Examples are Rani Rupmati pavilion (Mandu), Ashrafi Mahal (Mandu), Hindola mahal (Mandu), Jahaz Mahal (Mandu).

Jaunpur School of Architecture

- Developed by Sharqui Dynasty hence also called as sharqui style. It was influenced by the buildings of Tughlaq period.
- Prominent feature—Huge imposing propylon screens, filling the central and side bays of prayer hall.

MUGHAL PERIOD ARCHITECTURE

Babur

- Babur undertook the construction of a mosque in Panipat and Rohilkhand in 1526 A.D.
- His reign was too small for any new style and design but he was fond of formal gardens.

Humayun

- He succeeded Babur but the reign was filled with constant struggle and war with Sher Shah Suri.
- He led the foundation of a city named Dinpanah but he couldn't finish it.
- The first proper Mughal architecture was **Humayun's Tomb** in Delhi, built by his widow Hamida Banu Begum. Also known as a precursor of Taj Mahal in Agra and provided the prototype for Mausoleum of Jahangir at Shahdara, Lahore.
- Persian style was prominent during this period.
- Sikandar Lodhi's Tomb was the first garden-tomb built in India but it was the Humayun's Tomb which gave new vision to art.
- Some of the designing features were:
  - The tomb stands on a raised vast platform in the centre of a square garden.
  - Garden is divided into 4 parts by Charbagh (causeways), in the centre of which run shallow water-channels.
  - For the first time, red sandstone was used along with white (the white is used cleverly to emphasize, surround & underline doors and windows, strengthening the design).
  - On similar lines, square, red, sandstone; the double storeyed structure of the mausoleum rises over a high square terrace; raised over a series of cells; etc. were also introduced.

Sher Shah Suri (Sur Dynasty)

- His period is the transition from Lodhi style to the Mughal style of architecture.
- He built the **Quila-e-Quanah** (Mosque of the Old Fort) in Delhi.
- He built the famous **Rohtas Fort** in Pakistan.
- Constructed the **Sher Shah Suri Masjid** in Patna in Afghan style.
- He undertook the reconstruction and extension of an old Mauryan route and renamed it as Sadak-e-Azam which was later called as **Grand Trunk Road.** He ensured sarais and trees for travellers.
- His tomb was built at his birthplace Sasaram, Bihar, made up of red sandstone and situated inside a lake. Each side pierced by arches and halls mounted by a large dome.
- They made use of red and grey sandstone latticed screens, painted ceilings and coloured tiles.

Akbar

- He occupied the throne of Delhi in 1556, the golden period of Mughal art and architecture.
- Use of red sandstone was principle feature and he introduced the use of **Tudor arch** (four-centred arches).
- Some of the prominent construction under his reign are:

Agra Fort

- One of the first constructions during Akbar's reign.
- Made of red stone on the bank of river Yamuna.
- Some buildings inside are:
  - **Moti Masjid,** made by Shah Jahan
  - **Diwan-i-aam** (hall of public audience) by Shah Jahan
  - **Diwan-i-Khas** (hall of private audience) by Shah Jahan
  - **Jahangiri Mahal**
  - **Sheesh Mahal** (Turkish Bath)

Fatehpur Sikri

- This was the new capital city made by Akbar and was a new era of Indo-Islamic architecture.
- Described as 'frozen moment in history' as the buildings represented a unique combination of Hindu and Persian style.
- Some of the monuments here are:
  - **Buland Darwaza** (1576 A.D.)-built to commerate Akbar's victory over Gujrat. It is a 40 meters red sandstone structure and largest gateway of the world.
  - **Salim Chisti's tomb** (1581 A.D.)-jaali work in white marble and inscription of Quranic verses on the walls.
  - **Panch Mahal**-five storied structure inspired by Persian badger (wind-catcher).
  - **Jodha Bai's palace** or **Mariam-uz-Zamani's palace.**
  - **Ibadat Khana**-meeting with leaders of different religion for discussions.
  - **Pachisi Court**—courtyard where Akbar is said to have played chess.
  - **Hiran Minar**—built in the memory of Akbar's favourite elephant. Served as lighthouse for travellers.
- He built Temple of Govind dev in Vrindavan.

Jahangir

- He focused more on paintings and other art forms.
- Some of his noteworthy monuments were:
  - **Akbar's tomb** in Sikandra
  - His own tomb at Lahore
  - **Shalimar Bagh** in Kashmir
  - **Moti Masjid** at Lahore
  - **Tomb of Itmad-Ud-daulah,** father of Nur Jahan is an excellent example—it was first work during Mughal period which was made completely of white marble. Also with world's finest Pietra dura works.

Shah Jahan

- During his reign, architecture reached its height and some of the principle works were:

Taj Mahal

- The finest example of architecture and mark of Love.
- Constructed in the memory of his beloved wife Arzuman Bano Begum or Mumtaz Mahal.
- The features include calligraphy, pietra dura works (beautiful inlay work with precious multicolour stones), Charbagh style gardens, use of water in premises for decoration and foresightening technique.
- Jaali work is lace-like and carvings on marble were finely done.

Red Fort in Delhi

- He shifted his capital city from Agra to Delhi.
- He laid the foundation of **seventh city Shahjahanabad,** which had its famous citadel Red fort (begun in 1639 A.D.).
- Red Fort is an irregular octagon with its walls, gates, and a few other structures constructed in red sandstone, and marble used for the palaces.
- It consisted of Diwan-i-aam and Diwan-i-khas.
- **Jama Masjid** in Delhi
- **Shalimar bagh** at Lahore, also on the UNESCO world heritage list.
- **Peacock throne** is one of the finest examples of metal work.

Aurangzeb

- Mughal architecture started declining during his period.
- He didn't take any active interest in the pursuit of art and architecture.
- Some of his works were:
  - **Alamgiri gate** in Lahore fort, Lahore
  - **Badshahi Masjid,** Lahore–3rd largest in Pakistan and 7th largest in the world. Architecture plan is similar to Jama Masjid at Delhi.

Muhammad Azam Shah

- Last Mughal to undertake architectural constructions.
- **Biwi-ka-Maqbara**-poor imitation of Taj Mahal in memory of his mother Begum Rabia Durani wife of Aurangzeb situated in Aurangabad.
- **Zinat Mahal,** Delhi- in memory of his wife.

COLONIAL ARCHITECTURE-MODERN INDIA

- Portuguese established impressive churches in Iberian style of architecture for ex. churches of Goa. Francis Church at Cochin (1510) is believed to be the first church built by the Europeans in India.
- Portuguese used bricks as the main building material along with wooden roofs & stairs.
- British followed various architectural styles viz. Gothic, Imperial, Christian, Palladian and Victorian being prominent. Britishers used Red sandstone & coarse limestone as the main building material.
- Constantia, a building erected by General Martin (British) at Lucknow, is the best specimen of Palladian Style in India.
- Wittet designed the Gateway of India in Mumbai, borrowing several elements of Mughal style.
- Sardar Ram Singh, a master builder of Punjab, designed the Central Museum and the Senate House at Lahore (in Pakistan).

Victoria Terminus Station (Chhatrapati Shivaji station), Mumbai

- Designed by the British architect F.W. Stevens, the structure became the symbol of Bombay.
- Based on late medieval Italian models, the terminal was built over 10 years, starting in 1878.
- Bombay city was labelled as the 'Gothic City'.

Victoria Memorial Hall (Kolkata)

- Designed by William Emerson in late 19th century.
- To perpetuate the memory of Queen Victoria in India.

Revival of Delhi

- 1911—Transfer of capital from Calcutta (now Kolkata) to Delhi.
- Sir Edward Lutyens was made responsible for the overall plan of Delhi.
- He constructed India Gate and Rashtrapati Bhawan (Vice Regal Place).
- Vice regal palace appeared with a huge dome on the lines of a Buddhist stupa.
- Represent some elements of Hindu ornamentation & Islamic symmetry.

- Herbert Baker added South Block and North Block, which flank the Rashtrapati Bhawan.
- Englishman Robert Tor Tussell built the Connaught Place.

INDIAN PAINTING

- Painting is one of the most delicate forms of art giving expression to human thoughts and feelings through the medium of line and colour.
- The rocks have been painted by the cave dwellers to satisfy their aesthetic sensitivity and creative urge.
- Paintings in India was started in the ancient period, since the pre-historic era.
- The painting history has originated from rock paintings and carried through pottery, in textiles, miniature paintings and finally with modern paintings.
- The diversity in the style of paintings in different parts of the country indicates the diversity in culture as culture and livelihood being the themes of paintings and later dominated by Religion.
- The major inspiration for paintings in India was the birth of three religions—Hinduism, Buddhism and Jainism.
- Paintings in India projects the Spiritual contents, high ideals and common belief of the people.

Important Source of Information for Paintings

- Mudrarakshasa—Sanskrit play was written by Vishakhadutta–mentions many types of paintings during the 4th century period.
- Brahmanical Literature—the reference to the art of paintings with the representation of myths.
- Buddhist Literature—mentions different styles of paintings with various base and themes.
- Vinaya Pitaka—3rd and 4th century BC–houses containing paintings.

Pre-historic Paintings

- The pre-historic paintings are generally executed in rocks in the caves.
- The major themes are Animals like elephant, rhinoceros, cattle, snake, deer, etc., and other natural elements like plants.
- The pre-historic paintings are categorised into the three phases—Paleolithic, Mesolithic and Chalcolithic.

Wall Paintings

- The wall paintings in India has existed from the 2nd century BC to Medieval times.
- They are also referred to as **Mural paintings** as they are painted on the walls of solid structures.
- Natural caves and rock-cut chambers are the predominant places for wall paintings.
- Major Themes: Hinduism, Buddhism and Jainism.
- Examples: Ajanta caves, Ellora Caves, Bagh cave paintings, Ravan Chhaya rock paintings, etc.

Miniature Paintings

- Miniature paintings are characterised with small and detailed paintings.
- Human figures are mostly seen in side profile, bulging eyes, slim waist, pointed nose, etc.
- Different colours were used for different characters and the variety of base was used.
- Often painted on paper, clothes palm leaves, etc.
- Mostly developed after the 11th century AD and mostly concentrated on eastern and western regions.
- The arrival of Muslims changed the characteristics of miniature paintings to a great extent. The major changes have been earthy tones, the absence of primary colours, detached appearances, etc.
- The characteristics of Miniature painting was varied in different regions of the country.

Folk Paintings

- The Folk paintings have been existing since ancient times and the styles and patterns have the huge diversity in various regions of the country.
- Most of the folk paintings are pictorial representations and the subject varies from religion to natural things and also the day to day activities.
- Folk paintings generally use vibrant and natural colours with various natural ground substances.

INDIAN DANCES WITH STATES —FOLK & CLASSICAL

- India is known for its rich cultural heritage. Diversification is the identity of the country. Indian dance is one of the most revered identity of our culture. In India, dance forms can be broadly classified into two categories—classical and folk dance form. These dance forms have been originated from different parts of India as per the local tradition.

Dance Forms in India

- The two major dance form in India are classical and folk dance. The major difference between Classical and Folk dance is the origin.
- Classical dance has a deep-rooted relationship with the Natya Shastra where the specific features of each of the classical dance forms have been mentioned.
- Folk dance, on the other hand, emerged from the local tradition of the respective state, ethnic or geographic regions.

Classical Dance in India

- The Cultural Ministry of India has included Chhau into the list of classical dances that makes a total of 9 classical dance form.
- The list of classical dances in India is given below:

Type of Dance in India-Classical	*State of Origin*
Bharatnatyam	Tamil Nadu
Mohiniyattam	Kerala
Kathak	Uttar Pradesh
Odissi	Odisha
Sattriya	Assam
Manipuri	Manipur
Chhau	Odisha
Kuchipudi	Andhra Pradesh
Kathakali	Kerala

Folk Dances in India

State of Origin	*Folk Dance*
Bihar	Jata-Jatin, Bakho-Bakhain, Panwariya
Chattisgarh	Gaur Maria, Panthi, Raut Nacha, Pandwani, Vedamati, Kapalik
Gujarat	Garba, Dandiya Raas, Tippani Juriun, Bhavai
Goa	Tarangamel, Koli, Dekhni, Fugdi, Shigmo, Ghode, Modni, Samayi nrutya, Jagar, Ranmale
Andhra Pradesh	Vilasini Natyam, Bhama-kalpam, Veeranatyam, Dappu, Tappeta Gullu, Lambadi, Dhimsa, Kolattam.
Arunachal Pradesh	Buiya, Chalo, Wancho, Pasi Kongki, Ponung, Popir
Assam	Bihu, Bichhua, Natpuja, Maharas, Kaligopal, Bagurumba, Naga dance, Khel Gopal.
Haryana	Jhumar, Phag, Daph, Dhamal, Loor, Gugga, Khor.
Himachal Pradesh	Jhora, Jhali, Chharhi, Dhaman, Chhapeli, Mahasu
Jammu & Kashmir	Rauf, Hikat, Mandjas, Kud Dandi Nach
Jharkhand	Alkap, Karma Munda, Agni, Jhumar, Janani Jhumar, Mardana Jhumar, Paika, Phagua
Karnataka	Yakshagana, Huttari, Suggi, Kunitha, Karga
Rajasthan	Ghumar, Chakri, Ganagor, Jhulan Leela, Jhuma, Suisini, Ghapal
Sikkim	Chu Faat, Sikmari, Singhi Chaam or the Snow Lion, Yak Chaam, Denzong Gnenha, Tashi Yangku
Tamil Nadu	Kumi, Kolattam, Kavadi
Tripura	Hojagiri
Uttar Pradesh	Nautanki, Raslila, Kajri, Jhora, Chappeli
Uttarakhand	Garhwali, Kumayuni, Kajari, Jhora, Raslila
Kerala	Ottam Thullal, Kaikottikali
Maharashtra	Lavani, Nakata, Koli, Lezim, Gafa, Dahikala Dasavtar.
Madhya Pradesh	Jawara, Matki, Aada, Khada Nach, Phulpati, Grida Dance, Selalarki, Selabhadoni
Manipur	Dol Cholam, Thang Ta, Lai Haraoba, Pung Cholom
Meghalaya	Ka Shad Suk Mynsiem, Nongkrem, Laho
Mizoram	Cheraw Dance, Khuallam, Cháilam, Sawlakin, Chawnglaizawn, Zangtalam
Nagaland	Rangma, Bamboo Dance, Zeliang, Nsuirolians, Gethinglim
Odisha	Savari, Ghumara, Painka, Munari
Punjab	Bhangra, Giddha, Daff, Dhaman, Bhand

MULTIPLE CHOICE QUESTIONS

1. The nationalist demand for a Constituent Assembly was for the first time conceded by the British Government, though indirectly and with reservations in the:
A. Cripps proposals
B. August Offer
C. Cabinet Mission Plan
D. Act of 1935

2. The Constituent Assembly that finally framed India's Constitution was set up:
A. Under the Indian Independence Act
B. Under the Government of India Act, 1935
C. Under the Cabinet Mission Plan, 1946
D. By the Queen's Proclamation

3. Who was the head of the Drafting Committee of the Constitution?
A. Sachchidanand Sinha
B. B.N. Rao
C. Jawaharlal Nehru
D. B.R. Ambedkar

4. Who is considered to be the architect of the Indian Constitution?
A. B.R. Ambedkar B. Jawaharlal Nehru
C. Rajendra Prasad D. B.N. Rao

5. Who adopted the Constitution of India on the 26th November, 1949?
A. People of India
B. Parliament of India
C. Representative of the people of India in Constituent Assembly
D. Cabinet

6. Consider the following words:
(*i*) Socialist (*ii*) Democratic
(*iii*) Sovereign (*iv*) Secular

Choose the response that gives the correct order in which these words occur in the Preamble.

Codes:
A. (*iii*), (*i*), (*iv*), (*ii*) B. (*iii*), (*iv*), (*i*), (*ii*)
C. (*iii*), (*iv*), (*ii*), (*i*) D. (*iv*), (*i*), (*iii*), (*ii*)

7. Which one of the following statements regarding the Preamble is correct?
A. It is not enforceable in a Court of law
B. The Supreme Court has recently ruled that it is not a part of the Constitution
C. It has been amended twice
D. All the above are correct

8. The Preamble of our Constitution reads: India is a:
A. Sovereign, socialist, secular, democratic Republic
B. Sovereign, democratic, socialist, secular Republic
C. Socialist, democratic, secular Republic
D. Democratic, sovereign, secular, socialist Republic

9. The Preamble to the Constitution of India was amended by which Constitution Amendment Act?
A. 44th Constitutional Amendment Act
B. 42nd Constitutional Amendment Act
C. 56th Constitutional Amendment Act
D. It has never been amended

10. Which one of the following statements is incorrect?
A. Goa attained full statehood in 1987
B. Ibau is an island in the Gulf of Khambhat
C. Daman and Diu were separated from Goa by the 56th Amendment of the Constitution of India
D. Dadra and Nagar Haveli were under French colonial rule till 1954

11. Which of the following was ceded by the French to India?
A. Dadra & Nagar Haveli
B. Daman & Diu
C. Karaikal and Mahe
D. None of the above

12. When can citizenship not be terminated?
A. When there is Emergency
B. When there is war
C. When there are elections
D. It can be terminated regardless of conditions

13. Indian citizenship is lost when:
A. a person acquires a foreign citizenship
B. the person renounces the citizenship
C. the government deprives a citizenship for some cause
D. in all the above cases

14. There is a double citizenship is:
A. India B. England
C. USA D. Japan

15. The detailed provisions regarding acquisition and termination of Indian citizenship are contained in the Citizenship Act which was passed by:
A. the Indian Parliament in 1955
B. the Indian Parliament in 1950
C. the British Parliament in August 1948
D. the Constituent Assembly in 1949

16. The Constitution of India has provided for:
A. single citizenship B. multiple citizenship
C. double citizenship D. none of the above

17. The Constitution of India has introduced single citizenship on the pattern of:

A. Britain B. Canada
C. Both A and B D. United States

18. The authority to issue writs for the enforcement of Fundamental Rights rests with whom?
A. All the courts in India
B. The Parliament
C. The Supreme Court
D. The President of India

19. Which of the following Fundamental Rights have been deleted from our Constitution through a constitutional amendment?
A. Right against exploitation
B. Right to freedom of religion
C. Right to property
D. Freedom of speech and expression

20. Right to participate in government and equal opportunity to occupy the highest office by qualification gives the citizens:
A. national liberty B. political liberty
C. natural liberty D. civil liberty

21. Who is empowered to suspend the operation of Fundamental Rights?
A. Parliament B. Supreme Court
C. President D. Prime Minister

22. Who of the following does not constitute an exception to the provision of Article 14 (equality before the law)?
A. The President B. The Governor
C. The Prime Minister D. The Foreign diplomats

23. Which one of the following has been wrongly listed as a freedom provided to the Indian citizens under Article 19?
A. Freedom of speech and expression
B. Freedom of residence and settlement
C. Freedom of profession
D. Freedom of press

24. The Preventive Detention Act has a restraining effect on:
A. Right of Equality
B. Right to Freedom
C. Right to Religion
D. Right to Constitutional Remedies

25. Which one of the following sets or Articles in Part III of the Constitution emphasises its secular character?
A. Articles 8 to 11 B. Articles 25 to 28
C. Articles 45 to 48A D. Articles 14 to 19

26. Under the provision of which Article of the Constitution did the Government of India introduce Bharat Ratna and Padma Shri awards?
A. Article 14 B. Article 18
C. Article 25 D. Article 31

27. Which one of the following Articles of the Constitution prohibits censorship?
A. Article 19 B. Article 22
C. Article 32 D. None

28. Under which Article of the Constitution can an individual move the Supreme Court directly in case of any violation of a Fundamental Right?
A. Article 13 B. Article 14
C. Article 32 D. Article 34

29. The granting of fundamental rights to citizens aims at ensuring:
A. an independent judiciary
B. socialistic government
C. individual liberty
D. None of these

30. Which fundamental right is concerned with abolition of social distinctions?
A. Right to equality
B. Right against exploitation
C. Right to life and liberty
D. Cultural and educational rights

31. The Fundamental Rights have the sanction of:
A. the Supreme Court B. the Constitution
C. majority opinion D. the Government

32. Under the constitution, the Fundamental Rights of the citizen can be restricted but the final authority to decide whether these restrictions are reasonable or not rests with the:
A. Parliament B. Courts
C. Council of Ministers D. President

33. What is a Writ of Quo Warranto?
A. It is a writ from a superior court commanding some officer or particular authority to do a specific act
B. It is an order from a higher court to stop proceedings in a certain case
C. It is an order from the superior court to any official to show his right to the office
D. To produce the body of a person

34. Which one of the following writs literally means 'we command'?
A. Habeas Corpus B. Mandamus
C. Quo Warranto D. Certiorari

35. The writ of prohibition issued by the Supreme Court or a High Court is issued against:
A. judicial or quasi-judicial authorities
B. administrative and judicial authorities
C. administrative authorities only
D. administrative authorities and government

36. A uniform civil code mentioned in the Directive Principles of State Policy ensure:
A. economic equality

B. national security
C. national integration
D. support for weaker sections of society

37. Which Constitutional Amendment granted a position of primacy to all the Directive Principles over Fundamental Rights?
A. 24th B. 25th
C. 36th D. 42nd

38. The Directive Principles were accorded an overriding position over the Fundamental Rights under certain circumstances by:
A. The Constitution
B. The Forty-Second Amendment
C. The Forty-Fourth Amendment
D. The Twenty-Fifth Amendment

39. The enforcement of Directive Principles depends mostly on:
A. The Courts
B. An effective opposition in Parliament
C. Resources available to the Government
D. Public cooperation

40. Fundamental Duties were introduced in the Constitution by the:
A. 40th Amendment B. 42nd Amendment
C. 43rd Amendment D. 44th Amendment

41. When were the Fundamental Duties incorporated in the Constitution?
A. 1975 B. 1976
C. 1977 D. 1979

42. The Fundamental Duties of a citizen include:
A. respect for the Constitution, the National Flag and the National Anthem
B. respect for the President
C. respect for the Government
D. all the above

43. The Fundamental Duties were added to the Constitution:
A. to make the fundamental rights more effective
B. to check anti-national, subversive and unconstitutional agitations
C. to accord priority to the directive principles over fundamental rights
D. to achieve all the above objectives

44. The executive authority of the Union is vested by the Constitution in the:
A. Prime Minister B. President
C. Cabinet D. Union Legislature

45. The President takes an oath before assuming office in the presence of the Chief Justice of India. If the Chief Justice is not available, he takes the oath in the presence of:
A. The Vice-President
B. The senior most judge of the Supreme Court
C. The Attorney General
D. Election Commissioner

46. Disputes regarding the election of the President and Vice President are settled:
A. In the Supreme Court
B. By the Election Commission
C. By a Parliament Committee
D. In the Supreme Court or High Courts

47. Where can impeachment proceedings against the President be initiated?
A. In Lok Sabha
B. At a joint sitting of the two Houses specially called for the purpose
C. In either House of Parliament
D. In the Supreme Court

48. The Vice-President's letter of resignation is to be addressed to the:
A. Deputy Chairman of Rajya Sabha
B. Chief Justice of India
C. President
D. Speaker

49. The candidate for Vice Presidential election must possess the qualifications prescribed for the Presidential candidate except that he must be:
A. A citizen of India
B. Over 35 years of age
C. Holding no office of profit under the Government
D. Qualified to be a member of the Rajya Sabha

50. Who has the authority to remove the Vice President from his office before the expiry of his term?
A. Rajya Sabha B. Lok Sabha
C. Parliament D. Supreme Court

51. The President addresses his resignation letter to the:
A. Chief Justice of India
B. Speaker
C. Vice President
D. Prime Minister

52. If there is a vacancy in the offices of both President and Vice President, who has been empowered to function as President?
A. Chief Justice of India
B. Chief of Army Staff
C. A person appointed by Parliament
D. No one

53. The executive power is vested in the President but it is actually used by him on the advice of:
A. The Prime Minister
B. The Council of Ministers
C. Parliament
D. None of these

54. What function is specifically prescribed by the Constitution for the Vice-President of India?

A. Vice-Chancellorship of Universities
B. No function
C. To assist the President in times of emergency
D. None of the above

55. When the Vice-President acts as President he gets as emoluments of the:
A. President
B. Vice-President
C. Chairman of Rajya Sabha
D. President in addition to what he gets as Chairman of Rajya Sabha

56. The President may send the advice received from the Council of Ministers on a matter back to them for reconsideration. This power can be exercised by him ______ on the same matter.
A. Once B. Twice
C. Thrice D. Any number of times

57. The Ministers are individually responsible to:
A. The President
B. The House of the People
C. The Prime Minister
D. The House of which they are members

58. The Prime Minister is:
A. Elected by the Lok Sabha
B. Elected by the Parliament
C. Appointed by the President
D. Nominated by the party enjoying majority in Lok Sabha

59. The Prime Minister is said to hold office during the pleasure of the President but in reality he stays in office as long as he enjoys the confidence of:
A. The electorate
B. The Lok Sabha
C. The party to which he belongs
D. Parliament

60. The portfolios are allocated to the ministers by:
A. The President
B. The Prime Minister
C. Collective decision of the Council of Ministers
D. Individual choice

61. In practice the policy of the Government is shaped by:
A. All the ministers B. The Prime Minister
C. The Cabinet D. Special committees

62. That the Prime Minister acts as a channel of communication between the President and the Council of Ministers is provided by:
A. Convention B. Statute
C. Article 78 D. Article 75

63. The Attorney-General of India holds office during the pleasure of the:
A. President B. Prime Minister
C. Parliament D. Chief Justice

64. To whom does the President address his letter of resignation?
A. The Prime Minister B. The Vice President
C. The Speaker D. The Chief Justice

65. The President of the Union of India has the same constitutional authority as the:
A. British Monarch B. President of USA
C. President of France D. President of USSR

66. The President can be removed from his office before the expiry of his normal term only on the recommendation of:
A. The Supreme Court
B. The Chief Justice of India
C. Council of Ministers
D. The two Houses of Parliament

67. The Council of Ministers is responsible to:
A. The Prime Minister B. The President
C. The People D. The Parliament

68. How long can a person continue to be Minister of the Union Government/State Government without being a member of either House of Parliament/State Legislature?
A. One year B. Three months
C. Six months D. No time limit

69. Though the President of India is the executive head of the State, the real executive power vests in:
A. The Union Council of Ministers
B. The Prime Minister
C. The Civil servants
D. None of the above

70. The formation of the Council of Ministers starts with the appointment of:
A. The President B. The Speaker
C. The Prime Minister D. None of these

71. The meetings of the Council of Ministers are presided over by:
A. The President
B. The Vice President
C. The Prime Minister
D. The members of the Council of Ministers by rotation

72. The first Law Officer of the Government of India is the:
A. Chief Justice of Supreme Court
B. Law Minister
C. Attorney-General for India
D. None of the above

73. The election to the office of the President is conducted by:
A. The Speaker of Lok Sabha
B. The Prime Minister's Office
C. The Election Commission of India
D. The Minister for Parliamentary Affairs

74. The qualifications for the Chairman and other members of the Finance Commission:
A. are determined by the President
B. have been laid down in the Constitution
C. are determined by the President in consultation
D. are determined by the Parliament

75. The strength of the UPSC:
A. is determined by the President from time to time
B. is determined by the Parliament
C. has been permanently fixed by the Constitution
D. was determined by the Presidential Ordinance in 1952

76. National emergency remains in operation, with the approval of the Parliamentary, for:
A. a maximum period of three years
B. a maximum period of one year
C. a maximum period of six months
D. an indefinite period

77. How many times has the President of India declared financial emergency so far?
A. only once B. only twice
C. only thrice D. never

78. In a parliamentary democracy the:
A. Executive controls the Legislature
B. Executive and Legislature are strictly separate
C. Judiciary controls both Legislature and Executive
D. Legislature controls the Executive

79. The quorum of the Parliament is fixed at:
A. one-tenth of the membership of the House
B. two-thirds of the membership of the House
C. one-third of the membership of the House
D. one-eighth of the membership of the House

80. Money from the Contingency Fund of India can be withdrawn only after:
A. the Appropriation Act has been passed by the Parliament
B. the approval of the President
C. the Appropriation Bill is introduced in the Parliament
D. the prior approval of the Comptroller and Auditor General

81. Which of the following does not come under the public sector?
A. TISCO B. IISCO
C. SAIL D. Ordnance factories

82. Term loans to industry is provided by:
A. RBI B. EXIM Bank
C. IDBI D. NABARD

83. Among the steel plants, following has been built with Russian assistance:
A Rourkela B. Bhillai
C. Durgapur D. Kothagudam

84. The "Cafeteria approach" for family planning was put forward during:
A. Third plan B. Emergency
C. Annual plans D. Janata party rule

85. The Monopolies and Restrictive Trade Practice Act was passed in:
A. 1968 B. 1969
C. 1970 D. 1971

86. Inflation is caused by:
A. decrease in general spending
B. decrease in money supply
C. increase in industrial and agriculture output
D. increase in general spending or money supply

87. Among the following, quasi-governmental institution is:
A. EXIM Bank B. IDBI
C. ICICI D. UTI

88. The main purpose of UTI is:
A. mobilise and channelise small investors' savings
B. regulate the mutual fund industry
C. act as a stabilising agent in the share market
D. coordinate activities of other financial institution

89. White revolution refers to:
A. Cement industry
B. Dairying
C. Cotton textile industry
D. Marble industry

90. In India, the major means of irrigation is:
A. Wells & Tubewalls B. Canals
C. Tanks D. Animal drought

91. The major function of the Food Corporation of India is:
A. to distribute high yielding variety seeds
B. to extend credit to farmers
C. to control the demand side of foodgrains
D. to check the fluctuation in foodgrain prices by controlling supply

92. The largest population among the states is in:
A. Bihar B. Bengal
C. Uttar Pradesh D. Madhya Pradesh

93. Which of the following is referred as Sunrise industry?
A. Coffee B. Hi-technology
C. Small scale D. Heavy

94. Which of the following is not a measure of economic growth?
A. Per capita income B. Gross National Product
C. Net Domestic Product D. Money in circulation

95. Among the following, least revenue comes from:
A. Income tax B. Excise duty
C. Custom duty D. Wealth tax

96. A blue chip company is called so because:
A. it produces computer hardware
B. it produces computer software
C. it gives high rains and has low risk
D. it exports most of its produce

97. The Command Area Development Programme was a major step in the field of:
A. irrigation
B. plant protection measures
C. farm mechanisation
D. high yield variety seeds

98. Poverty line is defined on the basis of:
A. living conditions of people
B. the number of children per family
C. per capita family income
D. the requirement of calories per person

99. The oldest large scale industry of India is in the field of:
A. iron and steel sector B. jute sector
C. cotton textile sector D. sugar sector

100. Seasonal unemployment is maximum in:
A. Industrial sector B. Agricultural sector
C. Service sector D. Handloom sector

101. The oldest trade union organisation in India is:
A. Hind Mazdoor Sabha
B. Indian National Trade Union Congress
C. All India Trade Union Congress
D. Central Industrial Trade Union

102. Sindri, Haldia and Paradip have:
A. Sea-ports
B. Steel plants
C. Big Multipurpose dams
D. Fertilizer plants

103. The Export-Import Bank was set up in:
A. 1969 B. 1980
C. 1982 D. 1985

104. Which of the following state has been announced as 'a state of total organic farming'?
A. Karnataka B. Kelara
C. Sikkim D. Punjab

105. Which of the following does not contribute to the development of the Indian economy?
A. Rising industrial output
B. Exports' share decreased; imports' share increased; Modern technology
C. Exports' and imports' share increased; Green Revolution
D. Population growth

106. Which of the following has largest share in India's export?
A. Manufactured goods
B. Ores and minerals
C. Agriculture and allied products
D. Others

107. Which of the following has largest share in India's imports?
A. Food and allied products
B. Capital goods
C. Fertilizers
D. Fuel

108. Special Economic Zone Act was passed on:
A. February 2004 B. May 2006
C. May 2005 D. February 2007

109. The first steel project city in India was established at
A. Bhilai B. Jamshedpur
C. Kolkata D. Bokaro

110. Rupee was made convertible on current account in:
A. 1991 B. 1994
C. 1995 D. 1997

111. The Reserve Bank of India was established in—
A. 1927 B. 1947
C. 1935 D. 1949

112. The foodgrain production in the country in 2021-22 was
A. 172.64 million tonnes
B. 150.04 million tonnes
C. 160.43 million tonnes
D. 316.06 million tonnes

113. The foodgrain production is more during:
A. Rabi season
B. Kharif season
C. Between Kharif and Rabi season
D. No fixed season

114. Where is India's most prized tea grown?
A. Jorhat B. Darjeeling
C. Nilgiris D. Munnar

115. The ideal NPK ratio for fertilizers utilisation is:
A. 2 : 4 : 1 B. 2 : 1 : 4
C. 4 : 2 : 1 D. 1 : 2 : 4

116. Which is not having the status of 'Maharatna'?
A. NTPC B. NHPC
C. ONGC D. SAIL

117. "Green Revolution" began in India during the year—
A. 1972-73 B. 1977-78
C. 1967-68 D. 1980-81

118. The major source of revenue in India is through—
A. Internal Borrowings B. Direct Taxes
C. Indirect Taxes D. External Borrowings

119. The currencies has the highest value in terms of rupee is—
A. Pound B. Dollar
C. Euro D. Saudi Rial

120. VAT is related to:
A. Business Tax System B. Life Insurance
C. Banking Service D. Social Services

121. The maximum revenue comes from:
A. Excise duty
B. Customs duty
C. Income and Corporation Tax
D. Sales tax

122. Which amidst the following is not a credit rating agency?
A. CRISIL B. CARE
C. ICRA D. IFCI

123. The first steel project city in India was established at:
A. Bhopal B. Kolkata
C. Bokaro D. Bhilai

124. Which unit of valuation is known as "Paper gold"?
A. Euro dollar B. Petro dollar
C. GDK D. SDR

125. The crops grown after the summer monsoon are called?
A. Rabi B. Kharif
C. Annual D. Seasonal

126. During which plan, annual compound growth rates was maximum?
A. Second plan B. Sixth plan
C. Fourth plan D. Seventh plan

127. The maximum number of shares are being traded at:
A. BSE B. NSE
C. OTCEI D. DSE

128. Among the following, maximum disbursement has been by:
A. IRDI B. IDBI
C. ICICI D. IFCI

129. When was the National Small Scale Industries Corporation formed?
A. 1951 B. 1961
C. 1965 D. 1955

130. The finance minister to present five successive budgets was:
A. S.B. Chavan B. Pranab Mukherjee
C. Man Mohan Singh D. S.N. Patel

131. The paintings in the Ajanta and Ellora caves are indicative of the development of art under the:
A. Pallavas B. Chalukyas
C. Pandyas D. Rashtrakutas

132. Drupad Dhamar style of singing was started by:
A. Raja Man Singh Tomar
B. Tansen
C. Vishnu Digambar Paluskar
D. Amir Khusro

133. Which classical dance of the following is named after the village it was born from?
A. Kuchipudi B. Kathakali
C. Bharatanatyam D. Mohiniattam

134. Which one of the following is not a feature of North Indian temple architecture?
A. Sikhara B. Garbha Griha
C. Gopuram D. Pradakshina

135. Who composed the famous song "Sare Jahan Se Achha"?
A. Rabindranath Tagore
B. Jaidev
C. Mohammad Iqbal
D. Bankim Chandra Chattopadhyay

136. Sattriya is a classical dance form of which State?
A. Assam B. Kerala
C. Punjab D. Bengal

137. In which of the following festivals are boat races a special feature?
A. Pongal B. Navratri
C. Rongali Bihu D. Onam

138. Ramman is a religious festival and ritual theatre of ________?
A. Uttar Pradesh B. Bengal
C. Uttarakhand D. Haryana

139. 'Chauth' was:
A. Land tax levied by Shivaji on neighbouring states
B. Toll tax imposed by Shivaji
C. A religious tax imposed by Aurangzeb
D. Irrigation tax charged by Akbar

140. __________ is classical dance form of Uttar Pradesh.
A. Mohiniattam B. Kuchipudi
C. Kathakali D. Kathak

141. Which classical dance form is famous in Tamil Nadu?
A. Mohiniattam B. Kuchipudi
C. Bharatanatyam D. Kathakali

142. The famous Nabakalebara festival belongs to which of the following states?
A. Kerala B. Bihar
C. Rajasthan D. Odisha

143. Match List-I with List-II and select the correct answer by using the codes given below:

List-I	List-II
(*a*) Dhamar	1. Krishna theme/ Holi theme
(*b*) Thumri	2. Only rhythm is important
(*c*) Tarana	3. Words are important
(*d*) Tappa	4. Extinct

Codes:

	(*a*)	(*b*)	(*c*)	(*d*)
A.	1	2	3	4
B.	1	3	2	4
C.	4	3	2	1
D.	4	2	3	1

144. Consider the following statements:
1. Flute and Sexophone are wind instruments.
2. Dhol, Tabla, Mridanga are percussion instrument.
3. Piano, Sitar and Vina are chordophone.
4. Ghungru and Jaltarangs are percussion instruments.

Which of the above statements is/are correct?

A. 1 and 2 only B. 2 and 3 only
C. 2, 3 and 4 only D. All of the above

145. Match List-I with List-II and select the correct answer by using the codes given below:

List-I	List-II
(*a*) Sahitya Academy	1. 1954
(*b*) Sangeet Natak Academy	2. 1953
(*c*) National Book Trust	3. 1957
(*d*) National School of Drama	4. 1959

Codes:

	(*a*)	(*b*)	(*c*)	(*d*)
A.	1	2	3	4
B.	1	3	2	1
C.	4	3	2	1
D.	4	2	3	1

146. Match List-I with List-II and select the correct answer by using the codes given below:

List-I	List-II
(*a*) Bharatnatyam	1. Tamil Nadu
(*b*) Kathakali	2. Kerala
(*c*) Mohiniattam	3. Andhra Pradesh
(*d*) Odissi	4. Odisha

Codes:

	(*a*)	(*b*)	(*c*)	(*d*)
A.	1	2	3	4
B.	2	1	3	4
C.	1	4	3	2
D.	2	4	3	1

147. Consider the following statements:
1. Odisi dance related to Odisha.
2. Kathak belongs to North India (Uttar Pradesh)
3. Sattaria dance belongs to Assam.

Which of the statements given above is/are correct?

A. 1 and 2 only B. 2 and 3 only
C. 1 and 3 only D. All of the above

148. Match List-I with List-II and select the correct answer by using the codes given below:

List-I	List-II
(*a*) Chhau	1. Punjab
(*b*) Gatka	2. West Bengal & Jharkhand
(*c*) Dumhal	3. Kashmir
(*d*) Garba	4. Gujarat

Codes:

	(*a*)	(*b*)	(*c*)	(*d*)
A.	1	2	3	4
B.	2	1	3	4
C.	4	3	2	1
D.	4	2	3	1

149. Match List-I with List-II and select the correct answer by using the codes given below:

List-I	List-II
(*a*) Bhand pathar	1. Kashmir
(*b*) Swang	2. Haryana & U.P.
(*c*) Nautanki	3. Uttar Pradesh
(*d*) Naach	4. Madhya Pradesh

Codes:

	(*a*)	(*b*)	(*c*)	(*d*)
A.	1	2	3	4
B.	4	3	2	1
C.	4	2	3	1
D.	1	3	2	4

150. Match List-I with List-II and select the correct answer by using the codes given below:

List-I	List-II
(*a*) Mudiyettu	1. Kerala
(*b*) Burrakatha	2. Andhra Pradesh
(*c*) Therukoothu	3. Tamil Nadu
(*d*) Yakshagan	4. Karnataka

Codes:

	(*a*)	(*b*)	(*c*)	(*d*)
A.	1	2	3	4
B.	1	4	3	2
C.	4	3	2	1
D.	4	2	3	1

151. Consider the following statements:
1. Mudiyettu of Kerala enlisted in UNESCO.
2. It is performed in Kali temple.
3. It depicts the victory of Goddess Kail over Asur.

Which of the statements given above is/are correct?

A. 1 and 2 only B. 2 and 3 only
C. 1 and 3 only D. All of the above

152. Match List-I with List-II and select the correct answer by using the codes given below:

List-I	List-II
(*a*) String puppet	1. Kathputli (Rajasthan)
(*b*) Rod puppet	2. Putul Nautch (Bengal)
(*c*) Glove puppet	3. Kundhei Nach (Odisha)
(*d*) Shadow puppet	4. Ravanchhaya (Odisha)

Codes:

	(*a*)	(*b*)	(*c*)	(*d*)
A.	1	2	3	4
B.	4	3	2	1
C.	4	2	3	1
D.	1	3	2	4

153. Consider the following statements:
1. Tamasha, dialogue delivery and footwork at lightning speed belongs to Maharashtra.
2. Dashavatar, Vishnu's 10 Avatars is main theme belongs to Konkan & Goa.
3. Bhavai, Rare synthesis of devotional and romantic sentiment.

Which of the statements given above is/are correct?

A. 1 and 2 only B. 2 and 3 only
C. 1 and 3 only D. All of the above

154. Match List-I with List-II and select the correct answer by using the codes:

List-I	List-II
(*a*) Sitar	1. Pt. Ravi Shankar
(*b*) Tabla	2. Ustad Shafat Ahmed Khan
(*c*) Flute	3. Ustad Amjad Ali Khan
(*d*) Sarod	4. Hari Prasad Chaurasiya

Codes:

	(*a*)	(*b*)	(*c*)	(*d*)
A.	1	2	3	4
B.	1	2	4	3
C.	4	3	2	1
D.	4	2	3	1

155. Which among the following temples of India is known as Black Pagoda?

A. Brihadeeswara Temple, Tanjore
B. Sun Temple, Konark
C. Lord Jagannath Temple, Puri
D. Meenakshi Temple, Madurai

156. Tansen, a great musician of his time, was in the court of:

A. Jahangir B. Shahjahan
C. Akbar D. Bahadur Shah

157. Kathak is a classical dance of

A. Manipur B. Kerala
C. Tamilnadu D. North India

158. Which devotional saint was cobbler by profession?

A. Surdas B. Tulsidas
C. Raidas D. None of these

159. The Kala Ghoda Arts Festival is associated with which one of the following cities?

A. Delhi B. Mumbai
C. Haryana D. Kerala

160. Which Indian Academy is promoting dance, drama and music?

A. Sahitya Academy
B. Lalit Kala Academy
C. National School of Drama
D. Sangeet Academy

161. Pungi is a dance form related to the state:

A. Punjab B. Himachal Pradesh
C. Haryana D. Delhi

162. In which year National Anthem was first sung?

A. 1920 B. 1906
C. 1915 D. 1911

163. The word 'Sathyameva Jayate' is taken from ______.

A. Yajur Veda B. Atharva Veda
C. Mundaka Upanishad D. Sam Veda

164. The rock cut temples of Mahabalipuram and the temples of Kanchipuram are the achievements of the ________ rulers.

A. Chola B. Hoyasala
C. Vijayanagar D. Pallava

165. Who among the following was known as Bengal's Greata Garbo?

A. Amaravati B. Kanan Devi
C. Suchitra Sen D. Bharathi Shirodkor

166. Match List-I with List-II and select the correct answer by using the codes given below:

List-I	List-II
(*a*) Chong	1. Nagaland
(*b*) Goudi	2. Chattisgarh
(*c*) Mask dance	3. Arunachal Pradesh
(*d*) Yakshagan	4. Karnataka

Codes:

	(*a*)	(*b*)	(*c*)	(*d*)
A.	1	2	3	4
B.	1	3	2	4
C.	4	3	2	1
D.	4	2	3	1

167. Match List-I with List-II and select the correct answer by using the codes given below:

List-I	List-II
(*a*) Bidesia	1. Jharkhand
(*b*) Lajri	2. Uttarakhand
(*c*) Dangri	3. Himachal Pradesh
(*d*) Thullal	4. Kerala

Codes:

	(*a*)	(*b*)	(*c*)	(*d*)
A.	1	2	3	4
B.	2	1	4	3
C.	3	2	4	1
D.	3	4	1	2

168. Match List-I with List-II and select the correct answer by using the codes given below:

List-I (Tribes)	List-II (States)
(*a*) Baggarwal	1. Jammu and Kashmir
(*b*) Chencus	2. Andhra Pradesh
(*c*) Tharu	3. Jharkhand
(*d*) Bhumij	4. Uttar Pradesh

Codes:

	(*a*)	(*b*)	(*c*)	(*d*)
A.	1	2	3	4
B.	2	1	4	3
C.	3	2	1	4
D.	1	2	4	3

169. Match List-I with List-II and select the correct answer by using the codes given below:

List-I (Festival)	List-II (States)
(*a*) Ugadi	1. West Bengal
(*b*) Navbarsha	2. Gujarat
(*c*) Bhadra Purnima	3. Maharashtra
(*d*) Gudi Padwa	4. Andhra Pradesh

Codes:

	(*a*)	(*b*)	(*c*)	(*d*)
A.	4	1	2	3
B.	4	2	1	3
C.	3	2	1	4
D.	3	1	2	4

170. Consider the following statements:
1. Bharatnatyam is considered the mother art of most of the other classical dances of India.
2. 'Kathak' means the one who tells a story.
3. Kuchipudi derives its name from the Kuchipudi village of Andhra Pradesh.
4. Odissi is considered a dance of love, joy and intense passion, pure, divine and human.

Which of the statements given above is/are correct?
A. 1 and 2 only
B. 2 and 3 only
C. 1, 2 and 3 only
D. All of the above

171. Choose the correct chronological sequence.
A. Firoze Minar, Chand Minar, Char Minar, Qutub Minar
B. Chand Minar, Char Minar, Qutub Minar, Firoze Minar
C. Qutub Minar, Firoze Minar, Chand Minar, Char Minar
D. Char Minar, Qutub Minar, Chand Minar, Firoze Minar

172. Choose the correct sequence of location from north to south.
A. Monolithic Kailashnath Temple, Briha-diswara Temple, Modhera Sun Temple, Avantiswami Temple
B. Brihadiswara Temple, Avantiswami Temple, Monolithic Kailashnath Temple, Modhera Sun Temple
C. Avantiswami Temple, Modhera Sun Temple, Monolithic Kailashnath Temple, Brihadiswara Temple
D. Modhera Sun Temple, Avantiswami Temple, Brihadiswara Temple, Monolithic Kailashnath Temple

173. Consider the following statements:
Assertion (A) : Sunga sculpture were invariably carved in low-relief with flat surfaces.
Reason (R) : Because the sculptors had no knowledge of perspective.

Select the correct answer using the codes given below.
Codes:
A. (A) is correct, but (R) is incorrect.
B. (A) is incorrect, but (R) is correct.
C. Both (A) and (R) are correct.
D. Both (A) and (R) are incorrect.

174. Consider the following statements:
Assertion (A) : It would be logical to propose that social reality is integral to an artist's expression in the domain of visual arts.
Reason (R) : Because it is an inherent and natural instinct for human expression to seek contemporary relevance while formulating the visual image, both in form and content.

Select the correct answer using the codes given below.
Codes:
A. (A) is correct, but (R) is incorrect.
B. (A) is incorrect, but (R) is correct.
C. Both (A) and (R) are correct.
D. Both (A) and (R) are incorrect.

175. Consider the following statements:
Assertion (A) : Bronze sculptures are stronger than brass sculptures. It is the composition of alloys in bronze that makes it stronger.
Reason (R) : The high ratio of copper in bronze, with a little addition of lead, makes the material stronger and ensures greater pliability in the medium.

Select the correct answer using the codes given below.
Codes:
A. (A) is correct, but (R) is incorrect.
B. (A) is incorrect, but (R) is correct.
C. Both (A) and (R) are correct.
D. Both (A) and (R) are incorrect.

176. The ratio of width of our National flag to its length is
A. 3 : 5 B. 2 : 3
C. 2 : 4 D. 3 : 4

177. Rabindranath Tagore's 'Jana Gana Mana' has been adopted as India's National Anthem. How many stanzas of the said song were adopted?
A. Only the first stanza
B. The whole song
C. Third and Fourth stanza
D. First and Second stanza

178. 'Natya-Shastra' the main source of India's classical dances was written by:
A. Nara Muni B. Bharat Muni
C. Abhinav Gupt D. Tandu Muni

179. Dandia' is a popular dance of:
A. Punjab B. Gujarat
C. Tamil Nadu D. Maharashtra

180. The words 'Satyameva Jayate' inscribed below the base plate of the emblem of India are taken from:
A. Rigveda B. Satpath Brahmana
C. Mundak Upanishad D. Ramayana

ANSWERS

[illegible]	**2**	**3**	**4**	**5**	**6**	**7**	**8**	**9**	**10**
[illegible]	C	D	A	A	A	A	A	B	A
[illegible]	**12**	**13**	**14**	**15**	**16**	**17**	**18**	**19**	**20**
[illegible]	B	D	C	A	A	C	C	C	B
[illegible]1	**22**	**23**	**24**	**25**	**26**	**27**	**28**	**29**	**30**
C	C	D	B	B	B	D	C	C	A
31	**32**	**33**	**34**	**35**	**36**	**37**	**38**	**39**	**40**
B	B	C	B	A	C	D	B	C	B
41	**42**	**43**	**44**	**45**	**46**	**47**	**48**	**49**	**50**
B	A	B	B	B	A	C	C	D	C
51	**52**	**53**	**54**	**55**	**56**	**57**	**58**	**59**	**60**
C	A	B	B	A	A	A	C	B	B
61	**62**	**63**	**64**	**65**	**66**	**67**	**68**	**69**	**70**
C	C	A	B	A	D	D	C	B	C
71	**72**	**73**	**74**	**75**	**76**	**77**	**78**	**79**	**80**
C	C	C	D	A	D	D	D	A	A
81	**82**	**83**	**84**	**85**	**86**	**87**	**88**	**89**	**90**
A	C	B	D	B	D	C	A	B	A
91	**92**	**93**	**94**	**95**	**96**	**97**	**98**	**99**	**100**
D	C	B	D	D	C	A	D	C	B
101	**102**	**103**	**104**	**105**	**106**	**107**	**108**	**109**	**110**
C	D	C	C	D	A	D	C	D	B
111	**112**	**113**	**114**	**115**	**116**	**117**	**118**	**119**	**120**
C	D	A	B	C	B	C	B	D	A
121	**122**	**123**	**124**	**125**	**126**	**127**	**128**	**129**	**130**
C	D	C	D	B	B	A	B	D	C
131	**132**	**133**	**134**	**135**	**136**	**137**	**138**	**139**	**140**
B	D	A	C	C	A	D	C	A	D
141	**142**	**143**	**144**	**145**	**146**	**147**	**148**	**149**	**150**
C	D	B	D	A	A	D	B	A	A
151	**152**	**153**	**154**	**155**	**156**	**157**	**158**	**159**	**160**
D	A	D	B	B	C	D	C	B	D
161	**162**	**163**	**164**	**165**	**166**	**167**	**168**	**169**	**170**
B	D	C	D	C	A	A	D	A	D
171	**172**	**173**	**174**	**175**	**176**	**177**	**178**	**179**	**180**
D	C	A	C	A	B	A	B	B	C

4

INDIAN AGRICULTURE, COMMERCE & TRADE

INDIAN AGRICULTURE

IMPORTANCE OF AGRICULTURE

- The performance of the agricultural sector influences the growth of the Indian economy.
- As per the provisional estimates of national income released by CSO on 29th May, 2021, the share of agriculture and allied sectors in Gross value Added (GVA) of the country at current prices is 18.8 per cent for the year 2021-22.
- It accounts more than 48.9 per cent of the employment in the country.
- Apart from being the provider of food and fodder, its importance also stems from the raw materials that it provides to industry.
- The prosperity of the rural economy is also closely linked to agriculture and allied activities.
- Economic development without agricultural development creates bottlenecks and generate inflationary pressure. This is what has happened in India. Low rate of agricultural development resulted in shortage of food and essential raw materials leading to inflation. Therefore, agricultural development is essential to avoid inflation and to ensure growth with stability.

GREEN REVOLUTION

- After the drought of 1965-66 and 1966-67, the government enunciated the new agricultural strategy, and put to use the high yielding variety seeds.
- The Green Revolution came on the scene around the middle of the 1960s, beginning with the Kharif crop of 1966.
- The new agricultural strategy was put into practice for the first time in India in the Kharif season of 1966 and was termed High-Yielding Varities Programme (HYVP).
- The HYVP was introduced in the form of a package programme since it depended crucially on regular and adequate irrigation, fertilizers, high-yielding varieties of seeds, pesticides and insecticides.

Drawbacks of Green Revolution

- The spread of green revolution has remained limited to only a few regions. Excepting Punjab, Haryana and Western Uttar Pradesh practically the whole country has remained untouched by the green revolution.
- Intra-regional disparity has also increased, as not all, but 'only who could afford' took the advantage of new expensive package technology.
- Environmental degradation took as
  (*a*) Chemical fertilizers led to problems of entrochication etc.
  (*b*) Pesticides killed many nutrient enriching bacteria of the soil.
  (*c*) Bio-diversity decreased as monoculturisation introduced.
- Groundwater went down in areas where wells and tube wells sucked excess of water.
- Irrigation of fields, without proper drainage led to salinization and alkalization of soils.
- As a consequence of the concentration of the new technology in large farms, the inequalities have increased between the rich and the poor in the rural sector.

Second Green Revolution

- In 2004, a second green revolution policy was announced by the government, and even though the next, government at the Centre did not refer to it, the ingredients have been promoted in practice.
- The effort is to increase agricultural production, going beyond just some foodgrains to all sectors.

- It ranges across cropping patterns, diversification, checking post-harvest losses, sustainable practices, soil and water conservation, *et al.*
- It also includes encouraging use of bio-fertilisers, bio-pesticides, and organic farming.
- There is also the elements of improving infrastructure, storage, and value addition—agroprocessing.
- Indeed, the Eleventh Plan vision and strategy for agriculture was largely based on the holistic approach involving the 'second green revolution'.

RAINBOW REVOLUTION

The new agricultural policy promises Green Revolution, White Revolution, and Blue Revolution. The Rainbow Revolution also includes 'Foodchain Revolution' to put a check on destroying food-grains, vegetables and fruits. It has described as a policy of promising Rainbow Revolution.

- A focus on Price protection for farmers to suit their requirements.
- Dismantling of restrictions on movement of agricultural commodities.
- Involvement of private sector through Contract Farming.
- 4% targeted annual growth in the development of agriculture.

LAND REFORMS

- A land reforms package broadly involves the following components:
  1. abolition of intermediaries,
  2. tenancy reforms (i.e., providing security of tenure),
  3. ceiling and redistribution,
  4. consolidation, and
  5. updating of land records.

Abolition of Intermediaries

- Even during the struggle for independence, it was widely recognised that the stagnation in the Indian agricultural sector was primarily due to exploitative agrarian relations. Zamindars were the chief instrument of exploitation.
- Hence, abolition of zamindari system, along with other intermediary tenure systems, became the topmost priority of land reforms immediately after independence.
- The abolition of intermediaries started in 1948 with the enactment of legislation in Madras. In some other states, the legislations for abolition of intermediaries were passed before 1951.
- West Bengal, the state worst affected by the ravages of absentee landlordism, adopted the legislation in 1954-55. In this way, most of the states had passed the Acts related to abolition of intermediaries by the end of the First Plan.

Tenancy Reforms

- Tenants can be classified into (*i*) occupancy tenants, (*ii*) tenants-at-will, and (*iii*) sub-tenants.
- The rights of tenancy of the occupancy tenants are permanent and heritable. Hence, the occupancy tenants do not face the fear of eviction so long as they pay rent on time.
- But the position of tenants-at-will and sub-tenants is very precarious, since such tenants depend on the mercy of landlords.
- Hence, special laws have had to be enacted and implemented to protect these people.
- These laws relate to : (*i*) regulation of rent, (*ii*) security of tenure, and (*iii*) conferment of ownership rights on tenants.

(*i*) **Regulation of Rent:** The First and the Second Plans recommended that rents should not exceed one-fourth or one-fifth of the gross produce. Various states have passed necessary legislation in this regard, but there are large variations in the rates of rents fixed in different states.

(*ii*) **Security of Tenure :** Legislations have been passed in most of the states to protect tenants from ejectment and grant them permanent rights in land. The purpose of these legislations is to ensure that (*i*) ejectments are lawful, (*ii*) land assumed by an owner is only for personal cultivation, and (*iii*) the tenant is assured of a prescribed minimum area in case of resumption.

(*iii*) **Conferment of Ownership Rights on Tenants :** Legislative provisions have been made in many states for conferment of ownership rights on tenants. Some of the states have acquired ownership of land from landowners and transferred it to tenants. Sub-tenancies have generally been prohibited except in certain cases such as widows, members of armed forces, minors, unmarried women, persons suffering from disabilities, etc.

Ceilings on Agricultural Holdings

- The basic aim of the ceiling laws is to accomplish the elimination of excessive ownership of land.
- Till 2001, only about 73.66 lakh acres were declared surplus in India, out of which only about 53.79 lakh acres were redistributed. Further, different states had adopted different policies regarding land ceiling.
- To bring uniformity in land ceiling policies, a conference of chief ministers was held in 1972.
- A new land ceiling policy was evolved in this conference. The main features of the new policy were as follows:

  (*i*) lowering of ceilings to 18 acres of irrigated land and 54 acres of unirrigated land, (*ii*) making family and not the individual as the unit for determining land holding,

(*iii*) lowering ceiling for a family of five,

(*iv*) declaring benami transaction null and void, and

(*v*) including the land reform laws in the Ninth Schedule of the Constitution, which places them beyond any challenge in any courts of law on the grounds of infringement of Fundamental Rights.

- In the light of this policy, land ceiling legislations were enacted by all the states, except Goa and north-east states. But ceiling limits vary.

Consolidation of Land Holdings

- The basic purpose of consolidation of land holdings is that the owner of several scattered pieces of land be provided with land at one place and it should be equivalent to all pieces of land.
- All the States, except Kerala, Tamil Nadu and Andhra Pradesh have passed the law for consolidation of holdings.

Updating and Maintenance of Land Records

- With a view to assisting the States/Union Territories in the task of updating of land records, a Centrally-sponsored Strengthening of Revenue Administration and Updating of Land Records (SRA&ULR) scheme was started in 1987 with the following objectives:

(*i*) strengthening the existing survey and settlement organisations for early completion and preparation of land records in areas where this work still remains to be done;

(*ii*) setting up survey and settlement organisations, especially in north-eastern region, where no land records exist;

(*iii*) imparting pre-service and in-service training to revenue survey and settlement staff and strengthening of training infrastructure for this purpose;

(*iv*) providing facilities for modernisation of survey and settlement operations, printing cf survey maps, documents reports, copying and updating of land and crop records, and storage facilities by adopting the latest science and technology inputs; and

(*v*) strengthening revenue machineries at village and immediate supervisory levels on a selective basis so that workload of these functionaries is made manageable.

AGRICULTURAL FINANCE

- Finance is an essential requirement for every productive activity. However, agriculture is up against serious credit problems.
- Besides the large many of the rural folk are groaning under the burden of indebtedness.
- Three types of loans are provided to Indian farmers to meet their financial requirements–

  (*i*) Short term loans (*ii*) Medium term loans (*iii*) Long term loans
- Short term loans are provided for a period of less than 15 months to meet out expenses of routine farming and domestic consumptions. This type of loans is demanded by farmers for purchasing seeds, fertilizers and for meeting out family requirements.
- Medium term loans are provided for a period of 15 months to 5 years to purchase agricultural equipments, animals and for purchasing seeds, fertilizers and for meeting out family requirements.
- Long term loans are provided for a period of more than 5 years. This type of loan is taken by the farmers to purchase land and expensive agricultural equipments and for repayment of old loans.

Sources of Agricultural Finance

- The sources of agricultural finance can be divided into two parts: (*i*) institutional sources, and (*ii*) non-institutional sources.
- The Non-institutional sources include moneylenders, landlords, traders, relatives and commission agents.
- The institutional sources include cooperative societies, commercial banks, regional rural banks, NABARD and RBI.
- Non-institutional sources continue to be important, although their share in the total credit is on the decline.
- At the time of Independence, the most important source of agricultural credit was the moneylender.
- In 1951 moneylenders accounted for as much as 71.6 per cent of rural credit.
- As a result of the efforts undertaken by the government to expand the institutional sources of finance, the importance of non-institutional sources (especially moneylenders) in rural credit has declined significantly.

Co-operative Credit Societies

- The cooperative movement was initiated in 1904 through the establishment of co-operative credit societies.
- Cooperative Credit Societies are based on three-tier structure, except the states in north-east region.
- At the lowest tier are the village level Primary Agricultural Credit Societies (PACSs). PACSs can be formed by any ten or more than ten persons. PACSs provide loans generally for productive purposes.
- At the second tier are the District Central Co-operative Banks (DCBs). DCBs advance loans to the PACSs in time of so that they can fulfil the requirements of agriculture.

At uppermost tier are the State Co-operative Banks (SCBs). The SCBs advances loans to the DCBs in order to augment their capacity to provide loans to the PACSs. It also co-ordinates and regulates the working of DCBs. For long-term finance, there are land development banks.

Commercial Banks

- The credit supply by commercial banks has been on the increase particularly since the nationalisation of major banks in 1969.
- The share of commercial banks in rural credit was only 0.9 per cent in 1951 which rose to 71.29 per cent in 2019-20.

Regional Rural Banks

- On the basis of the recommendations of working group, five regional rural banks (RRBs) were initially set up in 1975.
- RRBs are sponsored by the government and the commercial banks. The regions for their operations (normally district) are specified.
- RRBs provide credits mainly to small and marginal farmers, rural artisans etc.

National Bank for Agriculture and Rural Development

- NABARD was set up in July 1982. NABARD is the apex bank for rural credit. Its head office is in Mumbai.
- The main functions of NABARD are as follows:
  - NABARD is responsible for the development, policy planning, operational matters, coordination, monitoring, research, training and consultancy, etc., relating credit.
  - It has authority to oversee the functioning of the co-operative sector through its Agricultural Credit Department.
  - It provides short-term credit (upto 18 months) to SCBs.
  - It provides refinance to DCBs and RRBs for medium term credit requirement.
  - It provides refinance for long-term credit requirement to SCBs, land development banks, RRBs and commercial banks.
  - It provides long-term loans to the state governments for a maximum period of 20 years, for contribution to share capital of co-operative credit societies.

Kisan Credit Card Scheme

- To provide adequate and timely support from the banking system to the farmers for their cultivation needs including purchase of all inputs in a flexible and cost-effective manner, a Kisan Credit Card (KCC) Scheme was introduced in August 1988 for short-and medium-term loans.
- NABARD had advised banks to extend coverage through expanding their outreach by lending to more farmers including non-wilful defaulters, oral lessees, tenant farmers, sharecroppers, who may have been outside the fold of the scheme, as also new farmers.
- The scheme now also covers borrowers of the long term co-operative credit structure.
- In order to safeguard the interests of KCC holders, NABARD has allowed banks the discretion to opt for any insurance company of their choice.
- The Kisan Credit Card (KCC) has been an important initiative for universal access of farmers to institutional credit.

COMMERCE AND TRADE

Business which includes trade and commerce have played a vital role since times memorial. India, had a golden past and the trading activities had a significant contribution to its prosperity and gains. The archaeological evidences have shown that trading activities were the mainstay of the economy in ancient times which were carried out by both water and land routes. Silk route and maritime trade were quite prominent in transporting goods and commodities for trading purposes.

The goods were traded both internally and to the foreign lands, which generated surplus income. As a result, the people were engaged in various economic activities such as agriculture and domestication of animals, weaving cotton, dyeing fabrics, making clay pots, utensils and handicrafts, sculpting, cottage industries, masonry, etc. Family based workshops [*karkhanas*], for manufacturing, were important components of economic life. This money was channelised into further investment, and led to the dominant growth of indigenous banking system to finance the trading activities.

An example of it is the use of age old *Hundi* and *Chitties* (used in southern region). These were used as documents to facilitate transfer of money from one hand to another for trading activities.

Many leading trade centres were developed in ancient times for the import and export of goods, some of them being Patliputra, Peshawar, Taxila, Indraprastha, Mithila, Madhuram, Surat, Ujjain and Kanchi. Major exports items were Spices, wheat, sugar, indigo, opium, sesame oil, cotton, parrot, live animals and animal products, etc. Major imports were Horses, animal products, Chinese silks, linen, wine, gold, silver, copper, etc. There were all kinds of towns—port towns, manufacturing towns, mercantile towns, the sacred centres, and pilgrimage towns. Their existence is an index of prosperity of merchant communities and professional classes.

Business activities led to the growth of different aids to trade such as transportation, banking, finance and communication which grew the prospects of trading activities. With the active contribution of Indian traders and other merchant communities, the Indian sub-continent was popularly called '*Swaran Bhoomi and Swaran Deep*' in the writings of many travellers, such as Megasthenes, Faxian (FaHien), Xuanzang (Huen Tsang), Al Beruni (11th century), Ibn Batuta (11th century), Frenchman Francois (17th century) and others. They repeatedly refer to the prosperity of the country.

Between the 1st and the 7th centuries CE, India is estimated to have the largest economy of the ancient and medieval world, controlling about one-third and one-fourth of the world's wealth.

Hundi as practised by Indian Merchant Communities

Name of Hundi	Broader classification	Functions of Hundi
Dhani-jog	*Darshani*	Payable to any person—no liability over who received payment.
Sah-jog	*Darshani*	Payable to a specific person, someone 'respectable'. Liability over who received payment.
Firman-jog	*Darshani*	*Hundi* made payable to order.
Dekhan-har	*Darshani*	Payable to the presenter or bearer.
Dhani-jog	*Muddati*	Payable to any person—no liability over who received payment, but payment over a fixed term.
Firman-jog	*Muddati*	*Hundi* made payable to order following a fixed term.
Jokhmi	*Muddati*	Drawn against dispatched goods. If goods lost in transit, the drawer or holder bears the coasts, and the Drawee carries no liability.

Major Trade Centres in Ancient Times

- ***Indraprastha:*** It was the commercial junction on the royal road where most routes leading to the east, west, south and north converged.
- ***Mathura:*** It was an emporium of trade and people here subsisted on commerce. Many routes from South India touched Mathura and Bharuch.
- ***Varanasi:*** It was well placed as it lay both on the Gangetic route and on the highway that linked North with the East. It grew as a major centre of textile industry and became famous for beautiful gold silk cloth and sandalwood workmanship. It had links with Taxila and Bharuch.
- ***Pataliputra:*** Known as Patna today, it was not only a commercial town, but also a major centre for export of stones.
- ***Peshawar:*** It was an important exporting centre for wool and for the import of horses. It had a huge share in commercial transactions between India, China and Rome in the first century A.D.
- ***Taxila:*** It served as a major centre on the important land route between India and Central Asia. It was also a city of financial and commercial banks. The city occupied an important place as a Buddhist centre of learning. The famous Taxila University flourished here.
- ***Madura:*** It was the capital of the Pandayas who controlled the pearl fisheries of the Gulf of Mannar. It attracted foreign merchants, particularly Romans, for carrying out overseas trade.
- ***Bharuch:*** It was the greatest seat of commerce in Western India. It was situated on the banks of river Narmada and was linked with all important marts by roadways.
- ***Kaveripatta:*** Also known as Kaveripatnam, it was scientific in its construction as a city and provided loading, unloading and stron" facilities of merchandise. Foreign traders had their headquarters in this city. It was a convenient place for trade with Malaysia, Indonesia, China and the Far East. It was the centre of trade for perfumes, cosmetics, scents, silk, wool, cotton, corals, pearls, gold and precious stones; and also for ship building.
- ***Tamralipti:*** It was one of the greatest ports connected both by sea and land with the West and the Far East. It was linked by road to Banaras and Taxila.
- ***Mithila:*** The traders of Mithila crossed the seas by boats, through the Bay of Bengal to the South China Sea, and traded at ports on the islands of Java, Sumatra and Borneo. Mithila established trading colonies in South China, especially in Yunnan,

- ***Ujjain:*** Agate, carnelian, muslin and mallow cloth were exported from Ujjain to different centres. It also had trade relations through the land route with Taxila and Peshawar.
- ***Surat:*** It was the emporium of western trade during the Mughal period. Textiles of Surat were famous for their gold borders (zari). It is noteworthy that Surat *hundi* was honoured in far off markets of Egypt and Iran.
- ***Kanchi:*** Today known as Kanchipuram, it was here that the Chinese used to come in foreign ships to purchase pearls, glass and rare stones and in return they sold gold and silk.

With the emergence of the British Empire roots in India the East India company used revenues generated by the provinces under its rule for purchasing Indian raw materials, spices and goods. This changed the condition of the Indian economy from being an exporter of processed goods to the exporter of raw materials and buyer of manufactured goods.

After independence the process of rebuilding the economy started and India embarked on planned development with the objective of achieving a self-reliant socialistic pattern of society. The measures taken towards the same was characterised by centralised economic planning and emphasis on public investment in basic and key industries.

As a result, India agreed to economic liberalisation in 1991.

A three pronged approach of stabilisation, restructuring and globalisation of Indian economy was adopted to address the changes in economic and business scenario and its integration with global economy. Government of India announced major economic reform packages aimed at restoring the growth momentum in the economy. Major policy changes were effected since 1991 w.r.t., fiscal, monetary, trade, industry, agriculture, infrastructure, foreign exchange and foreign investment since 1991.

The Indian economy is emerging as one of the faster growing economies in the world today and a preferred FDI destination. Rising incomes, savings, investment opportunities, increased domestic consumption and younger population ensures growth for decades to come. The high growth sectors have been identified, which are likely to grow at a rapid pace and the recent initiatives of the Government of India such as 'Make in India', Skill India', 'Digital India' is expected to help the economy in terms of exports and imports with steady and sustainable trade balance.

COMMERCE

While industry is concerned with the production of goods, commerce is concerned with making the same available to those who need them. In other words, commerce is mainly concerned with distribution of goods. It embraces all those functions which are essential for maintaining a free and uninterrupted flow of goods. Therefore, the term commerce includes 'trade' and 'aids to trade'.

TRADE

The term 'trade' is used to denote buying and selling. Therefore, one who buys and sells is a trader. A trader is a middleman between the producer and the consumer. Trade may be wholesale trade or retail trade. A wholesale trader purchases in large quantities from the producers, and sells in small quantities to the retail traders. A retail trader is one who purchases from the wholesale trader or sometimes directly from the producer, and sells in smaller quantities to the ultimate consumers.

AIDS TO TRADE (AUXILIARIES TO TRADE)

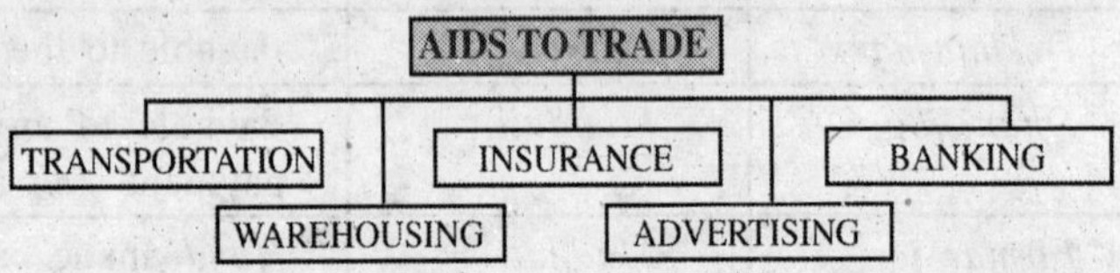

All activities that facilitate smooth flow of goods from manufacturing centres to the consumption centres are called aids or auxiliaries to trade. Aids to trade may be classified into five categories: (*i*) transportation, (*ii*) warehousing, (*iii*) insurance, (*iv*) advertising, and (*v*) banking. These are briefly explained below.

- **Transportation:** Selling all the goods produced at or near the production centres is not possible. Hence, goods are to be sent to different places where they are demanded. The medium which moves men and materials from one place to another is called transport.

  Transport can be of three types:

  (*i*) Land transport - road, rail

  (*ii*) Air transport - aeroplane

  (*iii*) Water transport - boat, ship

- **Warehousing:** Storage is indispensable in these days of mass production. The goods should be stored carefully from the time they are produced till the time they are sold, hence, the need for warehousing. Warehouses are also called godowns.
- **Insurance:** The goods may be destroyed while in production process or in transit due to accidents, or in storage due to fire or theft, etc. The businessmen would like to cover these risks. Insurance companies come to their rescue in this regard. They undertake to compensate the loss suffered due to such risks. For this purpose, the business has to take an 'insurance policy' and pay a certain amount regularly, called 'premium'.

- **Advertising:** Advertising is an effective aid in selling the goods. The producer, through advertisement, communicates all information about his goods, to the prospective consumers and create in them a strong desire to buy the product. Advertising can be carried in different ways. It can be indoor or outdoor. Communicating with people through advertising, when they are in their homes, is called indoor advertising. Examples of this type are advertising through newspapers, radio, 'television, etc. Communicating with people, when they go out from their homes, is called outdoor advertising. Examples of this type are advertisements in cinema theatre, wall posters, and hoardings at prominent places.
- **Banking:** Now-a-days we cannot think of business without banks. To start the business or to run it smoothly we require money. Banks supply money. A bank is an organization which accepts deposits of money from the public, withdrawable on demand or otherwise, and lends the same to those who need it. Banks also provide many services required for the business activity. Here, We have attempted to give just an overview of various business activities.

FOREIGN TRADE AND INVESTMENT

- Foreign trade has played a crucial role in India's economy growing at almost three times the growth of GDP during the last four years.
- India's exports cover a wide range of items including engineering goods, ores and minerals, chemicals and related products, gems and jewellery and of late, petroleum products.
- Imports have increased substantially, bulk of which comprise items like petroleum and crude products fertilizers, precious and semi-precious stones for export production, and capital goods, raw materials, consumables and intermediates for industrial production and technological upgradation.

Export Promotion Schemes

Export Processing Zones

- Before getting converted into Special Economic Zones (SEZs), these Export Processing Zones (EPZs) were playing important role in promoting exports of the country.
- These zones were created to develop such an environment in the economy which may provide capability of facing international competition.
- The Export Processing Zones (EPZs) set up as enclaves, separated from the Domestic Tariff Area by fiscal barriers, were intended to provide a competitive duty free environment for export production.
- All the 8 EPZs located at Kandla & Surat (Gujarat), Santa Cruz (Maharashtra), Cochin (Kerala), Chennai (Tamil Nadu), Vishakhapatnam (Andhra Pradesh), Faeta (West Bengal) and Noida (U. P.) have been converted into Special Economic Zones.

Export-Oriented Units

- Since 1981, the Government introduced a complementary plan of EPZ (Now converted into SEZ) scheme for promoting export units (making export of their cent per cent production).
- Under this scheme the Government provides various incentives to increase the production capacity of these units so as to increase exports of the country.
- This scheme offers a wider source of raw materials, hinterland facilities, availability of technological skills, existence of an industrial base and the need for a larger area of land for the project.

Export Houses, Trading Houses and Star Trading Houses

- To increase the marketable efficiency of exporters, the Government introduced the concept of export houses, trading houses and star trading houses.
- Those registered exporters who have shown good export performances over past few years have been given the status of export houses, and trading houses.
- These units are provided some special facilities and benefits by the Government.
- Since April 1, 1994 a new category named **Golden Super Star Trading** Houses was added by the Government which has the highest average annual foreign exchange earning.

Export Promotion Industrial Parks (EPIP)

- A Centrally-sponsored 'Export Promotion Industrial Park (EPIP)' scheme has been introduced in August 1994 with a view to involving the state governments in the creation of infrastructural facilities for export oriented production.
- It provides for 75% (limited to ₹ 10 crore) grant to state government towards creation of such facilities.

Export Development Centres

- The Government has made a plan to invest about ₹ 50,000 crore for developing infrastructure in 23 Export Development Centres identified by Union Commerce Ministry in 1995-96. The major portion of this investment will be made by the Private Sector.

Export Development Centres

1. Tirupur—Hosiery and Weaving Industry.
2. Moradabad—Brass Ware Handicraft.
3. Ludhiana—Heavy Machinery and Hosiery.

4. Surat—Gem and Jewellery.
5. Panipat—Handloom textiles.
6. Alleppi—Coconut and coir.
7. Jalandhar—Sport goods.
8. Ranipat (Amboor)—Leather.
9. Nagpur—Hand-made equipments.
10. Vishakhapatnam—Fish and Fish products.
11. Meerut—Sport goods.
12. Aligarh—Brass locks.
13. Agra—Leather shoes.
14. Khurja—Clay pots.
15. Kanchipuram—Silk.
16. Selam—Hand-made items.
17. Sivakashi—Match boxes.
18. Ambala—Scientific equipments.
19. Rajkot—Engine pump.
20. Wapi (Ankleshwar)—Chemicals
21. Jamnagar—Brass spare parts.
22. Batala—Machine equipment.
23. Bhagalpur—Weaving.

Agricultural Export Zones

- The EXIM policy 2001 introduced the concept of Agricultural Export Zones to give primacy to promotion of agricultural exports and effect a reorganisation of our export efforts on the basis of specific products and specific geographical areas.

Special Economic Zone

- With a view to creating an environment for achieving rapid growth in exports and to provide an internationally competitive and hassle-free environment for boosting exports, a Special Economic Zone Policy was announced in the EXIM Policy 2000.
- The SEZ Act 2005, supported by SEZ rules, came into effect on February 10, 2006.
- The salient features of SEZ schemes are:
  - A designated duty free enclave to be treated as foreign territory only for trade operations and duties and tariffs.
  - No license required for import.
  - Manufacturing, trading and service activities allowed.
  - SEZ units to be positive net foreign exchange earners within three years.
  - Full freedom for sub-contracting.
  - Domestic sales subject to full customs duty and import policy in force.
  - No routine examination by customs authorities of export/import cargo.

Foreign Investment

- Foreign investment is generally in the form of private foreign participation and government collaborations in certain sectors of the domestic economy.
- The main advantage of the form of assistance is that generally the foreign investor also brings with him technical expertise, machines, capital goods etc. which are scarce in under-developed countries.
- **Direct Foreign Investment :** Foreign capital can enter India in the form of direct investment. Sometimes companies of advanced countries start their subsidiary offices and affiliates in India. Alternately foreigners may subscribe to stocks and debentures of concerns in India. This is known as portfolio investment.
- **Foreign Collaboration :** There are three types of foreign collaborations— joint participation between private parties, between foreign firms and Indian Government and between foreign government and Indian Government.
- **Loans from International Institutions :** Since 1946, the World Bank and its affiliates have been important suppliers of capital to India. International Monetary Fund (IMF), Aid India Consortium, Asian Development Bank (ADB) and the World Bank have been the major sources of external assistance to India in recent years.
- **External Commercial Borrowing (ECB) :** India has also been tapping export credit agencies like the US Exim Bank, the Japanese Exim Bank, ECGC of the UK etc. to obtain a major portion of the commercial borrowing from the capital market.
- **Inter-Government Loans:** Since the second world war there has been a growing tendencies towards direct inter government loans and grants.

Foreign Exchange Convertibility

- Foreign exchange refers to the currencies of foreign countries that can be bought and sold on foreign exchange markets.
- Foreign exchange reserves are liquid assets held by a country's government or central bank to enable them to intervene in the foreign exchange market to influence the exchange rate.
- The exchange rate is the price of one currency in terms of another.
- For use in the external sector, the rupee is convertible into other currencies of the world. The central bank exchanges one country's currency for another.
- Till 1946, the rupee was linked to the British pound-sterling. However, when the International Monetary Fund (IMF) was set up (and India was a founder-member), as per IMF instructions, the external value of the rupee was fixed and maintained in terms of gold or the US dollar. The link with pound-sterling also continued.

- The IMF system of fixed exchange did not last long and in 1975 the Government of India delinked the rupee from pound-sterling and called upon the RBI to determine the exchange rate of the rupee in terms of the exchange rate movements of a basket of currencies—the pound, the US dollar, the yen and the deutsche mark.

Current Account Convertibility

- Current account convertibility means the freedom to buy or sell foreign exchange for the following international transactions: payments due in connection with foreign trade, current business, including services, and normal short-term banking and credit facilities; payments due as interest on loans, and as net income from other investments; payment of moderate amount of amortisation of loans or for depreciation of direct investments; and moderate remittances for family living expenses.
- However, full convertibility on current account does not mean abolition of all controls.
- The RBI can and does intervene to manage volatility, though it does not fix rate target.
- In order to prevent the rupee from appreciating too fast, RBI purchases dollars from the market and sells rupees in return.
- To control inflationary pressure, RBI sells some of the government securities it holds so as to draw out the rupees it has released in the economy.

Capital Account Convertibility

- Capital Account Convertibility (CAC) means freedom to convert local financial assets into foreign financial assets and vice versa at market determined rates of exchange.
- It is associated with changes of ownership in foreign/domestic financial assets and liabilities and embodies the creation and liquidation of claims on, or by, the rest of the world.
- Broadly, capital account convertibility would mean freedom for firms and residents to freely buy into overseas assets such as equity, bonds, property, and acquire ownership of overseas firms besides free repatriation of proceeds by foreign investors.
- The RBI chose a path of gradual and phased move towards capital account convertibility.

Foreign Exchange Reserves

- India's foreign exchange reserves comprise foreign currency assets (FCA), gold, special drawing rights (SDRs) and reserve tranche position (RTP) in the International Monetary Fund (IMF).

MULTIPLE CHOICE QUESTIONS

1. The chief producer of Soyabean in India is:
A. Gujarat B. Rajasthan
C. Madhya Pradesh D. Haryana

2. Of the total reporting area in India, the land under all foodgrains put together constitutes
A. 59.5 per cent B. 60.7 per cent
C. 84.2 per cent D. 74.4 per cent

3. The proportion of area under sugarcane to the total reporting area in the India is
A. 2.6 per cent B. 2.4 per cent
C. 11.0 per cent D. 3.0 per cent

4. The chief producer of groundnut in India is
A. Karnataka B. Andhra Pradesh
C. Maharashtra D. Gujarat

5. The leading state in wheat production is
A. Haryana B. Punjab
C. Uttar Pradesh D. Bihar

6. Difference between gross cropped area and the area sown represents
A. Area sown more than once
B. Wasteland area
C. Culturable area
D. Arable area

7. Which of the following state is the leading producer of tea?
A. Assam B. Karnataka
C. West Bengal D. Sikkim

8. In India, the main limiting factor for cultivation is
A. Small size of farms
B. Infertile soils
C. Length of growing season
D. Inadequacy of water supply

9. The Kharif season begins
A. In December
B. With the onset of South-West monsoon
C. At the end of the South-West monsoon
D. In March

10. Which cereal occupies the largest cropped area?
A. Rice B. Wheat
C. Maize D. Jowar

11. The portion of area under agricultural uses to the total geographical area in India is

A. 30.1 per cent B. 58.4 per cent
C. 77.2 per cent D. 46.6 per cent

12. Total area of land under crops counting the double cropped areas is called
A. Gross cropped area
B. Maximum area shown
C. Cropped area
D. Net area sown

13. Which of the following states leads in the production of maize?
A. Punjab B. U.P.
C. Karnataka D. Maharashtra

14. The production of wheat has increased mainly due to
A. Increase in prices
B. Increase in area under wheat
C. Increase in yield per hectare
D. Increase in demand for wheat

15. The crops of Kharif are
A. Barley B. Rice
C. Wheat D. Peas

16. Cotton cultivation is widespread in Maharashtra and Gujarat mainly because
A. Regur soils retain moisture
B. There is demand from local cotton mills
C. It requires moderate rainfall
D. It requires irrigation

17. India stands — in the production of tobacco
A. Second B. First
C. Third D. None of these

18. Agricultural yields in India are among the lowest in the world mainly because
A. Modern methods of cultivation are not extensively used
B. Prices are not remunerative to the farmers
C. Agricultural landholdings are small
D. People are illiterate

19. The largest producer of rice in India is
A. West Bengal B. Karnataka
C. Bihar D. Tamil Nadu

20. In rice production India's position in the world is
A. Fifth B. First
C. Second D. Third

21. Crops like barley, sugarbeat, date, rapeseed kale cotton etc., which can tolerate over 5,000 ppm salts are classified as
A. Salinity sensitive crops
B. Salinity tolerant crops
C. Resistant of salinity
D. Semi-tolerant to salinity

22. The top most Jute manufacturing centre in country is
A. Kolkata B. Patna
C. Mumbai D. Shillong

23. Only one crop of rice can be cultivated in a year in the following state
A. Tamil Nadu B. Kerala
C. Punjab D. West Bengal

24. Which state is the largest producer of tobacco?
A. Tamil Nadu B. Kerala
C. Andhra Pradesh D. Karnataka

25. The impact of the green revolution has been felt in
A. Increase in irrigated area
B. Increase in area under high yielding varieties
C. Increased yield per hectares
D. Increase in cropped area

26. Net agriculture is called for
A. Scientific agriculture
B. Single crop farming
C. Traditional subsistence agriculture
D. Crash crop

27. Which of the following states has the highest useful agricultural land?
A. U.P. B. Kerala
C. Bihar D. Maharashtra

28. Linear pattern of settlement is found along
A. Costal regions
B. Hills
C. Railways and Roadways
D. River valley

29. Operation flood is related to
A. Check the soil region
B. Milk production
C. Flood control
D. Fish production

30. Which of the following is the commercial crop in India?
A. Mustard B. Tobacco
C. Jute D. All of the above

31. Which Indian state produces the largest quantity of pulses?
A. Maharashtra B. Uttar Pradesh
C. Madhya Pradesh D. Rajasthan

32. What is the correct descending order of rice-producing states in India?
A. Punjab, West Bengal and Bihar
B. Punjab, Gujarat and West Bengal
C. Bihar, Punjab and West Bengal
D. West Bengal, Uttar Pradesh and Punjab

33. What is the correct descending order of food grain-producing states?
A. Uttar Pradesh, Madhya Pradesh and Punjab
B. Punjab, Uttar Pradesh and Madhya Pradesh
C. Uttar Pradesh, Punjab and Madhya Pradesh
D. Madhya Pradesh, Punjab and West Bengal

34. Which agency is responsible for the procurement, distribution, and storage of food grain production in India?
A. Ministry of Agriculture
B. Food Corporation of India
C. NAFED
D. TRIFED

35. Who approves the Fair and Remunerative Price (FRP) of sugarcane?
A. Cabinet Committee on Economic Affairs
B. Commission for Agricultural Costs and Prices
C. Directorate of Marketing and Inspection, Ministry of Agriculture
D. Agricultural Produce Market Committee

36. Which sector is the backbone of the Indian economy?
A. Service Sector B. Financial Sector
C. Tourism Sector D. Agriculture Sector

37. Which among the following is not a cereal?
A. Rice B. Wheat
C. Gram D. Maize

38. Which among the following does not belong to welfare schemes for the farmers?
A. Kisan Credit Card Scheme
B. SHG Bank Linkage Programme
C. National Agricultural Insurance Scheme
D. Employee Referral Scheme

39. When did the Government present Kisan Credit Card Scheme?
A. April 1853 B. August 1998
C. July 1991 D. November 1995

40. When were Kisan Call Centres established?
A. July 2000 B. March 2002
C. March 2004 D. January 2004

41. Sugarcane + Potato is an intercropping system of:
A. Autumn season B. Zaid season
C. Spring season D. Rainy season

42. Which crop requires the maximum amount of nitrogen?
A. Potato B. Wheat
C. Barley D. Sugarcane

43. Sprinkler irrigation is suitable, where the soil has:
A. Clayey texture
B. Loamy texture
C. Undulating topography
D. All of these

44. Covered smut of barley is a disease of:
A. Externally seed-borne
B. Internally seed-borne
C. Air-borne
D. None of these

45. The headquarters of the Indian Meteorological Department was established in 1875 at:
A. New Delhi B. Hyderabad
C. Pune D. Calcutta

46. How many agro-climatic zones (ACZ) are found in India?
A. 16 B. 18
C. 15 D. 20

47. The main function of NABARD is:
A. Farmers' loaning
B. Agricultural research
C. Refinancing to agricultural financing institutions
D. Development of agriculture

48. Rock phosphates are used in:
A. Saline soil B. Sodic soil
C. Acidic soil D. Neutral soil

49. Whiptail disease of cauliflower is caused by a deficiency of:
A. Nitrogen B. Boron
C. Molybdenum D. Zinc

50. The word 'Agriculture' is derived from:
A. Greek B. Latin
C. Arabic D. French

51. What is the main function of zinc in the plants?
A. Synthesis of nitrogen
B. Synthesis of phosphorus
C. Required for synthesis of Tryptophos
D. To increase the activity of the boron

52. Which of the following soil type is most suitable for garlic cultivation?
A. Loamy sand B. Sandy loam
C. Loam D. Clay

53. The main reason for the Irish Famine in Potato was:
A. Late Blight disease
B. Bacterial Blight disease
C. Blast disease
D. Ear Cockle disease

54. Farm Planning means:
A. Farm Budgeting
B. Cropping pattern
C. Type of enterprises
D. None of these

55. The main function of bio-fertilizer is:
A. To increase the chemical process
B. To increase the physiological process
C. To increase the biological process
D. To increase the photosynthesis process

56. A farming system in which airable crops are grown in alleys formed by trees or shrubs, to establish soil fertility and to enhance soil productivity, is known as:
A. Relay cropping B. Multiple cropping
C. Alley cropping D. Mixed cropping

57. Which among the following has the function of recommending Minimum Support Prices (MSP) for various commodities to the Government?
A. National Farmers Commission
B. Agriculture Cost & Price Commission
C. Central Statistical Organization
D. Department of Agriculture

58. The first state in India to launch a policy to establish Special Agriculture Zones (SAZs):
A. Uttar Pradesh B. Gujarat
C. Haryana D. Uttarakhand

59. At which among the following places, National Research Centre for Citrus is located?
A. Nagpur B. Kanpur
C. Surat D. Aurangabad

60. Which among the following is the largest foodgrain producing state of India?
A. Uttar Pradesh B. Punjab
C. Madhya Pradesh D. Rajasthan

61. Which of the following places India's First Agricultural University was established?
A. Pantnagar B. Kanpur
C. Lucknow D. Kolkata

62. Central Seed Testing and Referral Laboratory (CSTL) is located at:
A. Bhopal B. Varanasi
C. Lucknow D. Dehradun

63. Which one of the following sets of conditions is necessary for a good cultivation of wheat?
A. Low temperature and low rainfall
B. High temperature and moderate rainfall
C. High temperature and heavy rainfall
D. Moderate temperature and moderate rainfall

64. The Green Revolution has not been as green as it has been made out to be because
A. it created big farmers
B. it is confined to select regions
C. it is confined only to wheat
D. None of the above

65. Among the following states, which one has the most suitable climatic conditions for the cultivation of a large variety of orchids with minimum cost of production and can develop an export oriented industry in this field?
A. Arunachal Pradesh B. Madhya Pradesh
C. Andhra Pradesh D. Uttar Pradesh

66. Which among the following facilities has been started in India for refinance assistance for small irrigation, IRDP, dairy development and mechanisation of farms?
A. National Credit Stabilisation Fund
B. National Rural Credit Fund
C. National Credit Fund
D. Rural Infrastructure Development Fund

67. In India those farmers are called 'Marginal Farmers' who hold the land upto
A. 1 hectares B. 3 hectares
C. 5 hectares D. None of these

68. Rice, sorghum, maize, sunflower, berseem, onion, spinach, carrot, wheat, bajara etc. are classified as semi-tolerant to salinity, because they can tolerate salt concentration of
A. below 2,500 ppm
B. About 1,500 ppm
C. 2,500-5,000 ppm
D. above 5,000 ppm

69. In which of the following cakes the nitrogen content is highest?
A. Karanj cake B. Groundnut cake
C. Neem cake D. Mustard cake

70. Agricultural yields in India are among the lowest in the world mainly because
A. Modern methods of cultivation are not extensively used
B. Prices are not remunerative to the farmers
C. Agricultural landholdings are small
D. People are illiterate

71. Crops like barley, sugarbeat, date, rapeseed kale cotton etc., which can tolerate over 5,000 ppm salts are classified as
A. Salinity sensitive crops
B. Salinity tolerant crops
C. Resistant of salinity
D. Semi-tolerant to salinity

72. Only one crop of rice can be cultivated in a year in the following state
A. Tamil Nadu B. Kerala
C. Punjab D. West Bengal

73. The relative importance of various sources of irrigation in India is
A. Canals, wells, tanks
B. Tanks, canals, wells
C. Wells, tanks, canals
D. Canals, tanks, wells

74. The impact of the green revolution has been felt in
A. Increase in irrigated area
B. Increase in area under high yielding varieties
C. Increased yield per hectares
D. Increase in cropped area

75. Which state has the largest acreage under rubber?
A. Karnataka B. Maharashtra
C. Orissa D. Kerala

76. Net agriculture is called for
A. Scientific agriculture
B. Single crop farming
C. Traditional subsistence agriculture
D. Crash crop

77. Which of the following states has the highest useful agricultural land?
A. U.P. B. Kerala
C. Bihar D. Maharashtra

78. Trade between two countries can be useful if cost ratios of goods are:
A. Undetermined B. Decreasing
C. Equal D. Different

79. The term Euro Currency market refers to
A. The international foreign exchange market
B. The market where the borrowing and lending of currencies take place outside the country of issue
C. The countries which have adopted Euro as their currency
D. The market in which Euro is exchanged for other currencies

80. Which of the following theories suggests that firms seek to penetrate new markets over time?
A. Imperfect Market Theory
B. Product cycle theory
C. Theory of Comparative Advantage
D. None of the above

81. Dumping refers to:
A. Reducing tariffs
B. Sale of goods abroad at low a price, below their cost and price in home market
C. Buying goods at low prices abroad and selling at higher prices locally
D. Expensive goods selling for low prices

82. International trade and domestic trade differ because of:
A. Different government policies
B. Immobility of factors
C. Trade restrictions
D. All of the above

83. The margin for a currency future should be maintained with the clearing house by:
A. The seller
B. The buyer
C. Either the buyer or the seller as per the agreement between them
D. Both the buyer and the seller

84. The following statement with respect to currency option is wrong:
A. Foreign currency-Rupee option is available in India
B. An American option can be executed on any day during its currency
C. Put option gives the buyer the right to sell the foreign currency
D. Call option will be used by exporters

85. Govt. policy about exports and imports is called:
A. Commercial policy B. Fiscal policy
C. Monetary policy D. Finance policy

86. Which of the following is international trade?
A. Trade between countries
B. Trade between regions
C. Trade between provinces
D. Both (B) and (C)

87. Market in which currencies buy and sell and their prices settle on is called the:
A. International bond market
B. International capital market
C. Foreign exchange market
D. Eurocurrency market

88. Consider the following statements:
1. Trade in services denoted as invisible trade because they are not seen to cross national borders.
2. Total foreign trade (exports + imports) as a proportion of GDP is a common measure of the degree of openness of an economy.

Select the correct answer using the code given below.
A. 1 only B. 2 only
C. Both 1 and 2 D. Neither 1 nor 2

89. What does pegged exchange rate system mean?
A. The exchange rate is pegged at a particular level
B. The exchange rate is determined by the forces of market demand and supply
C. The exchange rate is fixed by bank consortium
D. The exchange rate is fixed by Govt together with private players.

90. Devaluation is said to occur when the exchange rate is ______?
A. Decreased B. Increased
C. Kept constant D. None of these

91. Which of the following Institutions are "The Bretton Woods System"?
A. IMF and WTO B. IMF and World Bank
C. IBRD and IDA D. WTO and World Bank

92. With reference to SDR, consider the following statement:
1. 'Reserve asset' created under the control of the IMF
2. At present, it is calculated daily as the weighted sum of the values in dollars of four currencies (euro, dollar, Japanese yen, and pound sterling)
3. Special Drawing Rights (SDRs) also known as 'paper gold'

Which of the statements given above is/are correct?
A. 1 and 2 only B. 2 only
C. 1, 2 and 3 D. 2 and 3 only

93. With mines not producing enough gold, ______ helped to economise on gold.
A. Fractional reserve banking (Paper currency was not entirely backed by gold)
B. Gold Standard
C. Fixed exchange rate system
D. Silver standard

94. The investment in productive assets and participation in management as stake holders in business enterprises is:
A. FDI B. FII
C. SDR D. Balance of payment

95. The portfolio investment by foreign institutional investors is called:
A. FDI B. FII
C. SDR D. Balance of payment

96. Which of the following is a part of capital account?
A. Private capital B. Banking capital
C. Official capital D. All the above

97. Which one among the following is the correct descending sequence of India's Export of commodities in terms of value in 2020-21?
A. Gems and Jewellery-Engineering goods-Drugs & Pharmaceuticals-Organic & inorganic chemicals-Petroleum products
B. Engineering goods-Drugs & Pharmaceuticals-Gems and Jewellery-Organic & inorganic chemicals- Petroleum products
C. Petroleum products-Gems and Jewellery-Drugs & Pharmaceuticals-Engineering goods-Organic & inorganic chemicals
D. Drugs & Pharmaceuticals-Gems and Jewellery-Engineering goods-Organic & inorganic chemicals-Petroleum products

98. Which of the following is not an objective of export promotion capital goods scheme?
A. Promote import of capital goods to enhance export
B. Promote exports from India
C. Reduce the customs duty collection from manufacturers
D. Infuse high technology capital equipment in the manufacturing sector

99. Which one of the following continents accounts for the maximum share in exports from India?
A. Asia B. Europe
C. Africa D. North America

100. Brent index is associated with
A. Crude oil prices B. Copper future prices
C. Gold future prices D. Shipping rate index

101. During 2020-21, which of the following items under manufacturing goods sector had the highest share in India's exports?
A. Gems and jewellery
B. Engineering goods
C. Chemical and related products
D. Handicrafts

102. What is the base year of newly introduced Consumer Price Index (CPI)
A. 2000 B. 2004
C. 2012 D. 2011

103. Most of India's foreign trade is carried through:
A. Land and sea B. Land and air
C. Sea and air D. Sea

104. Free international trade maximizes world output through ________.
A. Countries reducing various taxes imposed.
B. Countries specializing in production of goods they are best suited for.
C. Perfect competition between countries and other special regions
D. The diluting the international business laws & conditions between countries.

105. Domestic company limits it's operations to _____ political boundaries.
A. International B. National
C. Transnational D. Global

106. Trade between two or more than two countries is known as ________.
A. Internal Business B. External Trade
C. International Trade D. Unilateral Trade

107. _____ means selling the products at a price less than on going price in the market.
A. Quota B. Tariff
C. Subsidy D. Dumping

108. Commerce includes activities relating to trade and ______ to trade.
A. supporting B. subsidiaries
C. auxiliaries D. None of these

109. An economy that do not export or import from other country, is said to be....
A. Open economy B. Closed economy
C. Mixed economy D. Socialist economy

110. If import increase then the current account deficit of country is likely to:
A. Will remain constant
B. Is likely to increase
C. Is likely to decrease
D. All of the above

111. Which one of the following, clearly defines the meaning of the balance of payments of a country?
A. Balance in consolidated fund of the country
B. Balance with International Monetary Fund
C. Balance in World Bank
D. Record of foreign trade of the country

112. What is the effect of an increase in demand for exports on the foreign currency reserve of a country?
A. It will be Positive B. It will be Negative
C. It will be Neutral D. All of these

113. Which of the following is the part of the Balance of payments of a country?
A. Current account B. Capital account
C. Revenue accounts D. Both (A) & (B)

114. What will be effect of an increase in the debt of a country on current account deficit?
A. It shall be effected positively
B. It shall be effected negatively
C. It shall be effected neutrally
D. All of these

115. If the value of rupee declines rapidly with comparison to dollar, then the price of Indian goods will.
A. Indian goods will get cheaper for foreigners
B. Indian goods will get costlier for foreigners
C. Indian goods would remain at the same price
D. All the above

116. In which of the following account is borrowings from the World Bank be recorded in the balance of payments?
A. Capital account B. Visible goods
C. Current account D. Revenue account

117. In which of the following is, the visible items recorded for a country.
A. Capital account
B. The balance of trade
C. Foreign Exchange
D. Reserve Bank of India

118. Which of the following is the full form of IMF.
A. International Monetary Finance
B. International Money Federation
C. International Monetary Fund
D. International Monetary Function Committee

119. Which of the following is the full form of FDI?
A. Foreign direct investment
B. Foreign development investment
C. Fixed deposit interest
D. (B) and (C) of above

120. If balance of payments of country is in deficit, then:
A. Current account will be in deficit
B. Export shall increase
C. The country and borrow from abroad
D. (A) and (C) both

ANSWERS

1	2	3	4	5	6	7	8	9	10
C	D	B	D	C	D	A	D	B	A
11	**12**	**13**	**14**	**15**	**16**	**17**	**18**	**19**	**20**
C	D	C	C	B	A	A	A	A	C
21	**22**	**23**	**24**	**25**	**26**	**27**	**28**	**29**	**30**
B	A	C	C	C	C	A	C	B	D
31	**32**	**33**	**34**	**35**	**36**	**37**	**38**	**39**	**40**
D	D	A	B	A	D	C	D	B	D
41	**42**	**43**	**44**	**45**	**46**	**47**	**48**	**49**	**50**
A	D	D	B	D	C	C	C	C	B
51	**52**	**53**	**54**	**55**	**56**	**57**	**58**	**59**	**60**
C	B	A	B	C	C	B	D	A	A
61	**62**	**63**	**64**	**65**	**66**	**67**	**68**	**69**	**70**
A	B	D	C	A	D	A	C	B	A
71	**72**	**73**	**74**	**75**	**76**	**77**	**78**	**79**	**80**
B	C	A	C	D	C	A	D	B	B
81	**82**	**83**	**84**	**85**	**86**	**87**	**88**	**89**	**90**
B	D	D	D	A	A	C	C	A	B
91	**92**	**93**	**94**	**95**	**96**	**97**	**98**	**99**	**100**
B	C	A	A	B	D	A	C	A	A
101	**102**	**103**	**104**	**105**	**106**	**107**	**108**	**109**	**110**
A	C	C	B	B	A	D	C	B	B
111	**112**	**113**	**114**	**115**	**116**	**117**	**118**	**119**	**120**
D	A	D	B	A	A	B	C	A	D

5

POPULATION, ECOLOGY & URBANISATION

POPULATION

- Every year 11th July is celebrated as the World Population Day.
- The first census of India was done in 1872 during the reign of Viceroy Lord Mayo. But a series of census (After every ten years) was adopted in 1881 during the reign of Viceroy Lord Ripon.
- 2011 census is the 15th census of India, and the 7th census of free India.
- The entire census of 2011 exercise has been completed by March 15, 2011.
- The term density of population implies the average number of persons living per sq. km. It is denoted in the following way:

  The density of population

  $$= \frac{\text{Total population of a certain place}}{\text{Total area of the certain place}}$$

- No. of females in comparison to per 1000 males is known as sex ratio. It is denoted in the following way:

  $$\text{Sex Ratio} = \frac{\text{No. of Females}}{\text{No. of Males}} \times 1000$$

- No. of females in age group between 0-6 year, in comparison of per 1000 males of same age group is known as child sex ratio. It is denoted in the following way:

  Child Sex Ratio (0-6 year)

  $$= \frac{\text{No. of Females Children (0-6)}}{\text{No. of Males Children (0-6)}} \times 1000$$

- Birth Rate (or crude Birth Rate) is number of the birth per thousand of the population during a period, usually a year. Only live births are included in the calculation of birth rate.
- Death rate signifies the number of deaths in a year per thousand of the population. It is mostly known as crude death rate. Life expectancy is important determinant of death rate. A country having high life expectancy will have a high crude death rate.
- The term fertility refers to the actual bearing of children or 'occurrence of births'. Fertility rate measures the average number of the live births per 1000 women. This rate is one of the most important and useful aids to population projection. It helps in assessing population trends in the economy.
- Percentage of literates between the age of 7 and above of total population is called 'Literacy Rate'.
- The people between the age of 7 and above, who can understand, write and read any language are known as 'literate'.
- An urban area having population of 1,00,000 or above persons is known as a city.
- In the 2011 census, an urban area was defined as follows:
  - (*a*) All places with a municipal corporation, cantonment board or notified towns area committee, etc.
  - (*b*) All other places which satisfy the following criteria:
    - (*i*) Minimum population of 5,000 persons;
    - (*ii*) At least 75 per cent of male working population engaged in non-agricultural pursuits; and
    - (*iii*) A density of population of at least 400 persons per sq. km (1,000 persons per sq. mile).
- From the 1920s onwards, the rate of growth of population picked up. The year 1921 is termed as year of 'great divide'.
- High birth rate supplemented with improved health and medical facilities (which makes death rate fall) pushes the economy towards the state of "population explosion". India faces the same situation at present.
- An increasing difference between birth rate and death rate has created a scene of population explosion in India. This problem in India is not the result of declining death rate alone, which is actually an indicator of social development. But a simultaneous effort for reducing birth rate should have been made, where we have totally failed.
- The framework of the new population policy, 2000 was derived from recommendations of M.S. Swaminathan Committee. Three main objectives of this policy are:

2011 CENSUS OF INDIA : POPULATION DISTRIBUTION, POPULATION DENSITY AND LITERACY RATE

S. No.	State/ Union Territories	Population 2011			Population Density (per sq. km)	Literacy Rate 2011		
		Persons	Males	Females	2011	Persons	Males	Females
	INDIA	**1,21,08,54,977**	**62,32,70,258**	**58,75,34,719**	**382**	**73.0**	**80.9**	**64.6**
1.	Jammu and Kashmir	1,25,41,302	66,40,662	59,00,640	124	67.2	76.8	56.4
2.	Himachal Pradesh	68,64,602	34,81,873	33,82,729	123	82.8	89.5	75.9
3.	Punjab	2,77,43,338	1,46,39,465	1,31,03,873	551	75.8	80.4	70.7
4.	Chandigarh	10,55,450	5,80,663	4,74,787	9,258	86.0	90.0	81.2
5.	Uttarakhand	1,00,86,292	51,37,773	49,48,519	189	78.8	87.4	70.0
6.	Haryana	2,53,51,462	1,34,94,734	1,18,56,728	573	75.6	84.1	65.9
7.	Delhi	1,67,87,941	89,87,326	78,00,615	11,320	86.2	90.9	80.8
8.	Rajasthan	6,85,48,437	3,55,50,997	3,29,97,440	200	66.1	79.2	52.1
9.	Uttar Pradesh	19,98,12,341	10,44,80,510	9,53,31,831	829	67.7	77.3	57.2
10.	Bihar	10,40,99,452	5,42,78,157	4,98,21,295	1,106	61.8	71.2	51.5
11.	Sikkim	6,10,577	3,23,070	2,87,507	86	81.4	86.6	75.6
12.	Arunachal Pradesh	13,83,727	7,13,912	6,69,815	17	65.4	72.6	57.7
13.	Nagaland	19,78,502	10,24,649	9,53,853	119	79.6	82.8	76.1
14.	Manipur	28,55,794	14,38,586	14,17,208	128	76.9	83.5	70.2
15.	Mizoram	10,97,206	5,55,339	5,41,867	52	91.3	93.3	89.3
16.	Tripura	36,73,917	18,74,376	17,99,541	350	87.2	91.5	82.7
17.	Meghalaya	29,66,889	14,91,832	14,75,057	132	74.4	76.0	72.9
18.	Assam	3,12,05,576	1,59,39,443	1,52,66,133	398	72.2	77.8	66.3
19.	West Bengal	9,12,76,115	4,68,09,027	4,44,67,088	1,028	76.3	81.7	70.5
20.	Jharkhand	3,29,88,134	1,69,30,315	1,60,57,819	414	66.4	76.8	55.4
21.	Odisha	4,19,74,218	2,12,12,136	2,07,62,082	270	72.9	81.6	64.0
22.	Chhattisgarh	2,55,45,198	1,28,32,895	1,27,12,303	189	70.3	80.3	60.2
23.	Madhya Pradesh	7,26,26,809	3,76,12,306	3,50,14,503	236	69.3	78.7	59.2
24.	Gujarat	6,04,39,692	3,14,91,260	2,89,48,432	308	78.0	85.8	69.7
25.	Daman and Diu	2,43,247	1,50,301	92,946	2,191	87.1	91.5	79.5
26.	Dadra & Nagar Haweli	3,43,709	1,93,760	1,49,949	700	76.2	85.2	64.3
27.	Maharashtra	11,23,74,333	5,82,43,056	5,41,31,277	365	82.3	88.4	75.9
28.	Andhra Pradesh	4,93,86,799	2,47,38,068	2,46,48,731	308	67.4	74.8	60.0
29.	Karnataka	6,10,95,297	3,09,66,657	3,01,28,640	319	75.4	82.5	68.1
30.	Goa	14,58,545	7,39,140	7,19,405	394	88.7	92.6	84.7
31.	Lakshadweep	64,473	33,123	31,350	2,149	91.8	95.6	87.9
32.	Kerala	3,34,06,061	1,60,27,412	1,73,78,649	860	94.0	96.1	92.1
33.	Tamil Nadu	7,21,47,030	3,61,37,975	3,60,09,055	555	80.1	86.8	73.4
34.	Puducherry	12,47,953	6,12,511	6,35,442	2,547	85.8	91.3	80.7
35.	Andaman & Nicobar Island	3,80,581	2,02,871	1,77,710	46	86.6	90.3	82.4
36.	Telangana	3,51,93,978	17,704,078	17,489,900	308	66.5	75.0	57.9

(*i*) The immediate objective of this policy is to address the unmet needs of contraception, health infrastructure, health personnel and to provide integrated service delivery for basic reproductive and child healthcare.

(*ii*) The medium term objective is to bring the total fertility rates to replacement level by 2010.

(*iii*) The long-term objective is to achieve a stable population by 2045.

- The National Commission on Population (NCP) was constituted in May 2000 to review, monitor and give direction for the implementation of the National Population Policy (NPP), 2000.
- The National Commission of Population was reconstituted on 11th April, 2005 with 40 members under the chairmanship of the Prime Minister. Minister of Health and Family Welfare and the Deputy Chairman of the Planning Commission are Vice Chairmen of the Commission. The present membership also includes the Chief Ministers of the states of Uttar Pradesh, Madhya Pradesh, Rajasthan, Bihar, Jharkhand, Kerala and Tamil Nadu.
- According to the census 2011, total population of India is 1,21,08,54,977. Census 2011 makes India the second most populated country in the world.
- The growth rate of the population between 2001 and 2011 is 17.7 per cent. Meghalaya recorded the highest growth rate of 27.9 per cent while Nagaland the lowest –0.6 per cent.
- There were 623.27 million males and 587.58 million females according to Census 2011, making a ratio of 943 males per 1000 females. Kerala is the only state where females outnumber males. The sex-ratio these was 1084 females per 1000 males.
- According to census 2011, five most populous states (in descending order) are: Uttar Pradesh (19.9 crore), Maharashtra (11.2 crore), Bihar (10.4 crore), W. Bengal (9.12 crore) and Andhra Pradesh (8.4 crore).
- According to census 2011, three least populous states (in ascending order) are: Sikkim (6.10 lakh), Mizoram (10.9 lakh) and Arunachal Pradesh (13.8 lakh).
- According to census 2011, three most populous Union Territories (in descending order) are: Delhi, Puducherry and Chandigarh.
- According to census 2011, three least populous Union Territories (in ascending order) are: Lakshadweep, Daman and Diu, Dadra and Nagar Haveli.
- **Population Density:** In 2011, 382 persons were living in per square km area. Bihar was most densely populated state with a population density of 1,106 followed by West Bengal (1,028). Among the Union Territories, Delhi had the density of 11,320 and Chandigarh of 9,258. In Arunachal Pradesh, only 17 people were living in per sq. km area while in Mizoram 52.
- According to census-2011, 73.0 per cent of the country's population are literate. The male literacy rate (80.9%) is far more than the female literacy rate (64.6%). Kerala retains the top spot with 94.0 per cent literacy rate. Bihar is at the bottom with a literacy rate of 61.8 per cent.
- According to census 2011, five states with least sex ratio (in ascending order) are: Haryana (879), Jammu & Kashmir (889), Sikkim (890), Punjab (895), and Uttar Pradesh (912).
- According to census 2011, five states with most decadal growth rate (in descending order) are: Meghalaya (27.9%), Arunachal Pradesh (26%), Bihar (25.4), Jammu & Kashmir (23.6%), and Mizoram (23.5%).

ECOLOGY

Ecological system or ecosystem is an open space built by physical and biological components of an environment. Ecosystem is result of an active interaction between living and non-living components. Ecosystem is where community of plants, animals and their environment function as a whole, and relationship between organism and environment thrives blissfully. India is a vast country and possess many types of natural ecosystems.

TERRESTRIAL ECOSYSTEM IN INDIA

FORESTS

Tropical Evergreen or Rain Forests

- These are dense forests of luxuriant growth which look evergreen as their trees shed leaves at different times of the year.
- They are prevalent in areas where the annual rainfall is over 200 cm and the average annual humidity exceeds 77 per cent. The annual temperature is 25°C to 27°C on an average.
- Mahogany, Bamboo, Ivory Wood, Ebony, Rubber trees are the economically significant trees of these forests.
- Such forests are found in the north-east, eastern regions of subtropical Himalaya (Tarai), western portions of the Western Ghats and Andaman and Nicobar Islands. The forests are sub-divided as follows:

(a) ***Tropical Wet Evergreen Forests :*** They are found in areas where the annual rainfall is above 250 cm. The many storeyed forests have an undergrowth of bamboos, ferns, canes and climbers. They contain economically valuable species such as Ebony, Rosewood, Iron wood, Champa, Toon, etc. Such forest is found in the north-eastern states, the Andaman and Nicobar Islands and western parts of the Western Ghats.

(b) ***Tropical Semi-Evergreen Forests :*** Found in regions where the annual rainfall is below 200 cm, these forests have evergreen trees mixed with deciduous ones. The mean annual temperature in these forests ranges from 24°C to 27°C and humidity is about 80 per cent. Important trees include Champa, Canes, Ferns, Orchids, Rosewood, Benteak, Kadam, Semul, Laurel, etc. These forests occur in regions of upper Assam, lower eastern Himalaya, Odisha, and the Andaman and Nicobars.

(c) ***Tropical Moist Deciduous Forests :*** Also called the Monsoon forests, they occur where annual rainfall is 150 to 200 cm and the mean annual temperature is about 26-27°C. The forests are characterised by few species and the undergrowth is of canes and bamboos. Humidity varies from 60 to 80 per cent. They are found in the interior of the Indian Plateau and the Sivalik east of the Yamuna river. Sal, Teak, Tendu, Sissoo, Mahua, Sandal, Shisham are the important trees. The trees shed their leaves during spring and early summer.

(d) ***Littoral or Swamp Forests :*** Also called tidal forests, these occur in and around the tidal creeks and along the deltas of the rivers Ganga, Mahanadi, Krishna and Godavari. The trees, mainly evergreen, have profuse growth and stilt-like roots. The densest trees are found in the great Sunderban delta which has the sundari trees in abundance. Rhizophora and Nipa fruiticans (a type of palm) also grow in these forests. On the tropical tide-washed coasts where mud and silt have accumulated, dense mangrove forests flourish.

Dry Tropical Forests

- Such forests are mostly prevalent in regions with an annual rainfall of 90 to 130 cm, a mean annual temperature of 23 to 27°C and humidity ranging between 50 and 60 per cent.
- They are subdivided into following types.

  (a) ***Tropical Dry Deciduous Forests :*** They run from the Himalayan foothills to Kanyakumari and comprise important trees like Bijasal, Teak, Tendu, Amaltas, Khair, Palas, Rosewood and Axlewood. The tracts of these forests have a low canopy of grasses and shrubs in some places which has been cleared for agriculture or casuarina plantations.

  (b) ***Tropical Thorn Forests :*** These are mostly prevalent in those areas where rainfall is very low, i.e., 50 cm to 70 cm, the mean annual temperature is 25°C to 27°C and humidity is rather low, i.e., less than 47 per cent. Kutch, Saurashtra, Punjab, Haryana, Rajasthan, the Upper Ganga plains and the Deccan Plateau consist of such forests. Small trees such as Khair, Babul, Thor, Khejra, Kanju, Ak and Neem are found in these forests.

  (c) ***Tropical Dry Evergreen Forests :*** From Tamil Nadu to Nellore, such type of forests cover areas where the mean rainfall is about 100 cm, the annual temperature is 28°C and the mean annual humidity is 74 per cent. Trees are 12 m high with canopies. Bamboos are rare and the grass is not conspicuous. The important species of trees are Khirni, Jamun, Kokko, Toddy Palm, Casuarina, Neem, Cane, etc.

Riparian Forests

- They are common in wet places particularly along river banks and other wetlands where rainfall is less than 50 cm.
- Short trees and grasses such as Munj and Kans are abundant. Neem, Shisham, Pipal, Babul, Tamarind are common in such regions.

Subtropical Broad Leaved Hill Forests

- Such forests are common in the highlands of Bastar, Pachmarhi, Palani Hills, Khasi Hills on the lower slopes of the Himalaya in Assam and West Bengal.
- The mean annual temperature is about 18°C to 21°C, the mean annual rainfall is about 75 to 125 cm and the humidity is 80 per cent.
- With an abundance of evergreen trees, these forests are called Shola forests in southern India.

Montane Wet Temperate Forests

- Generally at a height of 1800-3000 m above sea level especially in the hills of Kerala, Tamil Nadu and the eastern Himalaya, the forests occur in regions with a mean annual temperature of about 11°C to 14°C and a mean annual rainfall of 150 to 300 cm.
- The important trees are Oaks, Magnolia, Chilauni, Birch, Plum, Michilus, Deodar and Hemlock.

Montane Moist Temperate Forests

- Such type of forests occur in the temperate eastern and western Himalaya, i.e., in Jammu and Kashmir, Himachal Pradesh, Punjab, Uttarakhand, Sikkim and Darjeeling.
- They are mainly composed of coniferous species generally 30 to 50 m high. Mosses and ferns grow on trees.
- The important trees are Pine, Deodar, Silver Fir, Oak, Beach, Rhododendrons, Maple, etc.

Alpine Forests

- As the name suggests, these forests cover the Alpine areas in the Himalayas, i.e., at a height of 2880 m to 3700 m.

- They constitute dwarf shrubs of Juniper, Fir, Pine, Birch and Rhododendrons. On the southern Himalayan slopes, the Alpine forests degenerate into a low evergreen scrub.
- On the northern slopes of the Himalaya, they represent a dry, xerophytic vegetation.

Grasslands

- Though the Indian grasslands are not comparable to the savanna or steppe, they do occur on wet soil ground and in the sal belt and some hilly areas.
- They are sub-divided as follows.
  - *(a)* ***Low-land Grasses :*** Occurring in regions receiving 31 to 200 cm of rainfall where the temperature is high during summers, they are found in the plains of upper India—Punjab, Uttar Pradesh, Haryana, Bihar and north-west Assam. These grasses grow on different soil type and are suitable for cattle-breeding.
  - *(b)* ***Upland or Hilly Grasses :*** They are found at a height of over 1,000 m in the Himalaya and in the cleared forest areas of the Western Ghats in the Karnataka region. They are found among small tracts of Shola forests in South India.
  - *(c)* ***Riverine Grasses :*** Found in the northern part of India, they form the Bhabar pastures which are important grazing grounds for buffaloes and cattle.

DESERTS

- The Thar desert in Rajasthan is an extension of the Sahara deserts through Arabian and Persian deserts.
- They extend from Punjab, Haryana, Rajasthan to Gujarat state.
- Indian deserts are divided into four main types: hills, plains with hills, marshes and plains with sand dunes.
- The distinct Rann of Kutchch-Bhuj in Gujarat forms a separate zone within Thar deserts due to its different climatic conditions. It represents vast saline flats.
- The region of sand dunes is most spectacular and covers an area of 100,000 sq. km nearly. It extends into Pakistan.
- The dunes are highly sandy and contain 0.12-0.18 mm size grain, 1.8 to 4.5% of clay and 0.4-1.3% of silt.
- There are only some thorn forests and dry open grasslands.
- Indira Gandhi canal which carries water through Punjab and Haryana enters into Rajasthan supports some vegetation.
- The main crops of desert are bajra, millet, wheat, barley, maize, jowar, guwar.
- Medicinal plants found here are mehndi, isabgole and gugal.
- Indian deserts support many threatened species of birds and mammals, such as Asiatic lion, wild ass, bats, scaly ant eater, desert fox, Indian gazzel, four horned antelope, white browed Bushchat, Great Indian Bustard, Cranes and Sandgrouse.
- Gulf of Kuchch is distinguished by the presence of living corals, pearl oyster, sea turtles and a large number of migratory birds like kingfisher, cranes ibis and herons.

MOUNTAINS

Physiographic Divisions of India

- The Indian sub-continent is characterised by a great diversity in its physical features. It may be divided in the following physiographic units:

The Northern Mountain

- The region extends all along the northern border of the country, from the eastern border of West Pakistan to the frontiers of Myanmar of about 2500 km. with an average width of about 240 km; occupied by the Himalayan ranges. This covers an area of about 5,00,000 km^2.
- It consists of the *Hindukush, Karakoram* and the *Himalayas* proper.
- Almost all the highest peaks of the world are in Karakoram and the Himalayas.
- There are three major fold axes represent the *Himadri* (Greater Himalaya), *Himachal* (Lesser Himalaya) and the *Shivaliks* (Outer Himalaya) extending almost uninterrupted throughout its length.
- The Himadri, the asymmetrical and the northern most range of the Himalaya owes its scenic beauty to glacier and lofty snowy peaks. Its average elevation is 6000 m.
- The Gangotri and Jamnotri are found in Himadri. This range has a granitic core, flanked by metamorphosed sediments.
- It has the credit of having the world's 14 highest peaks ranging between the Everest (8848m), Kanchenjunga (8,598m), Dhaulagiri (8,172m), Nanga Parbat (8,126m) and Nanda Devi (7,817m).
- The Himachal or the Lesser Himalayas forms the central chain composed mainly of highly compressed and altered rocks varying from Algonkian or pre-Cambrian to Eocene in age.
- In general, the alternating ranges and valleys acquire an elevation of about 3700 m and 4500 m respectively. Its asymmetrical structures at places provide it a more or less hogback look.
- The Shivaliks in the south, which extend from the Potwar Plateau on the west to the Brahmaputra valley on the east and have an average height of over 1,000m represent the outermost range of the system with roughly a hogback appearance, a steeply sloping southern and a gently sloping northern face.
- These newer and river-borne deposits derived from the rising Himalaya represent the most recent phase of the

Himalayan orogeny i.e., from Middle Miocene to the Lower Pleistocene.

- The range, bordered on the north by flat-floored structural-longitudinal or erosional valleys called the Doons is characterised by fault scarps, anticlinal valleys and synclinal ranges.

Regional Divisions of Himalayas

Apart from these longitudinal sub-divisions, the Himalaya exhibit regional characteristics and as such, the following regions have been identified :

(*a*) Kashmir or Northwestern Himalayas

- It comprise a series of ranges such as the Karakoram, Ladakh, Zaskar and Pir Panjal.
- The northeastern part of the Kashmir Himalayas is a cold desert, which lies between the Greater Himalayas and the Karakoram ranges.
- The famous Dal Lake of Kashmir lies between the Greater Himalayas and the Pir Panjal range.
- **Important Glaciers :** Baltoro and Siachen.
- **Important Passes :** Zoji La on the Great Himalayas, Banihal on the Pir Panjal, Jojila-Zaskar on the Zaskar and Khardung La on the Ladakh range.
- **Important Fresh Lakes :** Dal Lake, Wular lake and salt water lakes such as Pangong Tso and Tso Moriri.
- The river Indus, and its tributaries such as the Jhelum and the Chenab.
- **Duns :** The southernmost part of the region consists of longitudinal valleys known as 'duns'. Jammu dun and Pathankot dun are important examples.
- **Famous Places of Pilgrimage:** Vaishno Devi, Amarnath Cave, Charar-e-Sharif.

(*b*) The Himachal and Uttaranchal Himalayas

- This part lies approximately between the Sutluj in the west and the Kali (a tributary of Ghaghara) in the east.
- **Two Major River Systems,** the Indus and the Ganga. Tributaries of the Indus include the Ravi, the Beas and the Sutluj, and the tributaries of Ganga flowing through this region include the Yamuna, the Gomti and the Ghaghara.
- **Three Ranges of Himalayas** are prominent in this region, (*i*) Great Himalayan range, (*ii*) the Lesser Himalayas (which is locally known as Dhauladhar in Himachal Pradesh and Nagtibba in Uttarakhand) and (*iii*) the Shivalik range from the North to the South.
- **Tourism :** In this region, the Lesser Himalayas has altitude between 1,000-2,000 m. Some of the important hill stations are Dharamshala, Mussoorie, Shimla, Kaosani and the cantonment towns and health resorts such as Shimla, Mussoorie, Kasauli, Almora, Lansdowne and Ranikhet, etc.
- **Dun formations:** Some important duns located in this region are the Chandigarh-Kalka dun, Nalagarh dun, Dehradun, Harike dun and the Kota dun, etc. *Dehradun* is the largest of all the duns with an approximate length of 35-45 km and a width of 22-25 km.
- **Places of Pilgrimage** such as the Gangotri, Yamunotri, Kedarnath, Badrinath and Hemkund Sahib are also situated in this part. The region is also known to have five famous Prayags (river confluences).

(*c*) The Darjeeling and Sikkim Himalayas

- They are flanked by Nepal Himalayas in the west and Bhutan Himalayas in the east. It is relatively small but is a most significant part of the Himalayas.
- **Rivers :** It is known for its fast-flowing rivers such as Tista.
- **Mountain Peaks like** Kanchenjunga (Kanchengiri), and deep valleys.
- **Duar Formation :** In place of the Shivalik here, the 'duar formation' are important, which have also been used for the development of tea gardens. Duars like Dun's are also deposit filled Lacustrine valleys.

(*d*) The Arunachal Himalayas

- These extend from the east of the Bhutan Himalayas up to the Diphu pass in the east. The general direction of the mountain range is from southwest to northeast.
- **Important Mountain Peaks:** Kangtu and Namcha Barwa. These ranges are dissected by fast-flowing rivers from the north to the south, forming deep gorges. Brahmaputra flows through a deep gorge after crossing Namcha Barwa.
- **Important Rivers :** The Kameng, the Subansiri, the Dihang, the Dibang and the Lohit. These are perennial with the high rate of fall, thus, having the highest hydro-electric power potential in the country.

(*e*) The Eastern Hills and Mountains

- These are part of the Himalayan mountain system having their general alignment from the north to the south direction. They are known by different local names. In the north, they are known as Patkai Bum, Naga hills, the Manipur hills and in the south as Mizo or Lushai hills. These are low hills, inhabited by numerous tribal groups practising Jhum cultivation.
- **Rivers & Lakes :** The Barak is an important river in Manipur and Mizoram. 'Loktak' Lake in Manipur is at the centre.

Western Ghats

- It extends from the Tapi river in the north and Kanyakumari in the south and forms the western boundary of the Deccan Plateau. Its length is about 1600 km.

- The block mountains were formed due to the down warping of a part of the land into the Arabian Sea. Harishchandra, Mahabaleshwar, Kalsubai and Salher are important peaks in this region. Thalghat and Bhorghat are the important passes for roads and railways.
- It has average elevation of 1220 m. Few peaks are above 1500 m e.g. Kudremukh (1892) and Pushpagiri (1714).
- The Nilgiris (Eastern Ghats) join the Sahyadris (Western Ghats) to form a mountain knot where highest point is Doddabetta (2637m).
- In the south of Nilgiri lies the Palghat Gap which connects Tamil Nadu with Kerala. In the South of Palghat, Anaimudi (2695m) is a knot which is joined by three hills, viz. the Anaimalai hills (1800-2000m) in the north, the Palni hills (960-1200m) in the N.E. and the Cardamom or Elamalai hills in the south.
- The Anaimalai constitutes a series of plateau with rolling topography. Here hill slopes support tea, coffee, cinchona. Kodaikanal hill station (2195m) is located on the southern edge of the Palni hills, Tambraparni has it source near Agastya Malai forming a series of waterfalls (Bajiatirtham and Papanasam). The highest peak in the Western Ghats is Anaimudi with a height of 2,695 m. They rise steeply from the West Coast. The hills are continuous. All the rivers of the Deccan plateau rise in the Western Ghats.

Eastern Ghats

- It depict true Mountain characteristic between Mahanadi and Godavari (peaks are Nimalgiri at Koraput, Mahendragiri at Ganjam).
- In between the Krishna River and Chennai they continue as the Kondavidu hills mainly composed of Quartzites and Slates.
- The Nallamalai (900-1100m) and Palkonda hills are composed of Cuddapah and Kurnool formations.
- Nilgiris (blue mountains) provide the converging site for three mountain ranges: the Sahyadri joining opposite of the Makurti peak; the Southern Ghats across the Palghat in the south and the Eastern Ghats in the north eastern corner.
- The highest peak in the Eastern Ghats is Mahendragiri at, Vishakhapatnam with a height of 1,500 m. They rise gently from the east coast. The hills are discontinuous. Rivers cut the valleys through the Eastern Ghats. Two notable inlets in the western coastal plains are the Gulf of Kachchh and Gulf of Khambhat. The lake Vembanad, about 63 km in length is the largest lake.

AQUATIC ECOSYSTEM IN INDIA

Fresh Water Ecosystem

- Freshwater are terrestrial aquatic ecosystems. Lakes, flood ponds, reservoirs and rivers are its important components.
- The total freshwater area of India is about 7.6 million hectare.
- Lakes are naturally formed deep water bodies e.g. Sultanpur lake, Batkal lake (Haryana).
- Flood points are the places that undergo periodic flooding as a river channel overflows with flood water i.e. natural areas constituting shallow and seasonal water bodies.
- Bank of large rivers have flood points.
- Reservoir is manmade areas holding water irrigation and human use. e.g., reservoirs formed by dams used for irrigation.

Marine Ecosystem

- India has a long coastline of about 8000 km stretching along nine states and two island chains.
- At the coast a number of rivers form estuaries at their confluence with the sea.
- There are three gulfs - one on the east coast that is gulf of Mannar and two on the west coast i.e., gulf of Kutch and gulf of Khambhat.
- The tides are very important in determining the marine life.
- Nearly 14 species of sea grasses and 120 species of sea weeds are found along the coast.
- Corals are the most abundant and play a very important role.
- 199 Species of corals are known from Indian Ocean.
- The Coral reefs in India are mainly restricted to the Andaman and Nicobar Islands, Gulf of Mannar, Gulf of Kutch, Palk Strait and the Lakshadweep islands. All of these reefs are Fringing reefs, except Lakshadweep which are Atolls.
- The biodiversity in a coral reef is comparable to that of a tropical rain forest. Sea shore provides feeding and breeding ground to a number of birds also. Sea crows, whales and dolphins are the mammals that have secondarily invaded the sea.
- Marine fisheries constitute a highly productive sector in India. It is a source of food and employment to the coastal population.

THE THREATENED ECOSYSTEMS

Some of the natural ecosystems are very sensitive to misuse by humans and to natural disasters or calamities.

Estuaries

- An estuary is a place where a river or a stream opens into the sea (mouth of the river).
- It is a partially enclosed coastal area of brackish water (salinity varies between 0-35 ppt) with one or more rivers or streams flowing into it, and with a free connection to the open sea.

- At the estuaries, freshwater carrying fertile silt and runoff from the land mixes with the salty sea water.
- Estuaries form a transition zone (ecotone) between river environments and maritime environments.
- Examples of estuaries are river mouths, coastal bays, tidal marshes, lagoons and deltas.
- Estuaries are formed due to rise in sea level, movement of sand and sandbars, glacial processes and tectonic processes.
- All the plants and animals in the estuaries are subjected to variations in salinity to which they are adapted (osmoregulation).
- Estuaries are greatly influenced by tidal action. They are periodically washed by sea water once or twice a day based on the number of tides.
- In some narrow estuaries, tidal bores are significant. Tidal bores cause great damage to the estuarine ecology.
- India has 14 major, 44 medium and 162 minor rivers drains into the sea through various estuaries.
- Major estuaries occur in the Bay of Bengal. Many estuaries are locations of some of the major seaports.
- Most of India's major estuaries occur on the east coast. In contrast, the estuaries on the west coast are smaller (in environmental studies, deltas are considered as subsections of estuaries).
- Two typical examples of estuaries on the west coast are the Mandovi and Zuari estuaries.

Mangroves

- The mangrove tidal forests are found in the areas of coasts influenced by tides. Mud and silt get accumutated on such coasts. Dense mangroves are the common varieties with roots of the plants submerged under water.
- The deltas of the Ganga, the Mahanadi, the Krishna, the Godavari and the Kaveri are covered by such vegetation. In the Ganga Brahmaputra delta, sundari trees are found, which provide durable hard timber. Palm, coconut, keora, agar, etc., also grow in some parts of the delta.
- Royal Bengal Tiger is the famous animal in these forests. Turtles, crocodiles, gharials and snakes are also found in these forests.
- The Andhra Pradesh Government has constituted a seven-member committee for fulfilment of norms required for proposing the Godavari Mangroves (Mada forests), at Coringa, as a World Heritage Site.
- The mangrove forests in Andhra Pradesh are located in the estuaries of the Godavari and the Krishna rivers. The Godavari mangroves are located in the Godavari estuary of the East Godavari district.
- Mangrove habitats of Kochi in Kerala can store significant amounts of carbon for the long-term despite being heavily fragmented, but they need immediate attention.
- Crab density, mangrove leaf litter, and mangrove biomass shape the carbon sequestration potential of Kochi's mangrove habitats.
- The amount of sequestered carbon in Cochin (Kochi) mangroves is comparable to the amount stored in mangrove forests found globally.
- According to the Forest Survey of India, 2019, Mangroves' cover in the country increased by 54 sq km (91.10 per cent) in comparison to the 2017 assessment.

Islands

- The major islands groups of India are Andaman and Nicobar Archipelago (A chain of islands similar in origin) in Bay of Bengal and Lakshadweep islands in Arabian Sea.
- Two groups of islands also form part of India. Lakshadweep Islands are located in the Arabian Sea. These are coral islands located off the coast of Kerala. The Andaman and the Nicobar Islands lie to the southeast of the Indian mainland in the Bay of Bengal.
- These ecosystems are threatened mainly due to habitat destruction for resources and tourism.
- Although industrial pollution is much less on these islands, oil spills in oceans have greatly affected their fauna and flora.

Ecotone

- Ecotone is a zone of junction between two or more diverse ecosystems e.g. the mangrove forests.
- They represent an ecotone between marine and terrestrial ecosystem.
- Some more examples of ecotone are - grassland, estuary and river bank.

Characteristics of Ecotone

- It may be very narrow or quite wide.
- It has the conditions intermediate to the adjacent ecosystems. Hence ecotone is a zone of tension.
- It is linear as shows progressive increase in species composition of one in coming community and a simultaneous decrease in species of the other out going adjoining community.
- A well developed ecotones contain some organisms which are entirely different from that of the adjoining communities.
- Sometimes the number of species and the population density of some of the species is much greater in this zone than either community. This is called **edge effect**.
- The organisms which occur primarily or most abundantly in this zone are known as **edge species**.
- In the terrestrial ecosystems edge effect is especially applicable to birds.
- For example the density of song birds is greater in the mixed habitat of the ecotone between the forest and the desert.

Forest Cover of India in 2021

States/UTs	Geographical Area	VDF	MDF	OF	Total Forest Area	Percent of Geographical Area
Andhra Pradesh	1,62,968	1,994	13,929	13,861	29,784	18.28
Arunachal Pradesh	83,743	21,058	30,176	15,197	66,431	79.33
Assam	78,438	3,017	9,991	15,304	28,312	36.09
Bihar	94,163	333	3,286	3,762	7,381	7.84
Chhattisgarh	1,35,192	7,068	32,279	16,370	55,717	41.21
Delhi	1,483	6.72	56.60	131.68	195.00	13.15
Goa	3,702	538	576	1,130	2,244	60.62
Gujarat	1,96,244	378	5,032	9,516	14,926	7.61
Haryana	44,212	28	445	1,130	1,603	3.63
Himachal Pradesh	55,673	3,163	7,100	5,180	15,443	27.73
Jharkhand	79,716	2,601	9,689	11,431	23,721	29.76
Karnataka	1,91,791	4,533	20,985	13,212	38,730	20.19
Kerala	38,852	1,944	9,472	9,837	21,253	54.70
Madhya Pradesh	3,08,252	6,665	34,209	36,619	77,493	25.14
Maharashtra	3,07,713	8,734	20,589	21,475	50,798	16.51
Manipur	22,327	905	6,228	9,465	16,598	74.34
Meghalaya	22,429	560	9,160	7,326	17,046	76.00
Mizoram	21,081	157	5,715	11,948	17,820	84.53
Nagaland	16,579	1,272	4,449	6,530	12,251	73.90
Odisha	1,55,707	7,213	20,995	23,948	52,156	33.50
Punjab	50,362	11	793	1,043	1,847	3.67
Rajasthan	3,42,239	78	4,369	12,208	16,655	4.87
Sikkim	7,096	1,102	1,551	688	3,341	47.08
Tamil Nadu	1,30,060	3,593	11,034	11,792	26,419	20.31
Telangana	1,12,077	1,624	9,119	10,471	21,214	18.93
Tripura	10,486	647	5,212	1,863	7,722	73.64
Uttar Pradesh	2,40,928	2,627	4,029	8,162	14,818	6.15
Uttarakhand	53,483	5,055	12,768	6,482	24,305	45.44
West Bengal	88,752	3,037	4,208	9,587	16,832	18.96
A & N Islands	8,249	5,678	683	383	6,744	81.75
Chandigarh	114	1.36	13.51	8.01	22.88	20.07
Dadra & Nagar Haveli and Daman & Diu	602	1.40	85.56	140.79	227.75	37.83
Jammu & Kashmir* (54,624*)	2,22,236	4,155	8,117	9,115	21,387	39.15
Ladakh (1,68,055*)		2	512	1,758	2,272	1.35
Lakshdweep	30	0.00	16.09	11.01	27.10	90.33
Puducherry	490	0.00	17.53	35.77	53.30	10.88
Total	**32,87,469**	**99,779**	**3,06,890**	**3,07,120**	**7,13,789**	**21.71**

* *Includes Jammu & Kashmir area outside LoC that is under illegal occupation of Pakistan and China.*

BIODIVERSITY CONSERVATION

The Convention on Biological Diversity (CBD) is one of the key agreements adopted during the Earth Summit held in Rio de Janeiro in 1992. The objective of CBD are: conservation of biological diversity, sustainable use of its components, and fair and equitable sharing of benefits arising out of the use of genetic resources. Pursuant to the ratification of the CBD by India in 1994, several steps were initiated to meet the commitments under the Convention, and to realise the opportunities offered by the Convention. These efforts were aimed at bringing the legislative, administrative and policy regimes in tune with the three-fold objectives of the CBD. India enacted the Biological Diversity (BD) Act in 2002 to give effect to the provision of this Convention. India also prepared a National Biodiversity Action Plan (NBAP) in 2008, and an Addendum to NBAP in 2014 with 20 national targets on biodiversity.

The Nagoya Protocol on access and benefit sharing (ABS) adopted under the aegis of CBD in 2010, is aimed at fair and equitable sharing of benefits arising from the utilisation of genetic resources.

Biosphere Reserves

The idea of 'Biosphere Reserves' was initiated by UNESCO in 1973-74 under its Man and Biosphere (MAB) Programme. The MAB, launched in 1970 by UNESCO, is a broad-based ecological programme aimed to develop within the natural and social sciences a basis for the rational use and conservation of the resources of the biosphere and for the improvement of the relationship between man and the environment, to predict the consequences of today's actions on tomorrow's world and thereby to increase man's ability to manage efficiently the natural resources of the biosphere.

The Indian National Man and Biosphere (MAB) Committee identifies and recommends potential sites for designation as Biosphere Reserves, following the UNESCO's guidelines and criteria. There are 18 designated Biosphere Reserves (BRs) in all. Out of 18 Biosphere Reserves, 10 Biosphere Reserves have been included in the World Network of Biosphere Reserves of UNESCO.

BIOSPHERE RESERVES IN INDIA

S. No.	Name	Date of Notification	Area (in km^2)
1	Nilgiri	01.09.1986	5520
2	Nanda Devi	18.01.1988	5860.69
3	Nokrek	01.09.1988	820
4	Great Nicobar	06.01.1989	885
5	Gulf of Mannar	18.02.1989	10,500
6	Manas	14.03.1989	2837
7	Sunderbans	29.03.1989	9630
8	Simlipal	21.06.1994	4374
9	Dibru-Saikhowa	28.07.1997	765
10	Dehang-Dibang	02.09.1998	5111.50
11	Pachmarhi	03.03.1999	4926
12	Khangchendzonga	07.02.2000	2619.92
13	Agasthyamalai	12.11.2001	1828
14	Achanakamar - Amarkantak	30.3.2005	3835.51
15	Kachchh	29.01.2008	12,454
16	Cold Desert	28.08.2009	7770
17	Seshachalam Hills	20.09.2010	4755.997
18	Panna	25.08.2011	2998.98

Source: *Wildlife Institute of India*

Forest Policy

Forest Policy Division deals with the National Forest Policy, 1988, Indian Forest Act, 1927, and its amendments including policy matters and legislative matters of other ministries and state governments related to forests. The Division is the National Focal Division for the International Cooperation on United Nations Forum on Forestry (UNFF), Asia Pacific Forestry Commission (APFC), Asia Pacific Forest Invasive Species Network (APFISN), Committee on Forestry of FAO (COFO), UN-REDD and Centre for International Forestry Research (CIFOR) and International Poplar Commission of FAO.

Forest Protection

This Centrally Sponsored Scheme of intensification of Forest Management Scheme deals within forest fire management, to address the growing concern over adverse effects of forest fire. With this, the present Centrally Sponsored Scheme of Forest Fire Prevention and Management (FPM) was formulated.

WILDLIFE CONSERVATION

There is a Wildlife Division of the Ministry that has two subdivisions, namely, Project Elephant Division and Wildlife Division. In addition, there are three autonomous bodies. Wildlife Institute of India (WII) for wildlife research and training, Central Zoo Authority (CZA) for conservation and zoo management and National Tiger Conservation Authority (NTCA). The NTCA has been constituted by converting the Project Tiger Directorate into an autonomous body for tiger conservation. The National Zoological Park in the capital is also a part of the Wildlife Wing of the Ministry.

Asiatic Lion Conservation Project

This project was launched in January 2019, with an aim to protect and conserve the world's last ranging free population of Asiatic Lion and its associated ecosystem. It is aimed at strengthening the ongoing measures for conservation and recovery of Asiatic Lion with the help of state-of-the-art techniques/instruments, regular scientific research studies, disease management and modern surveillance/patrolling techniques.

Enhancement of Protected Area Network in the Country

The number of Protected Areas in the country has increased to 870 in 2019. The total area under Protected Areas is now 1,65,088.36 sq.kms.

Wildlife Crime Control Bureau

Wildlife Crime Control Bureau (WCCB) is a statutory multidisciplinary body established under the Ministry, to combat organised wildlife crime in the country. The Bureau has its headquarters in New Delhi and five regional offices at Delhi, Kolkata, Mumbai, Chennai and Jabalpur.

Central Zoo Authority

The Central Zoo Authority with its headquarters in New Delhi was established in 1992 under the provisions of the Wild Life (Protection) Act, 1972 to oversee the functioning of zoos in the country with the view to enhance their role in conservation. The main objective of the Central Zoo Authority is to enforce minimum standards and norms for upkeep and healthcare of animals in the Indian zoos; to control the mushrooming of ill-conceived, ill-planned zoos; to monitor and evaluate the existing zoos and to suggest ways and means for the improvement of zoos in the country so that they can be transferred into potent centres for ex-situ conservation of endangered wild fauna.

National Zoological Park

The National Zoological Park (NZP) was set up in 1959 under this Ministry. The main objective of the Park is to complement and strengthen the national efforts in conservation of the rich biodiversity of the country, particularly the wild fauna.

PROJECT ELEPHANT

Project Elephant (PE) was launched by the Government of India in 1991-92 as a centrally sponsored scheme with the objectives: to protect elephants, their habitat and corridors; to address issues of man-animal conflict; and ensure the welfare of domesticated elephants.

Project Tiger

Project Tiger was launched in 1973 for conserving the tiger. From 9 tiger reserves since its formative years, the Project Tiger coverage has increased to 53, spread out in 18 of tiger range states. These reserves are constituted on a core/ buffer strategy. The core areas have the legal status of a national park or a sanctuary, whereas the buffer or peripheral areas are a mix of forest and non-forest land, managed as a multiple use area. Due to the concerted efforts under the Project, India has the distinction of having the maximum number of tigers in the world - 2,967 - to be precise, as per the results of the 4th cycle of the All India Tiger Estimation.

International Tiger's Day is held every year on 29th July to raise public awareness and support regarding several issues related to tiger conservation. The idea behind such an event came up at the St. Petersburg Tiger Summit in 2010.

Famous National Parks in India

State/UT	*National Parks*
• **Andaman and Nicobar Islands**	Campbell Bay, Galathea Bay, Mahatma Gandhi Marine Wandoor, Middle Button Island, Mount Harriett, North Button Island, Rani Jhansi Marine, Saddle Peak, South Button Island
• **Andhra Pradesh**	Papikonda, Rajiv Gandhi (Rameswaram), Sri Venkateswara
• **Arunachal Pradesh**	Mouling, Namdapha
• **Assam**	Dibru-Saikhowa, Kaziranga, Manas, Nameri, Rajiv Gandhi Orang
• **Bihar**	Valmiki
• **Chhattisgarh**	Guru Ghasidas (Sanjay), Indravati (Kutru), Kanger Valley
• **Goa**	Mollem
• **Gujarat**	Vansda, Blackbuck (Velavadar), Gir, Marine (Gulf of Kutch)
• **Haryana**	Kalesar, Sultanpur
• **Himachal Pradesh**	Great Himalayan, Inderkillam, Khirganga, Pin Valley, Simbalbara
• **Jammu & Kashmir**	City Forest (Salim Ali), Dachigam, Hemis, Kishtwar
• **Jharkhand**	Betla
• **Karnataka**	Anshi, Bandipur, Bannerghatta, Kudremukh, Nagarahole (Rajiv Gandhi)
• **Kerala**	Anamudi Shola, Eravikulam, Mathikettan Shola, Pambadum Shola, Periyar, Silent Valley
• **Madhya Pradesh**	Bandhavgarh, Fossil, Kanha, Madhav, Panna, Indira Priyadarshini Pench, Sanjay, Satpura, Van Vihar

State/UT	National Parks
• Maharashtra	Chandoli, Gugamal, Nawegaon, Pench (Jawaharlal Nehru), Sanjay Gandhi (Borivilli), Tadoba.
• Manipur	Keibul-Lamjao
• Meghalaya	Balphakram, Nokrek Ridge
• Mizoram	Murlen, Phawngpui Blue Mountain
• Nagaland	Intanki
• Odisha	Bhitarkanika, Simlipal
• Rajasthan	Mukundra Hills, Desert, Keoladeo Ghana, Ranthambhore, Sariska
• Sikkim	Khangchendzonga
• Tamil Nadu	Guindy, Gulf of Mannar Marine, Indira Gandhi (Annamalai), Mudumalai, Mukurthi
• Telangana	Kasu Brahmananda Reddy, Mahaveer Harina Vanasthali, Mrugavani.
• Tripura	Clouded Leopard, Bison (Rajbari)
• Uttar Pradesh	Dudhwa
• Uttarakhand	Corbett, Gangotri, Govind, Nanda Devi, Rajaji, Valley of Flowers
• West Bengal	Buxa, Gorumara, Jaldapara, Neora Valley, Singalila, Sunderban

Famous Wildlife Sanctuaries in India

State/UT	Wildlife Sanctuaries
• Andhra Pradesh	Kolleru Lake, Nagarjuna Sagar, Sri Venkateswara, Pulicat
• Arunachal Pradesh	Mehao
• Assam	Sonai, Rupai, Pabha
• Bihar	Kaimur, Bhimbandha
• Chhattisgarh	Sitanadi
• Gujarat	Narayan Sarovar, (Wild Ass) Nal Sarovar
• Haryana	Sultanpur
• Himachal Pradesh	Kugti, Rupi Bhawa, Govind Sagar
• Jammu and Kashmir	Karakoram, Ramnagar
• Jharkhand	Hazaribagh, Dalma
• Karnataka	Ghatprabha, Dandili, Sharavathi, Ranganathittu, Ranebennur
• Kerala	Waynad, Mudimalai, ldukki
• Madhya Pradesh	Pachmarhi, Gandhi Sagar
• Maharashtra	Koyna, Chandoli, Radhanagari, Karnala, Gautalu, Yaval, Melghat
• Mizoram	Murien
• Nagaland	Fakim
• Odisha	Ushakothi, Karlapat, Chilka Lake, Bhittarkanika
• Punjab	Govind Sagar, Abohar, Harike
• Rajasthan	Mount Abu
• Tamil Nadu	Mundanthurai, Kodikkarai, Indira Gandhi, Vedantangal
• Telangana	Kawal, Eturnagram, Papikonda.
• Tripura	Trishna
• Uttarakhand	Kedarnath
• Uttar Pradesh	Katernighat, Sohagbarwa, Ranipur, Chandraprabha
• West Bengal	Jaldapara

INTERNATIONAL CONVENTIONS

Basel Convention

The Basel Convention on the Control of Transboundary Movements of Hazardous Wastes and their Disposal was adopted in 1989 in Basel, Switzerland. The overarching objective of the Basel Convention is to protect human health and the environment against the adverse effets of hazardous wastes.

Rotterdam Convention

The Rotterdam Convention on the prior informed consent procedure for certain Hazardous Chemicals and Pesticides in International Trade came into force in 2004. India acceded to the convention a year later. The Designated National Authorities (DNAs) for India are in Ministry of Agriculture and Farmers Welfare.

Stockholm Convention

The Stockholm Convention on Persistent Organic Pollutants (POPs) is a global treaty to protect human health and the environment from POPs. The Convention sought initially 12 chemicals, for restriction or elemination of the production and release. Now, the Convention covers 23 chemicals. The Convention came into force in 2004. India ratified the Convention in 2006.

Minamata Convention on Mercury

In February 2009, the Governing Council of UNEP adopted Decision 25/5 on the development of a global legally binding instrument on mercury. At the Conference of Plenipotentiaries held in 2013 in Minamata and Kumamoto, Japan, the "Minamata Convention on Mercury", a global treaty to protect human health and the environment from the adverse effects of mercury, was formally adopted.

Strategic Approach to International Chemicals Management

In 2006, over 190 countries including India acceded to the Strategic Approach to International Chemicals Management (SAICM), an international policy framework to foster sound management of chemicals.

National River Conservation Plan

The river conservation programme was initiated with the launching of the Ganga Action Plan (GAP) in 1985. The Ganga Action Plan was expanded to cover other rivers under National River Conservation Plan (NRCP) in 1995. The objective of NRCP is to improve the water quality of rivers, which are major water sources in the country.

National Plan for Conservation of Aquatic Ecosystems

The Wetlands Division of the Ministry looks after policies relating to the conservation and wise use of wetlands. The National Plan for Conservation of Aquatic Ecosystems (NPCA) is a single conservation programme for both wetlands and lakes.

Conservation of Wetlands

Wetlands are lifeline for a very large number of people and an important source of fresh water to mankind. They provide a host of ecosystem services to humanity, in addition to being host to rich biodiversity. However, due to anthropogenic activities, wetlands are getting degraded.

To control degradation and conserve wetlands, the National Wetland Conservation Programme (NWCP) was initiated in 1987 and financial assistance is being provided to the state governments for implementing action plans for conservation and management of identified wetlands.

Ramsar Convention

As a commitment for conserving potential wetlands, India became a signatory to the Ramsar Convention in 1982. As per this convention, India is committed for international cooperation and to take national action for conservation and wise use of wetlands. At present there are 26 Ramsar sites in India.

Wetlands (Conservation and Management) Rules

To implement the objectives of the convention, a regulatory mechanism was put in place through Wetlands (Conservation and Management) Rules in December 2010 vide GSR-951 (E). Central Wetland Regulatory Authority (CWRA) has been constituted under the Wetlands Rules, 2010. About 25 wetlands spread over 14 states have already been notified under these Rules.

National Afforestation and Eco-Development Board

In order to promote afforestation, tree planting, ecological restoration and eco-development activities in the country, the National Afforestation and Eco-Development Board (NAEB) was set up in 1992. Special attention is also given by NAEB to the regeneration of degraded forest areas and lands adjoining forest areas, national parks, sanctuaries and other protected areas as well as the ecologically fragile areas like the Western Himalayas, Aravallis, Western Ghats etc.

National Afforestation Programme Scheme

National Afforestation Programme (NAP) is a major afforestation scheme of the NAEB in the Government of India. Launched in 2000-02, the scheme has acquired a pan-India ambit over the last nine years of its implementation and was being implemented by the states of the country through a twin institutional set-up of Forest Development Agencies (FDAs) at the forest division level and Joint Forest Management Committees (JFMCs) at the village level.

Eco-Development Forces Scheme

Eco-Development Forces (EDF) Scheme was established in 1980s as a scheme being implemented through Ministry of Defence for ecological restoration of terrains, rendered difficult either due to severe degradation or remote location or difficult law and order situation. It is based on twin objectives of ecological regeneration in difficult areas, and promotion of meaningful employment to ex-servicemen.

National Mission for Green India

The National Mission for a Green India (GIM), one of the eight missions under the National Action Plan on Climate Change aims at protecting and enhancing India's diminishing forest cover to counter the perils of climate change. It envisages a holistic view of greening and focuses on multiple ecosystem services along with carbon sequestration and emission reduction as co-benefit.

Declaring Eco-Sensitive Areas in Western Ghats

The Western Ghats is a global biodiversity hotspot and a treasure trove of biological diversity harbouring many endemic species of flowering plants, fishes, amphibians, reptiles, birds, mammals and invertebrates. It is also the origin of Godavari, Krishna, Cauvery and a number of other rivers of Peninsular India, upon which much of the economy of the region is dependent. Therefore, there is a need to conserve and protect the unique biodiversity of Western Ghats, while allowing for sustainable and inclusive development of the region. The concept of Ecologically Sensitive Area (ESA) provides a mechanism to conserve biological diversity of an area while allowing for sustainable development to take place.

National Natural Resources Management System

The scheme "National Natural Resources Management System" (NNRMS) of the Ministry is a part of an umbrella scheme of the erstwhile Planning Commission-Planning Committee-National Natural Resources Management System (PC-NNRMS) and is in operation since 1985.

FORESTRY RESEARCH

Indian Council of Forestry Research and Education

Indian Council of Forestry Research and Education (ICFRE), Dehradun an apex body in the national forestry research system, has been undertaking the holistic development of forestry research, education and extension covering all aspects of forestry.

Major Institutes Engaged in Forest Research Include

Institutes	Place
Forest Research Institute	Dehradun
Institute of Forest Genetics and Tree Breeding	Coimbatore
Institute of Wood Science and Technology	Bengaluru
Tropical Forest Research Institute	Jabalpur
Rain Forest Research Institute	Jorhat
Arid Forest Research Institute	Jodhpur
Himalayan Forest Research Institute	Shimla
Institute of Forest Productivity	Ranchi
Institute of Forest Biodiversity	Hyderabad

Indira Gandhi National Forest Academy

The Academy was constituted in 1987 by upgrading and renaming the erstwhile Indian Forest College, established in 1938. The Academy imparts professional training to the Indian Forest Services (IFS) Probationers and has been accorded the status of "Staff College" for imparting mid-career training for officers of the Indian Forest Service (IFS).

Wildlife Institute of India

Wildlife Institute of India (WII) was established in 1986 in Dehradun as an autonomous institute of the Ministry. The Institute has emerged as a premier training and research institution in the field of wildlife and protected area management in South Asia and South east Asia.

National Green Corps Programme

National Green Corps (NGC) were formulated in 2001-02. The phenomenal response that NGC received has made the network more than 1,00,000 Eco-clubs across the country in 15 years, making it one of the largest conservation networks. Under NGC programme, 86,765 Eco-clubs were supported.

National Environmental Awareness Campaign

The National Environmental Awareness Campaign (NEAC) was launched in mid-1986 with the objective of creating environmental awareness at the national level. In this campaign, nominal financial assistance is provided to NGOs, schools, colleges, universities, research institutes, women and youth organisations, army units, government departments, etc., from all over the country for conducting awareness raising and action oriented activities.

GLOBE

Global Learning and Observations to Benefit the Environment (GLOBE) is a hands-on international environmental science and education programme that brings students, teachers and scientists together to study the global environment. MoEFCC and US Government signed an agreement in 2000 to implement the Globe programme in India. Indian Environmental Society, Delhi, is an implementing agency for Globe in India.

National Green Tribunal

The National Green Tribunal (NGT) was set up in 2010 under the NGT Act, 2010, for the purpose of effective and expeditious disposal of cases relating to environmental protection and conservation of forests and other natural resources including enforcement of any legal right relating to environment and giving relief and compensation for damages to persons and property and for matters connected therewith or incidental thereto.

NGT has five places of sitting, *i.e.*, the Principal Bench in Delhi and Zonal Benches in Pune, Kolkata, Bhopal and Chennai. Apart from this, the Tribunal holds three circuit Benches at Shimla, Shillong and Jodhpur.

National Adaptation Fund for Climate Change

National Adaptation Fund for Climate Change (NAFCC) is a central sector scheme under implementation in the 12th Five Year Plan with National Bank for Agriculture and Rural Development (NABARD) as National Implementing Entity (NIE).

Climate Change Action Programme

Ministry is implementing a scheme titled 'Climate Change Action Programme' since January 2014, with an objective to create and strengthen the scientific and analytical capacity for assessment of climate change in the country, putting in place appropriate institutional framework for scientific and policy initiatives and implementation of climate change related actions in the context of sustainable development. The NCAP is a major multi-institutional and multi-agency study.

OZONE CELL

Ozone Layer Protection

Ozone, a tri-atomic molecule of oxygen is formed from oxygen naturally in the upper levels of the earth's atmosphere by high energy ultraviolet (UV) radiation from the sun. The UV radiation breaks down oxygen molecules, releasing free atoms, some of which bond with other oxygen molecule to form ozone. About 90 per cent of ozone formed in this way lies between 10 and 50 kilometers above the earth's surface, called the Stratosphere. The ozone found in the part of the atmosphere is called the ozone layer.

The ozone layer absorbs all the harmful UV-B radiations emanating from the sun. It protects plant and animal life from UV-B radiation. The UV-B radiation has the potential to cause skin cancer, eye cataract, suppress body's immune system, decrease crop yield etc., which led to the adoption of the Vienna Convention for the Protection of the Ozone Layer in 1985 and the Montreal Protocol on Substances that Deplete the Ozone Layer in 1987. The mandate of the Montreal Protocol is to phase out the production and consumption of the Ozone Depleting Substances (ODSs).

Vienna Convention

The Vienna Convention for the Protection of the Ozone Layer and its Montreal Protocol on Substances that Deplete the Ozone Layer are the international treaties specific for the protection of the Stratospheric Ozone (Ozone layer). It has been universally ratified and all the 197 UN member countries of the world are the parties to the Vienna Convention and its Montreal Protocol.

United Nations Convention to Combat Desertification

India became a signatory to the United Nations Convention to Combat Desertification (UNCCD) in 1994. MoEFCC is the nodal ministry in the Government of India for the UNCCD, and Desertification Cell is the nodal point within MoEFCC to coordinate all issues pertaining to the convention.

United Nations Environment Programme (UNEP)

India is a member of UNEP and provides annual financial contribution of USD 100,000 to UNEP Environment Fund. Three of the thirty-three members on UNEP's International Resource Panel (IRP) are currently from India.

Global Environment Facility

India is a founding member of Global Environment Facility (GEF). Set up in 1991, GEF is the designated multilateral funding mechanism of 183 countries to provide incremental finance for addressing global environmental benefits which are also identified national priorities.

URBANISATION

URBANISATION IN INDIA

The level of urbanisation is measured in terms of percentage of urban population to total population. The level of urbanisation in India in 2011 was 31.10 per cent, which is quite low in comparison to developed countries. Total urban population has increased eleven-fold during the twentieth century. Enlargement of urban centres and emergence of new towns have played a significant role in the growth of urban population and urbanisation in the country. (Table). But the growth rate of urbanisation has slowed down during last two decades.

Table : India – Trends of Urbanisation 1901-2011

Year	Number of Towns/UAs	Urban Population (in Thousands)	% of Total Population	Decennial Growth (%)
1901	1,827	25,851.90	10.84	—
1911	1,815	25,941.60	10.29	0.35
1921	1,949	28,086.20	11.18	8.27
1931	2,072	33,456.00	11.99	19.12
1941	2,250	44,153.30	13.86	31.97
1951	2,843	62,443.70	17.29	41.42
1961	2,365	78,936.60	17.97	26.41
1971	2,590	1,09,114	19.91	38.23
1981	3,378	1,59,463	23.34	46.14
1991	4,689	2,17,611	25.71	36.47
2001	5,161	2,85,355	27.78	31.13
2011*	6,171	3,77,106	31.10	31.08

**Source: Census of India, 2011*

Classification of Towns on the Basis of Population Size

Census of India classifies urban centres into six classes as presented in Table. Urban centre with population of more than one lakh is called a city or class I town. Cities accommodating population size between one to five million are called metropolitan cities and more than five million are mega cities. Majority of metropolitan and mega cities are urban agglomerations. An urban agglomeration may consist of any one of the following three combinations:

(*i*) a town and its adjoining urban outgrowths,

(*ii*) two or more contiguous towns with or without their outgrowths, and

(*iii*) a city and one or more adjoining towns with their outgrowths together forming a contiguous spread.

It is evident from Table that more than 60 per cent of urban population in India lives in Class I towns. Out of 468 cities, 53 cities/ urban agglomerations are metropolitan cities. Six of them are mega cities with population over five million each. More than one-fifth (21.0%) of urban population lives in these mega cities.

Among them, Greater Mumbai is the largest agglomeration with 18.4 million people. Delhi, Kolkata, Chennai, Bengaluru and Hyderabad are other mega cities in the country.

Table : India — Class-wise number of towns and cities and their population, 2011

Class	Population Size	Number of Cities	Total Urban Population (in thousand)	% of Total Urban Population
I	1,00,000 and more	468	2,27,899	60.45
II	50,000 – 99,999	474	41,328	10.96
III	20,000 – 49,999	1,373	58,174	15.43
IV	10,000 – 19,999	1,683	31,866	8.45
V	5,000 – 9,999	1,749	15,883	4.21
VI	Less than 5,000	424	1,956	0.51

**Source: Census of India – 2011 and India, 2017, Ministry of Information and Broadcasting, GOI.*

Functional Classification of Towns

Apart from their role a central or nodal places, many towns and cities perform specialised services. Some towns and cities specialise in certain functions and they are known for some specific activities, products or services. However, each town performs a number of functions. On the basis of dominant or specialised functions, Indian cities and towns can be broadly classified as follows:

Administrative Towns and Cities

Towns supporting administrative headquarters of higher order are administrative towns, such as Chandigarh, New Delhi, Bhopal, Shillong, Guwahati, Imphal, Srinagar, Gandhinagar, Jaipur, Chennai, etc.

Industrial Towns

Industries constitute prime motive force of these cities, such as Mumbai, Salem, Coimbatore, Modinagar, Jamshedpur, Hugli, Bhilai, etc.

Transport Cities

They may be ports primarily engaged in export and import activities such as Kandla, Kochi, Kozhikode, Vishakhapatnam, etc., or hubs of inland transport, such as Agra, Dhulia, Mughalsarai, Itarsi, Katni, etc.

Commercial Towns

Towns and cities specialising in trade and commerce are kept in this class. Kolkata, Saharanpur, Satna, etc., are some examples.

Mining Towns

These towns have developed in mineral rich areas such as Raniganj, Jharia, Digboi, Ankaleshwar, Singrauli, etc.

Garrisson Cantonment Towns

These towns emerged as garrisson towns such as Ambala, Jalandhar, Mhow, Babina, Udhampur, etc.

Educational Towns

Starting as centres of education, some of the towns have grown into major campus towns, such as Roorki, Varanasi, Aligarh, Pilani, Allahabad, etc.

Religious and Cultural Towns

Varanasi, Mathura, Amritsar, Madurai, Puri, Ajmer, Pushkar, Tirupati, Kurukshetra, Haridwar, Ujjain came to prominence due to their religious/cultural significance.

Tourist Towns

Nainital, Mussoorie, Shimla, Pachmarhi, Jodhpur, Jaisalmer, Udagamandalam (Ooty), Mount Abu are some of the tourist destinations.

The cities are not static in their function. The functions change due to their dynamic nature.

Even specialised cities, as they grow into metropolises become multifunctional wherein industry, business, administration, transport, etc., become important. The functions get so intertwined that the city can not be categorised in a particular functional class.

SCHEMES/PROGRAMMES RELATED WITH HOUSING AND URBAN DEVELOPMENT

Pradhan Mantri Awas Yojana—Housing for All (Urban)

Mission Pradhan Mantri Awas Yojana (Urban) for ensuring housing for all in urban areas was launched in 2015 as a flagship mission and is to be implemented during 2015-22. The mission provides central assistance to all eligible families/ beneficiaries across all statutory towns for houses. States/UTs will have the flexibility to include the Planning Areas (to the exclusion of rural areas) as notified with respect to Statutory Towns and such Planning Areas (to the exclusion of rural areas) as notified by development authorities. To address Housing for All in urban area, the mission has four verticals: (*a*) *In-situ* Slum Redevelopment (ISSR) with participation of private developers using land as resource for providing housing to eligible slum dwellers; (*b*) affordable housing through credit-linked subsidy scheme (CLSS now renamed as CLSS for EWS/LIG); (*c*) Affordable Housing in Partnership (AHP) with public and private sectors; and (*d*) subsidy for beneficiary-led individual house construction/enhancements: size of house for Economically Weaker Section (EWS) is 30 sq. m., in carpet area but states have flexibility to enhance the size of houses in consultation with the Ministry. EWS family has been defined as the family with annual income up to ₹ 3 lakh and LIG with annual income between ₹ 3-6 lakh.

Jal Jeevan Mission (Urban)

In the Budget 2021-22, Jal Jeevan Mission (Urban) has been announced under the Housing and Urban Affairs Ministry to provide universal coverage of water supply to all households through functional taps in all statutory towns in accordance with Sustainable Development Goal-6. It complements the Jal Jeevan Mission (Rural) which envisages supply of 55 litres of water per person per day to every rural household through Functional Household Tap Connections (FHTC) by 2024.

Highlights

- 2.68 crore is the estimated gap in urban household tap connections that is proposed to be covered under JJM(U). Likewise, estimated gap in sewer connections/ septage in 500 AMRUT cities proposed to be covered in JJM(U) is 2.64 crore.
- Rejuvenation of water bodies to augment sustainable fresh water supply and creating green spaces and sponge cities to reduce floods and enhance amenity value through an Urban Aquifer Management plan are other key areas of the Mission.
- JJM(U) will promote circular economy of water through development of city water balance plan for each city focusing on recycle/reuse of treated sewage, rejuvenation of water bodies and water conservation. 20% of water demand to be met by reused water with development of institutional mechanism.
- A Technology Sub-Mission for water is proposed to leverage latest global technologies in the field of water.
- Information, Education and Communication (IEC) campaign is proposed to spread awareness among masses about conservation of water.
- Pey Jal Survekshan will be conducted in cities to ascertain equitable distribution of water, reuse of wastewater and mapping of water bodies with respect to quantity and quality of water through a challenge process.

PM Street Vendor's Atmanirbhar Nidhi (PM SVANIDHI): A Special Micro-Credit Facility for Street Vendors

The central government launched PM SVANIDHI- Pradhan Mantri Street Vendor's Atmanirbhar Nidhi- scheme on June 01, 2021. This special micro-credit facility scheme will provide affordable loans to street vendors. The scheme would benefit vendors, hawkers, thelewale and people involved in goods and services related to textiles, apparel, artisan products, barbers shops, laundry services etc. in different areas.

Highlights

- The vendors will be able to avail of a working capital loan of up to ₹ 10,000, which will be repayable in monthly instalments in the tenure of one year.
- On early or timely repayment of the loan, an interest subsidy at the rate of 7% per annum will be credited to the beneficiary's bank account through Direct Benefit Transfer (DBT) on six month basis.
- The Ministry also informed that if the beneficiaries repay the instalments earlier or on time, they will develop the credible score that will make him eligible for the higher amount of term loan to ₹ 20,000 or so on.

Smart Cities Mission

The Smart Cities Mission was launched in 2015. The objective of the Mission is to promote cities that provide core infrastructure and give a decent quality of life to its citizens, a clean and sustainable environment and application of 'smart' solutions. Some of the core infrastructure elements in a Smart City would include adequate water supply; assured electricity supply; sanitation; including solid waste management; efficient urban mobility and public transport; affordable housing, especially for the poor; robust IT connectivity and digitalisation; good governance, especially e-Governance and citizen participation; sustainable environment; safety and security of citizens, particularly women, children and the elderly; and health and education.

In the approach of the Smart Cities Mission, the objective is to promote cities that provide core infrastructure and give a decent quality of life to its citizens, a clean and sustainable environment and application of 'smart' solutions. Under it, 100 Smart Cities have been selected in 4 Rounds based on an All India Competition.

Census-2011: Rural and Urban Population

S. No.	State/UTs	Rural Population	Urban Population	Percentage of Rural Population	Percentage of Urban Population
1.	J&K	91,08,060	34,33,242	72.6	27.4
2.	Himachal Pradesh	61,76,050	6,88,552	90.0	10.0
3.	Punjab	1,73,44,192	1,03,99,146	62.5	37.5
4.	Chandigarh	28,991	10,26,459	2.7	97.3
5.	Uttarakhand	70,36,954	30,49,338	69.8	30.2
6.	Haryana	1,65,09,359	88,42,103	65.1	34.9
7.	Delhi	4,19,042	1,63,68,899	2.5	97.5
8.	Rajasthan	5,15,00,352	1,70,48,085	75.1	24.9
9.	Uttar Pradesh	15,53,17,278	4,44,95,063	77.7	22.3
10.	Bihar	9,23,41,436	1,17,58,016	88.7	11.3
11.	Sikkim	4,56,999	1,53,578	74.8	25.2
12.	Arunachal Pradesh	10,66,358	3,17,369	77.1	22.9
13.	Nagaland	14,07,536	5,70,966	71.1	28.9
14.	Manipur	20,21,640	8,34,154	70.8	29.2
15.	Mizoram	5,25,435	5,71,771	47.9	52.1
16.	Tripura	27,12,464	9,61,453	73.8	26.2
17.	Meghalaya	23,71,439	5,95,450	79.9	20.1
18.	Assam	2,68,07,034	43,98,542	85.9	14.1
19.	West Bengal	6,21,83,113	2,90,93,002	68.1	31.9
20.	Jharkhand	2,50,55,073	79,33,061	76.0	24.0
21.	Odisha	3,49,70,562	70,03,656	83.3	16.7
22.	Chhattisgarh	1,96,07,961	59,37,237	76.8	23.2
23.	Madhya Pradesh	5,25,57,404	2,00,69,405	72.4	27.6
24.	Gujarat	3,46,94,609	2,57,45,083	57.4	42.6
25.	Daman & Diu	60,396	1,82,851	24.8	75.2
26.	Dadra & N. Haveli	1,83,114	1,60,595	53.3	46.7
27.	Maharashtra	6,15,56,074	5,08,18,259	54.8	45.2
28.	Andhra Pradesh	3,99,70,761	1,46,10,410	66.6	33.4
29.	Karnataka	3,74,69,335	2,36,25,962	61.3	38.7
30.	Goa	5,51,731	9,06,814	37.8	62.2
31.	Lakshadweep	14,141	50,332	21.9	78.1
32.	Kerala	1,74,71,135	1,59,34,926	52.3	47.7
33.	Tamil Nadu	3,72,29,590	3,49,17,440	51.6	48.4
34.	Puducherry	3,95,200	8,52,753	31.7	68.3
35.	Andman & Nicobar Islands	2,37,093	1,43,488	62.3	37.7
36.	Telangana	2,15,85,313	1,36,08,665	61.33	38.64
	India	**83,37,48,852**	**37,71,06,125**	**68.9**	**31.1**

Jawaharlal Nehru National Urban Renewal Mission

The Jawaharlal Nehru National Urban Renewal Mission (JnNURM) was launched in 2005 as the first flagship scheme of this Ministry. JnNURM implemented by MoHUPA has two components: Basic Services for Urban poor (BSUP) and Integrated Housing and Slum Development Programme (IHSDP), which are aimed at integrated development of slums through projects for providing shelter, basic services and other related civic amenities with a view to providing utilities to the urban poor. Under BSUP, project cost is shared in the ratio of 50:50 for cities with population more than 1 million (as per Census 2001), 80:20 for other smaller Mission Cities and 90:10 for North Eastern and special category states. Entire cost of construction of Dwelling Units (DUs) and associated infrastructure was shared as per the above mentioned sharing pattern without any limitation. Under IHSDP, project cost is shared in the ratio of 80:20 for remaining smaller cities and 90:10 for North Eastern and special category states.

Atal Mission for Rejuvenation and Urban Transformation

The Atal Mission for Rejuvenation and Urban Transformation (AMRUT) was launched in 2015. In all, 500 cities have been included in the Mission. All Urban Local Bodies (ULBs) with a population of one lakh or more, all other capital cities of states/UTs and all Heritage City Development and Augmentation Yojana (HRIDAY) cities, identified cities on the stem of the main rivers, from hill states, islands and tourist destinations. Approximately 60 per cent of urban population in the country is covered under AMRUT. It is a centrally sponsored scheme with a total outlay of ₹ 1 lakh crore including a Central Assistance of ₹ 50,000 crore spread over 5 years, *i.e.*, from 2015-16 to 2019-2020. The balance share of ₹ 50,000 crore has to come from states and ULBs.

The Mission focuses on development of basic urban infrastructure in the specified cities with the following expected outcomes:

(*i*) universal coverage for access to potable water for every household;

(*ii*) substantial improvement in coverage and treatment capacities of sewerage;

(*iii*) developing city parks; and

(*iv*) reform implementation and capacity building.

Heritage City Development

The National Heritage City Development and Augmentation Yojana (HRIDAY), a central sector scheme of the Government of India was launched in 2015 with the aim of bringing together urban planning, economic growth and heritage conservation in an inclusive manner with the objective of preserving the heritage character of each Heritage City. By November 2018 and after a total outlay of ₹ 500 crore, the scheme is being implemented in 12 identified cities, namely, Ajmer, Amaravati, Amritsar, Badami, Dwarka, Gaya, Kanchipuram, Mathura, Puri, Varanasi, Velankanni and Warangal.

Deendayal Antyodaya Yojana

Ministry of Housing and Urban Affairs has been implementing a centrally sponsored scheme Deendayal Antyodaya Yojana-National Urban Livelihoods Mission (DAY-NULM) since 2013 for reducing the poverty and vulnerability of urban poor households. The Mission covers all the statutory towns in the country, which are to be decided by the state as per local need and capability.

Its major components include:

(*a*) Social Mobilization and Institutional Development (SM&ID)

(*b*) Employment through Skill Training and Placement (EST&P)

(*c*) Self-Employment Programme (SEP)

(*d*) Support to urban street vendors to support pro-vendor planning

(*e*) Innovative and Special Projects (I&SP)

MULTIPLE CHOICE QUESTIONS

1. As per 2011 census, the State in India with the largest rural population is:
A. Madhya Pradesh B. Maharashtra
C. Punjab D. Uttar Pradesh

2. As per 2011 Census, the State in India with the highest urban population is:
A. Madhya Pradesh B. Maharashtra
C. Punjab D. Uttar Pradesh

3. According to 2011 Census, the rural population of India comprises?
A. 62.48% B. 64.9%
C. 66.84% D. 68.84%

4. 2011 Census covered how many districts in India?
A. 610 B. 620
C. 630 D. 640

5. As per 2011 census, the literacy rate among Indians:
A. 67.04% B. 68.04%
C. 71.04% D. 73.00%

6. According to 2011 census, the Union Territory of India with lowest literacy rate:

A. Andaman & Nicobar Islands
B. Chandigarh
C. Dadra & Nagar Haveli
D. Puducherry

7. According to 2011 census, the literacy rate among women in India is:
A. 64.6% B. 66.46%
C. 67.46% D. 62.46%

8. According to 2011 census, the literacy rate among men in India is:
A. 80.9% B. 84.14%
C. 85.14% D. 86.14%

9. According to 2011 census, which one is the most populous Indian city?
A. Bengaluru B. Kolkata
C. Delhi D. Mumbai

10. As per 2011 census, the number of women per 1,000 men in India is:
A. 920 B. 930
C. 943 D. 950

11. As per 2011 census, the per cent of urban population in total population in India is:
A. 31.1% B. 33.36%
C. 35.36% D. 37.36%

12. The National Commission on population is headed by?
A. Prime Minister
B. President
C. Home Minister
D. Registrar General of India

13. ______ is the Census Commissioner, under whose guidance the 2011 Census has been conducted?
A. D.K. Sikri B. J.K. Banthia
C. Dr. C. Chandramouli D. Dr. M. Vijayanunni

14. Debang Valley, Arunachal Pradesh and Samba Valley J & K have?
A. Least population density
B. Least adult sex ratio
C. Least female literacy
D. Least child sex ratio

15. Which among the following pairs is/are not correctly matched?
A. Mizoram : Highest child sex ratio
B. Haryana : Lowest child sex ratio
C. Kerala : Highest literacy rate
D. Nagaland : Highest decennial growth

16. _______ was the Mascot of 2011 Indian Census?
A. A woman enumerator B. A helping hand symbol
C. A child and mother D. A teddy bear

17. The slogan of Census 2011 was?
A. One Census, Million Future
B. Our Census, Million Future
C. One Census, One Future
D. Our Census, Our Future

18. _____ is also called the "Year of Great Divide" in the demographic history of India?
A. 1921 B. 1901
C. 1931 D. 2011

19. Along with the highest sex ratio, Kerala also has the dubious distinction of highest?
A. Transgenders
B. Greying population
C. Handicapped population
D. Child marriages

20. The first ever Census in modern human history was conducted by?
A. UK B. USA
C. New Zealand D. India

21. The decadal growth of population for India as whole declined from ____ in 1981-91 to _____ in 2001-11?
A. 23.87, 17.7 B. 17.61, 10.61
C. 20.87, 10.61 D. 17.09, 9.61

22. Who was the First Registrar General and Census Commissioner of Independent India?
A. M.W.M. Yeatts B. J.H. Hutton
C. J.T. Marten D. E.A. Gait

23. The First Indian Registrar General and Census Commissioner of Independent India was?
A. Ashok Mitra B. R.B. Chari
C. A.R. Nanda D. R.A. Gopalaswami

24. The first modern regular census in India, was started in 1881 by?
A. Lord Ripon B. Lord Lytton
C. Lord Powell D. Lord Clive

25. Which one of the following pairs is not correctly matched?
A. Highest Sex Ratio – Kerala
B. Lowest Sex Ratio – Haryana
C. Highest Density – Bihar
D. Lowest Density – Sikkim

26. As per 2011 Census report, which among the following pairs is/are not correctly matched?
A. Hindus – 80.5% B. Muslims – 13.4%
C. Christians – 2.3% D. Sikhs – 1.5%

27. The Indian State with lowest density of population, according to 2011 census?
A. Arunachal Pradesh B. Himachal Pradesh
C. Manipur D. Nagaland

28. The Indian State with highest density of population, according to 2011 census?
A. Bihar B. Kerala
C. West Bengal D. Uttar Pradesh

29. The population of India, according to 2011 Census?
A. 1,210,854,977 B. 1,200,193,422
C. 1,190,193,422 D. 1,100,193,422

30. The Indian State with lowest population, according to 2011 Census?
A. Arunachal Pradesh B. Mizoram
C. Nagaland D. Sikkim

31. The Indian State with highest literacy rate, according to 2011 census?
A. Goa B. Kerala
C. Mizoram D. Tripura

32. The Indian State with lowest literacy rate, according to 2011 census?
A. Arunachal Pradesh B. Bihar
C. Jharkhand D. Rajasthan

33. The Union Territory in India with highest literacy rate, according to 2011 census?
A. Andaman - Nicobar B. Chandigarh
C. Lakshadweep D. Puducherry

34. According to 2011 Census, Urban population in India comprises?
A. 31.1% B. 32.36%
C. 33.36% D. 34.36%

35. As per 2011 census, number of women per every 1000 men was in Andhra Pradesh?
A. 982 B. 972
C. 974 D. 993

36. When was the first census conducted in India?
A. 1872 B. 1881
C. 1891 D. 1901

37. Second most populous country in the world is?
A. China B. India
C. USA D. Indonesia

38. Which one is the most populous Union Territory?
A. Delhi
B. Puducherry
C. Chandigarh
D. Andaman & Nicobar Islands

39. Which one is the least populous Union Territory?
A. Lakshadweep
B. Daman & Diu
C. Dadra & Nagar Haveli
D. Andaman & Nicobar Islands

40. Density of population is defined as the number of persons per square ....
A. Millimetre B. Centimetre
C. Decimetre D. Kilometre

41. As per Census 2011, the population density of India?
A. 325 B. 382
C. 482 D. 582

42. As per Census 2011, the population density of Andhra Pradesh?
A. 277 B. 308
C. 408 D. 508

43. Which state has become the most densely populated state with 1106 persons per square kilometer?
A. Bihar B. West Bengal
C. Kerala D. Uttar Pradesh

44. Total number of States/Union territories recorded in Census 2011 was?
A. 35 B. 27
C. 34 D. 31

45. As per census 2011, number of women per every 1000 men was in Uttar Pradesh?
A. 912 B. 915
C. 918 D. 905

46. As per census 2011, the population density of Uttar Pradesh is:
A. 824 B. 808
C. 829 D. 920

47. Environmental Studies are very important for :
A. getting clean drinking water
B. hygienic living conditions
C. clean and fresh air
D. All of the above

48. Which of the following is still a very important source of energy for millions of Indians living in villages?
A. Oil B. Coal
C. Fossil fuels D. Fuel wood

49. The characteristic/s of a community is/are :
A. diversity B. periodicity
C. dominance D. All of these

50. National Biodiversity Strategy and Action Plan (NBSAP) was established in :
A. 1986 B. 1988
C. 1999 D. 2004

51. Major pollutants of motor vehicular emission in India are :
A. Oxides of nitrogen and lead
B. Diesel particulates and carbon monoxide
C. Ozone and carbon dioxide, other toxics
D. All of the above

52. Exposure to UV radiations cause :
A. damage to eye sight
B. sun burn
C. cancer of skin
D. All of the above

53. Sewage water treatment that involves bacteria is called:
A. Primary treatment
B. Activated sludge treatment
C. Tertiary treatment
D. Cyclic treatment

54. Air pollution effects are mostly found on :
A. leaves B. flowers
C. stems D. roots

55. Most important causative pollutant in soil is :
A. Plastic B. Glass junk
C. Iron Junk D. Detergents

56. Green Petrol is :
A. Leaded petrol B. Unleaded petrol
C. Gasohol D. Low sulphur Diesel

57. When was NEPA (National Environmental Policy Act) enforced in India?
A. 1968 B. 1969
C. 1985 D. 1959

58. The composition of Compressed Natural Gas (CNG) is:
A. CH_4, C_2H_6 and C_4H_8 and other gases
B. CH_4, $(CO + H_2)$
C. $CO + N_2$
D. $LPG + H_2$

59. Land use planning must aim at :
A. minimal loss B. acceptable income
C. Both of the above D. None of the above

60. The most important cause for the loss of biodiversity is :
A. global warming B. climate change
C. ozone depletion D. None of these

61. Which pigment protects plants from UV radiation damage?
A. chlorophyll B. xanthophyll
C. carotenoids D. phycocyanin

62. Green Muffler is planting of trees and shrubs to reduce noise pollution. It is done :
A. on wastelands B. along roads
C. along canals D. on the slopes of hills

63. A crop helpful in *Dryland reclamation* is :
A. sunflower B. paddy
C. sugarcane D. cotton

64. An ozone depleting agent being used in fire extinguishers is
A. Nitrogen oxide
B. Halon
C. Chlorofluoro carbon
D. Methyl bromide

65. The Environmental Protection Act was enacted in :
A. 1986 B. 1985
C. 1987 D. 1972

66. The major stratospheric ozone layer over Antarctica was discovered in :
A. 1983 B. 1985
C. 1987 D. 1980

67. Nitrogen oxide can be absorbed by plants like :
A. Pinus B. Quercus
C. Junipers D. All of these

68. Carbon monoxide can be absorbed by plants like :
A. Bean B. Coleus
C. Carrot D. All of these

69. Photochemical smog bring about :
A. Floral bud shedding
B. Defoliation
C. Discolouration and curling of petals
D. Bleaching and blazing of foliage

70. Where is NEERI previously known as PHERI located?
A. Nagpur B. Shimla
C. Bengluru D. Cochin

71. Photochemical smog always contain :
A. ozone B. methane
C. CO D. PAN

72. Classical smog is :
A. Dark brown
B. Yellow brown
C. Los Angeles smog
D. Smog with sec. pollutants

73. Sulphurous smog is :
A. photochemical smog
B. oxidising smog
C. classical smog
D. Los Angeles smog

74. PAN (Peroxyacylnitrate) is a secondary pollutant and is found in :
A. smog B. fertilizer
C. herbicide D. pesticide

75. DDT is banned because it :
A. affects the reproduction in birds
B. has short half life
C. is uneconomical in use
D. is dangerous to animals and man

76. *Agent orange* contains
A. 2, 4-D
B. 2, 4, 5-T
C. Dioxin as contaminant/carcinogen
D. All of the above

77. Ozone increases :
A. photosynthesis B. transpiration
C. respiration D. Both (B) and (C)

78. In hospitals sterilization is brought by :
A. spraying DDT B. UV radiation
C. infrared radiation D. alpha radiation

79. Which secondary pollutant is produced by UV rays of sun light?
A. SO_2 B. CO
C. fluorides D. ozone

80. An ecosystem is :
A. different communities of plants, animals and microbes together with their physico-chemical environments
B. an interacting system of Biotic communities and their abiotic environment
C. open and closed depending upon community
D. All of the above

81. Temperature changes in the environment affect most of the animals which are :
A. Aquatic B. Desert
C. Poikilothermal D. Homoisothermal

82. Biome is :
A. The fauna of an ocean
B. The flora of land
C. Communities of organisms interacting with one another
D. The part of the earth and its atmosphere which is inhabited by living organisms

83. Ecological niche of an organism denotes :
A. Habitat of the organism
B. On whom the organism feeds
C. The status of an organism within a particular community
D. All of the above

84. Grassland biome for its maintenance requires :
A. Periodic fire B. Intensive grazing
C. Mowing D. All of the above

85. Which of the following is a biome :
A. Wheat field B. Rain water pond
C. Grass field D. Deciduous forest

86. Total organic matter present in an ecosystem is called:
A. Biomass B. Biome
C. Litter D. Food

87. The most important organisms for an ecosystem are :
A. Herbivores B. Carnivores
C. Green plants D. Protozoa

88. A food chain consists of :
A. Producers B. Consumers
C. Decomposers D. Both A and B

89. Primary consumers are :
A. Green plants B. Herbivores
C. Carnivores D. All of the above

90. Secondary consumers are :
A. Green plants B. Herbivores
C. Carnivores D. All of the above

91. Which one is inverted pyramid :
A. Pyramid of biomass in grassland
B. Pyramid of biomass in pond ecosystem
C. Pyramid of numbers in grassland ecosystem
D. Pyramid of energy in a pond ecosystem

92. Ecological pyramid which is never inverted :
A. Pyramid of energy
B. Pyramid of biomass
C. Pyramid of numbers
D. Pyramid of species richness

93. Ecological pyramids were given by:
A. Elton B. Haeckel
C. Odum D. Reiter

94. In pond ecosystem the shape of pyramid of number is:
A. Linear B. Irregular
C. Upright D. Inverted

95. Energy flow in an ecosystem is :
A. Unidirectional B. Bidirectional
C. Multidirectional D. All of the above

96. Tree ecosystem show inverted pyramid of numbers. It shows :
A. number of organisms go on increasing
B. size of individuals go on decreasing with each trophic level
C. Both (A) and (B)
D. None of these

97. Grassland of U.S.A. is referred to as :
A. Prairies B. Steppes
C. Pampas D. Veldts

98. Plankton, Nekton and Benthos are not the components of one of ecosystems which is :
A. Oceans B. Fresh water rivers
C. Grassland D. Pond or lake

99. A man-made microecosystem is :
A. Plants grown in a pond
B. Crop field
C. Tank formed naturally in your court yard
D. Lake in a forest

100. A treeless biome is :
A. Tundra B. Grassland
C. Desert D. All of the above

101. In an ecosystem, tropic level of man is :
A. Producer B. Herbivore
C. Omnivore D. Carnivore

102. Vegetation of Delhi is predominantly :
A. Halophytic B. Xerophytic
C. Mesophytic D. Hygrophytic

103. Ecosystem has two components :
A. Animals and humans
B. Plants and animals
C. Biotic and abiotic
D. Weeds and trees

104. Tropical plants *Prosopis, Acacia* and *Capparis* belong to :
A. Evergreen forest B. Deciduous forest
C. Grassland D. Thorn forest

105. First '*Earth Summit*' at Rio-de-Janeiro (Brazil) held in 1992 was related to :
A. soil fertility
B. soil erosion
C. prevention of afforestation
D. conservation of environment

106. **Red data book** (RDB) published by IUCN provides :
A. information of threatened species of flora and fauna

B. information on wildlife
C. information on toxic plants
D. a book on biota red sea

107. International day for Biological Diversity is observed on :
A. December 21 B. December 29
C. June 5 D. December 1

108. What should we do to save the existing species of the wildlife?
A. Protection of endangered species
B. Protection of wildlife *in situ* and *ex situ*
C. Preservation of useful plants and animals in protected areas
D. All of these

109. *Ex situ* conservation of natural resources can be obtained by :
A. controlling natural habits
B. inducing variations
C. establishing sanctuaries
D. protecting wildlife in Zoos and Botanical gardens

110. *In situ* conservation of natural resources is :
A. protection of wildlife in natural habitat/National parks
B. control of pollution
C. control of human interference in the biosphere
D. All of the above

111. Which programme is not for preservation of wildlife/ forests in India?
A. IUCN B. MAB
C. Project Tiger D. NEERI

112. Plant/animals species should be present because :
A. a species once lost can not be retrieved
B. zoologists study them
C. it can be useful to us
D. it is a creature of nature

113. National 'Wildlife Protection Act' was enacted by our government to declare hunting as unlawful act in the year :
A. 1979 B. 1972
C. 1962 D. 1982

114. The concept of biosphere reserve was evolved in 1986 by :
A. MAB programme of UNESCO
B. IUCN
C. WWF-N
D. Project Tiger

115. Where was the first biosphere reserve in India set up in 1986?
A. Nokrek B. Manas
C. Gulf of Mannar D. Nilgiri

116. National Park provides protection to :
A. fauna only B. flora only
C. Both A and B D. entire ecosystem

117. In Wildlife sanctuary :
A. only wild fauna (animals) are protected
B. private ownership is allowed
C. harvesting of trees for timber and forest products is permitted
D. All of these

118. **'Project Tiger'** was launched in April 1973. It is a :
A. conservation programme
B. afforestation programme
C. biosphere reserve
D. All of the above

119. Cutch (Katha) is obtained from:
A. *Acacia arabica* B. *A. senegal*
C. *A. catechu* D. *A. melanoxylon*

120. Mulching helps in:
A. Soil conservation
B. Jhooming
C. Moisture conservation
D. All of these

121. India's largest National Park is:
A. Corbett National Park, Uttarakhand
B. Desert National Park, Rajasthan
C. Nagarjuna Sagar National Park, Hyderabad Telangana
D. Sunderbans, W. Bengal

122. The area of semirural, low density population is called:
A. green area B. green belt
C. greenery D. greenland

123. Lesser Panda/Red Panda (*Ailurus fulgens*) is preserved at :
A. Dachigam National Park, J&K
B. Sasan Gir National Park, Gujarat
C. Khangchend Zonga National Park, Sikkim
D. Simlipal National Park, Odisha

124. Great Indian Bustard Sanctuary is located in :
A. Rajasthan B. Maharashtra
C. Karera (MP) D. Pakistan (Lahore)

125. Shivpuri Sanctuary in MP is asylum for :
A. Birds B. Tigers
C. Lions D. Snakes

126. Sariska Tiger Project is in Rajasthan in :
A. Alwar B. Savai Madhopur
C. Jaiselmer D. Bharatpur

127. Where is Nalabana Bird Sanctuary located?
A. Sultanpur Lake B. Dal Lake
C. Chilka Lake D. Silsit Lake

128. World Environment Day is observed on :
A. March 21st B. Dec. 1st
C. May 31st D. June 5th

129. World Earth Day is observed on :
A. April 22nd B. June 5th
C. March 21st D. May 31st

130. World forest day is celebrated on :
A. March 21st B. April 7
C. First week of Oct. D. April 22

131. When was the Forest Conservation Act passed in India?
A. 1960 B. 1970
C. 1980 D. 1950

132. When was the Environment Protection Act enforced in India?
A. 1980 B. 1986
C. 1982 D. 1988

133. When was the National Forest Policy formulated?
A. 1948 B. 1980
C. 1964 D. 1952

134. When was National Environment Policy Act (NEPA) was passed?
A. 1952 B. 1969
C. 1972 D. 1989

135. Which forest area in India was first brought under control and protection?
A. Malabar B. Konkan
C. Garhwal D. Sunderbans

136. Why is the *Silent Valley* so called?
A. It is silent during the night
B. It is silent during the day
C. It has nothing to do with silence
D. It is not a valley

137. Silent Valley of Kerala is preserved as :
A. it contains valuable timber trees
B. represents natural tropical rain forests with rich diversity
C. it is reservoir of rare wildlife
D. recreational value

138. Red data book is famous for :
A. extinct plants
B. endangered animals
C. endangered plants
D. endangered plants and animals

139. The science of the relations of all organisms all their environments is:
A. Ecology B. Ecosystem
C. Toxicology D. Cytology

140. In which year the term ecology was coined?
A. 1885 B. 1886
C. 1883 D. 1884

141. Father of plant ecology is Warming. Who is revered as father of ecology in India?
A. Father H. Santapan B. W. Dudgeon
C. Ramdeo Misra D. P. Maheshwari

142. The word Ecology (Oekologie) is derived from two Greek words which means :
A. the study of wildlife
B. the study of land and life
C. the study of life
D. the study of home

143. Term **bioecology** to study plant and animal ecology as integral branch, was coined by :
A. Odum
B. Reiter
C. Shelford and Clements
D. Kormondy

144. The study of interaction between living organisms and their environment is called :
A. Ecosystem B. Phytogeography
C. Phytosociology D. Ecology

145. The aspect considered to be most important in ecology is :
A. climate B. soil
C. environment D. man

146. Broad leaved deciduous forests are typical of :
A. Mid-altitude forests
B. Mediterranean region
C. Monsoon region
D. Coniferous region

147. Applied ecology deals with :
A. individual species
B. plant communities
C. physiological and genetic potentialities
D. man and biosphere

148. Consider the following statements:
1. An urban settlement may be linear, square, star or crescent shaped.
2. Towns and cities of developed or developing countries reflect marked differences in planning and development.
3. The form of the settlement, architecture and style of buildings are an outcome of its historical and cultural traditions.

Which of the above mentioned statements is/are correct?
A. 1 and 2 B. 1 and 3
C. Only 2 D. All the above

149. Consider the following statements about conurbation:
1. The term conurbation was coined by Patrick Geddes in 1915.
2. It is applied to a large area of urban development that resulted from the merging of originally separate towns or cities.

Which of the above mentioned statements is/are correct?
A. Only 1 B. Only 2
C. Both 1 and 2 D. Neither 1 nor 2

150. Consider the following statements:
1. A city may be regarded as a leading town, which has outstripped its local or regional rivals.

2. Cities are much larger than towns.
3. When the population crosses the one million mark it is designated as a million city.

Which of the above mentioned statements is/are correct?

A. 1 and 2 B. 1 and 3
C. Only 2 D. All the above

151. Consider the following statements:

1. Inadequate social infrastructure
2. Lack of educational and health facilities
3. Lack of employment
4. Male selective migration

Which of the above are the socio-cultural problems of cities in the developing countries?

A. 1 and 3 B. 1 and 2
C. 2, 3 and 4 D. All the above

152. Consider the following statements about Megalopolis:

1. The term 'Megalopolis' was popularised by Jean Gottman.
2. It is a region extending as union of conurbations.
3. Greater London, Manchester, Chicago and Tokyo are examples.

Which of the above mentioned statements is/are correct?

A. 1 and 2 B. 1 and 3
C. Only 2 D. All the above

153. "The theory of Demographic Transition suggests that population growth is linked to overall levels of economic development and that every society follows a typical pattern of development related population growth."

Choose the incorrect statement about Demographic Transition Theory.

A. The growth rate in phase I and phase II are high
B. The growth rate in phase II is high due to low death rate
C. The growth rate in phase I and phase III are low
D. The growth rate in phase III is approximately same as in phase I

154. "Considering from an urban point of view, the rapid growth in urbanization shows that the town or city has been acting as a magnet for the rural population."

Choose the incorrect statement about urbanisation in India.

A. Rural-to-urban migration has increased due to decline in common property resources
B. Cities offer anonymity to the poor and the oppressed castes
C. People go to cities in search of work
D. Urban areas are a decisive force in terms of political power dynamics

155. "Famines were also a major and recurring source of increased mortality".

Which of the following is not a cause of famines?

A. Continuing poverty and malnutrition in agroclimatic environment
B. Inadequate means of transportation and communication
C. Failure of entitlements
D. Increasing birth rate

156. Which policy was introduced by the Government of India that could increase the child-sex ratio in the country?

A. Beti-Bachao, Beti-Padhao
B. Sarva Shiksha Abhiyan
C. Mahatma Gandhi National Rural Employment Guarantee Act
D. Mid-day Meal Programme

157. "The pyramid for 2026 shows the estimated future size of the relevant age groups based on data on the past rates of growth of each age group. Such estimates are also called '______'."

A. Projections
B. Age pyramid
C. Demographic dividend
D. Rate of natural increase

158. This changes the age structure: relatively smaller proportions of the population are found in the younger age groups and larger proportions in the older age groups. This is also referred to as the ______.

A. Ageing of the population
B. Age structure
C. Population momentum
D. Demographic dividend

159. Which of the following is not one of the features of urban community?

A. Face-to-face relationships
B. Complex life
C. Materialistic
D. Glamour in life

160. Which among the following is not a cause of growth of cities?

A. Trade & commerce
B. Industrialism
C. Development of transport
D. Hygienic outlook of people

161. The movement of people from central cities to smaller communities in the surrounding area is known as...

A. Reverse migration B. Under urbanisation
C. Suburbanisation D. Over-urbanisation

162. The Sub-Mission for Basic Services to the Urban Poor is administered by the __________.

A. Ministry of Housing and Urban Poverty Alleviation
B. Ministry of Urban Development
C. HUDCO
D. Ministry of Human Resource

163. JNNURM was launched in the year: ________.

A. 2015 B. 2005

C. 2000 D. 1995

164. Which of the following is not a category for Urban Local Bodies in the country post 74th Amendment?

A. Nagar Palika (Municipality)

B. Mahanagar Nigam (Municipal corporation)

C. Nagar Panchayat (Notified Area council/City council)

D. Reserved area community (Reserved areas for high society)

165. The urban becomes the means by and through which ________ survives.

A. Socialism B. Communism

C. Capitalism D. Liberalism

ANSWERS

1	2	3	4	5	6	7	8	9	10
D	B	B	D	D	C	A	A	D	C
11	12	13	14	15	16	17	18	19	20
A	A	C	A	D	A	D	A	B	B
21	22	23	24	25	26	27	28	29	30
A	A	D	A	D	D	A	A	A	D
31	32	33	34	35	36	37	38	39	40
B	B	C	A	D	A	B	A	A	D
41	42	43	44	45	46	47	48	49	50
B	B	A	A	A	C	D	D	D	C
51	52	53	54	55	56	57	58	59	60
D	D	B	A	D	B	B	A	C	C
61	62	63	64	65	66	67	68	69	70
C	B	A	B	A	B	D	D	D	A
71	72	73	74	75	76	77	78	79	80
A	A	C	A	C	B	D	B	D	D
81	82	83	84	85	86	87	88	89	90
C	C	C	D	D	A	C	D	B	C
91	92	93	94	95	96	97	98	99	100
B	A	A	C	A	C	A	C	B	D
101	102	103	104	105	106	107	108	109	110
C	B	C	D	D	A	B	D	D	A
111	112	113	114	115	116	117	118	119	120
D	A	B	A	D	D	D	A	B	D
121	122	123	124	125	126	127	128	129	130
C	B	C	C	B	A	C	D	A	A
131	132	133	134	135	136	137	138	139	140
C	B	D	B	A	A	D	D	A	A
141	142	143	144	145	146	147	148	149	150
C	D	C	D	C	B	D	D	C	D
151	152	153	154	155	156	157	158	159	160
D	A	A	D	D	A	A	A	A	D
161	162	163	164	165					
C	A	B	D	C					

6

WORLD GEOGRAPHY, INDIAN GEOGRAPHY & ITS RESOURCES

WORLD GEOGRAPHY

THE UNIVERSE

- Existing matter and energy are together known as **Universe.**

Galaxy

- A galaxy is a huge system of billions of stars and clouds of dust and gases.
- Our solar system is a part of *Milky Way* galaxy.
- There are millions of galaxies that make the Universe.

Stars

- Stars account for 98 per cent of the matter in a galaxy. The stars nearest to the earth are *Proxima Centauri, Alpha Centauri, Barnard's Star, Sirius* and so on. Of these, *Sirius* is the brightest.

Light year

- Light year is the distance travelled by light in one year at a speed of 2,99,792.5 km. per second.

Solar System

- The Sun, eight planets, satellites and some other celestial bodies known as asteroids and meteoroids form the solar system.

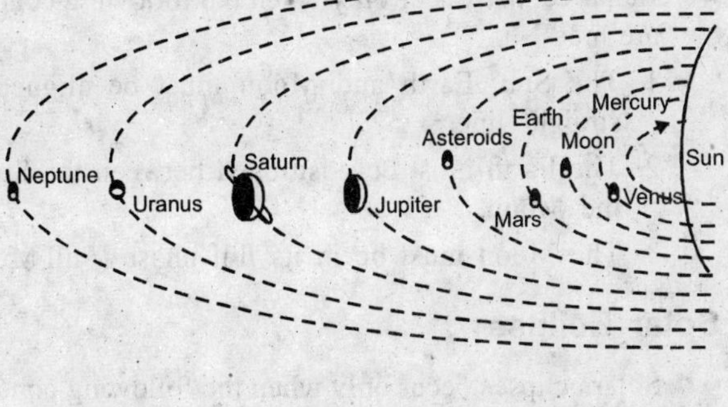

SUN

- The Sun is in the centre of the solar system.
- The Sun is a mixture of gases. It consists of 92% hydrogen, 7.8% helium and 0.2% other gases.
- The Sun is about 150 million km away from the earth.
- The sun is an ultimate source of energy for life on Earth.
- Sunlight takes 8 min 16.6 sec to reach earth.

Facts about Sun

Diameter	– 1.392×10^6 km
Volume	– 1.304 × 106 times the volume of earth
Temperature	– 6000°C at surface and 15 million degree C at the centre
Relative density	– 1.4
Gravitational Pull	– 28 times the gravitational pull of the earth

Facts about Planets

Closest to Sun	*Mercury*
Farthest from Sun	*Neptune*
Heaviest	*Jupiter*
Hottest	*Venus*
Inner	*Mercury, Venus, Earth, Mars*
Largest	*Jupiter*
Smallest	*Mercury*
Moons, None	*Mercury, Venus*
Moon; Largest	*Ganymede (Jupiter), larger than Mercury*
Nearest to Earth	*Venus*
Orbits; Order	*Mercury (closest to Sun), Venus, Earth, Mars, Jupiter, Saturn, Uranus, Neptune.*
Rings/largest number	*Saturn*
Spin; Backwards	*Venus (East to West)*

Comets

- It has a head and a tail. Its tail originates only when it gets closer to the sun. The tail can be 20-30 million km long. It always point away from the sun because of the force exerted by solar wind and radiation on the cometory material.

The Earth

- The earth is the third nearest planet to the Sun.
- From the outer space, the earth appears blue because its two-thirds surface is covered by water. It is, therefore, called a blue planet.
- It is the densest of all planets.
- Rotation is the movement of the earth on its axis. Due to this rotation, day and night occur.
- The earth takes about 23 hours 56 minutes and 4 seconds to complete one rotation around its axis.
- Earth takes 365¼ days (one year) to revolve around the sun.

The Earth: Facts and Figures

- *Mass of Earth*—5.880 × 10^{21} tonnes
- *Density of Earth*—5.517 times that of water
- *Volume of Earth*—1.083 × 10^{11} cubic km
- *Equatorial circumference*—4.007 × 104 km
- *Polar Diameter*—12,714 km
- *Equatorial Diameter*—12756 km
- *Polar or Meridional circumference*—4.0 × 10^4 km
- *Estimated Age*—At least 4600 million years
- *Land Surface*—148,951,000 sq km
- *Water Surface*—361,150,000 sq km (71 per cent of total area)
- *Highest Point of the land surface*—Mt. Everest (8,848 metres)
- *Lowest point of the land surface*—Shores of the Dead Sea (396 metres below the sea level)
- *Greatest Ocean depth*—Mariana Trench, East of Philippines (11,033 metres below the sea level)

The Moon

- Earth has only one satellite, that is, the moon.
- Its diameter is only one-quarter that of the earth. It is about 3,84,400 km away from us.
- The moon moves around the earth in about 27 days. It takes exactly the same time to complete one spin. As a result, only one side of the moon (only 59% of its surface) is visible to us on the earth.
- Moonlight takes 1.3 sec. to reach earth.

Latitude

- Imaginary lines drawn parallel to the equator. Measured as an angle whose apex is at the centre of the earth.
- The equator represents 0° latitude, while the North Pole is 90°N and the South Pole 90°S.
- 23½°N represents Tropic of Cancer while 23½°S represents Tropic of Capricorn.

Longitude

- It is the angular distance measured from the centre of the earth. On the globe the lines of longitude are drawn as a series of semicircles that extend from the North Pole to the South Pole through the equator. They are also called meridians.
- The distance between any two meridians is not equal. At the equator, 1 degree = 111 km. At 30°N or S, it is 96.5 km. It goes on decreasing this way until it is zero at the poles.

International Date Line

- It is the 180° meridian running over the Pacific Ocean, deviating at Aleutian Islands, Fiji, Samoa and Gilbert Islands.
- Travellers crossing the Date Line from west to east repeat a day and travellers crossing it from east to west lose a day.

Indian Standard Time (IST)

- Indian Standard Time is calculated on the basis of 82.5°E longitude which passes through Uttar Pradesh, Madhya Pradesh, Odisha, Chattisgarh and Andhra Pradesh.

Eclipses

- Sun is the only source of light for both the Earth and Moon. Eclipses occur when the light thus received is either blocked by the earth or by the Moon.
- Eclipses occur when either the Earth moves behind the Moon's shadow or the Moon moves behind the Earth's shadow.

Lunar Eclipse

- Lunar eclipse occur only when the following conditions are met.
  1. The Sun, Earth and Moon must be aligned in a straight line.
  2. The Earth must be positioned between the Sun and the Moon.
  3. The Moon must be in its full phase (Full Moon).

Solar Eclipse

- Solar eclipses occur only when the following conditions are met.

1. The Sun, Earth and Moon must be aligned in a straight line.
2. The Moon must be positioned between the Sun and the Earth.
3. Must be a New Moon day.

Rocks

- Rocks are composed of many minerals such as silica, aluminium, iron and magnesium. The nature of the rock is determined by the presence of its minerals.
- Rocks can be classified into three types:

1. ***Igneous rocks*** are formed by magma that reaches the earth's surface along deep cracks and at volcanic vents. e.g., Mica, Granite etc.
2. ***Sedimentary rocks*** are formed by the accumulation and cementation of mud, silt, or sand derived from weathered igneous rock fragments. e.g., Gravel, Peat, Gypsum etc.
3. ***Metamorphic rocks*** are igneous or sedimentary rocks that have been altered by heat and/or pressure, either because they have been buried and folded deep in the crust, or because they have come into contact with molten igneous rock, e.g., Gneiss, Marble, Quartzite etc.

Volcanoes

- Sudden eruption of hot magma (molten rock), gases, ash and other material from inside the Earth to its surface.
- ***Active*** which erupts frequently, e.g., Mauna Loa (Hawaii), Etna (Sicily), Vesuvius (Italy), Stromboli (Mediterranean Sea).
- ***Dormant*** Not erupted for quite sometime, e.g., Fujiyama (Japan), Krakatoa (Indonesia), Barren Island (Andamans).
- ***Extinct*** Not erupted for several centuries, e.g., Arthur's Seat, Edinburgh, Scotland.

Earthquakes

- Earthquakes are a form of wave energy that is transferred through bedrock. It is transmitted from the point of the earthquake focus, as spherical seismic waves. They travel in all directions outward.
- The intensity of earthquake waves is recorded by *Seismograph*.

LANDFORMS

- There are three major landforms: mountains, plateaus and plains.

Mountains

- A mountain can be defined as an area of land that rises abruptly from the surrounding region.
- There are three types of mountains- *Fold Mountains, Block Mountains* and the ***Volcanic Mountains***.
- Himalayas, Alps, Andes, Rockies, Atlas, etc are examples of Fold Mountains.
- The Aravali range in India is one of the oldest **fold mountain** systems in the world.
- The Rhine valley and the Vosges mountain in Europe are examples of such mountain systems.
- Volcanic mountains are formed due to volcanic activity.
- Mt. Kilimanjaro in Africa and Mt. Fujiyama in Japan are examples of such mountains.

Major Mountain Ranges of the World

Range	Location	Highest Peak (m)	Length (km)
Andes	South America	6,960	7,200
Himalayas-Karakoram-Hindukush	South Central Asia	8,848	4,800
Rockies	North America	4,401	4,800
Great Dividing Range	East Australia	2,228	3,600
Western Ghat	Western India	2,637	1,610
Caucasus	Europe	5,642	1,200
Alaska	USA	6,194	1,130
Alps	Europe	4,808	1,050
Apennines	Europe	2,912	—
Ural	Asia	1,895	—
Atlas	North West Africa	—	1,930

Plateaus

- A plateau is an elevated flat land. It is a flat-topped table land standing above the surrounding area.

Principal Mountain Peaks of the World

Mountains	Height in Metres
1. Mount Everest	8,848
2. K-2 (Godwin Austen)	8,611
3. Kanchenjunga	8,598
4. Lhotse	8,511
5. Makalu I	8,481
6. Dhaulagiri I	8,167
7. Mansalu I	8,156
8. Chollyo	8,153
9. Nanga Parbat	8,124
10. Annapurna I	8,091
11. Gasherbrum I	8,068
12. Broad Peak I	8,047
13. Gasherbrum II	8,034
14. Shisha Pangma (Gosainthan)	8,014
15. Gasherbrum III	7,952

Plains

- A relatively low-lying and flat land surface with least difference between its highest and lowest points is called a Plain.

OCEANS

- Oceans of the world is classified into four groups: the Pacific, the Atlantic, the Arctic and the Indian.
- The Pacific is the largest ocean, being twice the size of the Atlantic.
- It covers about a third of the Earth's surface, and contains more than half the water on the planet.

Oceans of the World

Names	Area (Sq. Km.)	Greatest Depth
Pacific	166,240000	Mariana Trench
Atlantic	86,560000	Puerto Rico Trench
Indian	73430000	Java Trench
Arctic	13230000	—

Major Gulfs of the World

Names	Area (Sq. Km.)
Gulf of Mexico	15,44,000
Gulf of Hudson	12,33,000
Arabian Gulf	2,38,000
Gulf of St. Lawrence	2,37,000
Gulf of California	1,62,000
English Channel	89,900

Important Lakes of the World

Lake	Location	Area (Sq. Km.)
Caspian	Russia and CIS	371000
Superior	Canada and USA	82414
Victoria	Tanzania (Africa)	69485
Huron	Canada and USA	59596
Michigan	USA	58016
Tanganyika	Africa	32892
Baikal	Russia (CIS)	31502
Great Bear	Canada	31080
Malawi	Malawi (Tanzania)	30044
Great Slave	Canada	28438

Major Rivers of the World

River	Origin	Falls in	Length (Km.)
Nile	Victoria lake	Mediterranean Sea	6,650
Amazon	Andes (Peru)	Atlantic Ocean	6,428
Yangtze	Tibetan Kiang Plateau	China Sea	6,300
Mississippi Missouri	Itaska lake (USA)	Gulf of Mexico (USA)	6,275
Yenisei	Tannu-Ola Mts.	Arctic Ocean	5,539
Hoang Ho	Kunlun Mts.	Gulf of Chibli	5,464
Ob	Altai Mts., Russia	Gulf of Ob	5,410
Congo	Lualaba & Luapula rivers	Atlantic Ocean	4,700
Amur	Northeast China	Sea of Okhotsk	4,444
Lena	Baikal Mts	Laptev Sea	4,400
Mekong	Tibetan Highlands	South China Sea	4,350
Mackenzie	Great Slave Lake	Beaufort Sea	4,241
Niger	Guinea	Gulf of Guinea	4,200

Important Straits of the World

Straits	Water Bodies joined	Area
Bab-al-Mandeb	Red Sea & Arabian Sea	Arabia & Africa
Bering	Arctic Ocean & Bering Sea	Alaska & Asia
Bosphorus	Black Sea & Marmara Sea	Turkey
Dover	North Sea & Atlantic Ocean	England & Europe
Florida	Gulf of Mexico & Atlantic Ocean	Florida & Bahamas Islands
Gibralter	Mediterranean Sea & Atlantic Ocean	Spain & Africa
Malacca	Java Sea & Bay of Bengal	India & Indonesia
Palk	Bay of Bengal & Indian Ocean	India & Sri Lanka
Magellan	South Pacific & South Atlantic Ocean	Chile
Sunda	Java Sea & Indian Ocean	Indonesia

Highest Waterfalls of the World

Name(s) (Foreign)	Location
Angel (Salto Angel)	Canaima National Park, Venezuela
Tugela	Natal National Park, South Africa
Utigord (Utigordsfoss)	Norway
Monge (Mongefoss)	Marstein, Norway
Gocta Cataracts	Chachapoyas, Peru
Mutarazi (Mtarazi)	Nyanga National Park, Zimbabwe
Yosemite	Yosemite National Park, California, U.S.
Espelands (Espelandsfoss)	Hardanger Fjord, Norway
Lower Mar Valley (Ostra Mardolafoss)	Eikesdal, Norway
Tyssestrengene	Odda, Norway

Important Cities on River Banks (World)

City	Country	River
Adelaide	Australia	Torrens
Amsterdam	Netherlands	Amsel
Alexandria	Egypt	Nile
Ankara	Turkey	Kazil
Bangkok	Thailand	Chao Praya
Basra	Iraq	Euphrates and Tigris
Baghdad	Iraq	Tigris
Berlin	Germany	Spree
Bonn	Germany	Rhine
Budapest	Hungary	Danube
Bristol	UK	Avon
Buenos Aires	Argentina	Laplata
Chittagong	Bangladesh	Majyani
Canton	China	Si-Kiang
Cairo	Egypt	Nile
Chung King	China	Yang-tse-kiang
Cologne	Germany	Rhine
Dandzing	Germany	Vistula
Dresden	Germany	Elbe
Dublin	Ireland	Liffy
Hamburg	Germany	Elbe
Kabul	Afghanistan	Kabul
Karachi	Pakistan	Indus
Khortoum	Sudan	Confluence of Blue & White Nile
Lahore	Pakistan	Ravi
Leningrad	Russia	Neva
Lisbon	Portugal	Tagus
Liverpool	England	Messey
London	England	Thames
Moscow	Russia	Moskva
Montreal	Canada	St. Lawrence
Nanking	China	Yang-tse-kiang
New Orleans	U.S.A.	Mississipi
New York	U.S.A.	Hudson
Ottawa	Canada	Ottawa
Paris	France	Seine
Philadelphia	U.S.A	Delaware
Perth	Australia	Swan
Prague	Czech Republic	Vitava
Quebec	Canada	St. Lawrence
Rome	Italy	Tiber
Rotterdam	The Netherlands	New Moss
Stalingrad	Russia	Volga
Shanghai	China	Yang-tse-kiang
Sidney	Australia	Darling
Saint Louis	U.S.A	Mississippi
Tokyo	Japan	Arakava
Vienna	Austria	Danube
Warsaw	Poland	Vistula
Washington D.C.	U.S.A.	Potomac
Yangoon	Myanmar	Irawaddy

World's Geographical Surnames

City of Sky-scrapers—New York
City of Seven Hills—Rome
City of Dreaming Spires—Oxford
City of Golden Gate—San Francisco
City of Magnificent Buildings—Washington D.C.
City of Eternal Springs—Quito (S. America)
China's Sorrow—Hwang Ho
Cockpit of Europe—Belgium
Dark Continent—Africa
Emerald Isle—Ireland
Eternal City—Rome
Empire City—New York
Forbidden City—Lhasa (Tibet)
Garden City—Chicago
Gate of Tears—Strait of Bab-el-Mandeb
Gift of the Nile—Egypt
Granite City—Aberdeen (Scotland)
Hermit Kingdom—Korea
Herring Pond—Atlantic Ocean
Holy Land—Jerusalem
Island Continent—Australia
Islands of Cloves—Zanzibar
Isle of Pearls—Bahrein (Persian Gulf)
Key to the Mediterranean—Gibralter
Land of Cakes—Scotland
Land of Golden Fleece—Australia
Land of Maple Leaf—Canada
Land of Morning Calm—Korea
Land of Midnight Sun—Norway
Land of the Thousand Lakes—Finland
Land of the Thunderbolt—Bhutan
Land of White Elephant—Thailand
Land of Thousand Elephants—Laos
Land of Rising Sun—Japan
Loneliest Island—Tristan De Gunha (Mid-Atlantic)
Manchester of Japan—Osaka
Pillars of Hercules—Strait of Gibraltar
Pearl of the Antilles—Cuba
Playground of Europe—Switzerland
Quaker City—Philadelphia
Queen of the Adriatic—Venice
Roof of the World—The Pamirs, Central Asia
Sugar bowl of the world—Cuba
Venice of the North—Stockholm
Windy City—Chicago
Whiteman's grave—Guinea Coast of Africa
Yellow River—Huang Ho (China)
Sickman of Europe—Turkey

Important Boundaries

Durand Line	Pakistan & Afghanistan
MacMohan Line	India & China
Radcliff Line	India & Pakistan
Maginot Line	France & Germany
Oder Niesse Line	Germany & Poland
Hindenberg Line	Poland & Germany (at the time of First World War)
38th Parallel	North & South Korea
49th Parallel	USA & Canada

Continents: Some Facts

Continent	Biggest Country	Highest Peak	Longest River
Asia	China	Mt. Everest (8848 m)	Yangtze Kiang
Africa	Algeria	Mt. Kilimanjaro (5895 m)	Nile
North America	Canada	Mt. Mckinley (6194 m)	Mississippi Missouri
South America	Brazil	Mt. Acancagua (6960 m)	Amazon
Europe	Russia	Mt. Elbrus (5642 m)	Ob
Australia	Australia	Mt. Kosciuszko (2228 m)	Darling
Antarctica	—	Vinson Massif (5140 m)	—

INDIAN GEOGRAPHY

AREA AND LOCATION

- India is in the southern parts of the Asian continent. In the west of India lies the Arabian Peninsula while in the east lies the Indo-China Peninsula.
- India extends between 8°4' N and 37°6' N latitudes and between 68°7' E and 97°25' E longitudes.
- India, has a total geographic area of 32,87,263 sq. km. This is only 2.42 % of the total geographic area of the world but holds 17 per cent of the world's population.
- The 23½°N, which is the Tropic of Cancer, runs across the country.
- India has a length of 3214 km from north to south and 2933 km from east to west. It has a land frontier of 15200 km.
- The total length of the coastline of the mainland, Lakshadweep Islands and Andaman and Nicobar Islands is 7,516.6 km.
- India is bordered on three sides by water and on one by land, it is also a peninsula.
- India shares its common border with Afghanistan and Pakistan in the north-west, China, Nepal and Bhutan in the north, and Bangladesh in the east. In the south, Sri Lanka is separated from India by a strait, known as the Palk Strait.
- There are 28 States, and 8 Union Territories in India.
- 82°30' E longitude is considered as the Indian Standard Meridian. The local time of this longitude is taken as the Indian Standard Time (IST). This is 5½ hours ahead of the Greenwich Mean Time.

The Indian States on International boundaries are:

- ***Bordering Pakistan:*** Jammu and Kashmir, Punjab, Rajasthan, Gujarat.
- ***Bordering China:*** Ladakh, Himachal Pradesh, Uttarakhand, Sikkim, Arunachal Pradesh.
- ***Bordering Nepal:*** Bihar, Uttarakhand, UP, Sikkim, West Bengal.
- ***Bordering Bangladesh:*** West Bengal, Mizoram, Meghalaya, Tripura, Assam.
- ***Bordering Bhutan:*** West Bengal, Sikkim, Arunachal Pradesh, Assam.
- ***Bordering Myanmar:*** Arunachal Pradesh, Nagaland, Manipur, Mizoram.
- ***Bordering Afghanistan:*** Jammu and Kashmir (Pakistan-occupied area).

Important Passes

Kashmir	Burzi-La, Banihal
Himachal Pradesh	Bara La, Cha-La, Shipki-La
Uttarakhand	Niti-La, Lipu-Lekh-La
Sikkim	Jelep-La, Nathu-La
Arunachal Pradesh	Bomdi-La

Heighest Mountain Peaks of India

Peaks	Elevation• (in mts.)
Godwin Austin (K2)	8611*
Kanchenjunga	8598
Nanga Parvat	8126*
Gasherbrum	8068*
Broad Peak	8047*
Dastegil	7885*
Masherbrum (East)	7821*
Nanda Devi	7817
Masherbrum (West)	7806*
Rakoposhi	7788*
Kamet	7756
Saser Kangdi	7672

• *Above mean sea level in metres.*
* *Situated in Pak occupied Kashmir (PoK).*

Waterfalls of India

Waterfall	Hgt (Mt.)	River	State
Kunchikal	455	Varahi	Karnataka
Jog/Gersoppa	260	Sharavati	Karnataka
Rakim Kund	168	Gaighat	Bihar
Chachai	127	Bihad	Madhya Pradesh
Kevti	98	Mahanadi	Madhya Pradesh
Sivasamudram	90	Cauveri	Karnataka

Important Lakes of India

Name of lake	State/UT
Pulicat Lake	Tamil Nadu & Andhra Pradesh Border
Sambhar Lake	Rajasthan
Tso Moriri Lake	Jammu & Kashmir
Vembanad Lake	Kerala
Wular & Dal Lakes	Jammu and Kashmir
Chilka Lake	Odisha
Kolleru Lake	Andhra Pradesh
Loktak Lake	Manipur
Lonar Lake	Maharashtra
Pangong Lake	Ladakh

Towns at River Banks

Town	River
Agra	Yamuna
Prayagraj	Confluence of the Ganges and the Yamuna
Ayodhya	Saryu
Badrinath	Alaknanda
Kolkata	Hooghly
Cuttuck	Mahanadi
Delhi	Yamuna
Dibrugarh	Brahmaputra
Ferozepur	Satluj
Guwahati	Brahmaputra
Hardwar	The Ganges
Hyderabad	Musi
Jabalpur	Narmada

Town	River
Kanpur	The Ganges
Kota	Chambal
Kurnool	Tungbhadra
Lucknow	Gomti
Ludhiana	Satluj
Nasik	Godavari
Pandharpur	Bhima
Patna	The Ganges
Sambalpur	Mahanadi
Srinagar	Jhelum
Srirangapattam	Cauveri
Surat	Tapti
Varanasi	The Ganges
Vijaywada	Krishna

Rivers of India

Name	Originates From	Falls Into
Yamuna	Yamunotri	Ganga
Chambal	Singar Chouri Peak, Vindhyan escarpment	Yamuna
Ghaghara	Matsatung Glacier	Ganga
Kosi	Near Gosain Dham Peak	Ganga
Sabarmati	Aravalis	Gulf of Khambat
Krishna	Western Ghats	Bay of Bengal
Godavari	Nasik district in Maharashtra	Bay of Bengal
Caurey	Brahmagir Range of Western Ghats	Bay of Bengal
Tungabharda	Western Ghats	Krishna
Ganges	Combines Sources	Bay of Bengal
Satluj	Mansarovar Rakas Lakes	Chenab
Indus	Near Mansarovar Lake	Arabian Sea
Ravi	Kullu Hills near Rohtang Pass	Chenab
Beas	Near Rohtang Pass	Sutlej
Jhelum	Verinag in Kashmir	Chenab
Son	Amarkantak	Ganga
Brahmaputra	Near Mansarovar Lake	Bay of Bengal
Narmada	Amarkantak	Gulf of Khambat
Tapti	Betul District in Madhya Pradesh	Gulf of Khambat
Mahanadi	Raipur District in Chhattisgarh	Bay of Bengal
Luni	Aravallis	Runn of Kutch
Ghaggar	Himalayas	Near Fatehabad
Betwa	Vindhyachal	Yamuna

Geographical Surnames

Bengal's Sorrow	Damodar River
City of Palaces	Kolkata
Gateway of India	Mumbai
Pink City	Jaipur
Paris of India	Jaipur
Manchester of India	Ahmedabad
Kashmir of South	Kerala
Son of Sea	Lakshadweep
Queen of Mountains	Mussourie
Iron City	Jamshedpur
Hollywood of India	Mumbai
Scotland of East	Meghalaya
City of Nawabs	Lucknow
City of Temples & Ghats	Varanasi
Land of Five Rivers	Punjab

City of Golden Temple	Amritsar	Ganga of South	Cauvery/Godavari
Garden of India	Bangaluru	Pitsburg of India	Jamshedpur
Spice Garden of India	Kerala	City of Bridges	Srinagar
City of Lakes	Srinagar	A Cross-road (Quadrivial) of National Highways	Kanpur
Twin City	Hyderabad-Secunderabad	Heart of India	Delhi
City of Seven Islands	Mumbai	Black River	Sharda
Diamond Harbour	Kolkata	City of Festivals	Madurai
Switzerland of India	Kashmir	Queen of Deccan	Pune
Rice Bowl	Chhattisgarh	Sorrow of Bihar	Kosi River
Fruit Bowl	Himachal Pradesh		

Some Major Irrigational and Multipurpose Projects

S.No.	Name of Project	Related State	River
1.	Bargi Project	Madhya Pradesh	Bargi
2.	Beas	Joint Venture of Haryana, Punjab and Rajasthan	Beas
3.	Bhadra	Karnakata	Bhadra
4.	Bhakra Nangal	Haryana, Punjab and Rajasthan	Sutluj
5.	Bhima I	Maharashtra	Pawana
6.	Bhima II	Maharashtra	Krishna
7.	Chambal	Joint Project of M.P. and Rajasthan	Chambal
8.	Damodar Valley Project	West Bengal and Bihar	Damodar
9.	Dulhasti Power Project	Jammu and Kashmir	Chenab
10.	Farakka	West Bengal	Hooghly
11.	Gandak	Bihar and U.P.	Gandak
12.	Ghataprabha	Karnataka	Ghataprabha
13.	Hasdeo Bango Project	Madhya Pradesh, Chhattisgarh	Hasdeo
14.	Hirakud	Odisha	Mahanadi
15.	Jayakwadi	Maharashtra	Godavari
16.	Kakrapara	Gujarat	Tapti
17.	Kangsbati	West Bengal	Kangsbati and Kumari
18.	Karjan	Gujarat	Karjan
19.	Kosi	Bihar	Kosi
20.	Koyana	Maharashtra	Koyana
21.	Krishna Project	Maharashtra	Krishna
22.	Kukadi	Maharashtra	Kukadi
23.	Left Bank Ghagra Canal	Uttar Pradesh	Ghagra
24.	Madhya Ganga Canal	Uttar Pradesh	Ganga
25.	Mahanadi Delta Scheme	Odisha	(The irrigation scheme will utilise releases from Hirakund Reservoir)
26.	Mahi	Gujarat	Mahi
27.	Malaprabha	Karnataka	Malaprabha
28.	Mayurakshi	West Bengal	Mayurakshi
29.	Nagarjunasagar	Andhra Pradesh	Krishna
30.	Panam	Gujarat	Panam
31.	Parambikulam Aliyar	Tamil Nadu and Kerala	Perimbikulam
32.	Pochampad	Andhra Pradesh	Godavari
33.	Pong Dam	Punjab	Beas

S.No.	Name of Project	Related State	River
34.	Ramganga	Uttarakhand	Ramganga
35.	Ranjit Sagar Dam (Thein Dam)	Punjab	Ravi
36.	Rihand	Uttar Pradesh	Rihand
37.	Sabarmati	Gujarat	Sabarmati
38.	Sharda Sahayak	U.P.	Ghagra
39.	Sone High Level Canal	Bihar	Sone
40.	Tawa	Madhya Pradesh	Tawa
41.	Tehri Dam	Uttarakhand	Bhagirathi
42.	Tungabhadra	Andhra Pradesh and Karnataka	Tungabhadra
43.	Upper Krishna	Karnataka	Krishna
44.	Upper Penganga	Maharashtra	Penganga
45.	Uri Power Project	Jammu and Kashmir	Jhelum
46.	Sardar Sarovar Dam	Gujarat, MP, Maharashtra, Rajasthan	Narmada

Major Indian Crops

Crops	Temp(°c)	Water(cm)	States where Produced
Wheat	15°-25°	60-90	Uttar Pradesh, Punjab, Haryana.
Rice	24°-26°	80-200	West Bengal, Uttar Pradesh, Andhra Pradesh, Bihar, Punjab
Maize	18°-21°	50-60	Bihar, Uttar Pradesh, Maharashtra
Jawar	20°-35°	40-60	Maharashtra, Madhya Pradesh, Karnataka
Soyabean	25°-27°	50-120	Madhya Pradesh
Cotton	20°-30°	80-150	Maharashtra, Gujarat, Karnataka, Madhya Pradesh
Tobacco	20°-25°	75-80	Andhra Pradesh, Gujarat, Karnataka, Maharashtra, Tamil Nadu, Bihar
Tea	24°-30°	100-200	Assam, West Bengal, Kerala, Tamil Nadu, Uttar Pradesh
Ground Nut	15°-25°	60-130	Gujarat, Maharashtra

Mineral Resources at a Glance (Metallic Minerals)

Mineral	Chief Producers
Bauxite	Odisha, Gujarat, Jharkhand
Chromite	Odisha, Karnataka
Coal	Jharkhand, West Bengal
Copper	Madhya Pradesh, Rajasthan
Diaspore	Uttar Pradesh, Madhya Pradesh
Gold	Karnataka
Iron	Odisha, Karnataka, Goa, Jharkhand, Chhattisgarh
Lead	Rajasthan, Andhra Pradesh
Lignite	Tamil Nadu
Manganese	Odisha, Karnataka
Natural Gas	Gujarat, Assam
Petroleum	Gujarat, Assam, Andhra Pradesh
Silver	Rajasthan, Andhra Pradesh, Jharkhand
Tungsten	Rajasthan
Zinc	Rajasthan, West Bengal

Zones and Headquarters of Indian Railways

S.N.	Zone	Headquarters
1.	Central	Mumbai (Victoria Terminus)
2.	Eastern	Kolkata
3.	Northern	New Delhi
4.	North-Eastern	Gorakhpur
5.	North-East Frontier	Maligaon, Guwahati
6.	Southern	Chennai
7.	South-Central	Secunderabad
8.	South-Eastern	Kolkata
9.	Western	Mumbai, Churchgate
10.	East Coast	Bhubaneswar
11.	East Central	Hajipur
12.	North Central	Prayagraj
13.	North Western	Jaipur
14.	South Western	Hubballi
15.	West Central	Jabalpur
16.	South East Central	Bilaspur
17.	Kolkata Metro Railway	Kolkata
18.	South Coast Railway	Vishakhapatnam (In Process)

Major National Highways

NH	Connects
NH 1	New Delhi-Ambala-Jalandhar-Amritsar
NH 2	Delhi-Mathura-Agra-Kanpur-Allahabad-Varanasi-Kolkata
NH 3	Agra-Gwalior-Nasik-Mumbai
NH 4	Thane and Chennai *via* Pune and Belgaum
NH 5	Kolkata-Chennai
NH 6	Kolkata-Dhule
NH 7	Varanasi-Kanyakumari (2369 km)
NH 8	Delhi-Mumbai (*via* Jaipur, Baroda and Ahmedabad)
NH 9	Mumbai-Vijaywada
NH 10	Delhi-Fazilka
NH 24	Delhi-Lucknow
NH 26	Lucknow-Varanasi
NH 44	Srinagar–Kanyakumari (3806 km)

Major Ports of Country

1. Syama Prasad Mookerjee (Kolkata)
2. Mumbai
3. J.L. Nehru Port (Nhava Sheva)
4. V.O. Chidambaranar (Tuticorin)
5. Chennai
6. Mormugao
7. New Mangalore
8. Paradeep,
9. Deendayal (Kandla)
10. Vishakhapatnam
11. Cochin
12. Kamarajar (Ennore).

Major International Airports in India

International Airports	City
Indira Gandhi International Airport	Delhi
Anna International Airport	Chennai
Sri Guru Ram Das Jee International Airport	Amritsar
Rajiv Gandhi International Airport	Hyderabad
Calicut International Airport	Kozhikode
Chhatrapati Shivaji International Airport	Mumbai
Kempegowda International Airport	Bengaluru
Veer Savarkar International Airport	Port Blair
Netaji Subash Chandra Bose International Airport	Kolkata
Thriuvananthapuram International Airport	Thiruvananthapuram
Lokpriya Gopinath Bordoloi International Airport	Guwahati
Sardar Vallabhbhai Patel International Airport	Ahmedabad

RESOURCES OF INDIA

MINERAL RESOURCES

- India is rich in mineral resources. But these are not equally distributed in the country.
- Most of the mineral resources found in the area of Deccan plateau, Chhattisgarh, Jharkhand, Madhya Pradesh, Odisha, Karnataka, Maharashtra and Tamil Nadu.

IMPORTANT MINERALS

Iron Ore

- China is the largest producer in the world. India ranks fourth in production.
- India produces four types of iron ores, Haematite, Magnetite, Limonite and Siderite.
- Karnataka has the Largest reserve of Magnetite ore followed by Odisha, Jharkhand, Chhattisgarh and Andhra Pradesh.
- Odisha has the largest reserve of haematite followed by Jharkhand, Chhattisgarh and Karnataka.

❑ **Odisha :** In Odisha main producing areas are Mayurbhanj, Keonjhar and Sundargarh.

❑ **Chhattisgarh:** Dantewada, Bastar, Durg, Rajnadgaon, Raigarh, and Bilaspur districts are main producers.

❑ **Karnataka :** Important areas are—Bellary, Chitradurga (Bababudan Hills) Chikmaglur, Bijapur, Dharwad, Tumkur and Shimoga districts.

❑ **Jharkhand :** Major producers are Noamundi and Gua in Singhbhum, Daltonganj in Palamau.

❑ **Andhra Pradesh and Telangana :** Anantpur, Khammam, Krishna, Kurnool, Cuddapha and Nellore.

❑ **Goa:** Pirna adol, Tolsia, Borgadogar, and Rivora are important regions, minings are open and mechanised, mainly exported to Japan.

Manganese

- Occur mainly in the Dharwar system of rocks.
- Odisha has the highest reserve followed by Karnataka, Madhya Pradesh, Maharashtra, and Goa.
- Odisha is the leading producer followed by Maharashtra, Madhya Pradesh and Karnataka.
  - **Odisha :** Keonjhar, Sundargarh, Koraput, Kalahandi and Bolangir.
  - **Maharashtra :** Main regions are—Nagpur-Bhandara Belt, and Ratnagiri.
  - **Madhya Pradesh :** Balaghat, Chhindwara, Jabalpur and Jhabua.
  - **Karnataka :** Bellary, Uttar kannad, Shimoga, Tumkur and Belgaum.
  - **Jharkhand :** Birmitrapur in Chaibasa, Singhbhum, Hazaribagh and Dhanbad districts.

Copper

- Important non-ferrous metal, earliest metal used by man.
- Highest reserve in Rajasthan followed by Madhya Pradesh, Jharkhand, Andhra Pradesh and Gujarat.
- Madhya Pradesh is largest producer followed by Rajasthan.
  - **Madhya Pradesh :** Malajkhand in Balaghat district, Sidhi and Jabalpur.
  - **Rajasthan:** Khetri Belt in Aravalli range, Kho Dariba near Alwar, Delwara and Debari in Udaipur districts are important mining centres.
  - **Jharkhand :** Mosabani, Rakha and Ghatshila
  - **Andhra Pradesh & Telangana :** Agnigumdala belt near Guntur.

Bauxite

- Mainly spread over the eastern ghats.
- Scattered in Laterite rocks.
- Odisha ranks first in reserve followed by Andhra Pradesh, Gujarat, Chhattisgarh and Maharashtra.
- Odisha is the largest producer followed by Gujarat, Jharkhand and Maharashtra.
  - **Odisha :** More than half of country's production comes from this state alone. Kalahandi-Koraput belt is famous for its production.
  - **Gujarat :** Another important producer in the country. Bhavnagar-Junagarh–Amreli Belt is the main region.
  - **Jharkhand :** Ranchi, Palamau, Lohardaga and Muri.
  - **Maharashtra :** production comes mainly from-Kolhapur, Ratnagiri, Thane, Satara and Kolaba.

Lead

- It occurs in the cambrian rocks and the vindhayan sediments.
  - **Rajasthan :** Reserves 88.61 per cent of the country's total mainly from the Zawar region of Udaipur. Other areas in Rajasthan include Rajpura-Dariba area of Bhilwara, Ajmer, Alwar, Banswara and Sawai Madhopur.
  - **Andhra Pradesh and Telangana :** Cuddapah, Guntur and Kurnool.
  - **Odisha :** Sambalpur, Kalahandi and Sundargarh.

Zinc

- Sphalerite is the chief ore.
- largely used for galvanising or coating iron and steel.
  - **Rajasthan** has a monopoly in zinc production. Main areas are–Zawar in Udaipur district. This area has two main zones of mineralisation.
    - (*i*) Pipli mine to Barla mine
    - (*ii*) Mochia Magra, Balaria.
  - Other producing areas are Bhilwara, Ajmer, Alwar and Sawai Madhopur.
  - Bhotang of Sikkim, Riasi of Jammu and Kashmir, Almora and Tehri Garhwal of Uttarakhand are other producing areas of the country.

Gold

- Karnataka is the largest producer of gold in the country. It has a monopoly in production of gold. Kolar, Hutti in Rachur and Gulbarga are main gold fields.
- Ramagiri in Andhra Pradesh
- Nilgiri and Coimbatore in Tamil Nadu
- Singhbhom in Jharkhand
- Kojhikod in Kerala
- Largest resources of gold ore (primamy) are located in Bihar, followed by Karnataka, Rajasthan, West Bengal, Andhra Pradesh and Madhya Pradesh.

Silver

- Silver is found in the galena ores that may have up to one per cent of the metalic mineral.
- Zawar mines in Udaipur, **Rajasthan**
- **Andhra Pradesh including Telangana** is one of the main producers of silver in the country. Guntur, Cuddapah, and Kurnool districts are important producers.
- **Jharkhand** including Bihar is the other important producer of silver. Singhbhum, Dhanbad and Dumka Districts are important producers.
- Vadodara in **Gujarat**, and
- Baramula in **Jammu and Kashmir**.

Mica

- India is the most important mica producing country in the world and it supplies 80 per cent of the world requirements of black mica.

- **Andhra Pradesh (including Telangana)** is the largest producer of mica in the country. Mica is extracted from Nellore in Gudur district. Kalichedu, Kalyanarama, Sitaram, Pallimita and Basayar are important mines. In less quantity it is found in Krishna, Visha, Khapatanam, and Anantpur districts.
- **Rajasthan** is the second largest producer in the country. Jaipur, Udaipur, Bhilwana, and Ajmer are important producers.
- In **Jharkhand** Mica is extracted from the Hazaribagh belt with Koderma. High quality mica is produced in Koderma district.
  - Gaya, Mungyr and Bhagalpur in **Bihar**
  - Hasan and Mysore in **Karnataka**.
  - Bastar and Bilaspur in **Chhattisgarh**
  - Balaghat and Chhindwara in **M.P**.
  - Ratnagiri in **Maharashtra**
  - Koraput, Mayurbhanj and Ganjam in **Odisha**.

Diamond

- Found in scattered crystals in an igneous rock called Kimberlite, also come from alluvial sources.
- Panna Belt of Madhya Pradesh, Raipur of Chhattisgarh and Kurnool in Anantpur district of Andhra Pradesh, are important producers.

Graphite

- Also called black lead, graphite occurs along with metamorphic rock.
- Arunachal Pradesh, Jammu & Kashmir, Jharkhand and Tamil Nadu possesses more reserve.

Gypsum

- A hydrated calcium sulphate found in the sedimentary rocks.
- Jodhpur region of Rajasthan, Coimbatore in Tamil Nadu and Uttarakhand are important producing regions.

Magnesite

- A refractory mineral, one of the important minerals of magnesium.
- A substantial quantities of resources are established in Uttarakhand, Rajasthan, Tamil Nadu, Andhra Pradesh, Himachal Pradesh and Jammu & Kashmir.

Lime stone

- Found in rocks constituting calcium carbonate.
- Karnataka is the leading state followed by Andhra Pradesh, Gujarat, Rajasthan, Meghalaya, Chhattisgarh, Madhya Pradesh and Odisha.

Dolomite

- Mainly produced in Chhattisgarh (Durg), Madhya Pradesh, Andhra Pradesh and Odisha (Birmitrapur, Bildih and Khatepur).

INDUSTRY

IRON AND STEEL INDUSTRY

- The location of iron and steel industry in India has been primarily influenced by considerations of transportational costs in procuring raw materials such as iron ore, coal and limestone.
- The country's richest iron ore deposits lie in the iron belt extending from Gurumahisani Hills in the Mayurbhanj region in Odisha to Singhbhum district of Jharkhand.
- Coal is another important raw material for the iron and steel industry. Raniganj (West Bengal) and Jharia (Jharkhand) have abundance of good quality coal.

ALUMINIUM INDUSTRY

- The location of the aluminium industry is governed mainly by the availability of bauxite.

Steel Plants in India

Name	Location	Owner
• Tata Iron and Steel Corporation (TISCO)	Jamshedpur (Jharkhand)	Tata Steel
• Visvesvaraya Iron and Steel Plant	Bhadravati (Karnataka)	SAIL
• Bhilai Steel Plant	Chhattisgarh	SAIL
• Durgapur Steel Plant	Durgapur (West Bengal)	SAIL
• Bokaro Steel Plant	Jharkhand	SAIL
• Chandrapur Ferro Alloy Plant	Chandrapur (Maharashtra)	SAIL
• IISCO Steel Plant	Asansol (West Bengal)	SAIL
• Salem Steel Plant	Tamil Nadu	SAIL
• Rourkela Steel Plant	Odisha	SAIL
• Vijaynagar Steel Plant (Karnataka) and Power	Hospet, Bellary	Jindal Steel
• Vishakhpatnam Steel Plant	Vishakhpatnam (A.P)	Rashtriya Ispat Nigam

- Hence, the aluminium industry is mostly located in areas producing bauxite and having cheaper availability of hydro-electricity as in West Bengal, Uttar Pradesh, Maharashtra, and Tamil Nadu.
- It was in the year 1938 that India for the first time Produce aluminium at Alupuram Reduction Works of the Indian Aluminium Company. This company was later on converted into a public company in 1944.

Indian Aluminium Company Limited (INDAL)

- The Indian Aluminium Company Limited is an integrated plant having three units at different places for the production of aluminium ingots into sheets.
- The reduction plant of alumina is located at Alupuram in Kerala and the fabrication plant at Belur manufactures aluminium sheets, rods, aluminium paste, electric conductors, domestic utensils, etc.
- In order to achieve the economics of scale, a second smelter was set up at Hirakud.

Hindustan Aluminium Corporation Limited (HINDALCO)

- The Hindustan Aluminium Corporation Limited is located at Renukoot near Mirzapur in Uttar Pradesh.

Bharat Aluminium Company (BALCO)

- The Bharat Aluminium Company has set up two units at Korba and Ratnagiri to utilise bauxite ores of Amarkantak in Madhya Pradesh and of Udaigiri-Dhargarvadi region in Maharashtra, respectively.
- Other important industrial units engaged in the smelting of aluminium include: Bharat Aluminium Company (MALCO) of Mettur, and the Aluminium Corporation of India at Jayakaynagar (near Asansol, West Bengal).

PAPER INDUSTRY

- Paper industry comes under the category of forest-based industry. Paper is made from cellulose or fibre.
- The first paper mill in the country was set up at Serampore (Bengal) in 1832, which failed.
- In 1870, a fresh venture was started at Ballygunj near Kolkata.
- The planned development of paper and paperboard industry began after independence.
- In 1950, there were 17 paper mills with installed capacity of 1.6 lakh tonnes. At present, there are nearly 850 mills in the country.
- The statewise distribution of paper industry is as follows.
  - **West Bengal :** The state had the advantage of an early start. Bamboo as the raw material was available from Assam, Bihar and Odisha in the vicinity and sabai grass from Madhya Pradesh. Major paper manufacturing centres in the state are Titanagar, Kakinara, Naihatti, Kolkata and Baranagore.
  - **Maharashtra :** Mumbai, Pune, Ballarpur and Kamptee produce paper and Vikhroli, Kalyan and Goregaon produce paper-boards here.
  - **Andhra Pradesh (including Telangana):** Rajamundry and Sirpur produce paper here.
  - **Madhya Pradesh :** Indore, Bhopal, Sehore and Shadol are the major paper-producing centres.
  - **Karnataka :** Belagola (using bagasse) and Shimoga are the main paper-producing centres.
- The other states known for paper production are Uttar Pradesh, Bihar, Odisha, Haryana, Tamil Nadu, Gujarat and Kerala.

CEMENT INDUSTRY

- Cement is made mainly from limestone and clay. Other raw materials include shale, coal and gypsum. Thus, cement factories are located near limestone deposits.
- The cement plants at **Bhadravati** (Karnataka) and **Chaibasa** (Jharkhand) use slag and the plant at **Sindri** uses sludge.
- At **Dalmia Dadri** in Haryana, there is a cement plant based on *kanker* (limestone nodules).
- The major cement producing Centres are as follow:
  - **Andhra Pradesh (including Telangana) :** Karimnagar, Kurnool, Vijaywada, Krishna, Sullupet and Anantpur.
  - **Rajasthan :** Bundi, Sawai Madhopur, Chittorgarh, Udaipur.
  - **Tamil Nadu :** Tirunelveli, Ramanathpuram, Tiruchirappalli, Salem and Coimbatore.
  - **Madhya Pradesh :** Jabalpur and Gwalior.
  - **Chhattisgarh :** Durg and Raipur.
  - **Gujarat :** Ahmedabad, Sikka, Sewree, Dwarka, Porbandar, Sewalia and Ankaleshwar.
  - **Jharkhand :** Sindri, Ranchi, Palamau, Chaibasa and Japla.
  - **Karnataka :** Shahbad, Wadi, Kurkunta, Bagalkot, Bhadravati and Tumkur.
- At present, there are 210 large cement plants.

SUGAR INDUSTRY

- After Brazil, India is the largest sugar producer in the world and it leads in sugarcane production.
- The major centres of sugar industries are as follows:
  - **Uttar Pradesh:** There are two belts—one in western Uttar Pradesh and the other in eastern Uttar Pradesh. The western belt includes Meerut, Saharanpur, Muzaffarnagar, Bijnor and Moradabad, and the eastern belt includes Gorakhpur, Deoria, Basti and Gonda.
  - **Bihar :** It is an extension of the eastern Uttar Pradesh belt, which includes Darbhanga, Saran, Champaran and Muzaffarpur.

- **Maharashtra :** Nasik, Pune, Satara, Sangli, Kolhapur, Sholapur are the centres well integrated in the cooperative sector in terms of cultivation and suagar factories.
- **Tamil Nadu :** In this state Nalikupuram, Pugulur, Coimbatore and Pandyarajpuram are famous for producing sugar.
- **Karnataka :** Munirabad, Shimoga and Mandya are the main centres.
- **Punjab :** mainly in the eastern side, in Phagwara and Dhuri.

COTTON TEXTILE INDUSTRY

- The first successful cotton textile mill was set up at Mumbai by Parsi entrepreneurs.
- The major centres of cotton textiles production are as follows:
  - **Maharashtra :** Mumbai is the focal point, the industry is spread in Sholapur, Kolhapur, Pune, Jalgaon, Akola, Sangli and Nagpur.
  - **Gujarat :** Besides Ahmedabad, other cotton textiles centres are Surat, Vadodara, Bharuch, Bhavanagar, Nadiad, Porbandar, Rajkot and Navsari.
  - **Tamil Nadu :** Coimbatore, Chennai, Tirunelvelli, Madurai, Tuticorin, Salem, Virudhnagar and Pollachi are the major cotton textile industry centres.
  - **Karnataka :** Bangalore and its hinterland have attracted cotton textiles industry.
  - **Uttar Pradesh :** The major cotton textiles producing centres are Kanpur, Etawah, Modinagar, Moradabad, Bareilly, Hathras, Agra, Meerut and Varanasi.
  - **Madhya Pradesh :** Indore, Gwalior, Mandsaur, Dewas, Ujjain, Nagda, Bhopal and Jabalpur.
  - **Chhattisgarh :** Rajnandgaon
  - **Rajasthan :** Kota, Jaipur, Sriganganagar, Bhilwada, Bhavanimandi, Udaipur and Kishengarh.
  - **West Bengal :** Kolkata, Howrah, Serampore, Shyamnagar, Murshidabad and Saikia.

WOOLLEN TEXTILE INDUSTRY

- The first woollen textiles mill was set up in 1876 at Kanpur.
- Most of the woollen textile mills are situated in **Punjab** along the Amritsar-Gurdaspur-Ludhiana belt, and at Patiala and Dhariwal.
- State–wise producers in the country are given below:
  - **Rajasthan :** Jaipur, Jodhpur, Bikaner
  - **Uttar Pradesh:** Kanpur, Agra, Mirzapur
  - **Madhya Pradesh :** Gwalior
  - **Gujarat :** Jamnagar, Ahmedabad, Vadodara
  - **Maharashtra :** Mumbai
  - **Karnataka :** Bangalore
  - **Jammu and Kashmir :** The state is a large producer of handloom woollen goods and manufacturing is centred around Srinagar.

SILK TEXTILE INDUSTRY

- India's silk industry is world's second largest after China.
- **Karnataka** is the largest producer of silk in the country. Major silk-producing centres in the state are Tumkur, Dodballapur, Bangalore and Mysore.
- Other silk-producing states are:
  - **Tamil Nadu :** Dharmapuram, Salem, Coimbatore, Tirunelveli.
  - **Andhra Pradesh (including Telangana) :** Karimnagar, Warangal, Mahbubnagar, Kurnool, Ongole, Adilabad.
  - **Jammu and Kashmir :** Srinagar.
  - **Punjab :** Amritsar.
  - **Maharashtra :** Chandrapur.
  - **Madhya Pradesh :** Raigarh.
  - **Uttar Pradesh :** Varanasi, Mirzapur.
  - **Bihar :** Katihar, Bhagalpur.
  - **Jharkhand :** Ranchi.
  - **West Bengal:** Malda, Murshidabad, Bankura.

JUTE INDUSTRY

- The first modern jute mill in India was set up at Rishra near Kolkata in 1854.
- India tops in production of raw jute and finished jute goods and second in export of jute goods.
- Nearly 85 per cent of the manufacturing capacity is located in a narrow belt about 100 km long and 3 km wide along River Hooghly.
  - (*i*) Soil and agronomic conditions suit jute cultivation.
  - (*ii*) The East India Company's initial efforts in and around Kolkata were of great advantage for the industry.
  - (*iii*) This belt is well connected through waterways and rail with the jute-growing areas.
- Other states are Bihar, UP and Odisha.

SYNTHETIC INDUSTRY

- Weaving of synthetic fibres began around 1920, when the first rayon plant was set up at Rayonpuram in Kerala.
- Mumbai, Ahmedabad, Delhi, Surat, Kolkata, Amritsar and Gwalior are the centres of this industry.

Other Industries in India

	Name	Location
1.	**Petro-chemical Industry**	Trombay, Koyali, Badodara, Chennai, Thane, Bongaigaon
2.	**Fertilizer Industry**	Nangal, Kanpur, Sindari, Talchar, Barauni, Korba, Alwai, Kalol.
3.	**Aircraft Manufacturing**	Lucknow, Kanpur, Koraput, Hyderabad, Nasik and Bengaluru.
4.	**Shipyard**	Kolkata, Vishakhapattnam, Cochin, Mumbai, Goa.
5.	**Electronic Goods**	Hyderabad, Bhopal, Haridwar, Sonipat, Patiala, Pune.
6.	**Shoftware Industry**	Bengaluru, Vishakhapattanam, Gurgaon, Noida, Gandhinagar, Bhubaneshwar.

ENERGY RESOURCES

COAL

- India is third largest producer of coal in the world after China and USA.
- In India, coal is the most abundantly available fossil fuel.
- India is highly dependent on coal for meeting its commercial energy requirements.
- In India coal occurs in rock series of two main geological ages, namely Gondwana, a little over 200 million years in age and in tertiary deposits which are only about 55 million years old.
- The major resources of Gondwana coal, which are metallurgical coal, are located in Damodar valley (West Bengal-Jharkhand). Jharia, Raniganj, Bokaro are important coalfields.
- The Godavari, Mahanadi, Son and Wardha valleys also contain coal deposits.
- Tertiary coals occur in the north eastern states of Meghalaya, Assam, Arunachal Pradesh and Nagaland.
  - It amounts to 60% of total electricity generated.
  - 67% of the commercial needs of energy.
  - Raniganj coal field is the oldest in India (1814).
- Important Coalfields
  - **Jharkhand :** Jharia, Bokaro, Giridih, Karanpura, Ramgarh.
  - **W. Bengal:** Raniganj.
  - **M.P., Chhattisgarh :** Singrauli, Korba.
  - **Andhra Pradesh (including Telangana) :** Godavari valley (Singareni) Kantapalli.
  - **Maharashtra:** Chanda, Kamte, Umrer and Bander.
  - **Odisha :** Talcher, Himgir.

LIGNITES

- Lignite deposits in India is confined to states of Tamil Nadu, Gujarat, Rajasthan, Pondicherry, Jammu & Kashmir and Kerala where coal is almost absent.

PETROLEUM

The mineral oil resources of India are distributed in three important basins.

- ***Upper Assam or the Naharkatia-Moran, Region* :** Major oil wells in this region are Digboi, Naharkatia, Moran, Lakwa, Sibsagar and Rudrasagar.
- ***Bombay High* :** This is an offshore source, lying 167 km to the north-west of Mumbai.
- ***Cambay Basin* :** This basin lies in the state of Gujarat and major oil-wells are Ankaleshwar, Kosamba, Kalol, Dhaka, Mahesana, Nawagam and Sobhasan.
- Some recently discovered oil-fields, include—
  1. South Heera, Neelam, Gandhar Phase II, Panna and Mukta in the Bombay High basin
  2. Ravva oil field in the offshore of Krishna- Godavari basin.
  3. Kaveri basin
  4. Arunachal Pradesh
  5. Andamans.

NATURAL GAS

- Most of the natural gas is found in association with crude oil. It is obtained as a by-product from petroleum refineries.
- The gasfield at Camaby (Gujarat) is the only non-associated source of natural gas.
- The Ankaleswar gasfield, Bombay High—a comparatively new source, and Morah and Naharkatiya gasfields in Assam are among the main sources.
- It is available as seepages in Nom-Chick, Miao Punga and Laptang Punga in Arunachal Pradesh, areas of the Baramura range in Tripura, and Jwalamukhi and Kangra in Himachal Pradesh.
- Natural gas has also been discovered in Punjab (Ferozepur district), Jammu and Kashmir (in parts of Mausar-Maradpur) and Tamil Nadu (Thanjavur and Chinglepet districts).

TIDAL ENERGY

- Tides are caused through a combination of forces created by the gravitational pull of the sun and the moon and the rotation of the earth.
- In India, the Gulf of Kutch and the Gulf of Cambay in Gujarat and the delta of the Ganaga in Sunderbans area of West Bengal have so far been known as potential sites for generating tidal power.

WIND ENERGY

- India has the fifth largest wind power installed capacity in the world.
- The coastal states of Tamil Nadu, Maharashtra, Gujarat and Rajasthan are better placed in regard to wind energy, as constant wind speeds above 10 km per hour are prevalent over coastal regions of these states.
- Tamil Nadu leads the wind power development accounting for about 35 per cent of the total capacity.

SOLAR ENERGY

- Solar Energy represents the earth's most abundant energy resource.
- In India, the average global radiation is around 4-7 kWh per sq m per day with about 2,300-3,200 sunshine hours per year, which can be judiciously exploited to meet our ever increasing energy requirements.
- On 16 May 2011, India's first 5 MW of installed capacity solar power project was registered under the Clean Development Mechanism. The project is in Sivagangai Village, Sivaganga district, Tamil Nadu.
- With regard to solar energy production, Rajasthan is one of India's most solar-developed states.
- The French group AREVA solar is currently engaged in constructing a 250 MW concentrated solar power (CSP) installation, which will become the largest CSP installation in Asia.
- A 4,000 MW Ultra Mega Green Solar Power Project (UMPP) is being built near Sambhar Lake in Rajasthan. Upon Completion, it would be world's largest Solar Power Plant.

NUCLEAR ENERGY

- Nuclear power is the fourth-largest source of electricity in India after thermal, hydroelectric and renewable sources of electricity.
- India has been making advances in the field of thorium-based fuels, working to design and develop a prototype for an atomic reactor using thorium and low-enriched uranium, a key part of India's three stage nuclear power programme.

Atomic Power Centres

	Name	Location
1.	Tarapur (India's first, 1969)	Maharashtra
2.	Kota	Rajasthan
3.	Naroura	Uttar Pradesh
4.	Kalpakkam	Tamil Nadu
5.	Kalkrapar	Gujarat
6.	Kaiga	Karnataka
7.	Kundankulam	Tamil Nadu

MULTIPLE CHOICE QUESTIONS

1. Who amongst the following was the first to state that the earth was spherical?
A. Copernicus B. Aristotle
C. Ptolemy D. Strabo

2. Name the Geographer who tried to show a meridian on the world map.
A. Erastosthenes B. Ptolemy
C. Herodotus D. Aristotle

3. Who wrote *the Almagest?*
A. Henry B. Marco polo
C. Ptolemy D. Al Idrisi

4. The study of physical geography in the past geological ages is included in:
A. Bio geography B. Historical geography
C. Paleography D. All of these

5. Who said about Humbaldt that "the greatest scientific travellers that ever lived"?
A. Varenius B. Carl Ritter
C. Immanual Kant D. Charles Drawin

6. Which one of the following is concerned with the study of glaciers?
A. Climatology B. Pedology
C. Hydrology D. Glaciology

7. Which of the following is matched wrongly?
I. 23 1/2° N latitude-Tropic of Cancer
II. 66 1/2° S latitude-Tropic of Capricorn
III. 23 1/2° S latitude-Arctic Circle
IV. 66 1/2° N latitude-Antarctic Circle
A. I B. II, III and IV
C. II and IV D. All of them

8. The North Pole is always in the light:
A. from September 23 to March 21
B. from March 21 to September 23
C. from June 21 to December 22
D. on June 21

9. The Tropic of Cancer does not pass through:
A. India B. Egypt
C. Mexico D. Iran

10. Igneous rocks are formed from molten rock material. Which one of the following is not an igneous rock?
A. Granite B. Quartz
C. Feldspar D. Slate

11. Which rocks could be formed by deposits of animal shells and skeletons?
A. Sandstone B. Limestone
C. Quartz D. Basalt

12. Magma that reaches earth's surface and then solidifies is called:
A. granite B. lava
C. quartz D. silicates

13. Gypsum, Saltpetre, Pyrite and Haematite all can be found in:
A. sedimentary rocks
B. igneous rocks
C. matamorphic rocks
D. sedimentary and igneous rocks

14. Platinum, diamond, iron, silver, gold, copper, manganese, lead and zinc are found in .... rock.
A. sedimentary B. metamorphic
C. igneous D. all

15. The capacity of rock to allow water to pass through it is called:
A. hardness B. joints
C. porosity D. permeability

16. The parent materials of soils are derived more frequently from:
A. igneous rocks B. metamorphic rocks
C. sedimentary rocks D. biological action

17. Which of the following help in aerating the soil?
A. Microfauna B. Mesofauna
C. Macrofauna D. All of the above

18. Soil profile refers to arrangement within a soil of:
A. its horizontal layers B. its vertical layers
C. groups of soil grains D. None of the above

19. Carbonaceous rocks which produce coal and oil belong to the category of rocks called:
A. metamorphic B. igneous
C. sedimentary D. inorganic

20. Formation of potholes in river beds is an example of:
A. corrosion B. corrasion
C. hydration D. erosion

21. The "cradles of civilization" have been:
A. valleys B. plains
C. plateaux D. hills

22. A narrow inlet of sea between cliffs or step slopes, especially associated with Scandinavia is:
A. Bay B. Gulf Stream
C. Fjord D. None of these

23. Which of these different kinds of soil is brought about by the depositional activity of winds?
A. Sandy soil B. Clayey soil
C. Black soil D. Yellow soil

24. Malaspine Glacier is in:
A. Karakoram Range B. Alps
C. Alaska D. Hindukush

25. Seasonal contrasts are maximum in:
A. low latitudes B. high latitudes
C. mid latitudes D. subtropics

26. A line drawn on a weather map connecting points that receive equal amounts of sunshine is:
A. Isohel B. Isobar
C. Isothere D. Isotherm

27. Most of the weather phenomena take place in the:
A. Ionosphere B. Stratosphere
C. Troposphere D. Mesosphere

28. Countries favourably influenced by Westerlies are:
A. British Columbia, East of U.S.A. and Western Europe
B. South Chile and South-West Africa
C. New Zealand
D. All the above

29. The lowest ever temperature was recorded in:
A. Antarctica B. Canada
C. Greenland D. Siberia

30. Why does temperature increase with increase in height in stratosphere?
A. Closeness of the sun
B. Decrease in atmospheric pressure
C. Concentration of ozone
D. None of these

31. Which of the following absorbs the insolation from the sun and preserves the earth's radiated heat, thus acting like a blanket allowing the earth neither to become too cold nor too hot?
A. Dust B. Water vapour
C. Ozone D. Nitrogen

32. Which one of the following is an area of evergreen forests?
A. Amazon basin B. Zaire basin
C. South-eastern Asia D. All of these

33. "Wood cellulose" is also known as:
A. Rayon B. Balata
C. Tanin D. Cork

34. Which of the following is not a minor product derived from forests?
A. Nuts and gums B. Tannin
C. Pitch and turpentine D. Pulp

35. Which one of these forests is mostly used for gathering?
A. Tundra B. Wet tropical
C. Dry tropical D. Temperate

36. Which of the most common areas of nomadic herding?
A. Cool humid region B. Rainy area
C. Dry areas D. Hot humid regions

37. Which product is formed by Coca leaves?
A. Cocoa beverage B. Cocaine
C. Quinine D. Camphor

38. Which one of the following is not a medicinal plant?
A. Chinchona B. Palm
C. Cocoa shrub D. Camphor

39. The coral reefs are the common characteristic of:
A. Indian Ocean B. Pacific Ocean
C. Atlantic Ocean D. Mediterranean Sea

40. Which one of the ocean touches the shores of Asia on one side and that of America on the other?
A. Indian Ocean B. Pacific Ocean
C. Atlantic Ocean D. Antarctic Ocean

41. Which of the following sub-races belong to Mongoloid?
A. Bantu B. Eskimoid
C. Nordic D. Alpine

42. What is the major cause of town-growth?
A. Natural growth
B. Low mortality rate
C. Rural-urban migration
D. None of these

43. The areas alongwith the congenial environment for human occupance are known as:
A. acumen areas B. agricultural areas
C. inhabited areas D. non-acumen areas

44. Agriculture probably began in about:
A. 4000 B.C. B. 7000 B.C.
C. 2000 B.C. D. 100 B.C.

45. The essential feature of shifting cultivation is:
A. rotation of crops
B. rotation of fields
C. single cropping
D. use of plenty of fertilizer

46. Cooperative farming has been successfully done in all the following countries except:
A. Norway B. Belgium
C. Denmark D. Russia

47. The leading producer of coffee in the world is:
A. Turkey B. Brazil
C. Venezuela D. Cuba

48. Collective farm of Ukraine is also known as:
A. Kolkhoz B. Dom
C. Ryckay Eczik D. Sovkhoz

49. Which one is the easiest and cheapest method of mining?
A. Open-cast mining B. Alluvial mining
C. Underground mining D. All of these

50. Shefield is famous for:
A. Meat packing B. Cutlery
C. Dairy D. Carpet

51. Oil is an undertaking engaged in:
A. Oil marketing B. Oil exploration
C. Oil importing D. Oil refining

52. Suez Canal links:
A. Mediterranean Sea and Caribbean Sea
B. Black Sea and Baltic Sea
C. Red Sea and Mediterranean Sea
D. Arabian Sea and Red Sea

53. Name the canal that joins the Red Sea and the Mediterranean sea?
A. Kiel Canal B. Panama
C. Suez Canal D. None of these

54. When was the Panama canal started?
A. 1914 B. 1915
C. 1918 D. 1869

55. Kiel canal joins:
A. Baltic sea to Mediterranean sea
B. Red sea to Mediterranean sea
C. North sea to Black sea
D. None of these

56. When did the EEC (European Economic Community) change into EU (European Union)?
A. 1992 B. 1995
C. 1996 D. 1991

57. When was the ASEAN formed?
A. 1966 B. 1967
C. 1976 D. 1977

58. The Arabian Sea lies to:
A. north-east of India B. south-east of India
C. south-west of India D. north-west of India

59. Palk Strait separates India from:
A. Pakistan B. China
C. Andaman Island D. Sri Lanka

60. Lakshadweep Islands are situated in:
A. Arabian Sea B. Palk Strait
C. Indian Ocean D. Bay of Bengal

61. The longest shore-line is along the state of:
A. Gujarat B. Maharashtra
C. Odisha D. Kerala

62. Which of the following States of India do not lie entirely in the Tropical Zone of the earth?
A. Kerala and Tamil Nadu
B. Gujarat
C. Karnataka
D. Maharashtra and Andhra Pradesh

63. Which of the following Indian islands lies between India and Sri Lanka?
A. Elephanta B. Nicobar
C. Rameshwaram D. Salsette

64. One of the states not bisected by the Tropic of Cancer is:

A. Odisha B. Gujarat
C. West Bengal D. Rajasthan

65. Of the following towns which one does not lie in the north of the Tropic of Cancer?
A. Prayagraj B. Patna
C. Bhopal D. Jhansi

66. Which of the following do not have a common boundary with Bangladesh?
A. Meghalaya B. Mizoram
C. Tripura D. Arunachal Pradesh

67. Which of the following mountains are the oldest according to geological history?
A. Nilgiris B. Satpura Range
C. Vindhyas D. Aravalli

68. Where mainly in India would you find denuded rocks?
A. Himalayan region B. Peninsular Plateau
C. Valleys D. Everywhere

69. The Garo, Khasi and Jaintia hills were formed in the same age as the:
A. Himalayas B. Shiwalik range
C. Malwa plateau D. Himachal range

70. What do the basalt layers of the Deccan indicate?
A. The influence of weathering
B. The immense erosional activity of the rivers
C. Huge volcanic eruptions in the distant past
D. All the above

71. The region on the southern side of the Shiwaliks is called the:
A. Dunes B. Bhabhar
C. Terai D. Khadar

72. The Cudappah range lie between:
A. Godavari and Palkonda range
B. Godavari and Jamshedpur
C. Palar and Cauveri
D. Satpura and Mohadeo-Maikal range

73. Which of the following is a trans-Himalayan river?
A. Ganga B. Yamuna
C. Sutlej D. Ravi

74. Which of the following rivers flows through a rift valley?
A. Luni B. Chambal
C. Son D. Tapti

75. Narmada originates from its source situated in the state of:
A. Maharashtra B. Uttar Pradesh
C. Madhya Pradesh D. Andhra Pradesh

76. The Jog fall is situated on the:
A. Tapti river B. Sharavati river
C. Cauvery river D. Bhima river

77. Beas flows through the State of:
A. Punjab, Haryana and Rajasthan
B. Punjab, Haryana and Jammu
C. Punjab and Himachal Pradesh
D. Punjab and Haryana

78. Ganga beyond Farakka, when it enters Bangladesh, is known as:
A. Padma B. Meghna
C. Hooghly D. Swaran Ganga

79. Which of the following river makes an estuary?
A. Cauvery B. Krishna
C. Narmada D. Ganga

80. River Tapti rises from:
A. Vindhyas B. Aravalis
C. Satpura range D. Amarkantak plateau

81. Which of the following rivers divides the Deccan Tableland from Northern India?
A. Chambal B. Krishna
C. Godavari D. Narmada

82. Tochi, Gilgit and Hunza are tributaries of:
A. Ganga B. Indus
C. Brahmaputra D. Yamuna

83. The right Ganga tributaries of the Plain do not include:
A. Alaknanda B. Yamuna
C. Son D. Tons

84. Which of the following is not a tributary of the Krishna?
A. Tungabhadra B. Malaprabha
C. Ghataprabha D. Amravati

85. The station likely to have the highest annual range of temperature is:
A. Hyderabad B. Srinagar
C. Chennai D. Jodhpur

86. Where would you experience a dry winter?
A. The Ganga plain B. North-eastern India
C. Kashmir D. Coromandal Coast

87. Which of the following is not one of the traditional Indian seasons?
A. Shisira B. Grishma
C. Varsha D. Margashirsha

88. How do dust storms in summer affect the temperature?
A. Increase it B. Decrease it
C. No effect D. Cannot say

89. At which place will you find maximum sunlight in December?
A. Kanyakumari B. Pune
C. Kolkata D. Leh

90. The Place in India receiving the lowest rainfall is:
A. Leh B. Jaisalmer
C. Bikaner D. Jodhpur

91. Among the following cities, which one is at the high altitude above mean sea level?

A. Bangalore B. Delhi
C. Jodhpur D. Nagpur

92. Which of the following does not get rains from the Arabian Sea current alone during the south west monsoon?
A. Gujarat B. Maharashtra
C. Punjab D. Western Ghats

93. The amount and intensity of monsoon rainfall is determined by the frequency of:
A. western disturbances B. dust-storms
C. cyclones D. tropical depressions

94. One of regions that receives rainfall from the North-easterly monsoon is:
A. Assam B. Kerala
C. West Bengal D. Tamil Nadu

95. Which of the following States has very little alluvial soil?
A. Bihar B. Madhya Pradesh
C. Tamil Nadu D. Punjab

96. Which of the following soils is formed under typical monsoonal conditions?
A. Black soils B. Red soils
C. Laterite soils D. None

97. Tropical moist deciduous vegetation is to be found in Sahyadris, north-east plateau of the Peninsula, and in the Shiwaliks. Which of the following is not a tree species of this group?
A. Teak B. Sal
C. Sandalwood D. Deodar

98. Which state has very little alluvial soil area?
A. Tamil Nadu B. Haryana
C. Madhya Pradesh D. West Bengal

99. Where is the greatest variety of flowers found?
A. Kerala B. Uttar Pradesh hills
C. Assam D. Sikkim

100. Khaddar soils are found:
A. in piedmont plains B. in flood plains
C. over low plateaux D. over steep stopes

101. Black soils is ideal for cultivation of cotton as:
A. it colour is black
B. it can retain moisture
C. it is made up of lava
D. it is found on plateau regions

102. The tropical deciduous plants special to the deccan are:
A. teak B. shisam
C. sandalwood D. sal

103. Mudumalai sanctuary, famous for elephants and deer, is situated in:
A. Assam B. Gujarat
C. Tamil Nadu D. Karnataka

104. Where would you not expect soil erosion through ravine erosion?
A. Andhra Pradesh
B. Uttar Pradesh
C. Rajasthan and Madhya Pradesh
D. Gujarat

105. The Indus Valley Civilization was based on the racial stocks of:
A. Mediterraneans B. Nordics
C. Negritos D. None of the above

106. The linguistic diversity in India gives information regarding:
A. regional differentiation
B. tribes
C. area of the country
D. climatic differences

107. What is the number of females per thousand males as per the 2011 census?
A. 967 B. 937
C. 936 D. 943

108. Bengali, Hindi, Gujarati and Marathi belong to the linguistic family:
A. Aryan B. Dravidian
C. Austric D. Sino-Tibetan

109. The Bhils and the Kols live:
A. along the Vindhya ranges
B. in the Nilgiris
C. in the North-East frontiers of India
D. all over India

110. The Mopla are to be found in:
A. Manipur B. Assam
C. Kerala D. Andhra Pradesh

111. According to the latest census figures sex ratio in India is:
A. declining B. stable
C. increasing D. fluctuating

112. Tribal settlement in India are usually concentrated:
A. on the plains
B. near big rivers
C. in the hilly and forested areas
D. on the periphery of townships

113. In which of the following states would you not find Bhils?
A. Gujarat B. Karnataka
C. Madhya Pradesh D. Uttar Pradesh

114. Where would you find Oraon, Munda, Santhal, Gonds and Asurs?
A. Madhya Pradesh B. Gujarat
C. Maharashtra D. Bihar

115. In which state women outnumber men?
A. Tamil Nadu B. Kerala
C. Himachal Pradesh D. Karnataka

116. Jarawas are tribes living in:
A. Madhya Pradesh B. Nagaland
C. Arunachal Pradesh D. Andaman and Nicobar

117. One of the chief effects of urbanization in India is:
A. overcrowding in cities
B. more jobs available
C. lower standard of living
D. stagnant agriculture

118. The maximum percentage of the tribal population in India consists of:
A. Santhals B. Bhils
C. Mundas D. Nagas

119. To which group do the tribals of central and southern India belong?
A. Negritos B. Proto-Australoids
C. Mongoloids D. Western Brachycephals

120. Where do Birhors live?
A. Madhya Pradesh B. Assam
C. Nagaland D. Tamil Nadu

121. In general, it is observed that the rate of population growth has been in the densely populated areas compared to sparsely populated areas:
A. low B. high
C. negligible D. almost the same

122. The Bhutia group of languages does not include:
A. Ladakhi B. Tibetan
C. Lepeha D. Sherpa

123. The Kosi project is aimed towards:
A. irrigation
B. drainage and power generation
C. power generation and flood control
D. irrigation, flood control and power generation

124. The Farakka project is mainly aimed towards:
A. irrigating more land in West Bengal
B. utilizing maximum of Ganga water
C. preserving the port of Kolkata
D. production of electricity

125. The Central Frozen Semen Bank at Bangalore was set up in order to help in:
A. producing high quality bulls
B. producing quality sheep
C. doing research in family planning and eugenics
D. all the above

126. Mahi Project will greatly benefit:
A. Maharashtra B. Punjab
C. Gujarat D. Uttar Pradesh

127. Which of the following projects is administered by more than one State?
A. Nagarjunasagar B. Kosi
C. Hirakud D. Tungabhadra

128. Which of the following is the biggest producer of cashewnut?
A. Karnataka B. Kerala
C. Tamil Nadu D. Kashmir

129. Which region in India is known as the 'Rice Bowl of India'?
A. Indo-Gangetic Plain
B. Krishna-Godavari Delta region
C. North-east region
D. Kerala and Tamil Nadu

130. Sheep with quality wool are reared in:
A. Jammu and Kashmir B. Andhra Pradesh
C. Punjab D. Nowhere in India

131. Which of the following hydro-electric stations is situated in Uttar Pradesh?
A. Mayurakshi B. Rihand
C. Kangsabati D. Hirakud

132. Which of the following crops will be beneficial in Rajasthan if adequate water supply through rivers and wells is provided?
A. Wheat B. Rice
C. Cotton D. Maize

133. Which of the following is not a project in Gujarat?
A. Panam B. Salal
C. Mahi D. Tawa

134. The multipurpose project irrigating maximum area in India is:
A. Beas B. Bhakra Nangal
C. Damodar Valley D. Hirakud

135. The Rajasthan Canal (now called the Indira Gandhi Canal) draws its water from the:
A. Yamuna B. Chambal
C. Sutlej D. Sutlej and Beas

136. Which one of the following is the leading producer of marine fish?
A. Gujarat B. Kerala
C. Maharashtra D. West Bengal

137. Gypsum is found in:
A. Rajasthan B. Odisha
C. Assam D. Madhya Pradesh

138. What is Bailadila famous for?
A. Bauxite B. Iron ore
C. Copper D. Coal

139. Gondwana coalfields are found in:
A. Assam B. Madhya Pradesh
C. Meghalaya D. Jammu & Kashmir

140. Which Central government agency is responsible for the mapping and exploration of minerals?
A. The Geological Survey of India
B. Surveyor-General of India
C. National Mineral Development Corporation Ltd.
D. Indian Bureau of Mines

141. Nickel ore deposits are found in:
A. Singhbhum (Bihar) B. Guntur (A.P.)
C. Keonjhar (Odisha) D. Khetri (Rajasthan)

142. The first machine-made paper was manufactured:
A. in 1870 near Kolkata B. in 1903 in Mumbai
C. in 1910 at Delhi D. after independence

143. Penicillin is produced at:
A. Bangalore B. Alwaye
C. Poona D. Pimpri

144. Passenger and merchant ships are constructed at:
A. Mazagon Docks
B. Hindustan Shipyard at Vishakhapatnam
C. no place; the Indian docks only make navy ships
D. Goa Shipyard

145. The first cement factory was built in India in 1904 at:
A. Ranchi B. Hazaribagh
C. Madras D. Hyderabad

146. The first shore-based integrated steel project in India is coming up at:
A. Ernakulam B. Tuticorin
C. Vishakhapatnam D. Mangalore

147. Which of the following iron and steel plants get coking coal from Jharia?
A. Bokaro and Burnpur
B. Durgapur and Jameshedpur
C. Bhilai and Rourkela
D. All of them

148. Which of the following fertilizer factories is not in the private sector?
A. Namrup B. Ennore
C. Kota D. Vadodara

149. The first coal mine in India was opened at:
A. Dhanbad B. Jharia
C. Raniganj D. Asansol

150. The state depending primarily on thermal power is:
A. Kerala B. West Bengal
C. Karnataka D. Tamil Nadu

151. The highest peak in Europe is:
A. Mont Blanc B. Andes
C. Monte Rosa D. Elburz

152. Land of the Rising Sun is:
A. Japan B. Norway
C. Assam D. Myanmar

153. Where was electricity supply first introduced in India?
A. Darjeeling B. Kolkata
C. Mumbai D. Delhi

154. Name the largest island in the world:
A. New Guinea B. Greenland
C. Madagascar D. Great Britain

155. Land of the Midnight Sun is:
A. Japan B. Myanmar
C. Norway D. Manipur

156. The longest river in the world is:
A. Nile B. Amazon
C. Yangtze D. Missouri-Mississippi

157. The Island Continent is:
A. Asia B. America
C. Africa D. Australia

158. Suez Canal joins:
A. London to Paris
B. Tokyo to Osaka
C. Mediterranean to the Red Sea
D. Rangoon to Philippines

159. The Radcliffe Line was drawn on 15th August, 1947 between:
A. India and Myanmar (Burma)
B. Pakistan and China
C. Pakistan and India
D. Pakistan and Nepal

160. New York is situated on the river bank of:
A. Rhine B. Thames
C. Hudson D. Amazon

161. Which place is called the land of Golden Fleece?
A. Australia B. Cuba
C. Austria D. Myanmar

162. Kiel is a:
A. renowned explorer
B. American antelope
C. big American sea bird
D. shipping canal between London and Baltic Sea

163. USA consists of so many States:
A. 30 B. 50
C. 20 D. 40

164. The Turan Type of Regions have the climate of extremes because:
A. These lie in the interior ports of the continent
B. These have either too much or too less rain
C. These are either on hills or near the deserts
D. None of the above

165. Which country tops in the mining of gold:
A. U.S.A. B. Canada
C. South Africa D. India

166. The largest Fresh water lake is:
A. Lake Superior B. Caspian Sea
C. Lake Baikal D. Hind Sea

167. ..... is the most important occupation of the people in the Monsoon Lands:
A. Forestry B. Agriculture
C. Industry D. Mining

168. There is the great variations of vegetation in the Monsoon Region because of:
A. It depends on nearness to forests, oceans mountains
B. Variation in the amount of rainfall in different places
C. The effect of rainfall is different in different regions
D. None of the above

169. In the Amur Valley of the Russia ..... is the most important economic activity:
A. agriculture B. animal rearing
C. mining D. industry

170. Which is the Land of White Elephants?
A. Korea B. Japan
C. Thailand D. Tanzania

171. The most important occupation of the people in the Turan Type of Regions is .....
A. agriculture B. cattle and animal rearing
C. mountaineering D. industry

172. Which is the City of Magnificent Buildings?
A. Tokyo B. New York
C. Washington D. Rome

173. In the West European Type of Regions, the summer temperature hardly exceeds ..... °C.
A. 10°C B. 16°C
C. 7°C D. 8°C

174. The extensive treeless tracts of North America, which are covered with tall coarse grass, are called: .
A. Savanna B. Tundras
C. Pampas D. Prairies

175. ....., ... and ..... are the important animal products of the Iran Type of Regions.
A. Skins and hides
B. Meat canning and export
C. Wool, meat and skins
D. Wool and hides

ANSWERS

1	2	3	4	5	6	7	8	9	10
B	C	C	C	D	D	C	B	D	D
11	**12**	**13**	**14**	**15**	**16**	**17**	**18**	**19**	**20**
B	B	A	C	D	C	B	A	C	B
21	**22**	**23**	**24**	**25**	**26**	**27**	**28**	**29**	**30**
B	C	A	C	C	A	C	D	D	C
31	**32**	**33**	**34**	**35**	**36**	**37**	**38**	**39**	**40**
B	C	A	D	B	C	B	B	B	B
41	**42**	**43**	**44**	**45**	**46**	**47**	**48**	**49**	**50**
B	C	A	B	B	D	B	A	A	B
51	**52**	**53**	**54**	**55**	**56**	**57**	**58**	**59**	**60**
D	C	C	A	C	B	C	C	D	A
61	**62**	**63**	**64**	**65**	**66**	**67**	**68**	**69**	**70**
A	B	C	A	C	D	D	B	C	C
71	**72**	**73**	**74**	**75**	**76**	**77**	**78**	**79**	**80**
B	A	C	D	C	B	D	A	C	C
81	**82**	**83**	**84**	**85**	**86**	**87**	**88**	**89**	**90**
D	B	A	D	C	A	D	B	A	A
91	**92**	**93**	**94**	**95**	**96**	**97**	**98**	**99**	**100**
A	C	D	D	B	C	D	C	B	B
101	**102**	**103**	**104**	**105**	**106**	**107**	**108**	**109**	**110**
B	C	C	A	A	A	D	A	A	C
111	**112**	**113**	**114**	**115**	**116**	**117**	**118**	**119**	**120**
A	C	D	D	B	D	A	A	B	A
121	**122**	**123**	**124**	**125**	**126**	**127**	**128**	**129**	**130**
A	C	D	C	A	C	D	B	B	A
131	**132**	**133**	**134**	**135**	**136**	**137**	**138**	**139**	**140**
B	D	D	D	D	B	A	B	B	A
141	**142**	**143**	**144**	**145**	**146**	**147**	**148**	**149**	**150**
C	A	D	B	C	C	D	A	C	B
151	**152**	**153**	**154**	**155**	**156**	**157**	**158**	**159**	**160**
D	A	A	B	C	A	D	C	C	C
161	**162**	**163**	**164**	**165**	**166**	**167**	**168**	**169**	**170**
A	D	B	A	C	A	B	B	A	C
171	**172**	**173**	**174**	**175**					
B	C	B	D	C					

2306

MATHEMATICS

1

Numbers System

Whole Numbers

In our System of numeration, numbers are written by using the symbols 0, 1, 2, 3, 4, 5, 6, 7, 8 and 9 with each symbol getting a value depending on the place it occupies. These symbols are called digits. A number related to the objects in a collection gives an idea of how many objects are there in the collection.

The number 789345126 can be represented as:

Ten crores	Crores	Ten Lacs (Millions)	Lacs	Ten Thousands	Thousands	Hundreds	Tens	Units
10^8	10^7	10^6	10^5	10^4	10^3	10^2	10^1	10^0
7	8	9	3	4	5	1	2	6

This number can be read as: "Seventy-eight crores, ninety-three lacs, forty-five thousands, one hundred twenty six".

1. **Natural Numbers or Positive Integers (N = 1, 2, 3, 4, 5 .....):** These are also called counting numbers. When two natural numbers are added or multiplied together, the result is always a natural number. Therefore, all positive integers, used for counting objects, are always **natural numbers** whereas zero together with negative integers and fractional numbers are not natural numbers.
2. **Whole Numbers: (W = 0, 1, 2, 3, 4, 5, ...):** The number '0' together with the natural numbers gives us the numbers which are called **whole numbers,** e.g., 0, 1, 2, 3, 4 ..... etc. whereas –10, –15, –12 ..... or $\frac{1}{5},\frac{2}{9},\frac{4}{5}$..... etc. are not whole numbers.
3. **Integers: (I = ..., –5, –4, –3, –2, –1, 0, 1, 2, 3, 4, 5, ...):** The negative numbers together with the whole numbers are called integers. The numbers –1, –2, –3, –4, –5, ... are called negative integers and 1, 2, 3, 4, 5, ..., *i.e.,* natural numbers are called positive integers. The number 0 is simply an integer, *i.e.,* it is neither positive nor negative.
4. **Rational Numbers:** A rational number is a number that can be put in the form $\frac{p}{q}$ where p and q are both integers and $q \neq 0$, e.g., 8, $-\frac{7}{5}$, $-\frac{3}{4}$, $\frac{1}{7}$, 0 .... are all rational numbers i.e. a rational number may be positive, zero or negative.
5. **Irrational Numbers:** An irrational number is a number that can not be put in the form $\frac{p}{q}$ where p and q are both integers and $q \neq 0$, e.g., $\sqrt{5}, \sqrt{11}, \sqrt{15}$, $3 + \sqrt{5}$ .... etc. are all irrational numbers.
6. **Real Numbers:** All those numbers which are either rational or irrational, are called real numbers, e.g., $\frac{11}{17}$, $\frac{19}{21}$, $-\frac{7}{8}$, $\sqrt{7}$, $8 + \sqrt{3}$ etc. are real numbers.
7. **Even Numbers:** All those numbers which are exactly divisible by 2, are called 'even numbers', e.g., 2, 8, 14, 28, 52 etc. are even numbers.
8. **Odd Numbers:** All those numbers which are not exactly divisible by 2, are called 'odd numbers', e.g., 1, 3, 5, 7, 9, 19 etc. are odd numbers.

9. **Composite Numbers:** The numbers which are divisible not only by 1 or themselves, but by some other numbers also, are called the 'composite numbers'. In other words, the numbers which have more than two factors are called 'composite numbers.', e.g., 4, 9, 15, 18, 27, ... etc. are composite numbers.
10. **Prime Numbers:** The numbers which have only two factors, 1 and the number itself are called 'prime numbers', e.g., 2, 5, 11, 19, 23, 31, ... etc. are prime numbers.
11. **Co-primes:** Two numbers which have only 1 as the common factor are called 'co-primes'. 5 and 7 are co-primes. So are 15 and 16.
12. **Twin Primes:** Two prime numbers which differ by 2, are called 'twin primes', e.g., 3, 5; 5, 7; 11, 13; 71, 73 are some pairs of twin primes.
13. **Consecutive Numbers:** The numbers which are following or coming after other numbers in regular order, are called consecutive numbers. 4, 6, 8, 10 are consecutive even numbers and 9, 11, 13, 15 are consecutive odd numbers. 3, 4, 5, 6, 7 ..... etc. are consecutive numbers in the natural order of the number series.

TESTS FOR DIVISIBILITY OF NUMBERS

1. **Divisibility by 2:** A number is divisible by 2, if its units digit is 0, 2, 4, 6 or 8. For example, each of the numbers 130, 244, 566, 278, ... etc. is divisible by 2.
2. **Divisibility by 3:** A number is divisible by 3, if the sum of its digits is a multiple of 3. For example, each of the numbers 312, 213, 456 is divisible by 3 since sum of digits in each of these numbers is (3 + 1 + 2 = 6), (2 + 1 + 3 = 6) and (4 + 5 + 6 = 15) respectively, each of which is a multiple of 3.
3. **Divisibility by 4:** A number is divisible by 4, if the number formed by its digits in ten's and unit's places is divisible by 4. For example, numbers formed by ten's and unit's digits of 1132, 1312, 1400 and 1348 are 32, 12, 00 and 48 respectively which are divisible by 4. Hence, these numbers also are divisible by 4.
4. **Divisibility by 5:** A number is divisible by 5, if its unit's digit is either 0 or 5. For example, each of the numbers 100, 205, 315, 435 is divisible by 5 since unit's digit in each of these numbers is either 0 or 5.
5. **Divisibility by 6:** A number is divisible by 6, if it is divisible by both 2 and 3.
6. **Divisiblity by 8:** A number is divisible by 8, if the number formed by its digits in hundred's, ten's and unit's places is divisible by 8. For example, numbers formed by hundred's, ten's and unit's digits of 1864, 1024, 2008 and 5000 are 864, 024, 008 and 000 respectively which are divisible by 8. Hence, these numbers also are divisible by 8.
7. **Divisibility by 9:** A number is divisible by 9, if the sum of its digits is a multiple of 9. For example, each of the numbers 23409, 454554, 66636 is divisible by 9 since sum of digits in each of these numbers is (2 + 3 + 4 + 0 + 9 = 18), (4 + 5 + 4 + 5 + 5 + 4 = 27) and (6 + 6 + 6 + 3 + 6 = 27) respectively, each of which is a multiple of 9.
8. **Divisibility by 10:** A number is divisible by 10, if its unit's digit is zero. For example, each of the numbers 50, 80, 1310, 1400 is divisible by 10 since unit's digit in each of these numbers is 0.
9. **Divisibility by 11:** A number is divisible by 11, if the difference of the sum of its digits in even places and the sum of its digits in odd places (starting from unit's place) is either 0 or a multiple of 11. For example, each of the numbers 909183, 540045 and 184712 is divisible by 11 since in each of the numbers difference of the sum of digits in even places and sum of the digits in odd places is [(9 + 9 + 8) – (0 + 1 + 3) = 22], [(5 + 0 + 4) – (4 + 0 + 5) = 0] and [(8 + 7 + 2) – (1 + 4 + 1) = 11] respectively, each of which is either '0' or a multiple of '11'.
10. **Divisibility by 12:** A number is divisible by 12, if it is divisible by 3 and 4 both.

    For example, take a number 769824

    (*i*) Sum of digits = 7 + 6 + 9 + 8 + 2 + 4 = 36, it is divisible by 3.

    (*ii*) The number has 24 as its last two digits, which is divisible by 4.

    Hence, 769824 is divisible by 3 and 4 both, so it is divisible by 12.
11. **Divisibility by 14:** A number is divisible by 14, if it is divisible by 2 and 7 both.
12. **Divisibility by 15:** A number is divisible by 15, if it is divisible by 3 and 5 both.
13. **Divisibility by 16:** A number is divisible by 16, if the number formed by its last four digits is divisible by 16.

    For example, take a number 9877856, the number formed by its last four digits is 7856, which is divisible by 16. Hence, the number 9877856 is divisible by 16.
14. **Divisibility by 24:** A number is divisible by 24, if it is divisible by 3 and 8 both.
15. **Divisibility by 40:** A number is divisible by 40, if it is divisible by 5 and 8 both.
16. **Divisibility by 80:** A number is divisible by 80, if it is divisible by 5 and 16 both.

[**Note:** If a number is divisible by two co-primes separately, then the number will be also divisible by the product of co-primes.]

EXERCISE

1. The difference between the squares of two consecutive numbers is 25. The numbers are—

A. 11, 12 B. 12, 13
C. 15, 14 D. 14, 13

2. The sum of two digits of a number is 15. If 9 is added to the number, the digits are reversed. The number is—

A. 78 B. 87
C. 69 D. 96

3. A number which when multiplied by 11 is as much above 180 as it was originally below it. The number is—

A. 25 B. 30
C. 40 D. 45

4. Divide ₹ 53 among X, Y, Z so that X may receive ₹ 7 more than Y, and Y may receive ₹ 8 more than Z.

A. 10, 15, 18 B. 18, 10, 25
C. 20, 12, 27 D. 25, 18, 10

5. If a = 16 and b = 15, then what is the value of $\frac{a^2+b^2+ab}{a^3-b^3}$ = ?

A. $\frac{1}{2}$ B. $\frac{1}{3}$
C. 1 D. 2

6. Find the number which when multiplied by 16 is increased by 225.

A. 13 B. 14
C. 15 D. 16

7. What is the largest number of four digits which is exactly divisible by 88?

A. 9999 B. 9988
C. 9944 D. 9998

8. If $\frac{a}{b} = \frac{4}{3}$, then $\frac{3a+2b}{3a-2b}$ = ?

A. 2 B. 3
C. 4 D. 5

9. If $\frac{x}{y} = \frac{3}{4}$, then the value of $\frac{6}{7}+\frac{y-x}{y+x}$ = ?

A. 1 B. 2
C. 3 D. 4

10. If the number $(10^n - 1)$ is divisible by 11, then n is—

A. odd number B. even number
C. any number D. multiple of 11

11. $\left(1-\frac{1}{3}\right)\left(1-\frac{1}{4}\right)\left(1-\frac{1}{5}\right)...\left(1-\frac{1}{n}\right)$ = ?

A. $\frac{42}{29}$ B. $\frac{n-1}{n}$
C. $\frac{2}{n}$ D. 0

12. $\left(2-\frac{1}{3}\right)\left(2-\frac{3}{5}\right)\left(2-\frac{5}{7}\right)...\left(2-\frac{997}{999}\right)$ = ?

A. $\frac{997}{999}$ B. ∞
C. $\frac{997}{3}$ D. $\frac{1001}{3}$

13. Divide 48 into two parts such that 7 times the first part added to 5 times the second part is 246. Find the first part.

A. 2 B. 3
C. 4 D. 5

14. The sum of a number and its reciprocal is thrice the difference of the number and its reciprocal. Find the number.

A. $\sqrt{2}$ B. $\sqrt{3}$
C. $\sqrt{5}$ D. $\sqrt{7}$

15. What should be added to the product of four consecutive odd numbers to make it a perfect square?

A. 13 B. 14
C. 15 D. 16

16. A boy was asked to find $\frac{7}{9}$ of a fraction. He made a mistake of dividing the fraction by $\frac{7}{9}$ and so got an answer which exceeded the correct answer by $\frac{8}{21}$. Find the correct answer.

A. 2/3 B. 5/7
C. 7/12 D. 7/15

17. If 40% of a number is 360, what will be 15% of 15% of that number?

A. 11.5 B. 20.25
C. 15.5 D. 21.75

18. The sum of two numbers is 25 and the difference of their square is 75. Find the difference between the numbers.

A. 2 B. 3
C. 4 D. 5

19. Ram eats 8 bananas in the morning, 5 in the afternoon and 2 in the evening. How many dozens of bananas does he eat in a day.

A. $1\frac{1}{4}$ B. $\frac{1}{4}$
C. $\frac{3}{13}$ D. $14\frac{17}{30}$

20. $47^{7.5} \div 47^{\frac{3}{2}} \times 47^{-3} = \left(\sqrt{47}\right)^?$ What should come in place of the question mark (?) in the following equation?

A. 5 B. 6
C. 7 D. 8

ANSWERS

1	2	3	4	5	6	7	8	9	10
B	A	B	B	C	C	C	B	A	B
11	12	13	14	15	16	17	18	19	20
C	D	B	A	D	C	B	B	A	B

EXPLANATORY ANSWERS

1. Let the numbers are x and $(x + 1)$

$\therefore \quad (x+1)^2 - x^2 = 25$

$\Rightarrow \quad x^2 + 1 + 2x - x^2 = 25$

$\Rightarrow \quad 2x + 1 = 25$

$\Rightarrow \quad 2x = 25 - 1 = 24$

$\therefore \quad x = \frac{24}{2} = 12$

$\therefore \quad x + 1 = 12 + 1 = 13$

Hence, the numbers are 12, 13.

2. Let x be the digit in units place. Digit in ten's place is then $15 - x$.

$\therefore$ The number $= 10\,(15 - x) + x$

The new number with reverse digits

$= 10 \times x + (15 - x)$

$\therefore \quad 10(15 - x) + x + 9 = 10x + 15 - x$

$\Rightarrow \quad 150 - 10x + x + 9 = 9x + 15$

$\Rightarrow \quad 18x = 144$

$x = \frac{144}{18} = 8$

The digit of ten's place $= 15 - 8 = 7$

$\therefore$ The required number = 78.

3. Let the number is x

$\therefore \quad 180 - x = 11x - 180$

$\Rightarrow \quad 180 + 180 = 11x + x$

$\Rightarrow \quad 360 = 12x,$

$\Rightarrow \quad x = \frac{360}{12} = 30.$

4. Let Y receives ₹ a. Then X receives ₹ $(a + 7)$ and Z receives ₹ $(a - 8)$

But, $a + 7 + a + a - 8 =$ ₹ 53

$\Rightarrow \quad 3a - 1 = 53,$

$\Rightarrow \quad 3a = 53 + 1$

$\Rightarrow \quad 3a = 54,$

$\therefore \quad a = \frac{54}{3} =$ ₹ 18. = Y's share

X's share $= a + 7 = 18 + 7 =$ ₹ 25

Z's share $= a - 8 = 18 - 8 =$ ₹ 10.

5. Given $a = 16$ and $b = 15$, then $\frac{a^2+b^2+ab}{a^3-b^3}$

$$= \frac{a^2+b^2+ab}{(a-b)\left(a^2+b^2+ab\right)} = \frac{1}{a-b} = \frac{1}{16-15} = 1$$

6. Let the required no. $= x$

then, $\quad 16x - x = 225$

$\Rightarrow \quad 15x = 225 \;\therefore\; x = 15$

7. The greatest no. of 4 digit = 9999

Now, after dividing 9999 by 88, we get Remainder = 55

Hence, the largest 4 digit no. = 9999 – 55 = 9944

8. $\frac{3a+2b}{3a-2b} = \frac{3\frac{a}{b}+2}{3\frac{a}{b}-2} = \frac{3\times\frac{4}{3}+2}{3\times\frac{4}{3}-2} = \frac{6}{2} = 3$

9. $\frac{6}{7} + \frac{y-x}{y+x} = \frac{6}{7} + \frac{1-x/y}{1+x/y} = \frac{6}{7} + \frac{1-3/4}{1+3/4} = \frac{6}{7} + \frac{1}{7} = 1$

10. n is even number.

11. $\frac{2}{3}\times\frac{3}{4}\times\frac{4}{5}\times\ldots\times\frac{n-1}{n} = \frac{2}{n}$

12. $\frac{5}{3}\times\frac{7}{5}\times\frac{9}{7}\times\ldots\times\frac{1001}{999} = \frac{1001}{3}$

13. Let the first part $= x$

then 2nd part $= (48 - x)$

By question, $\quad 7x + 5(48 - x) = 246$

$\Rightarrow \quad 2x = 246 - 240 \;\therefore\; x = 3$

14. Let the no. $= x$

then its reciprocal $= \frac{1}{x}$

By the question, $\left(x+\frac{1}{x}\right) = 3\left(x-\frac{1}{x}\right)$

$\Rightarrow \quad \frac{x^2+1}{x} = \frac{3\left(x^2-1\right)}{x}$

$\Rightarrow \quad x^2 + 1 = 3x^2 - 3$

$\Rightarrow \quad 3x^2 - x^2 = 3 + 1 \;\therefore\; x = \sqrt{2}.$

15. Let the four consecutive odd numbers be $(2x - 3)$, $(2x - 1)$, $(2x + 1)$ and $(2x + 3)$

$\therefore$ Their product $= (2x - 1)(2x + 1)(2x - 3)(2x + 3)$

$= (4x^2 - 1)(4x^2 - 9) = 16x^4 - 40x^2 + 9$

$= (4x^2 - 5)^2 - 16$

Hence, on adding 16, the result will be a perfect square.

16. Let the required fraction = x

then, by the question $x \div \frac{7}{9} - x \times \frac{7}{9} = \frac{8}{21}$

$\Rightarrow \quad x \times \frac{9}{7} - \frac{7x}{9} = \frac{8}{21} \Rightarrow \frac{32x}{63} = \frac{8}{21}$

$\Rightarrow \quad x = \frac{8}{21} \times \frac{63}{32} = \frac{3}{4}$

Hence, the correct answer $= \frac{3}{4} \times \frac{7}{9} = \frac{7}{12}$.

17. Let a number be x

then $\quad 40\%$ of $x = 360$

$\Rightarrow \quad \frac{40}{100} \times x = 360$

$\therefore \quad x = 360 \times \frac{100}{40} = 900$

Now by the question,

15% of 15% of 900 $= \frac{15}{100} \times \frac{15}{100} \times 900 = \frac{81}{4} = 20.25.$

18. Let two numbers are a and b

Given, $\quad a + b = 25$

and $\quad a^2 - b^2 = 75$

$\Rightarrow \quad (a + b)(a - b) = 75$

$\Rightarrow \quad (a - b) = \frac{75}{(a+b)} = \frac{75}{25} = 3.$

19. Total dozen of bananas Ram eats in a day

$= \frac{8}{12} + \frac{5}{12} + \frac{2}{12} = \frac{15}{12} = 1\frac{1}{4}$

20. $47^{7.5} \div 47^{\frac{3}{2}} \times 47^{-3} = (\sqrt{47})^{?}$

Let ? = x

then $\quad (47)^{\frac{15}{2}} \div (47)^{\frac{3}{2}} \times (47)^{-3} = (47)^{\frac{x}{2}}$

$\Rightarrow \quad (47)^{\frac{15}{2} - \frac{3}{2} - 3} = (47)^{\frac{x}{2}}$

$\Rightarrow \quad (47)^{\frac{6}{2}} = (47)^{\frac{x}{2}}$

$\therefore \quad x = 6.$

Decimal Fraction

FRACTION

The relation to represent some part of the body to the whole body is known *Fraction*. For example $\frac{2}{5}$ is a fraction where 2 is the numerator and 5 is the denominator.

Important Facts :

(i) A fraction is also called a rational number.

(ii) A fraction is unity when its numerator and denominator are equal.

(iii) When a fraction is reduced in its lowest term, its numerator and denominator are prime to each other, *i.e.*, they have no common factor.

(iv) The value of fraction is not altered by multiplying or dividing the numerator and the denominator by the same number.

Vulgar or Common Fraction : The fraction such as $\frac{2}{9}, \frac{7}{11}, \frac{3}{10}, \frac{9}{100}$ are called vulgar fraction.

Decimal Fraction : Fractions in which denomi-nators are power of 10 are called decimal fractions.

For example : $\frac{1}{10}, \frac{1}{100}, \frac{7}{1000}$ etc.

Here, $\frac{1}{10}$ is 1 tenths, written as .1

$\frac{1}{100} = .01$

$\frac{7}{1000} = .007$

$\frac{13}{100} = .13$ and so on.

Converting a Decimal into a Vulgar Fraction

First of all write down the given number as numerator without the decimal point, and for the denominator write 1 followed by as many zeros as many are there figures after the decimal point. Now reduce the fraction to its lowest terms.

Ex : *(i)* $0.63 = \frac{63}{100}$

(ii) $3.013 = 3\frac{013}{1000} = 3\frac{13}{1000}$

Addition and Subtraction of Decimal Fractions

First of all write down the numbers under one another. Other than the decimal point lies in one column. After arranging in this way, we add or subtract in usual fashion.

An example : Add $\quad 521 + 52.1 + 5.21 + 0.521$

Sol : 521.000
52.100
5.210
0.521 After adding we get 578.831

Multiplication of decimal fraction

1. To multiply by 10, 100, 1000, etc

Example : *(i)* $63.02 \times 10 = 630.2$

(ii) 63.02 × 100 = 6302

(iii) 63.02 × 1000 = 63020

2. To multiply of two or more decimal fractions.

An example : (i) 5.91 × 13 = 76.83

(ii) 6.32 × 0.59 = 3.7288

(iii) 63.2 × 0.01 = 0.632

Conclusion: First of all multiply the given numbers assuming them without the decimal point. Now mark off the decimal point from extreme right in the product as many places of decimal as is the sum of the number of decimal places in the given numbers.

DIVISION OF DECIMALS

1. When the divisor is a counting number

Example : (i) 4.309 ÷ 10 = 0.4309

(ii) 0.0182 ÷ 14 = 0.0013

(iii) 9.586 ÷ 100 = 0.09586

(iv) $0.05 \div 10^3 = 0.00005$

(v) 0.49 ÷ 7 = 0.07

Conclusion : *(i)* When divisor is the power of 10, then shift the decimal point to the left by as many places of decimal as is the power of 10, prefixing zero if necessary.

(ii) When divisor is other than power of 10, then divide as in the case of integers, and in quotient, put the decimal point to give as many places of decimal as are there in the dividend.

2. When the divisor is a decimal

Example:

(i) $0.00066 \div 0.11 = \frac{0.00066}{0.11} = \frac{0.066}{11} = 0.006$

(ii) $42 \div 0.07 = \frac{42}{0.07} = \frac{4200}{7} = 600$

(iii) $32.5 \div 0.0064 = \frac{32.5}{0.0064} = \frac{325000}{64} = 5078.125$

Recurring Decimal : If in a decimal number a digit or a set of digits is repeated again and again, the decimal is known as recurring decimal.

For example:

(i) $2.666... = 2.\overline{6}$

(ii) $1.363636... = 1.\dot{3}\dot{6}$ or $1.\overline{36}$

(iii) $7.3424242... = 7.3\dot{4}\dot{2}$ or $7.3\overline{42}$

Recurring decimal numbers are of two types:

(i) **Pure recurring decimals :** A decimal fraction in which all the figures after the decimal point are repeated is called a pure recurring decimal. For example, $0.\overline{3}$, $0.\overline{37}$, $3.\overline{4579}$ etc

(ii) **Mixed recurring decimals :** A decimal fraction in which at least one figure after the decimal point is not repeated is called a mixed recurring decimal. For example, $0.3\overline{59}$, $0.2\overline{954}$, $0.2\overline{7}$ etc.

Conversion of Recurring into Vulgar Fraction

1. Pure recurring decimals

Rule : Put as many 9's in the denominator at the number of digits under recurring and delete the recurring sign.

For example, $0.\overline{5} = \frac{5}{9}$

$0.\overline{35} = \frac{35}{99}$

$0.\overline{24} = \frac{24}{99} = \frac{8}{33}$

2. Mixed Recurring Decimals

For example,

(i) $0.1\overline{8}$

Here, numerator = 18 − 1 = 17

and denominator = 9 × 10 = 90

$\therefore \quad 0.1\dot{8} = \frac{18-1}{90} = \frac{17}{90}$

(ii) $0.2\overline{79}$

Here, numerator = 279 − 2 = 277

and denominator = 99 × 10 = 990

$\therefore \quad 0.2\overline{79} = \frac{279-2}{990} = \frac{277}{990}$

(iii) $0.3\overline{56} = \frac{356-3}{99 \times 10} = \frac{353}{990}$

(iv) $2.5\overline{36} = 2 + \frac{536-53}{9 \times 100} = 2 + \frac{483}{900}$

$= 2 + \frac{161}{300} = 2\frac{161}{300}$

(v) $0.43\overline{213} = \frac{43213-43}{999 \times 100}$

$= \frac{43170}{99900} = \frac{4317}{9990}$

Addition and Subtraction of recurring decimals

Example : (i) Add $3.\overline{76}$ and $1.4\overline{576}$ and subtract also.

3.7	676767	67
1.4	576576	57
(+) 5.2	253344	24 ⇒ $5.2\overline{253344}$
(−) 2.3	100191	10 ⇒ $2.3\overline{100191}$

(ii) Subtract $3.\overline{75}$ from $25.5\overline{473}$

25.5	473473	47
3.7	575757	57
21.7	897715	90

Hence, the required subtract = $21.7\overline{897715}$

Multiplication and Division of Recurring Decimal

Example 1:

(*i*) $7.\overline{63} \times 11 = 7\frac{63}{99} \times 11$

$= 7\frac{7}{11} \times 11 = \frac{84}{11} \times 11 = 84$

(*ii*) $0.\overline{09} \times 7.\overline{3} = \frac{9}{99} \times 7\frac{3}{9}$

$= \frac{1}{11} \times \frac{66}{9} = \frac{6}{9} = 0.\overline{6}$

(*iii*) $0.\overline{6} \times 7.\overline{3} = \frac{6}{9} \times 7\frac{3}{9}$

$= \frac{6}{9} \times \frac{66}{9} = \frac{44}{9} = 4.\overline{8}$

(*iv*) $0.\overline{06} \div 100 = 0.060606... \div 100 = 0.00\overline{06}$

(*v*) $0.73\dot{2} \div 0.02\dot{7} = 0.732\dot{3} \div 0.027\dot{7}$

$= \frac{7323-73}{99 \times 100} \div \frac{277-2}{99 \times 100}$

$= \frac{7250}{9900} \div \frac{275}{9900} = \frac{7250}{275} = \frac{290}{11} = 26.\overline{36}$

EXERCISE

1. Which of the following is equivalent to $\frac{15}{25}$?

A. $\frac{150}{25}$ B. $\frac{15}{250}$

C. $\frac{3}{5}$ D. $\frac{60}{75}$

2. If $\frac{9*3}{3*7}$ is equivalent to $\frac{9}{7}$, the sign * is replaced by

A. ÷ B. ×

C. + D. –

3. $\frac{5}{6}$ of an hour is equal to

A. half an hour B. 40 minutes

C. 50 minutes D. 55 minutes

4. An aircraft uses 2/5 of its fuel in flying 1,250 kilometres. The distance travelled on remaining fuel is

A. 1875 km B. 2125 km

C. 250 km D. 475 km

5. If $\frac{4}{3} * \frac{3}{4} = \frac{16}{9}$, then * means

A. + B. –

C. × D. ÷

6. Which of the following is the largest fraction?

$\frac{3}{15}, \frac{5}{20}, \frac{8}{64}, \frac{25}{1000}$

A. $\frac{3}{15}$ B. $\frac{5}{20}$

C. $\frac{8}{64}$ D. $\frac{25}{1000}$

7. Six times x increased by 12 is equal to

A. $\frac{x}{2}$ B. $2x$

C. $6x + 12$ D. $12x + 6$

8. Five times y diminished by 20 is equal to

A. $5y - 20$ B. $5y + 20$

C. $y/4$ D. $4y$

9. The number less than 15 by 7 is

A. $15x - 7$ B. 15/7

C. 15 D. 8

10. If 21 is add to four times a number, the result is 57. The number is

A. 7 B. 8

C. 9 D. 10

11. A number, the sum of whose fourth and fifth parts exceeds their third part by 28, is

A. 120 B. 240

C. 220 D. 160

12. Which fraction should be added to the sum of $5\frac{3}{4}$, $4\frac{4}{5}$ and $7\frac{3}{8}$ to make the result a whole number?

A. $\frac{1}{40}$ B. $\frac{2}{40}$

C. $\frac{3}{40}$ D. $\frac{4}{40}$

13. $\frac{1}{15} + \frac{3}{15} + \frac{5}{15} + \frac{6}{15} = ?$

A. $\frac{10}{15}$ B. $\frac{3}{5}$

C. $\frac{4}{5}$ D. 1

14. A number one-sixth of which exceeds its one-ninth by 100 is

A. 600 B. 900

C. 1500 D. 1800

15. The sum of 1/2, 1/4 and 1/8 of a number is 28. The number is

A. 28 B. 32

C. 36 D. 42

16. The sum of 1/9, 1/3, 1/6 and 7/18 of a number is 150. The number is

A. 120 B. 130

C. 140 D. 150

17. Which is the greatest?
.999, .1011, .1995, .9985
A. .999 B. .1011
C. .1995 D. .9985

18. In decimal system, $9\frac{1}{8}$ may be represented as
A. 9.18 B. 9.125
C. 9.025 D. 9.225

19. $2.205 \div 0.15 = ?$
A. 1.47 B. 14.7
C. 147 D. 0.147

20. G.C.M. of .24, 3.2 and 16.0 is
A. 80 B. 8
C. .8 D. .08

ANSWERS

1	2	3	4	5	6	7	8	9	10
C	B	C	A	D	B	C	A	D	C
11	**12**	**13**	**14**	**15**	**16**	**17**	**18**	**19**	**20**
B	C	D	D	B	D	A	B	B	D

EXPLANATORY ANSWERS

1. $\frac{15}{25} = \frac{3\times5}{5\times5} = \frac{3}{5}$

2. $\frac{9*3}{3*7} = \frac{9}{7}$, or, $\frac{9\times3}{7\times3} = \frac{9}{7}$, $\therefore$ The sign * is $\times$.

3. $\frac{5}{6}$ of 1 hr. $= \frac{5}{6}\times 60$ minutes = 50 minutes.

4. Remaining fuel $= 1-\frac{2}{5} = \frac{5-2}{5} = \frac{3}{5}$

Distance flown by $\frac{2}{5}$ of fuel = 1250 km.

Distance flown by full fuel $= \frac{1250}{2/5} = \frac{1250\times5}{2}$ km.

Distance flown by $\frac{3}{5}$ of fuel

$= \frac{1250\times5\times3}{2\times5} = 1875$ km.

6. $\frac{3}{15} = \frac{1}{5}, \frac{8}{64} = \frac{1}{8}, \frac{5}{20} = \frac{1}{4}, \frac{25}{1000} = \frac{1}{40}$

Now, the fractions are $\frac{1}{5}, \frac{1}{4}, \frac{1}{8}, \frac{1}{40}$

$\therefore$ The largest fraction is $\frac{1}{4} = \frac{5}{20}$

7. $x \times 6 + 12 = 6x + 12$

8. $5 \times y - 20 = 5y - 20$

9. $15 - 7 = 8$

10. Let the number be x

$\therefore$ $4x + 21 = 57$ or, $4x = 57 - 21 = 36$

Hence, $x = \frac{36}{4} = 9$

11. Let the number be x

$\therefore$ $\frac{x}{4}+\frac{x}{5} = \frac{x}{3}+28$

$\Rightarrow$ $\frac{9x}{20} = \frac{x}{3}+28 \Rightarrow \frac{9x}{20}-\frac{x}{3} = 28$

$\Rightarrow$ $\frac{27x-20x}{60} = 28 \therefore x = \frac{28\times60}{7} = 240.$

12. $5\frac{3}{4}+4\frac{4}{5}+7\frac{3}{8} = \frac{23}{4}+\frac{24}{5}+\frac{59}{8} = \frac{717}{40}$

717/40 becomes whole number when 3/40 is added to it, *i.e.*,

$\frac{717}{40}+\frac{3}{40} = \frac{720}{40} = 18$ which is a whole number.

13. $\frac{1}{15}+\frac{3}{15}+\frac{5}{15}+\frac{6}{15} = \frac{1+3+5+6}{15} = \frac{15}{15} = 1$

14. Let the number be x

$\frac{x}{6} = \frac{x}{9}+100$

$\Rightarrow$ $\frac{x}{6}-\frac{x}{9} = 100, \Rightarrow \frac{x}{18} = 100$

$\therefore$ $x = 100 \times 18 = 1800.$

15. Let the number be x

$\therefore$ $\frac{x}{2}+\frac{x}{4}+\frac{x}{8} = 28 \Rightarrow \frac{7x}{8} = 28$

$\therefore$ $x = \frac{28\times8}{7} = 32.$

16. Let the number be x

$\therefore$ $\frac{x}{9}+\frac{x}{3}+\frac{x}{6}+\frac{7x}{18} = 150$

$\Rightarrow$ $\frac{2x+6x+3x+7x}{18} = \frac{18x}{18} = 150 \therefore x = 150.$

17. .999 is the greatest.

18. $9\frac{1}{8} = 9+\frac{1}{8} = 9 + .125 = 9.125$

19. $2.205 \div 0.15 = \frac{2.205}{.15} = \frac{2205}{1000}\times\frac{100}{15} = \frac{2205}{150} = 14.7.$

20. G.C.M. of .24, 3.2 and 16.0

= G.C.M. of $\frac{24, 320 \text{ and } 1600}{100} = \frac{8}{100} = 0.08$

Relation Between Numbers

Simplification is a mathematical operation by which a complex expression of numbers or fractions is converted into a simpler or less difficult form. It is erroneous to solve this type of questions on random basis and a very appropriate method is to apply BODMAS Rule for arriving at the solution of such problems. Each of the letters of the word 'BODMAS' when explained serially, has following implications:

1.	B	→	Bracket	[{ (‾) }]
2.	O	→	of	of
3.	D	→	Division	÷
4.	M	→	Multiplication	×
5.	A	→	Addition	+
6.	S	→	Subtraction	–

Therefore, for simplification, we should remove the brackets first. Thereafter operation for 'of', then for 'division', after that the operation for 'multiplication' and thereafter for 'addition' and at last operation for 'subtraction' should be carried out.

Important Notes

A. In mathematical operations the word 'of' indicates multiplication.

B. While removing brackets, first of all bar bracket '–' and after that small bracket '( )' is removed. Thereafter the curly bracket '{ }' and at last square bracket [ ] is removed.

EXERCISE

1. The value of 51 ÷ 17 ÷ 3 is:

A. 9 B. 4
C. 3 D. 1

2. What will be the value of
40 × 2 ÷ 10 + 5 – 4?

A. 5 B. 8
C. 11 D. 9

3. The value of 28 × 104 ÷ (18 + 6) + 3 is:

A. $124\frac{1}{3}$ B. $104\frac{1}{3}$
C. $125\frac{1}{3}$ D. 128

4. If $75^2 - 65^2 = 2x$, then value of x is:

A. 715 B. 700
C. 688 D. 711

5. The value of 99 × 14 ÷ 11 ÷ 0.7 is:

A. 2.9 B. 1.6
C. 1.8 D. 2.8

6. If 45 – [28 – {37 – (15 – ?) }] = 58, then which of the following should replace the sign of interrogation (?)?

A. 18 B. 17
C. 13 D. 19

7. The value of $8\frac{1}{3}+5\frac{1}{4}\times 13\frac{1}{5}\div 6\frac{3}{5}$ is:

A. $19\frac{1}{3}$ B. $18\frac{5}{6}$
C. $21\frac{1}{3}$ D. $22\frac{1}{2}$

8. The value of $\frac{14}{3}$ of $\frac{5}{8}$ of 72 is:

A. 209 B. 217
C. 210 D. 199

9. What will be the value of
10 × 10 × 10 ÷ (20 ÷ 10 × 10 – 10) + 6?

A. 108 B. 111
C. 106 D. 114

10. What will be the value of $\dfrac{\frac{1}{3}\times 20\div 4}{\frac{1}{4}\times 25\div 5}$?

A. 7/3 B. 4/3
C. 5/3 D. 10/3

11. Which of the following is the standard form of $\dfrac{(24\times 13)+(28\div 7)}{(24+13)-\left(\frac{14}{3}\text{ of }\frac{5}{8}\right)}$?

A. $\frac{3792}{409}$ B. $\frac{4792}{309}$
C. $\frac{3792}{411}$ D. $\frac{3092}{409}$

12. If $\dfrac{144+32\div ?-8}{35\div \frac{1}{2}\text{ of }\frac{1}{2}} = 1$, then which of the following should replace the sign of interrogation?

A. 7 B. 6
C. 10 D. 8

13. What is the value of
$\dfrac{2.70\times 2.70+4.30\times 4.30+8.60\times 2.70}{2.70+4.30}$?

A. 6.8 B. 7.0
C. 7.6 D. 8.5

14. What will be the value of $\dfrac{\left(\sqrt{6}+\frac{1}{\sqrt{6}}\right)^2}{\frac{1}{2}\text{ of } 18 + 4}+\frac{2}{3}$?

A. 101/78 B. 104/71
C. 101/88 D. 99/57

15. 1150 ÷ 50 ÷ 23 + 15 = ?

A. 16 B. 20
C. 22 D. 18

ANSWERS

1	2	3	4	5	6	7	8	9	10
D	D	A	B	C	D	B	C	C	B
11	**12**	**13**	**14**	**15**					
A	D	B	A	A					

EXPLANATORY ANSWERS

1. $\because\ 51 \div 17 \div 3 = \frac{51}{17} \div 3 = 3 \div 3 = \frac{3}{3} = 1$

2. $\because\ 40 \times 2 \div 10 + 5 - 4$

$= 40 \times \frac{2}{10} + 5 - 4 = 8 + 5 - 4 = 9.$

3. $\because\ 28 \times 104 \div (18 + 6) + 3$

$= 28 \times 104 \div 24 + 3$

$= 28 \times \frac{104}{24} + 3 = 28 \times \frac{13}{3} + 3$

$= \frac{364}{3} + 3 = \frac{373}{3} = 124\frac{1}{3}$

4. $\because\ 75^2 - 65^2 = 2x$

$\Rightarrow (75 + 65)(75 - 65) = 2x$

$[\because a^2 - b^2 = (a + b)(a - b)]$

$\Rightarrow\ 140 \times 10 = 2x \Rightarrow x = 70 \times 10 = 700$

$\therefore$ Value of x is 700.

5. $\because\ .99 \times 14 \div 11 \div 0.7$

$= .99 \times \frac{14}{11} \div 0.7 = \frac{.99 \times 14}{11 \times 0.7} = 1.8$

6. $\because\ 45 - [28 - \{37 - (15 - ?)\}] = 58$

$\Rightarrow\ 45 - [28 - \{37 - 15 + ?\}] = 58$

$\Rightarrow\ 45 - [28 - \{22 + ?\}] = 58$

$\Rightarrow\ 45 - [28 - 22 - ?\} = 58$

$\Rightarrow\ 45 - 28 + 22 + ? = 58$

$\Rightarrow\ 39 + ? = 58$

$\Rightarrow\ ? = 58 - 39 = 19$

Therefore, the interrogation sign should be replaced by 19.

7. $\because\ 8\frac{1}{3} + 5\frac{1}{4} \times 13\frac{1}{5} \div 6\frac{3}{5}$

$= \frac{25}{3} + \frac{21}{4} \times \frac{66}{5} \div \frac{33}{5} = \frac{25}{3} + \frac{21}{4} \times \frac{66}{5} \times \frac{5}{33}$

$= \frac{25}{3} + \frac{21}{2} = \frac{50 + 63}{6} = \frac{113}{6} = 18\frac{5}{6}$

8. $\because\ \frac{14}{3}$ of $\frac{5}{8}$ of $72 = \frac{14 \times 5 \times 72}{3 \times 8} = 210$

9. $10 \times 10 \times 10 \div (20 \div 10 \times 10 - 10) + 6$

$= 10 \times 10 \times 10 \div \left(\frac{20}{10} \times 10 - 10\right) + 6$

$= 10 \times 10 \times 10 \div (20 - 10) + 6$

$= 10 \times 10 \times 10 \div 10 + 6$

$= 10 \times 10 \times \frac{10}{10} + 6$

$= 10 \times 10 \times 1 + 6 = 100 + 6 = 106$

10. $\because\ \frac{\frac{1}{3} \times 20 \div 4}{\frac{1}{4} \times 25 \div 5} = \frac{\frac{1}{3} \times 5}{\frac{1}{4} \times 5} = \frac{\frac{5}{3}}{\frac{5}{4}} = \frac{4}{3}$

11. $\because\ \frac{(24 \times 13) + (28 \div 7)}{(24 + 13) - \left(\frac{14}{3} \text{ of } \frac{5}{8}\right)} = \frac{312 + 4}{37 - \frac{35}{12}} = \frac{316}{\frac{409}{12}} = \frac{3792}{409}$

12. If $\frac{144 + 32 \div ? - 8}{35 \div \frac{1}{2} \text{ of } \frac{1}{2}} = 1 \Rightarrow \frac{144 + \frac{32}{?} - 8}{35 \div \frac{1}{4}} = 1 \Rightarrow \frac{136 + \frac{32}{?}}{\frac{35}{\frac{1}{4}}} = 1$

$\Rightarrow\ 136 + \frac{32}{?} = 35 \times 4 = 140$

$\Rightarrow\ \frac{32}{?} = 140 - 136 = 4 \Rightarrow ? = \frac{32}{4} = 8$

$\therefore$ Sign of interrogation (?) will be replaced by 8.

13. $\frac{2.70 \times 2.70 + 4.30 \times 4.30 + 8.60 \times 2.70}{2.70 + 4.30}$

$= \frac{(2.70)^2 + (4.30)^2 + 2 \times 4.30 \times 2.70}{2.70 + 4.30}$

$= \frac{(2.70 + 4.30)^2}{2.70 + 4.30}$ $[\because a^2 + b^2 + 2ab = (a + b)^2]$

$= 2.70 + 4.30 = 7.00$

14. $\therefore\ \frac{\left(\sqrt{6} + \frac{1}{\sqrt{6}}\right)^2}{\frac{1}{2} \text{ of } 18 + 4} + \frac{2}{3} = \frac{(\sqrt{6})^2 + \left(\frac{1}{\sqrt{6}}\right)^2 + 2.\sqrt{6}.\frac{1}{\sqrt{6}}}{9 + 4} + \frac{2}{3}$

$= \frac{6 + \frac{1}{6} + 2}{13} + \frac{2}{3} = \frac{\frac{49}{6}}{13} + \frac{2}{3} = \frac{49}{78} + \frac{2}{3} = \frac{101}{78}$

15. $1150 \div 50 \div 23 + 15$

$= \frac{1150}{50} \div 23 + 15 = 23 \div 23 + 15 = \frac{23}{23} + 15$

$= 1 + 15 = 16.$

2

Comparing Quantities

Percentage

The word 'per cent' or 'percentage' means 'for every one hundred'. In other words, it gives an indication of rate per hundred. It is denoted by the symbol %.

For example, 5% means 5 out of one hundred or $\frac{5}{100}$.

Remember:

(*i*) For converting a per cent into a fraction, divide it by 100.

(*ii*) For converting a fraction into a per cent, multiply it by 100.

(*iii*) For converting a per cent into a decimal, shift the decimal point two places to the left.

(*iv*) For converting one given quantity *(x)* as a percentage of another given quantity *(y)*, find $\frac{x}{y} \times 100$.

(*v*) There is no unit of percentage.

Important Facts—For quickly solving the problems related to percentage, remember following rules:

Rule 1:

(*a*) Of the given two numbers if the first is $x\%$ more than the second, then the second will be $\left(\frac{100 \times x}{100 + x}\right)\%$ less than the first.

(*b*) Of the given two numbers if the first is $x\%$ less than the second, then the second will be $\left(\frac{100 \times x}{100 - x}\right)\%$ more than the first.

(*c*) If two numbers are respectively $x\%$ and $y\%$ more than a third number, then the first number will be $\left(\frac{100 + x}{100 + y} \times 100\right)\%$ of the second.

(*d*) If two numbers are respectively $x\%$ and $y\%$ less than a third number, then the first number will be $\left(\frac{100 - x}{100 - y} \times 100\right)\%$ of the second.

Rule 2:

(*a*) If a number or quantity is increased by $x\%$ then in order to restore its original value it must be decreased by $\left[\frac{100 \times x}{100 + x}\right]\%$.

(*b*) If a number or quantity is decreased by $x\%$ then in order to restore its original value it must be increased by $\left[\frac{100 \times x}{100 - x}\right]\%$.

Rule 3:

(*a*) If a number is successively increased by $x\%$ and $y\%$ then a single equivalent increase in that number will be $\left(x + y + \frac{xy}{100}\right)\%$

(*b*) If two successive discounts of $x\%$ and $y\%$ are allowed on a particular amount, then a single discount that is equivalent to the two successive discounts will be $\left(x + y - \frac{xy}{100}\right)\%$

(*c*) If a number is successively increased by $x\%$, $y\%$ and $z\%$, then a single equivalent increase in that number will be

$$\left[(x + y + z) + \left(\frac{xy + yz + zx}{100}\right) + \frac{(xyz)}{10000}\right]\%$$

(*d*) If three successive discounts of $x\%$, $y\%$ and $z\%$ are allowed on an amount, then a single discount that is equivalent to the three successive discounts will be

$$\left[x + y + z - \frac{(xy + yz + zx)}{100} + \frac{xyz}{10000}\right]\%$$

Rule 4:

(*a*) If a number is increased by $x\%$ and thereafter reduced by $x\%$, then the number will be reduced by $\left(\frac{x^2}{100}\right)$ per cent.

(*b*) If a number is reduced by x% and thereafter increased by x% then the number will be reduced by $\left(\frac{x^2}{100}\right)$ per cent.

(*c*) If due to an increase of x% in the selling price of certain commodity the sell/consumption of the commodity decreases by y%, then gross receipts on account of sale of that commodity will be increased or decreased by $\left(x-y-\frac{xy}{100}\right)$%, where $x > y$ and will be decreased by $\left(y-x+\frac{xy}{100}\right)$%, where $y > x$.

EXERCISE

1. In the expression xy^2, the values of both variables x and y are decreased by 20%. By this, the value of the expression is decreased by

A. 40% B. 48.8%
C. 51.2% D. 80%

2. 15 litres of mixture contains 20% alcohol and rest water. If 3 litres of water be mixed in it, the percentage of alcohol in the new mixture will be:

A. 15 B. $16\frac{2}{3}$
C. 17 D. $18\frac{1}{2}$

3. The difference between 70% and 55% of a number is 72. The number is:

A. 370 B. 460
C. 480 D. 520

4. 20% of a number is 10% of:

A. half the number
B. double the number
C. ten times the number
D. twenty times the number

5. 75% of what area is 15 sq. metres?

A. 10 sq. metres B. 15 sq. metres
C. 20 sq. metres D. 25 sq. metres

6. In an examination 80% of the students passed in Mathematics and 70% passed in English, while 10% students failed in both the subjects. If 360 students passed in both the subjects, find the total number of students who appeared in the examination.

A. 400 B. 600
C. 630 D. 640

7. In an election, there are two candidates. A candidate secured 57% of the total votes polled and elected by a margin of 2100 votes. Find the total number of votes polled.

A. 15000 B. 17500
C. 18000 D. 21000

8. Electric tax is increased by 20% and its consumption is decreased by 20%. The change in the expenditure is:

A. 4% decrease B. 4% increase
C. 5% decrease D. 5% increase

9. A man loses 10% of his money, after spending 20% of the remainder he is left with ₹ 2160. Initially the man had:

A. ₹ 1800 B. ₹ 2500
C. ₹ 3000 D. ₹ 3200

10. In a school 55% of the students are below 9 years of age and the remaining 153 above 9 years of age. The total number of students in the school is:

A. 296 B. 300
C. 340 D. 1000

11. The selling price of certain commodity was reduced by 25%. As a result of it, the sales increased by 30%. What was the effect of it on cash collected by daily sales?

A. 2.5% decrease B. 2.5% increase
C. 5% decrease D. 5% increase

12. A cooler marked at ₹ 1500 is offered at ₹ 1350 due to off-season discount. Find the rate of off-season discount offered.

A. 9.5% B. 10%
C. 10.5% D. 12%

13. The number of Gypsy-cars sold in 2008 was 16,500 and that sold in 2007 was 16580. How much was the percentage decrease in sales of the Gypsy-cars from 2007 to 2008?

A. less than 1 per cent
B. more than 1 per cent
C. zero per cent
D. cannot be determined

14. A company decided to sell ₹ 50,000 T.V. set for ₹ 48,000 as a world cup offer. What is the percentage discount offered by the company?

A. 6.5 B. 7
C. 7.5 D. 4

15. 9% of a number is $\frac{81}{200}$, what is $\frac{2}{7}$ of that number?

A. $1\frac{1}{5}$ B. $1\frac{2}{7}$
C. $2\frac{1}{7}$ D. $2\frac{1}{5}$

ANSWERS

1	2	3	4	5	6	7	8	9	10
B	B	C	B	C	B	A	A	C	C
11	12	13	14	15					
A	B	A	D	B					

EXPLANATORY ANSWERS

1. Decrease in expression

$= xy^2 - \frac{80}{100}\times x\left(\frac{80}{100}y\right)^2 = xy^2 - \frac{64}{125}xy^2 = \frac{61xy^2}{125}$

Hence, decrease per cent

$= \frac{61xy^2}{125\times xy^2}\times 100 = 48.8\%$

2. Amount of alcohol $= \frac{20}{100}\times 15 = 3$ litre

Hence, required percentage $= \frac{3}{18}\times 100 = 16\frac{2}{3}\%$

3. Let the number be x; then

$(70 - 55)\times \frac{1}{100}\times x = 72$

$\therefore \quad x = \frac{100\times 72}{15} = 480$

4. Let number be 100, then 20% and 10% of the number be 20 and 10 respectively.

Hence, 20% of a number is 10% of double the number.

5. Let required area be x sq. metre; then

$\frac{75}{100}\times x = 15$

$\therefore \; x = \frac{15\times 100}{75} = 20$ sq metre

6. Here, percentage of students failed in Mathematics and English be 30% and 20% respectively.

Percentage of students failed either one or both subjects $= 30 + 20 - 10 = 40\%$

Hence, percentage of pass students $= 100 - 40 = 60\%$

Now, $\quad 60\% = 360$

$\therefore \quad 100\% = \frac{360}{60}\times 100 = 600$

7. Let total number of votes be x; then

$(57 - 43)\times \frac{1}{10}x = 2100$

$\therefore \quad x = \frac{100\times 2100}{14} = 15000$

8. Let initially electric tax is ₹ 100 and consumption = 100 units

Decrease in consumption

$= 100 \times 100 - 120 \times 80 =$ ₹ 400

Hence, decrease percentage $= \frac{400\times 100}{100\times 100} = 4\%$

9. Let initally the man had ₹ x, then

amount of money loses $= \frac{10}{100}\times x =$ ₹$\frac{x}{10}$

Remaining amount of money $= x - \frac{x}{10} =$ ₹$\frac{9x}{10}$

Money spent $= \frac{20}{100}\times\frac{9x}{10} =$ ₹$\frac{9x}{50}$

Now, $\frac{9x}{10} - \frac{9x}{50} = 2160 \Rightarrow \frac{36x}{50} = 2160$

$\therefore \; x = \frac{2160\times 50}{36} =$ ₹ 3000

10. Let total number of students be x, then

$\frac{45}{100}\times x = 153 \;\therefore\; x = \frac{100\times 153}{45} = 340$

11. Let the selling price of a commodity be ₹ 100 and number of sales = 100 units

Decrease in daily cash

$= 100 \times 100 - 75 \times 130 =$ ₹ 250

Hence, decrease percentage $= \frac{250\times 100}{100\times 100} = 2.5\%$

12. Discount per cent

$= \frac{1500-1350}{1500}\times 100 = \frac{150}{1500}\times 100 = 10\%$

13. Required decrease percentage

$= \frac{16580-16500}{16580}\times 100 = \frac{80}{16580}\times 100 = 0.48\%$

14. Discount per cent $= \frac{2000}{50,000}\times 100 = 4\%$

15. Let the number be x; then

$\frac{9}{100}\times x = \frac{81}{200} \;\therefore\; x = \frac{100\times 81}{9\times 200} = \frac{9}{2}$

Hence, $\frac{2}{7}x = \frac{2}{7}\times\frac{9}{2} = \frac{9}{7} = 1\frac{2}{7}$.

Discount

Market Price (M.P.)—The attached price is called the market price (M.P.) or list price (L.P.) of the article and the reduction allowed in the price is called the **discount**.

(*i*) Discount = M.P. – S.P.

(*ii*) $\text{Discount \%} = \frac{\text{Discount} \times 100}{\text{M.P.}}$

(*iii*) $\text{S.P.} = \text{M.P.} - \frac{\text{Discount\%} \times \text{M.P.}}{100}$

(*iv*) $\text{S.P.} = \text{M.P.} \times \left(1 - \frac{\text{Discount\%}}{100}\right)$

(*v*) $\text{M.P.} = \frac{100 \times \text{S.P.}}{100 - \text{Discount\%}}$

$\text{S.P.} = \text{M.P.} \left(\frac{100 - \text{Discount\%}}{100}\right)$

$\text{M.P.} - \text{S.P.} = \frac{\text{M.P.} \times \text{Discount\%}}{100}$

$\text{Discount\%} = \left(\frac{\text{M.P.} - \text{S.P.}}{\text{M.P.}}\right) \times 100$

EXERCISE

1. A cloth merchant offers 15% festival discount on every saree sold. If a certain saree is sold for ₹ 680, what is its marked price?

A. ₹ 800 B. ₹ 900
C. ₹ 1250 D. ₹ 1300

2. A shopkeeper offers 10% discount on an article and still makes a profit of 20%. What is the C.P. of the article if the marked price is ₹ 350?

A. ₹ 259.20 B. ₹ 262.50
C. ₹ 265.75 D. ₹ 272.5

3. A manufactures marks his goods in such a way that after allowing 20% discount, he makes a profit of 18%. What is the marked price of an item which costs him ₹ 200?

A. ₹ 295 B. ₹ 310
C. ₹ 315 D. ₹ 375

4. The marked price of a brand of coffee is ₹ 35 for 100g. But the shopkeeper gives a cup costing ₹ 7.50 free with it. Even then he gets a gain of 10%. What is the cost price of 100g of coffee?

A. ₹ 15 B. ₹ 25
C. ₹ 35 D. ₹ 65

5. A car is marked at ₹ 2,25,000. The manufacturer gives a discount of 10%. The dealer also gives a discount of 5%. What is the S.P. of the car?

A. ₹ 1,72,369 B. ₹ 1,64,370
C. ₹ 1,52,393 D. ₹ 1,92,375

6. A cycle merchant allows 25% commission on his advertised price and still makes a profit of 20%. If he gains ₹ 60 over the sale of one cycle. What is his advertised price?

A. ₹ 290 B. ₹ 310
C. ₹ 480 D. ₹ 520

7. The marked price of a shirt was ₹ 165 and it was at a discount of 12%. What the selling price of the shirt?

A. ₹ 145.20 B. ₹ 155.30
C. ₹ 165.20 D. ₹ 175.25

8. A trader marks his goods 40% above the cost price and gives a discount of 20% on the marked price. What is his gain per cent?

A. 8% B. 9%
C. 12% D. 15%

9. How much per cent more than the C.P. should a manufacturer mark his goods so that after allowing a discount of 20% on the marked price, he gains 10%.

A. 34.5% B. 27.5%
C. 37.5% D. 38.5%

10. A shopkeeper allows a discount of 10% to his customers and still gains 20%. What is the marked price of an article which costs ₹ 450 to the shopkeeper?

A. ₹ 600 B. ₹ 700
C. ₹ 800 D. ₹ 900

ANSWERS

1	2	3	4	5	6	7	8	9	10
A	B	A	B	D	C	A	C	C	A

EXPLANATORY ANSWERS

1. S.P. = ₹ 680, Discount = 15%

$\text{M.P.} = \frac{100 \times \text{S.P.}}{100 - \text{Discount\%}}$

$= \frac{100 \times 680}{100 - 15} = \frac{100 \times 680}{85} = ₹\ 800$

2. C.P. = ₹ x, 120% of x = 350 – 350 × 10%

$\frac{120}{100} \times x = 350 - 35 = 315.$

$x = \frac{315 \times 5}{6} = \frac{525}{2}$, C.P. = ₹ 262.50.

3. Let M.P. = ₹ x

$80\%\ x = 118\%$ of 200

$$\frac{80}{100}\times x = \frac{118}{100}\times 200 \Rightarrow x = \frac{236\times 5}{4} = ₹\ 295.$$

4. Let C.P. of 100 gm coffee = ₹ x

110% of x = 35 − 7.50 = 27.50

$$\frac{110}{100}\times x = 27.50$$

$$x = \frac{27.50\times 100}{110\times 100}$$

C.P. = ₹ 25.

5. M.P. = ₹ 225000

$$\text{1st S.P.} = 225000 - 225000 \times \frac{10}{100}$$

$= 225000 - 22500 = 202500$

$$\text{2nd S.P.} = 202500 - 202500 \times \frac{5}{100}$$

$= 202500 - 10125 = ₹\ 192375$

6. Let M.P. = 100

Commission = 25%

S.P. = 100 − 25 = 75

Profit = 20%

$$\text{C.P.} = \frac{100}{120}\times 75 = \frac{375}{6} = 62.50$$

Gain = 75 − 62.50 = ₹ 12.50

$$\text{M.P.} = \frac{100}{12.50}\times 60 = ₹\ 480$$

7. $$\text{S.P.} = \frac{\text{M.P.}(100-\text{Discount})}{100}$$

$$= \frac{165\times(100-12)}{100} = \frac{165\times 88}{100}$$

$= 33 \times 4.4 = ₹\ 145.20$

8. Let C.P. = 100, M.P. = 140, Discount = 20%

$$\text{S.P.} = 140 - 140\times\frac{20}{100} = 140 - 28 = 112$$

Profit = 112 − 100 = 12

$$\text{Profit }\% = \frac{12\times 100}{100} = 12\%$$

9. Let C.P. = ₹ x, S.P. = 110% of $x = \frac{110}{100}\times x = \frac{11}{10}x.$

Discount = 20%

$$\text{M.P.} = \frac{100\times\frac{11}{10}x}{100-20} = \frac{100\times\frac{11}{10}x}{80} = \frac{11}{8}x.$$

$$\text{Required }\% = \frac{\frac{11x}{8}-x}{x}\times 100 = \frac{3x\times 100}{8x} = 37.5\%$$

10. C.P. = 450, Gain = 20%

$$\text{S.P.} = 450 + 450\times\frac{20}{100} = 450 + 90 = 540$$

Discount = 10%

$$\text{M.P.} = \frac{100\times\text{S.P.}}{100-\text{Discount}} = \frac{100\times 540}{100-10}$$

$$= \frac{100\times 540}{90} = ₹\ 600$$

Profit & Loss

A consumer who goes to the market and buys certain goods. The buyer is called a customer and the shopkeeper who sells the goods to him is called a retailer. The retailer purchases goods in turn in bulk from a wholesaler who keeps a large stock of good and in this case, the retailer becomes the customer.

1. **Cost price (C.P.):** Cost price is that price at which a particular article is bought. Profit and loss both are marked at cost price.
2. **Selling Price (S.P.):** Selling price is that price at which a particular article is sold.
3. **Overheads:** The expenses incurred on transportation, maintenance, packaging, advertise-ments and the like are included as *Overhead.* These overheads and the profit when added to the cost price determine the selling price.
4. **Profit or Gain** : Whenever a person sells an article at price greater than the cost price he is said to have made a profit or gain.
   Profit or Gain = S.P. − C.P.
5. **Loss :** If S.P. is less than the C.P. there is loss.
   Loss = C.P − S.P

Some Basic Formulae:

(i) Gain = S.P. − C.P.

(ii) Loss = C.P. − S.P.

(iii) $\text{Gain }\% = \frac{\text{Gain}\times 100}{\text{C.P.}}$

(iv) $\text{Loss }\% = \frac{\text{Loss}\times 100}{\text{C.P.}}$

From these we can write direct expressions for S.P. and C.P.

(v) $\text{S.P.} = \left(\frac{100+\text{Gain}\%}{100}\right)\times\text{C.P.}$ in case of gain or profit

(vi) $\text{S.P.} = \left(\frac{100-\text{Loss}\%}{100}\right)\times\text{C.P.}$ in case of loss

These can be rewritten as

$\text{C.P.} = \frac{100}{100+\text{Gain}\%}\times\text{S.P.}$ in case of profit

$\text{C.P.} = \frac{100}{100-\text{Loss}\%}\times\text{S.P.}$ in case of loss *(vii)* If the C.P. of x goods = S.P. of y goods, then

(a) Gain % $= \frac{x-y}{y} \times 100$ [In case of $x > y$]

(b) Loss % $= \frac{y-x}{y} \times 100$ [In case of $y > x$]

(viii) When a man sells two things at the same price each and in this process his loss on first things is $x\%$ and gain on second things is $x\%$, then in such a type question, there is always a loss.

$$\text{Loss \%} = x\% \text{ of } x = \frac{x^2}{100} = \left(\frac{x}{10}\right)^2.$$

$$\text{and Loss} = \frac{2 \times \text{S.P.}}{\left(\frac{100}{x}\right)^2 - 1}$$

(ix) An article is sold at a profit of $x\%$. Had it been sold for ₹ a some more, $y\%$ would have gained. Then, C.P. of an article =

$$\frac{\text{More gain} \times 100}{\text{Difference in percentage profit}}$$

(x) A dishonest shopkeeper prefers to sell goods at his cost price but uses a false weight of x grams for each kilogram. Then his gain per cent,

$$\text{gain \%} = \frac{\text{Error}}{\text{True value} - \text{Error}} \times 100$$

$$= \frac{1000 - x}{x} \times 100$$

$$\text{or, gain \%} = \frac{\text{True weight} - \text{False weight}}{\text{False weight}} \times 100.$$

EXERCISE

1. Ashok bought 25 kg of rice at the rate of ₹ 6 per kg and 35 kg of rice at the rate of ₹ 7 per kg. He mixed the two and sold the mixture at the rate of ₹ 6.75 per kg. What was his gain or loss in the transaction?
   A. ₹ 16 gain B. ₹ 16 loss
   C. ₹ 10 gain D. None of these

2. A horse and a cow were sold for ₹ 12000 each. The horse was sold at a loss of 20% and the cow at a gain of 20%. The entire transaction resulted in
   A. no loss no gain B. loss of ₹ 1000
   C. gain of ₹ 1000 D. loss of ₹ 2000

3. Profit after selling a commodity for ₹ 425 is same as loss after selling it for ₹ 355. The cost of the commodity is :
   A. ₹ 285 B. ₹ 390
   C. ₹ 295 D. ₹ 400

4. Bhajan Singh purchased 120 reams of paper at ₹ 80 per ream. He spent ₹ 280 on transportation, paid octroi at the rate of 40 paise per ream and paid ₹ 72 to the coolie. If he wants to have a gain of 8%, what must be the selling price per ream?
   A. ₹ 86 B. ₹ 86.48
   C. ₹ 79 D. ₹ 90

5. Ram bought 4 dozen apples at ₹ 12 per dozen and 2 dozen at ₹ 16 per dozen. He sold all of them to earn 20%. At what price per dozen did he sell the apples?
   A. ₹ 14.40 B. ₹ 16.00
   C. ₹ 16.80 D. ₹ 16.20

6. Jimmy bought paper sheets for ₹ 7200 and spent ₹ 200 in transport. Paying ₹ 600 he had 330 boxes made, which he sold at ₹ 28 each. What is his profit percentage?
   A. 15.5 B. 40
   C. 50 D. None of these

7. A owns a house worth ₹ 10000. He sells it to B at a profit of 10% based on the worth of the house. B sells the house back to A at a loss of 10%. In this transaction A gets:
   A. no profit no loss B. profit of ₹ 1000
   C. profit of ₹ 1100 D. profit of ₹ 1200

8. At what price must Kantilal sell a mixture of 80 kg sugar at ₹ 6.75 per kg with 120 kg at ₹ 8 per kg to gain 20%?
   A. ₹ 7.50 per kg B. ₹ 8.20 per kg
   C. ₹ 8.35 per kg D. ₹ 9 per kg

9. Subhash purchased a taperecorder at $\frac{9}{10}$ of its selling price and sold it at 8% more than its S.P. His gain is:
   A. 8% B. 10%
   C. 18% D. 20%

10. A dealer marks his goods 20% above cost price. He then allows some discount on it and makes a profit of 8%. The rate of discount is :
    A. 12% B. 10%
    C. 6% D. 4%

11. A trader lists his articles 20% above C.P. and allows a discount of 10% on cash payment. His gain per cent is :
    A. 10% B. 8%
    C. 6% D. 4%

12. Tarun bought a T.V. with 20% discount on the labelled price. Had he bought it with 25% discount, he would have saved ₹ 500. At what price did he buy the T.V.?
    A. ₹ 5000 B. ₹ 8000
    C. ₹ 10000 D. ₹ 12000

13. While selling a watch, a shopkeeper gives a discount of 5%. If he gives a discount of 7%, he earns ₹ 15 less as profit. The marked price of the watch is :

A. ₹ 697.50 B. ₹ 712.50
C. ₹ 787.50 D. None of these

14. Kabir buys an article with 25% discount on its marked price. He makes a profit of 10% by selling it at ₹ 660. The marked price is :

A. ₹ 600 B. ₹ 700
C. ₹ 800 D. ₹ 885

15. A person bought an article and sold it at a loss of 10%. If he had bought it for 20% less and sold it for ₹ 55 more, he would have had a profit of 40%. The C.P. of the article is :

A. ₹ 200 B. ₹ 225
C. ₹ 250 D. None of these

ANSWERS

1	2	3	4	5	6	7	8	9	10
C	B	B	D	B	A	C	D	D	B
11	**12**	**13**	**14**	**15**					
B	B	D	C	C					

EXPLANATORY ANSWERS

1. C.P. of 60 kg mixture = ₹ (25 × 6 + 35 × 7) = ₹ 395

S.P. of 60 kg mixtire = ₹ (60 × 6.75) = ₹ 405

∴ Gain = ₹ (405 − 395) = ₹ 10

2. Loss % = $\left(\frac{20}{10}\right)^2 = (2)^2 = 4\%$

Total S.P. = ₹ 24000

and Total C.P. = ₹$\left(\frac{100}{96} \times 24000\right)$ = ₹ 25000

∴ Loss = ₹ (25000 − 24000) = ₹ 1000

3. Let C.P. = ₹ x, Then, $425 - x = x - 355$

⇒ $2x = 780$ ∴ x = ₹ 390

4. C.P. of 1 ream = $80 + \frac{280}{120} + \frac{72}{120} + 0.40$

$= 80 + \frac{7}{3} + \frac{3}{5} + \frac{2}{5}$ = ₹ $\frac{250}{3}$

∴ S.P. of 1 ream = ₹$\left(\frac{108}{100} \times \frac{250}{3}\right)$ = ₹ 90

5. C.P. of 6 dozen apples = ₹ (12 × 4 + 16 × 2) = ₹ 80

∴ S.P. = ₹$\left(\frac{120}{100} \times 80\right)$ = ₹ 96

∴ S.P. per dozen = ₹$\left(\frac{96}{6}\right)$ = ₹ 16

6. C.P. of 1 box = $\frac{7200 + 200 + 600}{330}$ = ₹ $\frac{800}{33}$

Hence, Gain% = $\frac{28 - \frac{800}{33}}{800/33} \times 100 = \frac{124}{800} \times 100 = 15.5\%$

7. Final C.P. for A = $\frac{110}{100} \times \frac{90}{100} \times$ ₹ 10000 = ₹ 9900

Hence, profit for A

= $\frac{10}{100}$ × ₹ 10,000 + ₹ (10,000 − 9900) = ₹ 1100

8. C.P. of 1 kg sugar = $\frac{80 \times 6.75 + 120 \times 8}{200}$ = ₹ 7.50

∴ S.P. of 1 kg = ₹$\left(\frac{120}{100} \times 7.50\right)$ = ₹ 9 per kg

9. Let S.P. = ₹ 100;

C.P. for Subhash = $\frac{9}{10} \times 100$ = ₹ 90 and S.P. = ₹ 108

Hence, gain % for Subhash = $\frac{108 - 90}{90} \times 100 = 20\%$

10. Let C.P. be ₹ 100; then Marked price = ₹ 120 and S.P. = ₹ 108

∴ Discount = $\left(\frac{12}{120} \times 100\right)\% = 10\%$

11. Let C.P. be ₹ 100

Then, marked price = ₹ 120

S.P. = ₹$\left(\frac{90}{100} \times 120\right)$ = ₹ 108

∴ Gain % = $\left(\frac{8}{100} \times 100\right)\% = 8\%$

12. Here, 5% = 500

∴ 100% = $\frac{500}{5} \times 100$ = ₹ 10,000

Hence, labelled price = ₹ 10,000

∴ S.P. = $\frac{80}{100}$ × ₹ 10,000 = ₹ 8000

13. Let the marked price = ₹ x

Then, $\frac{7x}{100} - \frac{5x}{100} = 15 \Rightarrow \frac{x}{50} = 15$ ∴ x = ₹ 750

14. C.P. = $\frac{100}{110} \times 660$ = ₹ 600

Hence, M.P. = $\frac{100}{75} \times 600$ = ₹ 800.

Simple Interest

Interest is the money paid for the use of money borrowed, *i.e.*, extra money paid for using other's money is called *interest.*

The sum borrowed is called the principal. The sum of interest and principal is called the *Amount.*

If the interest on a certain sum borrowed for a certain period is reckoned uniformly, then it is called simple interest, denoted by S.I.

Thus, if A = Amount, P = Principal, I = Interest, T = Time (in year), R = Rate per cent per annum, then

(*a*) $I = \frac{P \times R \times T}{100}$ (*b*) $P = \frac{100 \times I}{R \times T}$

(*c*) $T = \frac{100 \times I}{P \times R}$ (*d*) $R = \frac{100 \times I}{P \times T}$

(*e*) $P = \frac{100\,A}{100 + RT}$ (*f*) A = P + I.

EXERCISE

1. If the simple interest on a certain sum of money at 6% per annum for 3 years is ₹ 90, the sum will be:
A. ₹ 500 B. ₹ 450
C. ₹ 525 D. ₹ 560

2. If the simple interest on ₹ 1 for 1 month is 1 paise, the rate per cent p.a. will be :
A. 10% B. 8%
C. 12% D. 6%

3. A sum of money doubles itself in 20 years. In how many years will it triple itself at the same rate of simple interest?
A. 30 years B. 50 years
C. 40 years D. 45 years

4. If the simple interest on ₹ 500 for 4 years is ₹ 40, find the rate per cent p.a.
A. 3½% B. 2%
C. 2½% D. 3%

5. After what time will the sum of ₹ 2000 become ₹ 2240 at 4% per annum simple interest?
A. 3 years B. 2 years
C. 5 years D. 4 years

6. The simple interest on a certain sum of money is $\frac{25}{64}$ of the sum and the number of years equals the rate per cent p.a. The rate per cent p.a. will be :
A. $7\frac{1}{2}\%$ B. $5\frac{1}{4}\%$
C. $6\frac{3}{4}\%$ D. $6\frac{1}{4}\%$

7. A sum of money amounts to ₹ 1150 in 3 years and to ₹ 1250 in 5 years at a certain rate per cent p.a. simple interest. The rate per cent p.a. will be :
A. 5% B. 8%
C. 7% D. 6%

8. The simple interest on a sum of ₹ 892 lent out at 6% p.a. for 8 months will be :
A. ₹ 36.68 B. ₹ 35.68
C. ₹ 48.58 D. ₹ 33.38

9. If the simple interest on a certain sum of money at 6% p.a. for 4½ years is ₹ 81, the sum will be:
A. ₹ 325 B. ₹ 225
C. ₹ 300 D. ₹ 340

10. A sum of ₹ 1850 lent out for 5 years at 3% p.a. simple interest will amount to:
A. ₹ 2227.75 B. ₹ 2127.50
C. ₹ 2137.50 D. ₹ 2086.50

11. A lent a sum of ₹ 1250 to B at a certain rate of interest for 3 years and a sum of ₹ 1500 to C at the same rate of interest for 2 years. If he was paid total ₹ 258.75 as interest in both cases, find the rate of interest at which money was lent by him.
A. $4\frac{1}{6}\%$ B. $6\frac{1}{4}\%$
C. $2\frac{1}{7}\%$ D. $3\frac{5}{6}\%$

12. A invested ₹ 5000 at a certain rate of simple interest and ₹ 4000 for the same period at 1% higher rate of interest. If the interest in both cases is same, the former rate of interest is :
A. 3% B. 4%
C. 6% D. 5%

13. A man lends ₹ 500 for 4 years and ₹ 600 for 3 years at a certain rate of simple interest. If he gets total ₹ 190 as interest in both cases, the rate per cent per annum is:
A. 8% B. 5%
C. 10% D. 4%

14. What annual instalment should be paid to clear the debt of ₹ 645 in 4 years at the rate of 5% p.a. simple interest?
A. ₹ 160 B. ₹ 185
C. ₹ 180 D. ₹ 190

15. If a certain sum of money at simple interest amounts to ₹ 1900 in 3 years and to ₹ 2050 in 5 years, the rate per cent per annum is:
A. 4½% B. 3½%
C. 2½% D. 5¼%

ANSWERS

1	2	3	4	5	6	7	8	9	10
A	C	C	B	A	D	A	B	C	B
11	12	13	14	15					
D	B	B	C	A					

EXPLANATORY ANSWERS

1. $P = \dfrac{90 \times 100}{6 \times 3} = ₹\ 500$

2. $\text{Rate} = \dfrac{1 \times 100}{100 \times \frac{1}{12}} = 12\%.$

3. Let principal = ₹ x; Amount = ₹ $2x$;

then $I = 2x - x = ₹\ x$

$\therefore\ R = \dfrac{x \times 100}{x \times 20} = 5\%$

Again, if principal = ₹ x;

Amount = ₹ $3x$; then $I = 3x - x = ₹\ 2x$

Hence, $T = \dfrac{2x \times 100}{x \times 5} = 40$ years

4. $\text{Rate} = \dfrac{40 \times 100}{500 \times 4} = 2\%$

5. Here, I = 2240 − 2000 = ₹ 240

$\therefore\quad T = \dfrac{240 \times 100}{2000 \times 4} = 3$ years

6. Let, $R = T = x$; then

$\dfrac{25}{64}P = \dfrac{P \times x \times x}{100} \Rightarrow x^2 = \dfrac{25 \times 100}{64}$

$\therefore\quad x = \dfrac{5 \times 10}{8} = \dfrac{25}{4}$; $R = 6\frac{1}{4}\%$

7. Here, Simple interest for 2 years

= ₹ 1250 − ₹ 1150 = ₹ 100

$\therefore$ Simple interest for 3 years = $\dfrac{100 \times 3}{2} = ₹\ 150$

Hence, P = ₹ 1150 − ₹ 150 = ₹ 1000

$\therefore\quad \text{Rate} = \dfrac{50 \times 100}{1000 \times 1} = 5\%$

8. Here, $I = \dfrac{892 \times 6 \times \frac{2}{3}}{100} = ₹\ 35.68$

9. $P = \dfrac{81 \times 100 \times 2}{6 \times 9} = ₹\ 300$

10. $I = \dfrac{1850 \times 3 \times 5}{100} = ₹\ 277.50$

$\therefore$ Amount = ₹ 1850 + ₹ 277.50

= ₹ 2127.50

11. $\dfrac{1250 \times R \times 3}{100} + \dfrac{1500 \times R \times 2}{100} = 258.75$

$\Rightarrow\quad 6750\ R = 25875$

$\therefore\quad R = \dfrac{25875}{6750} = \dfrac{23}{6} = 3\frac{5}{6}\%$

12. Here, $\dfrac{5000 \times R \times T}{100} = \dfrac{4000 \times (R+1) \times T}{100}$

$\Rightarrow\quad 5R = 4R + 4 \therefore\ R = 4\%$

13. Here, $\dfrac{500 \times R \times 4}{100} + \dfrac{600 \times R \times 3}{100} = 190$

$\Rightarrow\quad 38R = 190$

$\therefore\quad R = \dfrac{190}{38} = 5\%.$

14. Let annual instalment be ₹ x; then

$x + \dfrac{x \times 3 \times 5}{100} + x + \dfrac{x \times 2 \times 5}{100} + x + \dfrac{x \times 1 \times 5}{100} + x = 645 + \dfrac{645 \times 4 \times 5}{100}$

$\Rightarrow 4x + \dfrac{3x}{10} = 774 \Rightarrow \dfrac{43x}{10} = 774$

$\therefore\quad x = \dfrac{774 \times 10}{43} = ₹\ 180$

15. Simple interest for 2 years

= ₹ 2050 − ₹ 1900 = ₹ 150

$\therefore$ Simple interest for 1 year

= ₹ $\dfrac{150}{2}$ = ₹ 75

Since simple interest for 3 years

= ₹ 75 × 3 = ₹ 225

$\therefore$ Principal = ₹ 1900 − ₹ 225 = ₹ 1675

Hence, $\text{Rate} = \dfrac{75 \times 100}{1675 \times 1} = 4½\%$

Compound Interest

In business transaction if interest as it becomes due is not paid to the lender but is added on to the principal, the money is said to be lent at *compound interest* and the total sum owed after a given time is called the amount at compound interest for that time.

After a certain period, the difference between the amount and the original principal is called the compound Interest (C.I.).

Some Important Formulae :

Let Principal = P, Time = n years

Rate = r% p.a.

then, the amount,

(*a*) when interest is compounded annually:

then, $\text{Amount} = P\left(1+\frac{r}{100}\right)^n$

(*b*) when interest is compounded half yearly:

then, $\text{Amount} = P\left(1+\frac{r/2}{100}\right)^{2n}$

(*c*) when interest is compounded quarterly :

then, $\text{Amount} = P\left(1+\frac{r/4}{100}\right)^{4n}$

(*d*) when time is fraction of a year, say $4\frac{1}{3}$ years,

then, $\text{Amount} = P\left(1+\frac{r}{100}\right)^4 \times \left(1+\frac{\frac{1}{3}r}{100}\right)$

(*e*) when rates are r_1%, r_2% and r_3% for Ist, IInd and IIIrd year respectively; then,

$\text{Amount} = P\left(1+\frac{r_1}{100}\right)\left(1+\frac{r_2}{100}\right)\left(1+\frac{r_3}{100}\right)$

EXERCISE

1. What will be the compound interest on ₹ 8000 for 3 years at 5% p.a.?
A. ₹ 1361 B. ₹ 1261
C. ₹ 1260 D. ₹ 1250

2. What will be the amount if a sum of ₹ 2500 is invested for 1 year at 4% per annum compound interest, interest being compounded half-yearly?
A. ₹ 2625 B. ₹ 2601
C. ₹ 2830 D. ₹ 2901

3. Find the compound interest on ₹ 2560 for ½ year at 12½% per annum, interest payable quarterly.
A. ₹ 3720.50 B. ₹ 2722.50
C. ₹ 2752.50 D. ₹ 2250.50

4. After how many years will ₹ 3375 become ₹ 4096 at $6\frac{2}{3}$% per annum compound interest?
A. 4 years B. 2 years
C. 2½ years D. 3 years

5. A certain sum of money placed at compound interest amounts to ₹ 110 in 1 year and to ₹ 121 in 2 years. The rate of interest per annum is :
A. 5% B. 10%
C. 8% D. 4%

6. The present population of a city is 80,000. If the rate of growth is 5% per year, find its population after 3 years.
A. 88,100 B. 95,600
C. 92,610 D. 84,600

7. First year's interest on a sum of money placed at compound interest at the rate of 8% per annum is ₹ 72. What will be interest for the second year?
A. ₹ 77.76 B. ₹ 78.66
C. ₹ 85.66 D. ₹ 78.76

8. The difference between compound and simple interest on a certain sum of money for 2 years at 5% per annum is ₹ 21. Find the sum.
A. ₹ 7200 B. ₹ 8400
C. ₹ 9200 D. ₹ 8500

9. In how many years will a sum of ₹ 19200 placed at 10% per annum compound interest yield an interest of ₹ 4032?
A. 1½ years B. 2½ years
C. 2 years D. 3 years

10. The compound interest on a certain sum of money invested for 3 years at 5% per annum is ₹ 1891.50. What will be the simple interest on the same sum at the same rate for 2 years?
A. ₹ 1700 B. ₹ 1200
C. ₹ 1500 D. ₹ 2100

11. The simple interest on a sum of ₹ 4800 for 2 years is ₹ 768. What will be the compound interest on the same sum at the same rate and for the same period?
A. ₹ 798.72 B. ₹ 870.75
C. ₹ 920.69 D. ₹ 884.20

12. A sum of money lent out at a certain rate of simple interest amounts to ₹ 6600 in 2 years and to ₹ 6900 in 3 years. What will be the compound interest on the same sum of money if lent out at the same rate for 2 years?
A. ₹ 605 B. ₹ 715
C. ₹ 615 D. ₹ 595

13. If the first year's interest on a certain sum of money placed at 5% p.a. compound interest is ₹ 1200, what will be the interest for the third year?

A. ₹ 1220 B. ₹ 1323
C. ₹ 1423 D. ₹ 1330

14. If a certain sum of money placed at compound interest amounts to ₹ 960 in 3 years and to ₹ 1000 in 4 years, find the rate of compound interest.

A. $4\frac{1}{6}\%$ B. $5\frac{1}{6}\%$
C. $2\frac{1}{3}\%$ D. 3%

15. What would be the compound interest on ₹ 3200 at 25% per annum for 3 years?

A. ₹ 2050 B. ₹ 2775
C. ₹ 3050 D. ₹ 3180

ANSWERS

1	2	3	4	5	6	7	8	9	10
B	B	B	D	B	C	A	B	C	B
11	**12**	**13**	**14**	**15**					
A	C	B	A	C					

EXPLANATORY ANSWERS

1. $\therefore$ $\text{C.I.} = 8000\left[\left(1+\frac{5}{100}\right)^3-1\right]$

$= 8000\left[\left(\frac{21}{20}\right)^3-1\right] = \frac{8000\times1261}{8000} = ₹\ 1261$

2. $A = 2500\left(1+\frac{2}{100}\right)^2 = 2500\left(\frac{51}{50}\right)^2 = \frac{2500\times51\times51}{50\times50}$

= ₹ 2601.

3. $\text{Amount} = 2560\left(1+\frac{25}{8\times100}\right)^2 = \frac{2560\times33\times33}{32\times32}$

= ₹ 2722.50

4. Here, $4096 = 3375\left(1+\frac{20}{3\times100}\right)^n$

$\Rightarrow \frac{4096}{3375} = \left(1+\frac{1}{15}\right)^n \Rightarrow \left(\frac{16}{15}\right)^3 = \left(\frac{16}{15}\right)^n$

$\therefore n = 3$ years

5. Here, simple interest of ₹ 110 for 1 year = 121 − 110 = ₹ 11

Hence, rate $= \frac{11\times100}{110\times1} = 10\%$

6. Population of the city after 3 years

$= 80{,}000\left(1+\frac{5}{100}\right)^3 = 80{,}000\times\frac{21}{20}\times\frac{21}{20}\times\frac{21}{20} = 92610$

7. Second year's interest = 72 + 8% of 72

$= 72+\frac{72\times8}{100} = 72 + 5.76 = ₹\ 77.76$

8. Here, $P\left[\left(1+\frac{5}{100}\right)^2-1\right]-\frac{P\times5\times2}{100} = 21$

$\Rightarrow P\left[\frac{441}{400}-1\right]-\frac{P}{10} = 21$

$\Rightarrow P\left[\frac{41}{400}-\frac{1}{10}\right] = 21 \Rightarrow P\times\frac{1}{400} = 21$

$\therefore P = 21 \times 400 = ₹\ 8400$

9. Amount = ₹ 19200 + ₹ 4032 = ₹ 23232

Now, $23232 = 19200\left(1+\frac{10}{100}\right)^n$

$\Rightarrow \frac{23232}{19200} = \left(\frac{11}{10}\right)^n \Rightarrow \frac{121}{100} = \left(\frac{11}{10}\right)^n$

$\Rightarrow \left(\frac{11}{10}\right)^2 = \left(\frac{11}{10}\right)^n$

$\therefore$ $n = 2$ years

11. $\text{Rate} = \frac{768\times100}{4800\times2} = 8\%$

$\therefore$ $\text{C.I.} = 4800\left[\left(1+\frac{8}{100}\right)^2-1\right]$

$= 4800\left[\left(\frac{27}{25}\right)^2-1\right] = \frac{4800\times104}{625} = ₹\ 798.72$

13. Required interest

$= 1200\left(1+\frac{5}{100}\right)^2 = 1200\times\frac{21}{20}\times\frac{21}{20} = ₹\ 1323$

14. Here, simple interest of ₹ 960 for 1 year = 1000 − 960 = ₹ 40

Hence, Rate $= \frac{40\times100}{960\times1} = \frac{25}{6} = 4\frac{1}{6}\%$

15. Compound interest

$= 3200\left[\left(1+\frac{25}{100}\right)^3-1\right] = 3200\left[\left(\frac{5}{4}\right)^3-1\right]$

$= \frac{3200\times61}{64} = ₹\ 3050.$

●●●

3

Ratio and Proportion

RATIO

In ratio we compare two quantities of the same kind and consider what multiple, part or parts one is of the other. In comparing 8 with 4, observe that it is 2 times 4. This comparison can be represented as $8 \div 4$ or $\frac{8}{4}$.

Hence, *ratio is that relation between two numbers which is expressed by the fraction, the numerator is which is the measure of the first quantity and denominator is the measure of the second quantity.*

If the terms of a ratio be multiplied or divided by the same quantity the value of the ratio remains unaltered.

Thus, 3 : 4 is the same as 9 : 12 and 9 : 12 is the same as 3 : 4.

PROPORTION

The equality of two ratio is called proportion.

Consider the two ratios:

Ist ratio	2nd ratio
5 : 15	7 : 21

Since, 5 is one-third of 15 and 7 is one-third of 21, the two ratios are equal. The equality of two ratios is called proportion and the numbers 5, 15, and 7, 21 are said to be in **proportion.**

The proportion may be written as 5 : 15 : : 7 : 21 (5 is to 15 as 7 is to 21)

$\Rightarrow \quad 5 : 15 = 7 : 21$

$$\Rightarrow \quad \frac{5}{15} = \frac{7}{21}$$

The numbers 5, 15, 7 and 21 are called the terms. 5 is the first term, 15 the second, 7 the third, and 21 the fourth.

The first and fourth terms, *i.e.*, 5 and 21 are called extremes (end terms), and the second and the third terms, *i.e.*, 15 and 7 are called the **means** (middle terms), 21 is called the fourth proportional.

Some Important Facts:

1. If a and b are two quantities, then

(a) Duplicate ratio of $a : b = a^2 : b^2$

(b) Sub-duplicate ratio of $a : b = \sqrt{a} : \sqrt{b}$

(c) Triplicate ratio of $a : b = a^3 : b^3$

(d) Sub-triplicate ratio $a : b = \sqrt[3]{a} : \sqrt[3]{b}$

(e) Inverse or reciprocal ratio of $a : b = \frac{1}{a} : \frac{1}{b}$

(f) Third proportional to 'a' and 'b' $= \frac{b^2}{a}$

2. If A : B = $x : y$ and B : C = $p : q$, then

(a) $A : C = \frac{x \times p}{y \times q}$

(b) A : B : C = $px : py : qy$

3. In what *ratio* the two kinds of tea must be mixed together one at ₹ x per kg and another at ₹ y per kg, so that the mixture may cost ₹ z per kg?

$$\text{Ratio} = \frac{z - y}{x - z}$$

4. A grey hound persues a hare as takes J_1 leaps for every J_2 leaps of the hare. If K_1 leaps of the hound are equal to K_2 leaps of the hare, then the Ratio of speeds of the hound and hare is

$$\frac{J_2 \times K_1}{J_1 \times K_2}$$

5. The incomes of two persons are in the ratio of $a : b$ and their expenditure are in the ratio of $x : y$. If the saving of each person is ₹ s, then income of each is ₹ $\frac{as(y - x)}{ay - bx}$ and ₹ $\frac{bs(y - x)}{ay - bx}$ respectively.

6. In a mixture of z litre, the ratio of milk and water is $x : y$. If another p litres of water is added to the mixture, the ratio of milk and water in the resulting mixture

$$= \frac{xz}{yz + p(x + y)}$$

7. There are four members a, b, c and d, then formula for

(a) What should be added to each of these numbers so that the remaining numbers may be proportional =

$$\frac{ad - bc}{(b+c)-(a+d)}$$

(b) What should be subtracted from each of these numbers so that the remaining numbers may be proportional $= \frac{ad - bc}{(a+d)-(b+c)}$

8. In a mixture the ratio of milk and water is $a : b$. If in this mixture another K litre of water is added, then the ratio of milk and water in the resulting mixture becomes $a : m$. Then the quantity of milk in the original mixture $= \frac{ak}{m-b}$ and quantity of water $= \frac{bk}{m-b}$

EXERCISE

1. If A : B = 6 : 7 and B : C = 8 : 9, then A : B : C is:
A. 24 : 28 : 63 B. 48 : 28 : 63
C. 48 : 56 : 63 D. None of these

2. The sum of two numbers is 20 and their difference is $2\frac{1}{2}$. What is the ratio of the numbers?
A. 11 : 7 B. 9 : 11
C. 9 : 7 D. None of these

3. If 0.7 of one number is equal to 0.075 of another, what is the ratio of the two numbers?
A. 6 : 14 B. 3 : 28
C. 5 : 7 D. None of these

4. If 10% of x is the same as 20% of y, then $x : y$ is equal to :
A. 1 : 2 B. 2 : 1
C. 5 : 1 D. 10 : 1

5. Two numbers are in the ratio 3 : 5. If each number is increased by 10, the ratio becomes 5 : 7. The numbers are:
A. 3, 5 B. 7, 9
C. 13, 22 D. 15, 25

6. The mean proportional between 0.32 and 0.02 is:
A. 0.34 B. 0.3
C. 0.16 D. 0.08

7. The sum of three numbers is 98. If the ratio between the first and second be 2 : 3 and that between the second and third be 5 : 8, then what is the second number?
A. 20 B. 30
C. 10 D. 40

8. One man adds 3 litres of water to 12 litres of milk and another 4 litres of water to 10 litres of milk. What is the ratio of the strenghts of the milk in the two mixtures?
A. 15 : 25 B. 25 : 28
C. 28 : 25 D. None of these

9. ₹ 425 is divided among 4 men, 5 women and 6 boys such that the share of a man, a woman and a boy may be in the ratio of 9 : 8 : 4. What is the share of a woman?
A. ₹ 34 B. ₹ 24
C. ₹ 44 D. None of these

10. A vessel contains liquids P and Q in the ratio 5 : 3. If 6 litres of the mixture are removed and the same quantity of liquid q is added, the ratio becomes 3 : 5. What quantity does the vessel hold?
A. 40 litres B. 50 litres
C. 30 litres D. None of these

11. A bucket contains a mixture of two liquids P and Q in the proportion 7 : 5. If 9 litres of the mixture is replaced by 9 litres of liquid Q, then the ratio of the two liquid becomes 7 : 9. How much of the liquid P was there in the bucket?
A. 11 litres B. 21 litres
C. 31 litres D. None of these

12. Three glasses P, Q and R with their capacities in the ratio 2 : 3 : 4 are filled with a mixture of spirit and water. The ratio of spirit to water in P, Q and R is 1 : 5, 3 : 5 and 5 : 7 respectively. If the contents of these glasses are mixed together, what is the ratio of spirit to water in the mixture?
A. 14 : 27 B. 23 : 47
C. 25 : 47 D. None of these

13. A and B are two alloys of gold and copper prepared by mixing metals in proportions 7 : 2 and 7 : 11 respectively. If equal quantities of the alloys are melted to form a third alloy C, the proportion of gold and copper in C will be
A. 5 : 9 B. 5 : 7
C. 7 : 5 D. 9 : 5

14. Gold is 19 times as heavy as water and copper 9 times as heavy as water. The ratio in which these two metals be mixed so that the mixtures is 15 times as heavy as water is:
A. 1 : 2 B. 2 : 3
C. 3 : 2 D. 19 : 135

15. The contents of two vessels containing water and milk are in the ratio 1 : 2 and 2 : 5 are mixed in the ratio 1 : 4. The resulting mixture will have water and milk in the ratio:

A. 21 : 54 B. 31 : 74
C. 27 : 74 D. None of these

16. One year ago, the ratio between Mahesh and Suresh's salaries was 3 : 5. The ratio of their individual salaries of last year and present year are 2 : 3 and 4 : 5 respectively. If their total salaries for the present year are ₹ 4300, what is the present salary of Mahesh?
A. ₹ 1800 B. ₹ 1900
C. ₹ 1600 D. None of these

17. The ratio of P's and Q's income last year was 3 : 4. The ratio of their own incomes of last year and this year is 4 : 5 and 2 : 3 respectively. If the total sum of their present income is ₹ 4160. What is the present income of P?
A. ₹ 1500 B. ₹ 1400
C. ₹ 1600 D. None of these

18. The monthly salary of A, B, C is in the proportion of 2 : 3 ; 5. If C's monthly salary is ₹ 1200 more than that of A, then B's annual salary is:
A. ₹ 14400 B. ₹ 24000
C. ₹ 1200 D. ₹ 2000

19. ₹ 1050 is divided among P, Q and R. The share of P is $\frac{2}{5}$ of the combined share of Q and R. Thus P gets:
A. ₹ 200 B. ₹ 300
C. ₹ 400 D. ₹ 420

20. The ratio between Sumit's and Prakash's age at present is 2 : 3. Sumit is 6 years younger than Prakash. The ratio of Sumit's age to Prakash's age after 6 years will be:
A. 1 : 2 B. 2 : 3
C. 3 : 4 D. 3 : 8

ANSWERS

1	2	3	4	5	6	7	8	9	10
C	C	B	B	D	D	B	C	A	A
11	**12**	**13**	**14**	**15**	**16**	**17**	**18**	**19**	**20**
B	C	C	C	B	A	C	C	B	C

EXPLANATORY ANSWERS

1. A : B = 6 : 7
B : C = 8 : 9
$\therefore$ A : B : C = 6 × 8 : 7 × 8 : 7 × 9 = 48 : 56 : 63

2. Ratio $= \dfrac{20 + \frac{5}{2}}{20 - \frac{5}{2}} = \dfrac{22.5}{17.5} = \dfrac{225}{175} = \dfrac{9}{7} = 9 : 7$

3. We have, $0.7x = 0.075\,y$

$\dfrac{x}{y} = \dfrac{0.075}{0.7} = \dfrac{75}{700} = \dfrac{3}{28} = 3 : 28$

4. 10% of x = 20% of y

$\Rightarrow \dfrac{10}{100}x = \dfrac{20}{100}y$

$\therefore \dfrac{x}{10} = \dfrac{y}{5} \Rightarrow \dfrac{x}{y} = \dfrac{10}{5} = \dfrac{2}{1} \Rightarrow x : y = 2 : 1$

5. Let the number be $3x$ and $5x$.

Then, $\dfrac{3x+10}{5x+10} = \dfrac{5}{7} \Rightarrow 7(3x + 10) = 5(5x + 10)$

$\Rightarrow 21x + 70 = 25x + 50 \Rightarrow 4x = 20 \Rightarrow x = 5$

So, the numbers are 15, 25.

6. Mean proportional $= \sqrt{0.32 \times 0.02} = \sqrt{0.0064} = 0.08$

7. The ratio among the three numbers is
2 : 3
5 : 8
and 10 : 15 : 24

$\therefore$ The second number $= \dfrac{98}{10+15+24} \times 15 = 30$

8. Strength of milk in the first mixture $= \dfrac{12}{12+3} = \dfrac{12}{15}$

Strength of milk in the second mixture $= \dfrac{10}{10+4} = \dfrac{10}{14}$

$\therefore$ The ratio of their strengths $= \dfrac{12}{15} : \dfrac{10}{14}$
$= 12 \times 14 : 15 \times 10 = 28 : 25$

9. The ratio of shares of group of men, women and boys
$= 9 \times 4 : 8 \times 5 : 4 \times 6 = 9 : 10 : 6$

$\therefore$ Share of 5 women $= \dfrac{425}{9+10+6} \times 10 = ₹\ 170$

$\therefore$ Share of 1 woman $= \dfrac{170}{5} = ₹\ 34$

10. Let the vessel contains $5x$ litres and $3x$ litres of liquid P and Q respectively. The removed quantity contains

$\dfrac{16}{5+3} \times 5 = 10$ litres of P

and 16 – 10 = 6 litres of Q.

Now, $(5x - 10) : (3x - 6 + 16) = 3 : 5$

$\Rightarrow \dfrac{5x-10}{3x+10} = \dfrac{3}{5} \Rightarrow 25x - 50 = 9x + 30$

$\Rightarrow 16x = 80 \Rightarrow x = 5$

$\therefore$ Vessel contains $8x = 8 \times 5 = 40$ litres.

11. Let the two liquids P and Q are $7x$ litres and $5x$ litres repectively.

Now, when 9 litres of mixture are taken out, P remains

$$7x-9\left(\frac{7}{7+5}\right) = 7x-\frac{9\times7}{12} = \left(7x-\frac{21}{4}\right)\text{ litres}$$

and Q remains

$$5x-9\left(\frac{5}{7+5}\right) = 5x-\frac{9\times5}{12} = \left(5x-\frac{15}{4}\right)\text{ litres}$$

Now, when 9 litres of liquid Q are added,

$$\left(7x-\frac{21}{4}\right):\left(5x-\frac{15}{4}+9\right) = 7:9$$

$$\Rightarrow \frac{7x-\frac{21}{4}}{5x-\frac{15}{4}+9} = \frac{7}{9}$$

$$\Rightarrow 63x-\frac{189}{4} = 35x+\frac{147}{4}$$

$$\Rightarrow 28x = \frac{189}{4}+\frac{147}{4} = \frac{336}{4} = 84$$

$$\Rightarrow x = \frac{84}{28} = 3 \Rightarrow 7x = 7\times3 = 21 \text{ litres.}$$

12. P : Q : R

2 : 3 : 4

Spirit : Water = 1 : 5, 3 : 5 and 5 : 7

When they are mixed, the ratio of spirit to water

$$= \left(2\times\frac{1}{1+5}+3\times\frac{3}{3+5}+4\times\frac{5}{5+7}\right):\left(2\times\frac{5}{1+5}+3\times\frac{5}{3+5}+4\times\frac{7}{5+7}\right)$$

$$= \left(\frac{1}{3}+\frac{9}{8}+\frac{5}{3}\right):\left(\frac{5}{3}+\frac{15}{8}+\frac{7}{3}\right) = \frac{25}{8}:\frac{47}{8} = 25:47$$

13. Gold in C $= \left(\frac{7}{9}+\frac{7}{18}\right) = \frac{21}{18} = \frac{7}{6}$

Copper in C $= \left(\frac{2}{9}+\frac{11}{18}\right) = \frac{15}{18} = \frac{5}{6}$

$\therefore$ Gold : Copper $= \frac{7}{6}:\frac{5}{6} = 7:5$

14. Let 1 gm of gold be mixed with x gm of copper to give $(1+x)$ gm of mixture.

Now, $1G = 19w$

and $1C = 9w$

and mixture $= 15w$

Now, 1 gm gold + x gm copper = $(1+x)$ gm mixture

$\therefore 19w + 9w\times x = (1+x)\times 15w$

Thus, $4w = 6wx$

$$\Rightarrow x = \frac{4w}{6w} = \frac{4}{6} = \frac{2}{3}$$

So, the required ratio is $1:\frac{2}{3}$, *i.e.*, 3 : 2.

15.

	Water	***Milk***
Vessel I	$\frac{1}{3}$	$\frac{2}{3}$
Vessel II	$\frac{2}{7}$	$\frac{5}{7}$

From vessel I, $\frac{1}{5}$ is taken and from vessel II, $\frac{4}{5}$ is taken. Therefore, the ratio of water to milk in the new vessel

$$= \left(\frac{1}{3}\times\frac{1}{5}+\frac{2}{7}\times\frac{4}{5}\right):\left(\frac{2}{3}\times\frac{1}{5}+\frac{5}{7}\times\frac{4}{5}\right)$$

$$= \left(\frac{1}{15}+\frac{8}{35}\right):\left(\frac{2}{15}+\frac{20}{35}\right) = \frac{31}{105}:\frac{74}{105} = 31:74$$

16. The ratio of Mahesh's salary for the two years = 2 : 3

The ratio of Suresh's salary for the two years = 4 : 5

We have also given that the ratio of their salary during the last year = 3 : 5

Now, we change the antecedents (2 and 4) of the first two ratios so that the antecedents in the first becomes 3 (antecedent of the third ratio) and the antecedent in the second becomes 5 (consequent of the third ratio).

Thus, $2:3 = 3:\frac{9}{2}$ and $4:5 = 4\left(\frac{5}{4}\right):5\left(\frac{5}{4}\right) = 5:\frac{25}{4}$

Now, it is clear that the ratio of their salaries for the present year is $\frac{9}{2}:\frac{25}{4} = 18:25$

$\therefore$ The present salary of Mahesh

$$= \frac{4300}{18+25}\times18 = ₹\ 1800$$

17. The ratio of present incomes

$$= 3\times\frac{5}{4}:4\times\frac{3}{2} = \frac{15}{4}:\frac{12}{2} = 30:48 = 5:8$$

$\therefore$ P's present income $= \frac{4160}{5+8}\times5 = ₹\ 1600$

18. Let the monthly salary of A, B, C be $2x$, $3x$ and $5x$

Then, $5x - 2x = 1200$

or, $3x = 1200$

$\therefore$ $x = 400$

B's monthly salary $= 3x = 3\times400 = ₹\ 1200$

19. P : (Q + R) = 2 : 5

$\therefore$ P's share $= ₹\left(1050\times\frac{2}{7}\right) = ₹\ 300$

20. Let their ages be $2x$ and $3x$ years.

$\Rightarrow$ $3x - 2x = 6 \Rightarrow x = 6$

Sumit's age = 12 years

Prakash's age = 18 years

After 6 years, Sumit's age = 18 years and Prakash's age = 24 years

$\therefore$ Ratio of their ages = 18 : 24 = 3 : 4

●●●

4

Algebra

Square Roots

Points To Remember

- A number n is a perfect square number, if $n = m^2$
- A perfect square number is never negative.
- A square number never ends in 2, 3, 7 or 8.
- The number of zeros at the end of a perfect square is even.
- The square of an even number is even.
- The square of an odd number is odd.
- There are no natural number p and q such that $p^2 = 2q^2$.
- A number m is a square root of n, if $n = m \times m = m^2$. Positive square root of n is written as $\sqrt{n}$.
- If p and q are perfect squares $(q \neq 0)$, then

  (*i*) $\sqrt{p \times q} = \sqrt{p} \times \sqrt{q}$

  (*ii*) $\sqrt{\dfrac{p}{q}} = \dfrac{\sqrt{p}}{\sqrt{q}}$
- A perfect squares leaves remainder 0 or 1 on division by 3.

  The following table gives the possible remainders for some other prime divisors.

Divisor	Possible Remainders
3	0, 1
5	0, 1, 4
7	0, 1, 2, 4
11	0, 1, 3, 4, 5, 9
13	0, 1, 3, 4, 9, 10, 12

- The unit's digit of the square of a natural number is the unit's digit of the square of the digit at unit's place of the given natural number.

Unit's digit of the number	Unit's digit of the square of the number
0	0
1 or 9	1
2 or 8	4
3 or 7	9
4 or 6	6
5	5

- For every natural number n,

  $(n + 1)^2 - n^2 = (n + 1) + n$

  e.g., $9^2 - 8^2 = 9 + 8 = 17$

  $19^2 - 18^2 = 19 + 18 = 37$
- The square of a natural number n is equal to the sum of first n odd natural numbers.

  e.g., $2^2 = 1 + 3$

  $4^2 = 1 + 3 + 5 + 7 = 16$

  n^2 = Sum of first n odd natural numbers.
- A triplet (m, n, p) of three natural numbers m, n and p is called a pythagorean triplet if $m^2 + n^2 = p^2$
- The square root of a perfect square number can be obtained by :

  (*i*) the prime factorization. (*ii*) the division method.
- If n is not a perfect square, then $\sqrt{n}$ is not a rational number.
- Squares of natural numbers having all digits 1 have a following pattern:

  $1^2 = 1$

  $11^2 = 1\ \mathbf{2}\ 1$

  $111^2 = 1\ 2\ \mathbf{3}\ 2\ 1$

  $1111^2 = 1\ 2\ 3\ \mathbf{4}\ 3\ 2\ 1$

$11111^2 = 1\ 2\ 3\ 4\ \mathbf{5}\ 4\ 3\ 2\ 1$
$111111^2 = 1\ 2\ 3\ 4\ 5\ \mathbf{6}\ 5\ 4\ 3\ 2\ 1$
$\vdots \quad \vdots \quad \vdots$
$111111111^2 = 1\ 2\ 3\ 4\ 5\ 6\ 7\ 8\ \mathbf{9}\ 8\ 7\ 6\ 5\ 4\ 3\ 2\ 1$

In this pattern the sum of the digits of every number on the right hand side is a perfect square at given below:

$1 + 2 + 1 = 4 = 2^2$
$1 + 2 + 3 + 2 + 1 = 9 = 3^2$
$1 + 2 + 3 + 4 + 3 + 2 + 1 = 16 = 4^2$
. . . .
$1 + 2 + 3 + 4 + 5 + 6 + 7 + 8 + 9 + 8 + 7 + 6 + 5 + 4 + 3 + 2 + 1 = 81 = 9^2$.

- Observe the following pattern

$11^2 = 121$
$101^2 = 10201$
$1001^2 = 1002001$
$10001^2 = 100020001$

- Observe the following pattern

$11^2 = 121$
$101^2 = 10201$
$10101^2 = 102030201$
$1010101^2 = 1020304030201$
$101010101^2 = 10203040504030201$

- **Short Cut Method to find Squares Column Method**

Using $(a + b)^2 = a^2 + 2ab + b^2$.

Make three columns: What is square of 86

$a = 8, b = 6$

Step	Column I (a^2)	Column II $2ab$	Column III b^2
I	$(8)^2 = 64$	$2 \times 8 \times 6 = 96$	$(6)^2 = 36$
II	64	96 + 3 **99**	3**6**
III	64 + 9 **73**	96 + 3 **9**9	36

The bold digits give the required square $86^2 = 7396$.

Square Root

Square root of a given number is that number which is multiplied by itself is equal to the given number.
For example, square root of 81 is 9 because
92 = 9 × 9 = 81.

Methods of Finding the square root

(*a*) **Prime Factorization Method**

(*i*) Prime Factorization Method
(*ii*) Group the Factors in Paris
(*iii*) Take one number from each pair of factors and then multiply them together.

Example: Find the square root of 4761?

Solution: $4761 = \underbrace{23 \times 23} \times \underbrace{3 \times 3}$

$\therefore \quad \sqrt{4761} = 23 \times 3 = 69.$

(*b*) **Method of Division:** This method is used when the number is large and the factors cannot be easily determined.

Example: Find the square root of 226576?

Solution:

```
        476
   4  226516
      16
  87    665
   7    609
 946     5676
   6     5676
            ×
```

$\sqrt[2]{226576} = 476.$

EXERCISE

1. $\sqrt{53824} = ?$

A. 202 B. 232
C. 242 D. 332

2. The value of $\sqrt{10+\sqrt{25+\sqrt{108+\sqrt{154+\sqrt{255}}}}}$ is:

A. 4 B. 6
C. 8 D. 10

3. Evaluate : $\sqrt{41-\sqrt{21+\sqrt{19-\sqrt{9}}}}$.

A. 3 B. 5
C. 6 D. 6.4

4. $\left(\frac{\sqrt{625}}{11} \times \frac{14}{\sqrt{25}} \times \frac{11}{\sqrt{196}}\right)$ is equal to:

A. 5
B. 6
C. 8
D. 11

5. If $x * y = x + y + \sqrt{xy}$, the value of 6*24 is:

A. 41 B. 42
C. 43 D. 44

6. $\sqrt{\frac{25}{81}-\frac{1}{9}} = ?$

A. $\frac{2}{3}$ B. $\frac{4}{9}$
C. $\frac{16}{81}$ D. $\frac{25}{81}$

7. The value of $\sqrt{0.01}+\sqrt{0.81}+\sqrt{1.21}+\sqrt{0.0009}$ is:
A. 2.03 B. 2.1
C. 2.11 D. 2.13

8. If $\sqrt{18225}$ = 135, then the value of

$\left(\sqrt{182.25}+\sqrt{1.8225}+\sqrt{0.018225}+\sqrt{0.00018225}\right)$ is:
A. 1.49985 B. 14.9985
C. 149.985 D. 1499.85

9. If $\sqrt{3^n}$ = 729, then the value of n is:
A. 6 B. 8
C. 10 D. 12

10. If $\sqrt{1+\frac{x}{169}}=\frac{14}{13}$, then x is equal to:
A. 1 B. 13
C. 27 D. None of these

11. If $\sqrt{1+\frac{55}{729}}=1+\frac{x}{27}$, then the value of x is:
A. 1 B. 3
C. 5 D. 7

12. The value of $\frac{\sqrt{80}-\sqrt{112}}{\sqrt{45}-\sqrt{63}}$ is:

A. $\frac{3}{4}$ B. $1\frac{1}{3}$
C. $1\frac{7}{9}$ D. $1\frac{3}{4}$

13. Given $\sqrt{2}=1.414$. The value of

$\sqrt{8}+2\sqrt{32}-3\sqrt{128}+4\sqrt{50}$ is:
A. 8.426 B. 8.484
C. 8.526 D. 8.876

14. $\sqrt{\frac{0.081\times 0.324\times 4.624}{1.5625\times 0.0289\times 72.9\times 64}}$ is equal to:
A. 0.024 B. 0.24
C. 2.4 D. 24

15. The value of $\sqrt{\frac{(0.03)^2+(0.21)^2+(0.065)^2}{(0.003)^2+(0.021)^2+(0.0065)^2}}$ is:
A. 0.1 B. 10
C. 10^2 D. 10^3

16. The square root of $\left(7+3\sqrt{5}\right)\left(7-3\sqrt{5}\right)$ is:
A. $\sqrt{5}$ B. 2
C. 4 D. $3\sqrt{5}$

17. $\left(\sqrt{3}-\frac{1}{\sqrt{3}}\right)^2$ simplifies to:

A. $\frac{3}{4}$ B. $\frac{4}{\sqrt{3}}$
C. $\frac{4}{3}$ D. None of these

18. $\left(\sqrt{2}+\frac{1}{\sqrt{2}}\right)^2$ is equal to :

A. $2\frac{1}{2}$ B. $3\frac{1}{2}$
C. $4\frac{1}{2}$ D. $5\frac{1}{2}$

19. If $3a = 4b = 6c$ and $a + b + c = 27\sqrt{29}$, then $\sqrt{a^2+b^2+c^2}$ is:
A. $3\sqrt{29}$
B. 81
C. 87
D. None of these

20. The square root of $0.\overline{4}$ is:
A. $0.\overline{6}$ B. $0.\overline{7}$
C. $0.\overline{8}$ D. $0.\overline{9}$

ANSWERS

1	2	3	4	5	6	7	8	9	10
B	A	C	A	B	B	D	B	D	C
11	**12**	**13**	**14**	**15**	**16**	**17**	**18**	**19**	**20**
A	B	B	A	B	B	C	C	C	A

EXPLANATORY ANSWERS

1.

```
    2 | 53824 (232
      | 4
   43 | 138
      | 129
  462 |  924
      |  924
      |   ×
```

$\therefore \sqrt{53824} = 232.$

2. Given exp. = $\sqrt{10+\sqrt{25+\sqrt{108+\sqrt{154+15}}}}$

$= \sqrt{10+\sqrt{25+\sqrt{108+\sqrt{169}}}}$

$= \sqrt{10+\sqrt{25+\sqrt{108+13}}} = \sqrt{10+\sqrt{25+\sqrt{121}}}$

$= \sqrt{10+\sqrt{25+11}} = \sqrt{10+\sqrt{36}}$

$= \sqrt{10+6} = \sqrt{16} = 4$

3. Given exp. = $\sqrt{41-\sqrt{21+\sqrt{19-3}}}$

$= \sqrt{41-\sqrt{21+\sqrt{16}}} = \sqrt{41-\sqrt{21+4}}$

$= \sqrt{41-\sqrt{25}} = \sqrt{41-5} = \sqrt{36} = 6$

4. Given exp. = $\frac{25}{11}\times\frac{14}{5}\times\frac{11}{14} = 5$

5. $6*24 = 6 + 24 + \sqrt{6\times 24} = 30+\sqrt{144} = 30+12 = 42$

6. $\sqrt{\frac{25}{81}-\frac{1}{9}} = \sqrt{\frac{25-9}{81}} = \sqrt{\frac{16}{81}} = \frac{\sqrt{16}}{\sqrt{81}} = \frac{4}{9}$

7. Given exp.

$= \sqrt{\frac{1}{100}}+\sqrt{\frac{81}{100}}+\sqrt{\frac{121}{100}}+\sqrt{\frac{9}{10000}}$

$= \frac{1}{10}+\frac{9}{10}+\frac{11}{10}+\frac{3}{100}$

$= 0.1 + 0.9 + 1.1 + 0.03 = 2.13$

8. Given exp.

$= \sqrt{\frac{18225}{10^2}}+\sqrt{\frac{18225}{10^4}}+\sqrt{\frac{18225}{10^6}}+\sqrt{\frac{18225}{10^8}}$

$= \frac{\sqrt{18225}}{10}+\frac{\sqrt{18225}}{10^2}+\frac{\sqrt{18225}}{10^3}+\frac{\sqrt{18225}}{10^4}$

$= \frac{135}{10}+\frac{135}{100}+\frac{135}{1000}+\frac{135}{10000}$

$= 13.5 + 1.35 + 0.135 + 0.0135 = 14.9985$

9. $\sqrt{3^n} = 729 = 3^6$

$\Leftrightarrow \left(\sqrt{3^n}\right)^2 = (3^6)^2$

$\Leftrightarrow 3^n = 3^{12}$

$\Leftrightarrow n = 12$

10. $\sqrt{1+\frac{x}{169}} = \frac{14}{13} \Rightarrow 1+\frac{x}{169} = \frac{196}{169}$

$\Rightarrow \frac{x}{169} = \left(\frac{196}{169}-1\right) = \frac{27}{169}$

$\Rightarrow x = 27.$

11. $\sqrt{1+\frac{55}{729}} = 1+\frac{x}{27}$

$\Rightarrow \sqrt{\frac{784}{729}} = \frac{27+x}{27}$

$\Rightarrow \frac{28}{27} = \frac{27+x}{27}$

$\Rightarrow 27 + x = 28 \Rightarrow x = 1$

12. $\frac{\sqrt{80}-\sqrt{112}}{\sqrt{45}-\sqrt{63}} = \frac{\sqrt{16\times 5}-\sqrt{16\times 7}}{\sqrt{9\times 5}-\sqrt{9\times 7}}$

$= \frac{4\sqrt{5}-4\sqrt{7}}{3\sqrt{5}-3\sqrt{7}} = \frac{4\left(\sqrt{5}-\sqrt{7}\right)}{3\left(\sqrt{5}-\sqrt{7}\right)} = \frac{4}{3} = 1\frac{1}{3}$

13. Given exp.

$= \sqrt{4\times 2}+2\sqrt{16\times 2}-3\sqrt{64\times 2}+4\sqrt{25\times 2}$

$= 2\sqrt{2}+8\sqrt{2}-24\sqrt{2}+20\sqrt{2}$

$= 6\sqrt{2} = 6 \times 1.414 = 8.484$

14. Given exp. = $\sqrt{\frac{81\times 324\times 4624}{15625\times 289\times 729\times 64}}$

$= \frac{9\times 18\times 68}{125\times 17\times 27\times 8} = \frac{3}{125} = 0.024$

15. Given exp. = $\sqrt{\frac{(0.03)^2+(0.21)^2+(0.065)^2}{\left(\frac{0.03}{10}\right)^2+\left(\frac{0.21}{10}\right)^2+\left(\frac{0.065}{10}\right)^2}}$

$= \sqrt{\frac{100\ [(0.03)^2+(0.21)^2+(0.065)^2}{(0.03)^2+(0.21)^2+(0.065)^2}}$

$= \sqrt{100} = 10$

16. $\sqrt{(7+3\sqrt{5})(7-3\sqrt{5})} = \sqrt{(7)^2-(3\sqrt{5})^2}$

$= \sqrt{49-45} = \sqrt{4} = 2$

17. $\left(\sqrt{3}-\frac{1}{\sqrt{3}}\right)^2 = \left(\sqrt{3}\right)^2 + \left(\frac{1}{\sqrt{3}}\right)^2 - 2\times\sqrt{3}\times\frac{1}{\sqrt{3}}$

$= 3+\frac{1}{3}-2 = 1+\frac{1}{3} = \frac{4}{3}$

18. $\left(\sqrt{2}+\frac{1}{\sqrt{2}}\right)^2 = \left(\sqrt{2}\right)^2 + \left(\frac{1}{\sqrt{2}}\right)^2 + 2\times\sqrt{2}\times\frac{1}{\sqrt{2}}$

$= 2+\frac{1}{2}+2 = 4+\frac{1}{2} = 4\frac{1}{2}$

19. $4b = 6c \Rightarrow b = \frac{3}{2}c$ and $3a = 4b$

$\Rightarrow \quad a = \frac{4}{3}b = \frac{4}{3}\left(\frac{3}{2}c\right) = 2c$

$a + b + c = 27\sqrt{29}$

$2c+\frac{3}{2}c+c = 27\sqrt{29}$

$\Rightarrow \quad \frac{9}{2}c = 27\sqrt{29}$

$\Rightarrow \quad c = 6\sqrt{29}$

$\therefore \sqrt{a^2+b^2+c^2}$

$= \sqrt{(a+b+c)-2(ab+bc+ca)}$

$= \sqrt{\left(27\sqrt{29}\right)^2 - 2\left(2c\times\frac{3}{2}c+\frac{3}{2}c\times c+c\times 2c\right)}$

$= \sqrt{(729\times 29)-2\left(3c^2+\frac{3}{2}c^2+2c^2\right)}$

$= \sqrt{(729\times 29)-2\times\frac{13}{2}c^2}$

$= \sqrt{(729\times 29)-13\times\left(6\sqrt{29}\right)^2}$

$= \sqrt{29(729-468)}$

$= \sqrt{29\times 261} = \sqrt{29\times 29\times 9}$

$= 29 \times 3 = 87$

20. $\sqrt{0.\bar{4}} = \sqrt{\frac{4}{9}} = \frac{2}{3} = 0.666.... = 0.\bar{6}$.

Basic Algebraic Identities of School Algebra & Elementary Surds

Algebric Identies

Some Important Formula

(*i*) $(a + b)^2 = a^2 + 2ab + b^2$

(*ii*) $(a - b)^2 = a^2 - 2ab + b^2$

(*iii*) $a^2 - b^2 = (a - b)(a + b)$

(*iv*) $(a + b + c)^2 = a^2 + b^2 + c^2 + 2ab + 2bc + 2ca$

(*v*) $(a + b - c)^2 = a^2 + b^2 + c^2 + 2ab - 2bc - 2ca$

(*vi*) $(a - b + c)^2 = a^2 + b^2 + c^2 - 2ab - 2bc + 2ca$

(*vii*) $(-a + b + c)^2 = a^2 + b^2 + c^2 - 2ab + 2bc - 2ca$

(*viii*) $(a + b)^3 = a^3 + b^3 + 3ab(a + b)$ or

$= a^3 + b^3 + 3a^2b + 3ab^2$

(*ix*) $(a - b)^3 = a^3 - b^3 - 3ab\ (a - b)$ or

$= a^3 - b^3 - 3a^2b + 3ab^2$

(*x*) $a^3 + b^3 = (a + b)\ (a^2 + b^2 - ab)$ or

$= (a + b)^3 - 3ab(a + b)$

(*xi*) $a^3 - b^3 = (a - b)\ (a^2 + b^2 + ab)$ or

$= (a - b)^3 + 3ab\ (a - b)$

(*xii*) $a^3 + b^3 + c^3 - 3abc$

$= (a + b + c)(a^2 + b^2 + c^2 - ab - bc - ca)$

If $a + b + c = 0$

$a^3 + b^3 + c^3 = 3abc$

(*xiii*) $(x + a)\ (x + b) = x^2 + (a + b)x + ab$

(*xiv*) $(a + b)^2 + (a - b)^2 = 2(a^2 + b^2)$

(*xv*) $(a + b)^2 - (a - b)^2 = 4ab$

(*xvi*) $(a + b)^3 + (a - b)^3 = 2(a^3 + 3ab^2)$

(*xvii*) $(a + b)^3 - (a - b)^3 = (2(b^3 + 3a^2b)$

(*xviii*) If $x+\frac{1}{x}=t$ Then, $x^2+\frac{1}{x^2}=t^2-2$

(*xix*) If $x-\frac{1}{x}=t$ Then, $x^2+\frac{1}{x^2}=t^2+2$

(*xx*) $x^3+\frac{1}{x^3}=\left(x+\frac{1}{x}\right)^3-3\left(x+\frac{1}{x}\right)$

(*xxi*) $x^2-\frac{1}{x^3}=\left(x-\frac{1}{x}\right)^3+3\left(x-\frac{1}{x}\right)$

(*xxii*) $x+\frac{1}{x}=\sqrt{x^2+\frac{1}{x^2}+2}$

(*xxiii*) $x-\frac{1}{x}=\sqrt{x^2+\frac{1}{x^2}-2}$

Factorization of Algebraic Expressions

Factorization : The process of writing an algebraic expression as the product of two or more algebraic expressions is called factorization.

Factors : The algebraic expressions that may be multiplied to obtain the given algebraic expressions are called factors of the given expression.

Factor Theorem : If $f(x)$ is completely divisible by $(x - a)$ then $f(a) = 0$, $(x - a)$ is called factor of $f(x)$, if and only if $f(a) = 0$

Remainder Theorem : If an expression $f(x)$ is divided by $(x - a)$ then the remainder is $f(a)$.

e.g., $f(x) = ax^3 + bx + cx + d$

$f(a) = a \cdot a^3 + b \cdot a + c \cdot a + d$ is known as remainder of the given polynomials.

Surds

Given a number, it is not always possible to find some whole number which when multiplied by itself will give the given number. In other words all given numbers are not perfect square numbers. For example, square root of 9, *i.e.*, $\sqrt{9}$ is 3, which is a whole number. But square root of 15, *i.e.*, $\sqrt{15}$ = 3.873, which is not a whole number.

Hence square roots of natural numbers which are not perfect squares are not rational numbers. These are irrational numbers and are called **Surds**.

For example, $\sqrt{3}$, $\sqrt{7}$, $2+\sqrt{11}$, $4+\sqrt{13}$ ..... etc. are Surds.

Given below are a few formulas which are quite helpful in solving the problems related to surds:

1. $\sqrt{a} \times \sqrt{a} = a$
2. $\sqrt{a} \times \sqrt{b} = \sqrt{ab}$
3. $\left(\sqrt{a} + \sqrt{b}\right)^2 = a + b + \sqrt[2]{ab}$
4. $\left(\sqrt{a} - \sqrt{b}\right)^2 = a + b - \sqrt[2]{ab}$
5. $x\sqrt{a} + x\sqrt{b} = x\left(\sqrt{a} + \sqrt{b}\right)$
6. $\dfrac{1}{\sqrt{a}+\sqrt{b}} = \dfrac{1}{\sqrt{a}+\sqrt{b}} \times \dfrac{\sqrt{a}-\sqrt{b}}{\sqrt{a}-\sqrt{b}} = \dfrac{\sqrt{a}-\sqrt{b}}{a-b}$
7. $\dfrac{1}{\sqrt{a}-\sqrt{b}} = \dfrac{1}{\sqrt{a}-\sqrt{b}} \times \dfrac{\sqrt{a}+\sqrt{b}}{\sqrt{a}+\sqrt{b}} = \dfrac{\sqrt{a}+\sqrt{b}}{a-b}$
8. $a + \sqrt{b} = c + \sqrt{d} \Rightarrow a = c$ and $b = d$
9. $\sqrt{2} = 1.41421$, $\sqrt{3} = 1.73205$, $\sqrt{5} = 2.23607$,

   $\sqrt{6} = 2.4494$ $\sqrt{7} = 2.64575$, $\sqrt{8} = 2.82842$,

   $\sqrt{10} = 3.16227$, $\sqrt{11} = 3.31662$

EXERCISE

1. $(28)^3 + (-15)^3 + (-13)^3 = ?$

A. 16380 B. 16250
C. 16420 D. 16280

2. If $x + \dfrac{1}{x} = 5$, What is the value of $x^3 + \dfrac{1}{x^3}$:

A. 120 B. 210
C. 110 D. 105

3. If $x^2 + \dfrac{1}{x^2} = 83$, what is the value of $x^3 - \dfrac{1}{x^3} = ?$

A. 756 B. 754
C. 856 D. 932

4. $23^3 - 17^3 = ?$

A. 7254 B. 7153
C. 7271 D. 7154

5. If $x + \dfrac{1}{x} = 15$, then the value of $x^2 + \dfrac{1}{x^2}$ will be:

A. 228 B. 230
C. 323 D. 223

6. If $x = 12$ and $y = 4$, the value of $(x + y)^{x/y}$ will be:

A. 4096 B. 3896
C. 4196 D. 5086

7. If $x + y = 2z$, then the value of $\left(\dfrac{x}{x-z} + \dfrac{z}{y-z}\right)$ will be:

A. 1 B. 4
C. 3/2 D. 2

8. If $x + y + z = 0$, then the value of $\dfrac{(x+y)(y+z)(z+x)}{xyz}$ will be:

A. –3 B. –2
C. 0 D. –1

9. If $x + \dfrac{1}{x} = 3$, the value of $x^4 + \dfrac{1}{x^4}$ will be:

A. 49 B. 47
C. 37 D. 42

10. If $\left(x + \dfrac{1}{x}\right)^2 = 0$, then the value of $\left(x^2 + \dfrac{1}{x^2}\right)$ will be:

A. 1 B. –1
C. 2 D. –2

11. If $\left(a + \dfrac{2}{a}\right) = 3$, then the value of $\left(a - \dfrac{2}{a}\right)$ will be:

A. ± 4 B. ± 5
C. ± 2 D. ± 1

12. If $\sqrt{a}+\frac{1}{\sqrt{a}} = 4$, then the value of $a^2 + \frac{1}{a^2}$ will be:

A. 194 B. 199
C. 178 D. 192

13. Factors of $x^2 - 25$ are:

A. $(x - 1)(x - 25)$
B. $(x + 25)(x - 1)$
C. $(x + 5)(x - 5)$
D. $(x - 5)(x - 5)$

14. Square of $\left(x-\frac{1}{x}\right)$ will be

A. $x^2 - 2 - \frac{1}{x^2}$ B. $x^2 - 2 + \frac{1}{x^2}$
C. $x^2 - 4 - \frac{1}{x^2}$ D. $x^2 - 2 + \frac{1}{x}$

15. Factors of $36 - 9x^2$ will be:

A. $(6 + 3x)(6 - 3x)$ B. $(3x - 6)(6 - 3x)$
C. $(3x + 6)(3x - 6)$ D. $(12x - 3x)(3 + 3x)$

ANSWERS

1	2	3	4	5	6	7	8	9	10
A	C	A	A	D	A	A	D	B	D
11	12	13	14	15					
D	A	C	B	A					

EXPLANATORY ANSWERS

1. Let $a = 28$, $b = -15$ and $c = -13$. Then

$$a + b + c = 28 - 15 - 13 = 0$$
$$a^3 + b^3 + c^3 = 3abc$$
$$(28)^3 + (-15)^3 + (-13)^3 = 3 \times 28 \times (-15) \times (-13) = 16380$$

2. $$x^3+\frac{1}{x^3} = \left(x+\frac{1}{x}\right)^3 - 3\left(x+\frac{1}{x}\right)$$
$$= (5)^3 - 3 \times 5 = 125 - 15 = 110.$$

3. If $x^2+\frac{1}{x^2} = 83$, what is the value of $x^3-\frac{1}{x^3} = ?$

$$\left(x-\frac{1}{x}\right)^2 = x^2+\frac{1}{x^2}-2$$
$$x-\frac{1}{x} = \sqrt{83-2} = \sqrt{81}$$
$$x-\frac{1}{x} = 9$$
$$\therefore \quad \left(x^3-\frac{1}{x^3}\right) = \left(x-\frac{1}{x}\right)^3 + 3\left(x-\frac{1}{x}\right)$$
$$= (9)^3 + 3 \times 9 = 729 + 27 = 756$$

4. $23^3 - 17^3 = (20 + 3)^3 - (20 - 3)^3 = 2(3^3 + 3 \times 20^2 \times 3)$

$$[\because (a + b)^3 - (a - b)^3 = 2(b^3 + 3a^2b)]$$
$$= 2(27 + 3600) = 54 + 7200 = 7254$$

5. $\because x+\frac{1}{x} = 15 \Rightarrow \left(x+\frac{1}{x}\right)^2 = (15)^2$

$$\Rightarrow x^2+\frac{1}{x^2}+2.x\frac{1}{x} = 225$$
$$\therefore \quad x^2+\frac{1}{x^2} = 225 - 2 = 223.$$

6. $(x+y)^{x/y} = (12+4)^{12/4} = (16)^3 = 4096.$

$[\because x = 12, y = 4]$

7. $\because x + y = 2z \Rightarrow x - z = z - y = -(y - z)$

$$\therefore \quad \frac{x}{x-z}+\frac{z}{y-z} = \frac{x}{-(y-z)}+\frac{z}{y-z} = \frac{z-x}{y-z} = 1.$$
$$[\because x - z = z - y]$$

8. $\because$ $x + y + z = 0 \Rightarrow x + y = -z$

$x + y + z = 0 \Rightarrow y + z = -x$

and $x + y + z = 0 \Rightarrow z + x = -y$

$$\therefore \quad \frac{(x+y)(y+z)(z+x)}{xyz} = \frac{(-z)(-x)(-y)}{xyz} = -1.$$

9. $\because x+\frac{1}{x} = 3 \Rightarrow \left(x+\frac{1}{x}\right)^2 = (3)^2$

$$\Rightarrow \quad x^2+\frac{1}{x^2}+2.x.\frac{1}{x} = 9$$
$$\Rightarrow \quad x^2+\frac{1}{x^2} = 9 - 2 = 7$$
$$\because \quad x^2+\frac{1}{x^2} = 7 \Rightarrow \left(x^2+\frac{1}{x^2}\right)^2 = (7)^2$$
$$\Rightarrow \quad x^4+\frac{1}{x^4}+2.x^2.\frac{1}{x^2} = 49$$
$$\therefore \quad x^4+\frac{1}{x^4} = 49 - 2 = 47.$$

10. $$\left(x+\frac{1}{x}\right)^2 = 0 \Rightarrow x^2+\frac{1}{x^2}+2x.\frac{1}{x} = 0$$
$$\Rightarrow \quad x^2+\frac{1}{x^2} = -2.$$

11. $\because \left(a-\frac{2}{a}\right)^2 = \left(a+\frac{2}{a}\right)^2 - 4.a.\frac{2}{a} = (3)^2 - 8 = 9 - 8 = 1$

$\therefore \left(a-\frac{2}{a}\right) = \pm\sqrt{1} = \pm 1.$

12. $\because \sqrt{a}+\frac{1}{\sqrt{a}} = 4 \Rightarrow \left(\sqrt{a}+\frac{1}{\sqrt{a}}\right)^2 = (4)^2$

$\Rightarrow a+\frac{1}{a}+2.\sqrt{a}.\frac{1}{\sqrt{a}} = 16 \therefore \left(a+\frac{1}{a}\right) = 14$

$\Rightarrow \left(a+\frac{1}{a}\right)^2 = (14)^2 \Rightarrow a^2+\frac{1}{a^2}+2.a.\frac{1}{a} = 196$

$\therefore a^2+\frac{1}{a^2} = 196-2 = 194.$

13. $x^2 - 25 = (x)^2 - (5)^2$, [which is of the form $a^2 - b^2$]

$= (x+5)(x-5).$

14. According to question:

Square of $\left(x-\frac{1}{x}\right) = \left(x-\frac{1}{x}\right)^2$

$= x^2 - 2.x.\frac{1}{x} + \left(\frac{1}{x}\right)^2$

$= x^2 - 2 + \frac{1}{x^2}.$

15. $36 - 9x^2 = (6)^2 - (3x)^2$ [which is of the form $a^2 - b^2$]

$= (6+3x)(6-3x).$

Graphs of Linear Equations

Linear Equation in One Variable

Definition: A linear equation in one variable is an equation of the form $ax + b = 0$ or, $ax = c$ where, a, b, c are real numbers, $a \neq 0$ and x is a variable. Its graph is a straight line.

(*i*) If equation is on X-axis, then Y = 0

(*ii*) If equation is on Y-axis, then X = 0

Linear Equation in Two Variables

Definition: An equation of the form $ax + by + c = 0$ or, $ax + by = c$ where, a, b, c are real numbers, $a \neq 0$, $b \neq 0$ and x, y are variables, is called a linear equation in two variables.

For example: (*i*) $2x + 3y = 12$ (*ii*) $x + 2y = 8$

The System of Equations

$a_1x + b_1y + c_1 = 0$ and $a_2x + b_2y + c_2 = 0$ may be either unique solution or no solution or infinitely many solutions.

Unique solution is known as consistent or not parallel. No solution is known as inconsistent or parallel, while many solutions are known as coincident or dependent.

(*a*) **For unique solution:** $\frac{a_1}{a_2} \neq \frac{b_1}{b_2}$

(*b*) **For no solution:** $\frac{a_1}{a_2} = \frac{b_1}{b_2} \neq \frac{c_1}{c_2}$

(*c*) **For many solutions:** $\frac{a_1}{a_2} = \frac{b_1}{b_2} = \frac{c_1}{c_2}$

Graph of linear equations

Graph of a linear equation in two variables x and y *i.e.*, the graph of the equation of the form

$ax + by + c = 0, a \neq 0, b \neq 0$

we consider the equation,

$2x + y = 6$

then, $y = 6 - 2x$

We find different values of this equation

x	0	1	2	3
y	6	4	2	0

Now, we plot these points (x, y) on a graph paper and then join these points

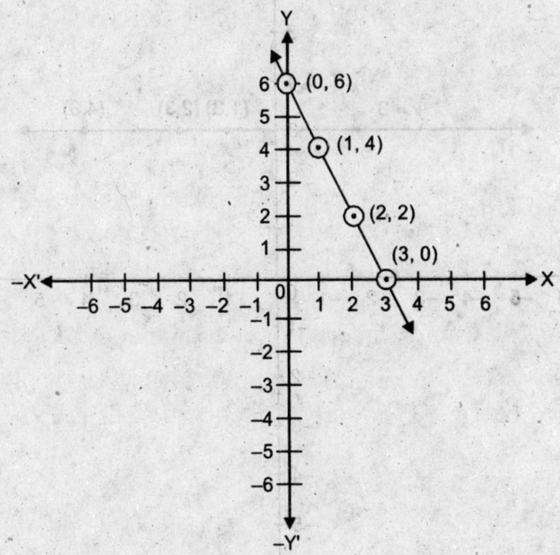

Hence, the line l is called the graph of the equation

$2x + y = 6$

Example 1: Draw the graph:

(*i*) $x = 2$, (*ii*) $y = 3$, (*iii*) $y = 0$

Solution: (*i*) The given equation, $x = 2$ does not contain y

Table of values

x	2	2	2	fixed
y	1	3	4	any value

ploting the points (2, 1), (2, 3) and (2, 4) and joining them

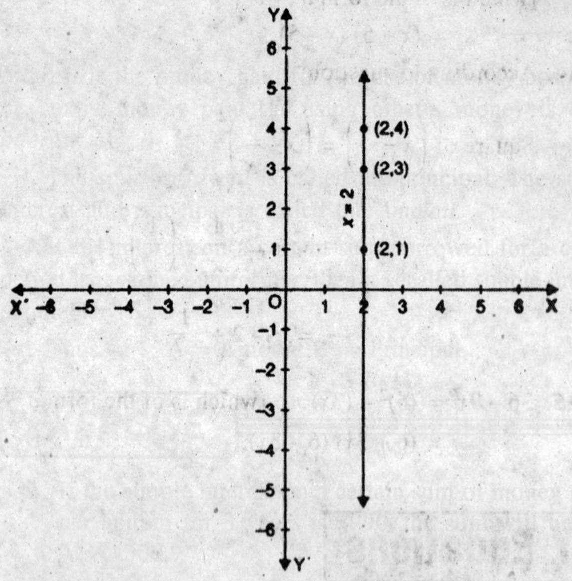

Hence, the graph of the given equation is a line parallel to y-axis

(*ii*) The given equation $y = 3$ does not contain x

Table of values

x	1	2	4	any value
y	3	3	3	fixed

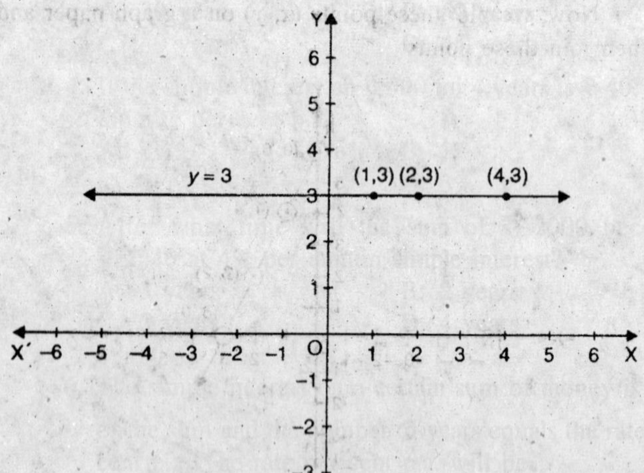

Hence, the graph of the given equation is a line parallel to x-axis.

(*iii*) The given equation is $y = 0$

Table of values

x	1	2	3	any value
y	0	0	0	fixed

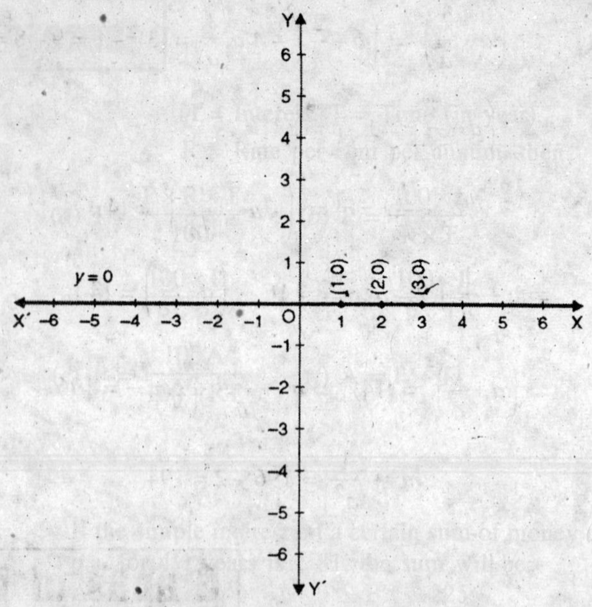

Hence, $y = 0$ is the equation of x-axis.

Example 2. Draw the graph of the line $x - 2y = 3$. From the graph find co-ordinates of the points when (*i*) $x = -5$, (*ii*) $y = 0$

Solution: The given equation is $x - 2y = 3$

Table of value

x	3	5	1
y	0	1	–1

$\because \quad 2y = x - 3$

$\therefore \quad y = \dfrac{x-3}{2}$

Plotting the points (3, 0), (5, 1) and (1, –1) on the graph paper and joining these points.

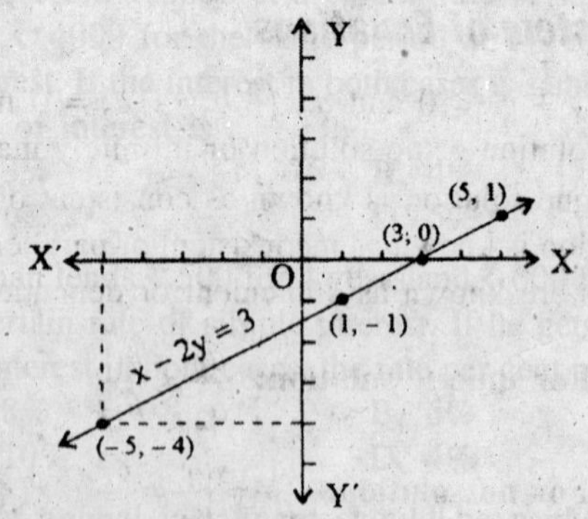

From the graph,

(*i*) when $x = -5$, then $y = -4$

(*ii*) when $y = 0$, then $x = 3$

Example 3. Draw the graph of the equations

$$5x + 3y = 4.$$

Solution: The given equation is $5x + 3y = 4$

$\Rightarrow \quad y = \dfrac{4-5x}{3}$

Table of values

x	–1	2	5
y	3	–2	–7

Plot the points (–1, 3), (2, –2) and (5, –7) on the graph paper and join these points.

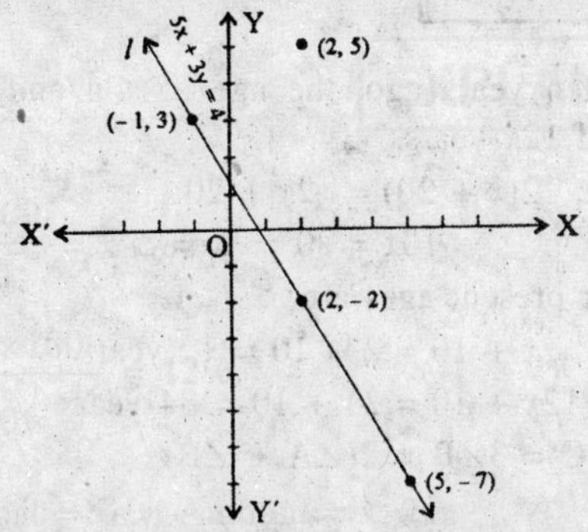

Hence, the line l is called the graph of the equation,

$$5x + 3y = 4$$

Example 4. Draw the graph of the equation

$$2x - 3y = -11.$$

Solution: The given equation is

$$2x - 3y = -11$$

$$\Rightarrow \quad 3y = 2x + 11$$

$$\Rightarrow \quad y = \frac{2x+11}{3}$$

Table of values

x	–1	2	–4
y	3	5	1

plot the points (–1, 3), (2, 5) and (–4, 1) on the graph paper and join these points

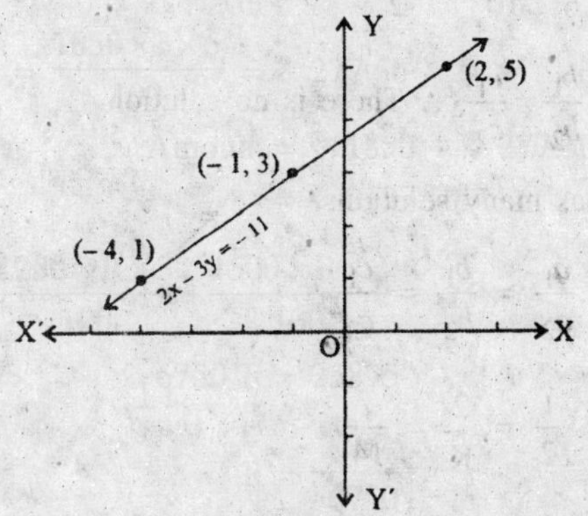

Hence, this line l is called the graph of the equation

$$2x - 3y = -11.$$

EXERCISE

1. The system of linear equations $2x + 3y = 7$ and $4x + 6y = 10$ has:

A. no solution
B. unique solution
C. infinite solution
D. no conclusion can be drawn

2. The value of k for which the system of equations $x + 2y + 7 = 0$ and $2x + ky + 14 = 0$ will have infinitely many solutions is:

A. 2 B. 4
C. 6 D. 8

3. For what value of α, the system of equations $\alpha x + 3y = \alpha - 3$ and $12x + \alpha y = \alpha$ will have a unique solution?

A. $\alpha \neq \pm 6$ B. $\alpha \neq \pm 3$
C. $\alpha \neq \mp 6$ D. None of these

4. For what value of k, the system of equations will represent the coincident lines $x + 5y - 7 = 0$ and $4x + 20y + k = 0$?

A. 28 B. –28
C. –26 D. None of these

5. A lady has 50 paise and ₹ 1 coins in her purse. If in all, she has 40 coins totally ₹ 25.50 how many of each type of coins does she have?

A. 26, 11 B. 11, 29
C. 29, 11 D. None of these

6. A father is three times as old as his son. After twelve years his age will be twice as the age of his son. Find their present ages in years.

A. 12, 26 B. 24, 36
C. 36, 12 D. None of these

7. Ten years ago, father was twelve times as old as his son. Ten years after, he will be twice as old as his son will be. Find their present ages in years.

A. 12, 36 B. 12, 24
C. 12, 34 D. None of these

8. The present age of a father is 3 years more than three times the age of son. Three years hence father's age will be 10 years more than twice the age of son. Determine their present ages in years.

A. 10, 33 B. 33, 10
C. 10, 30 D. None of these

9. In a triangle ABC, $\angle C = 3\angle B = 2(\angle A + \angle B)$. Find three angles in degrees.

A. 20°, 50°, 120° B. 30°, 40°, 120°
C. 20°, 40°, 120° D. None of these

10. The fraction becomes 2 when 1 is added to both the numerator and the denominator, and it becomes 3 when 1 is subtracted from both the numerator and denominator. The given fraction is :

A. 7/3 B. 4/7
C. 3/7 D. 7/4

ANSWERS

1	2	3	4	5	6	7	8	9	10
A	B	A	B	C	C	C	A	C	A

EXPLANATORY ANSWERS

1. $\frac{2}{4} = \frac{3}{6} \neq \frac{7}{10} \Rightarrow \frac{1}{2} = \frac{1}{2} \neq \frac{7}{10}$

$\frac{a_1}{a_2} = \frac{b_1}{b_2} \neq \frac{c_1}{c_2}$ $\therefore$ There is no solution.

2. Since, it has many solutions.

$\therefore \quad \frac{a_1}{a_2} = \frac{b_1}{b_2} = \frac{c_1}{c_2}$

$\frac{1}{2} = \frac{2}{K} = \frac{7}{14}$

$\frac{1}{2} = \frac{2}{K} \Rightarrow K = 4.$

3. Since, the given equations have unique solution.

$\therefore \quad \frac{a_1}{a_2} \neq \frac{b_1}{b_2}$

$\frac{\alpha}{12} \neq \frac{3}{\alpha}$

$\Rightarrow \quad \alpha^2 \neq 36 \Rightarrow \alpha \neq \pm 6$

4. Since, the given set of equations represent coincident lines.

then, $\frac{1}{4} = \frac{5}{20} = \frac{-7}{K} \Rightarrow K = -28$

5. Let, x be the number of 50 paise coins and y be the number of ₹ 1 coins.

According to the question,

$x + y = 40 \quad ...(i)$

and $\frac{x}{2} + y = 25.50$

$\Rightarrow \quad x + 2y = 51 \quad ...(ii)$

Subtracting equation (*i*) from (*ii*) and solving we get, $x = 29,\ y = 11$

6. Let, age of son = x years.

$\therefore$ age of father = $3x$ years.

According to the question,

$2(x + 12) = 3x + 12 \Rightarrow x = 12$

$\therefore$ Son's age = 12 years; Father's age = 36 years.

7. Let ten years ago, the age of son and father were x and $12x$ years.

Then, $2(x + 20) = 12x + 20$

$\Rightarrow \quad 10x = 20 \Rightarrow x = 2$

Their present ages are

$x + 10 = 2 + 10 = 12$ years

$12x + 10 = 24 + 10 = 34$ years.

9. $\therefore \angle C = 3\angle B = 2(\angle A + \angle B)$

$\angle A + \angle B = \frac{\angle C}{2}$

We have, $\angle A + \angle B + \angle C = 180°$

(Sum of angles of a triangle is 180°)

$\frac{\angle C}{2} + \angle C = 180°$

$3\angle C = 2 \times 180°$

$\angle C = \frac{2 \times 180°}{3} = 120°$

$3\angle B = \angle C$

$\angle B = \frac{\angle C}{3} = \frac{120°}{3} = 40°$

$\therefore \quad \angle A = 180° - (120° + 40°) = 180° - 160° = 20°.$

10. Let the fraction be $\frac{x}{y} \Rightarrow \frac{x+1}{y+1} = 2$

$\Rightarrow \quad x + 1 = 2y + 2$

$\Rightarrow \quad x - 2y = 1 \quad ...(i)$

Again $\frac{x-1}{y-1} = 3$

$\Rightarrow \quad x - 1 = 3y - 3$

$\Rightarrow \quad x - 3y = -2 \quad ...(ii)$

from (*i*) and (*ii*)

$x - 2y = 1$

$x - 3y = -2$

$- \quad + \quad +$

$y = 3$

Putting the value of y in (*i*) then we get, $x = 7$

$\therefore \quad \text{fraction} = \frac{x}{y} = \frac{7}{3}$

●●●

5

Average

The average of any number of quantities of the same kind can be found by dividing their sum by their number.

Thus,

$$\text{Average} = \frac{\text{Sum of quantities}}{\text{No. of quantities}}$$

Sum of quantities = Their average × Their number

$$\text{Number of quantities} = \frac{\text{Sum of quantities}}{\text{Their average}}$$

When a body coveres the same distance at two different speeds p km/hr and q km/hr, then its average speed for the whole journey is $\frac{2pq}{p+q}$ km/hr.

EXERCISE

1. The average of the fractions $1\frac{1}{2}$, $2\frac{1}{3}$, $3\frac{1}{3}$ and $4\frac{5}{6}$ is:

A. 2 B. $2\frac{1}{2}$
C. 3 D. 4

2. The average of first nine multiples of 3 is

A. 12.0 B. 12.5
C. 15.0 D. 18.5

3. The average of 13 numbers is 68, the average of first 7 numbers is 63 and the average of last 7 numbers is 70. What is the 7th number?

A. 43 B. 45
C. 47 D. 49

4. One-third of a certain journey was covered at the rate of 25 km per hour, one-fourth at the rate of 30 km per hour and the rest at the 50 km per hour. What is the average speed per hour for whole journey?

A. $33\frac{1}{3}$ kmph B. $44\frac{1}{4}$ kmph
C. $22\frac{1}{2}$ kmph D. 33 kmph

5. Nine men went to a hotel. Eight of them spent ₹ 3 for each over their meals and the ninth spent ₹ 2 more than the average expenditure of all the nine. What is the total money spent by them?

A. ₹ 29.25 B. ₹ 29.50
C. ₹ 29 D. ₹ 30

6. An establishment is permitted an average monthly contingency expenditure of ₹ 500 per month during the financial year. When a trial check was made at the end of the first nine months of the year it was found that the average monthly contingency expenditure worked out to be ₹ 511. What average monthly expenditure for the next three months should be aimed at in order to attain the permissible average of ₹ 500 per month for the whole year?

A. ₹ 567 B. ₹ 467
C. 367 D. ₹ 667

7. Average age of 8 persons increased by 2 years, when two men whose ages are 20 and 24 years are replaced by two women. What is the average age of women?

A. 30 years B. 31 years
C. 28 years D. 33 years

8. A man had seven children. When their average age was 12 years, the child who was 6 years of age died. What was the average of the surviving children 5 years after the death of the child?

A. 15 years B. 16 years
C. 17 years D. 18 years

9. The weight of a body, calculated as the average of seven different experiments is 53.735 grams. The average of the first three is 54.005 grams, the fourth was greater than the fifth by 0.004 gram, while the average of the sixth and seventh was 0.010 gram less than the average of the first three. What is the weight of the body as obtained by the fourth experiment?

A. 53.068 gm B. 53.078 gm
C. 53.086 gm D. 53.072 gm

10. A batsman has a certain average of runs for 16 innings. In the 17th innings, he makes a score of 85 runs thereby increasing his average by 3. What is the average after the 17th inning?

A. 33 runs B. 34 runs
C. 37 runs D. 36 runs

11. The average of 50 numbers is 38. If two numbers namely 45 and 55 are discarded, the average of the remaining numbers is

A. 36.5 B. 37
C. 37.5 D. 37.52

12. The average of 6 observations is 12. A new seventh observation is included and the new average is decreased by 1. The seventh observation is

A. 1 B. 3
C. 5 D. 6

13. A man whose bowling average is 12.4 takes 5 wickets for 26 runs and thereby decreases his average by 0.4. The number of wickets, taken by him, before his last match, is

A. 85 B. 78
C. 72 D. 64

14. The average of marks obtained by 120 candidates was 35. If the average of marks of passed candidates was 39 and that of failed candidates was 15, the number of candidates who passed the examination is

A. 100 B. 110
C. 120 D. 150

15. The average of three numbers is 42. The first is twice the second and the second is twice the third. The difference between the largest and the smallest number is

A. 18 B. 36
C. 54 D. 72

ANSWERS

1	2	3	4	5	6	7	8	9	10
C	C	C	A	A	B	A	D	D	C
11	**12**	**13**	**14**	**15**					
C	C	A	A	C					

EXPLANATORY ANSWERS

1. Average $= \frac{1}{4}\left(\frac{3}{2}+\frac{7}{3}+\frac{10}{3}+\frac{29}{6}\right)$

$= \left(\frac{9+14+20+29}{24}\right) = \frac{72}{24} = 3$

2. Average $= \frac{3(1+2+3+4+5+6+7+8+9)}{9} = \frac{135}{9}$

$= 15$

3. Average of 13 numbers = 68

$\therefore$ Total of 13 numbers = 13 × 68 = 884

Average of last 7 numbers = 70

$\therefore$ Total of last 7 numbers = 7 × 70 = 490

$\therefore$ Average of first 6 numbers

= 884 – 490 = 394

$\therefore$ Average of first 7 numbers = 63

$\therefore$ Total of first 7 numbers = 63 × 7 = 441

$\therefore$ 7th number = 441 – 394 = 47

4. Let the total distance covered during journey = 60 km

$\frac{1}{3}$ of the distance covered during journey

$= 60 \times \frac{1}{3} = 20$ km

$\frac{1}{4}$ of the distance covered during journey

$= \frac{1}{4} \times 60 = 15$ km

$\therefore$ The distance covered during the rest of journey = 60 – (20 + 15) = 25 km

Time taken to cover 20 km at 25 km/h

$= \frac{20}{25}$ hours $= \frac{4}{5}$ hour

Time taken to cover 15 km at 30 km/h

$= \frac{15}{30}$ hours $= \frac{1}{2}$ hour

Time taken to cover 25 km at 50 km/h

$= \frac{25}{50}$ hours $= \frac{1}{2}$ hour

Total time taken $= \frac{4}{5}+\frac{1}{2}+\frac{1}{2} = \frac{9}{5}$ hours

Hence average speed per hour

$= 60 \div \frac{9}{5} = \frac{60 \times 5}{9}$

$= \frac{100}{3}$ km/h $= 33\frac{1}{3}$ km/h

5. Let the average expenditure of all the nine

$= ₹\ x$

Now amount spent by eight

$= ₹\ 3 \times 8 = ₹\ 24$

and total spent by the ninth $= ₹\ x + 2$

$\Rightarrow \quad \frac{26 + x}{9} = x$

$\therefore$ Average amount spent by nine $= \frac{26 + x}{9}$

Total amount spent by nine $= 24 + x + 2 = 26 + x$

$\Rightarrow \quad 9x = 26 + x$

or, $\quad 8x = 26$

$\Rightarrow \quad x = \frac{26}{8} = ₹\ 3.25$

Hence total money spent

$= ₹\ (3.25 \times 9) = ₹\ 29.25$

6. Average monthly expenditure permitted = ₹ 500

Total expenditure permitted for 12 months

$= ₹\ 500 \times 12 = ₹\ 6000$

Expenditure incurred during the first nine months

$= ₹\ 511 \times 9 = ₹\ 4{,}599$

Expenditure for the last three month

$= ₹\ (6000 - 4599) = ₹\ 1{,}401$

$\therefore$ Average monthly expenditure for the three months

$= ₹\ \frac{1401}{3} = ₹\ 467$

7. Total increase in the age of 8 persons

$= 2 \times 8 = 16$ years

Total age of two men being replaced

$= 20 + 24 = 44$ years

Total of the age of two women $= 44 + 16 = 60$ years

$\Rightarrow$ The average age of women

$= \frac{60}{2} = 30$ years.

8. Average age of 7 children = 12 years

Total ages of 7 children $= 12 \times 7 = 84$ years

Age of 1 child who died = 6 years

Total ages of remaining 6 children

$= 84 - 6 = 78$ years

$\therefore$ Average age of 6 children $= \frac{78}{6} = 13$ years

$\therefore$ Average age of 6 children after 5 years

$= 13 + 5 = 18$ years

9. Total weight of 7 experiments

$= 53.735 \times 7 = 376.145$ gm

Total weight of first three

$= 54.005 \times 3 = 162.015$ gm

The average of the 6th and 7th was 0.010 gm less than that of the first three.

$\therefore$ Average of the 6th and 7th

$= 54.005 - 0.010 = 53.995$ gm

$\therefore$ Total of the 6th and 7th $= 53.995 \times 2 = 107.990$ gm

Thus, total of 4th and 5th

$= 376.145 - (162.015 + 107.990) = 106.140$ gm

The fourth was greater than the fifth by 0.004 gm

$\therefore \quad$ The fifth $= (106.140 - 0.004) \times \frac{1}{2} = \frac{106.136}{2}$

$= 53.068$ gm

Hence, the fourth $= 53.068 + 0.004$

$= 53.072$ gm

10. Average increase in the score of 17 innings

$= 3$ runs

Total increase in the score of 17 innings

$= 3 \times 17 = 51$ runs

$\therefore$ His average of 16 innings

$= 85 - 51 = 34$ runs

Hence, average after the 17th innings

$= 34 + 3 = 37$ runs

11. Total of 50 numbers $= 50 \times 38 = 1900$

Total of 48 numbers

$= 1900 - (45 + 55) = 1800$

$\therefore \quad$ Average $= \frac{1800}{48} = 37.5$

12. Seventh observation

$= (7 \times 11 - 6 \times 12) = 5$

13. Suppose the number of wickets taken before the last match $= x$

$\Rightarrow \quad \frac{12.4x + 26}{x + 5} = 12$

$\Rightarrow \quad 12.4x + 26 = 12x + 60$

$\Rightarrow \quad x = 85$

14. Let the number of candidates who passed $= x$

$\Rightarrow \quad 39 \times x + 15 \times (120 - x) = 120 \times 35$

$\Rightarrow \quad 24x = 4200 - 1800$

$\therefore \quad x = \frac{2400}{24} = 100$

15. Let the third number $= x$

Then, second number $= 2x$ and first number $= 4x$

$\therefore \quad \frac{x + 2x + 4x}{3} = 42$

$\Rightarrow \quad \frac{7x}{3} = 42 \Rightarrow x = \frac{42 \times 3}{7}$

$\Rightarrow \quad x = 18$

So, (largest) – (smallest) $= (4x - x) = 3x = 54$

●●●

6

Partnership Business

When two or more than two persons agree to invest money to run a business jointly, this association or deal is called *partnership* and those who invest money are called *pertners.* The total investment is called the *capital.*

Kind of partners : There are two kinds of partners.

1. **Working or active partner :** When a partner devotes his time for the business in addition to invest his money, he is called a working partner.

   With mutual agreement, the active partners get some fixed percentage of profit as *working allowance.*

2. **Sleeping or non-active partner :** A partner who simply invests money, but does not attend to the business is called a sleeping partner.

Kind of partnership :

(i) **Simple partnership :** If the capitals of several partners are invested for the same period, it is called a simple partnership.

(ii) **Compound or complex partnership :** If the capitals of the partners are invested for diffrent intervals of time, the partnership is called compound or complex.

EXERCISE

1. A and B started a business with the investment of ₹ 80000 and ₹ 60000 respectively. At the end of the year total profit in the business will be divided between them in the ratio of :

A. 2 : 3 B. 3 : 4
C. 2 : 1 D. 4 : 3

2. A and B started a business in partnership with the investment of ₹ 4000 and ₹ 6000 respectively. If at the end of the year total profit is ₹ 2250, what will each of them get?

A. ₹ 900, ₹ 1350
B. ₹ 800, ₹ 1450
C. ₹ 1000, ₹ 1250
D. ₹ 1200, ₹ 1050

3. Sonu, Monu and Mohit together start a business with the investment of ₹ 1800, ₹ 1500 and ₹ 1600 respectively. If at the end of the year, Monu gains a profit of ₹ 900 the total profit in the business is :

A. ₹ 2880 B. ₹ 2940
C. ₹ 3200 D. ₹ 3240

4. Omdutt started a business with a capital of ₹ 8000. After six months, Sanjay joined him with investment of some capital. If at the end of the year each of them gets equal amount as profit, how much did Sanjay invest in the business?

A. ₹ 18000 B. ₹ 17500
C. ₹ 16000 D. ₹ 16500

5. A, B and C buy a farm for ₹ 100000. A contributes ₹ 40000 in it. They sell it, and from the profit B gets ₹ 2750 and C gets ₹ 1750. What would be the profit of A?

A. ₹ 2780 B. ₹ 3000
C. ₹ 3280 D. ₹ 2785

6. A and B jointly invest ₹ 2100 and ₹ 3100 respectively in a firm. A is an active partner and hence he gets 25% of the profit separately. If their business yields them total ₹ 1040 as profit, what will be the gain of each of them?

A. ₹ 415, ₹ 625 B. ₹ 575, ₹ 465
C. ₹ 515, ₹ 525 D. ₹ 560, ₹ 480

7. Two partners invested ₹ 12500 and ₹ 8500 respectively in a business and decided that 60% of the profit incurred from the business will be equally divided between them while remaining profit will be assumed as interest on their capitals. If one of the partners gets ₹ 300 more profit than the other, what is the total profit in the business?

A. ₹ 3937.50 B. ₹ 4940.50
C. ₹ 3936.50 D. ₹ 4156

8. Neeraj and Birju are partners in a business. They divide between them the profit incurred in the business in such a proportion that $\frac{2}{5}$th portion of the profit gained by Neeraj is equal to $\frac{1}{3}$rd portion of the profit gained by Birju. If total profit in the business is ₹ 1210, find the profit earned by Birju.

A. ₹ 780 B. ₹ 660
C. ₹ 680 D. ₹ 590

9. A, B and C together took under lease a pasture ground for ₹ 888. If in this pasture ground A put his 20 sheep out to graze for 2½ months, B put his 30 sheep out to graze for 4 months and C put his 36 sheep out to graze for 3½ months, find the lease amount paid by each of them.

A. ₹ 205, ₹ 315, ₹ 378 B. ₹ 150, ₹ 360, ₹ 378
C. ₹ 170, ₹ 360, ₹ 358 D. ₹ 228, ₹ 360, ₹ 300

10. A, B and C started a business with the investment of ₹ 5000, ₹ 6000 and ₹ 4000 respectively. A is an active partner and therefore he gets 30% of the profit separately. Rest of the profit is divided in the ratio of their capitals. If at the end of year, A's profit is ₹ 200 more than the sum of the profits made by B and C, find the profit made by each of them.

A. ₹ 1620, ₹ 1242, ₹ 1178
B. ₹ 1720, ₹ 1252, ₹ 1228
C. ₹ 1510, ₹ 1187, ₹ 1133
D. ₹ 1600, ₹ 840, ₹ 560

11. Premchand, Nanak and Prabhat together rented a house for 2 years and settled to pay ₹ 1368 as rent. They lived together in this house for 5 months. Then Prabhat left the house and went away. 8 months after Nanak also went away and left the house for Premchand to live alone. How much did Premchand pay as rent of this house?

A. ₹ 1025 B. ₹ 950
C. ₹ 880 D. ₹ 780

12. A started a business with an investment of ₹ 4000. B joined him after 4 months and C joined him after 5 months. At the end of year they get profit in the ratio of 3 : 4 : 7. Find the ratio of capitals invested in the business by B and C.

A. 1 : 2 B. 2 : 1
C. 3 : 2 D. 1 : 3

13. Amit, Sumeet and Suresh started a business with capitals in the ratio of 2 : 3 : 4. Amit took back half of his investment after 3 months and Sumeet took back one-third portion of his investment after 4 months. If at the end of year, Suresh gets a profit of ₹ 3200, what is the total profit in the business?

A. ₹ $6076\frac{2}{3}$ B. ₹ $6066\frac{2}{3}$
C. ₹ 8000 D. ₹ $8333\frac{1}{3}$

14. A, B and C started a business in partnership. A invested ₹ 4000 for 8 months and ₹ 6000 for 4 months. B invested ₹ 3000 for 6 months and ₹ 5000 for next 6 months of the year while C invested ₹ 3000 for whole of the year. If at the end of year, total profit is ₹ 7000, what will be the shares of A, B and C in the profit?

A. ₹ 2800, ₹ 2400, ₹ 1800
B. ₹ 2500, ₹ 2600, ₹ 1900
C. ₹ 2600, ₹ 2500, ₹ 1900
D. ₹ 2000, ₹ 2700, ₹ 2300

15. A, B and C started a business in partnership with respective investment of ₹ 20000, ₹ 18000 and ₹ 12000. A and B are active partners and therefore they get an additional profit of 12% and 8% respectively for supervision and other related work they do for improvement of the trade. Rest of the profit is divided among them in the proportion of their capitals. If profit made by A is ₹ 648 more than B, find the profit earned by each of them.

A. ₹ 3960, ₹ 3312, ₹ 1728
B. ₹ 4960, ₹ 3312, ₹ 1728
C. ₹ 3690, ₹ 3132, ₹ 1820
D. ₹ 5960, ₹ 3600, ₹ 1750

16. Three labourers work for 5 hours, 6 hours and 7 hours respectively in a field and get wages in the proportion of time of working in the field. Three days after they increase their working hours by 1 hour. 4 days after they increase their working hours, work in the field gets finished. If their total wages is ₹ 276, find the share of wages earned by each of them.

A. ₹ 78, ₹ 92, ₹ 106 B. ₹ 88, ₹ 87, ₹ 101
C. ₹ 80, ₹ 90, ₹ 106 D. ₹ 81, ₹ 95, ₹ 100

17. A, B and C together took a pasture ground on rent at ₹ 16 per month with a view to graze their sheep in this ground. A, B and C owned 70, 50 and 40 sheep respectively. After 4 months A sold $\frac{2}{7}$th portion of his sheep to B and 3 month after that C sold $\frac{2}{5}$th portion of his sheep to A. How much will each of them pay as rent after the end of a year?

A. ₹ 70, ₹ 70, ₹ 52 B. ₹ 76, ₹ 76, ₹ 40
C. ₹ 80, ₹ 76, ₹ 36 D. ₹ 40, ₹ 76.30, ₹ 76

18. Samir and Saurabh started a joint firm. Samir's investment was thrice the investment of Saurabh and the period of his investment was two times the period of investment of Saurabh. If Saurabh got ₹ 4000 as profit, then their total profit is:

A. ₹ 16000 B. ₹ 20000
C. ₹ 24000 D. ₹ 28000

19. A, B and C together start a business. The amounts invested by A and B are in the ratio of 4 : 3 whereas the ratio of investments of B and C is 2 : 3. If the total profit earned is ₹ 46000, what is C's share in the profit?

A. ₹ 14000 B. ₹ 15000
C. ₹ 16000 D. ₹ 18000

20. Rani and Nisha started a business initially with ₹ 5100 and ₹ 6600 respectively. If the total profit is ₹ 2730, what is the Rani's share in the profit?

A. ₹ 1190 B. ₹ 1200
C. ₹ 1530 D. ₹ 1540

ANSWERS

1	2	3	4	5	6	7	8	9	10
D	A	B	C	B	B	A	B	B	D
11	**12**	**13**	**14**	**15**	**16**	**17**	**18**	**19**	**20**
B	A	B	A	A	A	B	D	D	A

EXPLANATORY ANSWERS

1. Ratio between their profits = 80000 : 60000 = 4 : 3.

2. Ratio of capitals of A and B = 4000 : 6000 = 2 : 3

A's share in the profit = $\frac{2}{5}\times 2250$ = ₹ 900

B's share in the profit = $\frac{3}{5}\times 2250$ = ₹ 1350

3. Ratio of their capitals

= 1800 : 1500 : 1600 = 18 : 15 : 16

Sum of proportionals = 18 +15 + 16 = 49

Monu's profit = ₹ 900

∴ Total profit in the business = $\frac{900}{15}\times 49$ = ₹ 2940

4. Investment by Omdutt for 1 month

= ₹ 8000 × 12 = ₹ 96000

Let Sanjay invested ₹ x for 6 months

∴ Capital of Sanjay for 1 month = ₹ $x \times 6$ = ₹ $6x$

Now, $6x = 96000$

∴ x = ₹ 16000

5. Here, ratio of capitals of A and (B + C)

= 40000 : 60000 = 2 : 3

Profit of (B + C) = 2750 + 1750 = ₹ 4500

Hence, A's profit = $\frac{4500}{3}\times 2$ = ₹ 3000

6. Separate profit for A = $\frac{1040\times 25}{100}$ = ₹ 260

Remaining profit = ₹ (1040 − 260) = ₹ 780

Ratio of capitals of A and B = 2100 : 3100 = 21 : 31

A's profit = $\frac{21}{52}\times 780$ = ₹ 315

B's profit = $\frac{31}{52}\times 780$ = ₹ 465

Total profit of A = ₹ (315 + 260) = ₹ 575

Therefore A and B will make profit of ₹ 575 and ₹ 465 respectively.

7. Ratio of their capitals = 12500 : 8500 = 25 : 17

Hence, sum of their ratios = 25 + 17 = 42 and difference of ratios = 25 − 17 = 8

Now total profit taken as interest

= $\frac{300}{8}\times 42$ = ₹ 1575

Hence, total profit in the business

= $\frac{100}{40}\times 1575$ = ₹ 3937.50

8. Let shares of Neeraj and Birju in profit are ₹ x and ₹ y respectively; then,

$\frac{2}{5}x = \frac{1}{3}y$ ∴ $x : y = 5 : 6$

Hence, share of Birju = $\frac{6}{11}\times 1210$ = ₹ 660

9. Ratio of their shares = (20 × 5/2) : (30 × 4) : (36 × 7/2) = 25 : 60 : 63

Sum of proportionals = 25 + 60 + 63 = 148

Total lease amount = ₹ 888

∴ Amount paid by A = $\frac{25}{148}\times 888$ = ₹ 150

Amount paid by B = $\frac{60}{148}\times 888$ = ₹ 360

Amount paid by C = $\frac{63}{148}\times 888$ = ₹ 378

10. Ratio of capitals of A, B and C = 5000 : 6000 : 4000 = 5 : 6 : 4

Let total profit in the business = ₹ x; then

$$\frac{30x}{100}+\frac{5}{15}\times\frac{70x}{100}-\frac{(6+4)}{15}\times\frac{70x}{100}=200$$

$$\Rightarrow \frac{8x}{15}-\frac{7x}{15}=200 \quad \therefore x = ₹\ 3000$$

Hence, A's profit = $\frac{8\times 3000}{15}$ = ₹ 1600;

B's profit = $\frac{6}{15} \times \frac{7 \times 3000}{10}$ = ₹ 840;

C's profit = $\frac{4}{15} \times \frac{7 \times 3000}{10}$ = ₹ 560

11. Rent for 1 month = $\frac{1368}{24}$ = ₹ 57

Total rent paid by Premchand

$= 5 \times \frac{57}{3} + 8 \times \frac{57}{2} + 11 \times 57$

= 95 + 228 + 627 = ₹ 950.

12. Let, B and C invest ₹ x and ₹ y respectively

∴ Ratio of their capitals = 48000 : $8x$: $7y$

But given ratio of the profits = 3 : 4 : 7

$$8x : 7y = 4 : 7 \Rightarrow \frac{x}{y} = \frac{1}{2}$$

Hence, $x : y = 1 : 2$

13. Ratio of capitals of Amit, Sumeet and Suresh

= (2 × 3 + 1 × 9) : (3 × 4 + 2 × 8) : (4 × 12)

= 15 : 28 : 48

Sum of the ratios = 15 + 28 + 48 = 91

∴ Total profit in the business

$= \frac{91}{48} \times 3200$ = ₹ $6066\frac{2}{3}$

14. Ratio of their capitals

= (4000 × 8 + 6000 × 4) : (3000 × 6 + 5000 × 6) : (3000 × 12)

= 56000 : 48000 : 36000 = 14 : 12 : 9

Sum of proportionals = 14 + 12 + 9 = 35

Share of A in the profit = $\frac{14}{35} \times 7000$ = ₹ 2800

Share of B in the profit = $\frac{12}{35} \times 7000$ = ₹ 2400

Share of C in the profit = $\frac{9}{35} \times 7000$ = ₹ 1800

15. Ratio of their capitals

= 20000 : 18000 : 12000 = 10 : 9 : 6

Let total profit in the business = ₹ x; then

$$\left(\frac{12x}{100} + \frac{10}{25} \times \frac{80x}{100}\right) - \left(\frac{8x}{100} + \frac{9}{25} \times \frac{80x}{100}\right) = 648$$

$$\Rightarrow \frac{11x}{25} - \frac{46x}{125} = 648 \Rightarrow \frac{9x}{125} = 648$$

$$\therefore \quad x = \frac{648 \times 125}{9} = ₹\ 9000$$

Hence, share of A = $\frac{11x}{25} = \frac{11 \times 9000}{25}$

= ₹ 3960;

Share of B = $\frac{46x}{125} = \frac{46 \times 9000}{125}$ = ₹ 3312

Share of C = $\frac{6}{25} \times \frac{80x}{100} = \frac{6}{25} \times \frac{4}{5} \times 9000$ = ₹ 1728

16. Ratio of their working hours

= (5 × 3 + 6 × 4) : (6 × 3 + 7 × 4) : (7 × 3 + 8 × 4)

= 39 : 46 : 53

Sum of proportionals = 39 + 46 + 53 = 138

∴ Wages for the 1st labourer = $\frac{39}{138} \times 276$ = ₹ 78

Wages for the 2nd labourer = $\frac{46}{138} \times 276$ = ₹ 92

Wages for the 3rd labourer = $\frac{53}{138} \times 276$ = ₹ 106

17. Number of sheep of A for 1 month

$= [70 \times 4 + (70 - \frac{2}{7} \times 70) \times 3 + (70 - \frac{2}{7} \times 70 + \frac{2}{5} \times 40) \times 5]$

= 280 + 150 + 330 = 760

Number of sheep of B for 1 month

$= [50 \times 4 + (50 + \frac{2}{7} \times 70) \times 8]$ = 200 + 560 = 760

Number of sheep of C for 1 month

$= [40 \times 7 + (40 - \frac{2}{5} \times 40) \times 5]$ = 280 + 120 = 400

Hence, ratio of their sheep

= 760 : 760 : 400 = 19 : 19 : 10

Sum of proportionals = 19 + 19 + 10 = 48

1 year's rent of the pasture ground = 16 × 12 = ₹ 192

∴ Rent to be paid by A = $\frac{19}{48} \times 192$ = ₹ 76

Rent to be paid by B = $\frac{19}{48} \times 192$ = ₹ 76

Rent to be paid by C = $\frac{10}{48} \times 192$ = ₹ 40

18. Ratio of Capitals of Samir and Saurabh

= (3 × 2) : (1 × 1) = 6 : 1

Saurabh's profit = ₹ 4000

Hence, total profit in the business

= 7 × ₹ 4000 = ₹ 28000

19. A : B = 4 : 3 and B : C = 2 : 3,

Therefore, A : B : C = 8 : 6 : 9

Hence, C's profit = $\frac{9}{23} \times 46000$ = ₹ 18000

20. Ratio of their Capitals = 5100 : 6600 = 17 : 22

Hence, Rani's profit = $\frac{17}{39} \times 2730$ = ₹ 1190

●●●

7

Mixture and Alligation

Alligation deals with calculation of values or properties of a mixture. Alligation is the rule that enables us—

(1) to find the proportion in which the two or more ingredients at the given prices must be mixed to yield a mixture at the given price. This is termed as "Alligation Alternate".

(2) to calculate the average or mean value of a mixture when the prices of two or more ingredients which are to be mixed together and proportion in which they are to be mixed are given. This is termed as "Alligation Medial".

1. Rule of Alligation:

$$\frac{\text{Amount of Cheaper ingredient}}{\text{Amount of Dearer ingredient}} = \frac{\text{Cost price of Dearer} - \text{Mean Price}}{\text{Mean Price} - \text{Cost Price of Cheaper}}$$

Here cost price of unit quantity of the mixture is called the *Mean Price.*

The above rule may be represented schematically as under:

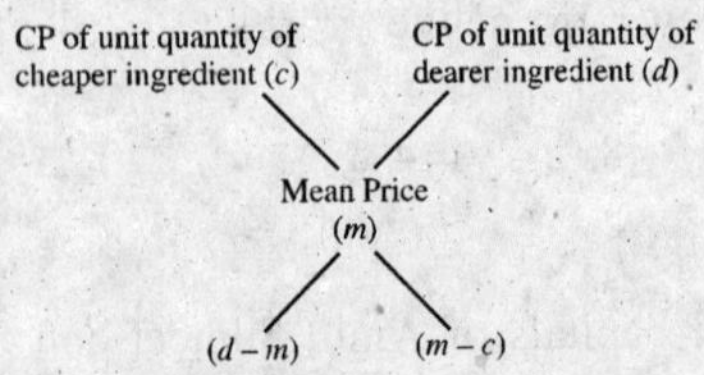

(Cheaper quantity) : (Dearer quantity) $= (d - m) : (m - c)$

This relationship is very helpful in solving problems on mixture involving percentage values, rates, prices, speeds etc.

2. m gm of sugar solution has x % sugar in it. To increase the sugar content in the solution to y %, quantity of sugar need to be added $= \dfrac{m(y-x)}{100-y}$

3. A vessel contains x litres of liquid A. y litres are withdrawn and replaced by liquid B. Next y litres of the mixture is withdrawn and again replaced by liquid B. This operation is repeated n times.

$$\frac{\text{Quantity of liquid A left after } n\text{th operation}}{\text{Whole quantity of liquid A initially present}} = \left(\frac{x-y}{x}\right)^n \text{ or } \left(1-\frac{y}{x}\right)^n$$

EXERCISE

1. In what proportion must tea at ₹ 62 per kg be mixed with tea at ₹ 72 per kg in order to obtain the mixture worth ₹ 65 per kg?

A. 4 : 6 B. 7 : 3
C. 2 : 3 D. 4 : 7

2. Find the quantity of rice @ ₹ 10 per kg. which should be mixed with 25 kgs of rice @ ₹ 8 per kg, so that on selling the mixture @ 15 per kg there is 80% profit.

A. 6 kgs B. 7 kgs
C. 3 kgs D. 5 kgs

3. A shopkeeper buys 26 kgs of milk @ ₹ 16 per kg. He also buys from another source an inferior quality of milk @ ₹ 10 per kg. How much quantity of the latter should he buy to mix it with the former so that he can sell the mixture @ ₹ 14 per kg without making any loss?

A. 13 kgs B. 12 kgs
C. 14 kgs D. 16 kgs

4. Two vessels A and B contain milk and water in the ratio 7 : 5 and 17 : 7 respectively. In what ratio mixtures from two vessels should be mixed to get a new mixture containing milk and water in the ratio 5 : 3?

A. 1 : 2 B. 2 : 1
C. 2 : 3 D. 3 : 2

5. Two vessels A and B contain mixture of milk and water in the ratio 4 : 1 and 9 : 11 respectively. They are mixed in the ratio of 3 : 2. Find the ratio of milk : water in the resulting mixture.
A. 34 : 16 B. 33 : 17
C. 16 : 34 D. 17 : 33

6. A person has two solutions of sugar with 30% and 50% concentration respectively. In what proportion should he mix two solutions to get 45% concentration in the resulting mixture?
A. 1 : 3 B. 3 : 1
C. 2 : 3 D. 3 : 2

7. 6 litres of milk and water mixture has 75% milk in it. How much milk should be added to the mixture to make it 90% pure?
A. 8 litres B. 9 litres
C. 10 litres D. 12 litres

8. In what ratio must water be added to spirit to gain 25% by selling it at cost price?
A. 1 : 4 B. 4 : 1
C. 3 : 4 D. 4 : 3

9. A shopkeeper has 50 kgs of rice. He sells a part of it at 20% profit and the rest at 40% profit. If he gains 25% on the whole, find the quantity of each part.
A. 12.5 kgs and 37.5 kgs B. 37.5 kgs and 12.5 kgs
C. 23.5 kgs and 21.5 kgs D. 21.5 kgs and 23.5 kgs

10. A shopkeeper has 100 kgs of tea. He sells a part of it at 20% profit and the rest at 5% loss. If his overall profit is 10%, find the quantity for each part.
A. 20 kgs B. 25 kgs
C. 30 kgs D. 40 kgs

11. A merchant has 160 kgs of wheat. He sells a part of it at 10% profit and the rest of 6% loss. If he incurs 4% loss on the whole, find the quantity for each part.
A. 120 kgs B. 140 kgs
C. 150 kgs D. 160 kgs

12. A man bought a certain quantity of sugar for ₹ 8000. He sells one-fourth of it at 20% loss. At what per cent profit should he sell the remainder stock so as to make an overall profit of 20%?
A. 20% B. 30%
C. 35% D. 40%

13. A person has ₹ 5000. He invests a part of it at 3% per annum and the remainder at 8% per annum simple interest. His total income in 3 years is ₹ 750. Find the sum invested at different rates of interest.
A. ₹ 2000 and ₹ 3000 B. ₹ 2500 and ₹ 2500
C. ₹ 3000 and ₹ 2000 D. ₹ 2750 and ₹ 2250

14. A person covers a dista2nce of 100 kms in 10 hours, partly by walking at 7 km/hr and rest by running at 12 km/hr. Find the distance covered in each part.
A. 48 kms B. 72 kms
C. 108 kms D. 124 kms

15. The average monthly salary of employees, consisting of officers and workers, of an organisation is ₹ 3000. The average salary of an officer is ₹ 10,000 while that of a worker is ₹ 2000 per month. If there are total 400 employees in the organisation, find the number of officers and workers separately.
A. 300, 100 B. 50, 350
C. 250, 150 D. 310, 90

16. The average daily wages of staff, consisting of supervisors and labourers, of a company is ₹ 50. The average wages of supervisors is ₹ 150 while that of labourers is ₹ 40 per day. If the number of supervisors is 15, find the number of labourers in the company.
A. 150 B. 175
C. 180 D. 200

17. ₹ 675 was divided among 75 boys and girls. Each boy gets ₹ 20 whereas a girl gets ₹ 5. Find the number of boys and girls.
A. 20, 55 B. 15, 60
C. 25, 50 D. 30, 45

18. A sum of ₹ 70 is divided among 10 children. Each boy gets ₹ 10 whereas a girl gets ₹ 5. If the number of boys is 4, find the number of girls.
A. 6 B. 7
C. 8 D. 9

19. From a cask of wine containing 25 litres, 5 litres are withdrawn and the cask is refilled with water. The process is repeated a second and then a third time. Find the quantity of wine left in the cask and also the ratio of wine to water in the resulting mixture.
A. 61 : 64 B. 16 : 46
C. 46 : 16 D. 64 : 61

20. A vessel contains 80 litres of milk. 16 litres of milk was taken out of the vessel and replaced by water. Then 16 litres of mixture was withdrawn and again replaced by water. The operation was repeated for third time. How much milk is now left in the vessel?
A. 96.40 litres B. 50.36 litres
C. 40.96 litres D. 32.76 litres

ANSWERS

1	2	3	4	5	6	7	8	9	10
B	D	A	B	B	A	B	A	B	D
11	**12**	**13**	**14**	**15**	**16**	**17**	**18**	**19**	**20**
B	B	C	B	B	A	A	A	D	C

EXPLANATORY ANSWERS

1. 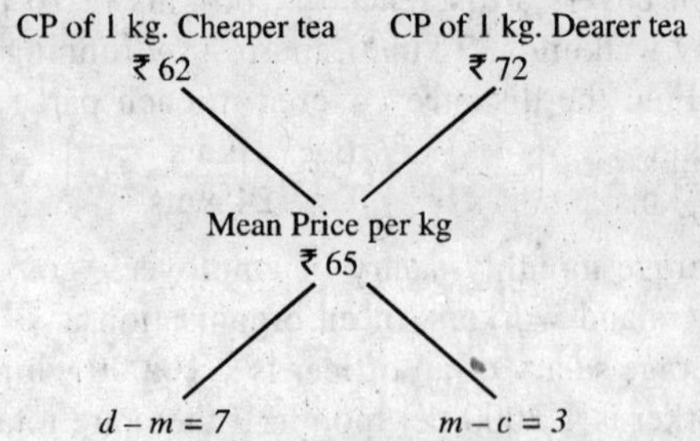

Using Alligation rule,

$$\frac{\text{Quantity of cheaper tea}}{\text{Quantity of dearer tea}} = \frac{d-m}{m-c} = \frac{7}{3}$$

Therefore, they must be mixed in the ratio of 7 : 3.

3. 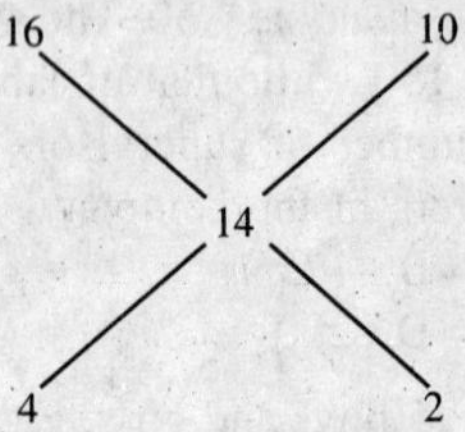

or 2 : 1 $\frac{\text{Quantity of milk @ ₹ 10 per kg}}{\text{Quantity of milk @ ₹ 16 per kg}} = \frac{1}{2}$

So, quantity of milk @ ₹ 10 per kg. = $\frac{26}{2}$ = 13 kgs.

5. Fraction is *Milk* *Water*

A : $\frac{4}{5}$ $\frac{1}{5}$

B : $\frac{9}{20}$ $\frac{11}{20}$

(3A + 2B) = A and B : $\left(\frac{12}{5}+\frac{9}{10}\right)$ $\left(\frac{3}{5}+\frac{11}{10}\right)$

$\frac{33}{10}$ $\frac{17}{10}$

So, Ratio of milk : water in the resulting mixture = 33 : 17.

6. 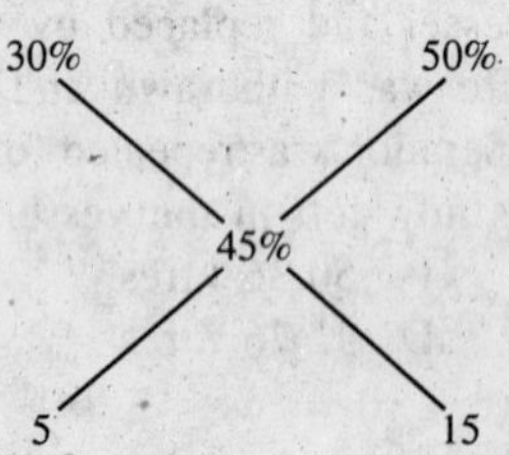

He should mix 30% and 50% in the ratio 5 : 15 or 1 : 3.

$\frac{\text{30\% Solution}}{\text{50\% Solution}} = \frac{1}{3}$ or 1 : 3

7. The given solution has 75% milk.
Milk to be added has 100% milk.

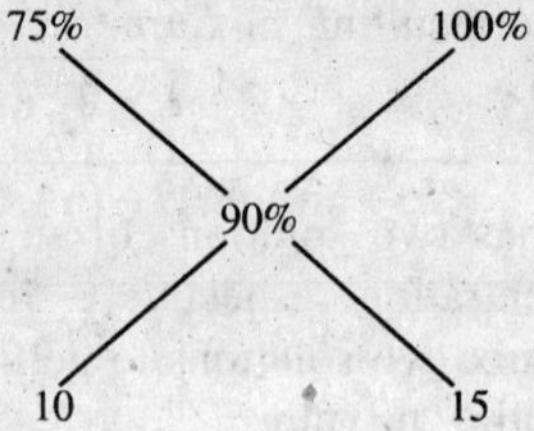

Milk should be added to the given mixture in the ratio 15 : 10 or 3 : 2.

∴ Quantity of milk to be added = $\frac{3}{2} \times 6$ = 9 litres.

8. Let cost price of spirit be ₹ 1 per litre.

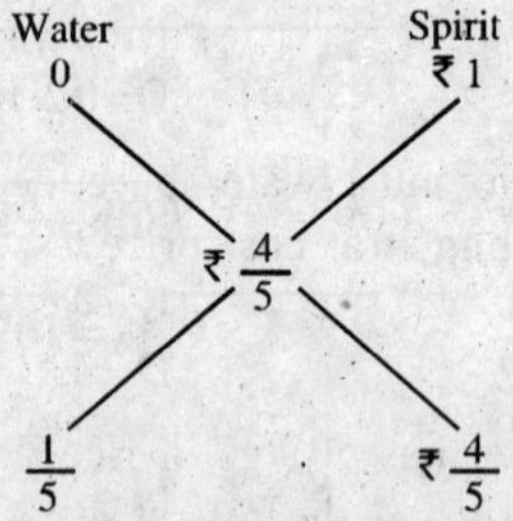

Then SP of mixture = ₹ 1 per litre
Gain = 25%

So, CP of mixture = $1 \times \frac{100}{125}$ = ₹ $\frac{4}{5}$

We assume that CP of water is zero.
Using alligation rule on cost price,

Water should be mixed to spirit in the ratio $\frac{1}{5} : \frac{4}{5}$ or 1 : 4.

9. 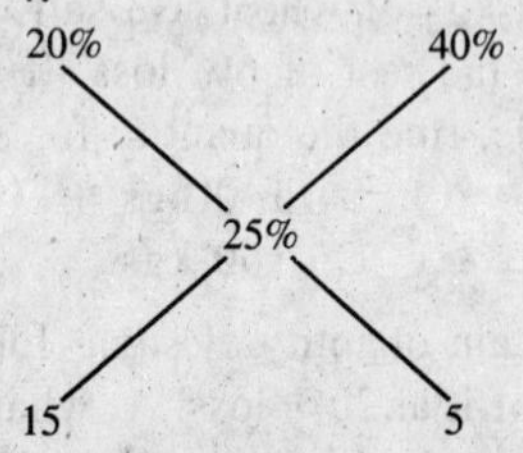

or 3 : 1

Quantity sold at 20% profit = $\frac{3}{3+1} \times 50$ = 37.5 kgs.

Quantity sold at 40% profit = (50 – 37.5) = 12.5 kgs.

10. 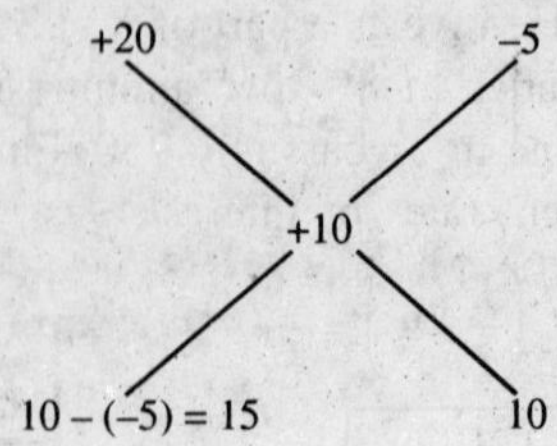

or 3 : 2

Quantity sold at 20% profit = $\frac{3}{3+2} \times 100$ = 60 kgs.

Quantity sold at 5% loss = (100 – 60) = 40 kgs.

11. 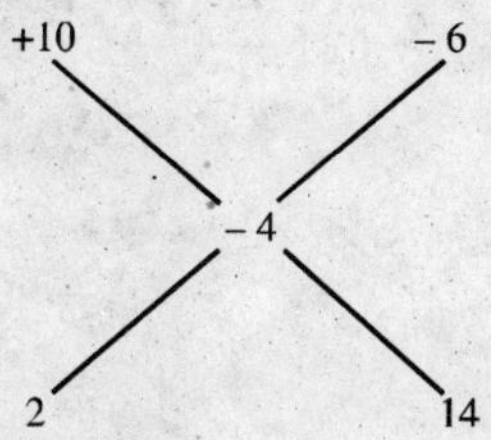

or 1 : 7

Quantity sold at 10% profit = $\frac{1}{1+7}$ × 160 = 20 kgs.

Quantity sold at 6% loss = 160 − 20 = 140 kgs.

12. Let the remainder stock be sold at x% profit.

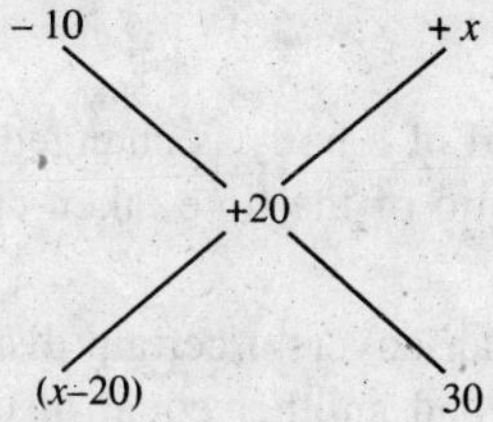

$\frac{x-20}{30} = \frac{1/4}{3/4}$ or $x - 20 = 30 \times \frac{1}{3}$

or $x = 20 + 10$, $x = 30\%$ profit.

13. Average rate of interest

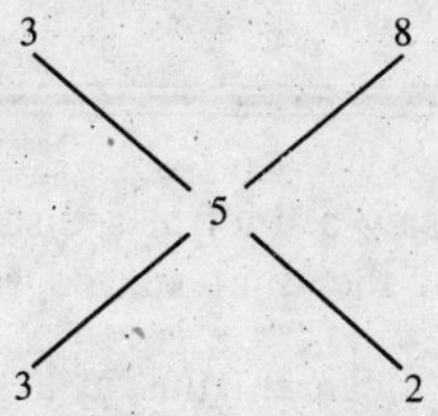

$= \frac{100 \times 750}{5000 \times 3} = 5\%$ per annum

Investment at 3% per annum = $\frac{3}{3+2} \times 5000$ = ₹ 3000

Investment at 8% per annum = $\frac{2}{3+2} \times 5000$ = ₹ 2000.

14. Average speed = $\frac{100}{10}$ = 10 km/hr.

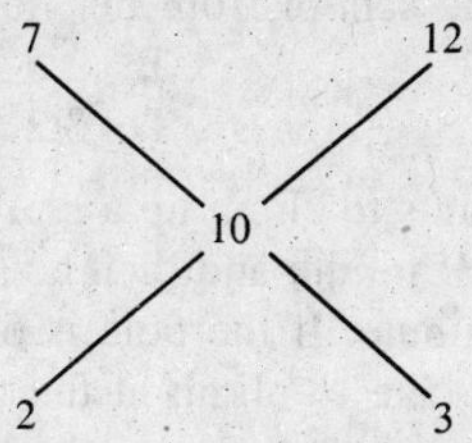

Ratio of time taken at 7 km/hr to 12 km/hr = 2 : 3

Time taken at 7 km/hr = $\frac{2}{2+3} \times 10$ = 4 hrs.

Distance covered at 7 km/hr = 7 × 4 = 28 km.

Distance covered at 12 km/hr = 100 − 28 = 72 km.

15. 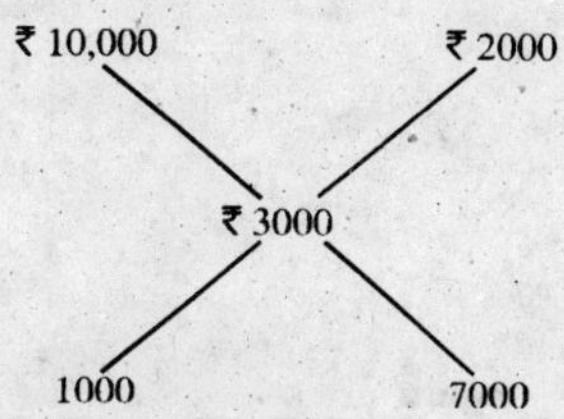

$\frac{\text{Number of officers}}{\text{Number of workers}} = \frac{1000}{7000} = \frac{1}{7}$

No. of officers = $\frac{1}{1+7} \times 400 = 50$

No. of workers = 400 − 50 = 350

16. 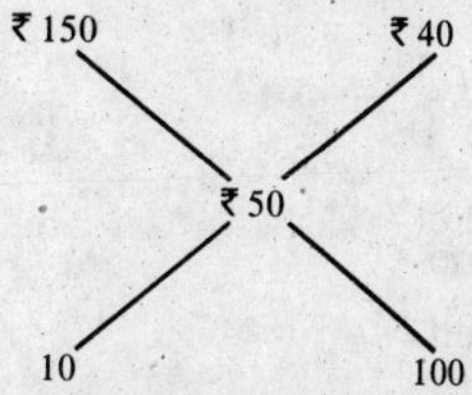

$\frac{\text{Number of supervisors}}{\text{Number of labourers}} = \frac{10}{100} = \frac{1}{10}$

Total number of labourers

= Total no. of supervisors × 10

= 15 × 10 = 150.

18. 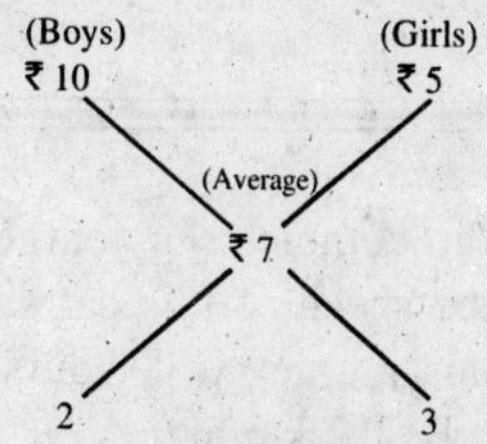

$\frac{\text{Number of girls}}{\text{Number of boys}} = \frac{3}{2}$

Number of girls = $\frac{3}{2} \times 4 = 6$

19. Here, quantity of wine left after third operation

$= \left(1 - \frac{5}{25}\right)^3 \times 25$

$= \left(\frac{4}{5}\right)^3 \times 25 = \frac{64}{125} \times 25 = \frac{64}{5} = 12\frac{4}{5}$ litres.

Final ratio of wine to water

$= \frac{(64/125)}{(1-64/125)} = \frac{64/125}{61/125}$

Wine : Water = $\frac{64}{61}$.

20. Amount of milk left

$= 80 \left(1 - \frac{16}{80}\right)^3 = 80 \left(\frac{4}{5}\right)^3 = 80 \times \frac{64}{125}$

= 40.96 litres.

●●●

8

Time and Distance

Important Formulae:

1. Speed = Distance ÷ Time
2. Distance = Time × Speed
3. Time = Distance ÷ Speed
4. x km/hr = $\left(x \times \frac{5}{18}\right)$ m/sec
5. x metres/sec = $\left(x \times \frac{18}{5}\right)$ km/hr.
6. If the speed of a body is changed in the ratio $m : n$, then the ratio of the time taken changes in the ratio $n : m$.
7. When a man covers a certain distance with a speed of x km/h and another equal distance at the rate of y km/h, then for the whole journey, the average speed is given by

   Average speed = $\frac{2xy}{x+y}$ km/h.

EXERCISE

1. A car moving at 48 km/hr completes a journey in 10 hours. By how much the speed of this car should be increased so as to do this journey in 8 hours?

A. 8 km/hr. B. 12 km/hr
C. 10 km/hr D. 15 km/hr

2. Starting from a point at a speed of 4 km/hr a man reaches at a cerain place and returns back to the point from where he had started journey on bicycle at the speed of 16 km/hr. His average speed during the entire journey will be:

A. 6.4 km/h B. 8.4 km/h
C. 5.4 km/h D. 10 km/h

3. A motorist covers a certain distance at a average speed of 48 km/h in 45 minutes. What speed in km/h he must maintain to cover the same distance in 30 minutes?

A. 66 km/h B. 79 km/h
C. 80 km/h D. 72 km/h

4. Two points A and B are 150 km apart. A man completes his onward journey from A to B in 3 hours 20 minutes and return journey from B to A in 4 hours 10 minutes. His average speed during the entire journey will be less than his average speed during the journey from A to B by:

A. 5 km/h B. 7.5 km/h
C. 9 km/h D. 3 km/h

5. A policeman saw a thief at a distance of 200 m. The policeman and the thief started running at the same time. If the policeman runs at a speed of $4\frac{1}{6}$ m per second and the thief at a speed of $3\frac{1}{3}$ m per second, after what time the policeman will catch the thief?

A. 12 min B. 10 min
C. 9 min D. 4 min

6. Kanchan walks from her home at 4 kms per hour and reaches her school 5 minutes late. If she walks at 5 kms per hour, she reaches the school 2½ minutes earlier. How far is the school from her home?

A. 3.5 kms B. 2.5 kms
C. 2.75 kms D. 3.2 kms

7. A monkey wants to climb up a glazed pole. He climbs 12 metres in 1 minute and then he slips back 3 metres in the next minute. If the pole is 63 metre high, how long does he take to climb at the top of the pole?

A. $11\frac{1}{4}$ min B. $12\frac{1}{2}$ min
C. $12\frac{3}{4}$ min D. $14\frac{3}{4}$ min

8. A and B start walking at the same time on a circular path with circumference 35 metre. If they walk in the same direction at 4 km/hr and 5 km/hr respectively, after what time will they meet together?

A. 35 hours B. 27 hours
C. 24 hours D. 40 hours

9. While walking at $\frac{3}{5}$ of his usual speed Kamalkant reaches at his destination late by 30 minutes. His usual time consumed in reaching to his destination is:
A. 32 min B. 40 min
C. 45 min D. 42 min

10. The distance between two stations A and B is 300 km. A train leaves the station A with a speed of 40 km/hr. At the same time another train departs from the station B with a speed of 50 km/hr. How much time will these two trains take to cross each other?
A. 3 hrs 40 min B. 3 hrs 20 min
C. 2 hrs 20 min D. 3 hrs 45 min

11. Gulshan starts from a place P at 2 p.m. and walks to Q at 5 km per hour. Tarun starts from P at 3 p.m. and follows Gulshan on bicycle at 10 km per hour. By when Tarun will catch Gulshan?
A. At 5.30 p.m. B. At 4.00 p.m.
C. At 4.30 p.m. D. At 6.00 p.m.

12. Nilesh goes to school from his village at the speed of 4 km/hr and returns from school to village at the speed of 2 km/hr. If he takes 6 hours in all, then what is the distance between the village and the school?
A. 8 km B. 6 km
C. 5 km D. 4 km

13. A school bus covers a distance from a village to school at the speed of 12 km/hr and reaches the school 8 minute late. The next day the bus covers the same distance at the speed of 20 km/hr and reaches the school 10 minutes early. What is the distance between village and the school?
A. 6 km B. 9 km
C. 12 km D. 15 km

14. By increasing the speed of the bus by 10 km/hr the time of journey for 72 km is reduced by 36 minutes. What was the original speed of the bus?
A. 30 km/hr B. 35 km/hr
C. 40 km/hr D. 45 km/hr

15. A car completes a fixed journey in 8 hours. It covers half distance at the speed of 40 km/hr and rest at the 60 km/hr, the distance of the journey is:
A. 400 km B. 420 km
C. 384 km D. 350 km

16. A car covers four consecutive extensions of 3 km each at the speeds of 10 km/hr, 20 km/hr, 30 km/hr and 60 km/hr. Its average speed of journey is:
A. 30 km/hr B. 25 km/hr
C. 20 km/hr D. 10 km/hr

17. A girl rides her bicycle 10 km at an average speed of 12 km/hr and another 12 km at an average speed of 10 km/hr. Her average speed for the entire journey is approximately:
A. 12.2 km/hr B. 11.2 km/hr
C. 10.8 km/hr D. 10.4 km/hr

18. Raman drove from home to a neighbouring town at the speed of 50 km/hr and on his returning journey, he drove at the speed of 45 km/hr and also took an hour longer to reach home. What distance did he cover each way?
A. 900 km B. 500 km
C. 450 km D. 225 km

19. A man takes 6 hours 35 minutes in walking to a certain place and riding back. He would have taken 2 hours less by riding both ways. What would be the time he would take to walk both ways?
A. 10 hours B. 8 hours 35 minutes
C. 8 hours 25 minutes D. 8 hrs

20. A man covers a distance of 6 km at the rate of 4 km/hr and other 4 km at 3 km/hr this average speed is
A. $3\frac{5}{9}$ km/hr B. $3\frac{9}{17}$ km/hr
C. $5\frac{9}{17}$ km/hr D. $9\frac{3}{17}$ km/hr

ANSWERS

1	2	3	4	5	6	7	8	9	10
B	A	D	A	D	B	C	A	C	B
11	**12**	**13**	**14**	**15**	**16**	**17**	**18**	**19**	**20**
B	A	B	A	C	C	C	C	B	B

EXPLANATORY ANSWERS

1. Let he has to increase his speed by x km/hr for given condition; then,

$$(48 + x) \times 8 = 48 \times 10$$

$$\Rightarrow \quad 48 + x = 60 \therefore x = 12 \text{ km/hr}$$

2. Average speed during the entire journey

$$= \frac{2xy}{x+y} = \frac{2\times4\times16}{4+16} = \frac{8\times16}{20} = 6.4 \text{ km/hr.}$$

3. Let required speed be x km/hr; then

$$x \times \frac{1}{2} = 48 \times \frac{3}{4} \quad \therefore x = 48 \times \frac{3}{4} \times 2 = 72 \text{ km/hr}$$

4. During onward journey from A to B:

$$\text{Average speed} = \frac{150}{10/3} = \frac{150\times3}{10} = 45 \text{ km/hr.}$$

During entire jouney:

$$\text{Average speed} = \frac{300}{\frac{10}{3}+\frac{25}{6}} = \frac{300\times 6}{45} = 40 \text{ km/hr.}$$

Hence, difference of average speed
= 45 – 40 = 5 km/hr.

5. Suppose the policeman will catch the thief after t sec

then, $\left(\frac{25}{6}-\frac{10}{3}\right)t = 200 \Rightarrow \frac{5}{6}t = 200$

$\therefore t = \frac{200\times 6}{5} = 240$ sec = 4 min.

6. Suppose the distance between her house to the school = x km

Difference of time = $\frac{5}{2} - (-5) = \frac{15}{2}$ min = $\frac{1}{8}$ hr.

$\frac{x}{4}-\frac{x}{5}=\frac{1}{8} \Rightarrow \frac{x}{20}=\frac{1}{8} \quad \therefore x = \frac{20}{8} = 2.5$ km

7. The monkey climbs 12 metres in 1 minute and then he slips back 3 metres in the next minute

∴ The monkey climbs in the first 2 minutes = 12 – 3 = 9 metres

∴ In the first 12 minutes the monkey climbs = 9 × 6 = 54 metres

Remaining height of the pole to be covered by the monkey = 63 – 54 = 9 metre

∴ The monkey will climb the height of 9 metres in the 13th minute

∵ The monkey climbs 12 metres in 1 minute

∴ The monkey will climb 9 metres in

$\frac{1}{12}\times 9 = \frac{3}{4}$ minute

∴ Time spent in climbing at the top of the pole

$= \left(12+\frac{3}{4}\right)$ minutes = $12\frac{3}{4}$ minutes

8. The two persons walk in the same direction

∴ Their relative speed = 5 – 4 = 1 km/hr

Distance covered in 1 round on the circular path = 35 km

∴ They will meet after $\frac{35}{1}$ = 35 hours.

9. Suppose usual speed of Kamalkant is v km/hr and his destination is at a distance of x kms; then usual time taken = $\frac{x}{v}$ hours.

$\frac{x}{3v/5}-\frac{x}{v}=\frac{1}{2} \Rightarrow \frac{2x}{3v}=\frac{1}{2} \quad \therefore \frac{x}{v}=\frac{3}{4}$ hour = 45 min.

10. The two trains are moving in the opposite directions

∴ Relative speed = 40 + 50 = 90 km/hr.

∴ Time taken to cross each other

$= \frac{300}{90} = 3\frac{1}{3}$ hours or, 3 hours 20 minutes.

11. Let Tarun will catch Gulshan after t hours the starting of Tarun; then, $10t = 5(t + 1)$

$\Rightarrow 5t = 5 \therefore t = 1$ hr

Hence, required time = 3 p.m. + 1 hr. = 4 p.m.

12. Let x km be the distance between village and the school; then

$\frac{x}{4}+\frac{x}{2}=6 \Rightarrow \frac{3x}{4}=6 \quad \therefore x = \frac{6\times 4}{3} = 8$ km

13. Let x km be the distance from village to school, then

$\frac{x}{12}-\frac{x}{20} = [8 - (-10)] \times \frac{1}{60}$

$\Rightarrow \frac{x}{30}=\frac{18}{60} \therefore x = \frac{18}{60}\times 30 = 9$ km

14. Let original speed of the bus be x km/hr; then

$\frac{72}{x}-\frac{72}{x+10}=\frac{36}{60} \Rightarrow \frac{72(x+10-x)}{x^2+10x}=\frac{3}{5}$

$\Rightarrow \quad 1200 = x^2 + 10x$

$\Rightarrow x^2 + 10x - 1200 = 0$

$\Rightarrow (x + 40)(x - 30) = 0$

$\therefore \quad x = 30$ or $x = -40$

Taking positive value only, so speed of the bus = 30 km/hr.

15. Let the distance of the journey be x km, then,

$\frac{x}{2\times 40}+\frac{x}{2\times 60} = 8 \Rightarrow \frac{5x}{240}=8$

$\therefore \quad x = 8 \times 48 = 384$ km

16. Total distance of the journey = 4 × 3 km = 12 km

Total time taken = $\frac{3}{10}+\frac{3}{20}+\frac{3}{30}+\frac{3}{60}=\frac{36}{60}=\frac{3}{5}$ hr.

Hence, average speed = $\frac{12}{3/5}=\frac{12\times 5}{3}$ = 20 km/hr.

17. Average speed

$= \frac{10+12}{\frac{10}{12}+\frac{12}{10}}=\frac{22}{61/30}=\frac{22\times 30}{61}=\frac{660}{61}$ = 10.8 km/hr

18. Let his distance of journey of each way be x km; then

$\frac{x}{45}-\frac{x}{50}=1 \Rightarrow \frac{x}{450} = 1$

$\therefore \quad x = 450$ km

19. Here, Walking to a certain place + riding back = 6 hrs 35 min. ...(i)

2 × riding the same distance = 4 hrs 35 min. ...(ii)

Multiplying equation (i) × 2 and subtracting (ii) we get

Time taken in walking both ways = 13 hrs 70 min – 4 hrs. 35 min = 8 hrs. 35 min.

20. His average speed = $\frac{6+4}{\frac{6}{4}+\frac{4}{3}}=\frac{10}{17/6}=\frac{60}{17}=3\frac{9}{17}$ km/hr

●●●

9

Time and Work

IMPORTANT FACTS:

1. If A can do a piece of work in n days, then work done by A in 1 day $= \frac{1}{n}$.
2. If work done by A in 1 day $= \frac{1}{n}$; then A can finish the whole work in n days.
3. If A is twice as good a workman as B then; Ratio of work done by A and B = 2 : 1
   Ratio of times taken by A and B to finish a work = 1 : 2.

EXERCISE

1. 12 boys can do a piece of work in 16 days. In how many days can 6 boys do the same work?

A. 16 days B. 32 days
C. 23 days D. 24 days

2. A can do a piece of work in 8 days while B can do the same work in 16 days. If they start working together, how long would they take to complete half portion of this work?

A. $2\frac{2}{3}$ days B. $3\frac{5}{7}$ days
C. $4\frac{1}{2}$ days D. $3\frac{1}{2}$ days

3. A can do a piece of work in 4 days. B is 50% more efficient than A. How long would B alone take to finish this work?

A. $3\frac{1}{3}$ days B. $5\frac{1}{4}$ days
C. $2\frac{2}{3}$ days D. $1\frac{2}{3}$ days

4. A and B working together complete a work in 35 days. If A takes 60 days to complete it, how long would B alone take to complete it?

A. 64 days B. 72 days
C. 81 days D. 84 days

5. A few children working together can do a piece of work in 18 days. If the number of children employed on the work is made double, how long would they take to complete half of the work?

A. $4\frac{1}{2}$ days B. $2\frac{1}{3}$ days
C. $8\frac{3}{4}$ days D. $6\frac{1}{2}$ days

6. 10 men or 18 boys can do a piece of work in 15 days. In how many days would 25 men and 15 boys complete the same work working together?

A. $5\frac{1}{2}$ days B. $4\frac{1}{2}$ days
C. $6\frac{2}{3}$ days D. $2\frac{1}{3}$ days

7. A can do a piece of work in 40 days. He starts working, but having some other engagements he drops out after 5 days. Thereafter B completes this work in 21 days. How many days would A and B take to complete this work working together?

A. 15 days B. 16 days
C. 17 days D. 11 days

8. Two persons A and B can complete a piece of work in 8 hours and 16 hours respectively. If they work at it alternately for an hour, A starting first, in how many hours will the work be finished?

A. $9\frac{1}{3}$ hours B. $10\frac{1}{2}$ hours
C. $11\frac{1}{2}$ hours D. $8\frac{1}{2}$ hours

ANSWERS

1	2	3	4	5	6	7	8
B	A	C	D	A	B	A	B

EXPLANATORY ANSWERS

1. $\because$ 12 boys can do a piece of work in 16 days.

$\therefore$ 1 boy will do the same piece of work in 16 × 12 days.

$\therefore$ 6 boys will do the same piece of work in

$\dfrac{16\times12}{6}$ days = 32 days.

2. (A + B)'s 1 day's work = $\dfrac{1}{8}+\dfrac{1}{16}=\dfrac{3}{16}$

Hence, (A + B) will do the whole work in $\dfrac{16}{3}$ days

So, they will do the half portion of the work in $\dfrac{16}{3\times2}$ days = $\dfrac{8}{3}=2\dfrac{2}{3}$ days.

3. A's 1 day's work $=\dfrac{1}{4}$;

Hence, B's 1 day's work = $\dfrac{150}{100}\times\dfrac{1}{4}=\dfrac{3}{8}$

So, B will do the whole work in $\dfrac{8}{3}=2\dfrac{2}{3}$ days.

4. (A + B)'s 1 day's work = $\dfrac{1}{35}$

and also, A's 1 day's work = $\dfrac{1}{60}$

Hence, B's 1 day's work

$=\dfrac{1}{35}-\dfrac{1}{60}=\dfrac{5}{420}=\dfrac{1}{84}$

So, B will do the whole work in 84 days.

5. Let number of children be x;

Now x children can do the work in 18 days.

Hence, $2x$ children will do $\dfrac{1}{2}$ of the work in

$\dfrac{18\times x}{2x\times2}=\dfrac{9}{2}$ days = $4\dfrac{1}{2}$ days.

6. 10 men ≡ 18 boys; 25 men ≡ $\dfrac{18}{10}\times25=45$ boys

Hence, 25 men + 15 boys = 45 + 15 = 60 boys

Now, 18 boys can do a piece of work in 15 days.

Hence, 60 boys will do a piece of work in

$\dfrac{15\times18}{60}=\dfrac{9}{2}$ days = $4\dfrac{1}{2}$ days.

7. A's 5 days' work = $5\times\dfrac{1}{40}=\dfrac{1}{8}$

Remaining work = $1-\dfrac{1}{8}=\dfrac{7}{8}$, which is done by B in 21 days.

Hence, B's 1 day's work = $\dfrac{7}{8\times21}=\dfrac{1}{24}$

Now, (A + B)'s 1 day's work = $\dfrac{1}{40}+\dfrac{1}{24}=\dfrac{8}{120}=\dfrac{1}{15}$

Hence, (A + B) will complete the work in 15 days.

8. In 2 hours the part of work = $\dfrac{1}{8}+\dfrac{1}{16}=\dfrac{3}{16}$ will be completed.

Hence, in 5 pairs of hours the part of work

$=5\times\dfrac{3}{16}=\dfrac{15}{16}$ will be completed

Remaining work = $1-\dfrac{15}{16}=\dfrac{1}{16}$ which will be done by A.

Time taken by A to complete the $\dfrac{1}{16}$ work

$=\dfrac{1/16}{1/8}=\dfrac{1}{2}$ hour.

Hence, required number of hours

$=10+\dfrac{1}{2}=10\dfrac{1}{2}$ hours.

●●●

10

L.C.M. & H.C.F.

LCM

Multiple : A number is said to be multiple of other when it is exactly divisible by the other.

Common multiple : A common multiple of two or more numbers is a number which is exactly divisible by each of them. For example, for 2 and 3, common multiples are 6, 12, 18, 24 and so on.

Explanation:

Consider the two numbers 2 and 3

Multiple of 2 are 2, 4, 6, 8, 10, 12, ...

Multiple of 3 are 3, 6, 9, 12, 15, ...

∴ Common multiples are 6, 12, 18, ...

Least Common Multiple (L.C.M.) : L.C.M. of two or more given numbers is the least number which is exactly divisible by each of them. For example,

6 is a common multiple of 2 and 3

12 is also common multiple of 2 and 3

18 is also common multiple of 2 and 3

But 6 is the least common multiple (L.C.M.) of 2 and 3.

Methods to find out L.C.M.

L.C.M. of two or more given numbers is determined by following two methods:

1. By prime factorization method

2. By division method

HCF

Factor : One number is said to be a factor of other when it divides the other exactly. Hence, 5 and 7 are factors of 35.

Common factor : A common factor of two or more numbers is a number that divides each of them exactly. Hence, 5 is a common factor of 15, 25, 35 and 55.

Highest Common Factor (H.C.F.) : H.C.F. of two or more numbers is the largest number by which each given number is divisible without leaving any remainder.

An example : It is required to find the H.C.F. of 6 and 8.

Factors of 6 are 1, 2, 3, 6 and

Factors of 8 are 1, 2, 4, 8.

The common factors are 1, 2, but highest of these is 2. Hence, 2 is the H.C.F.

Relationship Between Two Numbers and Their L.C.M. and H.C.F.

Product of the H.C.F. and the L.C.M. of two numbers is equal to the product of the given numbers.

i.e., 1st number × 2nd number = H.C.F. × L.C.M.

EXERCISE

1. The largest three-digit number, when divided by 6, 9 and 12 leaves 1 as remainder in each case, will be

A. 887 B. 987
C. 973 D. 730

2. Two numbers are in the ratio of 8 : 15. If their H.C.F. is 4, the numbers are

A. 32 and 60 B. 16 and 30
C. 80 and 150 D. 64 and 120

3. The largest number that will divide 226 and 272 leaving 1 and 2 as remainders respectively, is

A. 36 B. 45
C. 55 D. 59

4. Which of the following is the greatest common divisor of 1170 and 102?

A. 8 B. 4
C. 6 D. 3

5. A number, when 3 is added to it, becomes divisible by 36, 45 and 50. The smallest such number is

A. 987 B. 798
C. 986 D. 897

6. The least perfect square number which is completely divisible by 10, 20, 30 and 40 is

A. 4800 B. 3600
C. 4400 D. 2500

7. The product of two numbers is 2160 and their H.C.F. is 12. How many such pairs of numbers can be possibly formed?

A. 3 B. 1

C. 2 D. None

8. The greatest number that will divide 366, 513 and 324 leaving the same remainder in each case is

A. 21 B. 18

C. 27 D. 42

ANSWERS

1	2	3	4	5	6	7	8
C	A	B	C	D	B	C	A

EXPLANATORY ANSWERS

1. L.C.M. of 6, 9 and 12

$$\begin{array}{r|l} 3 & 6,\ 9,\ 12 \\ \hline 2 & 2,\ 3,\ 4 \\ \hline & 1,\ 3,\ 2 \end{array}$$

$\therefore$ LCM $= 3 \times 2 \times 3 \times 2 = 36.$

$\because$ Largest 3-digit number = 999

$$\begin{array}{l} 36\ )\ 999\ (\ 27 \\ \quad\ \ \underline{72} \\ \quad\ \ 279 \\ \quad\ \ \underline{252} \\ \quad\ \ \times\ 27 \end{array}$$

$\therefore$ Largest 3-digit number which is exactly divisible by 6, 9 and 12

$= 999 - 27 = 972$

$\therefore$ The required number $= 972 + 1 = 973$

2. Let the numbers be $8x$ and $15x$

$8x = 2 \times 2 \times 2 \times x$

$15x = 3 \times 5 \times x$

$\therefore$ LCM of $8x$ and $15x = 2 \times 2 \times 2 \times x \times 3 \times 5$

$= 120x$

Now, 1st number $\times$ 2nd number = HCF $\times$ LCM

$\Rightarrow \quad 8x \times 15x = 4 \times 120x$

$\Rightarrow \quad 120x^2 = 4 \times 120x$

$\Rightarrow \quad x = 4$

$\therefore$ Numbers are $8 \times 4 = 32$ and $15 \times 4 = 60$

3. $226 - 1 = 225$ and $272 - 2 = 270$

Now, HCF of 225 and 270

$$\begin{array}{l} 225\ )\ 270\ (\ 1 \\ \quad\quad\ \underline{225} \\ \quad\quad\ \ 45\ )\ 225\ (\ 5 \\ \quad\quad\quad\quad\ \ \underline{225} \\ \quad\quad\quad\quad\quad \times \end{array}$$

$\therefore$ The required number is 45.

4. $1170 = 2 \times 5 \times 3 \times 3 \times 13$

$102 = 2 \times 3 \times 17$

$\therefore$ Greatest common divisor $= 2 \times 3 = 6$

5. It is clear from the given conditions of the problem that the smallest number will be 3 less than the LCM of 36, 45 and 50.

$\therefore$ LCM of 36, 45 and 50

$$\begin{array}{r|l} 3 & 36,\ 45,\ 50 \\ \hline 2 & 12,\ 15,\ 50 \\ \hline 3 & 6,\ 15,\ 25 \\ \hline 5 & 2,\ 5,\ 25 \\ \hline & 2,\ 1,\ 5 \end{array}$$

$\therefore$ LCM $= 3 \times 2 \times 3 \times 5 \times 2 \times 5 = 900$

$\therefore$ Required number $= 900 - 3 = 897.$

6. LCM of 10, 20, 30 and 40

$$\begin{array}{r|l} 2 & 10,\ 20,\ 30,\ 40 \\ \hline 5 & 5,\ 10,\ 15,\ 20 \\ \hline 2 & 1,\ 2,\ 3,\ 4 \\ \hline & 1,\ 1,\ 3,\ 2 \end{array}$$

$\therefore$ LCM $= 2 \times 2 \times 5 \times 3 \times 2$

But the number is a perfect square number

$\therefore$ Required number $= 2 \times 2 \times 5 \times 5 \times 3 \times 3 \times 2 \times 2 = 3600.$

7. Product of two numbers = their HCF $\times$ their LCM

$2160 = 12 \times$ LCM

$\therefore \quad$ LCM $= \dfrac{2160}{12} = 180$

Therefore such pairs of numbers in which product of numbers is 2160 and HCF is 12 will be only 2. *i.e.*, 12×180 and 36×60.

8. Difference between 366 and 513

$= 513 - 366 = 147$

and difference between 513 and 324

$= 513 - 324 = 189$

$\therefore$ HCF of 147 and 189

$$\begin{array}{l} 147\ )\ 189\ (\ 1 \\ \quad\quad\ \underline{147} \\ \quad\quad\ \times\ 42\ )\ 147\ (\ 3 \\ \quad\quad\quad\quad\quad\ \underline{126} \\ \quad\quad\quad\quad\quad\ \times\ 21\ )\ 42\ (\ 2 \\ \quad\quad\quad\quad\quad\quad\quad\quad\ \underline{42} \\ \quad\quad\quad\quad\quad\quad\quad\quad\ \ \times \end{array}$$

$\therefore$ The required largest number is 21.

GENERAL SCIENCE

PHYSICS

Units and Measurement

Unit is that physical quantity which expresses the length, mass and time.

Types of Units: There are three systems of the fundamental units which are commonly used and internationally recognized these are:

(*i*) ***Metric System Unit (M.K.S.):*** In this system of unit 'M' stands for metre, 'K' for kilogram and S for second (time). Metre as unit of length, Kilogram as unit of mass and Second as unit of time.

(*ii*) ***C.G.S. System of unit:*** In this system 'C' stands for centimetre 'G' stands for gram and 'S' for Second. Centimetre is the unit of length, Gram is the unit of mass and Second is the unit of time.

(*iii*) ***F.P.S. System of Unit:*** In this system of unit 'F' stands for foot, 'P' stands for pound and 'S' for second. Foot is the unit of length, Pound is unit of mass, second is unit of time.

Scientific Instruments

1. **Altimeter:** It is used for measuring altitudes specially used in aircraft.
2. **Ammeter:** It is used for measuring the strength of the current in amperes.
3. **Barometer:** It is used for measuring the atmospheric pressure.
4. **Dynamo:** It is used to convert mechanical energy into electrical energy.
5. **Galvanometer:** It is used for detecting the presence of current.
6. **Hygrometer:** It is used for measuring humidity in air.
7. **Periscope:** A device to see the objects which are above the eye level of the observer.
8. **Potentiometer:** It is used for measuring or adjusting electrical potential.
9. **Sextant:** It is used for measuring angular elevation.
10. **Transformer:** It is used to decrease or increase the voltage of an alternating current.
11. **Thermocouple:** It is based on thermoelectricity used for measuring temperature.
12. **Thermometer:** It is used measuring temperature.
13. **Viscometer:** It is used for measuring viscosity of liquids.
14. **Voltmeter:** It measures the potential difference.

Mechanics

Branch of science dealing with the study of motion of object in called mechanics.

Distance: The length of path traversed by a particle in a given time is known as distance.

Displacement: The distance covered by a particle in a particular direction with respect to the point of reference is known as displacement.

Speed: The distance travelled by a particle in unit time is defined as its speed.

Average or Mean Speed: The ratio of the total distance travelled by a particle to the time taken to cover that distance is defined as its average speed.

Velocity: The ratio of the total displacement of a particle to the time taken to cover that displacement is defined as average velocity.

Acceleration: The change in velocity of a particle in unit time is defined as its average acceleration.

Retardation: The rate of decrease of velocity of a particle is defined as retardation. It is a negative acceleration.

Inertia: The property of a body by virtue of which it opposes any change in its state is defined as its inertia.

Mass: The quantity of matter contained in a body is defined as its mass.

(*a*) The mass of a body can never be zero.

(*b*) The mass of a body remains constant at all places of earth.

(*c*) It can be determined by a physical balance.

(*d*) There are two types of mass, *i.e.*, (*i*) gravitational mass, and (*ii*) inertial mass.

Gravitational Mass: The ratio of the weight of a body and acceleration due to gravity at that place is defined as gravitational mass. The mass determined by a chemical or physical balance is the gravitational mass.

Inertial Mass: The ratio of the force applied and the acceleration produced in a body at a place with zero gravity is defined as the inertial mass.

Force: The push or pull which one system exerts on another is defined as force.

Momentum: The product of mass and velocity of a moving body is known as its linear momentum.

Impulse: The product of applied force on a body and the time internal for which the force acts is defined as impulse.

Energy: The capacity of doing work is known as energy. Energy can be converted from one form to another form.

Mechanical Energy: The energy present in a body on account of its position or motion is defined as mechanical energy. This is of two type viz., (*i*) Potential energy and (*ii*) Kinetic energy.

Newton's Laws of Motion

(*i*) *First Law or Law of Inertia:* A body to be in its state of rest or of uniform motion until and unless it is acted upon by some external forces. This law defines forces.

(*ii*) *Second Law:* The force applied to a body is equal to the rate of change of its momentum.

(*iii*) *Third Law or Law of Action and Reaction:* To every action force there is an equai and opposite reaction force.

Gravitational Field: The region of space around a body in which gravitational force is experienced by other bodies is defined as the gravitational field of that body.

Newton's Law of Gravitation: Every particle in the universe attracts energy other particle with a force which is directly proportional to the product of their masses and inversely proportional to the square of distance between them.

Force of Gravity: The force with which earth attracts anybody towards its centre is defined as the force of gravity. The force exerted by earth on the body is known as the weight of the body.

Acceleration due to Gravity: The rate of change of velocity of a body falling freely due to earth's force of gravity is defined as acceleration due to gravity

Satellites: The bodies revolving around a planet in its gravitational field are defined as satellites.

Natural Satellites: The natural heavenly bodies which revolve around a planet are known as natural satellites, *e.g.*, moon is the natural satellite of earth.

Artificial Satellites: The man made bodies which are established in a particular orbit and are made to revolve around the earth are known as artificial satellites, *e.g.*, Aryabhatta, Rohini, Bhaskar.

Orbital Satellite: The satellites which always revolve in different orbits around earth are known as orbital satellites.

Communication Satellites: The satellite which remain stationary with respect to earth are known as communication satellites, *e.g.*, INSAT, 1B, 2A, 2E etc.

Power: The rate of doing work by a machine or a person is defined as power.

Law of Conservation of Momentum: In the absence of an external force, the total momentum of a system remains constant.

Deforming Force: The external force acting on a body on account of which is size or shape or both change is defined as the deforming force.

Elasticity: The property of a body, by virtue of which it regains its original form (size and shape) after the removal of external deforming force, is defined as elasticity.

Perfectly Elastic Body: The body which perfectly regains its original form on removing the external deforming force, is defined as a perfectly elastic body, *e.g.*, quartz.

Plastic Body: The body which does not have the property of opposing the external deforming force is known as a plastic body.

Elastic Limit: The maximum deforming force after which a body loses its property of elasticity and it gets permanently deformed, is defined as the elastic limit.

Stress: The internal reactional force per unit area developed as a result of applied external force is defined as stress.

Strain: The change in dimensions per unit original dimensions due to applied deforming force is defined as strain.

Hooke's Law: Within elastic limit, stress is directly proportional to strain.

Cohesive Force: The force of attraction acting between the molecules of same material is defined as cohesive force, *e.g.*, the force acting between water molecule.

Adhesive Force: The force of attraction acting between the molecules of two different materials is defined as adhesive force, *e.g.*, the force acting between the molecules of paper and ink.

Surface Tension: The property of a liquid, on account of which it lends to keep surface area in its free surface, is defined as surface tension.

Viscosity: The property of fluids, by virtue of which they oppose the relative motion between their different layers, is known as viscosity.

Heat

Temperature: Temperature of a body is that property which tells us that how much hot or cold a particular body is.

Scales of Temperature:

(*i*) Temperature in Kelvin = Temperature in Celsius + 273

(*ii*) 1°C temperature difference = 1° K

(*iii*) The temperature of –40°C is same in °C and °F

(*iv*) The temperature of a normal person is 37°C or 98.6°F.

Heat: Heat is a form of energy which is exchanged among various bodies or systems on account of temperature difference.

Latent Heat: The amount of heat used to change the state of matter, without changing its temperature is defined as latent heat.

Specific Heat: The amount of heat required to increase the temperature of 1 gm of material by 1°C is defined as its specific heat.

Boyles Law: At a constant temperature the volume of the given mass of gas is inversely proportional to its pressure.

Charle's Law: At constant pressure the volume of a given mass of gas is directly proportional to its absolute temperature. At constant pressure the volume of a given mass of gas increases by $\frac{1}{273}$ of its volume at 0°C for 1°C size in its temperature.

Gay Lussac's Law: At constant volume, the pressure of given mass of gas is directly proportional to its absolute temperature.

Graham's Law of Diffusion: At constant temperature and pressure, the rate of diffusion of a gas is inversely proportional to the square root of its density.

Dalton's Law of Partial Pressure: The total pressure exerted by the mixture of inactive gases in a vessel is equal to the sum of the partial pressures due to individual gas.

Avogadro's Law: If the temperature, pressure and volume of two gases are same then the number of molecules in them will also be equal.

Sound

Wave: A disturbance created in the medium which propagates in the forward direction with constant velocity without changing its shape, is defined as a wave.

Wave Motion: The mode of energy transfer in which a disturbance advances in the forward direction by affecting the medium without mass transfer, is defined as wave motion.

Characteristics of Wave Motion:

(*i*) The particle of the medium do not leave their mean positions rather they keep on vibrating about their mean positions.
(*ii*) The medium itself does not move.
(*iii*) The energy and momentum are transferred in the medium.
(*iv*) The phase of various particle of the medium keep on changing constantly.

Properties of Medium Necessary for Wave Propagation

(*i*) The medium should have the property of inertia.
(*ii*) The medium should posses the property of elasticity.
(*iii*) The medium should have low resistance.

Longitudinal Waves: In these waves the particles of the medium vibrate in the direction of propagation of waves.

Transverse Waves: In these waves the particles of the medium vibrate at right angles to the direction.

Ultrasonic Waves: The waves with frequency greater than that of sound, *i.e.*, 20×10^3 Hz are defined as Ultrasonic waves.

Shock Waves: When a sound source move with a velocity greater than that of sound then it leave behind it waves whose wave front is conical. These waves are defined as shock wave.

Terms Related to Wave Motion

(*i*) ***Displacement:*** The distance covered by a particle from mean position in a particular direction in SHM is known as displacement.
(*ii*) ***Amplitude:*** The maximum displacement of a particle executing SHM from its mean position, is defined as amplitude.
(*iii*) ***Time Period:*** The time taken by a particle in completing one vibration is defined as time period.
(*iv*) ***Frequency:*** The number of vibrations per second made by any particle of the medium is defined as its frequency.
(*v*) ***Wavelength:*** The distance between two nearest particles in one complete vibration is defined as the wavelength.
(*vi*) ***Wave Number:*** The number of wave present in unit length is defined as the wave number.
(*vii*) ***Wave Velocity:*** The velocity with which the crests and troughs or compression and rarefactions travel in medium, is defined as wave velocity.
(*viii*) ***Beats:*** When two waves of nearly same frequency, travelling in the same direction of the medium, superimpose over each other then the intensity at any point of the medium changes periodically with time. This phenomenon is defined as beats.
(*ix*) ***Beat Frequency:*** The number of beats heard per second is defined as beat frequency.
(*x*) ***Note:*** Any musical sound which is produced by the SHM of sound source is known as note.
(*xi*) ***Tone:*** Every component of musical sound is known as a tone. Every musical sound consists of a number of components of different frequencies. Every component is known as a tone.
(*xii*) ***Organ Pipe:*** The pipe filled with air and which when vibrated produces sound waves is known as organ pipe.
(*xiii*) ***Loudness:*** It is that characteristic of sound, on account of which the sound appears to be intense or slow is defined as loudness of sound or the power crossing per unit area at any point of the medium is defined as loudness.
(*xiv*) ***Pitch:*** It is that characteristic of sound on account of which it appears to be shrill or grave, is known as pitch.

Light

Light: The light is an electromagnetic radiation with the help of which our eyes experience the sensation of vision is known as light.

Ray of Light: The path of light energy from one point to another is known as a ray of light.

Properties of Light

(*i*) It propagates in straight line.

(*ii*) It exhibits the phenomenon of reflection, refraction, interference, diffraction, polarisation and double refraction.

(*iii*) The properties of the medium through which light passes remain unchanged.

(*iv*) Its velocity is different in different media. In rarer medium it is more and in denser medium it is less.

(*v*) Its velocity in vacuum is maximum whose value is 3×10^8 m/s.

Reflection of Light: The phenomenon of returning of incident light in the same medium is known as reflection.

Laws of Reflection:

(*i*) The incident ray, the reflected ray and the normal all lie in the same plane.

(*ii*) In regular reflection the angle of incidence is equal to the angle of reflection.

(*iii*) When light is reflected by a rarer medium then its phase remains unchanged whereas phase difference of a path difference of $\lambda/2$ or time difference T/2 is created when it is reflected by a denser medium. This is also known as Stoke's Law.

Refraction of Light: When a ray of light enters from one medium to another then at the boundary of separation it deviates from its initial path. This phenomenon is known as refraction.

Law of Refraction:

(*i*) The incident ray, the refracted ray and the normal all three lie in the same plane.

(*ii*) For given two media and for a given wavelength, the ratio of the sine of angle of incidence to the sine of angle of refraction always remain constant.

(*iii*) Light bends towards the normal if passes through rarer medium to denser medium.

(*iv*) Light bends away from the normal if passes through denser medium to rarer medium.

Critical Angle: When a ray of light enters from denser to rarer medium, then the angle of incidence corresponding to which the angle of refraction is 90°, is defined as the critical angle.

Total Internal Reflection: When a ray of light passes from a denser to rarer medium at an angle greater than the critical angle, then it gets totally reflected. This phenomenon is known as total internal reflection.

Refractive Index: The ratio of velocities of light in two media is defined as refractive index.

Dispersion of Light: The phenomenon of splitting of a ray of light into difference colours by a prism is defined as dispersion.

Spectrum: The whole band of colours from violet to red colour is known as spectrum. There are seven colours in the spectrum in the following order Violet, Indigo, Blue, Green, Yellow, Orange and Red or VIBGYOR.

Rainbow: The seven coloured curved strip formed as a result of dispersion of light through water droplets which keep suspended in the atmosphere after rains, is known as rainbow.

LASER (Light Amplification by Stimulated Emission of Radiation)

(*i*) The light amplification by induced emission of radiation is known as laser.

(*ii*) It is highly coherent and highly monochromatic light.

(*iii*) It is perfectly unidirectional and highly intense and powerful.

Polaroids: Microcrystals of iodo-sulphate of quinine are deposited on thin sheet of nitro-cellulose and then squeezed them out through a fine slit. In this process only the crystals having axes parallel to the slit pass through it and form a sheet. These sheets are kept between ordinary glass plates and called polaroids.

Uses of Polaroids: In winds screen; Window panes of aeroplanes; Camera filters and sun glasses in 3-D movies.

Luminous Flux: The luminous flux through a given surface is the amount of luminous energy that passes through the surface in one second in a direction normal to surface.

Lumen: One lumen is the amount of luminous flux emitted per unit solid angle by a source of light of luminous intensity one candela.

Luminous Intensity: The luminous intensity of a source is defined as the luminous flux emitted per unit solid angle by the source. It is also known as illuminating power.

Candela: One candela is the luminous intensity in a given direction due to a source, which emits monochromatic radiation of frequency 5.4×10^{14} Hz and whose radiant intensity in that direction is 1/683 watt per steradian.

Mirror: The highly polished reflecting surface is known as mirror. Mirror are of three types: Plane mirror; Concave mirror and Convex mirror.

Properties of Image Formed by Plane Mirror

(*i*) The image formed by a plane mirror is erect, virtual laterally reversed.

(*ii*) The size of image formed by it is equal to that of the object.

(*iii*) The image is formed behind the mirror at a distance equal to the distance of the object in front of mirror.

(*iv*) When the mirror is rotated through an angle θ, then the reflected ray rotates through an angle 2θ.

(*v*) When two mirrors are kept parallel to each other, then the number of images will be infinity as

Spherical Mirror: The smooth, polished spherical surface is known as spherical mirror, or the reflecting surface which is a part of a sphere is known as spherical mirror. It is of two types: (*i*) Concave mirror and (*ii*) Convex mirror

Magnification (m): The ratio of the size of image to size of object is defined as the magnification of spherical mirror, or *magnification* $= \frac{v}{u} = \frac{\text{Size of image}}{\text{Size of object}}$

or *magnification* $= \frac{\text{Length of image}}{\text{Length of object}}$

Use of Plane Mirrors:

(*a*) In dressing tables

(*b*) In looking-glass

(*c*) In scientific apparatus. Plane mirrors are used to bend the paths of rays of light in scientific apparatus.

Uses of Concave Mirror:

(*a*) As shaving and hair dressing mirrors.

(*b*) As reflectors—concave mirrors are used as reflectors in search lights and head light.

(*c*) The ENT specialists use concave mirror for viewing the inner parts of ear, nose and throat.

(*d*) In lighthouses in seas.

(*e*) In a torch for hunting purpose.

Use of Convex Mirror:

(*a*) To spread light on roads.

(*b*) As side mirrors on cars in order to view the vehicle following the cars.

(*c*) For decoration purpose as these form the very small images which look beautiful.

Lens: The part of an isotropic transparent medium by two spherical, cylindrical, parabolic or one plane and another spherical surfaces is defined as lens.

Lenses are of Two types:

(*i*) Concave lens or diverging lens.

(*ii*) Convex lens or converging lens.

Concave lenses are of three types:

(*i*) *Concave-concave lens:* Both of its surfaces are concave. The radii of curvature of its two concave surfaces may be same or different.

(*ii*) *Plano-concave lens:* Its one surface is plane and second surface is concave.

(*iii*) *Convexo-concave:* One of its surfaces is convex and another surface is concave. The radii of curvature of convex and concave surfaces are different.

Convex Lenses are of Three Types:

(*i*) *Convexo-convex:* Both of its surface are convex. The radii of curvature of its convex surfaces may be same or different.

(*ii*) *Plano-convex:* One of its surfaces is convex and another one is plane.

(*iii*) *Concavo-convex:* One of its surfaces is concave and another one is convex. The radii of its concave and convex surfaces are different.

Power of Lens:

(*i*) The power of a thin lens is equal to the reciprocal of its focal length measured in meter, *i.e.*, $P = \frac{1}{f}$.

The unit of power of lens is dioptre.

(*ii*) When two lenses are kept in contact then the power of compound lens is equal to the sum of power of two lenses, *i.e.*, $P = P_1 + P_2$.

(*iii*) When a concave lens and a convex lens of equal focal lengths are kept in contact then the power of the compound lens becomes zero, *i.e.*, it behaves like a plane glass plate.

(*iv*) Magnification: The ratio of the size of image formed by lens to the size of object is defined as its linear magnification.

Prism: An isotropic transparent medium closed by surfaces inclined at an angle is define as a prism.

Dispersion: The phenomen of splitting of a white ray of light into seven colours is defined as dispersion.

Visible Spectrum: The spectrum which can be viewed with the help of eye is known as visible spectrum. The spectrum spreads from violet and (wavelength 3500Å).

Magnetism

Magnet: A piece of matter, which when suspended freely rests in a particular direction (North-South) and which possesses a net magnetic moment and which attracts ferrous bodies towards it, is called a magnet.

Natural Magnet: The magnet which is found naturally in mines is called a natural magnet, *e.g.*, magnetite. Its shape and size are indefinite, hence it cannot be used for scientific purpose. Its magnetism is quite weak.

Artificial Magnet: The magnet which are artificially prepared are known as artificial magnets. There are generally made of iron, steel and nickel. Its shape and size are definite.

Bar Magnet: A system composed of two poles, equal in magnitude but opposite in polarity, plane, at a small displacement apart is known as a bar magnet. It is also known as a magnetic dipole.

Properties of a Magnet: Like pole repel and unlike pole attract each other; it can be magnetically saturated; it can be demagnetized by beating, mechanical jerks, heating and with lapse of time; it produces magnetism in other materials by induction.

Magnetism: It is the property of a magnet, by virtue of which it attracts ferromagnetic materials towards it and rests itself in North-South direction, is known as magnetism. The magnetism of materials is mainly due to the spin motion of its electrons.

Magnetic Poles: The two points at the ends of a magnet at which magnetism is maximum are defined as magnetic poles. The magnetic poles are of two types—(*i*) North pole, (*ii*) South pole.

Magnetic Axis: The imaginary line joining the two poles of a magnet is defined as magnetic axis.

Magnetic Meridian: An imaginary plane passing through the axis of a freely suspended stationary magnet is defined as magnetic meridian. It is not a particular plane rather it is the direction of earth's magnetic field.

Pole Strength: The strength of a magnetic pole to attract magnetic materials towards it is known as pole strength.

Magnetic Field: The space around a magnet in which a torque acts on a magnetic needle is known as magnetic field.

Magnetic Dipole: The structure, which tend to align along the direction of magnetic field, are known as magnetic dipoles.

Magnetic Flux: The number of lines of forces passing through a given area is defined as magnetic flux.

Magnetic Moment: The product of the pole strength of a magnet and its length is defined as its magnetic moment.

Electromagnetic Induction: The phenomenon of production of electromotive force on account of change in magnetic flux linked with a circuit, is defined as electromagnetic induction.

Induced emf: The emf generated on account of change in magnetic flux linked with a plane or a circuit, is defined as induced emf.

Induced Charge: The electric charge flowing in a closed circuit on account of induced current is defined as induced charge.

Transformer: The device based on the principle of mutual induction used to change the value of alternating voltage is defined as transformer. There are two types of transformer: (*a*) Step-up transformer, (*b*) Step-down transformer

Dynamo: The device used to convert mechanical energy into electrical energy is known as dynamo.

Electrostatics and Current Electricity

Electrostatics: The branch of physics in which we study charges at rest, is known as electrostatics.

Electric Charge: It is a fundamental property of matter which can never be isolated from matter.

Charges are of two types: (*a*) Positive charges; (*b*) Negative charges

Positive Charges: The deficiency of electron on a body or particle is known as positive charge.

Negative Charge: The excess of electrons on a body or a particle is known as negative charge. When a negative charge is given to a body then its mass some what increases.

Properties of Charges:

(*i*) Like charges repel and unlike charges attract each other.

(*ii*) A charged body attracts other uncharged light particles.

(*iii*) Total charge of an isolated physical system is always conserved.

Law of Conservation of Charge: Charges can neither be created nor be destroyed, rather these can be transferred from one body to another.

Coulomb's Law: The force of attraction or repulsion acting between two stationary point charges is directly proportional to the product of strengths of charges and inversely proportional to the square of distance between two charges. Its direction is along the line joining the two charges.

Electric Field: The region of space around a charge in which any other charge experiences coloumb forces is known as electric field.

Electric Intensity: The resultant coulomb force per unit test charge at any point in an electric field is defined as the intensity of electric field at that point.

Electromotive Force: The total work done in carrying a unit positive test charge around a closed path in an electric field, is defined as electromotive force.

Electric Potential: The work done against electric field in carrying a unit positive test charge from infinity to any point in electric field is defined as electric potential at that point.

Potential Difference: The negative of work done in carrying a unit positive test charge from one point to another point in an electric field is defined as electric potential difference between those two points.

Capacitance: It is numerically equal to that electric charge which raises its potential by unity. Unit of capacitance is farad.

Condenser: The pair of conductors of opposite charges, on which sufficient quantity of charge may be accommodated is defined as condenser.

Current: The rate of flow of charge in a circuit is defined as current. Electric current is equal to the charge that flow in one second.

Conductor: The materials, in which the number of free electron is very large are defined as conductors, *e.g.*, silver, copper, aluminium, etc.

Insulator: The materials, in which the number of free electrons at ordinary temperatures is negligible, are defined as insulators.

Resistance: The property of a conductor by virtue of which it opposes the flow of current in it is defined as resistance.

Ohm's Law: If the physical circumstances of the conductor (temperature, etc.) remains constant, then the applied potential difference is directly proportional to the current flowing in it.

Resistivity: The resistivity of a material is equal to the resistance of the wine of that material with unit cross-sectional area and unit length.

Conductivity : The reciprocal of specific resistance is defined as specific conductance.

Nuclear Physics

Isotopes: The elements which have same atomic number, same chemical properties, same electron number and same structure, but different mass is called isotopes.

Isobars: The elements which have same atomic mass, but different atomic number, physical and chemical properties is called isobars.

Photo-electric Cell: The device, by which light energy is directly converted into electrical energy, is known as the photo-electric cell.

X-rays: There are electromagnetic waves whose wavelength is more than that of γ-rays but less than that of ultraviolet rays, *i.e.*, these rays lie in between the ultraviolet region and γ-rays region of electromagnetic spectrum.

Mass Defect: When neutrons and protons combine to form a nucleus, then the mass of the nucleus is some what less than the sum of masses of its constituent particles.

Mass defect (Δm) = total mass of all the neutrons present inside nucleus + total mass of protons – mass of the nucleus.

Binding Energy: The minimum energy required to keep the neutrons and protons bound inside the nucleus, is defined as binding energy.

Nuclear Fission: The phenomenon in which a heavy unstable nuclear breaks into two parts of nearly same mass, is defined as nuclear fission.

Chain Reaction: The process of nuclear fission, which when once started, continues spontaneously is defined as chain reaction.

Nuclear Reactor: The device in which energy is generated by chain reaction of nuclear fission is known as nuclear reactor.

Nuclear Fusion: The process in which two or more than two lighter nuclei combine to form a heavier nucleus, is known as nuclear fusion.

Radioactivity: The phenomenon of spontaneous disintegration of nuclei of unstable atoms is defined as radioactivity.

Decay Constant: It is equal to the reciprocal of that time in which the number of radioactive atoms remains its initial value.

Half-life: The time, in which the number of atoms (N) reduces to half of its initial value is defined as the half-life of the element.

Mean-life: The time, for which a radioactive remains active, is defined as mean life of that material.

CHEMISTRY

Atoms and its Structure

Nucleus: The nucleus (atomic nucleus) is the center of an atom. It is composed of one or more protons and usually some neutrons as well. The simplest atom of all, hydrogen, has one proton in its nucleus.

Proton is a subatomic particle with a positive electric charge of 1.6×10^{-19} coulomb and a mass of 938 MeV ($1.6726231 - 10^{-27}$ kg, or about 1800 times the mass of an electron).

Neutron is a subatomic particle with no net electric charge and a mass of 940 MeV (very slightly more than a proton). The nucleus of most atoms consists of protons and neutrons.

Electron is a subatomic particle with a negative charge. In an atom the electrons surround the nucleus of protons and neutrons. The electron has a negative electric charge of -1.6×10^{-19} coulombs, and a mass of about 9.10×10^{-31} kg, which is 1/1800 of the proton mass.

Famous Inventions

Atomic Theory	**John Dalton**
Electron	**J.J. Thomson**
Proton	**Rutherford**
Neutron	**Masley**
Dynamite	**Alfred Nobel**
Atomic Number	**Chadwick**
Periodic Table	**Dmitry Mendeleyev**
Radioactivity	**Henri Becquerel**
Oxygen	**J. Priestly**
Hydrogen	**Cavendish**

Atomic Number: The number of protons in an atoms nucleus is called the atomic number (Z), and determines the element (for example, hydrogen, carbon, oxygen, etc.).

Atomic Weight (A): The atomic weight is the sum of neutrons and protons in the nucleus of the atom also called Mass Number.

Molecular Weight: The molecular weight of a molecule is the sum of the atomic weights of the atoms making up that molecule.

Isotopes: Isotopes are atoms of a chemical element whose nuclei have the same atomic number, Z, but different atomic weights, A.

Isobars: Isobars have the same isotopic mass but different atomic number, *e.g.*, Argon, Potassium and Calcium $^{18}Ar_{40}$, $^{19}K_{40}$, $^{20}Ca_{40}$.

Isotone : Isotone contains the same number of neutrons but different numbers of protons.

Elements

Elements are substances compose of same type of atom. Hydrogen, oxygen, chlorine, sodium, and iron are examples of elements. Ninety-two elements are known to occur in nature, and 22 more have been made artificially.

Some Common Elements and their Applications

Nitrogen: Nitrogen is the most abundant constituent in the atmosphere composes about four-fifths (78.03 per cent) by volume of the atmosphere. Nitrous oxide is known as laughing gas. Nitrous oxide is used as an anesthesia. Liquid nitrogen is used as coolant in cryogenics.

Oxygen: It was discovered by Joseph priestly. Oxygen composes 21 percent by volume of atmosphere. It is used in high-temperature welding torches, administered to patients whose breathing is impaired and oxygen-enriched air is used in open-hearth furnaces for steel manufacture. High-purity oxygen is used also in the metal-fabrication industries; in liquid form it is used in a propellant for guided missiles and rockets.

Argon: Argon is the third most prevalent gas in the earth atmosphere. Argon is also used in one type of neon lamp giving blue light whereas pure neon gives a red light. It is preferred because it requires a lower voltage than neon.

Hydrogen: Hydrogen exits as a gas at room temperature and is highly flammable. In stars, hydrogen nuclei combine with each other in nuclear reactions to form helium atoms. The isotopes of Hydrogen are Deuterium and Tritium. Spacecrafts use hydrogen as fuel that reacts with fluorine or oxygen. Nuclear plants use D_2O as a moderator.

Carbon dioxide: Carbon dioxide does not burn and support ordinary combustion; it is used in fire extinguishers. Solid carbon dioxide is known as Dry ice widely used as refrigerant. The presence of carbon dioxide in the blood stimulates breathing. For this reason, CO_2 is added to the oxygen in artificial respiration.

Methane: Methane also know as marsh gas, gas composed of carbon and hydrogen with formula CH_4, the first member of the paraffin or alkane series of hydrocarbons. It is lighter than air, colourless, odourless, and flammable. It occurs in natural gas, in coal mines, as a by-product of petroleum refining, and as a product of decomposition of matter in swamps.

Iron: Iron is a metal extracted from iron ore, and is hardly ever found in the free (elemental) state. Depending upon the carbon content Iron can be classified into: Pig Iron (4%–5%), Cast iron (2–3.5%), carbon steel (0.5–1.5%) and Wrought Iron (< 0.5%).

Sodium: Sodium is a constituent of table salt and baking soda. Sulfur, however, is a common impurity in fossil fuels used for home heating and the production of electricity. Large amounts of SO_2 are causing both local air pollution as well as acid rain.

The halogens: The halogens are: fluorine, chlorine, bromine, iodine, and astatine.

- Chlorine gas is greenish yellow. It is a powerful bleaching, and disinfecting agent. Chlorine is an important chemical in water purification.
- Bromine is a red volatile liquid at room temperature.
- Astatine is radioactive and heaviest of Halogens.
- Iodine is a bluish-black, lustrous solid. Potassium Iodide is used in Photography. Iodine 131 is used as a tracer in medicine.

Compound

Compound is a substance formed from two or more elements, *e.g.*, Water. **Mixture** is the product of a mechanical blending or mixing of chemical substances without other chemical change, so that each ingredient substance retains its own chemical properties. While there are no chemical changes in a mixture, physical properties of a mixture, such as its melting point, may differ from those of its components. Mixtures can usually be separated by mechanical means. There are different types of Compounds are Acids, Bases, Salts, Oxides and organic compounds.

Acids: An acid is a water-soluble, sour-tasting chemical compound. An acid always has a pH of less than 7 and turns litmus red. An acid reacts with a base in a neutralization reaction to form a salt.

Acid	Used as
Ascetic Acid	Vinegar
Amino Acid	Basis of protein
Ascorbic Acid	Vitamin C
Carbolic Acid/Phenol	Disinfectant
Citric Acid	Citrus fruits
Nitrohydrochloric Acid (Aqua Regia)	Dissolving gold and platinum
Tartaric Acid	Used in baking powder
Carbonic Acid	Carbonated beverages
Formic Acid	Ants
Lactic Acid	Sour milk
Malic Acid	Unripe apples
Nitric Acid/Aqua Fortis	Used in explosives and rocket fuels
Prussic Acid/ Hydrocynic Acid	Poison
Salicylic Acid	Basis of aspirin
Tannic Acid/Tannin	Found in tea
Uric Acid	In the urine of birds and reptiles
Oxalic Acid	Spinach

Bases : A base is a chemical compound that will neutralize an acid and form a salt and water. Bases are typically water-soluble, bitter tasting, turns litmus blue and always have a pH greater than 7 in solution, *e.g.*, baking soda , sodium carbonate etc.

Litmus: A mixture of pigments extracted from certain lichens that turns blue in basic solution and red in acidic solution.

Salt: A salt is a neutral compound composed of cations bound to anions. A cation is a positively charged ion. Metals typically form cations where as anions are negatively charged ion.

Organic compound: These contain carbon chemically bound to hydrogen. They often contain other elements (particularly O, N, halogens, or S).

Metals and Non-metals

Metals: Metals are shiny (lustre), high density, ductile and malleable, high melting point, hard, and conduct electricity and heat.

Ores: An ore is a mineral containing a metal as a proportion of its content, which is economical to extract its metallic component.

Substance	Important Ores
Aluminium	Bauxite
Antimony	Stibnite
Beryllium	Beryl, Crysoberyl
Calcium	Lime stone, Marble, Chalk, Gypsum, Flurosper
Chromium	Chromite
Cobalt	Smaltite
Copper	Cuprite, Bornite
Iron	Hematite, Magnatite
Lead	Galena, Masicot, Serusite
Magnicium	Magnesite, Dolomite, Carnallite
Manganese	Pyrolusite, Hausmannite
Mercury	Cinnabar
Molybdenum	Molybdenite and wulfenite
Nickel	Pantilandite and Gargnierite
Phosphorous	Phosphorite Apatite, Chlorapatite
Potassium	Carnelite, Saltpetre
Silver	Argentite
Sodium	Rock Salt, Chile Saltpetre
Sulphur	Galena, Copper Pyrites and Iron Pyrites
Tin	Cassiterite, Tin stone
Titanium	Rutile, Ilmenite
Uranium	Pitchblende
Zinc	Zinc Blends,Calamine

Some Important Processes

(*a*) ***Gravity separation:*** The heavier metal or metallic mineral particles separated from the lighter gangue. Gold and magnetite are separated in this way.

(*b*) ***Flotation:*** In this method, finely ground ore is mixed with a liquid. The metal or metallic mineral floats while the gangue sinks.

(*c*) ***Magnetic separation:*** Metals that have magnetic properties are separated from the gangue, *e.g.*, magnetite.

(*d*) ***Smelting:*** The ore is heated with a reducing agent and a flux to a high temperature. The reducing agent combines with the oxygen in a metallic oxide, leaving pure metal; and the flux combines with the gangue to form a slag that is liquid poured away from the metal. The production of pig iron extract copper, lead, nickel use this process.

(*e*) ***Amalgamation*** is a metallurgical process that utilizes mercury to dissolve silver or gold to form an amalgam.

(*f*) ***Electrolysis:*** In this process, the metal is deposited at the cathode from aqueous solutions or in an electrolytic furnace. Copper, nickel, zinc, silver, and gold are several examples of metals that are refined by deposition from aqueous solutions. Aluminium, barium, calcium, magnesium, beryllium, potassium, and sodium are metals that are processed in electrolytic furnaces.

Some Interesting Points

Osmium and iridium are the most dense metals, and lithium is the least dense. Bismuth has the lowest electrical conductivity of the metallic elements, and silver the highest at ordinary temperatures. Gallium, mercury, cesium, and rubidium are the only metal elements that melt near room temperature.

Metalloids have intermediate in properties between the metals and the non-metals. Most common is that metalloids are usually semiconductors rather than conductors. They are boron, silicon, germanium, arsenic, antimony, tellurium, polonium.

Non-metal: A non-metal is a substance that conducts heat and electricity poorly, is brittle or waxy or gaseous, and cannot be hammered into sheets or drawn into wire. The non-metals are: nitrogen, oxygen, fluorine, phosphorus, sulfur, chlorine, selenium.

Alkali metals: They are soft compared to other metals, have low melting points, and are so reactive that they are never found freely in nature, *e.g.*, lithium, sodium, potassium, rubidium, cesium, and francium. Francium exists only in a radioactive form.

Alkaline Earth Metals: They are brittle, the alkaline earth metals are malleable, conduct electricity and when heated, burn readily in air, *e.g.*, beryllium, magnesium, calcium, strontium, barium, and radium.

Alloys

An alloy is a compound, of two or more elements, at least one of which is a metal.

Alloy	Composition
Duraluminium	Aluminium, copper, magnesium, and manganese
Gun Metal	Copper, Tin
Steel	Iron, Carbon
Stainless Steel	Iron, carbon, chromium, tungsten
Petwar	Tin, Antimony and Copper
Bronze	Copper, Tin and Zinc
German Silver	Copper, Zinc and Nickel
Electrum	Gold and Silver
18 carat Gold	Gold, Silver and Copper
Dentist Amalgam	Mercury Copper
Yellow Brass	Copper Zinc
Brass	Copper and Zinc
Nichrome	Nickel and Chromium
Plumbers Solder	Lead and tin

Common Chemicals and their Chemical Names

Common Name	Chemical Name
grain alcohol	ethyl alcohol
wood Alcohol	methyl alcohol
alum	aluminum potassium sulfate
alumina	aluminum oxide
baking soda	sodium bicarbonate
bleaching powder	chlorinated lime
blue vitriol	copper sulfate
brimstone	sulfur
carbolic acid	phenol
carbonic acid gas	carbon dioxide
epsom salts	gypsum
hypo (photography)	sodium thiosulfate solution
gypsum	natural calcium sulfate
lime	calcium oxide
lime, slaked	calcium hydroxide
limewater	calcium hydroxide
lunar caustic	silver nitrate
magnesia	magnesium oxide
mercury oxide, black	mercurous oxide
methanol	methyl alcohol
methylated spirits	methyl alcohol
pearl ash	potassium carbonate

Important Points to Remember

- Temporary hardness of water is due to the presence of bicarbonates of calcium and magnesium in water. Whereas the permanent hardness is due to the presence of Calcium Sulphate, which can be eliminated by the use of Zeolites.
- The gas used in balloons is helium.
- Gobar gas is obtained by decomposition of vegetable matter and animal dung.
- L.P.G. (liquefied petroleum gas) consists of mainly propane and butane.
- Natural gas is composed primarily of methane and other light hydrocarbons.
- Ethylene gas is used for artificial fruit ripening.
- Sodium and potassium react vigorously with cold water so it is preserved under kerosene while phosphorus is spontaneously inflammable in air so preserved under water.
- Nitrous oxide is called laughing gas, in mild doses it is used as anesthetic.
- Nitric acid is used as fertilizers and explosives.
- Tri-nitro toluène and nitro glycerene are common explosives.
- Smelling salt is ammonium carbonate.
- Potassium nitrate or Nitre or Indian salt petre is used as Gun powder.
- The paste applied to the side of a match box is a mixture of Phosphorous Trisulphide, glass powder and sand to cause frictions and glue. The match head contains a readily combustible substance like atimony trisulphide, potassium chlorate which maintain the combustion and a binding material like glue.
- Marble is calcium carbonate.
- Methylated spirit is a mixture of methyl alcohol and ethyl alcohol.
- Urea is the first organic compound prepared in the laboratory.
- Carbonic acid is soda water.
- Mercaptans leakage in L.P.G. cylinders is easily detected.
- Hydrazine is used to propel rockets.
- Coke is obtained by healthy wood out of contact with air.
- Terylene and nylon arc synthetic fibres produced by a process of polymerization. Terylene is a polyester and Nylon a polymide.
- Pyrene is carbon tetrachloride specially used to extinguish electrical fires.
- Tincture iodine is a solution of iodine in alcohol.
- Nickel is used in conversion of oil into solid fat.
- Coal gas is the product of destructive distillation of coal *i.e.*, heating coal out of contact of air.
- Rust is hydrated ferric oxide.
- The chief component of pearl is ferric component.

BIOLOGY

The term *biology* derived from the Greek work, bios, "life" and the suffix-*logia*, "study of." **Biology** is a natural science concerned with the study of life and living organisms.

Branches of Biology

Apiculture	Culture of Bee
Cytology	Study of Cells
Dermatology	Study of Skin
Entomology	Study of Insects
Evolution	Study of Origin of new from old
Floriculture	Study of Flower Yielding Plants
Genetics	Study of Heredity and Variations
Gynaecology	Study of Female Reproductive Organ
Horticulture	Study of Garden Cultivation
Haematology	Study of Blood
Mycology	Study of Fungi
Nephrology	Study of Kidneys
Neurology	Study of Nervous System

Obstetrics	Branch of Medicine Dealing with Pregnancy
Ophthalmology	Study of Eyes
Ornithology	Study of Birds
Osteology	Study of Bones
Palaeontology	Study of Fossils
Phycology	Study of Algae
Pisciculture	Study of Fish
Pomology	Study of Fruits
Sericulture	Culture of Silk Moth and Pupa
Serpentology	Study of Snakes
Virology	Study of Virus

Cell

1. **Cell Membrane:** Cells are enclosed by a thin film like membrane called plasma membrane, cytoplasmic membrane or plasma lemma.
   Endocytosis: Taking substance inside the cell by the plasma membrane. It is of two types : *Phagocytosis :* Cell Eating. *Pinocytosis :* Cell drinking. *Exocytosis:* Reverse of Endocytosis.
2. **Cytoplasm:** It is a part of protoplasm lying between plasma membrane and nucleus.
3. **Cell Wall :** Cells of most fungi, prokaryotes (bacteria and blue-green algae) and plants (except gametes) are surrounded by the cell wall. It is absent in animals.
4. **Nucleus:** Discovered by Robert Brown. Nucleus controls the metabolic activities of the cell by controlling the synthesis of enzymes.
   - Contains nucleoplasm (nuclear sap) which contains chromatin.
   - Chromatin organizes itself into thread like structures called Chromosomes.
   - The function of chromosomes is to carry genetic information from one cell generation to another.
   - Nucleolus is also present which helps in the production of ribosomes.
5. **Chromosomes :** Waldeyer coined the term chromosome. Each chromosome is made up of DNA.
   - Chromosome number is constant for a particular species. Diploid number (2n) of chromosomes are present in somatic cells and haploid number (n) of chromosomes are there in gametes.
   - In humans, the diploid number is 46.
6. **Mitochondria :** Powerhouse of the cell and energy is stored as ATP
   - They are semi-autonomous organelles. They contain DNA.
   - Mitochondria is enclosed by a double-membraned envelope.
7. **Endoplasmic Reticulum :** Provides an increased surface area for various metabolic activities within the cell. Types: Rough ER and smooth ER.
8. **Golgi Complex :** Main function is secretion. Secretions are in the form of granules in cytoplasm.
9. **Lysosomes :** Also called Suicidal bags. Contain enzymes acid hydrolases which digest worn - out or unnecessary parts of the cell, or even whole cells by process called 'Autophagy'.
10. **Ribosomes :** Made of RNA and proteins in equal amounts. Sites of protein synthesis.
11. **Vacuoles :** Large vacuole found in plant cells. Membrane surrounding the vacuole is tonoplast. Regulation of water, in osmoregulation, in storage and in digestion.
12. **Plastids :** Found only in plant cells.
    - ***Chloroplast :*** Green contains the pigment chlorophyll.
    - ***Leucoplasts :*** Colourless, occur in large number in cells of fruits, seeds, etc. They store nutrients (*e.g.*, amyloplasts of potato store starch).
    - ***Chromoplasts :*** Coloured, containing fat soluble yellow, orange and red pigments. Found in flowers and fruits.
13. **Centrosome :** Found in animal cells and cells of lower plants (*e.g.*, Algae) only. The first indication that the cell is about to divide is generally given by the centrosome.

Balanced Diet

A Balanced Diet comprising of healthy and diverse foods is key to promoting good health. The components of food are:

1. **Carbohydrates:** Constitutes 3 elements: Carbon, Hydrogen and Oxygen. 1 gm gives 17 kJ of energy (or 4.1 kcal of energy). Carbohydrates form a better fuel than proteins and fats because their molecules have relatively more oxygen.
   - Cellulose is present in the cell-wall of plants.
   - D-fructose is the sweetest of sugars. It is found in Fruit Juices, Honey, etc.
   - Excess Sugar is stored as Glycogen in liver.
   - ***Sources of Carbohydrates are:*** Cereals (Wheat, Rice and Maize), Sugarcane, Milk (contains Lactose — a type of Sugar), Fruits, Honey, Beet, etc.
   - ***Types of Carbohydrates:*** **(*i*) Monosaccharides :** They are the simplest carbohydrates consist of one unit (*e.g.*, glucose, fructose, galactose). **(*ii*) Disaccharides :** Consist of 2 units of monosaccharides (*e.g.*, sucrose, lactose and 1 maltose). **(*iii*) Polysaccharides :** Consist of more than three monosaccharide units (*e.g.*, starch in plants and glycogen in animals).
2. **Fats:** Provides twice the energy of carbohydrates (1 gm provides 37 kJ or 9 kcal of energy). Acts as the reserve food material, excess fat is stored in the liver and adipose tissue.
   - ***Types of fatty acids :*** Saturated and Unsaturated. **(*i*) Saturated Fatty Acids :** Solids at room temperature. **(*ii*) Unsaturated Fatty Acids :** Liquids at room temperature.

- Excess of saturated fats increases the blood — cholesterol level and may cause arteriosclerosis (hardening of arteries). This may lead to heart attack.
- Essential Fatty Acids include Linoleic, Linolenic and Arachidonic Acids are present in Groundnut Oil, Sunflower Oil.
- ***Hydrogenation :*** Process by which unsaturated fatty acids are converted into saturated fatty acids by the addition of Hydrogen.

3. **Proteins** : Made up of Carbon, Hydrogen, Oxygen, Nitrogen and Sulphur. Important for growth and repair of the body (75% of our body is proteins only).
   - ***Types of Amino acids are:*** ***(i)*** **Essential Amino Acids :** They cannot be synthesised in the body, *e.g.*, isoleucine, leucine, lysine, methionine, phenylalanine, threonine, tryptophan and valine. ***(ii)*** **Non - Essential Amino Acids :** They are synthesized in the body, *e.g.*, Alanine, Arginine, Asparagine, Aspartic Acid, Cysteine, Glutamine, Glutamic Acid, Glycine, Histidine, Proline, Serine and Tyrosine.
   - ***Some Important Proteins are: Enzymes:*** *e.g.*, Pepsin, Trypsin. **Hormone:** *e.g.*, Insulin, Glucogon, **Carrier:** *e.g.*, Haemoglobin — Transports O_2 in blood, Myoglobin — Stores O_2 in muscles. **Contractile Proteins:** *e.g.*, Actin and Myosin. **Structural Proteins:** *e.g.*, Collagen — Component of Bones, Tendons, Cartilage. Keratin — Component of Skin, Feathers, Nails, Hair, Horn. **Protective Proteins:** *e.g.*, Gamma globulins. **Visual Proteins :** Rhodopsin and Iodopsin of rods and cones. (present in Retina of the eye).
   - ***Protein Energy Malnutrition:*** ***(i)*** **Kwashiorkar :** Due to deficiency of protein. Abdomen and feet swells, Skin becomes Dark and Scaly, Enlarged Liver, Anaemia. ***(ii)*** **Marasmus :** Deficiency of Proteins. Losing of body weight, wasting of muscles, ribs look prominent. (Oedema and skin pigmentation absent).
4. **Minerals:** Minerals maintain water balance and nutrition in the body
   - Although needed in very small quantities, mineral salts of various kinds are essential for the proper functioning of the body.
   - They yield no energy but are important constituents of certain tissues, besides playing a major role in the regulation of metabolic activities.
   - Calcium is the principal component of the skeleton.
   - Meat, eggs, milk, cheese and vegetables are important sources of minerals, and usually, the body gets adequate amounts of them from a normal diet.

Minerals Required in Human beings

Minerals	Sources	Functions	Deficiency
Macro Elements			
Calcium	Milk, Cheese	Formation of Teeth and Bones	Weak Teeth and Bones
Phosphorus	Milk, Meat	Component of ATP, DNA, RNA	Weak Teeth and Bones; Retarded Growth
Sulphur	Proteins of Food	Component of Amino Acids	Disturbed Protein Metabolism.
Potassium	Meat, Milk, Cereals, Fruits	Water Regulation	Weak Muscles; Risk of Paralysis
Chlorine	Table salt	Acid-Base Balance	Loss of Appetite; Muscle Cramps.
Sodium	Table salt	Acid - Base and Water Balances	Low Blood Pressure, Loss of Appetite;
Magnesium	Cereals, Green Vegetables	Cofactor of Enzymes	Affects Nervous Functions.
Iron	Meat, Eggs, Cereals	Component of haemoglobin	Anaemia, Weakness
Iodine	Sea Food, Iodized Salt	Component of Thyroxine	Goitre, Cretinism
Micro Elements			
Flourine	Drinking Water, Tea, Sea Food	Maintenance of Bones and Teeth	Weak Teeth,
Manganese	Dry Fruits, Cereals,	Cofactor of some Enzymes	Irregular Growth of Bones, Cartilages

Vitamins Required in Human beings

Vitamins : Discovered by Funk. It do not provide energy but help in different physiological processes.

Vitamin	Sources	Effect of Deficiency
Water - Soluble Vitamins		
B_1 (Thiamine)	Rice Bran, Whole Wheat Flour	Beri - beri
B_2 (Riboflavin)	Cheese, Eggs, Yeast,	Cheilosis Keratitis of Cornea
B_3 (Nicotinic Acid)	Fresh Meat, Liver, Fish,	Pellagra, Muscle Atrophy,
B_6 (Pyridoxine)	Milk, Cereals, Fish, Meat, Liver	Dermatitis, Convulsions, Nausea, Mental Disorders
B_5 (Pantothenic Acid)	Yeast, Liver, Kidneys, Eggs, Meat,	Dermatitis, Anaemia, Fatigue, Nausea.
H (Biotin)	Yeast, Vegetables, Fruits, Eggs,	Skin Lesions, Loss of Appetite, Hair Fall.
Folic Acid Group	Green Vegetables, Soyabean,	Retarded Growth.
B_{12} (Cyanocobabmine)	Meat, Fish, Liver, Eggs,	Pernicious Anaemia
C (Ascorbic acid)	Lemon, Orange	Scurvy
Fat - Soluble Vitamins		
A (Retinol)	Milk, Butter, Egg Yolk, Liver,	Xerophthalmia
D (Cholecalciferol)	Synthesized in skin cells	Rickets, Osteomalacia.
E (Tocopherol)	Green Vegetables	Causes sterility, Muscular dystrophy,
K (Phylloauinone)	Carrots, Lettuce	Haemorrhages, delayed blood clotting

Digestive System of Humans

The process of converting food into energy giving substances is carried out by this system.

1. **Buccal Cavity :** In the mouth salivary glands secrete saliva which contains the enzyme Ptyalin
   - ***Teeth :*** They are produced in two sets — Temporary and Permanent. The teeth are of four types : Incisors, Canines, Premolars and Molars.
   - ***Structure of a Tooth :*** A tooth consists of 3 Regions: Crown, Neck and Root. Enamel is the hardest substance in the human body.
   - ***Dental Formula :*** 2123 / 2123, means that there are 2 incisors, 1 canine, 2 Premolars and 3 molars in half of the upper jaw and exactly the same arrangement in half of the lower jaw.
   - In elephants, incisors of the upper jaw grow into huge tusks.
   - Canines are very large in predators such as cat, dog and lion.
   - Rabbit and squirrel lack canines. In walrus, the upper canines are enlarged into projecting tusks.
   - The last molars are called the wisdom teeth.
2. **Pharynx:** Links Buccal Cavity to Oesophagus. Food is carried by peristaltic movement. Trachea opens into Pharynx through an aperture called Glottis.
3. **Oesophagus:** 25 cm long tube. Longitudinal folds keep its cavity almost closed, except during swallowing of food.
4. **Stomach:** Oesophagus opens into it. In stomach, the food is called chyme. Has 3 Parts: Fundus, Cardiac and Pyloric. Gastric juices produced in the stomach help in digestion of food. Also contains HCl which provides acidic medium. Besides it activates pepsinogen to pepsin and prorennin to rennin.
   - Ruminents (Cattle, Buffaloes, Goats, Sheep, Deer, Camel) have their stomach consisting of 4 Chambers: Rumen, Reticulum, Omasum and Abomasum.
5. **Small Intestine:** Here the food from the stomach is mixed with bile and pancreatic juice.
   - Duodenum receives the bile — pancreatic duct formed by the union of bile duct and pancreatic duct.
   - Both jejunum and ileum have numerous figure like projections called the villi. The villi contain blood vessels to absorb digested food.
6. **Large Intestine:** It receives undigested material from the small intestine and absorbs water.
   - Caecum is the diverted part of intestine. Cellulose digestion takes place in it. It is very large in herbivores.
   - Vermiform appendix is a part of caecum. Both caecum and appendix are vestigial in humans.

Blood in Human Body

Blood is a fluid connective tissue. It is 6.8 litres in man and 500 ml less in woman. 6-8% of body weight (pH 7.4).

1. **Red Blood Corpuscles:** Also called Erythrocytes, disc - shaped (for increased Surface Area), no nucleus contains a pigment called Haemoglobin, which gives blood its Red Colour.
   - ***Amount of Haemoglobin*** is 14-15.6 gm/ 100 cc of blood (11-14 in woman).
   - Life of RBC is 120 days after which they are broken down in spleen or liver.

- Product of breakdown of haemoglobin is a pigment (yellow colour), called bilirubin. Retention of bilirubin leads to jaundice.

2. **White Blood Corpuscles:** Also called Leucocytes, rounded, with a nucleus, far less numerous than RBCs, life 3-4 days.
   - ***Types:*** Granulocytes (Basophils, Eosinophils, Neutrophils) and Agranulocytes (Monocytes, Lymphocytes).
   - ***Basophils :*** Take up basic stains. Have an S-shaped nucleus. Secrete an anti-coagulant Heparin, which prevents clots within the blood vessels.
   - ***Eosinophils or Acidophils :*** Take up acidic stains. Assists in defence mechanism.
   - ***Neutrophils :*** Most numerous of the WBCs (65-70%). Defence.
   - ***Monocytes :*** Largest of all. Very motile. Defence.
   - ***Lymphocytes :*** 25% of the WBC. Takes part in antigen and antibody formation.
3. **Platelets :** Also called Thrombocytes, formed in bone marrow, life 3-7 days, sets off blood clotting.

   Plasma (65%) : Watery part of blood, clear, yellow fluid. Contains about 90% water, proteins and organic salts.
   - ***Lymph :*** Lymph = Blood - RBC, *i.e.*, Plasma + WBC. All interchanges of nutrients and waste products between blood and tissue takes place through lymph only.
   - Spleen produces lymph. At the same time it also acts as the graveyard of lymph.

   Blood Groupings
   - ***Father of Blood Grouping:*** Karl Landsteiner. He discovered A, B and O blood groups in 1900.
   - Decastello and Sturle in 1902 discovered AB blood group.
   - ABO system of blood groups is based on antigens and antibodies.
   - AB: Universal recipient.
   - O: Universal donor.

RH Factor: It is based on Rh antigen. Discovered in 1940 by Landsteiner and A.S. Veiner. It discovered in Rhesus monkey. A person can be Rh^+ or Rh^-.

- In world population Rh^+ are 85% and Rh^- are 15% only.
- Blood transfusion technique was first developed by James Blundell in 1825.

Excretory System of Humans

Waste materials excreted in animals are of many kinds : Nitrogenous Substances, Carbon dioxide, Pigments, Excess Water, etc.

The Nitrogenous Waste can be excreted in the following forms :

- **Ammonia :** Highly Toxic. In aquatic animals (called Ammoniotelic).
- **Urea :** Far less toxic than ammonia In Mammals, Alligators, Turtles (called Ureotelic).
- **Uric Acid :** In animals where conservation of water is needed. In Birds, Insects, Land Reptiles (called Uricotelic).

Excretory System of Mammals

1. **Kidneys :**A kidney is composed of 1.2 million microscopic structural and functional units called nephrons or uriniferous tubules.
2. **Ureters :** Open into Urinary Bladder.
3. **Urinary Bladder :** Size depends upon the amount of mine in it (up to 700-800 ml).

   The lower part is guarded by 2 Sphinctors : inner involuntary and outer voluntary.
4. **Urethra :** Leads to the exterior. In females, it carries only urine. In males it carries urine as well as spermatic fluid.

   Nephron : Functional unit of kidney. It is a long tube differentiated into 4 regions.

1. **Bowman's Capsule :** Contains a globular bunch of capillaries, the glomerulus. In glomerular filtrate: water (99%), inorganic salts, amino acids, fatty acids, glucose, urea, uric acid, hormones, vitamins are present.
2. **Proximal Convoluted Tubule :** Starts from the neck of Bowman's capsule and is highly twisted. Almost whole of the glucose and vitamins, amino acids, Na and K, Ca and Mg and water is absorbed.
3. **Loop of Henle:** U-shaped. Consist of 2 straight limbs: descending and ascending. No water is absorbed in ascending limb.
4. **Distal Convoluted Tubule :** Greatly twisted. Reabsorbs some Na and Cl. Leads to Collecting Tubules which lead to ureters.
   - The yellow colour of urine is caused by the pigment urochrome, which is a breakdown product of haemoglobin from worn out RBCs.
   - The urine gives a pungent smell due to conversion of urea into ammonia by bacteria.
   - Kidney stones: Calcium Oxalate.

Respiratory System of Humans

I. **Anaerobic Respiration :** When nutrients are oxidized without using O_2 (also called fermentation). *e.g.*, Ascaris, Fasciola, Taenia also respire anaerobically. It is a low energy yielding process.

II. **Aerobic Respiration :** Cells utilize O_2 for oxidizing nutrients. It is found in most plants and animals. It involves:

1. **External Respiration:** Gaseous exchange of O_2 and CO_2 between blood and air (or water).
2. **Internal Respiration:** Gaseous exchange between blood and tissues.
3. **Cellular Respiration:** Oxidation of nutrients in the cells and liberation of energy.

Endocrine System of Humans

Formed by endocrine glands (or Ductless Glands). They secrete hormones directly into the blood stream.

Hypothalamus : Forms a part of fore-brain, secretes neurohormones, which effect the release of hormones from pituitary.

Pituitary Gland: Also called Master Gland. It is the smallest endocrine gland. It secretes:

1. ***Somatotrophic Hormone :*** Controls the general growth of the body. Hyper-secretion leads to acromegaly and gigantism and hyposecretion leads to dwarfness.
2. ***Gonadotrophic Hormone :*** Stimulates the primary sex hormones, *i.e.*, ovaries and testes.
3. ***Lactogenic Hormone :*** Initiates milk production in the pregnant females.
4. ***Thyrotrophic Hormone :*** Aids in the regulation of thyroid secretion.
5. ***Adrenocorticotrophic Hormone :*** Influences the secretion from the cortex of adrenal glands.
6. ***Oxytocin or Pitocin :*** Stimulates smooth muscle contractions during child birth. Also helps in the secretion of milk in females.
8. ***Vasopressin (Anti-Diuretic Hormone) :*** Regulates reabsorption of water from the kidney tubules, causing increase in Blood Pressure.

Thyroid Gland : It is the largest endocrine gland located in the neck between the trachea and larynx.

1. ***Thyroxine :*** Regulates physical, mental and sexual development.
   - Poor in iodine is insufficient for the synthesis of thyroxin, leads to simple goitre.
2. ***Thyrocalcitonin :*** It controls the amount of calcium in the body.
   - *Hashimoto Disease :* Due to age factor or injury in thyroid gland secretion of thyroid reduces.

Parathyroid Gland : Secretes Parathormone. It influences calcium and phosphorus metabolism.

Thymus Gland : Situated near the heart. Produces Thymine. Preventing development of gonads.

Pancreas : It is an exocrine as well as an endocrine gland. Its endocrine part is known as Islets of Langerhans. Beta cells secrete Insulin which controls the amount of sugar in the blood.

Adrenal Glands : Consists of 2 Distinct Parts: Outer cortex and Inner medulla.

1. Adrenal Medulla secretes Adrenaline or epinephrine which effects liberation of glucose from glycogen stored in liver.
2. Adrenal Cortex secretes two types of Hormones:
   (*a*) *Mineralo Corticoids :* Maintain electrolyte balance. Its hyposecretion results in Addison's disease.
   (*b*) *Gluco Corticoids :* It influences carbohydrate metabolism. Its hypersecretion leads to Cushing Disease.

Reproductive System of Humans

It is the process by which an individual multiplies in number by producing more individuals of its own type.

I. Asexual Reproduction: Asexual Reproduction is the process of multiplication of individuals without the formation or fusion of gametes.

Binary Fission : It involves the division of the nucleus followed by that of the cytoplasm, breaking the body into two young ones. *e.g.*, Amoeba, Euglena, Paramecium, etc.

II. Sexual Reproduction : The process of sexual reproduction involves the formation and fusion of gametes (Syngamy) and results in the formation of a new organism genetically different from parent.

Mammalian Reproductive System : The reproductive system of sexually reproducing animals consists of:

Sex	Primary Sex Organs	Secondary Sex Organs
Male	Testes	Epididymis, Vas deferens, Ejaculatory duct, Urethra Seminal vesicle, Prostate Gland Cowper's gland, Penis
Female	Ovary	Fallopian tubes, Uterus, Vagina, External Genitalia/ Vulva Bartholian's Gland, Mammary glands

Sensory Organs of Humans

Eye: Eye is made up of 3 Layers : Upper Sclerotic, Middle Choroids, Inner Retina.

1. ***Sclerotic Layer :*** The Transparent bulging, circular part of sclerotic layer which lies in the front is called cornea. Cornea is covered by the thin Conjunctiva.
2. ***Choroid Layer :*** Choroid layer starts from iris which is next to cornea. The circular aperture of iris is called pupil.
   - Lens is a proteinous. It is biconvex in nature.
3. ***Retina :*** Image of the object is formed on retina. Retina is composed of 2 types of Cells:
   - *Rod Cells :* Sensitive to dim light and contain the pigment Rhodopsin (in nocturnal animals more).
   - *Cone Cells :* Colour sensitive for 3 primary colours (Red, Blue and Green). They are found more in diurnal animals.

Yellow Spot (Macula Lutea) : On retina, finest image is formed here. Favea centralis is the depression in the middle of yellow spot.

Blind Spot : No image formation takes place here as the optic nerves innervate the eyeball here.

- Cornea is donated in Eye Donation.
- Eyes glow in animals due to tapetum.

Defects of Eye

1. ***Myopia:*** Cannot see distant objects, image formed before retina, concave lens is used.
2. ***Hypermetropia :*** Cannot see near objects, image formed behind retina, convex lens is used.
3. ***Astigmatism :*** Curvature of cornea becomes irregular and image is not clear cylindrical lens is used.
4. ***Cataract :*** Due to defective protein metabolism the lens becomes opaque Operation is needed.
5. ***Gloucoma :*** Due to defect in aqueous humour.
6. ***Presbiopia :*** In this, power of accommodation of lens decreases due to age factor and defected metabolism. Can be removed by bifocal lens.

Ear : Divided into 3 Parts :

1. ***External Ear:*** Pinna + External Auditary Meatus
   - Has wax glands which produce cerumen to trap dust particles.
2. ***Middle Ear:*** It encloses 3 Ear Ossicles : Malleus (Hammer-Shaped), Incus (Anvil- Shaped), Stapes (Stirrup-Shaped)

Fanastra Ovalis : Connects middle ear to internal ear. Middle ear is connected to the pharynx by Eustachian tube.

3. ***Internal Ear (Membranous Labyrinth) :*** Most delicate part. Enclosed by parotic bone. It perform two functions : Maintenance of balance and hearing.
   - In the internal ear are 3 semi-circular canals and utriculus which are filled with a fluid, endolymph.

Diseases in Human

Human Viral Diseases	Human Bacterial Diseases
Chickenpox	Cholera
Measles	Diphtheria
Polio	Tuberculosis
Rabies	Leprosy
Mumps	Tetanus
Influenza	Typhoid
Hepatitis	Plague
Herpes	Whooping Cough
AIDS	Sore Throat
Trachoma (of Cornea)	Pneumonia
Human Protozoans Diseases	Gonorrhoea
Amoebiasis	Syphilis
Malaria	Botulism
Sleeping Sickness	**Human Fungal Diseases**
Kalazar	Ringworm
Diarrhoea	Athlete's foot
Piarrhoea	Dhobie itch

Some Important Facts of Human Body

Length of Alimentary Canal	Approximately 8 metres
Number of Cells in Body	75 trillion
Longest Bone	Femur (Thigh bone)
Smallest Bone	Ear ossicle, stapes
Weight of Brain	1400 gms
Blood Volume	6.8 litres (in 70 kg body)
Normal B.P.	120/80 mm Hg
Number of R.B.C.	(*a*) In Male : 4.5-5.0 million/cubic mm. (*b*) In Female : 4.0-4.5 million/cubic mm
Life Span of R.B.C.	120 days
Normal W.B.C. Count	5000-1000/cubic mm
Life Span of W.B.C.	3-4 days
D.L.C. (Differential Leucocyte Count)	(*a*) Basophils : 0.5-1% (*b*) Eosinophils : 1-3% (*c*) Monocytes : 3-8% (*d*) Neutrophils : 40-70% (*e*) Lymphocytes : 2-25%
Blood Platelets Count	2,00,000-4,00,000/cubic mm
Haemoglobin	(*a*) In Male : 14-15.6 gm/100 c.c. of blood (*b*) In Female : 11-14 gm/100 c.c. of blood
Hb Content in Body	500-700 gm
Universal Blood Donor	O Rh–ve
Universal Blood Recipient	AB
Blood Clotting Time	2-5 minutes
Average Body Weight	70 kg
Normal Body Temperature	98.4°F or 37°C
Breathing Rate	16-20/minute

Dental Formula	Adult : 2123/2123 = 32; Child : 2120/2120 = 22 Milk Teeth
Number of Cranial Nerves	12 pairs
Number of Spinal Nerves	31 pairs
Largest Endocrine Gland	Thyroid
Gestation Period	9 months (253-266 days)
Normal Heart Beat	72-75/minute
Largest Gland	Liver
Largest Muscle in the Body	Gluteus maximus (Buttock Muscle)
Smallest Muscle in the Body	Stapedius
Largest Artery	Abdominal Aorta
Largest Vein	Inferior Venacava
Greatest Regeneration Power	In liver
Longest Nerve	Sciatic
Longest Cell	Neuron (Nerve Cell)
Minimum Regeneration Power	In Brain Cells
pH of Gastric Juice	1.4
pH of Urine	6.0
pH of Blood	7.35-7.45
Total Number of Muscles in the Body	639
Total Number of Bones in the Body	206

MULTIPLE CHOICE QUESTIONS

1. Which of the following is an antibiotic?
A. Aspirin B. Paracetamol
C. Penicillin D. Sulphadizine

2. Digestion of food starts in:
A. mouth B. liver
C. stomach D. intestines

3. By taking the pulse rate of the human body, a doctor determines:
A. heartbeat
B. functioning of heart valves
C. the amount of blood in body
D. the condition of liver

4. A thermostat is used to:
A. purify air
B. regulate humidity
C. regulate temperature
D. regulate air pressure

5. Heat from the sun reaches the earth by:
A. reflection B. conduction
C. convection D. radiations

6. Dew forms most readily on nights that are:
A. calm and clear B. stormy
C. windy D. cloudy

7. The full moon rises in the:
A. South B. North
C. East D. West

8. An aeroplane is able to fly because;
A. it is lighter than air
B. it is heavier than air
C. it is made of very light materials
D. moving air can lift objects

9. The souring of milk is caused by the action of:
A. a protozoa B. bacteria
C. viruses D. None of these

10. The smallest living thing that can cause disease in the human body is:
A. flea B. bacteria
C. a protozoa D. viruses

11. The most abundant gas in the air is:
A. oxygen B. carbon dioxide
C. nitrogen D. hydrogen

12. Which is the element common to brass and bronze
A. Copper B. Iron
C. Zinc D. Aluminium

13. The densest element known so far is:
A. iron B. mercury
C. osmium D. tungsten

14. The most ductile element is:
A. gold B. silver
C. iron D. aluminium

15. The metal having highest melting point is:
A. chromium B. tungsten
C. diamond D. silver

16. The gas which constitutes most of Venus's atmosphere is:
A. oxygen B. nitrogen
C. hydrogen D. carbon dioxide

17. The most common acid found in the nature is:
A. acetic acid B. citric acid
C. lactic acid D. hydrochloric acid

18. The bomb that cannot destroy the property but can damage the life only is:
A. atom bomb B. hydrogen bomb
C. fission bomb D. neutron bomb

19. The waves received by our Television sets are:
A. light waves B. radio waves
C. cosmic waves D. micro waves

20. Which of the following machines will fail to give satisfactory result in vacuum?
A. Bicycle B. Sewing machine
C. Fan D. Washing machine

21. Which of the following is the best conductor of electric current?
A. Aluminium B. Copper
C. Silver D. Gold

22. Tungsten is mainly used for making filament of electric bulbs because of its:
A. low cost
B. high melting point
C. high electrical conductivity
D. low thermal conductivity

23. The element common to bone and cement is:
A. silicon B. calcium
C. nitrogen D. phosphorus

24. The raw material common to cement and glass is:
A. soda B. rock
C. gypsum D. sand

25. What is essentially required to digest the food in stomach?
A. Air B. Water
C. Enzymes D. Minerals

26. Domestic electric meters record the consumption of electricity in:
A. Volts B. Amperes
C. Watts D. Ohms

27. Which of the following gases does not pollute air?
A. Carbon dioxide B. Carbon monoxide
C. Nitrogen dioxide D. Sulphur dioxide

28. Polio is a disease caused due to:
A. bacterial infection B. virus infection
C. protozoal infection D. food poisoning

29. Which form of gold is the softest?
A. 16 Carat B. 18 Carat
C. 20 Carat D. 22 Carat

30. Filtration of wastes from the blood in human body is done by:
A. heart B. lungs
C. kidney D. intestines

31. Speed of sound waves is maximum in:
A. vacuum B. gases
C. liquids D. solids

32. How many colours are there in the rainbow?
A. 7 B. 10
C. 12 D. 5

33. Barometer measures:
A. wind velocity B. atmospheric pressure
C. amount of rainfall D. atmospheric moisture

34. Anemometer measures:
A. amount of rainfall
B. atmospheric pressure
C. wind velocity
D. amperage of an electrical current

35. Sphygmomanometer measures:
A. specific heat, latent heat, heat of chemical combination and other thermal properties
B. intensity of light
C. distance covered, or steps taken, by a person walking
D. blood pressure

36. Meteorology is the study of:
A. meteors and meteorites
B. the climate
C. the weather
D. the measurement of length

37. Oil, water and gas can be present in a well in the ascending order of:
A. water, oil, gas B. gas, water, oil
C. water, gas, oil D. oil, water, gas

38. Vegetables can be cooked quickly in a pressure cooker because:
A. steam can boil vegetables faster than water
B. boiling point increases with the increase in pressure
C. high pressure lowers the boiling point
D. All the above

39. A person suffering from which of the following cannot see with clarity the horizontal and vertical lines simultaneously?
A. Myopia B. Hypermitropia
C. Astigmatism D. Squint

40. When a flake of ice melts in a water bowl, the level of water inside the bowl:
A. remains unchanged
B. goes down
C. increases
D. nothing can be said definitely

41. To an astronaut in a satellite the colour of the sky would appear to be:
A. black B. blue
C. grey D. white

42. A fuse wire is used for:
A. allowing high currents to flow harmlessly
B. breaking the electrical circuit
C. saving a man from receiving electric shocks
D. All the above

43. Excessive intake of alcohol damages a person's:
A. kidneys
B. liver
C. stomach
D. All the above to a certain degree

44. Which of the following is common in all acids?
A. Hydrogen B. Oxygen
C. Nitrogen D. None of the above

45. After boiling, rice grains grow in volume and weight because:
A. starch swells in water and heat
B. heat enlarges solid
C. rice is a fatty grain
D. All the above

46. Hygrometer is used for measuring:
A. temperature B. relative humidity
C. rainfall D. density of water

47. Phobos and Deimos are the satellites of:
A. Uranus B. Mars
C. Venus D. Saturn

48. Plants are grown along river banks in order to check:
A. siltage and floods B. pollution
C. rainfall D. All the above

49. Which one of the following signifies the optical technique of recording waves and amplitude?
A. Holography B. Bibliography
C. Audiography D. None of the above

50. People use iron ploughs now, instead of the old wooden ploughs. This change signifies:
A. advance technology
B. appropriate technology
C. obsolete technology
D. ultimate technology

51. Acetyl salicylic acid is used commonly as:
A. pain-reliever B. tear gas
C. chemical fertilizer D. preservative

52. In a village where fuel is not available and people are poor, which of the following measures is the most suitable to prevent disease through contaminated water from the wells?
A. Using chemicals to purify water
B. Boiling the water
C. Use of micro-organisms to purify water
D. None of the above

53. One of the main constituents of Gobar gas is:
A. thyamine B. methane
C. phosphate D. carbon monoxide

54. Quartz is softer than:
A. Diamond B. Corundum
C. Topaz D. All the above

55. Emerald and diamond are made of:
A. Beryllium and Carbon
B. Carbon
C. Silica
D. Silica and Beryllium

56. Human brain receives and sends signals as:
A. chemical impulses
B. physical impulses
C. electrical impulses
D. mechanical impulses

57. The ductless glands secreting hormones directly into human blood are known as:
A. exocrine glands B. endocrine glands
C. metabolic glands D. ductlands

58. Arrange the three forms of iron in descending order of carbon contents and other impurities in them:
I. wrought iron
II. cast iron
III. pig iron
A. III, II, I B. III, I, II
C. I, II, III D. II, I, III

59. Foot and mouth diseases attack:
A. cattle, sheep and pigs
B. cattle only
C. cattle and pigs only
D. cattle and sheep only

60. Which one of the following has maximum nitrogen content?
A. Sodium nitrate
B. Urea
C. Ammoniam sulphate
D. None of the above has enough nitrogen

61. Radio carbon dating is used for determining the age of:
A. fossils B. buildings
C. babies D. rocks

62. Pasteurization of milk means:
A. heating of milk upto 100°C
B. heating of milk at 65°C
C. cooling of milk at 100°C
D. cooling of milk upto 0°C

63. Ranikhet disease affects:
A. dogs B. cows
C. poultry D. sheep

64. Wisdom teeth appear in a human being between:
A. 17 and 20 years of age
B. 30 and 40 years of age
C. 10 and 17 years of age
D. 4 and 8 years of age

65. Decomposition of matter takes place due to the effect of:
A. bacteria B. virus
C. fungi D. algae

66. Bile is secreted by:
A. pancreas B. small intestine
C. stomach D. liver

67. Polio myelitis which causes polio is spread by:
A. mosquito B. virus
C. water D. adulterated food

68. Which of the following is a genetically transmitted disease?

A. Myopia B. Long sightedness
C. Colour blindness D. Night blindness

69. Which of the following is a metal?
A. Arsenic B. Sulphur
C. Potassium D. Carbon

70. How does weedicide remove weeds?
A. It removes the water required for growth
B. It destroys the roots of the weeds
C. It destroys the nutrients required for the growth of weeds
D. All of the above

71. A diamond is a:
A. form of fossilised mammal of ancient times
B. crystalline form of pure carbon
C. hard rolled under sea stone made into a diamond by the saliva of huge sea monsters and thereafter dug out from the mines
D. natural crystallized glass.

72. High heel and/or pointed shoes are harmful because:
A. they injure the feet
B. they weaken the eyesight
C. they cause polio
D. they cause backache and sleeplessness

73. When returning to the earth, spacecrafts have a communication blackout, the reason is:
A. the returning spacecraft is doing so against the force of gravity which interferes with the radio waves
B. during the re-entry period the density of the plasma generated by the intense frictional heat is so high that the operational frequencies used for communication becomes very much less than the plasma cut-off frequency resulting in a total blackout
C. stellar X-rays attract and absorb the sound waves
D. the sounds created by the whirring of the mechanism of the spacecraft renders the sounds inaudible

74. Respiration is:
A. to change the food into energy
B. the process during which food is oxidized and its chemical energy is transformed into useful form
C. a sort of exercise
D. interconversion of food and energy

75. Dialysis is:
A. the same process as osmosis
B. the diffusion of sugar molecules through water
C. the process involved in the diffusion of toxic substance through a membrane
D. the evaporation of surplus sugar

76. Mycology is the study of:
A. Mica
B. Ants
C. Changes of a structure as a result of environment
D. Fungi

77. In human body, quantity of water is about:
A. 10% B. 20%
C. 65% D. 80%

78. What does the urine of a man contain mainly?
A. Urea B. Sugar
C. Salt D. None of the above

79. The filament of electric bulb is made of:
A. iron B. tungsten
C. nichrome D. silver

80. The lightning rod used for protecting building from lightning is made of:
A. glass B. cement
C. wood D. copper

81. When a body becomes positively charged, it:
A. loses electrons
B. gains electrons
C. loses protons
D. None of the above is correct

82. During which season our body needs more fats?
A. Summer season B. Rainy season
C. Winter season D. Spring season

83. Deficiency of insulin causes:
A. Beri-Beri B. Fever
C. Cancer D. Diabetes

84. Iron is heavier than water, still the ship floats on the sea because:
A. weight of the ship is less than the weight of water in the sea
B. weight of the ship is more than sea water
C. weight of the ship is less than the weight of water that the ship displaces
D. weight of ship is equal to the weight of water that ship displaces

85. Photosynthesis results in:
1. release of oxygen
2. release of carbon dioxide
3. formation of carbohydrates
4. intake of carbon dioxide
A. 1, 2, 3 are correct B. 1,3,4 are correct
C. 2,3,4 are correct D. only 1 is correct

86. The Pythagorean Theorem states that:
A. in any triangle the square of the longest side equals the sum of the squares of the other sides
B. in any triangle the square of the longest side equals the square of the sum of the other sides
C. in a right-angled triangle the square of the hypotenuse equals the sum of the squares of the other two sides
D. in an isosceles triangle the third side equals the sum of the two equal sides

87. The formula for inter conversion of Centigrade, Fahrenheit and Reaumur scales is:
A. $\frac{F-32}{9}=\frac{C}{5}=\frac{R}{4}$ B. $\frac{F+32}{9}=\frac{C}{5}=\frac{R}{4}$
C. $\frac{F-32}{9}=\frac{C}{9}=\frac{R}{4}$ D. $\frac{F-32}{4}=\frac{C}{9}=\frac{R}{5}$

88. Which one of the following statements is incorrect?
A. The length of the days and nights is not the same all the year round
B. The axis of the earth is inclined at an angle of 66-1/2 to the plane of its orbit
C. Water pipes are apt to burst in very cold weather
D. Evaporation produces heat

89. Which of the following statements is correct?
A. Boiling of an egg is a chemical change
B. Freezing of ice cream is a chemical change
C. Burning of a candle is a physical change
D. Extracting the juice from an orange is a chemical change

90. When a bullet is fired why does the gun kick back?
A. Because the man firing the gun is light in weight
B. Because the gun is heavier than the firing soldier
C. Because the bullet goes out very fast
D. Because to every action there is an equal and opposite reaction

91. Which one of the following definitions is wrong?
A. *Amino Acids:* Large chemical substances containing carbon and oxygen
B. *Proteins:* Giant molecules of carbon, nitrogen and oxygen which are broken into small molecules during digestion
C. *Carbohydrates:* Big molecules used for getting energy
D. *Lipids:* A group of organic compounds found in living cells

92. The depth to which a floating body sinks in pure water is a measure of its
A. Density B. Weight
C. Inertia D. Viscosity

93. Which one of the following is a contagious disease?
A. Malaria B. Small pox
C. Cholera D. Tuberculosis

94. A pure (sun) spectrum is that in which:
A. only ultra violet and infra red rays are not seen
B. all the seven colours which combine to make up the sun light are clearly, distinctly and separately visible
C. all the seven colours are found
D. where the rainbow is found

95. What do fertilisers contain?
A. Calcium B. Sodium
C. Phosphorus D. Nitrogen

96. In which the purest form of carbon is found?
A. Coke B. Diamond
C. Graphite D. Coal

97. What is Tritium?
A. Compound of hydrogen
B. Isobar of hydrogen
C. Isotope of hydrogen
D. Oxide of hydrogen

98. How do the centripetal forces pull a body?
A. Upward B. Downward
C. Inwards D. Outwards

99. What does Mycology study?
A. Minerals B. Sound
C. Insects D. Fungus

100. DNA is concentrated in the:
A. Microsome B. Nucleus
C. Chromatin D. Cell wall

101. Vinegar is obtained by the fermentation process; what does it contain?
A. Acetic acid B. Formic acid
C. Nitric acid D. Oxalic acid

102. When the leaves of a plant show chlorosis, the possible cause can be:
A. increase in nitrate content in the soil
B. increase in chloride content in the soil
C. decrease in phosphorus content in the soil
D. deficiency of trace elements in the soil

103. Which of the properties of elements is a whole number?
A. Atomic number B. Atomic weight
C. Molecular weight D. Equivalent weight

104. What does the process in which a heavy nucleus breaks to give two or more small nuclei and large amount of energy is called:
A. electrolysis B. fission
C. fusion D. ionization

105. What is the process in which two or more small nuclei join to form a large nucleus with evolution of energy is called:
A. electrolysis B. fission
C. ionization D. diffusion

106. The main endocrine gland present in the human body is:
A. Adrenal gland B. Pituitary gland
C. Thyroid gland D. Pancreas gland

107. Which one is wrongly matched?
A. Phosphorus – Match
B. Potassium Sulphate – Fertilizer
C. Methyl Isocynate – Tyre
D. Silicon – Glass

108. Which one of the following pairs is incorrect?
A. Malaria – Mosquitoes
B. Small Pox – Virus
C. Typhoid – Fungi
D. Cholera – Water

109. Which one group of the following belongs to 'lichens'?
A. Algae and bacteria B. Virus and bacteria
C. Algae and fungi D. All the above

110. Arrange the following elements, present in human body, in the descending order of their percentage:
1. Oxygen
2. Nitrogen
3. Carbon
A. 1 and 2 only B. 1 and 3 only
C. 1, 3, 2 D. 2 and 3 only

111. Which one of the following is given to a typhoid patient?
A. Chloroquin B. Vitamin A
C. Chloromycetin D. Sulphur

112. Which one of the following is called a growth gland?
A. Adrenal B. Thyroid
C. Pituitary D. None of the above

113. Which one of the following is a rich source of vitamin A?
A. Potato tuber B. Carrot root
C. Onion bulb D. Maize grains

114. Of the following the best way to put out a petrol fire is to use:
A. water
B. rugs
C. soda water fire extinguisher
D. carbon tetrachloride extinguisher

115. Which type of nerves carry impulses from the sense organs in response to stimulus?
A. Motor B. Sensory
C. Secretory D. All the above

116. The gas which helps in burning is:
A. Carbon Monoxide B. Hydrogen
C. Oxygen D. Nitrogen

117. Which one of the following best defines IQ?
A. $\frac{\text{Actual Age}}{\text{Mental Age}} \times 100$ B. $\frac{\text{Mental Age}}{\text{Actual Age}} \times 100^2$
C. $\frac{\text{Actual Age}}{\text{Mental Age}} \times 10$ D. $\frac{\text{Mental Age}}{\text{Actual Age}} \times 1000$

118. Which one of the following is called 'red planet'?
A. Mercury B. Jupiter
C. Venus D. Mars

119. The instrument used to measure radio activity is called:
A. Gyroscope B. Nephoscope
C. Machmeter D. Geiger Counter

120. Which one is the most popular fodder for poultry?
A. Barley B. Maize
C. Wheat D. Bajra

ANSWERS

1	2	3	4	5	6	7	8	9	10
C	A	A	C	D	A	C	D	B	D
11	12	13	14	15	16	17	18	19	20
C	A	C	A	B	D	A	D	D	C
21	22	23	24	25	26	27	28	29	30
C	B	B	C	C	C	A	B	D	C
31	32	33	34	35	36	37	38	39	40
D	A	B	C	D	C	A	B	C	A
41	42	43	44	45	46	47	48	49	50
A	B	D	A	A	B	B	A	A	A
51	52	53	54	55	56	57	58	59	60
A	A	B	D	A	A	B	A	A	B
61	62	63	64	65	66	67	68	69	70
A	B	C	A	A	D	B	C	C	D
71	72	73	74	75	76	77	78	79	80
B	D	B	B	C	D	C	A	B	D
81	82	83	84	85	86	87	88	89	90
A	C	D	C	B	C	A	D	A	D
91	92	93	94	95	96	97	98	99	100
A	A	B	B	D	B	C	C	D	C
101	102	103	104	105	106	107	108	109	110
A	D	A	B	D	B	C	C	C	C
111	112	113	114	115	116	117	118	119	120
C	B	B	C	B	C	A	D	D	B

GENERAL AWARENESS

NATIONAL SYMBOLS

STATE EMBLEM

State Emblem of India is an adaptation from the Sarnath Lion Capital of Ashoka. It was adopted by the Government of India on January 26, 1950. In the adapted form, only three lions are visible, the fourth being hidden from the view. The wheel (Dharma Chakra) appears in relief in the centre of the abacus with a bull on the right and a horse on the left.

The bell-shaped lotus has been omitted. The words ''Satyameva Jayate'' meaning ''Truth alone triumphs'' are inscribed below the Emblem in Devanagari script.

NATIONAL FLAG

The National Flag of India is a horizontal tricolour of deep saffron (Kesari), white and dark green in equal proportion. In the centre of the white band there is a wheel in navy blue colour. It has 24 spokes. The ratio of the length and the breadth of the flag is 3 : 2. Its design was adopted by the Constituent Assembly of India on July 22, 1947.

NATIONAL ANTHEM

Rabindranath Tagore's song 'Jana-gana-mana' was adopted by the Constituent Assembly as the National Anthem of India on January 24, 1950.

Jana-gan-mana-adhinayaka jaya he, Bharata-bhagya-vidhata
Punjab-Sindh-Gujarat-Maratha-Dravida-Utkala-Banga
Vindhya-Himachala-Yamuna-Ganga Uchhala-jaladhi-taranga.
Tava subha name jage, Tava subha asisa mange,
Gahe tava jaya gatha,
Jana-gana-mangala-dayak, jaya he Bharata bhagya vidhata,
Jaya he, jaya he, jaya he, Jaya jaya jaya, jaya he.

NATIONAL SONG

Bankim Chandra Chatterji's 'Vande Mataram' which was a source of inspiration to the people in their struggle for freedom, has been adopted as National Song. It has an equal status with the National Anthem.

Vande Mataram
Sujalam, suphalam, malayaja-shitalam,
Shasya shyamalam, Mataram
Shubhrajyotsna,pulkita yaminim,
Phulla kusumita drumadalashobhinim,
Subhasinim sumadhura—bhashinim,
Sukhadam, Varadam, Mataram.

NATIONAL CALENDAR

It is based on the Saka era with Chaitra as its first month and a normal year of 365 days. It was adopted from March 22, 1957. Dates of the national calendar have a permanent correspondence with dates of Gregorian calendar as Chaitra I falls on March 22 in a normal year and March 21 in a leap year. In official communications, both Saka and Gregorian calendar dates are written. Months of the national calendar are Chaitra, Vaishakha, Jaishtha, Ashada, Shravan, Bhadra, Ashvina, Kartika, Margashirsha, Pausha, Magha and Phalguna.

NATIONAL ANIMAL

The magnificent tiger — Panthera tigris (Linnaeus) is the national animal of India. Tiger is found in several parts of the country and is known for its grace, strength, agility and enormous power. 'Project Tiger' was launched in 1973 to check their dwindling population in India.

NATIONAL BIRD

The Indian Peacock — Pavo Christatus (Linnaeus) is the national bird of India. It is a colourful, swan-sized bird with a fan-shaped crest of feathers on its head and a long-slander neck. The male species is more colourful with blue breast and a spectacular bronze-green train of around 200 elongated feathers.

National Flower—Lotus

National Tree—Banyan

National Fruit—Mango

National Currency—Rupee '₹' (One Rupee = 100 Paise)

National Aquatic Animal—Dolphin

BOOKS AND AUTHORS

Name of Book	Author
Ain-e-Akbari	Abul Fazal
Anand Math	Bankim Chandra Chatterjee
An Unknown Indian	Nirad C. Chaudhuri
Arthshastra	Kautilya
Coolie	Mulk Raj Anand
Das Kapital	Karl Marx

Name of Book	Author
Discovery of India	Jawaharlal Nehru
Eternal India	Mrs. Indira Gandhi
Godan	Prem Chand
Gitanjali	Rabindranath Tagore
Gora	Rabindranath Tagore
Geet Govinda	Jayadeva
Harsha Charit	Bana Bhatta
Hindu View of Life	Dr. S. Radhakrishnan
India Wins Freedom	Maulana Abul Kalam Azad
Jobs of Millions	V.V. Giri
Jungle Book	Rudyard Kipling
Kamayani	Jai Shankar Prasad
Kadambari	Bana Bhatta
Life Divine	Sri Aurobindo
Last days of Netaji	G.D. Khosla
Les Miserables	Victor Hugo
Mahabharat	Veda Vyas
Macbeth	William Shakespeare
Mein Kempf	Hitler
Meghduta	Kalidas
Mother (Maa)	Maxim Gorky
Mother India	Katherine Mayo
My Experiments with Truth	Mahatma Gandhi
My Presidential Years	R. Venkataraman

Name of Book	Author
Neeti Shatak	Bhartrihari
Nehru and His Vision	Dr. K.R. Narayanan
Old Man and the Sea	Ernest Hemingway
One World	Wendell Wilkie
Panchtantra	Vishnu Sharma
Paradise Lost	John Milton
Ramayana	Valmiki (in Sanskrit)
Raghuvansham	Kalidas
Rajtarangini	Kalhan
Ram Charit Manas	Tulsi Das
Abhijnan Shakuntalam	Kalidas
Satanic Verses	Salman Rushdie
Saket	Maithili Sharan Gupta
Speed Post	Shobha De
The God of Small Things	Arundhati Roy
Treasure Island	R.L. Stevenson
Twelfth Night	William Shakespeare
Train to Pakistan	Khuswant Singh
Uttara Ram Charitra	Bhava Bhuti
Vanity Fair	W.M. Thackeray
War and Peace	Leo Tolstoy
Wealth of Nations	Adam Smith
Wake up India	Annie Besant

INVENTIONS AND DISCOVERIES

Discovery	Discoverer
Geographical Discoveries	
America	Columbus
Brazil	Cabral
North Pole	Robert Peary
Everest (Conquered)	Tabie Junko
Planetary Motion	Kepler
Hawaiian Islands	Captain Cook
South Pole	Amundsen
Solar System	Copernicus
Chemistry and Physics	
Atom Bomb	Otto Hahn
Atomic Theory	Dalton
Atomic Numbers	Moseley
Cosmic Rays	R.S. Millikan
Dynamite	Alfred Nobel
Electrons Theory	Bohr
Electricity (current)	Volta
Electric Telegraphy (Code)	S. Morse
Gravitation	Newton
Gas Light	Murdock
Oxygen	J. Priestly
Photography	L. Daguerre

Discovery	Discoverer
Printing for the blind	Louis Braille
Radium	Madame Curie
Telegraph	Samuel Morse
Television	J.L. Baird
Telephone	Graham Bell
Wireless	G. Marconi
X-rays	W.K. Roentgen
Mechanical	
Aeroplane	Wright Brothers
Bicycle	Macmillan
Computer	Charles Babbage
Dynamo	Michal Faraday
Diesel Engine	Rudolf Diesel
Engine (Railway)	Stephenson
Fountain Pen	Waterman
Gramophone	Edison
Locomotive Power of Steam	James Watt
Helicopter	Brequet
Life Boat	Henry Greathead
Microscope	Z. Jansen
Printing Press	Gutenberg
Revolver	Colt

Discovery	Discoverer
Sewing Machine	Elias Howe
Thermometer	Fahrenheit
Transistor	W. Shockley
Typewriter	Sholes
Telescope	Hans Lippershey
Tank (Military)	Swinton
Medical	
Antiseptic Surgery	Lord Joseph Lister
Bacteria	Leeuwenhock
Circulation of Blood	William Harvey

Discovery	Discoverer
Homoeopathy (Discovered)	Hahnemann
Insulin	F. Banting
Penicillin	Alexander Flemming
Malaria Parasite	Dr. Ronald Ross
Stethoscope	Laennec
Vitamins	Funk
Anti-Rabies Treatment	Pasteur
General	
Nylon	Carouthers
Science of Geometry	Euclids

WORLD'S GEOGRAPHICAL SURNAMES

• City of Sky-scrapers—New York • City of Seven Hills—Rome • City of Dreaming Spires—Oxford • City of Golden Gate—San Francisco • City of Magnificent Buildings—Washington D.C. • City of Eternal Springs—Quito (S. America) • China's Sorrow—Hwang Ho • Cockpit of Europe—Belgium • Dark Continent—Africa • Emerald Isle—Ireland • Eternal City—Rome • Empire City—New York • Forbidden City—Lhasa (Tibet) • Garden City—Chicago • Gate of Tears—Strait of Bab-el-Mandeb • Gift of the Nile—Egypt • Granite City—Aberdeen (Scotland) • Hermit Kingdom—Korea • Herring Pond—Atlantic Ocean • Holy Land—Jerusalem • Island Continent—Australia • Islands of Cloves—Zanzibar • Isle of Pearls—Bahrein (Persian Gulf) • Key to the Mediterranean—Gibralter • Land of Cakes—Scotland • Land of Golden Fleece—Australia • Land of Maple Leaf—Canada • Land of Morning Calm—Korea • Land of Midnight Sun—Norway • Land of the Thousand Lakes—Finland • Land of the Thunderbolt—Bhutan • Land of White Elephant—Thailand • Land of Thousand Elephants—Laos • Land of Rising Sun—Japan • Loneliest Island—Tristan De Gunha (Mid-Atlantic) • Manchester of Japan—Osaka • Pillars of Hercules—Strait of Gibraltar • Pearl of the Antilles—Cuba • Playground of Europe—Switzerland • Quaker City—Philadelphia • Queen of the Adriatic—Venice • Roof of the World—The Pamirs, Central Asia • Sugar bowl of the world—Cuba • Venice of the North—Stockholm • Windy City—Chicago • Whiteman's grave—Guinea Coast of Africa • Yellow River—Huang Ho (China) • Sickman of Europe—Turkey

CURRENCIES OF DIFFERENT COUNTRIES

Country	Currency
Australia	Australian Dollar
Bangladesh	Taka
Belgium	Euro
Britain	Pound (Sterling)
Myanmar	Kyat
Canada	Canadian Dollar
Germany	Euro
Iran	Rial
India	Rupee
Sri Lanka	Rupee
China	Yuan
Czech Republic	Koruna
Denmark	Krone
France	Euro
Pakistan	Rupee

Country	Currency
Poland	Zloty
Spain	Euro
Indonesia	Rupiah
Iraq	Dinar
Italy	Euro
Japan	Yen
Mexico	Peso
The Netherland	Euro
European Union	Euro
Sweden	Krone
Switzerland	Swiss Franc
Turkey	Lira
U.A.E.	Dirham
U.S.A.	Dollar
Russia	Rouble

CAPITAL OF COUNTRIES

Country	Capital	Country	Capital
Austria	Vienna	Kenya	Nairobi
Afghanisatan	Kabul	Kuwait	Kuwait
Algeria	Algiers	Laos	Vientiane
Angola	Luanda	Lebanon	Beirut
Australia	Canberra	Mexico	Mexico City
Argentina	Buenos Aires	Malaysia	Kualalumpur
Bangladesh	Dhaka	Morocco	Rabat
Belgium	Brussels	Mozambique	Maputo
Bolivia	Lapaz	New Zealand	Welington
Bulgaria	Sofia	Netherlands	Amsterdam
Bhutan	Thimpu	Panama	Panama City
Brazil	Brasilla	Portugal	Lisbon
Canada	Ottawa	Poland	Warsaw
China	Beijing	Sri Lanka	Colombo
Cyprus	Nicosia	Sweden	Stockholm
Columbia	Bagota	Switzerland	Bern
Denmark	Copenhegan	Sudan	Khartoum
Ethiopia	Addis Ababa	Sierra Leone	Freetown
Finland	Helsinki	South Africa	Capetown
France	Paris	Saudi Arabia	Riyadh
Germany	Berlin	Spain	Madrid
Greece	Athens	Thailand	Bangkok
Guatemala	Guatemala City	Turkey	Ankara
Hungary	Budapest	Russia	Moscow
Iran	Tehran	Azerbaijan	Baku
India	New Delhi	Armenia	Yerevan
Indonesia	Jakarta	Latvia	Riga
Iraq	Baghdad	Ukrain	Kiev
Italy	Rome	U.S.A.	Washington
Ireland	Dublin	U.K.	London
Japan	Tokyo	Vietnam	Hanoi
Combodia	Phnom Penh	Zambia	Lusaka
Korea (North)	Pyong Yang		
Korea (South)	Seoul		

INDIAN CITIES AND THEIR RIVERS

City	State	River	City	State	River
Agra	U.P.	Yamuna	Kanpur	Uttar Pradesh	Ganga
Ahmedabad	Gujarat	Sabarmati	Ludhiana	Punjab	Sutlej
Prayagraj	U.P.	Confluence of the Ganga, Yamuna, and invisible Saraswati	Lucknow	Uttar Pradesh	Gomati
Alwaye	Kerala	Periyar	Nasik	Maharashtra	Godavari
Kolkata	West Bengal	Hooghly	Patna	Bihar	Ganga
Cuttack	Odisha	Mahanadi	Srinagar	J & K	Jhelum
Delhi	Delhi	Yamuna	Surat	Gujarat	Tapti
Haridwar	Uttarakhand	Ganga	Tiruchirapally	Tamil Nadu	Kaveri
			Ujjain	Madhya Pradesh	Shipra
			Vijayawada	Andhra Pradesh	Krishna
			Varanasi	Uttar Pradesh	Ganga

WONDERS OF THE WORLD

Seven Wonders of the Ancient World: (1) the Pyramids of Egypt, built in approximately 2700 BC; (2) the Hanging Gardens at Babylon; (3) the temple of Artemis at Emphesus; (4) the statue of Zeus at Olympia; (5) the tomb of Mausolus at Halicarnassus, built in nearly 350 BC; (6) the Colossus of Rhodes, built in nearly 280 BC; (7) the Pharos Lighthouse at Alexandria.

Seven Wonders of the Medieval World: (1) the Colosseum of Rome; (2) the Great Wall of China; (3) the Porcelain Tower of Nanking; (4) the Mosque at St. Sophia (Constantinople); (5) Stonehenge; (6) the Catacombs of Rome; (7) the Leaning Tower of Pisa.

Seven New Wonders of the World: (1) Taj Mahal of Agra (India); (2) Pyramid at Chichen Itza (Mexico); (3) Machu Picchu (Peru); (4) Statue of Christ The Redeemer (Brazil); (5) Great Wall of China; (6) Roman Colosseum, Italy; (7) Ruins of Petra, Jordan.

STATES OF INDIA (CAPITALS, PRINCIPAL LANGUAGES)

States Principal Languages	Capitals
Andhra Pradesh—*Telgu and Urdu*	Amaravati
Arunachal Pradesh—*Monpa, Adi, Nissi etc.*	Itanagar
Assam—*Assamese and Bengali*	Dispur
Bihar—*Hindi and Maithili*	Patna
Chattishgarh—*Hindi*	Raipur
Goa—*Konkani*	Panaji
Gujarat—*Gujarati*	GandhiNagar
Haryana—*Hindi*	Chandigarh
Himachal Pradesh—*Hindi and Pahari*	Shimla
Jharkhand—*Hindi*	Ranchi
Kerala—*Malyalam*	Thiruvananthpuram
Karnataka—*Kannada*	Bengluru
Madhya Pradesh—*Hindi*	Bhopal
Maharashtra—*Marathi*	Mumbai
Meghalaya—*Khashi, Jayantia and Garo*	Shillong
Manipur—*Manipuri*	Imphal
Mizoram—*Mizo and English*	Aizawl
Nagaland—*Naga, Assamese and English*	Kohima
Odisha—*Odiya*	Bhubaneshwar
Punjab—*Punjabi*	Chandigarh
Rajasthan—*Hindi, Rajasthani*	Jaipur
Sikkim—*Sikkimese and Gorkhali*	Gangtok
Tamil Nadu—*Tamil*	Chennai
Tripura—*Bengali, Tripuri and Manipuri*	Agartala
Uttar Pradesh—*Hindi*	Lucknow
Uttarakhand—*Hindi*	Dehradun
West Bengal—*Bengali*	Kolkata
Telangana—*Telgu and Urdu*	Hyderabad

Union Territories Principal Languages	Capitals
Andaman and Nicobar Islands—*Hindi, Nicobarese, Bengali, Malayalam, Tamil, Telugu*	Port Blair
Chandigarh—*Hindi, Punjabi, English*	Chandigarh
Dadar & Nagar Haveli and Daman and Diu—*Gujarati, Hindi*	Daman
Delhi—*Hindi, Punjabi*	Delhi
Jammu & Kashmir—*Kashmiri, Dongri, Urdu, Dardi and Pahari*	Srinagar (Summer) Jammu (Winter)
Lakshadweep—*Malayalam*	Kavaratti
Ladakh—*Urdu, Balti, Ladakhi*	Leh
Puducherry—*Tamil, Telugu, Malayalam, English and French*	Puducherry

HIGH COURTS IN INDIA

Name	Year	Territorial Jurisdiction	Seat
Allahabad	1866	Uttar Pradesh	Prayagraj (Bench at Lucknow)
Andhra Pradesh	2019	Andhra Pradesh	Amaravati
Bombay	1862	Maharashtra, Goa, Dadar & Nagar Haveli and Daman & Diu	Mumbai (Benches at Nagpur, Panaji and Aurangabad)
Calcutta	1862	West Bengal and Andaman & Nicobar	Kolkata (Circuit Bench at Port Blair)
Chhattisgarh	2000	Chhattisgarh	Bilaspur
Delhi	1966	Delhi	Delhi
Guwahati	1948	Assam, Nagaland, Mizoram and Arunachal Pradesh	Guwahati (Benches at Kohima, Aizawl and Itanagar)
Gujarat	1960	Gujarat	Ahmedabad
Himachal Pradesh	1971	Himachal Pradesh	Shimla
Jammu & Kashmir and ladakh	1928	Jammu & Kashmir, Ladakh	Srinagar and Jammu
Jharkhand	2000	Jharkhand	Ranchi
Karnataka	1884	Karnataka	Bengaluru (Circuit Benches at Dharwar and Gulbarga)
Kerala	1958	Kerala & Lakshadweep	Ernakulam
Madhya Pradesh	1956	Madhya Pradesh	Jabalpur (Benches at Gwalior and Indore)
Madras	1862	Tamil Nadu & Puducherry	Chennai (Bench at Madurai)
Orissa	1948	Odisha	Cuttack
Patna	1916	Bihar	Patna
Punjab and Haryana	1966	Punjab, Haryana and Chandigarh	Chandigarh
Rajasthan	1949	Rajasthan	Jodhpur (Bench at Jaipur)
Sikkim	1975	Sikkim	Gangtok
Uttarakhand	2000	Uttarakhand	Nainital
Tripura	2013	Tripura	Agartala
Telangana	2019	Telangana	Hyderabad
Meghalaya	2013	Meghalaya	Shillong
Manipur	2013	Manipur	Imphal

FAMOUS HILL STATION

	Station		State/UT
1.	Almora, Mussoorie Nainital	:	Uttarakhand
2.	Cherrapunji (Shillong), Khasi Hills (Shillong)	:	Meghalaya
3.	Ooty, Kodaikanal Yereaud	:	Tamil Nadu
4.	Dalhousie, Kassauli	:	Himachal Pradesh
5.	Darjeeling	:	West Bengal
6.	Gulmarg, Srinagar	:	Jammu and Kashmir
7.	Mahabaleshwar	:	Maharashtra
8.	Mt. Abu	:	Rajasthan
9.	Panchmarhi	:	Madhya Pradesh
10.	Ranchi	:	Jharkhand

FAMOUS NATIONAL PARKS

1. Corbett National Park : Nainital, Uttarakhand
2. Dudhwa National Park : Lakhimpur Kheri, UP
3. Kaziranga National Park : Jorhat, Assam
4. Kanha National Park : Jabalpur, Bhedaghat
5. Gir National Park : Rajkot, Junagarh, Gujarat
6. Guindy National Park : Guindy, Chennai, Tamil Nadu
7. Nagairhole National Park : Coorg, Karnataka
8. Bandipur National Park : Mysore, Karnataka

FAMOUS NATIONAL WILDLIFE SANCTUARIES

1. Dachigam Wildlife Sanctuary : Srinagar, Jammu and Kashmir
2. Sariska : Alwar, Rajasthan
3. Hazaribagh Wildlife Sanctuary : Hazaribagh, Jharkhand
4. Tiger Project : Sawai Madhopur, Rajasthan
5. Mudhumali Wildlife Sanctuary : Mudhumalia, Nilgiri, Tamil Nadu
6. Periyar Wildlife Sanctuary : Idukki, Kottayam, Kerala

HOLY PLACES IN INDIA

1. Amarnath	Kashmir
2. Ayodhya	Uttar Pradesh
3. Badrinath	Uttarakhand
4. Dwarka	Gujarat
5. Haridwar	Uttarakhand
6. Kancheepuram	Tamil Nadu
7. Kedarnath	Uttarakhand
8. Mathura	Uttar Pradesh
9. Puri	Odisha
10. Rameswaram	Tamil Nadu
11. Tirupati	Andhra Pradesh
12. Ujjain	Madhya Pradesh
13. Varanasi	Uttar Pradesh
14. Bodh Gaya	Bihar

SPORTS

Terms Associated With Sports :

Cricket : Ashes, Bye, Bodyline, Bowling, Break, Cover-point, Creases, Chinaman, Chucker, Drive, Duck, Follow on, Googly, Hit-Wicket, Hat-trick, Leg-before-wicket, Leg break, Leg-bye, Maiden over, No ball, Night-watchman, Runner, Run-out, Stumped, Silly-point, Slip.

Football : Handball, Corner kick, Dribble, Free Kick, Hat-trick, Off-side, Penalty Kick, Try, Throw in, Wembley.

Hockey : Bully, Carry, Corner kick, Corner, Penalty stroke, Off-side, Penalty, Roll in scoop, Sticks, Sudden death, Striking circle, Short Corner, Scoop, Tie-breaker, Under-cutting, Hat-trick.

Tennis : Backhand drive, Deuce, Fault, Half-volley, Net, Let, Volley, Smash, Service.

Billiards : Break, Cannons, Cue, Pot, Jigger, Scratch, In Bauk, In, Off.

Bridge : Dummy, Finesse, Grand-slam, Little Slam, Revoke, Ruff slam, Trump, Tricks, Vulnerable.

Volley Ball : Booster, Love, Service, Volley, Smasher.

Badminton : Smash, Drop, Let.

Chess : Check, Checkmate, Gambit, State-mate.

Golf : Bogy, Caddie, Hole, Links, Stymie, Tee, Put.

Polo : Chukker, Mallet, Bunder.

Baseball : Bunting, Diamond, Pitcher, Put-out, Strike, Home.

Boxing : Knockout, Punch, Upper-cut, Jab, Hook.

FAMOUS TROPHIES

Agha Khan Cup	Hockey
Beighton Cup	Hockey
Corbillion Cup	World Table Tennis (Women)
Davis Cup	Lawn Tennis
Duleep Trophy	Cricket
Durand Cup	Football
Ezra Cup	Polo
I.F.A. Shield	Football
Irani Cup	Cricket (India)
Jayalaxmi Cup	Table Tennis (Women)
Lady Rattan Tata Trophy	Hockey (Women)
Nehru Cup	Hockey (India)
Obaidullah Cup	Hockey
Ranji Trophy	Cricket (India)
Rangaswamy Cup	Hockey (India)
Rovers Cup	Football (India)
Santosh Trophy	Football (India)
Subroto Cup	Football
Thomas Cup	Badminton
Uber Cup	Badminton (Women)
Wellington Trophy	Rowing (India)

BIGGEST, LARGEST, TALLEST OF THE WORLD

Largest Desert	Sahara (Africa)
Tallest Statue	Statue of Unity (India)
Rainiest Place	Mowsynram near Cherrapunjee (Meghalaya, India)
Biggest Ocean	Pacific Ocean
Deepest Ocean	Pacific Ocean
Largest Mammal	Whale
Fastest Animal	Cheetah
Lightest Substance	Hydrogen gas
Longest River	Nile
Highest Waterfalls	Salto Angel Falls (Venezuela)
Tallest Animal	Giraffe
Largest Bird (Land)	Ostrich
Hardest Mineral	Diamond
Largest Delta	Sunderbans (W.B. India)
Largest Museum	American Museum of Natural History (New York)
Longest Day	June, 21
Shortest Day	December, 22
Biggest Army	People's Liberation Army, China
Largest Salt Water Lake	Caspian Sea
Highest Mountain Peak	Everest (8848 metre high)
Longest Wall	Great Wall of China
Largest Peninsula	India
Largest Planet	Jupiter
Coldest Place	Polus Nedostupnosti (Antarctica –58°C)
Smallest Continent	Australia
Largest Lake	Caspian Sea

Deepest Lake	Baikal, 3200 ft.
Finest Harbour	Sydney Harbour
Smallest Planet	Mercury
Largest Continent	Asia
Planet nearest to the Sun	Mercury
Longest Highway Tunnel	Laerdal Tunnel (Norway)
Highest Building	Burj Khalifa, Dubai
City Biggest in area	Mt. Isa (Australia)
Country Biggest	Russia (17075000 sq. km.)
Electorate, Largest	India (over 90 crores)
Longest Epic	Mahabharat
Island, Biggest in the World	Greenland
Population, Largest	China
Longest Railway Platform	Gorakhpur (India)
Swimming Course	English Channel

FIRST IN INDIA

Governor General of Independent India — Lord Mountbatten
Commander-in-chief of free India — General Roy Bucher
Cosmonaut — Sq. Ldr. Rakesh Sharma
Field Marshal — S.H.F.J. Manekshaw
Indian Governor General of Indian Union — C. Rajagopalachari
Indian I.C.S. Officer — Satyendra Nath Tagore
Indian to swim across English Channel — Mihir Sen
Indian Women to swim across English Channel — Miss Arti Saha
Man to climb Mount Everest — Tenzing Norgay
Man to climb Mount Everest without Oxygen — Phu Dorjee
Man to climb Mount Everest twice — Nwang Gombu
Nobel Prize Winner — Rabindra Nath Tagore
President of Indian National Congress — W.C. Banerjee
President of Indian Republic — Dr. Rajendra Prasad
Talkie Film — Alam Ara (1931)
Test Tube Baby (Documented) — Indira
Viceroy of India — Lord Canning
Woman Minister of Indian Union — Rajkumari Amrit Kaur
Woman Governor — Mrs. Sarojini Naidu
Woman President of Indian National Congress — Dr. Annie Besant
Woman Prime Minister — Mrs. Indira Gandhi
Chief of Defence Staff (CDS) — General Bipin Rawat
Woman Speaker of a State Assembly — Mrs. Shanno Devi
Prime Minister of India — Pt. Jawaharlal Nehru
Muslim President of Indian Union — Dr. Zakir Hussain
Speaker of Lok Sabha — G.V. Mavlankar
Women to Climb Mount Everest — Bachhendri Pal
Woman Judge in Supreme Court — Mrs. Meera Sahib Fatima Biwi
Women Chief Justice of a High Court — Smt. Leela Seth
The First Indian Weightlifter to Win bronze medal in Olympics — Karnam Malleshwari (Sydney, in 2000)
World Chess Champion — Vishwanathan Anand
India's First Woman Merchant Navy Officer — Sonali Banerjee
The First Woman Air Vice-Marshal — P. Bandopadhyaya
The First Indian to be appointed as United Nations Civilian Police Advisor — Ms. Kiran Bedi
The First Women to be appointed Deputy Governor of Reserve Bank of India — K.J. Udeshi
The First Indian Lady to win a medal in World Athletic Championship — Anju Bobby George
The First Sikh Prime Minister of India — Dr. Manmohan Singh

IMPORTANT DAYS

✶ January

5-11	Road Safety Week
12	National Youth Day
15	Army Day
23	National Day of Patriotism
26	Republic Day
30	Martyr's Day

✶ FEBRUARY

1-14	Oil Conservation Fortnight
14	Valentine's Day

✶ MARCH

4	National Safety Day
8	International Women's Day
15	Consumers' Day
21	World Forest Day
22	World Day for Water
24	World Meteorological Day

✶ APRIL

7	World Health Day
7-13	Handloom Week
14-20	Fire Service Week
18	World Heritage Day
22	World Earth Day

✶ MAY

1	May Day
5	National Labour Day
8	World Red Cross Day

11	National Technology Day
15	International Day of the Family
17	World Telecommunication Day
24	Commonwealth Day
31	World No-Tobacco Day

✶ **JUNE**

5	World Environment Day
21	International Day of Yoga
26	International Day against Drug Abuse and Illicit Trafficking

✶ **JULY**

11	World Population Day

✶ **AUGUST**

1-7	World Breast feeding Week
10	Sanskrit Divas
15	Independence Day
20	Sadbhavana Divas

✶ **SEPTEMBER**

1-7	National Nutrition Week
5	Teachers' Day
8	International Literary Day
14	Hindi Diwas
23	World Deaf Day
27	World Tourism Day

✶ **OCTOBER**

2	✶ Gandhi Jayanti
	✶ International Day of Non Violence
	✶ Anti-Leprosy Day
4	World Animal Day
6	World Habitat Day (Ist Monday)
8	Indian Air Force Day
14	World Standard Day
15	International Day of Rural Women
16	World Food Day
24	United Nations Day
27	Infantry Day
28	World Thrift Day
31	Anti-Terrorism Day

✶ **NOVEMBER**

2	All Saints Day
14	Children's Day
15-21	National Cooperative Week
19-25	Quami Ekta Week
20	Child Rights Day
26	Constitution Day

✶ **DECEMBER**

1	World AIDS Day
3	World Day for the Disabled
4	Naval Day
7	Flag Day
8	SMRC Day
10	Human Rights Day
14	National Energy Conservation Day

PARLIAMENTS OF IMPORTANT COUNTRIES

Afghanistan	—	Shora
Britain	—	Parliament House of Commons, House of Lords
Denmark	—	Folketing
The Netherlands	—	States General
India	—	Sansad
Israel	—	Knesset
Iran	—	Majlis
Ireland	—	Airetann
Iceland	—	Althing
Japan	—	Diet
Norway	—	Storting
Russia	—	Supreme Soviet
Spain	—	Cortes
Sweden	—	Riksdag
U.S.A.	—	Congress Senate
Germany	—	Bundestag

MINERAL RESOURCES OF THE WORLD

Articles	Producers	Articles	Producers
Aluminium	China	Asbestos	Russia
Boxide	Australia	Chromium	South Africa
Copper	Chile	Cobalt	Congo (Kinshasa)
Diamonds	Russia	Gold	China
Iron-ore	China	Lead	China
Platinum	South Africa	Silver	Mexico
Silicon	China	Sulfur	China
Tin	China	Titanium	China
Tungsten	China		

TEN LARGEST COUNTRIES AND THEIR AREAS

Rank by Area	Country	Area (sq. km.)
1.	Russia	17,075,400
2.	Canada	9,976,139
3.	China	9,561,000
4.	U.S.A.	9,363,123
5.	Brazil	8,511,965
6.	Australia	7,686,848
7.	India	3,287,263
8.	Argentina	2,776,889
9.	Kazakhstan	2,724,900
10.	Algeria	2,381,741

PRESIDENT OF INDIA

He is the constitutional head of the Republic but not the real executive.

Qualifications: (1) Indian citizen; (2) age not less than 35 years; (3) should have qualifications for election to Lok Sabha; (4) should not hold any office of profit; (5) should not be a Member of Parliament or State Legislature.

Election: He is elected by the elected Members of Parliament and State Legislative Assemblies in accordance with the system of proportional representation by means of single transferable vote.

Powers: He makes appointment to all the Constitutional posts. He can address either House of Parliament and send message to them. He can summon and prorogue either House of Parliament and dissolve Lok Sabha. All Bills passed by Parliament must receive his assent to become an Act. He issues Ordinance when Parliament is not in session. No money Bill can be introduced in Lok Sabha without his recommendation. He can grant pardon, reprieve or remit punishment and he can commute death sentences. He can declare national emergency, state emergency and financial emergency.

VICE-PRESIDENT OF INDIA

The Vice-President acts as the ex-officio Chairman of Rajya Sabha and acts as the President when the latter is unable to discharge his functions due to illness, absence or any other reason, or till the election of a new President when a vacancy is caused by the death, resignation or removal of the President.

The Vice-President is elected by an electoral college consisting of the members of both Houses of Parliament in accordance with the system of proportional representation by means of the single transferable vote. He must be a citizen of India, not less than 35 years of age, and should be eligible for election as a member of the Council of States.

COUNCIL OF MINISTERS

Council of Ministers is to aid and advise the President in exercise of his functions. Prime Minister and other ministers are appointed by the President.

Cabinet: Every member of the Council of Ministers is not a Cabinet Minister. Cabinet is a small body consisting of only senior members of Council of Ministers. The Cabinet functions like the executive committee of the Council of Ministers.

PRIME MINISTER OF INDIA

Art. 74(1) of our Constitution states that the Prime Minister shall be at the head of council of ministers. He has the power of selecting and advising the President to dismiss them individually. He is the chairman of the cabinet. Art. 78 provides that it shall be the duty of the Prime minister –

- To communicate to the president all the decisions of the council of ministers relating to the administration of the affairs of the union and proposals for legislation.
- To furnish such information relating to the administration of the affairs of the union and proposals for legislation as the president may call for and
- If the President so requires to submit for the consideration of the council of ministers any matter on which a decision has been taken by a minister but which has not been considered by the council.

THE SOLAR SYSTEM: SOME FACTS

Number of Planets: 8—Mercury, Venus, Earth, Mars, Jupiter, Saturn, Uranus and Neptune.

Largest most

Massive planet .... Jupiter
Brightest planet .... Venus
Brightest star .... Sirius
Fastest orbiting planet .... Mercury
Longest (Synodic) day .... Mercury
Planet with largest moon .... Jupiter
Greatest average density .... Jupiter
Tallest mountain .... Earth
Strongest magnetic fields .... Jupiter
Most circular orbit .... Venus
Shortest (synodic) day .... Jupiter
Hottest planet .... Venus
No moons .... Mercury, Venus
Planet with moon with most eccentric orbit ...... Neptune
Lowest average density .... Saturn
Greatest amount of liquid on the surface .... Earth

THE EARTH: FACTS AND DATA

Composition of the Earth: Aluminium (0.4%), Sulphur (2.7%), Silicon (13%), Oxygen (28%), Calcium (1.2%), Nickel (2.7%), Magnesium (17%), Iron (35%)

Surface area	: 510100500 sq km
Land Surface (29.1%)	: 148950800 sq km
Ocean Surface (70.9%)	: 361149700 sq km
Type of water	: 97% salt, 3% fresh
Total area of water	: 382672000 sq km
Equatorial diameter	: 12753 km
Equatorial Circumference	: 40066 km
Polar Circumference	: 39992 km
Polar diameter	: 12710 km
Equatorial radius	: 6376 km
Polar radius	: 6335 km

Mass (estimated weight)	: 594×10^{19} metric tons
Mean distance from the Sun	: 149407000 km
Earth's orbit speed (around sun)	: 107320 kmph
Period of Revolution (round the sun)	: 365 days 5 hrs 48 min. 45.51 seconds
Time of Rotation (on its axis)	: 23 hrs 56 min 4.09 seconds
Inclination of the axis (to the plane of the ecliptic)	: 23°27'

PRINCIPAL MOUNTAIN PEAKS OF THE WORLD

	Mountains	Height in Metres	Range	Date of First Ascent
1.	Mount Everest	8,848	Himalayas	May 29, 1953
2.	K-2 (Godwin Austen)	8,611	Karakoram	July 31, 1954
3.	Kanchenjunga	8,597	Himalayas	May 25, 1955
4.	Lhotse	8,511	Himalayas	May 18, 1956
5.	Makalu I	8,481	Himalayas	May 15, 1955
6.	Dhaulagiri I	8,167	Himalayas	May 13, 1960
7.	Mansalu I	8,156	Himalayas	May 9, 1956
8.	Chollyo	8,153	Himalayas	Oct. 19, 1954
9.	Nanga Parbat	8,124	Himalayas	July 3, 1953
10.	Annapurna I	8,091	Himalayas	June 3, 1950
11.	Gasherbrum I	8,068	Karakoram	July 5, 1958
12.	Broad Peak I	8,047	Karakoram	June 9, 1957
13.	Gasherbrum II	8,034	Karakoram	July 7, 1956
14.	Shisha Pangma (Gosainthan)	8,014	Himalayas	May 2, 1964
15.	Gasherbrum III	7,952	Karakoram	Aug. 11, 1975

POPULAR NICK NAMES OF SOME FAMOUS PERSONALITIES

Andhra Kesari	T. Prakasam
Anna	C.N. Anna Durai
Bang Bandhu	Sheikh Mujibur Rehman
Bapu	Mahatma Gandhi
Bard of Avon	William Shakespeare
Chachaji	Jawaharlal Nehru
Desh Bandhu	C.R. Das
Frontier Gandhi	Khan Abdul Gaffar Khan
Fuhrer	Adolf Hitler
G.B.S.	George Bernard Shaw
Grand Old Man of India	Dadabhai Naoroji
Grand Old Man of Britain	Gladstone
Guru Dev	Rabindra Nath Tagore
Guruji	M.S. Golwalkar
Iron Man of India	Sardar Patel
Lok Nayak	Jayaprakash Narayan
Lady with the Lamp	Florence Nightingale
Lal, Bal, Pal	Lala Lajpat Rai, Bal Gangadhar Tilak, Bipin Chandra Pal
Little Corporal	Napoleon Bonaparte
Lokmanya	Bal Gangadhar Tilak
Mahamana	Pt. Madan Mohan Malaviya
Maid of Orleans	Joan of Arc
Maiden Queen	Queen Elizabeth I
Missile Man	A.P.J. Abdul Kalam

Man of Destiny	Napoleon Bonaparte	Punjab Kesari	Lala Lajpat Rai
Netaji	Subhash Chandra Bose	Shastriji	Lal Bahadur Shastri
Nightingale of India	Sarojini Naidu	Uncle Ho	Ho Chi Minh
Panditji	Jawaharlal Nehru	Wizard of the North	Walter Scott

FAMOUS INTERNATIONAL ORGANISATIONS, HEADQUARTERS AND YEAR OF ESTABLISHMENT

International Organisations	*Headquarters*	*Year of Establishment*
United Nations Organisations (U.N.O.)	New York	1945
International Monetary Fund (I.M.F.)	Washington D.C.	1945
World Health Organisation (W.H.O.)	Geneva	1948
Food & Agricultural Organisation (FAO)	Rome	1945
International Labour Organisation (ILO)	Geneva	1919
UNESCO	Paris	1946
International Court of Justice	The Hague	1946
Universal Postal Union (UPU)	Berne	1874
International Civil Aviation Organisation (ICAO)	Montreal	1945
UNIDO	Vienna	1966
International Atomic Energy Agency (IAEA)	Vienna	1957
International Finance Corporation (IFC)	Washington	1956
United Nations Development Programme (UNDP)	New York	1965
UNICEF	New York	1946
International Maritime Organisation (IMO)	London	1948
World Meteorological Organisation (WMO)	Geneva	1950
International Telecommunication Union (ITU)	Geneva	1865
Arab League	Cairo	1945
Commonwealth of Nations	London	1949
World Trade Organisation (WTO)	Geneva	1995
International Development Association (IDA)	Washington D.C.	1960
International Bank for Reconstruction and Development (IBRD)	Washington D.C.	1945
World Intellectual Property Organisation (WIPO)	Geneva	1967
Organisation of Islamic Conference (OIC)	Jeddah (Saudi Arabia)	1969
European Union (EU)	Brussels	Changed form of EEC Established in 1958
Red Cross	Geneva	1863
Interpol	Lyons	1923
Asian Development Bank (ADB)	Manila	1966
North Atlantic Treaty Organisation (NATO)	Brussels	1949
Association of South East Asian Nations (ASEAN)	Jakarta	1967

BHARAT RATNA AWARD WINNERS

1. Dr. S. Radhakrishnan	1954	**8.** Dr. D.K. Karve	1958
2. C. Rajagopalachari	1954	**9.** Dr. Bidhan Chandra Roy	1961
3. Dr. C.V. Raman	1954	**10.** Purushottam Das Tandon	1961
4. Dr. Bhagwan Das	1955	**11.** Dr. Rajendra Prasad	1962
5. Dr. M. Visvesvaraya	1955	**12.** Dr. Zakir Hussain	1963
6. Jawaharlal Nehru	1955	**13.** Dr. Pandurang Vaman Kane	1963
7. Govind Ballabh Pant	1957	**14.** Lal Bahadur Shastri	1966

15. Indira Gandhi 1971
16. V.V. Giri 1975
17. K. Kamraj 1976
18. Mother Teresa 1980
19. Acharya Vinoba Bhave 1983
20. Khan Abdul Ghaffar Khan 1987
21. M.G. Ramachandran 1988
22. Dr. B.R. Ambedkar 1990
23. Dr. Nelson R. Mandela 1990
24. Rajiv Gandhi 1991
25. Sardar Vallabhbhai Patel 1991
26. Morarji R. Desai 1991
27. Maulana Abul Kalam Azad 1992
28. Jehangir Ratanji Dadabhai Tata 1992
29. Satyajit Roy 1992
30. Gulzari Lal Nanda 1997
31. Mrs. Aruna Asaf Ali 1997
32. Dr. A.P.J. Abdul Kalam 1998
33. M.S. Subbalakshmi 1998
34. C. Subramaniam 1998
35. Jaya Prakash Narayan 1999
36. Prof. Amartya Sen 1999
37. Pt. Ravi Shankar 1999
38. Gopinath Bardoloi 1999
39. Lata Mangeshkar 2001
40. Bismillah Khan 2001
41. Bhimsen Joshi 2008
42. C.N.R. Rao 2014
43. Sachin Tendulkar 2014
44. Madan Mohan Malaviya 2015
45. Atal Bihari Vajpayee 2015
46. Nanaji Deshmukh 2019
47. Bhupen Hazarika 2019
48. Pranab Mukherjee 2019

ART AND CULTURE

☞ Classical Dances

Dance	*State*	*Famous Artists*
Bharat Natyam	Tamil Nadu	Yamini Krishnamurthy, Rukmini Devi Arundale, Swapna Sundari, Sonal Mansingh, Vaijanti Mala, Mrinalini Sarabhai, Chandralekha, Indrani, Ram Gopal, Bal Saraswati
Kathakali	Kerala	Gopinath, K.K. Nayar, Kunju-Kurup, T.K. Chandu
Kuchipudi	Andhra Pradesh/ Telangana	Sapna Sundari, Raja Reddy, Shobha Nayar, Radha Reddy, Vedantam Satyanarayan, Vimpanti Chinna Satyam.
Kathak	North India	Birju Maharaj, Gopi Krishna, Shambhu Maharaj, Sitara Devi, Vishnu Sharma, Durga Lal, Shobhana Narayan
Odissi	Odisha	Kelucharan Mahapatra, Indrani Rehman, Madhavi Mudgal, Pratima Bedi, Samyukta Panigrahi, Sonal Mansingh, Debudas
Manipuri	Manipur	Uday Shankar, Bipin Singh, Suryamukhi, Darohra Jhaveri

☞ Famous Folk Dances

State	*Folk Dance*	*State*	*Folk Dance*
Andhra Pradesh/ Telangana	Dandari, Banjara	Madhya Pradesh	Lota Nritya, Jawara
Assam	Bihu, Keli Gopal, Sataria	Maharashtra	Tamasha, Dahi Handi, Gof, Deepak Dindi
Bihar	Chhau, Magahi, Durga dance	Manipur	Dhol Cholam
W. Bengal	Kirtan, Kalatri, Asweabadh, Brita, Kalidance	Meghalaya	Nongakarem
Chhattisgarh	Saila, Karama, Bhagoria	Nagaland	Bamboo dance
Gujarat	Garba, Rasalila, Tippani, Dandia,	Odisha	Chhau, Maya Shabari, Dalachai
Haryana	Damyal, Lahoor	Punjab	Gidda, Bhangra, Panihari
Himachal Pradesh	Dussehra dance, Hikat, Notio	Rajasthan	Thumar, Kathaputali, Tera Tali
J&K	Dumhal, Kud	Tamil Nadu	Terukalathu, Kabalatam, Kargam, Pulivesham
Ladakh	Spao, Jabro, Brokpa	Tripura	Hazagiri
Jharkhand	Jhau, Ghumakudia, Jadur, Sarhul, Soharai, Karama, Vaima, Loojhari, Jat-Jatin, Vidayat	Uttar Pradesh	Rasalila, Nautanki, Thali, Dhurang, Jhumela, Huraka, Bol.
Karnataka	Yakshagan, Dolu Kunitha	Uttarakhand	Kajari, Karan
Kerala	Mohini Attam, Padayuni	Goa	Dhode Modini

MUSIC

Main Schools of Classical Music

- There are two main schools of classical music, namely, the Hindustani and the Carnatic. The Hindustani school of classical music is in vogue in north-western India, eastern India and northern parts of the South India.

Musical Instruments

- *They are:* Tabla, Mridangam, Pakhawaj, Chandai, Dholak, Veena, Sitar, Sarod, Gootuvadhyam, Sarangi, Flute, Nadaswaram, Shehnai, Shringi and Turahi.

FAMOUS INTERNATIONAL AIR SERVICES

Air Service	*Name of Country*	*Air Service*	*Name of Country*
Air India	India	K.L.M. Royal Airlines	The Netherlands (Holland)
British Overseas Airways Corporation	Britain	Lufthansa Airlines	Germany
		Iraqi Airways	Iraq
Trans World Airlines	America	National Airlines	Iran
Russian Airlines	Russia	Quantas Airlines	Australia
Japan Airlines	Japan	Hong-Kong Airlines	Hong-Kong
Pakistan International Airlines	Pakistan	Egypt Airlines	Egypt
Malaysia Airlines	Malaysia	Slovak Airlines	Slovakia
Royal Nepal Airlines	Nepal	S.I.A.	Singapore
Swiss Airways	Switzerland	Garuda Airways	Indonesia
Air France	France	Bangladesh Viman Sewa	Bangladesh
Kuwait Airways	Kuwait	Air Lanka	Sri Lanka
Pan American World Airways	America	Elitalia Airlines	Italy
		Air Canada	Canada

FAMOUS RELIGIONS, FOUNDERS, HOLY BOOKS & PLACES OF WORSHIP

Religion	*Founder*	*Holy Books*	*Place of Worship*
Hinduism	Hinduism has no one Founder. (This religion is based upon the religion of original Aryan Settlers)	Ramayan, Vedas, Puranas and Geeta	Temple
Sikh	Guru Nanak Dev	Guru Grantha Sahib	Gurdwara
Christianity	Jesus Christ	Bible	Church
Islam	Prophet Mohammed	Koran (Quran)	Mosque
Parsi	Zoroaster	Zend Avesta	Fire Temple
Jainism	Adinath Rishavdev	Jain Granth	Jain Temple
Buddhism	Gautam Buddha	Tripitaka	Buddha Temple
Jew	Moosa	Torah	Synagogue

INTELLIGENCE AGENCIES OF SOME PROMINENT COUNTRIES

Country	*Intelligence Agency*	*Country*	*Intelligence Agency*
India	Research & Analysis Wing (RAW), Intelligence Bureau (I.B.),Central Bureau of Investigation (C.B.I.)	U.S.A.	Central Intelligence Agency, Federal Bureau of Investigation
Pakistan	Inter Service Intelligence (I.S.I.)	Britain	Military Intelligence (M.I.)-5 and 6, Special Branch, Ultra, Joint Intelligence Organisation

Country	Intelligence Agency	Country	Intelligence Agency
Israel	Mosad	Iran	Sabak
Egypt	Mukhabarat	Iraq	Al-Mukhabarat
Japan	Nicho	Australia	Australian Security and Intelligence Organisation
Russia	K.G.B. (Komitel Gosudars-tvennoy Bezopasnosty) (Committee for State Security)	France	S.D.E.C.E.
Canada	Security Intelligence Service	Spain	C.E.S.I.D.
S. Africa	Bureau of State Security	Cuba	D.G.I.

SOME PROMINENT RACES OF THE WORLD

Races	Country	Races	Country	Races	Country
Veddas	Sri Lanka	Bantu	Central and South Africa	Lapps	European Tundra
Somaid	West Siberia	Tartars	Siberia	Hausa	Nigeria
Masai	East Africa	Baddu	Arab's Desert	Kirghiz	Steppes (Russia)
Muree	New Zealand	Semang	Malaysia	Bushman	Kalahari Desert
Yakoot	Russian Tundra	Eskimo	Canada, Tundra Region	Red Indian	North America
Papuans	New Guyana				
Pygmy	Congo Basin				

FAMOUS STRAITS OF THE WORLD

Strait	Between	Country
Malacca Strait	Andaman Sea and South China Sea	Indonesia
Palk Strait	Mannar and Bay of Bengal	India-Sri Lanka
Magellan Strait	Pacific and South Atlantic Ocean	Chile
Dover Strait	English Channel and North Sea	England-France
Berring Strait	Berring Sea and Chukasi Sea	Alaska-Russia
Sugaroo Strait	Japan Sea and Pacific Ocean	Japan
Sunda Strait	Java and Indian Ocean	Indonesia
Gibralter Strait	Mediterranean Sea and Atlantic Ocean	Spain
Harmuj Strait	Persia and Bay of Oman	Oman-Iran
Hudson Strait	Bay of Hudson and Atlantic Ocean	Canada

FAMOUS NEWSPAPERS OF THE WORLD

Newspaper	Place of Publishing	Language	Newspaper	Place of Publishing	Language
Daily News	New York (America)	English	Hindu, Hindustan, Times of India, Tribune, Statesman, Indian Express, Economic Times	India	English
Guardian	London (Britain)	English	Hindustan, Nav Bharat Times, Dainik Bhaskar, Dainik Jagaran, Punjab Kesari	India	Hindi
Pravada	Moscow (Russia)	Russian			
Al-Ahram	Cairo (Egypt)	Arabic			
Merdeca	Jakarta (Indonesia)	Indonesian			
Times	London (Britain)	English			
People's Daily	Beijing (China)	Chinese			
New Statesman	Britain	English			
Daily Mirror	Britain	English			

IMPORTANT BOUNDARY LINES

Boundary Line	Countries	Boundary Line	Countries
Durand Line	Pakistan and Afghanistan	Seigfrid Line	Germany-France
Hindenberg Line	Germany-Poland	24th Parallel	India-Pakistan
Maginot Line	France and Germany	17th Parallel	The line which defined the boundary between North Viet-nam and South Vietnam before the two were united.
Mannerhein Line	Russia-Finland		
Mc Mahon Line	India-China		
Order Niesse Line	Germany-Poland	38th Parallel	North Korea and South Korea
Radcliff Line	India-Pakistan	49th Parallel	U.S.A. and Canada

SIGNALS/SIGNS AND MEANING

Signal/Sign	Meaning	Signal/Sign	Meaning
Red Triangle	Family Planning	White Flag	Treaty or Surrender
Red Cross	Medical Help	Yellow Flag	Vehicles with patients of contagious diseases
Red Light	Danger, 'Stop' for the movement of vehicles	Two Bones across with a Skull	Danger of electricity
Green Light	Go		
Olive Branch	Peace	Half mast flown Flag	National mourning
White Pigeon or Dove	Peace	Lotus and culture	Sign of civilization
Black Strip on Arm	(i) Opposition (ii) Sorrow	Wheel (Chakra)	Sign of Progress
Black Flag	Opposition	A blind folded woman with scale in hand	Sign of Justice
Red Flag	(i) Danger (ii) Revolution	Reversed flown	National calamity flag

NATIONAL EMBLEMS OF IMPORTANT COUNTRIES

Country	National Emblem	Country	National Emblem
Australia	Kangaroo	New Zealand	Kiwi, Fern Southern Cross
Ireland	Shamrock	Norway	Lion
Italy	White Lily	Nepal	Kukri
Israel	Candelabrum	Pakistan	Crescent
Iran	Rose	Poland	Eagle
Canada	White Lily	France	Lily
Great Britain	Rose	Belgium	Lion
Chile	Candor and Huemul	Bangladesh	Water Lily
Germany	Corn Flower	Mongolia	The Soyombo
Japan	Chrysanthemum	Russia	Double headed eagle
Zimbabwe	Zimbabwe Bird	Lebanon	Cedar Tree
Denmark	Beach	Sudan	Secretary Bird
Turkey	Crescent and Star	Syria	Eagle
The Netherlands	Lion	India	Lioned Capital

CONTINENTS : SOME FACTS

Continent	Biggest Counrty	Highest Peak	Longest River
Asia	China	Mt. Everest (8848 m)	Yangtze Kiang
Africa	Algeria	Mt. Kilimanjaro (5895 m)	Nile
North America	Canada	Mt. Mckinley (6194 m)	Mississippi Missouri
South America	Brazil	Mt. Acancagua (6960 m)	Amazon
Europe	Russia	Mt. Elbrus (5642 m)	Ob
Australia	Australia	Mt. Coscuisco (2228 m)	Darling
Antarctica	—	Vinson Massif (5140 m)	—

COMPUTER

The computer is the system of that electronic device through which various informations are processed on the basis of a definite set of instructions called program and mathematical (numerical) and non-mathematical both types of informations are processed.

The first mechanical computer was composed or fabricated by Blaise Pascal in 1642 and it is called Pascalene. But in 1833, Charles Babbage first time conceived an automatic calculator or computer. Charles Babbage is called the father of modern computer. Herman made an electronic tabulating machine based on punch cards which operates automatically.

In 1937, first mechanical computer mark-I was fabricated by Howard Akeen. The most outstanding contribution in the development of modern computer goes to John Wan Newmaan who brought the 2nd revolution in the area of computer in 1951. He discovered EDVAC (Electronic Discrete Variable Automatic Computer) and utilised the stored program and the binary number system in the computer.

FUNCTIONS OF COMPUTER

1. Collection and composition (input) of datas;
2. Storage of datas.
3. Processing of datas.
4. Retrieval or output of the proccessed informations and datas.

UNITS OF COMPUTER

1. Input unit.
2. Central processing unit–CPU.
3. External Memory unit.
4. Output unit.

The CPU of the computer is called brain of the computer and sometimes CPU is also called Micro Processor of the computer. The data is entered through the input unit in the computer and through the central processing unit with the help of External Memory Unit datas are arranged and processed. Ultimately by the output unit these datas or informations are issued or released.

PARTS OF COMPUTER

- **Monitor :** The monitor of the computer is like a television in which the picture appears in the form of doted points on the screen and these are called pixcels.
- **Hard Disc and Floppy Disc :** The Hard Disc is the permanent disc in the computers while the Floppy Disc is the disc utilised when datas or informations are to be transferred from one computer to another.
- **Mouse :** The mouse of the computer is like the remote control of TV through which computer is directly regulated or controlled without utilising the key-board.
- **Printer :** The printer is a device which prints any documents or processed informations of the computer.

SOME HIGH LEVEL LANGUAGES

1. **FORTRAN :** This language was developed for solving the mathematical formulae very quickly and conveniently.
2. **COBOL :** This language was developed for the commerical purposes. For the processing of this language a group of sentences is selected called paragraph and all paragraphs composed are called a section, while all sections composed are called a division.
3. **BASIC :** In basic a definite part of the prescribed instruction is only inserted in the computer.
4. **ALGOL :** This was basically fabricated and designed for the complex algebraic calculations.

5. **PASCAL :** It is an amplified and modified form of ALGOL.
6. **COMAL :** This computer language is used for the students of secondary level.
7. **LOGO :** This language is used for children and kids for drawing Graphic line diagrams.
8. **PROLOG :** This language is developed in 1973 in France and this language is used for Artificial Intelligence which is capable and equivalent to the logical program.
9. **FORTH :** This language was invented by Charles Mure which is frequently used in all types of the works in the computer.

COMPUTER VIRUS

The computer virus is an electronic code which is used to abolish or erradicate the inclusive informations or programs of the computer. Some important computer viruses are Micheleanjalo, Dork Avangor, kilo, filip, Macmug, Scores, Casecade, Jeruslem, Date crime, Coloumbs crime, Internet virus, Pachcom, Pach EXE, COM-EXE, Marizuana, C-brain, bloody, Chenge Mungu and Desi etc.

COMPUTER NETWORKING

There are two types of networkings which are usually occur—Local Area Networking (LAN) and Wide Area Networking (WAN). By LAN all the computers of the same buildings are connected like the computers of university premises, computers of offices etc.

By WAN all the comptuers of a large area are connected like the computers of all the offices of a city or town etc. In India a very large computer network namely INDONET has been installing through which all the main towns and cities has to be interlinked.

COMPUTER TERMINOLOGY

- **Bit :** The bit is a unit of measurement of the electronic data. One bit is either 0 or 1 but not both. On composing 8 bits, 1 byte is formed.
- **Bug :** The Bug is the error in the computer program or system and its eradication is called Debug.
- **Byte :** Total eight bits compose a byte. Thus 8 bits = 1 byte.
- **CD-ROM :** A CD like of music CD in which data can be stored substantially called CD-ROM. In a CD with comparison to floppy extremely more datas can be stored but one problem in it is that one time recorded data can not be deleted or modified.
- **Chip :** It is a thin slice on which by a special mechanism a circuit is designed which is normally made from Silicon.
- **Memory System :** The place where computer data and program are temporarily kept is called Memory system. Usually memory is implied from RAM.
- **Modem :** The device which converts digital signals into analogue signals and vice-versa is called Modem.
- **RAM :** It is Random Access Memory (a place) where datas to be processed are kept temporarily and it is unstable memory.
- **ROM :** It is Read Only Memory and it is stable or Non-valatile memory which doesn't ended after power off.
- **Scanner :** It is a device through which graphic image is transformed to digital image and the scanners are of usually two types one desktop and another hand operating.

PROGRAMING

Computers perform phenomenal feats of calculation, but they do not do so in a complicated way. They actually carry out very simple operations, such as addition and subtraction. They achieve their fantastic computing power by carrying out these operations at incredible speed.

The programme, or set of instructions for operating the computer, is therefore written as a sequence of very simple steps. (See box below) Several computer languages have been developed for different applications, including BASIC, COBOL, FORTRAN and PASCAL. Writing programmes is very skilled and time-consuming work. But for most typical computer applications ready-written programmes are available, called "packages".

☞ How A Programme Works

Without a programme to tell it what to do and how to do it, a computer is unable to function. If, for example, you wanted to know how many times the word 'the' appears in this paragraph, or in the whole book, it would not be enough merely to put the text into a computer and then ask it how many times the word appears. For the computer to accomplish the calculations it has to be told what to do in simple steps. The instructions might be:

1. Scan the text until a space followed by 'T' or 't' is found.
2. If the next letter is not 'h', go back to step 1.
3. If the letter is 'h', is the next letter 'e'?
4. If not, go back to step 1. If it is, go to step 5.
5. If 'e' is followed by a space, add 1 to the total.
6. Go back to step 1.

A full computer programme for this operation would need to be broken down into even more simple steps, but a series of such programmes could enable a computer to analyse any amount of text in great detail.

DEFENCE

The Supreme Command of the Armed Forces is vested in the hands of the President of the Country. The responsibility for national defence, however, rests with the Cabinet. All important questions having a bearing on defence are decided by the Cabinet Committee on Political Affairs, which is presided over by the Prime Minister. The Defence Minister is responsible to Parliament for all matters concerning the Defence Services. All the administrative and operational control of Armed Forces are exercised by the Ministry of Defence. The three services – Army, Navy and Air Force function through their respective service headquarters headed by the chief of Staff.

COMMISSIONED RANKS IN DEFENCE SERVICES

Army	*Navy*	*Air Force*
General	Admiral	Air Chief Marshal
Lieutenant-General	Vice-Admiral	Air Marshal
Major-General	Rear-Admiral	Air Vice-Marshal
Brigadier	Commodor	Air Commodor
Colonel	Captain	Group Captain
Lieutenant-Colonel	Commander	Wing Commander
Major	Lt.Commander	Squadron Leader
Captain	Lieutenant	Flight Lieutenant
Lieutenant	Sub-Lieutenant	Flying Officer

INTERNAL SECURITY ORGANISATIONS OF INDIA

S. No.	Name of Organisation	Year of Creation	Headquarters
1.	Assam Rifles (A.R.)	1835	Shillong
2.	Central Reserve Police Force (C.R.P.F.)	1939	New Delhi
3.	National Cadet Corps (N.C.C.)	1948	New Delhi
4.	Territorial Army	1948	In different States
5.	Indo-Tibetan Border Police	1962	New Delhi
6.	Home Guard	1962	In different States
7.	Coast Guard	1978	New Delhi
8.	Border Security Force (B.S.F.)	1965	New Delhi
9.	Central Industrial Security Force (C.I.S.F.)	1969	New Delhi
10.	National Security Guard	1984	New Delhi
11.	Police	—	In different States

COMMANDER-IN-CHIEFS OF INDIA

1. General Roy Bucher	Jan. 1, 1948 — Jan. 14, 1949
2. General K. M. Kariappa	Jan. 15, 1949 — Jan. 14, 1953
3. General Maharaj Rajendra Sinhji	Jan. 15, 1953 — March 31, 1955
4. First Marshal of the Indian Air Force — Arjan Singh	

FIRST CHIEFS OF STAFF OF INDIAN FORCES

1. General Maharaj Rajendra Sinhji (Army Staff)	April 1, 1955 — May 14, 1955
2. Vice Admiral R.D. Katari (Naval Staff)	April 22, 1958 — June 4, 1962
3. Air Marshal Sri Thomas Elmherst (Air Staff)	Aug. 15, 1947 — Feb. 21, 1950

FIRST CHIEF OF DEFENCE STAFF (CDS)

General Bipin Rawat—Jan. 01, 2020-Dec. 08, 2021

ARMY INSTITUTES

1. Sainik Schools upto +2 Level	33 places in India
2. Rashtriya Indian Military College (prepare for entrance to N.D.A)	Dehradun
3. National Defence Academy (three services)	Khadakwasla, Pune
4. Indian Military Academy (Army)	Dehradun
5. Officers Training Academy (3 services) Short Courses	Chennai
6. National Defence College	New Delhi
7. The College of Combat	Mhow
8. The College of Military Engineering	Kirkee
9. Military College of Telecommunication Engineering	Mhow
10. The armoured Corps Centre and School	Ahmed Nagar
11. The School Artillery	Deolali
12. The Infantry School	Mhow and Belgaum
13. College of Material Management	Jabalpur

AIR FORCE INSTITUTIONS

Air Force Academy	Hyderabad
Helicopter Training School	Hakimpet
Flying Instructors School	Tambaram, Chennai
The College of Air Warfare	Secunderabad
Air Force Administrative College	Coimbatore
Air Force Technical College	Jalahalli

DEFENCE PRODUCTION UNITS

1. Bharat Dynamites Ltd.	Hyderabad	8. Mazagaon Dock	Mumbai
2. Praga Tools	Hyderabad	9. Goa Shipyard	Marmugao
3. Mishra Dattu Nigam	Hyderabad	10. Hindustan Shipyard Ltd.	Vishakhapatnam
4. Bharat Electronics Ltd.	Bengaluru	11. Hindustan Aeronautics Ltd.	Bengaluru, Hyderabad, Nasik, Koraput, Kanpur, Lucknow
5. Bharath Earthmovers Ltd.	Bengaluru		
6. Heavy Vehicles Ltd.	Avadi, Chennai		
7. Garden Reach Ship Builders and Engineers Ltd.	Kolkata		

☞ Indian Army Commands

Command	HQ Location	Command	HQ Location
Eastern Command	Kolkata	Western Command	Chandigarh
Northern Command	Udhampur	Southern Command	Pune
Central Command	Lucknow	Training Command	Shimla
South-Western Command	Jaipur		

☞ Indian Air Force Commands

Command	HQ Location	Command	HQ Location
Western Air Command	New Delhi	South-Western Air Command	Gandhinagar
Central Air Command	Prayagraj	Eastern Air Command	Shillong
Southern Air Command	Thiruvananthapuram	Training Command	Bengaluru

☞ Indian Navy Commands

Command	HQ Location	Command	HQ Location
Eastern Naval Command	Vishakhapatnam	Western Naval Command	Mumbai
Southern Naval Command	Kochi		

☞ Missile and Other Weapons

Name	Class	Range	Name	Class	Range
✶ Agni I	SRBM	850 km	✶ Brahmos	Supersonic Cruise Missile	290 km
✶ Agni II	MRBM	2500 km	✶ Brahmos 2	Hypersonic Cruise Missile	290 km
✶ Agni III	IRBM	3500 km-5500 km	✶ Prithvi I	SRBM	150 km
✶ Agni IV *or* Agni II Prime	IRBM	4000 km	✶ Prithvi III	SRBM	350 km
✶ Agni V	ICBM	5000 km-6000 km	✶ Sagarika	SLBM	700 km-2200 km
✶ Agni VI	ICBM	8000 km-10000 km	✶ Shaurya	TBM	700 km-2200 km
✶ Agni 3SL	ICBM	5200 km-11600 km	✶ Astra	Air to Air Missile	80 km-100 km
✶ Dhanush	SRBM	350 km			
✶ Nirbhay	Subsonic Cruise Missile	1000 km			

MULTIPLE CHOICE QUESTIONS

1. Match List-I with List-II and select the correct answer from the codes given below the lists:

List-I

(*a*) Napoleon Bonaparte
(*b*) Jean Jacques Rousseau
(*c*) Croce
(*d*) Madame Roland

List-II

1. 'A history is contemporary history'
2. 'Liberty what crimes are committed in thy name'
3. 'Man is born free but everywhere he is in chains.'
4. 'I am the Child of Revolution'

Codes :

	(a)	(b)	(c)	(d)
A.	1	2	3	4
B.	4	3	1	2
C.	3	4	2	1
D.	3	4	1	2

2. Abraham Lincon was elected the President of United States in:
A. 1862 B. 1860
C. 1875 D. 1855

3. Who was known as the 'Prince of Humanists'?
A. Francisco Petrarch B. Dante
C. Boccacio D. Erasmus

4. D-Day is the day when:
A. Germany declared war on Britain
B. US dropped the atom bomb on Hiroshima.
C. Allied Troops landed in Normandy
D. Germany surrendered to the allies

5. Whose teachings inspired the French Revolution?
A. Locke
B. Rousseau
C. Hegel
D. Plato

6. At a time when empires in Europe were crumbling before the might of Napoleon which one of the following Governor-Generals kept the British flag flying high in India?
A. Warren Hastings B. Lord Cornwallis
C. Lord Wellesley D. Lord Hastings

7. Which one of the following statements regarding Fascism in Italy is *not* true?
A. The Fascists came to power as a result of popular uprising
B. In 1926, all political parties except Mussolini's party were banned
C. The Fascists suppressed the Socialist movement
D. The Fascists were hostile to the Communists

8. The fall of Czar Nicholas-II is known as:
A. Blood Sunday
B. Bolshevik Revolution
C. February Revolution
D. October Revolution

9. Industrial Revolution took place first in:
A. France B. Germany
C. United Kingdom D. Japan

10. The British Prime Minister at the outbreak of World War II was :
A. Churchill B. Baldwin
C. Attlee D. Chemberlain

11. The 'Great Depression' (1929) economic crisis was met by adopting the policy of
A. Stimulus B. Marshall Plan
C. New Deal D. Open Door

12. The slogan "No taxation without representation" was raised during the:
A. American War of Independence
B. Russian Revolution
C. French Revolution
D. Indian Freedom struggle

13. In the nineteenth century the people of Europe started moving from the villages to the cities due to the impact of :
A. Epidemics
B. War
C. Industrialisation
D. Population explosion in villages

14. The important cause of the Civil War in America was:
A. Abolition of slavery
B. Quest for freedom
C. Industrialisation
D. Rebellion by the native Americans

15. Industrial Revolution could not have come about without:
A. Merchant capitalism
B. The Enclosure Movement
C. The services of the proletariat class
D. An agricultural revolution

16. Consider the following statements :
The French Revolution came about mainly due to the :
1. Extreme poverty of the people
2. Impact of the works of great writers
3. Cruelty of the rulers
4. Impact of impulsive reaction

Which of the above statements are correct?

A. 1, 2 and 4 B. 2 and 3
C. 1, 3 and 4 D. 1, 2, 3 and 4

17. Asia's oldest and largest Buddhist monastery is situated in :

A. Tawang (Arunachal Pardesh)
B. Lhasa (Tibet)
C. Trincomallee (Sri Lanka)
D. Ulan Bator (Mongolia)

18. Who was the main architect of the Russian Revolution?

A. Karl Marx B. Lenin
C. Stalin D. Tolstoy

19. V.I. Lenin is associated with :

A. Russian Revolution of 1917
B. Chinese Revolution of 1949
C. German Revolution
D. French Revolution of 1789

20. Which one of the following statements is *not* correct?

A. Voltaire believed in Natural Religion
B. Rousseau wrote *Social Contract*
C. Montesquieu authored *The Spirit of Laws*
D. Necker believed in 'General Will'

21. 6th April, 1930 is well known in the history of India because this date is associated with..........

A. Dandi March by Mahatma Gandhi
B. Quit India Movement
C. Partition of Bengal
D. Partition of India

22. Which ruler enforced the system of 'Price Control' in India?

A. Mohammad Tughlak
B. Razia Begum
C. Alauddin Khilji
D. Sher Shah Suri

23. The concept of 'Din-e-Elahi' was founded by which king?

A. Dara Shikoh B. Akbar
C. Sher Shah Suri D. Shahjahan

24. Who are supposed to be the earliest inhabi-tants of India? Where did they come from?

A. Aryans from Central Asia
B. Dravidians from Mediterranean
C. Negroids from Africa
D. Bhils and the Santhals from West Asia

25. The one chief characteristic of temple architecture of the Gupta Age was :

A. Absence of dome
B. Huge size
C. Beautiful carvings
D. absence of a covered courtyard for the gathering of worshippers

26. The Rigveda consists of :

A. 1000 hymns B. 2028 hymns
C. 1028 hymns D. 1038 hymns

27. The central point in Ashoka's dharma was :

A. royalty to kings
B. peace and non-violence
C. respect to elders
D. religious tolerance

28. The social evil which was conspicuously absent during ancient India was :

A. *Sati*-System B. *Devadasi*-System
C. Polygamy D. *Purdah*-System

29. Which, among the following, can be accepted as a novelty introduced by Mughal emperors to their buildings?

A. Domes B. Minarets
C. Arches D. Attached gardens

30. The first ruler of India who defeated Muhammud of Ghur was :

A. Mularaja II of Gujarat
B. Prithviraja Chauhan of Delhi
C. Jayachand of Kannauj
D. Parmaldeva of Bundelkhand

31. What important event happened in India in 1911?

A. Bengal was partitioned
B. Non-Cooperation movement was launched
C. India's capital was shifted from Calcutta to Delhi
D. Mahatma Gandhi presided over the Congress session

32. The first phase of the Congress Party (1885-1905) was characterized by its efforts to secure:

A. limited independence
B. complete freedom
C. Indianization of services
D. constitutional reforms

33. The Muslim League demanded a separate homeland for the Indian Muslims openly for the first time at its annual session held in Lahore in the year :

A. 1931 A.D. B. 1936 A.D.
C. 1940 A.D. D. 1941 A.D.

34. Under whose governorship did the East India Company secure the Diwani Rights in Bengal, Bihar and Odisha from Emperor Shah Alam?

A. Lord Cornwallis
B. Lord William Bentinck
C. Lord Clive
D. Lord Wellesley

35. The Simon Commission was generally boycotted by the Indian political parties. What was the reason for this general non-cooperation?
A. the Commission aimed at dividing the people
B. it was an 'all white' Commission
C. it came after the Jallianwala Bagh carnage
D. it was an eye wash

36. Aligarh Muslim University was founded by :
A. Dr. Saifuddin Kitchlu
B. Mohammad Ali Jinnah
C. Sir Syed Ahmed Khan
D. Maulana Mohammad Ali

37. Ibn Batutah was an African traveller visiting India during the time of :
A. Alivardi Khan
B. Ala-ud-din Khalji
C. Iltutmish
D. Mohammad-bin-Tughlaq

38. The battle of Wandiawash was fought in :
A. 1726 B. 1760
C. 1818 D. 1857

39. The abolition of *Sati* by government regulation was at the time of :
A. Warren Hastings B. Lord Wellesley
C. Lord Bentinck D. Lord Ahmerst

40. Pick out the wrong combination :
A. Dilwara Temple : Mt. Abu
B. Pashupati Temple : Kathmandu
C. Padmanabh Temple : Bangalore
D. Minakshi Temple : Madurai

41. Match the following:
(a) Chanhudaro *(b)* Kalibangan
(c) Lothal *(d)* Surkotada
1. Alleged discovery of the skeleton of horse.
2. Bead making.
3. Traces of a dock and ship on seal.
4. Evidence of ploughing the fields.

The Correct code is :

	(a)	*(b)*	*(c)*	*(d)*
A.	2	4	3	1
B.	2	1	3	4
C.	1	2	3	4
D.	2	1	4	3

42. Match the Harappan settlements with the banks of rivers on which they were located :
(a) Harappa 1. Ravi
(b) Mohenjodaro 2. Indus
(c) Ropar 3. Sutlej
(d) Kalibangan 4. Ghaggar
(e) Lothal 5. Bhogava

Codes :

	(a)	*(b)*	*(c)*	*(d)*	*(e)*
A.	1	2	3	4	5
B.	1	2	3	5	4
C.	2	1	3	5	4
D.	2	1	4	3	5

43. The Goddess 'Kannagi' whose many temples were erected during the 'Sangam Age' was the goddess of:
A. Chastity B. Love
C. Prowess D. Wisdom

44. The Jain goal of life is to attain deliverance from the fetters of mudane existence, the way to which lies through three jewels. Which one of the following was not included among the 'three jewels' of Jainism?
A. Right faith B. Right action
C. Right knowledge D. Right conduct

45. The most striking feature of the Ashokan pillar is polish. Name the Ashokan pillar which is considered to be the most graceful of all Ashokan pillars.
A. Sarnath
B. Rampurva
C. Laurya-Nandangarh
D. Rummindei

46. Which are the correct statements?
1. The land grants, started in Satavahana period, paved the way for feudal developments in India.
2. Silk and spices were the Chief Indian export articles of Indo-Roman trade.
3. The Guptas issued the largest number of gold coins in ancient India.
4. The first memorial of a 'SATI' dated 510 A.D. is found at Eran in Madhya Pradesh.

A. 1 and 2 B. 1, 3, and 4
C. 1 and 4 D. 1, 2, 3 and 4

47. Who among the following patronised the 'Gandhara' (Indo-Greek style) School of Art?
A. Ashoka, the Great
B. Harsha Vardhana
C. Kanishka
D. Chandragupta Vikramaditya

48. The Sultanate of Delhi had five ruling dynasties. The dynasty having longest and shortest period were :
A. Ilbari and Khalji
B. Tughlaq and Khalji
C. Tughlaq and Sayyid
D. Ilbari and Lodis

49. Which one of the following events took place at the last during reign of Muhammad-bin-Tughlaq?
A. Introduction of token currency
B. Increase of land-revenue in Doab
C. Transfer of Capital from Delhi to Devagiri.
D. Conquest of Khurasan and Iraq

50. The most learned medieval Muslim ruler who was well versed in various branches of learning including astronomy, mathematics and medicine was :
A. Jalaluddin Khilji
B. Sikander Lodi
C. Ghiyasuddin Tughlaq
D. Muhammad-bin-Tughlaq

51. The 'Sufis' had 12 silsilas. They propounded the idea of Union with God through:
A. Love B. Rituals
C. Fasts D. Prayers

52. Match the following:
(*a*) Peshwa 1. Foreign affairs
(*b*) Panditrao 2. Audit and accounts
(*c*) Amatya 3. Providing grants to scholars
(*d*) Sumant 4. General supervision
5. Military affairs

Select the correct code :

	(*a*)	(*b*)	(*c*)	(*d*)
A.	2	3	4	5
B.	4	1	2	3
C.	4	3	2	1
D.	3	1	4	2

53. The Regulating Act of 1773 can be regarded as the first measure to :
A. assert the right of British Parliament to legislate for India
B. separate the legislature from the executive
C. separate the judiciary from the executive
D. centralise law-making

54. What was the exact constitutional status of the Indian Republic on 26th January, 1950?
A. A Democratic Republic
B. A Sovereign, Democratic Republic
C. A Sovereign, Secular, Democratic Republic
D. A Sovereign, Socialist, Secular, Democratic Republic

55. When the British obtained the grant of Diwani of Bengal, Bihar and Odisha they acquired the right to :
A. maintain law and order in these territories
B. administer civil justice and collect revenue in these territories
C. collect revenue and establish revenue administration in these territories
D. militarily defend these territories

56. Which of the following were responsible for the growth of nationalism in India during the British rule?
1. Economic exploitation of India.
2. Impact of western education.
3. Role of the Press.

Select the correct answer using the codes given below :
Codes:
A. 1, 2 and 3 B. 1 and 2
C. 2 and 3 D. 1 and 3

57. Which one of the following nationalist leaders has been described as being radical in politics but conservative on social issues?
A. G.K. Gokhale
B. B.G. Tilak
C. Lala Lajpat Rai
D. Madan Mohan Malviya

58. Provincial Autonomy in British India was envisaged by the :
A. Act of 1909 B. Act of 1919
C. Act of 1935 D. Act of 1947

59. Dyarchy means :
A. double government
B. a government in which the centre is very powerful
C. a government based on division of power between centre and provinces
D. None of the above

60. The Indian National Congress observed 'Independence Day' for the first time on 26th January in :
A. 1920 B. 1925
C. 1930 D. 1947

61. ....is situated near the banks of Sabarmati River
A. Bhavnagar B. Aurangabad
C. Ahmedabad D. Rajkot

62. Sericulture is:
A. science of the various kinds of serum
B. artificial rearing of fish
C. art of silkworm breeding
D. study of various cultures of a community

63. The most abundant constituents of earth's crust are:
A. Igneous rocks
B. Sedimentary rocks
C. Metamorphic rocks
D. Granite

64. Indian Standard Time is based on:
A. 80°E longitude B. 82½°E longitude
C. 110°E longitude D. 25°E longitude

65. Tides in the oceans are caused by :
A. Gravitational pull of the moon on the earth's surface including sea water
B. Gravitational pull of the sun on the earth's surface only and not on the sea water
C. Gravitational pull of the moon and the sun on the earth's surface including the sea water
D. None of these

66. Nagarjunasagar Project is situated on the river:
A. Tungabhadra
B. Cauvery
C. Krishna
D. Godavari

67. The difference between the Indian Standard Time and the Greenwich Mean Time is:
A. – 3½ hours B. + 3½ hours
C. – 5½ hours D. + 5½ hours

68. Which of the following dams is not on Narmada river?
A. Indira-Sagar Project
B. Maheshwar Hydel Power Project
C. Jobat Project
D. Koyna Power Project

69. Which of the following statements is **not true** about the availability of water on the earth, the crisis for which is going to increase in the years to come?
A. About 97.5 per cent of the total volume of water available on the earth is salty
B. 80 per cent of the water available to us for use comes in bursts as monsoons
C. About 2.5 per cent of the total water available on the earth is polluted water and cannot be used for human activities
D. Possibility is that some big glaciers will melt in the coming ten-fifteen years and sea level will rise by 3-4 metres all over the earth

70. Which of the following is **not** a cash crop?
A. Jute B. Paddy
C. Cashewnut D. Sugarcane

71. Through which States does Cauvery River flow?
A. Gujarat, M.P., Tamil Nadu
B. Karnataka, Kerala, Tamil Nadu
C. Karnataka, Kerala, Andhra Pradesh
D. M.P., Maharashtra, Tamil Nadu

72. Indian Standard Time is the local time of 82½°E which passes through :
A. Guntur B. Delhi
C. Allahabad D. Kolkata

73. The 17th parallel defines the boundary between:
A. North and South Korea
B. USA and Canada
C. North and South Vietnam
D. China and Russia

74. During the period of south-west monsoon, Tamil Nadu remains dry because:
A. the winds do not reach this area
B. there are no mountains in this area
C. it lies in the rain shadow area
D. the temperature is too high to let the winds cool down

75. Which of the following device measures depth of a sea?
A. Fathometer B. Anemometer
C. Altimeter D. Barometer

76. The biggest reserves of thorium are in :
A. India B. China
C. The Soviet Union D. U.S.A.

77. The Girnar Hills are situated in which of the following states?
A. Gujarat B. Karnataka
C. Madhya Pradesh D. Maharashtra

78. During December 22nd the sun is vertically over:
A. Tropic of Cancer
B. Tropic of Capricorn
C. The Equator
D. None of the above

79. Photosphere is described as the :
A. Lower layer of atmosphere
B. Visible surface of the sun from which radiation emanates
C. Wavelength of solar spectrum
D. None of the above

80. Broadly, there are three layers of the earth of the crust, the mantle and the core. The crust forms what percentage of the volume of the earth?
A. 0.5% B. 2.5%
C. 7.5% D. 12.5%

81. The grassland of Argentina is known as :
A. Pampas B. Campos
C. Savanna D. None of the above

82. Different seasons are formed because :
A. Sun is moving around the earth
B. of revolution of the earth around the Sun on its orbit
C. of rotation of the earth around its axis
D. All of the above

83. Eskers and Drumlins are features formed by:
A. underground water
B. running water
C. the action of wind
D. glacial action

84. Match List-I and List-II and select the correct answer using the codes given below the Lists :

List-I *(Rivers)*	**List-II** *(Towns)*
(*a*) Ghaghara	1. Lucknow
(*b*) Brahmaputra	2. Hoshangabad
(*c*) Narmada	3. Ahmedabad
(*d*) Sabarmati	4. Guwahati
	5. Ayodhya

	(a)	(b)	(c)	(d)
A.	4	5	1	2
B.	5	4	2	3
C.	5	4	3	1
D.	3	5	2	1

85. Which of the statements as regards the consequences of the movement of the earth is not correct?
A. Revolution of the earth is the cause of the change of seasons.
B. Rotation of the earth is the cause of days and nights.
C. Rotation of the earth causes variation in the duration of days and nights.
D. Rotation of the earth effects the movement of winds and ocean currents.

86. The world is divided into :
A. 12 time zones
B. 20 time zones
C. 24 time zones
D. 36 time zones

87. The 'Kiel' canal links the :
A. Pacific and Atlantic Oceans
B. Mediterranean Sea and Red Sea
C. Mediterranean Sea and Black Sea
D. North Sea and Baltic Sea

88. Match the following :

List-I	List-II
(a) Himadri	1. Outer Himalayas
(b) Shivalik	2. Inner Himalayas
(c) Himanchal	3. Middle Himalayas
(d) Sahyadri	4. Western Ghats

Codes:

	(a)	(b)	(c)	(d)
A.	1	2	3	4
B.	4	2	3	1
C.	2	1	3	4
D.	1	2	3	4

89. The term 'Regur' refers to:
A. Laterite soils
B. Black Cotton soils
C. Red Soils
D. Deltaic Alluvial Soils

90. Location of sugar industry in India is shifting from north to south because of:
A. cheap labour
B. expanding regional market
C. cheap and abundant supply of power
D. high yield and high sugar content in sugarcane

91. Consider the following statements :
1. Ozone is found mostly in the Stratosphere..
2. Ozone layer lies 55-75 km above the surface of the earth.
3. Ozone absorbs ultraviolet radiation from the Sun.
4. Ozone layer has no significance for life on the earth.

Which of the above statements are correct?
A. 1 and 3
B. 2 and 4
C. 2 and 3
D. 1 and 4

92. Which of the following is not a chemical coagulant used in water treatment?
A. Polyaluminium Chloride (PAC)
B. Nitrogen dioxide
C. Aluminium Sulfate (Alum)
D. Aluminium Chloride

93. Darjeeling and Dharamsala would be the right places to visit if one wanted to get a clear view respectively of :
A. Kanchanjunga and Dhauladhar ranges
B. Nandadevi and Dhauladhar ranges
C. Kanchanjunga and Nandadevi ranges
D. Nandadevi and Nanga Parvat

94. Atmosphere exists because:
A. The Gravitational force of the Earth
B. Revolution of the Earth
C. Rotation of the Earth
D. Weight of the gases of atmosphere

95. Victoria lake is located in the continent:
A. Africa
B. Asia
C. North America
D. South America

96. The famous Lagoon Lake of India is :
A. Dal Lake
B. Chilka Lake
C. Pulicat Lake
D. Mansarover

97. Where are most of the earth's active volcanoes concentrated?
A. Indian Ocean
B. Pacific Ocean
C. Aral Sea
D. Atlantic Ocean

98. Through which of the following states does the river Chambal flow?
A. U.P., M.P., Rajasthan
B. M.P., Gujarat, U.P.
C. Rajasthan, M.P., Bihar
D. Gujarat, M.P., U.P.

99. Which country is called the sugar bowl of the world?
A. Cuba B. India
C. Argentina D. USA

100. The area covered by forest in India is about:
A. 46% B. 33%
C. 23% D. 21.71%

101. A closed economy is the one which :
A. does not permit emigration or immigration
B. permits emigration but no immigration
C. engages in no foreign trade
D. engages in no foreign and domestic trade or transit

102. In a developed economy the major share of employment originates in the :
A. primary sector B. tertiary sector
C. secondary sector D. any of the above

103. The Economic and Social Commission for Asia and Pacific (ESCAP) is located at :
A. Bangkok B. Kuala Lumpur
C. Manila D. Singapore

104. Commercial vehicles are not produced by which of the following companies in India?
A. TELCO B. Ashok Leyland
C. DCM Daewoo D. Birla Yamaha

105. In India, the Public Sector is most dominant in:
A. transport
B. steel production
C. commercial banking
D. organised term-lending financial institutions

106. The main argument advanced in favour of small scale and cottage industries in India is that:
A. cost of production is low
B. they require small capital investment
C. they advance the goal of equitable distribution of wealth
D. they generate a large volume of employment

107. The most serious economic problems of India are:
A. Poverty and unemployment
B. Stagnation, not poverty
C. Unemployment, not poverty
D. Underdevelopment, not poverty

108. Which of the following is not one of the three central problems of an economy?
A. What to produce
B. How to produce
C. When to produce
D. For whom to produce

109. If saving exceeds investment, the national income will:
A. fall B. rise
C. fluctuate D. remain constant

110. In which of the following industries in India are the maximum number of workers employed?
A. Sugar B. Jute
C. Textiles D. Iron and Steel

111. Terrace Cultivation is practiced mostly:
A. in urban areas
B. on slopes of mountains
C. on tops of hills
D. in undulating tracts

112. Which of the following is a Selective Credit Control method?
A. Bank Rate
B. RBI directives
C. Cash Reserve Ratio
D. Open market operations

113. Which of the following taxes is not shared by the Central Government with the States?
A. Union excise duties
B. Customs duty
C. Income tax
D. Estate duty

114. ICICI is the name of a:
A. Financial Institution
B. Chemical Industry
C. Cotton Industry
D. Chamber of Commerce and Industry

115. Structural Unemployment arises due to
A. Deflationary conditions
B. Heavy industry bias
C. Shortage of raw material
D. Inadequate productive capacity

116. What is the full form of NPA in Context of Banking system?
A. Non-Performing Assests
B. National Productivity Authority
C. National Productivity Association
D. Non-Paying Assets

117. The largest public sector bank in India is:
A. Central Bank of India
B. Punjab National Bank
C. State Bank of India
D. Indian Overseas Bank

118. Which of the following statements best explains the term contraband goods?
A. Goods produced only for exports
B. Goods produced in joint sector only
C. Goods for the trading of which licence is not required
D. Goods that are forbidden, from export, import or even possession, by law

119. Price in the market is fixed by:
A. Stock exchange rates
B. The demand and supply ruling in the market at a particular time
C. The Finance Minister
D. None of the above

120. Devaluation of currency helps to promote:
A. National Income
B. Savings
C. Imports at lower cost
D. Exports

121. Balanced economic growth can be achieved only if:
A. All the sectors of economy grow at the same rate
B. Population growth is arrested
C. All the inter dependent sectors grow in harmony
D. Basic and heavy industries are assigned highest priority

122. P.V. Sindhu is associated with which of the following sport?
A. Badminton
B. Weightlifting
C. Swimming
D. Tennis

123. 'MODVAT' stands for:
A. Ad Valorem tax on output
B. Deduction of cost of inputs from the value of output
C. Reduction in import duties
D. Imposition of tax on professions

124. Who among the following is the first to receive 'Dada Saheb Phalke' award?
A. Shivaji Ganeson
B. Devika Rani
C. Dr. Raj Kumar
D. None of the above

125. The term 'devaluation' means:
A. Reducing the value of a currency in terms of another currency
B. Increasing the value of a currency
C. Revising the value of a currency
D. None of the above

126. Per capita net availability of pulses has shown a tendency of:
A. Increase over time
B. Decrease over time
C. Constant over time
D. First increase then decrease

127. National Income is the same as:
A. Net national product at market price
B. Net domestic product at market price
C. Net national product at factor cost
D. Net domestic product at factor cost

128. Which one of the following is not an example of indirect tax?
A. Goods and Services Tax
B. Excise duty
C. Customs duty
D. Expenditure tax

129. The major aim of devaluation is to:
A. encourage imports
B. encourage exports
C. encourage both exports and imports
D. discourage both exports and imports

130. Structural unemployment arises due to:
A. deflationary conditions
B. heavy industry bias
C. shortage of raw materials
D. inadequate productive capacity

131. When was the Family Planning Programme officially started in India?
A. 1950 B. 1952
C. 1956 D. 1962

132. When was the Reserve Bank of India nationalised?
A. 1947 B. 1949
C. 1950 D. 1951

133. Which of the following is *not* a feature of the Indian economy?
A. High rate of population growth
B. Disguised unemployment
C. Lowest rate of adult literacy
D. High rate of exports

134. The 'Relative Deprivation' approach for measuring poverty has been adopted by:
A. developing countries
B. developed countries
C. under-developed countries
D. None of the above

135. One of the main factors that led to rapid expansion of Indian exports is:
A. Imposition of import duties
B. Liberalisation of the economy
C. Recession in other countries
D. Diversification of exports

136. Sustainable economic development means an increase in the rate of growth of real:
A. total and per capita product
B. total and per capita product and level of literacy rate
C. total and per capita product and life expectancy at birth
D. total and per capita product, taking into account the cost of degradation of the quality of environment in this process

137. Functional unemployment occurs when:
A. unemployed have no qualification for job
B. people frequently change their job
C. people were thrown out from job due to recession
D. None of these

138. Which among the following does **not** have a 'free trade zone'?
A. Kandla B. Mumbai
C. Visakhapatnam D. Thiruvanantpuram

139. Sun Belt of USA is important for which one of the following industries?
A. Cotton textile
B. Petrochemicals
C. Hi-tech electronics
D. Food Processing

140. Commercial banking system in India is
A. unit banking B. branch banking
C. mixed banking D. None of the above

141. Who gives recognition to political parties in India?
A. Parliament
B. President
C. Supreme Court
D. Election Commission

142. The Quorum of the Legislative Council is :
A. one-fourth of its total membership
B. one-third of its membership
C. one-tenth of its membership
D. 25

143. The Indian Constitution is:
A. federal
B. unitary
C. a happy mixture of the federal and unitary
D. federal in normal times and unitary in times of emergency

144. Universal adult franchise implies a right to vote to all:
A. adult residents of the State
B. adult male citizens of the State
C. residents of the State
D. adult citizens of the State

145. When a resolution prefering a charge against the President has been passed by a specified majority in the House, it is sent to the other House for investigation. If, as a result of such an investigation, a resolution is passed through a specified majority by the other House, declaring that the charge has been sustained, the President shall leave his office. The specified special majority must not be less than :
A. two-third of the members present and voting
B. one-third of the members present and voting
C. three-fourth of the members present and voting and two-third of the total membership
D. two-third of the total membership

146. Which one of the following judicial powers of the President of India has been *wrongly* listed?
A. he appoints the Chief Justice and other judges of the Supreme Court
B. he can remove the judges of the Supreme Court on grounds of misconduct
C. he can consult the Supreme Court on any question of law or fact which is of public importance
D. he can grant pardon, reprieves and respites to persons punished under Union Law

147. The Vice-president of India can be removed from his office before the expiry of his term if :
A. the Rajya Sabha passes a resolution by a majority of its members and the Lok Sabha agrees with the resolution
B. if the Supreme Court of India recommends his removal
C. the President so desires
D. None of the above

148. The Chief Justice of a High Court in India is appointed by the :
A. Governor of the State
B. Prime Minister of India
C. Chief Justice of the Supreme Court
D. President of India

149. Which of the following statements is constitutionally, not true about the passing of the Union Budgets and Finance Bill in India?
1. Under the law, Finance Bill should be adopted by both the Houses of the Parliament within 45 days of its introduction.
2. If the Finance Bill is not adopted within specified period, the government loses its authority to levy the taxes proposed in the budgets.
3. In the absence of full budget, a vote-on-account gives the power to the government to spend.
4. Government cannot raise revenues without a proper approval of the Finance Bill

A. Only 2 B. Only 3
C. Only 4 D. Only 1, 2 and 3

150. Normally, on whose advice the President's Rule is imposed in a State?
A. Chief Minister
B. Legislative Assembly
C. Governor
D. Chief Justice of High Court

151. Which Article of the Indian Constitution deals with Amendment procedure?
A. Article 368 B. Article 358
C. Article 367 D. All of these

152. Government is the agency through which the will of:

A. the state is expressed

B. the people is expressed

C. the head of the state is expressed

D. the majority is expressed

153. In a unitary system of government :

A. The centre is all powerful

B. The centre is weaker than the states

C. The centre and states stand at par

D. The states and centre are supreme in their respective spheres

154. In Cabinet System of Government the real executive authority rests with :

A. The Council of Ministers

B. The Prime Minister

C. The Constitution

D. The Parliament

155. The Head of the State under a parliamentary government:

A. is an elected representative

B. is a hereditary person

C. is a nominated person

D. may be any one of the above

156. In the event of a ministerial proposal being defeated on the floor of the legislature, under the parliamentary system :

A. the government waits for a general no-confidence motion

B. the minister concerned is taken to task by the Prime Minister

C. the minister is forced to resign

D. the whole Council of Ministers resign

157. The "due process of law" is an essential characteristic of the judicial system of:

A. UK B. France

C. USA D. India

158. Under the Constitution it is :

A. obligatory for the President to accept the advice of the Council of Ministers but is not obliged to follow it

B. obligatory for the President to accept the advice of the Council of Ministers

C. not obligatory for the President to seek or accept the advice of the Council of Ministers

D. obligatory for the President to seek the advice of the Council of Ministers if his own party is in power

159. Which one of the following statements is correct?

A. the Presiding Officer of Rajya Sabha is elected every year

B. the Presiding Officer of Rajya Sábha is elected for a term of two years at a time

C. the Presiding Officer of Rajya Sabha is elected for a term of six years

D. the Vice-President of India is the ex-officio Presiding Officer of Rajya Sabha

160. The introduction of "no confidence" motion in the Lok Sabha requires the support of at least:

A. 50 members B. 70 members

C. 60 members D. 80 members

161. The High Court comes under :

A. State List B. Union List

C. Concurrent List D. None of the above

162. Which one of the following has been wrongly listed as a Fundamental Duty of the Indian citizens?

A. to develop scientific temper, humanism and spirit of inquiry and reform

B. to work for raising the prestige of the country in the international sphere

C. to protect and improve the natural environment

D. to strive towards excellence in all spheres of individual and collective activity

163. Which one of the following is not a Fundamental Duty as outlined in Article 51A of the Constitution?

A. to abide by the Constitution and respect its ideals

B. to defend the country and render national service when called upon to do so

C. to work for the moral upliftment of the weaker sections of society

D. to preserve the rich heritage

164. The main characteristics of the Directive Principles of State Policy given in the Indian Constitution are :

A. not enforceable by any court

B. fundamental in the governance of the country

C. 'Like instruments, instructions, political manifesto and a code of moral precepts which have to guide governors of the country'

D. no law can be passed, which is opposed to these principles

165. Of the following which are true?

A. In a State, the Legislative Council is dominant with regard to non-financial bills and the Legislative Assembly with regard to financial (money) bills

B. Vidhan Parishad can virtually block legisla-tion even if the same is passed by the Vidhan Sabha

C. In case of a tie between the two Houses, the Governor is duty-bound to call a joint session of the two Houses to have the issue settled on a majority verdict

D. If a Bill is twice approved by the Vidhan Sabha, it becomes law even if rejected by the Vidhan Parishad.

166. Which one of the following types of emergency can be declared by the President?
A. Emergency due to threat of war and external aggresion
B. Emergency due to break-down of constitu-tional machinery in a State
C. Financial emergency on account of threat to the financial credit of India
D. all the three emergencies

167. The chairman of which of the following parliamentary committees is invariably from the members of ruling party?
A. Committee on public undertakings
B. Public accounts committee
C. Estimates committee
D. Committee on delegated legislation

168. Which of the following is not a formally prescribed device available to the members of parliament?
A. Question hour
B. Zero hour
C. Half-an-hour discussion
D. Short duration discussion

169. Which of the following is not a tool of executive control over public administration?
A. Power of appointment and removal
B. Line agencies
C. Appeal to public opinion
D. Civil services code

170. If the Speaker of the State Legislative Assembly decides to resign, he should submit his resignation to the:
A. Judges of the High Court
B. Deputy Speaker
C. Chief Minister
D. Finance Minister

171. The President of India can nominate to the Rajya Sabha:
A. 6 members B. 9 members
C. 15 members D. 12 members

172. India is a Federal State because of:
A. dual judiciary
B. dual citizenship prevalent here
C. share of power between the Centre and the States
D. rigid Constitution

173. Residuary Subjects are those subjects which are:
A. contained in the State list
B. contained in the Union list
C. contained in the Concurrent list
D. not covered by any of the three lists

174. Which of the following writs can be issued, by the Supreme Court, to enforce Fundamental Rights?
A. Writ of Habeas Corpus
B. Writ of Mandamus
C. Writ of Quo Warranto
D. All of these

175. When the offices of both the President and the Vice-President of India are vacant, who will discharge their functions?
A. Prime Minister
B. Home Minister
C. Chief Justice of India
D. The Speaker

176. The Supreme Court tenders advice to the President of India on a matter of law or fact:
A. on its own
B. only when such advice is sought
C. only if the matter relates to some basic issue
D. only if the issue poses a threat to the unity and integrity of the country

177. Six months shall **not** intervene between two sessions of the Indian Parliament because :
A. it is the customary practice
B. it is the British convention followed in India
C. it is an obligation under the Constitution of India
D. None of the above

178. The States of the Indian Union can be recognised or their boundaries altered by:
A. the Union Parliament by a simple majority in the ordinary process of legislation
B. two-thirds majority of both the Houses of Parliament
C. two-thirds majority of both the Houses of Parliament and the consent of the legisla-tures of concerned States
D. an executive order of the Union government with the consent of the concerned State governments

179. The Basic Feature theory of the Constitution of India was propounded by the Supreme Court in the case of:
A. Minerva Mills Vs. Union of India
B. Golaknath Vs. State of Punjab
C. Maneka Gandhi Vs. Union of India
D. Keshavananda Vs. State of Kerala

180. Which one of the following writs is issued by a court in case of illegal detention of a person?
A. Habeas corpus
B. Mandamus
C. Certiorari
D. Quo-warranto

181. Name the instrument with the help of which a sailor in a submarine can see the objects on the surface of the sea.
A. Telescope B. Periscope
C. Gycroscope D. Stereoscope

182. 'HEMOPHILLIA' is the disease of ....
A. liver B. blood
C. brain D. bones

183. Vitamin A is abundantly found in ....
A. Brinjal B. Tomato
C. Carrot D. Cabbage

184. .... is not soluble in water.
A. Vitamin A B. Vitamin B
C. Vitamin C D. None of these

185. The blood vessels with the smallest diameter are called ....
A. capillaries B. arterioles
C. venules D. lymphatics

186. Out of the following .... has the greatest elasticity.
A. steel B. rubber
C. aluminium D. annealed copper

187. Cooking gas is a mixture of which of the following two gases?
A. Carbon Dioxide and Oxygen
B. Butane and Propane
C. Carbon Monoxide and Carbon Dioxide
D. Methane and Ethylene

188. The substance most commonly used as a food preservative is:
A. sodium carbonate B. tartaric acid
C. acetic acid D. benzoic acid

189. Normally, the substances that fight against diseases in human systems are known as:
A. dioxyribonucleic acids
B. carbohydrates
C. enzymes
D. antibodies

190. The SI unit of temperature is ....
A. Kelvin B. Celsius
C. Fahrenheit D. None of the above

191. One of the common fungal diseases of man is :
A. plague B. ringworm
C. cholera D. typhoid

192. A clear sky is blue because:
A. red light is scattered more than blue
B. ultraviolet light has been absorbed
C. blue light is scattered more than red
D. blue light has been absorbed

193. Jenner introduced the method of making people immune to :
A. small pox B. rabies
C. cholera D. polio

194. The largest cell in the human body is :
A. Nerve cell B. Live cell
C. Muscle cell D. Kidney cell

195. What is the device that steps up or steps down the voltage?
A. Dynamo B. Conductor
C. Inductor D. Transformer

196. The protein deficiency disease is known as :
A. Kwashiorker B. Cirrhosis
C. Eczema D. Clycoses

197. Iron deficiency causes :
A. rickets B. anaemia
C. cirrhosis D. goitre

198. Blood group of an individual is controlled by :
A. Haemoglobin B. Shape of RBC
C. Shape of WBC D. Genes

199. In a normal man the amount of blood pumped out by the heart per minute is about :
A. 1 litre B. 3 litres
C. 4 litres D. 5 litres

200. Red/green colour blindness in man is known as :
A. Protanopia
B. Deutetanopia
C. Both A and B above
D. Marfan's syndrome

201. The blue colour of the water in the sea is due to :
A. Reflection of the blue light by the impurities in sea water
B. Reflection of the blue sky by sea water and scattering of blue light by water molecules
C. Absorption of other colours by water molecules
D. None of the above

202. The image formed on the retina of the eye is:
A. upright and real
B. larger than the object
C. small and inverted
D. enlarged and real

203. Unit of loudness of sound is:
A. bel B. decibel
C. phon D. none of these

204. Oil rises up the wick in a lamp :
A. because oil is volatile
B. due to the capillary action phenomenon
C. due to the surface tension phenomenon
D. because oil is very light

205. The 'stones' formed in human kidney consist mostly of :
A. calcium oxalate
B. sodium acetate
C. magnesium sulphate
D. calcium

206. We hear the sound later, while the light is seen earlier:
A. because light's speed is more than that of sound
B. because lights travel in a straight direction while sound in a zigzag direction
C. because sound's frequency is lower than light
D. All of the above

207. Which part of an eye is transplanted?
A. Cornea B. Retina
C. Iris D. Sciera

208. The Universal donor group of blood is:
A. O B. A
C. B D. AB

209. The green colour of the leaf is due to :
A. Presence of Chloroplast
B. Presence of Chromium
C. Presence of Nicoplast
D. Presence of excess of oxygen

210. Voice of a child is more shrill than that of an elderly person because:
A. the pitch of the child's voice is higher than that of the person
B. the pitch is lower
C. the child is more energetic
D. None of the above

ANSWERS

1	2	3	4	5	6	7	8	9	10
B	C	D	C	B	C	A	C	C	D
11	**12**	**13**	**14**	**15**	**16**	**17**	**18**	**19**	**20**
C	A	C	A	A	D	A	B	A	D
21	**22**	**23**	**24**	**25**	**26**	**27**	**28**	**29**	**30**
A	C	B	C	D	C	B	D	D	B
31	**32**	**33**	**34**	**35**	**36**	**37**	**38**	**39**	**40**
C	D	C	C	B	C	D	B	C	C
41	**42**	**43**	**44**	**45**	**46**	**47**	**48**	**49**	**50**
A	A	A	B	C	D	C	B	B	D
51	**52**	**53**	**54**	**55**	**56**	**57**	**58**	**59**	**60**
A	C	A	B	B	A	B	C	A	C
61	**62**	**63**	**64**	**65**	**66**	**67**	**68**	**69**	**70**
C	C	B	B	C	C	D	D	D	B
71	**72**	**73**	**74**	**75**	**76**	**77**	**78**	**79**	**80**
B	C	C	C	A	A	A	B	E	A
81	**82**	**83**	**84**	**85**	**86**	**87**	**88**	**89**	**90**
A	B	D	B	C	C	D	C	B	D
91	**92**	**93**	**94**	**95**	**96**	**97**	**98**	**99**	**100**
A	B	A	A	A	B	B	A	A	D
101	**102**	**103**	**104**	**105**	**106**	**107**	**108**	**109**	**110**
C	B	A	D	D	D	A	C	D	C
111	**112**	**113**	**114**	**115**	**116**	**117**	**118**	**119**	**120**
B	B	B	A	D	A	C	D	B	D
121	**122**	**123**	**124**	**125**	**126**	**127**	**128**	**129**	**130**
C	A	A	B	A	D	C	D	B	D
131	**132**	**133**	**134**	**135**	**136**	**137**	**138**	**139**	**140**
B	B	D	A	B	D	B	D	D	C
141	**142**	**143**	**144**	**145**	**146**	**147**	**148**	**149**	**150**
D	C	D	D	D	B	A	D	C	C

151	152	153	154	155	156	157	158	159	160
A	B	A	A	A	D	C	B	D	A
161	162	163	164	165	166	167	168	169	170
B	B	C	B	D	D	C	B	B	B
171	172	173	174	175	176	177	178	179	180
D	C	D	D	C	B	C	A	D	A
181	182	183	184	185	186	187	188	189	190
B	B	C	A	A	A	B	D	D	A
191	192	193	194	195	196	197	198	199	200
B	C	A	A	D	A	B	D	D	A
201	202	203	204	205	206	207	208	209	210
B	B	B	B	A	A	A	A	A	A

2306

BIHAR GENERAL KNOWLEDGE

1. Which of the following inscription provide information about the Pala rulers?
A. Munger copper-plate inscription of Devapala
B. Bhagalpur copper-plate inscription of Narayanpala
C. Bangarh copper-plate inscription of Vigrahapala
D. All of the above

2. The earliest source for the history of Bihar is:
A. Upanishads B. Atharvaveda
C. Samaveda D. Aranayaks

3. Which of the following inscriptions belong to the Mauryas?
A. Lauriya Areraj B. Lauriya Nandangarh
C. Rampurva D. All of the above

4. Which of the following texts provide information regarding the mahajanpads in Bihar?
A. Vinay Pitaka B. Anguttaranikaya
C. Kalpasutra D. Dighanikaya

5. Which aspect has been covered by the Arthashastra of Kautilya?
A. Political B. Economic
C. Social D. Religious

6. The Panchobha copper plate inscription belongs to:
A. Skandagupta B. Chandragupta
C. Samgramagupta D. Samudragupta

7. The story of which epic has been depicted on the brick wall of a Vishnu temple excavated from Aphsad in Gaya district?
A. Ramayana
B. Mahabharata
C. Srimadbhagvadgita
D. The story of Nal-Damyanti

8. Who excavated the Nalanda Mahavihara at Baragaon in Nalanda?
A. Mckenzie B. Wheeler
C. Spooner D. Cunningham

9. The excavations at Saraitila in Nalanda have yielded:
A. Buddhist Vihara of Mauryan times
B. Buddhist Vihara of Pala times
C. Temples of Gupta period
D. Buddhist Vihara of Shunga period

10. Which Jaina canon gives an account of Lichhavis of Vaishali?
A. Bhagvati Sutra B. Kalpsutra
C. Kathakosa D. Parisisthaparvana

11. The Buddhist canons Digha Nikaya and Vinaya Pitaka gives an account of:
A. Monarchy of Magadha and republiç of Vaishali
B. Post-Mauryan Bihar
C. Both A and B
D. Neither A nor B

12. Which Buddhist text throws light on the political history of Bihar under the Guptas?
A. Dipavamsha
B. Mahavamsha
C. Aryamanjusrimulakalpa
D. Vinaya Pitaka

13. The Chalcolithic age remains have been found at:
A. Chechar (Vaishali) B. Chirand (Saran)
C. Sonpur and Maner D. All of the above

14. The evidences of the first appearance of human beings in Bihar are found at:
A. Munger and Nalanda
B. Gaya and Dehri
C. Chamaparan and Muzaffarpur
D. None of the above

15. Punch-marked coins which were found in abundance in Bihar were made of:
A. Gold B. Silver
C. Lead D. Copper

16. The early stone age site has been excavated at Paisara, located in the district of:
A. Munger B. Bhagalpur
C. Patna D. Gaya

17. From which neolithic site the antler bone tools have been unearthed?
A. Maner B. Barudih
C. Chechar D. Chirand

18. An ivory female-dancing figure with articulate limbs has been discovered at:
A. Champa B. Taradih
C. Maner D. Sonpur

19. An 80-pillared hall belonging to Mauryan period was excavated at:
A. Kurkihar B. Rampurva
C. Lauriya Areraj D. Kumrahar

20. Which of the following rulers did not issue a larger number of coins?
A. Palas B. Guptas
C. Mauryas D. Senas

21. Which text provides the crucial information about the Aryan expansion in North Bihar?
A. Rigveda B. Upanishads
C. Vayu Purana D. Satapatha Brahmana

22. The Aryans arrived in Bihar during:
A. Later Vedic period B. Rigvedic period
C. Mahajanapada period D. None of these

23. Which factor was responsible for the spread of the Aryans in Bihar as well as eastern India?
A. Extension of agriculture
B. Expansion of dynasties
C. Use of iron
D. Trade development

24. Which text mentions for the first time about the geographical area of Bihar?
A. Rigveda B. Shatapatha Brahmana
C. Vayu Purana D. Samaveda

25. The word Vratya mentioned in Atharvaveda refers to people of:
A. Anga B. Vajjis
C. Videha D. Magadha

26. Which of the following was an important state in the later vedic period in Bihar?
A. Vajji B. Videha
C. Magadha D. Anga

27. Who was the last ruler of Nanda dynasty and was a contemporary of Alexander?
A. Mahapadma Nanda B. Kalashoka
C. Pushyamitra D. Dhana Nanda

28. Which of the following Mahajanapadas was not situated in the region of modern Bihar?
A. Anga B. Vajji
C. Vatsa D. Magadha

29. In which regions of Bihar was the Anga Mahajanapada situated?
A. Bhagalpur and Munger
B. Muzaffarpur and Vaishali
C. Patna and Gaya
D. Hajipur and Siwan

30. The first capital of Magadha Mahajanapada was:
A. Pataliputra B. Girivraja
C. Gaya D. Champa

31. Which of the following ruling clan was not a part of Vajji republic?
A. Lichchavi B. Jnatrika
C. Chedi D. Videha

32. The capital of Lichchavi was:
A. Vaishali B. Kundagrama
C. Mithila D. Champa

33. Which river demarcated the Mahajanapadas of Magadha and Anga?
A. Assi B. Champa
C. Gandak D. Varuna

34. Which of the following Mahajanapadas in Bihar was a union of eight ruling clans?
A. Vajji B. Magadha
C. Anga D. All of the above

35. Patna and Gaya districts of Bihar were part of the Mahajanapada:
A. Anga B. Vajji
C. Asmak D. Magadha

36. The capital of Anga Mahajanapada was:
A. Gaya B. Girivraja
C. Vaishali D. Champa

37. Which of the following rulers permanently made Pataliputra the capital of Magadha?
A. Shisunaga B. Ajatashatru
C. Bimbisara D. Kalashoka

38. The founder of Nanda dynasty was:
A. Dhanananda B. Mahapadma Nanda
C. Munda D. None of the above

39. Bimbisara and Ajatashatru belonged to which dynasty?
A. Haryankas B. Sisungas
C. Nandas D. Brihadarathas

40. The last ruler of Haryanka dynasty was:
A. Udayin B. Anuruddha
C. Mundaka D. Nagadashka

41. Which dynasty established its rule after the fall of Haryanka dynasty?
A. Sisunaga dynasty B. Maurya dynasty
C. Nanda dynasty D. Gupta dynasty

42. Which of the following rulers established his capital at Vaishali?
A. Nagadashka B. Mahapadmananda
C. Shisunaga D. Kalashoka

43. Which ruler made a gift to Buddha of Venuvana (Bamboo-garden) near Rajagriha?
A. Bimbisara B. Ajatashatru
C. Shisunaga D. Udayin

44. Which of the following is considered as the real founder of Magadha dynasty?
A. Bimbisara B. Shisunaga
C. Jarasandha D. Mahapadma

45. Both Gautama Buddha and Mahavira died during the reign of:
A. Bimbisara B. Ajatashatru
C. Kalashoka D. Dhanananda

46. Which of the following rulers made Pataliputra the capital of Magadha for the first time?
A. Kalashoka B. Ajatashatru
C. Udayin D. Bimbisara

47. Who among the following was a contemporary of Gautam Buddha?
A. Nagarjuna B. Kanishka
C. Kautilya D. Mahavira

48. The concept of Anuvrata was advocated by:
A. Mahayana Buddhism B. Jainism
C. the Lokayata school D. Hinayana Buddhism

49. With which religion is Kaivalya associated?
A. Buddhism B. Jainism
C. Hinduism D. Sikhism

50. At which place did Gautama meet the five Brahmanas after achieving his enlightenment?
A. Sarnath B. Bodh Gaya
C. Kusinara D. Lumbini

51. Gautama gained enlightenment on the banks of the river:
A. Ganga B. Niranjana
C. Son D. Gandak

52. The famous Buddha disciple Sariputra was born in:
A. Gaya B. Vaishali
C. Patna D. Nalanda

53. The famous Mahabodhi temple was built at Bodh Gaya where:
A. Gautama Buddha was born
B. Gautama Buddha gave his first sermon
C. Gautama Buddha achieved englightenment
D. Gautama Buddha had died

54. The birth place of 12th Jaina Tirthankara was:
A. Champa B. Vaishali
C. Patna D. Gaya

55. Mahavira died at which place?
A. Vaishali B. Videha
C. Pavapuri D. Rajagriha

56. Mahavira's mother Trishala was a princess of:
A. Lichchavi B. Sarnath
C. Anga D. Videha

57. Mahavira's father Siddhartha was related to:
A. Kapilavastu B. Videha
C. Sarnath D. Vajji republic

58. Kundagrama, the birth place of Mahavira is situated in:
A. Patna B. Vaishali
C. Munger D. Champaran

59. The first Buddhist council was held at:
A. Rajagriha B. Vaishali
C. Pataliputra D. Kundalavana

60. The second Buddhist council was held during the reign of:
A. Ashoka B. Kalashoka
C. Kanishka D. Ajatashatru

61. Who was the founder of Ajivika sect?
A. Ajita Keshakambalin B. Makkhali Ghoshala
C. Pakudha Kaccayana D. Purana Kasyapa

62. Who was the founder of the Maurya dynasty?
A. Ashoka B. Chandragupta Maurya
C. Bindusara D. Dasaratha

63. Who helped Chandragupta Maurya in ascending the throne of Magadha?
A. Chanakya B. Seleucus
C. Megasthenes D. Radhagupta

64. The Greek ambassador Megasthenes lived in the court of:
A. Ashoka B. Bindusara
C. Chandragupta Maurya D. Kunala

65. During the reign of which Maurya King a 12-year long drought took place?
A. Ashoka B. Bindusara
C. Samprati D. Chandragupta Maurya

66. Who was the prime minister of Chandragupta Maurya?
A. Chanakya B. Radhagupta
C. Bhadrabahu D. Megasthenes

67. When did Ashoka invade Kalinga?
A. 298 B.C. B. 273 B.C.
C. 261 B.C. D. 232 B.C.

68. The Arthasastra is a treatise on which of the following?
A. Economics
B. Environment
C. Political Philosophy
D. Religion in Administration

69. Which one of the following edicts mentions the personal name of Ashoka?
A. Kalsi B. Rummindei
C. Bhabhru D. Maski

70. Who was the last ruler of Maurya dynasty in Bihar?
A. Brihadratha B. Samprati
C. Salisuka D. Kunala

71. The book written by Megasthenes is:
A. Arthasastra B. Indika
C. Mudrarakshasa D. Rajatarangini

72. Who was the successor of Bindusara?
A. Ashoka B. Tivara
C. Dasaratha D. Pushyamitra

73. Important evidence of the Maurya period has been found at which place?
A. Kumrahar B. Rajgir
C. Champa D. Sasaram

74. Who claimed that the affairs of the city of Pataliputra were conducted by a body consisting of 30 members which was divided into 6 boards of five members each?

A. Fa-hien B. Vishakhadatta
C. Taranath D. Megasthenes

75. The Greek ambassador Deimachus visited Magadha during the reign of:
A. Chandragupta Maurya B. Bindusara
C. Ashoka D. Brihadratha

76. Ptolemy Phillandelphus of Egypt sent Dionysius as his ambassador at the Mauryan court of:
A. Bindusara B. Chandragupta
C. Ashoka D. Dasaratha

77. Who built the famous temple named Gopika Kuha Bhawan in Nagarjuni Hills near Gaya?
A. Dasaratha B. Ashoka
C. Chandragupta D. Bindusara

78. The Mauryan palace excavated at Kumrahar was chiefly made of:
A. bricks B. stones
C. mud D. wood

79. During Ashoka's period there were 5 provinces after the addition of Kalinga. The capital of Kalinga (Prachyapatha) was at:
A. Pataliputra B. Tosali
C. Taxila D. Ujjaini

80. Which of the following edicts of Ashoka was not found in Bihar?
A. Lauriya Areraj B. Rummindei
C. Lauriya Nandangarh D. Rampurwa

81. In which district of Bihar, the edicts of Ashoka have been found?
A. Champaran B. Kaimur
C. Chhapra D. Bhagalpur

82. Which of the following sources mentions about the administration of Pataliputra?
A. Divyavadana B. Arthashastra
C. Indika D. Edicts of Ashoka

83. Which dynasty ruled Magadha after the fall of the Nandas?
A. Shungas B. Guptas
C. Mauryas D. Kushans

84. Megasthenes, who lived in the court of Chandragupta Maurya was the ambassador of:
A. Seleucus B. Alexander
C. Ptolemy D. Antiochus I

85. The central court of the Mauryas was situated at:
A. Pataliputra B. Avanti
C. Vaishali D. Suvarnagiri

86. Ashoka's Dhamma was:
A. a moral code
B. a religious law
C. an administrative system
D. a war code

87. The palace of Chandragupta Maurya was situated at:
A. Rajgriha B. Vaishali
C. Maner D. Kumrahar (Patna)

88. Who among the following had defeated the Hunas?
A. Chandragupta II B. Samudragupta
C. Skandagupta D. Ramagupta

89. Aryabhatta, the great mathematician and astrologer was related to which place?
A. Odantapura B. Pataliputra
C. Vaishali D. Nalanda

90. Gupta period coins have been found from which place?
A. Rajgir B. Vaishali
C. Sasaram D. Munger

91. Which Gupta ruler married Kumaradevi, a Lichchavi princess?
A. Chandragupta I B. Samudragupta
C. Chandragupta II D. Kumaragupta

92. The capital of Guptas was at:
A. Kanauj B. Ujjain
C. Pataliputra D. Allahabad

93. Nalanda University was established by the:
A. Mauryas B. Kushans
C. Palas D. Guptas

94. Nalanda University is famous for:
A. Medicine B. Philosophy
C. Buddhist Philosophy D. Physics

95. For how long did the Chinese pilgrim Fa-Hien stay in Pataliputra?
A. 3 months B. 1 year
C. 3 years D. 14 months

96. The Mahabodhi temple in Bodhgaya was established during the reign of:
A. Mauryas B. Palas
C. Guptas D. Later Guptas

97. The coronation ceremony Chandragupta-I took place at:
A. Prayag B. Banaras
C. Kanauj D. Pataliputra

98. The last ruler of the Later Guptas was:
A. Adityasena B. Jivitagupta II
C. Madhavagupta D. Kumaragupta III

99. In which one of the following inscriptions are Samudragupta's achievements mentioned?
A. Allahabad Pillar Inscription
B. Junagarh Rock Inscription
C. Mehrauli Iron Pillar Inscription
D. Hathigumpha Edict

100. In Sanskrit plays written during the Gupta period women and sudras speak:
A. Sanskrit B. Prakrit
C. Pali D. Sauraseni

101. Which one of the following is not a work of Kalidasa?
A. Ritusamhara B. Meghaduta
C. Kumarasambhava D. Dashakumaracharita

102. In Gupta period, the king's share of product was known as:
A. Bhaga B. Bhoga
C. Kara D. Hiranya

103. The largest grant of villages to temples and brahmanas was given by the ruling dynasty known as:
A. Guptas B. Palas
C. Rashtrakutas D. Pratiharas

104. Which university in Bihar was famous during the reign of Harshavardhan?
A. Vikramashila B. Gaya
C. Patna D. Nalanda

105. Which of the following authors stayed in Bihar and provided first hand information about the attacks of Bakhtiyar Khalji?
A. Minhas-us-Siraj B. Ziauddin Barani
C. Mullah Taqia D. Rizquallah

106. Which of the following books provide an account of land revenue in Bihar?
A. Tabakat-i-Nasiri B. Ain-i-Akbari
C. Akbarnama D. Tarikh-i-Firozshahi

107. The Arabic and Persian inscriptions in Bihar are predominantly found in:
A. Patna B. Sasaram
C. Bihar Sharif D. All of the above

108. Name the author of the book Corpus of Arabic and Persian Inscription of Bihar?
A. Cunningham B. Prof. Qyamuddin
C. Buchanan D. Z.A. Desai

109. The definite proof of minting of coins in Bihar comes from:
A. Tirhut-urf-Tughlaqpur B. Munger
C. Gaya D. Sasaram

110. Narsimhadeva was the king of:
A. Mithila B. Bhojpur
C. Sasaram D. Videha

111. Who founded the independent Karnat dynasty in Mithila?
A. Nanyadeva B. Narsimhadeva
C. Harisimha D. Devapala

112. Who founded the famous Odantapura Vihara?
A. Devapala B. Gopala
C. Rampala D. Narayanpala

113. Who was the last great king of Karnata dynasty?
A. Nanyadeva B. Harisimhadeva
C. Narsimhadeva D. None of the above

114. Who built the Sonapura Vihara in North Bengal?
A. Devapala B. Dharmapala
C. Gopala D. Vigrahapala

115. The Munger Copper Plate inscription belongs to which Pala King?
A. Devapala B. Gopala
C. Mahipala D. Dharmapala

116. The first important victory of Bakhtiyar Khalji in Bihar was:
A. Bihar Sharif (Oddantapuri)
B. Patna
C. Bhagalpur
D. Munger

117. Who destroyed the Nalanda University?
A. Mahmud Ghazni B. Bakhtiyar Khalji
C. Babar D. Muhammad Ghori

118. Who was the first ruler of Delhi Sultanate to invade Bihar?
A. Balban B. Alauddin Khalji
C. Aibak D. Iltutmish

119. At which place was Bakhtiyar Khalji buried?
A. Lakhnauti B. Munger
C. Bihar Sharif D. Rajgir

120. Who established the Turkish rule in Bihar?
A. Aibak B. Bakhtiyar Khalji
C. Iltutmish D. Malik Husam-ud-din

121. Which ruler established a mint-town at Tirhut which was also called Tughlaqabad-urf-Tirhut?
A. Ghiyasuddin Tughlaq
B. Firoz Tughlaq
C. Muhammad-bin-Tughlaq
D. Alauddin Khalji

122. Which Sultan ended the rule of Karnata dynasty?
A. Muhammad-bin-Tughlaq
B. Ghiyasuddin Tughlaq
C. Firoz Shah Tughlaq
D. Muhammad Tughlaq

123. Who defeated the Karnata dynasty ruler Harisimha Deva?
A. Ghiyasuddin Tughlaq B. Iltutmish
C. Firoz Tughlaq D. Alauddin Khalji

124. Which Sultan constructed a fort and a Jama Masjid in Darbhanga?
A. Firoz Tughlaq
B. Iltutumish
C. Ghiyasuddin Tughlaq
D. Muhammad-bin-Tughlaq

125. Which Sultan of Delhi conclusively controlled Bihar?
A. Tughlaqs B. Khaljis
C. Mamluks D. None of the above

126. In the 14th century Firoz helped in establishing the rule of which dynasty?
A. Karnata B. Vainvaar
C. Mitra D. Thakur

127. Who was the founder of Nuhani dynasty in Bihar?
A. Jalal Khan Nuhani B. Darya Khan Nuhani
C. Bahar Khan Nuhani D. Daulat Khan Lodhi

128. Who among the following was placed as the administrator of Bihar by Babar after removing Mahmud Lodhi?
A. Bahar Khan B. Jalal Khan
C. Farid Khan D. Hasan Khan

129. Who was deputed by Sikander Lodhi in 1495-96 as the head of Bihar?
A. Farid Khan B. Hasan Khan
C. Bahar Khan Nuhani D. Darya Khan Nuhani

130. The Sur dynasty was established by:
A. Sher Shah B. Hasan Khan
C. Muhammad Nuhani D. Darya Khan

131. Sher Khan's father Hasan Khan was a Jagirdar of:
A. Patna B. Gaya
C. Sasaram D. Arrah

132. Patna was made a provincial capital of Bihar by:
A. Ibrahim Lodhi B. Hasan Khan
C. Sher Shah D. Azim-us-Shaan

133. Sher Khan was appointed as the caretaker of which ruler of Bihar?
A. Darya Khan B. Jalal Khan
C. Hasan Khan D. Muhammad Nuhani

134. Sher Shah defeated Humayun in which of the following battles?
A. Kanauj or Bilgram B. Chausa
C. Both A and B D. None of the above

135. Who was the last Afghan ruler of Bihar?
A. Ibrahim Shah Sur
B. Ibrahim Lodhi
C. Dawood Khan Qararani
D. Sulaiman Qararani

136. Akbar merged Bihar and Bengal in Mughal empire in:
A. 1550 B. 1575
C. 1572 D. 1576

137. Who was the Governor of Bihar during Akbar's reign?
A. Munim Khan B. Baj Bahadur
C. Daud Khan D. None of the above

138. Who was the first Mughal ruler to be sworn in Patna?
A. Farrukhsiyar B. Bahadur Shah
C. Jahangir D. Shahjahan

139. Which Mughal ruler made his grandson as the Subedar of Bihar?
A. Akbar B. Shahjahan
C. Jahangir D. Aurangzeb

140. Who was the first Mughal Prince to be appointed as the governor of Bihar?
A. Prince Salim B. Prince Azim
C. Prince Parvez D. Prince Khurram

141. Raja Man Singh was appointed the governor of Bihar by:
A. Akbar B. Shah Jahan
C. Jahangir D. Aurangzeb

142. Who built the Shahi Idgah in Patna City?
A. Itiqad Khan B. Shaista Khan
C. Zulfiqar Khan D. Saif Khan

143. Who was the Dewan of Bihar when Prince Azim was the governor of Bihar?
A. Saadat Khan B. Safdarjung
C. Murshid Quli Khan D. Allahawardi Khan

144. Daud Khan was defeated by Akbar in the battle of:
A. Bahadurpur B. Munger
C. Rajmahal D. Chausa

145. The East India Company proclaimed the diwani rights of Bengal, Bihar and Odisha during the reign of:
A. Mir Qasim B. Shah Alam II
C. Farrukhsiyar D. Alivardi Khan

146. Who became the deputy Nawab of Bihar after the Battle of Plassey (1757)?
A. Mir Jafar B. Miran
C. Shujjat Khan D. Tabtabai

147. The first British traveller to visit Bihar was:
A. Bishop Heber B. Peter Mundy
C. John Marshall D. Raulf Fitch

148. Which Nawab of Bengal transferred his capital from Mushidabad to Munger?
A. Mir Jafar B. Siraj-ud-Daulah
C. Mir Qasim D. Alivardi Khan

149. In which year the Dutch established their first factory in Bihar?
A. 1620 B. 1651
C. 1609 D. 1632

150. In which year the Danes established their factory in Patna?
A. 1774 B. 1664
C. 1631 D. 1786

151. The Britishers established their first trading centre in 1620 Bihar at:
A. Munger B. Alamganj (Patna)
C. Purnea D. Champaran

152. Who among the following was the first to oppose the British rule in Bihar?
A. Ali Gauhar B. Haider Ali Khan
C. Kunwar Singh D. Mir Qasim

153. In which year was the Revenue Council of Patna established?
A. 1770 B. 1765
C. 1801 D. 1719

154. In which year did the company remove Dhiraj Narayan and replaced him with Raja Shitab Rai as the Naib Diwan of Bihar?
A. 1801 B. 1767
C. 1791 D. 1765

155. The Golghar in Patna was constructed during the reign of:
A. Warren Hastings B. Lord Hardinge
C. John Shore D. Lord Cornwallis

156. The first English magistrate of Patna was:
A. James Alexander B. Charles Francis Grand
C. Robert Palk D. John Vansittart

157. The battle of Buxar was fought on:
A. October 22, 1764 B. September 23, 1761
C. June 24, 1764 D. June 24, 1761

158. Who was the commander of British army in the battle of Buxar?
A. Clive B. Lord Hastings
C. Hector Munro D. Major Knox

159. Who emerged victorious in the battle of Buxar?
A. Shuja-ud-daulah B. East India Company
C. Shah Alam II D. Mir Qasim

160. Who was appointed as the Naib Diwan of Bihar by Robert Clive?
A. Omichand B. Shitab Rai
C. Raja Durlabh Rai D. Manik Chand

161. Which of the following is not related to Wahabi movement?
A. Syed Ahmad B. Shah Waliullah
C. Vilayat Ali D. Birsa Munda

162. In which year Wahabi movement was started?
A. 1820 B. 1830
C. 1840 D. 1850

163. Which of the following was/were the centres for the Wahabi Movement?
A. Patna B. Sittana
C. Both A and B D. None of these

164. Who led the Kol revolt?
A. Budhu Bhagat B. Sidhu and Kanhu
C. Birsa Munda D. Raja Porhat

165. Who led the Bhumij revolt?
A. Ganga Narayan B. Sidhu and Kanhu
C. Sayed Hasan D. Raja Porhat

166. Who among the following participated in the revolt of Tana Bhagat?
A. Ho tribe B. Munda tribe
C. Santhal tribe D. Oraon tribe

167. The Tana Bhagat movement was essentially a _______ movement.
A. religious B. political
C. social D. natural

168. The occupation of which of the following region led the HO uprising?
A. occupation of Singhbhum
B. occupation of Chhotanagpur
C. occupation of Kalahandi
D. None of the above

169. In which year Kol uprising began?
A. 1832 B. 1831
C. 1833 D. 1834

170. Who among the following was the leader of Ho tribals movement?
A. Raja Parhat B. Sidhu and Kanhu
C. Birsa Munda D. Budhu Bhagat

171. In which year Bhumij revolt started?
A. 1831 B. 1832
C. 1833 D. 1834

172. The term 'ulgulan' means:
A. Rebellion B. Courageous
C. Tribal movement D. Tribal song

173. Santhal uprising was led by:
A. Sidhu and Kanhu B. Birsa Munda
C. Budhu Bhagat D. None of them

174. Kunwar Singh was the King of:
A. Hamirpur B. Dheerpur
C. Jagdishpur D. Rampur

175. The leaders of the revolt of 1857 in Bihar was:
A. Maulvi Ahmadullah B. Tatya Tope
C. Nana Sahib D. Kunwar Singh

176. Who among the following had established an arms and ammunition factory at Jagdishpur?
A. Amar Singh B. Kunwar Singh
C. Pir Ali D. Harkishen Singh

177. Which region in Bihar was unaffected by the revolt of 1857?
1. Danapur 2. Patna
3. Ara 4. Muzaffarpur
5. Munger
Choose from the following options:
A. 4 and 5 B. Only 5
C. Only 4 D. 3, 4 and 5

178. The rulers of which state denied entry to Kunwar Singh in his state?
A. Rewa B. Azamgarh
C. Awadh D. Banda

179. Kunwar Singh fought his last war against which English captain?
A. Douglas B. Lugard
C. Le Grand D. Eyre

180. Who was the leader of Patna uprising in 1857?
A. Jaimangal Singh B. Inayat Ali
C. Vilayat Ali D. Pir Ali

181. Who arrested Amar Singh, the leader of revolt of 1857?
A. Lugard
B. Maharaja Jang Bahadur
C. Maharaja Rai Bahadur
D. Samuels

182. Kunwar Singh tried to meet which of the following leaders in October 1857?
A. Lakshmibai B. Liaqat Ali
C. Tatya Tope D. Begum Hazrat Mahal

183. Pir Ali, the leader of Patna rising was convicted and hanged on:
A. July 7, 1858 B. July 7, 1857
C. August 7, 1857 D. August 7, 1858

184. At which place in Bihar the revolt of 1857 started comprehensively for the first time?
A. Patna B. Munger
C. Muzaffarpur D. Rajgir

185. When did Kunwar Singh die?
A. 10 April, 1858 B. 23 April, 1858
C. 26 April, 1858 D. 20 June, 1858

186. Amar Singh initiated the guerilla war against the British in the hills of:
A. Rajgir B. Ranchi
C. Kaimur D. None of the above

187. The Zamindars of the following places helped the Company during the revolt of 1857?
A. Hathua B. Pandaul
C. Bettiah D. All of the above

188. Kunwar Singh captured which of the following districts on March 25, 1858?
A. Rewa B. Kanpur
C. Azamgarh D. Kalpi

189. Kunwar Singh helped Nana Saheb in the war of:
A. Lucknow B. Kanpur
C. Shahabad D. Jhansi

190. Who had invited Gandhiji in West Champaran district in Bihar?
A. Raj Kumar Shukla B. Mahadeo Desai
C. Rajendra Prasad D. Narhari Parikh

191. Which of the following Government Acts separated Odisha from Bihar province?
A. 1909 Act B. 1919 Act
C. 1935 Act D. 1948 Act

192. In Bihar, resolution for Non-cooperation Movement was passed in 1920 provincial meeting under the leadership of:
A. Rajendra Prasad B. Mazhar-ul-Haq
C. Shah Mohammad D. None of the above

193. In which year the period of Swarajist Movement started in Bihar?
A. 1920 B. 1922
C. 1921 D. 1923

194. The All India Congress Session in 1922, December was held in:
A. Patna B. Gaya
C. Bhagalpur D. Champaran

195. Which of the following movements is called first Civil Disobedience Movement?
A. Champaran B. Bhagalpur
C. Bardoli D. Gaya

196. Patna Yuvak Sangh was formed in:
A. 1929 B. 1926
C. 1928 D. 1927

197. Where was Anushilan Committee Branch established in Bihar?
A. Gaya B. Patna
C. Muzaffarpur D. Munger

198. When the British prince visited Bihar?
A. 1921 B. 1922
C. 1923 D. 1924

199. Who had formed Bihar Provincial Kisan Sabha (BPKS)?
A. Shahjanand Saraswati
B. Mohammad Zubair
C. Sri Krishna Singh
D. Rajendra Prasad

200. Champaran Satyagraha was against:
A. Tinkathiya system B. High rent
C. Outsiders D. Illegal transfer of land

201. When was Bihar Socialist Party established?
A. 1934 B. 1932
C. 1931 D. 1933

202. Who was the leader of Salt Satyagraha in Bihar?
A. Rajendra Prasad B. Jawaharlal Nehru
C. Gandhiji D. Professor Abdul Bari

203. Salt Revolt in Patna had started from which of the following dates?
A. 16th April, 1930 B. 18th April, 1930
C. 4th May, 1930 D. 3rd April, 1930

204. Which of the following physical features form the North-Western Part of Bihar?
A. Someshwar range B. Kaimur Plateau
C. Nawada hills D. Rajgir hills

205. In Bihar, Kaimur series of rocks are found in which district?
A. Bhojpur B. Aurangabad
C. Buxar D. Kaimur

206. Geologically southern plateau of Bihar was formed in the period.
A. Pre-cambrian B. Oligocene
C. Miocene D. Pleistocene

207. Mica deposits are found in which kind of rocks?
A. Dharwar B. Tertiary
C. Vindhyan D. Quaternary

208. The highest place of Bihar is:
A. Santpur B. Kaimur hills
C. Someshwar range D. Barabar hills

209. In which period was Ramnagar Dun formed?
A. Dharwar B. Quaternary
C. Vindhyan D. Tertiary

210. Bihar was maximum areal extent in which of the following natural regions?
A. Terai region of Shiwalik
B. North Gangetic Plan
C. South Gangetic Plan
D. None of the above

211. Chuars found in the Bihar plain are:
A. flooded plain B. levees
C. oxbow lakes D. highlands

212. In which district(s) of Bihar, gneiss, quartzite and schist rocks are found?
A. Munger B. Gaya
C. Sheikhpura D. All of these

213. The capital of the Shungas was at:
A. Sialkot B. Rajagriha
C. Kannauj D. Pataliputra

214. Out of the total geographical area of India, Bihar comprises:
A. 3.76% B. 6.76%
C. 4.02% D. 2.86%

215. The total geographical area of Bihar is:
A. 94,162 sq.km B. 94,163 sq.km
C. 94,164 sq.km D. 94,165 sq.km

216. Bihar forms an international boundary with which country?
A. Bhutan B. Bangladesh
C. Nepal D. China

217. Which district of Bihar has the longest border with Nepal?
A. West Champaran B. Sitamarhi
C. Kishanganj D. East Champaran

218. The highest part of Ramnagar Dun is:
A. Someshwar fort B. Santpur
C. Gridhkut D. Barabar

219. The length of Bihar from east to west is:
A. 483 km B. 362 km
C. 401 km D. 415 km

220. Harha valley which is located in north-western Bihar is also known as:
A. Ramnagar Dun B. Dun Valley
C. Someshwar Range D. None of the above

221. Which of the following ranges form a boundary between India and Nepal?
A. Kaimur Hills B. Ramnagar Dun
C. Someshwar Ranges D. None of the above

222. Gogaville Bird Sanctuary is situated in which district of Bihar?
A. Arwal B. Aurangabad
C. Araria D. Banka

223. Mandar Vidyapeeth is situated in:
A. West Champaran B. Vaishali
C. Darbhanga D. Banka

224. The Indian Oil Refinery is located in which district of Bihar?
A. Begusarai B. Sitamarhi
C. Katihar D. Supaul

225. Ustad Bismillah Khan was a native of:
A. Ara B. Dumraon
C. Darbhanga D. Sasaram

226. Bela Industrial Area is located at:
A. Sitamarhi B. East Champaran
C. Darbhanga D. Purnea

227. Raxaul town is also known as:
A. Gateway to Nepal
B. Gateway to Bangladesh
C. Gateway to Bhutan
D. None of these

228. Vishnupad Temple was rebuilt by:
A. Ahilya Bai Holkar B. Sher Shah
C. Kunwar Singh D. Kameshwar Thakhur

229. Where is Tal soil found in Bihar?
A. In terai region
B. In plains
C. In desert
D. In backwater belt of river Ganga

230. Tal soil extends from Buxar to:
A. Banka B. Gaya
C. Bhagalpur D. Champaran

231. What are the major crops that can be grown of Balthar soil?
A. Rice B. Jowar and Bajra
C. Sugarcane D. Pulses

232. Lowest temperature in Bihar is found in:
A. Gaya B. Buxar
C. Rohtas D. Darbhanga

233. Which type of soil is predominantly found in the plains of Ganga?
A. Residual soil B. Alluvial soil
C. Both A and B D. None of the above

234. In which district of Bihar Balsundari soil is found?
A. Saharsa B. Darbhanga
C. Muzaffarpur D. All of the above

235. The old alluvial soil is found in which of the following districts of Bihar:
A. Nalanda B. Munger
C. Bhagalpur D. All of the above

236. Which district of Bihar records the highest temperature?
A. Aurangabad B. Gaya
C. Saran D. Siwan

237. The Bhagar soil in Bihar is found in:
A. Gaya–Bodhgaya–East Champaran Bhagalpur area
B. Purnea–Saharsa–Darbhanga–Muzaffarpur area
C. Gaya–Nalanda–Bodhgaya–Saharsa area
D. East Champaran–Nalanda–Gaya–Sasaram area

238. The Old alluvial soil in Bihar is found in:
A. Rohtas–Gaya–Patna–Munger–Bhagalpur area
B. Purnea–Saharsa–Darbhanga–Muzaffarpur area
C. Saharsa–Darbhanga–Muzaffarpur–Saran area
D. None of the above

239. In which area of Bihar the concentration of lime in the soil is found:
A. North Bihar plain
B. South Bihar plain
C. North-West Bihar plain
D. South-East Bihar plain

240. Consider the following statements about Norwesters.
(*i*) It is a cyclonic wind
(*ii*) It brings rainfall of about 10 cm in Bihar plain
(*iii*) It is useful for crops like mango, litchi, rice and jute.
(*iv*) It is a hot wind blowing from west.

Which of the above statement/s is/are wrong?
A. (*i*), (*ii*) and (*iii*) B. Only (*iv*)
C. (*i*) and (*iv*) D. (*iii*) and (*iv*)

241. In which of the following districts Khadar soil is found?
A. Bhagalpur and Araria
B. Patna and Nalanda
C. Purnea and Saharsa
D. None of the above

242. What is the older alluvium of Ganga plains called?
A. Bhabhar B. Bangar
C. Khadar D. Balsundari

243. Which district of Bihar gets highest rainfall?
A. Araria B. Kishanganj
C. Gaya D. Aurangabad

244. The local winds loo blowing in Bihar has following wind velocity:
A. 10-16 km/hr B. 10-14 km/hr
C. 8-16 km/hr D. 12-16 km/hr

245. The rainfall during monsoon in Bihar is due to:
A. Eastern monsoon B. South-east monsoon
C. Southern monsoon D. South-west monsoon

246. Which of the following crops is grown in red and yellow soil?
A. Pulses B. Sugarcane
C. Rice D. Wheat

247. Usar soil is found in which district?
A. Saran B. West Champaran
C. Siwan D. Nawada

248. Which of the following Wildlife Sanctuaries has hot springs?
A. Bhimbandh B. Vikramshila
C. Sanjay Gandhi D. Kaimur

249. The tropical seasonal swamp forests (canebrakes) are predominantly found in:
A. Gopalganj B. East Champaran
C. Sitamarhi D. West Champaran

250. A Wildlife safari is being established at which place?
A. Rajgir B. West Champaran
C. Sasaram D. Jamui

251. Bhimbandh Wildlife Sanctuary is famous for:
A. Tiger B. Elephant
C. Leopard D. Resident Birds

252. Find the wrong match:

Wildlife Sanctuaries	**District**
A. Valmiki	West Champaran
B. Kaimur	Rohtas
C. Vikramshila	Begusarai
D. Bhimbandh	Munger

253. In which of the following wild life sanctuaries is Anupam lake situated?
A. Vikramshila B. Valmiki
C. Bhimbandh D. Kaimur

254. The largest wildlife sanctuary in Bihar is:
A. Bhimbandh
B. Valmiki
C. Sanjay Gandhi Udyan
D. Kaimur

255. Area of very dense forest is highest in:
A. West Champaran B. Siwan
C. Nawada D. East Champaran

256. The Vikramshila Gangetic Dolphin Sanctuary is located in:
A. Jamui B. Munger
C. Bhagalpur D. Vaishali

257. Kusheshwar Asthan Bird Sanctuary is located in:
A. Vaishali B. West Champaran
C. Samastipur D. Darbhanga

258. Gautam Buddha Bird Sanctuary is located in:
A. Rohtas B. Gaya
C. Nalanda D. Sasaram

259. Udaypur Vanya Prani Sanctuary is located in:
A. East Champaran B. Munger
C. West Champaran D. Rohtas

260. Baraila Jheel Salim Ali Jubba Sahni Bird Sanctuary is located in:
A. Vaishali B. Sheohar
C. Darbhanga D. Banka

261. The Bihar Government declared the Sanjay Gandhi Jaivik Udyan in Patna as protected forest in which year?
A. 1991 B. 1983
C. 1984 D. 1982

262. Nagi Dam Bird Sanctuary and Nakti Dam Bird Sanctuary are located in which district of Bihar?
A. Begusarai B. Siwan
C. Gaya D. Jamui

263. The Centre of Noise Pollution Control Board has been set up at:
A. Siwan B. Bhagalpur
C. Muzaffarpur D. Patna

264. The main vegetation of Bihar is:
A. Deciduous B. Tropical Evergreen
C. Mixed D. Alpine

265. In which of the following districts the Sal mixed deciduous forests are found?
A. Gaya B. Bhagalpur
C. West Champaran D. East Champaran

266. Which river is also known as Niranjana?
A. Gandak B. Phalgu
C. Sone D. Mahananda

267. Why is Bagmati considered as a dangerous river?
A. Due to its changing course
B. Due to its origin in the Himalayas
C. Due to its tendency to create floods
D. None of the above

268. ______ river emerges from Nampa of Nepal situated at Himalayan ranges.
A. Gandak B. Bagmati
C. Kamla D. Ghaghra

269. The North tributaries of the Ganga river are Gandak, Bagmati, Kosi Kalikosi and _____ .
A. Son B. Karmanasa
C. Punpun D. All of these

270. Durgavati and Chandraprabha are important tributaries of which of the following rivers?
A. Karmanasa B. Punpun
C. Phalgu D. Saryu

271. Which pair of springs of Bihar along with their places is not correctly matched?

	Springs	Places
A.	Sita Kund	Rajgir
B.	Rishi Kund	Munger
C.	Surya Kund	Rajgir
D.	Brahma Kund	Rajgir

272. Which river does not originate from Himalayas?
A. Bagmati B. Ganga
C. Kamla Balan D. Son

273. Triveni canal gets water from which river?
A. Son B. Kosi
C. Gandak D. Mayurakshi

274. Which of the following rivers of Bihar is almost dry in summer season?
A. Ganga B. Gandak
C. Punpun D. Kosi

275. Which of the following rivers has second longest length in the Bihar state?
A. Ganga B. Bagmati
C. Mahananda D. Burhi Gandak

276. Which river has the largest catchment area in Bihar?
A. Ganga B. Sone
C. Kiul Harohar D. Kosi

277. In which of the following districts river Ganga enters into Bihar?
A. Gopalganj B. Buxar
C. Rohtas D. Siwan

278. Which river is known as 'Sorrow of Bihar'?
A. Karmanasa B. Kosi
C. Son D. Subarnarekha

279. Which river is the sacred river for Hindus?
A. Punpun B. Phalgu
C. Karmanasa D. Sone

280. Name the bridge constructed over the river Ganga which connects Patna to Hajipur.
A. Mahatma Gandhi Setu
B. Hirakund Setu
C. Gopalganj Bridge
D. None of the above

281. Which river of Bihar does originate from the Someshwar hills and flows parallel to river Gandak?

A. Burhi Gandak B. Gandak
C. Kamla D. Bagmati

282. The deposits of manganese are found in the district(s) of:
A. Rohtas B. Kaimur
C. Darbhanga D. Patna and Gaya

283. Uranium is found in which of the following districts of Bihar?
A. Gaya B. Rohtas
C. Munger D. Banka

284. Gold is found in:
A. Munger B. Jamui
C. Siwan D. Saran

285. The deposits of Monazite are found in which districts of Bihar?
A. Siwan and Saran
B. Patna and Aurangabad
C. Gaya and Munger
D. Banka and Bhagalpur

286. Amjhor is famous for which of the following minerals?
A. Coal B. Pyrite
C. Mica D. Gold

287. Pyrite Phosphate and Chemicals Ltd. is located at:
A. Bihta B. Amjhor
C. Jamui D. Nawada

288. The least populous district of Bihar is:
A. Sheikhpura B. Madhubani
C. Saran D. Gaya

289. According to Census 2011, the child sex ratio of Bihar is:
A. 935 B. 938
C. 918 D. 925

290. Which among the following districts of Bihar has the lowest sex ratio?
A. Vaishali B. Arwal
C. Saran D. Siwan

291. Which among the following districts of Bihar has lowest population density?
A. Arwal B. Madhubani
C. Saran D. Kaimur

292. Which among the following districts of Bihar has the highest population density?
A. Sheohar B. Siwan
C. Saran D. Sitamarhi

293. The most populous district of Bihar is:
A. Patna B. Madhubani
C. Saran D. Gaya

294. As per Census 2011, the literacy rate of Bihar is:
A. 61.8% B. 71.2%
C. 52.5% D. 23.5%

295. As per Census 2011, the population density of Bihar is:
A. 223 B. 153
C. 1106 D. 123

296. According to Census 2011, what is the sex ratio of Bihar?
A. 918 B. 982
C. 972 D. 935

297. Which among the following districts of Bihar has the highest sex ratio?
A. Saran B. Sheohar
C. Madhubani D. Gopalganj

298. Which among the following districts of Bihar has the lowest child population?
A. Vaishali B. Arwal
C. Saran D. Siwan

299. According to Census 2011, the total population of Bihar is:
A. 10,40,99,452 B. 56,58,509
C. 68,70,997 D. 70,68,997

300. Highest production of wheat is recorded in which of the following districts?
A. Siwan B. Rohtas
C. Kaimur D. Muzaffarpur

301. Highest production of potato is recorded in which of the following districts?
A. Nalanda B. Patna
C. Saran D. Katihar

302. Sonaru Fish Seed Farm is being developed at which of the following places?
A. Badh B. Muzaffarpur
C. Gaya D. Fatuha

303. Which districts of Bihar has the highest population of goats?
A. Bhagalpur B. West Champaran
C. Araria D. East Champaran

304. Which district of Bihar is the leading produce of maize?
A. Katihar B. Madhepura
C. Khagaria D. Kaimur

305. The district of Bihar having the highest productivity (kg/hectare) of rice is:
A. Rohtas B. Lakhisarai
C. Sheikhpura D. West Champaran

306. A Fishery Research Centre has been established at which place:
A. Sonepur B. Fatuha
C. Mithapur D. Araria

307. The leading fish producing districts in Bihar are:
A. Kaimur, West Champaran, Madhubani
B. Madhubani, East Champaran, Darbhanga

C. Sitamarhi, Vaishali, Banka
D. Bhagalpur, Supaul, Saharsa

308. Which districts will be benefitted by the Budi Gandak–Noon-via-Ganga link scheme?
A. Samastipur, Begusarai, Khagaria
B. Jamui, Bhagalpur, Banka
C. Jamui, Banka, Lakhisarai
D. Kanpur, Rohtas, Aurangabad

309. The main cereal rops of Bihar are:
A. Groundnut, Coffee, Wheat
B. Sugarane, Tea, Barley
C. Rice, Wheat, Maize
D. None of the above

310. Which of the following district in Bihar is leader in terms of pulses production?
A. Patna B. Aurangabad
C. Nalanda D. Rohtas

311. Which of the following districts of Bihar has highest percentage of net sown area?
A. Siwan B. Gopalganj
C. Buxar D. Bhojpur

312. Which district of Bihar has the largest area under wheat cultivation?
A. East Champaran B. Rohtas
C. Kishanganj D. Siwan

313. Which district of Bihar has the largest area under rice cultivation?
A. Madhubani B. Samastipur
C. East Champaran D. Rohtas

314. Which district of Bihar has the largest area under maize cultivation?
A. Samastipur B. East Champaran
C. Begusarai D. Khagaria

315. Which district of Bihar has recorded highest productivity (kg/hectare) of sugarcane?
A. West Champaran B. Nalanda
C. Jehanabad D. East Champaran

316. Who has described agriculture as the Core Competence of Bihar?
A. APJ Abdul Kalam B. Pranab Mukherjee
C. Atal Behari Vajpayee D. M.S. Swaminathan

317. The marketing of dairy products in Bihar is done by which of the following organization?
A. KVIC B. COMFED
C. BIADA D. PMEGP

318. The medicine industry is situated in which of the following places?
A. Naryanpur B. Rampur
C. Bela D. Fatuha

319. The major implementing agency for Prime Minister Employment Generation Programme (PMEGP) is:
A. SIPB B. KVIC
C. KVI BOARD D. DIC

320. A Food Park is being established at which place?
A. Buxar B. Araria
C. Katihar D. Bettiah

321. In which year the Bihar State Milk Cooperative Federation was established?
A. 1984 B. 1981
C. 1980 D. 1983

322. Mukhyamantri Integrated Handloom Development Scheme was started in year:
A. 2011-12 B. 2012-13
C. 2013-14 D. 2014-15

323. The gun factory in Bihar is situated at which place?
A. Bhagalpur B. Sitamarhi
C. Munger D. Patna

324. In which five year plan was Barauni Oil Refinery in Bihar established?
A. Third B. Second
C. Fifth D. Fourth

325. In which district of Bihar the first Jute Park is being established?
A. Purnea B. Aurangabad
C. Begusarai D. Khagaria

326. At which place is Bihar Institute of Silk and Textiles located?
A. Nabinagar B. Fatuha
C. Bihta D. Nathnagar

327. The yarn produced under Mukhya Mantri Kosi Mulberry Scheme will be marketed under the brand name of:
A. Koshiki B. Mulberry Silk
C. Resham D. Tassar Silk

328. Which institute is the Cluster Monitoring and Technical Assistant (CMTA) for Bhagalpur Mega Handloom Cluster?
A. Rajendra Agriultural University, Pusa
B. NIFT, Patna
C. Bihar Institute for Silk and Textiles, Nathnagar
D. Bihar Agricultural University, Sabour

329. Match the corret pairs:

Cities	**Industry**
(*a*) Muzaffarpur	1. Tea
(*b*) Purnea	2. Tourism
(*c*) Kishanganj	3. Jute
(*d*) Gaya	4. Leather

Codes:

	(*a*)	(*b*)	(*a*)	(*d*)
A.	1	2	3	4
B.	4	3	2	1
C.	2	3	4	1
D.	4	3	1	2

330. In which of the following district of Bihar Castor Silk Development Project has been approved?
A. Purnea B. Katihar
C. Begusarai D. Kishanganj

331. The Plywood industry in Bihar is located in:
A. Hajipur B. Siwan
C. Muzaffarpur D. Motihari

332. Find out the incorrect pair:
A. Hajipur Plywood
B. Purnea Jute
C. Chakulia Leather
D. Samastipur Paper

333. Which city of Bihar is also known as Silk City?
A. Bhagalpur B. Purnea
C. Banka D. Madhubani

334. In which year was the sugar industry established in Bihar?
A. 1904 B. 1908
C. 1916 D. 1921

335. Which NGO is involved in the Tasar Silk Development at Chakai in Jamui?
A. Pahal B. Pradan
C. Prabandh D. Prarthna

336. The first diamond polishing unit in Bihar is being established at:
A. Patna B. Gaya
C. Muzaffarpur D. Samastipur

337. Mokama in Bihar is famous for:
A. Shoe factory B. Wagon of goods train
C. Brewery D. All of the above

338. The jute industry in Bihar is concentrated in which region:
A. North-western B. North-eastern
C. South-eastern D. Central

339. The Oil Refinery in Barauni was set up with the help of which country?
A. USA B. USSR
C. Britain D. Germany

340. The first radio station in Bihar was established at which place?
A. Muzaffarpur B. Patna
C. Darbhanga D. Sitamarhi

341. Abdul Bari Bridge is on the river Son at:
A. Koilwar B. Sonpur
C. Mokama D. Bhagalpur

342. The BSRTC was established in:
A. 1957 B. 1958
C. 1960 D. 1959

343. Which zone of Indian Railways lies in Bihar with its headquarters at Hajipur?
A. North-East Frontier Railways
B. East Central Zone
C. North-East Zone
D. Central Zone

344. Which two places in Bihar have international airports?
A. Patna and Muzaffarpur
B. Gaya and Bhagalpur
C. Patna and Gaya
D. Patna and Rajgir

345. Which National Highway in Bihar is a part of Golden Quadrangle project?
A. NH2 B. NH 31
C. NH 35 D. NH 38

346. The waterways present in river Ganga between Allahabad and Haldia is:
A. NW 2 B. NW 3
C. NW 1 D. NW 4

347. In which year was Bihar Rural Road Development Agency established?
A. 2004 B. 2003
C. 2002 D. 2001

348. A flying club is situated in which of the following places?
A. Nalanda B. Gaya
C. Patna D. Bhagalpur

349. Jaiprakash Narain International Airport is situated at:
A. Patna B. Nalanda
C. Bhagalpur D. Gaya

350. The capital of the Kanvas was at:
A. Ujjain B. Mathura
C. Pratishthan D. Pataliputra

351. Find the wrong pair:
A. Darbhanga – Nehru Setu
B. Bhagalpur – Vikramshila Setu
C. Mokama – Rajendra Setu
D. Patna – Gandhi Setu

352. In which of the following cities Vayudut service has been started?
A. Muzaffarpur B. Gaya
C. Raxaul D. Patna

353. Kataiya Hydro Power Project is located in which district of Bihar?
A. Supaul B. Katihar
C. Arwal D. Kishanganj

354. The highest installed capacity for power generation in Bihar is from:
A. Hydel Projects
B. Wind Projects
C. Thermal Power Projects
D. Nuclear Power Plants

355. In which district of Bihar an Ultra Mega Plant of 4000 MW capacity is being established?
A. Buxar B. Supaul
C. Katihar D. Banka

356. In which year was Bihar State Electricity Board established?
A. 2000 B. 1958
C. 1936 D. 1948

357. Find the wrong Match:
A. Nirmali Hydel Project Madhubani
B. Tejpura Hydel Projet Arwal
C. Rajpur Hydel Project Supaul
D. Amethi Hydel Projet Rohtas

358. Which of the following schemes have been launched by the central government for expanding the coverage of electricity supply?
A. IPDS B. DDUGJY
C. BRGF D. All of the above

359. Kosi Hydel Power Station is under the administration of:
A. BSHPC B. BREDA
C. BSEB D. None of the above

360. NABARD has identified how many districts in Bihar for promoting and financing women SHGs through positioning an anchor NGO in each identified district?
A. 15 B. 16
C. 17 D. 18

361. Which of the following reasons have been identified by NABARD for the dismal performance of SHGs in Bihar?
A. delays in opening SHG accounts
B. inadequate outreach in many regions
C. non-approval of repeat loans even when the first loans were repaired promptly
D. All of the above

362. Which of the following sectors are convered by RIDF?
A. Agriculture and Related sector
B. Social sectors
C. Rural connectivity
D. All of the above

363. Which district of Bihar has the highest participation of women in employment under MGNREGA?
A. Begusarai B. Darbhanga
C. Supaul D. Saharsa

364. The total number of Zila Parishads in Bihar are:
A. 36 B. 38
C. 41 D. 31

365. The chairperson of Zila Parishad is called:
A. Adhyaksha B. Mukhiya
C. Pramukh D. None of these

366. The Chairperson of Panchayat Samiti is called:
A. Mukhiya B. Adhyaksha
C. Pramukh D. Sarpanch

367. The Chairperson of Gram Panchayat is called:
A. Mukhiya B. Pramukh
C. Adhyaksha D. None of these

368. Bihar Panchayat Strengthening Project is being implemented with the help of:
A. SBI B. IMF
C. ADB D. World Bank

369. Which two cities of Bihar have received administrative approval for the implementation of Heritage City Development and Augmen-tation Yojana (HRIDAY)?
A. Ara and Sasaram B. Patna and Muzaffarpur
C. Gaya and Patna D. Gaya and Bodh Gaya

370. Which agency has been given the task of preparation of Detailed Project Report (DPR) for Patna Metro Rail Project?
A. CPWD B. DMRC
C. RITES Ltd. D. SE Railway

371. In which town of Bihar is Satyagraha Park being developed?
A. Motihari B. Bettiah
C. Ara D. Bhagalpur

372. Buddha Smriti Park is developed in which city of Bihar?
A. Vaishali B. Bhagalpur
C. Hajipur D. Patna

373. In which year was Bihar Urban Infrastructure Development Corporation (BUIDCO) established?
A. 2007 B. 2008
C. 2009 D. 2010

374. UIG and UIDSSMT are the sub-components of which of the following urban development programmes:
A. AMRUT
B. HRIDAY
C. Swachh Bharat Mission
D. Namami Ganga Scheme

375. The Namami Gange Scheme, a Central government programme aiming at the cleaning and rejuvenation of the river Ganga is being implemented in how many towns of Bihar:
A. 31 B. 20
C. 34 D. 35

376. The Support Programme for Urban Reforms (SPUR) is being implemented in 28 largest ULBs in Bihar with the support of:
A. USA B. Russia
C. France D. UK

377. Which three cities in Bihar have qualified to be developed under Phase I of Smart City Mission?
A. Patna, Bhagalpur, Muzaffarpur
B. Bhagalpur, Muzaffarpur, Gaya
C. Bhagalpur, Muzaffarpur, Biharsharif
D. Muzaffarpur, Biharsharif, Patna

378. The year for achieving the goals of Bihar Urban Agenda prepared by the state government is:
A. 2029 B. 2030
C. 2031 D. 2032

379. The first two towns in Bihar where property survey has been completed along with unique house numbering and number plate fixing:
A. Katihar, Banka B. Purnea, Banka
C. Katihar, Purnea D. Bhagalpur, Darbhanga

380. Which are the two mission cities in Bihar under the Urban Infrastructure and Governance (UIG) component of AMRUT?
A. Patna Urban Agglomeration, Bodhgaya
B. Gaya, Bodhgaya
C. Gaya, Jehanabad
D. Patna Urban Agglomeration, Gaya

381. JnNURM, a flagship programme for improving urban infrastructure in mission cities has been replaced by:
A. HRIDAY
B. Namami Gange Scheme
C. Swachh Bharat Mission
D. AMRUT

382. Which are the best three districts in Bihar in terms of availability of health infrastructure?
A. Sheohar, Sheikhpura, Sitamarhi
B. Jamui, Sheikhpura, Nawada
C. Bhagalpur, Banka, Bhojpur
D. Patna, Muzaffarpur, Darbhanga

383. In which district a new medical college Vardhamaan Ayurvigyan Sansthan, has been established?
A. Patna B. Samastipur
C. Bettiah D. Nalanda

384. Which of the following is incorrect?

A. IGIMS	Patna
B. Government Medical College	Bettiah
C. Narayan Medical college	Kishanganj
D. Vardhaman Ayurvigyan Sansthan	Nalanda

385. In which of the following districts of Bihar, Indira Gandhi Matritva Sahyog Yojana is operational?
A. East Champaran and West Champaran
B. Banka and Saharsa
C. Vaishali and Sitamarhi
D. Vaishali and Saharsa

386. Which of the following statement/statements is/are true regarding SABLA scheme?
A. It is a 100 per cent centrally sponsored shceme.
B. It is a comprehensive intervention for adolescent girls in the age group of 11-18 years.
C. It has a special focus on out-of-school girls.
D. All of the above

387. Consider the following statements regarding Janani Suraksha Yojana (JSY):
(*i*) It is an intervention for safe motherhood
(*ii*) It operates under National Health Mission
(*iii*) It is aimed at reducing maternal and neo-natal mortality by promoting institutional delivery among the poor women.

Which of the above statements are true regarding JSY?
A. (*i*) and (*ii*) B. (*ii*) and (*iii*)
C. (*i*) and (*iii*) D. All are true

388. Gargi Samhita mentions the attack of Greeks on Pataliputra. This attack took place during the reign of:
A. Vasudeva B. Dhanananda
C. Chandragupta II D. Pushyamitra

389. In which of the following district of Bihar the extent of institution delivery is highest?
A. Samastipur B. Purnea
C. Patna D. East Champaran

390. The bed occupancy rate means that the hospitals admit people with serious illness for their treatment. It reveals the availability of health infrastructure in a state. For Bihar as a whole, the bed occupancy rate is very high. Which of the following districts in Bihar has the highest bed occupancy rate?
A. Patna B. Bhojpur
C. Muzaffarpur D. Gaya

391. According to Manav Vikas Mission the target for Pupil-Teacher Ratio (PTR) in elementary education based on enrolment is:
A. 32 : 1 B. 40 : 1
C. 35 : 1 D. 30 : 1

392. The Mid-Day Meal Scheme (MDMS) covers the children belonging to classes:
A. I to VIII B. VI to VIII
C. I to V D. I to X

393. Bihar Education Project (Council) is the implementing agency for which of the following schemes:
A. Mid-Day Meal Scheme
B. Sarva Shiksha Abhiyan
C. Mission Gunwatta
D. None of the above

394. Pratham, a reputed non-government organization has been conducting learning assessment tests in every state, including Bihar. The results of these tests are presented in Annual Status of Education Report (ASER).

Consider the following results of ASER and identify which of the statement/statements is/are correct.

(*i*) In standard III, the percentage of students with satisfactory reading skills is lower in Bihar than the national average, while for mathematical skills it is nearly the same.

(*ii*) For standard V students, the percentage of students with satisfactory reading skills is same for both Bihar and India, however, for mathematics skills, the figures for Bihar are much higher.

A. Only (*i*) is correct
B. Only (*ii*) is orrect
C. None of them are correct
D. Both (*i*) and (*ii*) are correct

395. A high level committee has been constituted in Bihar under the chairmanship of Chief Secretary for the inclusion of which tribe in the category of scheduled tribe in Bihar.

A. Tharu B. Munda
C. Mal Pahariya D. Oraon

396. The Government of Bihar has decided to appoint Vikas Mitras at the Gram Panchayat and ward level for an effective implementation of various development and welfare schemes for a particular community. Name the community.

A. SC B. ST
C. Minorities D. Mahadalits

397. Which institution has been appointed as the nodal agency for imparting physical training to minority candidates for appearing in the examination of Bihar Police Service Recruitment?

A. Patna University
B. Mazharul Haque Arabi-Persian University
C. Magadha University
D. Tilka Manjhi University

398. The Government of Bihar has introduced reservation for women in panchayati raj institution and urban local bodies. How much reservation is provided?

A. 50 per cent B. 33 per cent
C. 51 per cent D. 75 per cent

399. In which of the following districts of Bihar, the state government operates AASRA, a 50-bedded special residential home for mentally challenged women and girls.

A. Samastipur B. Gaya
C. Siwan D. Patna

400. How much reservation is provided to women in direct recruitment for the posts of constable and in appointing junior inspector in the police force?

A. 33 per cent B. 50 per cent
C. 40 per cent D. 35 per cent

401. The objective of Samajik Punarvas Kosh Yojana which is in operation in all the districts of Bihar is:

A. to provide financial assistance to poor families at the time of marriage of girls who have attained the age of 18
B. to rehabilitate survivors of violene and human trafficking
C. to help mentally challenged women and girls
D. to provide free psychological legal of aid to victims and domestic violence

402. The state government operates speical schools for blind girls and a special school for deaf and dumb girls. These schools are respectively known as:

A. DRISHTI and KOSHISH
B. AASARA and SAHAYATA
C. DRISHTI and AASRA
D. SAHAYATA and KOSHISH

403. The state government has started a special school called KOSHISH, for deaf and dumb girls at:

A. Bettiah B. Motihari
C. Kishanganj D. Supaul

404. Which is the best district in terms of Mid-Day Meal Scheme Coverage?

A. Sitamarhi B. Sheohar
C. East Champaran D. Madhepura

405. Which of the following schemes are associated with drinking water and sanitation in Bihar?

A. Lohiya Swachhatta Yojana
B. Mukhyamantri Chapakal Yojana
C. Mukhyamantri Kshetra Vikas Yojana
D. All of the above

406. The head of state of Bihar, the Governor, is appointed by:

A. the President of India
B. the Chief Justice of India
C. Speaker of Lok Sabha
D. Speaker of Legislative Assembly

407. Governor holds office for a term of:

A. 5 years B. 4 years
C. 6 years D. 7 years

408. All the ministers are administered oath by:

A. Governor B. Chief Ministers
C. Speaker D. Deputy Chairman

409. Who was the first Governor of Bihar?

A. Sir James Sifton
B. Sir Maurice Garnier Hallett
C. Sir Thomas Alexander Stewart
D. Sir Thomas George Rutherford

410. Who appoints the Chief Minister?

A. Governor
B. President
C. Speaker of Legislative Assembly
D. Chairman of Legislative Council

411. After independence of India, who was the first Governor of Bihar?
A. Madhav Srihari Aney B. R.R. Diwakar
C. Jairamdas Daulatram D. Zakir Hussain

412. First Chief Justice of Patna High Court was:
A. Nand Lal Untwalia
B. D.P. Wadhwa
C. Vimal Chand Basak
D. Sir Edward Maynerd Champs Chamier

413. Bihar Public Service Commission (BPSC) is a body created by:
A. The Constitution of India
B. The extra constitutional provision
C. Legal provision
D. Administrative procedure

414. The Bihar Public Service Commission came into existence from:
A. 1st April, 1949 B. 1st April, 1950
C. 2nd April, 1953 D. 2nd April, 1951

415. The Bihar Public Service Commission initially began its functioning for the State of Bihar with its headquarters at:
A. Ranchi B. Patna
C. Gaya D. Muzaffarpur

416. Who was the first chairman of Bihar Public Service Commission?
A. Rajandhari Sinha B. Krishnakant Sahay
C. Bhupender Singh D. None of the above

417. The number of Divisions in Bihar are:
A. 6 B. 7
C. 8 D. 9

418. Gopalganj falls under which division:
A. Saran B. Tirhut
C. Magadha D. Patna

419. The total number of districts in Bihar are:
A. 27 B. 38
C. 37 D. 39

420. The sub-division is headed by SDM or SDO who is:
A. a newly recruited member of IAS
B. a member of state civil service
C. Both A and B
D. None of the above

421. Vaishali falls under which division:
A. Saran B. Tirhut
C. Bhagalpur D. Munger

422. A Panchyat Samiti is a local government body at which level?
A. Block level B. Village level
C. District level D. None of the above

423. What percentage of reservation has been provided to scheduled caste and scheduled tribe population in Panchayat election?
A. 1/2
B. 1/3
C. in proportion to their population
D. 1/5

424. The departments, not included under Panchayat Samiti work is:
A. Agriculture B. Education
C. Transport D. Social welfare

425. A Janpad Panchayat is constituted for each:
A. block B. village
C. district D. locality

426. Who is responsible for his work to the CEO of ZP?
A. BDO B. SDO
C. Sarpanch D. None of these

427. The schemes implemented by PRIs are financed by:
A. Backward Region Grants Fund (BRGF)
B. Grants from the Union Finance Commission
C. Grants from the State Finance Commission
D. All of the above

428. Panchayati Raj System was formalised in 1992 by which amendment to the Indian Constitution?
A. 73rd B. 74th
C. 75th D. 76th

429. Which of the following statement is true about panchayat election qualification:
A. must have 21 years age
B. must be qualified to be a member of legislature
C. Both A and B
D. None of the above

430. Which one of the following parts were added to the Constitution by 73rd Constitutional Amendment Act?
A. IXth B. Xth
C. XIth D. XIIth

431. The Panchayat Samiti is elected for a term of:
A. 5 years B. 3 years
C. 2 years D. 4 years

432. Zila Parishad has:
A. a President
B. a Vice President
C. a Chief Executive Officer
D. All of the above

433. The intermediate level of Panchayat is provided in which of the following state?
A. region with 10 lakh population
B. region with 15 lakh population
C. region with 20 lakh population
D. region with 25 lakh population

434. Bihar Panchayati Raj Act came in which year?
A. 2005 B. 2006
C. 2007 D. 2008

435. States appoints a finance commission to review the working of Panchayats:

A. every 2 year B. every 3 year
C. every 4 year D. every 5 year

436. The reservation for chairperson of Panchayats can be made by:

A. State B. Centre
C. Finance Commission D. Election Commission

437. The member of Block level Panchayat are:

A. ex-officials
B. elected by Gram Sabha
C. elected by Gram Panchayat
D. None of the above

438. The panchayat samiti is elected for a term of 5 years and is headed by:

A. A chairman and a deputy chairman
B. A chairman
C. A sarpanch
D. None of the above

439. How are the members of Zila Panchayat elected?

A. From the district on the basis of Adult Franchise
B. From the district on the basis of selection by the President
C. From the district on the basis of reommendation by the President
D. None of the above

440. Each Janpad Panchayat has a President, a Vice President and a:

A. Development Officer
B. Chief Executive Officer
C. Sarpanch
D. Both B and C

441. Which of the following statements is false about Karma dance?

A. It is performed mainly by tribes
B. It is mainly done at crop sowing and crop harvesting time
C. It is done to please Lord Karma
D. All of the above

442. The God worshipped in Karma dance form is:

A. Lord Rama B. Lord Krishna
C. Lord Indra D. Lord Karma

443. Find the incorrect match:

	Folk theatre	Main theme
A.	Bhakuli-Banka	Rural Life
B.	Domkuchh	Marriage
C.	Jat-Jatin	Child birth
D.	Kirtaniya	Krishna

444. Dhobia dance form is done in which region?

A. Bhojpur B. Gaya
C. Darbhanga D. Katihar

445. Hathiyar and Kalibanga are the two types of _______ dance.

A. Launda B. Chhau
C. Karma D. Kholdin

446. Sama Chakewa is organised in which month?

A. Kartik B. Magh
C. Phagun D. Shravan

447. Which of the following dance theatres has devotional theme?

A. Kirtaniya B. Jat-Jatin
C. Domkuchh D. Bhakuli-Banka

448. In which of the following festivals, Fagua songs are sung?

A. Holi B. Deepawali
C. Shravan D. Teej

449. Vidyapat dance is performed in:

A. Purnia B. Gaya
C. Siwan D. Saran

450. ________ dance is performed by ladies in moonlight in the month of Shravan to Kartik.

A. Jharni B. Jat-Jatin
C. Jogira D. Vidyapati

451. Pawadia dance form is performed on:

A. marriage B. child birth
C. gauna D. harvesting season

452. In which of the following regions, nunachar is sung?

A. Darbhanga B. Katihar
C. Nawada D. Gaya

453. Find the correct match:

	Dance Form	Occasion
A.	Kholdin	Child birth
B.	Karma	Harvesting
C.	Chhau	Holi
D.	Jogira	Marriage

454. Find the incorrect match:

	Dance Form	Occasion
A.	Jogira	Holi
B.	Kariya	Marriage
C.	Jharni	Muharram
D.	Launda	Child birth

455. Lalit Kala Manch is located at which place?

A. Gaya B. Patna
C. Muzaffarpur D. Darbhanga

456. Find the correct statement:

A. Chhau dance form has Veer Rasa and is performed at war time.
B. It is perfomed by males only
C. It is basically performed in South Bihar
D. None of the above

457. The Chief markets of Tikuli are:
A. Varanasi B. Patna
C. Kolkata D. All of these

458. Shah Daulat's tomb in Maner is best example of:
A. Mughal style B. Turks
C. Afghan D. None of these

459. Patna Kalam was an offshoot of:
A. Mughal painting B. Afghan painting
C. Pala painting D. None of the above

460. Yaksh and Yakshini statues are the examples of finest sculpture of Mauryan period, which has been obtained from:
A. Patna B. Darbhanga
C. Gaya D. Bihar Sharif

461. The tradition of carpet making in Bihar dates back to:
A. Buddhist and the Mauryan period
B. Mughal period
C. Later Mauryan period
D. Afghan period.

462. Sher Shah's tomb of Sasaram was built in which style?
A. Mughal style B. Afghan style
C. Jusks style D. Salve style

463. Manjusha Kala or Angika Art is another Bihari art form, practiced in the:
A. Vaishali region B. Magadh region
C. Anga D. None of the above

464. Madhubani painting depicts:
A. Nature and Hindu religious figures
B. Buddhist life
C. Marriage ceremony
D. None of the above

465. Tikuli works is a form of craft made from:
A. Broken glass B. Weeds
C. Applique D. Zari

466. Nalanda and Kurkihar has got evidence of which period?
A. Pala B. Mauryan
C. Post Mauryan D. None of these

467. Lacquer craft is famous for:
A. Bangles and stools B. Jewellery
C. Paintings D. Zari work

468. Which one is true?
A. Brass and stone statue gained prominence in Pala period
B. Dhiman and his son Vitthalpal had taken main role in its development
C. Both A and B
D. None of the above

469. Which is a very famous centre of wooden toy making?
A. Patna B. Gaya
C. Nawada D. Nalanda

470. Mandar hill features the unique image of which God from the Gupta period, in his man-lion incarnation?
A. Lord Vishnu B. Lord Shiva
C. Lord Ganesha D. None of the above

471. Patna Sahib is related to which of the following Sikh Gurus?
A. Guru Gobind Singh B. Guru Nanak
C. Guru Angad D. None of the above

472. In Saurath, in which month a fair on marriage is held?
A. Jayeshtha-Asharh B. Bhadrapada
C. Magha D. Kartik

473. Find the correct match:

	Fair		**District**
A.	Baunsi	-	West Champaran
B.	Saurath	-	Begusarai
C.	Brahmeshwamath	-	Buxar
D.	Simariya	-	Bhagalpur

474. Sonpur fair is held on which day?
A. Navami of Chaitra month
B. Kartik Purnima
C. Tryodashi of Chaitra Shukla
D. None of the above

475. Which one of the following fairs is celebrated by Tharu tribe?
A. Sahodhara B. Simaria
C. Saurath D. Baunsi

476. Singheswar fair is held in which district?
A. Supaul B. Madhepura
C. Katihar D. Purnia

477. Which of the following fairs is celebrated to Rama and Laxman arrival?
A. Buxar fair B. Sitamarhi fair
C. Sonpur fair D. None of these

478. When was Patna book fair held for the first time?
A. 1970 B. 1975
C. 1972 D. 1971

479. What does Mahalaya in Bihar mean?
A. Devpujan B. Govardhan
C. Pitrapaksha D. Ganeshapujan

480. Sitamarhi fair is celebrated for which occasion?
A. Saraswati Pooja B. Krishnashtami
C. Ramnavami D. Chhath

481. 'Jeutia' is celebrated on which day?
A. Ashwin Krishna Paksha Ashtami
B. Ashwin Shukla Paksha Ashtami
C. Kartik Krishna Paksha Ashtami
D. Kartik Shukla Paksha Ashtami

482. In which of the following places Loard Vishnu had taken holy bath?
A. Baunsi B. Simarya
C. Sitamarhi D. None of the above

483. In Chhath festival which God is offered Arghya?
A. Sun B. Vishnu
C. Shiva D. Rama

484. Which festival in Bihar is celebrated as a belief of the awakening of God after 4 months of sleep?
A. Chhath festival B. Govardhan
C. Mahalaya Amavasya D. Devotthan Ekadashi

485. Jeutia festival is celebrated by females for:
A. husband B. son
C. daughter D. none of these

486. Pitrapaksh fair in Gaya is held in which month?
A. Ashwin B. Kartik
C. Magh D. Chaitra

487. Brahmeshwarnath fair is basically:
A. an animal fair B. Jain's fair
C. Hindu's fair D. None of the above

488. Firangiya and Batohiya are written in which of the following languages?
A. Magadhi B. Maithili
C. Bhojpuri D. Angika

489. Which of the following languages is not a part of Munda language family?
A. Angika B. Vajjika
C. Maithili D. None of these

490. Which among the following languages in Bihar is included in the Eighth Schedule of the Indian Constitution by the 92nd Constitutional Amendment Act, 2003.
A. Maithili B. Magadhi
C. Bhojpuri D. Urdu

491. Urdu was granted second language in Bihar in which year?
A. 1980 B. 1985
C. 1984 D. 1989

492. 'Varn Ratnakar' is the first written com-position of which language?
A. Maithili B. Magadhi
C. Bhojpuri D. Angika

493. When was 'The Patna Times' started?
A. 1912 B. 1924
C. 1944 D. 1916

494. Who is the first poet of Magadhi/Magahi?
A. Ishan B. Siyaram
C. Manoranjan Singh D. Nagarjuna

495. Who have researched widely on the dialects of Bihar?
A. V.S. Smith B. George Grierson
C. William Taylor D. Jyon Dren

496. Ambpali was written by whom?
A. Ram Briksha Benipuri B. Vachaspati Mishra
C. Nagarjuna D. Vidyapati

497. Who among the following is not a Magadhi poet?
A. Chaturbhuj Mishra B. Yogeshwar Singh
C. Suresh Dubey D. Dariya Das

498. 'Gautam' Mahakavya was written in Magadhi language by whom?
A. Yamuna Pathak B. Yogeshwar Singh
C. Harihar Pathak D. Sridhar Mishra

499. Who wrote 'Kaikeyi' and 'Rituvansh' in Bhojpuri language?
A. Kapilmuni Pathak B. Ratneshwar Pathak
C. Pt. Kedarnath Mishra D. Suman Sahay

500. 'Bidesiya' is a work of:
A. Bhikhari Thakur B. Kedarnath Mishra
C. Dariya Das D. Dharti Das

501. Which of the following languages is not a part of Aryan family?
A. Maithili B. Magadhi
C. Vajjika D. Bhojpuri

502. Tej Narayan Kushwaha has contributed to which language?
A. Angika B. Magadhi
C. Vajjika D. Maithili

503. Bhim Rao Ambedkar University is situated in which district?
A. Buxar B. Darbhanga
C. Muzaffarpur D. Nawada

504. In which year was Magadha University established?
A. 1976 B. 1903
C. 1962 D. 1980

505. Patna University was established in:
A. 1917 B. 1919
C. 1915 D. 1916

506. Khuda Baksh Oriental Library is situated in:
A. Munger B. Gaya
C. Bhagalpur D. Patna

507. IGIMS, Patna was established in which year?
A. 1984 B. 1990
C. 1980 D. 1983

508. Arabic and Persian Research Institute is situated in:
A. Darbhanga B. West Champaran
C. Patna D. Bhagalpur

509. Jawaharlal Nehru Medical College is situated in:
A. Banka B. Bhagalpur
C. Katihar D. Kishanganj

510. Bhitarwara Asharam related to Gandhiji is situated in which district of Bihar?
A. West Champaran B. Patna
C. East Champaran D. Sitamarhi

511. Gandhiji experimented satyagraha at which place for the first time?

A. Siwan B. Saran
C. East Champaran D. West Champaran

512. At which place the highest Buddhist Stupa in India is located?
A. Nalanda B. Rajgir
C. Vaishali D. Kesariya

513. Ahirauli related to Ahilya is situated in which district of Bihar?
A. Saharsa B. Buxar
C. Darbhanga D. Gopalganj

514. Bodhgaya is religious palace of which religion?
A. Buddhism B. Hinduism
C. Jainism D. Islam

515. Kabar Jheel Bird Santuary is located in which district?
A. Begusarai B. Sitamarhi
C. Jamui D. Banka

516. Matsyagandha Tourism complex is located in which district of Bihar?
A. Supaul B. Saharsa
C. Sitamarhi D. Bhagalpur

517. Goraul Sharif a muslim pilgrimage, is situated in which district:
A. Supaul B. West Champaran
C. Sitamarhi D. Patna

518. Jarasandh's Akhara is situated at which of the following places?
A. Patna B. Rajgir
C. Vaishali D. Bodhgaya

519. Padri Ki Haveli was constructed in which year?
A. 1705 B. 1771
C. 1707 D. 1772

520. The Kundeshwari Devi Temple at Kundghat is situated at which place?
A. Jamui B. Banka
C. Kaimur D. Bhojpur

521. Which of the following tourist sites is located in Nalanda?
A. Vajrasana B. Guneri
C. Venuvana Vihara D. Vikramshila

522. The Vishwa Shanti Stupa is located at which place of Bihar?
A. Hajipur B. Rajgir
C. Bodhgaya D. Maner

523. Which of the following is an incorrect pair?
A. Maniar Math – Gaya
B. Vasokund – Muzaffarpur
C. Mandar Hill – Banka
D. Bisram – Bhojpur

524. Which is the most famous treasure of Patna Museum?
A. Shiva Statue B. Buddha Statue
C. Didarganj Yakshini D. Vishnu Statue

525. The tomb of Yahiya Maneri is situated in:
A. Bettiah B. Gaya
C. Manersharif D. Rajgir

526. Dargah of Makhdum Hazrat Sultan Ahmed Charampose is situated in which district?
A. Bihar Sharif (Nalanda) B. Gopalganj
C. Sitamarhi D. Nawada

527. Who wrote several collections of Hindi poems including 'Umang'?
A. Gopal Singh Nepali B. Naval Kishore Dhawal
C. Ramnarayan Sharma D. Bhikari Thakur

528. Who was the author of Chandrakantha?
A. Devkinandan Khatri
B. Navin Vilochan Sharma
C. Kedarnath Mishra
D. None of the above

529. Veer Kunwar Singh University is in which district?
A. Bhojpur B. Gaya
C. Siwan D. Saran

530. Swami Sahjananda Saraswati had set-up an Ashram at which place?
A. Arrah B. Patna
C. Muzaffarpur D. None of the above

ANSWERS

1	2	3	4	5	6	7	8	9	10
D	B	D	B	A	C	A	D	B	A
11	**12**	**13**	**14**	**15**	**16**	**17**	**18**	**19**	**20**
C	C	D	A	B	A	D	A	D	A
21	**22**	**23**	**24**	**25**	**26**	**27**	**28**	**29**	**30**
D	A	C	B	D	B	D	C	A	B
31	**32**	**33**	**34**	**35**	**36**	**37**	**38**	**39**	**40**
C	A	B	A	D	D	D	B	A	D
41	**42**	**43**	**44**	**45**	**46**	**47**	**48**	**49**	**50**
A	C	A	A	B	C	D	B	B	A

51	**52**	**53**	**54**	**55**	**56**	**57**	**58**	**59**	**60**
B	D	C	A	C	A	D	B	A	B
61	**62**	**63**	**64**	**65**	**66**	**67**	**68**	**69**	**70**
B	B	A	C	D	A	C	C	D	A
71	**72**	**73**	**74**	**75**	**76**	**77**	**78**	**79**	**80**
B	A	A	D	B	A	A	D	B	B
81	**82**	**83**	**84**	**85**	**86**	**87**	**88**	**89**	**90**
A	C	C	A	A	A	D	C	B	B
91	**92**	**93**	**94**	**95**	**96**	**97**	**98**	**99**	**100**
A	C	D	C	C	C	D	B	A	B
101	**102**	**103**	**104**	**105**	**106**	**107**	**108**	**109**	**110**
D	A	A	D	A	B	D	B	A	A
111	**112**	**113**	**114**	**115**	**116**	**117**	**118**	**119**	**120**
A	B	B	B	A	A	B	D	C	B
121	**122**	**123**	**124**	**125**	**126**	**127**	**128**	**129**	**130**
A	B	A	D	A	B	C	B	D	A
131	**132**	**133**	**134**	**135**	**136**	**137**	**138**	**139**	**140**
C	C	B	C	C	D	A	A	D	C
141	**142**	**143**	**144**	**145**	**146**	**147**	**148**	**149**	**150**
A	D	C	C	B	B	D	C	D	A
151	**152**	**153**	**154**	**155**	**156**	**157**	**158**	**159**	**160**
B	A	A	B	D	B	A	C	B	B
161	**162**	**163**	**164**	**165**	**166**	**167**	**168**	**169**	**170**
D	A	C	A	A	D	A	A	B	A
171	**172**	**173**	**174**	**175**	**176**	**177**	**178**	**179**	**180**
B	A	A	C	D	B	B	A	C	D
181	**182**	**183**	**184**	**185**	**186**	**187**	**188**	**189**	**190**
B	C	B	A	C	C	D	C	B	A
191	**192**	**193**	**194**	**195**	**196**	**197**	**198**	**199**	**200**
C	A	D	B	A	D	B	A	A	A
201	**202**	**203**	**204**	**205**	**206**	**207**	**208**	**209**	**210**
A	A	A	A	D	A	A	C	D	B
211	**212**	**213**	**214**	**215**	**216**	**217**	**218**	**219**	**220**
C	A	D	D	B	C	A	B	A	B
221	**222**	**223**	**224**	**225**	**226**	**227**	**228**	**229**	**230**
C	C	D	A	B	C	A	A	D	A
231	**232**	**233**	**234**	**235**	**236**	**237**	**238**	**239**	**240**
B	A	B	D	D	B	B	A	A	B
241	**242**	**243**	**244**	**245**	**246**	**247**	**248**	**249**	**250**
C	C	B	C	D	A	C	A	D	A
251	**252**	**253**	**254**	**255**	**256**	**257**	**258**	**259**	**260**
D	C	D	D	A	C	D	B	C	A
261	**262**	**263**	**264**	**265**	**266**	**267**	**268**	**269**	**270**
B	D	D	A	C	B	A	D	D	A
271	**272**	**273**	**274**	**275**	**276**	**277**	**278**	**279**	**280**
A	D	C	C	B	A	B	B	B	A
281	**282**	**283**	**284**	**285**	**286**	**287**	**288**	**289**	**290**
A	D	A	B	C	B	B	A	A	B
291	**292**	**293**	**294**	**295**	**296**	**297**	**298**	**299**	**300**
D	A	A	A	C	A	D	A	A	B

301	302	303	304	305	306	307	308	309	310
A	D	C	A	B	C	B	A	C	A
311	312	313	314	315	316	317	318	319	320
C	B	A	A	B	A	B	A	D	A
321	322	323	324	325	326	327	328	329	330
D	B	C	A	A	D	A	B	D	C
331	332	333	334	335	336	337	338	339	340
A	C	A	A	B	A	D	B	B	B
341	342	343	344	345	346	347	348	349	350
A	D	B	C	A	C	B	C	A	C
351	352	353	354	355	356	357	358	359	360
A	D	A	C	D	B	B	D	A	B
361	362	363	364	365	366	367	368	369	370
D	D	A	B	A	C	A	D	D	C
371	372	373	374	375	376	377	378	379	380
A	D	C	A	B	D	C	C	C	A
381	382	383	384	385	386	387	388	389	390
D	B	D	C	D	D	D	D	A	C
391	392	393	394	395	396	397	398	399	400
B	A	B	D	A	D	B	A	D	D
401	402	403	404	405	406	407	408	409	410
B	A	B	C	D	A	A	A	B	A
411	412	413	414	415	416	417	418	419	420
C	D	A	A	A	A	D	A	B	C
421	422	423	424	425	426	427	428	429	430
B	A	C	C	A	A	A	A	A	A
431	432	433	434	435	436	437	438	439	440
A	D	C	B	D	A	A	A	A	B
441	442	443	444	445	446	447	448	449	450
D	D	C	A	B	A	A	A	A	B
451	452	453	454	455	456	457	458	459	460
B	A	B	D	A	A	D	A	A	A
461	462	463	464	465	466	467	468	469	470
A	B	C	A	A	A	A	C	A	A
471	472	473	474	475	476	477	478	479	480
A	A	C	B	A	B	A	D	C	C
481	482	483	484	485	486	487	488	489	490
A	A	A	D	B	A	A	C	C	A
491	492	493	494	495	496	497	498	499	500
C	A	B	A	B	A	D	B	C	A
501	502	503	504	505	506	507	508	509	510
C	A	C	C	A	D	D	C	B	A
511	512	513	514	515	516	517	518	519	520
C	D	B	A	A	B	C	B	D	A
521	522	523	524	525	526	527	528	529	530
C	B	A	C	C	A	A	A	A	B

●●●